MULTI-ROBOT SYSTEMS, TRENDS AND DEVELOPMENT

Edited by **Toshiyuki Yasuda**
and Kazuhiro Ohkura

Multi-Robot Systems, Trends and Development
Edited by Toshiyuki Yasuda and Kazuhiro Ohkura

Published by InTech

Janeza Trdine 9, 51000 Rijeka, Croatia

Publishing Process Manager Ana Nikolic

Technical Editor Teodora Smiljanic

Cover Designer InTech Design Team

Additional hard copies can be obtained from orders@intechopen.com

Multi-Robot Systems, Trends and Development, Edited by Toshiyuki Yasuda and Kazuhiro Ohkura
p. cm.
ISBN 978-953-307-425-2

For EU product safety concerns:
IN TECH d.o.o., Prolaz Marije Krucifikse Kozulić 3, 51000 Rijeka, Croatia,
info@intechopen.com or visit our website at intechopen.com.

Meet the editors

Toshiyuki Yasuda received B.E., M.E., and Ph.D degrees, all in engineering, from Kobe University, in 2000, 2002, and 2006, respectively. He is an assistant professor of Graduate School of Engineering, Hiroshima University, Japan. He was a research assistant of Department of Electronics and Control Engineering, Tsuyama National College of Technology, from April 2006 to March 2007. He was a visiting researcher at School of Computer Science, University of Birmingham, UK, from July 2008 to March 2009. His research areas cover robotics and artificial intelligence.

Kazuhiro Ohkura received B.E., M.E., and Ph.D degrees, all in engineering, from Hokkaido University, in 1988, 1990, and 1996, respectively. From 1990 to 1993, he worked with FUJITSU Laboratories. In 1993, he became a research assistant of Kobe University. In 1997, he became an associate professor. He was a visiting research fellow, School of Informatics, University of Sussex, UK, from 1998 to 1999. He is currently a professor of Graduate School of Engineering, Hiroshima University, Japan. His research interests include evolutionary computation, reinforcement learning, multi-robot systems.

Contents

Preface

Multi robot systems have recently attracted considerable attention from roboticists as these offer the possibility of accomplishing a task that a single robot can not. A robot team may provide redundancy and perform assigned tasks in a more reliable, faster, or cheaper way.

This book is a collection of 29 excellent works and comprised of three sections: task oriented approach, bio inspired approach, and modeling/design. In the first section, applications on formation, localization/mapping, and planning are introduced. The second section is on behavior-based approach by means of artificial intelligence techniques. The last section includes research articles on development of architectures and control systems.

I wish everybody a pleasant and fruitful time reading this book, and, most importantly, that the readers learn something new by seeing things from a new perspective.

Finally I would like to express my gratitude to all authors for their invaluable contributions.

Toshiyuki Yasuda and Kazuhiro Ohkura

Hiroshima University
Japan

Part 1

Task Oriented Approach

1

Swarm Patterns: Trends and Transformation Tools

Blesson Varghese and Gerard McKee
School of Systems Engineering, University of Reading, Whiteknights Campus Reading, Berkshire, United Kingdom

1. Introduction

The domain of multi-robot systems incorporates research which is inspired by nature. The aim of this research is to design man-made systems which incorporate principles observed in multi-agent natural systems. The mapping of these principles to man-made systems is referred to as biomimetics (Habib et al., 2007) and the area within multi-robot systems that explores this mapping is generally referred to as swarm robotic systems (Sahin & Spears, 2005).

Research within swarm robotics includes self-organisation and an interesting aspect of self organisation is pattern formation (Camazine et al., 2003). The term pattern formation in literature is used in at least two different ways. Firstly, to define an area of study within multi robot systems that covers distinct aspects of patterns such as the establishment, maintenance and reconfiguration of patterns. Secondly, to report the natural phenomenon of flocking whereby loose or deformed geometric patterns emerge, and not necessarily strict geometric patterns (Arkin, 1998). In this chapter, the first usage of the term is adopted.

The research in this chapter is motivated by two observations based on an extensive review of literature based on pattern formation and swarm robotics. Firstly, it was noted that there are no mathematical models that exist for pattern formation in swarm robotic systems. Secondly, it was also noted that though pattern formation was a classic area of research, yet the challenges that have emerged in due course have not been addressed through a unifying model. Hence, it was necessary to address the need for a unifying mathematical model that can surmount the identified challenges in pattern formation.

The remainder of this chapter is organised as follows. The next section presents eight challenges identified in pattern formation. The second section sets the basic framework for mathematical modelling required to address the challenges. The fourth section presents a definition for transformation, four cases of transformation and tools for transformation. Simulation studies and a discussion are presented in the penultimate section. The last section concludes this chapter.

2. Challenges of pattern formation

With the progress of research in pattern formation a number of challenges have been identified by researchers. This section presents eight challenges which have been considered in exploring the need for a unifying mathematical model to address these challenges. The challenges were identified by reviewing extensive literature in swarm robotic systems, though only the most relevant of these are referenced here.

2.1 Establishment of a pattern

The problem of establishing patterns can be separated into two sub problems:

a. *Identification of robots forming a pattern,* which is based on the perceptual ability of the participating agents. The agents must recognize and establish communication with their peers with the goal of forming a single connected network (Poduri & Sukhtame, 2007). The search for peer robots in an environment can be performed by random walks, but at the expense of battery power; hence the random walk approach is more appropriate for a closed environment with specified boundaries.
b. *Positioning of the robots in the pattern* requires a referencing mechanism such as the unit centre reference, leader reference, virtual reference and neighbour reference (Balch & Arkin, 1998)(Michaud et al., 2002). In the Unit centre reference, each robot in a pattern computes a unit centre by averaging the x and y positions of other robots. In the leader, the formation position of a robot with respect to a lead robot position is determined. In the virtual reference mechanism, a virtual (or imaginary) point is referenced such that formation positions are based on this single point. In the neighbour reference mechanism, the formation position of a robot is determined with reference to one or more robots in close vicinity. Neighbour referencing can be based on a neighbour in the pattern that is the closest or farthest, or all detected neighbours.

2.2 Maintenance of a pattern

Once a pattern is established, the group of robots must move such that the pattern is maintained. Maintenance of a pattern can be considered as follows:

a. *Stability of the pattern* is challenged when an error is introduced into the pattern which is then propagated through the pattern resulting in the deformation of the pattern and possible failure in inter robot communication. String, mesh and leader to formation stability need to be studied in the context of patterns (Chen & Wang, 2005)(Naffin et al., 2004). String stability deals with the effect of disturbance propagations in platoon formations and a stable formation requires the dampening of disturbance while it travels from any source. Mesh stability is used for error attenuation. Leader to formation stability deals with how the leader behaviour affects the interconnection errors.
b. *Self-repairing* ability is challenged when an unpredicted or untimely failure occurs. In such cases the unaffected robots in the pattern must be capable of coping with the loss. The group can continue motion towards its goal if a restoration of pattern is not necessary. If fixture and refurbishment of the pattern is required, reassigning pivotal roles and transforming patterns or repositioning robots is appropriate. The self repairing property of patterns has been demonstrated by (Cheng et al., 2005). In the event of failure of a group of agents in the pattern, the remaining agents adjust their positions such as to maintain uniform density.

2.3 Obstacle avoidance

Most research work on obstacle avoidance are focused on avoiding stationary obstacles. The complexity of the problem of obstacle avoidance increases when obstacles are dynamic in the environment. The problem of obstacle avoidance can be separated into obstacle identification, sharing obstacle information across the group and responding appropriately to the obstacle.

Obstacle identification is related to the perceiving ability of the robotic agents in the pattern. For example, obstacles can be identified through vision mechanisms. Sharing obstacle information across the group can be achieved by broadcasting to all agents (global communication), or to a subset of a group, or the agents individually sense information of obstacles and respond locally. The solutions to these two problems provide the base for the appropriate response to the obstacle. Strategies employed for avoiding obstacles in patterns include potential field (Wang et al., 2006), dynamic window (Fox et al., 1997)(Seder & Petrovic, 2007)(Ogren & Leonard, 2003) and flow field method (Shao et al., 2006).

2.4 Collision avoidance

The chance of robots colliding against each other is yet another challenge in robot formations. Some researchers use the term collision avoidance synonymous with obstacle avoidance (Cai et al., 2007a)(Cai et al., 2007b). However, we treat the avoidance of inter robot collisions as collision avoidance.

Collisions are avoided by maintaining strict buffer distances and consistent communication between robots (Koh & Zhou, 2007). Maintaining strict buffer distances can challenge the flexibility of the pattern. Hence there is a trade off between flexibility and buffered distance for collision avoidance. Strict collision avoidance rules might prevent the establishment of a desired pattern.

2.5 Transformation of patterns

The transformation of patterns is synonymous with reconfiguration of patterns which is necessary when a swarm of robots need to respond to obstacles in the path of its motion (Chen & Wang, 2007b). Reconfiguration can be achieved by repositioning all or a few agents in the pattern and can lead to the deformation of a pattern or a change of shape of the pattern. When many robotic agents within a pattern attempt to reposition, chances of inter agent collisions increase. Hence collision avoidance discussed in the previous section is relevant while repositioning and may require path planning of individual robots.

However, we treat the transformation of patterns distinct from mere repositioning, since transformations are more geometry oriented. Repositioning of agents may be feasible only on flexible patterns while transformations can be achieved on both rigid and flexible patterns. The transformation of patterns, of primary focus in this chapter, is considered later in Section 4.

2.6 Role assignment

This challenge involves designating a role or assigning a job to a robot or a group of robots (Chaimowicz et al., 2002)(Chen & Wang, 2007a). Consider the example of a group of robots patrolling a secure area. It is possible that there exists a single assigned leader for the group. All the followers of the leader in the pattern perform a coordinated task and achieve the goal. But consider a team of robots in a soccer match. Each robot has its own specific role. At any instant, a robot would assume the role of a goal keeper, while some act as defenders or strikers. Hence, the role assigning module of a framework is of important consideration.

Group of robots in a pattern assigned roles should be capable to swap roles and accommodate heterogeneous robots in the pattern. Robust frameworks would require strategies to reassign roles at the event of agent failure or even while avoiding obstacles.

2.7 Scalability of patterns

Most pattern formation research is based on a finite number of robots and has proven to be not scalable. It is also interesting to note that the issue of scalability has been of little interest in most research work. It is practically impossible to study scalable formations on real world robot systems because of the cost factor. However, there is a need to derive models that facilitate scalability studies and are scalable.

Simulations would be an appropriate method to study scalability of patterns for which various numerical techniques and simulation environments are available. Robotic simulations necessarily need not be only performed on robotic development environments but may also employ physics, chemical or biological simulators. A particle physics based swarm simulation study is reported in (Varghese & McKee, 2008b).

2.8 Coordinating multiple patterns

Coordinating robots in a single group for a cooperative task has been of interest in swarm robotic research. It would also be interesting to consider multiple groups forming independent patterns for cooperative tasks. This includes coordination amongst groups of robots to merge and split to different patterns. Hence, the need for multiple role assignment strategies arises. Sharing of agents between groups at the event of agent failures could be a further consideration towards developing a robust strategy for multiple pattern coordination. The coordination of multiple teams (Hsu & Liu, 2004) and task assignment of multiple agents, pattern splitting and merging while accomplishing a task have been recently reported (Michael et al., 2008).

Researchers have attempted to address the eight challenges presented above with significant research contributions towards classic challenges such as obstacle and collision avoidance. However, it is noted that attempts towards developing a model that addresses most of the above challenges has been minimal. Hence, there exists a need to develop a mathematical model towards this end, such that the challenges presented above can be addressed.

3. A mathematical model for swarm patterns

This section proposes a mathematical model for swarm pattern formation based on the foundations of the Complex Plane and is shown in figure 1. The De Moivre's formula to obtain roots of an equation is used to represent the model. If $z = x + iy$ (Kreyszig, 2006) and is represented in the polar form as $z = r(\cos\theta + i\sin\theta)$ and r is called the absolute value or the modulus of z, then $z^n = r^n(\cos n\theta + i\sin n\theta)$ for n = 0, 1, 2, ... The nth root of z is obtained by $\sqrt[n]{z} = \sqrt[n]{r}\left(\cos\left[\frac{\theta+2k\pi}{n}\right] + i\sin\left[\frac{\theta+2k\pi}{n}\right]\right)$ where k = 0, 1, ..., (n − 1). The roots of the equation lie on a circle of radius $\sqrt[n]{r}$ with centre at the origin and constitute the vertices of a regular polygon of n sides. The result of joining the n roots is an n-sided polygon. The polygon is circumscribed by a circle otherwise referred as the circumcircle of the polygon. Mapping these results on to the area of multi-agent pattern formations, it is assumed that the robotic agents are positioned on the vertices of the polygon. Hence the robots form a closed polygonal pattern and the system is mobile with appropriate communication and coordination mechanism.

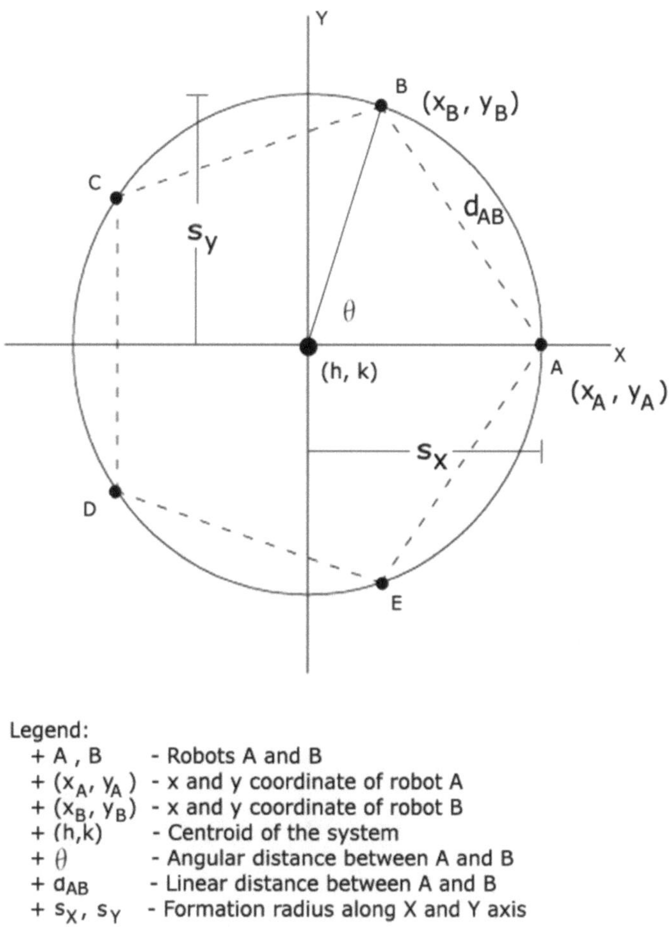

Fig. 1. Mathematical Model for Swarm Pattern Formation

Before proceeding further it is necessary to define a few terms such as microscopic and macroscopic primitives to articulate the mathematical model proposed in this section. The term primitive in this paper refers to an element used as a building block to define aspects of the model.

Microscopic primitives are specific to robots constituting the swarm and define the individual behaviours of swarm robotic agents. Microscopic primitives are employed in the research reported by (Chen et al., 2005)(Balch & Hybinette, 2000). It is also noted that behaviour based pattern formation approaches tend to be microscopic in nature and such models may not be scalable.

On the other hand macroscopic primitives of a group of robots are properties that affect the group behaviour of the system. They are abstract properties of a pattern, which when modified facilitates a change in the pattern. The control of a swarm of robot by varying abstract properties, namely variance and centroid is reported by Belta and Kumar (Belta & Kumar, 2004).

There are atleast four benefits of using macroscopic primitives. Firstly, implicit coordination, which refers to the coordination of a pattern comprising of mobile robots, need not be specified externally. Coordination is achieved as a result of varying the macroscopic primitives. Secondly, Group behaviour definition, which refers to the collective behaviour of the group, is possible by controlling the macroscopic primitives. The individual behaviour of the units is affected by the variation in the macroscopic primitive. Thirdly, Adaptability, which refers to the ability of the group to adjust to change of internal or external circumstances, can be affected by macroscopic primitives. Fourthly, Stability, which refers to the factor by which the robot group maintains a pattern, can be controlled by using macroscopic primitives to dampen the propagation of errors.

The mathematical model is realized by considering macroscopic primitives. The macroscopic primitives are separated into primary and secondary primitives. Primary macroscopic primitives are basic or fundamental elements. They are considered as input variables to the model and are irreducible to simpler parameters or expressions and therefore termed as independent primitives. Secondary macroscopic primitives are derived from other primitives of the mathematical model. Hence, these primitives are termed as dependent primitives.

The primary macroscopic primitives of the model proposed in this paper are the total number of robots, angular separation, formation radius and elongation. The total number of robots in a polygonal pattern, given by n, equates to the number of vertices of a polygon or the roots of the complex equation. Angular separation is an important factor that determines the coordinates for positioning robots in a polygonal pattern. Angular separation, denoted by θ, is a measure of the angular spacing between adjacent robots of a pattern. Formation radius, denoted by r, is the radius of the circumscribing circle of the polygonal pattern. This primitive determines the area occupied by the pattern. Elongation ratio of a pattern, denoted by e, is a ratio of magnitudes of the major and minor axis of the pattern and quantifies the shape transforming behaviour of a pattern. The symmetry of a pattern can also be described by the elongation ratio.

The secondary macroscopic primitives are linear distance and shaping radii. The distance between adjacent robots in the polygon is a constant if the polygon is regular. To compute the distance between robots, the coordinate positions of the robot need to be known. The centroid of the pattern, (h, k), is used to compute the coordinates of robots. Further, the Euclidean distance between adjacent robots A and B is given by $d_{AB} = \sqrt{(x_B - x_A)^2 + (y_B - y_A)^2}$. Hence, linear distance is dependent on the position coordinates of robots.

The shaping radii along the x and y axis, s_x and s_y respectively determine the measure of deflation or inflation of a pattern laterally and longitudinally. The magnitudes of elongation and formation radius are useful to determine the shaping radii of a pattern and are given by $s_x = re$ and $s_y = \frac{r}{e}$. The equations that define the shaping radii are also given by

$x_B = h + s_x cos\theta$ and $y_B = k + s_y sin\theta$. Hence, orientation radii are dependent on formation radius and elongation.

4. Pattern transformation

Having established a model for pattern formation in swarm systems it is also necessary to study and further develop the model to achieve transformation of patterns. This section defines the challenge of transformation and presents four cases of transformation.

4.1 Definition

Consider a rigid pattern P with geometric relationships represented as G_P which is macroscopic in nature such that the relationship G_P can be manipulated by varying some macroscopic parameter that relates to the pattern P. The pattern P comprises N robots such that their positions are given by $p_i(x_i, y_i)$ where $p_i \in R^2$ and $i = 1, 2, \ldots, N$. Pattern P transforms into the pattern Q with geometric constraints or relationships represented as G_Q which is macroscopic in nature such that the relationship G_Q can be manipulated by varying some macroscopic parameter that relates to the pattern Q. The pattern Q also comprises N robots such that the position of the robotic agents is given by $q_i(x_i, y_i)$ where $q_i \in R^2$ and $i = 1, 2, \ldots, N$.

The function which enables the transformation of the pattern P to Q is given by $f(P) = Q$. In other words, $f(p_1(x_1, y_1), p_2(x_2, y_2), \ldots, p_N(x_N, y_N)) = q_1(x_1, y_1), q_2(x_2, y_2), \ldots, q_N(x_N, y_N)$. The application of an inverse transformation function on the transformed pattern Q yields the pattern P, given by $f^{-1}(Q) = P$. The transformation on the pattern also results in a transformation of the geometrical relationships from to between the participating agents in the pattern.

4.2 Transformation cases

Four cases of transformation based on the above definition are derived by imposing restrictions on the geometrical constraints.

4.2.1 Case 1

$G_Q = G_P$ after a transformation that involves repositioning all agents. This case is relevant when robotic agents in the pattern have repositioned, yet the geometrical pattern has not changed. Such a transformation is termed as Elementary transformation in this paper. This term also refers to those transformations very basic in nature. For instance, a swarm could be rotated with respect to its centroid or translated such that all robotic agents have repositioned themselves. Though the orientation of the pattern has changed, the configuration of the pattern remains unaltered. Mathematically, the case of elementary transformation would be such that $G_Q = G_P$ and $\forall i : p_i(x_i, y_i) \neq q_i(x_i, y_i)$.

4.2.2 Case 2

$G_Q = G_P$ after a transformation without repositioning all agents. This case considers the rotation or translation of the swarm with respect to a few robotic agent whose position remains fixed. This case is also classified under elementary transformation, yet repositioning of all agents has not occurred. Mathematically, this case of elementary transformation would be such that $G_Q = G_P$ and $\exists i : p_i(x_i, y_i) = q_i(x_i, y_i)$.

4.2.3 Case 3

$G_Q \neq G_P$ after a transformation that involves repositioning all agents. This relates to the case when the geometrical constraints of the pattern have changed and a new pattern has emerged. It is termed a geometric transformation. This concept is relevant when robotic agents in the pattern reposition to result in a geometry change. For instance, the shape of a swarm could be geometrically transformed from a polygon to a line. It is interesting to note that the scaling of a pattern would result in a geometric transformation, since the geometrical constraints are dissimilar in both cases. Mathematically, the case of geometrical transformation would be such that $G_Q \neq G_P$ and $\forall i : p_i(x_i, y_i) \neq q_i(x_i, y_i)$.

4.2.4 Case 4

$G_Q \neq G_P$ after transformation without repositioning all agents. This case considers the geometric transformation such that the position of one or more than one robotic agent remains fixed. It is classified under geometric transformation, yet repositioning of all agents has not occurred. Mathematically, the case of geometrical transformation would be such that $G_Q \neq G_P$ and $\exists i : p_i(x_i, y_i) = q_i(x_i, y_i)$.

Cases 1 and 2 relate to elementary transformation of the pattern. In these cases, the pattern remains rigid in nature, since the geometric constraint or relationship persists even after elementary transformation. Cases 3 and 4 deal with geometric transformation and introduce flexibility into rigid patterns.

4.3 Tools for pattern transformation

This section considers two tools for pattern transformation, namely a macroscopic transformation tool and a mathematical transformation tool. Cases 1, 3 and 4 of transformation are considered in the both the transformation tools. To achieve geometrical transformation, a series of operations are performed in both methods. Case 2 of transformation will be reported elsewhere.

4.3.1 Tool 1: macroscopic transformation

The first transformation tool proposed in this section which is inclusive of both elementary and geometric transformations considers cases 1, 3 and 4 of transformation and are applied on the swarm model. This tool varies a macroscopic parameter, namely the formation radius (along x and y axis) of the swarm model to facilitate transformation. A sequence of operations is performed on the swarm model to obtain a transformed pattern and is shown in figure 2.

The set of operations are:

a. *Rotation*: The initial step of rotation of the model is performed to achieve collision avoidance during the next step. Apredefined angle offset is used to rotate the swarm. Though the robots are repositioned, the operation results in the same polygonal pattern with a different orientation from the former. Here, the concept of elementary transformation is introduced. Though all robots were repositioned in this operation, a geometric transformation is not evident since the shape of the pattern is retained. Though a geometric transformation is not evident, yet an elementary transformation of case 1 is achieved in this step.

b. *Macroscopic Parameter Operation*: Following a rotation operation, the macroscopic parameter is set to be modified. Deflating the model along the y-axis would result in a deformed polygonal pattern. The deflation of the model is performed by decrementing the magnitude of the formation radius along the y-axis. When deflation has reached its maximum value, the robotic agents have aligned themselves entirely along the x-axis. Maximum deflation is achieved when the formation radius value along any axis vanishes. An inflation operation along the other perpendicular axis simultaneously while deflating would result in a pattern with larger inter-linear distance between the agents (a measure for avoiding collisions). This variation is possible due to the notion of flexibility in rigid patterns.

c. *Further Rotation*: This step is performed to achieve equidistance between the participating agents. Though the pattern has transformed its shape by this step, the participating agents are still governed by the rules of the swarm model. A corrective rotation measure would ensure that the agents are loosely equidistant.

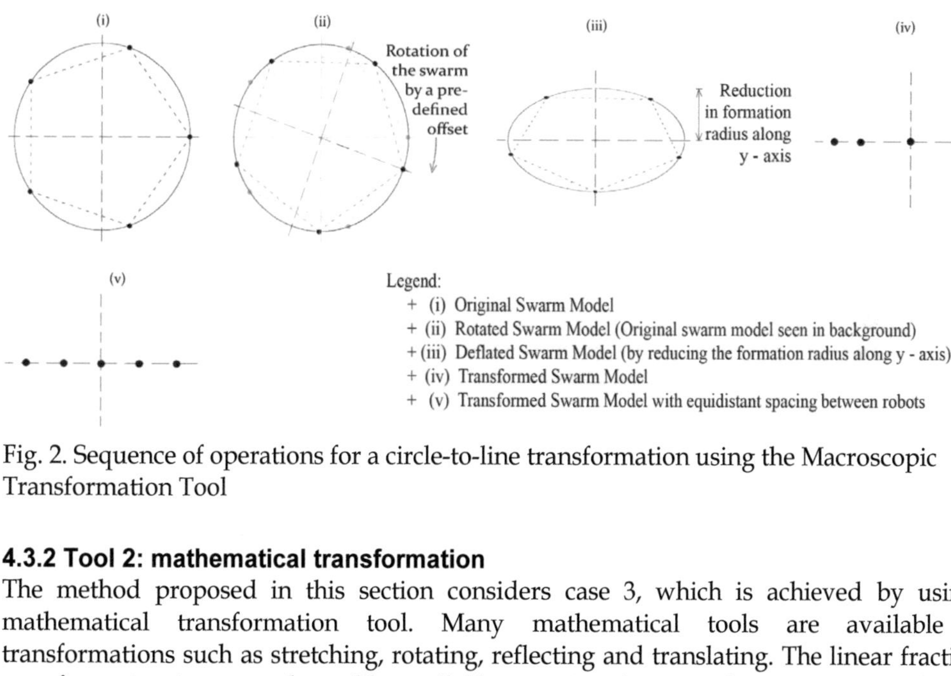

Fig. 2. Sequence of operations for a circle-to-line transformation using the Macroscopic Transformation Tool

4.3.2 Tool 2: mathematical transformation

The method proposed in this section considers case 3, which is achieved by using a mathematical transformation tool. Many mathematical tools are available for transformations such as stretching, rotating, reflecting and translating. The linear fractional transformation is one such readily available mapping function that maps a set of points from one plane to another. The transformation is given by $\frac{az+b}{cz+d}$, where z, a, b, c and d are complex numbers satisfying $ad - bc \neq 0$. The linear fractional transformation is also known as a Moebius transformation (Kreyszig, 2006).

The transformation functions are applied onto the swarm pattern which is polygonal in shape. Since the vertices of the polygonal pattern lie on the circle circumscribing the pattern, a circleto-line and a line-to-circle are the two transformation tools employed on the complex plane. However, the transformation function cannot be applied directly to the swarm pattern since the mathematical function is applicable on the local frame of reference and the swarm pattern in the proposed model is defined on the global frame of reference. Hence, a sequence of operations are performed on the swarm pattern to achieve transformation and is shown in figure 3. The set of operations are:

a. *Transformation from global to local frame of reference*: The frame of reference of the swarm is temporarily transformed from the global to a local frame. The local frame of reference considered is such that the circumscribing circle is divided into four equal quadrants. Hence the centroid of the pattern lies on the origin position of the local frame.

b. *Discrete Transformation*: This step applies the mathematical transformation function on the swarm model. The transformation of a circle to a line is obtained from $w = i\frac{1-z}{1+z}$. Applying the equation on the Euclidean plane, the mapping function is deduced as $\left(\frac{2y}{1+x^2+y^2}, \frac{1-x^2-y^2}{1+x^2+y^2}\right)$. The transformation from a line to a circle is applied by considering a special case of the Moebius transformation. The transformation $w = \frac{1}{z}$ maps every straight line or circle onto a circle or straight line. It is also known as the inversion in the unit circle or reciprocal transformation. Applying the equation on the Euclidean plane, the mapping function is otherwise written as $\left(\frac{x}{x^2+y^2}, \frac{y}{x^2+y^2}\right)$. The destination coordinates obtained by the mathematical functions are the coordinates to which individual robot agents need to reposition while the pattern transforms. However, it is evident that these transformation functions are discrete in nature yielding only one set of destination coordinate rather than sub-goals or intermediate destination coordinates.

c. *Transformation from local to global frame of reference with magnification*: The destination coordinates are obtained on the local frame of reference. Hence, the local frame needs to be shifted to the global frame of reference. Since the mathematical functions considered in operation (b) are reducing functions (destination coordinates reduce the span of the pattern), a magnification ratio is used in the local frame to achieve gain in the destination coordinates.

d. *Path planning by discretization*: Since the achieved destination coordinate set is discrete, the major challenge in repositioning agents is to plan their path to the destination coordinates. In this paper, the technique adopted to reposition robots is along straight line trajectories without collisions. The straight line path between the agent and its estimated destination is discretized. Figure 4 illustrates the straight line discretization process. The domain values of the path are sliced to extrapolate the range values. This relates to the underlying principle of Discrete Event Simulations (DEVS). The potential of DEVS in path planning for robots has been reported by (Arikan et al., 2001).

5. Simulation studies

Simulation studies were pursued to validate and visualize the mathematical model and tools employed for pattern transformation. The feasibility of the proposed approach was

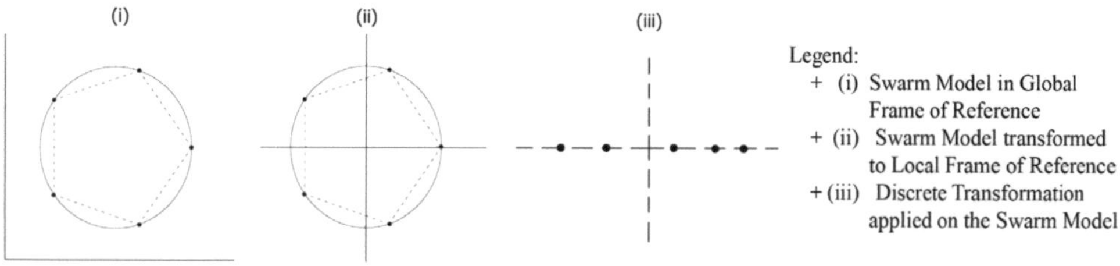

Fig. 3. Sequence of operations for a circle-to-line transformation using the Mathematical Transformation Tool

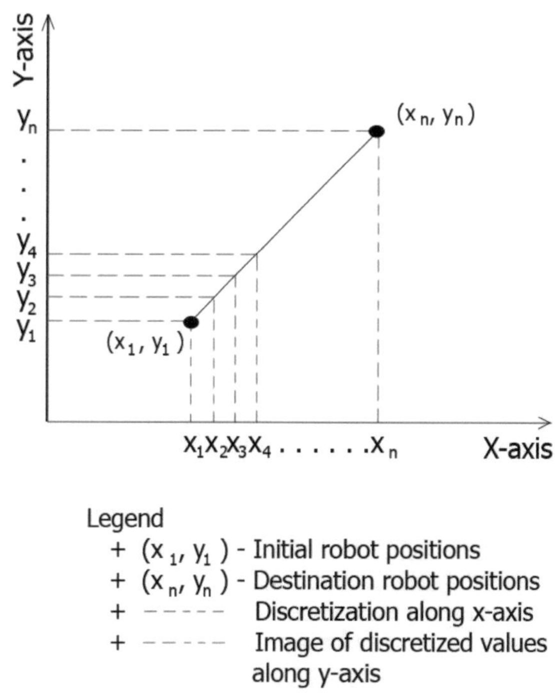

Fig. 4. Discretization of a straight line

validated on the Processing (Processing website, 2010) and Traer Physics (Traer Physics website, 2010) environment. Processing is an open source programming language and environment enabling visualizations for learning and prototyping, where as Traer Physics is a particle physics simulation engine for Processing.

The Traer physics library has provisions for modeling a particle system, particles, springs and attractive or repulsive forces (Traer Physics website, 2010). The particle system enables to prototype particles and forces. Particles represent objects which are stationary or dynamic in an environment and can be modelled using four properties, namely mass, position, velocity and age. Springs on the other hand can connect two particles and prevent collisions. Springs are characterized by three properties, namely rest length, strength and damping. Attractions or repulsions pull particles together or apart and have two properties, namely strength and minimum distance. The simulations reported in this paper employ the particle system, particles and attractive or repulsive forces.

5.1 Experimental setup

To establish a pattern, the particles of the pattern are modelled in an open environment such that they are acted upon by forces, namely macro and micro level forces of attraction and repulsion. The macro level forces include repulsive forces, which act on the centroid of the swarm and maintains the stability of the pattern. The forces of repulsion are generated from obstacles (modeled as forces) in the environment. All robotic agents align themselves around the centroid with respect to the forces forming a virtual structure polygonal pattern. Obstacles in the path of the pattern are detected by the computation of the net force acting on the group of robots. Beyond a maximum threshold of force, the pattern reacts appropriately by transforming its shape to avoid obstacles. The pattern regains its polygonal shape when the net force acting on the centroid decreases below a minimum threshold value, such as when the pattern has escaped from obstacles. The inter-agent bonding force and the forces of interaction with the centroid contributed to the micro level forces. The pattern generates a propulsive force to trace paths against repulsive forces.

The experimental setup comprised a tunnel through which the swarm had to displace. The walls of the tunnel generated repulsive forces and acted as the obstacle. The swarm initiated its motion from the left of the tunnel and aimed to reach a goal beyond the tunnel on the right side. While attempting to pass through the tunnel, the swarm transformed its shape to avoid obstacles and avoided collisions between agents. Both transformation tools discussed in the previous section were implemented.

First of all, the macroscopic transformation tool which consists of a sequence of three operations was implemented. Firstly, the swarm model was rotated to avoid collisions while deflating. Table 1 illustrates the different rotation angles that were applied on the swarm. Higher value angles resulted in collisions for most patterns. Angles less than 15 degrees proved effective for collision avoidance.

Secondly, the macroscopic parameters were varied. This variation resulted in deflation or inflation of the pattern (along x or y axis). Thirdly, a corrective rotation was applied to avoid agents from colliding against each other. Hence by transformation of the pattern, the swarm successfully displaced itself through the obstacle path. Figure 5 is a snapshot of the

Angle Offset / No. of Robots	15°	30°	45°	60°
3	-	-	-	1
4	-	-	2	-
5	-	1	-	-
6	-	3	-	3

Table 1. Rotation Values & Estimated Collisions

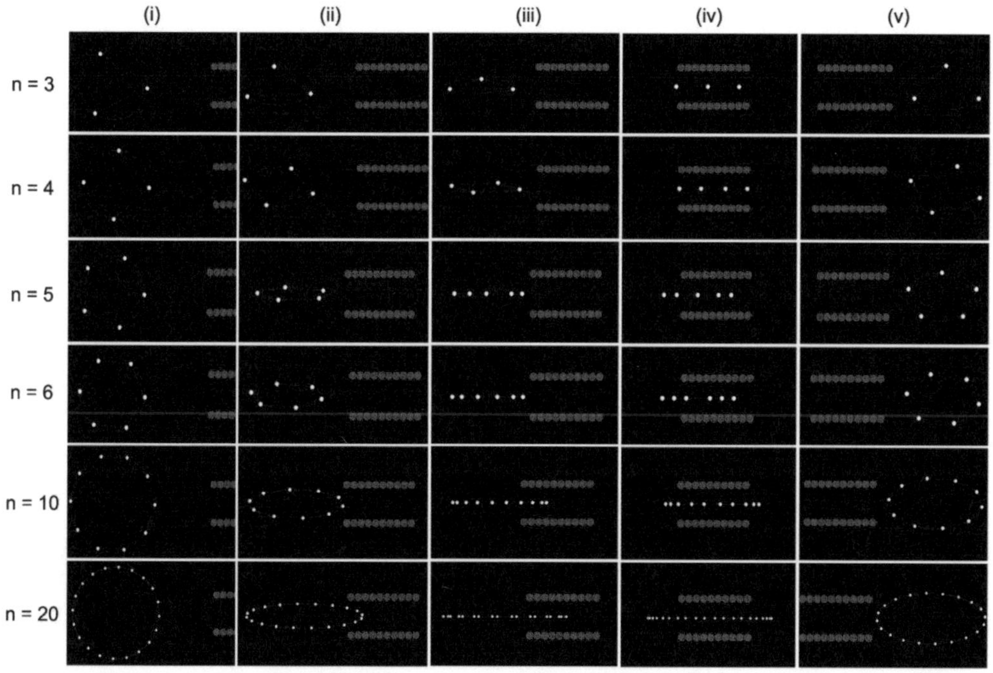

Fig. 5. Simulation results for transformation using Macroscopic Transformation tool. (i) Rotated swarm model for various number of robots, (ii) Deflation of the model along the y-axis (For n = 10 and 20, inflation along x-axis performed), (iii) Transformed pattern without corrective rotation measure, (iv) Transformed pattern after corrective rotation measure is applied (Except for n = 3 and 4, since equidistance is more or less achieved), (v) Inverse transformation by inflation back to original pattern.

simulation studies for n = 3 to 6, 10 and 20 robots transforming when the first transformation tool is employed.

It is observed that a geometric transformation is obtained by performing a sequence of operations which consists of an elementary transformation. A regular pattern transforms to an irregular polygonal pattern while reconfiguring.

Then, the mathematical transformation tool which consists of a sequence of four steps was implemented. Firstly, the swarm pattern was transformed from the global to a local frame such that the centroid of the pattern lies on the origin of local frame of reference. Hence, the pattern is equally spanned over the four quadrants in the local frame of reference, which was necessary for proper implementation of the transformation functions.

Secondly, the discrete transformation function was applied on the microscopic property, namely the position coordinates of the individual robots in the pattern. The transformation from a circle to line was employed in order for the pattern to pass through the tunnel in the environment. Beyond the obstacles, the transformation from a line to circle was employed. Both transformation operations yield a set of discrete destination coordinates for each robot.

Thirdly, transformation from the local to global frame of reference was performed. The destination coordinates obtained in the local frame of reference were such that the pattern radius is reduced. Hence a magnification of the coordinates in the local frame was performed and further mapped on to the global frame of reference.

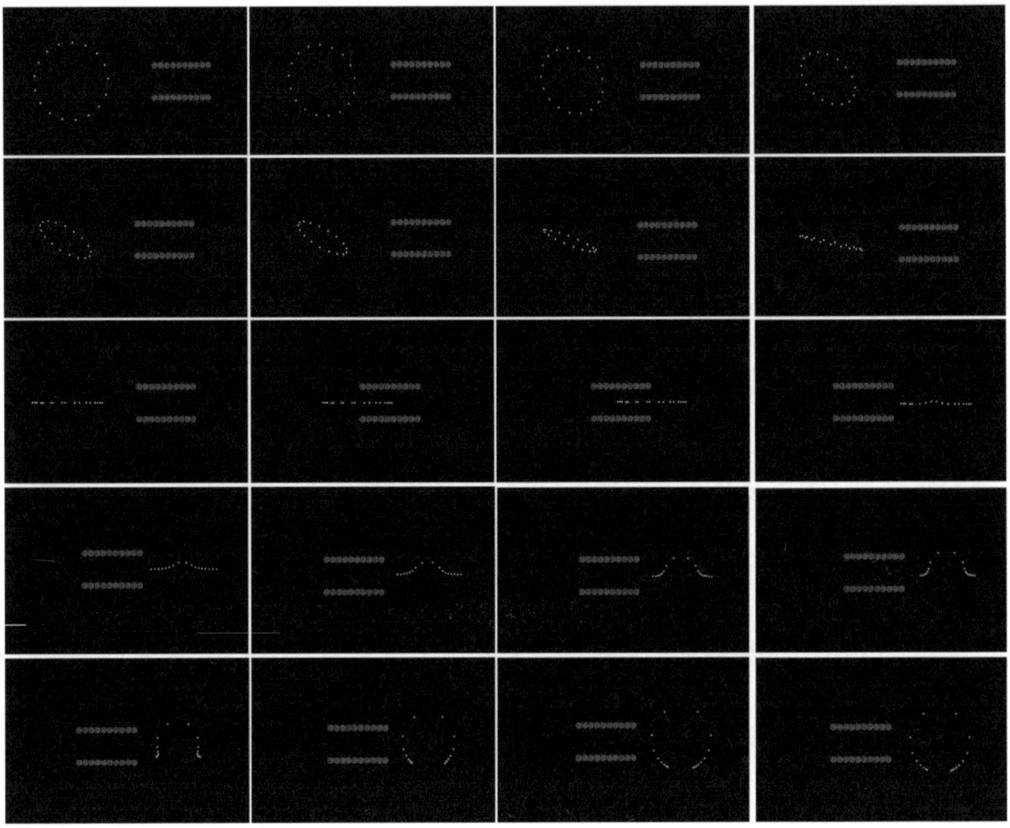

Fig. 6. Simulation studies for transformation using the Mathematical Transformation tool. Firstly, a circle to a line transformation (First three rows excluding the fourth sequence in the third row). Secondly, a line to circle transformation (Fourth sequence of the third row and last two rows).

Fourthly, path planning by discretization was executed. This step is essential to determine the sub goals or intermediate position coordinates. Repositioning the robots to sub-goals or intermediate coordinates is a computationally expensive process. Straight line trajectories from agents to calculated destination coordinates without collisions were considered in the work reported in paper. Figure 6 is a snapshot of the simulation studies for 17 robots that transform shape when the second transformation tool is employed.

It is observed that the circle to line transformation yielded a pattern in which robotic agents were loosely equidistant. The line to circle transformation employing the reciprocal transformation yielded a polygon irregular in nature. This was due to the nature of the reciprocal transformation which was anticipated.

It was observed that in both methods, the swarm successfully displaced itself through the obstacle path by transforming shape. The transformed patterns were loosely equidistant. Collision avoidance between repositioning agents is not implicitly guaranteed. Hence, atleast one operation in both methods ensured collision avoidance. The geometrical transformation of a circle to a line in both cases was achieved by transforming a regular polygonal pattern to an irregular pattern by repositioning agents. The observations are consistent with the theoretical studies presented in the previous section and according to the authors expectation.

5.2 Discussion

The transformation methods presented in this chapter are feasible tools for transforming patterns. However, it is noted that the mathematical tool employing Moebius transformation is not strictly macroscopic in nature; the microscopic properties of the swarm units are taken into consideration. For example, path planning of individual robots is necessary to reposition the robots. The method is not advantageous for small number of robots in the pattern. Moreover the mathematical transformation tool is a discrete transformation method. Hence, discretizing and quantizing the path for repositioning robots are required which are both computationally expensive operations unsupported and unwarranted on minimal processing swarm units. Therefore global planning is required thereby increasing wireless communication overheads. A high bandwidth for communication and synchronized and consistent communication with a centralized unit are challenges in realizing the mathematical tool in real time.

On the other hand, the macroscopic tool considers the group behaviour of the swarm system. Hence, individual robots need not be addressed, thereby eliminating microscopic parameter operations. For example, transformation using the macroscopic tool is obtained by a sequence of operations performed on the entire swarm pattern rather than considering individual robot path planning. The macroscopic tool is also observed to be consistent in the time taken for transformation, and is also continuous thereby reducing computations for individual robot planning. This tool would hence offer better synchronization between the swarm units since local planning is sufficient. Hence wireless communication overheads are relatively less compared to the mathematical tool.

By implementing an approach that could incorporate the macroscopic tool in a real time robot system, planning overheads for individual robots could be minimized. However, a mathematical transformation function is advantageous since it belongs to an analytical class of tools and mathematical analysis is possible. Therefore, this approach will also be explored in future work.

6. Conclusion

In summary, a review of the literature has revealed that there are at least eight challenges in pattern formation that need to be addressed. Further, a single mathematical model that aims to address these challenges are unavailable since research in this direction has not been a key focus. Hence, the work reported in this chapter is motivated by the need for developing a mathematical model that attempts to address the challenges in pattern formation. Particularly, transformation of patterns has been considered in this chapter. A mathematical model for pattern formation based on the complex plane is proposed. A definition for transformation, four cases of transformation and two tools for transforming patterns in the mathematical model are proposed. Simulation studies employing a particle physics simulation engine has incorporated the mathematical model. These studies have proven that most challenges in pattern formation can be addressed using the mathematical model, thereby validating the feasibility of the model. The challenge of role assignment, though not considered in this chapter, is reported elsewhere (Varghese & McKee, 2008a). Scalability studies are not presented in this chapter. Coordinating multiple patterns using the mathematical model need to be addressed in the future.

7. References

Arikan, O.; Chenney, S. & Forsyth, D. A. (2001). Efficient Multi-Agent Path Planning, *Proceedings of the Eurographic Workshop on Computer Animation and Simulation*, Manchester, UK, pp. 151- 162.

Arkin R. C. (1998). *Behavior-Based Robotics*. The MIT Press.

Balch, T. & Arkin, R. C. (1998). Behavior-based formation control for multi robot teams, *IEEE Transactions on Robotics and Automation*, pp. 926–939.

Balch, T. & Hybinette, M. (2000). Social potentials for scalable multi-robot formations, *Proceedings of the IEEE International Conference on Robotics and Automation*, pp. 73–80.

Belta, C. & Kumar, V. (2004). Abstraction and Control for Groups of Robots, *IEEE Transactions on Robotics*, pp. 865–875.

Cai, C.; Yang, C.; Zhu, Q. & Liang, Y. (2007). Collision avoidance in multi-robot systems, *Proceedings of the IEEE International Conference on Mechatronics and Automation*, pp. 2795–2800.

Cai, C.; Yang, C.; Zhu, Q. & Liang, Y. (2007). A Fuzzy-based collision avoidance approach for multi-robot systems, *Proceedings of the International Conference on Robotics and Biomimetics*, pp. 1012–1017.

Camazine S.; Deneubourg J. - L.; Franks N. R.; Sneyd J.; Theraulaz G. & Bonabeau E. (2003). *Self-Organization in Biological Systems*, Princeton University Press.

Chaimowicz, L.; Campos, M. F. M. & Kumar, V. (2002). Dynamic Role assignment for cooperative robots, *IEEE International Conference on Robotics and Automation*, pp. 293–298.

Chen, Y. Q. & Wang, Z. (2005). Formation control: a review and a new consideration, *Proceedings of the IEEE International Conference on Intelligent Robots and Systems*, pp. 3181–3186.

Chen, Y. - C. & Wang, Y. - T. (2007). Dynamic role assignment algorithm for robot formation control, *IEEE International Conference on Advanced Intelligent Mechatronics*, pp. 1–6.

Chen, Y. - C. & Wang, Y. - T. (2007). Obstacle avoidance and role assignment algorithms for robot formation control, *Proceedings of the IEEE International Conference on Intelligent Robots and Systems*, pp. 4201 - 4206.

Chen, P.; Song, Z.; Wang, Z. & Chen, Y. Q. (2005). Pattern formation experiments in mobile actuator and sensor, *Proceedings of the IEEE International Conference on Intelligent Robots and Systems*, pp. 735–740.

Cheng, J.; Cheng, W. & Nagpal, R. (2005). Robust and Self-Repairing Formation Control for Swarms of Mobile Agents, *Proceedings of the 20th AAAI National Conference on Artificial Intelligence*, pp. 59–64.

Fox, D.; Burgard, W. & Thrun, S. (1997). The dynamic window approach to collision avoidance, *IEEE Robotics and Automation Magazine*, pp. 23–33.

Habib, M. K.; Watanabe, K. & Izumi, K. (2007). Biomimetics Robots from Bio-inspiration to Implementation, *Proceedings of the 33rd Annual Conference of the IEEE Industrial Electronics Society*

Hsu, H. C. - H.&Liu, A. (2004). Multiple teams for mobile robot formation control, *Proceedings of the IEEE International Symposium on Intelligent Control*, pp. 168- 173.

Koh,W. L. & Zhou, S. (2007). An Extensible collision avoidance model for realistic self-driven autonomous agents, *Proceedings of the IEEE International Symposium on Distributed Simulation and Real- time applications*, pp. 7-14.

Kreyszig, E. (2006). *Advanced Engineering Mathematics*, 9th Edition, John Wiley & Sons Inc.

Michael, N.; Zavlanos, M. M.; Kumar, V. & Pappas, G. J. (2008). Distributed Multi-Robot task assignment and formation control, *Proceedings of the IEEE International Conference on Robotics and Automation*, pp. 128-133.

Michaud, F.; Letourneau, D.; Guilbert, M. & Valin, J.-M. (2002). Dynamic robot formations using directional visual perception, *Proceedings of the IEEE International Conference on Intelligent Robots and System*, pp. 2740-2745.

Naffin, D. J.; Akar, M. & Sukhatme, G. S. (2004). Lateral and Longitudinal Stability for Decentralized Formation Control, *Proceedings of the International Symposium on Distributed Autonomous Robotic Systems*, France.

Ogren, P. & Leonard, N. E. (2003). Obstacle avoidance in formation, *Proceedings of the IEEE International Conference on Robotics and Automation*, Taipei, pp. 2492-2497.

Poduri, S. & Sukhtame, G. S. (2007). Achieving Connectivity through Coalescence in Mobile Robot Networks, *Proceedings of the first International Conference on Robot Communication and Coordination*, Greece.

Processing website: http://www.processing.org

Sahin, E. & Spears W. M. (2005). *Swarm Robotics*, Springer Lecture Notes in Computer Science 3342.

Seder, M. & Petrovic, I. (2007). Dynamic Window based approach to mobile robot motion control in the presence of moving obstacles, *Proceedings of the IEEE International Conference on Robotics and Automation*, Italy, pp. 1986-1991.

Shao, J.; Wang, L. & Xie, G. (2006). Flexible Formation Control for Obstacle Avoidance Based on Numerical Flow Field, *Proceedings of the IEEE Conference on Decision and Control*, pp. 5986-5991.

Traer Physics website: http://www.cs.princeton.edu/ traer/physics

Varghese, B. & McKee, G. T. (2008). A Macroscopic Model for Multi-agent Pattern Formation, *Proceedings of the 6th EuropeanWorkshop on Multi-agent Systems*, Bath, UK, pp. 423-433.

Varghese, B. & McKee, G. T. (2008). A Mathematical Model, Implementation and study of a swarm conglomerate and its formation control, *Proceedings of the Towards Autonomous Robotic Systems Conference*, Edinburgh, pp. 156-162.

Wang, J.; Wu, X. - B. & Xu, Z. - L. (2006). Decentralized formation control and obstacle avoidance based on potential field method, *Proceedings of the fifth International Conference on machine Learning and Cybernetics*, pp. 803–808.

2

Formation and Obstacle Avoidance in the Unknown Environment of Multi-Robot System

Tao Zhang, Xiaqin Li, Yi Zhu, Song Chen, Yu Cheng and Jingyan Song
Department of Automation, Tsinghua University, Beijing 100084
Division of Control Science and Engineering, Tsinghua National Laboratory for Information Science and Technology, Beijing 100084
National Key Laboratory of Flight Vehicle Control Integrated Technology, Xi'an 710065
China

1. Introduction

Nowdays, formation and obstacle avoidance issue of multi-robot system has attracted many researchers' interests due to its application background. Originally, many algorithms have been proposed for obstacle avoidance of a single robot. With the increasing requests on the application of multi-robot system for complex tasks, the obstacle avoidance of multi-robot system becomes more and more crucial (Koivo, 1998). In addition, it is found that realizing obstacle avoidance of each robot in multi-robot system is not enough. Further, it requests multiple robots to have the ability to avoid obstacle while keeping formation. If a multi-robot system is in the unknown environment, it becomes more difficult to realize obstacle avoidance while keeping formation. This is just the topic of this paper.

Concerning about the formation of multi-robot system, there mainly have the following algorithms. (Ren, 2005)(Prijanian, 1999) proposed a behavior-based algorithm. In this algorithm, some expected essential behaviors are defined for robot. When the sensor of robot is stimulated by the outer environment, the output response of robot is the expected behavior according to the input of sensor information. The selection of behaviors of robot is based on some rules and each behavior has its specific purpose or task. The behavior-based algorithm can obtain real time feedback and it has complete distributed control structure. The collaboration of robot is implemented by sharing the knowledge of relative position, status, etc., among robots. Therefore, the merits of behavior-based algorithm are parallel, distributed and in real time. The disadvantage of this method is that, it is lack of clear definition of group behavior. It is hard to design the local basic behavior and control rule to synthesize nominated formation, and so on.

Another type of methods is virtual structure method (Anthony, 1997). This method assumes that there is a geometric shape among robots, which is called as virtual structure. During the movement of robots this structure is kept to fix. The merit of this method is that, it is easy to assign the group behavior of robot and it has feedback of formation. However, this method

limits the scale of movement due to the virtual structure and the formation is therefore not so flexible.
The third type of method is leader-following algorithm (Wang, 1991). In this research, this algorithm is adopted to keep the formation due to its merits. This method will be briefly introduced in section 2.
Concerning about obstacle avoidance, there are many algorithms. Artificial potential field algorithm is very suitable for real time control of robot due to its explicit physical implication and simple mathematical description. This method is adopted to realize obstacle avoidance in this research. The fundamental idea will be introduced in section 3.
This paper presents formation and obstacle avoidance in the unknown environment of multi-robot system. With the leader-following algorithm, multi-robot system can form and keep various formations and realize formation transformation. Through artificial potential field algorithm, multi-robot system can successfully avoid obstacle in the unknown environment while keeping formation. The proposed method not only can realize obstacle avoidance of multi-robot system with formation in the unknown environment, but also can be adopted in real time and applicable to many different situations. By means of Pioneer3 mobile robot platform, the simulation and experimental works, which considering various formations and unknown environments, demonstrate the effectiveness of the proposed method.
The organization of the chapter is as below. In section 2, the multi-robot system formation by means of leader-following algorithm is introduced. Section 3 presents the obstacle avoidance of multi-robot system with formation in the unknown environment by means of artificial potential field method. Section 4 shows the simulation and experimental results by use of Pioneer3 mobile robot platform. In the last section V the conclusion is drawn.

2. Multi-robot formation by means of leader-following algorithm

2.1 Leader-following algorithm

Leader-following algorithm is first proposed in (Wang, 1991), which is adopted for the formation control of mobile robot. The fundamental idea is that, in a group composed of multiple robots, one of robots is assigned as the leader and others are followers. The followers are keeping the position and direction with a certain distance to the leader. According to the relative position between leader and follower, it can form different network topology structures, i.e., different formations. In this algorithm, the collaboration of multi-robots is implemented based on the knowledge about the status of leader robot. The leader can control the motion trend of the system. Each follower is controlled with a formation through keeping the limitation of distance, direction angle, etc., with the leader.
The leader-following algorithm can be applicable to various situations. For example, either one leader or more leaders can be assigned. But the leader of the formation of group must be only one. Since the leader-following algorithm is based on the space geometric relation among robots, the merit of this algorithm is that, the behavior of the entire robot group can be controlled as long as the behavior or trajectory of the leader is given. It can simplify the control process of multi-robot system. However, this algorithm has two obvious disadvantages. One is that, there is no clear formation feedback because the leader does not consider other robots' movement during the course of motion. For example, if the leader moves too fast, or the follower is blocked by obstacle, the formation will be destroyed. Under the serious condition, the quality of fulfilling the task may be affected. The second

disadvantage is that, if the leader is failed, the entire formation can not be kept and the consequence will be very serious.

The leader-following algorithm is mainly adopted for the flight of spacecrafts with formation, the collaboration of robot manipulators in the production line, as well as searching in a region by multiple robots, etc.

2.2 Behavior of leader for formation

The task of leader is to lead the entire formation to the destination. By means of the idea of behavior-based algorithm, the control of leader has three behaviors. One is destination-oriented forward walking behavior. The second is obstacle avoidance behavior, which will be introduced in the next section. The third is lock-prevent behavior. The highest priority of the above three behaviors is lock-prevent behavior. And the lowest priority of them is destination-oriented forward walking behavior.

I. Destination-oriented forward walking behavior

In the destination-oriented forward walking behavior, a robot can be regarded as particle. The destination position of leader is defined as (x_{fg}, y_{fg}). The current position is (x_c, y_c). When leader does not reach the destination position, that is $(x_{fg} - x_c)^2 + (y_{fg} - y_c)^2 > \varepsilon$, the velocity of the leader is as below.

$$V_L = \frac{V}{\sqrt{(x_{fg} - x_c)^2 + (y_{fg} - y_c)^2}} \begin{bmatrix} x_{fg} - x_c \\ y_{fg} - y_c \end{bmatrix} \tag{1}$$

II. Lock-prevent behavior

In the process of robot movement to the destination in the environment with obstacles, robot may not continuously move and can not fulfil the task. At this moment, robot is staying at the status of locking. In order to assist robot escape from this status, it is better to define a lock-prevent behavior.

In this research, Pioneer3 mobile robot is adopted to test the proposed method. This kind of robot has defined a lock-prevent behavior, called ArActionStallRecover. When the wheel of the robot is locked, it can move by means of a series of pre-defined actions. Normally, this behavior is set with the highest priority.

2.3 Behavior of follower for formation

The task of follower is to reach the destination following the leader. It only needs to follow the leader and be able to avoid the obstacle, without knowing the position of destination and the route of formation. Therefore, one of important behaviors of follower is to keep the formation. According to (Shao, 2005), the motion function of single mobile robot is as below.

$$\begin{bmatrix} \dot{x}(t) \\ \dot{y}(t) \\ \dot{\phi}(t) \end{bmatrix} = \begin{bmatrix} \cos\phi(t) & 0 \\ \sin\phi(t) & 0 \\ 0 & 1 \end{bmatrix} \begin{bmatrix} v(t) \\ \omega(t) \end{bmatrix} \tag{2}$$

where (x, y, ϕ) denotes the robot position and motion direction in a certain inertial coordinate system. (v, ω) denotes the linear velocity and angular velocity of moving object. A certain point h at the place which has the distance L from the axis line of robot to the center of the object is considered as below. The reason to consider this point is that, this point is always the central position of the sensor of moving object in the experimental platform. The offset point of this axis center is defined as,

$$\begin{cases} x_h = x + L\sin\phi \\ y_h = y + L\cos\phi \\ \phi_h = \phi \end{cases} \tag{3}$$

It can be obtained as below after equation transformation.

$$\begin{bmatrix} \dot{x}_h(t) \\ \dot{y}_h(t) \\ \dot{\phi}_h(t) \end{bmatrix} = \begin{bmatrix} \cos\phi(t) & -L\sin\phi(t) \\ \sin\phi(t) & L\cos\phi t) \\ 0 & 1 \end{bmatrix} \begin{bmatrix} v(t) \\ \omega(t) \end{bmatrix} \tag{4}$$

Based on the above model, a simple leader-following system, illustrated by Fig.1, can be considered, where R_L denotes leader, R_F follower.

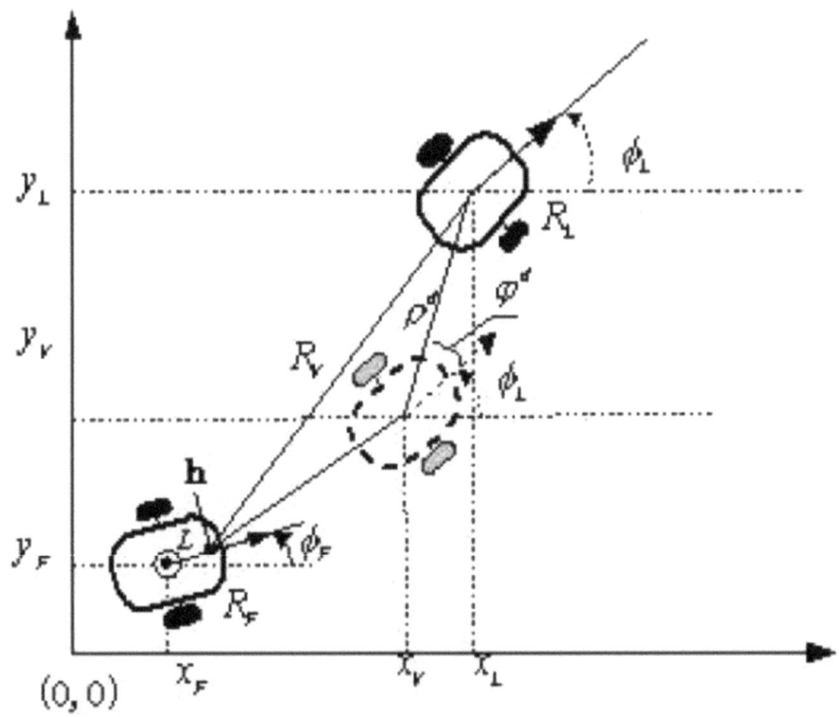

Fig. 1. Simple model of leader-following system

Since the aim of control is to keep the pre-defined distance ρ^d and angle φ^d between the follower R_F and the leader R_L, it can be assumed that there is a virtual leader R_V in the expected formation of the follower R_F. Therefore, what we need to do is to control the follower R_F to move following the virtual leader R_V. By referring to leader R_L, the motion function of R_V is as below.

$$\begin{aligned} \dot{x}_V &= v_L \cos\phi_L + \rho^d \sin(\varphi^d + \phi_L)\phi_L \\ \dot{y}_V &= v_L \sin\phi_L - \rho^d \cos(\varphi^d + \phi_L)\phi_L \\ \phi_V &= \omega_L \end{aligned} \tag{5}$$

Therefore, the tracking error between R_F and R_V is

$$\begin{aligned} \dot{\bar{x}} &= v_L \cos\phi_L - v_F \cos\phi_F + \rho^d \sin(\phi^d + \phi_L)\dot{\phi}_L + L\dot{\phi}_F \sin\phi_F \\ \dot{\bar{y}} &= v_L \sin\phi_L - v_F \sin\phi_F - \rho^d \cos(\phi^d + \phi_L)\dot{\phi}_L - L\dot{\phi}_L \cos\phi_F \\ \dot{\bar{\phi}} &= \omega_L - \omega_F \end{aligned} \tag{6}$$

Where $\bar{x} = x_V - x_F, \bar{y} = y_V - y_F, \bar{\phi} = \phi_V - \phi_F$

The next step is to choose a control law to reduce the tracking error. The control law is selected as below.

$$\begin{aligned} v_F &= v_L \cos\bar{\phi} + k_1(\rho\cos\varphi - \rho^d \cos(\varphi^d + \bar{\phi})) + \rho^d \omega_L \sin(\varphi^d + \bar{\phi}) \\ \omega_F &= \frac{1}{L}[v_L \sin\bar{\phi} - k_2(\rho\sin\varphi - \rho^d \sin(\varphi^d + \bar{\phi})) - \rho^d \omega_L \cos(\varphi^d + \bar{\phi})] \end{aligned} \tag{7}$$

(Shao, 2005) has proved the convergence of this algorithm.

3. Obstacle avoidance of multi-robot system with formation

3.1 Behavior of leader for obstacle avoidance

The behavior of leader for obstacle avoidance is based on artificial potential field (APF) algorithm. The APF algorithm is proposed by Khatib in 1986 (Khatib, 1986). Originally, this method is to solve the problem that manipulator can not bumps into working table when it moves to grasp the object. Later it is found that this method has good effect for mobile robot. It can generate very smooth moving trajectory. The basic idea of this method is to simplify the robot, obstacle and target to be a point respectively. Therefore, the moving space of robot becomes a two-dimensional space. If robot wants to reach the destination, it needs to continuously move to the destination. This movement process can be regarded as a motion in a virtual artificial field of force. The obstacle can generate repulsion to robot and the target point can generate attraction. The resultant of attraction and repulsion can control the moving direction of robot. Any moving direction of any position of robot in the space is determined by the total strengthen of field composed by repulsion field of obstacle and attraction field of target point. The attraction position field function is defined as,

$$U_{att}(X) = k\rho^2(X, X_g) \tag{8}$$

k is positive ratio gain coefficient of position. X, X_g respectively denote the position of robot and target point at the moving space. $\rho(X, X_g) = \|X - X_g\|$ denotes the F_{att} distance between robot and target point. The attraction force of target point is the negative gradient of attraction potential field. It is as below.

$$F_{att} = -\nabla[U_{att}(X)] = k\rho(X, X_g) \tag{9}$$

The repulsion potential field function is as,

$$U_{reg}(X) = \begin{cases} \eta(\frac{1}{\rho(X,X_0)} - \frac{1}{\rho_0})^2 & \rho(X, X_0) \leq \rho_0 \\ 0 & \rho(X, X_0) \geq \rho_0 \end{cases} \tag{10}$$

η is positive ratio gain coefficient of position. $\rho(X, X_0)$ is the shortest distance between robot and obstacle in the moving space. ρ_0 is the biggest distance of obstacle affecting the robot. Its value is determined based on the specific situation between obstacle and target point. Normally, this value is smaller than the half of the distance among each obstacle and the smallest distance between target point and each obstacle. When robot does not reach the target point, the repulsion of obstacle to the target point is as,

$$F_{rep}(X) = -\nabla\left[U_{rep}(X)\right] \begin{cases} -\frac{2\eta}{\rho(X, X)^2}(\frac{1}{\rho(X,X_0)} - \frac{1}{\rho_0}) & \rho(X, X_0) \leq \rho_0 \\ 0 & \rho(X, X_0) \geq \rho_0 \end{cases} \tag{11}$$

The resultant force of robot is as,

$$F = F_{att} + F_{rep} \tag{12}$$

This resultant force determines the moving direction. The graph of force is illustrated as below.

3.2 Behavior of follower for obstacle avoidance

Concerning about obstacle avoidance, assume that each robot has one virtual outer covering. The radius of this outer covering is determined by the maximal velocity of robot as well as braking ability. It is therefore called as protected shell. Any object and other robots should be avoided to enter into the region of this protected shell.

If follower detects out one obstacle in this protected shell, illustrated by Fig.3, it will turn a small angle to avoid the direction of this obstacle. And then it will turn an angle which is necessary to keep the formation. These two angles are combined to calculate the new expected angle φ'^d. The calculation equation is as below.

$$\varphi'^d = \varphi^d - \frac{\varphi^d - \gamma}{\|\varphi^d - \gamma\|} \arccos\sqrt{1 - \frac{(l^d - l)^2}{2(\rho^d)^2}} \tag{13}$$

where l denotes the shortest distance between the center of follower and obstacle. γ denotes the relative angle of the nearest point between the center of robot and obstacle. According to this strategy, follower can not be collided with the nearest obstacle while keeping the expected formation.

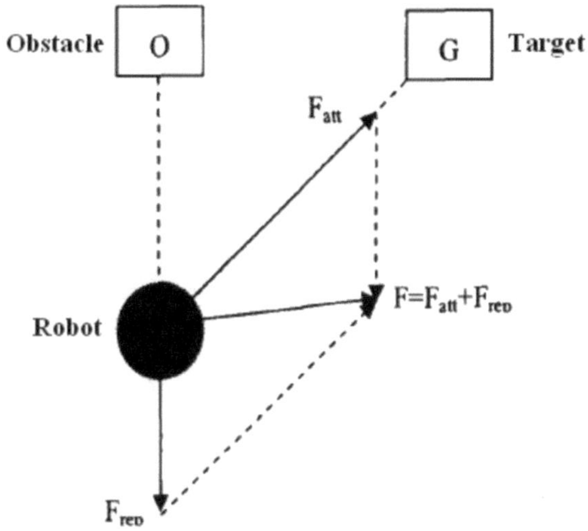

Fig. 2. Force of robot in the artificial potential field

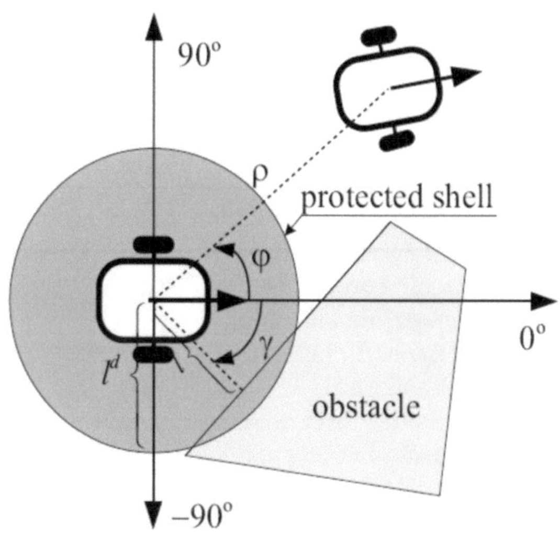

Fig. 3. Obstacle avoidance of follower

4. Simulation and experimental results

4.1 Pioneer3 mobile robot platform

As the simulation and experimental platform, Pioneer3 mobile robot is adopted, which has sonar and hodometers. Sonar is used as the device of measuring distance from obstacle to robot. Hodometer is used as the positioning device to obtain the current position relating to the starting point in real time. Pioneer3 robot has totally 2 sonar cycles, respectively at the front part and rear part of robot. Each sonar cycle has 8 transducers. In this research 8 transducers of front part of sonar cycle and 2 transducers of rear part of sonar cycle are used. The following Fig.4 is the sonar distribution and its identity coordinate of Pioneer3. When positioning concretely, the identity coordinate of Pioneer3 at the starting moment is regarded as the global coordinate for this path planning. In each simulation figure, G denotes target and S starting point.

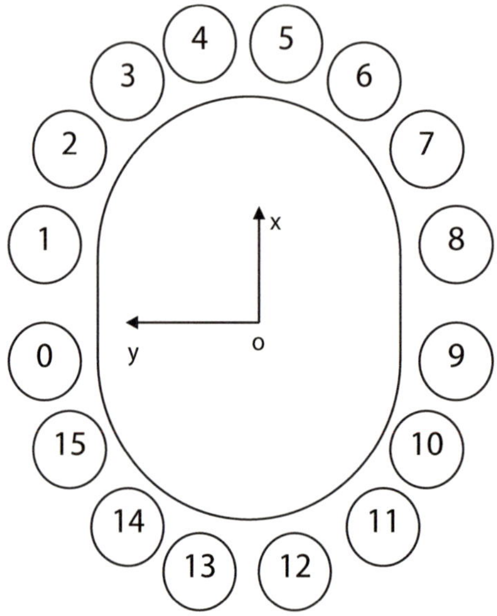

Fig. 4. Sonar distribution and its identity coordinate of Pioneer3

4.2 Simulation and experimental results

Pioneer3 mobile robot platform provides a simulation system MobileSim. In this system, a map can be installed and sensor information can be obtained. User can run the developed program in MobileSim before running on Pioneer3 mobile robot. Actually, it has same effect of running in MobileSim and Pioneer3 mobile robot.

In order to verify the proposed method, the following simulation and experimental works have been carried out by use of MobileSim.

Fig.5 is the simulation results about the obstacle avoidance of leader robot individually.

Fig.6 Illustrates the formation transformation among various formations in the environment without obstacle.

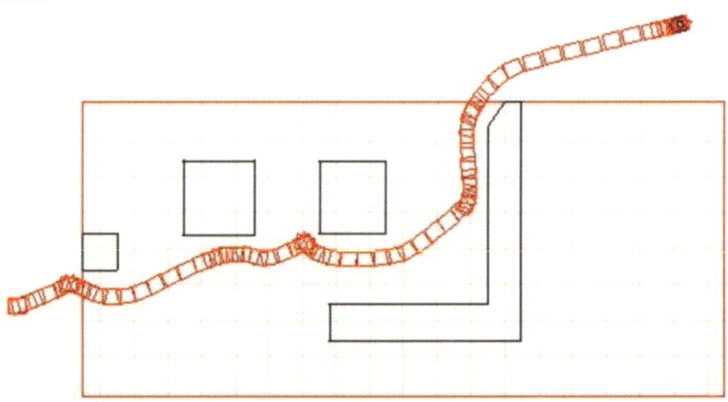

Fig. 5. Obstacle avoidance of leader robot individually

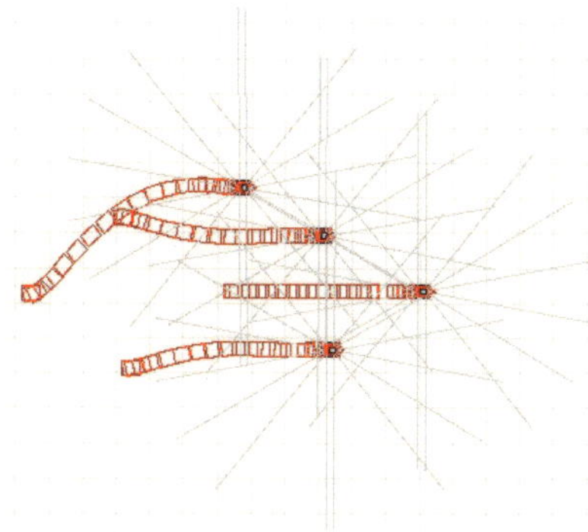

(a) From diamond to triangular formation

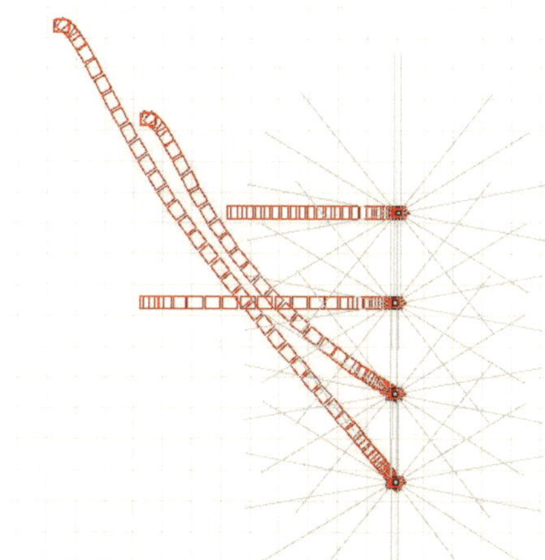

(b) From triangular to straight line formation

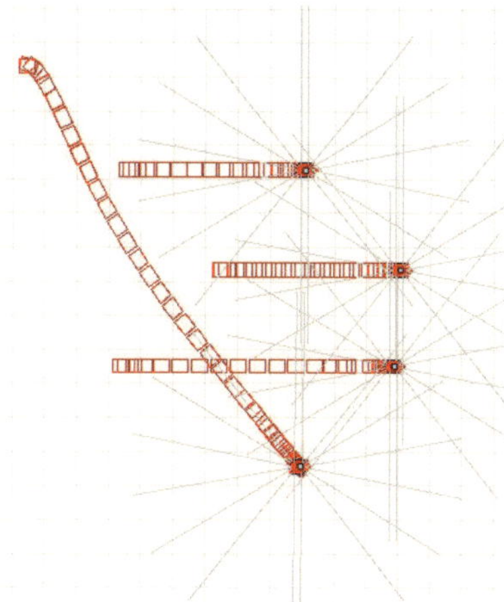

(c) From triangular to trapezoid formation

Fig. 6. Formation transformation

Fig.7 illustrates the simulation results of obstacle avoidance of two robots with formation. Fig.8 illustrates the experimental results of the proposed method in the Pioneer3 mobile robot.

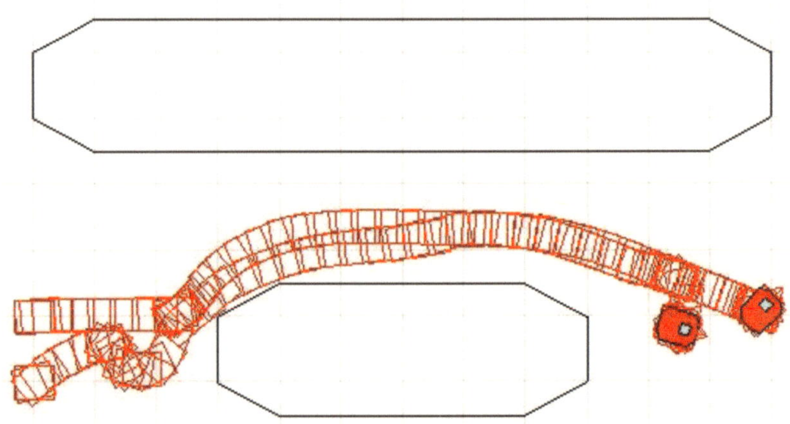

(a) Passing through a channel of two robots

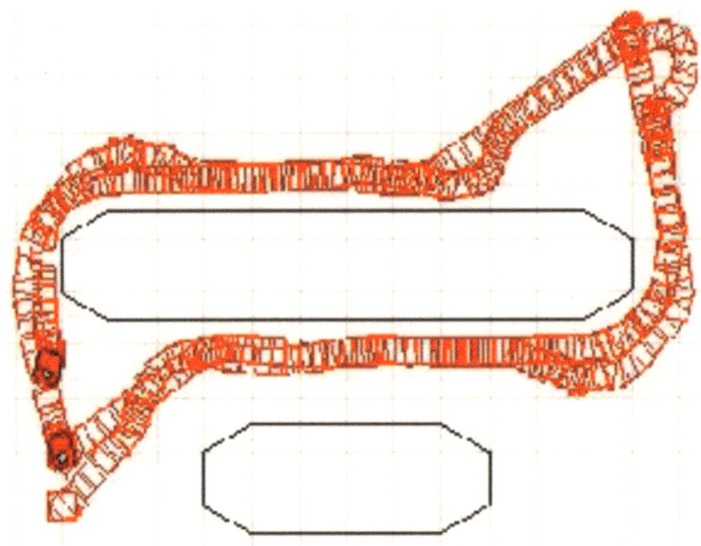

(b) Going there and back of two robots

Fig. 7. Obstacle avoidance of two robots

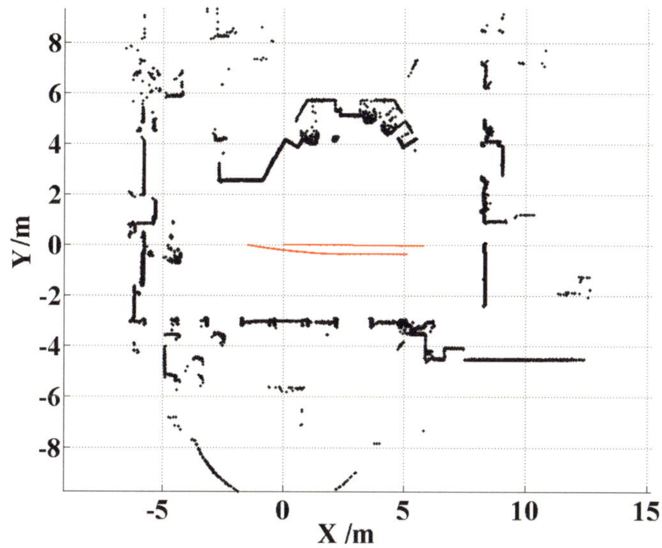

(a) Formation of two robots

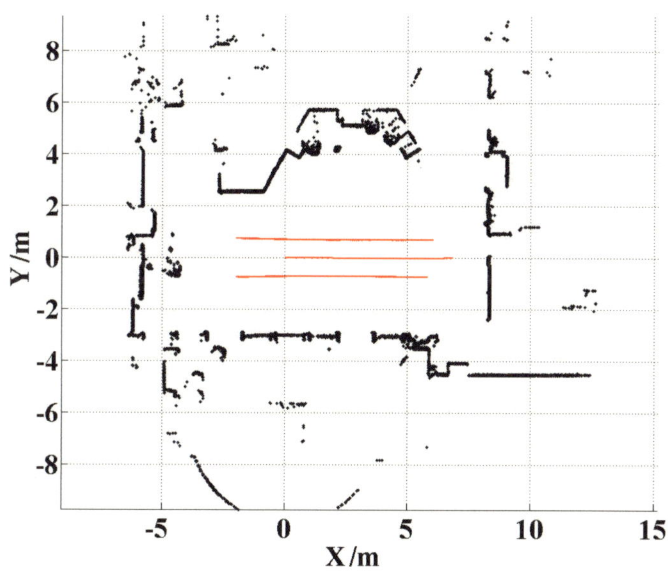

(b) Formation of three robots

Fig. 8. Experimental results

5. Conclusions

This paper introduces formation and obstacle avoidance in the unknown environment of multi-robot system. With the leader-following algorithm, multi-robot system can form and keep various formations and realize formation transformation. Through artificial potential field algorithm, multi-robot system can successfully avoid obstacle in the unknown environment while keeping formation. The proposed method not only can realize obstacle avoidance of multi-robot system with formation in the unknown environment, but also can be adopted in real time and applicable to many different situations. By means of Pioneer3 mobile robot platform, the simulation and experimental works, which considering various formations and unknown environment, demonstrate the effectiveness of the proposed method. In the future research, we will further consider more complicated environment with various types of obstacles. In addition, we will propose new method to optimize the movement of multiple robots with formation in order to improve autonomous and adaptive features of multi-robot system.

6. References

Anthony, L. M. & Tan, K. H. (1997). High precision formation control of mobile robots using virtual structures autonomous, *Autonomuous Robots*, Vol. 4, pp.260-266.

Khatib, O. (1986). Real-time obstacle avoidance for manipulators and mobile robot, *International Journal of Robotics Research*, Vol. 5, No. 1, pp. 90-98.

Koivo, A. J. & Bekey, G. A. (1998). Report of workshop on coordinated multiple robots: planning, control and application, *Robotic and Automation*, Vol. 14, No. 1, pp.91-93.

Pirjanian. (1999). Behavior coordination mechanisms state of the art, *Technical Report*, Institute of Robotics and Intelligent Systems, School of Engineering, University of Southern California.

Ren, D. H. & Lu, G. Z. (2005). Consideration on formation control, *Control and Decision Making*, Vol. 20, No. 6, pp.601-606. (in Chinese)

Shao, J.; Xie, G.; Yu, J.; et al. (2005). Leader-following formation control of multiple mobile robots, *Proceedings of the 2005 IEEE International Symposium on Intelligent Control*, pp.808-814.

Wang, P. K. C. (1991). Navigation strategies for multiple autonomous mobile robots moving in formation, *Journal of Robotic Systems*, Vol. 8, No. 2, pp. 177-195.

3

Distributed Adaptive Control for Networked Multi-Robot Systems

Abhijit Das and Frank L. Lewis
Automation and Robotics Research Institute, University of Texas at Arlington, Fort Worth USA

1. Introduction

Synchronization behavior among agents is found in flocking of birds, schooling of fish, and other natural systems. Synchronization among coupled oscillators was studied by (Kuramoto 1975). Much work has extended consensus and synchronization techniques to manmade systems such as UAV to perform various tasks including surveillance, moving in formation, etc. We refer to consensus and synchronization in terms of control of manmade dynamical systems. Early work on cooperative decision and control for distributed systems includes (Tsitsiklis 1984). The reader is referred to the book and survey papers (Ren & Beard 2008; Ren, Beard et al., 2005; Olfati-Saber et al., 2007; Ren, Beard et al., 2007). Consensus has been studied for systems on communication graphs with fixed or varying topologies and communication delays. See (Olfati-Saber & Murray 2004; Fax & Murray 2004; Ren & Beard 2005; Jadbabaie et al., 2003), which proposed basic synchronizing protocols for various communication topologies.

Early work on consensus studied leaderless consensus or the *cooperative regulator problem*, where the consensus value reached depends on the initial conditions of the node states and cannot be controlled. On the other hand, the *cooperative tracker problem* seeks consensus or synchronization to the state of a control or leader node. Convergence of consensus to a virtual leader or header node was studied in (Jadbabaie et al., 2003; Jiang & Baras 2009). Dynamic consensus for tracking of time-varying signals was presented in (Spanoset al., 2005). The pinning control has been introduced for synchronization tracking control of coupled complex dynamical systems et al., 2004; Z. Li et al., 2009). Pinning control allows controlled synchronization of interconnected dynamical systems by adding a control or leader node that is connected (pinned) into a small percentage of nodes in the network. Analysis has been done using Lyapunov and other techniques by assuming either a Jacobian linearization of the nonlinear node dynamics, or a Lipschitz condition, or contraction analysis. The agents are homogeneous in that they all have the same nonlinear dynamics.

The study of second-order and higher-order consensus is required to implement synchronization in most real world applications such as formation control and coordination among UAVs, where both position and velocity must be controlled. Note that Lagrangian motion dynamics and robotic systems can be written in the form of second-order systems. Moreover, second-order integrator consensus design (as opposed to first-order integrator node dynamics) involves more details about the interaction between the system dynamics/ control design problem and the graph structure as reflected in the Laplacian matrix. As such, second-order consensus is interesting because there one must confront more directly the interface between control systems and communication graph structure. See the book (Ren & Beard 2008) in Section III (Chapter 4-5). The article (Ren et al., 2007) studied the case of higher-order consensus for linear chained integrator systems. The detailed analysis there is performed for 3rd order systems but it extends to the higher order case. The paper (Zhu et al., 2009) studies the general second order consensus problem for double integrator systems. Ref. (Khoo et al., 2009) studied second order consensus in finite time using sliding mode error and a Lyapunov analysis. Papers (Bo & Huajing 2009; Yang et al., 2008; Su & Xiaofan Wang 2008) discuss consensus with time delays for second order integrator (Type II) systems. The article (Seo et al., 2009) proposed second order consensus using output feedback for agents with identical linear dynamics.

Few papers study second-order consensus for unknown nonlinear systems. Few papers study consensus for heterogeneous agents with different unknown nonlinear dynamics. Leaderless or uncontrolled synchronization with nonlinear non-identical passive systems is reported in (Chopra & Spong 2006), which provided a Lyapunov proof valid for balanced graph structures. By contrast, this Chapter concerns controlled consensus or the multi-agent tracker problem on general directed graphs.

Neural networks (NN) have a universal approximation property (Hornik et al., 1989) and learning capabilities that make them ideal for cooperative tracking control of multi agent systems with non-identical unknown nonlinear dynamics. Neural networks have been used since the 1990s to extend the abilities of adaptive controllers to handle larger classes of unknown nonlinear dynamical systems. Novel NN weight tuning algorithms have been developed to make NN suitable for online control of dynamical systems with real-time learning along the system trajectories. Rigorous proofs of convergence, performance, and stability have been offered. The reader is referred to (Qu 2009; Lewis et al., 1999; Lewis et al., 1996; Narendra 1992; Narendra & Parthasarathy 1990; F. -C Chen & Khalil 1992; Polycarpou 1996) for early works and the extensive literature since then is well known and hence not covered here. Neural adaptive control has not been fully explored for control of multiagent systems.

Distributed multiagent systems with unknown nonlinear non-identical dynamics and disturbances were studied in (Hou et al., 2009) where distributed neural adaptive controllers were designed to achieve robust consensus. That treatment assumed undirected graphs and solved the leaderless or uncontrolled consensus problem, that is, the nodes reach a steady-state consensus that depends on the initial conditions and cannot be controlled. Expressions for the consensus value were not given. Higher order consensus was proposed using a complex backstepping approach.

Many control system graph structures are nonsymmetric in that communication links are unidirectional, with information flowing only one way between subsystems. Moreover, in most problems it is important to be able to specify the desired synchronization trajectory. This corresponds to a multi-agent tracker problem. An example is the directed tree structure of formation control, where all agents sense (either directly or indirectly through intermediate neighbors) the state of the control node, but the control node sets the prescribed course and speed. Therefore, (Das & Lewis 2009) studied the cooperative tracker problem for agents on general digraphs having non-identical unknown dynamics and disturbances. First-order integrator dynamics were studied. A distributed adaptive control technique was given that used pinning control to achieve synchronization to a desired command trajectory. Performance and stability were shown using a Lyapunov approach.

In this Chapter we extend (Das & Lewis 2009) to consensus for agents having second order dynamics in Brunovsky form. We confront the second-order synchronization tracking problem for heterogeneous nodes with non-identical unknown nonlinear dynamics with unknown disturbances. Herein, 'synchronization control' means the objective of enforcing all node trajectories to follow (in a 'close-enough' sense to be made precise) the trajectory of a leader or control node. The communication structures considered are general directed graphs with fixed topologies. Analysis of digraphs is significantly more involved than for undirected graphs. The dynamics of the leader or command node are also assumed nonlinear and unknown. A distributed adaptive control approach is taken, where cooperative adaptive controllers are designed at each node. A parametric neural network structure is introduced at each node to estimate the unknown dynamics. The choices of control protocol as well as neural net tuning laws are the key factors in stabilizing the networked multi-agent systems. A Lyapunov analysis shows how to tune the neural networks cooperatively, and guarantees the stability and performance of the networked systems. The error bounds obtained from the Lyapunov proof are dependent on control design and NN tuning parameters which can be chosen to suitably manage the tracking error and estimation error. Simulation results for networked agents with Lagrangian dynamics are provided to show the effectiveness of the proposed method.
Section 2 is formulated the synchronization tracking control problem for second-order systems with non-identical unknown nonlinear dynamics. In Section 3 a Lyapunov technique is used to design cooperative adaptive controllers based on neural network approximation methods. Performance and stability guarantees are given for the networked systems. Section 4 presents simulation results.

2. Synchronization control formulation

Consider a graph $G=(V,E)$ with a nonempty finite set of N nodes $V=\{v_1,\cdots,v_N\}$ and a set of edges or arcs $E\subseteq V\times V$. We assume the graph is simple, e.g. no repeated edges and $(v_i,v_i)\notin E,\forall i$ no self loops. General directed graphs are considered. Denote the adjacency or connectivity matrix as $A=[a_{ij}]$ with $a_{ij}>0\; if\; (v_j,v_i)\in E$ and $a_{ij}=0$ otherwise. Note $a_{ii}=0$. The set of neighbors of a node v_i is $N_i=\{v_j:(v_j,v_i)\in E\}$, i.e. the set of nodes with arcs incoming to v_i. Define the in-degree matrix as a diagonal matrix $D=diag\{d_i\}$ with $d_i=\sum_{j\in N_i} a_{ij}$ the weighted in-degree of node i (i.e. i-*th* row sum of A). Define the graph laplacian matrix as $L=D-A$, which has all row sums equal to zero. Define $d_i^o=\sum_j a_{ji}$, the (weighted) out-degree of node i, that is the i-th column sum of A.
We consider directed communication graphs with fixed topologies and assume the digraph is strongly connected, i.e. there is a directed path from v_i to v_j for all distinct nodes $v_i,v_j\in V$. Then A and L are irreducible (Qu 2009), (Horn & Johnson 1994). That is they are not cogredient to a lower triangular matrix, i.e., there is no permutation matrix U such that

$$L=U\begin{bmatrix} * & 0 \\ * & * \end{bmatrix}U^T \tag{1}$$

The results of this Chapter can easily be extended to graphs having a spanning tree (i.e. not necessarily strongly connected) using the Frobenius form in (1).

2.1 Cooperative tracking problem for synchronization of multiagent systems

Consider second order node dynamics defined for the i-th node in Brunovsky form as

$$\begin{aligned} \dot{x}_i^1 &= x_i^2 \\ \dot{x}_i^2 &= f_i(x_i) + u_i + w_i \end{aligned} \tag{2}$$

where $x_i = [x_i^1 \; x_i^2]^T \in R^2$, $u_i(t) \in R$ is the control input and $w_i(t) \in R$ a disturbance acting upon each node. Note that each node may have its own distinct nonlinear dynamics. Standard assumptions for existence of unique solutions are made, e.g. $f_i(x_i)$ either continuously differentiable or Lipschitz. The overall graph dynamics is

$$\begin{aligned} \dot{x}^1 &= x^2 \\ \dot{x}^2 &= f(x) + u + w \end{aligned} \tag{3}$$

where the overall (global) state vector is $x^2 = \begin{bmatrix} x_1^2 & x_2^2 & \cdots & x_N^2 \end{bmatrix}^T \in R^N$,

$x^1 = \begin{bmatrix} x_1^1 & x_2^1 & \cdots & x_N^1 \end{bmatrix}^T \in R^N$, $x = \left(x^1, x^2\right)^T$, $f(x) = \begin{bmatrix} f_1(x_1) & f_2(x_2) & \cdots & f_N(x_N) \end{bmatrix}^T \in R^N$,

input $u = \begin{bmatrix} u_1 & u_2 & \cdots & u_N \end{bmatrix}^T \in R^N$, and $w = \begin{bmatrix} w_1 & w_2 & \cdots & w_N \end{bmatrix}^T \in R^N$.

If the states x_i^k are not scalars, this analysis carries over with the mere addition of the standard Kronecker product term (Das & Lewis 2009).

Definition 1. *The local neighborhood tracking synchronization errors (position and velocity) for node i are defined as* (Khoo et al., 2009)

$$e_i^1 = \sum_{j \in N_i} a_{ij}\left(x_j^1 - x_i^1\right) + b_i\left(x_0^1 - x_i^1\right) \tag{4}$$

and

$$e_i^2 = \sum_{j \in N_i} a_{ij}\left(x_j^2 - x_i^2\right) + b_i\left(x_0^2 - x_i^2\right) \tag{5}$$

with pinning gains $b_i \ge 0$, and $b_i > 0$ for at least one i. Then, $b_i \ne 0$ if and only if there exist an arc from the control node to the i-th node in G. We refer to the nodes i for which $b_i \ne 0$ as the pinned or controlled nodes.

Note that (4) and (5) represents the information that is available to any node i for control purposes.

The state $x_0 = [x_0^1 \; x_0^2]^T \in R^2$ of the leader or control node satisfies the (generally nonautonomous) dynamics in Brunovsky form

$$\begin{aligned} \dot{x}_0^1 &= x_0^2 \\ \dot{x}_0^2 &= f_0(x_0, t) \end{aligned} \tag{6}$$

This can be regarded as a command or reference generator. A special case is the standard constant consensus value with $\dot{x}_0^1 = 0$ and x_0^2 absent. Here, we assume that the control node can have a time-varying state.

The **Synchronization tracking control problem** confronted herein is as follows: Design control protocols for all the nodes in G to synchronize to the state of the control node, i.e. one requires $x_i^k(t) \to x_0^k(t)$, $k = 1,2, \forall i$. It is assumed that the dynamics of the control node is unknown to any of the nodes in G. It is assumed further that both the node nonlinearities $f_i(.)$ and the node disturbances $w_i(t)$ are unknown. Thus, the synchronization protocols must be robust to unmodelled dynamics and unknown disturbances.

2.2 Synchronization tracking error

Define the consensus disagreement error vector

$$\delta = \begin{bmatrix} \delta^1 & \delta^2 \end{bmatrix}^T = \begin{bmatrix} x^1 - \underline{1}x_0^1 & x^2 - \underline{1}x_0^2 \end{bmatrix}^T \tag{7}$$

From (4), the global error vector for network G is given by

$$e^1 = -(L+B)\left(x^1 - \underline{1}x_0^1\right) = -(L+B)\delta^1 \tag{8}$$

and

$$e^2 = -(L+B)\left(x^2 - \underline{1}x_0^2\right) = -(L+B)\delta^2 \tag{9}$$

where, $B = diag\{b_i\}$ is the diagonal matrix of pinning gains, and $e^k = \begin{bmatrix} e_1^k & e_2^k & \cdots & e_N^k \end{bmatrix}^T \in R^N$, $k = 1,2, \forall i$ and $\underline{1} \in R^N$ the vector of 1's.

Lemma 1. *Let the graph is strongly connected and* $B \neq 0$. Then

$$\left\|\delta^k\right\| \le \left\|e^k\right\| / \underline{\sigma}(L+B), \qquad k = 1,2 \tag{10}$$

with $\underline{\sigma}(L+B)$ *the minimum singular value of* $(L+B)$, *and* $e = 0$ *if and only if the nodes synchronize, that is*

$$x_i^k(t) = x_0^k(t), \; k = 1,2, \; \forall i. \tag{11}$$

2.3 Synchronization Control Design and Error Dynamics

Differentiating (8) and (9),

$$\dot{e}^1 = -(L+B)\left(x^2 - \underline{1}x_0^2\right) \tag{12}$$

and

$$\dot{e}^2 = -(L+B)\left(\dot{x}^2 - \underline{1}f_0(x_0, t)\right) \tag{13}$$

Note that $\dot{e}^1 = e^2$. Define sliding mode error for node i

$$r_i = e_i^2 + \lambda_i e_i^1 \tag{14}$$

or as a whole

$$r = e^2 + \Lambda e^1 \tag{15}$$

where $\Lambda = \mathrm{diag}(\lambda_i) > 0$. The next result follows directly.

Lemma 2. *The velocity error is bounded according to*

$$\left\| e^2 \right\| \le \left\| r \right\| + \bar{\sigma}(\Lambda) \left\| e^1 \right\| \tag{16}$$

Now differentiating r one obtains the error dynamics

$$\begin{aligned} \dot{r} &= -(L+B)\left(\dot{x}^2 - \underline{1} f_0(x_0,t)\right) - \Lambda(L+B)\left(x^2 - \underline{1} x_0^2\right) \\ &= -(L+B)\left(f(x) + u + w\right) + (L+B)\underline{1} f_0(x_0,t) + \Lambda e^2 \end{aligned} \tag{17}$$

Following the techniques in (Lewis et al., 1999; Ge et al., 1998), assume that the unknown nonlinearities in (2) are smooth and thus can be approximated on a compact set $S \in R$ by

$$f_i(x_i) = W_i^T \varphi_i(x_i) + \varepsilon_i \tag{18}$$

with $\varphi_i(x_i) \in R^{\eta_i}$ a suitable basis set of η_i functions at each node i with η_i number of neurons and $W_i \in R^{\eta_i}$ a set of unknown coefficients. According to the Weierstrass higher-order approximation theorem (Stone 1948), a polynomial basis set suffices to approximate $f_i(x_i)$ as well as its derivatives, when they exist, and moreover, the approximation error $\varepsilon_i \to 0$ uniformly as $\eta_i \to \infty$. According to the neural network (NN) approximation literature (Hornik et al., 1989), a variety of basis sets can be selected, including sigmoids, gaussians, etc. There $\varphi_i(x_i) \in R^{\eta_i}$ is known as the NN activation function vector and $W_i \in R^{\eta_i}$ as the NN weight matrix. Then it is shown that ε_i is bounded on a compact set. The ideal approximating weights $W_i \in R^{\eta_i}$ in (7) are assumed unknown. The intention is to select only a small number η_i of NN neurons at each node (see Simulations).

Here, to avoid distractions from the main issues being introduced, we assume a linear-in-the-parameters NN, i.e. the basis set of activation functions is fixed and only the output weights are tuned. It is straightforward to use a two-layer NN whereby the first and second-layer weights are tuned. Then one has a nonlinear-in-the-parameters NN and the basis set is automatically selected in the NN. Then, the below development can easily be modified as in (Lewis et al., 1999).

To compensate for unknown nonlinearities, each node will maintain a neural network locally to keep track of the current estimates for the nonlinearities. The idea is to use the information of the states from the neighbors of node i to evaluate the performance of the current control protocol along with the current estimates of the nonlinear functions. Therefore, select the local node's approximation $\hat{f}_i(x_i)$ as

$$\hat{f}_i(x_i) = \hat{W}_i^T \varphi_i(x_i) \tag{19}$$

where $\hat{W}_i \in R^{\eta_i}$ is a current estimate of the NN weights for node i , and η_i is the number of NN neurons maintained at each node i . It will be shown in Theorem 1 how to select the estimates of the parameters $\hat{W}_i \in R^{\eta_i}$ using the local neighborhood synchronization errors (4), (5). The global node nonlinearity $f(x)$ for graph G is now written as

$$f(x) = W^T\varphi(x) + \varepsilon = \begin{bmatrix} W_1^T & & & & \\ & W_2^T & & & \\ & & \ddots & & \\ & & & \ddots & \\ & & & & W_N^T \end{bmatrix} \underbrace{\begin{bmatrix} \varphi_1(x_1) \\ \varphi_2(x_2) \\ \vdots \\ \vdots \\ \varphi_N(x_N) \end{bmatrix}}_{\varphi(x)} + \begin{bmatrix} \varepsilon_1 \\ \varepsilon_2 \\ \vdots \\ \vdots \\ \varepsilon_N \end{bmatrix} \tag{20}$$

and the estimate $\hat{f}(x)$ as

$$\hat{f}(x) = \hat{W}^T\varphi(x) = \begin{bmatrix} \hat{W}_1^T & & & & \\ & \hat{W}_2^T & & & \\ & & \ddots & & \\ & & & \ddots & \\ & & & & \hat{W}_N^T \end{bmatrix} \underbrace{\begin{bmatrix} \varphi_1(x_1) \\ \varphi_2(x_2) \\ \vdots \\ \vdots \\ \varphi_N(x_N) \end{bmatrix}}_{\varphi(x)} \tag{21}$$

Consider an input

$$u_i = -\hat{f}_i(x_i) + \mu_i(x,t) \tag{22}$$

or

$$u \triangleq -\hat{f}(x) + \mu(x,t) \tag{23}$$

with $\mu_i(x,t)$ an auxiliary input for the i th node yet to be specified. Then using (12) the error dynamics (6) becomes

$$\dot{r} = -(L+B)\left(\tilde{f}(x) + \mu(x,t) + w\right) + (L+B)\underline{1} f_0(x_0,t) + \Lambda e^2 \tag{24}$$

where $\tilde{f}(x) = f(x) - \hat{f}(x) = \tilde{W}\varphi(x)$ with $\tilde{W} = \text{diag}\left(W_1 - \hat{W}_1, W_2 - \hat{W}_2, \cdots\cdots, W_N - \hat{W}_N\right)^T$.

3. Lyapunov design for cooperative adaptive tracking control

It is now shown how to select the auxiliary control $\mu(t)$ and NN weight tuning laws such as to guarantee that all nodes synchronize to the desired control node signal, i.e., $x_i(t) \to x_0(t), \forall i$. It is assumed that the dynamics $f(x_0,t)$ of the control node (which could represent its motion) are unknown to any of the nodes in G. It is assumed further that the node nonlinearities $f_i(x_i)$ and disturbances $w_i(t)$ are unknown. The Lyapunov analysis technique approach of (Lewis et al., 1999; Lewis et al., 1996) is used, though there are some complications arising from the fact that $\mu(x,t)$ and the NN weight tuning laws must be implemented as distributed protocols. This entails a careful selection of the Lyapunov function.

The maximum and minimum singular values of a matrix M are denoted $\bar{\sigma}(M)$ and $\underline{\sigma}(M)$ respectively. The Frobenius norm is $\|M\|_F = \sqrt{tr\{M^T M\}}$ with $tr\{\cdot\}$ the trace. The Frobenius inner product of two matrices is $\langle M_1, M_2 \rangle_F = \sqrt{tr\{M_1{}^T M_2\}}$.

The following Fact gives two standard results used in neural adaptive control (Lewis et al., 1999)

Fact 1. Let the nonlinearities $f(x)$ in (3) be smooth on a compact set $\Omega \subset R^N$. Then:

a. The NN estimation error $\varepsilon(x)$ is bounded by $\|\varepsilon\| \le \varepsilon_M$ on Ω, with ε_M a fixed bound (Hornik et al., 1989; Lewis et al., 1999).
b. Weierstrass higher-order approximation theorem. Select the activation functions $\varphi(x)$ as a complete independent basis (e.g. polynomials). Then NN estimation error $\varepsilon(x)$ converges uniformly to zero on Ω as $\eta_i \to \infty, i = 1, N$. That is $\forall \xi > 0$ there exist $\bar{\eta}_i, i = 1, N$ such that $\eta_i > \bar{\eta}_i, \forall i$ implies $\sup_{x \in \Omega} \|\varepsilon(x)\| < \xi$ (Stone 1948).

The following standard assumptions are required. Although the bounds mentioned are assumed to exist, they are not used in the design and do not have to be known. They appear in the error bounds in the proof of Theorem 1. (Though not required, if desired, standard methods can be used to estimate these bounds including [27].)

Assumption 1.

a. The unknown disturbance w_i is bounded for all i . Thus the overall disturbance vector w is also bounded by $\|w\| \le w_M$ with w_M a fixed bound.
b. Unknown ideal NN weight matrix W is bounded by $\|W\|_F \le W_M$.
c. NN activation functions φ_i are bounded $\forall i$, so that one can write for the overall network that $\|\varphi\| \le \phi_M$.
d. The unknown consensus variable dynamics $f_0(x_0, t)$ as well as the target output vector are bounded so that $\|f_0(x_0, t)\| \le F_M, \forall t$ respectively.
e. The target trajectory is bounded so that $\|x_0^1(t)\| < X_0^1, \|x_0^2(t)\| < X_0^2, \forall t$

The next definition for robust practical stability, or uniform ultimate boundedness, is standard and the following definition extends it to multi-agent systems

Definition 2. *Any vector time function $y(t)$ is said to be uniformly ultimately bounded (UUB) [27] if there exist a compact set $\Omega \subset R^N$ so that $\forall y(t_0) \in \Omega$ there exist a bound B_m and a time $t_f(B_m, y(t_0))$ such that $\|x(t) - y(t)\| \le B_m \; \forall t \ge t_0 + t_f$.*

Definition 3. *The control node state $x_0(t)$ is said to be cooperative uniformly ultimately bounded (CUUB) if there exist a compact set $\Omega \subset R$ so that $\forall\, (x_i(t_0) - x_0(t_0)) \in \Omega$ there exist a bound B_m and a time $t_f(B_m, x(t_0), x_0(t_0))$ such that $\|x_i(t) - x_0(t)\| \le B_m \; \forall i, \forall t \ge t_0 + t_f$.*

The next key constructive result is needed. An M-matrix is a square matrix having nonpositive off-diagonal elements and all principal minors nonnegative (Qu 2009; Horn & Johnson 1994).

Lemma 3. (Qu 2009) *Let L be irreducible and B have at least one diagonal entry $b_i > 0$. Then $(L + B)$ is a nonsingular $M-$matrix. Define*

$$q = \begin{bmatrix} q_1 & q_2 & \cdots & q_N \end{bmatrix}^T = (L + B)^{-1} \underline{1} \tag{25}$$

$$P = \operatorname{diag}\{p_i\} \equiv \operatorname{diag}\{1 / q_i\} \tag{26}$$

Then $P > 0$ *and the matrix Q defined as*

$$Q = P\left(L + B\right) + \left(L + B\right)^T P \tag{27}$$

is positive definite.

It is important that the matrix *P* is diagonal, as will be seen in the upcoming proof. The main result of the Chapter is now presented.

Theorem 1. Distributed Adaptive Control Protocol for Synchronization.

Consider the networked systems given by (3) under the Assumption 1. Let the communication digraph be strongly connected. Select the auxiliary control signal $\mu(x,t)$ *in (23) so that the local node control protocols are given by*

$$u_i = cr_i - \hat{f}_i(x_i) + \frac{\lambda_i}{d_i + b_i} e_i^2 \tag{28}$$

with $\lambda_i = \lambda > 0\ \forall i$, *control gains* $c > 0$, *and* $r_i(t)$ *defined in (14). Then*

$$u = cr - \hat{W}^T \varphi(x) + \lambda\left(D + B\right)^{-1} e^2 \tag{29}$$

with local node NN tuning laws be given by

$$\dot{\hat{W}}_i = -F_i \varphi_i r_i^T p_i (d_i + b_i) - \kappa F_i \hat{W}_i \tag{30}$$

with $F_i = \Pi_i I_{\eta_i}$, I_{η_i} *the* $\eta_i \times \eta_i$ *identity matrix,* $\Pi_i > 0$ *and* $\kappa > 0$ *scalar tuning gains, and* $p_i > 0$ *defined in Lemma 3. Define*

$$\lambda = \sqrt{\frac{\underline{\sigma}\left(D + B\right)}{\overline{\sigma}\left(P\right)\overline{\sigma}\left(A\right)}} \tag{31}$$

and select the control gain c and NN tuning gain κ *so that*

$$\begin{aligned} &i. \quad c = \frac{2}{\underline{\sigma}(Q)}\left(\frac{1}{\sqrt{\lambda}} + \lambda\right) > 0 \\ &ii. \quad \frac{1}{2}\varphi_m \overline{\sigma}\left(P\right)\overline{\sigma}\left(A\right) \le \kappa \le \lambda - 1 \end{aligned} \tag{32}$$

with $P > 0, Q > 0$ *define in Lemma 3 and* A *the graph adjacency matrix.*

Then there exist numbers of neurons $\bar{\eta}_i, i = 1, N$ *such that for* $\eta_i > \bar{\eta}_i, \forall i$ *the overall sliding mode cooperative error vector* $r(t)$, *the local cooperative error vectors* $e^1(t), e^2(t)$ *and the NN weight estimation errors* $\tilde{W}$ *are UUB, with practical bounds given by (53)-(55) respectively. Moreover the consensus variable* $x_0(t) = [x_0^1, x_0^2]^T$ *is cooperative UUB and all nodes synchronize such that* $\left\|x_i^1(t) - x_0^1(t)\right\| \to 0$, $\left\|x_i^2(t) - x_0^2(t)\right\| \to 0$. *Moreover, the bounds (53)-(55) can be made small by manipulating the NN and control gain parameters.*

Proof:

Part A: We claim that for any fixed $\varepsilon_M > 0$, there exist numbers of neurons $\bar{\eta}_i, i = 1, N$ such that for $\eta_i > \bar{\eta}_i, \forall i$ the NN approximation error is bounded by $\|\varepsilon\| \le \varepsilon_M$. The claim is proven in Part b of the proof. Consider now the Lyapunov function candidate

$$V = \frac{1}{2} r^T P r + \frac{1}{2} \tilde{W}^T F^{-1} \tilde{W} + \frac{1}{2} \left(e^1\right)^T e^1 \tag{33}$$

with $P = P^T > 0$ and $F^{-1} = F^{-T} > 0$. Then

$$\dot{V} = r^T P \dot{r} + tr\left\{\tilde{W}^T F^{-1} \dot{\tilde{W}}\right\} + \left(e^1\right)^T \dot{e}^1 \tag{34}$$

Using (24) and (29)

$$\dot{r} = -(L+B)\left(\tilde{f}(x) + cr + w\right) + (L+B)\underline{1} f_0(x_0,t) + A(D+B)^{-1} \Lambda e^2 \tag{35}$$

Therefore

$$\begin{aligned} \dot{V} = &-r^T P(L+B)\left(\tilde{W}^T \varphi(x) + \varepsilon + w + cr\right) + r^T P(L+B)\underline{1} f_0(x_0,t) + \\ &r^T PA(D+B)^{-1} \Lambda e^2 + tr\left\{\tilde{W}^T F^{-1} \dot{\tilde{W}}\right\} + \left(e^1\right)^T e^2 \end{aligned} \tag{36}$$

$$\begin{aligned} \dot{V} = &-r^T P(L+B)cr - r^T P(L+B)\tilde{W}^T \varphi(x) - r^T P(L+B)(\varepsilon + w) + \\ &r^T P(L+B)\underline{1} f_0(x_0,t) + r^T PA(D+B)^{-1} \Lambda e^2 + tr\left\{\tilde{W}^T F^{-1} \dot{\tilde{W}}\right\} + \left(e^1\right)^T \left(r - \Lambda e^1\right) \end{aligned} \tag{37}$$

$$\begin{aligned} \dot{V} = &-cr^T P(L+B)r - r^T P(L+B)\{\varepsilon + w - \underline{1} f_0(x_0,t)\} + \\ &r^T PA(D+B)^{-1} \Lambda e^2 + tr\left[\tilde{W}^T \left(F^{-1} \dot{\tilde{W}} - \varphi(x) r^T P(L+B)\right)\right] + \left(e^1\right)^T r - \left(e^1\right)^T \Lambda e^1 \end{aligned} \tag{38}$$

$$\begin{aligned} \dot{V} = &-cr^T P(L+B)r - r^T P(L+B)\{\varepsilon + w - \underline{1} f_0(x_0,t)\} + \\ &r^T PA(D+B)^{-1} \Lambda\left(r - \Lambda e^1\right) + tr\left[\tilde{W}^T \left(F^{-1} \dot{\tilde{W}} - \varphi(x) r^T P(L+B)\right)\right] + \left(e^1\right)^T r - \left(e^1\right)^T \Lambda e^1 \end{aligned} \tag{39}$$

$$\begin{aligned} \dot{V} = &-cr^T P(L+B)r - r^T P(L+B)\{\varepsilon + w - \underline{1} f_0(x_0,t)\} + tr\left[\tilde{W}^T \left(F^{-1} \dot{\tilde{W}} - \varphi(x) r^T P(D+B)\right)\right] + \\ &tr\left[\tilde{W}^T \varphi(x) r^T PA\right] + r^T PA(D+B)^{-1} \Lambda r - r^T PA(D+B)^{-1} \Lambda^2 e^1 + \left(e^1\right)^T r - \left(e^1\right)^T \Lambda e^1 \end{aligned} \tag{40}$$

Since L is irreducible and B has at least one diagonal entry b_i>0, then (L+B) is a nonsingular M-matrix. Thus, according to Lemma 3, one can write

$$\begin{aligned} \dot{V} = &-\frac{1}{2} cr^T Q r - r^T P(L+B)\{\varepsilon + w - \underline{1} f_0(x_0,t)\} + tr\left[\tilde{W}^T \left(F^{-1} \dot{\tilde{W}} - \varphi(x) r^T P(D+B)\right)\right] + \\ &tr\left[\tilde{W}^T \varphi(x) r^T PA\right] + r^T PA(D+B)^{-1} \Lambda r - r^T PA(D+B)^{-1} \Lambda^2 e^1 + \left(e^1\right)^T r - \left(e^1\right)^T \Lambda e^1 \end{aligned} \tag{41}$$

Adopt the NN weight tuning law $\dot{\hat{W}}_i = F_i \varphi_i r_i^T p_i (d_i + b_i) + \kappa F_i \hat{W}_i$. Taking norm both sides in (41) one has

$$\dot{V} \le -\frac{1}{2}c\underline{\sigma}(Q)\|r\|^2 + \bar{\sigma}(P)\bar{\sigma}(L+B)B_M\|r\| + \kappa W_M\|\tilde{W}\|_F - \kappa\|\tilde{W}\|_F^2 + \phi_M\bar{\sigma}(P)\bar{\sigma}(A)\|\tilde{W}\|_F\|r\| + \frac{\bar{\sigma}(P)\bar{\sigma}(A)\bar{\sigma}(\Lambda)}{\underline{\sigma}(D+B)}\|r\|^2 + \left(1+\frac{\bar{\sigma}(P)\bar{\sigma}(A)\bar{\sigma}(\Lambda^2)}{\underline{\sigma}(D+B)}\right)\|r\|\|e^1\| - \underline{\sigma}(\Lambda)\|e^1\|^2 \tag{42}$$

where $B_M = (\varepsilon_M + w_M + F_M)$. Then

$$\dot{V} \le -\begin{bmatrix}\|e^1\| & \|r\| & \|\tilde{W}\|_F\end{bmatrix}\begin{bmatrix}\underline{\sigma}(\Lambda) & \frac{1}{2}\left(1+\frac{\bar{\sigma}(P)\bar{\sigma}(A)\bar{\sigma}(\Lambda^2)}{\underline{\sigma}(D+B)}\right) & 0 \\ \frac{1}{2}\left(1+\frac{\bar{\sigma}(P)\bar{\sigma}(A)\bar{\sigma}(\Lambda^2)}{\underline{\sigma}(D+B)}\right) & \left(\frac{1}{2}c\underline{\sigma}(Q)-\frac{\bar{\sigma}(P)\bar{\sigma}(A)\bar{\sigma}(\Lambda)}{\underline{\sigma}(D+B)}\right) & \frac{1}{2}\phi_M\bar{\sigma}(P)\bar{\sigma}(A) \\ 0 & \frac{1}{2}\phi_M\bar{\sigma}(P)\bar{\sigma}(A) & \kappa\end{bmatrix}\begin{bmatrix}\|e^1\| \\ \|r\| \\ \|\tilde{W}\|_F\end{bmatrix} +$$

$$\begin{bmatrix}0 & \bar{\sigma}(P)\bar{\sigma}(L+B)B_M & \kappa W_M\end{bmatrix}\begin{bmatrix}\|e^1\| \\ \|r\| \\ \|\tilde{W}\|_F\end{bmatrix} \tag{43}$$

Write this as

$$\dot{V} \le -z^T H z + h^T z \tag{44}$$

Clearly $\dot{V} \le 0$ iff $H \ge 0$ and

$$\|z\| > \frac{\|h\|}{\underline{\sigma}(H)} \tag{45}$$

According to (33) this defines a level set of $V(z)$, so it is direct to show that $\dot{V} \le 0$ for V large enough such that (45) holds (Khalil 1996). To show this, according to (33) one has

$$\tfrac{1}{2}\underline{\sigma}(P)\|e\|^2 + \frac{1}{2\Pi_{\max}}\|\tilde{W}\|_F^2 + \frac{1}{2}\|e^1\|^2 \le V \le \tfrac{1}{2}\bar{\sigma}(P)\|e\|^2 + \frac{1}{2\Pi_{\min}}\|\tilde{W}\|_F^2 + \frac{1}{2}\|e^1\|^2 \tag{46}$$

$$\frac{1}{2}\begin{bmatrix}\|e^1\| & \|r\| & \|\tilde{W}\|_F\end{bmatrix}\underbrace{\begin{bmatrix}\underline{\sigma}(P) & & \\ & \frac{1}{\Pi_{\max}} & \\ & & 1\end{bmatrix}}_{S_1}\begin{bmatrix}\|e^1\| \\ \|r\| \\ \|\tilde{W}\|_F\end{bmatrix} \le V \le \frac{1}{2}\begin{bmatrix}\|e^1\| & \|r\| & \|\tilde{W}\|_F\end{bmatrix}\underbrace{\begin{bmatrix}\bar{\sigma}(P) & & \\ & \frac{1}{\Pi_{\min}} & \\ & & 1\end{bmatrix}}_{S_2}\begin{bmatrix}\|e^1\| \\ \|r\| \\ \|\tilde{W}\|_F\end{bmatrix} \tag{47}$$

with $\Pi_{\min}, \Pi_{\max}$ the minimum and maximum values of Π_i. Equation (47) is equivalent to

$$\tfrac{1}{2}z^T \underline{S} z \le V \le \tfrac{1}{2}z^T \bar{S} z \tag{48}$$

where $\underline{S} = \underline{\sigma}(S_1)$ and $\bar{S} = \bar{\sigma}(S_2)$. Then

$$\tfrac{1}{2}\underline{\sigma}(S)\|z\|^2 \le V \le \tfrac{1}{2}\bar{\sigma}(\bar{S})\|z\|^2 \tag{49}$$

Therefore,

$$V > \frac{1}{2}\frac{\bar{\sigma}(\bar{S})\|h\|^2}{\underline{\sigma}^2(H)} \tag{50}$$

implies (45).

For a symmetric positive definite matrix, the singular values will be equal to its eigenvalues.

Define $\Lambda = \lambda I, \lambda = \sqrt{\frac{\underline{\sigma}(D+B)}{\bar{\sigma}(P)\bar{\sigma}(A)}}$, $c = \frac{2}{\underline{\sigma}(Q)}\left(\frac{1}{\sqrt{\lambda}} + \lambda\right)$ and $\gamma = \frac{1}{2}\varphi_m\bar{\sigma}(P)\bar{\sigma}(A)$. Then (43) can be written as

$$\dot{V} \le -\begin{bmatrix}\|e^1\| & \|r\| & \|\tilde{W}\|_F\end{bmatrix}\underbrace{\begin{bmatrix}\lambda & 1 & 0\\ 1 & \lambda & \gamma\\ 0 & \gamma & \kappa\end{bmatrix}}_{H}\begin{bmatrix}\|e^1\|\\ \|r\|\\ \|\tilde{W}\|_F\end{bmatrix} + \begin{bmatrix}0 & \bar{\sigma}(P)\bar{\sigma}(L+B)B_M & \kappa W_M\end{bmatrix}\begin{bmatrix}\|e^1\|\\ \|r\|\\ \|\tilde{W}\|_F\end{bmatrix} \tag{51}$$

The transformed H matrix is symmetric and positive definite under assumption given by (32). Therefore from Gershgorin circle's theorem

$$\underline{\sigma}(H) \ge \kappa - \gamma \tag{52}$$

with $0 < \gamma \le \kappa \le \lambda - 1$. Therefore $z(t)$ is UUB (Khalil 1996).

In view of the fact that, for any vector z, one has $\|z\|_1 \ge \|z\|_2 \ge \cdots \ge \|z\|_\infty$, sufficient conditions for (45) are:

$$\|r\| > \frac{B_M\bar{\sigma}(P)\bar{\sigma}(L+B) + \kappa W_M}{\kappa - \frac{1}{2}\varphi_m\bar{\sigma}(P)\bar{\sigma}(A)} \tag{53}$$

or

$$\|e^1\| > \frac{B_M\bar{\sigma}(P)\bar{\sigma}(L+B) + \kappa W_M}{\kappa - \frac{1}{2}\varphi_m\bar{\sigma}(P)\bar{\sigma}(A)} \tag{54}$$

or

$$\|\tilde{W}\| > \frac{B_M\bar{\sigma}(P)\bar{\sigma}(L+B) + \kappa W_M}{\kappa - \frac{1}{2}\varphi_m\bar{\sigma}(P)\bar{\sigma}(A)} \tag{55}$$

Note that this shows UUB of $r(t), e_1(t), \tilde{W}(t)$. Therefore from Lemma 2, the boundedness of r and e^1 implies bounded e^2. Now Lemma 1 shows that the consensus error vector $\delta(t)$ is UUB. Then $x_0(t)$ is cooperative UUB.

Part B: See (Ge & C. Wang 2004)

According to (44) $\dot{V} \le -\underline{\sigma}(H)\|z\|^2 + \|h\|\|z\|$ and according to (49)

$$\dot{V} \le -\alpha V + \beta\sqrt{V} \tag{56}$$

with $\alpha \equiv 2\underline{\sigma}(H)/\bar{\sigma}(\bar{S})$, $\beta \equiv \sqrt{2}\|h\|/\sqrt{\underline{\sigma}(\underline{S})}$. Thence

$$\sqrt{V(t)} \le \sqrt{V(0)}e^{-\alpha t/2} + \tfrac{\beta}{\alpha}(1-e^{-\alpha t/2}) \le \sqrt{V(0)} + \tfrac{\beta}{\alpha} \tag{57}$$

Using (49) one has

$$\left\|e^1(t)\right\| \le \|z(t)\| \le \sqrt{\frac{\bar{\sigma}(\bar{S})}{\underline{\sigma}(\underline{S})}}\sqrt{\|e(0)\|^2 + \left\|\tilde{W}(0)\right\|_F^2 + \left\|e^1(0)\right\|^2} + \frac{\bar{\sigma}(\bar{S})}{\underline{\sigma}(\underline{S})}\frac{\|h\|}{\underline{\sigma}(H)} \equiv \rho$$

and

$$\|r(t)\| \le \|z(t)\| \le \sqrt{\frac{\bar{\sigma}(\bar{S})}{\underline{\sigma}(\underline{S})}}\sqrt{\|e(0)\|^2 + \left\|\tilde{W}(0)\right\|_F^2 + \left\|e^1(0)\right\|^2} + \frac{\bar{\sigma}(\bar{S})}{\underline{\sigma}(\underline{S})}\frac{\|h\|}{\underline{\sigma}(H)} \equiv \rho \tag{58}$$

Then from (8)

$$\left\|x^1(t)\right\| \le \frac{1}{\underline{\sigma}(L+B)}\left\|e^1(t)\right\| + \sqrt{N}\left\|x_0^1(t)\right\| \tag{59}$$

$$\left\|x^1(t)\right\| \le \frac{\rho}{\underline{\sigma}(L+B)} + \sqrt{N}X_0^1 \equiv h_0^1 \tag{60}$$

Similarly from (58) and using (16) in Lemma 2

$$\begin{aligned}\left\|e^2(t)\right\| &\le \lambda\left\|e^1(t)\right\| + \|r(t)\| \\ &\le \rho(1+\lambda)\end{aligned} \tag{61}$$

This implies

$$\left\|x^2(t)\right\| \le \frac{\rho(1+\lambda)}{\underline{\sigma}(L+B)} + \sqrt{N}X_0^2 \equiv h_0^2 \tag{62}$$

where $X_0^2 = \left\|x_0^2(t)\right\|$ and $\|h\| \le B_M\bar{\sigma}(P)\bar{\sigma}(L+B) + \kappa W_M$. Therefore, the state is contained for all times $t \ge 0$ in a compact set $\Omega_0 = \{x(t) \mid \left\|x^1(t)\right\| < h_0^1, \left\|x^2(t)\right\| < h_0^2\}$. According to the Weierstrass approximation theorem (Fact 1), given any NN approximation error bound ε_M there exist numbers of neurons $\bar{\eta}_i, i=1,N$ such that $\eta_i > \bar{\eta}_i, \forall i$ implies $\sup_{x\in\Omega}\|\varepsilon(x)\| < \varepsilon_M$.

□

Discussion:

If any one of (53), (54) or (55) holds, the Lyapunov derivative is negative and V decreases. Therefore, these provide practical bounds for the neighborhood synchronization error and the NN weight estimation error.

The elements p_i of the positive definite matrix $P = diag\{p_i\}$ required in the NN tuning law (30) are computed as $P^{-1}\underline{1} = (L+B)^{-1}\underline{1}$ (see Lemma 3), which requires global knowledge of the graph structure unavailable to individual nodes. However, due to the presence of the

arbitrary diagonal gain matrix $F_i > 0$ in (30), one can choose $p_i F_i > 0$ arbitrary without loss of generality.
It is important to select the Lyapunov function candidate V in (33) as a function of locally available variables, e.g. the local sliding mode error $r(t)$ and cooperative neighborhood error $e_1(t)$ in (15) and (18) respectively. This means that any local control signals $\mu_i(x,t)$ and NN tuning laws developed in the proof are distributed and hence implementable at each node. The use of the Frobenius norm in the Lyapunov function is also instrumental, since it gives rise to Frobenius inner products in the proof that only depend on trace terms, where only the diagonal terms are important. In fact, the Frobenius norm is ideally suited for the design of distributed protocols. Finally, it is important that the matrix P of Lemma 3 is diagonal.

4. Simulation result

For this set of simulations, consider the 5-node strongly connected digraph structure in Fig. 1 with a leader node connected to node 3. The edge weights and the pinning gain in (4) were taken equal to 1.

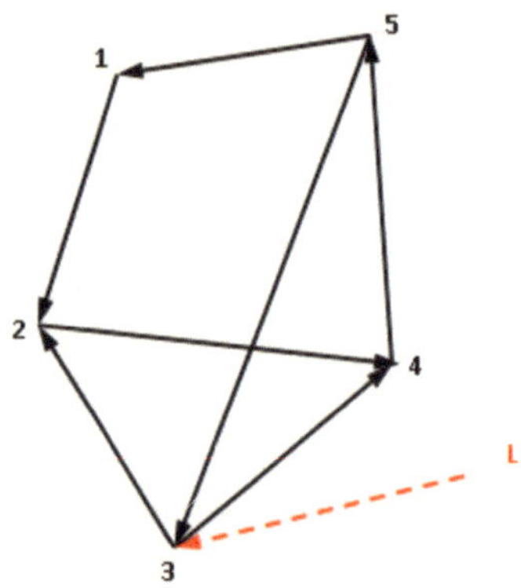

Fig. 1. Five-node SC digraph with one leader node
Consider the node dynamics for node i given by the second-order Lagrange form dynamics

$$\begin{aligned} \dot{q}_{1_i} &= q_{2_i} \\ \dot{q}_{2_i} &= J_i^{-1}\left[u_i - B_i^r q_{2_i} - M_i g l_i \sin(q_{1_i})\right] \end{aligned} \tag{63}$$

where $q_i = \left[q_{1_i}, q_{2_i}\right]^T \in R^2$ is the state vector, J_i is the total inertia of the link and the motor, B_i^r is overall damping coefficient, M_i is total mass, g is gravitational acceleration and l_i is the distance from the joint axis to the link center of mass for node. J_i, B_i^r, M_i and l_i are considered unknown and may be different for each node.
The desired target node dynamics is taken as the inertial system

$$m_0 \ddot{q}_0 + d_0 \dot{q}_0 + k_o q_0 = u_0 \tag{64}$$

with known m_0, d_0, k_0. Select the feedback linearization input

$$u_0 = -\left[K_1\left(q_0 - \sin(\beta t)\right) + K_2\left(\dot{q}_0 - \beta\cos(\beta t)\right)\right] + d_0\dot{q}_0 + k_0 q_0 + \beta^2 m_0 \sin(\beta t) \quad (65)$$

for a constant $\beta>0$. Then, the target motion $q_0(t)$ tracks the desired reference trajectory sin (βt). The cooperative adaptive control protocols of Theorem 1 were implemented at each node. As is standard in neural and adaptive control systems, reasonable positive values were initially chosen for all control and NN tuning parameters. Generally, the simulation results are not too dependent on the specific choice of parameters as long as they are selected as detailed in the Theorem and assumptions, e.g. positive. The number of NN hidden layer units can be fairly small with good performance resulting, normally in the range of 5-10. As in most control systems, however, the performance can be improved by trying a few simulation runs and adjusting the parameters to obtain good behavior. In on-line implementations, the parameters can be adjusted online to obtain better performance.

For NN activation function we use log-sigmoid of the form $\dfrac{1}{1+e^{-kt}}$ with positive slope parameter k. Number of neurons used at each node is 3. So, $\varphi_m \approx 1$ and $\gamma \approx 0.04$. NN gain parameter we selected as $\kappa = 1.5$. According to (32) the pinning gain should be selected large and it was taken as $c=1000$.

In the simulation plots we show tracking performance of positions (q_{1_i}) and velocities (q_{2_i}) for all i. At steady state all q_{1_i} and q_{2_i} are synchronized and follow the second order single link leader trajectory given by q_0 and $\dot{q}_0$ respectively.

Fig. 2 shows the tracking performance of the system. One can see from the figure that positions and velocities of all the five nodes are synchronized in two different final values which are given by the final values of $\left[q_0, \dot{q}_0\right]^T$. More specifically q_{1_i}'s are synchronized with q_0 and q_{2_i}'s are synchronized with $\dot{q}_0$ at steady state. The figure also shows the inputs u_i for all agents while tracking.

Fig. 3 describes the position and velocity consensus disagreement error vectors namely $\left(q_{1_i} - q_0, q_{2_i} - \dot{q}_0\right)^T, \forall i$ and also the NN estimation error in terms of $\left[f_i(x) - \hat{f}_i(x)\right]^T \forall i$. One can easily see that all the errors are minimized almost to zero.

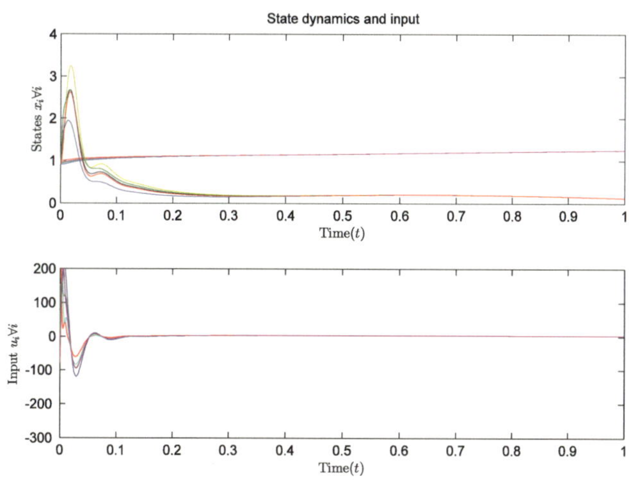

Fig. 2. Tracking performance (position and velocity) and control input

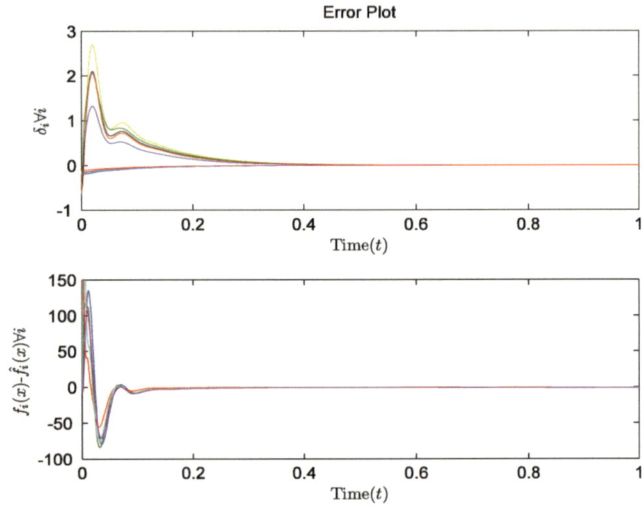

Fig. 3. Disagreement vector and NN estimation error vector

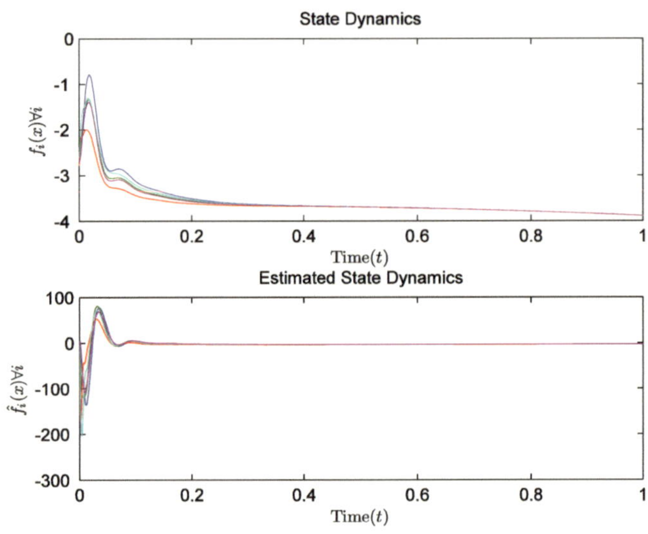

Fig. 4. Comarison of $f(x)$ and $\hat{f}(x)$

Fig. 4 describes the comparison of unknown dynamics $f(x)$ with estimated dynamics $\hat{f}(x)$. The figure also shows that the steady state values of $f(x)$ and $\hat{f}(x)$ are almost equal.

Fig. 5 shows the NN weight dynamics.

Fig. 6 is the phase plane plot of all agents, i.e. the plot of $q_{1_i} \forall i$ (along the x-axis) and $q_{2_i} \forall i$ (along the $y-$axis). At steady state the Lissajous pattern formed by all five nodes is the target node's phase plane trajectory.

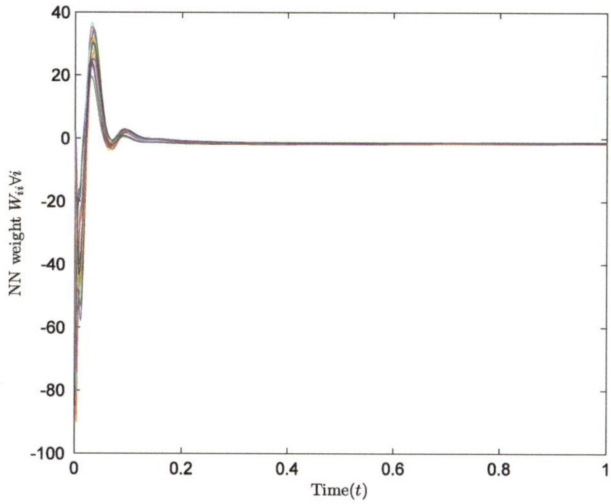

Fig. 5. NN weight dynamics

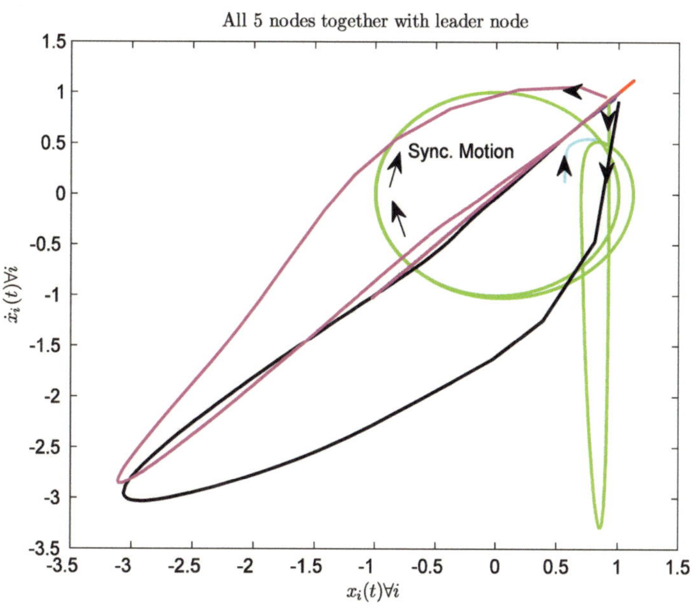

Fig. 6. Phase plane plot for all the nodes

5. Conclusion

This Chapter presents a method for synchronization control for multi-agent systems of order two with unknown dynamics. It gives the design of distributed adaptive controllers for second order nonlinear systems communicating on general strongly connected digraph network structures. The agent dynamics and command generator dynamics are considered unknown. Moreover the agent dynamics need not to be same. It is shown that with the use of pinning control based on the exchange of cooperative neighborhood errors among the agents, one can guarantee synchronization of all the robots to the single command trajectory. A simple neural network parametric approximator is introduced at each node to estimate the unknown dynamics and disturbances. The choices of control protocol as well as neural net tuning laws are selected through a Lyapunov formulation to induce synchronization within the networked multi-robot team. A Lyapunov-based proof shows the ultimate boundedness of the tracking error. Simulation results for Lagrangian agent dynamics are shown to illustrate the effectiveness of the proposed method.

6. Acknowledgements

This work is supported by AFOSR grant FA9550-09-1-0278, NSF grant ECCS-0801330, and ARO grant W91NF-05-1-0314.

7. References

Bo, Yang, and Fang Huajing. 2009. Second-Order Consensus in Networks of Agents with Delayed Dynamics. *Journal of Natural Sciences* 14, no. 2: 158-162.

Chen, F. -C, and H. K. Khalil. 1992. Adaptive control of nonlinear systems using neural networks. *Int. J. Control* 55, no. 6: 1299-1317.

Chopra, N., and M. W. Spong. 2006. Passivity-Based Control of Multi-Agent Systems. In *Advances in Robot Control*, 107-134. Springer Berlin Heidelberg.

Das, A., and F. L. Lewis. 2009. Distributed Adaptive Control for Synchronization of Unknown Nonlinear Networked Systems. *Submitted to Automatica* (December).

Fax, J. Alexander, and R. M. Murray. 2004. Information Flow and Cooperative Control of Vehicle Formations. *IEEE Trans. Automatic Control* 49, no. 9: 1465-1476.

Ge, S., and C. Wang. 2004. Adaptive neural control of uncertain MIMO nonlinear systems. *IEEE Trans. Neural Networks* 15, no. 3 (May): 674-692.

Ge, S. S., C. C. Hang, and T. Zhang. 1998. *Stable Adaptive Neural Network control*. Berlin: Springer.

Horn, Roger A., and Charles R. Johnson. 1994. *Matrix analysis*. Cambridge University Press.

Hornik, K., M. Stinchombe, and H. White. 1989. Multilayer Feedforward Networks are Universal Approximations. *Neural Networks* 20: 359-366.

Hou, Zeng-Guang, Long Cheng, and Min Tan. 2009. Decentralized robust adaptive control for the multiagent system consensus problem using neural networks. *IEEE Transactions on Systems, Man, and Cybernetics, Part B* 39, no. 3 (June): 636-647.

Jadbabaie, Ali, Jie Lin, and S. Morse. 2003. Coordination of Groups of Mobile Autonomous Agents Using Nearest Neighbor Rules. *IEEE Trans. Automatic Control* 48, no. 6: 988-1001.

Jiang, T., and J.S. Baras. 2009. Graph algebraic interpretation of trust establishment in autonomic networks. *Preprint Wiley Journal of Networks*.

Khalil, H. K. 1996. *Nonlinear Systems*. Prentice Hall.

Khoo, Suiyang, Lihua Xie, and Zhihong Man. 2009. Robust Finite-Time Consensus Tracking Algorithm for Multirobot Systems. *IEEE Transaction on Mechatronics* 14, no. 2: 219-228.

Kuramoto, Yoshiki. 1975. Self-entrainment of a population of coupled non-linear oscillators. In *International Symposium on Mathematical Problems in Theoretical Physics*, 39:420-422. Lecture Notes in Physics. Springer Berlin / Heidelberg.

Lewis, F., S. Jagannathan, and A. Yesildirek. 1999. *Neural Network Control of Robot Manipulators and Nonlinear Systems*. London: Taylor and Francis.

Lewis, F. L., A. Yesildirek, and K. Liu. 1996. Multilayer neural net robot controller with guaranteed tracking performance. *IEEE Trans. Neural Networks* 7, no. 2: 388-399.

Li, X., X. Wang, and G. Chen. 2004. Pinning a complex dynamical network to its equilibrium. *IEEE Trans. Circuits and Systems* 51, no. 10: 2074-2087.

Li, Z., Z. Duan, and G. Chen. 2009. Consensus of multi-agent systems and synchronization of complex networks: a unified viewpoint. *IEEE Trans. Circuits and Systems* (to appear).

Lu, J., and G. Chen. 2005. A time-varying complex dynamical network model and its controlled synchronization criteria. *IEEE Trans. Automatic Control* 50, no. 6: 841-846.

Narendra, K. S. 1992. *Adaptive Control of dynamical systems using neural networks*. Handbook of Intelligent Control. New York: Van Nostrand Reinhold.

Narendra, K. S., and K. Parthasarathy. 1990. Identification and control of dynamical systems using neural networks. *IEEE Transaction of Neural Networks* 1: 4-27.

Olfati-Saber, R., J. A. Fax, and R. M. Murray. 2007. Consensus and cooperation in networked multi-agent systems. *Proceedings of the IEEE* 95, no. 1: 215-233.

Olfati-Saber, R., and R. M. Murray. 2004. Consensus Problems in Networks of Agents with Switching Topology and Time-Delays. *IEEE Transaction of Automatic Control* 49, no. 9: 1520-1533.

Polycarpou, M. M. 1996. Stable adaptive neural control scheme for nonlinear systems. *IEEE Trans. Automat. Control* 41, no. 3: 447-451.

Qu, Z. 2009. *Cooperative Control of Dynamical Systems: Applications to Autonomous Vehicles*. New York: Springer-Verlag.

Ren, W., and R. W. Beard. 2005. Consensus Seeking in Multiagent Systems Under Dynamically Changing Interaction Topologies. *IEEE Trans. Automatic Control* 50, no. 5 (May): 655-661.

Ren, W., R. W. Beard. 2008. *Distributed Consensus in Multi-vehicle Cooperative Control: Theory and Applications*. London:Spring Verlag.

Ren, W., R. W. Beard, and E. M. Atkins. 2005. A Survey of Consensus Problems in Multi-agent Coordination. In *Proceedings of the 2005 American Control Conference*. Portland, OR, USA, June 8.

Ren, W., R. W. Beard, and E. M. Atkins. 2007. Information Consensus in Multivehicle Cooperative control. *IEEE Control Systems Magazine*.

Ren, W., K. L. Moore, and Y. Chen. 2007. High-order and model reference consensus algorithms
in cooperative control of multivehicle systems. *Journal of Dynamic Systems, Measurement, and Control* 129: 678-688.

Seo, Jin Heon, Hyungbo Shima, and Juhoon Back. 2009. Consensus of high-order linear systems using dynamic output feedback compensator: Low gain approach. *Automatica* 45, no. 11: 2659-2664.

Spanos, D. P., R. Olfati-Saber, and R. M. Murray. 2005. Dynamic consensus on mobile networks. In *2005 IFAC World Congress*.

Stone, M. H. 1948. The Generalized Weierstrass Approximation Theorem. *Mathematics Magazine* 21, no. 4,5: 167–184,237–254.

Su, Housheng, and Xiaofan Wang. 2008. Proceedings of the 7th World Congress on Intelligent Control and Automation. In . Chongqing, China, June 25.

Tsitsiklis, J. N. 1984. Problems in decentralized decision making and computation. Ph.D. dissertation, Massachusetts Institute of Technology, Cambridge, MA.

Wang, X., and G. Chen. 2002. Pinning control of scale-free dynamical networks. *Physica A* 310, no. 3: 521-531.

Yang, W., A. Bertozzi, and X. Wang. 2008. Proceedings of the 47th IEEE Conference on Decision and Control. In . Cancun, Mexico, December 9.

Zhu, J., Y.P. Tian, and J. Kuang. 2009. On the general consensus protocol of multi-agent systems with double-integrator dynamics. *Linear Algebra and its Applications* 431: 701-715.

4

Model-Based Nonlinear Cluster Space Control of Mobile Robot Formations

Ignacio Mas, Christopher Kitts and Robert Lee
Santa Clara University
USA

1. Introduction

Multi-robot systems have the potential to improve application-specific performance by offering redundancy, increased coverage and throughput, flexible reconfiguration, and/or spatially diverse functionality (Kitts & Egerstedt, 2008). For mobile systems, a driving consideration is the method by which the motions of the individual vehicles are coordinated. Centralized approaches have been successfully demonstrated (Yamaguchi & Arai, 1994; Tan & Lewis, 1996) and have been found to be useful for material transport, regional synoptic sampling, and sensing techniques where active stimulus and/or signal reception are spatially distributed (Hashimoto et al., 1993; Rus et al., 1995; Tang et al., 2006). Such approaches, however, typically suffer from limited scalability and the need for global information. As an alternative, decentralized approaches have been shown to hold great promise in addressing scalability and limited information exchange (Siljak, 1991; Ikeda, 1989; Yang et al., 2005); such approaches often employ control strategies that are behavioral (Balch & Hybinette, 2000; Flinn, 2005; Khatib, 1985), biologically-inspired (Murray, 2007), optimization-based (Dunbar & Murray, 2006), or potential field-based (Leonard & Fiorelli, 2001; Ogren et al., 2004; Justh & Krishnaprasad, 2004; Stipanovic et al., 2004). In this chapter, we present our work relating to the cluster space control technique for multi-robot systems, specifically its implementation using a nonlinear, model-based controller in both kinematic and dynamic forms. The cluster space state representation provides a simple means of specifying and monitoring the geometry and motion characteristics of a cluster of mobile robots without sacrificing flexibility in specifying formation constraints or limiting the ability to fully articulate the formation (Kitts & Mas, 2009). The cluster space control strategy conceptualizes the n-robot system as a single entity, a cluster, and desired motions are specified as a function of cluster attributes, such as position, orientation, and geometry. These attributes guide the selection of a set of independent system state variables suitable for specification, control, and monitoring. These state variables form the system's cluster space. Cluster space state variables are related to robot-specific state variables through a formal set of kinematic transforms. These transforms allow cluster commands to be converted to robot-specific commands, and for sensed robot-specific state data to be converted to cluster space state data. With the formal kinematics defined, the controller is composed such that desired motions are specified and control compensations are computed in the cluster space. For a kinematic controller, suitable for robots with negligible dynamics such as many low-speed wheeled robots, compensation commands are transformed to robot space through the inverse Jacobian relationship. For a dynamic controller, appropriate for clusters of marine and aerial robots, compensation commands are transformed to robot space through a Jacobian transpose relationship. In either case, the resulting robot-level commands are transformed to actuator commands through a vehicle-level inverse Jacobian. If robot space variables are sensed, they are transformed to the cluster space through the use of forward kinematic relationships in order to support control computations. Desired cluster space motions may be provided as regulation inputs, by a trajectory generator, by a realtime pilot, or by a higher-level application-specific controller. The Jacobian and inverse Jacobian matrices are functions of the cluster's pose and therefore must be updated at an appropriate rate. We have successfully used this control approach to demonstrate cluster-space-based versions of regulated motion (Ishizu, 2005), automated trajectory control (Connolley, 2006; To, 2006), human-in-the-loop piloting (Kalkbrenner, 2006; Tully, 2006), and both centralized and decentralized formation control (Mas & Kitts, 2010a). This work has included experiments with 2-, 3- and 4-robot planar land rover clusters (Mas et al., 2008; Mas, Acain, Petrovic & Kitts, 2009; Girod, 2008), with 2- and 3- surface vessel systems (Mahacek et al., 2009) and aerial blimps (Agnew, 2009), for robots that are both holonomic and non-holonomic, for robots negotiating obstacle fields (Kitts et al., 2009), and for target applications such as escorting and patrolling (Mahacek et al., 2009; Mas, Li, Acain & Kitts, 2009). In the following sections, we review the cluster space control strategy to include its formulation, the development of the appropriate kinematic relationships, and the composition of its control architecture. We also present the development of a kinematic and a dynamic nonlinear, model-based partitioned controller. For each case, we present experimental results that verify these techniques and demonstrate the capabilities of the cluster space control approach.

2. Cluster space framework

The cluster space approach to controlling formations of multiple robots was first introduced in (Kitts & Mas, 2009). The first step in the development of the cluster space control architecture is the selection of an appropriate set of cluster space state variables. To do this, we introduce a cluster reference frame and select a set of state variables that capture key pose and geometry elements of the cluster. Consider the general case of a system of n mobile robots where each robot has m DOF, with $m \leq 6$, and an attached body frame, as depicted in Fig. 1. Typical robot-oriented representations of pose use mn variables to represent the position and orientation of each of the robot body frames, $\{1\}, \{2\}, \cdots, \{n\}$, with respect to a global frame $\{G\}$. In contrast, consideration of the cluster space representation starts with the definition of a cluster frame $\{C\}$, and its pose. The pose of each robot is then expressed relative to the cluster frame. We note that the positioning of the $\{C\}$ frame with respect to the n robots is often critical in achieving a cluster space framework that benefits the operator/pilot. In practice, $\{C\}$ is often positioned and oriented in a manner with geometric significance, such as at the cluster's centroid and oriented toward the 'lead' vehicle or alternatively, coincident with a lead vehicle's body frame. An additional set of variables defining the shape of the formation complete the representation.

2.1 Selection of cluster space variables

We select as our state variables a set of position variables (and their derivatives) that capture the cluster's pose and geometry. For the general case of m-DOF robots, where the pose variables of $\{C\}$ with respect to $\{G\}$ are $(x_c, y_c, z_c, \alpha_c, \beta_c, \gamma_c)$ and where the pose variables

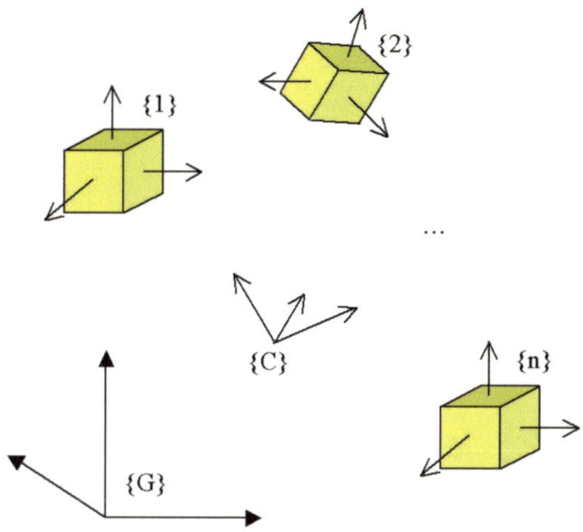

Fig. 1. Cluster and Robot Frame Descriptions with Respect to a Global Frame

for robot i with respect to $\{C\}$ are $(x_i, y_i, z_i, \alpha_i, \beta_i, \gamma_i)$ for $i = 1, 2, \cdots, n$:

$$\begin{aligned} c_1 &= f_1(x_c, y_c, z_c, \alpha_c, \beta_c, \gamma_c, x_1, y_1, z_1, \alpha_1, \beta_1, \gamma_1, \cdots, x_n, y_n, z_n, \alpha_n, \beta_n, \gamma_n) \\ c_2 &= f_2(x_c, y_c, z_c, \alpha_c, \beta_c, \gamma_c, x_1, y_1, z_1, \alpha_1, \beta_1, \gamma_1, \cdots, x_n, y_n, z_n, \alpha_n, \beta_n, \gamma_n) \\ &\vdots \\ c_{mn} &= f_{mn}(x_c, y_c, z_c, \alpha_c, \beta_c, \gamma_c, x_1, y_1, z_1, \alpha_1, \beta_1, \gamma_1, \cdots, x_n, y_n, z_n, \alpha_n, \beta_n, \gamma_n). \end{aligned} \tag{1}$$

The appropriate selection of cluster state variables may be a function of the application, the system's design, and subjective criteria such as operator preference. In practice, however, we have found great value in selecting state variables based on the metaphor of a virtual kinematic mechanism that can move through space while being arbitrarily scaled and articulated. This leads to the use of several general categories of cluster pose variables (and their derivatives) that specify cluster position, cluster orientation, relative robot-to-cluster orientation, and cluster shape. A general methodology for selecting the number of variables corresponding to each category given the number of robots and their DOF is described in (Kitts & Mas, 2009). Furthermore, an appropriate selection of cluster variables allows for centralized or distributed control architectures (Mas & Kitts, 2010a). As an example of cluster variables selection, consider a group of two robots that may be driven in a plane. The cluster space view of this simple multirobot system could be represented as a line segment at a certain location, oriented in a specific direction, and with a particular size. A pilot could "drive" the cluster along an arbitrary path while varying the orientation and size of the line segment. Similarly, a three-robot planar system could be represented as a triangle at a certain location, oriented in a certain direction, and with a specific shape. The pilot could "drive" this cluster along an arbitrary path while varying the shape and size of the triangle. The triangle could be "flattened" into a straight line while driving through a narrow passage. Overall, the cluster space approach allows the pilot to specify and monitor motions from the cluster space perspective, with automated kinematic transformations converting this point of view. This method can be thought as analogous to the cartesian or operational space control used for serial manipulator chains, where motions can be specified and monitor with respect to the end effector position, and kinematic transforms relate variables in operational space and joint space.

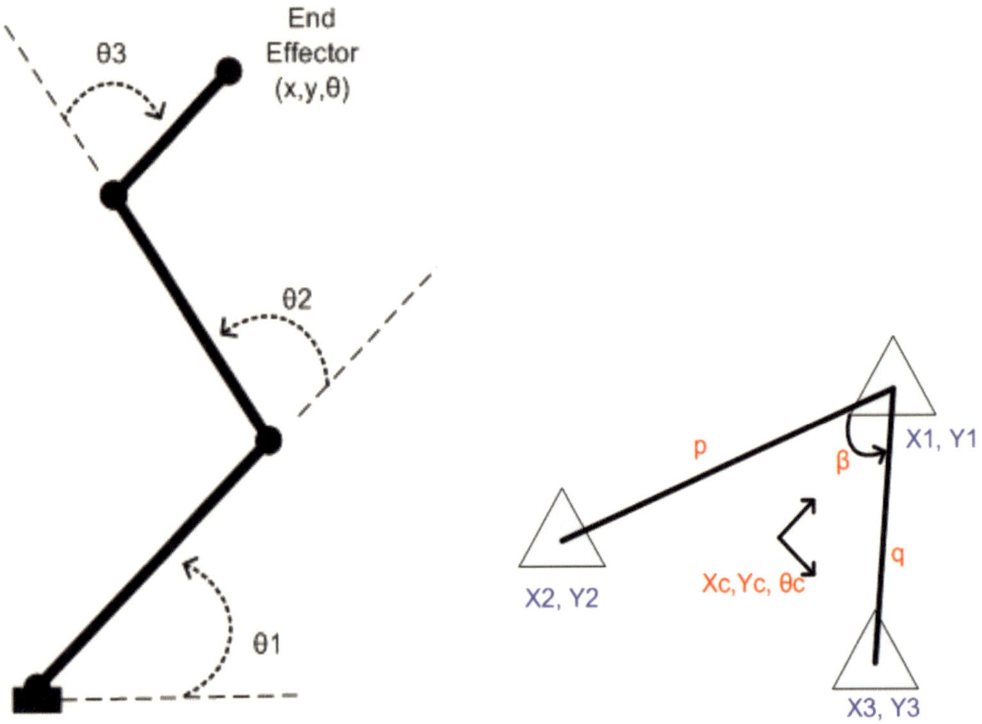

(a) Manipulator (b) Multirobot cluster

Fig. 2. Analogy between definition of variables for a serial chain manipulator and a mobile multirobot system. For manipulator chains, joint space variables are related to operational space variables through formal kinematics. In the cluster framework robot space variables–robot positions–are related to cluster space variables–cluster position, orientation and shape.

2.2 Cluster kinematic relationships

We wish to specify multi-robot system motion and compute required control actions in the cluster space using cluster state variables selected as described in the previous section. Given that these control actions will be implemented by each individual robot (and ultimately by the actuators within each robot), we develop formal kinematic relationships relating the cluster space variables and robot space variables. We can define $mn \times 1$ robot and cluster pose vectors, r and c, respectively. These state vectors are related through a set of forward and inverse position kinematic relationships:

$$c = KIN(r) = \begin{pmatrix} g_1(r_1, r_2, \cdots, r_{mn}) \\ g_2(r_1, r_2, \cdots, r_{mn}) \\ \vdots \\ g_{mn}(r_1, r_2, \cdots, r_{mn}) \end{pmatrix} \tag{2}$$

$$r \;= INVKIN(c) = \begin{pmatrix} h_1(c_1, c_2, \cdots, c_{mn}) \\ h_2(c_1, c_2, \cdots, c_{mn}) \\ \vdots \\ h_{mn}(c_1, c_2, \cdots, c_{mn}) \end{pmatrix}. \tag{3}$$

We may also consider the formal relationship between the robot and cluster space velocities, $\dot{r}$ and $\dot{c}$. From (2), we may compute the differentials of the cluster space state variables, c_i, and develop a Jacobian matrix, $J(r)$, that maps robot velocities to cluster velocities in the form of a time-varying linear function:

$$\dot{c} = J(r)\,\dot{r} \tag{4}$$

where

$$J(r) = \begin{pmatrix} \frac{\partial c_1}{\partial r_1} & \frac{\partial c_1}{\partial r_2} & \cdots & \frac{\partial c_1}{\partial r_{mn}} \\ \frac{\partial c_2}{\partial r_1} & \frac{\partial c_2}{\partial r_2} & \cdots & \frac{\partial c_2}{\partial r_{mn}} \\ \vdots & \vdots & \ddots & \vdots \\ \frac{\partial c_{mn}}{\partial r_1} & \frac{\partial c_{mn}}{\partial r_2} & \cdots & \frac{\partial c_{mn}}{\partial r_{mn}} \end{pmatrix}. \tag{5}$$

In a similar manner, we may develop the inverse Jacobian, $J^{-1}(c)$, which maps cluster velocities to robot velocities. Computing the robot space state variable differentials from (3) yields:

$$\dot{r} = J^{-1}(c)\,\dot{c} \tag{6}$$

where

$$J^{-1}(c) = \begin{pmatrix} \frac{\partial r_1}{\partial c_1} & \frac{\partial r_1}{\partial c_2} & \cdots & \frac{\partial r_1}{\partial c_{mn}} \\ \frac{\partial r_2}{\partial c_1} & \frac{\partial r_2}{\partial c_2} & \cdots & \frac{\partial r_2}{\partial c_{mn}} \\ \vdots & \vdots & \ddots & \vdots \\ \frac{\partial r_{mn}}{\partial c_1} & \frac{\partial r_{mn}}{\partial c_2} & \cdots & \frac{\partial r_{mn}}{\partial c_{mn}} \end{pmatrix}. \tag{7}$$

3. Cluster space kinematic control

Our initial work in nonlinear cluster space control used a kinematic controller in the cluster space. This controller specifies desired cluster space velocities for the multi-robot formation as a function of the errors in the cluster's position, orientation and shape. These velocities are transformed to robot-specific velocities, which serve as instantaneous command set-points for dynamic speed controllers that execute on each individual robot. This architecture is particularly appropriate for the formation control of robots that have such speed control functionality, which is the case for many commercially available wheeled robots (Schwager et al., 2009). The initial implementation of our nonlinear kinematic controller was developed in (Lee, 2007). Because each robot has an on-board velocity control system, a model of the closed loop dynamics is used rather than a model specific to the robot's physical parameters. This model is combined with the relevant kinematic and frame transforms in order to establish a relationship between the commanded cluster space velocity and the actual cluster space pose:

$$c = \int \dot{c}\,dt = \int J(r)\dot{r}\,dt = \int J(r)\,DYN\,\dot{r}_{cmd}\,dt = \int J(r)\,DYN\,J^{-1}(c)\,\dot{c}_{cmd}\,dt, \tag{8}$$

where DYN is the model of the closed loop dynamics. Given this mapping, a partitioned controller may be developed by inverting this relationship and substituting commanded cluster velocities with a proportional error-driven control term. With this accomplished, the control equation may be expressed in the form:

$$\dot{c}_{cmd} = \gamma\Big(M(c)K(c_{des} - c) + \beta(c)c\Big). \tag{9}$$

Our work in using this technique has been accomplished using both a dynamic model for each individual robot's translation and rotation as well as for dynamic models of each robot's individual actuators.

3.1 Model-based kinematic cluster control architecture

Kinematic control of the formation is performed by having the controller compute a cluster space velocity command, which is then transformed to a robot space velocity vector using (6). This computation exploits a partitioning strategy, which decomposes the control into a model-based portion and an idealized servo portion. The model-based term exploits knowledge of the formation's dynamics to cancel out nonlinearities and decouple the cluster parameters. Figure 3 shows the kinematic control architecture of the non-linear partitioned controller. The cluster's inverse Jacobian transform converts the controller's cluster space velocity output to the individual velocity commands for each robot in the formation.

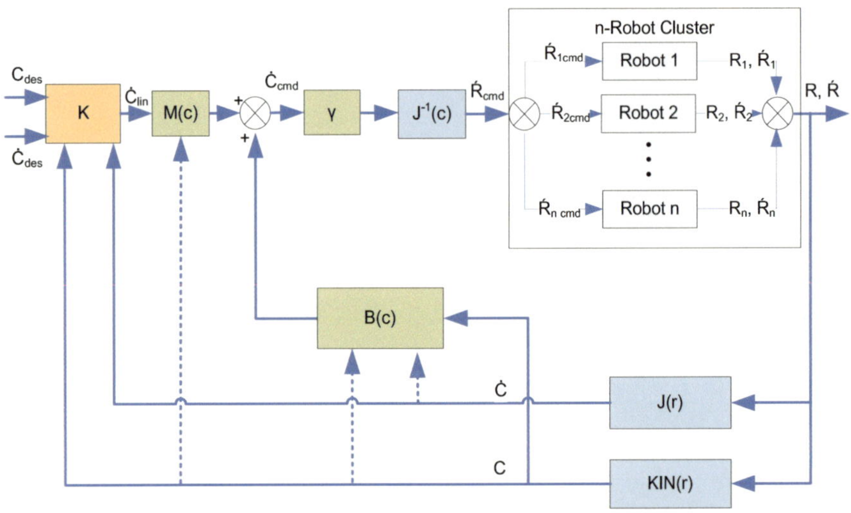

Fig. 3. Model-based kinematic cluster space control architecture for a mobile n-robot system. Desired control velocities are computed in cluster space and a partitioned control architecture decouples the system. The inverse Jacobian matrix converts the resulting cluster space velocities to robot space velocities that are then applied to the system. Robot sensor information is converted to cluster space through the Jacobian and kinematic relationships.

3.2 Experiments with a formation of two land rovers

Extensive verification of the nonlinear cluster space controller has been performed through both simulation and hardware experimentation. Here, we summarize a few of the experimental results conducted on a two-robot formation of custom-built omni-wheeled robots. As a two-robot system, the robot space pose is defined as:

$$r = (x_1, y_1, \theta_1, x_2, y_2, \theta_2)^T, \tag{10}$$

where $(x_i, y_i, \theta_i)^T$ defines the position and orientation of robot i. For this formation's cluster space formulation, the cluster frame $\{C\}$ was located at the midpoint of the cluster, as shown in Figure 4. The resulting cluster space pose is represented as:

$$c = (x_c, y_c, \theta_c, \phi_1, \phi_2, d)^T, \tag{11}$$

where $(x_c, y_c, \theta_c)^T$ is the position and orientation of the cluster, ϕ_i is the yaw orientation of robot i relative to the cluster, and d is the single required shape variable defined as half the separation between robots. The cluster space and robot space state variables may be related through a set of forward and inverse kinematic transforms. The derivative of these expressions leads to the forward and inverse velocity kinematic transforms, which are characterized by a Jacobian matrix. The derivation of these transforms are provided in (Lee, 2007). Experimental evaluation of this formulation was conducted with two holonomic,

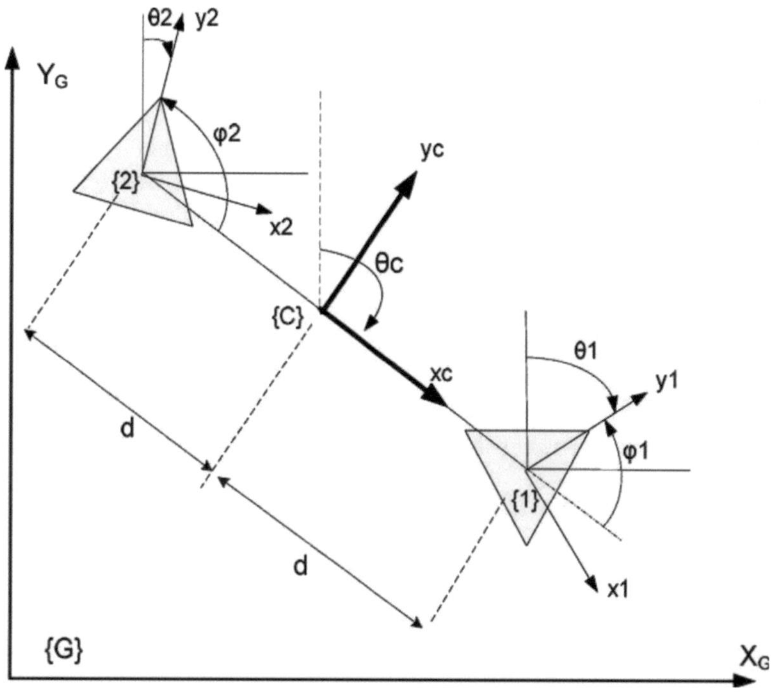

Fig. 4. Reference frame definition placing the cluster center at the center of the two robots

omni-wheeled robots operating in a plane. These student-developed robots consisted of a chassis with three omni-wheels, power components, a sonar suite, a 900 MHz serial radio-modem, and an Atmel AGMEGA128-based microcontroller for on-board control. The robots are capable of closed loop velocity control through the use of wheel encoders and industrial PID controller, with the vehicle-to-wheel inverse kinematic computation performed by the robot's microcontroller. The robots communicate with an off-board control computer for human interfacing and cluster space control computation, and an overhead camera system tracks robot position and orientation. Figure 5 shows the omni-wheeled robots used for experimentation.

Fig. 5. Omni-wheeled robots utilized for experimentation

3.3 Results

As the simplest of the two experimental systems discussed in this article, one test result from (Lee, 2007) is shown here to demonstrate the behavior of the controller. In this test, the two-robot cluster was given concurrent pose step inputs that required a both translation (a relocation of the cluster centroid) and a rotation through a 90 degree angle, while maintaining cluster size. For this experiment, cluster space sensing and control executed at a rate of approximately 2 Hz, and the accuracy of the overhead vision system was approximately +/- 5 cm over the 15 ft x 15 ft workspace. Results of the maneuver are shown in Figure 6. As can be seen, the cluster space variables of interest are each controlled (within the stated accuracy of the position tracking system) as if they were uncoupled, critically damped (with some initial saturation), 2nd order systems, which is the objective of our controller.

4. Cluster space dynamic control

For some robotic platforms, the kinematic model approximation described in the previous section may not hold true and a dynamic approach to modeling and control may be required. Examples of such robots are land rovers with non-negligible dynamics, aerial robots or marine robotic vehicles. For the development of a cluster space dynamic model, it is assumed that the robots composing the system are holonomic and that the formation stays away from singularities. Cluster space singular configurations are described in (Mas, Acain, Petrovic & Kitts, 2009). Next, we will show the relationship between cluster space generalized forces, composed of forces and torques in cluster space, and robot space generalized forces, composed of robot space forces and torques. This derivation is based on the work developed for operational space control of serial chain manipulators presented in (Khatib, 1987) and (Khatib, 1980) and the details are shown in (Mas & Kitts, 2010b). The dynamics of the system in cluster space can be represented by the Lagrangian $\mathcal{L}(c,\dot{c})$:

$$\mathcal{L}(c,\dot{c}) = T(c,\dot{c}) - U(c). \tag{12}$$

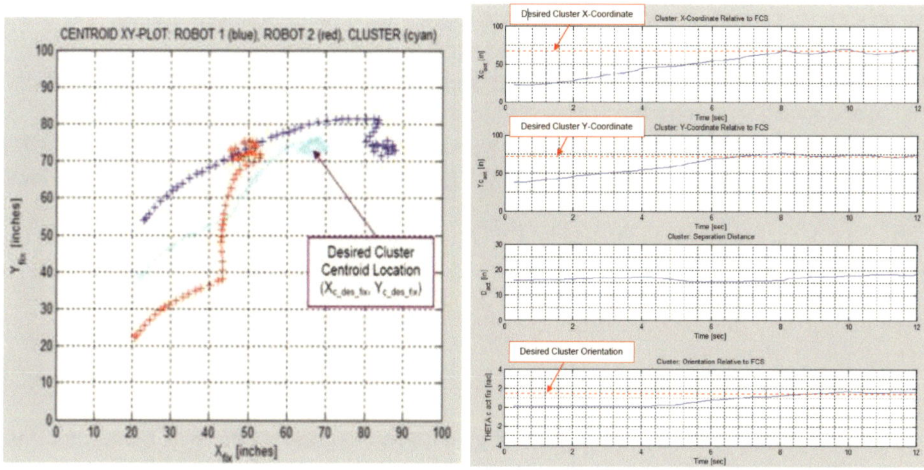

(a) Overhead View (b) Time History

Fig. 6. Kinematic cluster control experiment results with a formation of two holonomic robots. Position and orientation trajectories.

The kinetic energy of the system can be represented as a quadratic form of the cluster space velocities

$$T(c,\dot{c}) = \frac{1}{2}\dot{c}^T \Lambda(c)\,\dot{c}, \tag{13}$$

where $\Lambda(c)$ is the $mn \times mn$ symmetric matrix of the quadratic form, i.e., the kinetic energy matrix, and $U(c) = U(KIN(r))$ represents the potential energy due to gravity. For rovers on a plane, the gravity force is canceled out by the force normal to the surface and the gravitational potential energy term can be neglected. For other systems, including aerial unmanned vehicles (AUVs), underwater autonomous vehicles (UAVs) or planar rovers operating on an inclined plane, the gravity term must be included. Let $p(c)$ be the vector of gravity forces in cluster space

$$p(c) = \nabla U(c). \tag{14}$$

Using Lagrangian mechanics, the equations of motion in cluster space are given by

$$\frac{d}{dt}\left(\frac{\partial \mathcal{L}}{\partial \dot{c}}\right) - \frac{\partial \mathcal{L}}{\partial c} = F. \tag{15}$$

The equations of motion in cluster space can then be derived from (15) and written in the form

$$\Lambda(c)\,\ddot{c} + \mu(c,\dot{c}) + p(c) = F \tag{16}$$

where $\mu(c,\dot{c})$ is the vector of cluster space centrifugal and Coriolis forces and F is the generalized force vector in cluster space. The equations of motion (16) describe the relationships between positions, velocities, and accelerations of the formation location, orientation, and shape variables and the forces defined in cluster space acting on the formation. The dynamic parameters in these equations are related to the parameters of the robot dynamic models. The dynamics in robot space can by described by

$$A(r)\,\ddot{r} + b(r,\dot{r}) + g(r) = \Gamma \tag{17}$$

where $b(r,\dot{r})$, $g(r)$ and Γ represent, respectively, velocity dependent forces, gravity and generalized forces in robot space. $A(r)$ is the $mn \times mn$ robot space kinetic energy matrix. The relationship between the kinetic energy matrices $A(r)$ and $\Lambda(c)$ corresponding, respectively, to the robot space and cluster space dynamic models can be established (Khatib, 1980; Mas & Kitts, 2010b) by exploiting the identity between the expressions of the quadratic forms of the system kinetic energy with respect to the generalized robot and cluster space velocities,

$$\Lambda(c) = J^{-T}(r)\, A(r)\, J^{-1}(r). \tag{18}$$

The relationship between $b(r,\dot{r})$ and $\mu(c,\dot{c})$ can be established by the expansion of the expression of $\mu(c,\dot{c})$ that results from (15),

$$\mu(c,\dot{c}) = J^{-T}(r)\, b(r,\dot{r}) - \Lambda(r)\, \dot{J}(r,\dot{r})\, \dot{r}. \tag{19}$$

The relationship between the expressions of gravity forces can be obtained using the identity between the functions expressing the gravity potential energy in the two spaces and the relationships between the partial derivatives with respect to the variables in these spaces. Using the definition of the Jacobian matrix (6) yields

$$p(c) = J^{-T}(r)\, g(r). \tag{20}$$

Finally, we can establish the relationship between generalized forces in cluster space and robot space, F and Γ. Using (18), (19), and (20), the cluster space equations of motion (16) can be rewritten as

$$J^{-T}(r)\left[A(r)\, \ddot{r} + b(r,\dot{r}) + g(r)\right] = F. \tag{21}$$

Substituting (17) yields

$$\Gamma = J^{T}(r)\, F \tag{22}$$

which represents the fundamental relationship between cluster space forces and robots space forces. This relationship is the basis for the dynamic control of the robot formation from the cluster space perspective.

4.1 Model-based dynamic cluster control architecture

The dynamic control of the formation is performed by generating a cluster space generalized force vector F that is then transformed to a robot space force vector Γ using (22). In order to obtain such a control vector, we use a nonlinear dynamic decoupling approach (Craig, 2005). In this approach, we partition the controller into a model-based portion and a servo portion. The model-based portion uses the dynamic model of the cluster to cancel out nonlinearities and decouple the cluster parameters. The resulting control law then has the form

$$F = \Lambda(c)\, F_m + \mu(c,\dot{c}) + p(c). \tag{23}$$

where $\Lambda(c)$, $\mu(c,\dot{c})$ and $p(c)$ are the cluster space dynamic model parameters. F_m is the command force vector acting on an equivalent cluster space unit mass decoupled system, which we define as

$$F_m = \ddot{c}_{des} + K_p\, e_c + K_v\, \dot{e}_c, \tag{24}$$

where $e_c = c_{des} - c$ and $\dot{e}_c = \dot{c}_{des} - \dot{c}$ are, respectively, the cluster space position and velocity errors, and K_p and K_v are positive definite matrices. Figure 7 shows the dynamic control architecture of the non-linear partitioned controller.

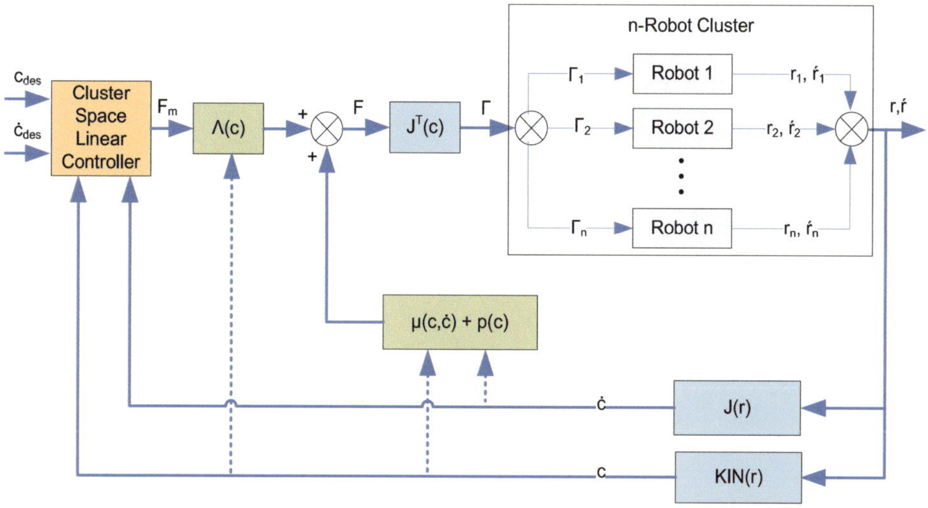

Fig. 7. Model-based dynamic cluster space control architecture for a mobile n-robot system.

4.2 Experiments with a formation of three surface vessel marine robots

To illustrate the functionality of the proposed formation control approach applied to systems with non-negligible dynamics, we conducted experimental tests with a group of three autonomous surface vessels (ASV). In order to apply the method to a planar three-robot system, the cluster space variables must be defined and the kinematic transforms must be generated. Figure 8 depicts the relevant reference frames for the planar three-robot problem. We have chosen to locate the cluster frame $\{C\}$ at the cluster's centroid, oriented with Y_c pointing toward robot 1. Based on this, the nine robot space state variables (three robots with three DOF per robot) are mapped into nine cluster space variables for a nine DOF cluster.

Given the parameters defined by Figure 8, the robot space pose vector is defined as:

$$\vec{r} = (x_1, y_1, \theta_1, x_2, y_2, \theta_2, x_3, y_3, \theta_3)^T, \tag{25}$$

where $(x_i, y_i, \theta_i)^T$ defines the position and orientation of robot i. The cluster space pose vector definition is given by:

$$\vec{c} = (x_c, y_c, \theta_c, \phi_1, \phi_2, \phi_3, p, q, \beta)^T, \tag{26}$$

where $(x_c, y_c, \theta_c)^T$ is the cluster position and orientation, ϕ_i is the yaw orientation of robot i relative to the cluster, p and q are the distances from robot 1 to robots 2 and 3, respectively, and β is the skew angle with vertex on robot 1. Given this selection of cluster space state variables, we can express the forward and inverse position kinematics of the three-robot system. These complete expressions can be found in (Mas, Li, Acain & Kitts, 2009). By differentiating the forward and inverse position kinematic equations, the forward and inverse velocity kinematics can easily be derived, obtaining the Jacobian and inverse Jacobian matrices. It should be noted that this particular selection of cluster space variables is not unique, and different sets of variables may be chosen following the same framework when more convenient for a given task. To validate the approach with experimental results, a testbed of three autonomous surface vessel (ASV) marine robots is used. Each robot is an off-the-shelf kayak retrofitted with two thrusters producing a differential drive behavior and an electronics box that includes motor controllers, GPS, a compass, and a wireless communication system. A remote central computer receives sensor information from the ASVs, executes the cluster

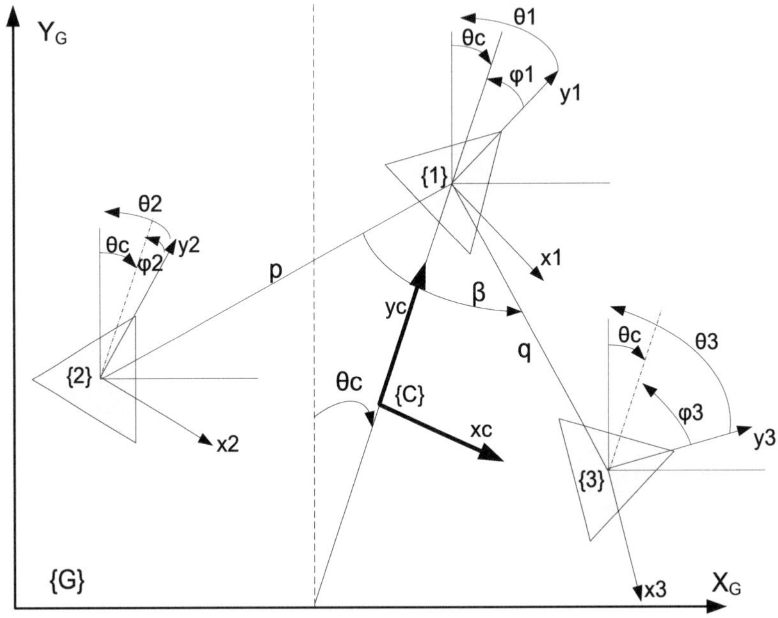

Fig. 8. Reference frame definition placing the cluster center at the triangle centroid

controller algorithms, and sends the appropriate compensation signals. A detailed description of this testbed can be found in (Mahacek et al., 2009). Figure 9 shows the ASVs used for the experiments. To accommodate for the non-holonomic constraints, a robot-level heading control inner-loop is implemented on each robot to achieve required bearings. The model-based partitioned controller makes use of a dynamic model of the cluster to compute the appropriate compensation. The cluster dynamic equation is obtained through the model parameters of the ASVs. Using (17), the parameters for the ith ASV are (Mahacek, 2009):

$$A_i(r) = \begin{pmatrix} 150kg & 0 & 0 \\ 0 & 150kg & 0 \\ 0 & 0 & 41kgm^2 \end{pmatrix}, \tag{27}$$

$$b_i(r,\dot{r}) = \begin{pmatrix} 100\frac{kg}{s}\dot{r}_x \\ 400\frac{kg}{s}\dot{r}_y \\ 25\frac{kgm^2}{srad}\dot{\theta} \end{pmatrix}, \tag{28}$$

$$g_i(r) = 0. \tag{29}$$

Using (18), (19), and the Jacobian matrices given by the cluster definition, the cluster dynamic parameters can be computed in execution time to produce dynamic compensation in the controller.

4.3 Results

Two experimental tests implementing the cluster dynamic controller are shown in this article. On the first one, the formation of ASVs follows a rectangular position trajectory, composed with a cluster rotation on the second half of it. The cluster shape parameters are held constant throughout the test. An overhead view of the resulting motions, and desired and measured

Fig. 9. Autonomous surface vehicles with propulsion systems and custom sensor and communication suites.

values for the cluster parameters over time are shown in Figure 10. In the second test, the position and orientation of the cluster are held constant and the shape parameters follow specified trajectories. An overhead view, and desired and measured values for the cluster parameters over time are shown in Figure 11. In both runs, the cluster parameters follow their desired values over time. Table 1 shows the mean squared errors for the cluster space parameters in both tests. Position sensing errors due to GPS receivers as well as errors in the estimation of the ASVs dynamic model parameters result in tracking errors during the experiments. In the second test, additional environmental disturbances introduced by wind and currents decreased the system performance. Overall, the experiments illustrate the basic functionality of the non-linear partition controlled model-based approach to cluster control of formations of mobile robots with non-negligible dynamics.

	MSE	
Cluster Parameter	Test 1 - Position Traj.	Test 2 - Shape Traj.
$x_c \quad (m^2)$	1.26065	9.65675
$y_c \quad (m^2)$	1.36074	4.58394
$\theta_c \quad (rad^2)$	0.00446	0.00003
$p \quad (m^2)$	0.53422	4.01754
$q \quad (m^2)$	0.17589	20.37102
$\beta \quad (rad^2)$	0.07355	0.00016

Table 1. Experimental Results. Mean Square Errors for Test 1–Position Trajectories–and Test 2–Shape Trajectories–.

5. Conclusions

The cluster space control approach for planar robots was briefly reviewed and two alternative model-based non-linear control architectures were presented. A kinematic approach to controlling formations of robots that have on-board closed-loop velocity control capabilities was presented. This controller exploits a partitioning strategy, which decomposes the control

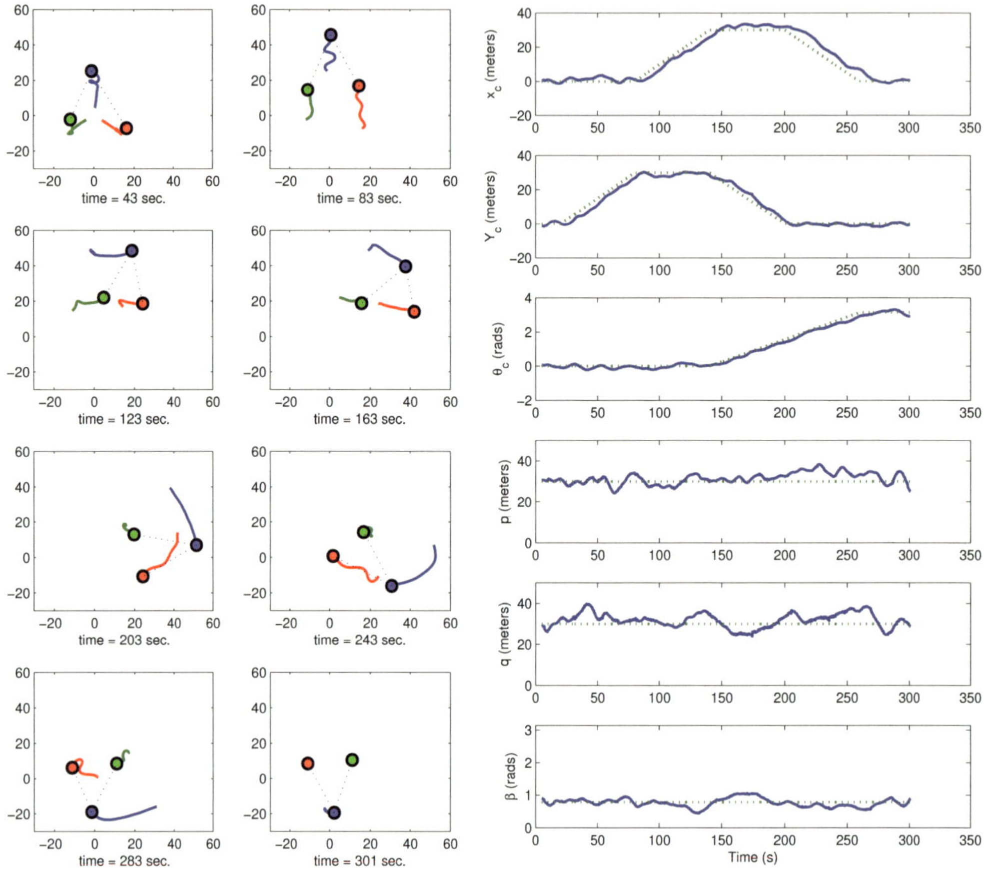

(a) Overhead View (b) Time History

Fig. 10. Dynamic cluster control experiment 1 results. Position and orientation trajectories.

into a model-based portion and an idealized servo portion. The model-based term exploits knowledge of the formation's dynamics to cancel out nonlinearities and decouple the cluster parameters. Experimental results using two omni-wheeled robots illustrate the effectiveness of the architecture. A dynamic approach to be used when the dynamics of the robots are not negligible was proposed and the equations of motion for the cluster space variables were derived. The parameters of the cluster space dynamics were then defined as a function of the dynamic parameters of the robots in the formation. It was shown that generalized forces in cluster space can be related to forces in robot space through the Jacobian transpose matrix. A non-linear cluster level dynamic partitioned controller was proposed. The model-based portion of such a controller cancels out the cluster space non-linear dynamics and allows for the cluster variables to be decoupled. The servo portion of the controller then effectively sees a set of decoupled unit mass plants. The proposed model-based dynamic controller was then applied to an experimental testbed composed of three ASVs. Results were presented in order to demonstrate the functionality of the system. The experiments showed the ability of the formation to navigate following position, orientation, and shape trajectories. Ongoing work includes the integration of obstacle avoidance methods and addressing in detail the

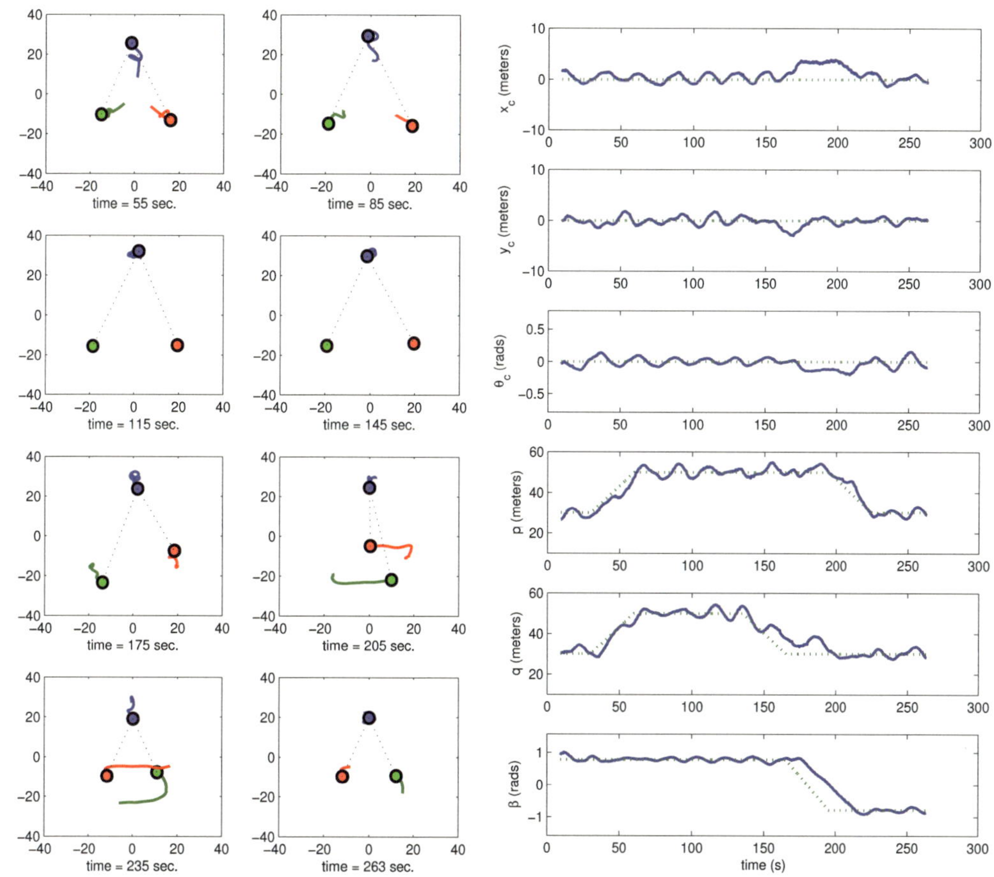

(a) Overhead View (b) Time History

Fig. 11. Dynamic cluster control experiment 2 results. Formation shape trajectories.

impact of errors in the estimations of the dynamic parameters of the robots. The study of alternative cluster definitions is being conducted under the assumption that they may be more convenient for specifying and monitoring requirements for different missions, they can be used to avoid singularities, and can be selected to reduce computational requirements. Future applications using the cluster space approach include marine environment survey via vehicle differential measurements and dynamic beamforming using cluster controlled smart antennae arrays (Okamoto et al., 2010).

6. Acknowledgments

The authors gratefully thank Paul Mahacek, Steve Li, Vincent Howard and Thomas Adamek for developing and managing the ASVs experimental testbed. This work has been sponsored through a variety of funding sources to include Santa Clara University Technology Steering Committee grant TSC131 and National Science Foundation Grant No. CNS-0619940. Any opinions, findings, and conclusions or recommendations expressed in this material are those of the authors and do not necessarily reflect the views of the National Science Foundation.

7. References

Agnew, S. (2009). *Cluster space control of a 2-robot aerial system*, Master's thesis, Santa Clara University.

Balch, T. & Hybinette, M. (2000). Behavior-based coordination of large-scale robot formations, *MultiAgent Systems, 2000. Proceedings. Fourth International Conference on* pp. 363–364.

Connolley, P. (2006). *Design and implementation of a cluster space trajectory controller for multiple holonomic*, Master's thesis, Santa Clara University.

Craig, J. (2005). *Introduction to Robotics, Mechanics and Control*, Pearson Prentice Hall, Third Edition.

Dunbar, W. & Murray, R. M. (2006). Distributed receding horizon control for multi-vehicle formation stabilization, *Automatica* 42(4): 549–558.

Flinn, E. (2005). Testing for the 'boids', *Aerospace America* 43(6): 28–29.

Girod, E. (2008). *Design and implementation of four robot cluster space control*, Master's thesis, Santa Clara University.

Hashimoto, M., Oba, F. & Eguchi, T. (1993). Dynamic control approach for motion coordination of multiple wheeled mobile robots transporting a single object, *Intelligent Robots and Systems '93, IROS '93. Proceedings of the 1993 IEEE/RSJ International Conference on* 3: 1944–1951 vol.3.

Ikeda, M. (1989). Decentralized control of large scale systems, *Three decades of mathematical system theory: A collection of surveys at the occasion of the 50th birthday of Jan C. Willems* pp. 219–242.

Ishizu, R. (2005). *The design, simulation and implementation of multi-robot collaborative control from cluster perspective*, Master's thesis, Santa Clara University.

Justh, E. W. & Krishnaprasad, P. S. (2004). Equilibria and steering laws for planar formations, *Systems and Control Letters* 52: 25 – 38.

Kalkbrenner, M. (2006). *Design and implementation of a cluster space human interface controller, including applications to multi-robot piloting and multi-robot object manipulation*, Master's thesis, Santa Clara University.

Khatib, O. (1980). *Commande Dynamique dans l'espace opérationnel des robots manipulateurs en présence d'obstacles*, Thése de docteur-ingénieur, Ecole Nationale Supérieure de l'aéronautique et de l'espace, Toulouse, France.

Khatib, O. (1985). The potential field approach and operational space formulation in robot control, *Proc. Fourth Yale Workshop on Applications of Adaptive Systems Theory, Yale University, New Haven, Connecticut* pp. 208–214.

Khatib, O. (1987). A unified approach for motion and force control of robot manipulators: The operational space formulation, *Robotics and Automation, IEEE Journal of* 3(1): 43 –53.

Kitts, C. A. & Mas, I. (2009). Cluster space specification and control of mobile multirobot systems, *Mechatronics, IEEE/ASME Transactions on* 14(2): 207–218.

Kitts, C. & Egerstedt, M. (2008). Design, control, and applications of real-world multirobot systems [from the guest editors], *Robotics & Automation Magazine, IEEE* 15(1): 8–8.

Kitts, C., Stanhouse, K. & Chindaphorn, P. (2009). Cluster space collision avoidance for mobile two-robot systems, *Intelligent Robots and Systems, IEEE/RSJ International Conference on* pp. 1941–1948.

Lee, R. (2007). *Model-based cluster-space control of multiple robot systems*, Master's thesis, Santa Clara University.

Leonard, N. & Fiorelli, E. (2001). Virtual leaders, artificial potentials and coordinated control of groups, *Decision and Control, 2001. Proceedings of the 40th IEEE Conference on*

3: 2968–2973 vol.3.

Mahacek, P. (2009). *Design and cluster space control of two autonomous surface vessels*, Master's thesis, Santa Clara University.

Mahacek, P., Mas, I., Petrovic, O., Acain, J. & Kitts, C. (2009). Cluster space control of autonomous surface vessels, *Marine Technology Society Journal* 43(1): 13–20.

Mas, I., Acain, J., Petrovic, O. & Kitts, C. (2009). Error characterization in the vicinity of singularities in multi-robot cluster space control, *2008 IEEE Robotics and Biomimetics, Bangkok, Thailand. IEEE International Conference on .*

Mas, I. & Kitts, C. (2010a). Centralized and decentralized multi-robot control methods using the cluster space control framework, *Advanced Intelligent Mechatronics, IEEE/ASME International Conference on - in press .*

Mas, I. & Kitts, C. (2010b). Dynamic control of mobile multi-robot systems: The cluster space formulation, *Mechatronics, IEEE Transactions on* p. Submitted.

Mas, I., Li, S., Acain, J. & Kitts, C. (2009). Entrapment/escorting and patrolling missions in multi-robot cluster space control, *Intelligent Robots and Systems. IEEE/RSJ International Conference on* pp. 5855–5861.

Mas, I., Petrovic, O. & Kitts, C. (2008). Cluster space specification and control of a 3-robot mobile system, *Robotics and Automation, 2008. ICRA 2008. IEEE International Conference on* pp. 3763–3768.

Murray, R. M. (2007). Recent research in cooperative control of multi-vehicle systems, *Journal of Dynamics Systems, Measurement and Control* 129(5): 571–583.

Ogren, P., Fiorelli, E. & Leonard, N. (2004). Cooperative control of mobile sensor networks:adaptive gradient climbing in a distributed environment, *Automatic Control, IEEE Transactions on* 49(8): 1292 – 1302.

Okamoto, G., Chen, C. & Kitts, C. (2010). Beamforming performance for a reconfigurable sparse array smart antenna system via multi-robot control, *Proceedings of the SPIE Defense, Security, and Sensing Conference.*

Rus, D., Donald, B. & Jennings, J. (1995). Moving furniture with teams of autonomous robots, *Intelligent Robots and Systems 95. 'Human Robot Interaction and Cooperative Robots', Proceedings. 1995 IEEE/RSJ International Conference on* 1: 235–242 vol.1.

Schwager, M., Rus, D. & Slotine, J. (2009). Decentralized, adaptive coverage control for networked robots, *The International Journal of Robotics Research* 28(3): 357–375.

Siljak, D. (1991). *Decentralized Control of Complex Systems*, New York: Academic.

Stipanovic, D. M., Inalhan, G., Teo, R. & Tomlin, C. J. (2004). Decentralized overlapping control of a formation of unmanned aerial vehicles.

Tan, K.-H. & Lewis, M. (1996). Virtual structures for high-precision cooperative mobile robotic control, *Intelligent Robots and Systems '96, IROS 96, Proceedings of the 1996 IEEE/RSJ International Conference on* 1: 132–139 vol.1.

Tang, C. P., Bhatt, R., Abou-Samah, M. & Krovi, V. (2006). Screw-theoretic analysis framework for cooperative payload transport by mobile manipulator collectives, *Mechatronics, IEEE/ASME Transactions on* 11(2): 169 –178.

To, T. (2006). *Automated cluster space trajectory control of two non-holonomic robots*, Master's thesis, Santa Clara University.

Tully, B. (2006). *Cluster space piloting of a non-holonomic multi-robot system*, Master's thesis, Santa Clara University.

Yamaguchi, H. & Arai, T. (1994). Distributed and autonomous control method for generating shape of multiple mobile robot group, *Intelligent Robots and Systems '94.*

'Advanced Robotic Systems and the Real World', IROS '94. Proceedings of the IEEE/RSJ/GI International Conference on 2: 800–807 vol.2.

Yang, T., Yu, H., Fei, M. & Li, L. (2005). Networked control systems: a historical review and current research topics, *Measurement and Control* 38(1): 12–16.

5

A Robust Nonlinear Control for Differential Mobile Robots and Implementation on Formation Control

Jie Wan and Peter C. Y. Chen
Department of Mechanical Engineering, National University of Singapore
Singapore

1. Introduction

The past three decades witness a long-term intensive interest in researching a variety of control methods on wheeled mobile robots (WMRs), although the general nonholonomic systems have been investigated for more than one and half a century (Kolmanovsky & McClamroch, 1995). It is well-known that usually WMRs are characterized by non-integrable kinematic constraints, namely the nonholonomic constraints. The consequence is that those constraints rule out the possibility of direct application of standard control theories, such as linear control system theory in this field. Furthermore, as pointed out in a landmark paper (Brockett, 1983), nonholonomic systems can not be stabilized by continuously differentiable, time invariant, state feedback control laws. To cope with the challenges arising in nonhonomic system control, a great number of approaches have been proposed and some selections of the vast amount of published literature are reflected in the survey paper (Kolmanovsky & McClamroch, 1995) and the book (Dixon et al., 2001) and in chapters (7 - 9) of the book (Wit & Siciliano, 1996). Several controls from experiment perspectives are examined and implemented in the work (Luca et al., 2001). Central to the WMR motion control are the tracking control problems. Normally there are two categories of tracking control: *posture tracking* and *point tracking*. The former aims to achieving stably tracking a moving reference posture (i.e., position and orientation) while the latter only concerns about position tracking. Nonlinear feedback control strategies (Wit & Sordalen, 1992),(Godhavn & Egeland, 1997),(Kanayama et al., 1990),(Closkey & Murray, 1997),(Teel et al., 1995) are often favored in dealing with tracking control problem to compensate disturbances and uncertainties although open-loop control laws are also workable (Murray & Sastry, 1990),(Lafferiere & Sussmann, 1991),(Brraquand & Latombe, 1989),(Brockett, 1981). In recent years, more and more attention have been drawn to the robustness of the controller in presence of uncertainties. In (Aguiar et al., 2000), the authors address the regulation control of WMR with parametric modelling uncertainty using Lyapunov functions. A robust new Kalman-based active observer controller for path following was proposed (Coelho & Nunes, 2005) in circumstances of uncertainties and disturbances. And the paper (Dixon et al., 1999) presents a controller robust to parametric uncertainty and additive bounded disturbance in the dynamic model through the use of a dynamic oscillator.

An autonomous multi-robot system comprises a group of (often homogeneous) robots, each has a certain degree of mobility and autonomy. Research interests in unmanned autonomous robots have been growing significantly in recent years, due to the potential that this type of robotic systems will be able to perform a variety of tasks in environments inaccessible or too dangerous to humans. One basic problem concerning multi-root systems is formation control, whereby a group of robots maintain a certain (usually 2D) geometry while in concerted motion. When encountering obstacles (either static or dynamic), the group must maneuver to avoid them while maintaining the overall formation geometry whenever possible.

In this chapter, we studied the robustness of a nonlinear feedback control law based on a kinematic model. A generic kind of feedback control laws which cover some commonly used methods and the associated stability are quickly reviewed in a new perspective by invoking Lyapunov stability theorems. A simple fact is then unveiled that the stability proof actually depends on perfect mathematical manipulation which requires some terms of the differential equations to be cancelled. However, in real world, the perfect will be ruined under some circumstances and the robustness issue has to be investigated. Invariance principles, rather than Lyapunov stability theorems, are the major tools in dealing with the imperfect cases in which no term cancellation can be reached. The stability issue and the robustness of this control law as well is analyzed and the results lead to stable zones for each given set of controller gains. It is found that under certain circumstances the closed-looped system may fail in reaching the desired control objectives and performance. Such insights into the stability zone for a given set of controller gains make it possible to improve the controller by choosing proper controller gains. This new robust control can overcome the drawbacks of the previous commonly used counterpart. Guidelines on designing improved control law are also provided to facilitate real implementation. The merits and benefits of this new control are also highlighted through comparisons with its prototype. The analysis shows that except the more robustness, the new control law is entitled to faster response if the controller gains are properly chosen. Matlab simulation results which show the benefit are presented.

Implementation of the proposed new control law on real robots is another major work of this chapter. An implementation on multiple robot formation control is reported including overview of the whole system structure, description of the robots used in the experiments, the vision system which is used for acquisition of the real-time position information of a group of robots moving on a test bed, and the background noise analysis of the vision system and so on. In the experiments, a group of mobile robots are requested to follow their corresponding visual leaders to form certain geometric patterns. A triangle formation with three robots and a square formation with four robots are demonstrated. The velocities/headings of robots during the formation control and other information are summarized in figures. The downside of robot locomotion mechanism, which is based on step motor and its effects on real implementation, such as misstep and dead zone are discussed. Suggestions and further improvements are discussed at the end of this chapter.

This chapter is organized as follows: in Section 2, the stability problem is reviewed in a new perspective. Section 3 deals with formulation the problem of robustness. In Section 4 robustness analysis and its benefits are addressed while the effectiveness of the new proposed robust control law is verified via simulation in Section 5. Implementation and experiments with multiple robots on the application of formation control are addressed in Section 6, followed by conclusions summarized in Section 7.

2. Problem statement

We consider the *point tracking* problem for a wheeled mobile robot which is depicted in Figure 1. In this scenario, a wheeled mobile robot is supposed to track a series of goal points denoted by the symbol q_g on a segment, which is a smooth curve in the world frame.

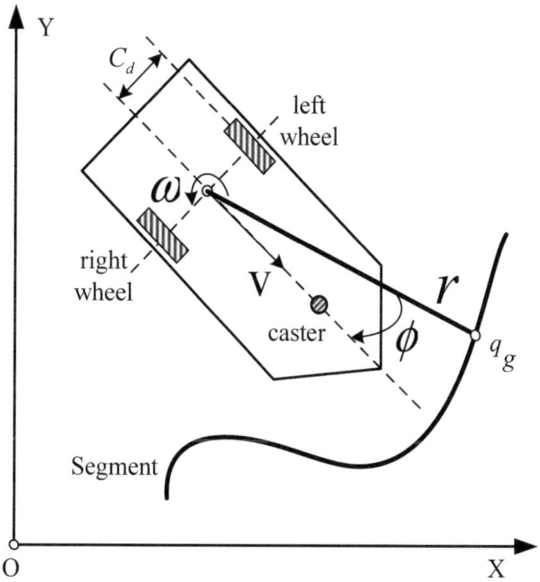

Fig. 1. Illustration of a wheeled mobile robot and its goal point q_g, which may be moving on a segment (smooth curve) in the world frame.

Referring to this figure, intuitively we refer to notations r and ϕ as "distance to target" and "misalignment angle" respectively.
As shown in Figure 2, in order to facilitate modelling kinematics of the wheeled mobile robot in a polar coordinate, specially we assign the origin to be the goal point (on the segment) for the robot to track. In this figure, a differential mobile robot, together with the associated notations, is illustrated in a polar coordinate. The separation between point (x,y) and center of each wheel is represented by C_d, which is a constant parameter for a given model of real robot. The heading of the robot is θ while its translational velocity and angular velocity are denoted by v and ω respectively. Notice that throughout this chapter, both ϕ and θ are defined in the domain $[-\pi, \pi]$.
Referring to Figure 2, motion of a differential mobile robot can be described by

$$\begin{bmatrix} \dot{\theta} \\ \dot{x} \\ \dot{y} \end{bmatrix} = \begin{bmatrix} 0 & 1 \\ \cos(\phi) & 0 \\ \sin(\phi) & 0 \end{bmatrix} \begin{bmatrix} v \\ \omega \end{bmatrix}. \tag{1}$$

To link this model with the notations in polar coordinate, we can calculate r and ϕ as

$$r = \sqrt{x^2 + y^2},$$

$$\phi = \pi + \theta - \varphi,$$

respectively.
A kinematic model of a differential robots in the polar coordinate can be derived as follows:

$$\begin{bmatrix} \dot{\theta} \\ \dot{r} \\ \dot{\phi} \end{bmatrix} = \begin{bmatrix} 0 & 1 \\ -\cos(\phi) & 0 \\ \frac{1}{r}\sin(\phi) & 1 \end{bmatrix} \begin{bmatrix} v \\ \omega \end{bmatrix}. \tag{2}$$

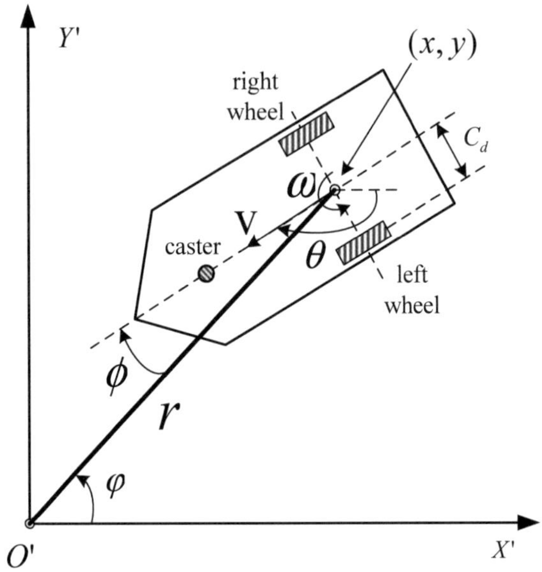

Fig. 2. Representation of a wheeled mobile robot in the polar coordinate frame with the origin O' (i.e., point q_g on Figure 1) being its goal point to track and the associated notations.

Detailed derivation procedures of Equation (2) can be found in the work (Lee et al., 1999) and are omitted for the sake of brevity in this chapter. This model is similar to the ones used in chapter 3 of (Siegwart & Nourbakhsh, 2004). From this model, specifically we have the relationship between $\dot{r}$, $\dot{\phi}$ and v, ω as

$$\begin{bmatrix} \dot{r} \\ \dot{\phi} \end{bmatrix} = \begin{bmatrix} -\cos(\phi) & 0 \\ \frac{1}{r}\sin(\phi) & 1 \end{bmatrix} \begin{bmatrix} v \\ \omega \end{bmatrix}. \tag{3}$$

Now we consider to derive a general form of control laws which can stabilize the robot in the sense of Lyapunov stability theorems. It requires that both r and ϕ tend to zero as time $t \to \infty$. One possible way is to choose control laws which lead to diagonalization of the matrix on the right hand side of Equation (3). To this end, we let v and ω being

$$\begin{bmatrix} v \\ \omega \end{bmatrix} = \begin{bmatrix} g_1(r,\phi) & 0 \\ 0 & g_2(r,\phi) \end{bmatrix} \begin{bmatrix} r \\ \phi \end{bmatrix} + \begin{bmatrix} 0 \\ -g_1(r,\phi)\sin(\phi) \end{bmatrix}, \tag{4}$$

where $g_1(r,\phi)$ and $g_2(r,\phi)$ are certain unexplicit functions to be determined.
Then by substituting the above equations into Equation (3), we can rewrite the Equation (3) into

$$\begin{bmatrix} \dot{r} \\ \dot{\phi} \end{bmatrix} = \begin{bmatrix} -\cos(\phi) & 0 \\ \frac{1}{r}\sin(\phi) & 1 \end{bmatrix} \begin{bmatrix} g_1(r,\phi) & 0 \\ 0 & g_2(r,\phi) \end{bmatrix} \begin{bmatrix} r \\ \phi \end{bmatrix} + \begin{bmatrix} 0 \\ -g_1(r,\phi)\sin(\phi) \end{bmatrix}. \tag{5}$$

A family of possible functions $g_1(r,\phi)$ and $g_2(r,\phi)$ can be chosen as follows:

$$\begin{aligned} g_1(r,\phi) &= K_1 r^n \phi^{2q} \left(\cos(\phi)\right)^{2p+1}, \\ g_2(r,\phi) &= -K_2 \phi^{2s}, \end{aligned} \tag{6}$$

where $n = 0,1,2,\cdots$, $p = 0,1,2,\cdots$, $q = 0,1,2,\cdots$ and $s = 0,1,2,\cdots$.

Accordingly Equation (4) can be rewritten into the following form:

$$\begin{aligned} v &= K_1 r^{n+1}\phi^{2q}\big(\cos(\phi)\big)^{2p+1}, \\ \omega &= -K_1 r^{n}\phi^{2q}\sin(\phi)\big(\cos(\phi)\big)^{2p+1} - K_2\phi^{2s+1}. \end{aligned} \tag{7}$$

Proposition 1 *The family of control laws given in Equation (7) asymptotically stabilizes a differential robot on its goal point.* □

Proof: The proof for this proposition is pretty straightforward by constructing a Lyapunov function candidate as

$$V = \frac{1}{2}r^2 + \frac{1}{2}\phi^2. \tag{8}$$

Simplifying Equation (5), we reach at

$$\begin{aligned} \begin{bmatrix} \dot{r} \\ \dot{\phi} \end{bmatrix} &= \begin{bmatrix} -g_1(r,\phi)\cos(\phi) \\ \frac{1}{r}g_1(r,\phi) + g_2(r,\phi) \end{bmatrix} \begin{bmatrix} r \\ \phi \end{bmatrix} + \begin{bmatrix} 0 \\ -g_1(r,\phi)\sin(\phi) \end{bmatrix} \\ &= \begin{bmatrix} -rg_1(r,\phi)\cos(\phi) \\ g_1(r,\phi)\sin(\phi) + \phi g_2(r,\phi) \end{bmatrix} + \begin{bmatrix} 0 \\ -g_1(r,\phi)\sin(\phi) \end{bmatrix} \\ &= \begin{bmatrix} -rg_1(r,\phi)\cos(\phi) \\ \phi g_2(r,\phi) \end{bmatrix}. \end{aligned} \tag{9}$$

Based on the results from Equation (9) and Equation (6), the first time derivative of V can be calculated readily as

$$\begin{aligned} \dot{V} &= r\dot{r} + \phi\dot{\phi} \\ &= -r^2 g_1(r,\phi)\cos(\phi) + \phi^2 g_2(r,\phi) \\ &= -K_1\phi^{2q}r^{n+2}\big(\cos(\phi)\big)^{2p+2} - K_2\phi^{2s+2} \leq 0, \end{aligned} \tag{10}$$

thus completes the proof. □

It should be noted that the general control law represented in Equation (7) can theoretically asymptotically stabilize the robot at its goal point. However the term ϕ^{2q} will greatly slow down the system response. Therefore for the sake of practical considerations, $q = 0$ is preferred. Let us focus on the control with simple structure. Obviously if we let $n = p = q = s = 0$, then the Equation (7) can be reduced into the simplest form as shown below:

$$\begin{aligned} v &= K_1 r\cos(\phi), \\ \omega &= -K_1\sin(\phi)\cos(\phi) - K_2\phi. \end{aligned} \tag{11}$$

However, it is noted that control in Equation (11) is actually not the "simplest". We can adopt another family of possible functions $g_1(r,\phi)$ and $g_2(r,\phi)$ as: $g_1(r,\phi) = K_1 r^n\phi^{2q}$, and $g_2(r,\phi) = -K_2\phi^{2s}$, where $n = 0,1,2,\cdots$, $p = 0,1,2,\cdots$ and $s = 0,1,2,\cdots$. Therefore a more simplified control law can be found as follows:

$$\begin{aligned} v &= K_1 r, \\ \omega &= -K_1\sin(\phi) - K_2\phi, \end{aligned} \tag{12}$$

by simply letting $n = q = s = 0$. The control law presented by Equation (12) is used in (Baillieul, 2005) with preliminary analysis results.

3. Robustness problem

Beneath the control law stated in Equation (11) exists a fundamental challenge, although the stability issue seems to be affirmatively guaranteed by Lyapunov stability theorem. We already noticed that the technique of term cancellation (i.e., $g_1(r,\phi)\sin(\phi)$) is used when simplifying Equation (9). One may be interested in the following question: what if the ideal cancellation fails and the gain K_1 in v and ω does not match with each other? To put it in details, it is to consider an alternative to the control law in Equation (11) as follows:

$$\begin{aligned} v &= K_1 r\cos(\phi), \\ \omega &= -K_3\sin(\phi)\cos(\phi) - K_2\phi, \end{aligned} \tag{13}$$

where K_3 is another independent variable and it may not be equal to K_1. In other words, it is equivalent to ask: "will the closed-loop system be stable if an alternative control represented in Equation (13) rather than the one in Equation (11) is applied to the system¿'.
In real world, there are numerous factors contributing to the such kind of "gain mismatching". Take the digital control for example, truncation error of numerical calculation of triangle functions of ϕ is unavoidable. More than that, in terms of real outputs of physical actuator, this "mismatching gain" phenomena may happen from time to time. To explain it, let v_L, v_R denote the tangent velocities of each wheel about the centers of rotation.

$$\begin{aligned} v &= \frac{v_L + v_R}{2}, \\ \omega &= \frac{v_R - v_L}{2C_d}, \end{aligned} \tag{14}$$

where C_d is the displacement from the point (x,y) to each wheel. We can establish the relationship between the vector $[v\ \omega]^T$ and $[v_L\ v_R]^T$ as follows:

$$\begin{bmatrix} v \\ \omega \end{bmatrix} = \frac{1}{2}\begin{bmatrix} 1 & 1 \\ \frac{1}{C_d} & \frac{1}{C_d} \end{bmatrix}\begin{bmatrix} v_L \\ v_R \end{bmatrix}, \tag{15}$$

$$\begin{bmatrix} v_L \\ v_R \end{bmatrix} = \begin{bmatrix} 1 & C_d \\ 1 & -C_d \end{bmatrix}\begin{bmatrix} v \\ \omega \end{bmatrix}. \tag{16}$$

The ideal case of control law Equation (11) is based on the assumption that we can make the equations

$$\begin{aligned} v_L &= K_1 r\cos(\phi) - C_d(K_1\sin(\phi)\cos(\phi) + K_2\phi), \\ v_R &= K_1 r\cos(\phi) + C_d(K_1\sin(\phi)\cos(\phi) + K_2\phi), \end{aligned}$$

strictly hold for each moment during the operation. However, in the real world, this turns out to be unrealistic. Apart from external disturbances, there are many factors that can ruin the perfect diagnosing shown in aforementioned context. For instance, each motor have different electro-mechanical characteristics. And each motor has its own nonlinearities (e.g. saturation) and so on. So in dynamic scenarios, we only have the real velocities $v_L^{'}$ and $v_R^{'}$ instead of the ideal counterparts v_L and v_R. It means that in the real world, we have the following relationship,

$$\begin{aligned} v^{'} &= (v_L^{'} + v_R^{'})/2, \\ \omega^{'} &= (v_R^{'} - v_L^{'})/(2C_d). \end{aligned} \tag{17}$$

Both $v^{'}$ and $\omega^{'}$ can be transformed into uncertainties in K_1 and K_2. To simplify the analysis, we consider uncertainties of K_1 caused by mismatching of ω with respect to v, which is the case with control in Equation (13). Substituting Equation (13) into Equation (2) in Part I of this chapter, we obtain

$$\begin{aligned}\begin{bmatrix}\dot{r}\\ \dot{\phi}\end{bmatrix} &= \begin{bmatrix}-\cos(\phi) & 0\\ \frac{1}{r}\sin(\phi) & 1\end{bmatrix}\begin{bmatrix}K_1 r\cos(\phi)\\ -K_3\sin(\phi)\cos(\phi)-K_2\phi\end{bmatrix}\\ &= \begin{bmatrix}-K_1(\cos(\phi))^2 r\\ -K_2\phi-(\frac{K_3-K1}{2})\sin(2\phi)\end{bmatrix}. \qquad (18)\end{aligned}$$

Through studying the stability of the closed-loop system described by Equation (18), we are entitled to investigating the robustness of the alternative control law given in Equation (13).

4. Robustness analysis

4.1 Stable zone

We refer to the model in Equation (18) as the real closed-loop system model. Then our problem is to analyze the stability and robustness of this real-world model. We can decompose this model into two subsystems as follows.

$$\begin{aligned}\dot{r} &= -K_1\big(\cos(\phi)\big)^2 r,\\ \dot{\phi} &= -K_2\phi-\left(\frac{K_3-K1}{2}\right)\sin(2\phi).\end{aligned}$$

Obviously except the special case with $\cos(\phi(t))\equiv 0$, $r(t)$ is at least asymptotically convergent to zero. As to $\phi(t)$, the situation is more complicated.
Let $K_4=(K_3-K_1)/2$, then we have

$$\dot{\phi}=-K_2\phi-K_4\sin(2\phi) \qquad (19)$$

As to the subsystem denoted by Equation (19), construct a Lyapunov candidate as $V=\frac{1}{2}\phi^2$. The derivative of V with respect to time is

$$\dot{V}=\phi\dot{\phi}=-K_2\phi^2-K_4\phi\sin(2\phi). \qquad (20)$$

As shown by the closed-loop system equation in Equation (18), this system is time invariant indicating that LaSalle's theorem is applicable. Therefore we are motivated to find out the invariant set Σ, which leads to negative $\dot{V}$ represented in Equation (20). The invariant set Σ can be calculated according to the following equation:

$$\Sigma=\big\{(K_1,K_2,K_3)|\dot{V}<0\big\}.$$

To this end we let $\dot{V}=0$, then we have to make either $\phi=0$ or $\phi=-K_4/K_2\sin(2\phi)$.
To find out the solution of $\phi=-K_4/K_2\sin(2\phi)$ for $\phi\in[0,\pi]$, we perform numerical calculation in Matlab environment. There are two scenarios: either $K_4/K_2\geq 0$ or $K_4/K_2<0$. The illustration of different solutions when $K_4/K_2>0$ is shown in Figure 3 while the case with $K_4/K_2<0$ is shown in Figure 4. The calculation shows that:

- if $K_4/K_2\geq 0$ when $0\leq K_4/K_2<c_1$, equation $\phi=-K_4/K_2\sin(2\phi)$ has only one solution, i.e., $\phi=0$.

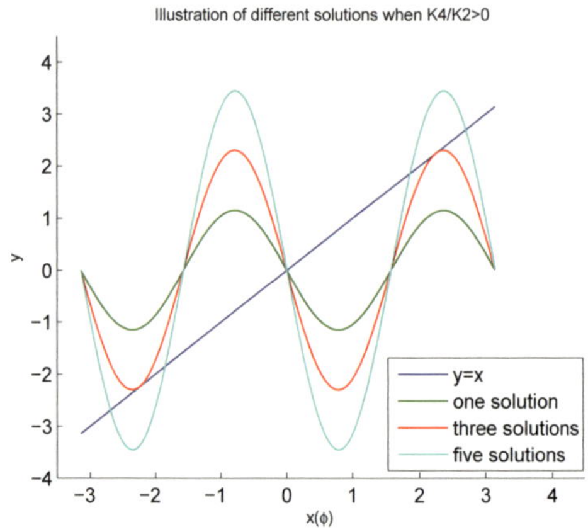

Fig. 3. Illustration of different solutions with $K_4/K_2 > 0$.

– if $K_{/}K_2 < 0$ when $c_2 < K_4/K_2 < 0$, equation $\phi = -K_4/K_2 \sin(2\phi)$ has only one solution, i.e., $\phi = 0$.

where c_1 and c_2 are constants. The numerical calculations offer approximation values of c_1 and c_2 as $c_1 \approx 2.30$ and $c_2 \approx -0.50$.
To sum up, the ratio K_4/K_2 should be within the range (c_2, c_1) to make subsystem Equation (19) asymptotically stable. Or in other words, the relationship among K_1, K_2, K_3 to make subsystem Equation (19) stable is: $K_1 + 2c_2K_2 < K_3 < 2c_1K_2 + K_1$ ($K_2 > 0$) or $2c_1K_2 + K_1 < K_3 < K_1 + 2c_2K_2$ ($K_2 < 0$).
In practise, K_2 is usually chosen to be positive. So we can further simplify the conclusions above. In this case, the whole stable range of K_3 is:

$$K_1 + 2c_2K_2 < K_3 < 2c_1K_2 + K_1. \tag{21}$$

The stable zone is shown in Figure 5. The stable zone is the whole wedge and is separated by a plane with $K3 = K1$. The upper part of this wedge has the property of $K4 > 0$ while the lower part with $K4 < 0$. Compared with the nominal sets of parameters in the plane $K3 = K1$,

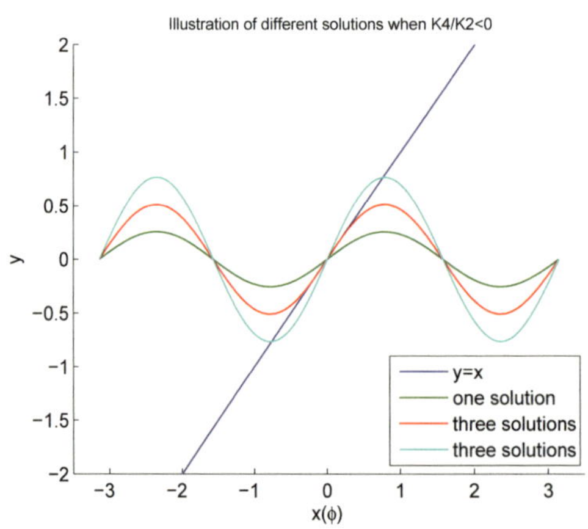

Fig. 4. Illustration of different solutions with $K_4/K_2 < 0$.

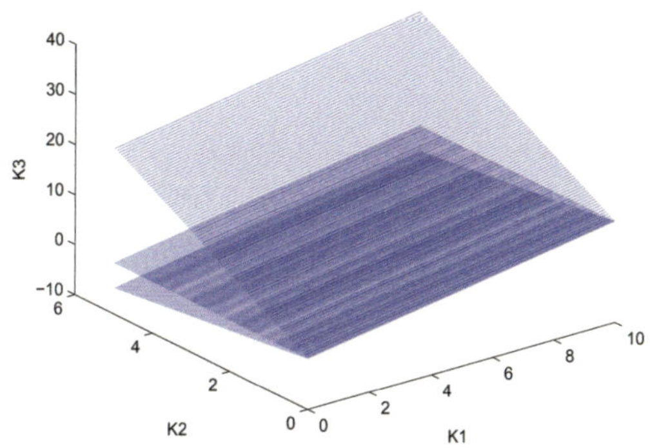

Fig. 5. Illustration of stable zone with practical concerns in the case when $K_1 > 0$ and $K_2 > 0$. Note that the whole zone is separated by a plane $K3 = K1$, i.e., $K4 = 0$.

the difference of those two parts of the zone is that the system response will be different as revealed by Proposition 3.

4.2 A new robust control and its benefits

Proposition 2 *If $K_4 \geq 0$, namely, $K_3 - K_1 \geq 0$, $r(t)$ is exponentially convergent to zero for arbitrary initial ϕ_0.* □

The proof is pretty straightforward and hence it is omitted here for the sake of brevity.

Proposition 3 *A Set of $(K1, K2, K3)$ in the upper part of the wedge in Figure 5 expedites the response of ϕ if $\phi_0 \in (0, \pi/2)$.* □

Proof: It is noted that equation

$$\dot{\phi} = -K_2\phi - K_4 \sin(2\phi)$$

has a unique solution on time interval $[0, t_1]$ for any $t_1 > 0$ because

$$f(\phi) = -K_2\phi - K_4 \sin(2\phi),$$

is locally Lipschitz. Let $p(t) = \phi^2(t)$, then

$$\begin{aligned} \dot{p}(t) &= 2\phi\dot{\phi} \\ &= -2K_2\phi^2 - 2K_4\phi\sin(2\phi) \\ &\leq -2K_2\phi^2 \\ &= -2K_2 p(t). \end{aligned}$$

Let $q(t)$ be the solution of the differential equation

$$\dot{q}(t) = -2K_2 q(t),$$

where $q(0) = \phi(0)$ then we arrive at

$$q(t) = \phi^2(0)e^{-2K_2 t}.$$

According to comparison principle, the solution $\phi(t)$ is defined for all $t \geq 0$ and satisfies

$$|\phi(t)| = \sqrt{p(t)} \leq |\phi(0)|e^{-K_2 t}, \forall t \geq 0,$$

thus completes the proof. □

According to the proposition above, we can deliberately choose $K_3 \geq K_1$ to make the system more robust. Specifically we can design control laws according to guidelines as follows:

1. As revealed in Figure 5, K_2 should not be too close to zero as the bigger K_2, the wider zone between upper bound and lower bound.
2. To maximize the stability zone for a given set of (K_1, K_2, K_3), it is desirable to choose $K_3 = K_1 + (c_1 + c_2)K_2$. In other words, (K_1, K_2, K_3) is within the plane in the middle of upper bound and lower bound as illustrated in Figure 5.
3. To obtain comparatively large stability zone for a given set of (K_1, K_2, K_3) while keep the converging rate from being negatively affected, it is desirable to choose $K_3 = K_1 + c_1 K_2$.

5. Simulation study

5.1 Mismatching K_3 and K_1

A simulation in Matlab is designed to show two cases of mismatching K_3 and K_1. In case one, initial conditions are set to be $\phi_0 = 1$ rad and $r_0 = 1$ and in case two $\phi_0 = \pi$ rad and $r_0 = 1$. The nominal gains are chosen as $K_1 = 20$ and $K2 = 1$. Suppose there is -6% deviation of K_3 with respect to K_1, i.e., $K_3 = 18.8$ in case one and a positive 24% deviation of K_3,i.e., $K_3 = 24.8$ in case two.

The simulation results of system response are depicted in Figure 6 with (a), (b) for case one and (c), (d) for case two. From this figure, it is obvious that in those two cases $\phi(t)$ fails to approach to zero due to -6% and 24% deviation of K_3 respectively. In other words, this is because both cases break the constraint described by Equation (21).

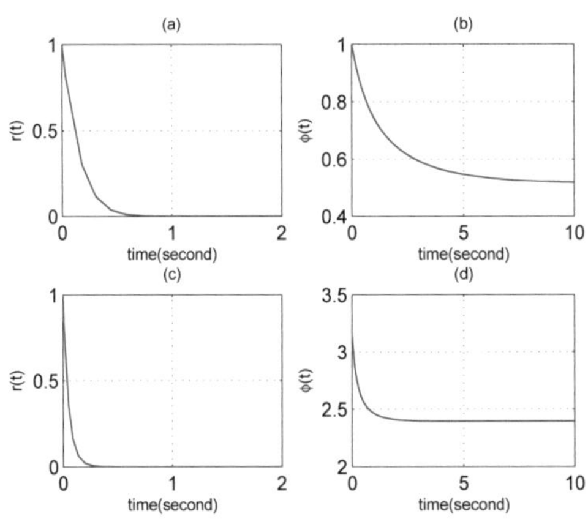

Fig. 6. Illustration of mismatching K_3 and K_1. In (a) and (b) initial conditions are $\phi_0 = 1$ rad and $r_0 = 1$ and gain $K_1 = 20$, $K2 = 1$ and $K3 = 18.8$ (i.e., -6% deviation). And in (c) and (d) initial conditions are $\phi_0 = \pi$ rad and $r_0 = 1$ and gain $K_1 = 20$, $K2 = 1$ and $K3 = 24.8$ (i.e., 24% deviation).

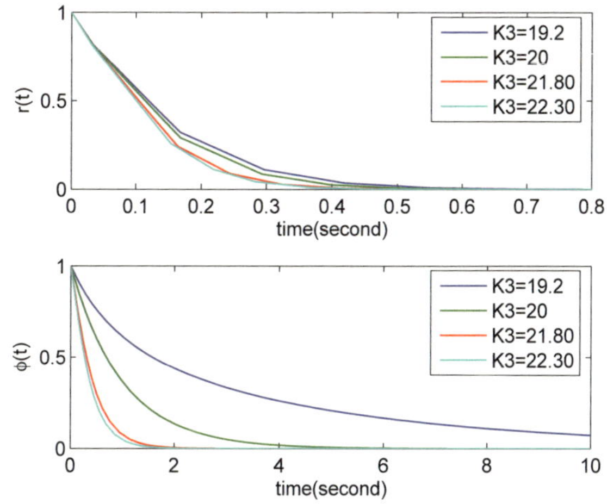

Fig. 7. Illustration of the effects of mismatching K_3 on system response. Initial conditions are $\phi_0 = 1$ rad and $r_0 = 1$ and gain $K_1 = 20$, $K2 = 1$ and $K3 = 19.2, 20, 21.80, 22.30$ respectively.

5.2 Effects of K_3 on system response

In this simulation we investigate the effects of mismatching K_3 on system response through simulation. Initial conditions are set to be $\phi_0 = 1$ rad and $r_0 = 1$ and gain $K_1 = 20$ and $K2 = 1$. We vary the value of K_3 with respect to K_1. Refer to the stable zone illustrated in Figure 5, we deliberately choose several sets of $(K1, K2, K3)$ from upper part, separation plane ($K_1 = K_3$) and lower part respectively. According to design guidelines, in this experiment, we choose $K_3 = 22.30, 21.8$ from upper part and $K_3 = 20$ for the nominal case and $K_3 = 19.2$ from the lower part. The results are depicted in Figure 7. From this figure, it is noticed that compared with $K_3 = 20$, a set in upper part of the wedge in Figure 5 contributes to expediting the system's response while a set in lower part of the wedge will negative affect the system's response. The most significant effects of mismatching K_3 is on the converging rate of term $\phi(t)$. Since they are all within the stable wedge, both $r(t)$ and $\phi(t)$ approach to zero as time $t \to 0$.
To compare the energy needed for each controller, we define a function J_n which is describe by

$$J_n = \int_0^t \left(v^2(\tau) + \omega^2(\tau) \right) d\tau.$$

In this simulation, the integral of the norm squared of the actual velocity signals for each controller is shown in Table 1. From the figures shown in this table, the control laws recommended by design guidelines seem to be more efficient than the nominal case with $K_3 = K_1$ and the one with negative deviation ($K_3 = 19.2$). And there is not significant difference between the two recommended control laws, i.e.,$K_3 = 21.80$ and $K_3 = 22.30$ respectively.

$K_3 = 19.2$	$K_3 = 20$	$K_3 = 21.80$	$K_3 = 22.30$
331.8	129.8	69.78	63.87

Table 1. Comparison of the integral of the norm squared of the velocity input signals $\int_0^{30} (v^2(t) + \omega^2(t))\, dt$.

6. Implementation and experiment

6.1 Overview of implementation

One picture of the real implementation is presented by Figure 8. In this figure, a 4m by 2.8m wooden test bed offers the field for a group of mobile robots. The MRKIT mobile robots presented in Figure 8 with on-board infrared sensors and compass, which are used in the experiments consist of the main platform to verify algorithms. Each robot has two independently controlled wheels driven by stepper motors. A GPS system is simulated by a vision system comprising vision frame grabber, CCD color camera with lens, a working station, and wireless communication modules. Two web-cam are mounted on the ceiling and can be used for robot tracking or video recording and only one is showed in Figure 8. The main parts of this implementation are connected as shown by Figure 10.

6.2 Parameters of MRKIT mobile robots

Each wheel of MRKIT robot is driven independently with step motor being controlled by on-board micro-controller. The velocity of wheel is controlled via PWM waveform and is determined by an internal time interval T in the micro-controller. The relationship between the velocity V of a wheel and T can be represented as

$$V = \frac{D\pi}{NP},$$

where $D = 54$ mm is the diameter of the wheel; $N = 400$ is the step of motor per revolution; P is the time (second) per step and

$$P = \frac{T \cdot 10^{-6}}{2.5}.$$

Fig. 8. Picture of real robots, test bed(on the floor), CCD color camera with wide-angle lens and one web-cam (mounted on the ceiling).

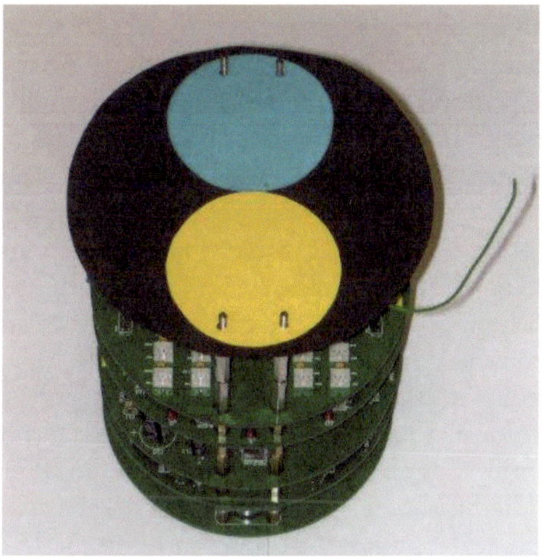

Fig. 9. Picture of one MRKIT mobile robot with on-board color pads.

Finally we arrive at

$$V = \frac{1060.288}{T} m/s,$$

and T is a 16-bit integer which can be set in micro-controller. Due to the finite length of T and physical limitations of motor, V has a minimum $V_{min} = 0.0162$ m/s and a maximum $V_{max} = 0.3$ m/s.

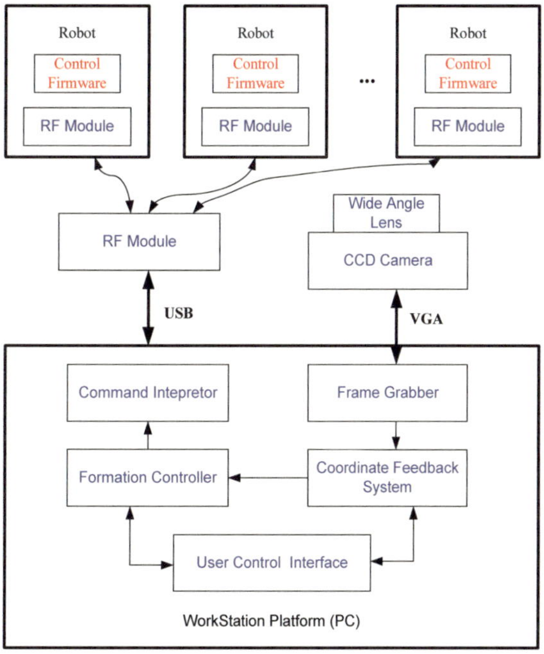

Fig. 10. Illustration of connection of the whole implementation.

6.3 Vision system: resolution and noise analysis

A vision system, comprising of CCD camera, lens, frame grabber and application program as shown in Figure 10, is developed for the tracking of mobile robots and detecting position/orientation of them. Its resolution is largely determined by the resolution of the CCD camera and the optical system. In the experiment, the CCD camera is mounted on a bracket fixed on the ceiling. Due to the limitation of ceiling's height, the viewable area on the test bed is of 1800mm by 2480mm. The CCD camera has a resolution of 576 by 768 pixels. We designate the x and y coordinate to the vision system and therefore we can calculate the real resolution of the vision system. The calculation results show that on the x axis, the resolution is 3.229mm per pix while on the y axis, 3.177mm per pix.

To identify the robot's position and orientation, a color pad is attached on the top of a robot as shown in Figure 9. Each color pad has two different color circles aligned in a line. Each color circle has a diameter of 65mm. One circle is painted blue and another one is yellow. The center of each circle can be calculated through the image processing hardware and software, namely the frame grabber and the corresponding vision processing software running on working station. We can use coordinates of the centers of the two color circles to calculate the position of the robot's center and its orientation as well. Let (x_a, y_a) and (x_b, y_b) denote the measured coordinates of the center of yellow circle and blue circle respectively. Hence, the coordinate of the robot's center can be represented as $(\frac{x_a+x_b}{2}, \frac{y_a+y_b}{2})$. Meanwhile the orientation of the robot can be calculated as

$$\theta = \cos^{-1}(\frac{x_a - x_b}{\rho}), \tag{22}$$

where

$$\rho = \sqrt{(x_a - x_b)^2 + (y_a - y_b)^2}.$$

The measurement of the position of each color circle is a resultant of its real position and the error signal together with noise. The position error is incurred by the hardware of the system. For instance the field is not even and can end up with position error. Another sample of the source of the error signal can be the optical system. The distortion of the lens on the margin of the viewable area is relatively salient and such distortion in fact affects the accuracy of the measurement. Roughly the measurement of position can be expressed in the following equation:

$$X_m = x_r + x_e + x_n,$$

where x_r is the real position; x_e is the system error and x_n the noise. It is of interest and practically importance to know the noise level of the measured signal. For any static robot on the test bed, its real position and system error are always constant and contribute no variation to the mean value of X_m and to the variance either. From this observation, it helps to sample the measurement for a certain period and then use the spectrum analysis tools to get the information of the noise signal. One convenient way is to use the FFT technique. It is well known that Microsoft Windows is not a real time operation system. For the purpose of FFT, it is required to evenly sample the data. To solve this conflict, a high resolution timer without accumulation error is in need. In this experiment, the multi-media timer is used. It is a high resolution timer with high accuracy and resolution while demands of the system resource are relatively low. We set the sampling rate to be 500 Hz. A period of 2 minutes is used to sample the data and the error signal along x-axis is presented in Figure 11. Figures of error signal along y-axis and the associated orientation error signal are shown in Figure 12 and 13 respectively. Then we apply the FFT technique to analyze its frequency components. It turns out that the noise signals on x, y and orientation all show on the feature of Gaussian noise. The analysis results show that $\delta_x = 0.142$ pix, $\delta_y = 0.154$ pix $\delta_\theta = 0.0122$ radius. Obviously compared with vision system's resolution, the noise level of position signal is relatively low.

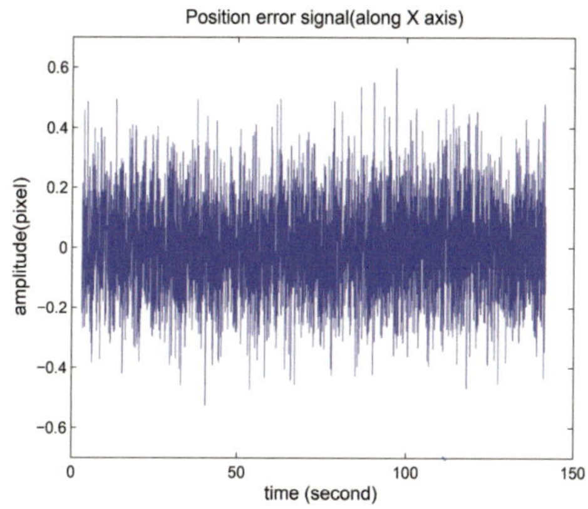

Fig. 11. Position error signal along x-axis with sample rate $f = 500$Hz.

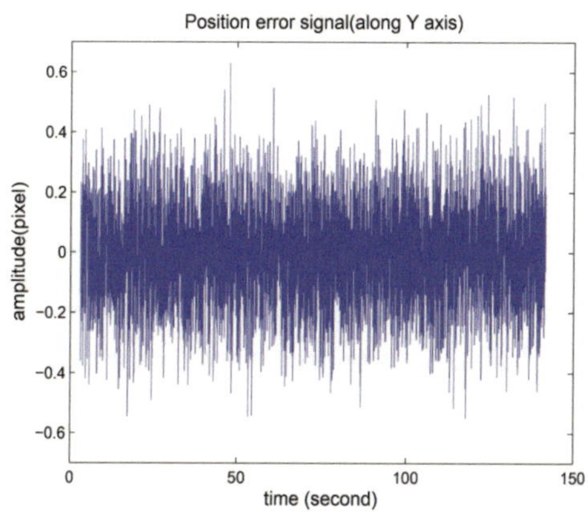

Fig. 12. Position error signal along y-axis with sample rate $f = 500$Hz.

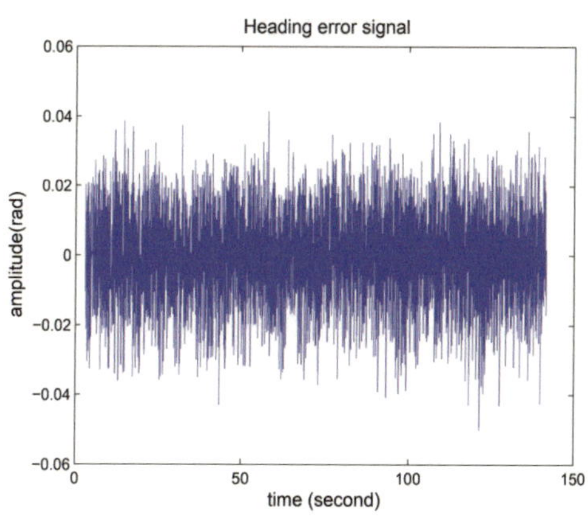

Fig. 13. Angular error signal with sample rate $f = 500$Hz.

6.4 Experiment-1: triangle formation of three robots

A scalable formation control scheme is introduced in (Ge & Fua, 2005). The idea is that, instead of being attracted to a predetermined point, each robot is to be attracted to the corresponding segment, and once there, move along the segment to distribute themselves along the trench in order to form a formation by maintaining the desired position in relation to other robots. To briefly review this idea, Figure 14 is presented to show the segments and the robots which are supposed to fall into certain assigned segment. Usually a segment S is a curve defined by some smooth (i.e., at least twice-differentiable) function in R^3 that passes through one or two formation vertices. And a robot will arrive at the nearest point on the segment and then move along the curve of the segment.

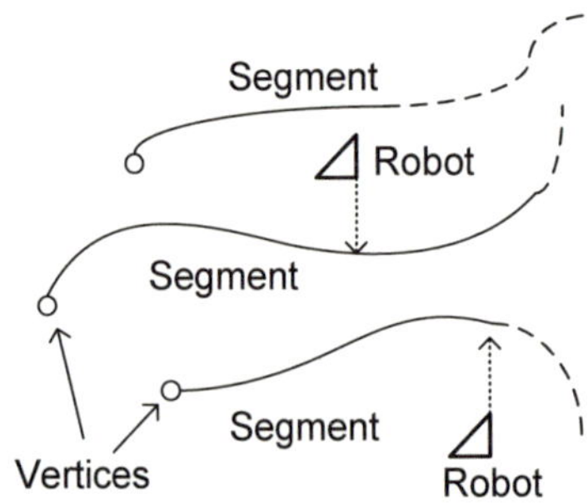

Fig. 14. Illustration of segments and robots falling into assigned segments.

In this experiment, suppose that assignment mechanism of segment is known and initially all robots are static. Three straight lines are assigned to three robots respectively. For the first 8 seconds, each robot will try to approach the nearest point on the segment and then three virtual points moving along segments are assigned to each robot. Those three virtual points form a triangle pattern and will stop at the vertices of segments. The velocity of virtual points are set to be 20 pix per second. During the process of formation, velocities and headings of each robot are depicted in Figure 15 - 18. Snapshots of video (taken by web-cam) are shown in Figure 19-22. The controller parameters are set to be $K_1 = 0.1$, $K_3 = 0.12$ and $K_2 = 1.0$. From those figures that all the robots are attracted to the segment for the first 8 seconds and later on form the triangular pattern while moving forward.

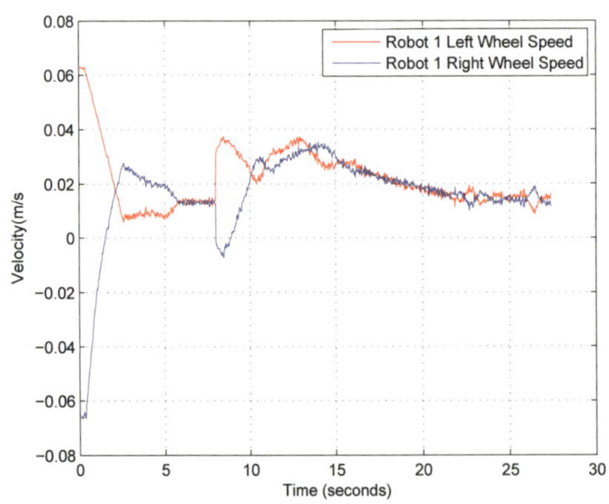

Fig. 15. Velocity of robot 1 during 3-robot triangle formation control.

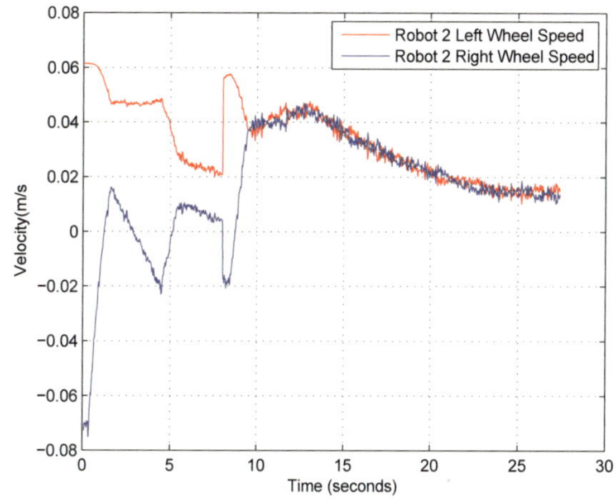

Fig. 16. Velocity of robot 2 during 3-robot triangle formation control.

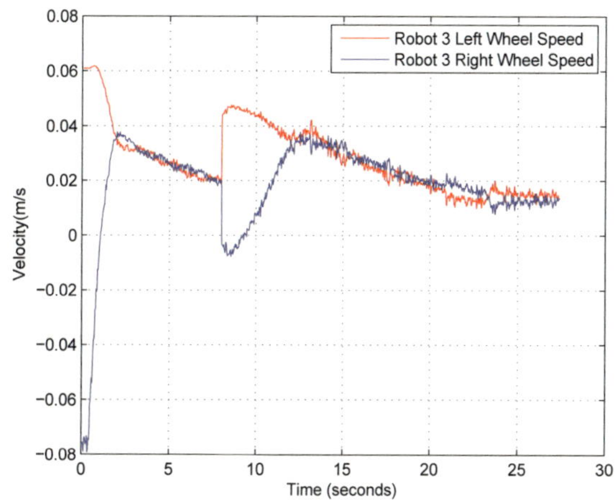

Fig. 17. Velocity of robot 3 during 3-robot triangle formation control.

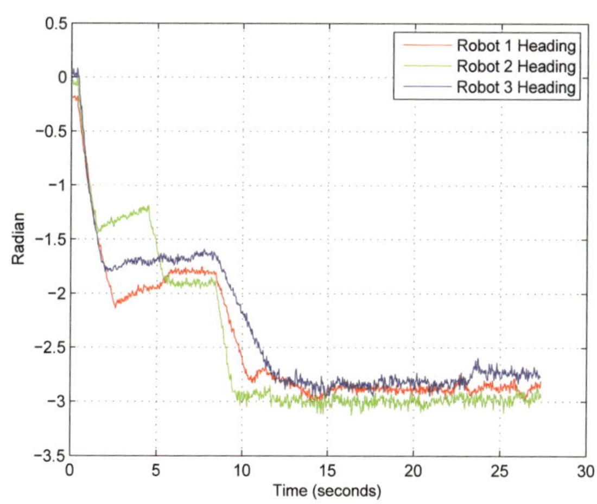

Fig. 18. Headings of all robots during 3-robot triangle formation control.

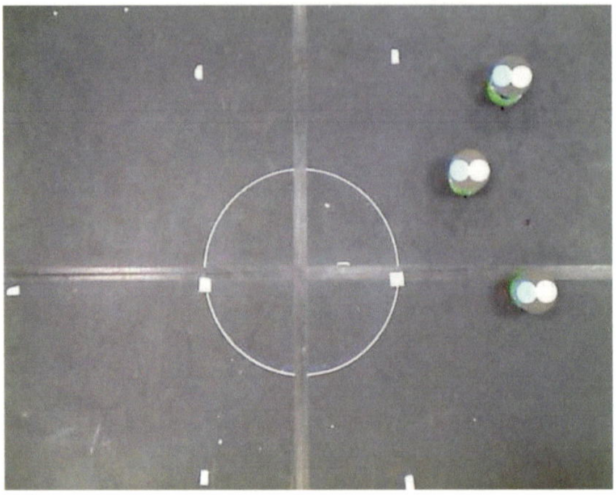

Fig. 19. Snapshot of initial conditions of 3-robot triangle formation control at $t = 0$.

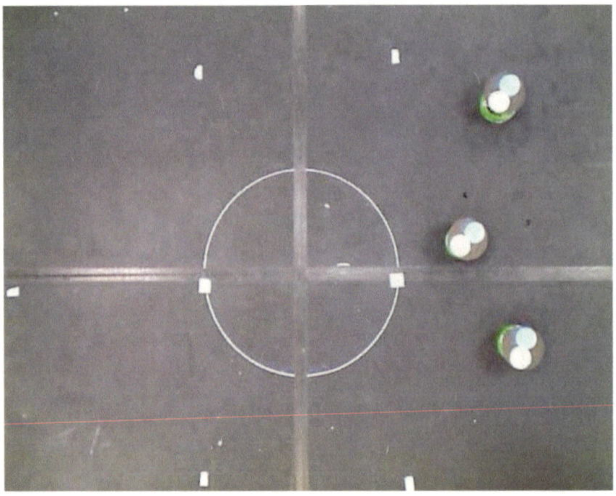

Fig. 20. Snapshot of 3-robot triangle formation control at ($t = 8$s).

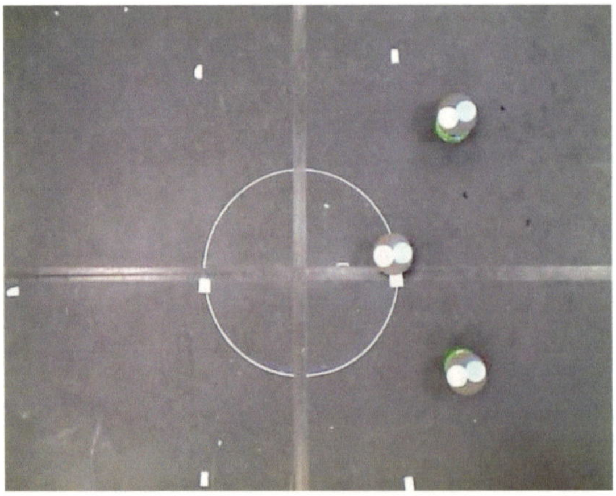

Fig. 21. Snapshot of 3-robot triangle formation control at ($t = 16$s).

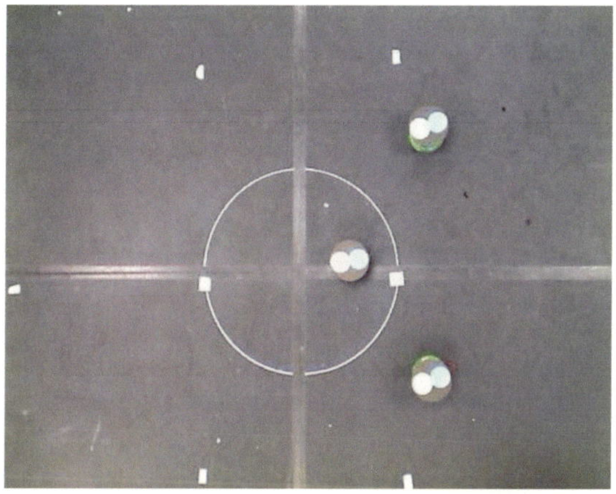

Fig. 22. Snapshot of 3-robot triangle formation control at ($t = 24$s).

6.5 Experiment-2: square formation of four robots

In this experiment, four robots which are initially randomly scattered are required to form a square patter. Two straight lines are assigned. For the first 3 seconds, each robot will try to approach the corresponding nearest point on the segment and then try to approach to four virtual points moving along segments are assigned to each robot. Those three virtual points form a triangle pattern and will stop at the vertices of segments. The velocity of virtual points are set to be 20 pix per second. During the process of formation, velocities and headings of each robot are depicted in Figure 23 - 27. Snapshots of video (taken by web-cam) are shown in Figure 28-30. The controller parameters are set to be $K_1 = 0.1$, $K_3 = 0.12$ and $K_2 = 1.0$. From those figures that all the robots are attracted to the segment for the first 3 seconds and later on form the square pattern while moving forward.

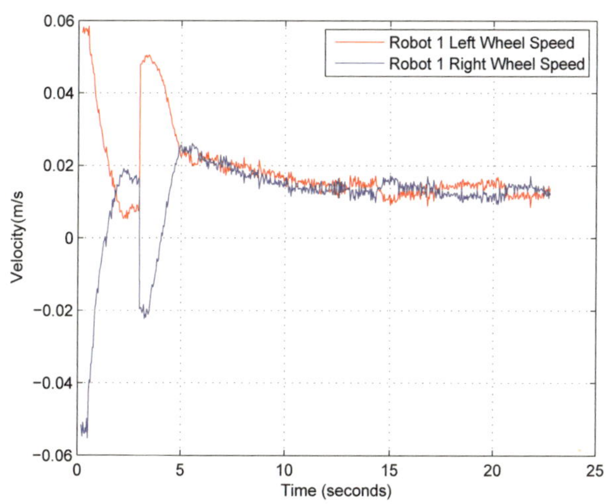

Fig. 23. Velocity of robot 1 during 4-robot square formation control.

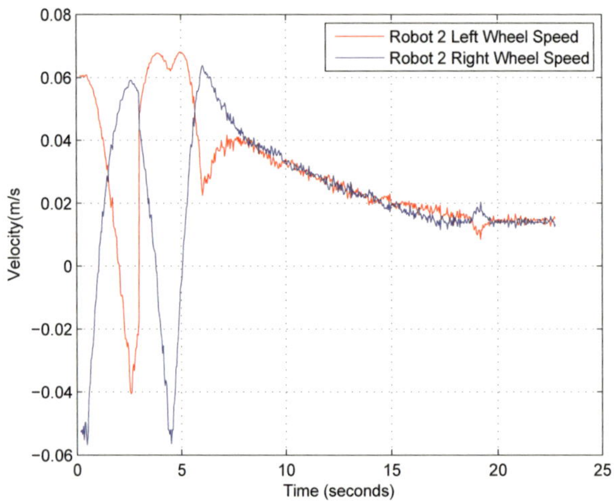

Fig. 24. Velocity of robot 2 during 4-robot square formation control.

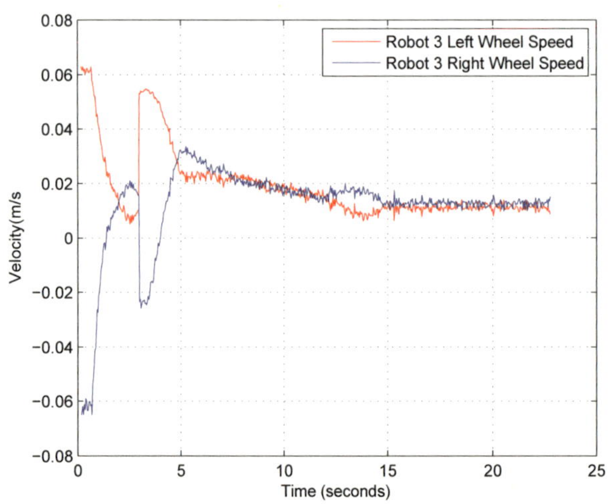

Fig. 25. Velocity of robot 3 during 4-robot square formation control.

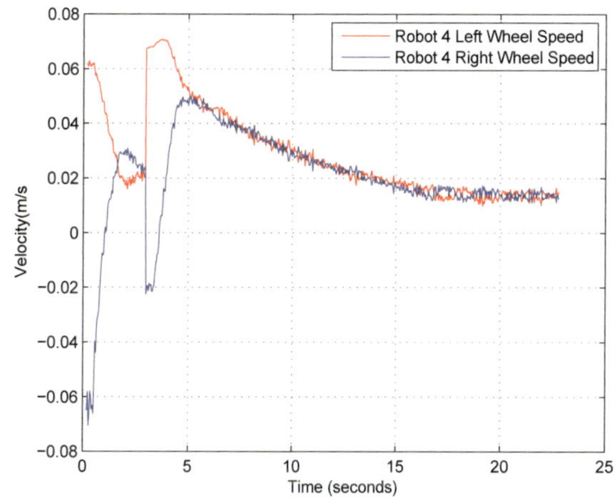

Fig. 26. Velocity of robot 4 during 4-robot square formation control.

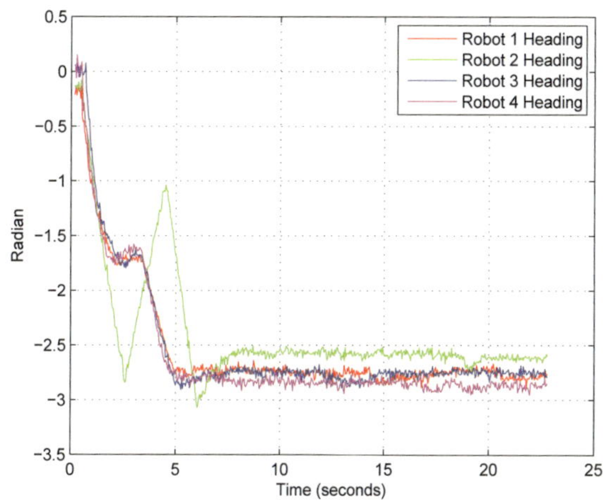

Fig. 27. Headings of all robots during 4-robot square formation control.

Fig. 28. Snapshot of 4-robot square formation control at ($t = 0$s).

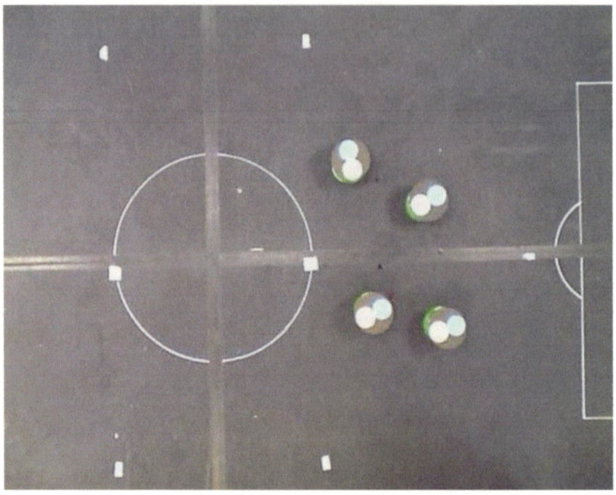

Fig. 29. Snapshot of 4-robot square formation control at ($t = 6$s).

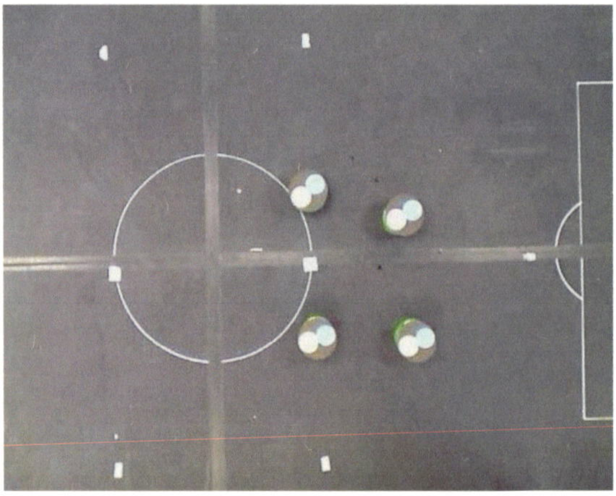

Fig. 30. Snapshot of 4-robot square formation control at ($t = 12$s).

6.6 Limitation of locomotion

Each wheel of MRKIT utilizes an independent step motor for locomotion. There are two outstanding drawbacks which impede implementation. As indicated by Equation (11), the desired velocity is proportional to the distance to goal point (i.e., r). If a robot is initially placed far away from its goal point, the desired velocity will be relatively high. However, step motor usually is weak on its maximum starting speed and starting torque. If the gain (K_1, K_2, K_3) is too high, a robot initially at standstill will immediately miss its step at the very beginning of formation control. The other shortcoming arises from the minimum speed of step motor. Due to the limitation of minimum speed, a wheeled mobile robot in fact can not reach a fixed goal point. Instead it will stop moving once it enters certain range with respect to its goal point. It results in a dead zone to which the robot is prohibited. To reduce dead zone, higher gain is demanded and thus increases the risk of missing steps. Trade-off has to be done for real implementation. To overcome such downside of locomotion, other motors with high starting torque such as permanent magnet brushless DC motor cater for real implementation.

7. Conclusion

In this chapter we first consider the stability issue of a generic form of nonlinear feedback control based on kinematic model in polar coordinate in a novel perspective. Some commonly used controls can be derived from this general form of a family of stable control laws. In addition to the commonly used stability analysis based on Lyapunov stability theorems, in this chapter we employe LaSalle's invariance theorem to investigate the robustness of a point tracking controller. Then the robustness problem of the control law (Lee et al., 1999) is investigated and successfully solved. Thanks to LaSalle's invariance theorem and Lyapunov's stability theorem as well, we are able to unveil the whole stable range of controller gains when velocity and angular velocity of each driving motor are not exactly what they are supposed to be in the real world. This study yields some exciting conclusions on converging rate than the counterpart. Based on the robustness analysis, we can propose useful and handy guidelines in determining controller gains and consequently a new robust control law is proposed. Improvement to this control law is achieved from the analysis results and is verified in Matlab simulation. Implementation with real robots has been done to demonstrate the application to multiple robot formation control. An implementation of multi-robot formation control has been done and discussed in details.

8. References

Kolmanovsky, I. & McClamroch, N.(1995).Developments in nonholonomic control problems, In: *IEEE Control Systems Magazine*, Vol.15, page numbers (20-36).

Brockett,R.W. (1983). Asymptotic stability and feedback stabilization, pp. 181-191, Boston, U.S., 1983, Birkhauser.

Dixon, W.E., Dawson, D.M., & Behal, A. (2001). *Nonlinear control of wheeled mobile robots*, Springer.

Wit,C., & Siciliano, B. (1996). *Theory of robot control*, Springer.

Luca, A.D., Oriolo,G., & M.Vendittelli, M. (2001). *Control of Wheeled Mobile Robots: An Experimental Overview. Lecture Notes in Control and Information Sciences 270*, Springer-Verlag, Berlin Heidelberg.

Wit, C. & Sordalen, O.J. (1992). Exponential stabilization of mobile robots with nonholonomic constraints. *IEEE Transcations on Automatic Control*, Vol.37, (Nov. 1992.) page numbers (1791-1797).

Godhavn, J. & Egeland, O. (1997). A lyapunov approach to exponentially stabilization of nonholonomic systems in power form. *IEEE Transcations on Automatic Control*, Vol.42, no. 7 page numbers (1028-1032).

Kanayama,Y., Kimura,Y., Miyazaki,F. & Noguchi, T. (1997). A stable tracking control method for an autonomous mobile robot. *in Proc. IEEE Conf. Robotics Automation*, page numbers (384-389).

Closkey,R.M and Murray, R. (1997). Exponentially stabilization of driftless nonlinear control systems using homogeneous feedback. *IEEE Transactions on Automatic Control*, Vol.42, (May 1997) page numbers (614-628).

Teel,A., Murray,R., & Walsh, C. (1995). Nonholonomic control systems: from steering to stabilization with sinusoids. *Int. Journal Control*, Vol.62,No. 4, page numbers (849-870).

Murray,R.M. & Sastry, S.S. (1990). Steering nonholonomic systems using sinusoids. *in Proc. IEEE Conf. Decision and Control*, Vol.62,No. 4, page numbers (2097-2101). Honolulu,

HI, Dec. 1990.

Lafferiere, G. & Sussmann, H.J. (1991). Motion planning for controllable system without drift. *in Proc. IEEE Conf. Robotics and Automation*, page numbers (1148-1153). Sacramento, CA, Apr. 1991.

Brraquand, J. & Latombe, J. (1989). On nonholonomic mobile robots and optimal maneuvering. *in Proc. IEEE Conf. Intelligent Control*, page numbers (340-347). Albany, NY, Sep. 1989.

Brockett,R.W. (1981). Control theory and singular riemannian geometry. *in New directions in applied mathematics*, NY,Springer-Verlag,1981.

Aguiar,A.P. Atassi,A. & Pascoal,A.M. (2000). Regulation of a nonhonomic dynamic wheeled mobile robot with parametric modelling uncertainty using lyapunov functions. *in Proc. IEEE Conf. Decision Control*, page numbers (2995-3000). Sydney, Australia, Dec. 2000.

Coelho,P. & Nunes,U. (2005). Path-following control of mobile robots in presence of uncertainties. *IEEE Transactions on Robotics*, Vol.21 (Apr. 2005) page numbers (252-261).

Dixon,W.E. Dawson,D.M. Zergeroglu,E. & Zhang,F. (1999). Robust tracking and regulation control for mobile robots. *in Proc. IEEE Conf. Control Applications*, page numbers (1015-1020). Kohala Coast-Island of Hawaii, U.S., Aug. 1999.

Lee,S.O. Cho,Y.J. B.,M.H. You,B.J. & Oh,S.R. (1999). A stable targettracking control for unicycle mobile robots. *in Proc. IEEE/RSJ Conf. Intelligent Robots and Systems*, page numbers (1822-1827). Takamatsu, Japan, 2000.

Siegwart,R. & Nourbakhsh,I. (2004). *Introduction to Autonomous Mobile Robots*, page numbers (13-46). MIT Press, 2004.

Baillieul,J. (1999). The Geometry of Sensor Information Utilization in Nonlinear Feedback Control of Vehicle Formations. *Lecture Notes in Control and Information Sciences 309: Cooperative Control*, Berlin Heidelberg: Springer-Verlag, 2005.

Ge,S. S. and Fua,C.-H. (2005). Queues and artificial potential trenches for multi-robot formations. *IEEE Transactions on Robotics*, Vol.21(4) (Aug. 2005) page numbers (646-656).

6

Building Visual Maps with a Team of Mobile Robots

Mónica Ballesta, Arturo Gil, Óscar Reinoso and Luis Payá
Miguel Hernández University
Elche

1. Introduction

This paper tackles the problem of Simultaneous Localization and Map Building (SLAM) carried out by a team of robots. Particularly these robots build landmark-based maps by extracting interest points from the environment. These points are characterized by a local descriptor and a 3D position on the environment, constituting the visual landmarks. In this approach we consider the situation in which the robots start their mapping task independently. That is to say, the path followed by the robots and the observations are estimated independently. After a while, there is a set of independent local maps that can be fused in order to obtain a global map. For that reason, we have also solved the problem of aligning and fusing visual maps. Finally, once a global map is obtained, the robots continue the map building task jointly. Regarding the sensors used in order to extract information from the environment, some authors use range sensors such as SONAR (Wijk & Christensen, 2000; Kwak et al., 2008) or LASER (Leonard & Durrant-Whyte, 1991; Thrun, 2001). However, in the last years, there is a great interest on using cameras as sensors. This approach is denoted as visual SLAM (Valls-Miró et al., 2006). The cameras are less expensive than laser and offer a higher amount of information from the environment. This advantage makes it possible to incorporate additional applications to the robot, such as face recognititon. Additionally, 3D information can be obtained from the environment when using stereo vision (Murray & Little, 2000; Gil, Reinoso, Fernández, Vicente, Rottmann & Martínez-Mozos, 2006). Most approaches using visual information are landmark-based. A process to extract these visual features with accuracy is required. In these sense, several detection and description methods appear in the literature such as the Harris Corner Detector (Davison & Murray, 2002), Harris-Laplace (Jensfelt et al., 2006), SIFT (Gil, Reinoso, Martínez-Mozos, Stachniss & Burgard, 2006; Little et al., 2002) and SURF (Murillo et al., 2007). In (Gil et al., 2009; Ballesta, Gil, Reinoso & Úbeda, 2010) we performed an evaluation comparing several detection and description methods in order to obtain the most suitable feature extractor for visual SLAM. As a result, we obtained that the Harris Corner Detector in combination with the u-SURF descriptor satisfied our requirements in visual SLAM. The task of building a map of the environment while simultaneously localizing in it can be performed by a single robot. However, it will be carried out with more efficiency if there is a team of robots which collaborates in this task. This approach is denoted as multi-robot SLAM (Konolige et al., 2003). In this field, two main solutions can be found. On the one hand, in some proposals the robots build a unique global map (Gil, Reinoso, Martínez-Mozos, Stachniss & Burgard, 2006; Fenwick et al., 2002). In this case, the exploration task can be performed more efficiently since the robots have a global notion of the environment. However, the initital pose of the robots must be known, which may not be possible in practice. On the other hand, some authors present the approach in which each robot builds its own map indepentently (Roumeliotis & Bekey, 2002; Stewart et al., 2003; Zhou & Roumeliotis, 2006). In this case, it is not necessary to know the initial positions of the robots. Nevertheless, a process of merging the data of the different robots is needed. In the situation that we set out, the robots start from different positions and build their maps independently. Therefore, the initial position of the robots is unknown. After a while, these independent local maps can be fused into a global map. Before fusing the local maps, the transformation that relates the different reference systems of the robots should be computed. This previous step is called map alignment. Then, once the relative positions of the robots is known and the maps can be expressed in the same reference sytem, the maps are fused into a global map. After solving the alignment problem, we propose that the robots continue their navigation tasks jointly. To sum up, the robots initially build their maps independently and then, once they manage to align and fuse their maps, the continue the map building together. In order to build the map, we propose a Rao-Blackwellized particle filter, firstly for a single robot and then extended to the multi-robot case. The paper is structured into three parts according to the approach proposed. First, in Section 2 we concentrate on the independent stage of the proposal, i.e., there is a team or robots that begins tis navigation tasks independently. In this case, we describe the particle filter used to solve the SLAM problem (Section 2.2). Logically, since the robots act indepdendently, the algorithm has been implemented for a single robot. Secondly, we concentrate in the fusion stage in Section 3. At this moment there is a set of local maps, independently built, that have to be aligned and merged into a global map. Finally, the third stage consist of the multi-robot map building (Section 4). After the fusion stage, the robots build together the map of the environment. In this case, the estimate of the map and the paths is performed jointly. For this purpose, we propose an extension of the previous particle filter to the multi-robot case. Finally, we present some experiments that validate the proposal (Section 5) and the main conclusions in Section 6.

2. Independent map building

In the first stage of the approach presented in this paper, there is a team of robots in which each one builds its map independently. The map building is performed by means of a Rao-Blackwellized particle filter, known with the general term FastSLAM (Montemerlo, 2003). The robots may start at different positions and they have no knowledge about their relative poses. After a while, the robots will have built several local maps that can be fused into a global map. This is done even if the relative initial positions of the robots are unknown. In addition, the robots compare their maps and compute the relative position between them, based on the descriptor simmilarity of the landmarks. In the following, we describe, in detail, the steps of the FastSLAM algorithm used by each robot independently. Then we focus on the map alignment step in which the relative position of the robots is obtained. Finally, it is explained how the local maps are fused into a global one.

2.1 Visual landmarks

In this paper we focus on a visual SLAM approach. Particularly, the robots observe distinctive points in the environment. These points are then located in a global reference system. In this case, the reference system of each robot is located in its initial position. The process of obtaining distinctive points from the environment is tackled by a feature extractor, i.e., the combination of a detector and a descriptor, that obtains suitable features. At the detection stage, it is desirable that the points can be detected from different viewpoints, due to the fact that the robots, while navigating, will observe the same from different position. As a result of a previous work (Gil et al., 2008), the Harris Corner detector (Harris & Stephens, 1998) was selected as the most suitable for this kind of maps, since it extracts stable points. Then, the description stage is also crucial for the extraction of good visual features. It is very important that the points are distinguishable enough, since this influences in the solution of the data association problem. When a robot performs an observation, it should be able to distinguish whether it is a new landmark or a landmark that was previously integrated in the map. This aspect was also studied in (Gil et al., 2008) and the u-SURF descriptor was the best choice (Bay et al., 2006).

2.2 3D visual fastSLAM

Initially, as the robots builds the maps independently, each one uses an independent particle filter. Then, after fusing the local maps, the robots continue the map building by means of a joint particle filter. In this section, we concentrate on the first case, i.e., FastSLAM for a single robot. In order to build the map, each robot is equiped with a stereo camera system, which enables them to obtain relative measurements to landmarks detected in the environment. In addition, these landmarks are characterized by means of a descriptor using visual information. In this context, each robot explores the environment while it observes visual landmarks. At time t the robot performs an observation $z_t = (v_t, d_t)$, where $v_t = (X_c, Y_c, Z_c)$ is three dimensional vector relative to the left camera reference frame and d_t is the visual descriptor associated to the landmark. The map L is represented by a collection of N landmarks $L = \{l_1, l_2, \ldots, l_N\}$. Each landmark is represented as: $l_k = \{\mu_k, \Sigma_k, d_k\}$, where $\mu_k = (X_k, Y_k, Z_k)$ is a vector describing the position of the landmark red to a global reference frame, with associated covariance matrix Σ_k. Furthermore, each landmark l_k is differentiated from others by means of a descriptor d_k. The robot pose at time t is denoted as x_t and movement of the robot at time t as u_t. On the other hand, $x^t = \{x_1, x_2, \ldots, x_t\}$ represents the robot path until time t, $z^t = \{z_1, z_2, \ldots, z_t\}$ is the set of observations made by the robot until time t and the set of actions $u^t = \{u_1, u_2, \ldots, u_t\}$. The solution to the SLAM problem consists in determining the location of the landmarks in the map L and the robot poses x^t from a set of measurements z^t and robot actions u_t. The set of data association performed until time t is denoted as $c^t = \{c_1, c_2, \ldots, c_t\}$. Each time the robot performs an observation, it has to determine whether this observation corresponds to a landmark previously incorporated in the map ($c_t \in [1 \ldots N]$) or to a new one ($c_t = N + 1$). The main idea of the FastSLAM algorithm is that the SLAM problem can be separated into two main subproblems: the estimate of the trayectory of the robot and the estimate of the map (Montemerlo & Thrun, 2003). This can be expressed as:

$$p(x^t, L | z^t, u^t, c^t) = p(x^t | z^t, u^t, c^t) \prod_{k=1}^{N} p(l_k | x^t, z^t, u^t, c^t) \tag{1}$$

This equation states that the SLAM posterior is decomposed into two parts: the estimate of the robot path and N independent estimators of the landmark positions, each conditioned to the path estimate. We approximate $p(x^t | z^t, u^t, c^t)$ by means of a set of M particles. Thus, each particle has N independent landmark estimators (implemented as EKFs), one for each landmark. Each particle is therefore defined as:

$$S_t^{[m]} = \{x^{t,[m]}, \mu_{t,1}^{[m]}, \Sigma_{t,1}^{[m]}, d_1^{[m]}, \ldots, mu_{t,N}^{[m]}, \Sigma_{t,N}^{[m]}, d_N^{[m]}\}, \tag{2}$$

where $\mu_{t,k}^{[m]}$ is the best estimation at time t for the position of landmark l_k based on the path of the particle m and $\Sigma_{t,k}^{[m]}$ the associated covariance matrix. The visual descriptor associated to the landmark j is represented by $d_j^{[m]}$. The particle set $S_t = \{S_t^{[1]}, S_t^{[2]}, \ldots, S_t^{[M]}\}$ is calculated incrementally from the set S_{t-1} in time $t-1$ and the control u_t. Each particle is sampled from a proposal distribution $x_t^{[m]} \sim p(x_t|x_{t-1}, u_t)$ that models the noise in the odometry of the robot. Then, a weight is assigned to each particle according to (Montemerlo & Thrun, 2003):

$$\omega_t^{[m]} = \frac{1}{\sqrt{|2\pi Z_{c_t}|}} e^{\{-\frac{1}{2}(v_t - \hat{v}_{t,c_t})^T [Z_{c_t}]^{-1} (v_t - \hat{v}_{t,c_t})\}} \tag{3}$$

where v_t is the actual measurement and $\hat{v}_{t,c_t}$ is the predicted measurement for the landmark c_t based on the pose $x_t^{[m]}$. The matrix Z_{c_t} is the covariance matrix associated with the innovation $(v_t - \hat{v}_{t,c_t})$. Note that it is assumed that each measurement v_t has been associated to the landmark c_t of the map. In short, the algorithm proposed in this paper is based on a Rao-Blackwellized particle filter that enables the robot to build a map and localize in an environment by means of the detection of three dimensional visual features. This algoritm can be decomposed in four basic steps:

a. Generating a new particle set.
b. Updating the estimate of the landmarks based on the observations.
c. Calculating a weight for each particle.
d. Resampling based on the weight of each particle.

In the following, we describe the previous steps of the FastSLAM algorithm.

2.2.1 New particle set generation

In the first step a new set of hypothesis S_t is obtained based on teh set S_{t-1}. That is to say, we obtain a new pose $x_t^{[m]}$ for the robot by sampling from a motion model:

$$x_t^{[m]} \sim p(x_t|x_{t-1}, u_t), \tag{4}$$

where $p(x_t|x_{t-1}, u_t)$ defines the movement model of the robot. This movement model is applied to each of the poses of each particle separately, based on the movement performed by the robot. Figure 1 shows the application of Equation 4. The figures show the path of three robots that work independently. Solid lines represent the real path followed by the robots, whereas dashed lines represent the odometry readings. It can be observed that, at the begining, all the particles are concentrated on the same point. After applying the movement model, we obtain a set of particle clouds that represent the probability of the pose of each robot at each time step.

2.2.2 Landmark estimate

The landmark update is performed based on the pose of the robot that performed the observation $z_t = \{v_t, d_t\}$ with data association c_t. This is done independently for each landmark l_k by means of the standard *EKF* equations presented below:

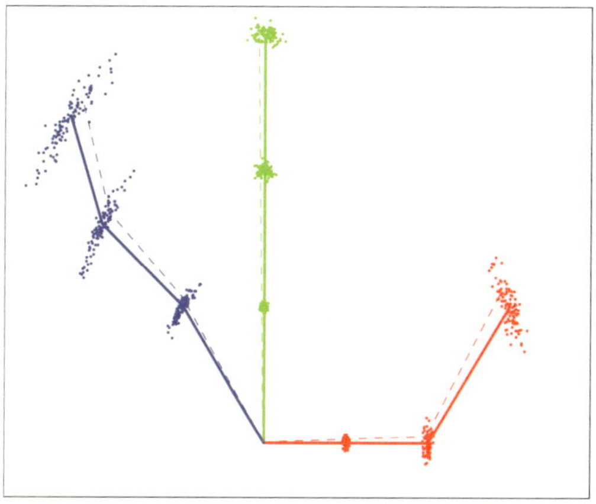

Fig. 1. The figure shows a new set of particles generated by sampling from the motion model.

$$\hat{v}_t = g(x_t^{[m]}, \mu_{c_t,t-1}^{[m]}) \quad (5)$$

$$G_{l_{c_t}} = \nabla_{l_{c_t}} g(x_t, l_{c_t})_{x_t = x_t^{[m]}; l_{c_t} = \mu_{c_t,t-1}^{[m]}} \quad (6)$$

$$Z_{c_t,t} = G_{l_{c_t}} \Sigma_{c_t,t-1}^{[m]} G_{l_{c_t}}^T + R_t \quad (7)$$

$$K_t = \Sigma_{c_t,t-1}^{[m]} G_{l_{c_t}}^T Z_{c_t,t}^{-1} \quad (8)$$

$$\mu_{c_t,t}^{[m]} = \mu_{c_t,t-1}^{[m]} + K_t(v_t - \hat{v}_t) \quad (9)$$

$$\Sigma_{c_t,t}^{[m]} = (I - K_t G_{l_{c_t}}) \Sigma_{c_t,t-1}^{[m]} \quad (10)$$

where $\hat{v}_t$ is the prediction for the current measurement v_t assuming that it has been associated with landmark c_t in the map. The observation model $g(x_t, l_{c_t})$ is linearly approximated by the Jacobian matrix $G_{l_{c_t}}$. It is assumed here that the noise in the observation is Gaussian and can be modeled with the covariance matrix R_t. Equation (9) represents the update of the estimate of the landmark c_t: $\mu_{c_t,t-1}^{[m]}$ based on the innovation $v = (v_t - \hat{v}_t)$. Finally, Equation (10) updates the covariance matrix $\Sigma_{c_t,t}^{[m]}$, which is associated to the m particle and the landmark c_t. Note that we implicitly assume that the observation z_t corresponds to the landmark l_{c_t} in the map. By now we assume this correspondence to be known.

2.2.3 Asigning weights to the particles and resampling

As seen in Section 4, the set of particles is generated by the movement model and distributed according to $p(x_t|x_{t-1}, u_t)$, which is known as proposal distribution. However, our aim is to estimate the posterior $p(x^t, L|z^t, u^t, c^t)$ which includes all the information from odometry and sensors until time t. This is known as target distribution. The difference between the proposal distribution and the target distribution is corrected with a process denoted as importance resampling (SIR). This process works as follows. A weight is assigned to each particle based on the quality of the current observation and the map matches. Then, a new set of particles S_t is created by sampling from S_{t-1}. Each particle is included in the new set with probability proportional to its weight. Assuming that a robot performs a single measurement z_t with data association c_t, the weight $w_t^{[m]}$ associated with the particle m as:

$$\omega_t^{[m]} = \frac{1}{\sqrt{|2\pi Z_{c_t}|}} e^{\{-\frac{1}{2}(v_t-\hat{v}_{t,c_t})^T[Z_{c_t}]^{-1}(v_t-\hat{v}_{t,c_t})\}} \quad (11)$$

Then, the weights are normalized to approximate a probability density function $\sum_{i=1}^{M} \omega_t^{[i]} = 1$. In this way, the set of particles represent a set of hipothetical paths that the robot may follow. Conditioned to each path, there is a set of 3D estimated landmarks, each one represented by a Kalman filter. Finally, in order to choose the path and map that best represents the true trajectories and environment, a logartihmic sum over the global weights of the particles is maintained. The most probable particle is selected as follows:

$$\hat{m} = \underset{m}{argmax} \sum_{t=1}^{A} \log(w_t^{[m]}) \quad (12)$$

3. Map fusion

In the previous section we have seen how each robot is able to estimate a map of the environment by means of a particle filter. This task is initially performed individually. The result is a set of local maps whose landmarks are red to each robot system. At a specific moment, the fusion of these local maps into a global map may be required. In this section we concentrate on the map merging problem. This task is tackled in two subproblems: map alignment and map merging. These steps are described in detail in the following.

3.1 Map alignment

Aligning two maps means estimating the transformation between those maps. Concretely, three parameters are computed: a translation in x and y (t_x, t_y) and a rotation θ. In our case, each map is refered to the local reference system of the robot, which is located in its origin. In addition, the maps are landmark-based, thus the alingment is obtained by looking for correspondences based on the descriptor simmilarity. Afterwards, the landmarks of different maps can be expressed in the same reference system. In a previous work (Ballesta, Reinoso, Gil, Payá & Juliá, 2010), we studied, in detail, the problem of aligning three dimensional landmark-based maps. For this purpose, we compared a set of aligning methods suitable for this kind of maps. Particularly, we evaluated the following methods: RANSAC (RANdom SAmple Consensus), SVD (Singular Value Decomposition), ICP (Iterative Closest Point) and ImpICP (Improved ICP). The last one is an *ad-hoc* implementation. The experiments were carried out with simulated data as well as real maps built by the robots. Figures 2(a) and 2(b) show the results obtained. The experiments consisted of testing the behaviour of the aligning methods at different stages of the SLAM process. That is to say, initially the maps are smaller and obtaining the alignment is therefore more difficult. However, as the size of the maps is bigger, the common landmarks between those maps may increase, and thus the aligment can be succesfully found. This is represented in the figures that show the error obtained in the estimate of the aligning parameters. Figure 2(a) shows the error in the estimate of the translation parameters (t_x, t_y) when the alignment is obtained. Analogously, Figure 2(b) show the error in rotation (θ). Paying attetion to both figures, it is noticeable that RANSAC obtains the best results. The error is practically zero independently of the size of the maps. An example of the performance of RANSAC is illustrated in Figure 3. This figure shows how the common landmarks are indentified and matched.

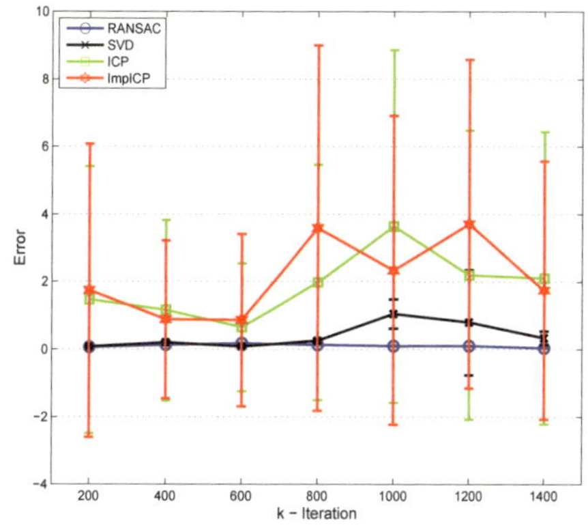

(a)

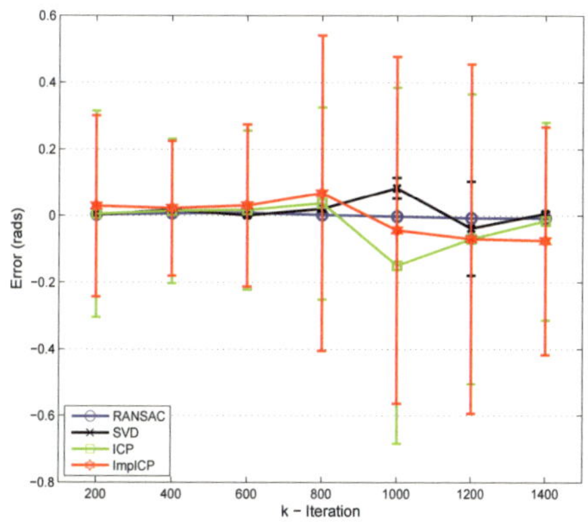

(b)

Fig. 2. (a) Traslation error. (b) Rotation error.

3.2 Map merging

In this section we focus on the map merging problem. Once the alignment is performed, we will have the local maps expressed in the same ence system and the common landmarks between these maps identified. In this situation the local maps can be merged into a global one. As described previously, the maps built by the robots consist of a set of landmarks $L = \{l_1, l_2, \ldots, l_N\}$. Each landmark l_k is defined as $l_k = \{\mu_k, \Sigma_k, d_k\}$, where $\mu_k = (X_k, Y_k, Z_k)$ represents the position of the landmark by means of a three dimensional vector. Then Σ_k and d_k are the covariance matrix and the descriptor associated to each landmark. When merging two maps, the uncertainty in the estimate of the landmarks should be considered. We therefore propose a *Multivariable Stationary Kalman Filter* in order to fuse this data. Given two maps, map_1 and map_2, and using the nomenclature described previously, the following formulation is used to merge these maps:

$$K_{\{i\}} = \Sigma_{1\{i\}} \cdot (\Sigma_{1\{i\}} + \Sigma_{2\{i\}})^{-1} \tag{13}$$

$$\mu_{G\{i\}} = \mu_{1\{i\}} + K_{\{i\}} \cdot (\mu_{1\{i\}} - \mu_{2\{i\}}) \tag{14}$$

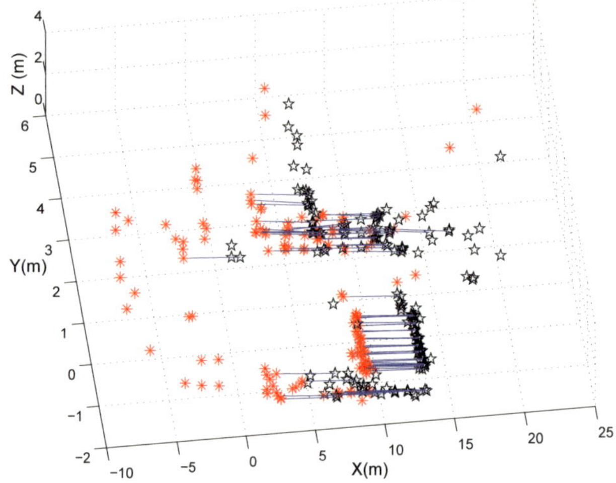

Fig. 3. Example of alignment.

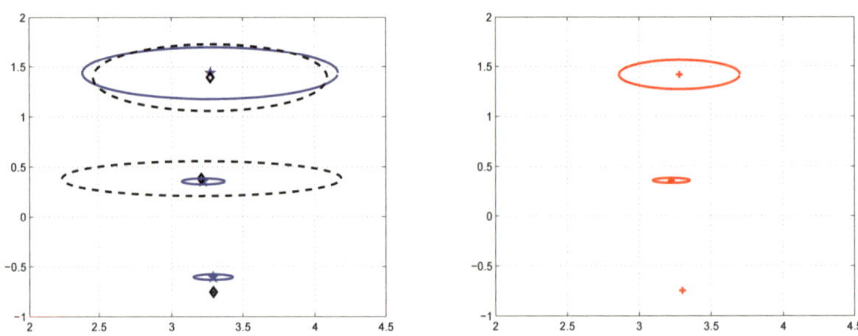

(a) (b)

Fig. 4. (a) Position and uncertainty of 3 aligned landmarks from map_1 and map_2 (b) Same landmarks after fusion. Uncertainty is represented by an ellipse.

$$\Sigma_{G\{i\}} = (I - K_{\{i\}}) \cdot \mu_{1\{i\}} \tag{15}$$

where i is an index ($i \in \{1, N\}$) that denotes each matched landmark. N is the total number of matched landmarks between both maps (1 and 2). K_i represents the Kalman gain. $\mu_G\{i\}$ indicates the 3D coordinates of landmark i in the global map. This landmark is the result of matching and merging a common landmark between both local maps, map_1 and map_2. μ_1 are the 3D coordinates of map_1 and μ_2 the 3D coordinates of map_2 expressed in the map_1's reference system (i.e. after the alignment process). Finally, Σ_G,Σ_1 and Σ_2 are the 3×3 covariance matrices, which represent the uncertainty in the location of the landmarks in map_G, map_1 and map_2 respectively. The covariance matrices of map_2 (Σ_2) have been also transformed to the map_1's reference system. In Fig. 4, the uncertainty of the landmarks are represented with an ellipse. It can be observed that in the alignment process, we transform not only the position of the landmarks but also the error ellipse. This is done by means of a rotation matrix as follows:

$$\Sigma_2 = R^T \cdot \Sigma_{20} \cdot R \tag{16}$$

where Σ_{20} is the covariance matrix of map_2 before being aligned with map_1. And R is the transformation matrix which is:

$$R = \begin{pmatrix} \cos\theta & -\sin\theta & 0 \\ \sin\theta & \cos\theta & 0 \\ 0 & 0 & 1 \end{pmatrix} \tag{17}$$

Finally, as far as the visual descriptor is concerned, we computed the mean between the descriptors in the local maps and incorporate the resulting descriptor to the global map.

4. Multirobot SLAM

Once the global map is obtained and the relative positions of the robots is known, the SLAM problem is solved jointly. That is to say, from the fusion of the local maps on, the robots perform the map building together. To do this, we propose the Rao-Blackwellized Kalman Filter extended to the multi-robot case. In this sense, the equation of the SLAM posterior is:

$$\begin{aligned} & p(x^t_{\langle 1:K\rangle}, L | z^t_{\langle 1:K\rangle}, u^t_{\langle 1:K\rangle}, c^t) = \\ & p(x^t_{\langle 1:K\rangle} | z^t_{\langle 1:K\rangle}, u^t_{\langle 1:K\rangle}, c^t) \prod_{k=1}^{N} \quad p(l_k | x^t_{\langle 1:K\rangle}, z^t_{\langle 1:K\rangle}, u^t_{\langle 1:K\rangle}, c^t) \end{aligned} \tag{18}$$

This probability function is a way to estimate a set of K paths $x^t_{\langle 1:K\rangle}$ and a map L conditioned to the case in which the robots perform a number of movements $u^t_{\langle 1:K\rangle}$ and a series of observations $z^t_{\langle 1_K\rangle}$ associated to landmarks in the map c^t. As it can be observed this expression is analogous to the equation 1, so the estimate of the map and the estimate of K paths can be separated into two parts: $p(x^t_{\langle 1:K\rangle} | z^t_{\langle 1:K\rangle}, u^t_{\langle 1:K\rangle}, c^t)$, which is estimated using a particle filter and the map L which is estimated using N independent estimates conditioned to the paths $x^t_{\langle 1:K\rangle}$. Analogously to Equation 2, the estimate of the posterior is done by means of M particles, each one represented as:

$$S_t^{[m]} = \{x^{t,[m]}_{\langle 1:K\rangle}, \mu^{[m]}_{1,t}, \Sigma^{[m]}_{1,t}, d^{[m]}_1, \cdots, \mu^{[m]}_{N,t}, \Sigma^{[m]}_{N,t}, d^{[m]}_N\} \tag{19}$$

Unlike the particle defined in (2), in this case the state that we would like to estimate is composed by the pose (x, y, θ) of K robots, thus $x^t_{\langle 1:K\rangle} = \{x_{t,\langle 1\rangle}, x_{t,\langle 2\rangle}, \cdots, x_{t,\langle K\rangle}\}$. As a result, we propose a joint estimation over a path state of dimension $3K$. According to (Thrun et al., 2005), the number of particles needed to obtain a good estimation increases exponentially with the dimension of the state. However, the results that we present here show that the approach works perfectly for robot teams of 2–3 members using a reasonable number of particles. In the case presented, the same map is shared by all the robots, which means that an observation performed by a particular robot affects the map of the whole robot team. For example, a robot does not need to explicitly close a loop to reduce the uncertainty in its pose. On the contrary, the robot can reduce its uncertainty if it observes landmarks previously seen by other robots. In consequence, one member of the team may observe a landmark previously mapped by a different robot and update its estimate. The formulation of the multi-robot FastSLAM algorithm proposed here is presented in algorithm 1.

Algorithm 1 Summary of the proposed algorithm.

$S = \emptyset$
$[z_{t,\langle 1\rangle}, z_{t,\langle 2\rangle}, z_{t,\langle 3\rangle}]$ = ObtainObservations()
InitialiseMap$(S, x_{0,\langle 1:3\rangle}, z_{t,\langle 1:3\rangle})$
for $t = 1$ to numMovements **do**
  $[z_{t,\langle 1\rangle}, z_{t,\langle 2\rangle}, z_{t,\langle 3\rangle}]$ = ObtainObservations()
  $[S, \omega_{t,\langle 1\rangle}]$ = FastSLAMMR$(S, z_{t,\langle 1\rangle}, R_t, u_{t,\langle 1\rangle})$
  $[S, \omega_{t,\langle 2\rangle}]$ = FastSLAMMR$(S, z_{t,\langle 2\rangle}, R_t, u_{t,\langle 2\rangle})$
  $[S, \omega_{t,\langle 3\rangle}]$ = FastSLAMMR$(S, z_{t,\langle 3\rangle}, R_t, u_{t,\langle 3\rangle})$
  $\omega_t = \omega_{t,\langle 1\rangle}\omega_{t,\langle 2\rangle}\omega_{t,\langle 3\rangle}$
  S = ImportanceResampling(S, ω_t) //Sample randomly from S according to $\omega_t^{[m]}$
end for

function $[S_t]$ = **FastSLAMMR**$(S_{t-1}, z_{t,\langle i\rangle}, R_t, u_{t,\langle i\rangle})$
$S_t = \emptyset$
for $m = 1$ to M {For every particle} **do**
  $x_{t,\langle i\rangle}^{[m]} \sim p(x_{t,\langle i\rangle} | x_{t-1,\langle i\rangle}, u_{t,\langle i\rangle})$
  for $n = 1$ to $N_{t-1}^{[m]}$ //Loop over all possible data associations **do**
    $\hat{v}_{t,\langle i\rangle} = g(x_{t,\langle i\rangle}^{[m]}, \mu_{n,t-1}^{[m]})$
    $G_{l_n} = \nabla_{l_{c_t}} g(x_t, l_n)_{x_{t,\langle i\rangle} = x_{t,\langle i\rangle}^{[m]}; l_{c_t} = \mu_{c_t,t-1}^{[m]}}$
    $Z_{n,t} = G_{l_n} \Sigma_{n,t-1}^{[m]} G_{l_n}^T + R_t$
    $D(n) = (v_{t,\langle i\rangle} - \hat{v}_{t,\langle i\rangle})^T [Z_{n,t}]^{-1} (v_{t,\langle i\rangle} - \hat{z}_{t,\langle i\rangle})$
    $E(n) = (d_{t,\langle i\rangle} - d_n)^T (d_{t,\langle i\rangle} - d_n)$
  end for
  $D(N_{t-1}^{[m]} + 1) = D_0$
  $j = find(D \leq D_0)$ {Find candidates below D_0}
  $c_t = argmin_j E(n)$ {Find minimum among candidates}
  if $E(c_t) > E_0$ // Create a new landmark? **then**
    $c_t = N_{t-1}^{[m]} + 1$
  end if
  if $c_t = N_{t-1}^{[m]} + 1$ //New landmark **then**
    $N_t^{[m]} = N_{t-1}^{[m]} + 1$
    $\mu_{c_t,t}^{[m]} = g^{-1}(x_{t,\langle i\rangle}^{[m]}, z_{t,\langle i\rangle})$
    $\Sigma_{c_t,t}^{[m]} = G_{l_{c_t}}^T R_t^{-1} G_{l_{c_t}}$
    $\omega_t^{[m]} = p_0$
  else
    $N_t^{[m]} = N_{t-1}^{[m]}$ //Old landmark
    $K_t = \Sigma_{c_t,t-1}^{[m]} G_{L_{c_t}}^T Z_{c_t,t}^{-1}$
    $\mu_{c_t,t}^{[m]} = \mu_{c_t,t-1}^{[m]} + K_t(v_{t,\langle i\rangle} - \hat{v}_{t,\langle i\rangle})$
    $\Sigma_{c_t,t}^{[m]} = (I - K_t G_{l_{c_t}}) \Sigma_{c_t,t-1}^{[m]}$
  end if
  $\omega_{t,\langle i\rangle}^{[m]} = \frac{1}{\sqrt{|2\pi Z_{c_t}|}} e^{\{-\frac{1}{2}(v_{t,\langle i\rangle} - \hat{v}_{t,c_t})^T [Z_{c_t}]^{-1} (v_{t,\langle i\rangle} - \hat{v}_{t,c_t})\}}$
  add $\{x_{t,\langle i\rangle}^{[m]}, N_t^{[m]}, \mu_{1,t}^{[m]}, \Sigma_{1,t}^{[m]}, d_{1,t}^{[m]}, \cdots, \mu_{N_t^{[m]},t}^{[m]}, \Sigma_{N_t^{[m]},t}^{[m]}, d_{N_t^{[m]},t}^{[m]}, \omega_t^{[m]}\}$ to S_t
end for
return S_t

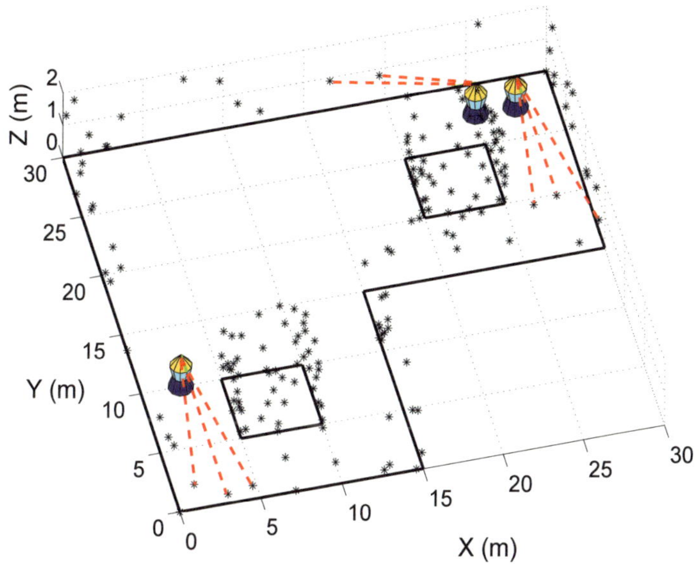

Fig. 5. Simulated environment. The robots perform observations of simulated landmarks located in walls. These walls are represented by a line. It can be observed that the walls restrict the visibility of the visual landmarks placed behind.

5. Experiments

In order to test the SLAM algorithm proposed, we have created a simulated environment as shown in figure 5. In this figure there are three robots building a map of the environment. This environment is represented by walls (line) with landmarks randomly located in them. In the figure we can see which landmarks are the robots currently observing. This is represented by dashed lines. In the experiments performed we have test the computational cost of the algorithm as well as the RMS error in the estimate of the error. Regarding the computational time, two parameteres are mainly influencing: the number of particles used (M) and the number of observations integrated as each time step (B). In order to decrease the computational cost, we can reduce the number of observations that each robot reduces at each iteration of the algorithm. For example, we consider that each robot obtains B/K observations. That is to say, if we had three robots and $B = 15$, then each robot would integrate $B = 5$ observations. Figure 6(a) shows the results obtained if robots perform B/K observations. In this case, it can be observed that the computational cost is simmilar regardless of the number of robots, for any number of particles. The total number of observations integrated in the filter is the same for the case of 1, 2 or 3 robots. On the other hand, in Figure 6(b) we evaluate the error in the map, using the previous restriction (B/K observations). As the figure shows, the estimate of the map and the paths improves when more robots are used. It can be deduced, from these figures, that good results can be obtained even if we reduce the number of observations performed by each robot.

6. Conclusion

This paper presents a posible solution to the multi-robot SLAM problem in the visual context. Particularly, the approach proposed begins with an independent map building part, in which

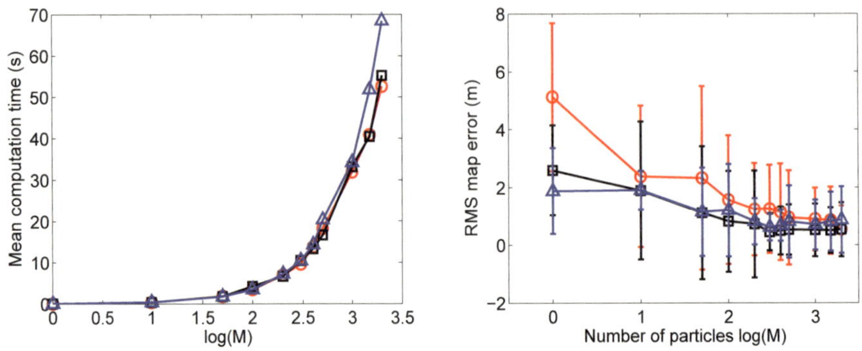

(a) (b)

Fig. 6. Figure (a) shows the mean computation time at each iteration of the algorithm for different number of particles $M = \{1\ 10\ 50\ 100\ 200\ 300\ 400\ 500\ 1000\ 1500\ 2000\}$. Figure (b) shows the RMS error in the map when B/K observations are used. We show simultaneously results with one robot (◯), two robots (□) and three robots (△).

each robot builds its own map independently. In this case, the relative positions of the robots are not necessary. This is an advantage in practice, since this data could be unknown. As a consequence, the robots build their own local maps regardless of other robots' poses and observations. The map building is carried out by means of a Rao-Blackwellized particle filter. Since the robots work independently, this algorithm has been implemented for a single robot. At some point, the robots may share the information collected and fused the local maps into a single one. For this reason, the map fusion problem has been tackled in this paper. First, we paid attention to the alignment problem in which a common reference system for the local maps is obtained. Then, we concentrated on the map merging problem. In this case, the common landmarks are identified based on the descriptor similarity and fused, taking into account the uncertainty in the estimate of those landmarks. To do this, we use a *Multivariable Stationary Kalman Filter*. The results show that the uncertainty of the fused landmarks is reduced. Finally, once the relative positions of the robots are known and a global map is computed, the SLAM process is continued by means of an extension of the previous particle filter. This time, we implemented a multi-robot particle filter in such a way that the robots estimate their trajectories and the map jointly. The results obtained show the good performance of the algorithm in simulation. As future work, it is desirable to evaluate this algorithm in a real environment.

7. References

Ballesta, M., Gil, A., Reinoso, O. & Úbeda, D. (2010). Análisis de detectores y descriptores de características visuales en slam en entornos interiores y exteriores, *Revista Iberoamericana de Automática e Informática Industrial (RIAII)* 7(2): 68–80.

Ballesta, M., Reinoso, O., Gil, A., Payá, L. & Juliá, M. (2010). Evaluation of aligning methods for landmark-based maps in visual slam, *INTECH* . To appear.

Bay, H., Tuytelaars, T. & Van Gool, L. (2006). Surf: Speeded up robust features, *Proceedings of the ninth European Conference on Computer Vision*.

Davison, A. J. & Murray, D. W. (2002). Simultaneous localisation and map-building using active vision, *IEEE Transactions on Pattern Analysis and Machine Intelligence* .

Fenwick, J. W., Newman, P. M. & Leonard, J. J. (2002). Cooperative concurrent mapping and localization, *Proceedings of the 2002 IEEE International Conference on Robotics and Automation* pp. 1810–1817.

Gil, A., Martínez Mozos, O., Ballesta, M. & Reinoso, O. (2009). A comparative evaluation of interest point detectors and local descriptors for visual slam, *Machine Vision and Applications Journal* .

Gil, A., Martínez-Mozos, ., Ballesta, M. & Reinoso, . (2008). A comparative evaluation of interest point detectors and local descriptors for visual slam, *Machine Vision and Applications* .

Gil, A., Reinoso, O., Fernández, C., Vicente, M. A., Rottmann, A. & Martínez-Mozos, O. (2006). Simultaneous localization and mapping in unmodified environments using stereo vision, *Proceedings of the 3rd International Conference on Informatics in Control, Automation and Robotics*, Setúbal, Portugal.

Gil, A., Reinoso, O., Martínez-Mozos, O., Stachniss, C. & Burgard, W. (2006). Improving data association in vision-based SLAM, *Proc. of the IEEE/RSJ Int. Conf. on Intelligent Robots and Systems (IROS)*, Beijing, China.

Harris, C. G. & Stephens, M. (1998). A combined corner and edge detector, *Alvey Vision Conference.*

Jensfelt, P., Kragic, D., Folkesson, J. & Björkman, M. (2006). A framework for vision based bearing only 3D SLAM, *IEEE Int. Conf. on Robotics & Automation*, Orlando, FL, USA.

Konolige, K., Fox, D., Limketkai, B., Ko, J. & Stewart, B. (2003). Map merging for distributed robot navigation, *Proc. of the 2003 IEEE/RSJ International Conference on Intelligent Robots and Systems.*

Kwak, N., Kim, G.-W., Ji, S.-H. & Lee, B.-H. (2008). A mobile robot exploration strategy with low cost sonar and tungsten-halonen structural ligth, *Journal of Intelligent and Robotic Systems* 51(1): 89–111.

Leonard, J. J. & Durrant-Whyte, H. F. (1991). Mobile robot localization by tracking geometric beacons, *IEEE Transactions on Robotics and Automation* 7(4).

Little, J., Se, S. & Lowe, D. (2002). Global localization using distinctive visual features, *Proc. of the IEEE/RSJ Int. Conf. on Intelligent Robots and Systems (IROS)*, Lausanne, Suiza.

Montemerlo, M. (2003). *FastSLAM: A Factored Solution to the Simultaneous Localization and Mapping Problem with Unknown Data Association*, PhD thesis, Robotics Institute, Carnegie Mellon University, Pittsburgh, PA.

Montemerlo, M. & Thrun, S. (2003). Simultaneous localization and mapping with unknown data association using FastSLAM, *Proc. of the IEEE Int. Conf. on Robotics & Automation (ICRA)*, Taipei, Taiwan.

Murillo, A. C., Guerrero, J. J. & Sagüés, C. (2007). Surf features for efficient robot localization with omnidirectional images, *Proc. of the IEEE Int. Conf. on Robotics & Automation (ICRA)*, San Diego, CA, USA.

Murray, D. & Little, J. J. (2000). Using real-time stereo vision for mobile robot navigation, *Autonomous Robots* 2(8): 161–171.

Roumeliotis, S. & Bekey, G. (2002). Distributed multi-robot localization, *IEEE Transactions on Robotics and Automation* 18(5): 781–795.

Stewart, B., Ko, J., Fox, D. & Konolige, K. (2003). A hierarchical bayesian approach to mobile robot map structure estimation, *Proceedings of the Conference on Uncertainty in AI (UAI)*, Acapulco, Mexico.

Thrun, S. (2001). A probabilistic online mapping algorithm for teams of mobile robots,

Int. Journal of Robotics Research 20(5): 335–363.

Thrun, S., Burgard, W. & Fox, D. (2005). *Probabilistic Robotics*, The MIT Press. ISBN: 0-262-20162-3.

Valls-Miró, J., Zhou, W. & Dissanayake, G. (2006). Towards vision based navigation in large indoor environments, *Proc. of the IEEE/RSJ Int. Conf. on Intelligent Robots and Systems (IROS)*, Beijing, China.

Wijk, O. & Christensen, H. I. (2000). Localization and navigation of a mobile robot using natural point landmarks extracted from sonar data, *Robotics and Autonomous Systems* 1(31): 31–42.

Zhou, X. S. & Roumeliotis, S. I. (2006). Multi-robot slam with unknown initial correspondence: The robot rendezvous case, *Proc. of the 2006 IEEE/RSJ International Conference on Intelligent Robots and Systems, Beijing, China, pp. 1785-1792.*

7

Multirobot Cooperative Model applied to Coverage of Unknown Regions

Eduardo Gerlein and Enrique González
Pontificia Universidad Javeriana
Colombia

1. Introduction

This chapter describes the problems of robotic exploration and coverage, and also presents the main characteristics that must include a multirobot platform in order fulfill such task in terms of general architecture, goals and cooperativeness. It is described a validated model for multirobot exploration called Backtracking Spiral Algorithm - Cooperative Multirobot, BSA-CM.

Exploration and coverage of unknown regions are tasks that have been developed by human beings throughout history. Nevertheless, tasks that imply lands under hazardous or hostile circumstances such as planetary exploration (Menzel, 2000), humanitarian demining (Freese et al., 2007), environmental cleaning (Tilden, 1996) of dangerous materials as radioactive or military remainders leads to delegating such exercise to robots. The main issue is to protect human life at all cost. In this particular case, by unloading the people of tasks in daily routine that implies covering of regions.

Exploration of unknown areas and lands, and also execution of complex tasks in unknown or partially structured regions, is an extremely complex job for an independent robot, given the nature of the algorithms and intelligence and reasoning levels whereupon are equipped the robots (Murphy, 2000). Nevertheless, the possibility of having robotic platforms able to explore these spaces is becoming more and more a fundamental necessity in the development of autonomous mobile robots. The subject of covering and exploration with robotic entities has been boarded from different optical but in case of multi-robot systems, the challenge just begins.

Systems that involve several robots can present advantages over those that include a single robot of great power, processing capacity and cost. First of all, a robot team can cover an area more quickly than a single robot. On the other hand, the exploration performed by a set of robots is robust due to the added redundancies and allows to have a notion of the best next point of view to gain information of the area where a single system would fail (Balch & Parker, 2002).

After a review of different approaches to the coverage problem with robots, it is possible to conclude that such solutions are subscribed in one of two main groups depending on the movement strategy chosen to solve the problem of coverage: those that use Non-Structured trajectories, where the navigation of the robots depends on the search of the best next point of view that derives in the elimination of borders of the unknown world, or, by means of

probabilistic methods. The other family involves Structured trajectories, where a sweeping of simple regions is made by deterministic movements following zig-zag or spirals paths.
The study of multi-robot coverage solutions allows to determine the relevant characteristics in order to be considered at the time of designing a coverage system that fulfill the requirements such as reliability, robustness and efficiency and also to determine the cooperative characteristics needed to allow the robots to act as a team. The focus of this chapter is the description and tests of BSACM - Backtracking Spiral Algorithm Cooperative Multi-robot, which is an upgraded version of a single robot coverage procedure, implemented under a multi-agent cooperative systems approach as an example of a model that includes the requirements described. It is presents the multi-agent cooperative coverage with robotic entities, and the internal agent architecture designed. The algorithm is tested in an event-driven multi-agent environment, which includes multitasking, multithread, and a continuous space robot simulator. Tests and simulation results show the convenience of using robot teams for coverage tasks and multi-agent approach to coordinate their actions.
In this chapter the reader will find:

- In section 2, the reader will find a deep analysis of cooperation in multiagent systems as a basis of multirobot platforms. Based on the theory compilation it is possible to determine, discriminate and group the intrinsic characteristics that a cooperative system must achieve in order to fulfill a successfully coverage task.
- Section 3 presents a review referred to a coverage models with a single robot, and summarize some of the multirobot solutions. It is presented a comparative analysis of those approaches. As a result it is possible to determine requirements related to architecture, world modeling and in general, the algorithms used in multirobot coverage systems.
- Section 4 presents the design, implementation and tests of BSA-CM as a case of study of a system that includes the requirements described in previous subchapters and that achieve a complete coverage with a team of robots.

2. Cooperation in multiagent systems

In this particular case, the task of region coverage will have a multiagent cooperation approach. The main goal is to give a general frame for region coverage using multirobot teams in terms of requirements and indicators that must be present and evidenced in the system. This analysis allows a designer to build the architecture in terms of cooperation since the beginning of the process. This section aims to define an agent and its architecture in the context of a multiagent system; finally, a brief description of communication, task allocation, and information access leads to the identification of the requirements that have to be taken into account to design a cooperative system.

2.1 Agents

Although there is not an enough generalized definition for what an agent represents, it is possible to mention a common characteristic between the different approaches which is the capacity to do "tasks" for the user under a certain degree of discernment, given by a basic level of intelligence which allows it to interact with the environment in an autonomous way, requiring the user intervention just in certain cases. In other words, an agent is an "entity" immerse in an environment capable of perceiving and taking actions according to those perceptions. In most of the cases, an agent can modify the state of its environment.

Following this general definition, we can include human beings, animals, software, robots as being agents. From now, we can refer to an agent as an entity created and designed by humans, limiting this category to software and robots.
An agent is considered autonomous if the type of developed actions comes from the experience of interaction with its environment and not from the previous knowledge given by the designer, even though this a priori knowledge is necessary. Agents require:

- **goals**, which orient them to the main objective and provide feedback about the progress of the general task;
- **sensors**, which allow to capture data from the environment;
- **intelligence**, in order to interpret data and orient behaviors to accomplish the main goal;
- **actuators**, which allow the agents to take actions which result in the accomplishment of the task.

2.2 Agent architecture

An agent is designed under a basic structure or architecture that answers to the fashion in which the agent is organized internally. It involves, besides sensors and actuators drivers, a main program which includes certain level of intelligence in order to interpret data from the sensors and to give directions to the actuators based in the data process to adapt itself or modify the environment. Given the extensive theory about agents and multiagent systems, there are many architectures proposed, however, it has to be taken into account how the world representation is related with the new perceptions, and how they trigger decisions about future actions (Ferber, 1999).
Thus, the mapping mechanism between perceptions and actions depends entirely on the main goal or task that the agent is designed for. For example, it is possible to analyze a scheme where certain perception is related to one or a set of actions. In this case, the designer has to analyze all the possible perceptions and situations that the agent will find. If the agent is confronted to unknown or none determined situations, it can be derived in malfunction or inactivity. When different actions could apply for a situation, it is also possible to established priority mechanisms or to identify special actions for special situations.

2.3 Multiagent Systems (MAS)

A multiagent system is formed by a set of agents that coordinate and conjugate their abilities and resources to solve particular or global problems (Ferber, 1999). A MAS can be defined by the following intuitive items:

- An environment E.
- A set of objects O located in E.
- A set of agents A, $(A \subset O)$ which are the active objects capable of perceive, create and modify other objects and communicate with other agents.
- A set of relations $\Re$, which relate the objects.
- A set of operations *Op*, defined to allow the agents to perceive, transform and manipulate the passive objects in O.
- A set of universal laws, that determine the consequences of *Op* in the particular world.

In such mutiagent context, cooperation is the key to achieve a common goal by a set of agents. The goals of a cooperative agent have to be aligned with those of the team. From now, any reference to an agent is oriented to physical cooperative agents, in other words, to a software agent that controls a robotic hardware in a cooperative multiagent context.

2.4 Cooperation

Cooperation between physical agents or robots is a complex control problem that implies a high degree of information exchange between them in order to accomplish the team goal. Any approach to the problem requires a global knowledge about the environment to be able to consider all the possible states. Centralized approaches have inherent limitations (Ferber, 1999), meanwhile distributed solutions are more efficient.

Cooperation between agents implies a shared main goal and mechanisms of avoidance or managing of conflicts in order to help other agents if necessary. This concept of "benevolence" (Balch & Parker, 2002) is applicable when all agents belong to the same user or organization. There are MAS that are not necessary cooperative in where the agents are only interested in their particular tasks and do not share goals neither information, even the taken actions can generate conflicts. One can conclude that cooperative robotics is oriented in designing autonomous societies that include robots capable to recognize, identify and solve problems inside their environment and look for negotiation of tasks in such situations.

The decomposition of a global task in particular tasks depends on the agent's abilities and resources availability. However, it is possible that the sum of abilities and resources results insufficient. In some cases, particular tasks can be incompatible even if all agents are pursing the same global goal.

The MAS can be intentionally cooperative since at early stages of design it is included this characteristic in the programming or cooperative behaviors can merge during its operation described by an external observer in a reactive way, but in both cases one can say that the system is cooperative if an *a posteriori* analysis evidence one of two conditions (Ferber, 1999):

- Adding a new member to the team increases the global performance. To accomplish this criterion, the system is in a "collaborative situation".
- Agent actions are designed to prevent or solve current or potential conflicts. To accomplish this criterion, the system is in a "conflict solving situation".

In the *intentional cooperation,* agents have the intention of cooperation at a cognitive level, and the cooperation is a mechanism to achieve concrete goals. In *reactive or merging cooperation,* a collective behavior satisfies at least one of the previous criterions; even thought there is no explicit intention of cooperation. It means that one can talk about cooperation even if the agents do not have knowledge about their environment and other agents. For this reason, cooperation implies simultaneous operation to oblation a common benefit (Jung, 1998).

2.5 Cooperation Indicators

According to Ferber, a MAS to be considered as cooperative it must exhibit some important characteristics: grouping, multiplication, specialization, collaboration, communications and conflict resolution.

- Grouping implies and homogeneous array of agents along the space.
- Multiplication brings an increment in the number of agents that will be reflected in a performance and reliability improvement. Multiplication will imply also the emergence of conflicts for physical space.

- Specialization refers to the adaptation degree of agents to perform their tasks. It can be a gradual process if the system includes learning mechanisms.
- Collaboration is determined by the strategy used by the system to assign and distribute tasks. Task allocation can be determined by centralized methods, where a central agent assign duties after a corresponding analysis (i.e. contract nets with one trader and several bidders) or by means of a "yellow pages" system which eliminates the hierarchy relations and tasks are located in a common board. Also there is a distributed approach which eliminated the concept of a central agent as in acquaintance nets or distributed contract nets.
- Communications are fundamental in a cooperative system, and can be seen as an extra perception capability trough the agents are able to exchange information, request actions and interpret the world in a global way.
- Conflict resolution is close related with collaboration since the tasks distribution mechanism must include negotiation procedures. Conflicts can emerge for physical space, resources, communication channel, access to data and information, etc.

Coordination of actions, supported in communication systems, avoid conflicts for access to resources caused by grouping and multiplication of agents. In multiagent systems emerge relations and dependencies that determine actions of the agent. Resources will be always limited, thus agents must include mechanisms that allow to share and to access to them avoiding obstructions, optimizing operating costs, and reducing redundant actions. Coordination is the set of activities subjacent to the main goal that allow the execution of particular actions in time and space, in a coherent and synchronized way, which derives in the increasing of the global performance and the avoidance of conflicts.

Rules that determine coordination between agents are determined by the environment in which the MAS operates. For example, a system for flight control in an airport, the coordination rules will be designed to a division of resources physical (tracks, hangars, access points, etc.); for a coverage robot team, coordination rules will look forward to make an efficient distribution of the agents along the surface.

2.6 Requirements for a Cooperative Multiagent System

In the previous sections, the basic concepts of agents and multiagent systems have been introduced, so now it is possible to define the requirements that a multiagent system must incorporate to be considered as cooperative. Designing a cooperation strategy will be based on them; the requirements have to be covered one by one, independent of the chosen methods to manage communications, coordination and synchronization.

A single cooperation model can be implemented for a diverse set of tasks, but in order to reveal and determine the cooperation level; those requirements must be measurable in a certain way in terms of existence or inexistence or by means of ratios and numeric values in order to be evaluated on subsequent stages of implementation on simulated and/or real platforms.

Deployment: it is referred to the spatial distribution of the agents. For the particular task of coverage, the physical space is a resource and a goal at the same time. The capability of the agents of getting closer or establish wide distributed arrays will determine the communication strategy. Some applications need the agents as close as possible, but others look for exactly the opposite situation improving the coverage efficiency. A harvest system for example will implement mechanism of grouping and deployment both synchronized in time.

Multiplication: as a cooperation indicator, multiplication is desired since adding new members to the team will increase the global performance and efficiency of the system. In physical environments, the addition of agents will imply the use of space and the merging of obstructions, so an efficient task allocation mechanisms must be implemented. Multiplication can offer some advantages depending on the system and the main task the system is designed for; in some cases it is desired to have some redundant task, but in others, it can affect directly the final efficiency.

Communications: for intentional cooperation, the designer must implement explicit and intentional communications between agents that informs their internal states and and the new acquired data of the world. At the same time, agents must be in capacity to interpret all the communicative acts in order to transform them in useful information for the achievement of the task. Communications are the base in the operation. It is possible that the system presents robustness to communication failures adding redundant tasks; however, communications must be present to consider the system as cooperative. Communication mechanisms, messages nature and conversational structures must be independent from the chosen channel and protocol.

Totipotence: it is referred to the capacity of the agents to execute a wide range of tasks; totipotence is the opposite feature to specialization. Agents that have this characteristic are in capacity to assume other's roles in case of obstructions or failures. Even though specialization will emerge in cases where agents develop certain skills to perform particular subtasks, and in systems with some level of learning mechanisms; however, a very high level of specialization will affect the system's robustness to agent failures.

Collaboration: this is one of the fundamental requirements in cooperation, since implies tasks distribution according to abilities and availability. It is necessary to implement a task distribution mechanism that increases the global efficiency while aiming to balance operation loads and avoiding agent inactivity.

Coordination: coordination mechanisms must synchronize actions of multiple agents at early stages to improve the efficiency of the collaboration techniques. It is necessary to implement global planning as a mean of organization and articulation of particular tasks.

Conflict solving: it is important to design and implement mechanisms of negotiation and arbitrage in case of merging of incompatible goals or insufficient resources. For region coverage, conflicts will be determined for physical space, exploration routes, obstructions, and communication channel interference.

Competence: cooperation levels can be increased if competitive relations are implemented between agents since the assignation of a particular task can be determined by the profit that certain agent will obtain doing it, understanding profit as benefit minus cost. In this way, resources as energy can be optimized.

Functional Architecture: agents must be in capacity of develop those tasks that the primary goal requires. At functional level, agents must incorporate abilities according to the task and environment the system is designed to operate for. Physical agents (robots) designed for region coverage must incorporate adequate locomotion mechanisms, also sensorial systems to navigate and interpret the world, and sufficient communications modules.

World representation: the system must incorporate mechanisms to interpret data obtained from sensors as a representation of the environment and also the agent's location in the space. Precision of this representation will determine future decisions. Also the system must be able to interpret the world in a global way based on particular information from the agents. More complex mechanisms of world representation can include prediction of future states of the environment and probabilistic models that aid the decision making processes.

Robustness: the global system must accomplish the main goal and react adequately in case of failures of communications or agents. However, it is necessary to establish the minimum operation conditions in which the system continues working.

Efficiency: the system must incorporate means to measure its efficiency in terms of resource wasting, time, number of agents, and balance of loads.

It is expected that the described requirements would be present and evidenced during the system operation. As was previous mentioned, some of them must be measurable in terms of its presence or absence, while others can be expressed as a quantity or a ratio. To measure the accomplishment of the requirements in a cooperation model allow to evaluate how the system is been benefited with the cooperation strategies. But even more than just to measure the final efficiency in terms of goal accomplishment, it is necessary to create measure systems that can be implemented over real or simulated platforms under controlled conditions to determine how a system take advantage of the cooperative potentials.

3. Multirobot cooperation for exploration/coverage

The goals of the exploration and coverage tasks can be quite different: construct an incremental representation of the explored region or generate a safe navigation path; however, from the structural point of view, both tasks have to assure completeness. The subject of covering and exploration with single robotic entities has been boarded from different optical but in case of multi-robot systems, the challenge just begins.

Systems that involve several robots can present advantages over those that include a single robot of great power, processing capacity and cost. First of all, a robot team can cover an area more quickly than a single robot. On the other hand, the exploration performed by a set of robots is robust because of the added redundancies and allows having a notion of the best next point of view/coverage to gain information of the area where a single system would fail (Balch & Parker, 2002).

After a revision of different approaches to coverage with robots, it is possible to conclude that such solutions are subscribed in one of two main ways to solve the problem of coverage based on the chosen movement strategy: those that choose Non-Structured trajectories (Doty & Harrison, 1993) (Pirzadeh & Snyder, 1990), where the navigation of the robots depends on the search of the best next point of view that derives in the elimination of borders of the unknown world, or, by means of probabilistic methods. The other family involves Structured trajectories (Choset & Pignon) (Zelinsky, et al., 1992) (González, et al. 1996) (Gabriely & Rimon, 2002) (Gonzalez, et al., 2005), where a sweeping of simple regions is made by deterministic movements in zig-zag or spirals paths.

The work proposed by Choset (Choset, et al., 2004), presents an extension of the covering system described in previous projects, where a parallel sweeping is made by means of boustrophedic trajectories, subdividing the team and the exploration area as the obstacles are found. This system could not guarantee complete coverage if one of the members of the team does not complete its task. The collaboration is evidenced by means of parallel navigation paths.

Simmons (Simmons, et al., 2000) presents a multi-robot exploration approach driven by the elimination of borders with a protocol based on a bidding criterion. Depending on the assignation algorithm it is possible to obtain optimal results if the plans only consider what will happen in the near future. This system requires constant communication with a central agent, otherwise the complete system will fail.

Zlot (Zlot, 2002) describes an efficient and robust distributed exploration method using a robot team derived from the model of markets or contract net, maximizing the obtained data by the agents and reducing the execution costs as collective trip distance of the system. This system is robust since the exploration is completely distributed nevertheless, although a map is constructed with telemetric sensors it does not arrive at all the reachable points of the exploration area.

Wagner (Wagner, Lindenbaum & Bruckstein, 1999) presents a coverage system that does not require explicit communication between the robots. On the contrary, the system uses volatile signs in order to mark cells already visited. It is a useful system in a region with dynamic topology; nevertheless it does not construct a final representation of the world.

Butler (Butler, Rizzi & Hollis, 2000) shows an evolution of a single-robot algorithm presented in previous works to a multi-robot system. They present zig-zag trajectories and a cell division of the region denominated "Generic Rectilinear Decomposition". The system is efficient making maps integration and making the decomposition of the exploration area. Nevertheless, it holds a high re-sweeping rate and it is necessary to include methods of conflict solving caused by obstructions.

Howard (Howard, Mataric & Sukhtme, 2002) presents a system that looks for a robot deployment over the structure or area trying to maximize the sensors coverage. The algorithm is designed to be used in searching/rescuing operations and emergency zones monitoring. Nevertheless, it is limited to the number of robots because the deployment is performed in line of view.

The study of multi-robot systems allows to determine the relevant characteristics in order to be considered at the time of designing a coverage system that fulfill the requirements such as reliability, robustness and efficiency.

3.1 MAS coverage characteristics

When analyzing the coverage systems described below, it is possible to identify common characteristics. Those criteria must be included in a MAS designed for the execution of a surface covering algorithm.

In order to design a cooperative model for a coverage MAS, it is necessary to clearly establish the parameters that, in last instance, become the requirements for an ideal algorithm. Those criteria are:

Task Sensor Requirements: the task the system is designed for, determines the sensorial equipment to be embedded in the robots. Telemetric and contact sensors seem to be indispensable, however in an exploration task more complex and powerful sensors must be integrated, for example long range lasers or artificial vision systems.

Extension from a Single-Robot System: it is possible to use an algorithm validated on single-robot platforms in order to design a cooperative surfaces sweeping algorithm and adding the multi-agent perspective. Some of the most efficient approaches comes from single-robot solutions. The sweeping strategy must be robust to shape, size and configuration of the environment and the obstacles. The good features of a single robot algorithm are usually inherited by the multirobot one.

World Representation: it is indispensable that the system implements a world representation model used as tool for task planning; this representation is also going to be one of the final result of the coverage procedure. One of the main goals of a coverage algorithm is to create global maps that represent the sweeping area. It is necessary also to determine the a priori information that the system must incorporate previous to the algorithm execution (i.e. shape and size of the environment and obstacles, self-location, etc.).

Trajectories: they can be planned (i.e. zig-zag or spirals) or random (systematic border elimination). Random trajectories present a high re-sweeping rate although the procedure results simple and fast. Planned structured trajectories require higher processing capacity but decrease the re-sweeping rates. Zig-Zag or spiral like trajectories implement systematic and deterministic navigation procedures, they overcome in efficiency random trajectories but imply complex design and a reliable localization system. The indicator of trajectories quality is related with the re-sweeping rate expressed as the percentage of the accessible surface that is visited more than once.

Operation Time: a general objective of a cooperative multi-agent system is based in the fact that a team of agents must reduce the operation time for the task compared with a single entity.

Completeness: it is mandatory that the system shows a complete coverage of 100% of the area, which implies to visit to all the reachable points of the region.

Competition: with the implementation of competitive relations between the team members. It is possible to increase the cooperation level since the assignment of a particular task is assigned to the agent that can get a better profit.

Architecture: at functional level, the agents must own such abilities according with the primary objective, the task and the topology of the area. In particular, physical agents must have adequate means of locomotion, sensorial systems in order to perform navigation and interpretation of the world. Also, communication systems are needed to fulfill the requirements previously mentioned.

Robustness: the system must be robust fulfilling the task and maintaining the operation even if there are communications or agents failures.

A Priori Knowledge: it is desirable that the system does not have any priori knowledge of the world, which means that the sweeping algorithm must be robust to the geometry of the accessible surface.

Initial Condition: before starting the task, the system must assume certain minimal operational conditions. When structured paths are used, usually some certain conditions as the knowledge of the initial position of the other team members are required.

End Condition: there must be a set of well-defined end conditions of the algorithm in order to determine the culmination and the success of the task. End conditions usually are associated to the covering of all the borders of the non-visited areas or the lack of reachable unknown points.

4. BSA coverage algorithm

The Backtracking Spiral Algorithm was first proposed for a single robot approach (Gonzalez, et al., 2005). This algorithm decomposed the accessible surface in regions that can be covered by structured spiral paths. Once the basic BSA algorithm is introduced, in this chapter, its multirobot extension is presented.

4.1 Single Robot BSA Algorithm

The basic BSA algorithm introduced in (Gonzalez, et al., 2005). assures the complete coverage of non-occupied cells. The map is represented by a coarse-grain occupancy grid, where cells

are of the size of the robot. BSA uses two main concepts: covering of regions using a structured spiral-like path and linking of these regions using a backtracking mechanism. The model of the accessible surface is constructed incrementally as the robot navigates. Initially, all cells are marked as "unkown". When a cell is covered by the robot, it is marked as a "virtual obstacle"; these ones are not accessible to the robot while executing a spiral path. Cells with obstacles, even partially occupied ones, are marked as a "real obstacle".
Spiral structured paths are formed by concentric rings that generate a continuous path from the region's boundary (nearby obstacles) to a central spiral ending point. Before starting a spiral path the robot is placed nearby an obstacle (real or virtual), which is located at its Reference Lateral Side (RLS); RLS indicates the relative direction where obstacles have to be referenced during the spiral filling procedure. The Opposite Lateral Side (OLS) identifies the antipode of the RLS. The following set of reactive rules drive the robot to generate a spiral coverage path:

RS1 IF (obstacles_all_around)
THEN ending_spiral_point_detected
RS2 IF (NOT obstacle_in_RLS)
THEN turn_to(RLS) and move_forward
RS3 IF (obstacle_in_front) THEN turn_to(OLS)
RS4 OTHERWISE move_forward

Remark that the cells already marked as virtual obstacles are considered as real obstacles when evaluating the rules. At the end of the algorithm, the virtual obstacles will represent non-occupied covered regions. A backtracking mechanism is used to return to areas that have not been visited, where a new spiral procedure is performed. Backtracking points (BP) are detected and stored during the execution of a normal spiral path: a BP is a cell that could be the starting point of a future alternative path.
At the end of a spiral path, the robot must go to the nearest BP to start a new sweeping procedure. The robot builds the shortest path using a distance propagation algorithm; only already covered (virtual obstacles) cells are considered to generate the route from the end of the current spiral to the best BPs. During this path, the robot traverses only already visited cells; they are known to be free ones as they have already been covered. BSA finishes when there is no more possible BP, which means that there are no more uncovered surfaces.
An example of a typical BSA coverage is shown in Figure 1. Spiral paths are represented by continuous lines; notice that spirals starts as open paths nearby the obstacles that finally are "trapped", forming real spiral trajectories, in the concavities formed by obstacles. The paths used to go to the BPs are illustrated by doted lines; the BPs are always cells nearby the frontier of the already covered areas.
In the basic algorithm only the cells that are completely free of obstacles are considered as accessible. An extension of this algorithm has also been developed that also covers the partially occupied cells. In fact, these cells are covered by a wall following procedure during the first spiral ring nearby the real obstacles.

4.2 Multi robot BSA algorithm

The multi-robot coverage problem is solved using a multi-agent systems (MAS) approach; where a robot is seen as an entity that can perceive and modify its environment, and communicate with others to fulfill the goals of the system. Assuming such a cooperative and

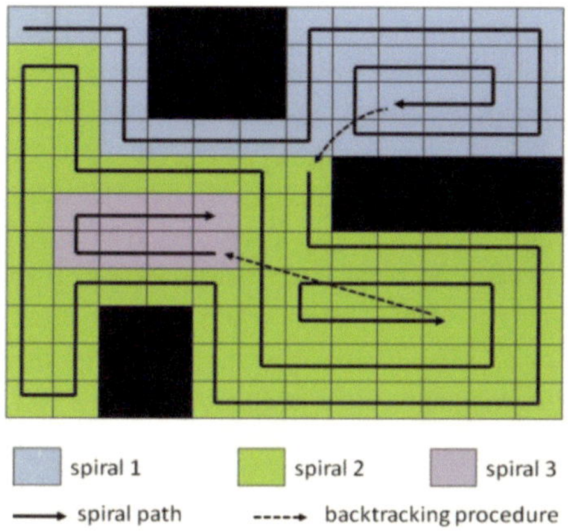

Fig. 1. Example of the basic BSA algorithm.

concurrent posture allows improving the productivity of each agent, since increasing the number of parallel tasks supposes a reduction in the total exploration time.

The BSA Conceptual framework has been extended to a cooperative multi-agent system environment in BSA-CM, where a team of robots, controlled by an agent software, are executing a sweeping procedure following the basic rules of BSA. As in the single robot algorithm, robots perform spiral paths detecting and marking backtracking points (BPs) in the map. When a robot arrives to the ending cell of a spiral path, it negotiates one of the remaining BPs. The BP that maximizes a utility function is assigned, and the robot moves to this BP and starts a new spiral path procedure.

In BSA-CM, robots must know the absolute initial position of all team members. This condition can be implemented by several methods such as: line of view, fixed positions, landmarks, etc. The robots have an identical copy replicated map; as a robot modifies a cell in its map, this information is sent to all robots; in this way, the robot team is building and sharing the same map in a cooperative way. Each robot is in one of three possible states: "inactive", "spiral" or "return" mode; robots shall know and store the state of every team member. Normal communications are considered as "prove of life" in order to determine the activity of other robots.

A potential conflict appears while crossing from one cell to another, as several robots could try to get the same cell at the same time. A coordinated reservation mechanism is used to avoid this problem, just before traveling to the next cell, each robot broadcasts a message that includes its state, information about its current position in the map, recently discovered BPs and the next cell that is going to be reached. As in this case, all the communicative acts in the cooperative system will concern to all team members. Robots also reserve BPs once they are assigned after the negotiation process succeeds. In coverage, the main conflicting resource is the physical space, death lock situations can appear when the cell to which a robot goes is occupied or reserved by other robot. A real blocking condition will appear only in corridors or halls when both robots are in "return" mode. To solve these conflicts a role exchange procedure has been implemented.

The designed negotiation mechanism allows robots to identify the nearest backtracking points, which reduces navigation time, processing and use of resources such as energy. A robot initiates a negotiation process as soon it reach the end of a spiral path. The selection to find the best backtracking point (BBP) available, that the robot will try to negotiate, is made by means of a simulation of the estimated cost of travelling from the cell where the spiral path has finished to the candidates BPs. This simulation procedure is done only once using the current map; all the candidates BPs are ordered based on this estimated cost function and stocked in a list. Then, the bidding process starts, the goal is to determine if the cost to reach the particular BBP, the first BP on the list, is smaller than the estimated cost of any other robot to reach this BBP. If this is the case, the robot that initiates the negotiation obtains the lower cost, it will win the right to cover the BBP and the region around it. On the contrary, if the cost is greater, the bidder must select its next available best BP and starts the negotiation again. If the negotiation of the entire candidates of BP fails, the bidder robot shall select the nearest BP in order to avoid inactivity.

In order to initiate the negotiation, the bidder sent to all the other n-1 robots a message that includes the BPP and its estimated cost. Once these messages have been sent, the bidder starts a timeout counter and waits for one of these three possible situations:

a. n-1 "approval" messages have been returned (n is the number of active robots).
b. 1 o more "deny" messages arrived, which means that a smaller cost has been detected by another robot.
c. a timeout event occurs, which implies that at least one robot of the team has failed to answer in a reasonable time; in this case, it will be assumed that the backtracking point in negotiation is the best choice for the bidder robot.

During a negotiation process, the robots in "return" mode shall give automatic "approval" since its current BP assignment corresponds to the best choice available for them; in other words, a robot that is just trying to get a BP that has won during a recent negotiation process does not participate in a new auction initiated by another robot. The cost estimation for the other robots, those in "spiral" mode, is based on an optimistic assumption. First, the cost to finish the actual spiral path is evaluated by a simulation procedure that assumes all the unknown cells as non-occupied; then, the Manhattan distance from the simulated spiral end point to the BP in negotiation is calculated. The total estimated cost is the sum of these two partial costs. If this total cost is smaller than the one estimated by the bidder, the robot answers with a "deny", otherwise it gives an "approval".

5. Validation of BSA-CM in a simulation context

The validation of the cooperative model includes the implementation of BSA-CM in a multi-agent platform. An experimental protocol has been designed and applied in order to characterize the correctness of the extended multirobot BSA algorithm.

5.1 Implementation of BSA-CM in a multiagent platform

The system is implemented in JAVA over a multi-agent framework called BESA, which includes real time operation, multitasking, multithread and a continuous space robot simulator with uncertainly.

BESA is based in three fundamental concepts: an event-driven control approach implementing a select like mechanism, a modular behavior-oriented agent architecture, and a social-based support for cooperation between agents. The BESA architecture is composed of three levels: agent level, social level and system level. The internal architecture of an agent integrates two important features: a modular composition of behaviors and an event selector mechanism as shown in the figure 2.

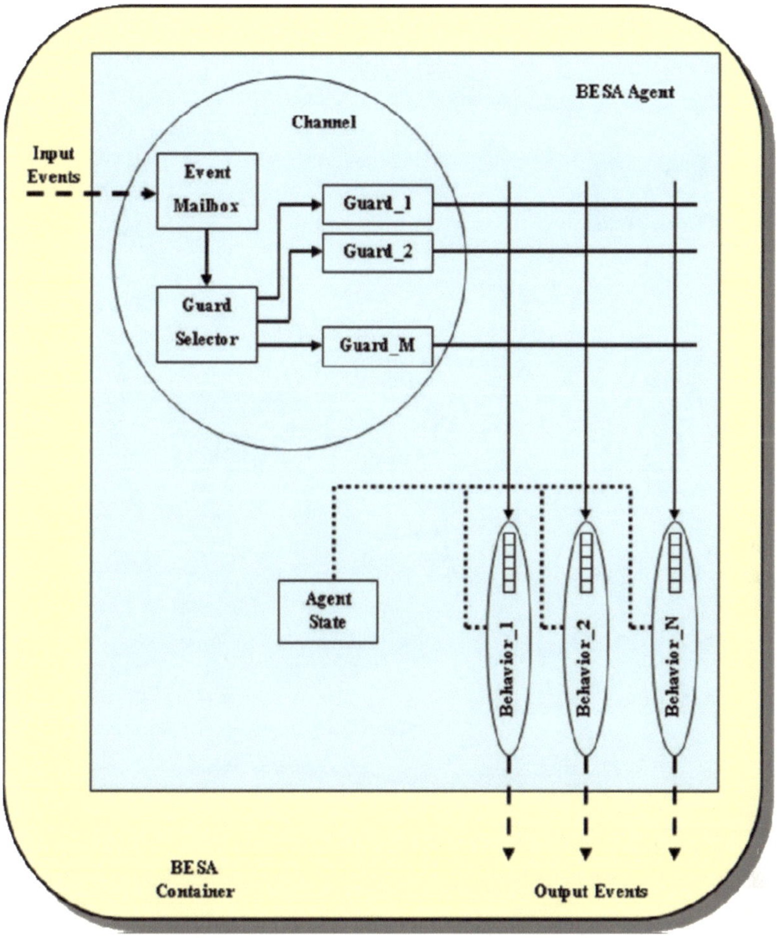

Fig. 2. General internal architecture of an agent in BESA.

The MAS for BSA-CM includes only one type of agent role, called "Explorer". In order to identify the agent internal behaviors, as well as the events associated to those behaviors, it is necessary to define the goals of the agent.

In the "spiral" mode, the robot objectives are:

a. to complete a spiral path following the simple exploration rules of BSA.
b. to identify and mark in the map: real obstacles, backtracking points (non-occupied cells in the OLS), and virtual obstacles (already covered cells).
c. to initiate a negotiation when a spiral path is finished.

In the "return" mode, the robot objectives are:

a. to select a return route through the cells previously visited.
b. to arrive to the selected BP avoiding obstacles.
c. to detect and solve corridor conflicts.

Once the particular objectives have been identified, it is possible to construct a diagram of internal modules (behaviors) and interactions of the explorer agent. This model intends to control the robot in a real time environment by executing several concurrent behaviors in a parallel way. The architecture of the AgentExplorer is shown in figure 3.

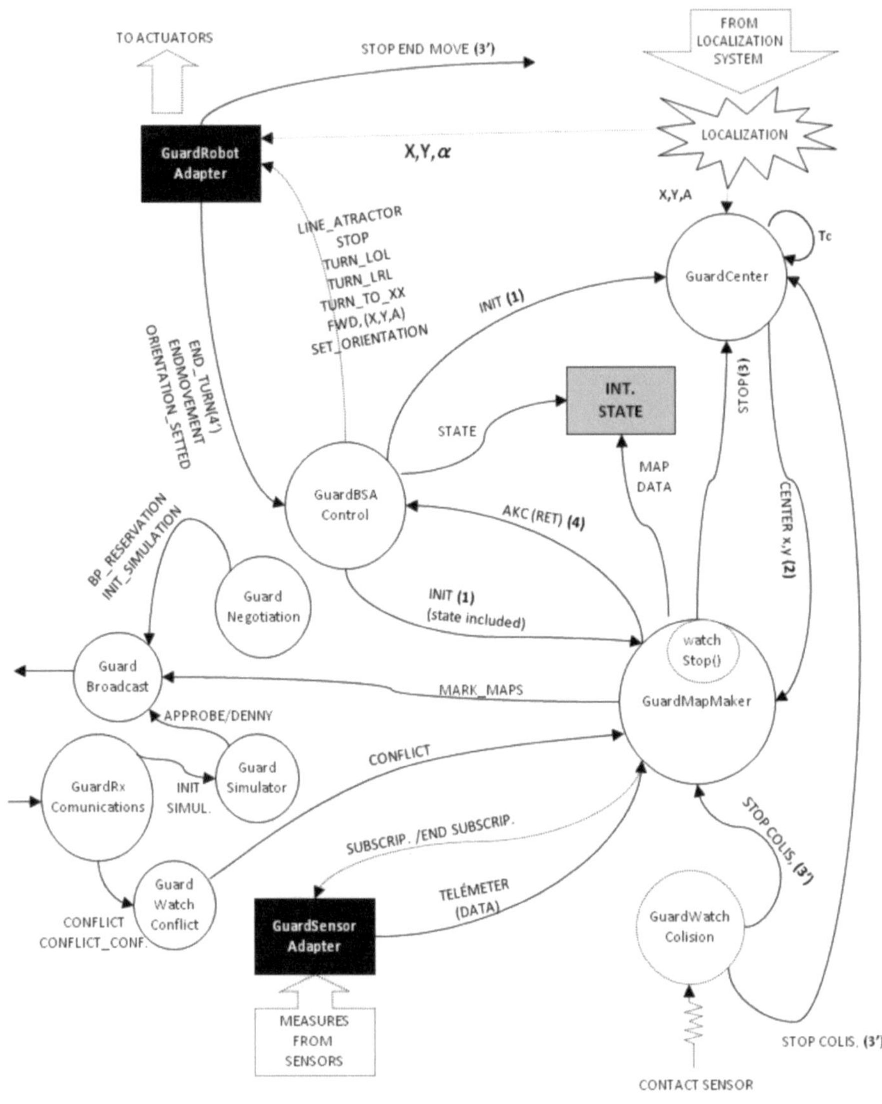

Fig. 3. Cooperative Architecture of AgentExplorer.

The internal architecture, based on a multi-agent approach, is designed to accomplish the agent objectives. It includes a main control behavior which organizes the internal interactions, sets the robot states and evaluates the BSA rules. It also includes one adapter to control the robot actuators and other adapter to acquire and manage information coming from the sensors. Additionally, each agent has several behaviors in charge of the following procedures: map marking, arriving to a cell centre detection, negotiation and simulation of spiral paths involving in the biddings, monitoring of stop conditions, detection of conflicts, and management of communications. For each defined event, a guard procedure is programmed:
GuardBSAControl: is in charge of controlling the correct execution of the algorithm.

GuardMapMaker: marks the maps by processing the sensor information and verifying stop conditions.
GuardCenter: checks the position of the agent periodically in order to broadcast the required information at every cell´s centre, before crossing to the following cell.
GuardNegotiation: negotiates the BPs and builds a return path once a backtracking point is reseved.
GuardSimulator: simulates a spiral and determines the cost for a negotiated BP.
GuardBroadcast: will send all messages concerning the team.
GuardRxCommunications: is in charge of receiving the information from other agents; it also calls the appropriate functions to treat the incoming events and information.
GuardWatchColision, GuardRobotAdapter and GuardSensor-Adapter: will supervise the contact sensors, actuators and telemetric sensors respectively.
According to the internal robot cooperation model described in the previous section, is its necessary to identify the different messages, modeled as events, exchanged by the agents. In Table 1, each event type and the attached information to it is described.

EVENT	WHEN	DATA
Anouncement_Mov	Before a movement to the next cell	Send_State
		Send_Next_Cell
Anouncement_VO	At arriving of any cell center	Send_State
	After evaluate it	Send_Actual_Position
	New robot state if it changes	
Anouncement_BP	as identified after the respective analysis	Send_BeachID
		Send_BP
Anouncement_Colision	In a collision	Send_State
		Send_Real_Obstacle
INIT_SIMULATION	At the end of a spiral path	Request_BP
		ID_Negot_Initiator
		Send_Cost
DENNY	At the end of a cost simulation	Send_Denny
	If my cost is less than the negotiated one.	ID_Negot_Initiator
		Send_BeachID
APPROVE	At the end of a cost simulation	Send_Approve
	If my cost is grater than the negotiated one.	ID_Negot_Initiator
		Send_BeachID
Reserve_BP	when aprove_total is received	ID_Robot
		Send_BP_reserved
Reset_Reservation	My cost for a BP in negotiation is less	Clear_Reserva_BP
	I am un RETURN	ID_Negot_Initiator
	After winning a negotiation	
Total_Approve	After receive n-1 approves or	Send_Total_Approve
	After time out in negotiation	ID_Robot_Ofertante
	No more BP to negotiate	
Conflict	Conflict detected in RETURN	Conflict_Anouncement
	My next cell y reserved	ID_Robot_In_Conlfict
	Tho other robot is in Conflict	ID_Conlfict_Initiator
Conflict_Confirmation	Once ID is verified	Confirm_Conflict
	After verify the robot´s cell	

Table 1. Event messages exchanged between robot agents.

5.2 Test and results

The performance of the algorithm was tested in a simulation environment using 20 "worlds" with different shape, complexity and granularity previously designed in order to test basic BSA as proposed in (Gonzalez, 2005). Each test is compared with the results in the same "world" covered by a single robot. Tests are performed also with the robots starting in two different initial positions: (a) parallel fashion - aligned close to each other and with the same heading - and (b) random distributed initial positions over the accessible surface.

The initial parallel positions can be achieved easily by real robotic platforms; this approach represents a low cost alternative to know the initial state of the robots. Figure 4 presents one of the test worlds with initial parallel positions.

Tests in each world were performed adding one robot at a time to the team until the average time of coverage is higher than the previous simulated case; in other words, the number of robots is incremented progressively until the task performance does not improve anymore.

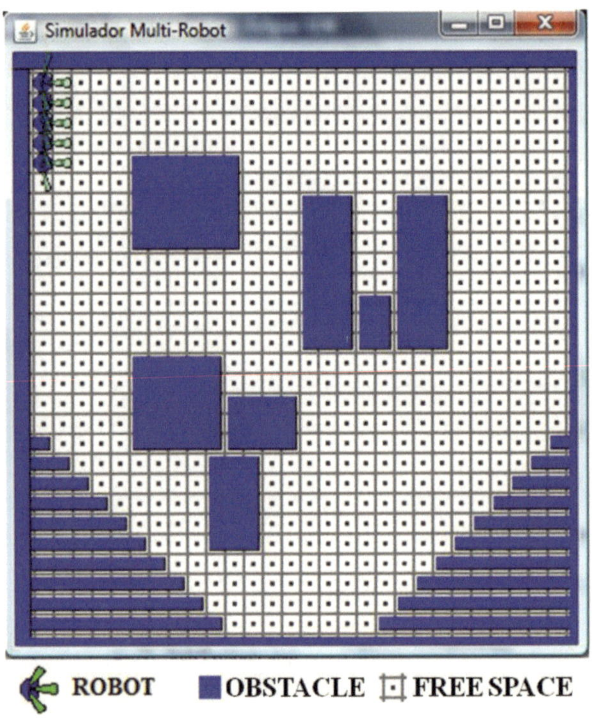

Fig. 4. Typical simulation "world" with parallel initial positions.

Total Time: is the average between all exploration times in each map. The average exploration time in all words with 1, 2, 3, 4, 5 and 6 robots is shown in figure 5. It can be noted a significant reduction of operating time with 2 robots and 3 robots. Adding members to the team reduces the time. Test with 6 robots in parallel initial positions increases the total time due to obstructions between the agents. The improvement of the performance depends on the number of robots but also on the nature and size of the world.

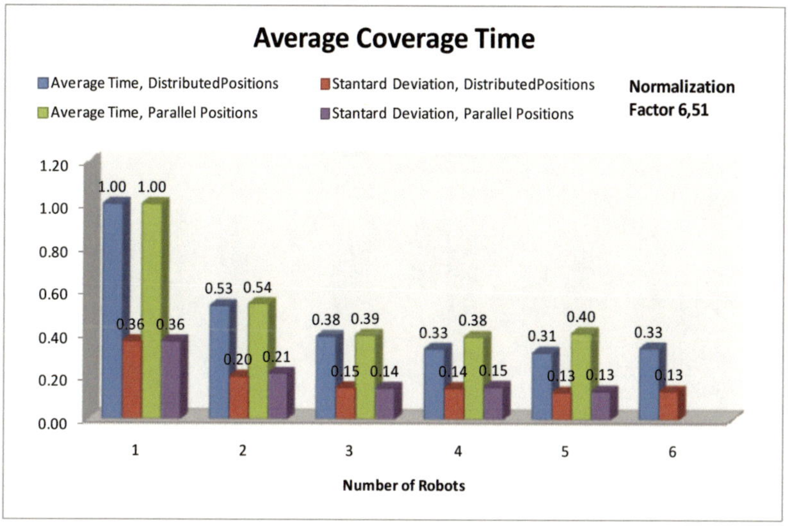

Fig. 5. Time of exploration results.

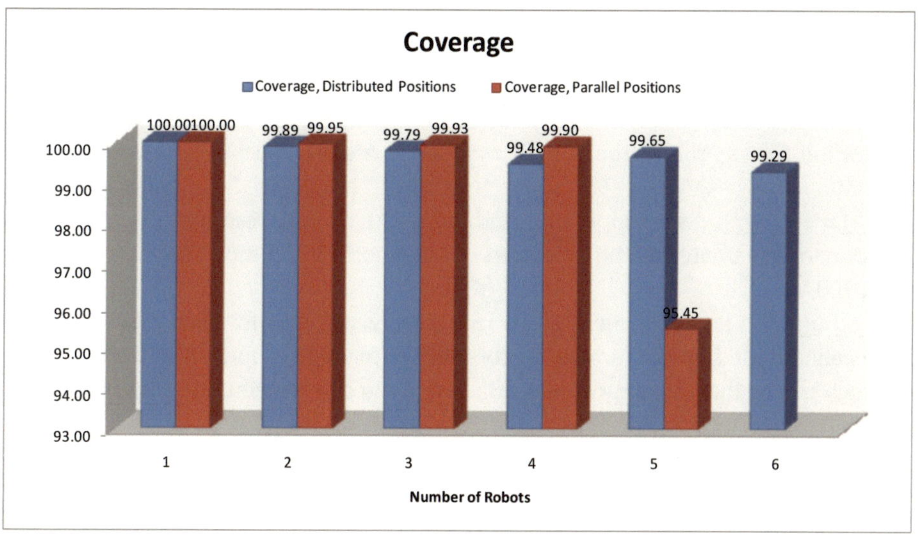

Fig. 6. Total Coverage Percentage results.

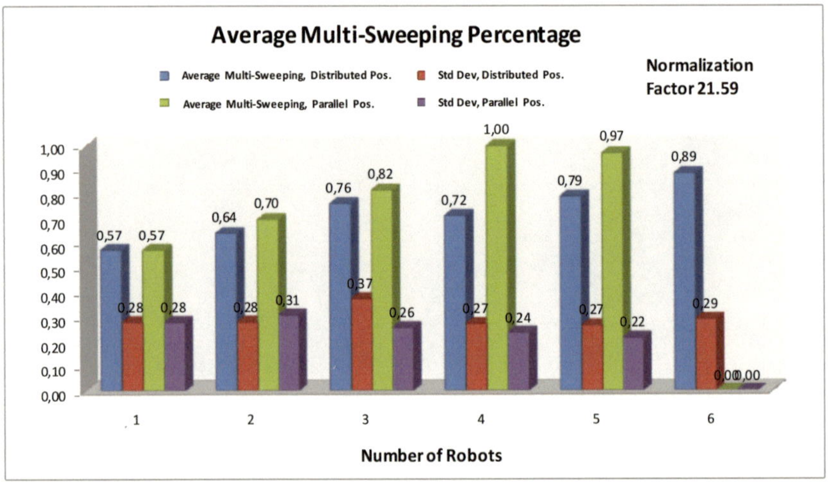

Fig. 7. Average Multi-Sweeping Percentage results.

Coverage: the percentage of covered cells is presented in figure 6. It was observed that in some cases, the robots tend to group in the same zone at the end of the algorithm, causing conflicts and obstructions.

Average of Multi-Sweeping: multi-sweeping shows the number of cells that are covered more than once. Multi-sweeping is expected because the return paths are constructed over visited cells. The average multi-sweeping percentage (figure 7) is higher in the parallel initial position case as robots finish their first spiral sooner, causing the execution of more return paths.

Conflict Management: As a cooperation indicator, the conflict resolution rate indicates the number of conflicts treated in the execution of the algorithm. In most of cases, this indicator is near to 100%.

Task Distribution: it is represented by the ratio of covered cells for each robot and the total available cells divided by the number of robots. The average of indicators is near to 1 in all cases, which means that the algorithm is efficient in the task distribution (figures 8a and 8b).

6. Final discussion

In order to cover the entire accessible surface, a sweeping algorithm must eliminate systematically all the known frontier by driving the robot to explore and eventually cover the non-visited regions adjacent to this frontier. Structured trajectories tend to provide a more efficient covering procedure, in terms of reducing the multi-sweeping rate; they also guarantee the detection of the uncovered points nearby the known frontier.

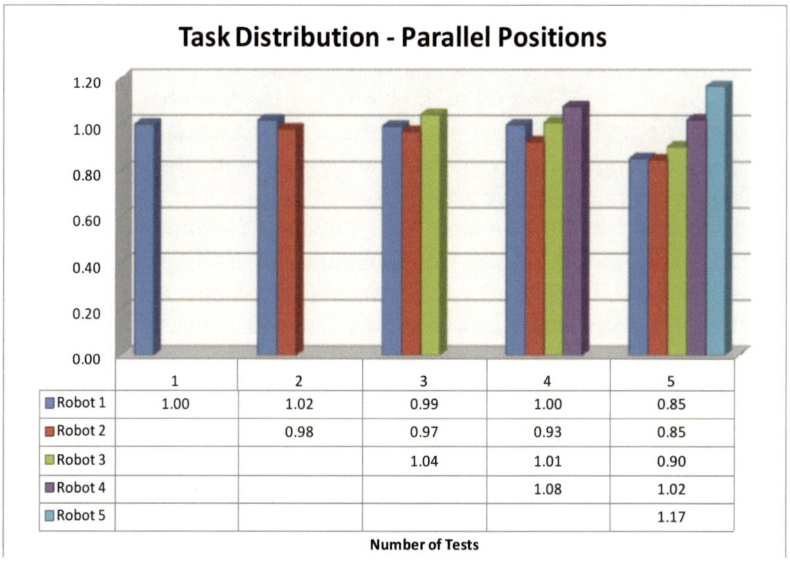

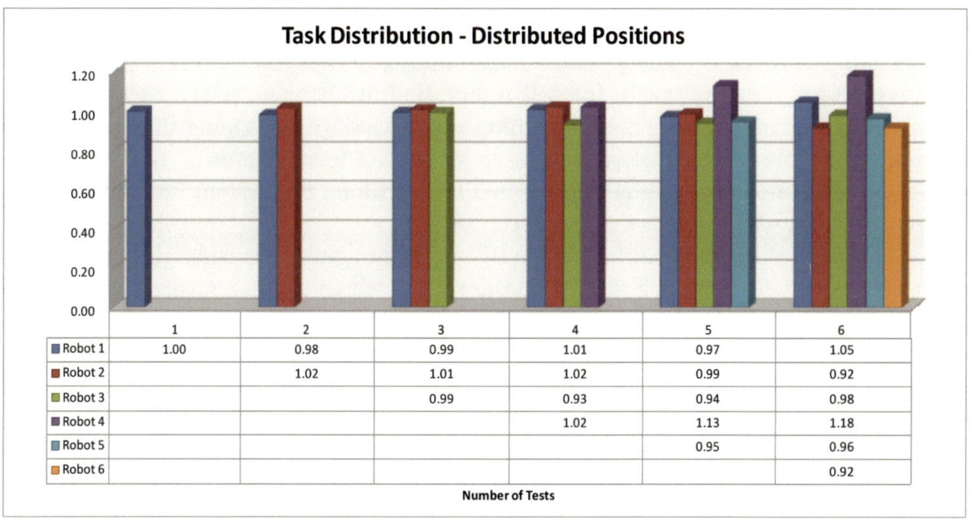

Fig. 8. Average Task Distribution in (a)Parallel and (b) Distributed initial positions.

BSA-CM achieves the deployment of the team all over the exploration area by means of backtracking point assignation using the described negotiation mechanism. In fact, robots will be ready to reserve the nearest missions. In this first version of BSA-CM, only homogenous agents have been used; however, it will be easy to extend the algorithm to deal with a team of heterogeneous robots. Coordination and collaboration have been implemented by the proposed distributed mechanism for task assignation. The existence of a task for conflict supervision allows detecting conflicts at early stages, and the mechanism of "role exchange" solves these deadlock situations.

From the point of view of the proposed agency model, the agents are modeled as autonomous entities, which are (a) proactive since they work continuously to achieve their goals following a spiral path or executing a return path, (b) cooperative since the agent's goals depend on team's goals, and (c) each member of the team have a role which defines agent's responsibilities and partial temporal goals. The system develops relations with the environment and other agents since each robot interact with the world by means of its sensors and elaborate communicative acts with clear semantics in the application context to inform new discoveries in the coverage task. Cooperation under this agency model is evidenced since the purposes of the semantic interactions are task allocation, synchronization between agents and conflict identification and resolution. The protocols designed for the interaction allow the agents to have well-formed conversations including enough information and optimization of the communication channel. In fact, messages in BSA-CM include negotiation of BPs, cell entry protocols and role swapping.

From the point of view of the proposed cooperation model, there are three main aspects to be analyzed: task allocation understood as collaboration, synchronization understood as coordination, and conflict resolution. Collaboration is present as BSA-CM implements a decomposition of the coverage task in simple regions covered by each agent using spiral paths starting from assigned BPs; the negotiation mechanism allows to select the best robot for each particular available BP. Evidence of synchronization is present in the shared replicated map which is constructed incrementally and synchronized as the robots perform their particular spirals. The messages include relevant information via multicast about obstacles and new BPs. Finally, conflict resolution, where the physical space is the conflictive resource, is present in the cell reservation mechanism, which only allows one robot in a cell at any moment; this solution also gives to the agents the possibility of planning future movements taking into account all the team members' actions. Besides, when a deadlock in return paths is presented as corridors, the system implements a role exchange protocol which solves the space conflict.

The use of an optimistic cost function in the BP negotiation produces relations of competence between the robots. The use of a greedy decision approach generates a greater benefit for the agent in particular and also for the team in general. Robustness, understood as the fulfillment of the task even if there are communications or agent failures, is also assured; in these conditions, the coverage will be performed by all the active robots all over the area; experiments have demonstrated this behavior when there is no communications at all.

Future work includes a complete evaluation of BSA-CM using real robot platforms. Then, the algorithm must be extended to cover also partially occupied cells in a similar way as the basic BSA extension does. Moreover, as the decision of classifying a cell as occupied or free can generate differences between the readings, it is required a method to assign a value of certainty to a particular cell - by means of Bayesian updating model (Martin & Moravec, 1996) for example. It is also important to compare the requirements and indicators with other multi-robot coverage algorithms.

7. References

Menzel, P.(2000). *Robo-sapiens evolution of a new species*. The MIT press, 2000

Ferber, J. (1999). *Multiagent Systems: An Introduction to Distributed AI*, Addison – Wesley Longman. 1ra. ed.

Maes, P. (1994). *Modeling Adaptative Autonomous Agents*, Artificial Life Journal, v. 1, MIT Press.

Rusell, N. (1996). *Artificial Intelligence : A modern approach*, Prentice Hall.

Tolosa G. & Bordignon F. (1999). *Review: Technology of agents of software*, Ci. Inf., Brasilia, v. 28, set./dez.

Wooldridge, M. & Jennings,N.(1998). *Agent Technology – Foundations, Applications, and Markets*. Springer - UNICOM.

Wolldrige, M. (2009) *An introduction to Multiagent Systems*. Ed John Whiley & Sons. 2 ed. ISBN : 978-0470519462

Usategui, J.; Romero, S. & Angulo, I. (1999). *Microbótica: Tecnología, Aplicaciones y Montaje Práctico*. Ed. Thompson. 2 ed. Madrid.

Weiss, G. (2001). *Multiagent Systems: a modern approach to distributed artificial intelligence*. MIT press, ISBN: 0262731312.

Lui, J. & Jianbing, W. (2001). *Multiagent Robotic Systems*. Ed CRC PRESEE. 2001. ISBN : 0-8493-2288-X

Balch, T. & Parker, E. (2002). *Robot Teams*. AK Peters, Canada. ISBN : 1-56881-115-1.

Miriad E. (1992). Approcher la notion de collectif. *En Actes des journées multiagents du PRC-IA*, Nancy.

Jung, D. (1998). *An Architecture for Cooperation among Autonomous Agents*. Intelligent Robotics Laboratory, Department of Computer Science, University of Wollongong.

Murphy, R. (2000). *Introduction to AI Robotics*. Ed The MIT Press. ISB : 0-262-13383-0

Choset, H. (2004). *Principles of robot motion theory, algorithms, and implementation*. MIT Press. ISBN 0-262-03327-5

Hopgood, A. (2001). *Intelligent Systems for Engineers and Scientist*. Boca Raton, Florida ; London : 2nd ed CRC.

Tilde, M.W. (1996) Yuma proving grounds Automatic Uxo Detection using Biomorphic Robots. *Test Teschnology Symposium*. US Army Test & Evaluation Com.

Doty K. & Harrison R. (1993). Sweep Strategies for a Sensory-Driven, Behavior-Based Vacuum Cleaning Agent. *AAAI Fall Symposium Series*.

Choset, H. & Pignon, P. *Coverage Path Planning: The Boustrophedon Cellular Decomposition*. unpublished

Zelinsky A. et al. (1992). A mobile robot exploration algorithm. *Robotics and Automation, IEEE Transactions on*. Volume 8, Issue 6, Page(s):707 - 717

Pirzadeh, A. & Snyder W. (1990). A unified solution to coverage and search in explored and unexplored terrains using indirect control. *Robotics and Automation, Proceedings. IEEE International Conference on*. Page(s):2113 - 2119 vol.3.

González E. et al. (1996). Complementary Regions: a Surface Filling Algorithm. *ICRA96*, pp. 909-914..

Gabriely Y.; & Rimon E. (2002). Spiral-STC: an on-line coverage algorithm of grid environments by a mobile robot. *IEEE International Conference on Robotics and Automation*,. Proceedings. ICRA 2002. Volume 1, Page(s):954 – 960.

Gonzalez, E., et al. (2005). BSA: A Complete Coverage Algorithm. *Robotics and Automation, 2005. ICRA 2005. Proceedings of the 2005 IEEE International Conference on*. Pages: 2040 - 2044

Martin, M.C. & Moravec, H. (1996) *Robot Evidence Grids*. The Robotics Institute. Carnegie Mellon Univ.. USA, CMU-RI-TR-96-06.

Choset, H., et al. (2004) Towards sensor based coverage with robot teams. *Robotics and Automation, 2004. Proceedings. ICRA '04. 2004 IEEE International Conference on.* Volume 4, Page(s):3462 - 3468 Vol.4

Simmons R. Et al. (2000). Coordination for multirobot exploration and mapping. *Proceedings of the National Conference on Artificial Intelligence. AAAI*, 2000

Dias, M.B. et al. (2006). Market-based multirobot coordination: A survey and analysis. *Proceedings of the IEEE*, pages: 1257-1270..

Wagner, I.A.; Lindenbaum, M. & Bruckstein, A.M. (1999). Distributed covering by ant-robots using evaporating traces. *Robotics and Automation, IEEE Transactions on*, Volume 15, Issue 5, Page(s):918 - 933.

Butler Z.J.; Rizzi, A.A. & Hollis, R.L. (2000). Cooperative Coverage of Rectilinear Enviroments. *Robotics and Automation, 2000. Proceedings. ICRA '00. IEEE International Conference on*, Volume 3, 24-28 Page(s):2722 - 2727 vol.3

Howard; Mataric & Sukhtme. (2002). An Incremental Deployment Algorithm for Mobile Robot Team. *IEEE/RSJ International conference in Robotics and Intelligent Systems.* Switzerland.

Gerlein E., Gonzalez E.. (2009) BSA-CM: A Multi-Robot Coverage Algorithm. *2009 IEEE/WIC/ACM International Conference on Intelligent Agent Technology.*

Gonzalez E., et.al. (2008) *Development of Applications based on Multi-Agent Systems*. Editorial Javeriana, Colombia 2008.

Rizzi, A.; Gowdy, J. & Hollis, L.. (1997) Contact sensor-based coverage of rectilinear environments. *Proc. Of IEEE Int'l. Conf. on Robotics and Automation*. Pp 1511-1516.

Zlot R., et al. (2002);. Multi-robot exploration controlled by a market economy. Conference on Robotics and Automation, 2002. Proc. ICRA '02. IEEE International.

8

Cooperative Global Localization in Multi-robot System

Luo Ronghua
School of Computer Science and Engineering, South China University of Technology
China

1. Introduction

With the development of robotic technology, the application areas of robots have been greatly widened. The robots may serve as assistants (Elena et al., 2004), rescuers (Robert & Arvin, 2003) and explorers (Schenker et al., 2003). In many cases a multi-robot system has to be used, since many tasks cannot be completed with a single robot and multi-robot system can finish the tasks much more efficiently. As in a single robot system, knowing their relative positions and their global positions in the environment are the preconditions for performing tasks and coordination. Since a robot can determine the location of another robot relative to its own when they see each other, both robots can refine their internal beliefs based on the other robot's estimate. In this way cooperative localization of multiple robots can greatly improve the localization precision and efficiency (Fox et al., 2000; Trawny et al., 2009). An area that has received some attentions in the single-robot case and very little attention in the multi-robot case is active localization (Fox et al., 1998). In active localization, the robot(s) may actively choose actions so as to aid in localization. Active localization has the potential to increase the speed and accuracy of localization further. In this chapter a mechanism of making robots coordinate their action actively during localization is proposed. In order to determine the exploration strategy, the ability to stably track multi-hypotheses of the robot's own position and his partners' positions is very important in active localization. However using traditional particle filters for localization tends to produce premature convergence, i.e. the hypothesis represented by particle filters converge to a small area of the state space with high likelihood too quickly. To overcome this problem a new version of particle filters termed co-evolution particle filters (CEPF) is proposed. Another problem of using particle filters in multi-robot localization system is the communication problem. When several robots want to share their estimates they have to transmit a large set of samples from one robot to another, so a great bandwidth is needed. To solve this problem the reduced set density estimator (RSDE) (Girolami & Chao, 2003) is used to estimate the density over robots' pose, so that only a small sub-set of the original samples should be transmitted between robots, which can reduce the communication data considerably.

2. Related works

2.1 Robot localization

Localization is a basic problem of mobile robot systems. Whenever the robots explore in an unknown environment or a known one, determining their own positions is of great importance for them. Localization in unknown environments is called simultaneous localization and mapping (SLAM) (Dissanayake et al., 2001; Guivant & Nebot, 2001; Dasvison & Murray, 2002), whose purpose is to estimate the pose of robot so as to build a consistent map of the environment. The most popular method for SLAM is extended Kalman filter (EKF). Cooperative simultaneous localization and mapping (CSLAM) in multi-robot system has also been studied in recent years (Fenwick et al., 2002; Wu et al., 2009; Gil et al., 2010) . Compared with SLAM of single robot system, CSLAM can improve the mapping efficiency and localization precision based on the information sharing. Localization in known environment can be divided into two sub-problems: pose tracking and global localization. In pose tracking, the initial robot pose is known, and localization seeks to identify small, incremental errors in a robot's odometry. Global localization is a more challenging problem, in which the robot is required to estimate its pose by local and incomplete observed information under the condition of uncertain initial pose. Most recently, several approaches based on probabilistic theory have been proposed for global localization, including grid-based approaches (Burgard et al., 1996), topological approaches (Dayoub & Duckett, 2008; Kaelbling et al., 1996), particle filters (PF) based approaches (Dellaert et al., 1999) and multi-hypothesis tracking (Jensfelt & Kristensen, 2001). Since exploring actively can get more useful information for global localization, several methods for active localization in single robot system are proposed: a method using entropy to evaluate the utility of the robot's action was proposed (Hongjun & Shiyeyuki, 2002), Jensfelt proposed a active localization method with a topological map (Jensfelt & Kristensen, 2001) and a method based on Bayes network was proposed for sensor planning in localization (Kaelbling et al., 1996). In multi-robot system, the ability to exchange information is particularly attractive in global localization, in which the fusion of information can reduce the uncertainty in the estimated location. Particle filters are applied to localization in multi-robot system (Fox et al., 2000). But it is a passive localization method with no mechanism for the robots to actively determine their locations. In this paper we mainly discuss the active localization of multi-robots in a known environment based on a new version of particle filters.

2.2 Particle filter

Over the last years, particle filters have been applied successfully in many areas for state estimation (Doucet et al., 2000; Arulampalam et al., 2002). The key idea of particle filters is to represent the posterior density with a set of weighted samples. Particle filters include the following three steps:

- Re-sampling: resample N samples randomly from sample set S_{t-1} , according to the distribution defined by weights of samples w_{t-1};
- Importance Sampling: sample pose $x_t^{(j)}$ from $p(x_t|x_{t-1}^{(j)}, u_{t-1})$ for each of the N possible pose $x_{t-1}^{(j)}$, and evaluate the importance factor $w_t^{(j)} = p(y_t|x_t^{(j)})$.
- Summary: normalize the importance factors $w_t^{(j)} = w_t^{(j)} / \sum_{k=1}^{N} w_t^{(k)}$; and calculate the statistic property of sample set S_t to estimate the pose of the robot.

By representing probability densities with samples and using the sequential Monte Carlo importance sampling (Arulampalam et al., 2002), particle filters can represent non-linear and non-Gaussian models well and especially can focus the computational resources on regions with high likelihood, where things really matter. Particle filters have been successfully used in single robot localization (Dellaert et al., 1999) and have also been tried for multi-robot localization (Fox et al., 2000). But using traditional particle filters for multi-robot localization has some shortcomings. Since samples are actually drawn from a proposal density, if the observation density moves into one of the tails of the proposal density, most of the samples' non-normalized importance factors will be small (Doucet et al., 2001). So a large sample size is needed to represent the true posterior density to ensure stable and precise localization. However in multi-robot cooperative localization, since all the samples should be transmitted from one robot to another, large sample size will not only lead to a heavy computational burden but also a heavy communication burden. Another problem of particle filters is that samples often converge to a single, high likelihood pose too quickly. In active localization this will not only lead to erroneous localization but also lead to inefficient exploration strategy. How to improve efficiency and to prevent premature convergence of particle filters are the key concerns of the researchers. To make the samples represent the posterior density better, Thrun et al. proposed mixture-MCL (Thrun et al., 2001), but it needs much additional computation in the sampling process. To improve the efficiency of MCL, a method adjusting sample size adaptively over time has been proposed (Fox, 2003), but it increases the probability of premature convergence. Although clustered particle filters are applied to solve premature convergence (Milstein et al., 2002), the method loses the advantage of focusing the computational resources on regions with high likelihood because it maintains the same sample size for all clusters.

3. Dynamic architecture of cooperative localization

We assume that robots can determine their relative positions when they see each other. And the relative positions between robots will also be updated according to their motion model for some time after one robot disappears from the sight of the other robots. Our active localization approach utilizes a dynamically evolving coordination architecture. At each point of time, the state of the system can be summarized by a graph structure where the nodes are individual robots and the edges represent the relationship between robots (see Fig.1). An isolated node represents that the robot doesn't know its relative positions to the other robots and cannot communicate with the other robots, in this case the robot tries to determine its global position by itself as in a single robot system. Another kind of relationship between robots is that they do not know their relative positions but they can communicate with each other, which is represented by dotted line in Fig.1 (for example robot 2 and robot 3). In this case there may be several hypotheses of their relative positions. In order to actively verify their relative positions, the two robots are arranged to meet each other at a rendezvous point. As is shown in the left picture of Fig.1, robot 2 will manage to meet robot 3 so as to determine its position using the information gotten by robot 3. If the robots fail to meet, the hypothesis will be rejected and they continue to select the other hypothesis to verify. A key sub-structure of our architecture is the connected group indicated by the shade areas in Fig.1. In the connected group, two robots that know their relative positions and can communicate with each other are connected with a solid line. The robots in a connected group can fuse their sensor information to improve the precision of localization. And each group determines one robot as a leader to be responsible for coordination of their exploration (for example robot 4 and robot 9). But if the poses of the robots in a connected group are merged to form a single state for coordination, it is infeasible for a small number of robots due to the too high dimensional state space. So a hierarchical structure is proposed in which each robot maintains its own belief function, i.e. the information of its position estimated by other robots will be fused by each robot itself. Only several summarized hypotheses of their global positions will be transmitted to their

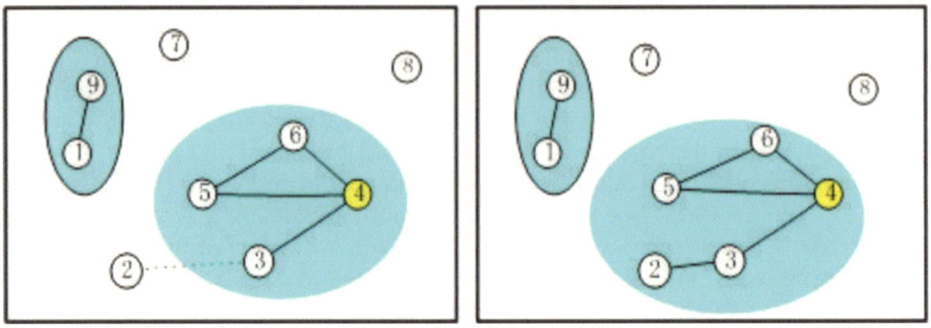

Fig. 1. The dynamic relationship between robots

leader, and the leader will estimate the most likely positions where the robots are located. Then the leader will choose an action for each robot to maximize utility-cost trade-off of the group. The active coordination structure of multi robots is shown in Fig.2. In order to reduce the communication data between robots, a density estimator is used before the data transmission.

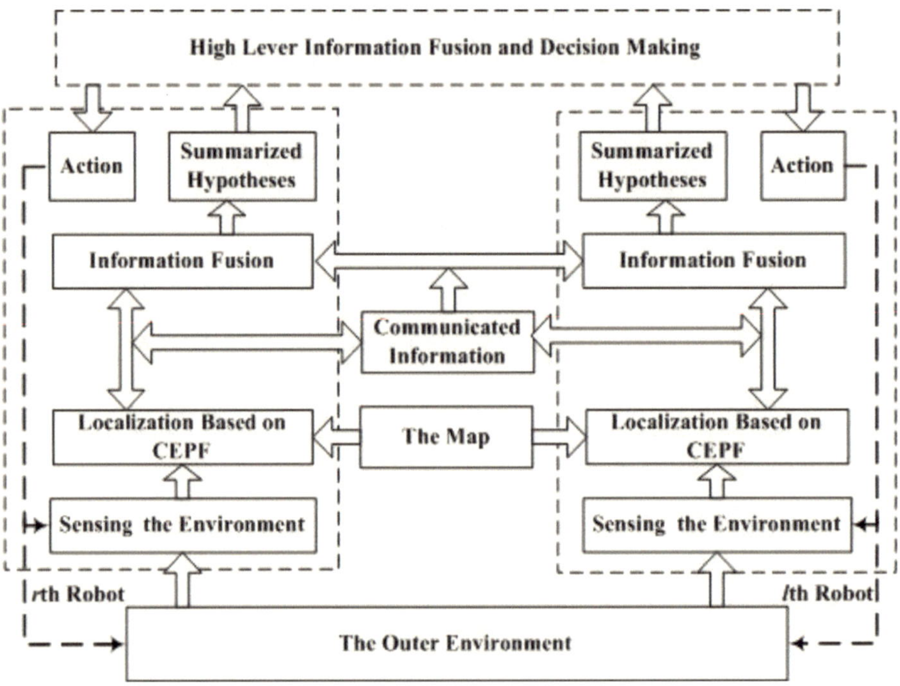

Fig. 2. Multi-robot active localization architecture

4. Cooperative localization based on co-evolution particle filters

In this section we discuss multi-robot localization based on a new version of particle filters called co-evolution particle filters (CEPF). In the first sub-section we present co-evolution particle filters; in the second sub-section, the algorithm of cooperative localization of multiple robots based on CEPF is described, in which an efficient communication mechanism is proposed to reduce the data that should be transmitted between robots.

4.1 Co-evolution particle filters

In order to satisfy the needs of the dynamic architecture of active localization and overcome the limitations of particle filters, samples are clustered into groups which are also called species. And a co-evolutionary model derived from the competition of ecological species is introduced to make the species evolve cooperatively, so the premature convergence can be prevented. And genetic operators are used for intra-species evolution to search for optimal samples in each species. So the samples can represent the desired posterior density better, and precise localization can be realized with a small sample size. The improved version of particle filters is termed co-evolution particle filters (CEPF).

1) Inter-Species Competition

The concept of co-evolution is derived from ecologic science. In ecology, much of the early theoretical work on the interaction between species started with the Lotka-Volterra model of competition (Shang & Cai, 1996). The model itself was a modification of the logistic model of the growth of a single population and represented the result of competition between species by the change of the population size of each species. It is simple and easy to use the model although it could not embody all the complex relations between species and it has been accepted by most of the ecologists. In this paper, Lotka-Volterra model is merged into particle filters to solve the premature problem of particle filters. Let us assume the samples of the r-th robot can be clustered into $\Omega_r^{(t)}$ species (clusters) at time t. Inspired by ecology, when competing with other species the population growth of species can be modeled using the Lotka-Volterra competition model. The Lotka-Volterra competition model for two species, which are denoted using species 1 and species 2, includes two equations of population growth, one for each of the two competing species.

$$\frac{dN_r^{(1)}}{dt} = \eta_r^{(1)} N_r^{(1)} \left(1 - \frac{N_r^{(1)} + \alpha_r^{(12)} N_r^{(2)}}{K_r^{(1)}}\right) \tag{1}$$

$$\frac{dN_r^{(2)}}{dt} = \eta_r^{(2)} N_r^{(2)} \left(1 - \frac{N_r^{(2)} + \alpha_r^{(21)} N_r^{(1)}}{K_r^{(2)}}\right) \tag{2}$$

Where $\eta_r^{(1)}$ and $\eta_r^{(2)}$ are the maximum possible rates of population growth, $N_r^{(1)}$ and $N_r^{(2)}$ are the population sizes, $K_r^{(1)}$ and $K_r^{(2)}$ are the upper limit of population size the environment resources can support of species 1 and species 2 respectively, and $\alpha_r^{(12)}$ refers to the impact of an individual of species 2 on population growth of species 1. Actually, The Lotka-Volterra model of inter-specific competition also includes the effects of intra-specific competition on population of the species. When $\alpha_r^{(12)}$ or $N_r^{(2)}$ equals 0, the population of the species 1 will grow according to the logistic growth model which models the intra competition between individuals in a species. These equations can be used to predict the outcome of competition over time. To do this, we should determine equilibria, i.e. the condition that population growth of both species will be zero. Let $dN_r^{(1)}/dt = 0$ and $dN_r^{(2)}/dt = 0$. If $\eta_r^{(1)} N_r^{(1)}$ and $\eta_r^{(2)} N_r^{(2)}$ do not equal 0, we get two line equations which are called the isoclines of the species. They can be plotted in four cases, as are shown in Fig. 3. According to the figure, there are four kinds of competition results determined by the relationship between $K_r^{(1)}$, $K_r^{(2)}$, $\alpha_r^{(12)}$ and $\alpha_r^{(21)}$.

1. When $K_r^{(2)}/\alpha_r^{(21)} < K_r^{(1)}, K_r^{(1)}/\alpha_r^{(12)} > K_r^{(2)}$, species 1 will always win and the balance point is $N_r^{(1)} = K_r^{(1)}, N_r^{(2)} = 0$.
2. When $K_r^{(2)}/\alpha_r^{(21)} > K_r^{(1)}, K_r^{(1)}/\alpha_r^{(12)} < K_r^{(2)}$, species 2 will always win and the balance point is $N_r^{(1)} = 0, N_r^{(2)} = K_r^{(2)}$.
3. When $K_r^{(2)}/\alpha_r^{(21)} < K_r^{(1)}, K_r^{(1)}/\alpha_r^{(12)} < K_r^{(2)}$, they can win each other; the initial population of them determines who will win.
4. When $K_r^{(2)}/\alpha_r^{(21)} > K_r^{(1)}, K_r^{(1)}/\alpha_r^{(12)} > K_r^{(2)}$, there is only one balance point and they can coexist with their own population size.

For an environment that includes Ω species, the competition equation can be modified as:

$$\frac{dN_r^{(i)}}{dt} = \eta_r^{(i)} N_r^{(i)} \left(1 - \frac{N_r^{(i)} + \sum_{j=1, j\neq i}^{\Omega} \alpha_r^{(ij)} N_r^{(j)}}{K_r^{(i)}}\right). \quad (3)$$

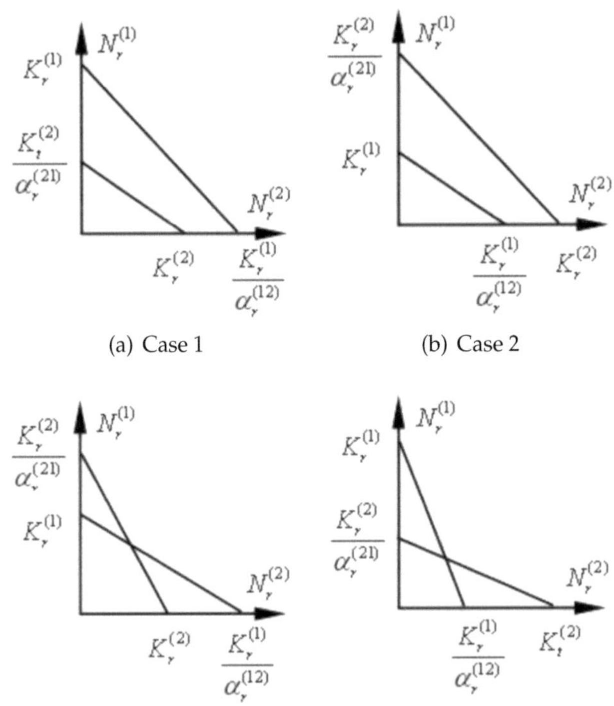

(a) Case 1 (b) Case 2

(c) Case 3 (d) Case 4

Fig. 3. The isoclines of two co-evolution species

2) Intra-Species Evolution

Since genetic algorithm and particle filters have many common aspects, Higuchi(Higuchi, 1997) has merged them together. In CEPF the genetic operators, crossover and mutation, are applied to search for optimal samples in each species independently. The intra-species evolution will interact with inter-species competition: the evolution of individuals in a species will increase its ability for inter-species competition, so as to survive for a longer time. Because the observation density $p(o_r^{(t)}|x_r^{(t)})$ includes the most recent observed information of the robot, it is defined as the fitness function. The two operators: crossover and mutation, work directly over the floating-points to avoid the trouble brought by binary coding and decoding. The crossover and mutation operator are defined as the following: Crossover: for two parent samples $(x_{r1}^{(t)}, w_{r1}^{(t)})$, $(x_{r2}^{(t)}, w_{r2}^{(t)})$from the samples of a species of the r-th robot. The crossover operator mates them by Equation 4 to generate two children samples.

$$\begin{cases} x'^{(t)}_{r1} = \xi x^{(t)}_{r1} + (1-\xi) x^{(t)}_{r2}, \\ x'^{(t)}_{r2} = (1-\xi) x^{(t)}_{r1} + \xi x^{(t)}_{r2}, \\ w'^{(1)}_{r} = p(o_r^{(t)}|x^{(t)}_{r1}), \\ w'^{(t)}_{r2} = p(o_r^{(t)}|x^{(t)}_{r2}). \end{cases} \tag{4}$$

Where$\xi \sim U[0,1]$, and $U[0,1]$represents uniform distribution. And two samples with the largest importance factors are selected from the four samples for the next generation. Mutation: for a parent sample $(x_{r1}^{(t)}, w_{r1}^{(t)})$ from the samples of a species of the r-th robot, the mutation operator on it is defined by Equation 5.

$$\begin{cases} x'^{(t)}_{r1} = x^{(t)}_{r1} + \tau, \\ w'^{(t)}_{r1} = p(o_r^{(t)}|x^{(t)}_{r1}). \end{cases} \tag{5}$$

Where $\tau \sim N(0,\Sigma)$ is a three-dimensional vector and $N(0,\Sigma)$ represents normal distribution. The sample with larger importance factor is selected from the two samples for next generation. In CEPF, the crossover operator will perform with probability p_c and mutation operator will perform with probability p_m. Because the genetic operator can search for optimal samples, the sampling process is more efficient and the number of samples required to represent the posterior density can be reduced considerably.

3) Splitting and Merging of Species

We assume the samples of the r-th robot are clustered into $\Omega_r^{(t)}$ species at time step t and each sample is a n-dimensional point. Samples of the i-th species $S_{ri}^{(t)} = \{({}_i x_{rj}^{(t)}, {}_i w_{rj}^{(t)})|j = 1,\cdots,N_r^{(i)}\}$ are contained in a sub-domain $D_r^{(i)}$ which is an hypercube of the state space. If the sub-domains of two species such as sub-domain $D_r^{(i)}$ and $D_r^{(j)}$ cover each other, the two species will be merged and the their corresponding sub-domain will also be merged. We call this the merging process. Let us assume there are $\Omega'^{(t)}_r$ species after the merging process. In the splitting process the sub-domain $D_r^{(i)}$ of the i-th species is partitioned into small hyper-rectangular grids of equal size. And samples in the i-th species are mapped into the grids. The weight of each grid is the average importance factor of the samples that fall in it. A threshold $T = \mu$is used to classify the grids into two groups; here the coefficient$\mu \in (0,1)$. Grids with weight larger than T are picked out to form a grid set V. Using the network defined through neighborhood relations between the grids, the set V is divided into connected regions (i.e. sets of connected grids). Assuming there are $B_r^{(i)}$ connected regions, these connected regions are used as seeds for the clustering procedure. A city-block distance is used in the network of grids. As in image processing field, the use of distance and seeds permits to define influence zones, and the boundary between influence zones is known as SKIZ (skeleton by influence zone) (Serra, 1982). So the sub-domain $D_r^{(i)}$ will be split into B_r^i parts. This process will perform for each species and the number of species of t+1 step is $\Omega_r^{(t+1)} = \sum_{i=1}^{\Omega'^{(t)}_r} B_r^i$. The merging and splitting process is shown in Table 1.

Input: $\Omega_r^{(t)}$ species of time step t;

Output: the new $\Omega_r^{(t+1)}$ species;

$\Omega'^{(t)}_r := \Omega_r^{(t)}$;

for all species **do**

  if $D_r^{(i)}$ and $D_r^{(j)}$ cover each other;

    merge($S_{ri}^{(t)}$,$S_{rj}^{(t)}$);

    $\Omega'^{(t)}_r := \Omega'^{(t)}_r - 1$; // Update the number of species

  end if

end for

$\Omega_r^{(t+1)} := 0$;

for $i := 1$ to $\Omega'^{(t)}_r$ **do** //Split the species

  split the domain $D_r^{(i)}$ into grids;

  calculate the weight of each grids;

  select the grids whose weight larger than T to form set V;

  calculate $B_r^{(i)}$; //the number of connected regions in V

  split D_r^j into $B_r^{(i)}$ sub-regions and samples in each sub-region form a new species;

  $\Omega_r^{(t+1)} := \Omega_r^{(t+1)} + B_r^{(i)}$; //Update the number of species;

end for

end

Table 1. Merging-splitting process of species

4.2 Cooperative localization based on CEPF

Multi-robot localization is to integrate measurements taken at different platforms. The simplest way for integrating the information from different platforms is to maintain a single state for all the robots i.e. if there are R robots the state of the system will be of $3R$ dimension. But using particle filters for state estimation the dimension of state of the system should be small, thus estimating the distribution of the pose of all the robots is infeasible for a few robots. So a distributed representation is used in our system similar to the approach proposed by Fox (Fox et al., 2000), in which each robot maintains its own belief function that models its own uncertainty. The posterior of position is given by:

$$p(x_1^{(t)}, \cdots, x_R^{(t)} | d^{(t)}) = p(x_1^{(t)} | d^{(t)}) \cdot \cdots \cdot p(x_R^{(t)} | d^{(t)}), \tag{6}$$

Where R is the number of the robots, $d^{(t)}$is the data items collected by all robots up to time t. The distributed representation enables the estimation of the posteriors to be conveniently carried out locally on each robot. When the$l$-th robot knows the position of the r-th robot relative to itself, information is transmitted from the l-th robot to the r-th robot and integrated in the following way:

$$\begin{aligned} p(x_r^{(t)}|d^{(t)}) &= p(x_r^{(t)}|d_r^{(t)})p(x_r^{(t)}|d_l^{(t)}) \\ &= p(x_r^{(t)}|d_r^{(t)}) \int p(x_r^{(t)}|x_l^{(t)},o_{lr}^{(t)})p(x_l^{(t)}|d_l^{(t)})dx_l^{(t)}. \end{aligned} \tag{7}$$

Where $o_{lr}^{(t)}$ is the relative positions between the two robots estimated by the l-th robot. Two cases are considered in the calculation of $o_{lr}^{(t)}$: (1) the l-th robot can see the r-th robot; (2) the r-th robot has just gone out the eyesight of the l-th robot. In the first case, $o_{lr}^{(t)}$ is observed by the l-th robot, and $p(x_r^{(t)}|x_l^{(t)},o_{lr}^{(t)})$ is the detection model of the l-th robot. In the second case, $o_{lr}^{(t)}$ is calculated using their odometry data. Since the relative positions of the two robots according to their odometry data are much more certain than the global positions, the information of their relative positions is used to refine their global positions. In both cases $p(x_r^{(t)}|x_l^{(t)},o_{lr}^{(t)})$ is learned from data. CEPF can be applied to solve Equation 7. Since samples in $S_r^{(t)}$and $S_l^{(t)}$are drawn randomly, it is not straightforward to establish correspondence between individual samples in $p(x_r^{(t)}|d_r^{(t)})$ and $\int p(x_r^{(t)}|x_l^{(t)},o_{lr}^{(t)})p(x_l^{(t)}|d_l^{(t)})dx_l^{(t)}$. And the sample set which represents the position of the r-th robot in the eyes of the l-th robot will be transmitted from the l-th robot to the r-th robot. If the sample size is large, a too wide band is needed for communication. These problems can be solved, if we turn the discrete density represented by a large set of samples into continuous density function represented by much fewer parameters or a small sub-set of samples. This can be implemented by many density estimation methods such as Gaussian mixture density estimation, SV based density estimation. But density estimation is a time- consuming process, in order to satisfy the real time requirement we choose reduced set density estimator (RSDE) (Girolami & Chao, 2003). RSDE is a kernel-based density estimator which is optimal in L_2 sense. The advantage of RSDE is that it only requires $O(n^2)$ optimization routines to estimate the required kernel coefficients, but the SV based method requires $O(n^3)$ optimization routines. The general form of density estimation using a sample set with N samples can be denoted as:

$$\hat{p}(x;h,\gamma) = \sum_{i=1}^{N} \gamma_i \kappa_h(x,x_i) \tag{8}$$

Where $\kappa_h(x,x_i)$ are kernel functions, and γ are weighting coefficients and h is the window width. For a fixed window width h, process of estimation in RESDE is to find the parameters $\hat{\gamma}$ which provides the minimum integrated squared error (ISE):

$$\begin{aligned} \hat{\gamma} &= \arg\min_{\gamma} \int_{R^d} |p(x) - \hat{p}(x;h,\gamma)|^2 dx \\ &= \arg\min_{\gamma} \int_{R^d} \hat{p}^2(x;h,\gamma)dx - 2E_{p(x)}\{\hat{p}(x;h,\gamma)\} \end{aligned} \tag{9}$$

Where $\int_{R^d} p^2(x)dx$ has been dropped from the above due to its independence of the γgarameters and $E_{p(x)}\{\hat{p}(\cdot)\}$ denotes the expectation with respect to the desired density $p(x)$. Equation 9 can be represented in the following form:

$$\hat{\gamma} = \arg\min_{\gamma} \sum_{i,j=1}^{N} \gamma_i\gamma_j \int_{R^d} \kappa_h(x,x_i)\kappa_h(x,x_j) - 2\sum_{i=1}^{N} \gamma_i E_{p(x)}\{\kappa_h(x,x_i)\} \tag{10}$$

Since the required optimization of ISE will cause many of the $\gamma_i$terms to be driven to zero, the desired density can be presented with a small sub-set of samples. An example of density estimation based on RESDE is shown in Fig. 4, in which the density represented by 500 samples shown in Fig.4(a) can be estimated using 90 samples shown in Fig.4(b). Suppose the position of the r-th robot estimated by the l-th robot is represented by ${}^{l}N_r$ samples ${}^{l}S_r^{(t)} = \{({}^{l}x_{rj}^{(t)}, {}^{l}w_{rj}^{(t)}) | j = 1, \cdots, {}^{l}N_r\}$ after using RSDE, the algorithm of cooperative localization is shown in Table 2.

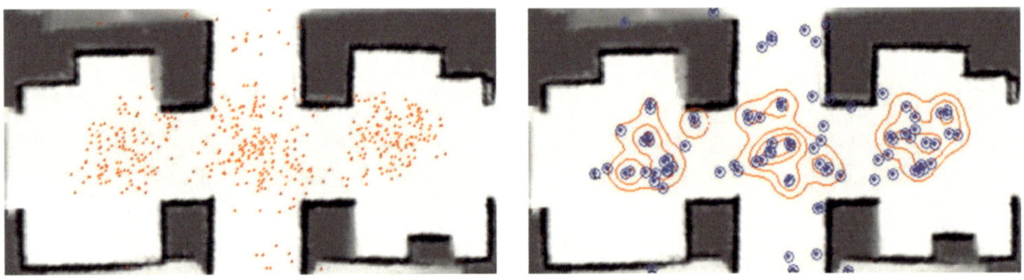

(a) Original samples (b) Sub-set of samples after density estimation

Fig. 4. Density estimation based on RDSE

5. Decision-theoretic active localization

In this section we propose a strategy based on decision theory to coordinate the robots actively. For a robot that is in a connected group, the strategy includes two steps. In the first step, the leader of a connected group will determine the position of the group (i.e. the most likely position of the robots) according to summarized global position hypotheses of robots in the group; in the second step, each robot will generate several candidate actions according to the position of the connected group and the utility and cost of the actions are calculated, then the leader will solve the conflictions between robots and choose the next action for each robot so as to maximize the utility-cost trade-off. For a robot that is not connected with any other robots, it will summarize its global position using the species with the largest average importance factor, and will explore actively taking itself as the leader.

5.1 Position estimation of the connected group

In multi-robot cooperative localization based on CEPF, each species represents a hypothesis of the position of the robot. In order to estimate the position of the connected group, the summarized hypotheses of positions and the relative positions between robots are transmitted to their leader. And the position of the leader will be estimated according to the information from other robots. Suppose the leader of a group is the l-th robot and the r-th robot is a member under its leadership. The probability that the leader will be in the position represented by the hypothesis $h_{li}^{(t)}$according to the data collected by the r-th robot and the relative positions between them can be represented by the following equation:

$$p(h_{li}^{(t)} | d_r^{(t)}) = \sum_{j=1}^{\Omega_r^{(t)}} p(h_{li}^{(t)} | h_{rj}^{(t)}, o_{rl}^{(t)}) p(h_{rj}^{(t)} | d_r^{(t)}) \tag{11}$$

Input: NULL

Output: the position hypotheses summarize from the species;

1. cluster samples into $\Omega_r^{(0)}$ species,$dN_r^{(i)}/dt := 0$ and t:=1; //Initialization

2. **for** i:=1 to $\Omega_r^{(t)}$ **do**

3. $S_{ri}^{(t)} := \phi$;

4. normalize importance factors of species i ; // Importance factor normalization

5. $N_r^{(i)} := \max(N_r^{(i)} + dN_r^{(i)}/dt, 0)$ //Calculate the sample size

6. resample $N_r^{(i)}$ samples from $S_{ri}^{(t-1)}$; // Resampling from species i

7. **for** j:=1 to $N_r^{(i)}$ **do** // Importance sampling

8. sample ${}_i x_{rj}^{(t)}$ from $p(x_t|{}_i x_{rj}^{(t-1)}, u_{t-1})$; // Predict next state using motion

9. ${}_i w_{rj}^{(t)} := p(o_r^{(t)}|{}_i x_{rj}^{(t)})$; // Calculate importance factor

1. $S_{ri}^{(t)} = S_{ri}^{(t)} \cup ({}_i x_{rj}^{(t)}, {}_i w_{rj}^{(t)})$ //Incorporate the sample to $S_{ri}^{(t)}$

10. **end for**

11. intra-species evolution of sample set $S_{ri}^{(t)}$; // Intra-species evolution

12. **end for**

13. **if** the r-th robot should send information to the l-the robot

14. estimate the state of the l-the robot and perform density estimation;

15. **end if**

16. **if** the robot receives the position information estimated by the l-th robot ;

17. Merge the information from the l-th robot;

18. **end if**

19. **if** not end

20. $t = t+1$ goto step 2;

21. **end**.

Table 2. Cooperative localization of multi robots based on CEPF

Where $h_{li}^{(t)}$ is a hypothesis of position summarized by the species i of the l-th robot, $h_{rj}^{(t)}$ is a hypothesis of position summarized by the species j of the r-th robot, $\Omega_r^{(t)}$ is the number of species of the r-th robot, $o_{rl}^{(t)}$ is the relative position between the l-th robot and the r-th robot which may not be observed directly but may be calculated according to the relative positions between the other robots in the cluster, $p(h_{rj}^{(t)}|d_r^{(t)})$ represents the probability that the r-th robot is at the position $h_{rj}^{(t)}$ and $p(h_{li}^{(t)}|h_{rj}^{(t)}, o_{rl}^{(t)})$ is a probability model learned from experiment data. The probability that the l-th robot is at the position represented by the hypothesis $h_{li}^{(t)}$ according to the data collected by all the robots in the connected group will be:

$$p(h_{li}^{(t)}|d^{(t)}) = \alpha \sum_{r=1}^{R} p(h_{li}^{(t)}|d_r^{(t)}) \tag{12}$$

Where α is a normalization parameter to make probability of all hypotheses sum to 1, and R is the number of robots in the group. The hypothesis $h_{l\max}^{(t)}$ with the largest probability is supposed to be the position of the l-th robot. We call $h_{l\max}^{(t)}$ the position of the connected group. The hypothesis $h_{r\max}^{(t)}$ that has the largest value of $p(h_{l\max}^{(t)}|h_{rj}^{(t)},o_{rl}^{(t)})$ is supposed to be the position of the r-th robot:

$$h_{r\max}^{(t)} = \arg\max_{h_{rj}^{(t)}} p(h_{l\max}^{(t)}|h_{rj}^{(t)},o_{rl}^{(t)}) \tag{13}$$

5.2 Exploration strategy

The world model in our system is represented by a hybrid map of grid and topology. For a grid map a Voronoi Diagram is produced using an approach similar to the one proposed by Thrun (Thrun, 1998). The grid map is partitioned into disjoint regions using the critical lines, as shown in Fig.5(a), and each region corresponds to one or more topological nodes which is the furcate point of Voronoi Diagram or the middle point if there is no furcate point as shown in Fig.5(b).

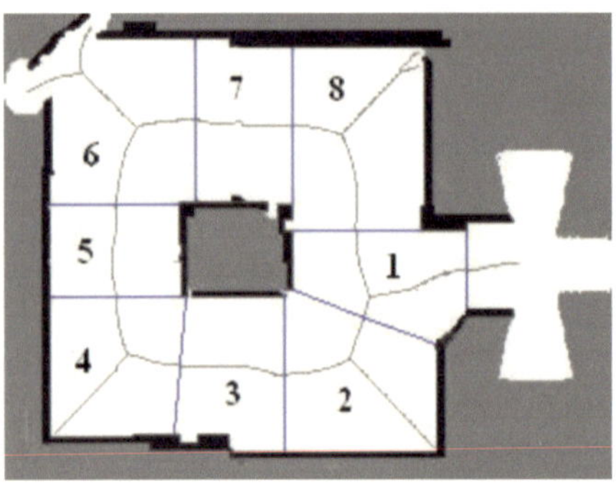

(a) Disjoint regions of grid map

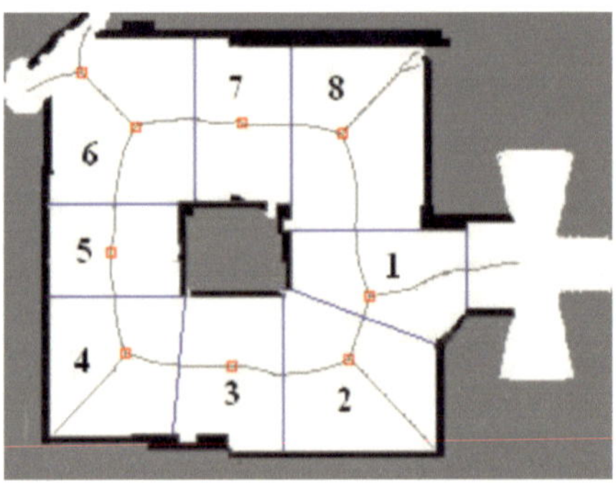

(b) Topological nodes in Voronoi Diagram

Fig. 5. Hybrid map of grid and topology

By using the position hypothesis $h_{l\max}^{(t)}$, we can get the topological nodes in the environment around the group. At any point of time the robot in each group can be assigned either to a topological node or to a rendezvous point of another robot. Coordination can be phrased as the problem of finding the assignment that maximizes the utility-cost trade-off similar to the method in (Burgard et al., 2000). More specifically, let E denote an assignment that determines the exact target (topological nodes and rendezvous point) of each robot and $E(r,j)$=1 if the r-th robot in the connected group is assigned to the j-th target. Among all assignments we choose the one that maximizes expected utility and minus expected cost:

$$E^* = \arg\max_{E} \sum_{(i,j)\in E} E(r,j)(U(r,j) - C(r,j)) \tag{14}$$

The utility and cost of each robot target pair (r,j) can be calculated as the following. **Utility:** The entropy of the belief, obtained by the following formula:

$$H(x_r^{(t)}) = \sum_{i=1}^{N_r^{(t)}} p(x_{ri}^{(t)}) \log p(x_{ri}^{(t)}), \tag{15}$$

measures the uncertainty in the robot position. Suppose the position of the r-th robot is $h_{r\max}^{(t)}$ at time point t, and it was assigned to the target j. If command a can drive the robot from the position $h_{r\max}^{(t)}$ to the target, we can measure the utility $U(r,j)$ of performing an action a by the decrease in uncertainty:

$$U(r,j) = H(x_r^{(t)}) - E_a(H(x_r^{(t+1)})). \tag{16}$$

If the target is a topological node, $E_a(H(x_r^{(t+1)}))$ denotes the expected entropy after having performed action a and having fired the sensors of the robot.

$$\begin{aligned} E_a(H(x_r^{(t+1)})) &= \sum_s H(x_r^{(t+1)}|s,a)p(s|a) \\ &= -\sum_s \sum_{x_r^{(t+1)}} p(s|x_r^{(t+1)})p(x_r^{(t+1)}|a) \log \frac{p(s|x_r^{(t+1)})p(x_r^{(t+1)}|a)}{p(s|a)} \end{aligned} \tag{17}$$

Where s is the sensor information. If the target is a rendezvous point with another robot that is not in the group, $E_a^{(}H(x_r^{(t+1)}))$ is the expected entropy after having performed action a and having received the information from the other robot.

$$\begin{aligned} E_a(H(x_r^{(t+1)})) &= \sum_{o_{rk}} H(x_r^{(t+1)}|d^{(t+1)},o_{rk})p(o_{rk}|a) \\ &= \sum_{o_{rk}} \sum_{x_r^{(t+1)}} p(o_{rk}|a)p(x_r^{(t+1)}|d^{(t+1)},o_{rk}) \log p(x_r^{(t+1)}|d^{(t+1)},o_{rk}). \end{aligned} \tag{18}$$

Where $p(o_{rk}^{|}a)$ represents the probability that the relative position between the r-th robot and the k-th robot is o_{rk} after having performed the action a and the probability $p(x_r^{(t+1)}|d^{(t+1)},o_{rk})$ can be calculated by:

$$p(x_r^{(t+1)}|d^{(t+1)},o_{rk}) = p(x_r^{(t)}|d_r^{(t)}) \int p(x_r^{(t+1)}|x_k^{(t+1)},o_{rk}^{(t+1)})p(x_k^{(t+1)}|d_k^{(t)})dx_k^{(t+1)}. \tag{19}$$

Cost: using the occupancy grid map we can get the cost-optimal path from the current location of the robot to the target location. And we use the cost of following the optimal path as the cost of assigning the r-th robot to the target j. Let $p_{occ}(x_r^{(t+1)})$ denote the probability that location $x_r^{(t+1)}$ is blocked by an obstacle. The robot has to compute the probability that the target point is occupied. Recall that the robot does not know its exact location; thus it must estimate the probability that the point relative to the robot according to the action a is occupied:

$$p_{occ}(a) = \sum_{x_r^{(t+1)}} p(x_r^{(t+1)})p_{occ}(f_a(x_r^{(t+1)})). \tag{20}$$

Where $f_a(x_r^{(t+1)})$ represents the location relative to the robot after performing action a when the robot is at the position $x_r^{(t+1)}$. Based on $p_{occ}(a)$, the expected path length and the cost-optimal policy can be obtained through value iteration. And the cost $C(r,j)$ can be calculated according to the length of the optimal path.

6. Experiment results

In this section we present experiments conducted using three robots: one is the HIT-Pioneer2 which is equipped with 16 sonar sensors and a CCD camera; one is the HIT-Pioneer3 which is equipped with 16 sonar sensors, a front laser range finder and a CCD camera and the third one is the HIT-Ghost which is equipped with two cameras (see Fig.6). The robots can detect each other using their CCD cameras, and communicate with each other using wireless Ethernet. Experiments are carried out in our lab building, and the map of the environment is shown in Fig.7(a). In the topological map are created before experiment (see Fig.7(b)). And some color marks are pasted on the wall or on the floor near the topological nodes so that HIT-Ghost can localize with visual information. Since even in multi-robot system the robots have to perform

Fig. 6. Picture of robots used for experiment

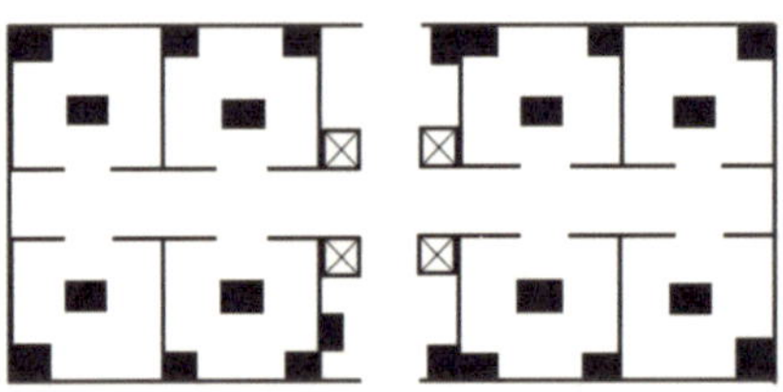

(a) The map drawn by hand

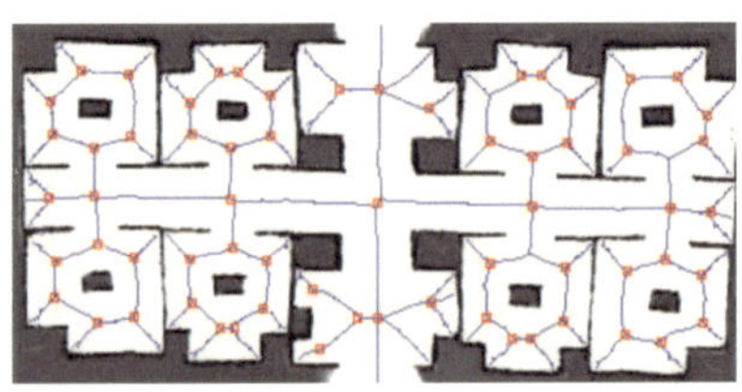

(b) The map built by robot

Fig. 7. The map of the environment

localization by itself when they do not connect with each other, we first evaluate the quality of CEPF for single robot localization. The HIT-Pioneer3 was placed in one of the rooms and its destination is the door of the building. During the process of going to its destination, the initial position of the robot is unknown and it has to make global localization using the laser range finder (see Fig.8(a)). After randomly running several meters, most of the samples will move to several small areas because of the symmetry of the environment, so CEPF can cluster the samples into clusters naturally (see Fig.8(b)). And the robot can make decision according to the estimated location of the species. At the moment shown in Fig.8(a), the robot will make a right turning and go to another corner of the rooms to determine the room it will be in as is shown in Fig.8(c). Then the robot will go to the door of the room and only two most likely hypotheses are remained (see Fig.8(d)). Then we evaluated the multi-robot localization

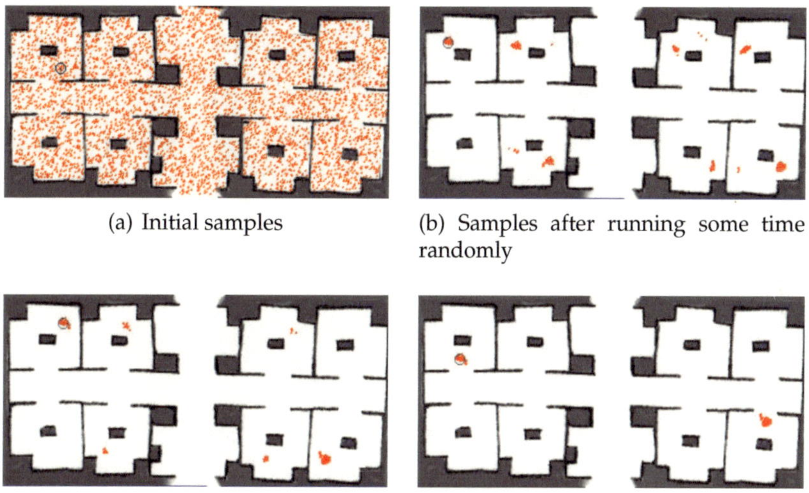

(a) Initial samples

(b) Samples after running some time randomly

(c) Samples after making one decision

(d) Samples after making another decision

Fig. 8. Active localization of a single robot

based on CEPF with 1500 samples for each robot. The three robots are randomly placed in the environment and explore actively by themselves as in single robot localization at the first stage (see Fig.9). In figure 9 HIT-Pioneer3 is represented by red particles, HIT-Pioneer2 is represented by green particles and HIT-Ghost is represented by blue particles. When the two HIT-Pioneer robots can communicate with each other, a rendezvous point R is determined by them to manage to meet each other (see Fig.9(a)). When they can see each other their observation information will be exchanged, so their global positions can be refined and only two localization hypotheses are remained for each robot (see Fig.9(b)). And HIT-Pioneer3 is assigned to be the leader to coordinate their actions to go to an optimal topological node (see Fig.9(c)). Since the color marks in the environment are sparse and specious, the global position of the HIT-Ghost is very uncertain. When the HIT-Ghost can communicate with the two HIT-Pioneer robots, the utility to meet the other two robots is much larger than go to a topological node, so the HIT-Ghost will manage to meet the HIT-Pioneer3 (see Fig.9(d)). The time to determine the global position of the robots using no-cooperative localization, cooperative localization and cooperative active localization based on CEPF, which are termed CEPF, CCEPF and CACEPF for short respectively, are compared. In 20 times of experiments, the time needed for localization of CACEPF and CCEPF are 62% and 89% of that of CEPF respectively.

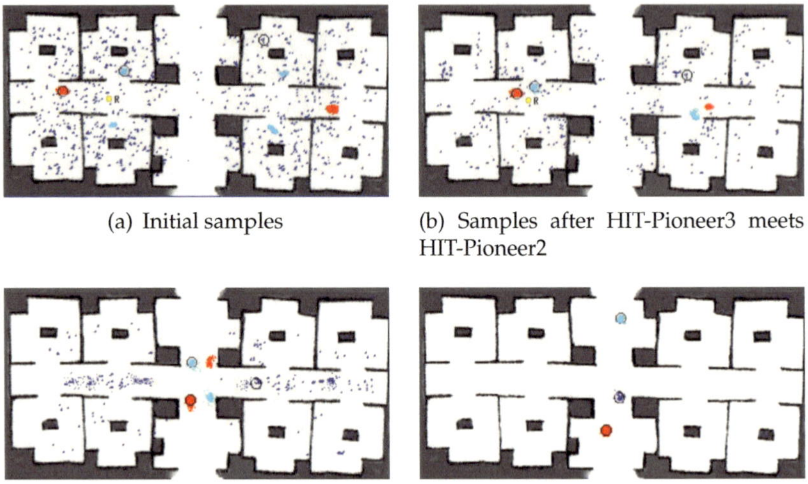

(a) Initial samples

(b) Samples after HIT-Pioneer3 meets HIT-Pioneer2

(c) Samples after making a active exploration

(d) Samples after HIT-Ghost meets HIT-Pioneer3

Fig. 9. Multi-robot active localization based on CEPF

7. Conclusion

A novel method for active localization of multi-robot is proposed. Based on the new version of particle filters called co-evolution particle filters (CEPF) the problem of premature convergence can be solved, so the hypothesis of the robots' positions can be tracked stably. And the decision theory- based coordination strategy can efficiently coordinate the action of the robots so as to maximize the utility-cost trade-off. Experimental results have proved the efficiency of the method of the active localization in multi-robot system.

8. References

Arulampalam, S. M., Maskell, S., Gordon, N. & Clapp, T. (2002). A tutorial on particle filters for online nonlinear/non-gaussian bayesian tracking, *IEEE Trans. Signal processing* Vol. 50(No. 2): 174–187.

Burgard, W., D. Fox, M. M., Simmons, R. & Thrun, S. (2000). Collaborative multi-robot exploration, *Proceedings of IEEE International Conference on Robotics and Automation*, Vol. Vol. 1, San Francisco, USA, pp. 476 – 481.

Burgard, W., Fox, D., Hennig, D. & Schmidt, T. (1996). Estimating the absolute position of a mobile robot using position probability grids, *Proceedings of Thirteenth National Conference on Artificial Intelligence*, Oregon, USA, pp. 896–901.

Dasvison, A. J. & Murray, D. W. (2002). Simultaneous localization and map-building using active vision, *IEEE Trans. Pattern Analysis and Machine Intelligence* Vol. 24(No. 3): 865–880.

Dayoub, F. & Duckett, T. (2008). An adaptive appearance-based map for long-term topological localization of mobile robots, *Proceedings of IEEE/RSJ International Conference on Intelligent Robots and Systems*, Nice, France, pp. 3364–3369.

Dellaert, F., Fox, D., Burgard, W. & Thrun, S. (1999). Monte carlo localization for mobile robots, *Proceedings of IEEE International Conference on Robotics and Automation*, Michigan,

USA, pp. 1322–1328.

Dissanayake, G., Newman, P. M., Durrant-Whyte, H. F. & Csorba, M. (2001). A solution to the simultaneous localization and map building (slam) problem, *IEEE Trans. Robotics and Automation* Vol. 17(No. 3): 229–241.

Doucet, A., Freitas, D. N. & Gordon, N. (2001). *Sequential Monte Carlo in Practice*, Springer-Verlag,, New York.

Doucet, A., Godsill, S. & Andrieu, C. (2000). On sequential monte carlo sampling methods for bayesian filtering8, *Statist. Computing* Vol. 10(No. 3): 19–20.

Elena, L. M., Rafael, B., Miguel, B. L. & Soledad, E. M. (2004). A human-robot cooperative learning system for easy installation of assistant robots in new working environments, *J. Intelligent and Robotic Systems* Vol. 40(No. 3): 233–265.

Fenwick, J. W., Newman, P. M. & Leonard, J. J. (2002). Cooperative concurrent mapping and localization, *Proceedings of IEEE International Conference on Robotics and Automation*, Vol. Vol. 2, IEEE, Washington, DC, USA, pp. 1810–1817.

Fox, D. (2003). Adapting the sample size in particle filters through kld-sampling, *Internat. J. Robotic Res* Vol. 22: 985–1004.

Fox, D., B., W., Kruppa, H. & Thrun, S. (2000). A probabilistic approach to collaborative multi-robot localization, *Autonomous Robots* Vol. 8(No. 3): 325–344.

Fox, D., Burgard, W. & Thrun, S. (1998). Active markov localization for mobile robots, *Robotics and Autonomous Systems* Vol. 25(No. 3-4): 195–207.

Gil, A., Reinoso, ı., Ballesta, M. & Juliá, M. (2010). Multi-robot visual slam using a rao-blackwellized particle filter, *Robotics and Autonomous Systems* Vol. 58(No. 1): 68–80.

Girolami, M. & Chao, H. (2003). Probability density estimation from optimally condensed data samples, *IEEE Trans. Pattern Analysis and Machine Intelligence* Vol. 25(No. 10): 1253–1264.

Guivant, J. E. & Nebot, E. M. (2001). Optimization of the simultaneous localization and map-building algorithm for real-time implementation, *IEEE Trans. Robotics and Automation* Vol. 17(No. 3): 242–257.

Higuchi, T. (1997). Monte carlo filtering using genetics algorithm operators, Vol. 59: 1–23.

Hongjun, Z. & Shiyeyuki, S. (2002). Sensor planning for mobile robot localization using bayesian network representation and inference., *Proceedings of IEEE/RSJ International Conference on Intelligent Robots and Systems*, Lausanne, Switzerland, pp. 440–446.

Jensfelt, P. & Kristensen, S. (2001). Active global localization for a mobile robot using multiple hypothesis tracking, *IEEE Trans. Robotics Automation* Vol. 17: 748–760.

Kaelbling, L. P., Cassandra, A. R. & Kurien, J. A. (1996). Acting under uncertainty: Discrete bayesian models for mobile-robot navigation, *Proceedings of IEEE/RSJ International Conference on Intelligent Robots and Systems*, Vol. Vol. 2, Osaka, Japan, pp. 963–972.

Milstein, A., Sanchez, J. N. & Wiamson, E. (2002). Robust global localization using clustered particle filtering, *Proceedings of Eighteenth National Conference on Artificial Intelligence*, Edmonton, Canada, pp. 581–586.

Robert, L. D. & Arvin, A. (2003). Simulation and control of distributed robot search teams, *Computers and Electrical Engineering* Vol. 29(No. 5): 625–642.

Schenker, S. P., Terry, L., Pirjanian, H. P., Bamgartner, E. T. & Tunsrel, E. (2003). Planetary rover developments supporting mars exploration, *Autonomous Robots* Vol. 14(No. 2-3): 103–126.

Serra, J. (1982). *Image Analysis and Mathematical Morphologym*, New York: Academic Press.

Shang, Y. & Cai, X. (1996). *Common Ecology (in Chinese)*, Beijing University Press, Beijing.

Thrun, S. (1998). Learning metric-topological maps for indoor mobile robot navigation, Vol. 99(No. 1): 21–71.

Thrun, S., Fox, D., Burgard, W. & Dellaert, F. (2001). Robust monte carlo localization for mobile robots, *Artificial Intelligence* Vol. 128: 99–141.

Trawny, G. H. N., Mourikis, A. & Roumeliotis, S. (2009). On the consistency of multi-robot cooperative localization, *Proceedings of 2009 Robotics: Science and Systems Conference*, Seattle, Washington.

Wu, M., Huang, F., Wang, L. & Sun, J. (2009). Cooperative multi-robot monocular-slam using salient landmarks, *Proceedings of the 2009 International Asia Conference on Informatics in Control, Automation and Robotics*, IEEE Computer Society, Washington, DC, USA, pp. 151–155.

9

Cooperative Localization and SLAM Based on the Extended Information Filter

Francesco Conte[1], Andrea Cristofaro[2],
Alessandro Renzaglia[2] and Agostino Martinelli[2]
[1]*Università degli Studi dell'Aquila*
[2]*INRIA Rhône-Alpes*
[1]*Italy*
[2]*France*

1. Introduction

Simultaneous Localization and Mapping (SLAM) requires a mobile robot to autonomously explore the environment with its on-board sensors, gain knowledge about it, interpret the scene, build an appropriate map and localize itself relative to this map. Many approaches have been proposed both in the framework of metric and topological navigation. A very successful metric method is the stochastic map (26) where early experiments (4) (16) have shown the quality of fully metric SLAM.
Currently, the SLAM has two contrasting problems to be solved, which are often faced with a trade-off:

- The map precision;
- The computational requirement for real-time/real-world implementation

Dissanayake et al. (5), proved the convergence of an algorithm based on the Kalman filter theoretically. However, the proof is based on the strong hypothesis of a linear observation. Julier and Uhlmann (13) and Castellanos et al. (2) proved that the conventional EKF based $SLAM$ (from now on $EKF - SLAM$) yields an inconsistent map (in particular, in (13) was shown that this happens even for the special case of a stationary vehicle with no process noise). The map inconsistency arises from the linearization introduced by the Extended Kalman Filter (EKF) as clearly pointed out by Castellanos et al. (2). Indeed, this approximation only holds if the difference between the estimated state and the ground truth is small. Now, in any map representation, the corresponding vehicle location will drift (if no loop is closed). This is a consequence of the fact that the absolute location is derived from a composition of many relative measurements. Therefore, when the drift is large enough, the linearization is not a possible approximation. Additionally, even by solving SLAM with an EKF (i.e. by adopting a linearization) the computational complexity becomes prohibitive since it grows up squarely in the features number.
In 2006 Eustice *et al,* (see (6)) introduced an approach called *Exactly Sparse Delayed-State Filters* (from now on ESDF). Basing on the Information Filter (from now on IF or EIF with linearization) and only introducing negligible approximations on the the state recovery, this technique solves the SLAM problem through a constant-time filtering algorithm. This means that the ESDF computational cost does not grow up with the environment size.

Therefore, ESDF is considered as the solution to the scalability problem for arbitrately large environments.
Because of this optimal computational behaviour, the ESDF cannot be improved in terms of computational cost through a Filter-based solution to SLAM. On the other hand, the EIF used by the ESDF method suffers from the same limitation of the EKF-SLAM in terms of map accuracy. In particular, as well as the EKF, the EIF is based on the linear approximation of the analyzed system. Hence, the estimation process could become inconsistent if the environment is large enough.
Recently, a new strategy has emerged that offers the possibility to solve the SLAM problem without any linear approximation. This approach is called Graph-based approach. It consists in facing the SLAM as a non linear optimization problem: *find the robot trajectory and the map with the greatest probability, given the sensor measurements.* In the works realized by Olson (22) and Grisetti (9) non linear optimization algorithms are proposed in order to solve the SLAM problem. These suggested algorithms are able to build very accurate maps, with a low computational cost. In the first part of this chapter, we illustrate a new approach to SLAM which combines an EIF and a non linear optimizer. In particular, we suggest a hybrid solution to SLAM which consists in using a suitable modification of the ESDF filtering algorithm when the system non linearities are supposed to be negligible, and switching to a non linear optimizer when the system non linearities are stronger (e.g. loop closure). An analogous strategy was proposed in (18) in the context of the Relative Map Approach to solve SLAM.
In the second part of this chapter we will focus our attention on the cooperative case, i.e. when the estimation process is performed simultaneously by a team of agents. In particular, we consider the case of flying vehicles. In recent years, flying robotics has received significant attention from the robotics community. The ability to fly allows easily avoiding obstacles and quickly having an excellent birds eye view. These navigation facilities make flying robots the ideal platform to solve many tasks like exploration, mapping, reconnaissance for search and rescue, environment monitoring, security surveillance, inspection etc. In the framework of flying robotics, micro aerial vehicles (MAV) have a further advantage. Due to the small size they can also be used in narrow out- and indoor environment and they represent only a limited risk for the environment and people living in it. One of the main prerequisite for the successful accomplishment of many tasks is a precise vehicle localization. Since micro aerial vehicles are equipped with low computational capabilities an efficient solution must be able to distribute the computation among all the agents in order to exploit the computational resources of the entire team. Distributing the computation has also another key advantage. It allows us to make the solution robust with respect to failures. On the other hand, distributing the computation must also account the limited communication capabilities.
The cooperative localization problem has been faced by many authors so far. Fox and collaborators (7) introduced a probabilistic approach based on Markov localization. Their approach has been validated through real experiments showing a drastic improvement in localization speed and accuracy when compared to conventional single robot localization. Other approaches take advantage of relative observations for multi-robot localization (8; 10; 15; 23; 24; 27). In (10) a method based on a combination of maximum likelihood estimation and numerical optimization was introduced. This method allows to reduce the error in the robot localization by using the information coming from relative observations among the robots in the team. In (24), a distributed multi robot localization strategy was introduced. This strategy is based on an Extended Kalman Filter to fuse proprioceptive and exteroceptive sensor data. In (17), the same approach was adapted in order to deal with any kind of relative

observations among the robots. In (24), it was shown that the equations can be written in a decentralized form, allowing the decomposition into a number of smaller communicating filters. However, the distributed structure of the filter only regards the integration of the proprioceptive data (i.e. the so called prediction phase). As soon as an observation between two robots occurs, communication between each member of the team and a single processor (which could be embedded in a member of the team) is required. The same communication skill is required when even an exteroceptive measurements which only regards a single robot occurs (e.g. a GPS measurement). Furthermore, the computation required to integrate the information coming from this observation is entirely performed by a single processor with a computational complexity which scales quadratically with the number of robots. Obviously, the centralized structure of the solution in dealing with exteroceptive observations becomes a serious inconvenient when the communication and processing capabilities do not allow to integrate the information contained in the exteroceptive data in real time. In particular, this happens as soon as the number of robots is large, even if each robot performs very few exteroceptive observations. In (20) this problem was considered. However, the structure of the filter was maintained the same as in (24) (namely centralized in dealing with exteroceptive data). Each robot was supposed to be equipped with several sensors and the optimal sensing frequencies were analytically derived by maximizing the final localization accuracy. The limit of this approach is that as the number of robots increases, the sensing frequencies reduce. In other words, by performing the estimation process in a centralized fashion it is necessary to reduce the number of observations to be processed as the number of robots increases. Hence, distibuting the entire estimation process can provide a great improvement.

The information filter is very appealing in this framework since the integration of the exteroceptive data is very simple and could be easily distributed. On the other hand, the equations which characterize the prediction step are much more complex and their distributed implementation seems to be forbidden. This is a serious inconvenient since the proprioceptive data run at a very high frequency.

Eustice et al. (6) and Caballero et al. (1) have recently shown that by using a delayed state also the prediction step has some nice properties. In particular, in (6) a solution to the SLAM problem by using an Extended Information Filter (EIF) to estimate a delayed state has been proposed. In (1) the tracking problem has been considered.

In the second part of this chapter we present the problem of cooperative localization in $3D$ when the MAVs are equipped with inertial sensors and exteroceptive sensors (e.g. range sensors and GPS). We adopt a delayed state and we perform its estimation by using an Extended Information Filter. We introduce a simple trick which allows us to mathematically express the quantities measured by the IMU (Inertial Measurement Unit) as a function of the delayed state (i.e. the state to be estimated). In other words, by using this trick, the link between sensor-state for the IMU (which are typically proprioceptive sensors) has the same mathematical expression of the one which characterizes an exteroceptive observation. This allows us to use the equations of the integration of the exteroceptive data also to integrate the IMU data. In this way the equations of the EIF prediction step are never used and the overall estimation process can be easily distributed.

When dealing with a $3D$ environment, another important issue arises. The orientation of a MAV which moves in $3D$ is provided by 3 parameters. On the other hand, the MAV dynamics become very easy by adopting quaternions. However, this parameterization is redundant. This means that part of the information is frozen in a geometrical constraint. Without using this constraint part of the information is not exploited and the overall precision gets worse.

To this regard a new filter, the projection filter, has been introduced (21); this filter permits us to consider the geometrical constraint (expressing that the quaternion must be unitary) as an ideal observation.

2. A brief overview on extended information filter

Consider an arbitrary system driven by the discrete equations

$$x_i = f(x_{i-1}, u_i)$$

$$z_i = h(x_i)$$

Let us denote with Σ and ξ the information matrix and the information vector respectively; we recall that information matrix and information vector are related to covariance matrix P and mean value μ as follows

$$\Sigma = P^{-1}, \quad \xi = P^{-1}\mu.$$

2.1 Estimation with EIF: integration of exteroceptive data

Let R be the covariance matrix characterizing the measurement error for an exteroceptive sensor. The update equations at the time step i are (see (28)):

$$\Sigma_i = \overline{\Sigma}_i + \Sigma_{obs}, \qquad \Sigma_{obs} = H_i^T R^{-1} H_i, \tag{1}$$

$$\xi_i = \overline{\xi}_i + \xi_{obs}, \qquad \xi_{obs} = H_i^T R^{-1} \left[z_i - h(\overline{\mu}_i) + H_i \overline{\mu}_i \right], \tag{2}$$

where $\overline{\Sigma}_i, \overline{\xi}_i$ are the predicted information matrix and information vector, $\overline{\mu}_i = \overline{\Sigma}_i^{-1} \overline{\xi}_i$ is the predicted mean value and H_i is the Jacobian of the observation function $h(\cdot)$ evaluated at $\overline{\mu}_i$.

2.2 Estimation with EIF: integration of proprioceptive data

Denoting by Q a noise term affecting the system dynamics, the prediction steps are given by

$$\overline{\Sigma}_i = \left[F_i \Sigma_{i-1}^{-1} F_i^T + Q \right]^{-1}, \tag{3}$$

$$\overline{\xi}_i = \overline{\Sigma}_i F_i \Sigma_{i-1}^{-1} \xi_{i-1}, \tag{4}$$

where F_i is the Jacobian of the dynamics $f(\cdot,\cdot)$ evaluated at the estimated mean value (μ_{i-1}, u_i), where $\mu_{i-1} = \Sigma_{i-1}^{(-1)} \xi_{i-1}$.

2.3 EIF and delayed-states

In a multi robot scenario Σ and ξ characterize the probability distribution of several robots; in (1) it is shown that delayed-states allow us to distribute the estimation process over the entire network. In particular the authors explain how to recover the global belief from the local belief of each network node and remark that the same operation with standard (non delayed) states is not possible at all.

Definition 1 *A delayed-state is a dynamic vector X whose entries at time step i are the current robot coordinates x_i together with all the past poses $x_0, x_1, ..., x_{i-1}$.*

For example, a delayed-state for a 2D robot having coordinates assigned by $x_i = (r_{x,i}, r_{y,i}, \theta_i)$ is given by the vector

$$X_i = (r_{x,0}, r_{y,0}, \theta_0, r_{x,1}, r_{y,1}, \theta_1, ..., r_{x,i}, r_{y,i}, \theta_i).$$

As already mentioned, a distributed algorithm for the implementation of update equations (1)-(2) can be designed (see (1)). The structure of such equation is very simple as the update consists only in summing the new information from the exteroceptive sensors to the predicted values. On the other hand, the prediction equations (3)-(4) are more complicated and they cannot be easily distributed. Nevertheless we will show that, once a delayed-state is considered, data obtained from proprioceptive sensors can be integrated using only the update equations (1)-(2).

3. SLAM problem for a single 2D robot

3.1 Advantages and drawbacks in the ESDF-approach

In 2006 Eustice *et al.* (6) introduced the innovative technique called *Exactly Sparse Delayed-state Filters*. The ESDF algorithm succeeds in exploiting the benefits of the EIF by maintaining a sparse structure of the information matrix (covariance inverse), without any approximation. This is obtained through a *state-augmentation* technique and yields a constant-time computational cost per iteration. In the following we will summarize the ESDF method pointing out some of its key properties.

Let us represent the robot motion and perception by the following equations:

$$x_i = f(x_{i-1}, u_i + w_i) \tag{5}$$

$$z_i = h(x_i, m) + v_i \tag{6}$$

where x_i is the robot pose at the time step i, u_i is the control input (proprioceptive measurement), z_i is the exteroceptive measurement available at the time step i, m is the environment map, f is the robot motion function, h is the observation function, and w_i and v_i are the proprioceptive and exteroceptive measurements errors, respectively.

The ESDF key idea is to extend the estimated state vector each time an observation occurs. Specifically, at the time step i the current estimated vector is:

$$X_i^T = \begin{pmatrix} x_i^T & M^T \end{pmatrix} \tag{7}$$

where M is a vector carrying all the maintained old poses and the map m. In the following we will often talk about the size of X_i as the environment size.

Basing on the information form and the state augmentation, the ESDF technique solves the SLAM problem by performing the following tasks: *motion update*, *state augmentation* and *observation update*. If we suppose that the current state mean μ_i is available at each iteration (i.e. the state recovery problem is supposed to be solved), the three mentioned tasks have constant-time computational costs (i.e. independent of the environment size). This is possible thanks to the estimated state structure, defined in (7). For a detailed proof, the reader is referred to (6).

On the other hand, the ESDF suffers from a strong limitation about the map precision. To be more precise, it suffers from the same limitations of every Gaussian-Filter-based solution to SLAM. The crucial problem is that a Gaussian-filter generally is a linear estimator. Unfortunately, the SLAM is a strong non linear problem, i.e. the robot motion function f in (5) and the observation function h in (6) are strongly non linear. This leads to the use of the linear approximation of both the robot kinematics and observations. In this way the estimation accuracy is obviously made worse.

3.1.1 Estimation process with the EIF

The estimation process is performed using update and prediciton steps given by (1)-(2) and (3)-(4). We introduce the two following assumptions.

Assumption 1 (Sparse Observation) *The observation function h only depends on q components of X_i and q is independent of the size of X_i.*

Assumption 2 (Easy State Recovery) *It is possible to recover the estimated state X_i (i.e. obtain μ_i) from the information quantities (ξ_i, Σ_i) with a complexity independent of the size of X_i.*

Under the previous assumptions we obtain the following property characterizing the complexity of the observation update.

Property 1 (Observation Update Complexity) *Under the assumptions 1 and 2 the observation update defined by the equations (1) and (2) can be computed with a complexity independent of the size of X_i, i.e. the observation update has a constant-time cost.*

Proof: if the observation function h depends on q elements of X_i, at any time step k, the integration of the information from the corresponding measurement requires to update only q entries of ξ_i and q^2 entries of Σ_i (actually even less $\left(\frac{q(q+1)}{2}\right)$ because of the symmetry of Σ_i). Furthermore, the overall complexity is proportional to q^2. In the assumption 1 we suppose that q is independent of the size of X_i. Therefore, if we suppose that the mean value $\overline{\mu}_i$ is available (assumption 2) the cost to implement the equations (1) and (2) is independent of the size of X_i. In the following we will suppose that the state recovery problem is solved, i.e. we suppose that the assumption 2 is always satisfied. In (6) it is shown that it is possible to recover the mean value in a constant-time but its value will be approximated (see (6) for more details). Moreover, at any time, the robot typically makes a limited number, q, of relative observations to individual landmarks, i.e. a limited number of elements of the state X_i. This means that the assumption 1 is satisfied. From property 1 we obtain that the ESDF observation update task has a constant-time computational cost.

3.2 Using relative coordinates in ESDF

In this subsection we describe how to use the relative coordinates in the ESDF framework. In particular, we define the new coordinates to represent the same quantities estimated by ESDF, i.e. the robot poses and the landmark locations.

Before introducing the new coordinates, we define the structure of the new estimated state as it follows:

$$D_i^T = \left(D_i^{R^T} D_i^{L^T} \right) \tag{8}$$

where D_i^R contains all the stored robot poses, and D_i^L contains all the landmark locations.

3.2.1 Robot pose coordinates

Instead of defining the robot poses in a common global reference frame, each robot pose is defined in the frame of the robot at the previous time step. Let us indicate with d_i^R the robot pose at the time step k in the reference of the robot at the time step $k-1$, i.e. $x_i = x_{i-1} \oplus d_i^R$, where $\oplus$ is the composition operator between two robot poses. Therefore, the portion D_i^R of the estimated state has the following structure:

$$D_i^{R^T} = (d_i^{R^T} d_{i-1}^{R^T} \cdots d_1^{R^T}) \tag{9}$$

Now, let us focus on the robot motion function f, defined in (5). It describes the relation between the current robot pose x_i with the old robot pose x_{i-1} and the proprioceptive measurement u_i, which is available at each time step. We can generally express this relation in the following way:

$$x_i = f(x_{i-1}, u_i + w_i) = x_{i-1} \oplus (u_i + w_i) \tag{10}$$

We are assuming that the proprioceptive measurements contain the necessary information to provide the shift and the rotation of the robot occurred at every step. This is for instance the case of the wheel encoders. From the definition of the new coordinates of the robot pose d_i^R and the equation (10) it follows that:

$$u_i = d_i^R + w_i \tag{11}$$

The expression in (11) allows us to consider u_i as a measurement of the estimated state. The idea is that the proprioceptive measurement can be considered as an observation of the estimated state: $u_i = \tilde{h}(D_i) + w_i$ and hence the proprioceptive measurement information can be integrated via the observation update defined in (1) and (2), applied to the measurement u_i. Furthermore, in our special case, the measurement function defined in (11) satisfies the hypothesis of sparse observation (assumption 1). This means that we can integrate the considered information with a constant-time computational cost.

3.2.2 Landmark coordinates

Instead of defining the coordinates of each landmark in a global and unique reference frame, the new state defines a given landmark by its coordinates in the frame of the robot pose where it was observed for the first time. Let us indicate with $d_i^{L_j}$ the coordinates of the landmark j in the reference attached to the robot pose at the time step k, i.e. we suppose that the landmark j is observed at the time step k for the first time. When the robot, at a given time step $l > k$ observes again this landmark, the relative measurement can be expressed by the following expression:

$$z_l = h(x_l, m_j) \tag{12}$$

where m_j represents the coordinates of the landmark j in the global frame. Since we are considering a relative measurement, the inputs of the function h in (12) can be expressed in any reference frame (provided that it is the same for both inputs). By choosing the frame attached to the robot pose x_i we have:

$$z_l = h(d_{i+1}^R \oplus \cdots \oplus d_l^R, d_i^{L_j}) \tag{13}$$

With the exception of the loop closure, the function h depends on a number of elements of the estimated state which is independent of the size of the environment. To this regard, a loop closure event is defined as follows.

Definition 2 (Loop Closure) *The loop closure is the re-observation of a landmark after a while large enough to have at least one of the two following conditions:*

- $l - i$ *i.e. the number of elements* d^R_{i+q} $(q = 1, \ldots, l - i)$ *in (13), is large enough to make the execution of the observation update not possible in real time;*
- *the linearization of (13) makes the estimation process inconsistent.*

In order to detect the previous two conditions we propose the following criteria.
Regarding the first condition, we simply set a threshold on the computational time. As soon as the time required by the information filter to integrate a landmark re-observation exceeds this threshold, we consider the re-observation a loop closure.
Regarding the second condition, we propose the following criterion. Since we base on local relative coordinates we expect the innovation norm $\| z_i - h(\overline{\mu}_i) \|$ will be bounded by a given threshold. Once defined σ^2 as the max eigenvalue of the innovation covariance matrix, a possible threshold value can be 2σ. Indeed, in a linear estimation process we know that the mentioned norm is bounded by 2σ with 0.95 likelihood. On the other hand, the non linearities could lead the innovation norm to overtake this threshold. When the norm is really bounded we are sure about the estimation consistency. On the contrary, when the innovation norm overtakes the threshold, we cannot say the same. Thus, this overtake event can be considered as a loop closure. Unfortunately, since we base on the information filter, the innovation covariance matrix is not available. However, basing on the measurements covariance matrices, we can build an approximated innovation covariance matrix whose norm is larger than that of the real one. In this way, we have a consistent threshold since it is larger than the theoretical one.
When a loop is closed, new coordinates corresponding to the re-observed landmark are introduced in the state. They are the coordinates of the landmark in the frame of the robot pose where the landmark is re-observed. Thus, in this approach there are landmarks whose configuration is defined in more than one frame. This means that there are geometrical dependencies among state elements. These geometrical dependencies contain the information gained at the loop closure. We can say that by adding redundant coordinates we just freeze the loop closure information in these geometrical dependencies. This allows us to maintain the estimation process of the relative coordinates consistent and totally unaffected by the system non linearities. The exploitation of the information at the loop closure, namely of the previous geometrical dependencies, will be performed separately by a suitable non linear optimizer. We point out that this optimization can be computed only once, even if more than one loop closure event occurs.

3.3 Combining ESDF with a non linear optimizer

The basic idea consists in introducing a cost function. Such a cost function must carry the loop closure information, which is kept by the geometrical dependencies among the estimated state elements. Hence, it must be based on this geometrical information.
In order to simplify the notation, let us indicate the estimated state D_i with r, the corresponding mean value with $\hat{r}$ and the information vector and matrix with ξ and Σ, respectively. Furthermore, we indicate with P the estimate error covariance matrix (i.e. inverse of Σ). We remark that both ξ and Σ are provided by our ESDF modification algorithm. Let us focus on the example represented in figure 1. When the robot re-observes a landmark a loop is closed. The blue edges and the red dashed one represent all the relative quantities carried by the estimated vector r. The quantity represented by the red dashed

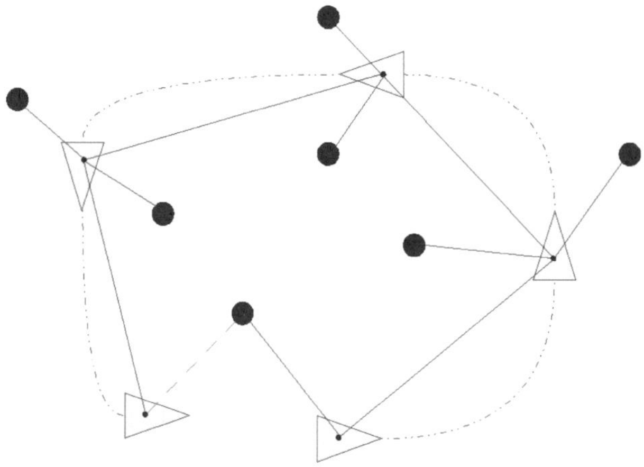

Fig. 1. The loop closure information. The blue discs represent the landmarks, the triangles represent the robot poses, the edges (blue and red dashed) represent the relative coordinates stored in the estimated state.

edge can be expressed as a function of some of the other quantities, i.e. there are geometrical dependencies among state elements. In order to exploit this information, we introduce a new state containing only independent quantities. Possible choices are:

- the independent relative coordinates (e.g. the ones represented by the blue edges in figure 1);
- the global coordinates of both robot poses and landmarks in a common frame.

Let us indicate this state with τ. As said, the quantities in r can be expressed as a function of the components of τ. Let us indicate this function with $\psi(\tau)$ (i.e. $r = \psi(\tau)$).
Our goal is to evaluate τ starting from Σ and ξ. Let us indicate the best evaluation of τ with τ_{best}. τ_{best} minimizes the following cost function:

$$c(\tau) = (\hat{r} - \psi(\tau))^T \; P^{-1} \; (\hat{r} - \psi(\tau)) \tag{14}$$

namely $\tau_{best} = argmin_{\tau} c(\tau)$.
By expanding the expression of $c(\tau)$ and dropping the part independent of τ, we obtain:

$$c(\tau) = \psi(\tau)^T \Sigma \, \psi(\tau) - 2\psi(\tau)^T \xi \tag{15}$$

This last expression is very important since it shows that the computation of the cost function is based on the information quantities ξ and Σ, namely it does not require to invert Σ.
Our method can now be completed by optimizing the cost function in (15) through a suitable optimization method. Literature provides lots of methods able to find a local minimum (or maximum) for a non linear function. We decided to use the well known *quasi-Newton*.
In order to use an optimization method we need to provide the cost function (15) computed for a given value of τ and the corresponding gradient. To do this, we must exactly define the meaning of the τ components and find the relation expressed by the function $\psi(\tau)$.
For our simulation, whose results can be found in section 5, we defined τ as the global coordinates of both the robot poses and the landmarks in a common frame. Therefore, the function $\psi(\tau)$ we obtained is made by inverse compositions which return the relative coordinates, given the absolute coordinates in τ. Moreover, we observed that such a function

is linear on the robot and landmarks location components of τ, and non linear on the robot orientation components. This makes the cost function in (15) quadratic for the first mentioned portion of τ and non linear for the second portion. Thanks to this particular property, we minimized on the first portion through a suitable algebraical method (i.e. by solving a system of linear equations). Then, we minimized on the second portion through the non linear optimizer. This algebraical manipulation reduced the dimension of the space in which the optimization algorithm had to move, making the optimization significantly faster.

4. Localization problem for MAV systems

4.1 A single MAV system

We provide here a mathematical description of our system. We introduce a global frame, whose z-axis is the vertical one. Let us consider a MAV equipped with IMU proprioceptive sensors (an accelerometer and a gyroscope) as well as some suitable exteroceptive sensors (GPS, range sensors). In the following we assume that the IMU data are unbiased. From a practical point of view, unbiased data can be obtained by continuously calibrating the IMU sensors (see for instance (11)). The configuration of the MAV is described by a vector $(r,v,\theta) \in \mathbf{R}^9$ where $r = (r_x,r_y,r_z) \in \mathbf{R}^3$ is the position, $v = (v_x,v_y,v_z) \in \mathbf{R}^3$ is the speed and $\theta = (\theta_{\mathrm{r}},\theta_{\mathrm{p}},\theta_{\mathrm{y}}) \in \mathbf{R}^3$ assignes the MAV orientation: θ_{r} is the roll angle, θ_{p} is the pitch angle and θ_{y} is the yaw angle. We will adopt lower case letters to express a quantity in the global frame, while capital letters for the same quantity exptressed in the local frame (i.e. the one attached to the MAV).The system description can be simplified adopting a quaternions framework. We recall that the quaternions space $\mathbf{H}$ is the noncommutative set of elements

$$\mathbf{H} = \left\{ q_t + q_x i + q_y j + q_z k : \quad q_t, q_x, q_y, q_z \in \mathbf{R}, \quad i^2 = j^2 = k^2 = ijk = -1 \right\}.$$

For an arbitrary quaternion $q = q_t + q_x i + q_y j + q_z k$, we define the conjugate element $q^* = q_t - q_x i - q_y j - q_z k$ and the norm $||q|| = \sqrt{qq^*} = \sqrt{q^*q} = \sqrt{q_t^2 + q_x^2 + q_y^2 + q_z^2}$.
Denoting by A,Ω the accelerometer and the gyroscope values respectively and by a_g the gravity acceleration (i.e. $a_g = -(0,0,g)$ with $g \simeq 9.81 m/s^2$), the continuous-time dynamics of the MAV is given by the following system of ordinary differential equations

$$\dot{r} = v \tag{16}$$

$$\dot{v} = q \cdot A \cdot q^* + a_g \tag{17}$$

$$\dot{q} = \frac{1}{2} q \cdot \Omega \tag{18}$$

where r,v,Ω,A are purely imaginary quaternions, while q is a unitary quaternion. The following relations for roll, pitch and yaw angles $\theta_{\mathrm{r}},\theta_{\mathrm{p}},\theta_{\mathrm{y}}$ hold

$$\theta_{\mathrm{r}} = \frac{q_t q_x + q_y q_z}{1 - 2(q_x^2 + q_y^2)}$$

$$\theta_{\mathrm{p}} = q_t q_y - q_x q_z$$

$$\theta_{\mathrm{y}} = \frac{q_t q_z + q_y q_x}{1 - 2(q_y^2 + q_z^2)}.$$

During the exploration, the MAV performs measurements thanks to its exteroceptive sensors equipment; such measurements can be individual (i.e. GPS-based measurements) as well as relative to other MAVs poses or to the position of fixed landmarks. The general single MAV observation equation is given by

$$z = h(r,v,q) \tag{19}$$

where $h(\cdot,\cdot,\cdot)$ is a known function.
In the case the exteroceptive sensor is a GPS, the observation equation is very simple as it is linear

$$z_{GPS} = r. \tag{20}$$

4.1.1 Estimation with the EIF: the integration of the proprioceptive data

Let us introduce the delayed-state

$$X_i = (r_0, q_0, r_1, ..., r_i, q_i)$$

containing all MAV poses until the i-th time step. The discretization of the dynamics equations over a Δt time-step interval gives

$$r_{i+1} = r_i + v_i \Delta t \tag{21}$$

$$v_{i+1} = v_i + q_i \cdot \int_i^{i+\Delta t} A dt \cdot q_i^* + a_g \Delta t \tag{22}$$

$$q_{i+1} = q_i + \frac{1}{2} q_i \cdot \int_i^{i+\Delta t} \Omega dt \tag{23}$$

From Equation (21) we can get

$$v_i = (r_{i+1} - r_i)/\Delta t$$

and hence the following recursive formula holds

$$r_{i+1} = 2r_i - r_{i-1} + \Delta t \left(q_i \cdot \int_i^{i+\Delta t} A dt \cdot q_i^* + a_g \Delta t \right), \tag{24}$$

corresponding to a second order continuous-time evolution. The system dynamics can be written in terms of delayed-states as

$$X_{i+1} = \mathcal{F}(X_i),$$

where $\mathcal{F}$ is a suitable function obtained from (23)-(24). Setting

$$\tilde{A}_i = \int_i^{i+\Delta t} A dt \tag{25}$$

and

$$\tilde{\Omega}_i = \int_i^{i+\Delta t} \Omega dt, \tag{26}$$

the proprioceptive measurements can be regarded as delayed-state dependent functions:

$$\tilde{A}_i = h_A(r_{i-2}, r_{i-1}, r_i, q_i) = \frac{q_i^*(-a_g \Delta t^2 + r_i - 2r_{i-1} + r_{i-2}) q_i}{\Delta t}$$

$$\tilde{\Omega}_i = h_\Omega(q_{i-1}, q_i) = 2 q_{i-1}^* (q_i - q_{i-1}).$$

In other words, $\tilde{A}_i$ and $\tilde{\Omega}_i$ are functions of the state X_i to be estimated; moreover, since we are considering the discrete dynamics given by (23)-(24), there is no need to include the MAV speed v into the state vector X_i.
Due to these considerations, we are allowed to integrate proprioceptive data using (1)-(2) instead of (3)-(4), with a consequent reduction of computational cost in the estimation algorithm.
For nonlinear measurements equation (2) involves the mean value and hence information matrix inversion is required; nevertheless in many situation, due to the sparsity of such matrix, a partial state recovery is sufficient in order to guarantee a good estimate (see (6)). Whole state recovering can be obtained using for example the Conjugate Gradients algorithm (see (25)) or the Givens rotations factorization (see (14)). We point out that at any update step, i.e. when a true exteroceptive measurement is performed, the size of the delayed-state vector X increases of $3+4=7$.

4.1.2 Projection filter: integration of ideal constraints

As mentioned in the introduction, the quaternion structure is redundant for the problem we are considering and this may lead to a loss of information. To avoid this problem we have assumed that the quaternion q is unitary. On the other hand, if the discrete dynamics (23) is considered, such property is no longer preserved. Anyway, we can take into account the norm invariance of q_i imposing an ideal constraint with a fake observation given by the function

$$h_0(q) = 1 - q_t^2 + q_x^2 + q_y^2 + q_z^2;$$

in other words, we can regard the norm constraint as the measurement

$$z_i = h_0(q_i) = 0.$$

Integration of such fake measurement can be performed with the projection filter (see (21)).

4.2 The cooperative case

We consider now the problem of cooperaive localization for a multi robot system.

4.2.1 The system

We consider now a fleet of $N > 1$ MAVs, each one having the characteristics described in Section 4.1. Let us denote by $(r^{(k)}, q^{(k)})$ the coordinates of the k-th MAV; the discrete dynamics is given by

$$r_{i+1}^{(k)} = 2r_i^{(k)} - r_{i-1}^{(k)} + \Delta t \left(q_i^{(k)} \cdot \int_i^{i+\Delta t} A^{(k)} dt \cdot (q_i^{(k)})^* + a_g \Delta t \right) \tag{27}$$

$$q_{i+1}^{(k)} = q_i^{(k)} + \frac{1}{2} q_i^{(k)} \cdot \int_i^{i+\Delta t} \Omega^{(k)} dt. \tag{28}$$

Each MAV, in addition to the measurement model (19), may perform relative observation; the general multi robot observation equation can be written as

$$z_i^{(k)} = h^{(k)}(r_i^{(1)}, q_i^{(1)}, \ldots, r_i^{(k)}, q_i^{(k)}, \ldots, r_i^{(N)}, q_i^{(N)}). \tag{29}$$

Simple and common examples of relative observations are distance measures. If the k-th MAV measures its own distance from the j-th MAV, the observation is given by

$$z_i^{(k)} = (r_{i,x}^{(k)} - r_{i,x}^{(j)})^2 + (r_{i,y}^{(k)} - r_{i,y}^{(j)})^2 + (r_{i,z}^{(k)} - r_{i,z}^{(j)})^2.$$

4.2.2 The distributed EIF

When the exploration starts, each MAV begins to integrate the information provided by its own sensors by equation (1)-(2) as described before. In particular for any measurement, the incoming data are stored in the bottom-right block of the information matrix and, as a consequence, in the last entries of the information vector:

$$\Sigma_{i-1} \to \Sigma_i = \begin{pmatrix} \Sigma_{i-1} & 0^{7(i-1)\times 7} \\ 0^{7\times 7(i-1)} & 0^{7\times 7} \end{pmatrix} + \begin{pmatrix} 0^{7(i-3)\times 7(i-3)} & 0^{7(i-3)\times 21} \\ 0^{21\times 7(i-3)} & \Sigma_{obs} \end{pmatrix}$$

$$\xi_{i-1} \to \xi_i = \begin{pmatrix} \xi_{i-1} \\ 0^{7\times 1} \end{pmatrix} + \begin{pmatrix} 0^{7(i-3)\times 1} \\ \xi_{obs} \end{pmatrix}.$$

Suppose that after i_1 updating time-steps for the j_1-th MAV and i_2 steps for the j_2-th MAV a relative measurement occurs and for sake of semplicity suppose that $j_1 < j_2$. Each MAV has to increase the size of the information matrix and information vector in order to store the new data. The process is carried out following the steps described below:

1. *State augmentation.* The states of the two MAVs are increased in order to have the same size $7(i_1 + i_2)$; this can be done adding a suitable number of zeros in the information matrix and information vector.

$$\Sigma_{(j_1),i_1} \to \begin{pmatrix} \Sigma_{(j_1),i_1} & 0^{7i_1\times 7i_2} \\ 0^{7i_2\times 7i_1} & 0^{7i_2\times 7i_2} \end{pmatrix}, \quad \xi_{(j_1),i_1} \to \begin{pmatrix} \xi_{(j_1),i_1} \\ 0^{7i_2\times 1} \end{pmatrix}$$

$$\Sigma_{(j_2),i_2} \to \begin{pmatrix} 0^{7i_1\times 7i_1} & 0^{7i_1\times 7i_2} \\ 0^{7i_2\times 7i_1} & \Sigma_{(j_2),i_2} \end{pmatrix}, \quad \xi_{(j_2),i_2} \to \begin{pmatrix} 0^{7i_1\times 1} \\ \xi_{(j_2),i_2} \end{pmatrix}$$

2. *Relative estimation.* The information from relative observations are integrated using the standard update equations (1)-(2). Correlation between the estimates on the last poses of the MAVs may appear, so that the updated matrices may be not block-diagonal.

$$\Sigma_{(j_1),i_1} \to \begin{pmatrix} \Sigma_{(j_1),i_1} & * \\ ** & * \end{pmatrix}, \quad \xi_{(j_1),i_1} \to \begin{pmatrix} \xi_{(j_1),i_1} \\ ** \end{pmatrix}$$

$$\Sigma_{(j_2),i_2} \to \begin{pmatrix} * & * \\ ** & \Sigma_{(j_2),i_2} \end{pmatrix}, \quad \xi_{(j_2),i_2} \to \begin{pmatrix} * \\ \xi_{(j_2),i_2} \end{pmatrix}$$

3. *Data fusion.* A communication is established between the MAVs and they exchange their stored data. The data fusion scheme is a non negligible theoretical issue: as a matter of fact, if the process is carried out taking simply the sum of the contributions from each MAV, estimation errors may arise due to adding several times the same information. Following (1), we have adopted a fusion algorithm based on a convex combination of the data:

$$\Sigma_{(j_1),i_1} \rightarrow \omega\Sigma_{(j_1),i_1} + (1-\omega)\Sigma_{(j_2),i_2}, \qquad \xi_{(j_1),i_1} \rightarrow \omega\xi_{(j_1),i_1} + (1-\omega)\xi_{(j_2),i_2}$$

$$\Sigma_{(j_2),i_2} \rightarrow (1-\omega)\Sigma_{(j_1),i_1} + \omega\Sigma_{(j_2),i_2}, \qquad \xi_{(j_2),i_2} \rightarrow (1-\omega)\xi_{(j_1),i_1} + \omega\xi_{(j_2),i_2}$$

As proved in (12), for any $0 < \omega < 1$, the above convex combinations lead to unbiased and consistent estimates, i.e. no overconfident estimate is performed and there is no overlapping of information.

5. Performance Evaluation

In order to validate our approach we have performed simulations. We have considered a conventional scenario defined by a few parameters which regard the robot(s) perception and the environment properties. All our simulations are implemented in Matlab and tested on a computer with 1 Intel Pentium CPU M 1.70GHz, 512MB of memory.

5.1 Single robot SLAM

5.1.1 Simulated scenario

In our simulations we consider a two-wheels robot moving in a $110m$x$110m$ rectangular area in which many point landmarks are randomly distributed. Let us indicate the average landmark density with ρ_L, the robot average speed with v, and the distance traveled by the robot with d. The data associations ere supposed to be given. We consider a robot equipped with wheel encoders which provide the proprioceptive measurements. We base on the Chong-Kleeman ((3)) error model. According to this model, the translation of the right/left wheel as estimated by the odometry sensors is generated as a Gaussian random quantity satisfying the following relations:

$$\begin{aligned} \delta\rho^{R/L} &= \delta\rho^{aR/L}\delta_{R/L} + \nu^{R/L} \\ \nu^{R/L} &\sim N(0, K|\delta\rho^{aR/L}|) \end{aligned} \tag{30}$$

In other words, both $\delta\rho^R$ and $\delta\rho^L$ are assumed Gaussian random variables, whose mean values are given by the actual values (respectively, $\delta\rho^{aR}$ and $\delta\rho^{aL}$), and whose variance also increases linearly with the travelled distance. In our simulation we set $K = 0.00001m$, which corresponds to an indoor environment (19). Finally, the frequency is $100Hz$.
The simulated exteroceptive sensor provides bearings and ranges of the landmarks whose distance does not exceed $12m$. Furthermore, the sensor angle of view is $360deg$. Both the bearings and the distances are generated as Gaussian quantities with variances equal to σ_R^2 and σ_B^2, respectively. The frequency is $0.2Hz$.

5.1.2 Results

Figures 2(a)-2(b) illustrate the results provided by a given simulation in which the robot closes a loop in counter clockwise direction. Let us point out that the loop closure does not consist of the trajectory closure but it consists of the re-observation of landmarks located close to the starting point. We implemented both our method and the ESDF one. As said in section 3.3, the minimization is carried out through a *quasi-Newton* method. We set $\sigma_B = 1deg$, $\sigma_R = 1cm$, $\rho_L = 0.02m^{-2}$, $v = 1ms^{-1}$, $d = 180m$. The simulation time is $T_s = 180s$.
Figures 2(a) and 2(b) show the results obtained before the loop closure. In each figure, we represent the true robot trajectory and the true landmark locations (ground truth) by a

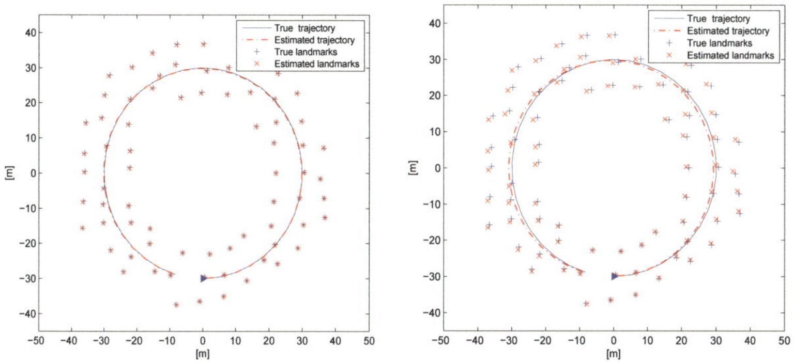

(a) Simulation 1: estimation results of our method before the loop closure.

(b) Simulation 1: ESDF estimation results before the loop closure.

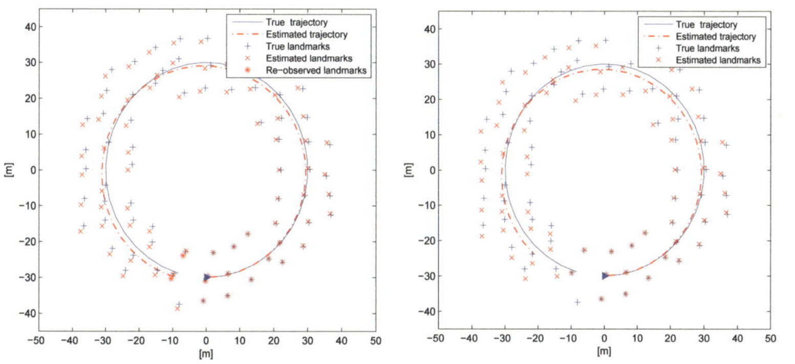

(c) Simulation 1: estimation results of our method after the loop closure.

(d) Simulation 1: ESDF estimation results after the loop closure.

Fig. 2. Pictures for the results of Simulation 1

solid blue line and cross blue markers, respectively. Moreover, the estimated trajectory and landmark locations are represented by a dash-dotted red line and red x-markers, respectively. In order to provide quantitative results, we consider the error on the estimated map by computing for all the landmarks the distance between the estimated location and the corresponding true location. Then, the mean value on all the landmarks is taken. We refer to this mean value as the *map error* (E_m^{bl} before the loop closure and E_m^{al} after the loop closure). The behavior of our estimation process and that of the ESDF one are very similar. However, the map errors are $E_m^{bl} = 1.30m$ for our method and $E_m^{bl} = 2.02m$ for the ESDF. Therefore, our method shows a better behavior also before the loop closure.

Figures 2(c) and 2(d) show the results after the loop closure. The correction we obtained through the non linear optimizer clearly outperforms the one computed by the ESDF method. This is confirmed by the map errors: $E_m^{al} = 0.15m$ for our method and $E_m^{al} = 1.01m$ for the ESDF. The total computation time needed for the estimation process is $Tc = 16.20s$ for our method (5.45s for the filtering process and 10.75s for the optimization) and $Tc = 39.67s$ for the ESDF.

The results provided by a second simulation are shown in Figures 3(a)-3(b): the robot closes a loop in counter clockwise direction and than goes on re-traversing a region for a long time. The parameters of this simulation are: $\sigma_B = 1deg$, $\sigma_R = 1cm$, $\rho_L = 0.02m^{-2}$, $v = 1.2ms^{-1}$,

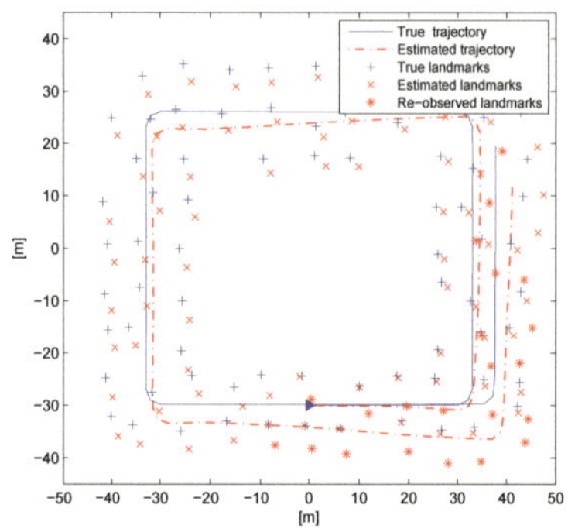

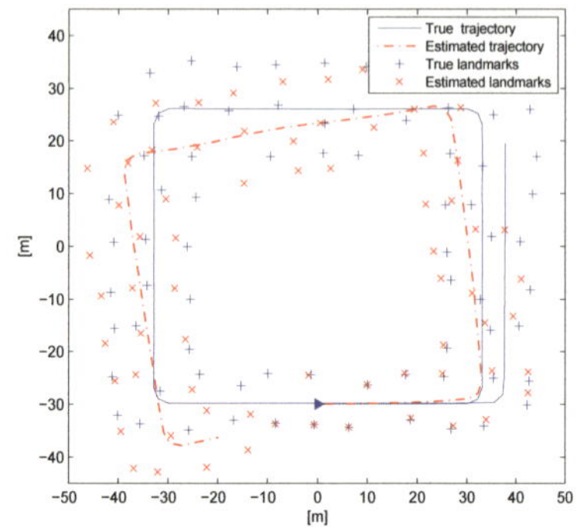

(a) Simulation 2: estimation results of our method before the loop closure.

(b) Simulation 2: ESDF estimation results before the loop closure.

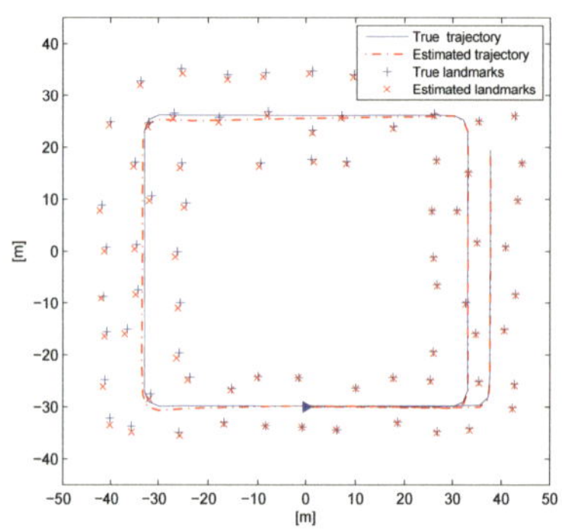

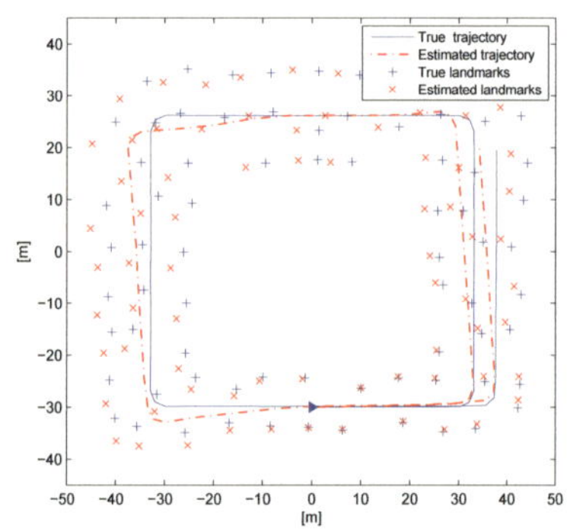

(c) Simulation 2: estimation results of our method after the loop closure.

(d) Simulation 2: ESDF estimation results after the loop closure.

Fig. 3. Pictures for the results of Simulation 2

$d = 325m$. The simulation time is $T_s = 270s$. Figs. 3(a) and 3(b) show the two methods before exploiting the loop closure information. Concerning our method, as said in section 3.3, a loop closure does not necessary activate the optimization . Indeed, in this case the estimation process goes on considering the re-observed landmarks as new landmarks. In Figure 3-(a) these phantom landmarks are represented by star red markers. As the figures clearly show, our estimation process outperforms the ESDF one. This is confirmed by the map errors: $E_m^{bl} = 3.17m$ for our method and $E_m^{bl} = 3.91m$ for the ESDF.
Figure 3(c) shows the results obtained through the non linear optimizer which is activated only once, after a long time from the first loop closure. Moreover, Figure 3(d) shows the results of the correction computed by the ESDF technique after the loop closure. The comparison of these two last figures clearly shows the success of our hybrid approach in improving the ESDF performances. This is confirmed by the map errors: $E_m^{al} = 0.38m$ for our method and $E_m^{al} = 0.58m$ for the ESDF.
The total computation time needed for the estimation process is $Tc = 46.36s$ for our method (13.67s for the filtering process and 32.70s for the optimization) and $Tc = 91.44s$ for the ESDF.

5.2 Cooperative MAV localization

5.2.1 The simulated environment

The trajectories of the MAVs are generated randomly and independently one each other. In particular, for every MAV, the motion is generated by generating randomly the linear and angular acceleration at $100Hz$. Specifically, at each time step, the three components of the linear and the angular acceleration are generated as Gaussian independent variables with mean values μ_a and $\mu_{\dot{\Omega}}$ and with covariance matrices P_a and $P_{\dot{\Omega}}$. By performing many simulations we remarked that the precision of the proposed strategy is almost independent of all these parameters. The simulations provided in this section are obtained with the following settings: $\mu_a = \mu_{\dot{\Omega}} = [000]^T$,

$$P_a = \begin{bmatrix} (5ms^{-2})^2 & 0 & 0 \\ 0 & 0 & 0 \\ 0 & 0 & 0 \end{bmatrix}$$

and

$$P_{\dot{\Omega}} = \begin{bmatrix} (10deg\, s^{-2})^2 & 0 & 0 \\ 0 & (10deg\, s^{-2})^2 & 0 \\ 0 & 0 & (10deg\, s^{-2})^2 \end{bmatrix}$$

We adopt many different values for the initial MAV positions orientations and speeds. We also consider different scenarios corresponding to a different number of MAVs.

Starting from the accomplished trajectories, the true angular speed and the linear acceleration are computed at each time step of $0.01s$ (respectively, at the time step i, we denote them with Ω_i^{true} and A_i^{true}). Starting from them, the IMU sensors are simulated by generating randomly the angular speed and the linear acceleration at each step according to the following: $\Omega_i = N\left(\Omega_i^{true}, P_{\Omega_i}\right)$ and $A_i = N\left(A_i^{true} - A_{g\,i}, P_{A_i}\right)$ where N indicates the Normal distribution whose first entry is the mean value and the second one its covariance matrix and P_{Ω_i} and P_{A_i} are the covariance matrices characterizing the accuracy of the IMU; finally, A_g is the gravity acceleration expressed in the local frame. In all the simulations we set both P_{A_i} and P_{Ω_i} diagonal matrices. In the results here provided they are set as follows:

$$P_{A_i} = \begin{bmatrix} (0.1ms^{-2})^2 & 0 & 0 \\ 0 & (0.1ms^{-2})^2 & 0 \\ 0 & 0 & (0.1ms^{-2})^2 \end{bmatrix}$$

and

$$P_{\Omega_i} = \begin{bmatrix} (10deg\, s^{-1})^2 & 0 & 0 \\ 0 & (10deg\, s^{-1})^2 & 0 \\ 0 & 0 & (10deg\, s^{-1})^2 \end{bmatrix}$$

for every step i.

The MAVs are also equipped with GPS and range sensors. The GPS provides the position of the MAV with a Gaussian error whose covariance is a diagonal matrix and whose components are equal to $25m^2$. The GPS data are delivered at $5Hz$. Finally, the range sensors provide the distances among the MAVs at $2Hz$ and the measurement errors are normally distributed with variance $(0.01m)^2$.

5.2.2 Results

We provide some of the results obtained with the previous settings and by simulating N MAVs. In particular, we consider the case of $N = 3$ and $N = 5$. Furthermore, we consider separately the cases when the estimation is performed by only integrating the IMU data, by combining the IMU data with the GPS data and by combining all the sensor data. Finally, in order to evaluate the benefit of using the projection filter discussed in Section 4.1.2, we consider separately the cases when this filter is adopted and when it is not adopted.
Figs. 5(a)-5(b) show the results obtained with three MAVs. The blue dots represent the ground truth. In Fig. 5(a) the magenta dots represent the GPS data and the black circles the trajectories estimated by only integrating the IMU data. It is clear that both IMU and GPS are very noisy and cannot be used separately to estimate the MAV trajectories. In Fig. 5(b) the green dots represent the trajectories estimated by fusing the IMU data and the GPS data with our proposed approach (EIF and projection filter). Finally, the red dots represent the result obtained by also fusing the range measurements. We remarked that the use of the range measurements further reduce the error. In particular, for the simulation in fig. 1a-b the position error averaged on all the three MAV and on all the time steps is equal to $0.6m$ without the range measurements and $0.45m$ with them. As expected, this improvement is still larger by increasing the number of MAVs. In Figs. 4(c)-4(d) the results obtained by using 5 MAVs is shown. The position error obtained by also fusing the range measurements reduces to $0.2m$.
Fig. 4 shows the benefit of using the Projection filter discussed in Section 4.1.2. In particular, in Fig. 4(a) the red circles represent the trajectories estimated by fusing all the sensor data and by running the Projection Filter at $5Hz$ while in Fig. 4(b) the red circles represent the trajectories estimated without the use of the Projection Filter. As in the previous figures, the ground truth is represented with blue dots and the black dots represent the trajectories obtained by a simple integration of the IMU data.

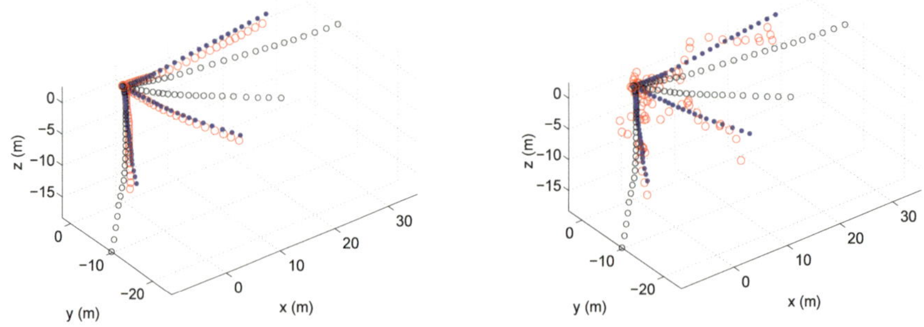

(a) (b)

Fig. 4. Blue points represent true MAVs trajectories, balck circles are the estimated trajectories via odometry and red circles are the estimated trajectories with the EIF. Figure 4(a) represents the simulation of a 3-MAV system; Figure 4(b) represents the same scenario without taking into account the information provided by the projection filter.

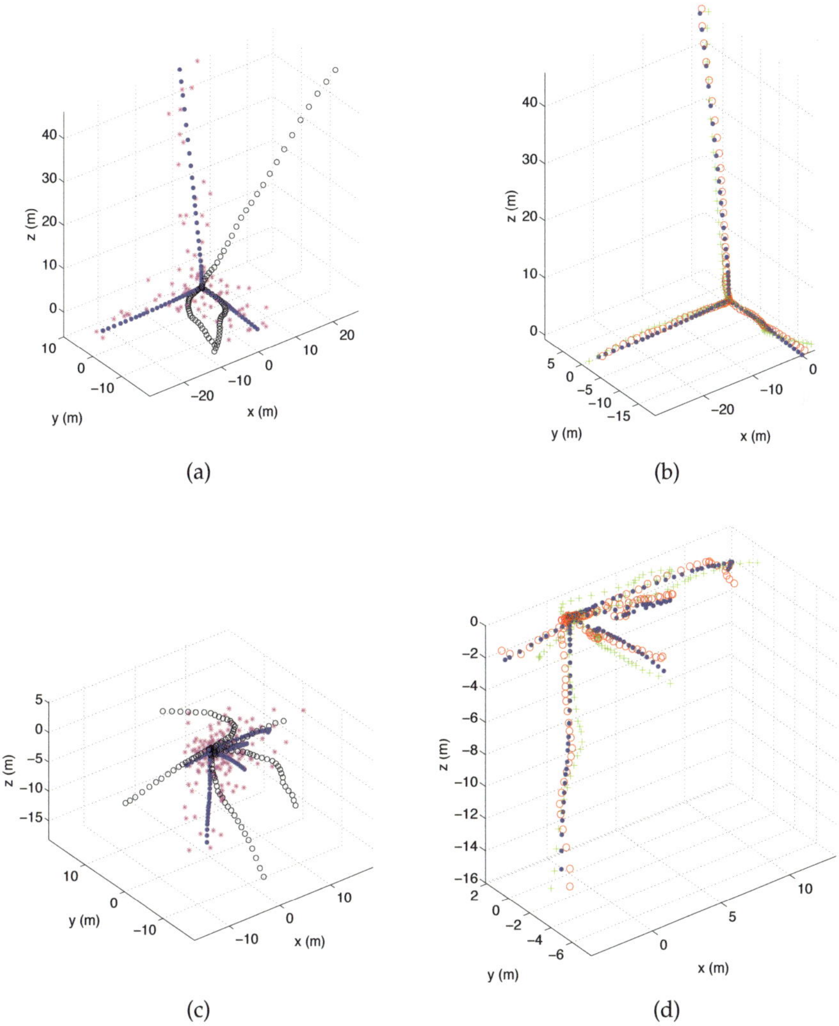

Fig. 5. Blue points represent true MAVs trajectories, black circles are the trajectories with only odometric estimates, magenta stars are the GPS data, green stars are the trajectory estimates without taking into account relative observations and red circles are the estimates with the complete distributed EIF. Figures 5(a)-5(b) are the simulation of 3-MAV scenario, while in Figures 5(c)-5(d) is plotted the evolution of a 5-MAV system.

6. Conclusions

In this chapter we considered the problem of cooperative localization and SLAM by using an Extended Information Filter.
We started by considering the ESDF technique (6) which makes possible a real-time/real-world implementation for any kind of environment. The only drawback of this technique is the use of the linear approximation which could become not consistent when the environment is large enough.
Therefore, we proposed a method able to combine a suitable modification of the ESDF with a non linear optimizer. This solution allows us to use the modified ESDF when the non linearities are negligible and to switch to the optimizer when the non linearities are not negligible.
Furthermore, we considered the cooperative case, i.e. when the estimation process is performed simultaneously by a team of agents. In this case, two original contributions have been introduced. The former consists of a simple trick which allowed us to avoid the equations which characterize the prediction phase of the extended information filter. In particular, the information contained in the data provided by the inertial sensors is exploited by using the equations which characterize the perception step of the EIF. This allowed us to easily distributing the entire estimation process over all the team members. The latter contribution is the use of a projection filter which allowed exploiting the information contained in the geometrical constraints which arise as soon as the MAV orientations are characterized by unitary quaternions.
The performance of the proposed approaches has been evaluated by using synthetic data.

7. Acknowledgment

The research leading to these results has received funding from the European Community's Seventh Framework Programme (FP7/2007-2013) under grant agreement n. 231855 (sFly).

8. References

[1] J. Capitan, L. Merino, F. Caballero and A. Ollero, Delayed-state Information Filter for Cooperative Decentralized Tracking, *ICRA*, 2009, Kobe, Japan, pages 3865-3870
[2] J.A. Castellanos, J. Neira and J.D. Tardos, Limits to Consistency of the EKF-based SLAM, *Intelligent Autonomous Vehicle*, 2004, Lisbon, Portugal
[3] K.S. Chong and L. Kleeman, Accurate Odometry and Error Modelling for a Mobile Robot, *IEEE International Conference on Robotics and Automation (ICRA97)*, 1997, Albuquerque, New Mexico, USA
[4] Crowley, J.L., (1989). World Modeling and Position Estimation for a Mobile Robot Using Ultrasonic Ranging. IEEE International Conference on Robotics and Automation (ICRA), Scottsdale, AZ
[5] Dissanayake, Newman, Clark, Durrant-Whyte and Csorba, 2001, A Solution to the Simultaneous Localization and Map Building (SLAM) problem, IEEE Trans. On Rob. And Aut. Vol 17, No.3, June 2001
[6] R.M. Eustice, H. Singh and J.J. Leonard, Exactly Sparse Delayed-State Filters for View-Based SLAM, *IEEE Trans. on Robotics*, vol. 22, n. 6, 2006, pages 1100-1114
[7] D. Fox, W. Burgard, H. Kruppa, S. Thrun, 2000, A Probabilistic Approach to Collaborative Multi-Robot Localization, Autonomous Robots 8, 2000, pages 325-344
[8] R. Grabowski, L.E. Navarro-Serment, C.J.J. Paredis, P.K. Khosla, 2000, Heterogeneous

Teams of Modular Robots for Mapping and Exploration, Autonomous Robots, Vol. 8, n. 3, June 200?, pages 325-344

[9] G. Grisetti, C. Stachniss, s. Grzonka and W. Burgard, A Tree Parametrization for Efficiently Computing Maximum Likelihood Maps Using Gradient Descent, *Robotics: Science and Systems (RSS07)*, 2007, Atlanta, Georgia, USA

[10] A. Howard, M.J. Mataric and G.S. Sukhatme, "Localization for Mobile Robot Teams Using Maximum Likelihood Estimation", *International Conference on Inteligent Robot and Systems (IROS02)*, Volume: 3 , 30 Sept.-5 Oct. 2002,Lausanne, pages 2849-2854

[11] E. Jones, A. Vedaldi and S. Soatto, Inertial Structure from Motion with Autocalibration, *ICCU Workshop*, 2007

[12] S.J. Julier and J.K. Uhlmann, A Non-divergent Estimation Algorithm in the Presence of Unknown Correlations, *American Control Conference*, 1997, Albuquerque, New Mexico, pages 2369-2373

[13] S.J. Julier and J.K. Uhlmann, A Counterexample to the Theory of Simoultaneous Localization and Map Building, *IEEE International Conference on Robotics and Automation (ICRA01)*, 2001, Seoul, Korea

[14] M. Kaess, A. Ranganathan and F. Dellaert, iSAM: Incremental Smoothing and Mapping, *IEEE Trans. on Robotics*, vol. 24, n.6, 2008, pages 1365-1378

[15] K. Kato, H. Ishiguro, M. Barth, "Identifying and Localizing Robots in a Multi-Robot System Environment" *International Conference on Inteligent Robot and Systems (IROS99)* 1999

[16] J.J. Leonard, H.F. Durrant-Whyte, "Directed Sonar Sensing for Mobile Robot Navigation," *Kluwer Academic Publishers*, Dordrecht, 1992

[17] A. Martinelli, F. Pont and R. Siegwart , "Multi-Robot Localization Using Relative Observations" *IEEE International Conference on Robotics and Automation (ICRA05)*, 2005, Barcellona, Spain

[18] A. Martinelli and R. Siegwart, Exploiting the Information at the Loop Closure in SLAM, *IEEE International Conference on Robotics and Automation (ICRA07)*, 2007, Rome, Italy

[19] A. Martinelli, N. Tomatis and R. Siegwart, Simultaneous Localization and Odometry Self-Calibbration for Mobile Robot, *Autonomous Robots*, 2007, 22, pp. 75-85

[20] A.I. Mourikis, S.I. Roumeliotis, "Optimal Sensing Strategies for Mobile Robot Formations: Resource-Constrained Localization", Robotics: Science and Systems June 8-11, 2005 Massachusetts Institute of Technology Cambridge, Massachusetts, USA

[21] P. Newman, On the structures and solution of simultaneous localization and mapping problem, PhD thesis, Australian Center for Field Robotics, Sidney, 1999

[22] E. Olson, J. Leonard and S. Teller, Fast Iterative Alignment of Pose Graphs with Poor Initial Estimates, *IEEE International Conference on Robotics and Automation (ICRA06)*, 2006, Orlando, Florida, USA

[23] I.M. Rekleitis, G. Dudek and E.E. Milios, "Multi-robot cooperative localization: a study of trade-offs between efficiency and accuracy " *International Conference on Inteligent Robot and Systems (IROS02)* Lausanne, Switzerland

[24] S.I. Roumeliotis and G.A. Bekey, 2002, Distributed Multirobot Localization, IEEE Transaction On Robotics And Automation Vol 18, No.5, October 2002

[25] J. Schewchuk, An Introduction to Conjugate Gradient Method without Agonizing Pain, Carnegie-Mellon University, Pittsburgh, PA, Tech. Report CMU-CS-94-125, 1994

[26] Smith, Self, et al. (1988) "Estimating uncertain spatial relationships in robotics" *Uncertainty in Artificial Intelligence 2* Elsevier Science Pub: 435-461

[27] J.R. Spletzer and C.J. Taylor, "A Bounded Uncertainty Approach to Multi-Robot Localization" *International Conference on Inteligent Robot and Systems (IROS03)* Las Vegas, USA, 2003
[28] S. Thrun, W. Burgard and D. Fox, Probabilistic Robotics, MIT Press, Cambridge, MA, 2005

10

Multi-Robot SLAM: A Vision-Based Approach

Hassan Hajjdiab[1] and Robert Laganiere[2]
[1]*Abu Dhabi University*
[2]*University of Ottawa*
[1]*Abu Dhabi, United Arab Emirates*
[2]*Ottawa, Canada*

1. Introduction

The robot is said to be truly autonomous (Dissanayake et al. (2001)), if it has the ability to start at an unknown location in an unknown environment and then simultaneously build a map of the environment and localize it self in the map. Thus the robot has to solve the simultaneous localization and mapping (SLAM) problem. The information used are sequences of relative observations captured by the mobile robot. Many approaches has been proposed to solve the SLAM problem.

Se et al. (2001) proposed an approach for a robot equipped with a trinocular stereo system (Murray & Little (1998)) and an odometer. The algorithm starts by detecting feature points (Lowe (1999)) in the three images. Then these feature points are matched using the epipolar and disparity constraints thats exist between the three cameras. Assuming known camera intrinsic parameters, the 3D position of each matched feature point is estimated. As the robot moves, the odometry readings are used to provide a rough estimate about the motion. This estimate can be employed in matching feature points among consecutive frames. The 3D position of each newly detected feature point is estimated and the motion of the robot is localized using a least-squares minimization scheme (Lowe (1991)). Finally, a map is built for the 3D positions of the detected feature points and the location graph of the robot is computed.

Other SLAM methods are based on evaluating some probabilistic models of the robot motion and sensed data from the environment. It is assumed that the robot can sense landmarks relative to its local coordinate frame. The landmarks may be naturally occurring in the environment like trees or artificially added like steel poles.

Smith & Cheeseman (1986) use extended Kalman filters (EKF) to estimate the posterior distribution over the robot pose. The problem they solved can be stated as follows: Given a measurement of the environment $\mathbf{z}^t = [z_1, z_2, ..., z_t]$ and a set of control inputs $\mathbf{u}^t = [u_1, u_2, ..., u_t]$, determine the robot pose $\mathbf{s}^t$ and the location of all the k landmarks $\mathbf{m} = [m_1, m_2, ..., m_k]$. In probabilistic terms, this can be expressed as the posterior:

$$p(\mathbf{s}^t, \mathbf{m}/\mathbf{z}^t, \mathbf{u}^t) \tag{1}$$

where the superscript ^{t} refer to a set of variables at time t.

The extended kalman filters (EKFs) are relatively slow when estimating maps with very large number of landmarks. Murphy (99) and Montemerlo et al. (03) proposed more capable approach. They proposed algorithms to solve the SLAM problem by integrating particle filter and Kalman filter representation to solve the posterior function in Equation(1).

When a team of robots are sharing the same worksite, the SLAM problem becomes more challenging. The robots has to build a joint map of the environment and be able to localize their positions in the joint map in order to coordinate the navigation and minimize the overlap in information.

Thrun et al. (2000) presented a multi-robot SLAM algorithm based on likelihood maximization to find the maps that are maximally consistent with the sensor data. The sensor data used are laser scanners to sense the environment and odometers to estimate the robot motion. The exact initial pose of all robots relative to each other is assumed to be known. The localization process starts as follows: Each robot collects a sequence of its own odometry and sensor measurements (like laser scans). Using these measurements, each robot incrementally constructs a maximum likelihood estimate for its position and a maximum likelihood estimate for the location of surrounding objects and a posterior function to determine its location in the map. To build a joint map, the posterior estimation component is used. The relative location of robots is unknown; however, each robot in the team starts within a map of a specific robot called the team leader. Using the posterior estimation, each robot localizes it self in the team leader's map and thus a unified map for the team is built.

Simmons et al. (2000) introduced similar approach but with known approximate initial pose of the robots (within 1 meter distance and 20° orienation). Each robot in the team incrementally constructs the likelihood and posterior estimates as in the approach proposed by Thrun et al. (2000).

However, to build a joint map, each robot in the team sends its sensed data (laser range scans and odometer readings) to the team leader. Since the initial approximate pose of each robot is known, the team leader localizes the robots relative to each other.

When the initial pose of the robots is unknown, an important question is raised:

> *If two robots in the team sensing similar data in the environment, are they actually sensing the same part of the environment or are they sensing different parts that look alike?*

Liu & Thrun (2003) presented an approach to solve the multi-robot SLAM problem assuming unknown initial positions and ambiguous landmarks. Each robot in the team builds a local map similar to ones discussed in Thrun et al. (2000) and Simmons et al. (2000). The joint map is built by fusing the maps acquired by the robots into one map. First, the landmarks between different local maps are matched. Correspondences found in this matching process provide an estimate of the rotation and translation between local maps. Using this estimate, a global map of the environment may be built by estimating a posterior similar to the one defined in Equation(1) evaluated over all robot poses and all landmarks from all available data. Liu and Thrun applied the algorithm using a single vehicle equipped with laser range finder and an odometer in an outdoor environment. Features in the map are the stems of trees detected by the laser range finder. The multi-robot case is demonstrated by splitting the data acquired by the vehicle into 8 disjoint sequences and then the proposed multi-robot SLAM algorithm is applied.

In this chapter, we propose to solve the multi-robot SLAM problem by using a collection of sparse views of the scene. The originality of our approach is that it uses purely vision sensors (single camera on each robot) and that no special landmarks are assumed to exist in the environment. Moreover, no assumptions are made on the initial relative pose of the robots. The robot location is estimated from sparse views, this makes the estimation much more accurate. In contrast, method based on small incremental displacements are more affected by noise and inaccuracies and are thus more subject to error accumulation. In our proposed

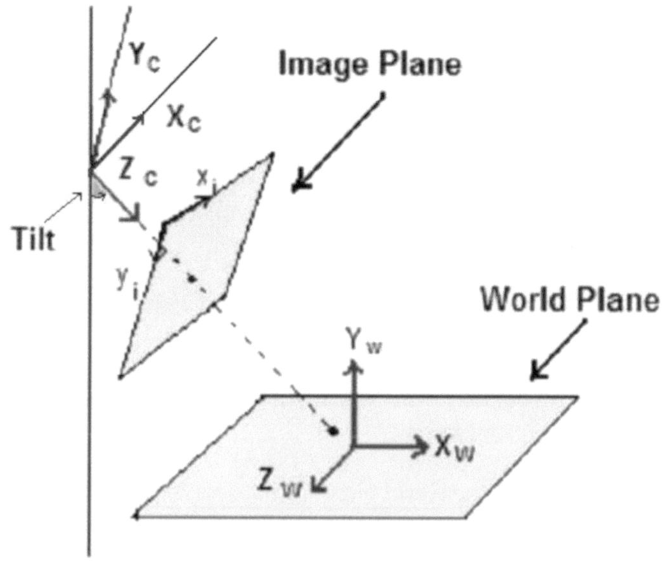

Fig. 1. Geometry of the system.

algorithm, each robot in the team starts at an arbitrary unknown location and incrementally builds a local map of the environment with the ability to localize itself in the map. When an overlap occurs between any two robots, a joint map can be built between them and the two robots are able to localize themselves in the joint map for all their previous as well as future locations without the need for a new overlap. Under this approach a joint map of the team can be built if each robot has at least one overlap with any other robot in the team.
In our approach we simply assume that each robot is equipped with a single camera and the robots are operating on a planar surface. We also assume that the height of the camera with respect to the ground plane as well as its orientation are known. Note that the tilt angle does not have to be accurate since this one is simply used as an initial approximation and will be re-estimated by the algorithm. However, a good accuracy in the height measure could be required since robot localization will be specified in terms of height units.

2. Robot localization

2.1 Estimating the camera motion

In our work, the overhead views are used to match images and get the homography. The matching is done without depending on known patterns, moving objects on the plane or manual registration, instead the algorithm is based on features that have to be matched between views. However when a plane is observed by a tilted camera the features lying on it are subject to important perspective deformations. In the context of sparse views, this makes the features difficult to match using the usual correlation schemes. Applying the overhead view transformation will undo the perspective deformation which will make the apparent features differing only by a similarity transformation.
Figure 1 shows the structure of the coordinate systems of the world, camera and image coordinate systems. The ground plane surface is at $Y = 0$, the optical axis of the camera is aligned with the Z axis and the camera is rotated around the X axis by an angle α. The camera height from the world plane is h.

(a) (b)

Fig. 2. Overhead view: (a) The image of a planar surface taken with tilt = 33°, (b) The corresponding generated overhead view.

The projective relation between the world plane and the corresponding overhead image point can be represented as follows:

$$\begin{bmatrix} x_i \\ y_i \\ 1 \end{bmatrix} = \mathbf{H}_O \begin{bmatrix} X_W \\ Z_W \\ 1 \end{bmatrix} \tag{2}$$

When the geometry of the system is as shown in Figure 1, the 3×3 homography matrix $\mathbf{H}_O$ can be described as follows (Laganière (2000)):

$$\mathbf{H}_O = \begin{bmatrix} f & x_0 \cos(\alpha) & x_0 h \cos(\alpha) \\ 0 & f \sin(\alpha) + y_0 \cos(\alpha) & y_0 h \cos(\alpha) - f h \sin(\alpha) \\ 0 & \cos(\alpha) & h \cos(\alpha) \end{bmatrix} \tag{3}$$

where f represents the focal length, x_0 and y_0 are coordinates of the principal point, α is the tilt angle and h is the height of the camera.

This transformation is inversible such that the overhead view can be generated from a perspective or vice versa. Figure 2(a) shows an image taken with a tilt = 33°, the corresponding overhead view image is shown in Figure 2(b).

2.2 Overhead view mosaic

In this section the composition of overhead view mosaics is discussed. The method is based on estimating the homography transformation of the set of images with respect to a certain plane in the scene (for example the ground plane). The overhead view mosaic is finally built by rectifying the images using an overhead transformation with respect to a reference image. One of the images (say image 0) is selected as a reference frame. The homographic transformation between the reference view 0 and a view i is:

$$\mathbf{x}_i = \mathbf{H}_{0i} \mathbf{x}_0 \tag{4}$$

For known camera parameters, the image to plane homography $\mathbf{H}_O$ between the reference view (view 0) and the ground plane can be calculated as described in Equation(3). The two matrices $\mathbf{H}_{0i}$ and $\mathbf{H}_O$ can be used to calculate the homography transformation between a view

i and the composted overhead view as follows:

$$\mathbf{H}_{iO} = \mathbf{H}_O^{-1}\mathbf{H}_{0i}^{-1} = \begin{bmatrix} h_{11} & h_{12} & h_{13} \\ h_{21} & h_{22} & h_{23} \\ h_{31} & h_{32} & h_{33} \end{bmatrix} \tag{5}$$

Armed with all these homographic transformations, it is possible to produce an overhead mosaic representing the environment under study. When combining the information coming from different images, two strategies can be considered. The first one consists in determining the value of each pixel in the mosaic by selecting the pixel from the source image that has the best resolution as described by Laganière (2000). For a world point $[X,Y,1]^T$ the mosaic pixel is selected from the source image that best samples the segment between points $[X,Y,1]^T$ and $[X+\Delta_X, Y+\Delta_Y, 1]^T$ where Δ_X and Δ_Y are small increments in the X and Y directions respectively. The relation between a point $[X,Y,1]^T$ in world plane and a point $[x,y,1]^T$ in the image plane is:

$$X = h_X(x,y) = \frac{h_{11}x + h_{12}y + h_{13}}{h_{31}x + h_{32}y + h_{33}} \tag{6}$$

$$Y = h_Y(x,y) = \frac{h_{21}x + h_{22}y + h_{23}}{h_{31}x + h_{32}y + h_{33}} \tag{7}$$

The image resolution is determined by a measure called *instantaneous sampling rate*. For a world point $[X,Y,1]^T$ the sampling rate at the X direction is the number of source images between points $[X,Y,1]^T$ and $[X+\Delta_X,Y,1]^T$ divided by the distance between them. The instantaneous horizontal sampling rate is as follows:

$$s_X = \sqrt{\left(\frac{\delta h_X(x,y)}{\delta x}\right)^2 + \left(\frac{\delta h_X(x,y)}{\delta y}\right)^2} \tag{8}$$

Similarly the instantaneous vertical sampling rate is:

$$s_Y = \sqrt{\left(\frac{\delta h_Y(x,y)}{\delta x}\right)^2 + \left(\frac{\delta h_Y(x,y)}{\delta y}\right)^2} \tag{9}$$

The instantaneous sampling rate is defined as follows:

$$s = s_X s_Y \tag{10}$$

The mosaic pixel at point (x,y) is selected from the source image that have the highest sampling density s.

Figure 3 shows a set of images of a ground plane scene; the reference image is Figure 3(a). Figure 4(a) shows the mosaic obtained for this set of images. As it can be seen, when obstacles are visible in the source image, these ones interfere with the ground plane representation. In order to cope with this problem, we have to discard the source pixels that contains intensities that belong to the obstacles. To do so, we propose the following algorithm:

Fig. 3. Set of images of a ground plane scene.

- **Step 1**: For each point on the ground plane apply the appropriate transformation to obtain the corresponding image point in each view.
- **Step 2**: Compute the mean *RGB* value of the pixels and the pixel that deviates the most from this mean value is discarded.
- **Step 3**: Repeat steps 1 and 2 until half of the points are discarded.
- **Step 4**: The mean *RGB* value of the remaining points is then used in the mosaic composition.

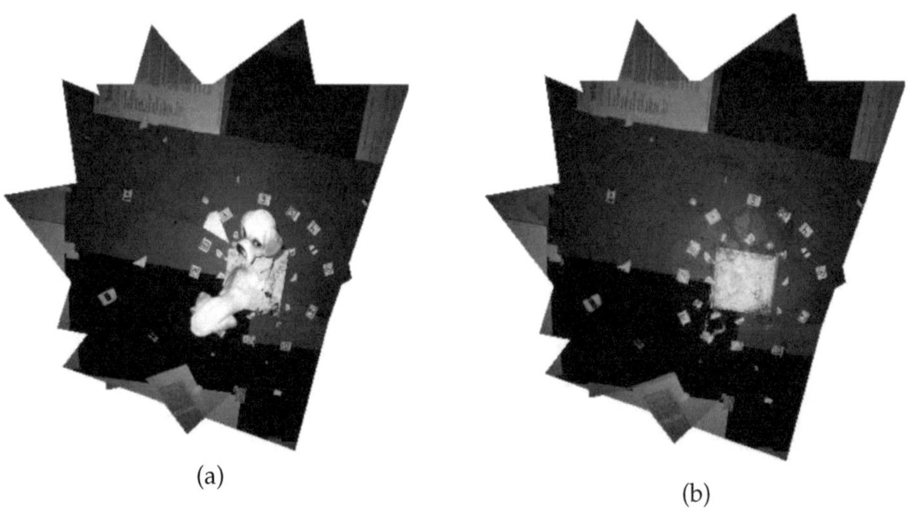

Fig. 4. Mosaic of the set of images in Figure 3 : (a) selecting points with best resolution. (b) discarding points that belong to the obstacle.

The result obtained using this algorithm is shown in Figure 4(b). An appropriate representation is thus obtained that could be used as a ground plane model of the environment. We show in the next section how it is possible to obtain the inter-image transformations ($\mathbf{H}_{ij}$) necessary to build such overhead view mosaic. This is done by matching the different available views, however taken from widely separated viewpoints.

2.3 Matching two widely separated views

The idea of this proposed technique is to use the overhead view images in the matching process. The procedure first starts by detecting corners on the original perspective images (Figure 5 (a) and (b))and the corners are then mapped to the overhead view images(Figure 5 (c) and (d)).

The two views in Figure 5 (a) and (b) are subjected to a projective deformation which makes image matching more challenging and subject to false matches. However, the two corresponding overhead views in Figure 5 (c) and (d) are only related by a similarity transformation (i.e. translation and rotation). This makes matching corner points using the overhead views more favorable. The matching process can be summerized as follows:

- **Step 1**: detect corners on the two images to be matched (Figure 5 (a) and (b))
- **Step 2**: use Equation 3 to calculate the overhead views of the two images (Figure 5 (c) and (d))
- **Step 3**: Match overhead views to calculate the similarity transformation $H_{S_{ij}}$
- **Step 4**: Homography transformation between (Figures 5 (a) and (b)) can be calculated as: $H_{ij} = H_{Oi}^{-1} H_{S_{ij}} H_{Oj}$

The reader is referred to Hajjdiab & Laganière (2004) for more details of the matching process. The inter-image homography transformation H_{ij} for two cameras C_i and C_j viewing a planar scene can be expressed as:

$$\mathbf{H}_{ij} = \mathbf{K}_j \left[\mathbf{R} - \frac{\mathbf{t}\mathbf{n}^T}{d} \right] \mathbf{K}_i^{-1} \tag{11}$$

where $\mathbf{K}_i$ and $\mathbf{K}_j$ are the matrices containing the intrinsic parameters of cameras C_i and C_j respectively, $\mathbf{R}$ is the rotation between the two cameras, $\mathbf{n}$ is the normal to the plane under consideration and $\mathbf{t}$ is the translation. Finally d is the distance from the camera to the ground. The optical axis of the two cameras are along the Z-axis as described in Figure 1, then the rotation between the two cameras can be expressed as follows (Altmann (1986)):

$$\mathbf{R} = \begin{bmatrix} \cos(\theta) & -\sin(\theta)\cos(\alpha_i) & -\sin(\theta)\sin(\alpha_i) \\ \cos(\alpha_j)\sin(\theta) & \cos(\theta)\cos(\alpha_j)\cos(\alpha_i) + \sin(\alpha_j)\sin(\alpha_i) & \cos(\alpha_j)\sin(\alpha_i)\cos(\theta) - \cos(\alpha_i)\sin(\alpha_j) \\ \sin(\alpha_j)\sin(\theta) & \sin(\alpha_j)\cos(\theta)\cos(\alpha_i) - \cos(\alpha_j)\sin(\alpha_i) & \cos(\theta)\sin(\alpha_j)\sin(\alpha_i) + \cos(\alpha_j)\cos(\alpha_i) \end{bmatrix} \tag{12}$$

where α_i and α_j are the angle of cameras C_i and C_j with respect to the ground plane.
The normal to the ground plane $\mathbf{n}$ can be expressed with respect to camera C_i as follows:

$$\mathbf{n} = \begin{bmatrix} 0 \\ -\sin(\alpha_i) \\ \cos(\alpha_i) \end{bmatrix} \tag{13}$$

The motion parameters can be estimated using SVD decomposition as proposed by Triggs (1998) as follows:

Let the coordinates of camera C_i be the reference frame, the projection matrices of cameras C_i and C_j are respectively:

$$\mathbf{P}_i = [\mathbf{I} \mid \mathbf{0}] \tag{14}$$

$$\mathbf{P}_j = \mathbf{R}[\mathbf{I} \mid -\mathbf{t}] \tag{15}$$

where $\mathbf{R}$ is the rotation matrix, $\mathbf{t}$ is translation vector and $\mathbf{I}$ is the 3×3 identity matrix.
The inter-image homography matrix $\mathbf{H}_{ij}$ can be decomposed as follows:

$$\mathbf{H}_{ij} = \mathbf{R}\left[\mathbf{I} - \frac{\mathbf{t}'\mathbf{n}^T}{d}\right] \tag{16}$$

where $\mathbf{t} = -\mathbf{R}\mathbf{t}'$.
For $\frac{\mathbf{n}^T}{d} = 1$, Equation (16) can be expressed as follows:

$$\mathbf{H}_{ij} = \mathbf{R}\left[\mathbf{I} - \mathbf{t}'\right] = \mathbf{R}\mathbf{H}^*_{ij} \sim \mathbf{P}_j \tag{17}$$

The motion can be estimated from the SVD's $\mathbf{H}_{ij}$ and $\mathbf{H}^*_{ij}$.

$$\begin{aligned} \mathbf{H}_{ij} &= \mathbf{USV} \\ \mathbf{H}^*_{ij} &= \mathbf{U_1SV} \end{aligned} \tag{18}$$

where $\mathbf{U}$ and $\mathbf{V}$ are 3×3 rotation matrices denoted by the columns $\mathbf{U} = [\mathbf{u}_1, \mathbf{u}_2, \mathbf{u}_3]$ and $\mathbf{V} = [\mathbf{v}_1, \mathbf{v}_2, \mathbf{v}_3]$, $\mathbf{S} = diag(s_s, s_2, s_3)$ is a diagonal matrix and $\mathbf{U} = \mathbf{R}\mathbf{U}_1$.
The motion between the two cameras $(\mathbf{R}, \mathbf{t}')$ can be estimated as follows:

$$\mathbf{t}' = \frac{\beta_1}{s_1}\mathbf{v}_1 + \frac{\beta_2}{s_3}\mathbf{v}_3 \tag{19}$$

$$\mathbf{R} = \mathbf{U}\mathbf{U}_1^T \tag{20}$$

where $\beta_1 = \pm\sqrt{1 - s_3^2}$ and $\beta_2 = \pm\sqrt{s_1^2 - 1}$
In general, the SVD approach gives two distinct solutions. This indetermination can be resolved if additional information about the scene is known. In our case, the normal vector to the ground plane is known (Equation (13)) and is used to eliminate the ambiguity.
In the following section an experiments is performed to estimate the motion parameters between two cameras. The internal camera parameters are assumed to be known.

2.3.1 Experiment: motion estimation

In this section the details of calculating the motion between two camera is provided. The carpet example in Figures 5(a) and (b) is used here to calculate $\mathbf{R}$ and $\mathbf{t}$. The homography is calculated as described in section 2.3 as follows:

$$\mathbf{H}_{ij} = \begin{bmatrix} 0.599 & -0.883 & 213.665 \\ 0.270 & 0.946 & -39.851 \\ 0 & 0 & 1 \end{bmatrix} \tag{21}$$

The SVD approach is applied to the matrix in Equation (21). The following two solutions were obtained:

Solution 1:

$$\mathbf{n} = \begin{bmatrix} -0.039 \\ -0.697 \\ 0.715 \end{bmatrix} \quad \mathbf{R} = \begin{bmatrix} 0.787 & 0.413 & 0.457 \\ -0.43 & 0.899 & -0.07 \\ -0.44 & -0.141 & 0.886 \end{bmatrix} \quad \mathbf{t} = \begin{bmatrix} -0.798 \\ -0.045 \\ -0.016 \end{bmatrix} \tag{22}$$

Solution 2:

$$\mathbf{n} = \begin{bmatrix} 0.709 \\ 0.683 \\ 0.17 \end{bmatrix} \quad \mathbf{R} = \begin{bmatrix} 0.613 & 0.772 & -0.164 \\ -0.787 & 0.585 & -0.189 \\ -0.05 & 0.245 & 0.968 \end{bmatrix} \quad \mathbf{t} = \begin{bmatrix} -0.289 \\ -0.505 \\ 0.548 \end{bmatrix} \tag{23}$$

The solution is the one with normal vector that satisfies the normal to the plane **n** as defined in Equation (13). In this case **Solution** 1 is selected.
The SVD algorithm is used to calculate the camera motion for the images in Figures 5, 6 and 7. The results are shown in Table 1.
In the next section, the robot localization algorithm is presented. The algorithm is applied on Table 1 and the localization results are presented.

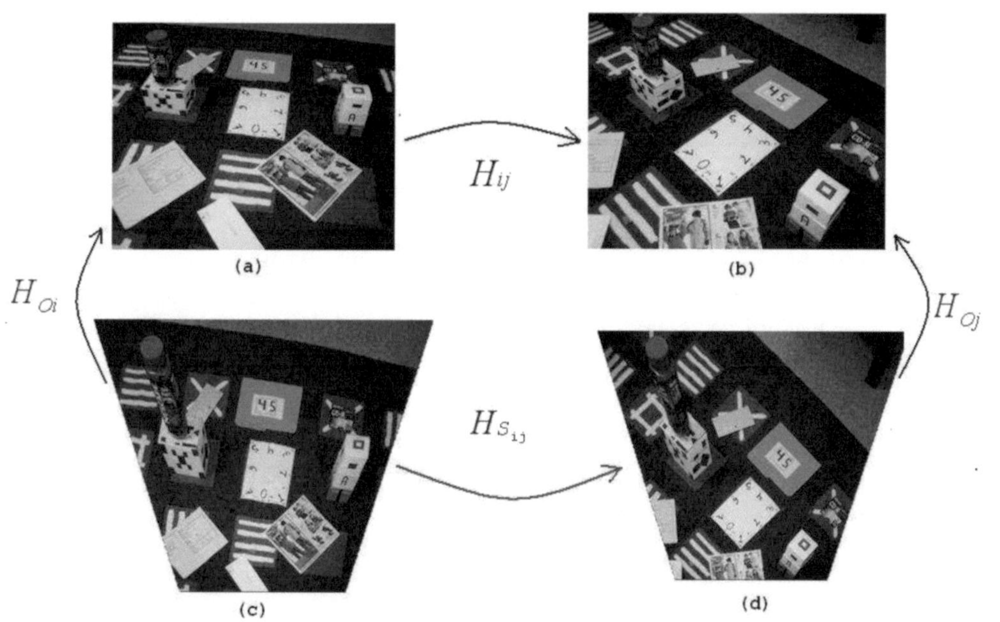

(a)

Fig. 5. Two views of a *carpet* scene taken with camera tilt of 45°. (a) The first image (Image i)(b) The second image (Image j). (c) and (d) The overhead view transformations of images in i and j respectively mapped.

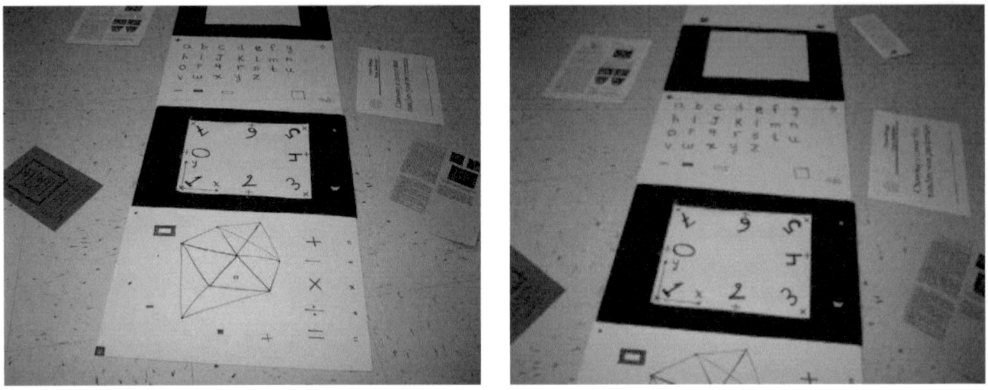

(a) (b)

Fig. 6. Floor images (a)and (b) images for a floor taken at tilt of 45°.

Scene	Motion estimated from $\mathbf{H}_{ij}$
carpet	$\mathbf{R} = \begin{bmatrix} 0.787 & 0.413 & 0.457 \\ -0.43 & 0.899 & -0.07 \\ -0.44 & -0.141 & 0.886 \end{bmatrix}$, $\mathbf{t} = [-0.798\ -0.045\ -0.016]^T$, $\mathbf{n} = [-0.039\ -0.697\ 0.715]^T$
floor	$\mathbf{R} = \begin{bmatrix} 0.999 & 0.025 & 0.028 \\ -0.026 & 0.999 & 0.016 \\ -0.028 & -0.016 & 0.999 \end{bmatrix}$, $\mathbf{t} = [-0.082\ -0.256\ -0.209]^T$, $\mathbf{n} = [-0.013\ -0.661\ 0.75]^T$
vase	$\mathbf{R} = \begin{bmatrix} 0.852 & 0.474 & 0.221 \\ -0.424 & 0.873 & -0.237 \\ -0.306 & 0.108 & 0.945 \end{bmatrix}$, $\mathbf{t} = [-0.289\ 0.239\ 0.15]^T$, $\mathbf{n} = [-0.01\ -0.377\ 0.926]^T$

Table 1. Camera motion estimation using the homography transformations.

2.4 Locating the Robots

The localization problem is formalized as shown in Figure 8. This can be parameterized by the triplet $\Gamma = [\rho, \phi_1, \phi_2]$. Where ρ is the Euclidean distance between the two robots, ϕ_1 is the angle of *Robot*2 with respect to *Robot*1 and ϕ_2 is the angle of *Robot*1 with respect to *Robot*2. The robot locations with respect to one another may be expressed by projecting the two 3D

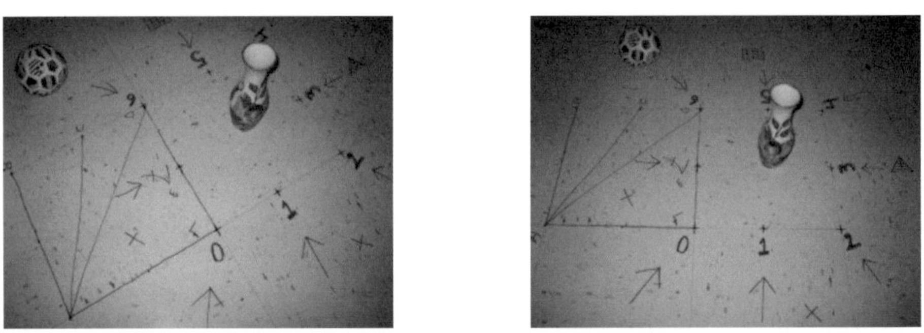

(a) (b)

Fig. 7. Vase images: (a) tilt $= 22^o$ and (b) tilt $= 33^o$.

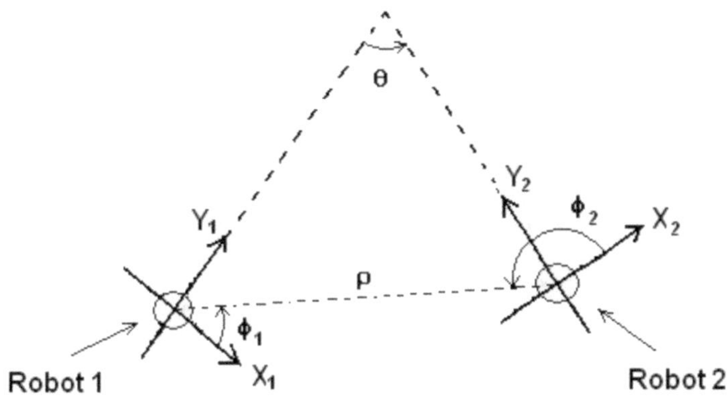

Fig. 8. The Robot angles.

camera coordinate systems on *Robot*1 and *Robot*2 on a 2D coordinate systems. The location of *Robot*2 with respect to *Robot*1 is at (x_1, y_1) defined as follows:

$$x_1 = -t_{x_1} \tag{24}$$

$$y_1 = \sqrt{t_{y_1}^2 + t_{z_1}^2}\sin(\alpha_1 + \beta_1) \tag{25}$$

$$\rho_1 = \sqrt{x_1^2 + y_1^2} \tag{26}$$

where $\beta_1 = \tan^{-1}\frac{t_{y_1}}{t_{z_1}}$
Similarly, the location of *Robot*1 with respect to *Robot*2 is at (x_2, y_2) defined as follows:

$$x_2 = -t_{x_2} \tag{27}$$

$$y_2 = \sqrt{t_{y_2}^2 + t_{z_2}^2}\sin(\alpha_2 + \beta_2) \tag{28}$$

$$\rho_2 = \sqrt{x_2^2 + y_2^2} \tag{29}$$

where $\beta_2 = \tan^{-1}\frac{t_{y_2}}{t_{z_2}}$
Finally, the location vector Γ is defined as follows:

$$\Gamma = [\rho, \phi_1, \phi_2] = \left[\frac{\rho_1 + \rho_2}{2}, tan^{-1}\left(\frac{y_1}{x_1}\right), tan^{-1}\left(\frac{y_2}{x_2}\right)\right] \tag{30}$$

The value of ρ in Equation (30) is calculated in term of camera height units. For a known camera height h in cm, the value of Γ can be expressed as follows:

scene	h	$d_{measured}$	Γ	$\|\Delta_d\|$
carpet	78 *cm*	61.5 *cm*	$[0.79, -3.18^o, 138.76^o]$	0.12 *cm*
floor	80 *cm*	27 *cm*	$[0.33, -75.99^o, 101.76^o]$	0.6 *cm*
vase	78 *cm*	32 *cm*	$[0.40, 44.09^o, 102.06^o]$	0.8 *cm*

Table 2. The calculated robot position from the estimated homographies

$$\Gamma = [\rho h \, \text{cm}, \phi_1, \phi_2] \tag{31}$$

The information in Table 1 is used to localize the robots in the *carpet*, *floor* and *vase* scenes. The localization results are shown in Table 2. The camera height h and the measured distance between the cameras for each scene are shown in columns 2 and 3 respectively. The location vectors Γ are calculated as described in this section and the results are shown in column 4, the discrepancy between the calculated and the measured locations are shown in column 5.

3. SLAM Experiments

In this section two experimental examples are provided for a robot traversing a work site. The objective is that the robot is capable of calculating its pose with respect to its previous position.

3.1 Single-robot SLAM

Figure 9 shows a set of images collected by a robot moving on a planar surface, the tilt with the ground is set manually to 33° and the height of the cameras is measured to be $h = 82\text{cm}$. First, the matching algorithm discussed in the previous section is applied and the inter-image homographies are calculated between consecutive robot locations. The homography transformations calculated are: $\mathbf{H}_{01}$, $\mathbf{H}_{12}$, $\mathbf{H}_{23}$, $\mathbf{H}_{34}$, $\mathbf{H}_{45}$, $\mathbf{H}_{56}$ and $\mathbf{H}_{67}$. These homographies are used to incrementally build a location graph. At each new location, the robot pose is calculated with respect to its previous position, the resulting location graph is shown in Figure 10. To estimate the accumulated error in estimating the pose between consecutive locations, the pose between the initial location (Robot0) and last location (Robot 7) is estimated by concatenating the calculated inter-image homography transformations as follows:

$$\mathbf{H}_{07} = \mathbf{H}_{67}\mathbf{H}_{56}\mathbf{H}_{45}\mathbf{H}_{34}\mathbf{H}_{23}\mathbf{H}_{12}\mathbf{H}_{01} \tag{32}$$

Any error in estimating any of the matrices in the right hand side of Equation(32) will influence the estimation of $\mathbf{H}_{07}$. In Figure 10 the value of r_1 represents the measured distance between Robot 7 and Robot 0, the estimated distance using $\mathbf{H}_{07}$ is represented by r_2.

The error in estimating the distance between Robot 0 and Robot7 can be evaluated by $d_r = |r_1 - r_2|$ as shown in Figure 10. The value of d_r is $11.5cm$ for a total displacement error of 2.95%.

The global overhead view map of the environment can be built by combining the overhead transformation and the inter-image homographies as described in Section 2.2. The result is shown in Figure 11.

In the next section, our single-robot SLAM algorithm is generalized to the multiple-robot case.

3.2 Multi-robot SLAM

In this section we provide an example of two mobile robots *RobotA* and *RobotB* moving in the same work site. The camera tilt on robots *RobotA* and *RobotB* are set manually to 33° and 45° respectively, the height of the camera from the ground plane is $55cm$. Figure 12 shows the images captured by *RobotA* and Figure 13 shows the images captured by *RobotB*. The two robots start at arbitrary unknown locations (location $A0$ for *RobotA* and location $B0$ for *RobotB*). Each of the robots starts building a local location graph and a local map of the environment as discussed in the single-robot SLAM case, the local locations graphs are shown in Figure 14(a) and (b). When an overlap occurs between the two robots, a joint location graph

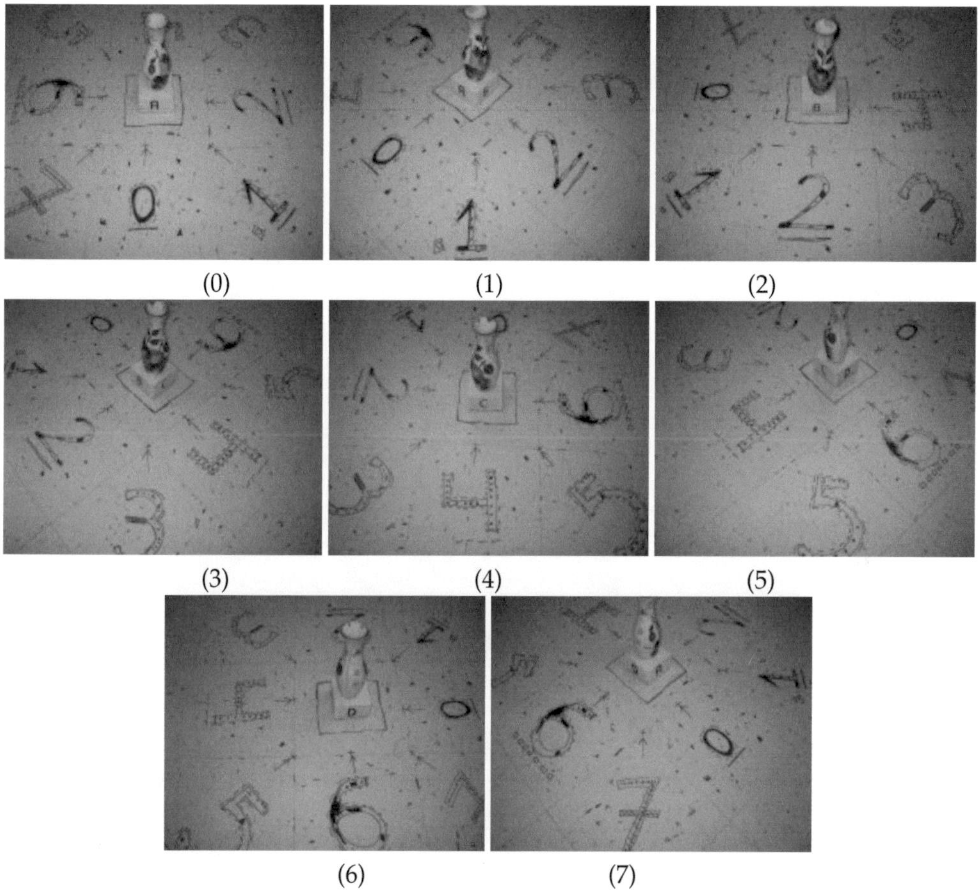

Fig. 9. Single-robot SLAM: Image set collected by the robot.

and environment map can be build by calculating the relative pose of the two robots. The approach used to determine the overlap between two robots is presented in the next section. At location *A7* for *RobotA* and location *B8* for *RobotB* the two robots are viewing the same scene, this overlap can be verified by comparing image *A7* in Figure 12 and image *B8* in Figure 13. The relative pose of the two robots is estimated by the inter-image homography between the two images and a joint location graph can be built. Figure 14(c) shows the joint location graph which relates all the robot locations with *A7* selected as the reference frame. The joint map of the environment is shown in Figure 15.

3.3 Overlapping view detection

In order to determine if two cameras are viewing the same scene, the images have to be compared. One approach is to calculate the inter-image homography as discussed in Section 2.3 and then determine the validity of this transformation. The validity may be checked by mapping the corner points from one image to the other. If there exist a large number of matches then this transformation is considered to be a valid transformation and accepted otherwise it is rejected.

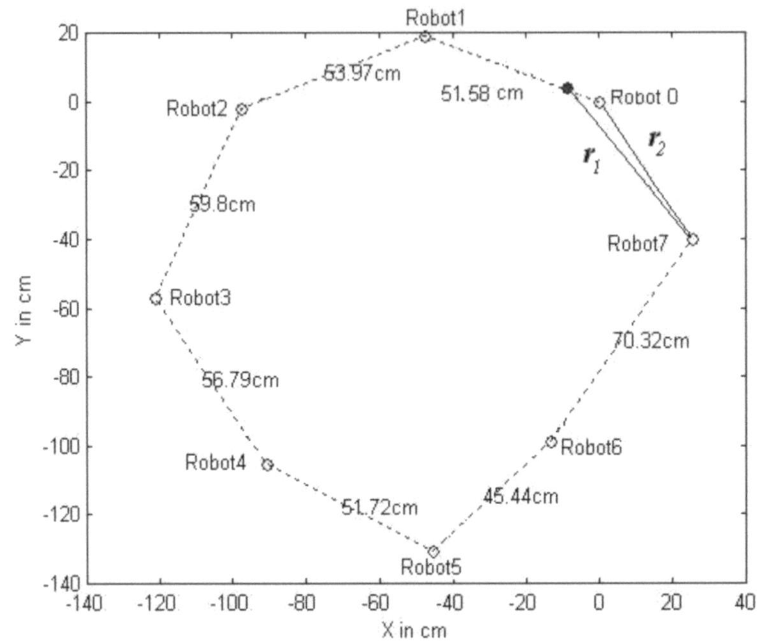

Fig. 10. Single-robot SLAM: Location graph.

For two robots, this approach requires calculating the inter-image homography for every possible combination of images. For N images captured by each robot, a complexity of $O(N^2)$ of inter-image homography calculations is required. To improve the efficiency, the homography between any two images is only calculated if there is a potential for match. To do so, we propose a method based on color histogram distance.

The color histograms are commonly used to compare images based on their overall appearance (Pass et al. (1996)). Because they are computationally efficient, they have been used in many applications like image retrieval (Brown et al. (1995); Flicker (1995); Olga & Stonebraker (1995); Pentland et al. (1996)) and object identification(Swain & Ballard (1991)).

The histogram $\mathbf{h}$ of an image is a vector consisting of n bins as follows:

$$\mathbf{h} = [h_1, \ldots, h_n] \tag{33}$$

Each bin $h_i \in \mathbf{h}$, $1 \leq i \leq n$, contains the number of pixels of color i in the image. Two images $\mathbf{I}$ and $\mathbf{I}'$ of histograms $\mathbf{h}$ and $\mathbf{g}$ can be compared based on the inter-bin distance $d(\mathbf{h}, \mathbf{g})$ between their histograms. Images $\mathbf{I}$ and $\mathbf{I}'$ are considered similar if $d(\mathbf{h}, \mathbf{g})$ is minimized. The histogram is trivially computed compared to the inter-image homography. We propose an algorithm to use histogram distance to determine the most likely overlap and then use-inter image homography transformation to validate such an overlap. The algorithm is stated as follows:

Let $\mathbf{A} = \{\mathbf{I}_1, \ldots, \mathbf{I}_{N_A}\}$ and $\mathbf{B} = \{\mathbf{I}'_1, \ldots, \mathbf{I}'_{N_B}\}$ be the sets of images collected by *RobotA* and *RobotB* respectively. With set $\mathbf{A}$ contains N_A images and set $\mathbf{B}$ contains N_B images. The problem to solve is to find, using color histogram distance, an image $\mathbf{I}_a \in \mathbf{A}$ and an image $\mathbf{I}'_b \in \mathbf{B}$ such that $\mathbf{I}_a$ and $\mathbf{I}'_b$ are most likely the overlap images if such an overlap exists between the two robots.

Fig. 11. Single-robot SLAM: generated map of the site

Let $Hist(\mathbf{I})$[1] denotes the histogram of the overhead view of image **I** and C_{Hist} and C_{Homog} denote the cost of computing the histogram distance d and the inter-image homography between two images. The algorithm we propose is summarized as follows:

Step 1: **For** $k = 1$ to N_A
    For $l = 1$ to N_B
        calculate $d(Hist(\mathbf{I}_k), Hist(\mathbf{I}'_l))$
        If d is minimized **then**
            $\mathbf{I}_a = \mathbf{I}_k$ and $\mathbf{I}'_b = \mathbf{I}'_l$
        End
    End
End
Step 2: Calculate the inter-image homography $\mathbf{H}_{ab}$ between images $\mathbf{I}_a$ and $\mathbf{I}'_b$
Step 3: Accept/reject $\mathbf{H}_{ab}$ based on the validation test.

In Step 1, the histogram distances between all the images acquired by the two robots are calculated. The outcome is the two images ($\mathbf{I}_a$ and $\mathbf{I}'_b$) whose histogram distance is the global minimum. In Step 2, the inter-image homography ($\mathbf{H}_{ab}$) is calculated for the two images.

[1]throughout this chapter all the histograms are calculated using the overhead view images

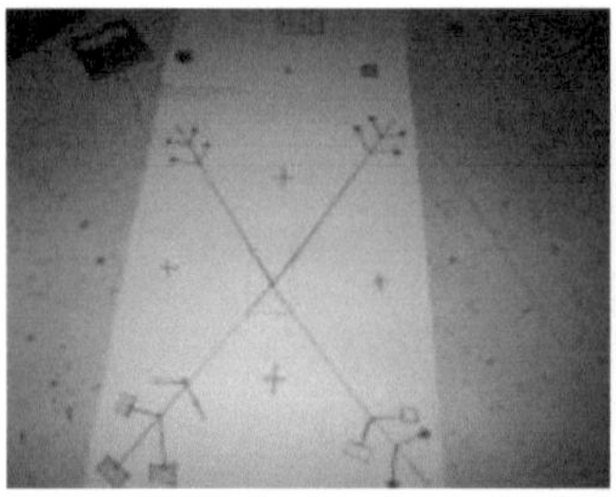
(A_0)

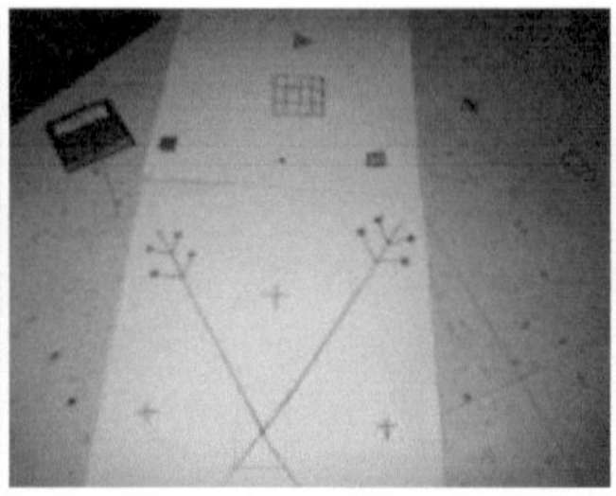
(A_1)

(A_2)

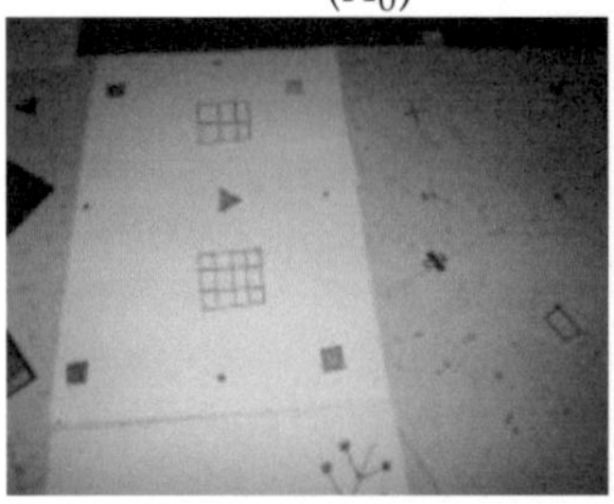
(A_3)

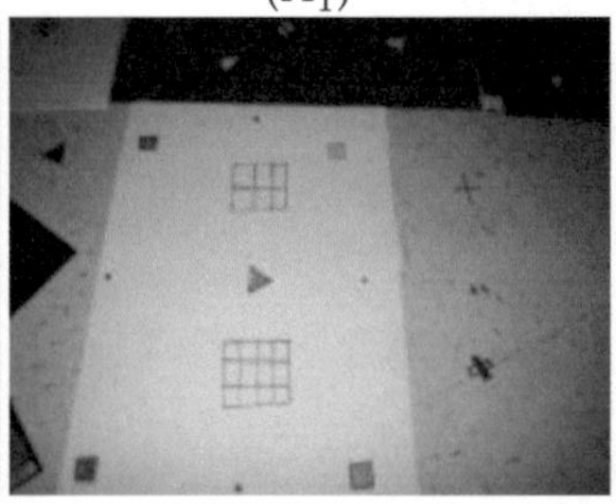
(A_4)

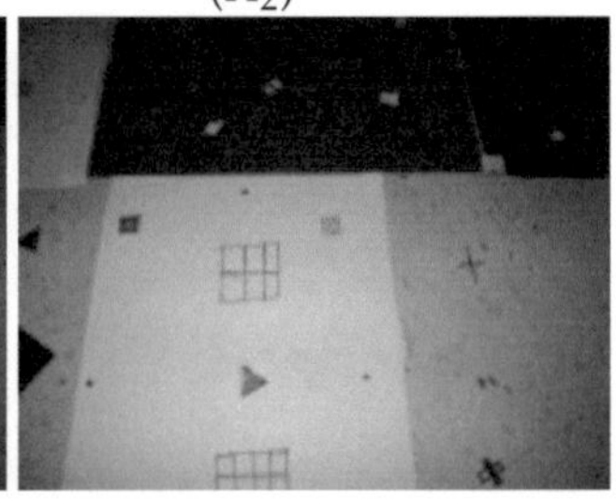
(A_5)

(A_6)

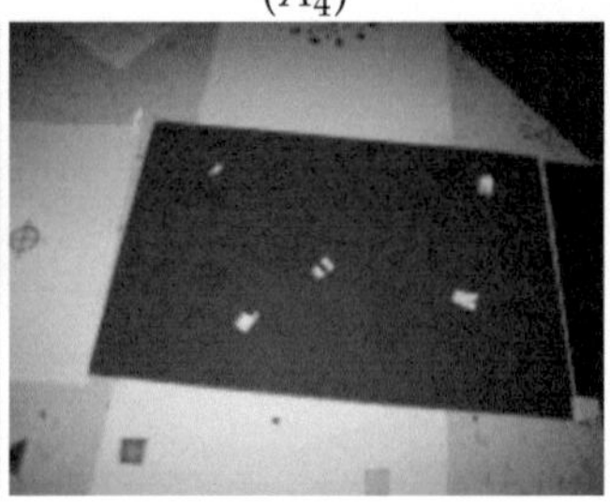
(A_7)

(A_8)

(A_9)

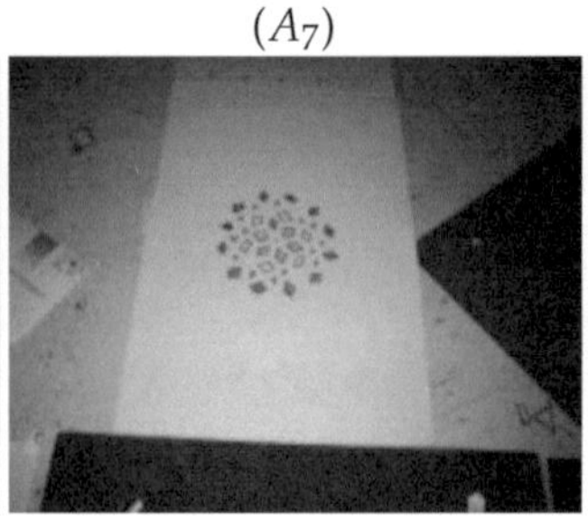
(A_{10})

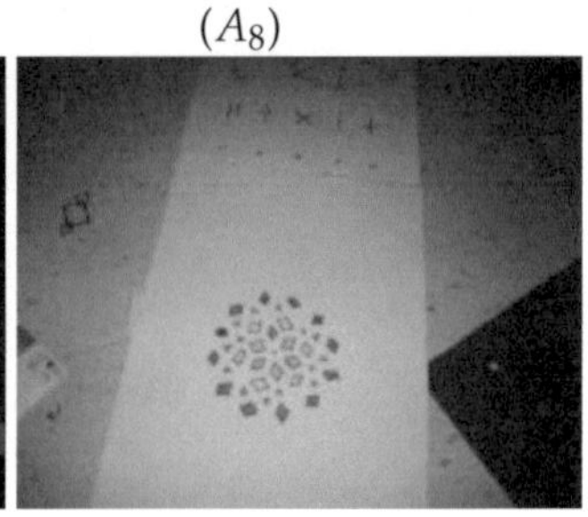
(A_{11})

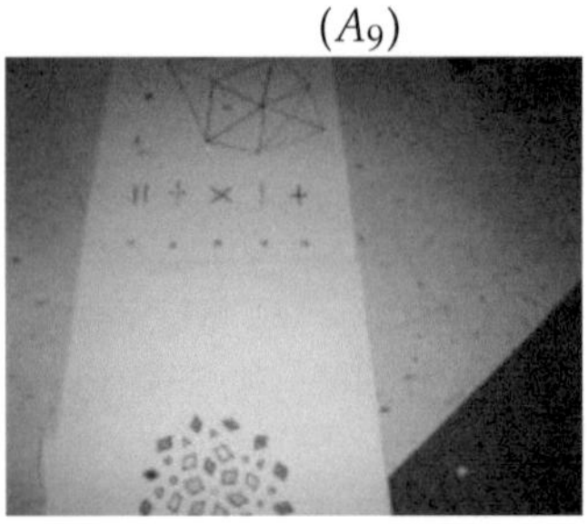
(A_{12})

Fig. 12. Image set collected by the *Robot A*.

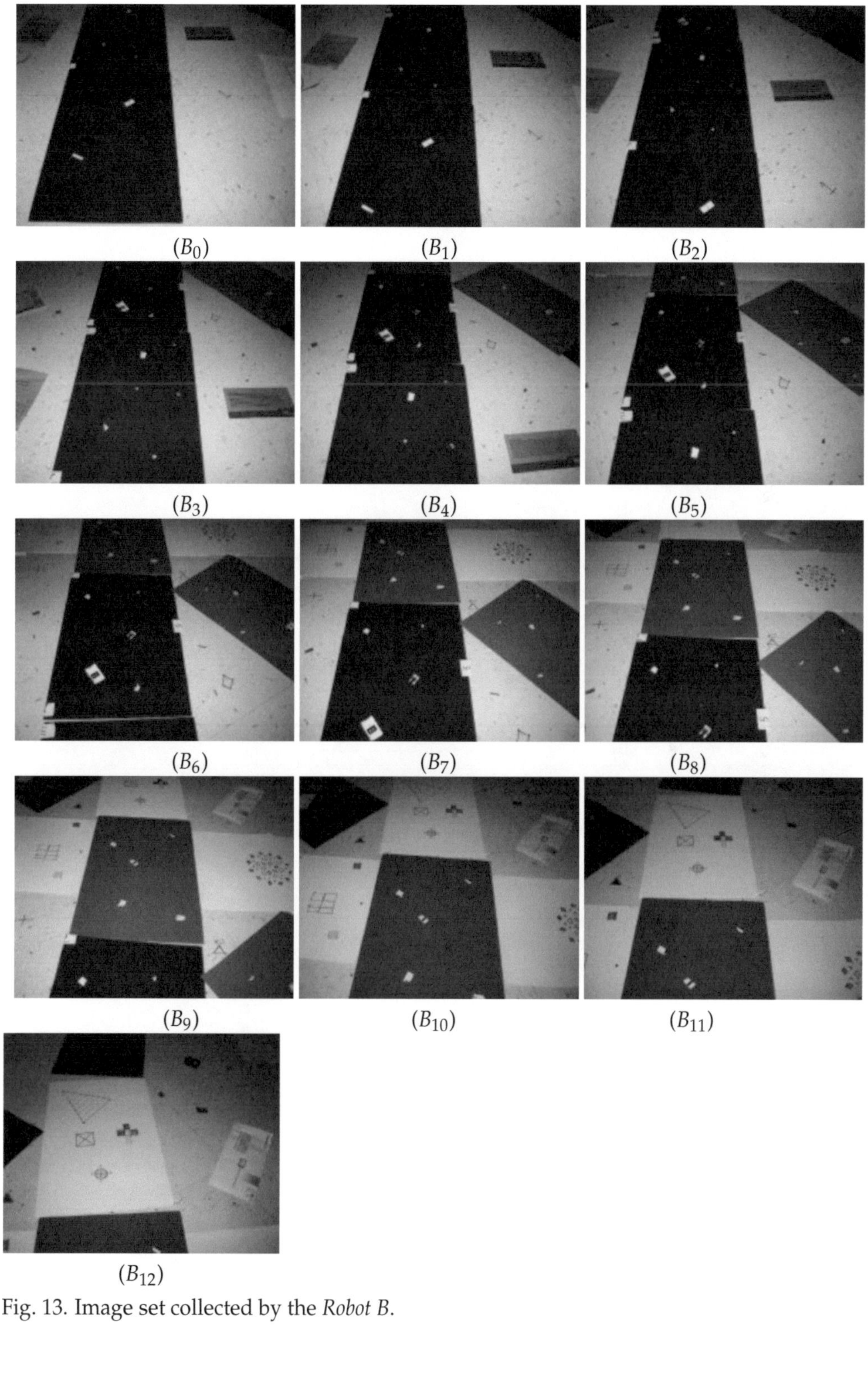

(B_0) (B_1) (B_2)

(B_3) (B_4) (B_5)

(B_6) (B_7) (B_8)

(B_9) (B_{10}) (B_{11})

(B_{12})

Fig. 13. Image set collected by the *Robot B*.

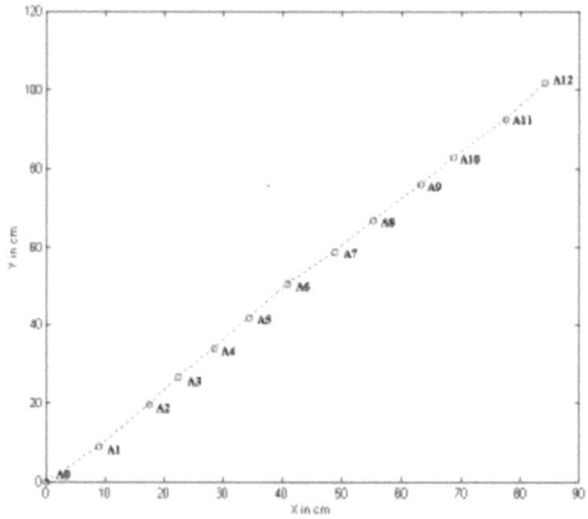

(a)

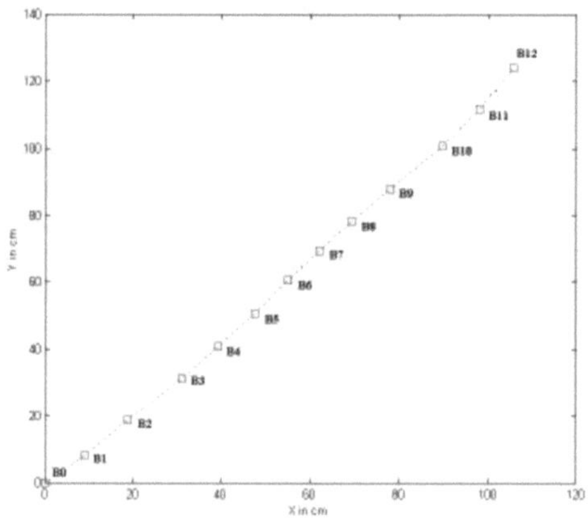

(b)

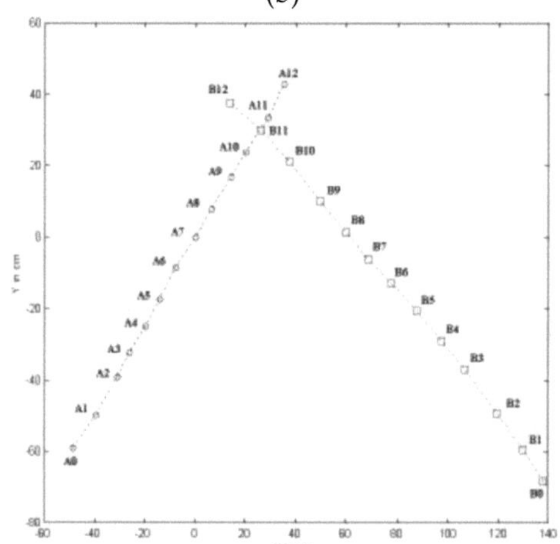

(c)

Fig. 14. Multi-Robot Localization: (a) location graph generated by *RobotA* (b) location graph generated by *RobotB* (c) the joint location graph

Fig. 15. The map generated from images collected by *Robot A* and *Robot B*.

Finally, in Step 3, $\mathbf{H}_{ab}$ is validated, if there exist a high number of matches between corners in image $\mathbf{I}_a$ and corners in image $\mathbf{I}'_b$ then the homography $\mathbf{H}_{ab}$ is accepted.

4. Summary

We have presented a vision-based technique to solve the multi-robot SLAM problem. The different robot locations are computed by finding the transformations that relate together the captured images of the scene. The camera motions are estimated from the computed inter-image homographies and each robot is localized with respect to a local map. To build a global map, the inter-image homographies have to be calculated between different robots in the team. To do so, an overlapping view detection technique is presented. The technique is based on color histogram distances between images collected by the team of robots. When two images from two robots have similar color histograms, a potential overlapping between the two robots is assumed. The inter-image homography is calculated to verify if this overlapping is valid. If the such an overlapping exist, then it is possible to build a common map of the environment inside which the robots are evolving.

5. References

Altmann, S. (1986). *Rotations, Quaternions, and Double Groups*, Oxford University Press, Oxford.

Brown, M., Foote, J., Jones, G., Jones, K. & Young, S. (1995). Automatic content-based retrieval of broadcast news, *ACM Multimedia conference*.

Dissanayake, G., Newman, P., Durrant-Whyte, H., Clark, S. & Csobra, M. (2001). A solution to the simultaneous localization and map building (slam) problem, *IEEE Trans. on Robotics and Automation* 17(3): 229–241.

Flicker, M. (1995). Query by image and video content: The qbic system, *IEEE computer*, Vol. 28 of 9, pp. 23–32.

Hajjdiab, H. & Laganière, R. (2004). Vision-based multi-robot simultaneous localization and mapping, *in Proceedings of the* 1st *Canadian Conference on Computer and Robot Vision, CCCRV'04*, London,Ontario,Canada.

Laganière, R. (2000). Composing a bird's eye view mosaic, *Vision Interface* pp. 382–386.

Liu, Y. & Thrun, S. (2003). Gaussian multi-robot slam, *submitted to NIPS* .

Lowe, G. (1991). Fitting parameterized three-dimensional models to images, *IEEE Trans. Pattern Analysis and Mach. Intell, PAMI*, Vol. 13, pp. 441–450.

Lowe, G. (1999). Object recognition from local scale invariant features, *Proceedings of the* 7th *International conference on Computer Vision*, Kerkyra, Greece, pp. 1150–1157.

Montemerlo, M., Thrun, S., Koller, D. & Wegbreit, B. (03). Fastslam2.0: An improved particle filtering algorithm for simultaneous localization and mapping that provably converges, *IJCAI* .

Murphy, K. (99). Bayesian map learning in dynamic environments, *NIPS* .

Murray, D. & Little, J. (1998). Using real-time stereo vision for mobile robot navigation, *Proceedings of the IEEE Workshop on Perception for Mobile Agents*, Santa Barbara, CA.

Olga, V. & Stonebraker, M. (1995). Chabot: Retrieval from a relational database of images, *IEEE computer*, Vol. 28 of 9, pp. 40–48.

Pass, G., Zabih, R. & Miller, J. (1996). Comparing images using color coherence vectors, *In Proceedings of ACM Multimedia 96*, Boston, Ma, USA, pp. 65–73.

Pentland, A., Picard, R. & Sclaroff, S. (1996). Photobook: Content-based manipulation of image database, *International Journal of Computer Vision* 18(3): 233–254.

Se, S., Lowe, D. & Little, J. (2001). Vision-based mobile robot localization and mapping using scale-invariant features, *Proceedings of the IEEE International Conference on Robotics and Automation (ICRA)*, Seoul, Korea, pp. 2051–2058.

Simmons, R., Apfelbaum, D., Burgard, W., Fox, M., Moors, D., Thrun, S. & Younes, H. (2000). Coordination for multi-robot exploration and mapping, *In Proceedings of the AAAI National Conference on Artificial Intelligence*, Austin, TX.

Smith, R. & Cheeseman, P. (1986). On the representation and estimation of spatial uncertainty, *Int. J. Robotics Research* 5(4).

Swain, M. & Ballard, D. (1991). Color indexing, *International Journal of Computer Vision* 7(1): 11–32.

Thrun, S., Burgard, W. & Fox, D. (2000). A real-time algorithm for mobile robot mapping with application to multi-robot and 3d mapping, *in Proceedings of the IEEE International Conference on Robotics and Automation*.

Triggs, B. (1998). Autocalibration from planar scenes, *In Proc. European Conference on Computer Vision*, pp. 89–105.

11

Probabilistic Map Building, Localization and Navigation of a Team of Mobile Robots. Application to Route Following.

L. Payá, O. Reinoso, F. Amorós, L. Fernández and A. Gil
Miguel Hernandez University
Spain

1. Introduction

The applications that require the navigation of a robot or a team of robots through an environment need an internal representation (or map) of this environment. Thanks to it, the robots can estimate their position and orientation using the information captured with the different sensors the robots are equipped with. Despite the fact that there are several kinds of sensors to carry out that task, omnidirectional visual systems can be stood out due to the richness of the information they provide and the relatively low cost they have.

A typical problem in collaborative robotics implies a path following, e.g. to perform a surveillance task in an office environment or an assembly or delivery task in an industrial environment. Also, the problem of formations, where a team of robots must navigate keeping a relative position in a structure of robots can be seen as a problem of path following, where one or several robots must follow the path the leader is recording with an offset either in space or in time.

Classical researches into mobile robots provided with vision systems have focused on the extraction of natural or artificial landmarks from the image to build the map and carry out the localization of the robot (Booij et al., 2007; Burschka & Hager, 2001; Thrun, 2003). Nevertheless, it is not necessary to extract such kind of landmarks to recognize where the robot is. Instead of this, we can process the image as a whole. These approaches (known as *appearance-based*) are especially useful for complicated scenes in unstructured environments where appropriate models for recognition are difficult to create. As an example, (Matsumoto et al., 1999) address a method for route following where several low-resolution images along the route are stored, and (Payá et al., 2007) use an incremental compression method of the scenes that permits online multi-robot route following.

In the appearance-based approaches, images are saved without extracting any local feature, and the comparison is made directly, working with the whole information of the scenes. So the problem of finding the position of the robot in the environment consists in getting the best match for the current image among the reference images. Since no relevant information is extracted, an important problem of such approaches is the high computational cost they suppose. That is the reason why often it is necessary to apply some compression techniques.

Different researchers have shown how a manifold representation of the environment using some compression techniques can be used. For example, PCA (Principal Components Analysis) is a widely used method that has demonstrated being robust applied to image processing, as (Kröse et al., 2004) do to create a database using a set of views with a probabilistic approach for the localization inside this database. Conventional PCA methods do not take profit of the amount of information that omnidirectional cameras offer, because they cannot deal with rotations in the plane where the robot moves. (Uenohara & Kanade, 1998) studied this problem with a set of rotated images, and (Jogan and Leonardis, 2000) applied these concepts to an appearance-based map of an environment. Despite its complexity and computational cost, it has the advantage of being a rotationally invariant method due to the fact that it takes into account the images with other orientations apart from the stored one. The approach consists in creating an eigenspace that takes into account the possible rotations of each training image, trying to keep a good relationship between amount of memory, time and precision of the map

Other authors use the Discrete Fourier Transform (DFT) as a generic method to extract the most relevant information from an image. In this field, (Menegatti et al., 2004) define the Fourier Signature for panoramic images, which is based on the 1D Discrete Fourier Transform of the image rows and gets more robustness dealing with different orientations and (Rossi et al., 2008) use spherical Fourier transform of the omnidirectional images.

On the other hand, (Dalal and Triggs, 2005) used a method based on the Histogram of Oriented Gradients (HOG) to pedestrians detection, proving that it could be a useful descriptor for computer vision and image processing using the objects' appearance.

In some applications, the use of a team of robots may help to make the achievement of the task quicker and more reliable. In such situations, each robot works with incomplete and changing information that has, also, a high degree of uncertainty. This way, only a suitable choice of the representation and an effective communication between the members of the team can provide the robots with a complete knowledge of the environment where they move. As an example, (Thrun, 2001) presents a probabilistic EKF algorithm where a team of robots builds a map online, while simultaneously they localize themselves. In (Ho & Newman, 2005) a map is build using visual appearance. From sequences of images, acquired by a team of robots, subsequences of visually similar images are detected and finally, the local maps are joined into a single map.

In this work, we present a framework that permits carrying out multi-robot route following, where an appearance-based approach is used to represent the environment and a probabilistic approach is used to compute the localization of the robot. Each robot carries out an omnidirectional camera in a fixed position on its top, and the localization and navigation tasks are carried out using a descriptor of the global appearance of the omnidirectional images captured by this camera. Along the chapter, we study and compare some alternatives to build an efficient appearance descriptor. We compare the descriptors in terms of computational cost, size of memory and its validity in localization tasks. We use three different approaches to build these descriptors: the Discrete Fourier Transform, Principal Components Analysis and Histogram of Oriented Gradients.

The remainder of the paper is organized as follows. In section 2, the main features of the multi-robot route-following system are addressed. In section 3, some methods to describe the appearance of the scenes are detailed. The performance of these descriptors is tested in section 4 in a map building task, and in section 5 in a localization task. In both sections, the results of the experiments are commented. At last, the conclusions are presented.

2. Multi-robot route following

The main goal of the work is to present an architecture to carry out multi-robot route following using just visual information and with an appearance-based approach.

In this application, we work with a team of Pioneer P3-AT robots (fig. 1(a)) that are equipped with a catadioptric system (fig. 1(b)) consisting on a forward-looking camera and a parabolic mirror that provides omnidirectional images of the environment. To work with this information in an efficient way, the omnidirectional images are transformed to panoramic images, as shown on fig. 1(c). The size of these panoramic images is 41x256 pixels.

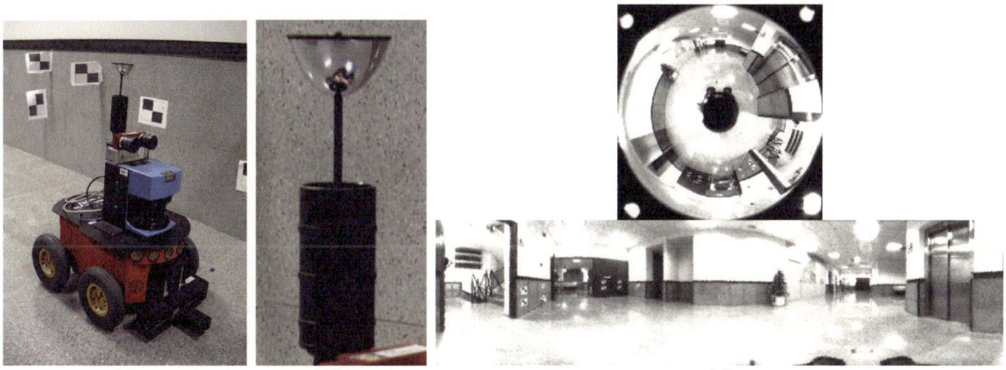

(a) (b) (c)

Fig. 1. (a) Pionner P3-AT robot and (b) catadioptric system that provides omnidirectional images. (c) Omnidirectional and (d) panoramic view of the environment captured by the catadioptric system.

In a multi-robot route following task, a leader robot goes through the desired route while a team of robots follow it with an offset in space or in time. To accomplish this goal, the leader robot performs a *learning* task while the follower robots perform an *autonomous navigation* task. The *learning* task consists in tele-operating the leader robot through the route to follow while it stores some general visual information along this route. In a general way, new omnidirectional images are continuously acquired, but a new image is stored only when its correlation with the previously stored image goes down a threshold. This way, images are stored more frequently when the information changes quicker (i.e. turnings and non structured environments) and fewer images are stored when the new information is quite similar. In this step, it is important to define correctly the representation of the environment to permit that any robot can follow the route of the leader one with an offset either in space or/and in time in an efficient way. In this work, we propose the use of appearance-based methods to describe globally the information in the scenes. In section 3 we show how we build an efficient descriptor to represent this visual information.

Fig. 2 shows a sample route in an indoor environment. The points where a new omnidirectional image has been stored are drawn as red dots. Each omnidirectional image has been transformed to the panoramic format, as show in the figure. In a posterior phase, a single descriptor per image will be computed. All these descriptors will constitute the database or map.

On the other hand, once the leader robot has created the database or while it is being built, the follower robots perform the *autonomous navigation* task. Before starting this process, the follower robot is situated in a point near the learned route. Then, it has to recognize which of the stored positions is the nearest to the current one and drive to tend to the route, following it till the end. This task must be carried out just comparing its current visual information with the information stored in the database. Two processes must run

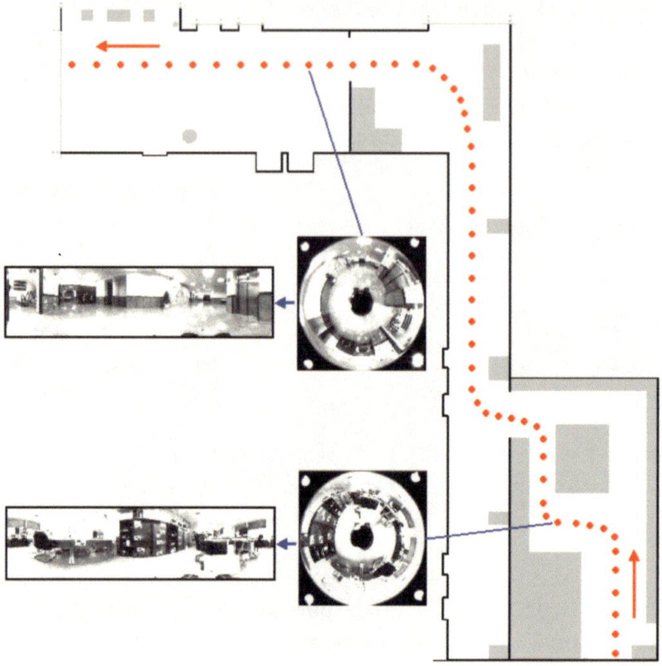

Fig. 2. Sample route including a hall, a corridor and a laboratory. The red dots show the places where the robot has acquired omnidirectional images to form the database.

successively: *auto-location* and *control*. During the *auto-location*, the current visual information is compared with the information in the database, and the most similar point is taken as the current position of the robot. This decision must be made taking into account the aperture problem in office environments. This way, the new position of the robot must be in a neighbourhood of the previous one, depending on the speed of the robot. Once we have a new matching, in the *control phase*, the current visual information must be compared with the matched information of the database, and from this comparison, a control law must be deducted so that the robot tends to the route and follows it till the end.
Once the principles of our route-following architecture have been exposed, in the next subsections each process in described in deep.

2.1 Task 1: learning the map

The map is built gradually while the leader robot is going through the route to record. This robot captures a new omnidirectional image when the correlation respect to the previous one goes down a threshold. This way, our database is composed of a set of omnidirectional views.
As our proposal consists in working with global appearance methods, that imply using the information in the images as a whole, we do not perform any feature extraction. This fact becomes a problem due to the growing size of the memory for long routes and the high computational cost in the localization phase to find the best match between the current image and all the images stored in the database. That is the reason why a compression method must be used to extract the most relevant information from the set of images.
When a new omnidirectional image is captured, first it is transformed into the panoramic image and then, the information is compressed to build a global descriptor of each

panoramic image. This way, each 41x256 image is compressed to a sequence of M numbers that constitute the descriptor of the image.

Each image $X_j \in \Re^{RxC}; j = 1...N$, being *R* the number of rows and *C* the number of columns, is transformed into a vector $\vec{z}_j \in \Re^M; j = 1...N$, being *M* the size of the global descriptor, *M* << *RxC*.

While building the descriptor $\vec{z}_j$, some principles must be taken into account. It must extract the most relevant information from the image, and its length must be as small as possible. Also, each image must be described as the leader robot is capturing them; the descriptor must be computed in an incremental procedure (i.e. the descriptor of each image must be computed independently of the rest of images). At last, the descriptor must contain enough information so that the follower robot can estimate the control law that makes it tend to the route. In section 3 we present some approaches to build the descriptor and we make a complete set of experiments to decide the optimal procedure to build it in our route-following application.

2.2 Task 2: robot navigation

After the *learning* task, the leader robot has created a database consisting of some feature vectors that are labelled as positions *1,..., N*. For each position, a descriptor represents the visual information taken at that position. The descriptors are $\vec{z}_j \in \Re^M; j = 1...N$.

Now, a different robot (the follower robot) can follow the same route carrying out successively two processes: *auto-location* and *control*.

2.2.1 Auto-location

When the follower robot captures a new image X_t, first, the global descriptor of this image $\vec{z}_t$ must be computed. Then, using this information, the robot must be able to compute which of the stored points is the closest one. With this aim, the distance between the descriptor of the current images and all the descriptors in the database is computed. We propose using the Euclidean distance as a measure. The distance between the descriptor of the current image $\vec{z}_t$ and the descriptors $\vec{z}_j$ in the database is:

$$d_{tj} = \sqrt{\sum_{l=0}^{M} \left(\vec{z}_t(l) - \vec{z}_j(l)\right)^2}; \quad j = 1...N \tag{1}$$

To normalize the values of the distances, a degree of similarity between descriptors is computed with eq. (2). The image of the database that offers the maximal value of γ_{tj} is the matching image, and then, the current position of the robot (the nearest one) is *j*.

$$\gamma_{tj} = \frac{\left(d_t^{\max} / d_{tj}\right) - 1}{\left(d_t^{\max} / d_t^{\min}\right) - 1}; \quad \gamma_{tj} \in [0,1]; \quad j = 1...N \tag{2}$$

where $d_t^{\max} = \max_{j=1}^{N}\left(d_{tj}\right)$ and $d_t^{\min} = \min_{j=1}^{N}\left(d_{tj}\right)$.

However, in office environments that present a repetitive visual appearance, this simple localization method tends to fail often as a result of the aperture problem (aliasing). This means that the visual information captured at two different locations that are far away can be very similar. To avoid these problems, we propose the use of a probabilistic approach, based on a Markov process (Thrun et al., 2005) to solve the problem.

In this localization task, we are interested in the estimation of the nearest point of the database, i.e. the state x_t at time t using a set of measurements $\vec{z}_{1:t} = \{\vec{z}_1, \vec{z}_2, ..., \vec{z}_t\}$ from the environment and the movements $u_{1:t} = \{u_1, u_2, ..., u_t\}$ of the robot. In this notation, we consider that the robot makes a movement u_t from time *t-1* to time t and next obtains an observation $\vec{z}_t$. In this document the localization problem has been stated in a probabilistic way: we aim at estimating a probability function $p(x_t \mid \vec{z}_{1:t}, u_{1:t})$ over the space of all possible localizations, conditioned on all the data available until time t, the observations $\vec{z}_{1:t}$, movements performed $u_{1:t}$ and the map. In a probabilistic mobile robot localization, the estimation process is usually carried out in two phases:

Prediction phase:

In the Prediction Phase the motion model is used to compute the probability function $p(x_t \mid \vec{z}_{1:t-1}, u_{1:t})$, taking only motion into account. The motion model is a probabilistic generalization of robot kinematics. In this work the value of u is an odometry reading. Generally, we assume that the current state x_t depends only on the previous state x_{t-1} and the movement u_t. The motion model is specified in the form of the conditional density $p(x_t \mid x_{t-1}, u_t)$. As we have a set of discrete localizations, the probability function at the next step is obtained by the summation:

$$p(x_t \mid \vec{z}_{1:t-1}, u_t) = \sum p(x_t \mid x_{t-1}, u_t) \cdot p(x_{t-1} \mid \vec{z}_{1:t-1}, u_{1:t-1}) \tag{3}$$

where the function $p(x_t \mid x_{t-1}, u_t)$ represents the probabilistic movement model.

When the robot moves, the uncertainty over its pose generally increases. This is due to the fact that the odometry sensors are not precise. In consequence, the function $p(x_t \mid x_{t-1}, u_t)$ describes the probability over the variable x_t given that the robot was at the pose x_{t-1} and performed the movement u_t.

Update phase:

In the second phase, a measurement model is used to incorporate information from the sensors and obtain the posterior distribution $p(x_t \mid \vec{z}_{1:t}, u_{1:t})$. In this step, the measurement model $p(\vec{z}_t \mid x_t)$ is employed, which provides the likelihood of obtaining the observation $\vec{z}_t$ assuming that the robot is at pose x_t. The posterior $p(x_t \mid \vec{z}_{1:t}, u_{1:t})$, can be calculated using Bayes' Theorem:

$$p(x_t \mid \vec{z}_{1:t}, u_{1:t}) = \eta \cdot p(\vec{z}_t \mid x_t) \cdot p(x_t \mid \vec{z}_{1:t-1}, u_t) \tag{4}$$

where $p(x_t \mid \vec{z}_{1:t-1}, u_t)$ denotes the probability that the robot is on the position x_t before observing the image whose descriptor is $\vec{z}_t$. This value is estimated using the previous information and the motion model (eq. 3). $p(\vec{z}_t \mid x_t)$ is the probability of observing $\vec{z}_t$ if the position of the robot is x_t. This way, a method to estimate the observation model must be deducted. In this work, the distribution $p(\vec{z}_t \mid x_t)$ is modelled through a sum of Gaussian kernels, centred on the n most similar points of the route:

$$p(\vec{z}_t \mid x_t) = \frac{1}{n} \cdot \sum_{i=1}^{n} \left(\gamma_{ti} \cdot e^{-\left(\frac{x_t - x_i}{\sigma}\right)^2} \right) \tag{5}$$

Each kernel is weighted by the value of confidence γ_{ti} (eq. 2). Once the prediction and the update phase have been computed, the new position is considered at the point with highest probability contribution. After the update phase, this process is repeated recursively.
The knowledge about the initial state at time t_0 is generally represented by $p(x_0)$. In this case two different cases are generally considered. When the initial pose of the mobile robot is totally unknown, the initial state at time t_0, $p(x_0)$, is represented by a uniform distribution on the map. Then we say we are in the case of global localization. But if the initial pose of the mobile robot is partially known, the case of local localization or tracking, the function $p(x_0)$ is commonly represented by a Gaussian distribution centred at the known starting pose of the robot. In our route-following application, as the initial position is usually unknown, we use a uniform distribution to model $p(x_0)$.

2.2.2 Control

Once the robot knows its position, it has to compute its heading, comparing to the heading that the leader had when it captured the image at that position. This information must be computed from the comparison between the image descriptors. We suppose that the descriptor of the current image is $\vec{z}_t$. After the probabilistic localization process, the descriptor of the corresponding location in the database is $\vec{z}_i$. If we suppose we can retrieve the relative orientation θ_t between the heading of the leader robot when it captured the image X_t and the heading of the follower robot when it captured the image X_i, then, a control action can be computed to control the robot. We propose the use of a controller with the following expression:

$$\begin{aligned} \omega_t &= k_1 \cdot \theta_t + k_2 \cdot [\theta_t - \theta_{t-1}]. \\ v_t &= k_3 \cdot p(x_t). \end{aligned} \tag{6}$$

where ω_t is the steering speed and v_t the linear speed that must be applied to the robot. For the calculation of the steering speed, we propose to use a proportional and derivative controller. The linear velocity will be proportional to the probability $p(x_t)$, what means that when the robot is bad localized (due to the aperture problem or to the fact that it is far from the route), the linear velocity is low to allow correcting the trajectory, but when the robot is well localized (i.e. the robot is following the route quite well and no aliasing is produced), the robot goes quicker.
Since the most important parameter to control the robot is the relative orientation of the robot, θ_t, in section 5 we make a detailed experimental study to determine how efficient is each descriptor when computing the relative orientation of the robot.

3. Representation of the environment through a set of omnidirectional images with appearance-based methods

In this section, we outline some techniques to extract the most relevant information from a set of panoramic images, captured from several positions along the route to follow. We have grouped these approaches in three families: DFT (Discrete Fourier Transform), PCA (Principal Components Analysis) and HOG (Histogram of Oriented Gradients) methods. The last technique has proved previous promising results, although not in localization functions. This section completes the study presented in (Paya et al., 2009).

3.1 DFT-based techniques

As shown in (Menegatti et al., 2004), when working with panoramic images, it is possible to use a Fourier-based compact representation for the scenes. It consists in expanding each row of the panoramic image $\{a_n\} = \{a_0, a_1, \ldots, a_{N_y-1}\}$ using the Discrete Fourier Transform into the sequence of complex numbers $\{A_n\} = \{A_0, A_1, \ldots, A_{N_y-1}\}$.

This Fourier signature presents the same properties as the 2D Fourier Transform. The most relevant information concentrates in the low frequency components of each row, and it presents rotational invariance. However, it exploits better this invariance to ground-plane rotations in panoramic images. These rotations lead to two panoramic images which are the same but shifted along the horizontal axis (fig. 3). Each row of the first image can be represented with the sequence $\{a_n\}$ and each row of the second image will be the sequence $\{a_{n-q}\}$, being q the amount of shift, that is proportional to the relative rotation between images. The rotational invariance is deducted from the shift theorem, which can be expressed as:

$$\Im\left[\{a_{n-q}\}\right] = A_k e^{-j \cdot \frac{2\pi q k}{N_y}}; \qquad k = 0, \ldots, N_y - 1 \tag{7}$$

where $\Im\left[\{a_{n-q}\}\right]$ is the Fourier Transform of the shifted sequence, and A_k are the components of the Fourier Transform of the non-shifted sequence. According to this expression, the amplitude of the Fourier Transform of the shifted image is the same as the original transform and there is only a phase change, proportional to the amount of shift q.

Fig. 3. Two panoramic images captured in the same point of the environment but with different heading for the robot.

Then, with this method, a descriptor $\vec{z}_j$ can be built with the modules and the angles of the Fourier signature of the panoramic image I_j, retaining only the f first columns where the most relevant information is stored.

3.2 PCA-based techniques

When we have a set of N images with M pixels each, $I_j \in \Re^{Mx1}; j = 1 \ldots N$, each image can be transformed in a feature vector (also named 'projection' of the image) $\vec{z}_j \in \Re^{Kx1}; j = 1 \ldots N$, being K the PCA features containing the most relevant information of the image, $K \leq N$ (Kirby, 2000). The PCA transformation can be computed from the singular value decomposition of the covariance matrix C of the data matrix, X that contains all the training images arranged in columns (with the mean subtracted). If V is the matrix containing the K principal eigenvectors and P is the reduced data of size K x N, the dimensionality reduction is done by $P = V^T \cdot X$, where the columns of P are the projections of the training images, $\vec{z}_j$.
However, if we apply PCA directly over the matrix that contains the images, we obtain a database with information just with the orientation of the robot when capturing those images but not for other possible orientations. Some authors have studied how to build an appearance-based map of an environment using a variation of PCA that includes information not only about the localizations where the images were taken but also about all the possible orientations at that points (Jogan et al., 2000). However, in previous works we have proved that the computational cost of such techniques does not permit to use them in an online task. Instead of using these rotational invariant techniques, what we propose in this chapter is to build the descriptor $\vec{z}_j$ by applying PCA over the Fourier Signature components instead of the original image, obtaining the compression of rotational invariant information, joining the advantages of PCA and Fourier techniques.

3.3 HOG-based techniques

The Histogram of Oriented Gradient (HOG) descriptors (Dalal and Triggs, 2005) are based on the orientation of the gradient in local areas of an image. The first step to apply HOG to an image is to compute the spatial derivatives of the image along the x and y-axes (U_x and U_y). We have obtained these derivatives by calculating the convolution of the images with Gaussian filters with different variance. Once the convolution of the image is made, we can get the magnitude and direction values of the gradient at each pixel:

$$|G| = \sqrt{U_x^2 + U_y^2} \qquad \theta = \arctan\left(U_x / U_y\right) \tag{8}$$

After that, we compute the orientation binning by dividing the image in cells, and creating the histogram of each cell. The histogram is computed based on the gradient orientation of the pixels within the cell, weighted with the corresponding module value. The number of histogram divisions is 8 in our experiments, and the angle varies between -90º and 90º. Each image is represented through the histogram of every cell ordered into a vector.
An omnidirectional image contains the same pixels in a row although the image is rotated, but in a different order. We can take profit of this characteristic to carry out the location of the robot by means of calculating the histogram with cells having the same width as the image (fig. 4). This way, we obtain an array of rotational invariant characteristics.
However, to know the relative orientation between two rotated images vertical windows (cells) are used, with the same height of the image, and variable width and distance (fig. 4). Ordering the histograms of these windows in a different way, we obtain the same results as calculating the histogram of an image rotated a proportional angle to the D distance. The angle resolution that can be got between two shifted images is proportional to that distance:

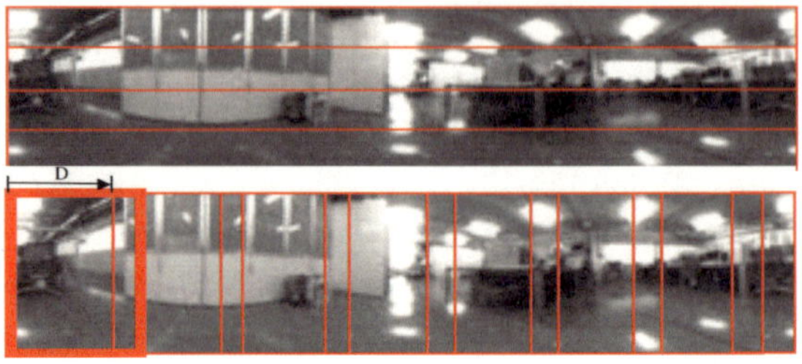

Fig. 4. Cells used to compute the current position and the orientation of the robot.

$$Angle(^{\circ}) = \frac{D * 360}{Width \quad of \quad the \quad image} \tag{9}$$

4. Performance of the descriptors in a map building task

In this section, the different methods to build the images' descriptors are compared using a database made up of a set images that were collected in several living spaces under realistic illumination conditions. It has been got from Technique Faculty of Bielefeld University (Möller et al., 2007). The images were captured with an omnidirectional camera, and later converted into panoramic ones with 41x256 pixels size. All the images belong to inner living spaces. Specifically, there are examples from a living room (L.R.), a kitchen and a combined area (C.A.), all of them structured in a 10x10 cm rectangular grid. Fig. 5 shows an example of image corresponding to each area. The objective is to test the memory requirements and computational cost of each descriptor when representing an environment.
The number of images that compose the database varies depending on the experiment, since, in order to assess the robustness of the algorithms, the distance between the images of the grid we take will be expanded, getting less information. I.e., instead of using all the images in the database to make up the map, we use just every two, three or four available images. In table 1 the size of the grid and the number of elements appear depending on the selected grid.

	Size	10x10	20x20	30x30	40x40
L.R.	22x11	242	66	32	18
Kitchen	12x9	108	30	12	9
C.A.	36x11	396	118	48	27
TOTAL		**746**	**204**	**92**	**54**

Table 1. Size of the database and number of images selected depending on the grid.

Fig. 5. Living room, kitchen and combined area sample images.

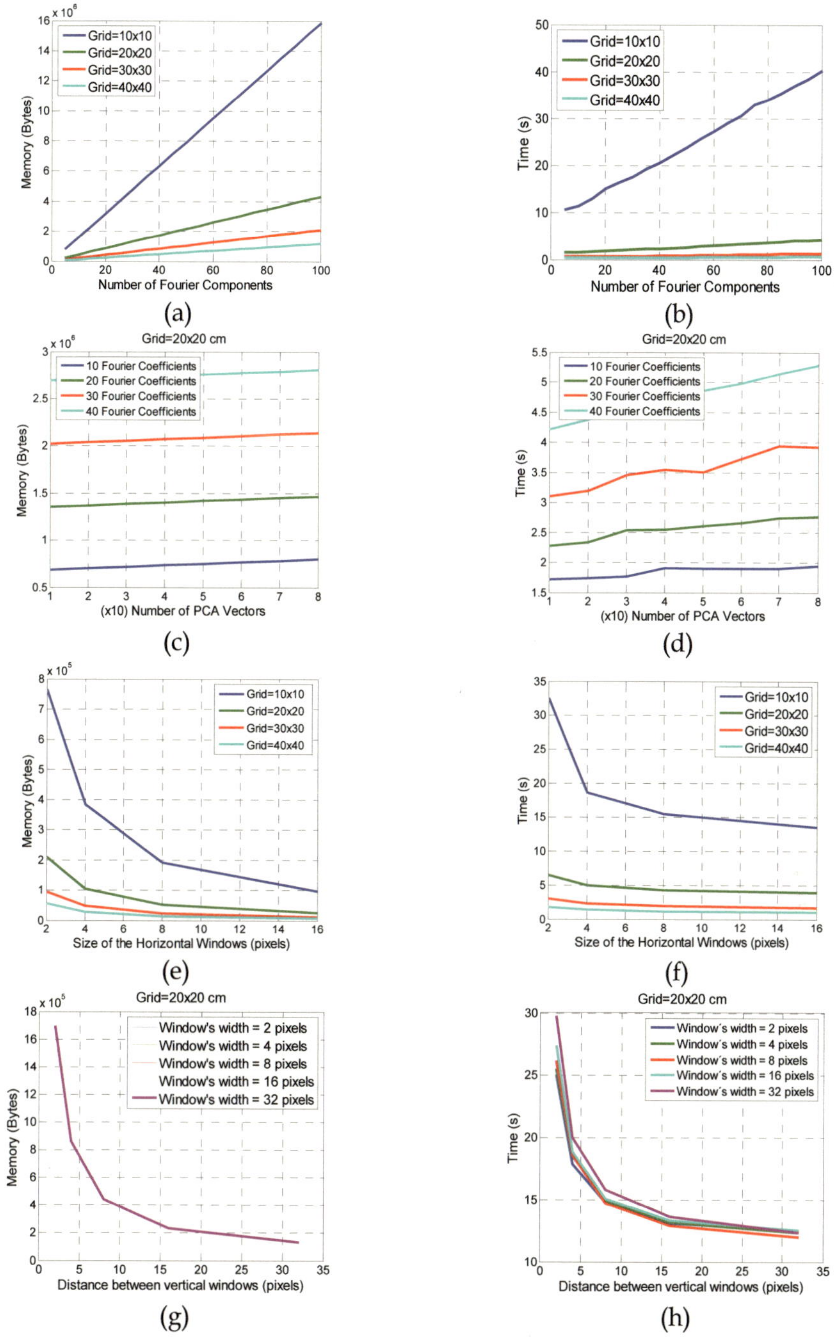

Fig. 6. (a) Amount of memory and (b) processing time to build the map with the Fourier-based algorithm. (c) Amount of memory and (d) processing time to build the map using PCA over Fourier Signature method. (e) Amount of memory and (f) processing time to build the map with HOG, varying horizontal windows parameters. (g) Amount of memory and (h) processing time to build the map with HOG, varying vertical windows parameters.

Once the images of the map are selected, we compute the image descriptors using each method to obtain a dataset, which represents the map of the environment.
Fig. 6 shows the amount of memory and time necessary to build the map, depending on the number of images and/or the different parameters that affect each algorithm as described in the previous section. These parameters are, in the case of Fourier signature, the number of Fourier coefficients per row (f). In the case of PCA over the Fourier signature, they are the number of vectors selected from the PCA decomposition (K), apart from the number of Fourier coefficients (f). At last, in the case of HOG, both the size and separation between windows must be decided in the case of the horizontal (position estimation) and the vertical (orientation estimation) windows.
Fig. 6(a) and 6(b) show the memory requirements and processing time to build the map with the Fourier method. Naturally, there is a proportional increase of the memory and time requirements as we get more coefficients of each row (since more information is computed and stored), and a decrease of both parameters when the grid step increases (since it supposes fewer images in the map).
Fig. 6(c) and 6(d) show the results when applying PCA to the Fourier Signature for a 20x20 cm grid. The results are more dependent on the number of Fourier coefficients than on the number of PCA components. In all the experiments, the processing time is larger than in the first method if the same number of Fourier components is taken, due to the fact that apart from calculating the Fourier signature, it is necessary to compute the PCA algorithm too.
Fig. 6(e) and 6(f) show the results when using HOG and varying the size of the horizontal windows and grid step. In these experiments, the vertical windows have a fixed width and gap of 8 pixels (i.e., degree step of 11,25º). These figures show a strong correlation between the size of the horizontal window and the memory and time requirements, since the bigger is the window, the lesser windows exist (no overlapping is used in horizontal windows).
Fig. 6(g) and 6(h) show the results when using HOG and varying the size of and the distance between the vertical windows, for a 20x20 grid step. In this case, overlapping between windows is allowed. In these figures, we appreciate that the number of windows is much more influential in the results than its size. That is because calculating the histogram of a bigger window is computationally less expensive than computing the histogram of a new cell. In fig. 6(g) the graphs are overlapped because the information stored (the histogram of each cell) has the same size although the windows get bigger.

5. Performance of the descriptors in a localization task

Apart from studying the performance of the descriptors when representing the scenes, it is also necessary to test the accuracy they offer when computing the position and the orientation of the robot in the environment, since both results are crucial in the localization and control phases of the route-following aplication. In this section, we measure this accuracy. When a new image arrives, the position and orientation the robot had when capturing it must be computed comparing the descriptor of the new image with the descriptors in the map. To carry out the experiments, we use as test images all the available images in the database, independently of the grid selected to make the map, and 15 artificial rotations of each one (every 22.5º). So, the total number of test images is 11,936.
We study separately the computation of the position and the orientation of the robot. Position is studied as binary results, considering if we obtain the best possible match or not,

and the information is showed with recall and precision measurements (Gil et al., 2009). Each chart shows the information about if a correct location is in the Nearest Neighbour (N.N.), i. e., if it is the first result selected, or between Second or Third Nearest Neighbours (S.N.N or T.N.N). Regarding the rotation, we represent the results accuracy in bar graphs depending on how much they differ from the correct ones. If the experiment error is bigger than ±10 degrees, it is considered as a failure. The processing time to calculate the position and orientation of the robot is shown in different tables, in seconds.

5.1 Fourier signature technique

The map obtained with the Fourier signature descriptor is represented with two matrices per image: the module and the phase of the Fourier coefficients. When a new image arrives, the first step is to compute its Fourier signature. Then, the location is estimated calculating the Euclidean distance between its module matrix and the module matrices stored in the map. The best match is obtained as the image in the map with minimun distance. Once the position of the robot is known, the phases' matrix associated to the most similar image is used to compute the relative orientation of the robot. Table 2 shows the processing time depending on the images grid step and the number of Fourier components per row. There is a bigger dependency on the number of components than on the grid step (i.e. the number of images in the map). This is due to the orientation estimation, since it is the most computational heavy part of the algorithm and it depends only on the number of components per row.

GRID	2 Comp	5 Comp	10 Comp	20 Comp
10x10	0.0099	0.0130	0.0219	0.0487
20x20	0.0072	0.0107	0.0192	0.0446
30x30	0.0070	0.0104	0.0187	0.0440
40x40	0.0069	0.0103	0.0185	0,0438

Table 2. Processing time (in seconds) of the position and orientation estimation using the Fourier signature, varying the number of components per row and the grid step.

Fig. 7 shows recall and precision measures. When more components per row are taken, the location is better, but there is a limit over which it is not interesting to raise the number of components because the results do not improve. In this case, with 10 components the location is successful. The phase accuracy also improves when more coefficients are used to compute the angle, although it is quite constant when we take 8 or more components.

5.2 PCA over fourier signature

After applying PCA over the Fourier signature modules matrix, we obtain another matrix containing the main eigenvectors, and the projection of the training images onto the space made up with that vectors. These projections are used to calculate the position of the robot. On the other hand, we keep the phases matrix of the Fourier signature directly to estimate the orientation.

To know where the robot is, first the Fourier signature of the current image must be computed. After retaining the desired number of components per row, the vector of modules is projected onto the eigenspace. The most similar image in the map is obtained by

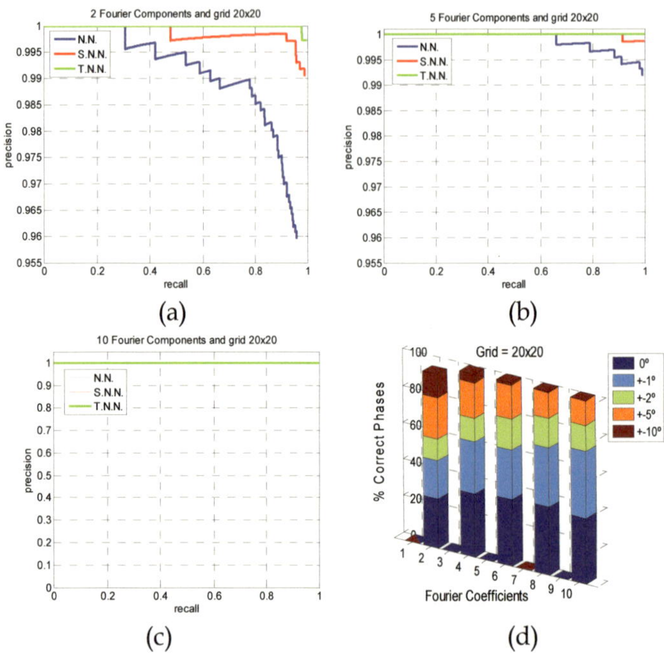

Fig. 7. (a), (b), (c) Recall-Precision charts with Nearest Neighbour (N.N.), Second Nearest Neighbour (S.N.N.) and Third Nearest Neighbour (T.N.N) and (d) accuracy in the calculation of the orientation using the Fourier Signature method.

GRID	2 Comp	5 Comp	10 Comp	20 Comp
10x10	0.1113	0.2420	0.2844	0.3362
20x20	0.0355	0.0613	0.0985	0.1462
30x30	0.0233	0.0483	0.0838	0.1321
40x40	0.0205	0.0459	0.0815	0.1294

Table 3. Processing time (in seconds) of the pose estimation using PCA over Fourier signature when selecting 10 PCA components.

GRID	2 Vectors	5 Vectors	10 Vectors	20 vectors
10x10	0.1505	0.1492	0.1497	0.1497
20x20	0.1294	0.1293	0.1300	0.1295
30x30	0.1278	0.1280	0.1271	0.1273
40x40	0.1272	0.1273	0.1272	0.1270

Table 4. Processing time (in seconds) of the pose estimation using PCA over Fourier signature when selecting 40 Fourier coefficients per row.

calculating the minimum Euclidean distance of the new image's projection and the map ones. When the position is known, the phase is calculated in the same way than when we do not apply PCA since the phase matrix is not projected.
Table 3 presents the processing time to get the position and the orientation of the robot from the moment the current image arrives. To measure this time, the number of eigenvectors we keep is constant. The results show that the elapsed time rises as the number of images in the map or the components in the Fourier signature increase. However, except in the first case, the number of coefficients we take has more influence since the computation of the phase is computationally more expensive than the localization, and it depends on this parameter.
Table 4 shows the processing time when applying PCA over Fourier signature, varying the number of eigenvectors. These results show again that the number of vectors is not very influential since the time spent in the algorithm does not change significantly. Moreover, as far as PCA effects are concerned, there are no important variations in the time when the grid step varies, i.e. projecting the characteristic vector onto the eigenspace is a fast process and there are no important differences when having more images or using more vectors to build the projection space.
As we can see in fig. 8, if a high accuracy in the localization task is needed, it is required a high number of PCA eigenvectors, what means loosing the advantages of applying this method. Moreover, in the majority of experiments, the number of Fourier coefficients we need is bigger than when we do not use PCA, incrementing the memory requirements.
Phase results are not included because the results are exactly the same as showed in fig. 4 since its calculation method does not vary.

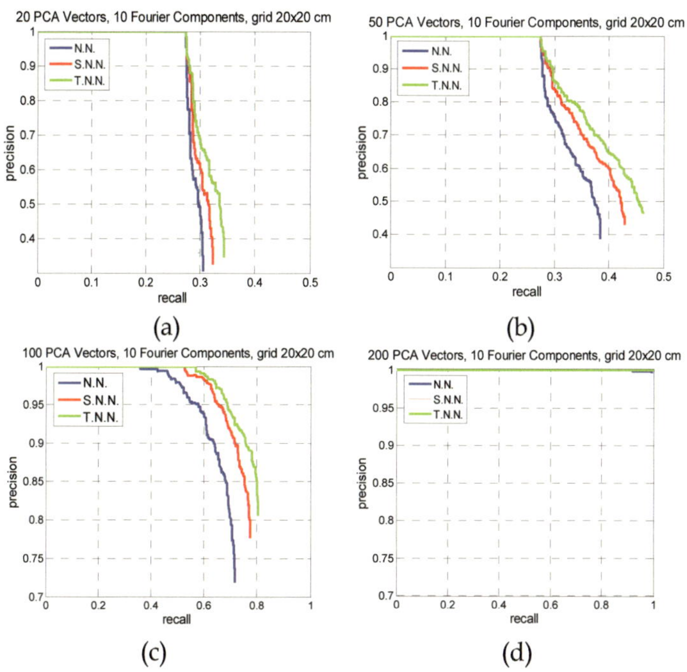

Fig. 8. Recall-Precision charts with Nearest Neighbour (N.N.), Second Nearest Neighbour (S.N.N.) and Third Nearest Neighbour (T.N.N) using PCA over Fourier Signature varying the number of PCA vectors.

5.3. Histogram of oriented gradient

When a new image arrives, first, its histogram of oriented gradient is computed using cells (windows) with the same size as when the map was built. So, the time needed to find the pose of the robot varies depending on both vertical and horizontal cells. To find the position of the robot, the horizontal cells information is used, whereas to compute the phase it is necessary to use the information in the vertical cells. In both cases, the information is found by calculating the Euclidean distance between the histogram of the new image and the stored ones in the map.

GRID	2 pixels	4 pixels	8 pixels	16 pixels
10x10	0.1113	0.2420	0.2844	0.3362
20x20	0.0355	0.0613	0.0985	0.1462
30x30	0.0233	0.0483	0.0838	0.1321
40x40	0.0205	0.0459	0.0815	0.1294

Table 5. Processing time (in seconds) in the pose estimation using HOG, varying horizontal cells height.

GRID	2 pixels	4 pixels	8 pixels	16 pixels
10x10	0.6599	0.5259	0.4979	0.4857
20x20	0.2777	0.1598	0.1240	0.1136
30x30	0.2546	0.1301	0.0982	0.0866
40x40	0.2497	0.1247	0.0943	0.0822

Table 6. Processing time (in seconds) in the pose estimation using HOG, varying vertical cells distance.

When a smaller cells' size is used, more windows appear, so more histograms have to be computed. So, when we reduce the height of the cells, the processing time is bigger (table 5). Moreover, when the map is made up of more images, we have to make more comparisons to find the nearest image, what means to spend more time. But with fewer cells, it is more difficult to recognise the correct position, as shown in fig. 9.

In table 6 the effect of varying the distance between vertical cells is assessed. This parameter conditions the phase computation. The more distance we have, the less time we need, because the number of histograms to compute is lower. However, to improve the angle accuracy, that distance must be reduced.

6. Conclusion

In this paper, we have presented an appearance-based multi-robot route following scheme. The proposed solution uses low resolution panoramic images obtained through a catadioptric system that is mounted on each robot in the system, and appearance based methods to build the map and compute the localization.

In our approach, a leader robot goes through the desired rote while it creates a database with some visual information captured along the route. This database is shared with the follower robots, which have to follow this route from a distance (as in space or in time). To

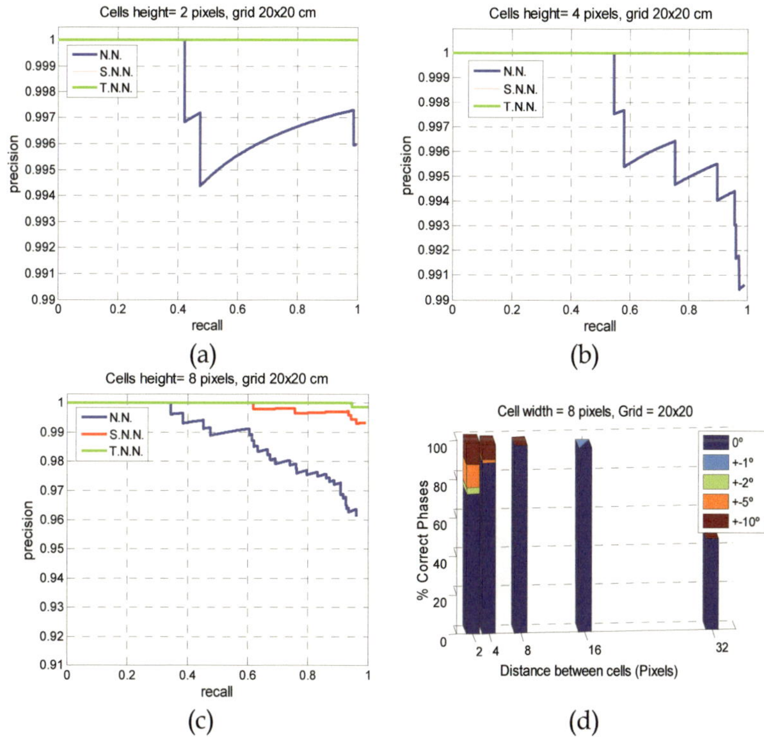

Fig. 9. (a), (b), (c) Recall-Precision charts with Nearest Neighbour (N.N.), Second Nearest Neighbour (S.N.N.) and Third Nearest Neighbour (T.N.N). (d) Phase accuracy using HOG.

do it, a probabilistic algorithm, based on a Markov process has been implemented to calculate their current position among those that the leader has stored, and a controller has been implemented, also based on the appearance of the scenes, to calculate the linear and turning speeds of the robot. To allow a new robot can follow the route that another robot is recording at the same time, an incremental algorithm is presented.

The work is mainly focused in the study of the feasibility of the techniques based on the global appearance of the panoramic scenes to solve the problem. With this aim, we use dimensionality reduction to extract the most relevant information from the environment and build a robust and efficient descriptor of each scene.

We have compared the performance of three different approaches when working with panoramic images: Fourier signature, Principal Components Analysis applied to the Fourier signature and Histogram of Oriented Gradients. Our contribution in the comparison of these three methods is twofold. First, we have studied their performance when representing the environment. We have carried out a set of experiments to test the computational cost to compute each kind of descriptor and the memory requirements to store them. Secondly, we have also studied their validity in localization tasks. In this case, the experiments have allowed us to know the efficiency in calculating the position and the orientation of the robot by comparing its current visual information with all the descriptors previously stored in the database.

All the description methods have demonstrated to be valid to represent the environment and to carry out the estimation of the pose of a robot inside the map. However, the Fourier signature has proved to be the most efficient method since with few components of the Fourier Transform of each row we obtain good results. So, the map does not need a huge amount of memory to be stored, and the comparison is not a computationally heavy process. No advantage has been found in applying PCA to the Fourier signature, since creating the eigenspace is a computationally expensive task, and in order to have good results it is needed to keep the great majority of the eigenvectors obtained. Moreover, because we need more Fourier coefficients, the size of the map is not reduced. Regarding HOG, although the results demonstrate it is a robust method, it is not very flexible due to its time and memory requirements, since the histogram computation is a time-consuming task, and if we want to improve the orientation accuracy, the map's memory increases notably.

This paper shows again the wide range of possibilities of appearance-based methods applied to mobile robotics, and its promising results encourage us to continue studying them in deep, looking for new available techniques. Our future work includes studying how to build more sophisticated topological maps of the environment and how to cope with some typical problems in indoor environments such as occlusions, changes in the lighting conditions and changes in the position of some objects of the scene. Also, these new maps will require the use of new probabilistic localization methods, such as Monte Carlo approaches, whose applicability to appearance-based data must be explored.

7. Acknowledgements

This work has been supported by the Spanish government through the project DPI2010-15308. 'Exploración integrada de entornos mediante robots cooperativos para la creación de mapas 3D visuales y topológicos que puedan ser usados en navegación con 6 grados de libertad'.

8. References

Booij, O.; Terwijn, B.; Zivkovic, Z. & Kröse, B. (2007). Navigation using an Appearance Based Topological Map. *Proceedings of IEEE International Conference on Robotics and Automation*, pp. 3297-3932, ISBN 1-4244-0602-1, Roma, Italy, IEEE

Burschka, D. & Hager, G. (2001). Vision-Based Control of Mobile Robots, *Proceedings of IEEE International Conference on Robotics and Automation*, pp. 1707-1713, ISBN 0-7803-6578-X, Seoul, Korea, May 2001, IEEE

Dalal, N. & Triggs, B. (2005). Histograms of Oriented Gradients for Human Detection. *Proceedings of the IEEE Conference on Computer Vision and Pattern Recognition*, pp. 886-893, ISBN: 0-7695-2372-2, San Diego, USA, Jun. 2005. IEEE Press.

Gil, A.; Martinez, O.; Ballesta, M. & Reinoso, O. (2009). A comparative evaluation of interest point detectors and local descriptors for visual SLAM. *Machine Vision and Applications*, (Apr. 2009) ISSN: 0932-8092.

Ho, K. & Newman, P. (2005). Multiple Map Intersection Detection using Visual Appearance. *Proceedings of 3rd International Conference on Computational Intelligence, Robotics and Autonomous Systems*, Singapore, Dic. 2005.

Jogan, M. & Leonardis, A. (2000). Robust Localization Using Eigenspace of Spinning-Images. *Proceedings of IEEE Workshop on Omnidirectional Vision*, pp. 37-44, ISBN 0-7695-0704-2, Hilton Head Island, USA, Jun 2000, IEEE.

Kirby, M. (2000). *Geometric data analysis. An empirical approach to dimensionality reduction and the study of patterns*, Wiley Interscience, ISBN 0-4712-3929-1

Kröse, B.; Bunschoten, R.; Hagen, S.; Terwijn, B. & Vlassis, N. (2004). Household robots: Look and learn. *IEEE Robotics & Automation magazine*, Vol. 11, No. 4, (Dec 2004) 45-52, ISSN 1070-9932

Matsumoto, Y.; Ikeda, K.; Inaba, M. & Inoue, H. (1999). Visual Navigation Using Omnidirectional View Sequence. *Proceedings of IEEE International Conference on Intelligent Robots and Systems*, pp. 317-322, ISBN: 0-7803-5184-3, New York, USA, Oct 1999, IEEE Press

Menegatti, E.; Maeda, T. & Ishiguro, H. (2004). Image-based memory for robot navigation using properties of omnidirectional images. *Robotics and Autonomous Systems*. Vol. 47, No. 4, (Jul 2004), 251-276, ISSN 0921-8890

Möller, R.; Vardy, A.; Kreft, S. & Ruwisch, S. (2007). Visual homing in environments with anisotropic landmark distribution. *Autonomous Robots*, Vol. 23, No. 3, (Oct. 2007) pp. 231-245, ISSN: 0929-5593.

Payá, L.; Fernández, L.; Reinoso, O.; Gil, A. & Ubeda, D. (2009). Appearance-based Dense Maps Creation: Comparison of compression techniques with panoramic images, *Proceedings of 6th International Conference on Informatics in Control, Automation and Robotics*, pp. 250-255, ISBN: 978-989-674-000-9, Milan, Italy, Jun. 2009, INSTICC Press.

Payá, L.; Reinoso, O.; Gil, A.; Pedrero, J. & Ballesta, M. (2007). Appearance-Based Multi-Robot Following Routes Using Incremental PCA. *Lecture Notes in Artificial Intelligence. Knowledge-Based Intelligent Information and Engineering Systems*. Vol. 4693, (Sep. 2007) pp. 1170-1178, ISSN: 0302 -9743.

Payá, L.; Reinoso, O.; Gil, A. & Sogorb. J. (2008). Multi-robot route following using omnidirectional vision and appearance-based representation of the environment. *Lecture Notes in Artificial Intelligence. Hybrid Artificial Intelligence Systems*, Vol. 5271, (Sep 2008) pp. 680-687, ISSN 0302-9743.

Rossi, F.; Ranganathan, A.; Dellaert, F. & Menegatti, E. (2008). Toward topological localization with spherical Fourier transform and uncalibrated camera. *Proceedings of International Conference on Simulation, Modeling and Programming for Autonomous Robots*, pp. 319-330, ISBN 978-88-95872-01-8, Venice, Italy, Nov 2008.

Thrun, S. (2001). A probabilistic online mapping algorithm for teams of mobile robots. *International Journal of Robotics Research*, Vol. 20, No. 5, (May. 2001), pp. 335-363, ISSN: 0278-3649.

Thrun, S. (2003). Robotic Mapping: A Survey, In: *Exploring Artificial Intelligence in the New Milenium*, 1-35, Morgan Kaufmann Publishers, ISBN 1-55860-811-7, San Francisco, USA

Thrun, S.; Burgard, W. & Fox D. (2005). *Probabilistic Robotics*. MIT Press, ISBN: 0-262-20162-3, Cambridge, USA.

Ueonara, M. & Kanade, T. (1998). Optimal approximation of uniformly rotated images: relationship between Karhunen-Loeve expansion and Discrete Cosine Transform. *IEEE Transactions on Image Processing*. Vol. 7, No. 1, (Jan. 1998) pp. 116-119, ISSN: 1057-7149.

Vasudevan, S.; Gächter, S.; Nguyen, V. & Siegwart, R. (2007). Cognitive maps for mobile robots - an object based approach. *Robotics and Autonomous Systems*, Vol. 55, No. 5, (May. 2007) pp. 359-371, ISSN 0921-8890.

12

Graph-based Multi Robot Motion Planning: Feasibility and Structural Properties

Ellips Masehian and Azadeh H. Nejad
Tarbiat Modares University
Iran

1. Introduction

Future generation autonomous agents are expected to operate in remote and dangerous places like outer space, undersea, hazardous waste sites, and are therefore anticipated to be far more self-directed than today's existing agents. The ability of an agent to plan its own motion is pivotal to its autonomy. For over more than three decades, agent motion planning in general, and robot motion planning in particular, have attracted much research in various fields and have become central topics in autonomous agents and artificial intelligence. Although today the term 'motion planning' is considered to cover a wide variety of problems, we will use it for the problem of planning collision-free motions for an autonomous robot moving among obstacles.

The necessity of planning the motions of autonomous agents originally arose in early 1970's, when the first industrial robots were to perform automatic tasks of manipulation and navigation. Soon it was realized that the complexity of the robot motion planning problem is PSPACE-hard and NP-complete since the size of the solution space grows exponentially and gets extremely complicated, especially for high degrees of freedom (Canny, 1988).

Many techniques have been developed for solving the robot motion planning problem, including the 'Skeleton' or 'Roadmap' approach (Choset et al., 2005). In this approach, the continuous workspace is mapped into a one-dimensional graph with vertices including the start and goal of the robot, and edges as paths between vertices. This graph is then searched to find a collision-free start-to-goal path.

Visibility Graph is a type of roadmap which is the collection of lines in the free space connecting vertices of an object to those of another (Fig. 1(a)). There are $O(n^2)$ edges in the Visibility Graph, and it can be constructed in $O(n^2)$ time and space in 2D, where n is the number of vertices.

Voronoi Diagram is another roadmap defined as the set of points equidistant from two or more objects (Fig. 1(b)). The Voronoi Diagram partitions the space into regions, where each region contains one object. For each point in a region, the object within the region is the closest to that point than any other object. There are only $O(n)$ edges in the Voronoi Diagram, and it can be efficiently constructed in $\Omega(n\log n)$ time, where n is the number of objects (Hwang & Ahuja, 1992).

When multiple moving robots share a common workspace, the motion planning task becomes even more difficult and cannot be performed for just one robot without considering others. In this kind of problems, while pursuing their individual (local) goals,

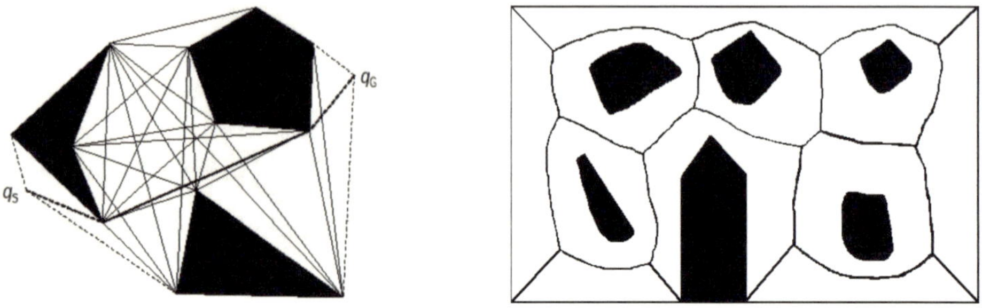

(a) (b)

Fig. 1. (a) Visibility Graph, and (b) Voronoi Diagram

robots must coordinate their motions with each other in order to avoid collisions with obstacles and one another, thus contributing to the task of achieving a global goal, which might be minimizing the total time or distance. This problem is called Multi Robot Motion Planning (MRMP) problem. In MRMP, each robot is regarded as a dynamic obstacle for other robots, and therefore the element of time plays a major role in planning, especially because of its irreversible nature (Latombe, 1991).

Although classic roadmaps like Visibility Graph and Voronoi diagram have proved to be effective for single-robot problems, they do not provide straightforward solutions to MRMP problems, including the corridor-like environment shown in Fig. 2(a). This kind of environments is prevalent in large warehouses, plants, and transportation systems, where Automatic Guided Vehicles (AGVs) convey material and products (Fig. 2(b)).

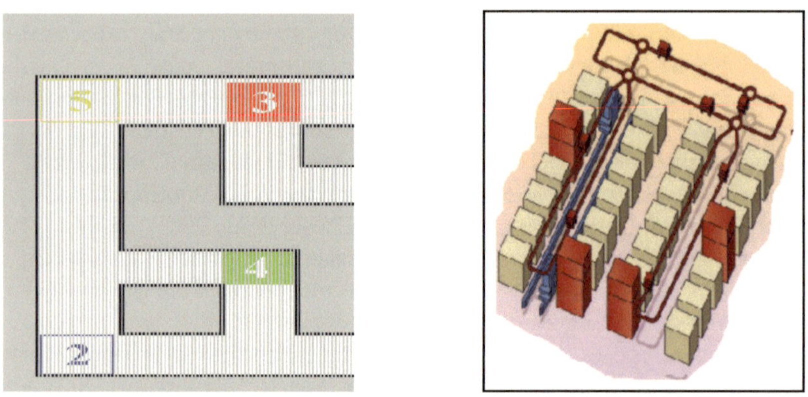

(a) (b)

Fig. 2. (a) Each robot must move toward its final destination while allowing other robots to reach their goals. (b) Planning the motions of AGVs to different locations in a shop floor or warehouse is a real-world application of MRMP

Space is the most limiting constraint in a typical MRMP problem: often, because of lack of sufficient space around moving robots, they cannot reach their destinations without obstructing each other's way, causing deadlocks. Deadlocks are situations in which two (or more) robots intercept each other's motions and are prevented from reaching their goals. This happens generally in narrow passageways where autonomous moving robots cannot pass by each other. To resolve such a deadlock, one of the robots should leave and evacuate the passageway (by usually backtracking), and let the opposite robot move out of the passage.

A well-known cooperative behaviour of robots is following independent start-to-goal paths while resolving deadlocks by reshuffling, circumnavigating, detouring, and speed regulating, which is also known as Velocity Tuning and is first developed in (Kant & Zucker, 1986). Another approach developed for resolving deadlocks is the Prioritized Planning, in which the robots are sorted by their moving priorities (Bennewitz et al., 2001). Higher-priority robots are planned first, whereas lower-priority robots plan their motion subsequently by considering higher-priority robots as dynamic obstacles.

By reducing the workspace into a graph with vertices including the starts and goals of all robots, the MRMP problem can turn into a sequencing problem where the robots are planned to move sequentially (or concurrently) toward their destinations, without colliding with each other. The graph structure stipulates them to remain on predefined routes (i.e. graph edges), and so avoid static obstacles existing in the workspace.

The main question in designing a predefined graph, however, is to find out whether the graph is 'reachable' (solvable) for any initial and final configurations. Solvable Graphs allow the transition of any initial configuration of agents (e.g. pebbles (beans), robots, or vehicles) to a final state via their sequential moves along the graph's edges.

Wilson in (Wilson, 1974) worked out a relation between the number of pebbles (k) and the number of vertices (n) of only bi-connected graphs as $k = n - 1$. Kornhauser in (Kornhauser et al., 1984) improved this result through generalizing the decision problem for all graphs and any number of agents. (Auletta et al., 1999) studied the above problem as pebble motion problem by following the generalization of the 15-puzzle and presented a linear algorithm for deciding the reachability of trees. Ryan in (Ryan, 2008) studied the possibility of reaching destinations of connected sub-graphs by simplifying the multi robot motion planning between the sub-graphs. He worked on predefined sub-graphs like stack, clique and hall. In (Onn & Tennenholtz, 1997) it is demonstrated that the environment can be shown through any two-connected graph which has a routing with a practical social law for motion planning.

To our knowledge, the problem of deciding whether a graph is always solvable for a specific number of robots for any initial and final configuration has never been mentioned or addressed in the literature prior to our work (Masehian & Hassan Nejad, 2009). The problem of determining the smallest solvable graph (in terms of vertices) for a certain number of robots has also been remained untackled.

Graphs can be categorized into two general classes: cyclic, and acyclic: cyclic graphs have loops and are more convenient for moving of multiple robots (or agents), while acyclic graphs (i.e. trees) provide less manoeuvrability for the agents moving on it. That's why MRMP on trees can serve as a basis for MRMP on general cyclic graphs. MRMP on trees has real-world applications in maze-like environments, indoor corridors, parking lots, railway networks, etc.

In this chapter, we specifically deal with tree-type (acyclic) graphs, and set forth the following questions: What is the maximum number of robots a tree can accommodate such that any final configuration can be reached from any initial configuration? What topology a tree must have to be solvable for a specific number of robots? and What is the 'smallest' tree solvable for a specific number of robots?

After presenting some basic definitions in section 2, in section 3 the conditions for a tree to be solvable are investigated and the maximum number of robots located on it is determined.

The concept of Minimal Solvable Trees is introduced in Section 4, and a practical shop-floor problem is presented in Section 5 to demonstrate the application of theoretical results. Some discussions and conclusions are presented in Section 6.

2. Definitions and assumptions

As mentioned earlier, reducing (or mapping) the configuration space into a graph is very helpful regarding the significant savings in required time and memory. In order to lay a proper mathematical foundation for expressing and investigating the properties of graphs, we adopt the standard terminology used in Graph Theory (Diestel, 2000). In addition, some definitions and symbols have been introduced and defined specifically for this work, all presented in Table 1. A number of these concepts are illustrated in Fig. 2.

Generally, an MRMP in a continuous space is composed of the following phases:

a. Constructing a network (graph) with nodes (vertices) including the robots' initial and final stopping locations, together with all the locations the robots should be able to temporarily stop at and offer a service. The arcs (edges) of the graph must pass through free spaces (e.g. unoccupied rooms or corridors) such that no obstacle may be collided with during the robots' motions along the edges.
b. Planning the robots' motions along the arcs of the network from their starting to final locations, such that a cost criterion (e.g. time, distance, or expense) is minimized.

Term/Symbol	Description
Order, $\lvert G \rvert$	The number of vertices of the Graph $G = (V, E)$.
$\lVert G \rVert$	The number of edges on G.
Path	A non-empty graph $P = (V, E)$ of the form $V = \{v_0, v_1, ..., v_k\}$, $E = \{v_0v_1, v_1v_2, ..., v_{k-1}v_k\}$, where all v_i 's are distinct.
Cycle	A non-empty graph of the form $V = \{v_0, v_1, ..., v_k\}$, $E = \{v_0v_1, v_1v_2, ..., v_{k-1}v_k, v_kv_0\}$, where all v_i 's are distinct.
Cycle Edge	An edge on a cycle.
Tree	An acyclic graph.
Leaf, L	A vertex with a degree $d = 1$.
Cycle Vertex, C	A vertex located on a cycle.
Internal Vertex, I	A vertex with a degree $d > 1$ which is not a Cycle Vertex.
Stem, S	The longest path in the graph with its one end (or both ends, if located between two cycles) connected to a cycle vertex and including it, and not containing any Cycle Edge. None of the edges of the Stem are cycle edges. If not unique, the Stem is selected arbitrarily. The number of vertices on the Stem (i.e. its order) is shown by $\lvert I_S \rvert$.
Configuration	An arrangement of robots on the graph vertices such that no vertex is occupied by more than one robot.

Table 1. Definitions of used terms and symbols

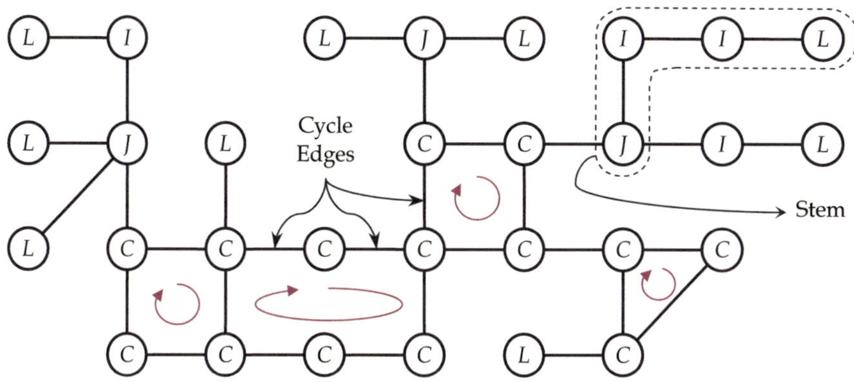

Fig. 3. Some concepts illustrated: *L*, *I*, *J* and *C* denote Leaf, Internal vertex, junction and Cycle-vertex, respectively. The symbol ↻ indicates a cycle, and the dashed area designates the Stem

When designing a graph or network of routes, it is always important to consider current transportation demands, as well as future developments of the system. In the context of MRMP, this consideration requires that the system designer decides the proper topology of the network, the number of agents (as mobile robots or vehicles) required to move along the routes, and the possibilities of expanding the network for future increased transportation traffic.

Concerned about these issues, we have comprehensively investigated the concept of Solvable Graphs. To date, the notion of graph solvability has been essentially dependent to the initial and final configurations (situations) of the moving objects. For instance, the question whether a tree-like graph is solvable for a given initial and final configuration of pebbles is solvable or not is addressed in (Auletta et al., 1999). However, no work exists in the literature for all types of graphs, and never has the problem of deciding if a graph is always solvable for a specific number of robots for any initial and final configuration been mentioned or addressed.

In this chapter, we just focus on the first phase of MRMP, that is, graph construction, and propound some related problems of broad scope, such as:

- What is the maximum number of robots a graph can accommodate such that any final configuration can be reached from any initial configuration?
- What topology must a graph have to be solvable for a specific number of robots?
- What is the 'smallest' graph solvable for a specific number of robots?

Before dealing with the answers to the above questions, three new fundamental and correlated notions are presented:

Definition 1. A Solvable Graph is a graph on which any configuration of at most m robots can be reached from any initial configuration through their moves on graph edges, and is shown by SG^m.

Definition 2. A Partially Solvable Graph is a graph on which only some configurations of m robots can be reached from any initial configuration through their moves on graph edges, and is shown by PSG^m.

Definition 3. A Minimal Solvable Graph is the smallest graph on which any configuration of at most m robots can be reached from any initial configuration through their moves on graph edges, and is shown by MSG^m. In this definition, 'smallest' can be expressed and measured in terms of the number of either vertices or edges.

Graphs can be categorized into two general classes: (1) Cyclic graphs, and (2) Acyclic graphs. Cyclic graphs have loops and provide alternative ways to access a specific node, and therefore are more convenient for planning the motions of multiple robots. On the other hand, Acyclic graphs (i.e. trees) do not have any loops, and the shortest path between every pair of vertices is unique. As such, trees provide fewer options and less manoeuvrability for robots, and are much harder to solve than cyclic graphs. Actually, MRMP on trees can serve as a basis for MRMP on cyclic graphs, and the solution of an MRMP on a tree is also valid for the MRMP problem on a cyclic graph which is the superset of that tree. In view of this, and considering its NP-hardness, we found the MRMP problem on trees a worthwhile and challenging problem to be solved efficiently.

2.1 Assumptions

In the phase of graph construction, the topological (and not geometric) features of the world are important; features like the number and degrees of vertices, existence of edges between certain pairs of vertices, existence of loops and their sizes, etc. Nevertheless, the geometrical features of the world, such as the exact coordinates of the vertices, the lengths of edges, etc. become decisive in the phase of motion planning.

In this chapter some simplifying (yet not limiting) assumptions about the graph and robots are made as following:

1. An essential assumption is that the designed graph is finite, connected, planar, acyclic, and represents the free space. This means that edges intersect only at vertices.
2. The graph is undirected, and a path exists from any vertex v to u and vice versa.
3. The initial and final locations of all robots lie on the graph and are known.
4. All robots share the same graph and can (and may) move on the edges of the graph and stay on the vertices of the graph. A Move is defined as transferring a robot from a vertex to its neighbouring vertex via their connecting edge.
5. Two or more robots may not simultaneously occupy the same vertex in the graph. That is, the vertices are supposed to be spaced sufficiently far apart so that two robots can occupy any two distinct vertices without having collision.
6. Robots have sequential (i.e. one at a time) movements on edges of the graph. In other words, a robot at vertex v can move to its neighbouring Leaf or Internal vertex u only if u is unoccupied. Robots occupying other vertices in the graph do not affect this movement.

3. Solvable trees

Since junctions are vertices in the tree where different branches and Leaves meet (just as squares or crossroads which connect avenues and streets), they enable the robots to change their course of motion and shift from one branch or Leaf to another branch or Leaf.

Therefore, Leaves and junctions' branches can be used for robots' manoeuvres and interchanges, and serve as places for situating the robots permanently or temporarily during the motion planning task, aiming to make the start-to-goal paths of robots as free as possible and facilitate the robots' moves toward their goals.

On the other hand, the exchangeability of robots at and around a junction also depends on the number of vertices not occupied by robots at the initial configuration. We call these empty vertices '*Holes*', and their number, H, is calculated by $H = |G| - m$, where $|G|$ is the order of the graph.

In this section, for obtaining the solvability conditions of trees, first the simplest trees called 'Stars' are introduced and their solvability is investigated. The results are then generalized to more complicated trees. It is noted that we are trying to find the *maximum* number of robots for which a tree is solvable. Obviously, any tree solvable for m robots is also solvable for $k < m$ robots since there will be more empty vertices and so deadlocks can be resolved more easily.
The basic requirement for the solvability of a graph is expressed as follows:
Lemma 1. *A graph is SG^m iff any two robots located on it can exchange their positions.*
Proof. Suppose that m robots have to move from their initial positions to specified final positions. We represent the exchange of two robots r_i and r_j by $X(r_i, r_j)$ and denote the act of moving a robot r_i to an empty vertex by $M(r_i, h)$, and assume that robots' exchanges are possible while the initial and final positions of all other robots remain unchanged. It is noted that while the premise of the lemma deals with exchanging of two robots, moving a robot to an empty vertex is a direct ramification of it since it is equivalent to exchanging a real robot with a dummy one.
The planning of start-to-goal motions of all robots can be decomposed into a sequence of 2-robot exchanges, as follows:

Stage 1:	$M(r_1, h)$	or	$X(r_1, r_i)$,	$\forall\, i \in \{2, 3, \ldots, m\}$,
Stage 2:	$M(r_2, h)$	or	$X(r_2, r_i)$,	$\forall\, i \in \{3, 4, \ldots, m\}$,
…				
Stage $m-1$:	$M(r_{m-1}, h)$	or	$X(r_{m-1}, r_i)$,	$\forall\, i \in \{m\}$,
Stage m:	$M(r_m, h)$.			

Note that for accomplishing each Stage numerous steps (i.e. moves) might be necessary. It follows that if according to the premise of the lemma any 2-robot (either real or dummy) exchange is possible, then any m-robot exchange is also possible, which means that the graph is solvable.
Conversely, if a graph is solvable, then any configuration is reachable from any initial configuration—a special case of which could be the exchanging of just two robots. This shows that graph solvability and 2-robot exchanging are logically equivalent. □

3.1 Solvability of star trees

A *Star*^{k} is a complete bipartite graph with only one vertex in one part and k vertices in the other part. Stars are trees with diameters equal to 2, and have only one junction. Fig. 4(a) illustrates a 6-Leaf Star.
An *Extended Star* (ES^k) is a graph comprised of a single junction connected to k vertices, some or all of which are connected to 'chains' of internal vertices, such that there are no other junctions in the graph. A typical Extended Star is shown in Fig. 4(b).
Lemma 2 investigates the solvability of Stars:

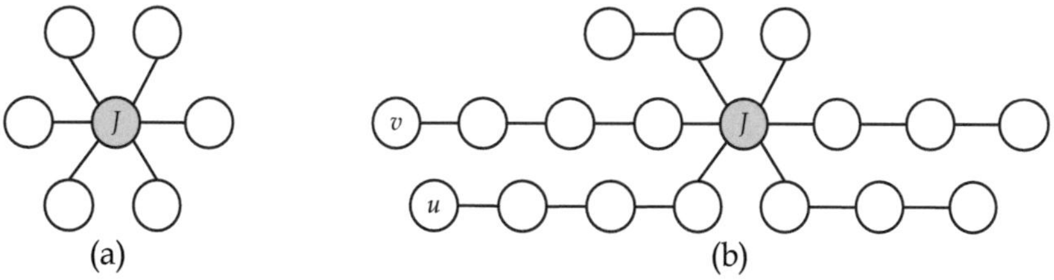

Fig. 4. (a) A 6-leaf Star, and (b) an Extended Star with $\|S\| = 4$

Lemma 2. *A Star with k leaves is Solvable iff $H \geq 2$, where H is the number of Holes.*
Proof. A $Star^k$ has $k + 1$ vertices (as can be seen in Fig. 4(a) for $k = 6$), and when $H = 2$, these two Holes may either be (*i*) on two leaves, or (*ii*) on a leaf and the junction. Now for proving the solvability of the Star, various possibilities of initial and final configurations of robots can be considered in the form of four Scenarios enlisted in Table 2.

	G1: The goals of all robots are on leaves	G2: The goals of all robots are on leaves except for one that is on the junction
S1: The starts of all robots are on leaves	Scenario 1	Scenario 2
S2: The starts of all robots are on leaves except for one that is on the junction	Scenario 3	Scenario 4

Table 2. Possible scenarios for robots' configurations on Stars

Scenario 1: In this scenario a Leaf and the junction are initially empty (case (*ii*)). If the empty Leaf is the goal of a robot, then it should be occupied by that specific robot either directly (if there is a free path for the robot), or indirectly (after freeing the path by other robots). So the Star is solvable.
Scenario 2: In this scenario the case (*ii*) holds again. The robots should occupy their goals in the same manner as in the Scenario 1, with the consideration that occupying the junction should be the last move. The Star is therefore solvable.
Scenario 3: In this scenario, initially one robot is on the Star's junction and $m-1$ robots are on the Leaves, and so the case (*i*) holds true. Through a single move of the robot located on the junction to an arbitrary empty Leaf, the Scenario 1 is attained, and the subsequent moves for solving the problem can be done in the same manner.
Scenario 4: The case (*i*) applies for this scenario. Again by moving the robot on the junction to an empty Leaf, this scenario converts to the Scenario 2, and the problem can be solved accordingly.
If $H > 2$, then the situation for the solvability of the Star is more favourable and the Star is definitely solvable. Conversely, if $H < 2$, then the robots located on leaves can just move to the junction and cannot locate on another leaf, so the graph is not salvable. □

Lemma 3 deals with the solvability of Extended Stars:

Lemma 3. *An Extended Star is solvable iff $H \geq \|S\| + 1$, where H is the number of Holes and $\|S\|$ is the length of the graph's Stem.*
Proof. According to the Lemma 1, in order for the graph to be solvable, any two robots must be able to exchange their positions. On the other hand, the worst case of exchanging occurs when a robot r_i located on the vertex v with the maximum distance to the junction, (i.e. on the leaf of the graph's Stem) has to exchange its position with robot r_j located on the furthest vertex u of the second longest chain (with a length of at most $\|S\|$) as shown in Fig. 4(b). Since there are no cycles or other junctions in the graph, the only way for robot r_i to get to another chain of the graph is to reach the junction (as proved in the Lemma 2) and then enter the destination chain. This is possible only by evacuating the path connecting the vertex v to the junction (if the path is not initially empty) plus an additional vertex

connected to the junction, by removing all obstructing robots onto the graph's empty vertices. The additional empty vertex beyond the junction serves as a 'parking', so that after locating the robot r_i on it, the destination chain can be evacuated completely by moving its robots toward the empty Stem through the junction. This means that at least $\|S\| + 1$ vertices in the graph should be empty.

Conversely, if $H < \|S\| + 1$, the robot r_i could at most reach the junction, and not farther, toward other chains. Thus the graph would be unsolvable. □

Regarding the pivotal role of junction vertices in solvability of graphs, at this point we present a new concept, the *Influence Zone* (*IZ*) of a junction as the set of vertices and edges around a junction. Mathematically:

Definition 4. The Junction Influence Zone ($IZ_J^{\,i}$) of the junction J^i is the subgraph satisfying the following condition:

$$IZ_J^{\,i} = \left\{ (v,e) \in (V,E) \,\middle|\, Dist(J^i, v) \le H - 1 \right\} \qquad (1)$$

which means that $IZ_J^{\,i}$ contains the junction J^i plus all vertices with distances to J^i less than or equal to $H - 1$, together with all their connecting edges.

Fig. 5 illustrates Junction Influence Zones of a tree with $H = 3$ holes. In this example, the vertices in Influence Zones are: $IZ_J^{\,1} = \{J^1, J^4, v_3, v_4, v_7, v_8, v_9\}$; $IZ_J^{\,2} = \{J^2, v_1, v_2, v_6, v_{10}, v_{11}, v_{12}, v_{16}\}$; $IZ_J^{\,3} = \{J^3, v_{13}, v_{14}, v_{15}, v_{17}, v_{18}\}$; $IZ_J^{\,4} = \{J^4, J^1, v_7, v_{11}, v_{12}, v_{13}, v_{14}\}$.

By comparing the definitions of the Extended Star and Junction Influence Zone, and regarding the results of the Lemmas 2 and 3, the following corollary can be proposed about the general condition for a Junction IZ to be solvable:

Corollary 1. *Any Junction Influence Zone having at least* $\|S\|$ *+ 1 Holes is solvable.*

Proof. Considering the following two facts:

i. Junction Influence Zones (IZ_J) may contain multiple junctions whereas Extended Stars (ES) do not contain any junction (other than the central junction, as seen in Fig. 4(b)); and,

ii. Junctions in a graph provide possibilities for robots' exchange and temporary residence,

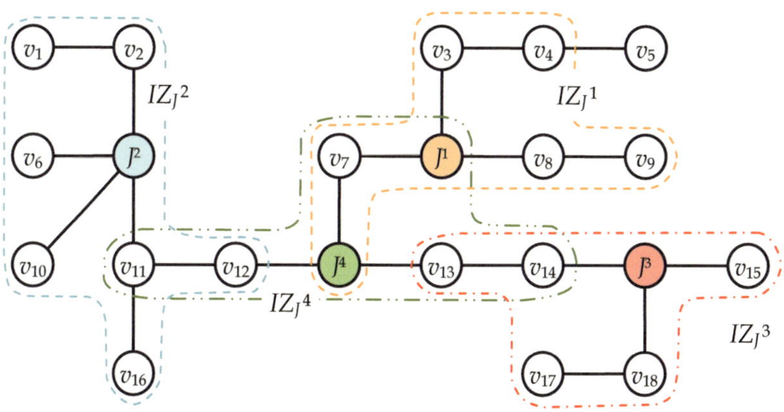

Fig. 5. Junction Influence Zones of a tree with $H = 3$ holes

it is concluded that the topology of an IZ_J with just one junction is analogous to that of an ES, and since there are less possibilities in ES for robot's exchanges (due to the existence of just one junction), the condition for an ES to be solvable is at least as hard as the condition for an IZ_J to be solvable. In other words, if an ES with at least $H = \|S\| + 1$ Holes is solvable, then a Junction IZ_J with at least $H = \max\{Dist(J^i, v) + 1; \forall v \in V\} = \|S\| + 1$ Holes would also be solvable. □

3.2 Solvability of general trees

A general tree usually has multiple junctions, and so can be partitioned into a number of zones formed around each junction, based on the Definition 4. Note that this decomposition is unique for any tree with a specified number of Holes.

After determining the Junction Influence Zones of a general tree, its solvability can be assessed in two phases:

1. checking the possibility of robots' exchanges within a zone, and
2. verifying the possibility of robots' exchanges between multiple zones.

The first phase (i.e. the solvability of a Zone) was discussed in the Corollary 1, the results of which are now generalized to the general trees. In this subsection, we will specify the conditions for global exchanges of robots, based on which the solvability of general trees can be proved.

As mentioned in the Lemma 1, all robots can access all vertices in a solvable graph. In fact, in the second phase we intend to verify the condition for a typical robot to expand the scope of its movements beyond the limits of the Influence Zone(s) within which it is located. Such an expansion of movements would essentially start with 'penetrating' into *Adjacent* zones. The concept of Adjacency is defined in Definition 5:

Definition 5. Any two junctions (J^p and J^q) are considered Adjacent if there is no other junction (J^r) between them. That is,

$$\left\langle J^p \leftrightarrow J^q \right\rangle \xleftrightarrow{\text{if}} \left\langle \nexists J^r \in Path(J^p, J^q); \quad \forall J^p, J^q, J^r \in J(G) \right\rangle, \tag{2}$$

in which the symbol '↔' stands for Adjacency. In other words, two junctions are Adjacent if there is no other junction on their connecting shortest path. Two Influence Zones are considered as *Adjacent* if their junctions are Adjacent (see Fig. 6).

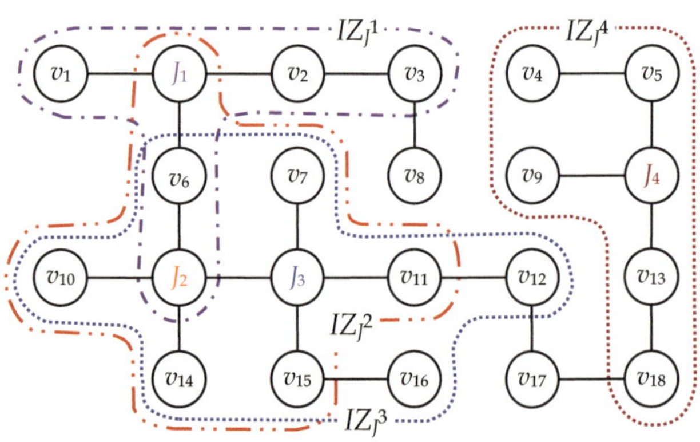

Fig. 6. Influence Zones of the junctions of a sample tree with $H = 3$. Note that v_8 and v_{17} do not belong to any IZ.

In addition to the Adjacency concept, the new notion of *Interconnectedness* is also introduced here to work out the solvability conditions of a general tree (i.e. with multiple Influence Zones), as defined in Definition 6:

Definition 6. Two Influence Zones (IZ^p and IZ^q) are Interconnected if

$$\left\langle IZ^p \equiv IZ^q \right\rangle \xleftrightarrow{\text{if}} \left\langle IZ^p \leftrightarrow IZ^q \right\rangle \wedge \left\langle Dist(X^p, X^q) \le H-2;\ \ X^p, X^q \in J(G) \right\rangle, \quad (3)$$

In which the symbol '≡' indicates Interconnectedness. This means that the maximum distance between the junctions of two Influence Zones must be at most $H-2$. Note that every two Interconnected IZs are Adjacent, but the reverse is not true. For instance in Fig. 6, $IZ_J^1 \equiv IZ_J^2$, and no other IZs are Interconnected.

Now the conditions for exchangeability of any two robots located in Interconnected Influence Zones are investigated, which will lead to the solvability of general trees. Obviously, the results for Interconnected zones can be generalized to trees with multiple zones due to the transitive property of sets (in this case, IZs). Theorem 1 deals with the conditions for exchanges of robots in Interconnected Influence Zones:

Theorem 1. *Any robot located on an Influence Zone can access any vertex in its Adjacent Influence Zone if the two Zones are Interconnected.*

Proof. We will prove the theorem by indirect proof. Suppose that the two Adjacent Influence Zones IZ^p and IZ^q are not interconnected. We will prove that this supposition is not true.

If the two Influence Zones are not Interconnected, then $Dist(J^p, J^q) > H-2$, being at least $(H-1)$. Fig. 7 shows two Adjacent IZs with $H = 5$ and $Dist(J^p, J^q) = 4$. The worst case of accessibility occurs when the robot on vertex 1 wants to access the vertex 7. To make this possible, the path connecting the two junctions (inclusive) and the destination vertex 7 should be empty (or able to be emptied by removing all the robots occupying the path); that is, vertices 2, 3, 4, 5, 6, and 7 in the figure.

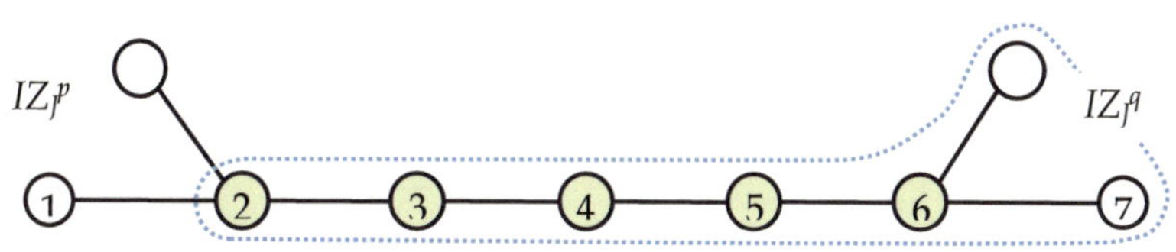

Fig. 7. Illustration for the proof of Theorem 1. Dashed areas designate Influence Zones, and dark vertices show Holes.

Therefore, the required number of Holes would be:

$$H^* = |Path(J^p, J^q)| + 1 = H + 1 \quad (4)$$

in which $|Path(J^p, J^q)| = Dist(J^p, J^q) + 1$. Since (4) is in contradiction with the assumption of existing H Holes, it is concluded that $Dist(J^p, J^q) \le H-2$, in which case IZ^p and IZ^q will be Interconnected according to (3). □

By combining the results of the Theorem 1 and the Lemma 1, it is possible to work out the solvability conditions of any general compound graph with multiple influence zones, as exhibited in Theorem 2. Note that this theorem also holds true for graphs with a single influence zone.

Theorem 2. *Any graph with multiple Influence Zones is solvable if and only if the following conditions are satisfied:*

i. All two Adjacent Influence Zones are Interconnected,

ii. All vertices belong to at least one Influence Zone.

Proof of 'if'. We will first prove the following statement: "*A:= if the conditions (i) and (ii) hold, then a graph is solvable*" by direct proof. Regarding the Lemma 1, the solvability of a graph is equivalent to the possibility of exchanging any two robots on it while the arrangement of all other robots remains unchanged. Therefore, alternatively, we want to prove that "*A':= if the conditions (i) and (ii) hold, then any two robots can exchange while the arrangement of other robots remain unchanged*".

If an arbitrarily selected robot is located on any vertex, then this vertex belongs to at least one IZ (regarding to (*ii*)), and the robot not only can move to anywhere in its IZ (regarding Corollary 1), but also to any vertex in its Interconnected IZ (according to the Theorem 1).

We define the expression $X\left(\frac{r_i}{IZ^m}, \frac{r_j}{IZ^n}\right)$ as the act of exchanging the positions of robots r_i and r_j located in the IZ^m and IZ^n Influence Zones, respectively. Now suppose that a graph has k Influence Zones with the order of $IZ^1, IZ^2, \ldots, IZ^k$ being mutually interconnected, as affirmed by the condition (*i*). It can be shown straightforwardly that the $X\left(\frac{r_1}{IZ^1}, \frac{r_k}{IZ^k}\right)$ can be expressed by a series of consecutive intermediate exchanges between two Adjacent IZs, as follows:

$$(IZ^1 \equiv IZ^2) \wedge (IZ^2 \equiv IZ^3) \wedge \ldots \wedge (IZ^{k-1} \equiv IZ^k) \quad \Rightarrow$$

$$X\left(\frac{r_1}{IZ^1}, \frac{r_k}{IZ^k}\right) = X\left(\frac{r_1}{IZ^1}, \frac{r_2}{IZ^2}\right) \to X\left(\frac{r_1}{IZ^2}, \frac{r_3}{IZ^3}\right) \to \cdots \to X\left(\frac{r_1}{IZ^{k-1}}, \frac{r_k}{IZ^k}\right) \to$$
$$X\left(\frac{r_k}{IZ^{k-1}}, \frac{r_{k-1}}{IZ^{k-2}}\right) \to X\left(\frac{r_k}{IZ^{k-2}}, \frac{r_{k-2}}{IZ^{k-3}}\right) \to \cdots \to X\left(\frac{r_k}{IZ^2}, \frac{r_2}{IZ^1}\right).$$

As a result of the above operations, only the robots r_i and r_j exchange while all other robots maintain their initial positions. Thus, it is concluded that any pair of robots can exchange their positions and so any robot has access to any IZ of the graph. On the other hand, since according to (*ii*) all vertices in the graph are located within at least one IZ, the robot can therefore reach any vertex in the graph. This means that the graph is solvable.

Proof of 'only if'. Now we prove the following statement: "*B := If a graph is solvable, then the conditions (i) and (ii) hold*" by indirect proof (i.e. proof by contradiction), and for each condition separately:

i. If we assume that at least two Adjacent Influence Zones in a graph are not Interconnected (i.e., condition (*i*) revoked), then according to the Theorem 1, exchanging some robots located on two Adjacent—but not Interconnected—IZs would not be possible, and so the graph would not be solvable. This contradicts with the premise of *B*, and so the condition (*i*) holds.

ii. Now we assume that there is a vertex v which does not belong to any Influence Zone (i.e., condition (*ii*) revoked). In this case, the distance of v to the nearest junction J^p

would be $Dist(v, J^p) \geq H$, which contains $H + 1$ vertices (refer to Definition 4). According to the proof of Lemma 3, in order for a robot on v to move to a vertex connected to J^p, all the vertices between v and J^p (excluding v but including J^p) plus the destination vertex must be empty or able to be emptied (compare to the Fig. 7). Therefore, the total number of required Holes would be

$$H^* = [\,|Path(v, J^p)| - 1] + 1 = [(H + 1) - 1] + 1 = H + 1 \tag{5}$$

which is in contradiction with the assumption of existing H Holes in the statement B.
Thus, it is concluded that any vertex in the graph must belong to at least one IZ, and the condition (*ii*) holds. □

A direct ramification of the Theorem 2 is proposed in Corollary 2:

Corollary 2. *The maximum number of robots for which a tree is solvable is* $m = |G| - \|S\| - b$, *in which* $|G|$ *is the order of the graph,* $\|S\|$ *is the length of the Stem, and*

$$b = \begin{cases} 2 & \text{if both ends of the Stem are junctions} \\ 1 & \text{if only one end of the Stem is a junction} \end{cases}$$

Proof. Recall that $H = |G| - m$, in which m is the number of robots on the graph. If we assume that the graph is solvable, then the maximum distances between all its Adjacent junctions cannot exceed $H - 2$. As a result, the length of the longest sequence of Internal Vertices including the two vertices connected to its ends (i.e. the Stem) is bound by $\|S\| \leq H - 2$.

Depending on the types of end-vertices of a Stem, the number of Holes and thus the maximum number of robots in a Solvable Graph is determined as follows:

If the Stem's both end-vertices are junctions, then based on (3):

$$\|S\| \leq H - 2 \;\Rightarrow\; \|S\| \leq |G| - m - 2 \;\Rightarrow\; m \leq |G| - \|S\| - 2.$$

If the Stem's end-vertices are a junction and a leaf, then based on (1):

$$\|S\| \leq H - 1 \;\Rightarrow\; \|S\| \leq |G| - m - 1 \;\Rightarrow\; m \leq |G| - \|S\| - 1.$$ □

4. Minimal Solvable Trees

For a specific number of robots (m), a notable subclass of Solvable Trees ST^m is the set of Minimal Solvable Trees (MST^m) which have the minimum number of vertices necessary for accommodating m robots. Considering that the complexity of graph searching operations is directly influenced from the graph size, finding Minimal Solvable Trees would significantly ease the tasks of graph designing and multi robot motion planning. In this section the topologies of Minimal Solvable Trees are introduced. It is noted that for m robots, there can be a number of MSTs with different topologies.

4.1. Minimal stars

As introduced in section 3.1, a $Star^k$ is a tree with k leaves and has a diameter of 2. According to the Lemma 2, in order for a $Star^k$ to be solvable for m robots, it must have at least $H = 2$ Holes. This means that the order of the tree must be

$$|Star^k| = k + 1 \geq m + 2. \quad (6)$$

For verifying this equation we resort to the proof by contradiction: Let's assume that a $Star^m$ is not minimally solvable for m robots. Then a Star with a smaller order (i.e. $|Star^m| < m + 2$) should be minimally solvable. If $|Star^m| \leq m$, then there are no vertices for moving the robots, and so this Star is not solvable. If $|Star^m| = m + 1$, then a robot on a Leaf cannot move to another Leaf since its moves are limited to just one Leaf and the only junction. Therefore, all final configurations are not reachable, and so the graph is not solvable. We conclude that for a Star to be Minimally Solvable for m robots it must have $m + 1$ Leaves, and its order should be

$$|Star^m| = m + 2. \quad (7)$$

4.2 Minimal Extended Stars

An Extended Star (ES^k) has a total of k leaves and internal vertices, all vertices of which belong to the only Influence Zone formed around the only junction. Since according to the Lemma 3 the longest path from the junction (inclusive) must be empty (which is the Stem, S), then $H \geq \|S\| + 1$, or equivalently, $H \geq |S|$. Therefore, the minimum number of vertices of an Extended Star is:

$$|ES^k| = m + |S|. \quad (8)$$

4.3 Minimal General Trees

In a General tree, multiple junctions, and therefore, multiple Influence Zones can exist. According to Theorems 1 and 2, in any solvable tree we have: $Dist(J^p, J^q) \leq H - 2$. The minimum value that H can take to produce a positive distance is $H = 3$. Thus, the order of a Minimal General Tree with at least two junctions is:

$$|G| = m + 3. \quad (9)$$

Any tree not satisfying the conditions of the Theorem 2 is definitely not solvable for m robots, and may be either a non-solvable tree, or a Partially Solvable Tree for m robots (PST^m). Also, regarding the proof of minimality of General Trees, if $m < |T| < m + 3$, then the tree is PST^m. Note that while not being Solvable Trees, PSTs are still solvable for a limited class of problems: those which require only Local Interchanges within either a single Influence Zone, or an Interconnected Influence Zone.

5. Application

Although the results of the previous sections are theoretical in nature, they can be used straightforwardly in real-world applications, such as designing and reshaping transportation networks, railways, traffic roads, AGV routes, and robotic workspaces for multiple moving agents such as trains, vehicles, and robots. On the other hand, in order for a graph to be utilized as the structure of a real network, its topology must be suited to the application it is designed for. Thus, efficiency is an important issue in designing and tailoring applied graphs.

A graph can be considered as efficient if, in addition to being solvable, has no or very few redundant edges and vertices. Lacking redundant elements (i.e. edges and vertices) in a solvable graph becomes substantially significant particularly when the cost of constructing real world counterparts of graph elements (such as roads, railways, canals, etc.) is remarkably high.

Based on the above discussions, designing an efficient graph encompasses two phases:

a. *Compatibility* phase, and
b. *Rightsizing* phase.

In the Compatibility phase, the given graph is made compatible with the needs and constraints of the application. This may include making the graph solvable for the specified number of agents (or robots) by expanding it (if it is not solvable), or reducing the size of the graph if it is solvable for an excessive, unnecessary number of robots. The output of this phase is a Solvable Graph for exactly the predefined number of robots, e.g., m.

In the Rightsizing phase, the Solvable Graph is further examined to find redundant edges or vertices for pruning. We will call the resultant graph a 'Lean' graph since it is fully operational and optimized for the application at hand.

As discussed in Corollary 2, the maximum number of robots for which a graph can be solvable is determined by the order of the graph, $|G|$, the length of the Stem, $\|S\|$ and the type of vertices on the Stem's ends. On the other hand, sometimes it is desirable to modify a given Solvable Graph SG^m in order to accommodate larger or smaller numbers of moving robots. This happens for instance when the graph represents the routes of Automatic Guided Vehicles (AGVs) on plant floor, or railways connecting urban or rural districts.

Converting an SG^m to $SG^{m'}$ has two aspects:

1. If $m' > m$, then the SG^m is Partially Solvable for m' robots (i.e., it is a $PSG^{m'}$). In this case, some vertices and/or edges must be inserted or relocated to produce an $SG^{m'}$.
2. If $m' \le m$, then the SG^m is solvable for m' robots. In this case, there might be some redundant vertices and/or edges in the graph which can be truncated or relocated to produce a smaller $SG^{m'}$.

Apparently the first case, i.e. the problem of converting an SG^m into an $SG^{m'}$ for $m' > m$, is interesting, in which $n = m' - m$ additional robots should navigate on the graph. Regarding that in an SG^m the maximum number of robots is $m = |G| - \|S\| - b$ (b = 1 or 2), accommodating n additional robots requires that the difference $|G| - \|S\|$ be increased by n, or the value of b decreased by 1, if possible.

The graph's expansion or modification is done through four basic operations: Vertex Insertion, Vertex Relocation, Edge Insertion, and Edge Relocation. It should be noted that increasing the number of robots by decreasing the value of b is possible only via Edge Insertion and Edge Relocation operations.

In expanding the size of the graph in the Compatibility phase special care must be taken to comply with the limitations and conditions of the application. For example, there might be no sufficient space for inserting a vertex or edge, or inserting an edge could be economically or technically infeasible. Whenever the graph is not capable of accommodating the specified number of agents, a possible engineering solution could be either reducing the number of agents or inserting the required graph elements such that the sustained expense is minimized.

On the other hand, in reducing/pruning the graph, some vertices might be indelible as they are essential to the system, as the positions for loading, feeding, or parking machines or vehicles. Therefore, possible operations in the Rightsizing phase are Vertex Deletion and Edge Deletion operations, and Vertex/Edge Relocation and Insertion are not considered.

It must be noted that although deletion of redundant vertices or edges from the graph may reduce the overall cost of network design and construction, it may lead to higher costs of agents' movements as well, since by possessing a more limited space for manoeuvring and reshuffling, agents may be forced to travel/stop more frequently for resolving deadlocks.

5.1 An example

Now a practical illustrative example is provided for demonstrating a typical application of the results of the previous sections. Specifically, it is shown how designing a Solvable Graph and then optimizing it might help solving an industrial shop floor problem.
Suppose that a factory is consisted of a workshop and two warehouses, one for raw material and one for finished products. The production area accommodates 3 milling, 2 turning, 1 drilling, and 1 grinding machines, as well as a heat treatment line and an assembly station. Each of these machines or departments requires certain amount of raw material (or unfinished parts) to be loaded, processed, unloaded and then transported to other divisions of the factory. The layout of the factory and the loading/unloading positions for each machine and department are shown in Fig. 8.

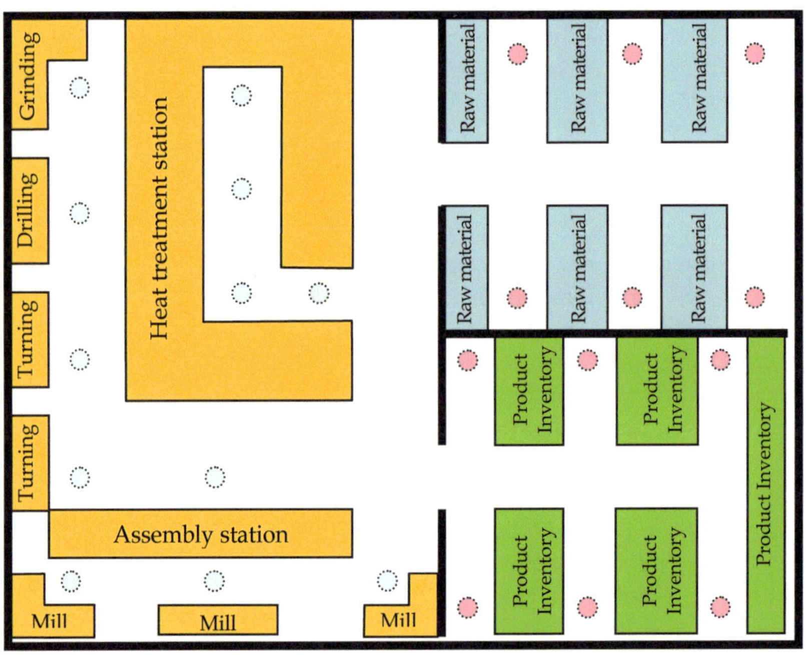

Fig. 8. Layout of the factory. The specific locations for loading/unloading parts and material are shown with small circles

The materials and products are currently carried manually by carts and pallets. However, the management decides to upgrade the factory's transportation system and utilize

Automatic Guided Vehicles (AGVs). However, there are a number of constraints and conditions in this regard.

Constraints:

1. The AGVs can only move along predefined paths realized by embedding special type of wires in the floor and covering them with epoxy resins for safety and durability.
2. Due to space limitation, no two AGVs can move along a single passageway or corridor side by side, and should therefore wait until the passageway (i.e. the wire track) is evacuated and emptied from other AGVs.
3. AGVs can only stop at certain locations for loading/unloading or changing their tracks. They cannot stop at any point on the track other than the predefined spots.
4. Since the factory's production system is Job-Shop, the volume of interdepartmental transportation is high. Therefore, all AGVs need to have access to all points of the transportation network. In other words, all AGVs must be able to reach any destination from any initial position.
5. Each AGV is equipped with some batteries that actuate it and provide power for its sensors and control unit, and therefore needs to be recharged daily. The recharging is done during the factory's idle times, i.e. at nights. However, for safety reasons, recharging hubs are located in warehouses so that AGVs can be recharged and kept secured at nights.
6. The cost of laying out wire tracks is proportionate to their lengths. Also, situating each stop point requires additional expense due to the special sensors and circuits needed. These initial costs are much higher than the costs of increased movements the AGVs need to make for avoiding collisions or deadlocks.
7. The management has decided to mechanise the material handling system through two phases: in the first phase, 10 AGVs are planned to operate in the factory, and in the second phase, in parallel with increasing the production volume and variety, the number of AGVs will be increased to 15.

Problem:

The problem is to design a network of wire tracks and stopping stations such that the total cost of upgrading is minimized while the above constraints are fulfilled. In other words, it is desired to plan a Solvable Graph for 10 AGVs (for the first phase) which is efficient (minimal) in terms of the number of vertices and edges.

Solution:

As a starting point, the Voronoi Diagram of the factory is calculated, which is the collection of points equidistant from two or more facilities or walls (refer to Section 1 for more details). Implementing the Voronoi Diagram is quite proper since it yields the safest paths passing through narrow corridors and production facilities. Fig. 9 depicts the Voronoi Diagram of the factory. As can be seen in the Fig. 9, the Voronoi diagram has some small redundant edges connected to concave corners of the workspace. These edges, however, can be easily pruned (removed) from the diagram. Also, there are some vertices very close to each other (as shown in the dashed circle) which can be merged for simplicity and practicality.

The next step is to modify the pruned Voronoi Diagram to comply with the requirements of loading/unloading stations imposed by the constraint 3. This is done by superimposing the Voronoi Diagram and the stations' locations, as illustrated in Fig. 10.

Nearly all stopping stations situate at proper positions on the Voronoi Diagram, except for the lower-left corner, for which we proposed a simplifying solution, as depicted in Fig. 11.

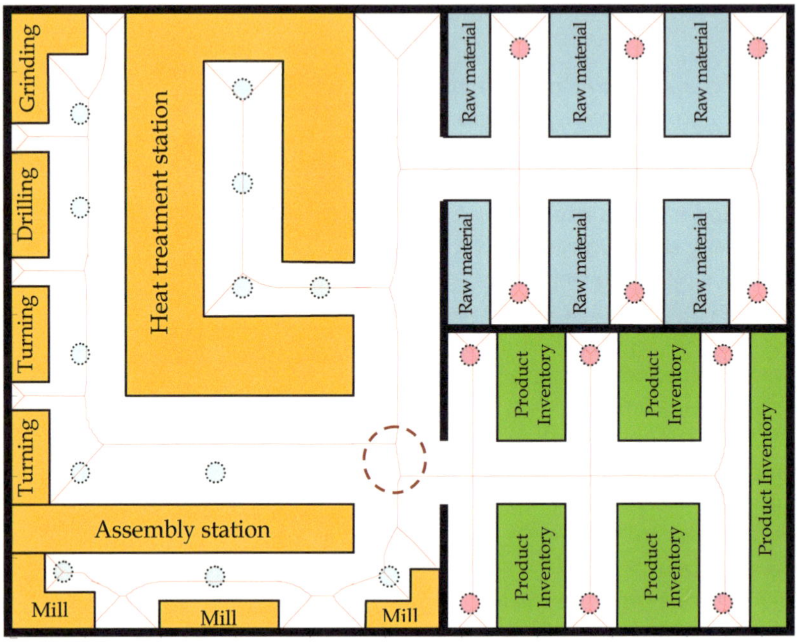

Fig. 9. Voronoi Diagram of the factory, which is the collection of safest paths amid facilities.

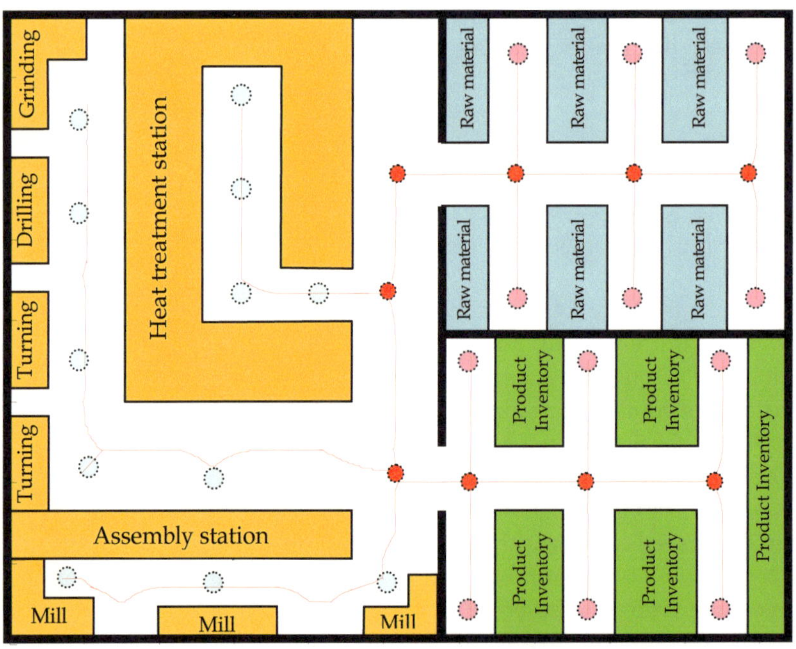

Fig. 10. Superimposition of the pruned Voronoi Diagram and the stopping stations

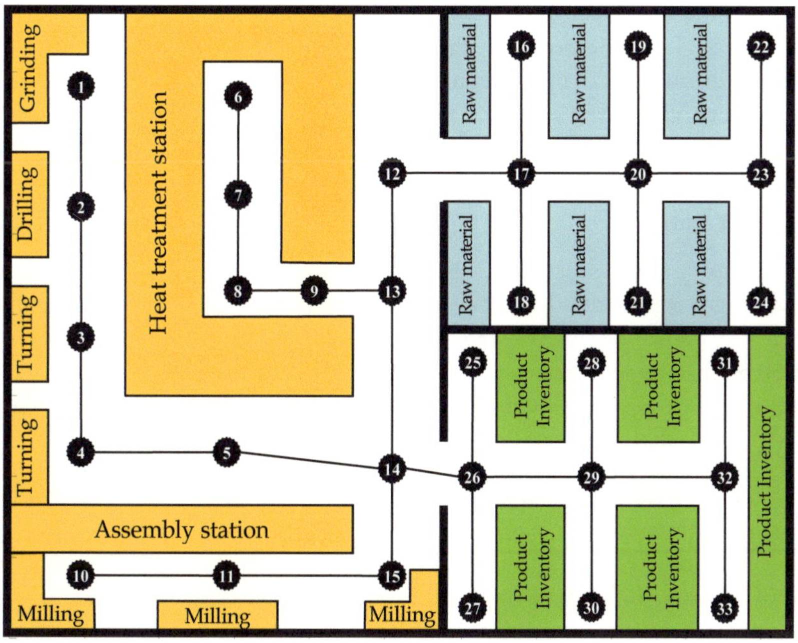

Fig. 11. A simplified AGV transportation network for the factory

In the Fig. 11 there are 8 junctions and the vertices v_1, v_2, v_3, v_4, v_5 and v_{14} constitute the Stem. As stated in the constraint 7 above, the management has decided to operate the network for 10 AGVs in the first phase. By taking into consideration all possible vertices of the network and according to the Corollary 2, the maximum number of AGVs that can travel in the whole factory is $m = |G| - \|S\| - 1 = 33 - 5 - 1 = 27$. Although this implies that a large number of AGVs can operate, they have to make use of all vertices (including those in warehouses) for accessing all stations, which may make their travels long and unnecessary, and will cause disorder and insecurity in the warehouses.

The engineering team responsible for designing the network recommends limiting the scope of the AGVs' motions to the production workshop, such that no AGV can enter the warehouses except for material loading or unloading, and therefore is only allowed to travel in the production area for resolving deadlocks with other AGVs. In this case, the maximum number of AGVs able to move will be $m = 15 - 5 - 1 = 9$. Since this number is less that the required number of AGVs the management has planned, the vertex v_{26}, which is the nearest vertex in the warehouses to the production area, is selected to be included in the operational network. This resolution will not affect the size of the network's Stem, and so the number of operational AGVs will increase to $m = 16 - 5 - 1 = 10$, which will make the network compatible with the requirements of the management.

In order to increase the production volume and variety, the number of AGVs is planned to increase to 15. For this phase, two possible scenarios among others are:

1. By utilizing 5 additional vertices located in the warehouse areas, such as v_{17}, v_{20}, v_{23}, v_{29} and v_{32}, the maximum number of AGVs will increase to $m = (16 + 5) - 5 - 1 = 15$.
2. By merging the vertices v_8 and v_9, and converting the vertex v_3 into a junction, the Stem size will be $\|S\| = 3$. Moreover, by utilizing 3 additional warehouse vertices such as v_{17}, v_{20} and v_{29}, the number of operational AGVs will increase to $m = (16 + 3) - 3 - 1 = 15$.

Evidently, each of the above solutions should undergo financial and technical feasibility studies to be selected and finalized.

6. Concluding remarks

The time complexity of the proposed method for verifying the solvability of a graph without explicitly solving it is in $O(n)$ which is spent on identifying the Stem, where n is the number of graph vertices. Also, calculating the maximum number of robots operable on a given graph can be performed in the same time order.

In contrast, investigating the solvability of a Multi Robot Motion Planning problem of m robots on a graph with n vertices through exhaustive enumeration will require

$$p = \frac{n!}{(n-m)!} \tag{10}$$

different permutations of robots to be checked, which is far beyond the linear time order of the presented algorithm.

Moreover, verifying whether a graph is SG^m would require

$$\sum_{i=1}^{m} \left(\frac{n!}{(n-i)!} \right)^2 \tag{11}$$

operations to be checked, for any initial and final configurations, which is again exponentially time consuming. These figures demonstrate the effectiveness of our findings in terms of required time and memory.

In designing transportation networks for multiple autonomous agents (such as mobile robots, AGVs, cars, etc.) which can merely move along the network's arcs, it is important to make sure that the graph has a proper topology and sufficient number of vertices (relative to the number of agents) to enable the agents' motion planning. This chapter dealt with the topology of Solvable Graphs and introduced the new concept of Minimal Solvable Graphs and investigated their properties, which are the smallest graphs that satisfy the feasibility conditions for multi robot motion planning for any initial and final configurations of robots. Finding Minimal Solvable Trees will significantly ease the motion planning task for multiple robots on trees.

In this chapter we assumed that the robots move sequentially on internal vertices and leaves of the tree. For further research it is possible to assume all moves to be concurrent and find the minimum sequence of moves to reach the final configuration with different edge lengths and robots velocities. Also, further research is underway for working out solvability conditions for Cyclic Graphs and Partially Solvable Graphs.

7. References

Auletta, V.; Monti, A.; Parente, D. & Persiano, G. (1999). A Linear-Time Algorithm for the Feasibility of Pebble Motion on Trees, Algorithmica, Vol. 23, No. 3, pp. 223-245, ISSN 0178-4617.

Bennewitz M.; Burgard, W. & Thrun, S. (2001). Optimizing schedules for prioritized path planning of multi-robot systems, *Proceeding of the IEEE International Conference on Robotics and Automation (ICRA)*, pp. 271-276, ISBN 0-7803-6576-3, Seoul, Korea, May 2001, IEEE, New Jersey.

Canny, J. F. (1988). *The Complexity of Robot Motion Planning*, The MIT Press, ISBN 978-0-262-03136-3, Cambridge, Mass.

Choset, H.; Lynch, K. M.; Hutchinson, S.; Kantor, G.; Burgard, W.; Kavraki, L. E. & Thrun, S. (2005). *Principles of Robot Motion: Theory, Algorithms, and Implementations*, The MIT Press, ISBN 978-0-262-03327-5, Boston.

Diestel, R. (2000). *Graph Theory*, Springer-Verlag, ISBN 978-3-642-14278-9, Heidelberg.

Hwang, Y. K. & Ahuja, N. (1992). Gross motion planning - A survey, *ACM Computing Surveys*, Vol. 24, No. 3, pp. 219-291, ISSN 0360-0300.

Kant, K. & Zucker, S. W. (1986). Toward efficient trajectory planning: the path-velocity decomposition, *International Journal of Robotic Research*, Vol. 5, No. 3, pp. 72-89, ISSN 0278-3649.

Kornhauser, D.; Miller G. & Spirakis, P. (1984). Coordinating pebble motion on graphs, the diameter of permutations groups and applications, *Proceedings of the 25th IEEE Symposium on Foundations of Computer Science*, pp. 241-250, ISBN 0-8186-0591-X, Singer Island, FL, October 1984, IEEE, New Jersey.

Latombe, J. C. (1991). *Robot Motion Planning*, Kluwer Academic Publishers, ISBN 978-0792392064, London.

Masehian, E. & Hassan Nejad, A. (2009). Solvability of multi robot motion planning problems on trees, *Proceedings of the International Conference on Intelligent Robots and Systems (IROS)*, pp. 5936-5941, ISBN 978-1-4244-3803-7, St. Louis, USA, October 2009, IEEE, New Jersey.

Onn, S. & Tennenholtz, M. (1997). Determination of social laws for agent mobilization, *Artificial Intelligence*, Vol. 95, 1997, pp. 155-167, ISSN 0004-3702.

Ryan, M. R. K. (2008). Exploiting subgraph structure in multi-robot path planning, *Journal of Artificial Intelligent Research*, Vol. 31, No. 1, pp. 497-542, ISSN 1076-9757.

Wilson, R. M. (1974). Graph puzzles, homotopy, and the alternating group, *Journal of Combinatorial Theory*, Series B, Vol. 16, pp. 86-94, ISSN 0095-8956.

13

Target Tracking for Mobile Sensor Networks Using Distributed Motion Planning and Distributed Filtering

Gerasimos G. Rigatos
Industrial Systems Institute
Greece

1. Introduction

The problem treated in this research work is as follows: there are N mobile robots (unmanned ground vehicles) which pursue a moving target. The vehicles emanate from random positions in their motion plane. Each vehicle can be equipped with various sensors, such as odometric sensors, cameras and non-imaging sensors such as sonar, radar and thermal signature sensors. These vehicles can be considered as *mobile sensors* while the ensemble of the autonomous vehicles constitutes a *mobile sensor network* (Rigatos, 2010a),(Olfati-Saber, 2005),(Olfati-Saber, 2007),(Elston & Frew, 2007). At each time instant each vehicle can obtain a measurement of the target's cartesian coordinates and orientation. Additionally, each autonomous vehicle is aware of the target's distance from a reference surface measured in a cartesian coordinates system. Finally, each vehicle can be aware of the positions of the rest $N-1$ vehicles. The objective is to make the unmanned vehicles converge in a synchronized manner towards the target, while avoiding collisions between them and avoiding collisions with obstacles in the motion plane. To solve the overall problem, the following steps are necessary: (i) to perform distributed filtering, so as to obtain an estimate of the target's state vector. This estimate provides the desirable state vector to be tracked by each one of the unmanned vehicles, (ii) to design a suitable control law for the unmanned vehicles that will enable not only convergence of the vehicles to the goal position but will also maintain the cohesion of the vehicles ensemble.
Regarding the implementation of the control law that will allow the mobile robots to converge to the target in a coordinated manner, this can be based on the calculation of a cost (energy) function consisting of the following elements : (i) the cost due to the distance of the i-th mobile robot from the target's coordinates, (ii) the cost due to the interaction with the other $N-1$ vehicles, (iii) the cost due to proximity to obstacles or inaccessible areas in the motion plane. The gradient of the aggregate cost function defines the path each vehicle should follow to reach the target and at the same time assures the synchronized approaching of the vehicles to the target. In this way, the update of the position of each vehicle will be finally described by a gradient algorithm which contains an interaction term with the gradient algorithms that defines the motion of the rest $N-1$ mobile robots. A suitable tool for proving analytically the convergence of the vehicles' swarm to the goal state is Lyapunov stability theory and particularly LaSalle's theorem (Rigatos, 2008a),(Rigatos, 2008b).
Regarding the implementation of distributed filtering, the Extended Information Filter and the Unscented Information Filter are suitable approaches. In the Extended Information

Filter there are local filters which do not exchange raw measurements but send to an aggregation filter their local information matrices (local inverse covariance matrices) and their associated local information state vectors (products of the local information matrices with the local state vectors) (Rigatos & Tzafestas, 2007). The Extended Information Filter performs fusion of the local state vector estimates which are provided by the local Extended Kalman Filters (EKFs), using the *Information matrix* and the *Information state vector* (Lee, 2008b), (Lee, 2008a), (Vercauteren & Wang, 2005), (Manyika & Durrant-Whyte, 1994). The Information Matrix is the inverse of the state vector covariance matrix and can be also associated to the Fisher Information matrix (Rigatos & Zhang, 2009). The Information state vector is the product between the Information matrix and the local state vector estimate (Shima et al., 2007). The Unscented Information Filter is a derivative-free distributed filtering approach which permits to calculate an aggregate estimate of the target's state vector by fusing the state estimates provided by Unscented Kalman Filters (UKFs) running at the mobile sensors. In the Unscented Information Filter an implicit linearization is performed through the approximation of the Jacobian matrix of the system's output equation by the product of the inverse of the estimation error covariance matrix with the cross-covariance matrix between the system's state vector and the system's output. Again the local information matrices and the local information state vectors are transferred to an aggregation filter which produces the global estimation of the system's state vector.

Using distributed EKFs and fusion through the Extended Information Filter or distributed UKFs through the Unscented Information Filter is more robust comparing to the centralized Extended Kalman Filter, or similarly the centralized Unscented Kalman Filter since, (i) if a local filter is subject to a fault then state estimation is still possible and can be used for accurate localization of the target, (ii) communication overhead remains low even in the case of a large number of distributed measurement units, because the greatest part of state estimation is performed locally and only information matrices and state vectors are communicated between the local filters, (iii) the aggregation performed also compensates for deviations in the state estimates of the local filters (Rigatos, 2010a).

The structure of the paper is as follows: in Section 2 the problem of target tracking in mobile sensor networks is studied. In Section 3 a distributed motion planning approach is analyzed. This is actually a distributed gradient algorithm, the convergence of which is proved using LaSalle's stability theory. In Section 4 distributed state estimation with the use of the Extended Information Filter approach is proposed. In section 5 distributed state estimation with the use of the Unscented Information Filter is studied. In Section 6 simulation experiments are provided about target tracking using distributed motion planning and distributed filtering. Finally, in Section 7 concluding remarks are stated.

2. Target tracking in mobile sensor networks

2.1 The problem of distributed target tracking

It is assumed that there are N mobile robots (unmanned vehicles) with positions $p_1, p_2, ..., p_N \in R^2$ respectively, and a target with position $x^* \in R^2$ moving in a plane (see Fig. 1). Each unmanned vehicle can be equipped with various sensors, cameras and non-imaging sensors, such as sonar, radar or thermal signature sensors. The unmanned vehicles can be considered as mobile sensors while the ensemble of the autonomous vehicles constitutes a mobile sensors network. The discrete-time target's kinematic model is given by

$$\begin{aligned} x_t(k+1) &= \phi(x_t(k)) + L(k)u(k) + w(k) \\ z_t(k) &= \gamma(x_t(k)) + v(k) \end{aligned} \tag{1}$$

where $x_t \in R^{m\times 1}$ is the target's state vector and $z_t \in R^{p\times 1}$ is the measured output, while $w(k)$ and $v(k)$ are uncorrelated, zero-mean, Gaussian zero-mean noise processes with covariance matrices $Q(k)$ and $R(k)$ respectively. The operators $\phi(x)$ and $\gamma(x)$ are defined as $\phi(x) = [\phi_1(x), \phi_2(x), \cdots, \phi_m(x)]^T$, and $\gamma(x) = [\gamma_1(x), \gamma_2(x), \cdots, \gamma_p(x)]^T$, respectively.

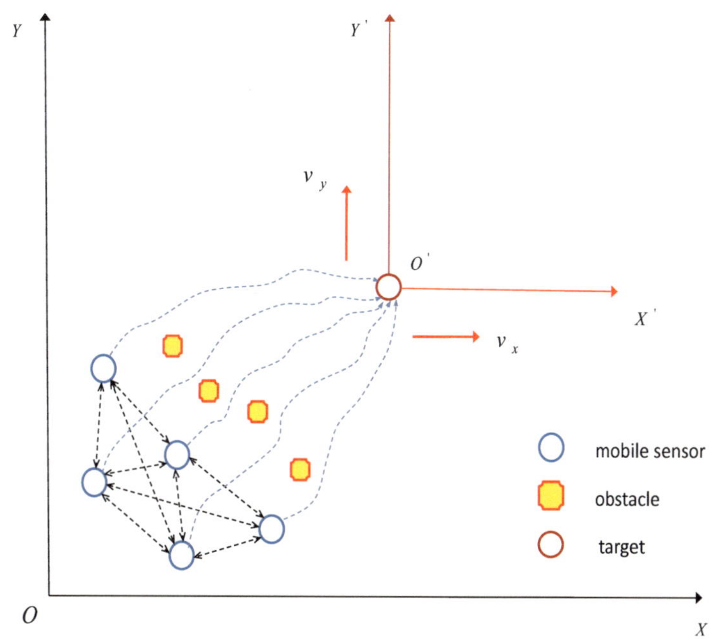

Fig. 1. Distributed target tracking in an environment with inaccessible areas.

At each time instant each mobile robot can obtain a measurement of the target's position. Additionally, each mobile robot is aware of the target's distance from a reference surface measured in an inertial coordinates system. Finally, each mobile sensor can be aware of the positions of the rest $N-1$ sensors. The objective is to make the mobile sensors converge in a synchronized manner towards the target, while avoiding collisions between them and avoiding collisions with obstacles in the motion plane. To solve the overall problem, the following steps are necessary: (i) to perform distributed filtering, so as to obtain an estimate of the target's state vector. This estimate provides the desirable state vector to be tracked by each one of the mobile robots, (ii) to design a suitable control law that will enable the mobile sensors not only converge to the target's position but will also preserve the cohesion of the mobile sensors swarm (see Fig. 2).

The exact position and orientation of the target can be obtained through distributed filtering. Actually, distributed filtering provides a two-level fusion of the distributed sensor measurements. At the first level, local filters running at each mobile sensor provide an estimate of the target's state vector by fusing the cartesian coordinates and bearing measurements of the target with the target's distance from a reference surface which is measured in an inertial coordinates system (Vissière et al., 2008). At a second level, fusion

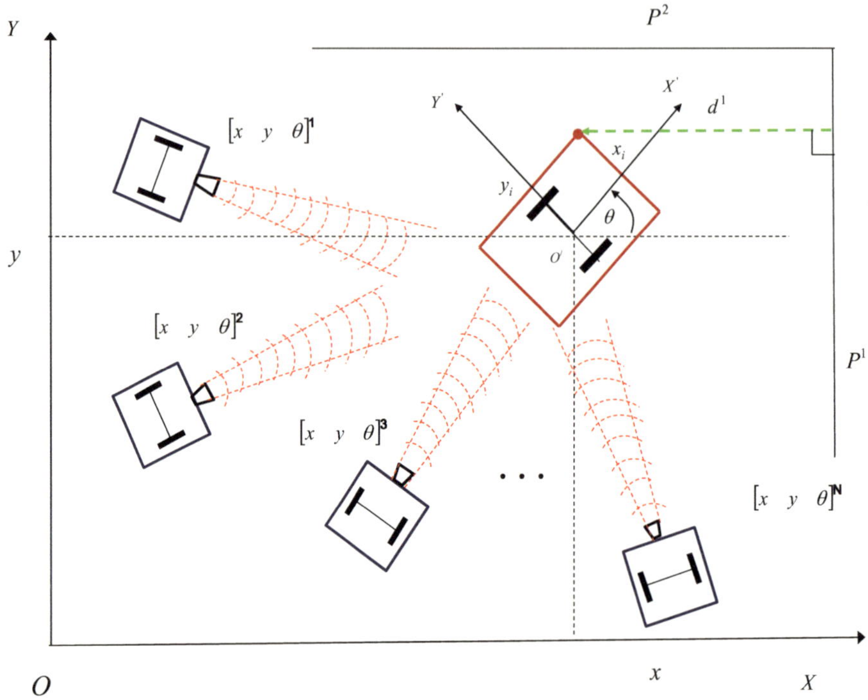

Fig. 2. Mobile robot providing estimates of the target's state vector, and the associated inertial and local coordinates reference frames

of the local estimates is performed with the use of the Extended Information Filter and the Unscented Information Filter. It is also assumed that the time taken in calculating the selection of data and in communicating between mobile robots is small, and that time delays, packet losses and out-of-sequence measurement problems in communication do not distort significantly the flow of the exchanged data.
Comparing to the traditional centralized or hierarchical fusion architecture, the network-centric architectures for the considered multi-robot system has the following advantages: (i) Scalability: since there are no limits imposed by centralized computation bottlenecks or lack of communication bandwidth, every mobile robot can easily join or quit the system, (ii) Robustness: in a decentralized fusion architecture no element of the system is mission-critical, so that the system is survivable in the event of on-line loss of part of its partial entities (mobile robots), (iii) Modularity: every partial entity is coordinated and does not need to possess a global knowledge of the network topology. However, these benefits are possible only if the sensor data can be fused and synthesized for distribution within the constraints of the available bandwidth.

2.2 Tracking of the reference path by the target

The continuous-time target's kinematic model is assumed to be that of a unicycle robot and is given by

$$\begin{aligned}\dot{x}(t) &= v(t)cos(\theta(t))\\ \dot{y}(t) &= v(t)sin(\theta(t))\\ \dot{\theta}(t) &= \omega(t).\end{aligned} \tag{2}$$

The target is steered by a dynamic feedback linearization control algorithm which is based on flatness-based control (Léchevin & Rabbath, 2006),(Rigatos, 2010b),(Fliess & Mounier, 1999),(Villagra et al., 2007):

$$\begin{array}{c} u_1 = \ddot{x}_d + K_{p_1}(x_d - x) + K_{d_1}(\dot{x}_d - \dot{x}) \\ u_2 = \ddot{y}_d + K_{p_2}(y_d - y) + K_{d_2}(\dot{y}_d - \dot{y}) \\ \dot{\xi} = u_1 cos(\theta) + u_2 sin(\theta) \\ v = \xi, \ \omega = \frac{u_2 cos(\theta) - u_1 sin(\theta)}{\xi} \ . \end{array} \tag{3}$$

The dynamics of the tracking error is given by

$$\begin{array}{c} \ddot{e}_x + K_{d_1}\dot{e}_x + K_{p_1}e_x = 0 \\ \ddot{e_y} + K_{d_2}\dot{e}_x + K_{p_2}e_y = 0 \end{array} \tag{4}$$

where $e_x = x - x_d$ and $e_y = y - y_d$. The proportional-derivative (PD) gains are chosen as K_{p_i} and K_{d_i}, for $i = 1,2$. The dynamic compensator of Eq. (3) has a potential singularity at $\xi = v = 0$, i.e. when the target is not moving. It is noted however that the occurrence of such a singularity is structural for non-holonomic systems. It is assumed that the target follows a smooth trajectory $(x_d(t), y_d(t))$ which is persistent, i.e. for which the nominal velocity $v_d = (\dot{x}_d^2 + \dot{y}_d^2)^{1/2}$ along the trajectory never goes to zero (and thus singularities are avoided). The following theorem assures avoidance of singularities in the proposed flatness-based control law (Oriolo et al., 2002):

Theorem: Let λ_{11}, λ_{12} and λ_{21}, λ_{22} be respectively the eigenvalues of the two equations of the error dynamics, given in Eq. (4). Assume that for $i = 1,2$ it is $\lambda_{i1}, \lambda_{i2} < 0$ (negative real eigenvalues), and that λ_{i2} is sufficiently small. If

$$min_{t \geq 0} ||(\begin{pmatrix} \dot{x}_d(t) \\ \dot{y}_d(t) \end{pmatrix})|| \geq \begin{pmatrix} \dot{e}_x^0 \\ \dot{e}_y^0 \end{pmatrix} \tag{5}$$

with $\dot{e}_x^0 = \dot{e}_x(0) \neq 0$ and $\dot{e}_y^0 = \dot{e}_y(0) \neq 0$ then the singularity $\xi = 0$ is never met.

3. Distributed motion planning for the multi-robot system

3.1 Kinematic model of the multi-robot system

The objective is to lead the ensemble of N mobile robots, with different initial positions on the 2-D plane, to converge to the target's position, and at the same time to avoid collisions between the mobile robots, as well as collisions with obstacles in the motion plane. An approach for doing this is the *potential fields theory*, in which the individual robots are steered towards an equilibrium by the gradient of an harmonic potential (Rigatos, 2008c),(Groß, et al.),(Bishop, 2003),(Hong et al., 2007). Variances of this method use nonlinear anisotropic harmonic potential fields which introduce to the robots' motion directional and regional avoidance constraints (Sinha & Ghose, 2006),(Pagello et al., 2006),(Sepulchre et al., 2007),(Masoud & Masoud, 2002). In the examined coordinated target-tracking problem the equilibrium is the target's position, which is not a-priori known and has to be estimated with the use of distributed filtering.

The position of each mobile robot in the 2-D space is described by the vector $x^i \in R^2$. The motion of the robots is synchronous, without time delays, and it is assumed that at every time instant each robot i is aware about the position and the velocity of the other $N-1$ robots. The cost function that describes the motion of the i-th mobile robot towards the target's position

is denoted as $V(x^i): R^n \rightarrow R$. The value of $V(x^i)$ at the target's position in $\nabla_{x^i} V(x^i) = 0$. The following conditions must hold:
(i) The cohesion of the mobile robot's ensemble should be maintained, i.e. the norm $||x^i - x^j||$ should remain upper bounded $||x^i - x^j|| < \epsilon^h$,
(ii) Collisions between the robots should be avoided, i.e. $||x^i - x^j|| > \epsilon^l$,
(iii) Convergence to the target's position should be succeeded for each mobile robot through the negative definiteness of the associated Lyapunov function $\dot{V}^i(x^i) = \dot{e}^i(t)^T e^i(t) < 0$, where $e = x - x^*$ is the distance of the i-th mobile robot from the target's position.
The interaction between the i-th and the j-th mobile robot is

$$g(x^i - x^j) = -(x^i - x^j)[g_a(||x^i - x^j||) - g_r(||x^i - x^j||)] \quad (6)$$

where $g_a()$ denotes the attraction term and is dominant for large values of $||x^i - x^j||$, while $g_r()$ denotes the repulsion term and is dominant for small values of $||x^i - x^j||$. Function $g_a()$ can be associated with an attraction potential, i.e. $\nabla_{x_i} V_a(||x^i - x^j||) = (x^i - x^j) g_a(||x^i - x^j||)$. Function $g_r()$ can be associated with a repulsion potential, i.e. $\nabla_{x_i} V_r(||x^i - x^j||) = (x^i - x^j) g_r(||x^i - x^j||)$. A suitable function $g()$ that describes the interaction between the robots is given by (Rigatos, 2008c),(Gazi & Passino, 2004)

$$g(x^i - x^j) = -(x^i - x^j)(a - be^{\frac{||x^i - x^j||^2}{\sigma^2}}) \quad (7)$$

where the parameters a, b and c are suitably tuned. It holds that $g_a(x^i - x^j) = -a$, i.e. attraction has a linear behavior (spring-mass system) $||x^i - x^j|| g_a(x^i - x^j)$. Moreover, $g_r(x^i - x^j) = be^{\frac{-||x^i - x^j||^2}{\sigma^2}}$ which means that $g_r(x^i - x^j)||x^i - x^j|| \leq b$ is bounded. Applying Newton's laws to the i-th robot yields

$$\dot{x}^i = v^i, \;\; m^i \dot{v}^i = U^i \quad (8)$$

where the aggregate force is $U^i = f^i + F^i$. The term $f^i = -K_v v^i$ denotes friction, while the term F^i is the propulsion. Assuming zero acceleration $\dot{v}^i = 0$ one gets $F^i = K_v v^i$, which for $K_v = 1$ and $m^i = 1$ gives $F^i = v^i$. Thus an approximate kinematic model for each mobile robot is

$$\dot{x}^i = F^i. \quad (9)$$

According to the Euler-Langrange principle, the propulsion F^i is equal to the derivative of the total potential of each robot, i.e.

$$\begin{aligned}
F^i &= -\nabla_{x^i}\{V^i(x^i) + \tfrac{1}{2}\textstyle\sum_{i=1}^N \sum_{j=1, j\neq i}^N [V_a(||x^i - x^j|| + V_r(||x^i - x^j||)]\} \Rightarrow \\
F^i &= -\nabla_{x^i}\{V^i(x^i)\} + \textstyle\sum_{j=1,j\neq i}^N [-\nabla_{x^i} V_a(||x^i - x^j||) - \nabla_{x^i} V_r(||x^i - x^j||)] \Rightarrow \\
F^i &= -\nabla_{x^i}\{V^i(x^i)\} + \textstyle\sum_{j=1,j\neq i}^N [-(x^i - x^j) g_a(||x^i - x^j||) - (x^i - x^j) g_r(||x^i - x^j||)] \Rightarrow \\
F^i &= -\nabla_{x^i}\{V^i(x^i)\} - \textstyle\sum_{j=1,j\neq i}^N g(x^i - x^j).
\end{aligned}$$

Substituting in Eq. (9) one gets in discrete-time form

$$x^i(k+1) = x^i(k) + \gamma^i(k)[h(x^i(k)) + e^i(k)] + \sum_{j=1, j\neq i}^{N} g(x^i - x^j), \; i = 1,2,\cdots,M. \quad (10)$$

The term $h(x(k)^i) = -\nabla_{x^i} V^i(x^i)$ indicates a local gradient algorithm, i.e. motion in the direction of decrease of the cost function $V^i(x^i) = \frac{1}{2} e^i(t)^T e^i(t)$. The term $\gamma^i(k)$ is the algorithms step while the stochastic disturbance $e^i(k)$ enables the algorithm to escape from local minima. The term $\sum_{j=1,j\neq i}^{N} g(x^i - x^j)$ describes the interaction between the i-th and the rest $N-1$ stochastic gradient algorithms (Duflo, 1996),(Comets & Meyre, 2006),(Benveniste et al., 1990).

3.2 Stability of the multi-robot system

The behavior of the multi-robot system is determined by the behavior of its center (mean of the vectors x^i) and of the position of each robot with respect to this center. The center of the multi-robot system is given by

$$\begin{gathered}\bar{x} = E(x^i) = \frac{1}{N}\sum_{i=1}^{N} x^i \Rightarrow \dot{\bar{x}} = \frac{1}{N}\sum_{i=1}^{N} \dot{x}^i \Rightarrow \\ \dot{\bar{x}} = \frac{1}{N}\sum_{i=1}^{N}[-\nabla_{x^i} V^i(x^i) - \sum_{j=1,j\neq i}^{N}(g(x^i - x^j))]\end{gathered} \tag{11}$$

From Eq. (7) it can be seen that $g(x^i - x^j) = -g(x^j - x^i)$, i.e. $g()$ is an odd function. Therefore, it holds that $\frac{1}{N}(\sum_{j=1,j\neq i}^{N} g(x^i - x^j)) = 0$, and

$$\dot{\bar{x}} = \frac{1}{N}\sum_{i=1}^{N}[-\nabla_{x^i} V^i(x^i)] \tag{12}$$

Denoting the target's position by x^* , and the distance between the i-th mobile robot and the mean position of the multi-robot system by $e^i(t) = x^i(t) - \bar{x}$ the objective of distributed gradient for robot motion planning can be summarized as follows:
(i) $lim_{t\to\infty}\bar{x} = x^*$, i.e. the center of the multi-robot system converges to the target's position,
(ii) $lim_{t\to\infty}x^i = \bar{x}$, i.e. the i-th robot converges to the center of the multi-robot system,
(iii) $lim_{t\to\infty}\dot{\bar{x}} = \dot{x}^*$, i.e. the center of the multi-robot system stabilizes at the target's position.
If conditions (i) and (ii) hold then $lim_{t\to\infty}x^i = x^*$. Furthermore, if condition (iii) also holds then all robots will stabilize close to the target's position.
It is known that the stability of local gradient algorithms can be proved with the use of Lyapunov theory (Benveniste et al., 1990). A similar approach can be followed in the case of the distributed gradient algorithms given by Eq. (10). The following simple Lyapunov function is considered for each gradient algorithm (Gazi & Passino, 2004):

$$V_i = \frac{1}{2}{e^i}^T e^i \Rightarrow V_i = \frac{1}{2}||e_i||^2 \tag{13}$$

Thus, one gets

$$\dot{V}^i = {e^i}^T \dot{e}^i \Rightarrow \dot{V}^i = (\dot{x}^i - \dot{\bar{x}})e^i \Rightarrow$$

$$\dot{V}^i = [-\nabla_{x^i} V^i(x^i) - \sum_{j=1,j\neq i}^{N} g(x^i - x^j) + \frac{1}{M}\sum_{j=1}^{N}\nabla_{x^j} V^j(x^j)]e^i.$$

Substituting $g(x^i - x^j)$ from Eq. (7) yields

$$\dot{V}_i = [-\nabla_{x^i} V^i(x^i) - \sum_{j=1,j\neq i}^{N}(x^i - x^j)a + \sum_{j=1,j\neq i}^{N}(x^i - x^j)g_r(||x^i - x^j||) + \frac{1}{N}\sum_{j=1}^{N}\nabla_{x^j} V^j(x^j)]e^i$$

which gives,

$$\begin{aligned}\dot{V}_i = \; & -a[\sum_{j=1,j\neq i}^{N}(x^i - x^j)]e^i + \\ & +\sum_{j=1,j\neq i}^{N} g_r(||x^i - x^j||)(x^i - x^j)^T e^i - [\nabla_{x^i} V^i(x^i) - \frac{1}{N}\sum_{j=1}^{M}\nabla_{x^j} V^j(x^j)]^T e^i\end{aligned}$$

It holds that $\sum_{j=1}^{N}(x^i - x^j) = Nx^i - N\frac{1}{N}\sum_{j=1}^{N}x^j = Nx^i - N\bar{x} = N(x^i - \bar{x}) = Ne^i$, therefore

$$\dot{V}_i = -aN||e^i||^2 + \sum_{j=1,j\neq i}^{N} g_r(||x^i - x^j||)(x^i - x^j)^T e^i - [\nabla_{x^i}V^i(x^i) - \frac{1}{N}\sum_{j=1}^{N}\nabla_{x^j}V^j(x^j)]^T e^i \quad (14)$$

It assumed that for all x^i there is a constant $\bar{\sigma}$ such that

$$||\nabla_{x^i}V^i(x^i)|| \leq \bar{\sigma} \quad (15)$$

Eq. (15) is reasonable since for a mobile robot moving on a 2-D plane, the gradient of the cost function $\nabla_{x^i}V^i(x^i)$ is expected to be bounded. Moreover it is known that the following inequality holds:

$$\sum_{j=1,j\neq i}^{N} g_r(x^i - x^j)^T e^i \leq \sum_{j=1,j\neq i}^{N} be^i \leq \sum_{j=1,j\neq i}^{N} b||e^i||.$$

Thus the application of Eq. (14) gives:

$$\dot{V}^i \leq aN||e^i||^2 + \sum_{j=1,j\neq i}^{N} g_r(||x^i - x^j||)||x^i - x^j|| \cdot ||e^i|| + ||\nabla_{x^i}V^i(x^i) - \tfrac{1}{N}\sum_{j=1}^{M}\nabla_{x^j}V^j(x^j)||||e^i||$$

$$\Rightarrow \dot{V}^i \leq aN||e^i||^2 + b(N-1)||e^i|| + 2\bar{\sigma}||e^i||$$

where it has been taken into account that

$$\sum_{j=1,j\neq i}^{N} g_r(||x^i - x^j||)^T ||e^i|| \leq \sum_{j=1,j\neq i}^{N} b||e^i|| = b(N-1)||e^i||,$$

and from Eq. (15),

$$||\nabla_{x^i}V^i(x^i) - \tfrac{1}{N}\sum_{j=1}^{N}\nabla_{x^i}V^j(x^j)|| \leq ||\nabla_{x^i}V^i(x^i)|| + \tfrac{1}{N}||\sum_{j=1}^{N}\nabla_{x^i}V^j(x^j)|| \leq \bar{\sigma} + \tfrac{1}{N}N\bar{\sigma} \leq 2\bar{\sigma}.$$

Thus, one gets

$$\dot{V}^i \leq aN||e^i|| \cdot [||e^i|| - \frac{b(N-1)}{aN} - 2\frac{\bar{\sigma}}{aN}] \quad (16)$$

The following bound ϵ is defined:

$$\epsilon = \frac{b(N-1)}{aN} + \frac{2\bar{\sigma}}{aN} = \frac{1}{aN}(b(N-1) + 2\bar{\sigma}) \quad (17)$$

Thus, when $||e^i|| > \epsilon$, $\dot{V}_i$ will become negative and consequently the error $e^i = x^i - \bar{x}$ will decrease. Therefore the tracking error e^i will remain in an area of radius ϵ i.e. the position x^i of the i-th robot will stay in the cycle with center $\bar{x}$ and radius ϵ.

3.3 Stability in the case of a quadratic cost function

The case of a convex quadratic cost function is examined, for instance

$$V^i(x^i) = \frac{A}{2}||x^i - x^*||^2 = \frac{A}{2}(x^i - x^*)^T(x^i - x^*) \quad (18)$$

where $x^* \in R^2$ denotes the target's position, while the associated Lyapunov function has a minimum at x^*, i.e. $V^i(x^i = x^*) = 0$. The distributed gradient algorithm is expected to converge to x^*. The robotic vehicles will follow different trajectories on the 2-D plane and will end at the target's position.

Using Eq.(18) yields $\nabla_{x^i} V^i(x^i) = A(x^i - x^*)$. Moreover, the assumption $\nabla_{x^i} V^i(x^i) \leq \bar{\sigma}$ can be used, since the gradient of the cost function remains bounded. The robotic vehicles will concentrate round $\bar{x}$ and will stay in a radius ϵ given by Eq. (17). The motion of the mean position $\bar{x}$ of the vehicles is

$$\begin{array}{c} \dot{\bar{x}} = -\frac{1}{N}\sum_{i=1}^{N} \nabla_{x^i} V^i(x^i) \Rightarrow \dot{\bar{x}} = -\frac{A}{N}\sum_{i=1}^{N}(x^i - x^*) \Rightarrow \\ \dot{\bar{x}} = -\frac{A}{N}\sum_{i=1}^{N} x^i + \frac{A}{N} N x^* \Rightarrow \dot{\bar{x}} - \dot{x}^* = -A(\bar{x} - x^*) - \dot{x}^* \end{array} \tag{19}$$

The variable $e_\sigma = \bar{x} - x^*$ is defined, and consequently

$$\dot{e}_\sigma = -A e_\sigma - \dot{x}^* \tag{20}$$

The following cases can be distinguished:
(i) The target is not moving, i.e. $\dot{x}^* = 0$. In that case Eq. (20) results in an homogeneous differential equation, the solution of which is given by

$$\epsilon_\sigma(t) = \epsilon_\sigma(0) e^{-At} \tag{21}$$

Knowing that $A > 0$ results into $lim_{t \to \infty} e_\sigma(t) = 0$, thus $lim_{t \to \infty} \bar{x}(t) = x^*$.
(ii) the target is moving at constant velocity, i.e. $\dot{x^*} = a$, where $a > 0$ is a constant parameter. Then the error between the mean position of the multi-robot formation and the target becomes

$$\epsilon_\sigma(t) = [\epsilon_\sigma(0) + \frac{a}{A}] e^{-At} - \frac{a}{A} \tag{22}$$

where the exponential term vanishes as $t \to \infty$.
(iii) the target's velocity is described by a sinusoidal signal or a superposition of sinusoidal signals, as in the case of function approximation by Fourier series expansion. For instance consider the case that $\dot{x^*} = b \cdot sin(at)$, where $a, b > 0$ are constant parameters. Then the nonhomogeneous differential equation Eq. (20) admits a sinusoidal solution. Therefore the distance $\epsilon_\sigma(t)$ between the center of the multi-robot formation $\bar{x}(t)$ and the target's position $x^*(t)$ will be also a bounded sinusoidal signal.

3.4 Convergence analysis using La Salle's theorem

From Eq. (16) it has been shown that each robot will stay in a cycle C of center $\bar{x}$ and radius ϵ given by Eq. (17). The Lyapunov function given by Eq. (13) is negative semi-definite, therefore asymptotic stability cannot be guaranteed. It remains to make precise the area of convergence of each robot in the cycle C of center $\bar{x}$ and radius ϵ. To this end, La Salle's theorem can be employed (Gazi & Passino, 2004),(Khalil, 1996).
La Salle's Theorem: Assume the autonomous system $\dot{x} = f(x)$ where $f: D \to R^n$. Assume $C \subset D$ a compact set which is positively invariant with respect to $\dot{x} = f(x)$, i.e. if $x(0) \in C \Rightarrow x(t) \in C \ \forall \ t$. Assume that $V(x): D \to R$ is a continuous and differentiable Lyapunov function such that $\dot{V}(x) \leq 0$ for $x \in C$, i.e. $V(x)$ is negative semi-definite in C. Denote by E the set of all points in C such that $\dot{V}(x) = 0$. Denote by M the largest invariant set in E and its boundary by L^+, i.e. for $x(t) \in E: lim_{t \to \infty} x(t) = L^+$, or in other words L^+ is the positive limit set of E. Then every solution $x(t) \in C$ will converge to M as $t \to \infty$.
La Salle's theorem is applicable in the case of the multi-robot system and helps to describe more precisely the area round $\bar{x}$ to which the robot trajectories x^i will converge. A generalized Lyapunov function is introduced which is expected to verify the stability analysis based on

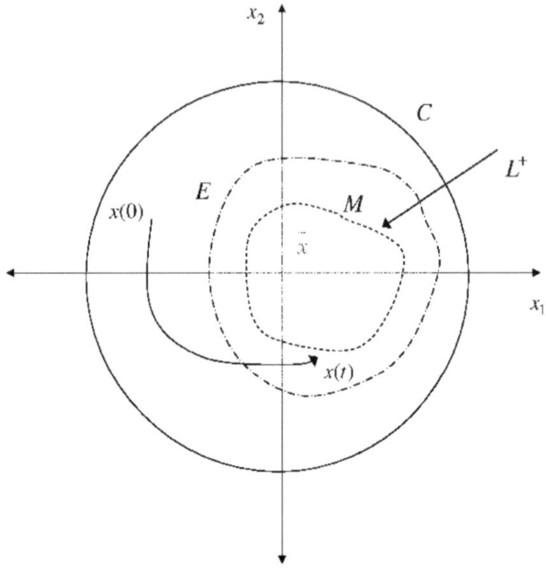

Fig. 3. LaSalle's theorem: C: invariant set, $E \subset C$: invariant set which satisfies $\dot{V}(x) = 0$, $M \subset E$: invariant set, which satisfies $\dot{V}(x) = 0$, and which contains the limit points of $x(t) \in E$, L^+ the set of limit points of $x(t) \in E$

Eq. (16). It holds that

$$V(x) = \sum_{i=1}^N V^i(x^i) + \tfrac{1}{2}\sum_{i=1}^N \sum_{j=1, j\neq i}^N \{V_a(||x^i - x^j|| - V_r(||x^i - x^j||)\} \Rightarrow$$
$$V(x) = \sum_{i=1}^N V^i(x^i) + \tfrac{1}{2}\sum_{i=1}^N \sum_{j=1, j\neq i}^N \{a||x^i - x^j|| - V_r(||x^i - x^j||)$$

and

$$\nabla_{x^i} V(x) = [\sum_{i=1}^N \nabla_{x^i} V^i(x^i)] + \tfrac{1}{2}\sum_{i=1}^N \sum_{j=1, j\neq i}^N \nabla_{x^i}\{a||x^i - x^j|| - V_r(||x^i - x^j||)\} \Rightarrow$$
$$\nabla_{x^i} V(x) = [\sum_{i=1}^N \nabla_{x^i} V^i(x^i)] + \sum_{j=1, j\neq i}^N (x^i - x^j)\{g_a(||x^i - x^j||) - g_r(||x^i - x^j||)\} \Rightarrow$$
$$\nabla_{x^i} V(x) = [\sum_{i=1}^N \nabla_{x^i} V^i(x^i)] + \sum_{j=1, j\neq i}^N (x^i - x^j)\{a - g_r(||x^i - x^j||)\}$$

and using Eq. (10) with $\gamma^i(t) = 1$ yields $\nabla_{x^i} V(x) = -\dot{x}^i$, and

$$\dot{V}(x) = \nabla_x V(x)^T \dot{x} = \sum_{i=1}^N \nabla_{x^i} V(x)^T \dot{x}^i \Rightarrow \dot{V}(x) = -\sum_{i=1}^N ||\dot{x}^i||^2 \leq 0 \qquad (23)$$

Therefore it holds $V(x) > 0$ and $\dot{V}(x) \leq 0$ and the set $C = \{x : V(x(t)) \leq V(x(0))\}$ is compact and positively invariant. Thus, by applying La Salle's theorem one can show the convergence of $x(t)$ to the set $M \subset C$, $M = \{x : \dot{V}(x) = 0\} \Rightarrow M = \{x : \dot{x} = 0\}$.

4. Distributed state estimation using the extended information filter

4.1 Extended kalman filtering at local processing units

As mentioned, to obtain an accurate estimate of the target's coordinates, fusion of the distributed sensor measurements can be performed either with the use of the Extended

Information Filter or with the use of the Unscented Information Filter. The distributed Extended Kalman Filter, also know as Extended Information Filter, performs fusion of the state estimates which are provided by local Extended Kalman Filters. Thus, the functioning of the local Extended Kalman Filters should be analyzed first. The following nonlinear state-space model is considered again (Rigatos & Tzafestas, 2007), (Rigatos, 2009b):

$$\begin{aligned} x(k+1) &= \phi(x(k)) + L(k)u(k) + w(k) \\ z(k) &= \gamma(x(k)) + v(k) \end{aligned} \tag{24}$$

where $x \in R^{m \times 1}$ is the system's state vector and $z \in R^{p \times 1}$ is the system's output, while $w(k)$ and $v(k)$ are uncorrelated, Gaussian zero-mean noise processes with covariance matrices $Q(k)$ and $R(k)$ respectively. The operators $\phi(x)$ and $\gamma(x)$ are $\phi(x) = [\phi_1(x), \phi_2(x), \cdots, \phi_m(x)]^T$, and $\gamma(x) = [\gamma_1(x), \gamma_2(x), \cdots, \gamma_p(x)]^T$, respectively. It is assumed that ϕ and γ are sufficiently smooth in x so that each one has a valid series. Taylor expansion. Following a linearization procedure, ϕ is expanded into Taylor series about $\hat{x}$:

$$\phi(x(k)) = \phi(\hat{x}(k)) + J_\phi(\hat{x}(k))[x(k) - \hat{x}(k)] + \cdots \tag{25}$$

where $J_\phi(x)$ is the Jacobian of ϕ calculated at $\hat{x}(k)$:

$$J_\phi(x) = \frac{\partial \phi}{\partial x}|_{x=\hat{x}(k)} = \begin{pmatrix} \frac{\partial \phi_1}{\partial x_1} & \frac{\partial \phi_1}{\partial x_2} & \cdots & \frac{\partial \phi_1}{\partial x_m} \\ \frac{\partial \phi_2}{\partial x_1} & \frac{\partial \phi_2}{\partial x_2} & \cdots & \frac{\partial \phi_2}{\partial x_m} \\ \vdots & \vdots & \vdots & \vdots \\ \frac{\partial \phi_m}{\partial x_1} & \frac{\partial \phi_m}{\partial x_2} & \cdots & \frac{\partial \phi_m}{\partial x_m} \end{pmatrix} \tag{26}$$

Likewise, γ is expanded about $\hat{x}^-(k)$

$$\gamma(x(k)) = \gamma(\hat{x}^-(k)) + J_\gamma[x(k) - \hat{x}^-(k)] + \cdots \tag{27}$$

where $\hat{x}^-(k)$ is the estimation of the state vector $x(k)$ before measurement at the k-th instant to be received and $\hat{x}(k)$ is the updated estimation of the state vector after measurement at the k-th instant has been received. The Jacobian $J_\gamma(x)$ is

$$J_\gamma(x) = \frac{\partial \gamma}{\partial x}|_{x=\hat{x}^-(k)} = \begin{pmatrix} \frac{\partial \gamma_1}{\partial x_1} & \frac{\partial \gamma_1}{\partial x_2} & \cdots & \frac{\partial \gamma_1}{\partial x_m} \\ \frac{\partial \gamma_2}{\partial x_1} & \frac{\partial \gamma_2}{\partial x_2} & \cdots & \frac{\partial \gamma_2}{\partial x_m} \\ \vdots & \vdots & \vdots & \vdots \\ \frac{\partial \gamma_p}{\partial x_1} & \frac{\partial \gamma_p}{\partial x_2} & \cdots & \frac{\partial \gamma_p}{\partial x_m} \end{pmatrix} \tag{28}$$

The resulting expressions create first order approximations of ϕ and γ. Thus the linearized version of the system is obtained:

$$\begin{aligned} x(k+1) &= \phi(\hat{x}(k)) + J_\phi(\hat{x}(k))[x(k) - \hat{x}(k)] + w(k) \\ z(k) &= \gamma(\hat{x}^-(k)) + J_\gamma(\hat{x}^-(k))[x(k) - \hat{x}^-(k)] + v(k) \end{aligned} \tag{29}$$

Now, the EKF recursion is as follows: First the time update is considered: by $\hat{x}(k)$ the estimation of the state vector at instant k is denoted. Given initial conditions $\hat{x}^-(0)$ and $P^-(0)$ the recursion proceeds as:

– *Measurement update.* Acquire $z(k)$ and compute:

$$\begin{array}{l} K(k) = P^{-}(k)J_{\gamma}^{T}(\hat{x}^{-}(k))\cdot[J_{\gamma}(\hat{x}^{-}(k))P^{-}(k)J_{\gamma}^{T}(\hat{x}^{-}(k)) + R(k)]^{-1} \\ \hat{x}(k) = \hat{x}^{-}(k) + K(k)[z(k) - \gamma(\hat{x}^{-}(k))] \\ P(k) = P^{-}(k) - K(k)J_{\gamma}(\hat{x}^{-}(k))P^{-}(k) \end{array} \tag{30}$$

– *Time update.* Compute:

$$\begin{array}{l} P^{-}(k+1) = J_{\phi}(\hat{x}(k))P(k)J_{\phi}^{T}(\hat{x}(k)) + Q(k) \\ \hat{x}^{-}(k+1) = \phi(\hat{x}(k)) + L(k)u(k) \end{array} \tag{31}$$

The schematic diagram of the EKF loop is given in Fig. 4.

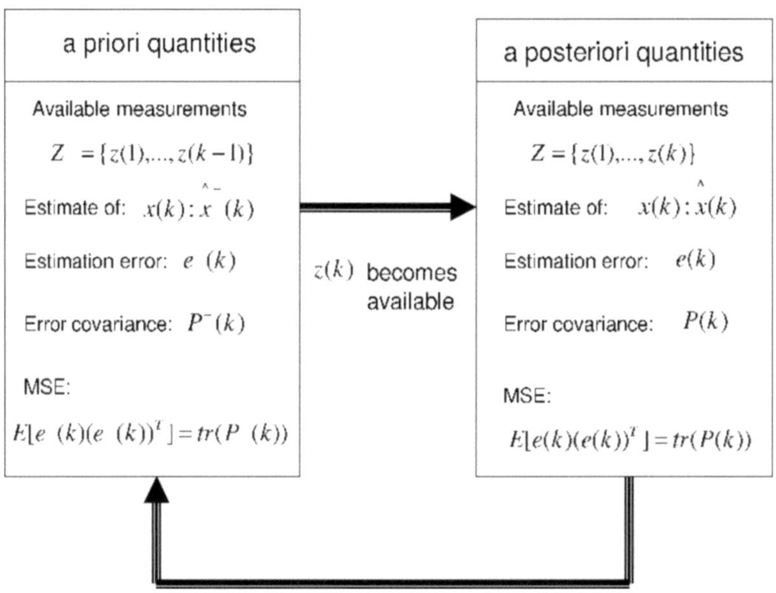

Fig. 4. Schematic diagram of the EKF loop

4.2 Calculation of local estimations in terms of EIF information contributions

Again the discrete-time nonlinear system of Eq. (24) is considered. The Extended Information Filter (EIF) performs fusion of the local state vector estimates which are provided by the local Extended Kalman Filters, using the *Information matrix* and the *Information state vector* (Lee, 2008b), (Lee, 2008a), (Vercauteren & Wang, 2005), (Manyika & Durrant-Whyte, 1994). The Information Matrix is the inverse of the state vector covariance matrix, and can be also associated to the Fisher Information matrix (Rigatos & Zhang, 2009). The Information state vector is the product between the Information matrix and the local state vector estimate

$$\begin{array}{c} Y(k) = P^{-1}(k) = I(k) \\ \hat{y}(k) = P^{-}(k)^{-1}\hat{x}(k) = Y(k)\hat{x}(k) \end{array} \tag{32}$$

The update equation for the Information Matrix and the Information state vector are given by

$$\begin{array}{rl} Y(k) = & P^{-}(k)^{-1} + J_{\gamma}^{T}(k)R^{-1}(k)J_{\gamma}(k) \\ & = Y^{-}(k) + I(k) \end{array} \tag{33}$$

$$\hat{y}(k) = \hat{y}^-(k) + J_\gamma^T R(k)^{-1}[z(k) - \gamma(x(k)) + J_\gamma \hat{x}^-(k)] = \hat{y}^-(k) + i(k) \tag{34}$$

where

$$\begin{aligned} I(k) &= J_\gamma^T(k) R(k)^{-1} J_\gamma(k) \text{ is the associated information matrix and} \\ i(k) &= J_\gamma^T R(k)^{-1}[(z(k) - \gamma(x(k))) + J_\gamma \hat{x}^-(k)] \text{ is the information state contribution} \end{aligned} \tag{35}$$

The predicted information state vector and Information matrix are obtained from

$$\begin{aligned} \hat{y}^-(k) &= P^-(k)^{-1} \hat{x}^-(k) \\ Y^-(k) = P^-(k)^{-1} &= [J_\phi(k) P^-(k) J_\phi(k)^T + Q(k)]^{-1} \end{aligned} \tag{36}$$

The Extended Information Filter is next formulated for the case that multiple local sensor measurements and local estimates are used to increase the accuracy and reliability of the estimation of the target's cartesian coordinates and bearing. It is assumed that an observation vector $z^i(k)$ is available for N different sensor sites (mobile robots) $i = 1, 2, \cdots, N$ and each sensor observes a common state according to the local observation model, expressed by

$$z^i(k) = \gamma(x(k)) + v^i(k),\ i = 1, 2, \cdots, N \tag{37}$$

where the local noise vector $v^i(k) \sim N(0, R^i)$ is assumed to be white Gaussian and uncorrelated between sensors. The variance of a composite observation noise vector v_k is expressed in terms of the block diagonal matrix

$$R(k) = diag[R(k)^1, \cdots, R^N(k)]^T \tag{38}$$

The information contribution can be expressed by a linear combination of each local information state contribution i^i and the associated information matrix I^i at the i-th sensor site

$$\begin{aligned} i(k) &= \sum_{i=1}^N J_\gamma^{i\,T}(k) R^i(k)^{-1}[z^i(k) - \gamma^i(x(k)) + J_\gamma^i(k)\hat{x}^-(k)] \\ I(k) &= \sum_{i=1}^N J_\gamma^{i\,T}(k) R^i(k)^{-1} J_\gamma^i(k) \end{aligned} \tag{39}$$

Using Eq. (39) the update equations for fusing the local state estimates become

$$\begin{aligned} \hat{y}(k) &= \hat{y}^-(k) + \sum_{i=1}^N J_\gamma^{i\,T}(k) R^i(k)^{-1}[z^i(k) - \gamma^i(x(k)) + J_\gamma^i(k)\hat{x}^-(k)] \\ Y(k) &= Y^-(k) + \sum_{i=1}^N J_\gamma^{i\,T}(k) R^i(k)^{-1} J_\gamma^i(k) \end{aligned} \tag{40}$$

It is noted that in the Extended Information Filter an aggregation (master) fusion filter produces a global estimate by using the local sensor information provided by each local filter. As in the case of the Extended Kalman Filter the local filters which constitute the Extended information Filter can be written in terms of *time update* and a *measurement update* equation.
Measurement update: Acquire $z(k)$ and compute

$$\begin{aligned} Y(k) &= P^-(k)^{-1} + J_\gamma^T(k) R(k)^{-1} J_\gamma(k) \\ \text{or } Y(k) &= Y^-(k) + I(k) \text{ where } I(k) = J_\gamma^T(k) R^{-1}(k) J_\gamma(k) \end{aligned} \tag{41}$$

$$\begin{aligned} \hat{y}(k) &= \hat{y}^-(k) + J_\gamma^T(k) R(k)^{-1}[z(k) - \gamma(\hat{x}(k)) + J_\gamma \hat{x}^-(k)] \\ \text{or } \hat{y}(k) &= \hat{y}^-(k) + i(k) \end{aligned} \tag{42}$$

Time update: Compute

$$Y^-(k+1) = P^-(k+1)^{-1} = [J_\phi(k) P(k) J_\phi(k)^T + Q(k)]^{-1} \tag{43}$$

$$y^-(k+1) = P^-(k+1)^{-1} \hat{x}^-(k+1) \tag{44}$$

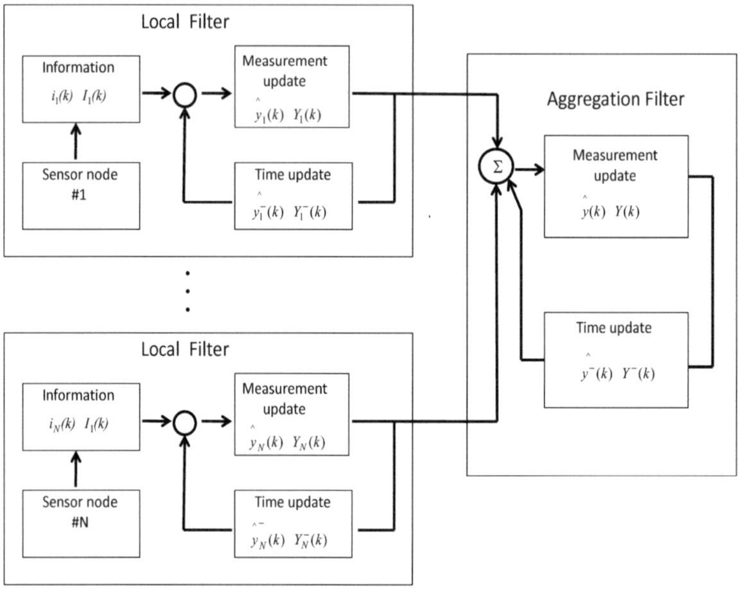

Fig. 5. Fusion of the distributed state estimates of the target (obtained by the mobile robots) with the use of the Extended Information Filter

4.3 Extended information filtering for state estimates fusion

In the Extended Information Filter each one of the local filters operates independently, processing its own local measurements. It is assumed that there is no sharing of measurements between the local filters and that the aggregation filter (Fig. 5) does not have direct access to the raw measurements feeding each local filter. The outputs of the local filters are treated as measurements which are fed into the aggregation fusion filter (Lee, 2008b), (Lee, 2008a), (Vercauteren & Wang, 2005). Then each local filter is expressed by its respective error covariance and estimate in terms of information contributions given in Eq.(36)

$$\begin{array}{c} P_i^{-1}(k) = P_i^-(k)^{-1} + J_\gamma^T R(k)^{-1} J_\gamma(k) \\ \hat{x}_i(k) = P_i(k)(P_i^-(k)^{-1}\hat{x}_i^-(k)) + J_\gamma^T R(k)^{-1}[z^i(k) - \gamma^i(x(k)) + J_\gamma^i(k)\hat{x}_i^-(k)] \end{array} \tag{45}$$

It is noted that the local estimates are suboptimal and also conditionally independent given their own measurements. The global estimate and the associated error covariance for the aggregate fusion filter can be rewritten in terms of the computed estimates and covariances from the local filters using the relations

$$\begin{array}{c} J_\gamma^T(k)R(k)^{-1}J_\gamma(k) = P_i(k)^{-1} - P_i^-(k)^{-1} \\ J_\gamma^T(k)R(k)^{-1}[z^i(k) - \gamma^i(x(k)) + J_\gamma^i(k)\hat{x}^-(k)] = P_i(k)^{-1}\hat{x}_i(k) - P_i(k)^{-1}\hat{x}_i(k-1) \end{array} \tag{46}$$

For the general case of N local filters $i = 1, \cdots, N$, the distributed filtering architecture is described by the following equations

$$\begin{array}{c} P(k)^{-1} = P^-(k)^{-1} + \sum_{i=1}^N [P_i(k)^{-1} - P_i^-(k)^{-1}] \\ \hat{x}(k) = P(k)[P^-(k)^{-1}\hat{x}^-(k) + \sum_{i=1}^N (P_i(k)^{-1}\hat{x}_i(k) - P_i^-(k)^{-1}\hat{x}_i^-(k))] \end{array} \tag{47}$$

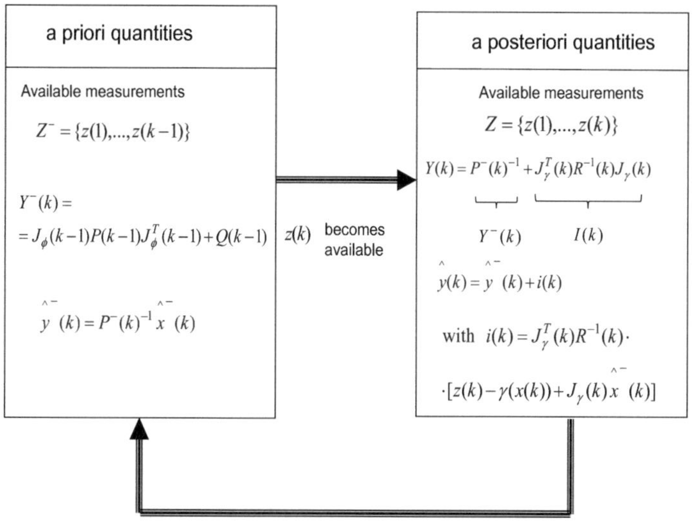

Fig. 6. Schematic diagram of the Extended Information Filter loop

It is noted that the global state update equation in the above distributed filter can be written in terms of the information state vector and of the information matrix

$$\begin{aligned} \hat{y}(k) &= \hat{y}^{-}(k) + \textstyle\sum_{i=1}^{N}(\hat{y}_i(k) - \hat{y}_i^{-}(k)) \\ \hat{Y}(k) &= \hat{Y}^{-}(k) + \textstyle\sum_{i=1}^{N}(\hat{Y}_i(k) - \hat{Y}_i^{-}(k)) \end{aligned} \tag{48}$$

The local filters provide their own local estimates and repeat the cycle at step $k+1$. In turn the global filter can predict its global estimate and repeat the cycle at the next time step $k+1$ when the new state $\hat{x}(k+1)$ and the new global covariance matrix $P(k+1)$ are calculated. From Eq. (47) it can be seen that if a local filter (processing station) fails, then the local covariance matrices and the local state estimates provided by the rest of the filters will enable an accurate computation of the system's state vector.

5. Distributed state estimation using the unscented information filter

5.1 Unscented kalman filtering at local processing units

It is also possible to estimate the cartesian coordinates and bearing of the target through the fusion of the estimates provided by local Sigma-Point Kalman Filters. This can be succeeded using the Distributed Sigma-Point Kalman Filter, also known as *Unscented Information Filter* (UIF) (Lee, 2008b), (Lee, 2008a). First, the functioning of the local Sigma-Point Kalman Filters will be explained. Each local Sigma-Point Kalman Filter generates an estimation of the target's state vector by fusing the estimate of the target's coordinates and bearing obtained by each mobile robot with the distance of the target from a reference surface, measured in an inertial coordinates system. Unlike EKF, in Sigma-Point Kalman Filtering no analytical Jacobians of the system equations need to be calculated as in the case for the EKF (Julier et al., 2000), (Julier & Uhlmann, 2004), (Särrkä, 2007). This is achieved through a different approach for calculating the posterior 1st and 2nd order statistics of a random variable that undergoes a

nonlinear transformation. The state distribution is represented again by a Gaussian random variable but is now specified using a minimal set of deterministically chosen weighted sample points. The basic sigma-point approach can be described as follows:
1. A set of weighted samples (sigma-points) are deterministically calculated using the mean and square-root decomposition of the covariance matrix of the system's state vector. As a minimal requirement the sigma-point set must completely capture the first and second order moments of the prior random variable. Higher order moments can be captured at the cost of using more sigma-points.
2. The sigma-points are propagated through the true nonlinear function using functional evaluations alone, i.e. no analytical derivatives are used, in order to generate a posterior sigma-point set.
3. The posterior statistics are calculated (approximated) using tractable functions of the propagated sigma-points and weights. Typically, these take on the form of a simple weighted sample mean and covariance calculations of the posterior sigma points.
It is noted that the sigma-point approach differs substantially from general stochastic sampling techniques, such as Monte-Carlo integration (e.g Particle Filtering methods) which require significantly more sample points in an attempt to propagate an accurate (possibly non-Gaussian) distribution of the state. The deceptively simple sigma-point approach results in posterior approximations that are accurate to the third order for Gaussian inputs for all nonlinearities. For non-Gaussian inputs, approximations are accurate to at least the second-order, with the accuracy of third and higher-order moments determined by the specific choice of weights and scaling factors.
The Unscented Kalman Filter (UKF) is a special case of Sigma-Point Kalman Filters. The UKF is a discrete time filtering algorithm which uses the unscented transform for computing approximate solutions to the filtering problem of the form

$$\begin{array}{c} x(k+1) = \phi(x(k)) + L(k)U(k) + w(k) \\ y(k) = \gamma(x(k)) + v(k) \end{array} \tag{49}$$

where $x(k) \in R^n$ is the system's state vector, $y(k) \in R^m$ is the measurement, $w(k) \in R^n$ is a Gaussian process noise $w(k) \sim N(0, Q(k))$, and $v(k) \in R^m$ is a Gaussian measurement noise denoted as $v(k) \sim N(0, R(k))$. The mean and covariance of the initial state $x(0)$ are $m(0)$ and $P(0)$, respectively.
Some basic operations performed in the UKF algorithm (*Unscented Transform*) are summarized as follows:
1) Denoting the current state mean as $\hat{x}$, a set of $2n+1$ sigma points is taken from the columns of the $n \times n$ matrix $\sqrt{(n+\lambda)P_{xx}}$ as follows:

$$\begin{array}{c} x^0 = \hat{x} \\ x^i = \hat{x} + [\sqrt{(n+\lambda)P_{xx}}]_i, \ i = 1, \cdots, n \\ x^i = \hat{x} - [\sqrt{(n+\lambda)P_{xx}}]_i, \ i = n+1, \cdots, 2n \end{array} \tag{50}$$

and the associate weights are computed:

$$\begin{array}{cc} W_0^{(m)} = \frac{\lambda}{(n+\lambda)} & W_0^{(c)} = \frac{\lambda}{(n+\lambda)+(1-\alpha^2+b)} \\ W_i^{(m)} = \frac{1}{2(n+\lambda)}, \ i = 1, \cdots, 2n & W_i^{(c)} = \frac{1}{2(n+\lambda)} \end{array} \tag{51}$$

where $i = 1, 2, \cdots, 2n$ and $\lambda = \alpha^2(n+\kappa) - n$ is a scaling parameter, while α, β and κ are constant parameters. Matrix P_{xx} is the covariance matrix of the state x.

2) Transform each of the sigma points as

$$z^i = h(x^i) \quad i = 0, \cdots, 2n \tag{52}$$

3) Mean and covariance estimates for z can be computed as

$$\begin{aligned} \hat{z} &\simeq \sum_{i=0}^{2n} W_i^{(m)} z^i \\ P_{zz} &= \sum_{i=0}^{2n} W_i^{(c)} (z^i - \hat{z})(z^i - \hat{z})^T \end{aligned} \tag{53}$$

4) The cross-covariance of x and z is estimated as

$$P_{xz} = \sum_{i=0}^{2n} W_i^{(c)} (x^i - \hat{x})(z^i - \hat{z})^T \tag{54}$$

The matrix square root of positive definite matrix P_{xx} means a matrix $A = \sqrt{P_{xx}}$ such that $P_{xx} = AA^T$ and a possible way for calculation is Singular Values Decomposition (SVD).
Next the basic stages of the *Unscented Kalman Filter* are given:
As in the case of the Extended Kalman Filter and the Particle Filter, the Unscented Kalman Filter also consists of prediction stage (time update) and correction stage (measurement update) (Julier & Uhlmann, 2004), (Särrkä, 2007).
Time update: Compute the predicted state mean $\hat{x}^-(k)$ and the predicted covariance $P_{xx}{}^-(k)$ as

$$\begin{aligned} [\hat{x}^-(k), P_{xx}^-(k)] &= UT(f_d, \hat{x}(k-1), P_{xx}(k-1)) \\ P_{xx}^-(k) &= P_{xx}(k-1) + Q(k-1) \end{aligned} \tag{55}$$

Measurement update: Obtain the new output measurement z_k and compute the predicted mean $\hat{z}(k)$ and covariance of the measurement $P_{zz}(k)$, and the cross covariance of the state and measurement $P_{xz}(k)$

$$\begin{aligned} [\hat{z}(k), P_{zz}(k), P_{xz}(k)] &= UT(h_d, \hat{x}^-(k), P_{xx}^-(k)) \\ P_{zz}(k) &= P_{zz}(k) + R(k) \end{aligned} \tag{56}$$

Then compute the filter gain $K(k)$, the state mean $\hat{x}(k)$ and the covariance $P_{xx}(k)$, conditional to the measurement $y(k)$

$$\begin{aligned} K(k) &= P_{xz}(k) P_{zz}^{-1}(k) \\ \hat{x}(k) &= \hat{x}^-(k) + K(k)[z(k) - \hat{z}(k)] \\ P_{xx}(k) &= P_{xx}^-(k) - K(k) P_{zz}(k) K(k)^T \end{aligned} \tag{57}$$

The filter starts from the initial mean $m(0)$ and covariance $P_{xx}(0)$. The stages of state vector estimation with the use of the Unscented Kalman Filter algorithm are depicted in Fig. 7.

5.2 Unscented information filtering

The Unscented Information Filter (UIF) performs fusion of the state vector estimates which are provided by local Unscented Kalman Filters, by weighting these estimates with local Information matrices (inverse of the local state vector covariance matrices which are again recursively computed) (Lee, 2008b), (Lee, 2008a), (Vercauteren & Wang, 2005)]. The Unscented Information Filter is derived by introducing a linear error propagation based on the unscented transformation into the Extended Information Filter structure. First, an augmented state vector $x_\alpha{}^-(k)$ is considered, along with the process noise vector, and the associated covariance matrix is introduced.

$$\hat{x}_\alpha^-(k) = \begin{pmatrix} \hat{x}^-(k) \\ \hat{w}^-(k) \end{pmatrix}, \quad P^{\alpha-}(k) = \begin{pmatrix} P^-(k) & 0 \\ 0 & Q^-(k) \end{pmatrix} \tag{58}$$

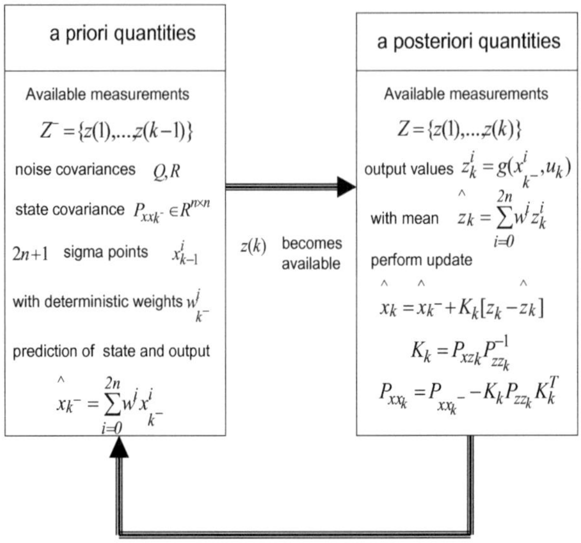

Fig. 7. Schematic diagram of the Unscented Kalman Filter loop

As in the case of local (lumped) Unscented Kalman Filters, a set of weighted sigma points $X^{i-}_{\alpha}(k)$ is generated as

$$\begin{aligned} X^-_{\alpha,0}(k) &= \hat{x}^-_{\alpha}(k) \\ X^-_{\alpha,i}(k) &= \hat{x}^-_{\alpha}(k) + [\sqrt{(n_\alpha+\lambda)P^-_{\alpha}(k-1)}]_i,\ i=1,\cdots,n \\ X^-_{\alpha,i}(k) &= \hat{x}^-_{\alpha}(k) + [\sqrt{(n_\alpha+\lambda)P^-_{\alpha}(k-1)}]_i,\ i=n+1,\cdots,2n \end{aligned} \tag{59}$$

where $\lambda = \alpha^2(n_\alpha + \kappa) - n_\alpha$ is a scaling, while $0 \leq \alpha \leq 1$ and κ are constant parameters. The corresponding weights for the mean and covariance are defined as in the case of the lumped Unscented Kalman Filter

$$\begin{aligned} W^{(m)}_0 &= \frac{\lambda}{n_\alpha+\lambda} & W^{(c)}_0 &= \frac{\lambda}{(n_\alpha+\lambda)+(1-\alpha^2+\beta)} \\ W^{(m)}_i &= \frac{1}{2(n_\alpha+\lambda)},\ i=1,\cdots,2n_\alpha & W^{(c)}_i &= \frac{1}{2(n_\alpha+\lambda)},\ i=1,\cdots,2n_\alpha \end{aligned} \tag{60}$$

where β is again a constant parameter. The equations of the prediction stage (measurement update) of the information filter, i.e. the calculation of the information matrix and the information state vector of Eq. (36) now become

$$\begin{aligned} \hat{y}^-(k) &= Y^-(k)\Sigma_{i=0}^{2n_\alpha} W^m_i X^x_i(k) \\ Y^-(k) &= P^-(k)^{-1} \end{aligned} \tag{61}$$

where X^x_i are the predicted state vectors when using the sigma point vectors X^w_i in the state equation $X^x_i(k+1) = \phi(X^{w-}_i(k)) + L(k)U(k)$. The predicted state covariance matrix is computed as

$$P^{-}(k)=\sum_{i=0}^{2n_{\alpha}} W_i^{(c)}[X_i^{x}(k)-\hat{x}^{-}(k)][X_i^{x}(k)-\hat{x}^{-}(k)]^T \tag{62}$$

As noted, the equations of the Extended Information Filter (EIF) are based on the linearized dynamic model of the system and on the inverse of the covariance matrix of the state vector. However, in the equations of the Unscented Kalman Filter (UKF) there is no linearization of the system dynamics, thus the UKF cannot be included directly into the EIF equations. Instead, it is assumed that the nonlinear measurement equation of the system given in Eq. (24) can be mapped into a linear function of its statistical mean and covariance, which makes possible to use the information update equations of the EIF. Denoting $Y_i(k)=\gamma(X_i^x(k))$ (i.e. the output of the system calculated through the propagation of the i-th sigma point X^i through the system's nonlinear equation) the observation covariance and its cross-covariance are approximated by

$$\begin{aligned} P_{YY}^{-}(k) &= E[(z(k)-\hat{z}^{-}(k))(z(k)-\hat{z}^{-}(k))^T] \\ &\simeq J_{\gamma}(k)P^{-}(k)J_{\gamma}(k)^T \end{aligned} \tag{63}$$

$$\begin{aligned} P_{XY}^{-}(k) &= E[(x(k)-\hat{x}(k)^{-})(z(k)-\hat{z}(k)^{-})^T] \\ &\simeq P^{-}(k)J_{\gamma}(k)^T \end{aligned} \tag{64}$$

where $z(k)=\gamma(x(k))$ and $J_{\gamma}(k)$ is the Jacobian of the output equation $\gamma(x(k))$. Next, multiplying the predicted covariance and its inverse term on the right side of the information matrix Eq. (35) and replacing $P(k)J_{\gamma}(k)^T$ with $P_{XY}^{-}(k)$ gives the following representation of the information matrix (Lee, 2008b), (Lee, 2008a), (Vercauteren & Wang, 2005)

$$\begin{aligned} I(k) &= J_{\gamma}(k)^T R(k)^{-1} J_{\gamma}(k) \\ &= P^{-}(k)^{-1}P^{-}(k)J_{\gamma}(k)^T R(k)^{-1} J_{\gamma}^{-}(k)P^{-}(k)^T(P^{-}(k)^{-1})^T \\ &= P^{-}(k)^{-1}P_{XY}^{-}(k)R(k)^{-1}P_{XY}^{-}(k)^T(P^{-}(k)^{-1})^T \end{aligned} \tag{65}$$

where $P^{-}(k)^{-1}$ is calculated according to Eq. (62) and the cross-correlation matrix $P_{XY}(k)$ is calculated from

$$P_{XY}^{-}(k)=\sum_{i=0}^{2n_{\alpha}} W_i^{(c)}[X_i^{x}(k)-\hat{x}^{-}(k)][Y_i(k)-\hat{z}^{-}(k)]^T \tag{66}$$

where $Y_i(k)=\gamma(X_i^x(k))$ and the predicted measurement vector $\hat{z}^{-}(k)$ is obtained by $\hat{z}^{-}(k)=\sum_{i=0}^{2n_{\alpha}} W_i^{(m)}Y_i(k)$. Similarly, the information state vector i_k can be rewritten as

$$\begin{aligned} i(k) &= J_{\gamma}(k)^T R(k)^{-1}[z(k)-\gamma(x(k))+J_{\gamma}(k)^T\hat{x}^{-}(k)] \\ &= P^{-}(k)^{-1}P^{-}(k)J_{\gamma}(k)^T R(k)^{-1}[z(k)-\gamma(x(k))+J_{\gamma}(k)^T(P^{-}(k))^T(P^{-}(k)^{-1})^T\hat{x}^{-}(k)] \\ &= P^{-}(k)^{-1}P_{XY}^{-}(k)R(k)^{-1}[z(k)-\gamma(x(k))+P_{XY}^{-}(k)(P^{-}(k)^{-1})^T\hat{x}^{-}(k)] \end{aligned} \tag{67}$$

To complete the analogy to the information contribution equations of the EIF a "measurement" matrix $H^T(k)$ is defined as

$$H(k)^T = P^{-}(k)^{-1}P_{XY}^{-}(k) \tag{68}$$

In terms of the "measurement" matrix $H(k)$ the information contributions equations are written as

$$\begin{aligned} i(k) &= H^T(k)R(k)^{-1}[z(k)-\gamma(x(k))+H(k)\hat{x}^{-}(k)] \\ I(k) &= H^T(k)R(k)^{-1}H(k) \end{aligned} \tag{69}$$

The above procedure leads to an implicit linearization in which the nonlinear measurement equation of the system given in Eq. (24) is approximated by the statistical error variance and its mean

$$z(k) = \gamma(x(k)) \simeq H(k)x(k) + \bar{u}(k) \tag{70}$$

where $\bar{u}(k) = \gamma(\hat{x}^-(k)) - H(k)\hat{x}^-(k)$ is a measurement residual term.

5.3 Calculation of local estimations in terms of UIF information contributions

Next, the local estimations provided by distributed (local) Unscented Kalmans filters will be expressed in terms of the information contributions (information matrix I and information state vector i) of the Unscented Information Filter, which were defined in Eq. (69) (Lee, 2008b), (Lee, 2008a), (Vercauteren & Wang, 2005). It is assumed that the observation vector $\bar{z}_i(k+1)$ is available from N different sensors, and that each sensor observes a common state according to the local observation model, expressed by

$$\bar{z}_i(k) = H_i(k)x(k) + \bar{u}_i(k) + v_i(k) \tag{71}$$

where the noise vector $v_i(k)$ is taken to be white Gaussian and uncorrelated between sensors. The variance of the composite observation noise vector v_k of all sensors is written in terms of the block diagonal matrix $R(k) = diag[R_1(k)^T, \cdots, R_N(k)^T]^T$. Then one can define the local information matrix $I_i(k)$ and the local information state vector $i_i(k)$ at the i-th sensor, as follows

$$\begin{aligned} i_i(k) &= H_i^T(k)R_i(k)^{-1}[z_i(k) - \gamma^i(x(k)) + H_i(k)\hat{x}^-(k)] \\ I_i(k) &= H_i^T(k)R_i(k)^{-1}H_i(k) \end{aligned} \tag{72}$$

Since the information contribution terms have group diagonal structure in terms of the innovation and measurement matrix, the update equations for the multiple state estimation and data fusion are written as a linear combination of the local information contribution terms

$$\begin{aligned} \hat{y}(k) &= \hat{y}^-(k) + \Sigma_{i=1}^N i_i(k) \\ Y(k) &= Y^-(k) + \Sigma_{i=1}^N I_i(k) \end{aligned} \tag{73}$$

Then using Eq. (61) one can find the mean state vector for the multiple sensor estimation problem.

As in the case of the Unscented Kalman Filter, the Unscented Information Filter running at the i-th measurement processing unit can be written in terms of *measurement update* and *time update* equations:

Measurement update: Acquire measurement $z(k)$ and compute

$$\begin{aligned} Y(k) &= P^-(k)^{-1} + H^T(k)R^{-1}(k)H(k) \\ \text{or } Y(k) &= Y^-(k) + I(k) \text{ where } I(k) = H^T(k)R^{-1}(k)H(k) \end{aligned} \tag{74}$$

$$\begin{aligned} \hat{y}(k) &= \hat{y}^-(k) + H^T(k)R^{-1}(k)[z(k) - \gamma(\hat{x}(k)) + H(k)\hat{x}^-(k)] \\ \text{or } \hat{y}(k) &= \hat{y}^-(k) + i(k) \end{aligned} \tag{75}$$

Time update: Compute

$$\begin{aligned} Y^-(k+1) &= (P^-(k+1))^{-1} \\ \text{where } P^-(k+1) &= \Sigma_{i=0}^{2n_\alpha} W_i^{(c)}[X_i^x(k+1) - \hat{x}^-(k+1)][X_i^x(k+1) - \hat{x}^-(k+1)]^T \end{aligned} \tag{76}$$

$$\begin{aligned} \hat{y}(k+1) &= Y(k+1)\Sigma_{i=0}^{2n_\alpha} W_i^{(m)} X_i^x(k+1) \\ \text{where } X_i^x(k+1) &= \phi(X_i^w(k)) + L(k)U(k) \end{aligned} \tag{77}$$

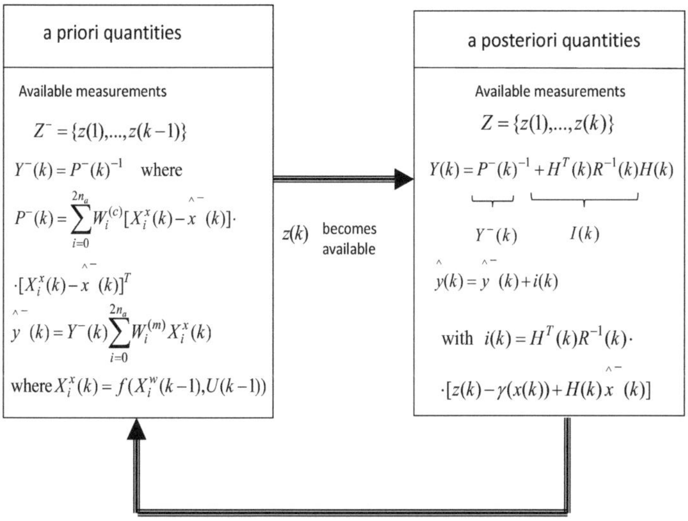

Fig. 8. Schematic diagram of the Unscented Information Filter loop

5.4 Distributed unscented information filtering for state estimates fusion

It has been shown that the update of the aggregate state vector of the Unscented Information Filter architecture can be expressed in terms of the local information matrices I_i and of the local information state vectors i_i, which in turn depend on the local covariance matrices P and cross-covariance matrices P_{XY}. Next, it will be shown that the update of the aggregate state vector can be also expressed in terms of the local state vectors $x_i(k)$ and in terms of the local covariance matrices $P_i(k)$ and cross-covariance matrices $P^i_{XY}(k)$. It is assumed that the local filters do not have access to each other row measurements and that they are allowed to communicate only their information matrices and their local information state vectors. Thus each local filter is expressed by its respective error covariance and estimate in terms of the local information state contribution i_i and its associated information matrix I_i at the i-th filter site. Then using Eq. (61) one obtains

$$\begin{array}{c} P_i(k)^{-1} = P_i^-(k)^{-1} + H_i^T(k)R_i(k)^{-1}H_i(k) \\ \hat{x}_i = P_i(k)(P_i^-(k)\hat{x}_i^-(k) + H_i^T(k)R_i(k)^{-1}[z_i(k) - \gamma^i(x(k)) + H_i(k)\hat{x}^-(k)]) \end{array} \tag{78}$$

Using Eq. (78), each local information state contribution i_i and its associated information matrix I_i at the i-th filter are rewritten in terms of the computed estimates and covariances of the local filters

$$\begin{array}{c} H_i^T(k)R_i(k)^{-1}H_i(k) = P_i^{-1}(k) - P_i^-(k)^{-1} \\ H_i^T(k)R_i(k)^{-1}[z_i(k) - \gamma^i(x(k)) + H_i(k)\hat{x}^-(k)]) = P_i(k)^{-1}\hat{x}_i(k) - P_i^-(k)^{-1}\hat{x}_i^-(k) \end{array} \tag{79}$$

where according to Eq.(68) it holds $H_i(k) = P_i^-(k)^{-1}P^-_{XY,i}(k)$. Next, the aggregate estimates of the distributed Unscented Information Filtering are derived for a number of N local filters $i = 1, \cdots, N$ and sensor measurements, first in terms of covariances (Lee, 2008b),(Lee, 2008a),(Vercauteren & Wang, 2005).

$$\begin{aligned} P(k)^{-1} &= P^{-}(k)^{-1} + \sum_{i=1}^{N}[P_i(k)^{-1} - P_i^{-}(k)^{-1}] \\ \hat{x}(k) &= P(k)[P^{-}(k)^{-1}\hat{x}^{-}(k) + \sum_{i=1}^{N}(P_i(k)^{-1}\hat{x}_i(k) - P_i^{-}(k)^{-1}\hat{x}_i^{-}(k))] \end{aligned} \tag{80}$$

and also in terms of the information state vector and of the information state covariance matrix

$$\begin{aligned} \hat{y}(k) &= \hat{y}^{-}(k) + \sum_{i=1}^{N}(\hat{y}_i(k) - \hat{y}_i^{-}(k)) \\ Y(k) &= Y^{-}(k) + \sum_{i=1}^{N}[Y_i(k) - Y_i^{-}(k)] \end{aligned} \tag{81}$$

State estimation fusion based on the Unscented Information Filter (UIF) is fault tolerant. From Eq. (80) it can be seen that if a local filter (processing station) fails, then the local covariance matrices and local estimates provided by the rest of the filters will enable a reliable calculation of the system's state vector. Moreover, the UIF is computationally more efficient comparing to centralized filters and results in enhanced estimation accuracy.

6. Simulation tests

6.1 Estimation of target's position with the use of the extended information filter

The number of mobile robots used for target tracking in the simulation experiments was $N = 10$. However, since the mobile robots ensemble (mobile sensor network) is modular a larger number of mobile robot's could have been also considered. It is assumed that each mobile robot can obtain an estimation of the target's cartesian coordinates and bearing, i.e. the target's position $[x, y]$ as well as the target's orientation θ. To improve the accuracy of the target's localization, the target's coordinates and bearing are fused with the distance of the target from a reference surface measured in an inertial coordinates system (see Fig. 2 and 9).

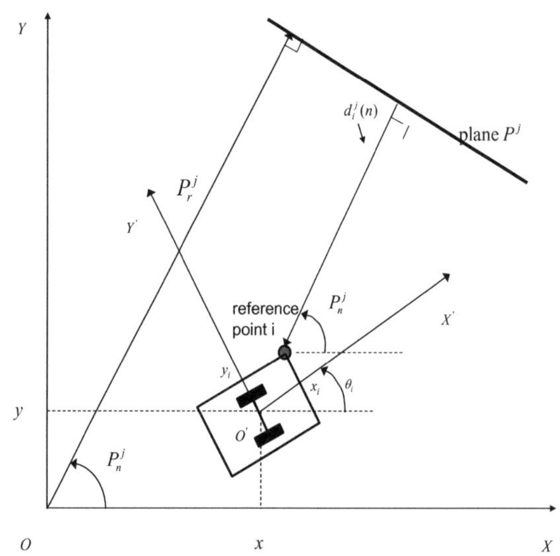

Fig. 9. Distance of the target's reference point i from the reference plane P^j, measured in the inertial coordinates system OXY

The inertial coordinates system OXY is defined. Furthermore the coordinates system $O'X'Y'$

is considered (Fig. 2). $O'X'Y'$ results from OXY if it is rotated by an angle θ (Fig. 2). The coordinates of the center of the wheels axis with respect to OXY are (x,y), while the coordinates of the reference point i that is mounted on the vehicle, with respect to $O'X'Y'$ are $x_i^{'},y_i^{'}$. The orientation of the reference point with respect to $OX'Y'$ is $\theta_i^{'}$. Thus the coordinates of the reference point with respect to OXY are (x_i,y_i) and its orientation is θ_i, and are given by:

$$\begin{aligned} x_i(k) &= x(k) + x_i^{'}sin(\theta(k)) + y_i^{'}cos(\theta(k)) \\ y_i(k) &= y(k) - x_i^{'}cos(\theta(k)) + y_i^{'}sin(\theta(k)) \\ \theta_i(k) &= \theta(k) + \theta_i \end{aligned} \tag{82}$$

Each plane P^j in the robot's environment can be represented by P_r^j and P_n^j (Fig. 9), where (i) P_r^j is the normal distance of the plane from the origin O, (ii) P_n^j is the angle between the normal line to the plane and the x-direction.
The target's reference point i is at position $x_i(k),y_i(k)$ with respect to the inertial coordinates system OXY and its orientation is $\theta_i(k)$. Using the above notation, the distance of the reference point i, from the plane P^j is represented by P_r^j,P_n^j (see Fig. 9):

$$d_i^j(k) = P_r^j - x_i(k)cos(P_n^j) - y_i(k)sin(P_n^j) \tag{83}$$

Assuming a constant sampling period $\Delta t_k = T$ the measurement equation is $z(k+1) = \gamma(x(k)) + v(k)$, where $z(k)$ is the vector containing target's coordinates and bearing estimates obtained from a mobile sensor and the measurement of the target's distance to the reference surface, while $v(k)$ is a white noise sequence $\sim N(0,R(kT))$. The measure vector $z(k)$ can thus be written as

$$z(k) = [x(k) + v_1(k), y(k) + v_2(k), \theta(k) + v_3(k), d_1^j(k) + v_4(k)] \tag{84}$$

with $i = 1,2,\cdots,n_s$, $d_i^j(k)$ to be the distance measure with respect to the plane P^j and $j = 1,\cdots,n_p$ to be the number of reference surfaces. By definition of the measurement vector one has that the output function $\gamma(x(k))$ is given by $\gamma(x(k)) = [x(k),y(k),\theta(k),d_1^1(k)]$.
To obtain the Extended Kalman Filter (EKF), the kinematic model of the target described in Eq. (2) is discretized and written in the discrete-time state-space form of Eq.(24) (Rigatos, 2009a),(Rigatos, 2010b).
The *measurement update* of the EKF is

$$\begin{aligned} &K(k) = P^-(k)J_\gamma^T(\hat{x}^-(k))[J_\gamma(\hat{x}^-(k))P^-(k)J_\gamma^T(\hat{x}^-(k)) + R(k)]^{-1} \\ &\hat{x}(k) = \hat{x}^-(k) + K(k)[z(k) - \gamma(\hat{x}^-(k))] \\ &P(k) = P^-(k) - K(k)J_\gamma^T P^-(k) \end{aligned}$$

The *time update* of the EKF is

$$\begin{aligned} &P^-(k+1) = J_\phi(\hat{x}(k))P(k)J_\phi^T(\hat{x}(k)) + Q(k) \\ &\hat{x}^-(k+1) = \phi(\hat{x}(k)) + L(k)U(k) \end{aligned}$$

where

$$L(k) = \begin{pmatrix} Tcos(\theta(k)) & 0 \\ Tsin(\theta(k)) & 0 \\ 0 & T \end{pmatrix}$$

and

$$J_{\phi}(\hat{x}(k)) = \begin{pmatrix} 1 & 0 & -v(k)sin(\theta)T \\ 0 & 1 & -v(k)cos(\theta)T \\ 0 & 0 & 1 \end{pmatrix}$$

while $Q(k) = diag[\sigma^2(k),\sigma^2(k),\sigma^2(k)]$, with $\sigma^2(k)$ chosen to be 10^{-3} and $\phi(\hat{x}(k)) = [\hat{x}(k),\hat{y}(k),\hat{\theta}(k)]^T$, $\gamma(\hat{x}(k)) = [\hat{x}(k),\hat{y}(k),\hat{\theta}(k),d(k)]^T$, i.e.

$$\gamma(\hat{x}(k)) = \begin{pmatrix} \hat{x}(k) \\ \hat{y}(k) \\ \hat{\theta}(k) \\ P_r^j - x_i(k))cos(P_n^j) - y_i(k)sin(P_n^j) \end{pmatrix} \quad (85)$$

The vector of the control input is given by $U(k) = [v(k),\omega(k)]^T$. Assuming one reference surface in the target's neighborhood one gets

$$J_{\gamma}^T(\hat{x}^-(k)) = [J_{\gamma_1}(\hat{x}^-(k)),J_{\gamma_2}(\hat{x}^-(k)),J_{\gamma_3}(\hat{x}^-(k)),J_{\gamma_4}(\hat{x}^-(k))]^T, \text{i.e.}$$

$$J_{\gamma}^T(\hat{x}^-(k)) = \begin{pmatrix} 1 & 0 & 0 \\ 0 & 1 & 0 \\ 0 & 0 & 1 \\ -cos(P_n^j) & -sin(P_n^j) & \{x_i^{'}cos(\theta - P_n^j) - y_i^{'}sin(\theta - P_n^j)\} \end{pmatrix} \quad (86)$$

The use of EKF for fusing the target's coordinates and bearing measured by each mobile robot with the target's distance from a reference surface measured in an inertial coordinates system provides an estimation of the state vector $[x(t),y(t),\theta(t)]$ and enables the successful tracking of the target's motion by the individual mobile robots (mobile sensors).

The tracking of the target by the swarm of the autonomous vehicles was tested in the case of several reference trajectories, both for motion in an environment without obstacles as well as for motion in a plane containing obstacles. The proposed distributed filtering scheme enabled accurate estimation of the target's state vector $[x,y,\theta]^T$ through the fusion of the measurements of the target's coordinates and orientation obtained by each mobile robot with the measurement of the distance from a reference surface in an inertial coordinates frame. The state estimates provided by the Extended Kalman Filters running at each mobile sensor were fused into one single state estimate using Extended Information Filtering. The aggregate estimated coordinates of the target $(\hat{x}^*,\hat{y}^*)$ provided the reference setpoint for the distributed motion planning algorithm. Each mobile sensor was made to move along the path defined by $(\hat{x}^*,\hat{y}^*)$. The convergence properties of the distributed motion planning algorithm were described in Section 3. The tracking of the target's trajectory by the mobile robots ensemble as well as the accuracy of the two-level sensor fusion-based estimation of the target's coordinates is depicted in Fig. 10 to Fig. 14. The target is marked as a thick-line rectangle and the associated reference trajectory is plotted as a thick line.

It is noted that using distributed EKFs and fusion through the Extended Information Filter is more robust comparing to the centralized EKF since (i) if a local processing unit is subject to a fault then state estimation is still possible and can be used for accurate localization of the target, as well as for tracking of target's trajectory by the individual mobile sensors (autonomous vehicles), (ii) communication overhead remains low even in the case of a large number of distributed mobile sensors, because the greatest part of state estimation procedure is performed locally and only information matrices and state vectors are communicated

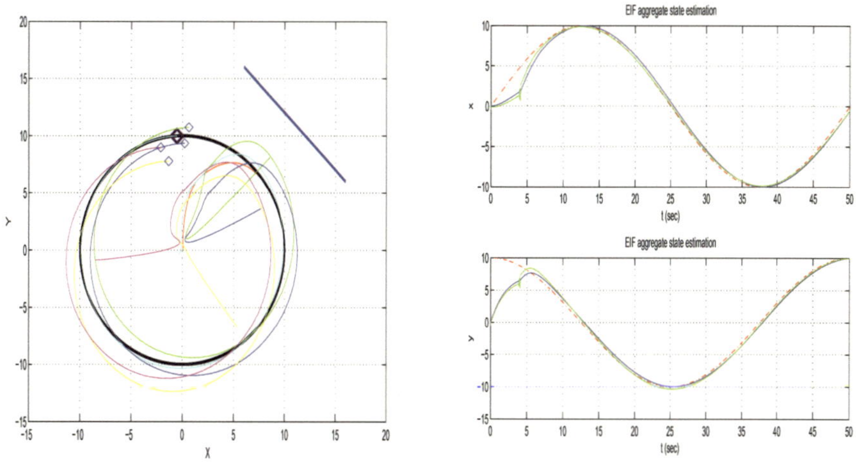

(a) (b)

Fig. 10. (a) Distributed target tracking by an ensemble of autonomous vehicles when the target follows a circular trajectory in an obstacles-free motion space, (b) Aggregate estimation of the target's position with the use of Extended Information Filtering (continuous line) and target's reference path (dashed line).

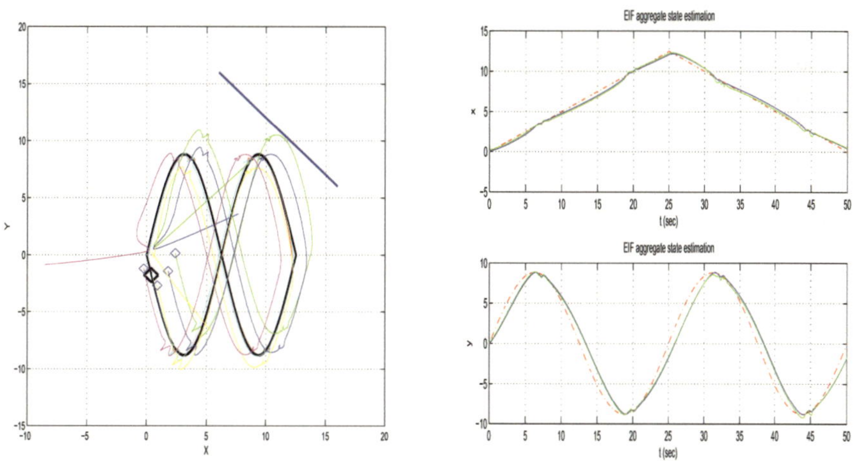

(a) (b)

Fig. 11. (a) Distributed target tracking by an ensemble of autonomous vehicles when the target follows an eight-shaped trajectory in an obstacles-free motion space, (b) Aggregate estimation of the target's position with the use of Extended Information Filtering (continuous line) and target's reference path (dashed line)

.

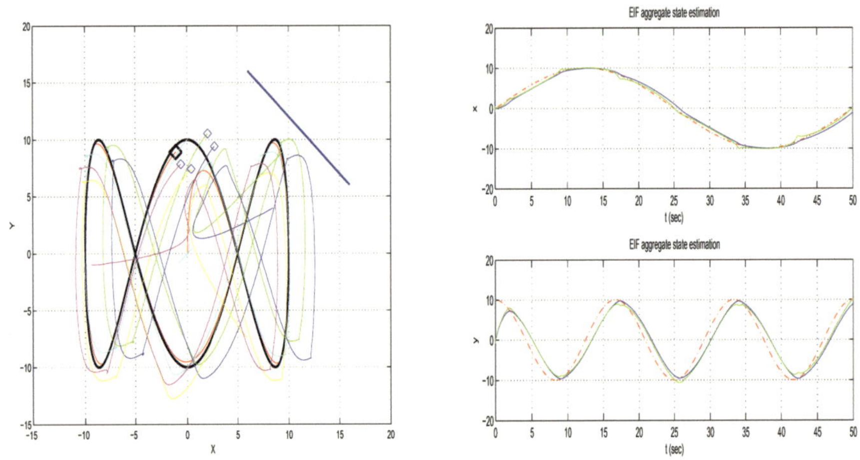

(a) (b)

Fig. 12. (a) Distributed target tracking by an ensemble of autonomous vehicles when the target follows a curve-shaped trajectory in an obstacles-free motion space, (b) Aggregate estimation of the target's position with the use of Extended Information Filtering (continuous line) and target's reference path (dashed line).

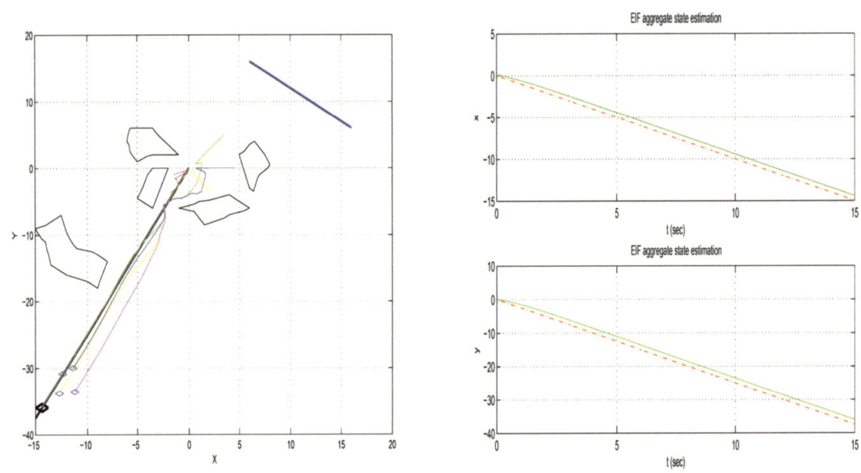

(a) (b)

Fig. 13. (a) Distributed target tracking by an ensemble of autonomous vehicles when the target follows a line path in a motion space with obstacles, (b) Aggregate estimation of the target's position with the use of Extended Information Filtering (continuous line) and target's reference path (dashed line).

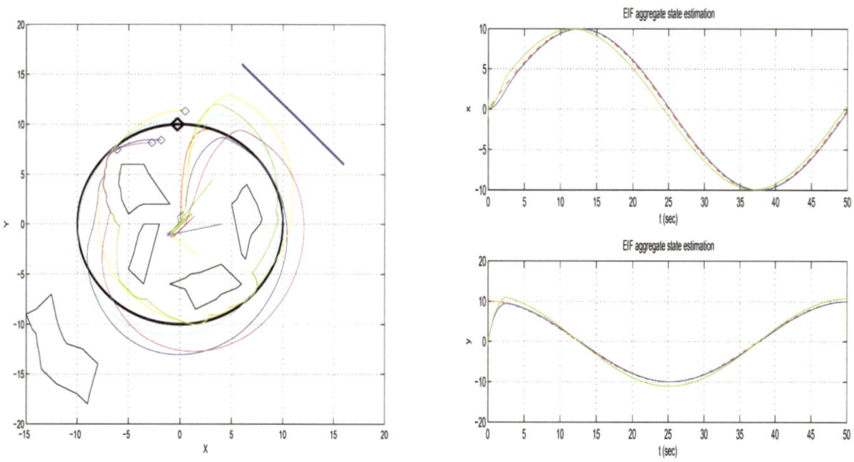

(a) (b)

Fig. 14. (a) Distributed target tracking by an ensemble of autonomous vehicles when the target follows a circular path in a motion space with obstacles, (b) Aggregate estimation of the target's position with the use of Extended Information Filtering (continuous line) and target's reference path (dashed line).

between the local processing units, (iii) the aggregation performed on the local EKF also compensates for deviations in state estimates of local filters (which can be due to linearization errors).

6.2 Estimation of target's position with the use of unscented information filtering

Next, the estimation of the target's state vector was performed using the Unscented Information Filter. Again, the proposed distributed filtering enabled precise estimation of the target's state vector $[x,y,\theta]^T$ through the fusion of measurements of the target's coordinates and bearing obtained by each mobile sensor with the distance of the target from a reference surface measured in an inertial coordinates system. The state estimates of the local Unscented Kalman Filters running at each mobile sensor (autonomous vehicle) were aggregated into a single estimation by the Unscented Information Filter. The estimated coordinates $[\hat{x}^*,\hat{y}^*]$ of the target were used to generate the reference path which was followed by the mobile robots. The tracking of the target's trajectory by the mobile robots ensemble as well as the accuracy of the two-level sensor fusion-based estimation of the target's position is shown in Fig. 15 to Fig. 19.

As previously analyzed, the Unscented Information Filter is a derivative-free distributed filtering approach in which the local Unscented Kalman Filters provide estimations of the target's coordinates using the update in-time of a number of suitably chosen sigma-points. Therefore, unlike the Extended Information Filter and the local Extended Kalman Filters contained in it, in the Unscented Information Filter there is no need to calculate Jacobians through the computation of partial derivatives. Additionally, unlike the case of local Extended Kalman Filters there is no truncation of higher order Taylor expansion terms and

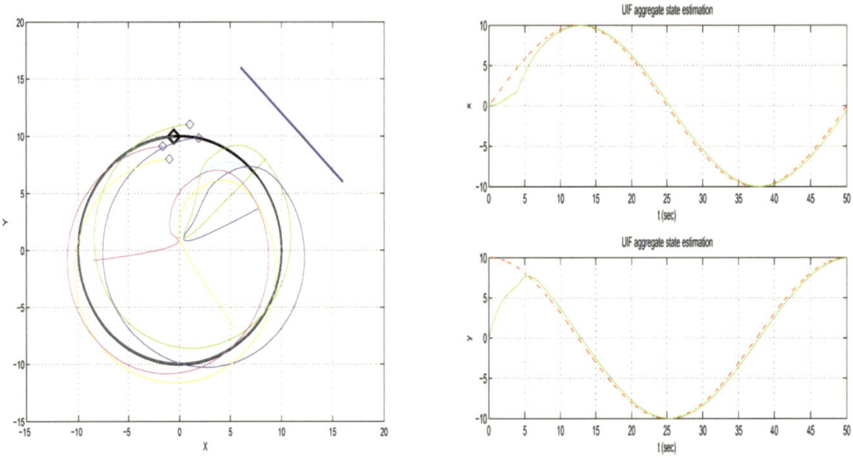

(a) (b)

Fig. 15. (a) Distributed target tracking by an ensemble of autonomous vehicles when the target follows a circular trajectory in an obstacles-free motion space, (b) Aggregate estimation of the target's position with the use of Unscented Information Filtering (continuous line) and target's reference path (dashed line)

no linearization errors are introduced at the local estimators. In that sense the Unscented Information Filter provides a robust distributed state estimation and enables accurate tracking of the target by the mobile sensors (autonomous vehicles).

7. Conclusions

The paper has examined the problem of coordinated tracking of a target by an ensemble of mobile robots (unmanned ground vehicles). Each mobile robot was able to obtain measurements of the target's cartesian coordinates and orientation while a measurement of the target's distance from a reference surface in an inertial coordinates frame was also communicated to the mobile robots. The state estimates of local Extended Kalman Filters running at each mobile robot were fused into one single estimate using the Extended Information Filter. Similarly, the state estimates of local Unscented Kalman Filters running at each mobile sensor were aggregated by the Unscented Information Filter into one single estimation. The estimated coordinates of the target $[\hat{x}^*, \hat{y}^*]$ were used to generate the reference path which was followed by the mobile robots. Next, a suitable motion planning algorithm was designed. The algorithm assured not only tracking of the reference path by the individual autonomous vehicles but also permitted (i) convergence of the autonomous vehicles to the target in a synchronized manner and (ii) avoidance of collisions with obstacles in the motion plane as well as avoidance of collisions between the autonomous vehicles. The performance of the distributed tracking algorithm was tested through simulation experiments.
Comparing to the traditional centralized or hierarchical fusion architecture, the network-centric architecture proposed by the paper has significant advantages which

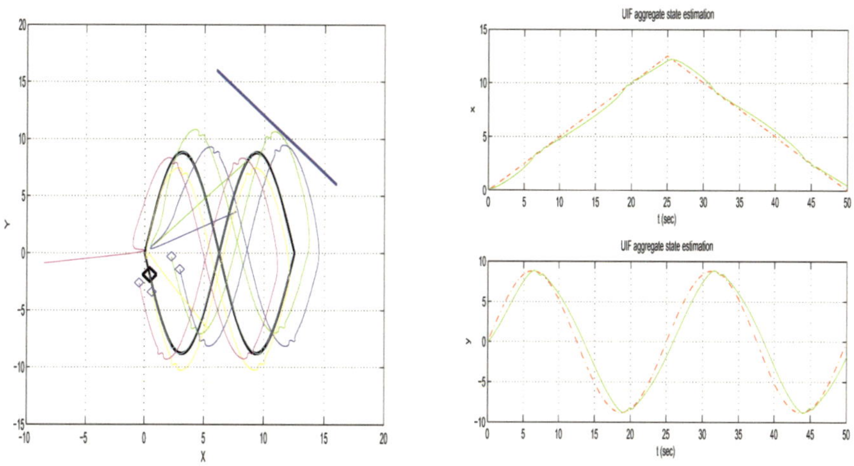

(a) (b)

Fig. 16. (a) Distributed target tracking by an ensemble of autonomous vehicles when the target follows an eight-shaped trajectory in an obstacles-free motion space, (b) Aggregate estimation of the target's position with the use of Unscented Information Filtering (continuous line) and target's reference path (dashed line).

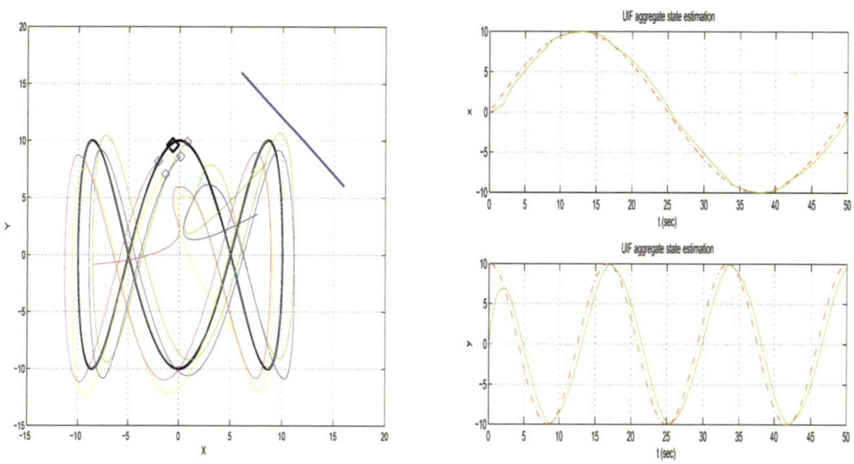

(a) (b)

Fig. 17. (a) Distributed target tracking by an ensemble of autonomous vehicles when the target follows a curve-shaped trajectory in an obstacles-free motion space, (b) Aggregate estimation of the target's position with the use of Unscented Information Filtering (continuous line) and target's reference path (dashed line).

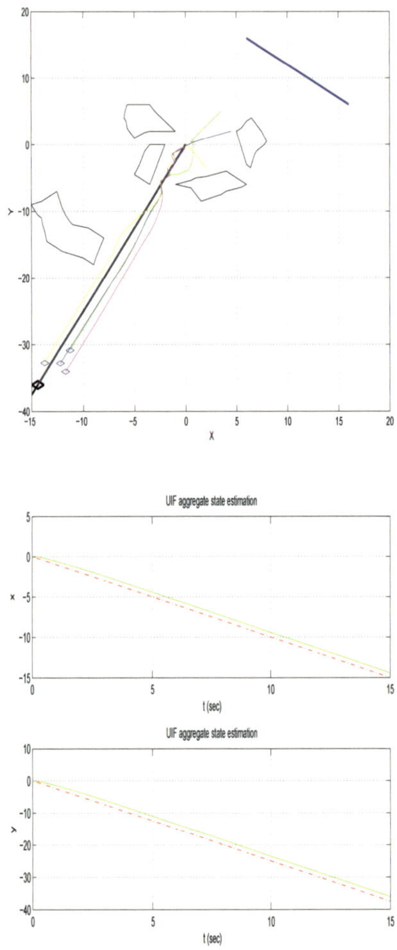

(a) **(b)**

Fig. 18. (a) Distributed target tracking by an ensemble of autonomous vehicles when the target follows a line path in a motion space with obstacles, (b) Aggregate estimation of the target's position with the use of Unscented Information Filtering (continuous line).

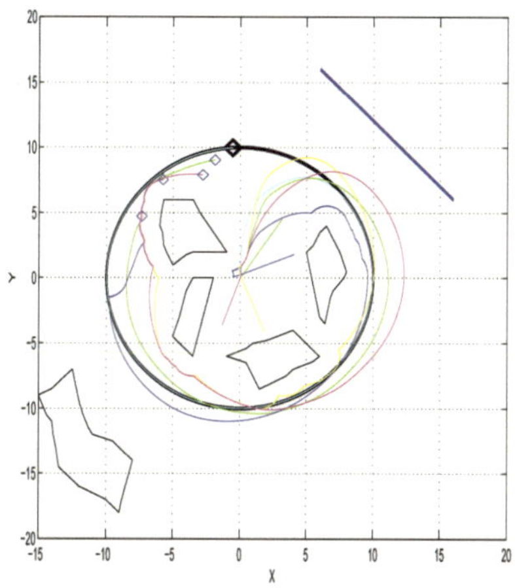

(a)

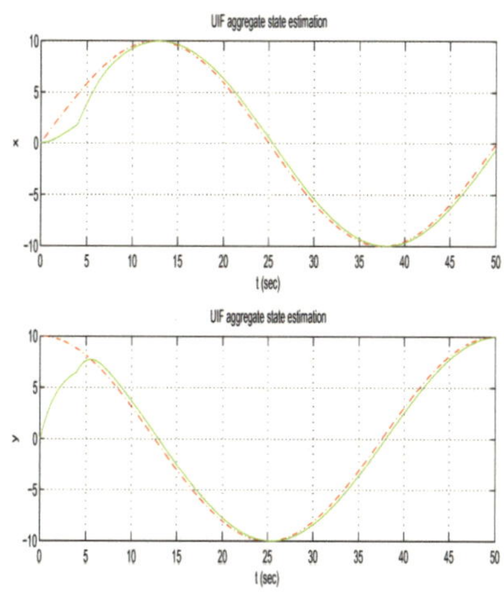

(b)

Fig. 19. (a) Distributed target tracking by an ensemble of autonomous vehicles when the target follows a circular path in a motion space with obstacles, (b) Aggregate estimation of the target's position with the use of Unscented Information Filtering (continuous line) and target's reference path (dashed line).

are summarized as follows: (i) Scalability: since there are no limits imposed by centralized computation bottlenecks or lack of communication bandwidth, every mobile robot (mobile sensor) can easily join or quit the system, (ii) Robustness: in a decentralized fusion architecture no element of the system is mission-critical, so that the system is survivable in the event of on-line loss of part of its partial entities (mobile robots), (iii) Modularity: every partial entity is coordinated and does not need to possess a global knowledge of the network topology.

Using distributed EKFs or UKFs and fusion through the Extended Information Filter and the Unscented Kalman Filter respectively, is more robust comparing to the centralized EKF and centralized UKF since (i) if a local processing unit is subject to a fault then state estimation of the target's position is still possible and can be used for planning of the mobile robot's motion towards the target, (ii) communication overhead remains low even in the case of a large number of mobile robots, because the greatest part of state estimation is performed locally and only information matrices and state vectors are communicated between the local processing units.

8. References

Benveniste, A.; Métivier, M. & Priouret, P. (1990). *Adaptive algorithms and stochastic approximations*, Springer.

Bishop, B.E. (2003). On the use of redundant manipulator techniques for control of platoons of cooperative robotic vehicles. *IEEE Transactions on systems, Man and Cybernetics - Part A*, Vol. 33, No. 5, pp. 608-615, 2003.

Comets, F. & Meyre, T. (2006). *Calcul stochastique et modèles de diffusions*. Dunod, 2006.

Duflo, M. (1996). *Algorithmes stochastiques*, Mathématiques et Applications. Vol. 23, Springer, 1996.

Elston, J. & Frew, E. (2007). Net-centric cooperative tracking of moving targets. *American Institute of Aeronautics and Astronautics (AIAA) 2007 Conference and Exhibit*, California, USA, May 2007.

Gazi, V. & Passino, K. (2004). Stability analysis of social foraging swarms. *IEEE Transactions on Systems, Man and Cybernetics - Part B: Cybernetics*, Vol. 34, No. 1, pp. 539-557, 2004.

Groß,R.; Bonani, M.; Mondada, F. & Dorigo, M. (2006). Autonomous self-assembly in swarm-bots, *IEEE Transactions on Robotics*, Vol. 22, No.6, pp. 1115-1130, 2006.

Hong, Y.; Gao, L.; Cheng, D. & Hu, J. (2007). Luapunov-based approach to multi-agent systems with switching jointly connected interconnection. *IEEE Transactions on Automatic Control*, Vol.52, No.5, pp. 943-948, 2007.

Fliess, M. & Mounier, H. (1999). Tracking control and π-freeness of infinite dimensional linear systems. *Dynamical Systems, Control, Coding and Computer Vision*, G. Picci and D.S. Gilliam (Eds.), Vol. 258, pp. 41-68, Birkhaüser, 1999.

Julier, S.; Uhlmann, J. & Durrant-Whyte, H.F. (2000). A new method for the nonlinear transformations of means and covariances in filters and estimators. IEEE Transactions on Automatic Control, Vol.45, No.3, pp. 477-482, 2000.

Julier, S.J. & Uhlmann, J.K. (2004). Unscented Filtering and Nonlinear Estimation. *Proceedings of the IEEE*, Vol.92, pp. 401-422, 2004.

Khalil, H. (1996). *Nonlinear Systems*, Prentice Hall, 1996.

Léchevin, N. & Rabbath, C.A. (2006). Sampled-data control of a class of nonlinear flat systems with application to unicycle trajectory tracking. *ASME Journal of Dynamical Systems, Measurement and Control*, Transactions of the ASME, Vol. 128, No. 3, pp. 722-728, 2006.

Lee, D.J. (2008a). Nonlinear estimation and multiple sensor fusion using Unscented Information Filtering. *IEEE Signal Processing Letters*, Vol. 15, pp. 861-864, 2008.

Lee, D.J. (2008b). Unscented Information Filtering for Distributed Estimation and multiple sensor fusion. *AIAA Guidance, Navigation and Control Conference and Exhibit*, Hawai, USA, Aug. 2008.

Manyika, J. and Durrant-Whyte, H. (1994). *Data fusion and sensor management: a decentralized information theoretic approach*. Englewood Cliffs, NJ, Prentice Hall, 1994.

Masoud, S.A. & Masoud, A.A. (2002). Motion planning in the presence of directional and regional avoidance constraints using nonlinear, anisotropic, harmonic potential fields: a physical metaphor. *IEEE Transactions on Systems, Man and Cybernetics - Part A*, Vol. 32, No.6, pp. 705-723, 2002.

Olfati-Saber, R. (2005). Distributed Kalman Filter with Embedded Consensus Filters. *In: Proc. 44th IEEE Conference on Decision and Control*, pp. 8179-8184, Seville, Spain, 2005.

Olfati-Saber, R. (2007). Distributed tracking for mobile sensor networks with information-driven mobility. *American Control Conference, ACC 2007*, pp.4606-4612, New York, USA, 2007.

Oriolo, G.; De Luca, A. & Vendittelli, M. (2002). WMR Control Via Dynamic Feedback Linearization: Design, Implementation and Experimental Validation. *IEEE Transactions on Control Systems Technology*, Vol. 10, No.6, pp. 835-852, 2002.

Pagello, E.; D' Angelo, A. & Menegatti, E. (2006). Cooperation issues and distributed sensing for multi-robot systems. *Proceedings of the IEEE*, Vol. 94, No. 7, pp. 1370-1383, 2006.

Rigatos, G.G. & Tzafestas, S.G. (2007). Extended Kalman Filtering for Fuzzy Modeling and Multi-Sensor Fusion. *Mathematical and Computer Modeling of Dynamical Systems*, Taylor and Francis, Vol. 13, No. 3, 2007.

Rigatos, G.G. (2008a). Distributed gradient and particle swarm optimization for multi-robot motion planning. *Robotica*, Cambridge University Press, Vol. 26, No 3, pp. 357-370, 2008.

Rigatos,G.G. (2008b). Coordinated motion of autonomous vehicles with the use of a distributed gradient algorithm. *Journal of Applied Mathematics and Computation*, Elsevier, Vol. 199, N. 2, pp. 494-503, 2008.

Rigatos, G.G. (2008c). Distributed gradient and particle swarm optimization for multi-robot motion planning. *Robotica*, Cambridge University Press, Vol. 26, No. 3, pp. 357-370, 2008.

Rigatos, G.G. (2009a). Particle Filtering for State Estimation in Nonlinear Industrial Systems. *IEEE Transactions on Instrumentation and Measurement*, Vol. 58, No. 11, pp. 3885-3900, 2009.

Rigatos, G.G. (2009b). Sigma-point Kalman Filters and Particle Filters for integrated navigation of unmanned aerial vehicles. *Intl. Workshop on Robotics for Risky Interventions and Environmental Surveillance, RISE 2009*, Brussels, Belgium, Jan. 2009.

Rigatos, G. & Zhang, Q. (2009) Fuzzy model validation using the local statistical approach. *Fuzzy Sets and Systems*, Elsevier, Vol. 60, No.7, pp. 882-904, 2009.

Rigatos, G.G. (2010a). Distributed particle filtering over sensor networks for autonomous navigation of UAVs. *In: "Robot Manipulators"*, SciYo Publications, Croatia, 2010.

Rigatos, G.G. (2010b). Extended Kalman and Particle Filtering for sensor fusion in motion control of mobile robots. *Mathematics and Computers in Simulation*, Elsevier, doi:10.1016/j.matcom.2010.05.003, 2010.

Särrkä, S. (2007). On Unscented Kalman Filtering for state estimation of continuous-time nonlinear systems. *IEEE Transactions on Automatic Control*, Vol.52, No.9, pp.1631-1641, 2007.

Sepulchre, R., Paley, D.A. & Leonard, N.E. (2007). Stabilization of planar collective motion: all to all communication, *IEEE Transactions on Automatic Control*, Vol. 52, No.5, pp. 811-824, 2007.

Shima,T.; Rasmussen, S.J. & Chandler, P. (2007). UAV team decision and control using efficient collaborative estimation. *Journal of Dynamic Systems, Measurement and Control*, Transactions of the ASME, Vol. 129, No. 5, pp. 609-619, 2007.

Sinha, A. & Ghose, D. (2006). Generalization of Linear Cyclic Pursuit with Application to Rendezvous of Multiple Autonomous Agents. *IEEE Transactions on Automatic Control*. Vol.51, No. 11, pp. 1819-1824, 2006.

Vercauteren, T. & Wang, X. (2005). Decentralized Sigma-Point Information Filters for Target Tracking in Collaborative Sensor Networks. *IEEE Transactions on Signal Processing*. Vol.53, No.8, pp. 2997-3009, 2005.

Villagra, J.; D'Andrea-Novel, B.; Mounier, H.; & Pengov, M. (2007). Flatness-based vehicle steering control strategy with SDRE feedback gains tuned via a sensitivity approach. *IEEE Transactions on Control Systems Technology*, Vol. 15, 554-565, 2007.

Vissière, D.; Bristeau, P.-J.; Martin, A.P. & Petit, N. (2008). Experimental autonomous flight of a small-scaled helicopter using accurate dynamics model and low-cost sensors. *Proceedings of the 17th World Congress The International Federation of Automatic Control Seoul*, Korea, July 6-11, 2008.

14

Multi-robot Path Planning

Pavel Surynek
Charles University in Prague
Czech Republic

1. Introduction

This chapter is devoted to a problem of *path planning for multiple robots* (Ryan, 2008; Surynek, 2010a). Consider a group of mobile robots that can move in some environment (for example in the 2-dimensional plane with obstacles). Each robot of the group is given an initial and a goal position in the environment. The question of our interest is how to determine a sequence of motions for each robot of the group such that all the robots reach their goal positions starting from the initial ones. Physical limitations must be respected by robots: robots must not collide with each other and they must avoid obstacles in the environment during their movements.

The problem of multi-robot path planning is motivated by many practical tasks. Various problems of navigating a group of mobile robots can be formulated as multi-robot path planning. However, the primary motivations for the problem are tasks of moving certain entities within an environment with a limited free space. Hence, the formulation of the problem is not limited to the case where robots are actually represented by mobile robots. The constraint of limited free space represents a key aspect that makes the problem interesting and non-trivial. It is quite intuitive to see that the problem becomes easier with a lot of free space in the environment. The interaction between robots (which corresponds to the probability of collisions) is low in such a case. Thus, it is possible to plan movements of each robot relatively independently with respect to other robots. Then the problem reduces almost to the series of simple single source path finding (Cormen et al., 2001) for each robot; potentially with finding alternative paths if a collision still occurs.

On the other hand, if there is limited free space in the environment the problem becomes harder. Consider the situation where the space occupied by robots is comparable to the free space or even the situation where robots occupy larger space than the space that remains unoccupied in the environment. The interaction between robots (that is, the probability of collisions) is so high in such a case that finding a path for each robot independently no longer works. Therefore, different methods must be used.

One of the aims of this chapter is to explain solving methods for these cases. Notice, that it is desirable to reason about the case with limited free space since practical tasks typically has this property. Such real-life examples include rearranging of shipping containers in warehouses (a robot is represented by a shipping container - see Fig. 1) or coordination of vehicles in dense traffic (robot = vehicle). Additionally, our reasoning should not be limited to physical entities only. A robot may be represented by a virtual entity or by a piece of commodity too. Thus, many tasks such as planning of data transfer between communication nodes with limited storage capacity (robot = data packet), commodity transportation in the commodity transportation network (robot = certain amount of commodity), or even the motion planning of large groups of virtual agents in the computer-generated imagery can be expressed as the problem of multi-robot path planning.

Fig. 1. *An illustration of shipping container rearranging.* This problem can be formulated as path planning for multiple robots where robots are represented by containers.

We would like also to emphasize that an approach to solving tasks of multi-robot path planning presented in this chapter is substantially different from the multi-agent approach where the final plan is constructed in a distributed manner through communication between individual agents. A robot in our case is not regarded as an autonomous agent with communication ability. The plan for individual robots is constructed by the centralized mechanism (that is represented by a solving method in our case), which is capable of observing the whole environment and all the robots. The individual robots merely execute the centrally created plan.

2. Formal abstraction

When dealing with the problem of multi-robot path planning it will soon turn out to be necessary to work with the problem at the highly abstract level. Nevertheless, even with the high abstraction the problem remains computationally hard. Let us now introduce abstract formulations of the problem where the environment is modeled as a graph. Vertices of the graph represent locations in the environment. Time is modeled as a structure of discrete time steps isomorphic to the structure of natural numbers (including zero). Robots are placed in vertices of the graph while there is at most one robot in each vertex. Robots can move between neighboring vertices in a single step. That is, an edge represents an unobstructed way between locations in the environment represented by connected vertices that can be travelled by a robot in a single time step. At least one vertex is left unoccupied to allow robots to move. An initial and a goal arrangement of robots are also given to specify the task.

There are two different approaches to the dynamicity of the problem. One approach is that a move is allowed to a currently unoccupied vertex only - this variant of the problem is known as coordinating *pebble motion on a graph* (Wilson, 1974; Kornhauser et al., 1984) . Another approach is to allow moves into currently vacated vertices. This allows a group of robots to move like a train where only the leading robot must move into an unoccupied vertex; the other robots directly follow it. As this variant of the problem is closer to the reality of how robots are required to move, it is called *multi-robot path planning* (Surynek, 2010a). Following definitions describes both variants of the problem formally.

Definition 1. ***(problem of pebble motion on a graph).*** Let $G = (V, E)$ be an undirected graph. Next, let $P = \{\bar{p}_1, \bar{p}_2, ..., \bar{p}_\mu\}$ where $\mu < |V|$ be a set of pebbles. The graph models an environment in which the pebbles are moving. An ***initial arrangement*** of the pebbles is defined by a uniquely invertible function $S_P^0 : P \longrightarrow V$ (that is $S_P^0(p) \neq S_P^0(q)$ for every $p, q \in P \in$ with $p \neq q$). A ***goal arrangement*** of the pebbles is defined by another uniquely invertible function $S_P^+ : P \longrightarrow V$ (that is $S_P^+(p) \neq S_P^+(q)$ for $p, q \in P$ with $p \neq q$). A problem of ***pebble motion on a graph*** is the task to find a number ξ and a sequence $\mathcal{S}_P = [S_P^0, S_P^1, ..., S_P^\xi]$ where $S_P^k : P \longrightarrow V$ is a uniquely invertible function for every $k = 1,2, ..., \xi$. Additionally, the following conditions must hold for the sequence $\mathcal{S}_P$:

i. $S_P^\xi = S_P^+$; that is, all the pebble reaches their destination vertices.

ii. Either $S_P^k(p) = S_P^{k+1}(p)$ or $\{S_P^k(p), S_P^{k+1}(p)\} \in E$ for every $p \in P$ and $k = 1,2, ..., \xi - 1$; that is, a pebble can either stay in a vertex or move into the neighboring vertex between each two successive time steps.

iii. If $S_P^k(p) \neq S_P^{k+1}(p)$ (that is, the pebble p moves between time steps k and $k + 1$) then $S_P^k(q) \neq S_P^{k+1}(p)$ $\forall q \in P$ such that $q \neq p$; must hold for every $p \in P$ and $k = 1,2, ..., \xi - 1$; that is, a pebble can move into an unoccupied neighboring vertex only. This constraint together with unique invertibility of functions forming $\mathcal{S}_P$ implies that no two pebbles can enter the same target vertex at the same time step.

The instance of the problem of pebble motion on a graph is formally a quadruple $\Pi = (G, P, S_P^0, S_P^+)$. Sometimes, the solution of the problem Π will be denoted as $\mathcal{S}_P(\Pi) = [S_P^0, S_P^1, ..., S_P^\xi]$. □

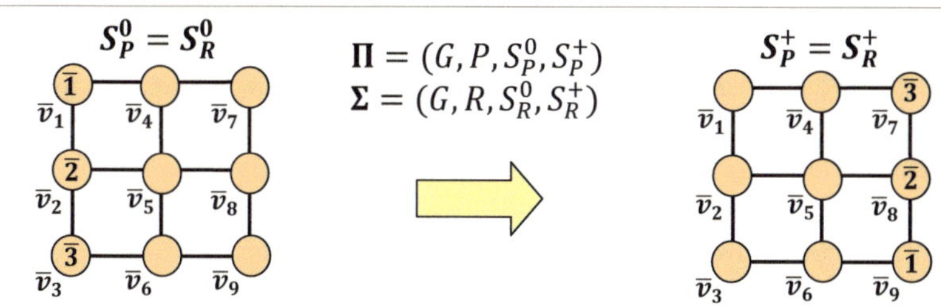

Solution of the problem of *pebble motion on a graph* Π with $P = \{\bar{1}, \bar{2}, \bar{3}\}$

$\xi = 6$ P	S_P^0	S_P^1	S_P^2	S_P^3	S_P^4	S_P^5	$S_P^6 = S_P^+$
$\bar{1}$	$\bar{v}_1$	$\bar{v}_4$	$\bar{v}_7$	$\bar{v}_8$	$\bar{v}_9$	$\bar{v}_9$	$\bar{v}_9$
$\bar{2}$	$\bar{v}_2$	$\bar{v}_2$	$\bar{v}_1$	$\bar{v}_4$	$\bar{v}_7$	$\bar{v}_8$	$\bar{v}_8$
$\bar{3}$	$\bar{v}_3$	$\bar{v}_3$	$\bar{v}_3$	$\bar{v}_2$	$\bar{v}_1$	$\bar{v}_4$	$\bar{v}_7$

Solution of the problem of *path planning for multiple robots* Σ with $R = \{\bar{1}, \bar{2}, \bar{3}\}$

$\zeta = 4$ R	S_R^0	S_R^1	S_R^2	S_R^3	$S_R^4 = S_R^+$
$\bar{1}$	$\bar{v}_1$	$\bar{v}_4$	$\bar{v}_7$	$\bar{v}_8$	$\bar{v}_9$
$\bar{2}$	$\bar{v}_2$	$\bar{v}_1$	$\bar{v}_4$	$\bar{v}_7$	$\bar{v}_8$
$\bar{3}$	$\bar{v}_3$	$\bar{v}_2$	$\bar{v}_1$	$\bar{v}_4$	$\bar{v}_7$

Fig. 2. *An illustration of problems of* ***pebble motion on a graph*** *and* ***multi-robot path planning***. Both problems are illustrated on the same graph with the same initial and goal positions. The task is to move pebbles/robots from their initial positions specified by S_P^0/S_R^0 to the goal positions specified by S_P^+/S_R^+. A solution of the makespan 6 ($\xi = 6$) is shown for the problem of pebble motion on a graph and a solution of the makespan 4 ($\zeta = 4$) is shown for the problem of multi-robot path planning. Notice the differences in parallelism between both solutions.

The notation with a stripe above the symbol is used to distinguish a constant from a variable (for example, $p \in P$ is a variable while $\bar{p}_2$ is a constant; sometimes a constant parameterized by a variable or by an expression will be used - for example $\bar{p}_i$ denotes a constant parameterized by an index $i \in \mathbb{N}$; the parameterization by an expression will be clear from the context).

When speaking about a move at time step k, it is referred to the time step of commencing the move (exactly, the move is performed between time steps k and $k+1$). A problem of multi-robot path planning is a relaxation of the problem of pebble motion on a graph. The condition that the target vertex of a pebble/robot must be vacated in the previous time step is relaxed. Thus, the motion of a robot entering the target vertex that is simultaneously vacated by another robot is allowed in multi-robot path planning. However, there must be some leading robot initiating such chain of moves by moving into an unoccupied vertex.

Definition 2 ***(problem of multi-robot path planning).*** Again, let $G = (V, E)$ be an undirected graph. Now a set of robots $R = \{\bar{r}_1, \bar{r}_2, \dots, \bar{r}_\nu\}$ where $\nu < |V|$ is given instead of the set of pebbles. Similarly, the graph models an environment in which the robots are moving. The ***initial arrangement*** of the robots is defined by a uniquely invertible function $S_R^0: R \longrightarrow V$ (that is $S_R^0(r) \neq S_R^0(s)$ for $\forall r, s \in R$ with $r \neq s$). The ***goal arrangement*** of the robots is defined by another uniquely invertible function $S_R^+: R \longrightarrow V$ (that is $S_R^+(r) \neq S_R^+(s)$ for $\forall r, s \in R$ with $r \neq s$). A problem of ***multi-robot path planning*** is the task to find a number ζ and a sequence $\mathcal{S}_R = [S_R^0, S_R^1, \dots, S_R^\zeta]$ where $S_R^k: R \longrightarrow V$ is a uniquely invertible function for every $k = 1,2,\dots,\zeta$. The following conditions must hold for the sequence $\mathcal{S}_R$:

i. $S_R^\zeta = S_R^+$; that is, all the robots reaches their destination vertices.
ii. Either $S_R^k(r) = S_P^{k+1}(r)$ or $\{S_R^k(r), S_R^{k+1}(r)\} \in E$ for every $r \in R$ and $k = 1,2,\dots,\zeta - 1$; that is, a robot can either stay in a vertex or move to the neighboring vertex at each time step.
iii. If $S_R^k(r) \neq S_R^{k+1}(r)$ (that is, the robot r moves between time steps k and $k+1$) and $S_R^k(s) \neq S_R^{k+1}(r)$ $\forall s \in R$ such that $s \neq r$ (that is, no other robot s occupies the target vertex at time step k), then the move of r at the time step k is called to be ***allowed*** (that is, the robot r moves into an unoccupied neighboring vertex - a ***leading*** robot). If $S_R^k(r) \neq S_R^{k+1}(r)$ and there is $s \in R$ such that $s \neq r \wedge S_R^k(s) = S_R^{k+1}(r) \wedge S_R^k(s) \neq S_R^{k+1}(s)$ (that is, the robot r moves into a vertex that is being left by the robot s) and the move of s at the time step k is allowed, then the move of r at the time step k is also ***allowed***. All the moves of robots at all the time steps **must be allowed**. And analogically, this condition together with the requirement on unique invertibility of functions forming $\mathcal{S}_R$ implies that no two robots can enter the same target vertex at the same time step.

The instance of the problem of multi-robot path planning is formally a quadruple $\Sigma = (G, R, S_R^0, S_R^+)$. The solution of the problem Σ will be sometimes denoted as $\mathcal{S}_R(\Sigma) = [S_R^0, S_R^1, \dots, S_R^\zeta]$. □

The numbers ξ and ζ are called ***makespan*** of the solution of pebble motion on a graph and multi-robot path planning respectively. The makespan needs to be distinguished from the ***size*** of the solution, which is the total number of moves performed by pebbles/robots.

3. Properties of problems and complexity issues

Let us now summarize several basic properties of the solutions of instances of problems of pebble motion on graphs and multi-robot path planning.

Notice that a solution of the problem of pebble motion on a graph as well as a solution of the problem of multi-robot path planning allows a pebble/robot to stay in a vertex for more than a single time step. It is also possible that a pebble/robot visits the same vertex several times within the solution. Hence, a sequence of moves for a single pebble/robot does not necessarily form a simple path in the input graph. Notice further that both problems intrinsically allow parallel movements of pebbles/robots. That is, more than one pebble/robot can perform a move in a single time step. However, multi-robot path planning allows higher motion parallelism due to its weaker requirements on robot movements (the target vertex is required to be unoccupied only for the leading robot in the previous time step - see Fig. 2). More than one unoccupied vertex is necessary to obtain parallelism in the problem of pebble motion on a graph. On the other hand, it is sufficient to have a single unoccupied vertex to obtain parallelism within the solution of multi-robot path planning problem (consider for example robots moving around a cycle).

The following proposition puts in relation the solution of an instance of multi-robot path planning and the solution of the corresponding instance of pebble motion on a graph (the instance of multi-robot path planning problem consists of the same graph, the set of robots is represented by the set of pebbles, and the initial/goal positions of robots are the same as in the case of pebbles). As the proof is easy, it is left as an exercise.

Proposition 1 *(problem correspondence).* Let $\Pi = (G, P, S_P^0, S_P^+)$ be an instance of the problem of pebble motion on a graph and let $\mathcal{S}_P(\Pi) = [S_P^0, S_P^1, \dots, S_P^\xi]$ be its solution. Then $\mathcal{S}_R(\Sigma) = \mathcal{S}_P(\Pi)$ is a solution of an instance of the problem of path planning for multiple robots $\Sigma = (G, P, S_P^0, S_P^+)$. ■

There is a variety of modifications of the defined problems. A natural additional requirement is to produce solutions with **makespan** as small as possible (that is, the numbers ξ or ζ respectively are required to be as small as possible). Unfortunately, this requirement makes the problem of pebble motion on a graph intractable. It is shown in (Ratner & Warmuth, 1986) that the optimization variant of a special case of the problem of pebble motion on a graph is NP-hard (Garey & Johnson, 1979). The restriction forming the special case adopted in (Ratner & Warmuth, 1986) works with a graph that can be embedded in plane as a square grid and where there is a single unoccupied vertex - this case is known as $N \times N$ *puzzle* (also known as $N^2 - 1$ *puzzle*). Hence, the general optimization variant of the problem of pebble motion on a graph is NP-hard as well.

A restriction of both types of problems on *bi-connected graphs* (West, 2000) (for the precise definitions see Section 4.1) represents important subclass with respect to the existence of a solution. Hence, it is a reasonable question what is the complexity of these classes of problems. Since the grid graph forming the mentioned $N \times N$ puzzle is bi-connected, the immediate answer is that the optimization variant of the problem of pebble motion on a bi-connected graph with a single unoccupied vertex is again NP-hard.

However, it is not possible to simply make any similar statement about the complexity of the optimization variant of multi-robot path planning based on the above facts. The situation here is complicated by the inherent parallelism, which can reduce the makespan of the solution significantly. Constructions used for the $N \times N$ puzzle in (Ratner & Warmuth, 1986) thus no longer work. It has been shown recently in (Surynek, 2010a) that the optimization variant of multi-robot path planning is *NP*-hard as well. As the proof of this result is technically complicated and not all the details fit into the conference paper (Surynek, 2010a) we refer the reader to technical report (Surynek, 2010b) for further reading.

Observe that above difficult cases of the problem of pebble motion on a graph have a single unoccupied vertex. This fact may raise the question how the situation is changed when there are more than one unoccupied vertices. More unoccupied vertices may simplify the problem. Unfortunately, it is not the case. The pebble motion problem on a general graph with the fixed number of unoccupied vertices is still NP-hard since multiple copies of the $N \times N$ puzzle can be used to add as many unoccupied vertices as needed.

Without the requirement on the optimality of the makespan of solutions the situation is much easier; the problem of pebble motion on a graph is in the P class as it is shown in (Wilson, 1974; Kornhauser et al., 1984). Due to Proposition 1, the problem of path planning for multiple robots is in the P class as well. Moreover, it is shown in (Kornhauser et al., 1984) that a solution of the size of $O(|V|^3)$ can be generated for $\Pi = (G = (V, E), P, S_P^0, S_P^+)$. Hence, it provides us a polynomial upper bound on size of the oracle in the content to guess in non-deterministic model. Thus, it is possible to conclude that decision versions of optimization variants of both pebble motion on a graph as well as of multi-robot path planning are NP-complete problems (Garey & Johnson, 1979). By the decision version it is meant a yes/no question whether there is a solution of Π/Σ of the makespan smaller than the given bound. As constructions proving the membership of the problem of pebble motion on a graph into the P class used in (Wilson, 1974; Kornhauser et al., 1984) generate solutions that are too long, we will show an alternative solving algorithm proposed in (Surynek, 2009a, 2009b).

4. Solving algorithm

This section is devoted to a sub-optimal algorithm for solving problems of motion on a graph in polynomial time. The algorithm presented in the following text is designed for the problem of pebble motion on a graph. As we have Proposition 1, algorithm for pebble motion on a graph applies also for multi-robot path planning. However, the practice of solving multi-robot path planning problems using algorithms for pebble motion on a graph does not reflect the possibility of higher parallelism in multi-robot path planning. Particularly, parallelism in the form of the "train like" movement of a queue of robots is never produced in this way. This drawback can be augmented by a post-processing step that increases parallelism which is discussed in Section 5.

The *BIBOX* algorithm that will be presented below comes from (Surynek, 2009a). The input instance of the problem of pebble motion on a graph should consist of a so called *non-trivial bi-connected graph* with exactly **two unoccupied** vertices. Overcoming some of these assumptions is discussed in Section 4.4.

4.1 Graph-theoretical preliminaries

Several notions from graph theory (Tarjan, 1972; West, 2000) are introduced in this section. Following definitions establish the notion of bi-connectivity upon that the *BIBOX* algorithm is built. Several useful properties of bi-connected graph will be also discussed.

Definition 3 *(connected graph).* An undirected graph $G = (V, E)$ is ***connected*** if $|V| \geq 2$ for any two vertices $u, v \in V$ such that $u \neq v$ there is an undirected path consisting of edges from E connecting u and v. □

Definition 4 (*bi-connected graph, non-trivial*). An undirected graph $G = (V, E)$ is ***bi-connected*** if $|V| \geq 3$ and the graph $G' = (V', E')$, where $V' = V \setminus \{v\}$ and $E' = \{\{u, w\} | u, w \in V \wedge u \neq v \wedge w \neq v\}$, is connected for every $v \in V$. A bi-connected graph not isomorphic to a cycle will be called ***non-trivial*** bi-connected graph. □

Observe that, if a graph is bi-connected, then every two distinct vertices are connected by at least two *vertex disjoint paths* (equivalently, there is a cycle containing both vertices; only internal vertices of paths are considered when speaking about vertex disjoint paths - vertex disjoint paths can intersect in their *start points* and *endpoints*). If a graph is not bi-connected then it is either disconnected or there exists a vertex which removal partitions the graph into at least two connected components - this vertex is called an *articulation point*. Several examples of bi-connected graphs are shown in Fig. 3.

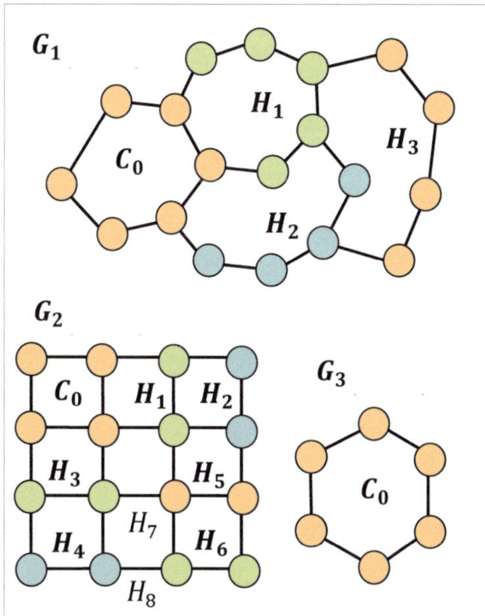

Fig. 3. *Examples of* ***bi-connected graphs***. Three bi-connected graphs G_1, G_2, and G_3 and their handle decompositions are shown using colors (handles H_7 and H_8 of the decomposition of G_2 consist of a single edge).

Bi-connected graphs have an important property, which is exploited within the algorithm. Each bi-connected graph can be constructed from a cycle by an operation of *adding a handle* to the graph. Consider a graph $G = (V, E)$; the new handle with respect to G is a sequence $L = [u, w_1, w_2, \ldots, w_l, v]$ where $l \in \mathbb{N}_0$, $u, v \in V$ (called *connection vertices*) and $w_i \notin V$ for $i = 1,2, \ldots, l$ (w_i are new vertices). The result of the addition of the handle L to the graph G is a new graph $G' = (V', E')$ where $V' = V \cup \{w_1, w_2, \ldots, w_l\}$ and either $E' = E \cup \{\{u, v\}\}$ in the case of $l = 0$ of $E' = E \cup \{\{u, w_1\}, \{w_1, w_2\}, \ldots, \{w_{l-1}, w_l\}, \{w_l, v\}\}$ in the case of $l \geq 0$. Let the sequence of handles together with the initial cycle be called a *handle decomposition* of the given graph. See Fig. 3 for examples.

Lemma 1 ***(handle decomposition)*** (Tarjan, 1972). Any bi-connected $G = (V, E)$ graph can be obtained from a cycle by a sequence of operations of adding a handle. Moreover, the corresponding handle decomposition of the graph G can be effectively found in the worst case time of $O(|V| + |E|)$ and worst case space of $O(|V| + |E|)$. ■

An important property of the construction of a bi-connected graph according to its handle decomposition is that the currently constructed graph is bi-connected at any stage of the construction. This property is substantially exploited in the design of the *BIBOX* algorithm.

The *BIBOX* algorithm is presented using a pseudo-code as Algorithm 1 (the algorithm is illustrated with pictures for easier understanding). The algorithm starts with the last handle of the handle decomposition and proceeds to the original cycle. Pebbles, which goal positions are within the last handle, are moved to their goal positions within this handle. The instance of the problem now reduces to the instance of the same type indeed on a smaller bi-connected graph. That is, the last handle is not considered any more since its pebbles do not need to move any more. This process is repeated until the original cycle of the decomposition remains.

Let $\Pi = (G = (V,E), P, S_P^0, S_P^+)$ be an instance of the pebble motion problem. The following notation is used in the formalization of the algorithm. The handle decomposition of the graph G is formally a sequence $\mathcal{D} = [C_0, H_1, H_2, \dots, H_d]$, where C_0 is the initial cycle and H_c is a handle for $c = 1,2,\dots,d$. The order of handle additions in construction of G corresponds to their positions in the sequence (that is, H_1 is added to C_0 first; and H_d is added as the last to the currently constructed graph). A handle $H_c = [u^c, w_1^c, w_2^c, \dots, w_{h_i}^c, v^c]$ for $c \in \{1,2,\dots,d\}$ can be assigned a cycle $C(H_i)$ if the input graph G is connected. The cycle $C(H_c)$ consists of the sequence of vertices on a path connecting v^c and u^c in a graph before the addition of H_c followed by vertices $w_1^c, w_2^c, \dots, w_{h_i}^c$. Specially, it is defined that $C(C_0) = C_0$. The following lemma is important for the design of the algorithm.

Lemma 2 *(two paths existence).* Let $G = (V,E)$ be a bi-connected graph and let $u_1, u_2 \in V$ and $v_1, v_2 \in V$, where u_1, u_2, v_1, v_2 are pair-wise distinct, be two pairs of vertices. Then either the first or the second of the following claims holds:

a. There exist two vertex disjoint paths φ and χ such that they connect u_1 with v_1 and u_2 with v_2 in G respectively.
b. There exist two vertex disjoint paths φ and χ such that they connect u_1 with v_2 and u_2 with v_1 in G respectively. ■

Notice that the above lemma states that individual vertices in the input pair of vertices are indifferent with respect to connecting by vertex disjoint paths.

Proof. The idea of the proof is to proceed inductively according to the size of the handle decomposition of the graph $G = (V,E)$. Let $\mathcal{D} = [C_0, H_1, H_2, \dots, H_d]$ be a handle decomposition of the graph G. A function $c_{\mathcal{D}}: V \longrightarrow \mathbb{N}_0$ is defined as follows: $c_{\mathcal{D}}(v) = 0$ if $v \in C_0$ and $c_{\mathcal{D}}(v) = c$ if $v \in H_c$ for some $c \in \{1,2,\dots,d\}$ (v is one of the internal vertices of the handle L_c). Observe, that $c_{\mathcal{D}}$ is a correctly defined function.

A given 4-tuple of vertices (u_1, u_2, v_1, v_2) is assigned a 4-tuple of integers defined using the function $c_{\mathcal{D}}$: $(c_{\mathcal{D}}(u_1), c_{\mathcal{D}}(u_2), c_{\mathcal{D}}(v_1), c_{\mathcal{D}}(v_2))$. The mathematical induction will proceed according to the lexicographic ordering of the 4-tupules assigned using the function $c_{\mathcal{D}}$ sorted in descending order. Several cases must be distinguished.

Case (i): Let the 4-tuple of vertices (u_1, u_2, v_1, v_2) is assigned a 4-tuple of numbers (1,1,1,1), that is, all the vertices u_1, u_2, v_1, v_2 are located within the initial cycle C_0. Then the following juxtapositions of vertices u_1, u_2, v_1, and v_2 within C_0 with respect to the positive orientation of the cycle can occur: (u_1, v_1, v_2, u_2), (u_1, v_2, v_1, u_2), (v_1, u_1, v_2, u_2), (v_1, v_2, u_1, u_2), (v_2, u_1, v_1, u_2), and (v_2, v_1, u_1, u_2) (vertices are listed according to the positive orientation of the cycle; there is in total $4! = 24$ candidates for juxtapositions of 4 vertices; however, the remaining juxtapositions are isomorphic to the listed ones using a rotation along the cycle). In all the cases either the claim (a) or the claim (b) holds. See Fig. 4 for detailed case analysis - for example in the juxtaposition (u_1, v_1, v_2, u_2), u_1 should be connected in positive orientation with v_1 and u_2 should be connected in negative orientation with v_2.

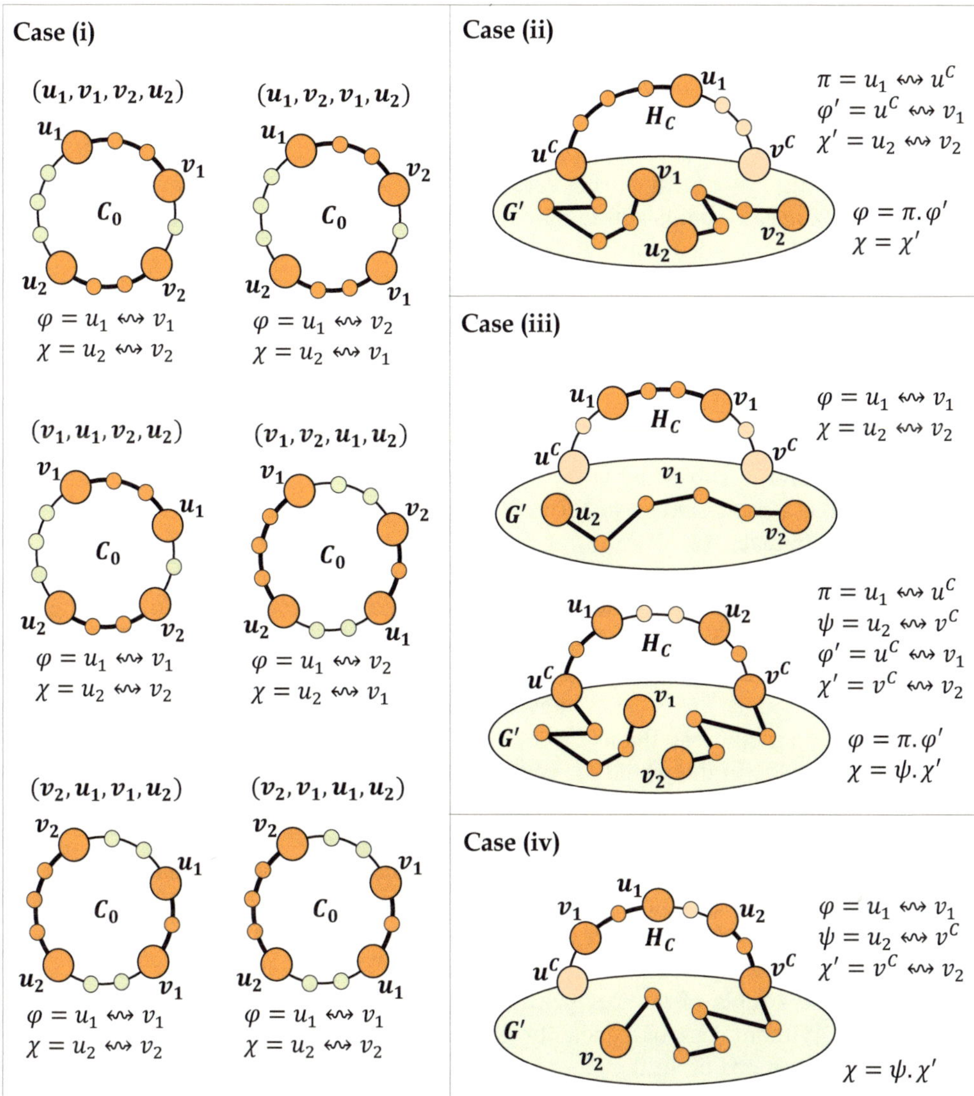

Fig. 4. *An illustration of the existence of* ***two vertex disjoint paths*** *connecting two pairs of vertices in a bi-connected graph.* The figure illustrates the case analysis from the proof of Lemma 2 which states that there exist two vertex disjoint paths φ and χ connecting a pair of vertices u_1 and u_2 with a pair of vertices v_1 and v_2 in a bi-connected graph G. The proof proceeds as mathematical induction according to the size of the handle decomposition of the graph G.

Case (ii): Let the 4-tuple of vertices (u_1, u_2, v_1, v_2) is assigned a sorted 4-tuple (C, c_2, c_3, c_4) where $C > c_2 \wedge C > c_3 \wedge C > c_4$. Using the interchangeability of vertices u_1, u_2, v_1, v_2, it is possible to suppose that $c_{\mathcal{D}}(u_1) = C$ without loss of generality. Let $H_C = [u^C, w_1^C, w_2^C, \dots, w_{l_C}^C, v^C]$, then there exists a path π connecting u_1 and u_C consisting of the internal vertices of L_C. Since the sorted 4-tuple $(c_{\mathcal{D}}(u^C), c_{\mathcal{D}}(u_2), c_{\mathcal{D}}(v_1), c_{\mathcal{D}}(v_2))$ is lexicographically strictly less than (C, c_2, c_3, c_4), the induction hypothesis implies that the lemma holds for the 4-tuple of vertices u^C, u_2, v_1, v_2 and the graph G without the internal vertices of the handle H_C; let this smaller graph be denoted as G'. That is either (a) or (b) holds in G'. Without loss of generality, suppose that (a) holds. Then there exist vertex disjoint paths φ' and χ' connecting u^C with v_1 and u_2 with v_2 in G' respectively. The path π is vertex disjoint with χ' and it shares exactly one vertex u^C with φ. Let φ be a path formed by the concatenation of π with φ' (the vertex u^C is used only once) and let $\chi = \chi'$. Then φ and χ are vertex disjoint paths substantiating the claim (a) for 4-tuple of vertices u_1, u_2, v_1, v_2 in G. See Fig. 4 for detailed illustration of the case.

Case (iii): The next case is that the 4-tuple of vertices (u_1, u_2, v_1, v_2) is assigned a sorted 4-tuple (C, C, c_3, c_4) where $C > c_3 \wedge C > c_4$. Again using the interchangeability of vertices only some of all the case are interesting. The first case is that $c_{\mathcal{D}}(u_1) = C$ and $c_{\mathcal{D}}(v_1) = C$ (that is, a pair of vertices to connect is within the handle H_C) and the second case is that $c_{\mathcal{D}}(u_1) = C$ and $c_{\mathcal{D}}(u_2) = C$ (that is, one vertex of a pair to connect is within the handle and the other is outside the internal vertices of the handle). In the first case, it is sufficient to construct a path φ connecting u_1 and v_1 consisting of the internal vertices of H_C and a path χ connecting u_2 and v_2 in G' (G' is a connected graph). The constructed paths φ and χ are vertex disjoint and hence they substantiate the claim (a) of the lemma. In the second case, it is necessary to distinguish between two juxtapositions of u_1 and u_2 within H_C with respect to the positive orientation of the handle: (u_1, u_2) and (u_2, u_1). In the case of juxtaposition (u_1, u_2), a path π connecting u_1 and u^C and a path ψ connecting u_2 and v^C are constructed (with the exception of u^C and v^C only the internal vertices of L_C are used). The second juxtaposition just interchanges u_1 and u_2. The sorted 4-tuple $(c_{\mathcal{D}}(u^C), c_{\mathcal{D}}(v_C), c_{\mathcal{D}}(v_1), c_{\mathcal{D}}(v_2))$ is lexicographically strictly less than (C, C, c_3, c_4), hence the lemma holds for the 4-tuple of vertices u^C, v^C, v_1, v_2 in the graph G'. Without loss of generality suppose that the case (a) holds; that is, there exists a path φ' that connects u^C with v_1 in G' and a path χ' that connects v^C with v_2 in G' while φ' and χ' are vertex disjoint. Observe, that π and ψ are vertex disjoint as well. It is sufficient to set a path φ to be a concatenation of π and φ' and a path χ to be a concatenation of ψ and χ'. Then φ and χ are the paths substantiating the claim (a) of the lemma for the 4-tuple of vertices u_1, u_2, v_1, v_2 in G. Again, see Fig. 4 for the detailed illustration of the case.

Case (iv): Let the 4-tuple of vertices (u_1, u_2, v_1, v_2) is assigned a sorted 4-tuple (C, C, C, c_4) where $C > c_4$. Without loss of generality, suppose that $c_{\mathcal{D}}(v_2) = c_4$. Then the following interesting juxtapositions of vertices u_1, u_2, and v_1 within the handle L_C with respect to the positive orientation can occur: (v_1, u_1, u_2), (u_1, v_1, u_2), and (u_1, u_2, v_1) (interchangeability of u_1 and u_2 is used to rule out the second half of juxtapositions). All the cases can be treated in the same way, thus it is sufficient to show only one case – for example the case of (v_1, u_1, u_2). Let φ be a path connecting v_1 and u_1 consisting of the internal vertices of the handle H_C. Next, let ψ be a path connecting u_2 with v^C that uses internal vertices of the handle H_C and the vertex v^C. Let χ' be a path connecting v^C and v_2 in G' (such a path exists since G' is a connected graph). Observe, that φ is vertex disjoint with ψ as well as with χ'. Thus, if χ is set to be a concatenation of ψ and χ', then φ and χ substantiate the claim (a) of the lemma for the 4-tuple of vertices u_1, u_2, v_1, v_2 and the graph G. Again, see Fig.4 for illustration of the case.

Case (v): The last case occurs if a sorted 4-tuple (C, C, C, C) where $C > 1$ is assigned to the 4-tuple of vertices (u_1, u_2, v_1, v_2). This case reduces to the case with all the vertices of the input 4-tuple located within the original cycle of the handle decomposition. However, instead of the original cycle a cycle $C(H_C)$ should be used. ■

4.2 Pseudo-code of the *BIBOX* algorithm

Several primitives are introduced to express the *BIBOX* algorithm in an easier way. Except functions S_P^0 and S_P^+ there is a function $S_P: P \longrightarrow V$ that represents the current arrangement of pebbles in the graph. Additionally, there are functions $\Phi_P^0: V \longrightarrow P \cup \{\bot\}$, $\Phi_P^+: V \longrightarrow P \cup \{\bot\}$, and $\Phi_P: V \longrightarrow P \cup \{\bot\}$ which are generalized inverses of S_P^0, S_P^+, and S_P respectively with the symbol $\bot$ is used to represent an unoccupied vertex (that is, $(\forall p \in P)\Phi_P(S_P(p)) = p$ and $\Phi_P(\bot) = \bot$ if $(\forall p \in P)S_P(p) \neq v$). Next, each undirected cycle appearing in the handle decomposition of the input graph is assigned a fixed orientation. Let C be an undirected cycle (a set of vertices of the cycle), then the orientation of C is expressed by functions $next_{\circlearrowleft}$ and $prev_{\circlearrowleft}$ where $next_{\circlearrowleft}(C, v)$ for $v \in C$ is the vertex following v (with respect to positive orientation) in the cycle C and $prev_{\circlearrowleft}(C, v)$ is the vertex preceding v (with respect to positive orientation). The orientation of a cycle given by $next_{\circlearrowleft}$ and $prev_{\circlearrowleft}$ is respected as well when vertices of the cycle are explicitly enumerated in the code. Auxiliary operations *Lock* (X) and *Unlock*(X) locks or unlocks a set of vertices X. Each vertex of the input graph is either locked or unlocked. The state of a vertex is used to determine whether a pebble can move into a vertex. Typically, a pebble is not allowed to enter a locked vertex (see the pseudo-code for details). Finally, there is assumed a potentially infinite sequence of functions $S_P^0, S_P^1, S_P^2, \ldots$ which finite prefix is used to form a solution. Actually, these variables are not needed to be stored in the memory; the output solution can be directly printed to the output. For convenience, several variables such as those representing handle decomposition are global; that is, they are shared among all the functions and procedures in the pseudo-code.

It is assumed that for the number of pebbles it holds that $|V| = \mu - 2$, where $|P| = \mu$ (that is, there are exactly two unoccupied vertices in the graph G). Furthermore, it is required for the successful progression of the algorithm that the unoccupied vertices within the goal arrangement are located in the first two vertices of the original cycle (according to the positive orientation) of the handle decomposition. This requirement is treated by a function *Transform-Goal* and a procedure *Finish-Solution*. The function *Transform-Goal* determines two vertex disjoint paths from unoccupied vertices in the goal arrangement to first two vertices in the original cycle of the handle decomposition. Since the unoccupied vertices are indifferent, it does not matter what unoccupied vertex is associated with the first or with the second vertex of the initial cycle. Thus, preconditions of Lemma 2 are satisfied and hence the existence of mentioned two vertex disjoint paths is ensured.

The goal arrangement is changed by the function *Transform-Goal* so that finally unoccupied vertices are located in the original cycle. This is done by shifting pebbles within the goal arrangement along the two determined paths. After the modified instance is solved, the function *Finish-Solution* moves unoccupied vertices back to their goal positions given by the original unmodified goal arrangement. This final placement of unoccupied vertices is done by shifting pebbles along the two paths determined by the function *Transform-Goal* in the opposite direction.

Several upper level primitives are exploited by the *BIBOX* algorithm. It is possible to make any vertex unoccupied in a connected graph (especially in a bi-connected graph). The process of making a given vertex unoccupied is implemented by a procedure *Make-Unoccupied*. Let v be a vertex to be made unoccupied. A path ϕ connecting v and some of the unoccupied vertices avoiding the locked vertices is found. Then pebbles along the path ϕ are shifted using swapping pebbles towards the currently unoccupied vertex.

An operation of swapping pebbles itself is implemented using a procedure *Swap-Pebbles-Unoccupied*. The procedure moves a pebble into a neighboring unoccupied vertex and the next member S_P^{ξ} of the output solution sequence is constructed together with the update of functions S_P and Φ_P according to the new arrangement of pebbles.

Algorithm 1. *The **BIBOX** algorithm.* It solves a given pebble motion problem on a **non-trivial bi-connected** graph with exactly **two unoccupied** vertices. The algorithm proceeds inductively according to the handle decomposition of the graph of the input instance. The two unoccupied vertices are necessary for arranging pebbles within the original cycle of the handle decomposition.

---

function *BIBOX-Solve*$(G = (V, E), P, S_P^0, S_P^+)$: **pair**

/* Top level function of the BIBOX algorithm; solves a given problem of pebble motion on a graph.
Parameters: G - a graph modeling the environment,
P - a set of pebbles,
S_P^0 - a initial arrangement of pebbles,
S_P^+ - a goal arrangement of pebbles. */

let $\mathcal{D} = [C_0, H_1, H_2, \dots, H_d]$ be a handle decomposition of G
$(S_P^+, \varphi, \chi) \leftarrow$ Transform-Goal(G, P, S_P^+)
$S_P \leftarrow S_P^0$
$\xi \leftarrow 1$
for $c = d, d-1, \dots, 1$ **do**
    if $|H_c| > 2$ **then**
        Solve-Regular-Handle(c)
Solve-Original-Cycle
Finish-Solution(φ, χ)
return $(\xi, [S_P^0, S_P^1, \dots, S_P^{\xi}])$

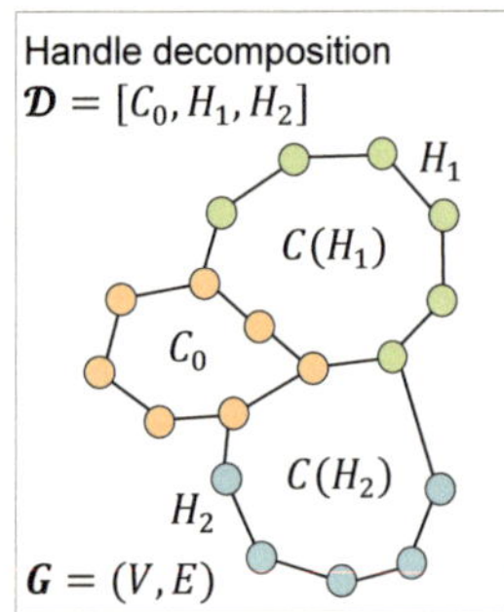

procedure *Solve-Regular-Handle*(c)

/* Places pebbles which destinations are within a handle H_c; pebbles placed in the handle H_c are finally locked so they cannot move any more.
Parameters: c – the index of a handle */

let $[u^j, w_1^j, w_2^j, \dots, w_{h_c}^j, v^j] = H_j \ \forall j \in \{1, 2, \dots, d\}$
/* Both unoccupied vertices must be located outside the currently solved handle. */
let $w, z \in V \setminus \bigcup_{j=c}^{d} (H_j \setminus \{u^j, v^j\})$ such that $w \neq z$
Make-Unoccupied(w)
Lock $(\{w\})$
Make-Unoccupied(z)
Unlock $(\{w\})$
for $i = h_c, h_c - 1, \dots, 1$ **do**
    Lock$(H_c \setminus \{u^c, v^c\})$
    /* A pebble to be placed is outside the handle H_c. */
    if $S_P(\Phi_P^+(w_i^c)) \notin (H_c \setminus \{u^c, v^c\})$ **then**
        Move-Pebble$(\Phi_P^+(w_i^c), u^c)$
        Lock$(\{u^c\})$

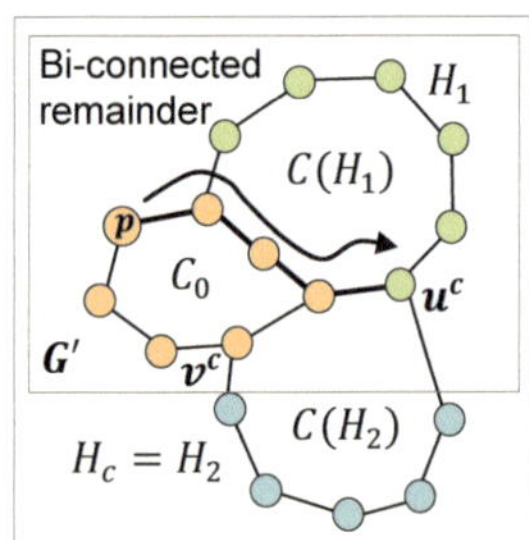

Pebble $p = \Phi_P^+(w_i^c)$ is outside H_c; move p to u^c.

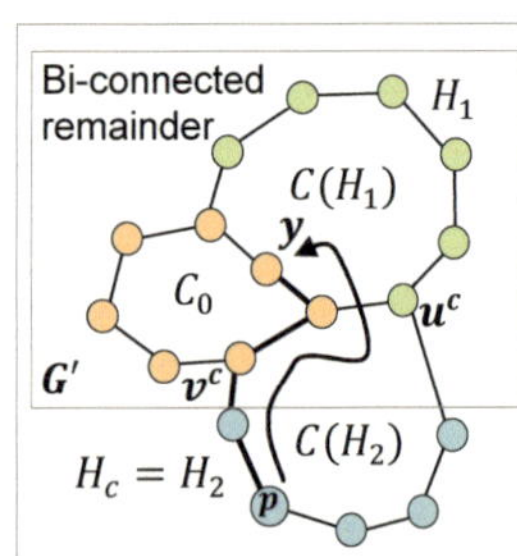

Pebble $p = \Phi_P^+(w_i^c)$ is inside H_c; move p outside $C(H_c)$.

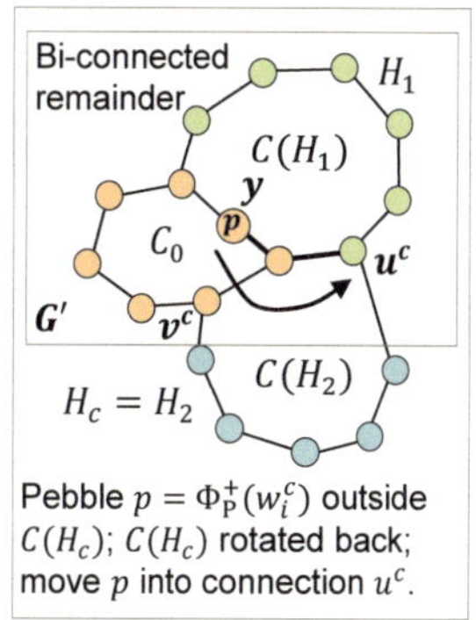

Pebble $p = \Phi_P^+(w_i^c)$ outside $C(H_c)$; $C(H_c)$ rotated back; move p into connection u^c.

Make-Unoccupied(v^c)
Unlock(H_c)
Rotate-Cycle⁺($C(H_c)$)
/* A pebble to be placed is inside the handle H_c. */
else
Make-Unoccupied(u^c)
Unlock(H_c)
$\rho \leftarrow 0$
while $S_P(\Phi_P^+(w_i^c)) \neq v^c$ **do**
Rotate-Cycle⁺($C(H_c)$)
$\rho \leftarrow \rho + 1$
Lock($H_c \setminus \{u^c, v^c\}$)
let $y \in V \setminus (\bigcup_{j=c+1}^{d}(H_j \setminus \{u^j, v^j\}) \cup C(H_c))$
Move-Pebble($\Phi_P^+(w_i^c), y$)
Lock ($\{y\}$)
Make-Unoccupied(u^c)
Unlock(H_c)
while $\rho > 0$ **do**
Rotate-Cycle⁻($C(H_c)$)
$\rho \leftarrow \rho - 1$
Unlock($\{y\}$)
Lock($H_c \setminus \{u^c, v^c\}$)
Move-Pebble($\Phi_P^+(w_i^c), u^c$)
Lock ($\{u^c\}$)
Make-Unoccupied(v^c)
Unlock(H_c)
Rotate-Cycle⁺($C(H_c)$)
Lock($H_c \setminus \{u^c, v^c\}$)

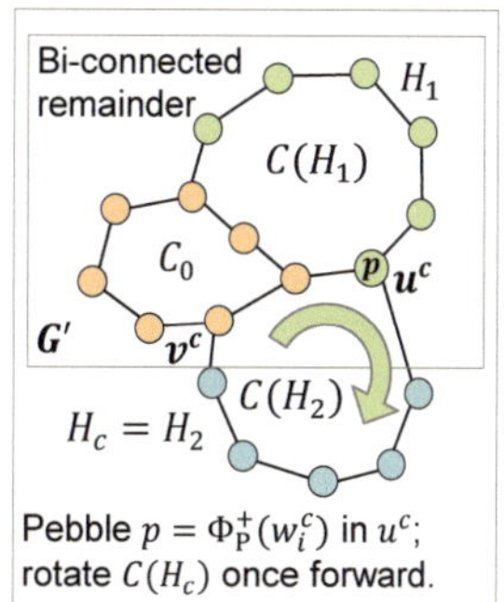

Pebble $p = \Phi_P^+(w_i^c)$ in u^c; rotate $C(H_c)$ once forward.

procedure *Solve-Original-Cycle*
/* Places pebbles which destinations are within the original cycle;it is assumed that unoccupied vertices of the goal arrangement of pebbles are located within the original cycle. */
let $u \in C_0$ and $v \in V \setminus C_0$ such that $\{u, v\} \in E$
let $[w_1^0, w_2^0, \ldots, w_l^0] = C_0$
/* According to the assumption on the goal arrangement it holds that $\Phi_P^+(w_1^0) = \perp$ and $\Phi_P^+(w_2^0) = \perp$. */
for $i = 3,4,\ldots,l$ **do**
Make-Unoccupied(w_1^0)
Lock($\{w_1^0\}$)
Make-Unoccupied(w_2^0)
Unlock($\{w_1^0\}$)
if $\Phi_P^+(w_i^0) \neq \Phi_P(w_i^0)$ **then**
Exchange-Pebbles ($\Phi_P^+(w_i^0), \Phi_P(w_i^0), u, v$)
Make-Unoccupied(w_1^0)
Lock($\{w_1^0\}$)
Make-Unoccupied(w_2^0)
Unlock($\{w_1^0\}$)

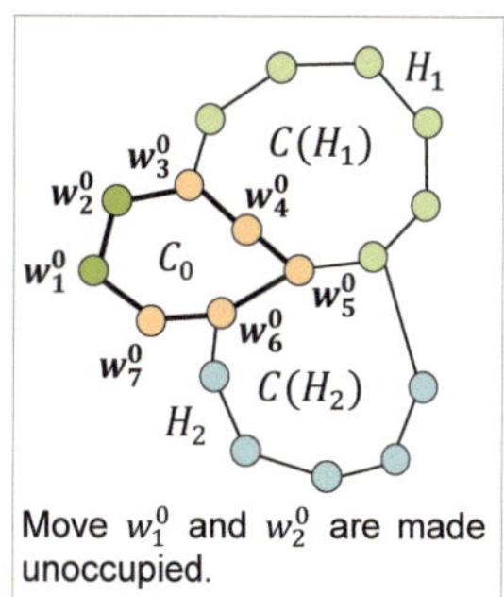

Move w_1^0 and w_2^0 are made unoccupied.

procedure *Exchange-Pebbles*(p, q, u, v)

/* Exchanges a pair of pebbles within the initial cycle of the handle decomposition.
Parameters: p, q - a pair of pebbles to be exchanged,
u, v - a pair of neighboring vertices where v is used as a storage space. */

$r \leftarrow \Phi_P(v)$
Make-Unoccupied(u)
Swap-Pebbles-Unoccupied(v, u)
while $S_P(p) \neq u$ **do**
| Rotate-Cycle$^+(C_0)$
Swap-Pebbles-Unoccupied(u, v)
Lock $(\{u\})$
Make-Unoccupied$(next_{\circlearrowleft}(C_0, u))$
Unlock $(\{u\})$

/* Subsequent rotation must use u as the unoccupied vertex. */

Lock$(C_0 \setminus \{u\})$
$\rho \leftarrow 0$
while $S_P(q) \neq next_{\circlearrowleft}(C_0, u)$ **do**
| Rotate-Cycle$^+(C_0)$
| $\rho \leftarrow \rho + 1$
Swap-Pebbles-Unoccupied(v, u)
Unlock $(C_0 \setminus \{u\})$
Make-Unoccupied$(prev_{\circlearrowleft}(C_0, u))$
Swap-Pebbles-Unoccupied$(u, prev_{\circlearrowleft}(C_0, u))$
Swap-Pebbles-Unoccupied$(next_{\circlearrowleft}(C_0, u), u)$
Swap-Pebbles-Unoccupied(u, v)
Unlock$(\{u\})$
Lock$(C_0 \setminus \{u\})$
while $\rho > 0$ **do**
| Rotate-Cycle$^-(C_0)$
| $\rho \leftarrow \rho - 1$
Swap-Pebbles-Unoccupied(v, u)
while $S_P(r) \neq u$ **do**
| Rotate-Cycle$^+(C_0)$
Swap-Pebbles-Unoccupied(u, v)
Unlock(C_0)

procedure *Make-Unoccupied*(v)

/* Makes a vertex v unoccupied while locked vertices remain untouched.
Parameters: v - a vertex to be made unoccupied. */

let $u \in V$ such that $\Phi_P(u) = \perp$ and u is not locked
let $\phi = [u = w_1, w_2, \ldots, w_j = v]$ be a (shortest) path
| connecting u and v in G not containing locked vertices
for $i = 1, 2, \ldots, j - 1$ **do**
| Swap-Pebbles-Unoccupied(w_{i+1}, w_i)

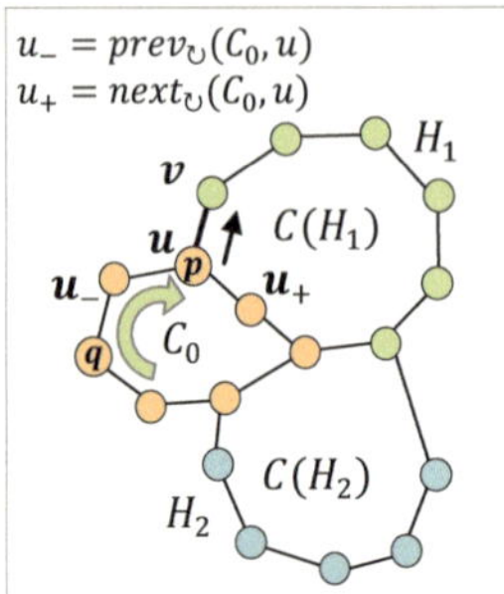

Move p into v; rotate C_0 forward such that q appears in u_+.

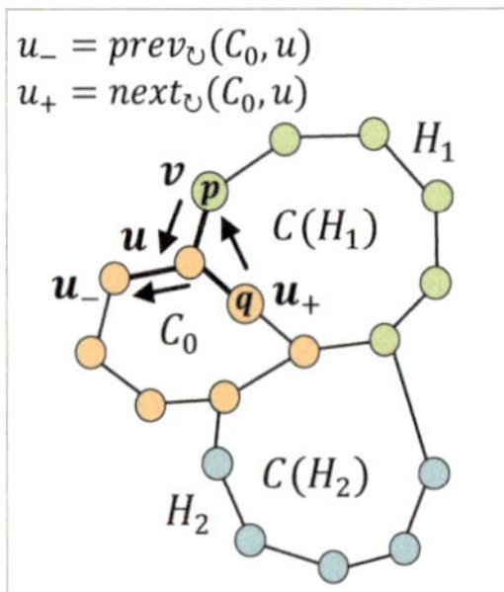

Exchange p and q (p appears in u_-).

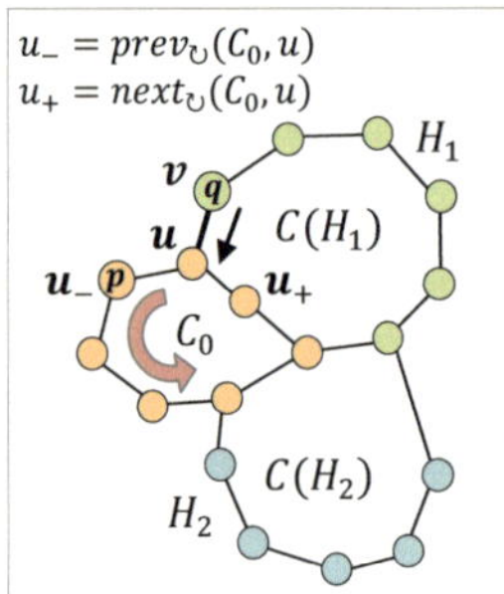

Rotate C_0 back; move q from v to u.

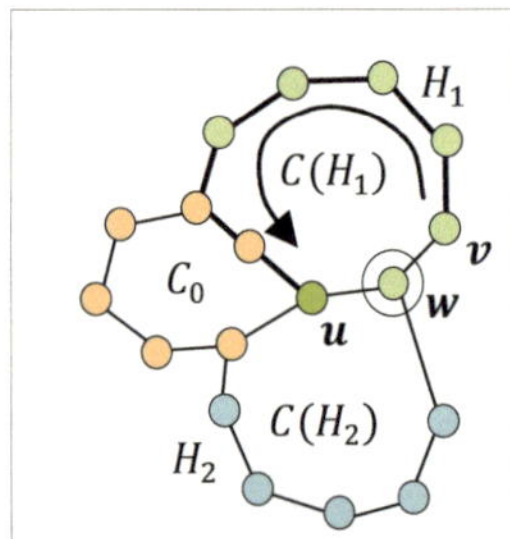

Vertex w is locked; u is unoccupied; pebbles are shifted along cycle $C(H_1)$ to make v unoccupied.

procedure *Move-Pebble*(p, v)

/* Moves a pebble p into a vertex v avoiding locked vertices.
Parameters: p - a pebble to move,
v - a target vertex.*/

/* complexity issues impose special selection of φ */

let $\varphi = [S_P(p) = w_1^\varphi, w_2^\varphi, \ldots, w_{j_\varphi}^\varphi = v]$ be a path
  connecting $S_P(p)$ and v in G not containing
  locked vertices such that an alternative vertex
  disjoint path $\chi = [S_P(p) = w_1^\chi, w_2^\chi, \ldots, w_{j_\chi}^\chi = v]$
  not containing locked vertices exists

for $i = 1,2,\ldots, j_\varphi - 1$ **do**
  Lock $(\{w_i^\varphi\})$
  Make-Unoccupied(w_{i+1}^φ)
  Unlock$(\{w_i^\varphi\})$
  Swap-Pebbles-Unoccupied$(w_i^\varphi, w_{i+1}^\varphi)$

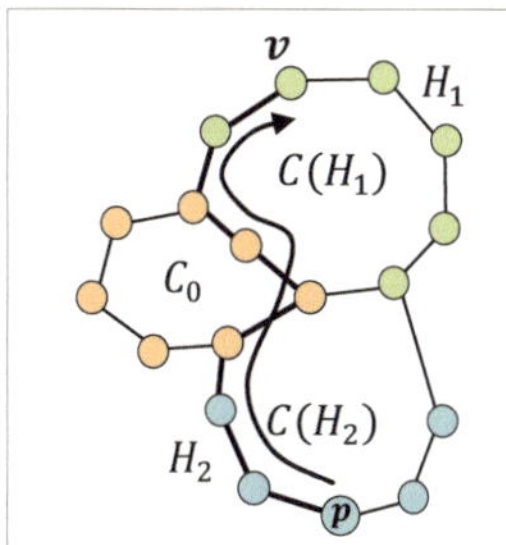

Pebble p is moved to v through cycles $C(H_2)$, C_0, and $C(H_1)$.

procedure *Rotate-Cycle*$^+(C)$

/* Rotates pebbles in a cycle C in the positive direction; the vertex locking mechanism allows to select which one of unoccupied vertices should be used. At least one unlocked unoccupied vertex must be located in C.
Parameters: C - a cycle to rotate. */

let $w \in C$ such that $\Phi_P(w) = \perp$ and w is not locked

for $i = 1,2,\ldots,|C|$ **do**
  Swap-Pebbles-Unoccupied$(prev_\circlearrowleft(C, w), w)$
  $w \leftarrow prev_\circlearrowleft(C, w)$

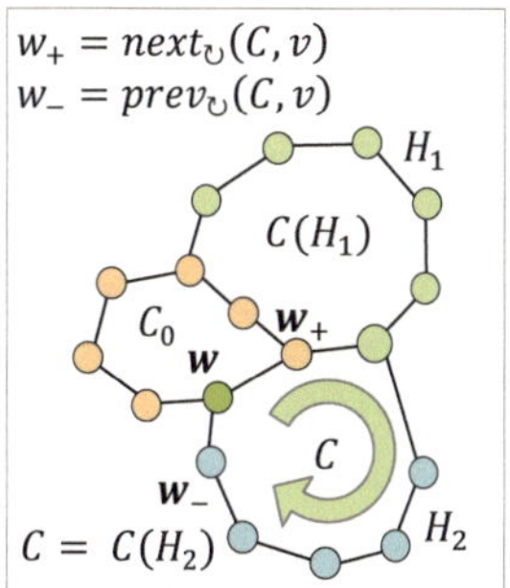

Vertex w is unoccupied; $C(H_2)$ is rotated in the positive direction.

procedure *Rotate-Cycle*$^-(C)$

/* Rotates pebbles in the cycle C in the negative direction; again an unoccupied vertex to use can be selected by the vertex locking mechanism. At least one unlocked unoccupied vertex must be located in C.
Parameters: C - a cycle to rotate. */

let $w \in C$ such that $\Phi_P(w) = \perp$ and w is not locked

for $i = 1,2,\ldots,|C|$ **do**
  Swap-Pebbles-Unoccupied$(next_\circlearrowleft(C, w), w)$
  $w \leftarrow next_\circlearrowleft(C, w)$

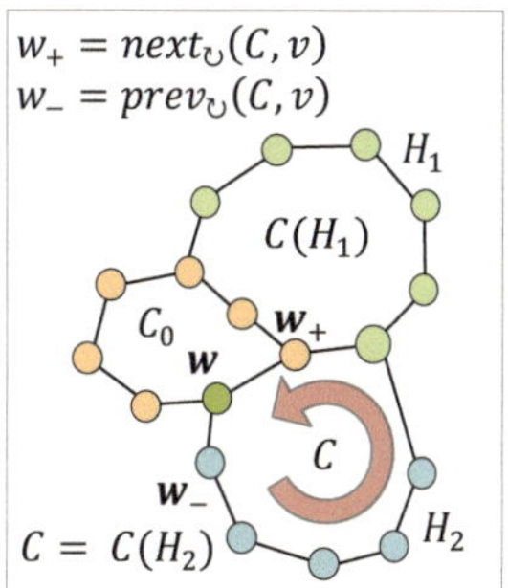

Vertex w is unoccupied; $C(H_2)$ is rotated in the negative direction.

procedure *Swap-Pebbles-Unoccupied*(u, v)

/* Swaps pebbles in vertices u and v; vertex v is supposed to be unoccupied.
Parameters: u, v – vertices in which pebbles are swapped. */

$S_P(\Phi_P(u)) \leftarrow v$
$\Phi_P(v) \leftarrow \Phi_P(u)$
$\Phi_P(u) \leftarrow \perp$
$S_P^\xi \leftarrow S_P$
$\xi \leftarrow \xi + 1$

The next important process is moving a pebble into a given target vertex. This is implemented by a procedure *Move-Pebble*. Let a pebble p is moved to a vertex v. A path φ is found such that is connects vertices $S_P(p)$ (which is a vertex currently occupied by p) and v and there exists an alternative vertex disjoint path χ connecting the same pair of vertices. The existence of the alternative is ensured by Lemma 2. Indeed, the proof of Lemma 2 provides the construction such a path. Parameters of the lemma should be set as follows: u_1 is $S_P(p)$, u_2 is a neighboring vertex to u_1 in the same bi-connected component, v_1 is v, and v_2 is a neighboring vertex to v_1 in the same bi-connected component (it can be determined which of the neighboring vertices belong into the same bi-connected component from the knowledge of the handle decomposition). Vertex disjoint paths φ' and χ' resulting from Lemma 2 together with edges $\{u_1, u_2\}$ and $\{v_1, v_2\}$ form the required φ and χ. In case (a): $\varphi = \varphi'$ and $\chi = [u_1].\chi.[u_2]$; in case (b): $\varphi = [u_1].\chi'$ and $\chi = \varphi'.[u_2]$.
Subsequently, edges of φ are traversed in the following way. The first vertex of the edge is locked so paths to be searched must avoid this vertex. An invariant holds, that p is located in the first vertex of the edge at the beginning of each traversal step and thus it cannot move. Then the second vertex of the edge is made unoccupied (the alternative path χ is used for this task); the first vertex of the edge is unlocked and the pebble p is moved to the second vertex of the edge which is now unoccupied.
The last basic operation exploited by the algorithm is a rotation of pebbles along a cycle. This operation is implemented by procedures *Rotate-Cycle*$^+$ and *Rotate-Cycle*$^-$. The former rotates pebbles in the positive direction and the latter rotates pebbles in the negative direction. It supposed the at least one vertex in the given input cycle is unoccupied. The rotation is done using an unlocked unoccupied vertex located in the cycle.
During movement of an unoccupied vertex and during movement of a pebble to another vertex, the arrangement of pebbles located in vertices that are locked is preserved while the arrangement of pebbles located in unlocked vertices is generally not preserved. This behavior helps to control finished parts of the goal arrangement. On the other hand, moving pebbles must be done in a precise way so that required unlocked paths always exist.
The process of placing pebbles according to the given goal arrangement will be described now using the primitives discussed above. Pebbles, which goal positions are within the currently solved handle, are placed in a stack like manner. This process is carried out by a procedure *Solve-Regular-Handle* (iteration through the handle is at lines 7-37). Let $H_c = [u^c, w_1^c, w_2^c, \dots, w_{h_c}^c, v^c]$ for $c \in \{1,2,\dots,d\}$ be a current handle. Suppose that a pebble which goal position is in w_i^c for $i \in \{1,2,\dots,h_c\}$, that is a pebble $\Phi_P^+(w_i^c)$, is processed in the current iteration. Inductively suppose that pebbles $\Phi_P^+(w_{h_c}^c), \Phi_P^+(w_{h_c-1}^c), \dots, \Phi_P^+(w_{i+1}^c)$ are located in vertices $w_{h_c-i-1}^c, w_{h_c-i-2}^c, \dots, w_1^c$ respectively. An analogical situation for the next pebble $\Phi_P^+(w_{i+1}^c)$ must be produced at the end of the iteration.
The pebble $\Phi_P^+(w_i^c)$ is moved to the vertex u^c and then the cycle $C(H_c)$ is positively rotated once which causes that the pebble $\Phi_P^+(w_i^c)$ moves to w_1^c and pebbles $\Phi_P^+(w_{h_c}^c), \Phi_P^+(w_{h_c-1}^c), \dots, \Phi_P^+(w_{i+1}^c)$ plunge in the cycle so that they are located in $w_{h_c-i}^c$, $w_{h_c-i-1}^c, \dots, w_2^c$. The described process represents one iteration of stacking pebbles into the handle H_c. However, the process is not that easy. At least, two major cases must be distinguished within this process. In both cases, the first step is that internal vertices of the handle H_c are locked (line 8 of *Solve-Regular-Handle*).
If the pebble $\Phi_P^+(w_i^c)$ is not located in the internal vertices of the handle H_c (line 9-14 of *Solve-Regular-Handle*), it is just moved to u^c. This is possible since an invariant holds that both

unoccupied vertices are located outside the internal vertices of the handle and the graph without the internal vertices of the handle is connected. This holds at the beginning, since both unoccupied vertices are explicitly moved outside the handle H_c (lines 2-6 of *Solve-Regular-Handle*) and it is preserved through all the iterations. Observe that these movements do not affect pebbles already stacked in the handle. The pebble $\Phi_P^+(w_{h_c}^c)$ is fixed in u^c by locking u^c and then an unoccupied vertex is moved to v^c which makes the rotation of the cycle $C(H_c)$ possible. The positive rotation of $C(H_c)$ finishes the iteration.

If the pebble $\Phi_P^+(w_i^c)$ is already located in some of the internal vertices of the handle H_c (lines 15-37 of *Solve-Regular-Handle*), the above process is reused but it must be preceded by getting the pebble $\Phi_P^+(w_{h_c}^c)$ outside the handle. Notice, that it is not possible for the pebble $\Phi_P^+(w_i^c)$ to intermix with already stacked pebbles $\Phi_P^+(w_{h_c}^c), \Phi_P^+(w_{h_c-1}^c), \ldots, \Phi_P^+(w_{i+1}^c)$. The vertex u^c is made unoccupied and the cycle $C(H_c)$ is positively rotated until the pebble $\Phi_P^+(w_i^c)$ gets outside the internal nodes of H_c; that is, $\Phi_P^+(w_i^c)$ appears in v^c. This series of rotations preserves the order of the already stacked pebbles. To restore the situation however, the cycle must be rotated back the same number of times. A vertex w outside the already finished part of the graph (that is outside $C(H_c)$ and outside H_j for $j > c$) is selected; the pebble $\Phi_P^+(w_i^c)$ is moved into w and it is fixed there by locking. The vertex u^c is made unoccupied again since the preceding process may move some pebble into it (this is possible since w alone cannot rule out the existence of a path from an unoccupied vertex to u^c in the bi-connected graph; there is always an alternative path). The cycle is rotated back so that inductively supposed placement of $\Phi_P^+(w_{h_c}^c), \Phi_P^+(w_{h_c-1}^c), \ldots, \Phi_P^+(w_{i+1}^c)$ is restored. The situation is now the same as in the previous case with $\Phi_P^+(w_i^c)$ outside the handle.

After the last iteration within the handle H_c it holds that the pebbles $\Phi_P^+(w_{h_c}^c), \Phi_P^+(w_{h_c-1}^c), \ldots, \Phi_P^+(w_1^c)$ are located in vertices $w_{h_c}^c, w_{h_c-1}^c, \ldots, w_1^c$ respectively. Moreover it holds that unoccupied vertices are both outside the internal vertices of H_c. Thus, the solving process can continue with the next handle in the same way while the already solved handles remain unaffected by subsequent steps. Notice, that only one unoccupied vertex is sufficient for stacking pebbles into handles.

The initial cycle C_0 of the handle decomposition must be treated in a different way. Here, the second unoccupied vertex is utilized. An arrangement of pebbles within C_0 can be regarded as a permutation. The task is to obtain the right permutation corresponding to the goal arrangement. This can be achieved by exchanging several pairs of pebbles. More precisely, if a pebble residing in a vertex of C_0 differs from a pebble that should reside in this vertex in the goal arrangement, this pair of pebbles is exchanged. The process is implemented by a procedure *Solve-Original-Cycle* and by auxiliary procedure *Exchange-Pebbles* for exchanging a pair of pebbles.

The procedure *Exchange-Pebbles* expects that first two vertices of the initial cycle are unoccupied in the current arrangement. However, the function generally does not preserve this property. Hence, the vacancy of the first two vertices of the initial cycle must be repeatedly restored (lines 4-7 and 10-13 of *Solve-Original-Cycle*). The process of exchanging a pair of pebbles p and q itself exploits a pair of vertices u and v which are connected by an edge and $u \in C_0 \wedge v \notin C_0$. The vertex v is used as a storage place. The need of two unoccupied vertices is imposed by the fact that a pebble from C_0 to be stored in v must be rotated into u first. During this process, some vertex of the cycle must be unoccupied to make the rotation possible and the vertex v must be unoccupied as well to make storing possible.

When exchanging the pair o pebbles p and q it is necessary to preserve ordering of the remaining pebbles. First, a pebble occupying the vertex v is moved into the cycle C_0 in order to make v vacant (lines 1-3 of *Exchange-Pebbles*). Then the cycle is rotated until the pebble p appears in u (since there was a pebble in u at the beginning of the rotation, there is always some pebble in u after all the rotations) and the pebble p is stored in v (lines 4-6 of *Exchange-Pebbles*). Next, the cycle C_0 is rotated positively so that q appears in $next_{\circlearrowright}(C_0, u)$ (the next vertex to u with respect to the positive orientation) while the number of rotations is recorded (lines 7-14 of *Exchange-Pebbles*). However, the second unoccupied vertex must not interfere with counting of rotations, thus it is located $next_{\circlearrowright}(C_0, u)$ at the beginning (that is, outside the sequence of pebbles between p and q which length is being counted in fact) and then moved to $prev_{\circlearrowright}(C_0, u)$ in the positive direction (the movement of the second unoccupied in the negative direction is not possible here, since u is locked at the moment). At this moment, pebbles p and q are exchanged using two unoccupied vertices so that ordering of p in the cycle C_0 is the same as of q before the exchange (lines 15-20 of *Exchange-Pebbles*). Then, the cycle is rotated in the negative direction recorded number of times so that place within the cycle where p was originally ordered appears in u; thus q is ordered here (lines 21-26 of *Exchange-Pebbles*). Finally, the pebble that was located in v before the exchange of pebbles p and q has been commenced is put back into v (lines 27-30 of *Exchange-Pebbles*). Since the process of exchange of a pair of pebbles is quite complicated, the detailed case analysis is given within the proof of correctness of the process in (Surynek, 2010c).

4.3 Summary of properties of the *BIBOX* algorithm

Several theoretical properties of the *BIBOX* algorithm regarding the time and space complexity are summarized in the following propositions. Propositions are presented without proofs. The detailed proofs can be found in (Surynek, 2010c). Nevertheless, it can be briefly stated that the algorithm is polynomial in all the aspects.

Proposition 2 *(BIBOX - soundness and completeness).* The *BIBOX* algorithm is sound and complete. That is, the algorithm always terminates and produces a solution of a given input instance of the problem of pebble motion on a graph $\Pi = (G = (V, E), P, S_P^0, S_P^+)$. ■

Proposition 3 *(BIBOX – worst case time complexity).* The worst case time complexity of the *BIBOX* algorithm is $O(|V|^3)$ with respect to an input instance of the problem pebble motion on a graph $\Pi = (G = (V, E), P, S_P^0, S_P^+)$. ■

Proposition 4 *(BIBOX – makespan of the solution).* The makespan of a solution in the worst case produced by the *BIBOX* algorithm (that is, the number ξ) for an input instance of the problem of pebble motion on a graph $\Pi = (G = (V, E), P, S_P^0, S_P^+)$ is $O(|V|^3)$. ■

Proposition 5 *(BIBOX – worst case space complexity).* The worst case space complexity of the *BIBOX* algorithm is $O(|V| + |E|)$ with respect to an input instance of the problem pebble motion on a graph $\Pi = (G = (V, E), P, S_P^0, S_P^+)$. ■

4.4 Extensions and the real-life Implementation

The natural question is how to apply the *BIBOX* algorithm if there are more than two unoccupied vertices in input instance (that is, $\mu - 2 \leq |V|$). The algorithm can be used directly if the graph is filled by dummy pebbles. The instance with dummy pebbles is solved by the algorithm as it is and finally movements of dummy pebbles are filtered out from the solution in an additional post-processing step. An adaptation of the solving algorithm for sparse instances of the pebble motion problem is out of scope of this chapter. Nevertheless, a straightforward adaptation is to replace the non-deterministic selection of an unlocked unoccupied vertex (such as that at line 1 of *Make-Unoccupied*) by the selection of the most promising one. For example, an unlocked unoccupied vertex that is nearest to the vertex that is to be made unoccupied can be selected.

Some further optimizations should be used in the real-life implementation to reduce the makespan of the produced solution. Various preconditions are explicitly enforced in order to make the presented pseudo-code simpler (for example, the precondition of having first two vertices of the initial cycle of the handle decomposition unoccupied before a pair of vertices is exchanged within the cycle - lines 4-6 of *Solve-Original-Cycle*). This approach should be avoided and a lazier approach should be adopted in the real-life implementation (in the case of exchanging pebbles, locations of unoccupied vertices should be detected implicitly in subsequent steps by more sophisticated branching of the code).

The real-life implementation of procedures *Solve-Regular-Handle* and *Solve-Original-Cycle* should use opportunistic selection of vertices to store pebbles (vertex y - line 23 of *Solve-Regular-Handle* and vertices u, v - line 1 of *Solve-Original-Cycle*). The nearest vertex to the target pebble should be always selected. Moreover, selection of these vertices within the procedure *Solve-Original-Cycle* should be done not only at the beginning but also in every iteration of its main loop.

5. Improving makespan by increasing parallelism

This section is devoted to a method for increasing parallelism of solutions. In fact, this method represents a major technique how to utilize parallelism allowed by the definition of the problem of multi-robot path planning. The presented algorithm does not utilize the possibility of parallel movements. It solves the problem of pebble motion on a graph in fact. The method presented below is intended as a post-processing technique that should be applied on a solution produced by the *BIBOX* algorithm.

Definition 5 (*sequential solution*). A solution $\mathcal{S}_R(\Sigma) = [S_R^0, S_R^1, \ldots, S_R^\zeta]$ of multi-robot path planning problem $\Sigma = (G = (V,E), R = \{\bar{r}_1, \bar{r}_2, \ldots, \bar{r}_\nu\}, S_R^0, S_R^+)$ is called ***sequential*** (ζ is the length of the solution) if for each $k = 1,2, \ldots, \zeta - 1$ there exists $j \in \{1,2, \ldots, \nu\}$ such that $S_R^k(\bar{r}_j) \neq S_R^{k+1}(\bar{r}_j)$ and $S_R^k(\bar{r}_l) \neq S_R^{k+1}(\bar{r}_l)$ for each $l = 1,2, \ldots, \nu \wedge l \neq j$ (at time step k a robot $\bar{r}_j$ is moved; all the other robots do not move at the time step). □

A move of a robot r from a vertex u to a vertex v will be denoted using the notation $r: u \rightarrow v$. The sequential solution of multi-robot path planning problem can be equivalently represented as a sequence of moves of the form $r: u \rightarrow v$. That is, a sequence $\mathcal{S}_R^{\prec}(\Sigma) = [r_1: u_1 \rightarrow v_1, r_2: u_2 \rightarrow v_2, \ldots, r_\zeta: u_\zeta \rightarrow v_\zeta]$ determines sequential solution (r_i are variables with the domain $\{\bar{r}_1, \bar{r}_2, \ldots, \bar{r}_\nu\}$; $\bar{r}_i$ are constants). Notice, that $u_k \neq v_k$ for each $k = 1,2, \ldots, \zeta$ which is ensured by the definition of the sequential solution. In other words, a solution is sequential if there is just one move at each step. This, however, may prolong makespan significantly, which is not desirable.

Suppose a sequential solution $\mathcal{S}_R^{\prec}(\Sigma) = [r_1: u_1 \rightarrow v_1, r_2: u_2 \rightarrow v_2, \ldots, r_\zeta: u_\zeta \rightarrow v_\zeta]$ of an instance of multi-robot path planning $\Sigma = (G = (V,E), R = \{\bar{r}_1, \bar{r}_2, \ldots, \bar{r}_\nu\}, S_R^0, S_R^+)$. This form of the solution of the problem will be more convenient for reasoning about the possible parallelism. The following definitions refer will to $\mathcal{S}_R^{\prec}(\Sigma)$.

Definition 6 (*interfering moves*). A move $r_h: u_h \rightarrow v_h$; $h \in \{1,2, \ldots, \zeta - 1\}$ is ***interfering*** with a move $r_k: u_k \rightarrow v_k$; $k \in \{1,2, \ldots, \zeta - 1\}$ if $|\{u_h, v_h\} \cap \{u_k, v_k\}| \geq 1$. □

Typically, interfering moves cannot be executed in parallel. However, the situation is not so straightforward. Following definitions are trying to capture which pairs of interfering moves can be undoubtedly executed in parallel and which not.

Definition 7 (*potentially concurrent moves*). A move $r_k: u_k \rightarrow v_k;\ k \in \{1,2,\dots,\zeta\}$ is ***potentially concurrent*** with a move $r_h: u_h \rightarrow v_h;\ h \in \{1,2,\dots,\zeta\}$ with $h < k$ if $r_h \neq r_k,\ u_h = v_k \wedge v_h \neq u_k$, and there is no other move $r_{\hbar}: u_{\hbar} \rightarrow v_{\hbar}$ in $\mathcal{S}_R^{\prec}(\Sigma)$ such that $h < \hbar < k$ interfering with $r_h: u_h \rightarrow v_h$ or $r_k: u_k \rightarrow v_k$. The notation is that $r_h: u_h \rightarrow v_h \preccurlyeq r_k: u_k \rightarrow v_k$. □

The definition captures the fact that although the moves are interfering they can be executed at the same time step according to the definition of a solution of the instance of multi-robot path planning problem. The relation of potential concurrence is anti-reflexive due to the requirement on different robots involved ($r_h \neq r_k$) and anti-symmetric due to the ordering of moves within the sequential solution ($h < k$).

Definition 8 (*trivially dependent moves*). A move $r_k: u_k \rightarrow v_k;\ k \in \{1,2,\dots,\zeta\}$ is ***trivially dependent*** on a move $r_h: u_h \rightarrow v_h;\ h \in \{1,2,\dots,\zeta\}$ with $h < k$ if these moves are interfering, $r_h = r_k$ or $u_h \neq v_k \vee v_h = u_k$, and there is no other move $r_{\hbar}: u_{\hbar} \rightarrow v_{\hbar}$ in $\mathcal{S}_R^{\prec}(\Sigma)$ such that $h < \hbar < k$ interfering with $r_h: u_h \rightarrow v_h$ or $r_k: u_k \rightarrow v_k$. The notation is that $r_h: u_h \rightarrow v_h \prec r_k: u_k \rightarrow v_k$. □

The definition captures the fact that trivially dependent moves cannot be executed at the same time step. Notice, that the condition $r_h = r_k$ or $u_h \neq v_k \vee v_h = u_k$ is the negation of the condition $r_h \neq r_k$ and $u_h = v_k \wedge v_h \neq u_k$ from the definition of the potential concurrence. Observe that, when $|\{u_h, v_h\} \cap \{u_k, v_k\}| \geq 1$ (interfering moves), the condition $u_h \neq v_k \vee v_h = u_k$ can be equivalently expressed as a disjunction of several cases as follows: $(u_h \neq u_k \wedge v_h = v_k)$ or $(u_h = u_k \wedge v_h \neq v_k)$ or $(u_h = u_k \wedge v_h = v_k)$ or $(u_h = v_k \wedge v_h = u_k)$ or $(u_h \neq v_k \wedge v_h = u_k)$ (original and target vertices of each move are different; thus, each of the conjunctions defines the situation unambiguously with respect to involved vertices). Observe, that none of the cases is actually possible if $r_h = r_k$ and with no middle move $r_{\hbar}: u_{\hbar} \rightarrow v_{\hbar}$ allowed. The relation of trivial dependence of moves is reflexive and anti-symmetric due to the ordering of moves within the sequential solution ($h < k$).

The notions of potential concurrence and trivial dependence are to be used as building blocks of a process that constructs parallel solution of the instance of the problem of multi-robot path planning.

Proposition 6 (*execution order*). Let each move of a sequential solution $\mathcal{S}_R^{\prec}(\Sigma)$ is assigned a time step of its execution by a function $t: \bigcup \mathcal{S}_R^{\prec}(\Sigma) \longrightarrow \{1,2,\dots,\zeta-1\}$. Let t satisfies the following constraint: if $r_h: u_h \rightarrow v_h \prec r_k: u_k \rightarrow v_k$ then $t(r_h: u_h \rightarrow v_h) < t(r_k: u_k \rightarrow v_k)$ and if $r_h: u_h \rightarrow v_h \preccurlyeq r_k: u_k \rightarrow v_k$ then $t(r_h: u_h \rightarrow v_h) \leq t(r_k: u_k \rightarrow v_k)$. Then a standard (parallel) solution $\mathcal{S}_R(\Sigma)$ constructed from $\mathcal{S}_R^{\prec}(\Sigma)$ using the function t forms a (correct) solution of Σ (sequence of arrangements of robots in $\mathcal{S}_R(\Sigma)$ reflects changes induced by moves at time steps determined by the function t). ■

Proof. The proof will proceed by induction according to the length of the sequential solution $\mathcal{S}_R^{\prec}(\Sigma)$. If the sequence $\mathcal{S}_R^{\prec}(\Sigma)$ consists of a single element, the proposition holds. Suppose that $\mathcal{S}_R^{\prec}(\Sigma) = [r_1: u_1 \rightarrow v_1, r_2: u_2 \rightarrow v_2, \dots, r_\zeta: u_\zeta \rightarrow v_\zeta]$ is of non-trivial length. From induction hypothesis, the proposition holds for the sequence of moves $\mathcal{S}_R^{\prec}(\Sigma') = [r_1: u_1 \rightarrow v_1, r_2: u_2 \rightarrow v_2, \dots, r_{\zeta-1}: u_{\zeta-1} \rightarrow v_{\zeta-1}]$. In other words, there is a function $t': \bigcup \mathcal{S}_R^{\prec}(\Sigma') \longrightarrow \{1,2,\dots,\zeta-1\}$ such that it determines a correct parallel solution of an instance Σ' which is almost the same as Σ except the goal arrangement which differs by the last move $r_\zeta: u_\zeta \rightarrow v_\zeta$.

If there is some move $r_i: u_i \rightarrow v_i$ with $1 \leq i \leq \zeta$ such that $r_\zeta: u_\zeta \rightarrow v_\zeta$ is trivially dependent on it, then t should satisfy that $t(r_i: u_i \rightarrow v_i) < t(r_\zeta: u_\zeta \rightarrow v_\zeta)$. Properties of trivial dependency ensure that execution of $r_\zeta: u_\zeta \rightarrow v_\zeta$ after $r_i: u_i \rightarrow v_i$ does not violate correctness of the solution.

If there is some move $r_j: u_j \rightarrow v_j$ with $1 \leq j \leq \zeta$ such that $r_\zeta: u_\zeta \rightarrow v_\zeta$ is potentially concurrent with it, then t should satisfy that $t(r_j: u_j \rightarrow v_j) \leq t(r_\zeta: u_\zeta \rightarrow v_\zeta)$. The relation of potential concurrence ensures that execution of $r_\zeta: u_\zeta \rightarrow v_\zeta$ at the same time step or after the time step with $r_i: u_i \rightarrow v_i$ does not violate correctness of the solution.
Let $t(r_h: u_h \rightarrow v_h) = t'(r_h: u_h \rightarrow v_h)$ for $h = 1,2, \dots, \zeta - 1$. The function will be defined for the last element of $\mathcal{S}_R^{\prec}(\Sigma)$ specially to satisfy above inequalities with respect to all the trivially dependent and potentially concurrent moves with respect to $r_\zeta: u_\zeta \rightarrow v_\zeta$. Let $t'_{\prec} = \max\{t'(r_i: u_i \rightarrow v_i) \mid r_i: u_i \rightarrow v_i \prec r_\zeta: u_\zeta \rightarrow v_\zeta \wedge i \in \{1,2,\dots,\zeta-1\}\}$ be the time step assigned to the last trivially dependent move. Similarly, let $t'_{\preccurlyeq} = \max\{t'(r_j: u_j \rightarrow v_j) \mid r_j: u_j \rightarrow v_j \preccurlyeq r_\zeta: u_\zeta \rightarrow v_\zeta \wedge j \in \{1,2,\dots,\zeta - 1\}\}$ be the time step assigned to the last potentially concurrent move. Let $t(r_\zeta: u_\zeta \rightarrow v_\zeta) \geq \max\{t'_{\prec} + 1, t'_{\preccurlyeq}\}$. The function t defined as above satisfies the proposition. ■

The parallelized solution will be constructed according to Propopsition 6. To obtain small makespan and high parallelism of the solution, low execution times for execution should be assigned to the individual moves. Thus, it is recommended to assign the time step for the execution of the newly added move in the proposition as follows: $t(r_\zeta: u_\zeta \rightarrow v_\zeta) = \max\{t'_{\prec} + 1, t'_{\preccurlyeq}\}$.
The process is formalized in pseudo-code as Algorithm 2. The method described above is also known as *critical path method* in different contexts (Russel & Norvig, 2003). The algorithm consists of three functions: *Increase-Parallelism*, *Earliest-Execution-Time*$^{\prec}$, and *Earliest-Execution-Time*$^{\preccurlyeq}$. The main framework of the algorithm is represented by the function *Increase-Parallelism*. The function successively includes moves into the constructed parallel solution while trivial dependency and potential concurrence with respect to already included moves is calculated. The function is build over the array *step* which is indexed by time steps. The cell *step*$[t]$ contains a set of moves that are to be executed at the time step t. Functions *Earliest-Execution-Time*$^{\prec}$ and *Earliest-Execution-Time*$^{\preccurlyeq}$ calculates earliest execution time for the newly included move with respect to already included trivially dependent moves and potentially concurrent moves.

Algorithm 2. *The **parallelism increasing** algorithm.* The algorithm produces a parallelized solution of an instance of multi-robot path planning problem from the given sequential solution. The idea of the algorithm is inspired by the **critical path method** (Russel & Norvig, 2003).

---

function *Increase-Parallelism*$(\mathcal{S}_R^{\prec}(\Sigma), S_R^0)$: **pair**

/* A function for producing standard solution of multi-robot path planning problem instance from the sequential one.
Parameters: $\mathcal{S}_R^{\prec}(\Sigma)$ - a sequential solution of Σ,
S_R^0 - a initial arrangement of robots. */

let $\mathcal{S}_R^{\prec}(\Sigma) = [r_1: u_1 \rightarrow v_1, r_2: u_2 \rightarrow v_2, \dots, r_\zeta: u_\zeta \rightarrow v_\zeta]$
step$[1] \leftarrow \{r_1: u_1 \rightarrow v_1\}$
$\omega \leftarrow 1$
for $k = 2,3, \dots, \zeta - 1$ **do**
  $t'_{\prec} \leftarrow$ Earliest-Execution-Time$^{\prec}(r_k: u_k \rightarrow v_k)$
  $t'_{\preccurlyeq} \leftarrow$ Earliest-Execution-Time$^{\preccurlyeq}(r_k: u_k \rightarrow v_k)$
  $t \leftarrow \max\{t'_{\prec} + 1, t'_{\preccurlyeq}\}$
  step$[t] \leftarrow$ *step*$[t] \cup \{r_1: u_1 \rightarrow v_1\}$

| $\omega \leftarrow \max\{\omega, t\}$
$S_R \leftarrow S_R^0$
$\zeta \leftarrow 1$
for $i = 1,2, \ldots, \omega$ **do**
| **for each** $(r: u \rightarrow v) \in step[i]$ **do**
| | $S_R(r) \leftarrow v$
| | $S_R^i \leftarrow S_R$
return $(\omega, [S_R^0, S_R^1, \ldots, S_R^\omega])$

function *Earliest-Execution-Time*$^{\prec}(r_k: u_k \rightarrow v_k, \omega)$: **integer**
/* Calculates earliest execution time for a given move
with respect to the relation of trivial dependency.
Parameters: $r_k: u_k \rightarrow v_k$ - a move for that
a time step is calculated,
ω - currently last time step. */
for $i = \omega, \omega - 1, \ldots, 1$ **do**
| **for each** $(r: u \rightarrow v) \in step[i]$ **do**
| | **if** $r: u \rightarrow v \prec r_k: u_k \rightarrow v_k$ **then**
| | | **return** k
return 1

function *Earliest-Execution-Time*$^{\preccurlyeq}(r_k: u_k \rightarrow v_k, \omega)$: **integer**
/* Calculates earliest execution time for a given move
with respect to the relation of potential concurrence.
Parameters: $r_k: u_k \rightarrow v_k$ - a move for that
a time step is calculated,
ω - currently last time step. */
for $i = \omega, \omega - 1, \ldots, 1$ **do**
| **for each** $(r: u \rightarrow v) \in step[i]$ **do**
| | **if** $r: u \rightarrow v \preccurlyeq r_k: u_k \rightarrow v_k$ **then**
| | | **return** k
return 1

Proposition 7 *(increasing parallelism).* The algorithm for increasing parallelism has the worst case time complexity of $\mathcal{O}(|\mathcal{S}_R^{\prec}(\Sigma)|^2)$ for the input sequential solution $\mathcal{S}_R^{\prec}(\Sigma) = [r_1: u_1 \rightarrow v_1, r_2: u_2 \rightarrow v_2, \ldots, r_\zeta: u_\zeta \rightarrow v_\zeta]$. The worst case space complexity of the algorithm is $\mathcal{O}(|\mathcal{S}_R^{\prec}(\Sigma)|)$. ■

Proof. Each call of *Earliest-Execution-Time*$^{\prec}$ and *Earliest-Execution-Time*$^{\preccurlyeq}$ requires time of $\mathcal{O}(|\mathcal{S}_R^{\prec}(\Sigma)|)$. Both functions are called $|\mathcal{S}_R^{\prec}(\Sigma)|$ times, thus the overall worst case time complexity is $\mathcal{O}(|\mathcal{S}_R^{\prec}(\Sigma)|^2)$. A space of the size $\mathcal{O}(|\mathcal{S}_R^{\prec}(\Sigma)|)$ is required to store the input sequential solution $\mathcal{S}_R^{\prec}(\Sigma)$. A space of the same size is necessary for storing the array *step*. ■

6. Discussion and conclusions

The graph theoretical abstraction of the problem of path planning for multiple robots has been introduced in this chapter. The abstraction consists in modeling the environment where robots are moving as an undirected graph with vertices standing for locations and edges representing an unblocked way from one location to another. At most one robot is placed in each vertex and at least one vertex remains unoccupied to allow robots to move.

The solving algorithm called *BIBOX* has been shown. It can be used to solve instances of the problem over bi-connected graphs with at least two unoccupied vertices. The algorithm produces a solution of the cubic makespan with respect to the number of vertices of the input graph. The technique how to increase the parallelism and consequently the makespan of solutions has been also presented. A more sophisticated algorithm called *BIBOX-θ* has been developed in (Surynek, 2010c). It is again designed for solving multi-robot path planning over bi-connected graphs. Contrary to the *BIBOX* algorithm, it suffices with just one unoccupied vertex.

There are still some open questions for the future work. The method represented by the *BIBOX* algorithm is suitable for instances with relatively small number of unoccupied vertices where there is high probability of collisions. On the other hand there exists methods suitable for instances with lot of unoccupied space (Wang & Botea, 2008; Wang, 2009). These methods are based on search for shortest paths between initial and goal positions of individual robots. Eventual collisions between robots are resolved by search for alternative paths. The interesting question is under what circumstances one or the other of these two approaches is more advantageous.

Another interesting question regarding the complexity of the optimization variant of the multi-robot path planning problem is whether it is possible to construct a solution with the makespan constant time worse than the optimum in pseudo-polynomial time (= polynomial time with respect to the size of the input and the given constant).

7. References

Cormen, T. H.; Leiserson, C. E.; Rivest, R. L.; Stein, C. (2001). *Introduction to Algorithms, Second Edition.* The MIT Press, ISBN 978-0-262-03293-3.

Garey, M. R.; Johnson, D. S. (1979). *Computers and Intractability: A Guide to the Theory of NP Completeness.* W. H. Freeman & Co., ISBN: 978-0716710455.

Kornhauser, D.; Miller, G. L.; Spirakis, P. G. (1984). *Coordinating Pebble Motion on Graphs, the Diameter of Permutation Groups, and Applications.* Proceedings of the 25th Annual Symposium on Foundations of Computer Science (FOCS 1984), pp. 241-250, West Palm Beach, FL, USA, IEEE Press, 1984.

Ratner, D.; Warmuth, M. K. (1986). *Finding a Shortest Solution for the N×N Extension of the 15-PUZZLE Is Intractable.* Proceedings of the 5th National Conference on Artificial Intelligence (AAAI 1986), pp. 168-172, Philadelphia, PA, USA, Morgan Kaufmann Publisher.

Russell, S.; Norvig, P. (2003). *Artificial Intelligence: A Modern Approach (second edition).* Prentice Hall, ISBN: 978-0137903955

Ryan, M. R. K. (2008). *Exploiting Subgraph Structure in Multi-Robot Path Planning.* Journal of Artificial Intelligence Research (JAIR), Volume 31, pp. 497-542, AAAI Press.

Surynek, P. (2009a). *A Novel Approach to Path Planning for Multiple Robots in Bi-connected Graphs.* Proceedings of the 2009 IEEE International Conference on Robotics and Automation (ICRA 2009), pp. 3613-3619, ISBN 978-1-4244-2789-5, Kobe, Japan, IEEE Press.

Surynek, P. (2009b). *An Application of Pebble Motion on Graphs to Abstract Multi-robot Path Planning.* Proceedings of the 21st International Conference on Tools with Artificial Intelligence (ICTAI 2009), pp. 151-158, ISBN 978-0-7695-3920-1, Newark, NJ, USA , IEEE Press.

Surynek, P. (2009c). *Towards Shorter Solutions for Problems of Path Planning for Multiple Robots in Theta-like Environments.* Proceedings of the 22nd International FLAIRS Conference (FLAIRS 2009), pp. 207-212, ISBN 978-1-57735-419-2, Sanibel Island, FL, USA, AAAI Press.

Surynek, P. (2010a). *An Optimization Variant of Multi-Robot Path Planning is Intractable.* Proceedings of the 24th AAAI Conference on Artificial Intelligence (AAAI 2010), pp. 1261-1263, ISBN 978-1-57735-463-5, Atlanta, GA, USA, AAAI Press.

Surynek, P. (2010b). *Abstract Path Planning for Multiple Robots: A Theoretical Study.* Technical Report, http://ktiml.mff.cuni.cz/~surynek/index.html.php?select=publications, Charles University in Prague, Czech Republic.

Surynek, P. (2010c). *Abstract Path Planning for Multiple Robots: An Empirical Study.* Technical Report, http://ktiml.mff.cuni.cz/~surynek/index.html.php?select=publications, Charles University in Prague, Czech Republic.

Tarjan, R. E. (1972). *Depth-First Search and Linear Graph Algorithms.* SIAM Journal on Computing, Volume 1 (2), pp. 146-160, Society for Industrial and Applied Mathematics.

Wang, K. C. (2009). *Bridging the Gap between Centralised and Decentralised Multi-Agent Path-finding.* Proceedings of the 14th Annual AAAI/SIGART Doctoral Consortium (AAAI-DC 2009), pp. 23-24, AAAI Press, 2009.

Wang, K. C.; Botea, A. (2008). *Fast and Memory-Efficient Multi-Agent Path-finding.* Proceedings of the Eighteenth International Conference on Automated Planning and Scheduling (ICAPS 2008), pp. 380-387, ISBN 978-1-57735-386-7, Australia, AAAI Press, 2008.

West, D. B. (2000). *Introduction to Graph Theory, second edition.* Prentice-Hall, ISBN 978-0130144003.

Wilson, R. M. (1974). *Graph Puzzles, Homotopy, and the Alternating Group.* Journal of Combinatorial Theory, Ser. B 16, pp. 86-96, Elsevier.

15

Object Path Planner for the Box Pushing Problem

Ezra Federico Parra-Gonzalez and José Gabriel Ramírez-Torres
Cinvestav-Tamaulipas
México

1. Introduction

Researchers generally agree that multi-robot systems have several advantages over single-robot systems (E. Parker & Tang, 2006). The most common motivations for developing multi-robot system solutions are that:

1. The task complexity is too high for a single robot to accomplish.
2. The task is inherently distributed.
3. Building several resource-bounded robots is easier than having a single powerful robot.
4. Multiple robots can solve problems faster using parallelism.
5. The introduction of multiple robots increases robustness through redundancy.

The *box-pushing problem*, as defined in (Gerkey & Mataric, 2002), consists to cooperatively move a box, relatively large when compared to the size of the robots, from an initial position to another goal location using robots that can only make pushing movements.
This problem has many practical applications, among them we can emphasize the next ones:

- Rescue of people.
- Carrying out dangerous works.
- Automatization of industrial processes.
- Carrying out attendance works.
- Movement of heavy objects.

Nevertheless, the most motivating aspect of this problem is that it represents an interesting challenge for the development of coordination schemes in multiagent systems. Indeed, the displacement of the object cannot be realized if cooperation between the different members of the community does not exist.
The *box-pushing problem* is related to the well-known "Piano Mover's Problem"(Schwartz & Sharir 1983) (Gerkey et al., 1995): given an arbitrary rigid polyhedral environment, find a continuous collision-free path taking this object from a source configuration to a desired destination configuration. In the *box-pushing problem*, the object B must be moved by N mobile robots toward the goal position T, with pushing movements only. Then the fundamental research problem is to design the appropriate control laws in order to obtain the desired global behavior by the community of robots (Figure 1). It was shown (Reif, 1979) that this problem is PSPACE-hard, which implies NP-hard.

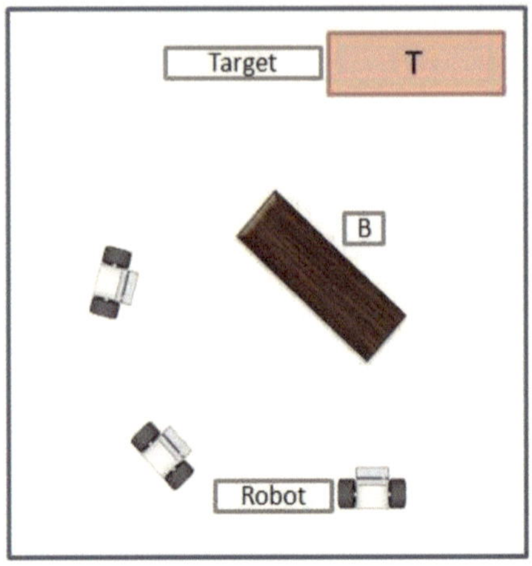

Fig. 1. Basic scheme of the "box-pushing" problem.

The object transportation task made by a cooperative community of several mobile robots involves different problems, for example: collisions avoidance, stable manipulations, path planning for robots and for the object, etc. In the most complex cases robots will have to manipulate the object and to change not only their position, they will have to change also their orientation in order to be able to move the object in the narrower places of the environment.
In this chapter we review some of the outstanding works that has been done in the area and we present a new strategy (collisions avoidance, stable manipulations, object path planning, etc.) to solve this problem. The solution that we design was inspired from the wavefront algorithm but includes certain original considerations which help to obtain trajectories that facilitate the movement of the object by unspecialized robots.

2. Related work

At present, there exist several approaches to the object transportation problem by a community of mobile robots. For example, some works have been developed so all communication needs are omitted and replaced by behavioral mechanisms based on local information (Yamada & Saito, 2001), on the other hand, there are works in which the communication is fundamental to improve the behavior of multi-robot systems (Muñoz Melendez & Drogoul, 2004).
There are some well-known strategies like the "Object closure" (Wang & Kumar, 2002; Guilherme A. S. et al., 2002) where the object position can be controlled by a team of robots that surround the object, so the box position will be controlled by the movement of each robot that surrounds and pushes the object. Another common approach is the "Pusher-Watcher" (Gerkey & Mataric, 2002; Kovac et al., 2004) where a robot (watcher) beholds the movement of the object, while coordinating the operations of the robot team (pushers) that physically manipulate the box.
Some recent works use the "swarm intelligence" model, (Li & Chen, 2004) where self-organized systems of homogeneous robots are built around simple behaviors, obtaining a decentralized and intelligent global behavior. Also, some approaches are based on Artificial Intelligence tools, as the reinforcement learning or "Q-Learning" (Wang & W. de Silva, October 2006). For more complex task of manipulation, some authors propose the use of specialized robots in manipulation tasks (Gupta & Huang, 2003; Inoue et al., 2007).

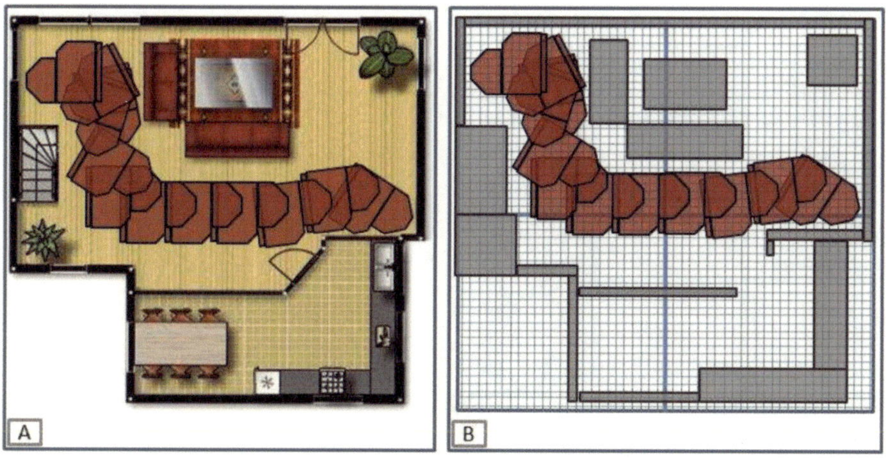

Fig. 2. Path example for moving an object from a starting point to another final.

The proposed strategy in this document obtains a feasible path for the object, computing a discrete representation of the configuration-space (C-space). There exist some works using a similar approach (Gene et al., 2005; Jed et al., 1990; MIYOSHI et al., 2008), but in addition, our strategy focus in obtaining a feasible path for the object, such the displacements (maneuvers or *reconfigurations*) of the pushing robots around it is kept to a minimum.

3. Object path planner

The path planning problem can be defined as follows: given an initial and a final configurations, find a feasible continuous collision free trajectory between them (Figure 2). Path planning algorithms are responsible for maintaining many essential aspects of plausible agent behavior, including collision avoidance and goal satisfaction. Path planning also consumes a significant part of the computation time for many simulations, particularly in highly dynamic environments where most of the agents are moving at the same time.

The main objective of this work is to compute trajectories for objects that will be moved by communities of not specialized mobile robots in cluttered environments[1]. The fundamental contribution is the development of new solving strategies for the collision-free path-planning problem for the object, that take into account some criteria in order to allow the robots to carry out the task precisely and faster.

When using unspecialized robots, each change of direction during the displacement of the box requires that the robots modify their position around the object before starting a new pushing movement (robot reconfiguration). These reconfigurations require certain time to be completed; if the total number of reconfigurations is small, the time required for the displacement is improved.

In this work we will consider that robots are not specialized in manipulation tasks, in other words, they only can push the box, but not to pull it. Therefore, it is important to obtain trajectories for the object that, besides being a solution to the path planning problem, the number of robot reconfigurations during the movement tend to be minimal. This is obtained

[1]A cluttered environment will be considered as a complex work area that contains many obstacles.

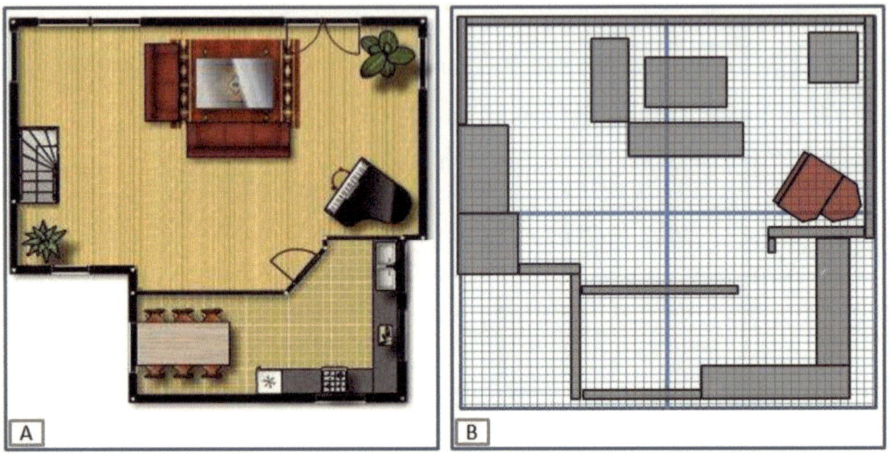

Fig. 3. Polygonal description of the object and the obstacles in a same coordinate system.

finding trajectories that reduce the number of changes of object direction, that is to say, trajectories that have a greater "continuity".

4. Proposed method

The proposed approach computes a discrete representation of the configuration space (C-space) for the box in the cluttered environment. In this representation, an heuristical search is performed, in order to obtain a trajectory with the minimal number of changes of direction. The main characteristics of the solution are listed below.

1. Find the shortest trajectories.
2. Look for trajectories with the smaller number of robot reconfigurations.
3. Preference to certain box rotations, in order to improve the pushing points.

The method is realized in four main stages: 1) Obtain the correct space representation from a predefined map; 2) Find intersection between polygons (collision detection); 3) Build the C-space in which valid positions (free of collisions) and invalid positions (collision) are split; 4) Generate the object path trajectory using alternative heuristics which reduces the robot reconfiguration and look for the shortest paths.

4.1 Object and environment representation

The environment and the box are represented by a set of convex polygonal objects, each described as a set of linear constraints (see Equation 1):

$$a_i x + b_i y \leq d_i, i = 1...P_k \tag{1}$$

where P_k is the number of faces of object k and for each $(a_i, b_i); a_i \neq 0$ or $b_i \neq 0$.
A representative example of this polygonal representation is shown in (Figure 3).

4.2 Finding intersections between polygons (collisions)

We need a method to verify whether there is an intersection between 2 given polygons. This can be achieved if we find at least a segment of a line which satisfies the sets of constraints of both polygons.

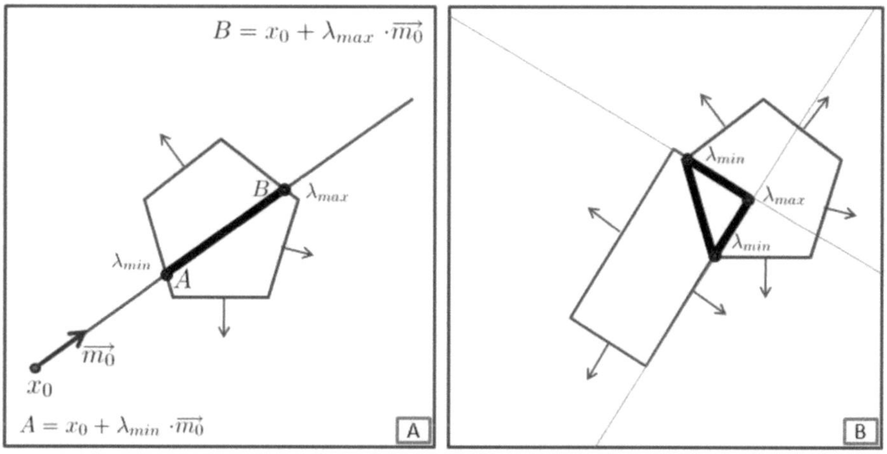

Fig. 4. A)Obtaining a segment of a line that satisfies the polygon's restrictions. B) Example of 3 segments that satisfy both sets of constraints of the polygons.

The general concept to make this evaluation is the following one: Given a line, defined by a point x_0 and a vector $\overrightarrow{m_0}$, we can compute the intersection between this line and a set of linear constraints by finding the intersection of the line with each single constraint and use them to determine the limits of the segment (figure 4A).
To verify the intersection between two polygons we use the previous method as follows. Given 2 polygons verify for each single constraint $n_i x \leq d_i$ if there is a segment on the line $n_i x = d_i$ (edges) which verifies both sets of constraints at the same time.
In figure 4B an example of an intersection between two polygons is shown, as we can see there exist three edges over the constraints that satisfies the restrictions of both polygons.

4.3 C-space and wavefront algorithm

Assuming we have the mathematical representation of all the involved objects and the capacity to identify if an intersection exist between two polygons, the following step is the formal construction of the C-space.
From the polygonal representation of the environment, the free space has to be computed, since the trajectory must belong to it. For this, we use a discrete representation of the configuration space. The C-space is the set of all possible configurations that an object (even articulated) can have in a given space (Lozano-Pérez, 1983).
Computing the precise limits of the free configurations is a difficult problem (Reif, 1979; Reif & Sharir, 1985). A very common representation of the C-space is to consider only the configurations on a grid, obtaining a discrete C-space. The configuration of the object is defined by the 3-tuple (x,y,θ) that represents the degrees of freedom of the box. The pair (x,y) is the position of a fixed point on the object, and θ is the orientation of the box and will take values in interval $[0,2\pi]$ (Figure 6) The main advantage of the C-space representation, is that the objet is reduced to a single point (the configuration), thus simplifying the motion planning.
Each voxel of the C-space 3D matrix represents a given configuration of the box. This matrix is filled using the collision detection algorithm in order to obtain a binary description of both free and occupied spaces. In the figure 5B, the binary layer corresponding to figure 5A is presented.

The precision of C-space is linked to the amount of configurations that were defined in the work area (discretization resolution), nevertheless, a greater precision will not only affect the computational times, it will also affect the storage requirements.
In order to obtain feasible trajectories, a virtual size expansion is applied to the object. Indeed, since the object must be pushed along the whole trajectory, a minimal distance between the object and the obstacles must be guaranteed, so the robots can always push the box suitably. In Figure 7 an example of the virtual object expansion is shown, as we can see, before start the calculation of the C-space, the object is expanded in such a way that the new size includes the robots size that surround it.

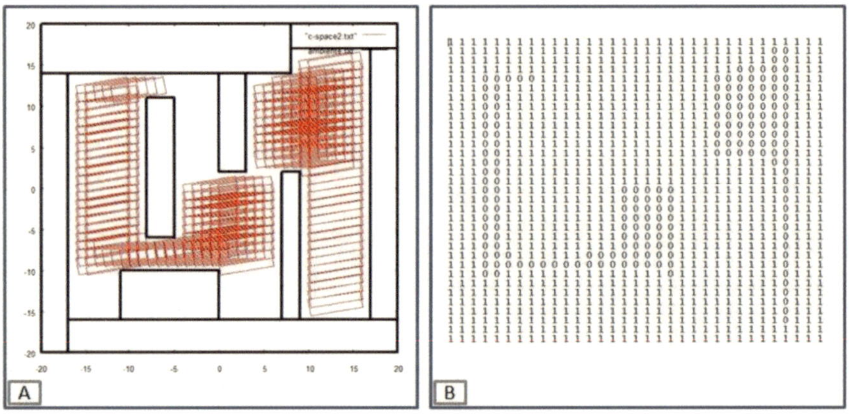

Fig. 5. A) Graphical representation of the C-space when the box is rotated 10 degrees; the positions where the box is not in collision are drawn. B) C-space binary layer that corresponds to figure A.

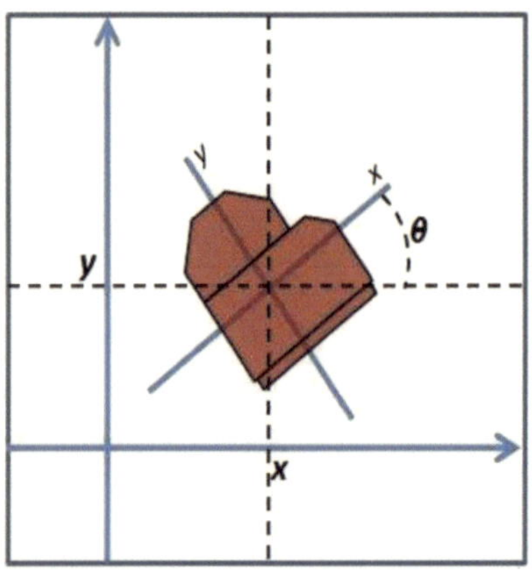

Fig. 6. Configuration of the object.

Once the C-space resolution has been established, the construction is made by verifying in each cell if a collision exist between the object and, at least, one of the obstacles of the environment. This action is made by testing each voxel [x][y][c] of the matrix by moving the object to the (x,y) position and rotate (c * resolution of rotation) degrees. Finally it is necessary to apply the collision detection function in order to verify if the configuration is collision-free ([x][y][c] = 0) or if a collision exists ([x][y][c] = 1) with any obstacle.

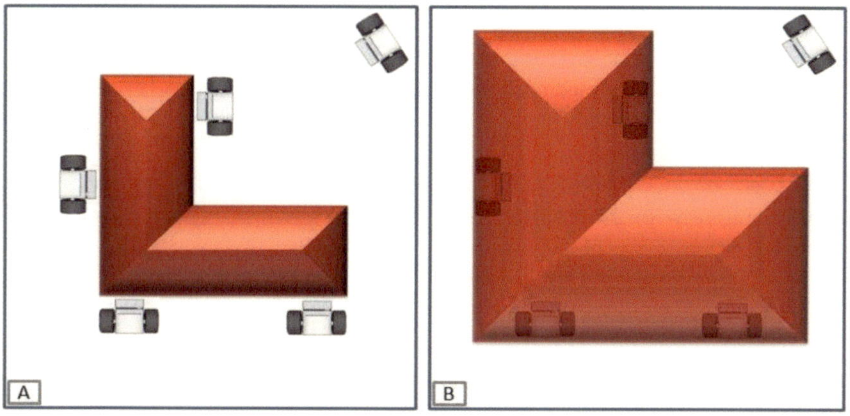

Fig. 7. Sample of the virtual object expansion.

Because there exists a direct relationship between solution quality and the size of the "C-space" (bigger size allows to find more precise paths) it is important define the correct size for the "C-space", however, there exist also a relationship between the size of "C-space" and computing requirements (a bigger size needs a larger number of intersect evaluations) then we need to improve the performance of the "C-space" construction by reducing the number of intersect evaluations in order to have better results in less time.

To reduce the number of intersect evaluations we apply a preprocessing based on the concept of " Bounding boxes" introduced by Cohen (Cohen et al., 1995) which basically works getting the square of minimum area that contains the object (polygon) within it. This action allows determine the possibility of having an intersection between two polygons and decide if is necessary to evaluate intersections with other objects or skip this step. This preprocessing technique has prove to perform well in practice (Suri et al., 1998) and in our tests showed his efficiency by reducing in some cases the 50 percent of the intersections evaluations.

As a result of this step we will have a binary 3D matrix that represents the discrete C-space, where each voxel represents if a given configuration of the object is in collision with the environment or not.

With a 3D-grid representation of the free configurations, is natural to apply an artificial potential field to compute the feasible paths. The wavefront algorithm is widely used for path planning of mobile robots: The algorithm determines if a free collision trajectory exists or not, unlike methods based on classical potential fields, the wavefront algorithm does not have local minima and it guarantees to find the shortest path between the origin and the destiny.

- The algorithm determines if a free collision trajectory exists or not.
- Unlike methods based on classical potential fields, the wavefront algorithm does not have local minima.
- This method guarantees to find the shortest path between the origin and the destiny under the chosen neighborhood criteria.

The construction of a wavefront, according to LaValle (LaValle, 2006), is made in the following way. Suppose that the minimum common cost between each state is i, and having a set of states organized in a wavefront, W_i. The start point of the wave front is W_0 and it represents the objective state X_G. The algorithm will assign the cost of optimal move of 1 for all the states that can be reached from W_0 in a single step. The states that receive cost of 1 can be

organized in a wavefront like W_1. The unexplored neighbors of W_1 will have an assigned cost of 2. This process will be repeated from i to $i+1$ until all the reachable states have been visited. All the unreachable states will be assigned with the value of $\phi(x) = \infty$. The optimal cost to move from a state to another one will be calculated in time $O(n)$, where n is the number of reachable states.
When the wavefront is computed, the robot must follow the descendent gradient selecting the neighboring state with the smaller cost, this process will be repeated until reaching the objective state X_G:

$$u^* = argmin_{u \in U(x)} \left\{ \phi(f(x,u)) \right\}$$

where $U(x)$ is the set of actions (movements) neighboring to the present state x towards which the robot can be moved. u^* represents the following state and $f(x,u)$ is the transition function of action for the action u applied to the state x.

4.4 Path generation

With an artificial potential field, there exist many different solutions to the object path planning problem. In order to find a well suited solution for the box-pushing problem we have developed three different heuristics to find trajectories where the number of robot reconfigurations are minimal. These strategies are based on the concept of "reaching measure". The reaching measure is basically the number of cells (voxels) of the C-space that are valid (decreasing value and free) following a specific direction. The path segment with the greatest reaching measure is used to construct the trajectory.

4.4.1 Trajectory computation with reaching measure (TCMR)

As was stated before, working with non specialized mobile robots (in pushing task) it is necessary, along the path, to modify their position respect to the box (reconfiguration) to be able to obtain a valid pushing position.
The reduction of robots reconfigurations throughout the trajectory, allows in first instance to guarantee an important reduction of time, simply because the change of pushing points is a process that needs some time to be completed. Another aspect that can be improved when the robots reconfigurations are reduced is the increase of the precision of the movements. The continuous movements of the robots around the box can increase the possibilities of having collisions among them, and of course, the increase of the odometry errors by the constant movement of the robots can affect the precision of the pushes.
Our first strategy is a greedy approach, trying to reduce as much as possible the number of robot reconfigurations using the concept of "reaching measure", choosing among the possible directions of movement from a given configuration, the one which allows to move closer to the goal configuration.
This heuristic is based on the conventional "wavefront algorithm" and works in the following way: Once the wavefront matrix is computed, starting from initial configuration, validate all the neighbors (north, south, east, west, up and down). If at least 2 neighbors had an smaller value than the value of the starting point, the next step would be to measure the reach of all the possible routes, following the direction of these neighbors. For instance, if we start from a defined point with a value of 99 and it has only two neighbors with smaller values, west with a value of 98 and up with a value also of 98, the following step is to evaluate and count the strictly decreasing cells in the up and west directions. Finally we compare the number of

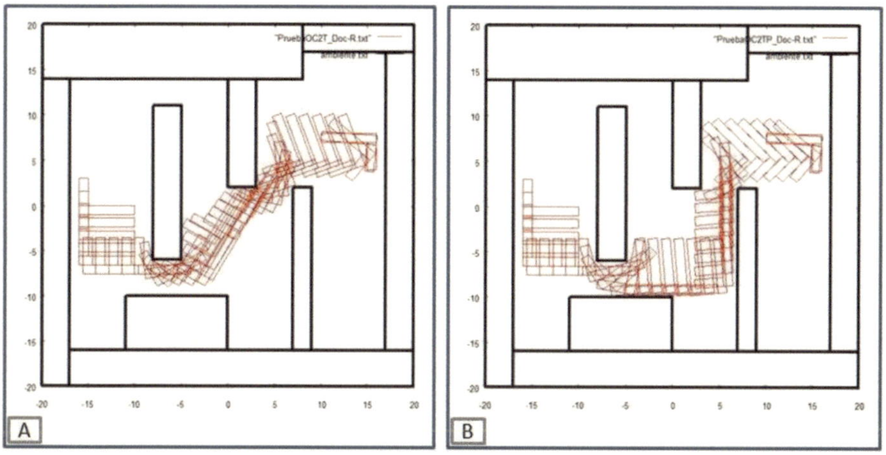

Fig. 8. A) Graphical representation of the box trajectory obtained without any heuristic to select the neighbors. B) Graphical representation of the box trajectory obtained with the proposed heuristic to reduce the reconfigurations.

squares in both directions and follow the one that had the greatest value (moving the robot closer to the goal).

In Figure 8A we can see a sample of a path obtained without using any heuristic, it was calculated by selecting the first cell neighbor that lead us closer to the objective. In Figure 8B we can appreciate another sample path but calculated using the proposed heuristic. If we compare both trajectories we can verify that using the proposed approach we can reduce the changes of the box direction and also reduce the number of required robot reconfigurations.

4.4.2 Trajectory computation with layer validation (TCLV)

Since the obtained trajectories are composed by vertical, horizontal movements and pure rotations, there may be some orientations that are best suitable for pushing than others, given the geometry of the box (e.g. 0, 90, 180 and 270 degrees for a rectangular box). This strategy is similar to the previous one, but the path is generated so these particular orientations of the box are prefered. This improvement will help to obtain a greater precision in the pushing task. Compared with the first heuristic (TCMR) that use the "reach measure" to reduce as most as possible the maneuvers of the object, this alternative uses again the "reach measure" but with some modifications that helps to construct paths having some specific object rotations.

The difference between "TCMR" and this alternative is that "TCLV" will repeat the "reach measure" every time the algorithm detects that it is being evaluated a cell that pass over a privileged layer. This action allows to find new longer path segments on certain layers in spite of following an specified direction. Another modification is to give an extra values to some layers (or even cells), this action helps even more to select some specific "C-space" layers.

Applying these changes helps to find alternative paths that in most cases uses the layers that we privileged, but the fact of place new measurement points and give extra values to some cells can increase (sensibly) the quantity of robot reconfigurations.

For example: If we were paced in a square that has 3 possible directions to follow: north, west and up and after making the neighbor measurement we found that the reach of the routes is: north 21, west 19 and up 11. If we do not privilege any layers clearly the route to follow would be the one that has the north direction. The proposed change is to validate if the route that is going by the superior layer pass through some of the privileged layers, if it occurs, the value can be increased. In the present implementation the value of the route is duplicated ($11 * 2 = 22$), that is why the route with up direction will be followed to construct the final route. With this, the algorithm can conclude that the trajectory can be pursued with the prefered orientation.

4.4.3 Route graph (RG)

The fist two approaches are greedy so in order to find better solutions, the third strategy uses a graph representation of possible trajectories. This change allows to evaluate more possible trajectories before selecting one. In this *route graph strategy*, each node represents a change of direction of the object. Within this graph, a search is done to identify the path with the minimal number of reconfigurations. In Figure 9, an example of the route graph obtained from a configuration space marked with the wavefront algorithm is shown.
The route graph is constructed as follows (c.f. Algorithm 1):

- Start from the initial configuration and add it as the root node n_i of the route graph.
- Compute the reaching measures for all possible directions of movement.
- The reachable configurations are added as nodes, linked to the root node.
- Steps 2 and 3 are repeated, for each of the new nodes, recursively.
- The construction of the route graph is finished when all the branches converge to the final configuration n_f.

Algorithm 1 "Route graph" strategy

```
Input: Wave front matrix and origin node n_i
Output: Path from n_i to n_f (if it exist)
OriginPos ← origin node n_i
Insert OriginPos node on node[0]
x ← 1
while node[x] ≠ ∅ do
  OriginPos ← position of node[x]
  for All the neighbors of node[x] do
    if Neighbor of node[x] is valid then
      dir ← direction to reach the neighbor of node[x]
      NeighborPos ← position of the neighbor of node[x]
      while Neighbor of NeighborPos on direction dir is valid do
        NeighborPos ← position of the neighbor of NeighborPos
      end while
      Insert node NeighborPos on node[]
    end if
  end for
  x++
end while
return Route graph path
Generate the path based on the final node of smaller depth
```

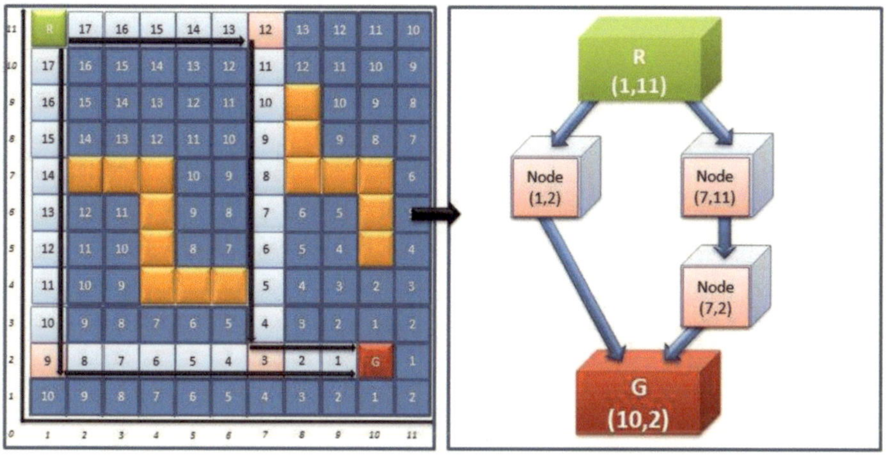

Fig. 9. Example of the route graph construction.

4.4.4 Modified A* algorithm (A*RR)

In order to realize the pertinent comparisons of the proposed heuristics, we implement a modified version of the A-Star algorithm (A*). This algorithm was presented in 1968 by Hart (Hart et al., 1968), and is extensively used for path planning.

The A* algorithm combines the capacities of the Dijkstra algorithm with some characteristics of the breadth-first search (BFS) algorithms, since it looks for the shortest routes like Dijkstra does and in addition it includes an heuristic as in the BFS to quickly converge to the objective. The efficiency secret of the A* algorithm is that it combines pieces of Dijkstra's information (favoring the selection of nodes near the origin) with BFS's information (favoring nodes that are close to their destination). In the A* standard terminology $g(n)$ represents the cumulative cost of the path from the initial position to any node n, and $h(n)$ represents the estimated cost by the heuristics from n to the final position. The algorithm balance the two values as it moves from origin to destination and maintains two lists: one open and one closed where the closed list stores the nodes that have been already evaluated, and the open list contains the nodes that have not been. Each time that the algorithm starts a new cycle, it moves the current position to the node n that has the lower $f(n)$ ($f(n) = g(n) + h(n)$).

The alternative A* heuristic that we propose works by replacing the function $g(n)$, which now will have an additional cost associated to the amount of changes of direction and not to the distance cost from the origin to n (as happen in the classical A* heuristic).

In the Figure 10 we can compare two paths that uses the two different A* heuristics. In Figure 10.A, we shown a route obtained by using the classical A* heuristic. In Figure 10.B we can see the resulting path using the A* alternative cost function. As we can see, the classical heuristic built a shorter trajectory but it requires 18 changes of direction to transport the object, while the modified A* algorithm finds a path with less reconfigurations (only 9), but longer.

5. Tests and results

In this section we will tackle the related aspects to the final implementation of the proposed methods and we will present the obtained results of the testing set.

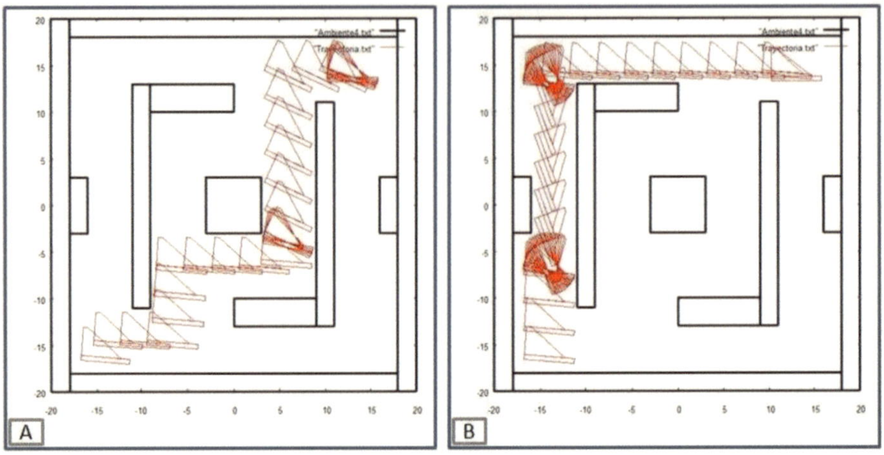

Fig. 10. A) Path planning with classical A* algorithm. B) Path planning with modified A* algorithm.

5.1 Description of the tests

The total set of tests was constituted by the computation of 2539 random routes divided in 5 different test environments and 2 different resolutions for the C-space. For the tests we implemented 7 heuristics: our 3 proposed heuristics, as well as 4 classical heuristic for comparative effects. The implemented heuristics are the following:

1. Wavefront selecting randomly the neighbor (WRN): Each time it moves from a cell, this algorithm randomly select the neighbor to follow (from all possibles).
2. Wavefront with predefined evaluation of neighbor (WPN): Each time it moves from a cell, this algorithm evaluates the possible neighbors following a predetermined order and select the first valid.
3. Classical A* algorithm (A*C): It uses the classical heuristic to reduce distance.
4. Modified A* algorithm (A*RR): It uses the proposed A* heuristic to reduce maneuvers.
5. Trajectory computation with reaching measure (TCMR)
6. Trajectory computation with layer validation (TCLV)
7. Route graph (RG)

The heuristics 1, 2 and 3 are oriented to reduce distance and the rest to the reduce reconfigurations. To cover a wide range of test cases were developed five different environments that vary in complexity, number of obstacles and in the percentage of free space (Figure 11).

The first test environment (Figure 11(a)) was designed to test that the routes are able to displace the object while the box is going away from the target area. This is useful to evaluate that the heuristics do not fall into local minima.

The second (Figure 11(b)) and third environments (Figure 11(c)) were designed with narrow corridors to test that despite having a smaller number of possible solutions, the heuristics are able to construct valid routes. It is also important to mention that this type of environments are very complex to solve by some techniques, for example those based on Probabilistic Road Maps (PRM).

The 4th environment (Figure 11(d)) is symmetric and with a higher percentage of free space. This environment was created to compare the strategies, those that reduces the distance against those that reduce the maneuvers. The central corridors allow the construction of shorter routes, but more complex.
In the fifth environment (Figure 11(e)) were added small obstacles and placed uniformly on the map, this was designed to evaluate the strategies in environments that have multiple solutions.
The chosen metrics to compare the strategies were:

- Number of reconfigurations: After the paths were computed, the number of changes of direction were counted. This value represents the number of necessary robot reconfigurations for the trajectory.
- Time: Related to the computing time required by each heuristic to find the paths.

The statistic metrics used to analysis the results are:

- Average value
- Max value
- Minimum value
- Standard deviation

It is important to state that for our approach it is more attractive obtain trajectories with a smaller number of direction changes. Tables 1 and 2 shows the results for one of the set of tests.

Method	Average	Max val	Min val	Standard dev.
WRN	22.08	51	4	11.02
WPN	12.16	27	2	8.06
A*C	13.1	40	3	8.65
A*RR	6.98	14	3	2.29
TCRM	5.84	12	2	2.39
TCLV	5.94	13	2	2.4
GR	5.2	10	2	1.92

Table 1. Comparison of path planning methods by number of reconfigurations

As we can see (Table 1), the heuristics "WRN", "WPN" and "A*C" were not competitive compared with the other four strategies. Nevertheless, this situation is congruent because these heuristics do not include any strategy to reduce the number of changes of direction, which is the case of the other 4 strategies.
The results show that the "GR" have the best overall results, however, it was overcome by the heuristic "A*RR" in the situations where to find the paths that have the minimum number or reconfigurations it is necessary to move the object away from the objective (see Figure 10). This situation is consistent because the proposed heuristics use the wavefront matrix to build their solutions, then it is impossible for the heuristics find the trajectories that moves the object away from goal.
In Table 2 we show the computing time needed by the heuristics to build a path. The time values in the table are in milliseconds.
The strategies bases on "A*" algorithms were affected in computing time, this is because they must handled and stored many information to calculate the trajectories. As we can see in

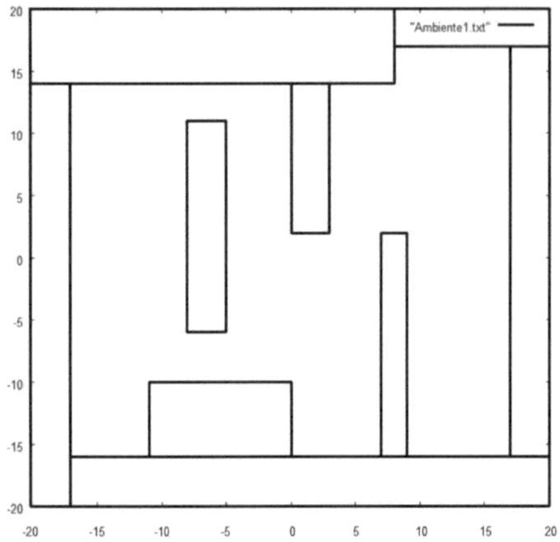

(a) Environment 1 (44.4% free space)

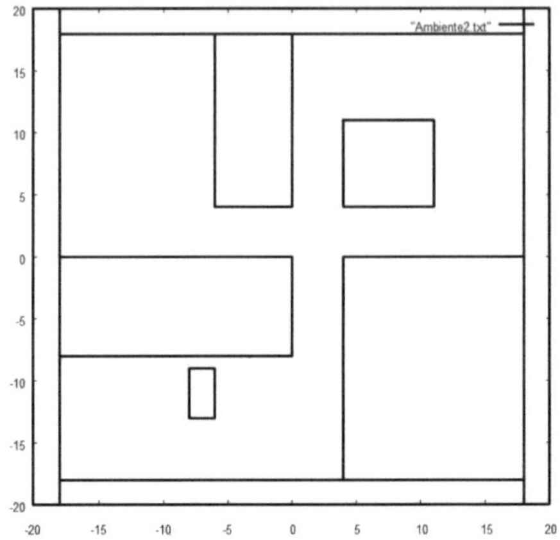

(b) Environment 2 (49% free space)

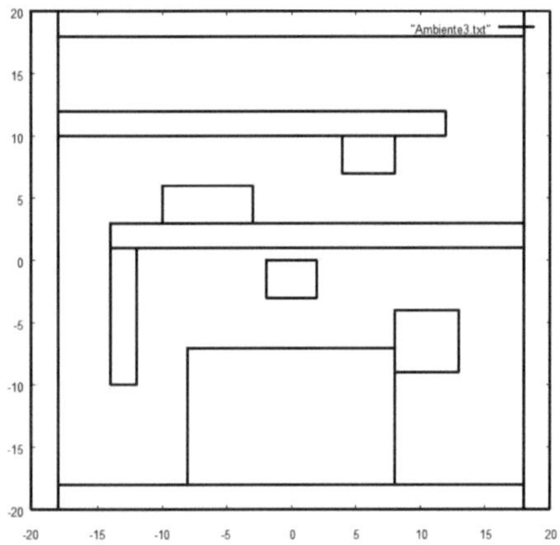

(c) Environment 3 (56.4% free space)

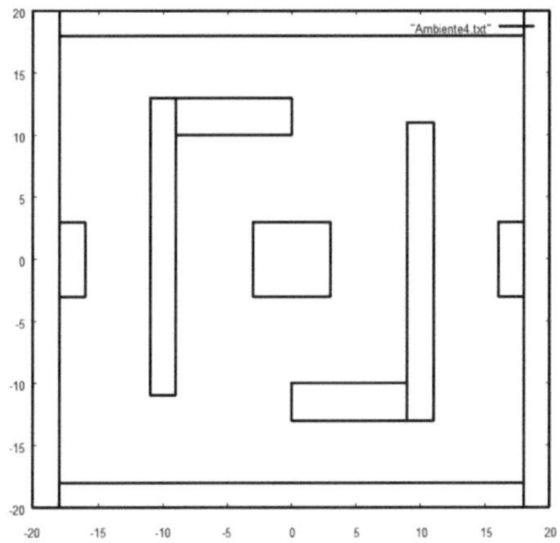

(d) Environment 4 (67.9% free space)

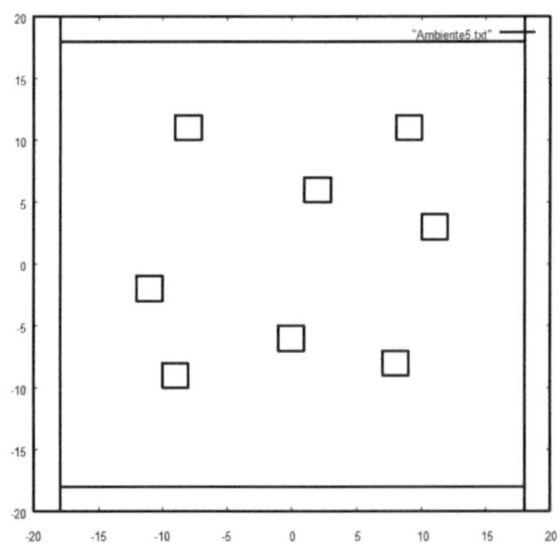

(e) Environment 5 (79% free space)

Fig. 11. All test environments used in tests.

Method	Average	Max val	Min val	Standard dev.
WRN	375.08	377	375	0.34
WPN	375	375	375	0
A*C	24948.3	272625	1	53531.45
A*RR	1174.34	10062	1	2109.2
TCRM	375.02	376	375	0.14
TCLV	375.02	376	375	0.14
GR	421	438	406	9.78

Table 2. Comparison of path planning methods by computing time (*ms*)

Table 2 the best computing times correspond to the heuristics "WRN", "WPN", "TCRM" and "TCVL", in that order. In this case the results favor the greedy strategies because they do not store any information and they just make desitions based on local information. Nevertheless, the time for the heuristic "GR" was very competitive and give better results for the number of reconfigurations. Thus, the "GR" strategy shows the best compromise between computing time and solution quality.

5.2 Discussion and conclusions

According to the numerical experiments, we can conclude that, although exist situations in which the "A*RR" algorithm can obtain trajectories with smaller number of changes of direction (thus, better results), the proposed heuristics "TCRM" , "TCVL" and particularly the "GR" obtain a better balance between quality of the solution and the required computing effort.
It is important to emphasize that the specialization of heuristic "GR" had a slight increase in the computing time. Nevertheless, we can conclude that the balance between number of reconfigurations, length of trajectories and computing time clearly benefits to heuristic "Route Graph".

6. Future work

In future works the resulting paths will be used to determine (by an optimization strategy) the best combination of robots and pushing points in each sub trajectory to reduce the travel distance for each individual robot during the reconfiguration phase.
Also, we would like to consider the problem of advantageous location of the robots, in order to place the robots which are not participating in a sub trajectory in a favorable position for another sub trajectory. Our main goal is to obtain a coordination strategy able to conclude the task in an efficient way.

7. References

Cohen, J. D., Lin, M. C., Manocha, D. & Ponamgi, M. (1995). I-collide: an interactive and exact collision detection system for large-scale environments, pp. 189–ff.

E. Parker, L. & Tang, F. (2006). Building multirobot coalitions through automated task solution synthesis, *Proceedings of the IEEE* 94(7): 1289–1305.

Gene, E. J., Tong-Ying, J., Jun-Da, H., Chien-Min, S. & Chih-Yung, C. (2005). A fast path planning algorithm for piano mover's problem on raster, *Advanced Intelligent Mechatronics. Proceedings, 2005 IEEE/ASME International Conference on* pp. 522–527.

Gerkey, B. P. & Mataric, M. J. (2002). Pusher-watcher: An approach to fault-tolerant tightly-coupled robot coordination, *Robotics and Automation, 2002. Proceedings. ICRA '02. IEEE International Conference on* 1: 464–469.

Gerkey, B. P., Mataric, M. J. & Simsarian, K. (1995). Cooperative multi-robot box-pushing, *Proceedings, IROS-95* pp. 556–561.

Guilherme A. S., P., Vijay, K., John, S., Camilo J., T. & Mario F. M., C. (2002). Cooperative transport of planar objects by multiple mobile robots using object closure, *in Experimental Robotics VIII* pp. 275–284.

Gupta, A. & Huang, W. (2003). A carrying task for nonprehensile mobile manipulators, *Intelligent Robots and Systems, 2003. (IROS 2003). Proceedings. 2003 IEEE/RSJ International Conference on* pp. 2896–2901.

Hart, P., Nilsson, N. & Raphael, B. (1968). A formal basis for the heuristic determination of minimum cost paths, *Systems Science and Cybernetics, IEEE Transactions on* 2: 100–107.

Inoue, Y., Tohge, T. & Iba, H. (2007). Cooperative transportation system for humanoid robots using simulation-based learning, *Appl. Soft Comput.* 7(1): 115–125.

Jed, L., Mark, R., Bruce, R. D. & Donald, P. G. (1990). Real-time robot motion planning using rasterizing computer graphics hardware, *SIGGRAPH '90: Proceedings of the 17th annual conference on Computer graphics and interactive techniques* pp. 327–335.

Kovac, K., Zivkovic, I. & Dalbelo Basic, B. (2004). Simulation of multi-robot reinforcement learning for box-pushing problem, *Electrotechnical Conference, 2004. MELECON 2004. Proceedings of the 12th IEEE Mediterranean* 2: 603– 606.

LaValle, S. M. (2006). *Planning Algorithms*, Cambridge. Available on `http://planning.cs.uiuc.edu/`.

Li, Y. & Chen, X. (2004). Modeling and simulation of a swarm of robots for box-pushing task, *12th Mediterranean Conference on Control and Automation, Kusadasi, Aydin, Turkey* .

Lozano-Pérez, T. (1983). Spatial planning: A configuration space approach, *Computers, IEEE Transactions on* pp. 108–120.

MIYOSHI, T., KAWAKAMI, S. & TERASHIMA, K. (2008). Cooperative transportation system for humanoid robots using simulation-based learning, *Journal of Mechanical Systems for Transportation and Logistics* 1(1): 134–145.

Muñoz Melendez, A. & Drogoul, A. (2004). Analyzing multi-robot box-pushing, *Avances en la Ciencia de la Computación. Memoria de los Talleres del Quinto Encuentro Internacional de Computación ENC'04. Universidad de Colima* 1: 530–539.

Reif, J. H. (1979). Complexity of the mover's problem and generalizations, *Annual IEEE Symposium on Foundations of Computer Science* pp. 421–427.

Reif, J. & Sharir, M. (1985). Motion planning in the presence of moving obstacles, *26th Annual IEEE Symposium on Foundations of Computer Science* pp. 144–154.

Suri, S., Hubbard, P. M. & Hughes, J. F. (1998). Analyzing bounding boxes for object intersection.

Wang, Y. & W. de Silva, C. (October 2006). Multi-robot box-pushing single-agent q-learning vs team q-learning, *Intelligent Robots and Systems, 2006 IEEE/RSJ International Conference on* pp. 3694–3699.

Wang, Z. & Kumar, V. (2002). Object closure and manipulation by multiple cooperating mobile robots, *Robotics and Automation, 2002. Proceedings. ICRA '02. IEEE International Conference on* 1: 394–399.

Yamada, S. & Saito, J. (2001). Adaptive action selection withouth explicit communication for multi-robot box-pushing, *Systems, Man and Cybernetics, Part C: Applications and Reviews, IEEE Transactions on* 31(3): 398–404.

16

Time-Invariant Motion Planner in Discretized C-Spacetime for MRS

Fabio M. Marchese
Università degli Studi di Milano-Bicocca
Italy

1. Introduction

In this work, a new class of planners for MRS is introduced: Time-invariant Motion Planners, a class of planners that operate indifferently in forward or in backward planning-time direction. Thanks to the specular symmetry (with respect to the timeline) of the motion operators, the planning algorithm can operate both in top-down way (from the goal to the starting pose) or vice versa bottom-up (from the starting pose to the goal) addressing different types of problems.
The planner underlying mechanism is an artificial field over a lattice (CAs), where the robots are shrunk to points subjected to attractive and repulsive forces (Lagrangian mechanics). Building a regular manifold of potential values and following its minimum valleys, a trajectory in the spacetime is extracted, corresponding to a robot movement (geometrization of the motion). The potential manifold is constructed on the base of the motion operators. These are the atomic (non interruptible) moves over the space and the time lattice and the set of all of them represents the entire kinematics of a robot. Every robot has its own set and there are contemporarily robots with different kinematics. The manifold emerges from the interaction of the set of operators, the world model and the representation of the robots' shapes. Using a discretized C-Spacetime, the definition of velocity of a robot becomes an intrinsical (geometrical) property emerging from the interaction between the motion operators and the spacetime.
It is fundamental for the correctness of the planning to take care of the actual robot occupancy during an atomic move to avoid collisions with other robots/obstacles. It derives the definition of *Motion Silhouette*, a conceptual evolution of the *Sweeping Silhouette* (2002), which is itself an evolution of the Obstacles Enlargement concept by Lozano-Pérez in 1983. To avoid the problem of the swapping of two robots, it is important to take in consideration of the well-known Shannon's Theorem in the discretization phase of the C-Spacetime and consequently in the definition of *Motion Silhouette*.

2. Multi robots systems motion planning

The basic problem is how to make a flock of robots to navigate coordinately to achieve a common task. The robot(s) navigation can be shortly described as follow (question, process, result):

1. Where have I been?	Map making	➢ World Representation
2. Where am I?	Localization	➢ Robot(s) Pose(s)
3. Where am I going?	Task/Mission planning	➢ Goal pose(s)
4. What's the best way there?	Path/Motion planning	➢ Trajectory/Movement
5. How am I going to get there?	Path/Movement exec.	➢ Moves/Motion Commands

Therefore, Multi Robots Systems Motion Planning is a phase of the overall MRS Coordinated Navigation problem.
Many approaches have been proposed to solve the Path/Motion Planning problem for single and multiple robots in the last thirty years. A model-based solution has been proposed since 1979 (Lozano-Pérez & Wesley, 1979, Lozano-Pérez, 1983) where a geometrical description of the environment is given.
To address the problem in a dynamical world, some authors proposed the Artificial Potential Fields Methods. Khatib first proposed a method for the real-time collision avoidance problem of a manipulator in a continuous space (Khatib, 1986). Jahanbin and Fallside introduced a wave propagation algorithm in the Configuration Space (C-Space) on discrete maps (*Distance Transform,* Jahanbin & Fallside, 1988). In the '90s, Barraquand et al. used the Numerical Potential Field Technique over the C-Space to build a generalized Voronoi Diagram (Barraquand et al., 1992). Zelinsky extended the *Distance Transform* to the *Path Transform* (Zelinsky, 1994). Marchese in 1996 first introduced the Cellular Automata paradigm in robot path planning problem (Marchese, 1996) for non-holonomic rototranslating robots. Tzionas et al. in (Tzionas et al., 1997) described a VLSI implementation for a CA based algorithm for diamond-shaped translating holonomic robot in a static environment. For multiple robot motion planning, in (Warren, 1990) the coordination of robots is solved using a discretized 3D C-Spacetime (2D Workspace plus Time) for translating robots with same shapes (only square and circle). In (LaValle & Hutchinson, 1998) the authors apply the concepts of the Game Theory and multi-objective optimization to the centralized and decoupled planning. A solution in the C-Spacetime is proposed in (Bennewitz et al., 2001), where the authors use a decoupled and prioritized path planning in which they repeatedly reorder the robots to try to find a solution. It can be proven that these approaches are not complete.

3. MRS motion planning in a discretized world

A MRS is a set (a flock, a team) of robots with a common task. Robots not sharing the same task are insulated or own to different MRSs with different tasks. The condivision of a task is an important issue: it implies that the robots access to the same resources.
In particular, MRS Motion Planning is a concurrent task, where the shared resource is the common workspace.
In this work, we want to design a motion planner for a set of heterogeneous mobile robots, in order to determine the motions of mobile agents and able to avoid collisions with (statical or dynamical with a designed movement) obstacles and with other robots.
We have adopted Cellular Automata as formalism for merging a grid model of the world (Occupancy Grid) with the C-Spacetime of multiple robots and Artificial Potential Fields Methods, with the purpose to give a simple and fast solution.

3.1 Prioritized planning

While the path planning problem for a single robot has a polynomial complexity, in 1979 Reif established that the problem for a team of robots is PSPACE-hard (Reif, 1979) which implies it is NP-hard. Canny later established that the problem lies in the PSPACE and therefore the general motion planning problem is PSPACE-complete (Canny, 1988). Even a Warehouseman's problem on a discrete 2D grid is PSPACE-hard (Culberson, 1998).

In general, for a N rigid robots problem the number of dimensions of the C-Spacetime would be: $C_{ST} = C^1 \times C^2 \times \cdots \times C^N \times T$ where C^i is the C-Space of the ith robot. If the robots are moving on a 2D surface (manifold), the C-Space of a single robot is $\mathbb{R}^2 \times SO(2)$, thus the overall C-Spacetime has $3\,N + 1$ dimensions. Even for small MRS, the cardinality of the space makes the problem untreatable. Therefore it is necessary to reduce the number of dimensions, adopting the Prioritized Planning technique (a description in LaValle, 2006).

It is a case of Decoupled Planning for multiple robots, where the interaction robot to robot is ignored in the first phase of motion design. Then the interactions are taken into account to constrain the options available. The problem arises when no option remains, because this approach is not reversible, thus losing the completeness. The typical example is shown in Fig. 1. The two robots have to exchange their positions in the corridor. The red one has the highest priority and has to pass first, occluding the lateral space that would be useful for the green robot to overtake the red one.

Nevertheless, the Prioritized Planning is very practical and solves most of the situations.

In the prioritized approach, an order of robot planning (*priority*) is given, starting to plan with the high-priority robot first. Robots with lower priority view the higher-priority robots as moving obstacles with designed trajectories.

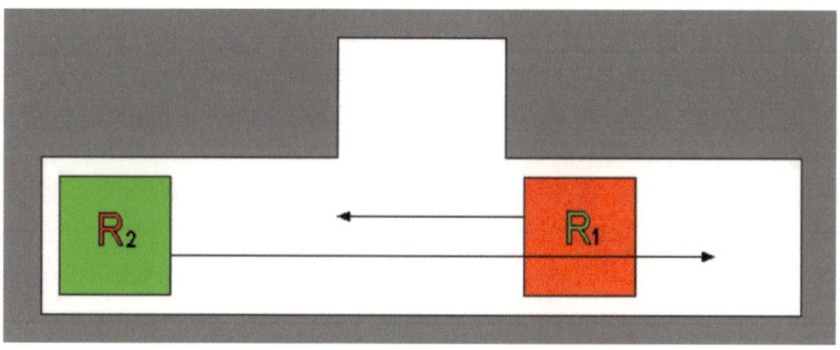

Fig. 1. Priority planning counterexample: red robot moves first

In Fig. 2 is shown an example of the approach in the Spacetime: the blue object is a static obstacle, while two robots (red and green) turn around it, leaving a helicoidal temporal trace.

The planning phases are:

1. Establish an order of priority for the robots.
2. Plan the motion for the robot with the highest priority not yet planned (single robot motion planning).
3. Using the Coordination Space, select one collision-free movement from the set of all movements found.
4. Trace the robot (mark the configurations as not available) in the Coordination Space (the robot becomes a dynamical obstacle for all the other robots with lower priority).
5. Goto step 2 until the robot with the lowest priority has been planned.

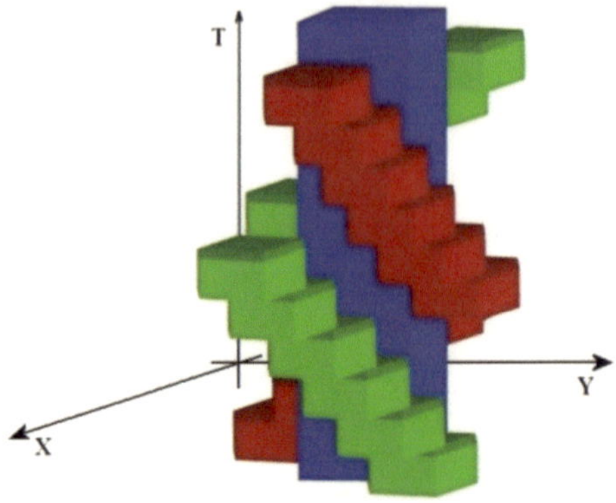

Fig. 2. Spatiotemporal traces of three objects: a static obstacle (blue) and two robots (red and green)

If no collision-free movement can be found for a robot, many recovery strategies can be adopted. The simpler is to eliminate the robot from the space and from the problem. Another strategy consists in considering the robot as a static object standing in the starting pose (as the blue object in Fig. 2). A more complex strategy is to let the robot at the starting pose, with the final goal to stay in that pose, but reducing its priority. In this case, the robot can move away if another robot (with a higher priority) has to pass in that pose, and then it get back to the initial pose.
The Motion Planning components needed for a well-posed problem are:

- World description
- MRS description: shapes & kinematics of all the robot
- Problem description: starting events (timed poses) and goal events of all the robots.

In this case, we use a discretized description of all the components.

3.2 Discrete world representation

The world representation consists in a Regular Decomposition map, i.e. a grid of cells, marked as full or empty (Occupancy grid). Because of the temporal evolution of a dynamical world, even the world map is a 2D workspace with a discrete time axis (Fig. 3).

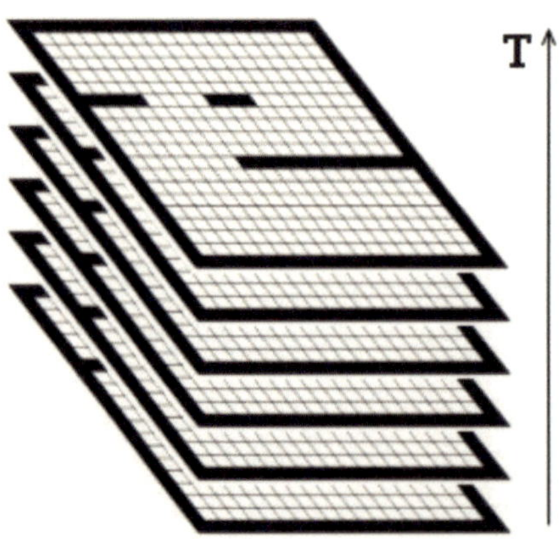

Fig. 3. Spatiotemporal world representation

From this representation derives the most important data structure: the C-Spacetime which, in our case, coincides with the Coordination Space. It is a 4D discretized space composed by the 2D workspace, the orientation axis and the time axis, and it is fundamental for the prioritized planning.

3.3 Robot discrete representation: the motion silhouette

In Regular Decomposition world models, the robot is often represented as a point (usually the robot cinematic center) as in the Lagrangian mechanics, a point moving from one free cell to a neighbor free one. To take into account of its real extension, the well-known technique of enlarging the obstacles by a given quantity has been considered.
Lozano-Pérez et al. at the end of the '70s first introduced this method using the robot maximum radius and approximating its shape to a cylinder with the consequence of losing a great amount of space around the obstacles and a loss of executable trajectories. Then they improved it using an anisotropic enlargement (Lozano-Pérez & Wesley, 1983), i.e. using a different obstacles enlargement for each robot orientation, to solve (only partially) the problem for robots with asymmetric shapes: counter-examples (fig.4.c) can be found in which the robot still collides with obstacles (a peg in the example) due to the sliding of its silhouette between two consecutive poses. In 2002 we proposed a different and more precise approach to address this problem (Marchese, 2002), introducing the *Sweeping Silhouette* defined as the whole space covered during the movement between two consecutive poses (Fig.4.d).

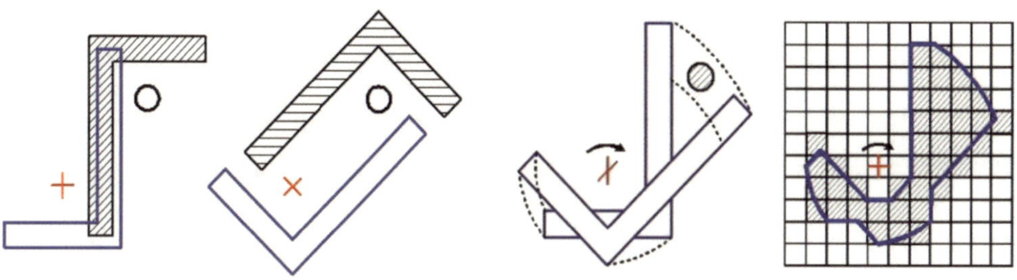

a) b) c) d)

Fig. 4. Silhouette sweeping: a-b) expanded obstacle (hatched) for two robot poses (white); c) a counter-example due to a coarse discretization of the orientation; d) *Sweeping Silhouette* (hatched cells) obtained sweeping the robot silhouette between the two poses

The *Sweeping Silhouette* is not sufficient in a spatiotemporal representation: it is necessary a finer representation that takes into account of the position of the robot in every time slice during an atomic movement. The problem is similar to the previous one that brought to define the *Sweeping Silhouette*: a coarse discretization of the time axis could result in undesired effects. For example, two thin and fast robots could swap their positions between two time ticks, passing one through each other. In the same way, a small robot could pass through a thin wall (tunneling).
The necessity of a finer modeling of the motion carries to the definition of a new feature: the *Motion Silhouette*. It is a stack (a sequence) of silhouettes along the time, modeling an atomic move of the robot (e.g. in Fig. 6). Every move has a corresponding *motion silhouette*, or the *motion silhouette* is a conceptual extension of the move where the shape and the physical size of the robot are considered.

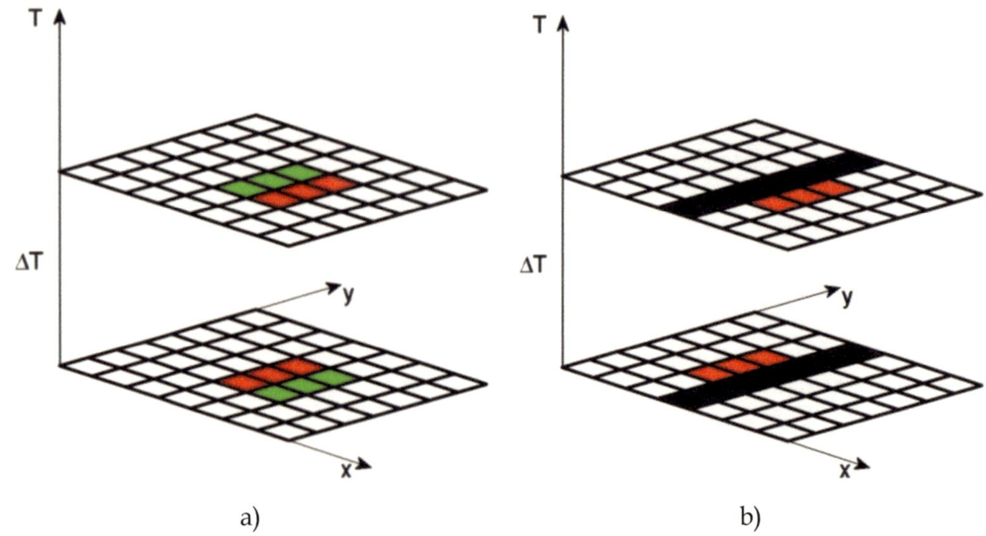

Fig. 5. Examples of undesired effects: a) robots swapping (red move (+1, 0, 0, ΔT), green move (-1, 0, 0, ΔT)); b) robot passing through the wall (red move (+2, 0, 0, ΔT))

To be consistent with the Shannon's Theorem it is sufficient to apply a sampling of the time at a twice frequency, i.e., the timeline must have a time unit half of the other timelines. In particular, the twice sampling has to be applied in the space where the collisions are detected: the Coordination Space. This guarantees an adequate representation of all the obstacles along the time, static (e.g., walls) and dynamical (e.g., other robots, opening doors, etc.). This assumption also ensures to avoid the problem of Fig. 5 of robots tunneling the walls or other robot through.

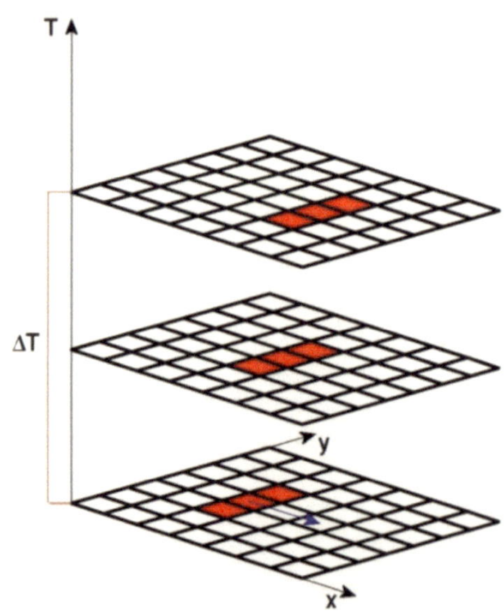

Fig. 6. The *Motion Silhouette* for the translational move (+2, 0, 0, ΔT))

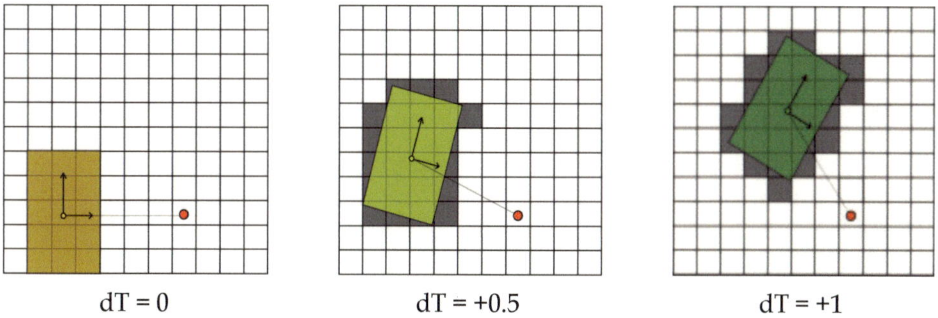

Fig. 7. The *Motion Silhouette* for a rototranslation

3.4 Robot discrete kinematics: the spatiotemporal discrete move

To define properly the behavior of a robot in a discretized world is mandatory to define accurately its kinematics. A discretized kinematics is a set of atomic moves defined on the base of single moves along the coordinate axes.

In a discretized spatiotemporal space Z^4 for a robot moving on a 2D manifold, the definition of *spatiotemporal move* is the 4-tuple: $(\Delta x, \Delta y, \Delta\theta, \Delta t)$, where Δ is a finite variation, $(\Delta x, \Delta y) \in Z^2$, $\Delta\theta \in S^1$, $\Delta t \in Z$ and with the obvious constraint $\Delta t > 0$ (an example in Fig. 8).

This definition has two main interpretations:

- $(\Delta x, \Delta y, \Delta\theta)$ are finite increments of the spatial coordinates during the finite time interval Δt. It entails the following space metrics Δs:

$$\text{move} \cong \frac{(\Delta x, \Delta y, \Delta \theta)}{\Delta t} \quad \Rightarrow \quad \Delta s^2 = \Delta x^2 + \Delta y^2 + r^2 \cdot \Delta\theta^2$$

- $(\Delta x, \Delta y, \Delta\theta, \Delta t)$ are finite increments of the spatiotemporal coordinates, inducing the following metrics:

$$\text{move} \cong (\Delta x, \Delta y, \Delta\theta, \Delta t) \Rightarrow \Delta S^2 = \Delta x^2 + \Delta y^2 + r^2 \cdot \Delta\theta^2 + v_\tau{}^2 \cdot \Delta t^2 = \Delta s^2 + v_\tau{}^2 \cdot \Delta t^2$$

Where ΔS is the "distance" between two events of the spacetime, r is a dimensional constant, v_τ is the "speed" of spontaneous translation along the time axis.

It is easier to see it if considering a robot standing in a place (a static object), then the *temporal speed* results to be:

$$\text{Move} \cong (0,\ 0,\ 0,\ \Delta t) \qquad \Delta S^2 = v_\tau{}^2 \cdot \Delta t^2 \qquad |v_\tau| = \sqrt{\Delta S^2 / \Delta t^2}$$

Because of this definition of *spatiotemporal move*, the movement of a rigid body becomes a trajectory in the spacetime executed by means of a sequence of finite moves, and where the necessity to indicate the speed disappears (it becomes an intrinsic factor), thus we have the concept of geometrization of the movements.

The speed is computed as usual, but it is a rational value:

$$\Delta s^2 = \Delta x^2 + \Delta y^2 + r^2 \cdot \Delta\theta^2 \qquad |v| = \left|\frac{\Delta s}{\Delta t}\right| = \sqrt{\frac{\Delta x^2 + \Delta y^2 + r^2 \cdot \Delta\theta^2}{\Delta t^2}} = \sqrt{v_x^2 + v_y^2 + r^2\omega^2}$$

For example, (+2, 0, 0, +1) is a move with double speed (x direction) or (+1, 0, 0, +2) represent a move at a half speed with respect to normalized units.

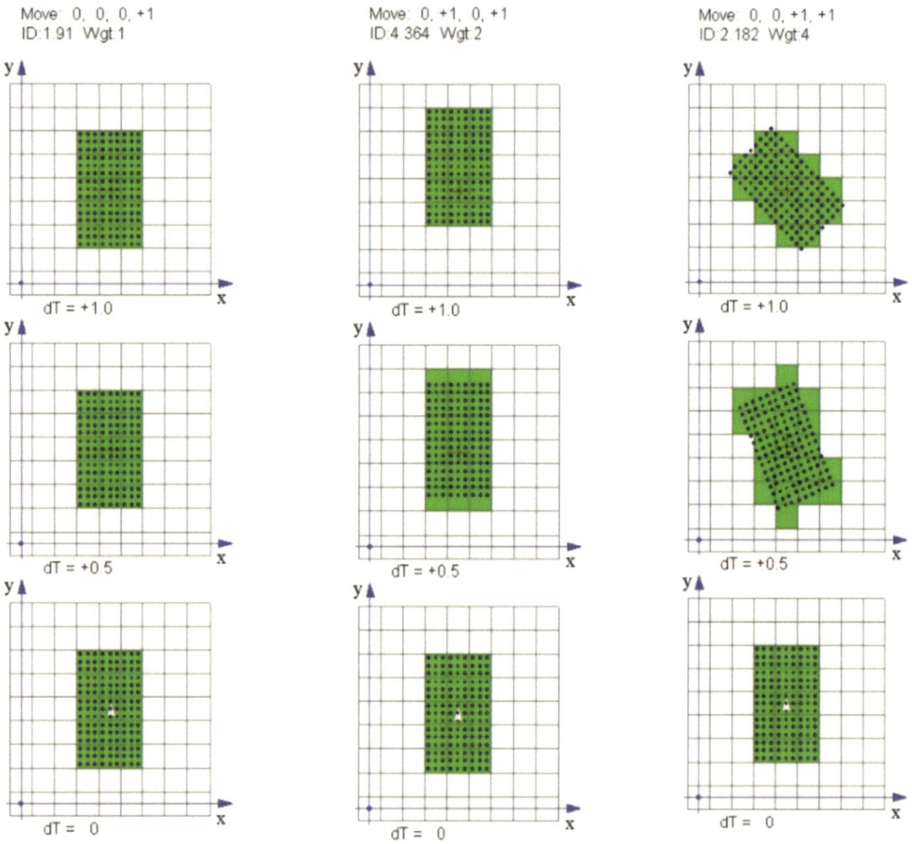

a) Move (0, 0, 0, +1) - a standing robot

b) Move (0, +1, 0, +1) - robot moving forward along y direction

c) Move (0, 0, +1, +1) - robot turning left

Fig. 8. An example of three moves for a rectangular robot

3.5 T-invariant planning and dual motion planning problem

First we have to define the *move dualization* operation. It is thought to simplify the top-down planning (from the goal pose to the starting pose). Every move of the kinematics is dualized inverting the sign of each component of the *spatiotemporal move* (see Fig. 9).

$$\text{Move} \cong (\Delta x,\ \Delta y,\ \Delta\theta,\ \Delta t) \ \Rightarrow\ \text{dualMove} \cong (-\Delta x,\ -\Delta y,\ -\Delta\theta,\ -\Delta t)$$

The dual kinematics is the set of all the dual moves computed from the original kinematics. Using the dual moves, it is easy to plan a movement from the goal to the start. It is a top-down planning or backward planning, but using the dual moves it becomes a forward planning (bottom-up) where the "bottom" is the goal and the "up" is the starting pose. Thus it is easy to solve the dual problem as it would be a forward planning.

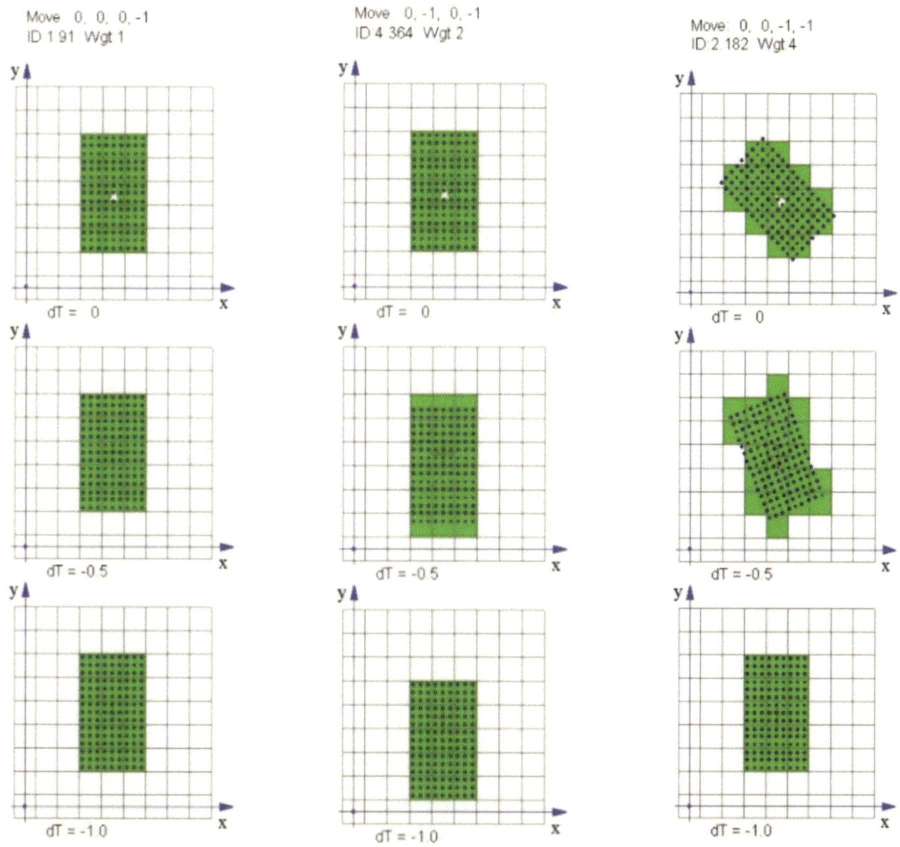

a) dualMove (0, 0, 0, -1) - a standing robot

b) Move (0, -1, 0, -1) - backward move along y & t direction

c) Move (0, 0, -1, -1) - right turning and backward along time direction

Fig. 9. Examples of the dual moves of Fig. 8

Exchanging the start with the goal and dualizing the two sets of moves we have the dual problem (Fig. 10). To be able to solve even this problem we should relax a constraint: we must consider that moves with $\Delta t < 0$ have to be admissible. It could seem quite strange that a body could run backward in the past, but it is only a logical operation of remapping the original problem to the dual problem. In any case, we do not intend to affirm that the robot could navigate back in the Time! Rather, it would seem as a kind of retrograde motion, but in the real spacetime any robot will always move forward in the Time.

If we relax the constraint $\Delta t > 0$, and we admit any *spatiotemporal move* (Δx, Δy, $\Delta \theta$, Δt) with any sign of delta, the set of moves is said to be closed under the dualization operation. Thus the Moves set and the dualMoves set belongs to the same superset that it will be called *dMoves set*.

The definition of the *dMoves set* makes any motion planning problem and any dual motion planning problem the same problem embedded in the same space: the C-Spacetime. They are both solved with the same algorithm, unifying them in a unique problem: *the motion planning problem over the C-Spacetime.*

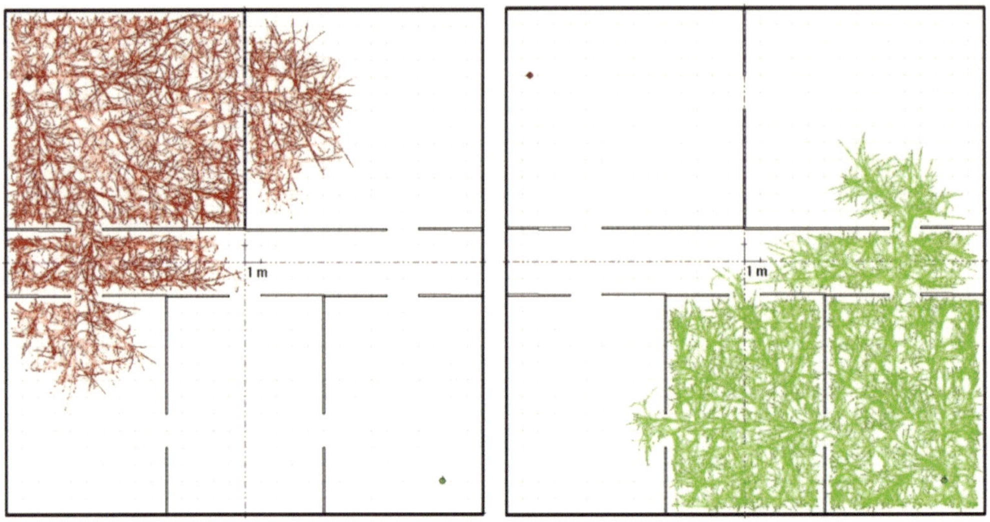

a) Top-down planning b) Bottom-up planning

Fig. 10. Examples of search trees in path planning, from the goal (red tree) and from the start (green tree)

It is a Time-invariant Motion Planner. Because the top-down and the bottom-up planning are both solved by the same algorithm and thus are perfectly equivalent, it has the property of T-invariance concerning the planning time (not the robot time). It means that the solution of a problem is invariant with respect to the starting time of the planning, but even if we invert the time axis direction the solution found is the same. It is possible to plan a movement from the goal to the starting pose or, vice versa, from the starting pose to the goal and we will find the same motion.

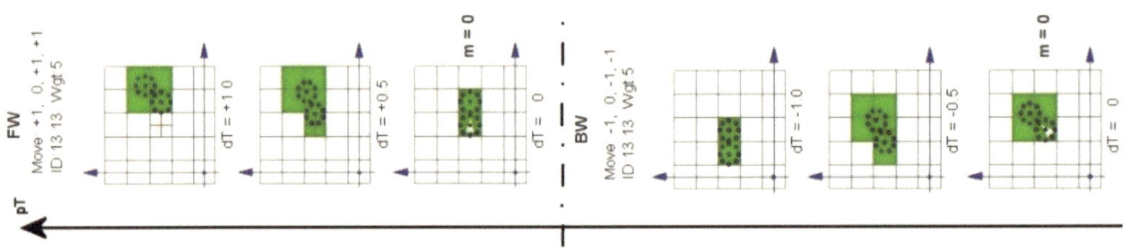

Fig. 11. Time specularity of the dMove operator with respect to the dot-dashed axis

The time-invariance emerges from the property of temporal specularity of the dMove operators with respect to the planning time (pT). In Fig. 11 an example is shown for a simple robot (only two cells size). The dMove (+1, 0, +1, +1) and the dual move (-1, 0, -1, -1) are specular with respect to the dot-dashed axis, unless a spatial shift (because the dMove are always invariant with respect to any space displacement, this shift is not relevant). The meaning is: during the planning, the dMoves are applied from right to left (starting with m = 0 grid). The dMoves are specular with respect to the planning order (time) of application, while are complementary with respect to the time T (the real time of motion of the robot). For the latter consideration, the composition of the two operators generates an identity mapping (applying both in sequence, the robot get back to the original event).

3.6 Attraction Space

The Attraction Space is the substrate on which a discrete representation of a potential function is built (C-Potential function U(q)) in the metaphor of the Artificial Potential Fields. The C-Potential function generates a potential bowl (Fig. 12) in the free space (avoiding and surrounding the obstacles) with a global minimum in the goal cell that attracts the robot with a force -grad(U). If it is correctly defined (it is always possible), no local minima are generated and there is only one global minimum.

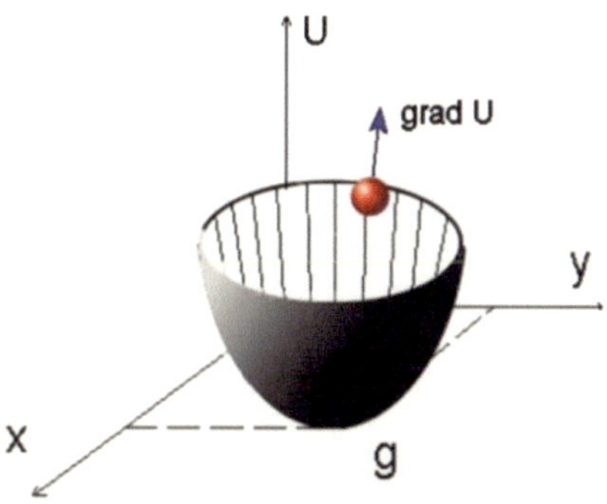

Fig. 12. Potential bowl

The potential value represents the integer "distance" of a cell c from the goal cell along the shortest collision-free path, or more simply it is the cost to reach the goal from the cell c. To evaluate the entire path cost, every basic robot movement (spatiotemporal move) has its own positive weight. Even the "move" along the time axis has its cost.
It is easy to demonstrate two main properties: the termination of the propagation of the potential values through the C-Spacetime and the absence of local minima. The later property ensures that the robot does not enter in obstacles concavities and stall (unless the goal is inside the concavity). In Fig. 13.b, it is shown a simplified example of potential

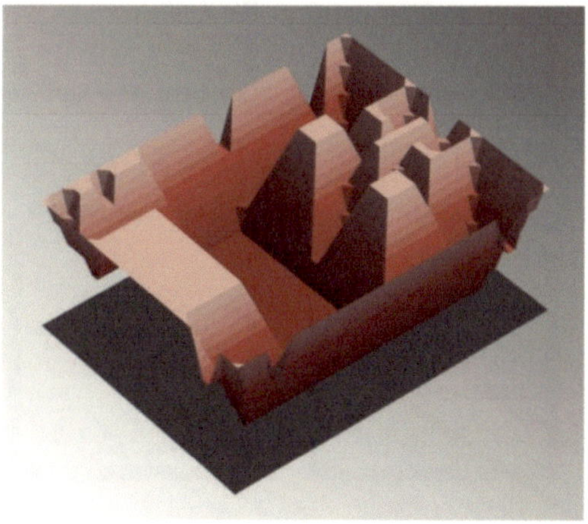

a) Repulsive field

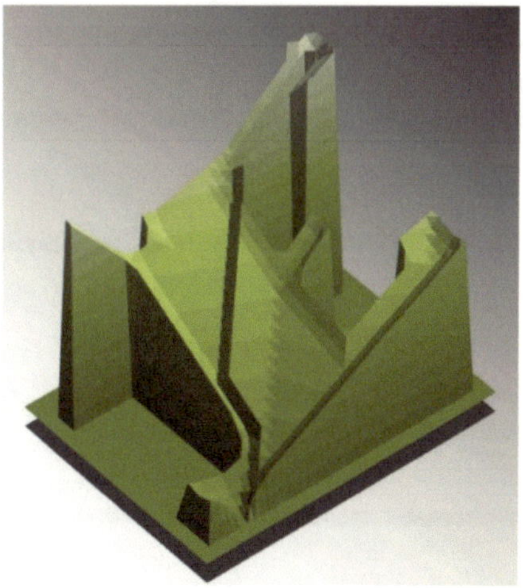

b) Attraction field

Fig. 13. Potentials fields

surface generated from the goal and surrounding the obstacles. The real surface is embedded in a 5D discrete space ($Z^2 \times S^1 \times Z \times Z$), where also the Time is represented.
Every single robot has its own Attraction Space, which is computed depending on the obstacles distribution and the temporal traces of the robots with higher priorities.

3.7 Coordination space or repulsive space

It is a unique space for all the MRS, where the interaction robot-robot and robot-obstacle are modeled. By the way, it is the C-Spacetime and it represents the evolution in the time of the environment. Another metaphor for this space is the Repulsive Space. In this space, repulsive forces are generated by the obstacles to take the robot away from them. It is very useful for the coordination of the robots in a prioritized planning: after the planner has computed the movement for a robot, its passing points (configurations) are marked as unavailable in the Coordination Space. The remaining robots will plan their movements only in the free space, avoiding any unavailable configuration. As stated before, to

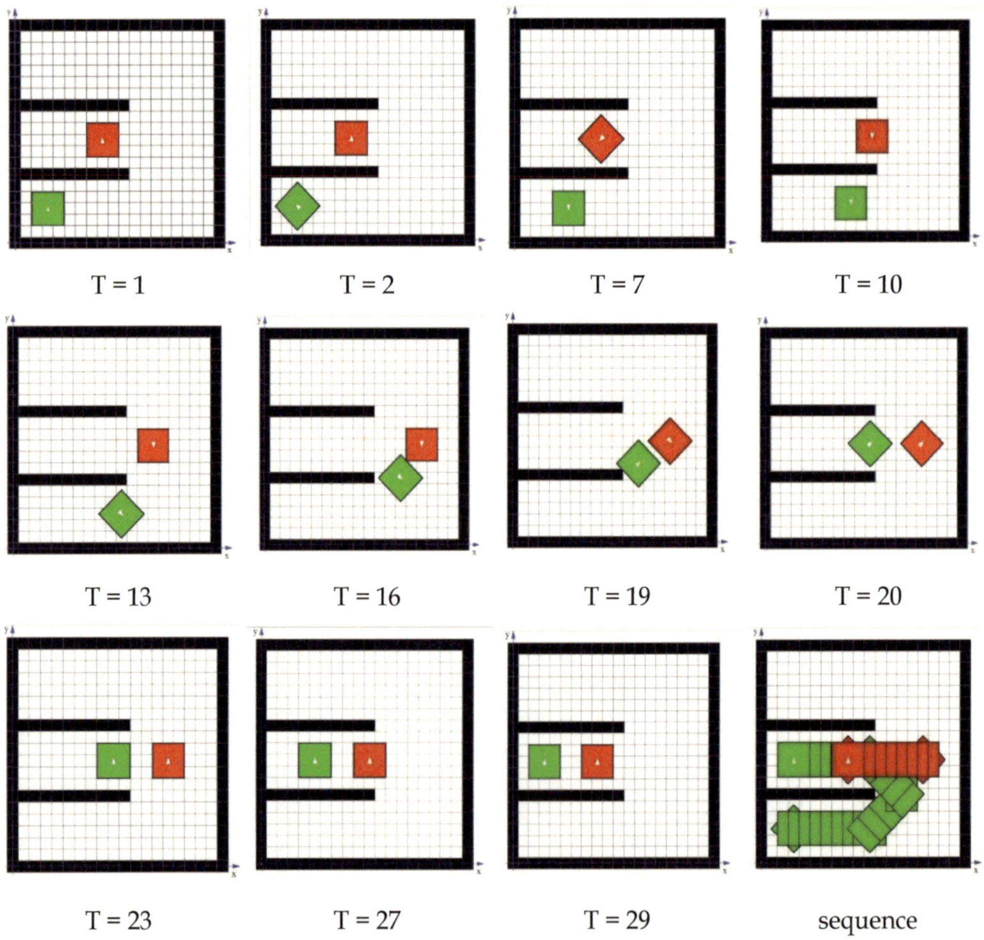

Fig. 14. Example with two robots with same shapes and kinematics (priority order: green, red)

guarantee the Shannon's Theorem, the time unit must be half of the time unit of the Attraction Space. A simplified version of repulsive potential surface is shown in Fig. 13.a (the repulsive force is maximum over the obstacles); the real surface is embedded in a 5D discrete space ($Z^2 \times S^1 \times Z \times Z$).

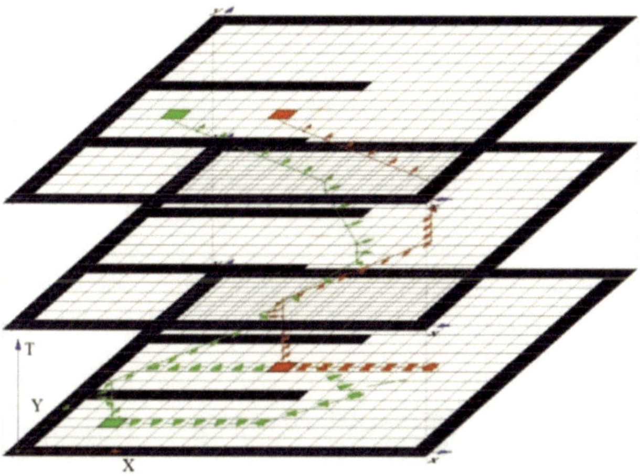

Fig. 15. Spacetime representation of the robots movements of Fig. 14

4. Experimental results

In the example of Fig. 14, two robots with particular kinematics move in a simple environment. The target for the green one (GRobot) is to get inside of a corridor closed by the red RRobot. The RRobot has only to rest in the same place. Thus the GRobot having a higher priority, forces the red one to get outside, enters inside, and then lets the RRobot to return to the original pose. The kinematics is quite strange: the two robots can rest, turn counterclockwise or move aside on their left. Kinematics definition for GRobot and RRobot: $\{(0, 0, 0, +1), (0, 0, +1, +1), (0, +1, 0, +1)\}$. Even with a quite limited kinematics, a solution is found.

In Fig. 15, it is shown the Spacetime and the movements of the robots (colored lines). The Spacetime should be 4D: to reduce it to 3D, the robot orientations have been represented with arrows. The robot trajectories are represented on the plane T = 0 (orthogonal projection of the movements along the time direction).

In the example of Fig. 16, three O-ring robots move one inside the others (matrioska). The robots have different shapes and sizes, but all have the same kinematics: $\{(0, 0, 0, +1), (0, 0, +1, +1)\}$. The difficulty of this example is the coordination of the movements of the three robots to avoid the collision one with each others: thus the green one start first to let enough space to the red one to move without to collide with it. The red robot also has to move to let the space to the blue robot. At the end of the motions, they all stack against the pegs.

In the example of figure Fig. 18, there are two robot with different shapes and kinematics. GRobot kinematics: $\{(0, 0, 0, +1), (+1, 0, 0, +1), (-1, 0, 0, +1)\}$ (forward and backward translations).

RRobot kinematics: $\{(0, 0, 0, +1), (0, 0, +1, +1), (0, 0, -1, +1)\}$ (clockwise and counterclockwise rotations).

To let the GRobot to pass, the RRobot has to turn until the vertical orientation and then it has to stay fixed till the green one is close to it. When the GRobot has overtaken the red one, the latter can complete the motion.

5. Conclusion

An important result is the following: the potential field over the spatiotemporal domain is not conservative (not irrotational). The spatiotemporal lines connecting the starting event and the goal event over the spacetime are not equivalent: not every geometrical solution (movement) is admissible. The dependency arises from the interaction between robots with finite size shapes (it would be conservative for robots smaller then a cell).
The overall algorithm works with any polygonal obstacles, with multiple robots, with any type of kinematics (holonomic, non-holonomic, omnidirectional, car-like, etc.) and any shapes (non-connected, with convexities, concavities and holes). It plans the optimal motions for robots (even one inside another), facing different types of problems without stalling inside the concavities.

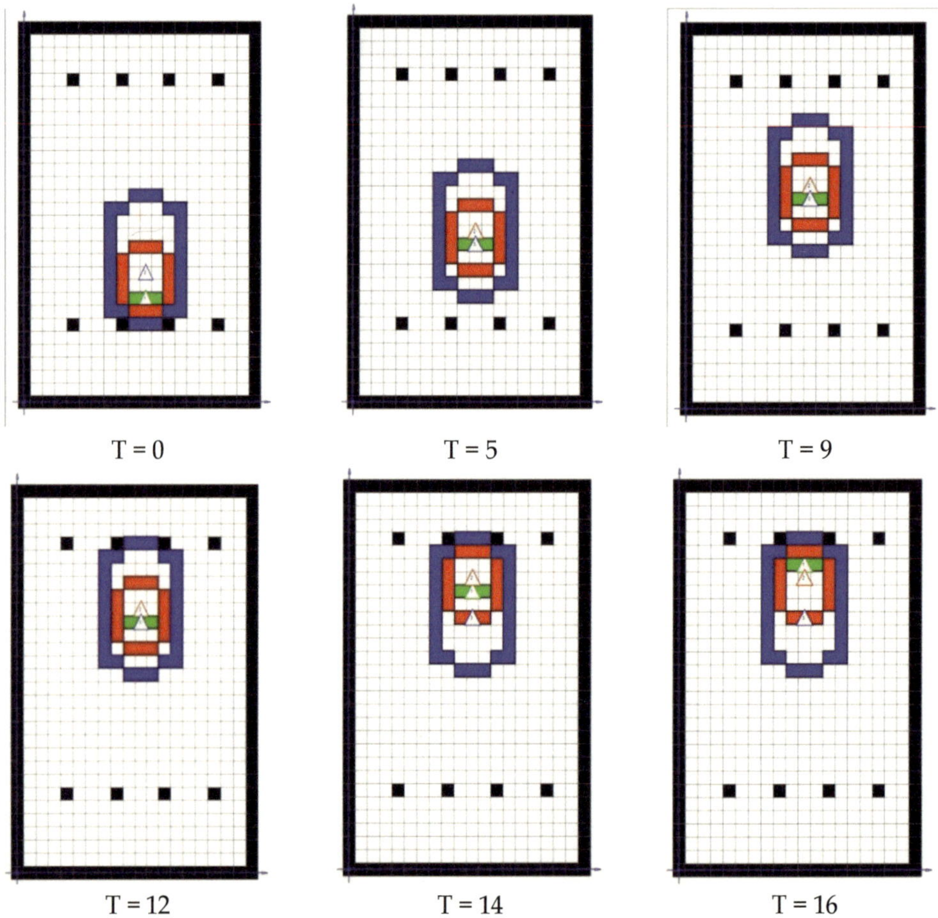

Fig. 16. Matrioska example (priority order: green, red, blue)

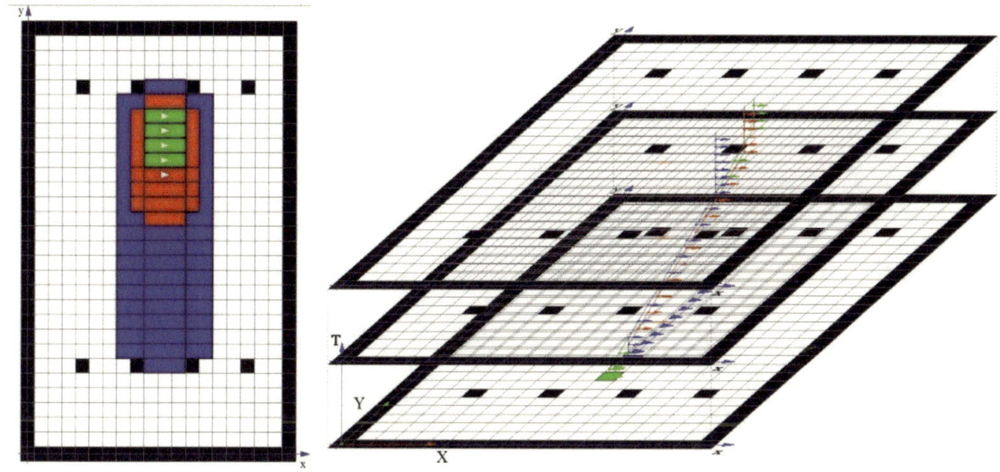

Fig. 17. Silhouettes sequences and Spacetime of example of Fig. 16

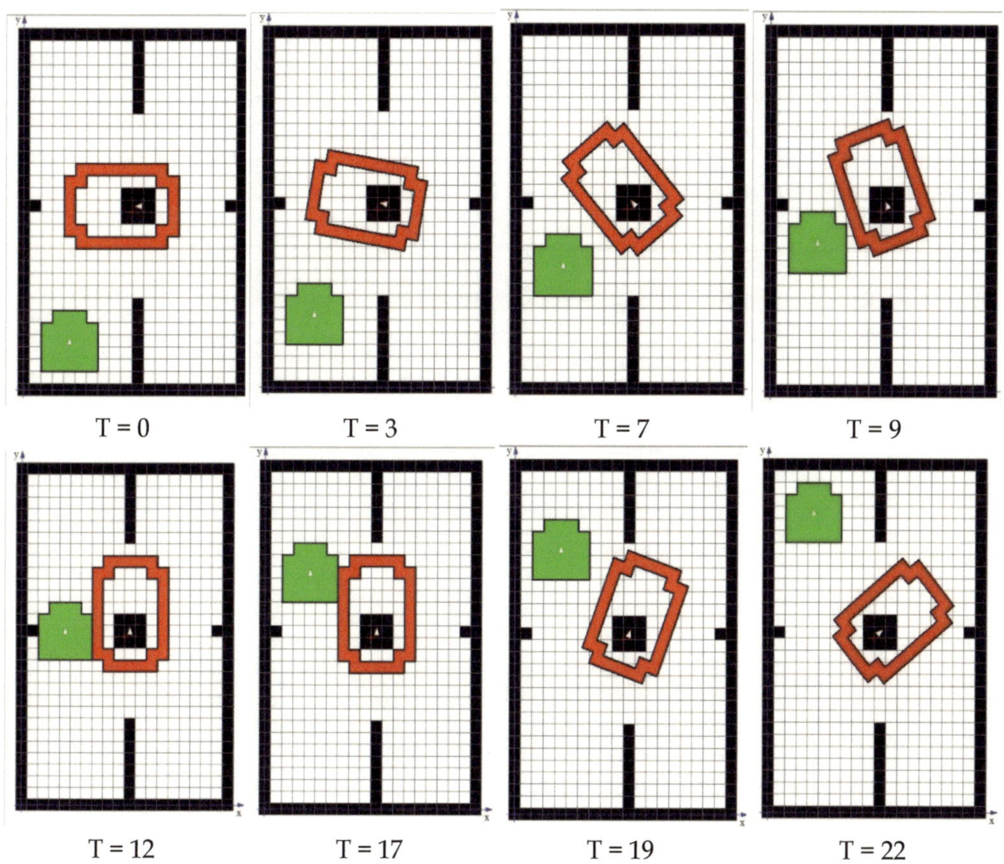

Fig. 18. Example with robots with completely different shapes and kinematics (priority order: green, red)

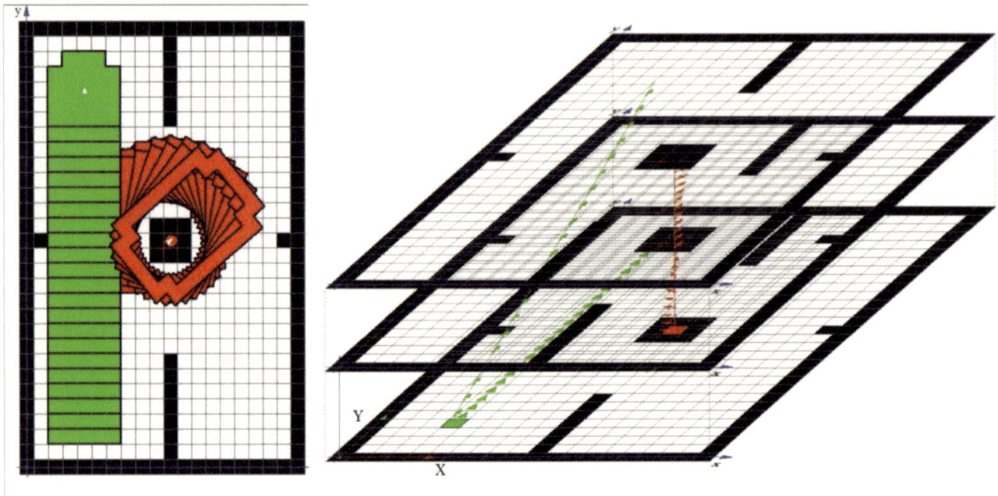

Fig. 19. Silhouettes sequences and Spacetime of example of Fig. 18

In this work, only the solutions satisfying the Dirichlet (or first-type) boundary condition are searched. In other words, we search the motion connecting a starting event with a goal event in a 4D Spacetime (initial and final conditions) in the case of a single robot. For MRS, a vector of starting events (one for each robot) and a vector of goal events are specified. Many other problems can be studied, for example specifying a range of starting time (interval) and a range of arrival time for each robot, relaxing the temporal constraints and searching the best time of arrival (or leaving time).

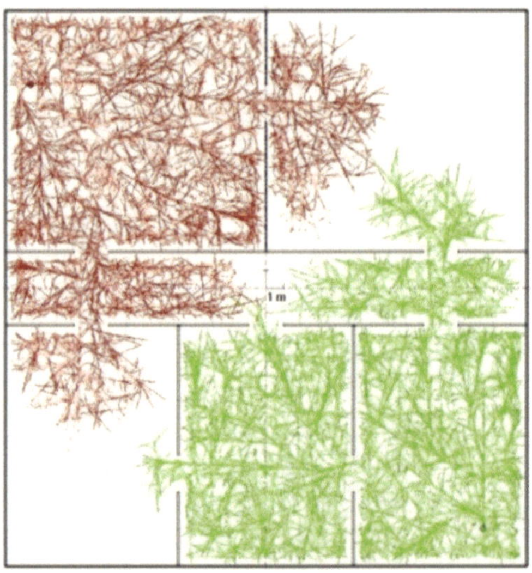

Fig. 20. Search trees growing one against the other (bidirectional planning)

A future development will regard the simultaneous growing of the search trees, one from the goal and the other from the start, as in Fig. 20, intersecting somewhere in the middle of the search space (bidirectional planning). The task is to reduce the planning time, but still maintaining the optimality of the solutions found.

6. References

Barraquand, J.; Langlois, B. & Latombe, J. C. (1992). Numerical potential field techniques for robot path planning, *IEEE Trans. on Systems, Man and Cybernetics*, Vol. 22, No. 2, pp. 224-241, ISSN 0018-9472

Bennewitz, M.; Burgard, W. & Thrun, S. (2001). Optimizing schedules for prioritized path planning of multi-robot systems, *Proceedings of IEEE Int. Conf. on Robotics and Automation (ICRA)*, pp. 271-276, Seoul (Korea), May 2001

Canny, J. F. (1988). *The Complexity of Robot Motion Planning*, MIT Press, ISBN 978-0-262-03136-3, Cambridge, MA

Culberson, J. C. (1998). Sokoban is pspace-complete. *Proceedings of the International Conference on Fun with Algorithms (FUN98)*, pp. 65-76, Waterloo, Ontario, Canada, June 1998, Carleton-Scientific

Erdmann, M. & Lozano-Perez, T. (1987). On multiple moving obstacles, *Algorithmica*, Vol. 2, No. 1-4, pp. 477-521, ISSN 0178-4617, Springer-Verlag, New York, NY, USA

Jahanbin, M. R. & Fallside, F. (1988). Path planning using a wave simulation technique in the configuration space, In: *Artificial Intelligence in Engineering: Robotics and Processes*, J. Gero S. (Ed.), Computational Mechanics Inc., ISBN 0-931215-98-6, Billerica, MA, USA

Kathib, O. (1986). Real-time obstacle avoidance for manipulators and mobile robots, *Int. J. of Robotics Research*, Vol. 5, No. 1, pp. 90-98, ISSN 0278-3649

Lamound, J. P. (1998). Robot Motion Planning and Control, *Lectures Notes in Control and Information Sciences*, No. 229, Springer-Verlag, ISBN 3-540-76219-1, New York, NY, USA

Latombe, J. C. (1991). *Robot Motion* Planning, Kluwer Academic Publishers, ISBN 079239206X, Boston, MA

LaValle, S. M. (2006). *Planning Algorithms*, Cambridge University Press, ISBN 0521862051, New York, NY, USA

LaValle, S. M. & Hutchinson, S. A. (1998). Optimal motion planning for multiple robots having independent goals, *IEEE Trans. on Robotics and Automation*, Vol. 14, No. 6, (December 1998), pp. 912-925, ISSN 1042-296X

Lozano-Pérez, T. & Wesley, M. A. (1979). An Algorithm for Planning Collision-Free Paths Among Polyhedral Obstacles, *Communications of the ACM*, Vol. 22, No. 10, (October 1979), pp. 560-570, ISSN 0001-0782

Lozano-Pérez, T. (1983). Spatial Planning: A Configuration Space Approach, *IEEE Trans. on Computers*, Vol. C-32, No. 2, (February 1983), pp. 108-120, ISSN 0018-9340

Marchese, F, (1996). Cellular automata in robot path planning, *Proc. of the 1st Euromicro Workshop on Advanced Mobile Robots (EUROBOT)*, pp. 116-125, ISBN 0-8186-7695-7, Kaiserslautern (G), October 1996, IEEE Computer Society

Marchese, F. M. (2002). A Path-Planner for Mobile Robots of Generic Shape with Multi-Layered Cellular Automata, In: *Cellular Automata - 5th Int. Conf. on Cellular Automata for Research and Industry (ACRI 2002)*, Bandini, S.; Chopard, B.; Tomassini, M., (Eds.), LNCS, Vol. 2493, (October 2002), pp. 178-189, Springer-Verlag, Berlin/Heidelberg, Germany, ISBN 978-3-540-44304-9, ISSN 0302-9743

Marchese, F. M. (2008). Spatiotemporal MCA Approach for the Motion Coordination of Heterogeneous MRS, In: *Recent Advances in Multi Robot Systems*, Lazinica, A. (Ed.), pp. 123-138, Tech Ed. and Publ., ISBN 978-3 902613-24-0

Murphy, R. R. (2000). *An Introduction to AI Robotics*, MIT Press, ISBN 978-0-262-13383-8, Cambridge, MA, USA

Reif, J. H. (1979). Complexity of the mover's problem and generalizations, *Proc. of 20th Annual Symposium on Foundations of Computer Science (FOCS 1979)*, pp. 421-427, October 1979, IEEE Computer Society, ISSN 0272-5428, Washington, DC, USA

Sheu, P. C. Y. & Xeu, Q. (1993). Intelligent Robotic Planning Systems, *World Scientific Series in Robotics and Automated Systems*, World Scientific Publishing, ISBN 9810207581, River Edge, NJ, USA

Tzionas, P. G.; Thanailakis, A. & Tsalides, P. G. (1997). Collision-free path planning for a diamond-shaped robot using two-dimensional cellular automata, *IEEE Trans. on Robotics and Automation*, Vol. 13, No. 2, pp. 237-250, ISSN 1042-296X

Warren, C. (1990). Multiple robot path coordination using artificial potential fields, *Proceedings of IEEE Int. Conf. on Robotics and Automation*, pp. 500-505, ISBN 0-8186-9061-5, Cincinnati, OH, USA, May 1990

Zelinsky, A. (1994). Using Path Transforms to Guide the Search for Findpath in 2D, *Int. J. of Robotics Research*, Vol. 13, No. 4, pp. 315-325

Part 2

Bio Inspired Approach

17

Coordinated Hunting Based on Spiking Neural Network for Multi-robot System

Xu Wang, Zhiqiang Cao, Chao Zhou, Zengguang Hou and Min Tan
Laboratory of Complex Systems and Intelligence Science
Institute of Automation, Chinese Academy of Sciences
Beijing 100190
China

1. Introduction

Multi-robot systems have been extensively studied and the coordination among the robots becomes a hotspot. Among the typical research tasks of multi-robot system, coordinated hunting with unknown irregular motion of the evader or target has attracted more and more attentions due to its potential application to military, safe guard etc.

The spiking neural network (SNN), considered as the third generation of neural network (Maass & Bishop, 1999), has attracted many attentions. Spikes (pulses) are used to deliver the information between neurons, i.e. SNN processes the information in the form of spikes, which brings temporal structure and extends the functionality of SNN (Kasabov, 2010). Besides the rate coding, inspired by the results of biological experiments, some coding strategies based on spike timing have been proposed, such as time-to-first-spike coding, phase coding, correlations/synchrony coding et al. (Maass & Bishop, 1999). Also, Maass et al. present some useful spiking neuron models, such as spike response model (SRM), integrate-and-fire model (IF), Hodgkin-Huxley Model and so on (Maass & Bishop, 1999). For these coding methods and neuron models, the Hebb learning is proposed to adapt the weights between neurons based on the temporal difference between input and output spikes (Kempter et al., 1999). Nowadays, the controllers based on SNN have been introduced to many applications, such as phase/frequency correlations recognizing (Kiselev, 2009), movement prediction from real-world images (Burgsteiner et al., 2005), movement generation of the robot arm (Joshi & Maass, 2005), etc. Especially, SNN has been applied to the control of the mobile robot (Floreano & Mattiussi, 2001; Roggen et al., 2003; Hagras, 2004; Qu et al., 2009).

In this chapter, a robot controller based on spiking neural network (SNN) is proposed for the coordinated hunting of multi-robot system. The controller utilizes 12 direction-sensitive modules to encode and process the inputs including the environment, target and coordination information by the time-to-first-spike coding and then, the motor neurons generate the control signals for the motors according to the winner-take-all strategy. Also, the Hebbian learning with a stochastic form is applied to adjust the connection weights.

The rest of the chapter is organized as follows. In Section 2, the structure of the controller is given and the inputs encoding, coordination between robots and motor neurons are described in detail. Section 3 demonstrates the simulations. Finally, Section 4 concludes the work.

2. The controller based on spiking neural network

2.1 The structure of the controller

The SNN based controller is composed of 12 modules, denoted by $M_i, i=1,\cdots,12$, as well as four motor neurons, as shown in Figure 1(a). The module M_i is direction-sensitive and it is

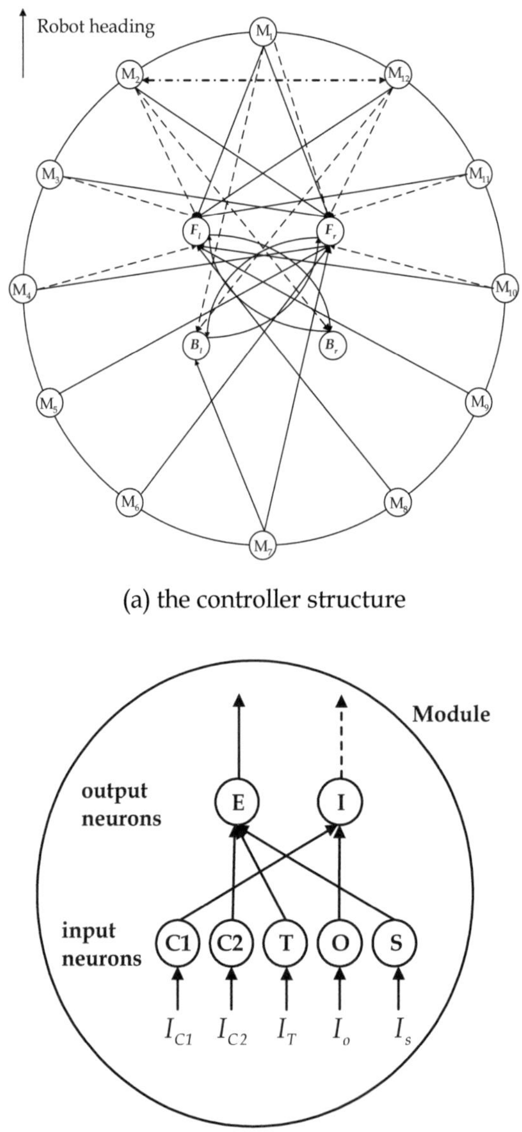

Fig. 1. The frame of the controller

corresponding to the direction $\frac{(i-1)\pi}{6}$ with respect to the heading of the robot, such that they are considered to be uniformly distributed around the robot. The module is shown in Figure 1(b), and it consists of two layers. Layer 1 is composed of input neurons {S, O, T, C1, C2} that encode the sensor input I_s, obstacle input I_o, target input I_T, coordination inputs I_{C1} and I_{C2} according to the time-to-first-spike coding, respectively. Layer 2 generates the outputs with two output neurons E (excitory) and I (inhibitory) that represent that the robot should turn to or away from the direction of the module, respectively. In Figure 1(a), the lines denote the connections from the neuron E of every module to the motor neurons, while dashed lines represent the connections from the neuron I to the motor neurons.

The four motor neurons denoted by (F_l, B_l, F_r, B_r) represent left forward motor neuron, left backward motor neuron, right forward motor neuron and right backward motor neuron, respectively. They are divided into two pairs (F_l, B_l) and (F_r, B_r) according to the related motor. There exist connections between two pairs for the information transmission.

The motor neurons corresponding to each motor receive the outputs of the modules along with the outputs of other motor neurons and fire spikes to generate the control signal by the winner-take-all strategy.

2.2 Input signals of the module

The input signals are encoded into corresponding spikes by time-to-first-spike coding and can be formulated as follows:

a. Sensor input I_s

I_s is encoded according to the formula

$$t_s = round(T(1-\frac{I_s}{I_{\lim}}))+1 \tag{1}$$

where t_s is the time when the spike is generated with the constant T=100*ms*, and the input I_s is the data from the corresponding sensor bounded by an up-bound $I_{\lim}$. Here, we assume that there are 16 ultrasonic sensors evenly distributed on the peripheral ring of the robot and "corresponding" means the sensor is closest to the direction of the module. Also, the sensor data caused by the target is filtered such that the target does not affect the sensors information. The function round (•) adjusts the variable into its nearest integer.

b. Obstacle input I_o

I_o also comes from the corresponding sensor, and it is encoded by

$$t_T = round(\frac{5T}{I_{\lim}}\max(I_o - I_{thred}, 0))+1 \tag{2}$$

where $I_o = I_s$, and the constant I_{thred} can be considered as the threshold for the obstacle neuron. The function max(•) makes sure that $t_T \geq 1$.

c. Target input I_T

I_T is the relative angle θ_T between the module direction and the line from the target to the robot. It is encoded to the spike time t_T as

$$t_T = round(T(1-\frac{\max(f(\theta_T),0)}{0.8}))+1 \tag{3}$$

with

$$f(x) = 2e^{(-\frac{\pi x^2}{4})} - 1.2e^{(-\frac{\pi x^2}{16})}$$

where t_T only concerns the relative angle and does not care about the relative distance. Obviously, $\max_x(f(x)) = 0.8$ and we divide the function by 0.8 to normalize the result. The function $f(\bullet)$ makes the module sensitive to the target near the direction of the module.

d. Coordination input I_{C1}

I_{C1} is introduced to prevent the robots from being close to each other. It contains two parts: the relative angle θ_C^j between the direction of the module and one detected robot R_j and the relative distance d_C^j between the two robots.

$$t_{C1} = round(T(1 - \min(\max(\sum_j \frac{g(d_C^j)f(\theta_C^j)}{0.8}, 0), 1))) + 1 \quad (4)$$

with

$$g(x) = e^{-(\frac{x}{2500})^2}$$

where $f(\bullet)$ as mentioned above deals with the relative angle θ_C^j while $g(\bullet)$ is responsible for the relative distance d_C^j. Eq. (4) makes the module be more sensitive to the companion robots near its direction.

e. Coordination input I_{C2}

I_{C2} is activated only when there exists at least one neighboring robot R_n whose Boolean attraction tag is 1. Every robot has its own table of all robots' attraction tags and neighboring robots topology. By broadcasting, each robot sends its information including whether it detects the target, its tag and neighbor information such that the tables of robots can be updated. The attraction tag of a robot is updated as follows:

If some neighborships among the robots break or some robots lose the track of the target based on the updated table
{
    If there exists a route from it to the target according to the neighboring robots topology
    { its tag is 1; }
    Else
    { its tag is 0; }
}
Else
{
If one tag of its neighbors is 1 or it detects the target
{ the tag is 1; }
Else

{ the tag is 0; }

}

When I_{C2} is activated, it can be encoded as

$$t_{C2} = round(T(1 - \min(\max(\sum_n \frac{g(d_C^n - 3000) f(\theta_C^n)}{0.8}, 0), 1))) + 1 \quad (5)$$

where the relative distance d_C^n between the robots is encoded with a translation, as shown in $g(d_C^n - 3000) = e^{-(\frac{d_C^n - 3000}{2500})^2}$.

2.3 The weights and outputs of the module

For a module, the weights between neurons represent the delay from neurons to neurons. Thus, when delay is small, the connection between neurons is considered to be strong. For every module, the initial weights for the neurons in the module are nearly the same, which will be shown in the simulation section. The output neurons E_i and I_i of the module $M_i, i = 1, \cdots, 12$ fire at the time t_E^i and t_I^i (when their first input spikes arrive). t_E^i and t_I^i can be calculated as follows:

$$t_j^i = \min_k (t_k^i + w_{k,j}^i), j = E, I; k = S, O, T, C1, C2 \quad (6)$$

where $w_{k,j}^i$ is the corresponding weight (i.e. delay) from the input neuron k to the output neuron j in the module M_i.

Furthermore, there exist mutual inhibitions between the module M_2 and M_{12} (dot and dash line in Figure 1(a)), which can be calculated as follows:

$$\begin{cases} t_I^{12} = 10T & t_I^2 < t_I^{12} \\ t_I^2 = t_I^{12} = 10T & t_I^2 = t_I^{12} \\ t_I^2 = 10T & t_I^2 > t_I^{12} \end{cases} \quad (7)$$

2.4 The motor neuron

The motor neurons fire at the time $t_i^j, i = r, l; j = f, b$ when their first input spikes arrive. t_i^j is bounded by T. Especially, when there is no input spike during the period (0, T], t_i^j is set to be T. Furthermore, there are mutual connections between the left forward motor neuron F_l and the right backward motor neuron B_r, as well as the right forward motor neuron F_r and the left backward motor neuron B_l. Thus, the information from one side can pass to the other side. The motor neurons are divided into two pairs according to the motor they belong to. The competence (i.e. winner-take-all strategy) is used in each pair to decide whether the motor rotates forward or backward. Then we have

$$v_i = \frac{10 \operatorname{sgn}(t_i^b - t_i^f)(1 - \min(t_i^f, t_i^b) / T)}{4}, i = r, l \quad (8)$$

where v_i is the velocity of the motor i.

2.5 Learning

For the SNN based controller, the weights are adjusted by the Hebbian learning (Kempter et al., 1999) in a stochastic form. Denote w_{ij} the weight from the neuron j to neuron i. When learning occurs, a random number ς is generated following the uniform distribution in the [0, 1].
If ς is smaller than $|2r_{learn}W(t_i - t_j)|$ with

$$W(\Delta t) = \begin{cases} \exp(\frac{\Delta t}{\tau^{syn}})[(1-\frac{\Delta t}{\tilde{\tau}_+}) - (1-\frac{\Delta t}{\tilde{\tau}_-})] & \Delta t \geq 0 \\ \exp(-\frac{\Delta t}{\tau_+}) - \exp(-\frac{\Delta t}{\tau_-}) & \Delta t < 0 \end{cases} \quad (9)$$

the weight will be adjusted. Here constants $\tau^{syn} = 5$, $\tau_+ = 1$, $\tau_- = 20$. Considering that weights are integers, the change of weight is also an integer. In this controller, the weight will change by 1 or -1, i.e.

$$w_{ij} = \begin{cases} w_{ij} - 1 & \varsigma < |2r_{learn}W(t_i - t_j)|, t_i > t_j \\ w_{ij} + 1 & \varsigma < |2r_{learn}W(t_i - t_j)|, t_i < t_j \\ w_{ij} & otherwise \end{cases} \quad (10)$$

where $r_{learn} = 0.001$ is the learning rate.

3. Simulations

In this part, the simulations will be given to testify the feasibility of the proposed controller based on SNN. The mobile robots are modeled as two-wheel mobile robots and can be seen as circles with a diameter 500mm. The target (evader) is also considered as a circle. The target has the same controller structure as shown in Figure 1(a), and each module has a repulsing input to make it be away from the robots just like I_{C1} with $g(x) = e^{-(\frac{x}{3000})^2}$ while there are no coordination inputs and target input. The parameters of the controller in simulations are as follows: $I_{\lim} = 2000mm$ and the maximum range of detecting other robots is 5000mm; $I_{thred} = 200mm$ for M_1 and $300mm$ for other modules.
The initial weights between the input neurons and the output neurons in the module are as follows: {S→E, O→I, T→E, C1→I, C2→E} are {38,8,13,8,18}, {40,10,15,11,20}, {40, 10,15,13,20}, {40,10,15,16,20}, {40,10,15,10,20}, {40,10,15,10,20}, {40,10,15,10,20}, {40,10,15,10,20}, {40,10,15,10,20}, {40,10,15,16,20}, {40,10,15,13,20}, {40,10,15,11,20} for modules M_1 to M_{12}, respectively. The initial values of the weights connecting the modules to the motor neurons are 10, while the initial values are 4 for the weights of the motor neurons' mutual connections.

In following simulations, the start points of the robots are denoted by "S", while "G" represents the stop points. When the distance between the target and a robot is smaller than 1000mm, the hunting task is considered to be completed.

In simulation 1, we consider three robots to complete the hunting task in an environment which is enclosed by 4 walls (the black line in the Figure 2). The result of simulation 1 is shown in Figure 2, and the states of the robots are shown in Figure 3. Every robot has three states: 0, 1, 2. State 2 represents the target being observed by the robot itself and state 1 depicts that the robot builds a neighborship route with a robot that observes the target while the target is not detected by itself, otherwise, its state is 0. At first, only robot 3 can observe the target. The target is out of the detection range of robot 1 and robot 2. Then, robot 2 will follow robot 3 according to the updated tag table which includes the information that robot 3 can observe the target. After that, robot 1 also follows robot 2 because it finds that the tag of robot 2 is 1. A route from robot 1 to the target in the neighboring robots topology is built. After the robot 2 observes the target by itself, the target is pursued by robots 2 and 3, while robot 1 is still in following. Finally, the target is caught successfully.

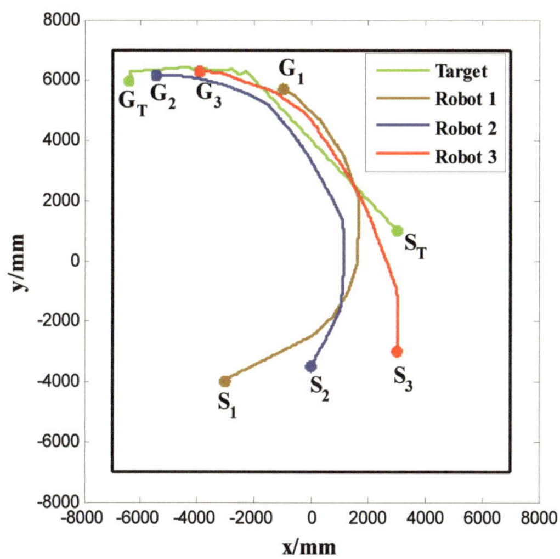

Fig. 2. The trajectories of the robots in simulation 1

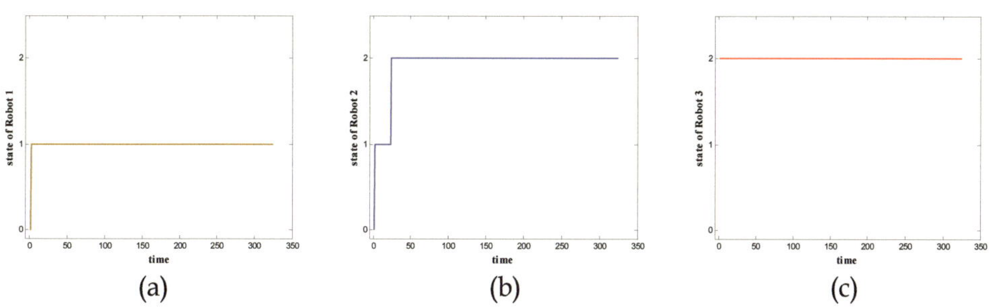

Fig. 3. The states of the robots in simulation 1

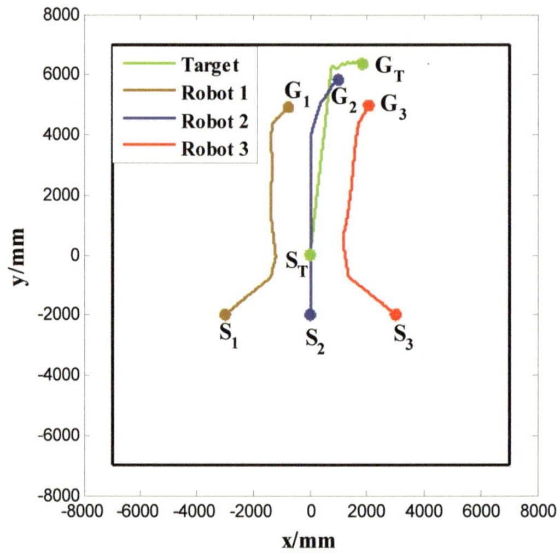

Fig. 4. The trajectories of the robots in simulation 2

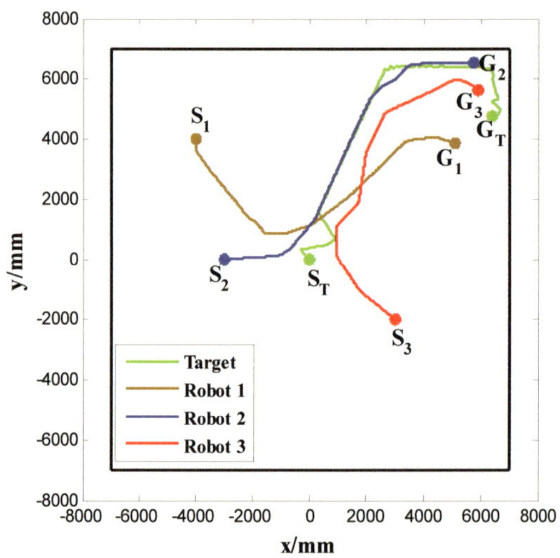

Fig. 5. The trajectories of the robots in simulation 3

In simulation 2, all three robots can observe the target at the beginning. The trajectories of the robots are presented in Figure 4. In simulation 3, the robots 2 and 3 observe the target at the beginning and robot 1 follows robot 2. The corresponding trajectories of the robots and their states are given in Figures 5 and 6, respectively.
The simulation 4 considers the still target with an obstacle between the target and the robots, as shown in Figures 7 and 8.

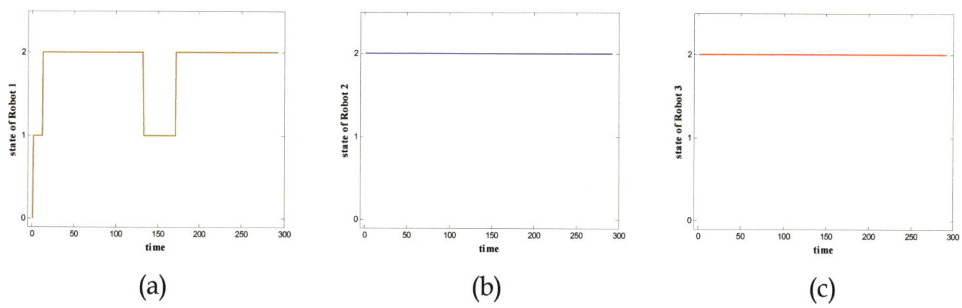

Fig. 6. The states of the robots in simulation 3

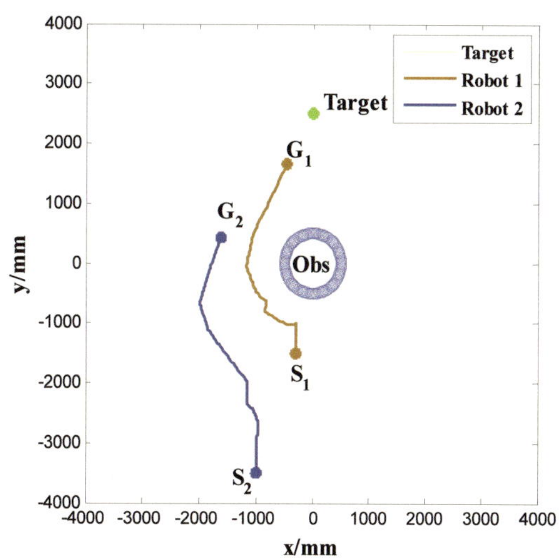

Fig. 7. The trajectories of the robots in simulation 4

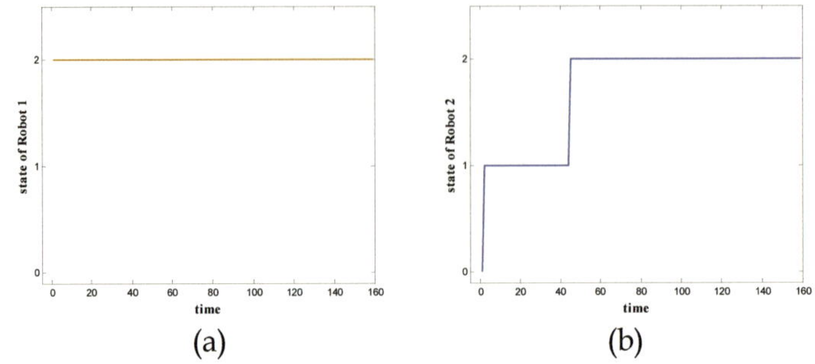

Fig. 8. The states of the robots in simulation 4

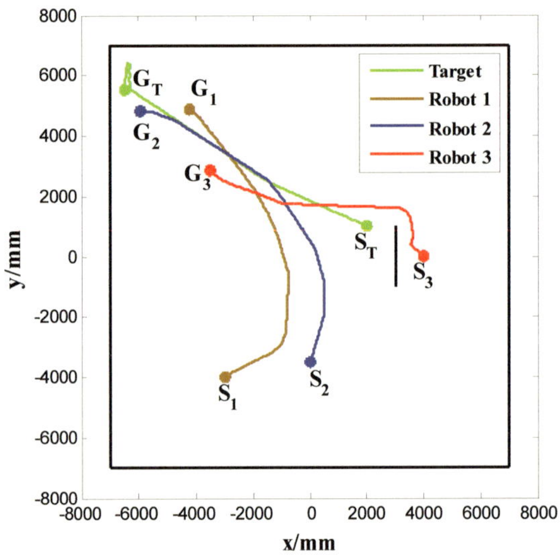

Fig. 9. The trajectories of the robots in simulation 5

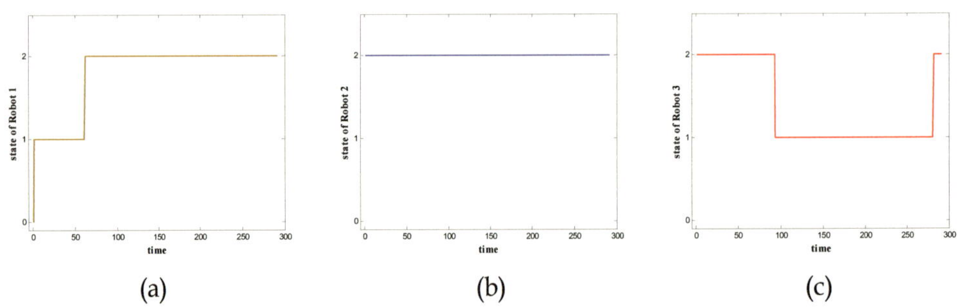

Fig. 10. The states of the robots in simulation 5

In simulations 5 shown in Figures 9 and 10, initially, the robots 2 and 3 observe the target. After robot 1 observes the target, all the robots pursue the target. For robot 3, because of the obstruction of the obstacle, it loses the target and its state is from 2 to 1. Finally, the hunting task is completed.

4. Conclusion

In this work, the controller based on SNN is applied to the hunting task for the multi-robot system. By using time-to-first-spike coding and winner-take-all strategy, the controller with 12 direction-sensitive modules and four motor neurons can make the robots coordinate with each other to finish the hunting task, as demonstrated in the simulations. In this work, the function $f(\bullet)$ is the same for all the modules, which, in fact, may be different for different modules. The will be considered in the future work.

5. Acknowledgement

This work is supported in part by the National Natural Science Foundation of China under Grants 60805038, 60725309, and the National High Technology Research and Development Program of China (863 Program) under Grant 2009AA043901-1.

6. References

Burgsteiner, H.; Kroll, M.; Leopold A. & Steinbauer G. (2005). Movement prediction from real-world images using a liquid state machine, *Proceedings of Lecture Notes In Computer Science, Proceedings of the 18th international conference on Innovations in Applied Artificial Intelligence*, pp. 121-130, Bari, Italy

Floreano, D. & Mattiussi, C. (2001). Evolution of spiking neural controllers for autonomous vision-based robots, In: *Evolution Robotics. From Intelligent Robotics to Artificial Life*, Lecture Notes in Computer Science, Vol. 2217, pp. 38-61, Springer, ISBN 978-3-540-42737-7, Berlin / Heidelberg

Hagras, H.; Cornish, A.P.; Colley, M.; Callaghan, V. & Clarke, G. (2004). Evolving spiking neural network controllers for autonomous robots, *IEEE International Conference on Robotics and Automation*, pp. 4620-4626

Joshi, P. & Maass, W. (2005). Movement generation with circuits of spiking neurons, *Neural Computation*, Vol. 17, No. 8, pp. 1715-1738

Kasabov, N. (2010). To spike or not to spikes: probabilistic spiking neuron models, *Neural Networks*, Vol.23, No.1, pp. 16-19

Kiselev, M.V. (2009). Self-organized spiking neural network recognizing phase/frequency correlations, *Proceedings of International Joint Conference on Neural Networks*, pp. 1633-1639, Altanta, Georgia, USA

Maass, W. & Bishop, C. M. (1999). *Pulsed Neural Networks*, MIT-Press, Cambridge, MA

Qu, H.; Yang, S.X.; Willms, A.R. & Yi, Z. (2009). Real-time robot path planning based on a modified pulse-coupled neural network model, *IEEE Transaction on Neural Networks*, Vol. 20, No. 11, pp.1724-1739

Roggen, D.; Hofmann, S.; Thoma, Y. & Floreano, D. (2003). Hardware spiking neural network with run-time reconfigurable connectivity in an autonomous robot, *NASA/DOD Conference on Evolvable Hardware*, pp. 189-198

Kempter, R.; Gerstner, W. & Van Hemmen, J.L. (1999). Hebbian learning and spiking neurons, *Physical Review E*, Vol. 59, No. 4, pp. 4498-4514

18

Multi-robot Information Fusion and Coordination Based on Agent

Bo Fan and Jiexin Pu
Electronic Information Engineering College
Henan University of Science & Technology, 471003 Luoyang
P.R.China

1. Introduction

With the rapid progress of modern science and technology, robots' development and application extend ceaselessly. For different tasks and environment, especially to large complex tasks and environment, the problems of capability limitation of single robot become more and more obvious, such as information gathering and processing, controlling and so on. Therefore, the multi-robot coordination and cooperation are required to improve these abilities.

Nowadays, the multi-robot system has been paid much attention. It has the prominent property of multidisciplinary intercrossing and fusion. Based on multi-agent system, and with the introduction of multi-agent system's architecture, coordination and cooperation, this dissertation gives a thorough and systematic research on the information fusion of multi-robot system, the tasks distribution and programming of multi-robot coordination, and the multi-robot under oppositional environment.

2. Multi-agent decision fusion based on evidence reasoning and its application to multi-robot system

The overall goal of the research described in this section is to investigate a problem of distributed artificial intelligence introducing evidence theory for decision making in uncertain environment. Such problems arise, for example, in multi-sensor information fusion systems, and in multi-agent decision systems and in the situation assessment problem with distributed artificial intelligence.

The evidence reasoning is applied effectively to intelligent decision systems and specialist systems, which not only accords with people's reasoning manner and decision process but also gives the rational explanation based on information theory to reasoning. In this paper, evidence theory is introduced to the multi-agent system and the Multi-Agent Decision System Based on the Evidence Reasoning is presented. This system is composed of agents, fusion center and decision center. The distributed agents do not interact with environment and do not communicate with each other but only with a fusion center. Each agent extracts the feature information and educes the basic beliefs about local environment. The fusion center combines all agents' beliefs and acquires the beliefs about global environment. The decision center produces the pignistic probabilities that are used to make decision.

2.1 Distributed decision system

a. System architecture

A general multi-agent distributed system consists of a group of distributed intelligent agents that have to coordinate their knowledge, goals, skills, and plans in order to make decisions, take actions, and solve problems. Agents in a distributed system may have different areas of expertise, specific a priori knowledge, and different decision functions. They may be able to observe only certain characteristics of the environment; they may observe different spatio-temporal regions of the environment. Since no one agent has complete information about the environment and observations, they have to cooperate to achieve their goals. There have been many coordination schemes developed in the field of distributed artificial intelligence (Galina Rogova & Pierre Valin., 2005).

In this paper, we investigate a problem of decision making in a hierarchical multi-agent system. Agents do not communicate with each other but only with a fusion center. Each agent has its own internal structure including domain knowledge, a set of hypotheses to be considered, and the basic belief assignment for each hypothesis. They transmit these beliefs to the fusion center. The fusion center combines each agent's beliefs and produces the combined beliefs about the global environment. The decision center acquires pignistic probabilities of the hypotheses under consideration and maps them into actions. Based on this idea, we present the distributed decision system architecture in Figure 1.

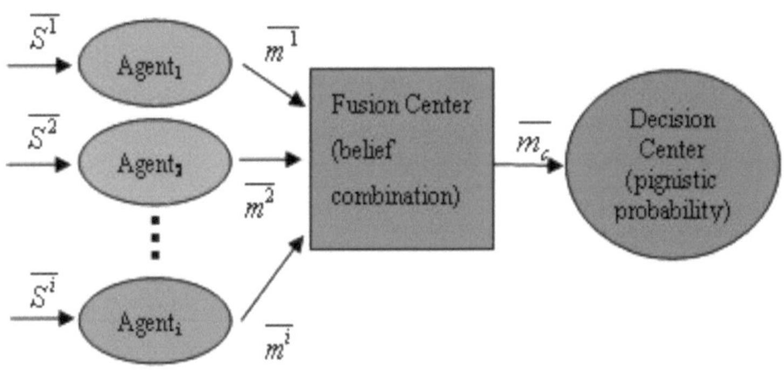

Fig. 1. Distributed decision system architecture

b. Agent model

Each agent i ($1 \le i \le I$, I is the number of agent) is able to observe states of environment and extracts a particular type of information from it, which represented by a feature vector $\overline{S}^i = (s_1^i, s_2^i, ..., s_{N_i}^i)$ (Ni is the dimension of a feature vector. Let $\Theta = \{\theta1, \theta2,, ..., \theta n\}$ be a frame of discernment, where θ_k (k=1,...,n) is the element of the frame of discernment and belongs to class k. of the hypothesis.

For the feature vector which each agent i extract from environment and each class k, a proximity measure function $\Phi(\overline{S}^i, \theta_k)$ is defined to map the evidence (feature vector) to the basic belief assignment of the element of Θ. $\Phi(\overline{S}^i, \theta_k)$ is a decreasing function, $0 \le \Phi(\overline{S}^i, \theta_k) \le 1$, which can be considered as a simple support function with focal element θ_k.

$$m_k^i(\theta_k) = \Phi(\overline{X^i}, \theta_k) \tag{1}$$

$$m_k^i(\Theta) = 1 - \Phi(\overline{X^i}, \theta_k) \quad (2)$$

$$m_k^i(A) = 0 \qquad \forall A \neq \theta_k \subset \Theta \quad (3)$$

Combining all the m_k^i according to the Dempster rule of combination (Dempster, A. P., 1967), the basic belief assignment of agent i can be obtained (Shafer, G., 1976):

$$m^i(\theta_k) = \frac{m_k^i \prod_{j\neq k}(1 - m_j^i)}{\sum_k m_k^i \prod_{j\neq k}(1 - m_j^i) + \prod_j (1 - m_j^i)} \quad (4)$$

Each agent i extracts the feature vector from environment as the input, produces the simple support function of each hypothesis of Θ by the measure function Φ, and acquires its basic belief assignment using (4) as the output: $m^i(\theta_1), m^i(\theta_2), ..., m^i(\theta_n), m^i(\Theta)$. This is shown in Figure 2.

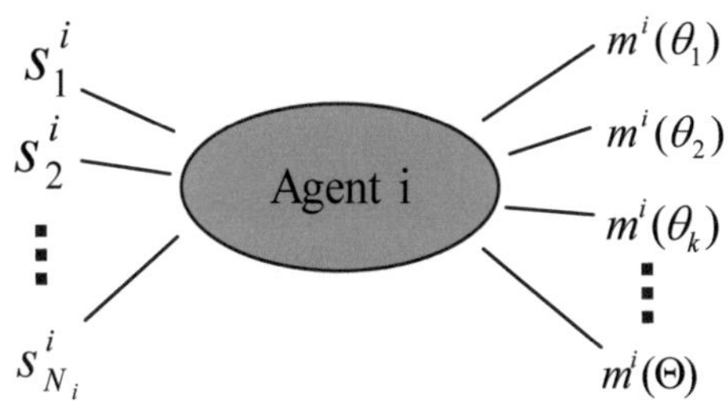

Fig. 2. Agent model

c. Fusion Center

The function of the fusion center is to combine beliefs of all the agents in all the hypotheses with the Dempster rule of combination. However, the fusion center confront with two problems: how to deal with the agents' beliefs when they have the different internal structure, which means that the agents have the different and compatible frame of discernment; and how to resolve the relative reliability of different agents.

In our system (Figure 1.), the fusion center is able to combine the various kinds of the evidence. However, the Dempster rule of combination is based on the single frame of discernment, which obviously can handle one part of the information. In some situation, we have to appeal to the different conception and change the frame of discernment for evidence reasoning in order to solve the some special kinds of evidence. Coarsening and refinement are the transform methods to satisfy this demand. If the agents have different internal structure, i.e. the different and compatible frame of discernment, we can resolve their beliefs combination by coarsening and refinement.

Agent_i and agent_j are assumed to own the different and compatible frame of discernment $\Theta = \{\theta_1^i, \theta_2^i, ..., \theta_n^i\}$ and $\Omega = \{\theta_1^j, \theta_2^j, ..., \theta_m^j\}$. The map, $\sigma: 2^\Theta \rightarrow 2^\Omega$, is a refining from Θ to Ω, then: $\forall A \subset \Theta, B \subset \Omega \quad \sigma(A) = B$

Let m_1 and m_2 are the basic belief assignments of Θ and Ω, they can be transformed and transferred as follow:

$$\forall B \subset \Omega \qquad m_2(B) = \sum_{A \subset \Theta : \sigma(A) = B} m_1(A) \tag{5}$$

where the sum is 0 when no A satisfies the constraint. m_2 is called the vacuous extension of m_1 on Ω (Philippe Smets., 2005).

Reliability, i.e. our opinion about the 'value' of a agent, various from agent to agent. The idea is to weight more heavily the information produced by the 'best' agents and conversely for the 'bad' ones. For α [0, 1], let (1-α) be the degree of 'confidence' we assign to the agent. It can be encoded into a basic belief assignment defined on the set {reliable, unreliable} such that (Elouedi, Z. et al., 2004):

$$m(reliable) = 1 - \alpha \tag{6}$$

$$m(unreliable) = \alpha \tag{7}$$

Suppose m is the basic belief assignment on Θ. The result of combining m with the 'confidence' is a new belief, defined as:

$$m^{\alpha}(A) = (1-\alpha) \cdot m(A) \qquad for \qquad A \subset \Theta \tag{8}$$

$$m^{\alpha}(\Theta) = \alpha + (1-\alpha) \cdot m(\Theta) \tag{9}$$

This operation is called a discounting by Shafer and the coefficient α is called the discounting factor. The larger α, the closer mα is from the vacuous belief function.

The fusion center combines the all agent's basic belief assignment to acquire the global environment information. With the coarsening and refinement, the basic belief assignments between the different and compatible frames of discernment are transformed and transferred. Moreover, the fusion center considers the relative reliability of agents, so it distributes the discounting to each agent's basic belief assignment. Let m_i is the basic belief assignment of agent i, and is transferred on the same frame of discernment. Let αi is the discounting factor of agent i. The Dempster rule of combination (Rogova G., 2003) is used to combine the all agent's beliefs:

$$\begin{aligned} m_c(\theta_k) &= c \sum_{\substack{A_i \subset \Theta \\ \bigcap_{i=1}^{I} A_i = \theta_k}} m^{1,\alpha_1}(A_1) \cdot m^{2,\alpha_2}(A_2) \cdots m^{I,\alpha_I}(A_I) \quad {\scriptstyle i=1,2,\cdots,I} \\ c &= \Big(\sum_{\substack{A_i \subset \Theta \\ \bigcap_{i=1}^{I} A_i \neq \varnothing}} m^{1,\alpha_1}(A_1) \cdot m^{2,\alpha_2}(A_2) \cdots m^{I,\alpha_I}(A_I) \Big)^{-1} \quad {\scriptstyle i=1,2,\cdots,I} \end{aligned} \tag{10}$$

So the fusion center produces the beliefs in all hypothesis of the frame of discernment $\Theta = \{\theta_1, \theta_2, \ldots, \theta_k\}$: $\{m_c(\theta_1), m_c(\theta_2), \ldots, m_c(\theta_k)\}$ and $m_c(\Theta)$.

d. Decision Center

The agents shown in Figure 1 extract the environment information and derive their corresponding beliefs. The fusion center combines the ensemble of agent beliefs into a set of combined basic probability assignments defined over the frame of discernment. From the fusion center's output, decision center adopts pignistic probability transformation to compute pignistic probabilities of each hypothesis. The transformation is based on the generalized Insufficient Reason Principle according to which $\forall A \subseteq \Theta$ the mass of belief m(A) is distributed equally among the elements of A (Philippe Smets., 2005).

$$BetP_k = BetP(\theta_k) = \sum_{\substack{\theta_k \in A \\ A \subseteq \Theta}} \frac{m_c(A)}{|A|} \tag{11}$$

2.2 Experiments and results

The approach described in the papers is problem independent and does not impose any restrictions on the kind of features or information used by each agent. We use SimuroSot, one of FIRA simulation game, to evaluate the performance of this decision system.
SimuroSot is FIRA's robot football simulation match. The simulation system provides playground information: robots' position and rotation information of both sides and ball's position information. The strategy system assesses the situation based on the information and makes the responsive game (shown in Figure 3). From analyzing SimuroSot, we think that the strategy system must focus on two types of important information: the state of the ball and the strategy of opponent. The multi-agent decision system based on evidence reasoning of this paper is applied to the match situation assessment of SimuroSot, aiming at the ball state information and opponent's strategy information.

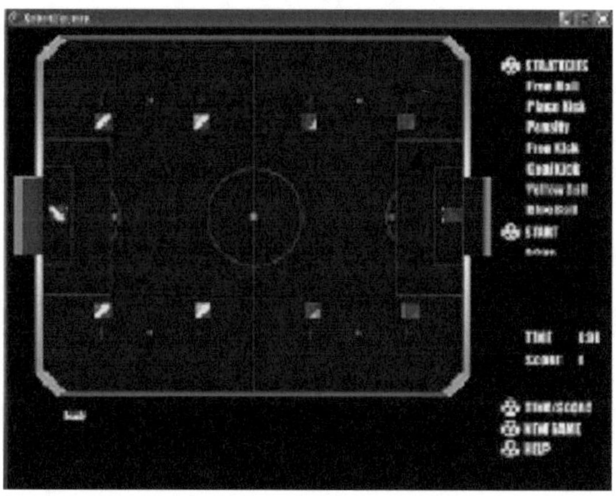

Fig. 3. the interface of SimuroSot platform

The ball state information is observed by agent p and agent d respectively. The two agents have different internal structure.
Agent p extracts ball's position features, the feature vector is ball's position coordinates: $\overline{S_p} = \{x, y\}$, and produces beliefs in each hypothesis of Θ_p = {threat, sub-threat, sub-good, good}, which is the frame of discernment of agent p. Base on the playground's property, there are four representative vector defined: $\omega_p^1, \omega_p^2, \omega_p^3, \omega_p^4$. So the measure function is as follow:

$$\Phi(\overline{S_p}, \theta_p^k) = \exp(-\gamma^k(d^k)) \tag{12}$$

where k=1,2,3,4, $\gamma^k > 0$, $d^k = \left\| \overline{S_p} - \omega_p^k \right\|$

Agent d extracts ball's movement direction features, the feature vector is ball's direction angle: $\overline{S_d} = \{\phi\}$, and produces beliefs in each hypothesis of Θ_d = {towards us, backwards us}, which is the frame of discernment of agent d. The goals of both sides are considered as reference point. Let the angle from ball's direction to goal home is φh, $0^o \le \phi_h \le 180^o$, and to goal opponent is φo, $0^o \le \phi_o \le 180^o$. We can define the measure function:

$$\Phi(\overline{S_d}, \theta_k^d) = \tfrac{1}{2}(\cos\phi_k + 1) \tag{13}$$

The fusion center takes the two agent's beliefs as input. The fusion center confirms the combination beliefs frame of discernment, Θf = {threat, sub-threat, sub-good, good}. So the beliefs of agent d must be transferred. Let $\sigma_1 : 2^{\Theta_d} \to 2^{\Theta_f}$ is a refining from Θ_d to Θ_f. During the transform, several rules are added according to the need of application, which is based on the area (area1, area2, area3) of ball to judge.

if ball is area$_1$*, then* σ_1*({towards us}) = {threat} and* σ_1*({backwards us}) = {sub-threat, sub-good, good},*
if ball is area$_2$*, then* σ_1*({towards us}) = {threat, sub-threat} and* σ_1*({backwards us}) = {sub-good, good},*
if ball is area$_3$*, then* σ_1*({towards us}) = {threat, sub-threat, sub-good} and* σ_1*({backwards us}) = {good},*
also $\sigma_1(\Theta_d) = \Theta_f$.

The fusion center also considers the two agents' belief reliability. Let αp and αd are the discounting factor of agent p and agent d, respectively. During the simulation, we design that, when ball is in middle-ground, α_p = 0.6 and α_d = 0.1; when ball is near the base line, α_p = 0.1 and α_d = 0.8

With the Dempster rule of combination, the fusion center leads to the basic probability assignment for hypotheses under consideration. The decision center computes pignsitic probabilities of each hypothesis based on combined beliefs. We can use these probabilities to judge the ball states.

Figure 4 describes the five different game states information. If the right side is us, the decision of game state is made by pignistic probability: $BetP_1$(threat), $BetP_2$(sub-threat), $BetP_3$(sub-good) and $BetP_4$(good). Table 1 shows that only agent p is used to observe the match and receive the game state. Table 2 shows the game state with the fusion of the observation of agent p and agent d. We can find that the distributed system makes the fusion of each agent's information and produces the more accuracy and more effective game state.

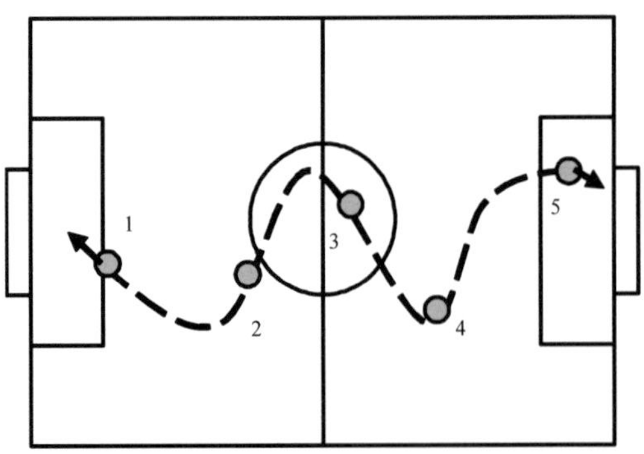

Fig. 4. Ball state: five cases (● is ball)

Game State	Pignistic probability			
	***BetP**$_1$*	***BetP**$_2$*	***BetP**$_3$*	***BetP**$_4$*
case 1	0.072856	0.159931	0.224461	0.542753
case 2	0.058579	0.220646	0.617479	0.103296
case 3	0.021759	0.856901	0.103349	0.017991
case 4	0.203953	0.457638	0.251437	0.086973
case 5	0.639409	0.172916	0.126939	0.060736

Table 1.

Game State		Pignistic probability			
		***BetP**$_1$*	***BetP**$_2$*	***BetP**$_3$*	***BetP**$_4$*
case 1	L	0.051437	0.108067	0.147387	0.693109
	R	0.083047	0.183288	0.258486	0.475180
case 2	L	0.078714	0.081742	0.617399	0.222144
	R	0.216245	0.505598	0.139411	0.138746
case 3	L	0.119005	0.123862	0.579351	0.177782
	R	0.054978	0.837930	0.054657	0.052435
case 4	L	0.125516	0.125686	0.506824	0.241973
	R	0.241554	0.596728	0.081055	0.080663
case 5	L	0.506455	0.240708	0.172812	0.080025
	R	0.636418	0.176342	0.127544	0.059696

Table 2. (L and R are two direction)

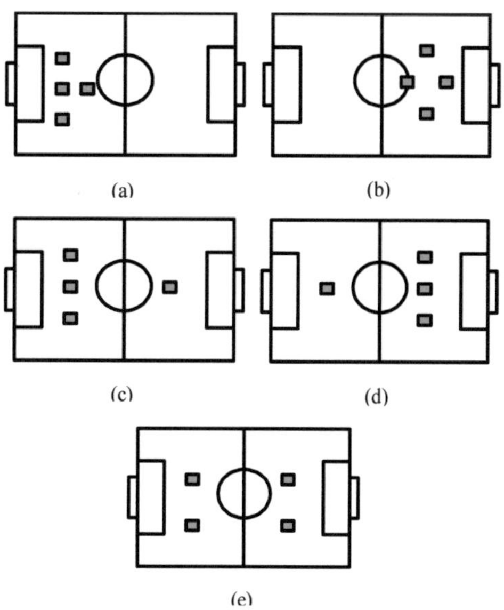

Fig. 5. Five kinds of opponent strategy formation(■ is opponent robot)

Opponent's strategy is the other focus. Each robot's information of opponent team has to be obtained. With the information, opponent's formation and decision are estimated. This is the important foundation of our decision-making. On basis of application to SimuroSot, the four agents are designed to observe the opponent's four robots except the goalkeeper. These agents have a common internal structure including domain knowledge, a set of hypothesis to be considered, and a procedure for assigning a level of belief to each hypothesis. Let Θr = {attack, balance, defense} be the frame of discernment. Each agent produces beliefs from opponent's robot position information, the feature vector is opponent robot's position coordinates: $\overline{S_i} = \{x_i, y_i\}$. The fusion center combines beliefs of the four agents in all the hypotheses with the Dempster rule and computes combined beliefs. Based on them, the decision center produces pignistic probabilities of each hypothesis, so that opponent strategy is estimated.
The five typical strategy formations is shown in Figure 5. If the right side is us, we can judge the opponent's strategy using decision center's output, pignistic probability: $BetP_1$(attack), $BetP_2$(balance) and $BetP_3$(defense), shown in Table 3.

Opponent strategy formation	**Pignistic probability**		
	***BetP*₁**	***BetP*₂**	***BetP*₃**
formation a	0.150022	0.849978	0.849978
formation b	0.814607	0.185393	0.185393
formation c	0.282619	0.717381	0.717381
formation d	0.634057	0.365943	0.365943
formation e	0.470250	0.529750	0.529750

Table 3.

2.3 Summary

The method of distributed decision based on TBM is presented in this paper. In the system architecture, the agents may be homogeneous, or may be heterogamous and do not communicate with each other. Each agent is independent and does not be imposed any restrictions on the kind of features or information used by itself. The fusion center integrates the information provided by all agents and computes the global environment beliefs. The decision center uses the probability transformation to produce the final conclusion.
In the application, we find that there are two key factors of the system operation performance: how to choose the frame of discernment and how to extract the features from the environment. Therefore, the multi-agent decision system of this paper should depend on the practicality characters to design agent's extracting features and to choose appropriate frame of discernment. The decision system must aim at the property of application and assign the rational discount factors to agents to improve the accuracy and effectively of this system.

3. Multi-agent learning reward function based on knowledge

Markov games and reinforcement learning are main research methods to Multi-Agent System (MAS) ((M. L. Littman., 2001) & (Bowling M.; Veloso M., 2004)). Markov game can fit for dealing with MAS coordination and building the dynamic model of multi-agent's interaction. Reinforcement learning is an interactive learning. Q-learning (C. J. C. H. Watkons & P. Dayan., 1992), one of reinforcement learning, is the dynamic programming learning based on Markov Decision Process (MDP). Applied to multi-agent system, reinforcement learning is extended to Markov games. Although reinforcement learning is focused on widely by its convergence and biology relativity, it does not work well in practice, especially to application to robot.

Reinforcement learning does not provide the mapping of state and action. After choosing an action, an agent is signaled the effect but do not know which is the optimal. Therefore, the agent depends on the interacting with environment to collect states, actions, the transition of states and reward in order to get the optimal policy. However, in practice, the reward received from environment is not immediate, but delayed, so learning becomes more difficult within the time-limited. Currently, how to design the reinforcement function, which maybe the most difficult to reinforcement learning, is seldom discussed. M. J. Matalic designs the reinforcement function by reinforcing multiple goals and using progress estimators (M. J. Mataric, 2001). Kousuk INOUE presents reinforcement learning is accelerated by using experience information to distill the general rules (Kousuke INOUE, et al., 2000). L. P. Kaelbling decomposes the learning task and combines the prior knowledge to direct reinforcement learning (W. D. Smart & L. P. Kaelbling., 2002).

Most research on reinforcement function is depended on application environment. Based on environment's property, learning system reduces complexity and introduces relative information to enrich reinforcement function so that the learner can obtain more knowledge about environment and itself to process reinforcement learning by. We have the same opinion. We design reinforcement function including two aspects: the information of goal state and the agent's action effect. The former is provided by environment, which is the interaction information between an agent and environment for accomplishing the special task, the latter is that the agent evaluates action effect, which depends on its domain knowledge of action ability. In this paper, the simulation game of Robot Soccer is applied.

3.1 Multi-agent reinforcement learning

In this section some basic principle of MDP is reviewed and then the formalisms of Markov games, which is an extension of MDPs. Q-learning algorithm is also presented, which is used to solve MDPs. Minmax-Q algorithm is proposed to solve Markov games.

a. MDP and Q-learning Algorithm

Let us consider a single agent interacting with its environment via perception and action. On each interaction step the agent senses the current state s of the environment, and chooses an action to perform. The action alters the state s of the environment, and a scalar reinforcement signal r (a reward or penalty) is provided to the agent to indicate the desirability of the resulting state.

Formally, a MDP is represented by a 4-tuple $<S, A, r, T>$: S is a set of states, A is a set of actions, r is a scalar reinforcement function, $r: S \times A \rightarrow R$, T is a state transition function, $T: S \times A \rightarrow S$.

The goal of the agent in the most common formulation of the reinforcement learning problem is to learn an optimal policy of actions that maximizes an expected cumulative sum of the reinforcement signal for any starting state. The task of an agent with RL is thus to learn a policy $\pi: S \rightarrow A$ that maps the current state s into the desirable action a to be performed in s.

The action policy π should be learned through trial-and-error interaction of the agent with the environment, which means that the learner must explicitly explore its environment.
There is at least one optimal policy π^* that is stationary and deterministic. One strategy to learn the optimal policy π^* when the model (T and r) is not known in advance is to allow the agent to learn the evaluation function Q: $S \times A \rightarrow R$. Each Q(s, a) value (or action value for pair s, a) represents the expected cost incurred by the agent when taking action at state s and following an optimal policy thereafter.
Q-learning algorithm iteratively approximates Q, provided the system can be modeled as a MDP, the reinforcement function is bounded, and actions are chosen so that every state-action pair is visited an infinite number of times. Q-learning rules (C. J. C. H. Watkons & P. Dayan, 1992) are:

$$Q(s,a) \leftarrow Q(s,a) + \alpha(r + \beta \max_{a'} Q(s',a') - Q(s,a)) \tag{14}$$

Where s is the current state, a is the action performed in s, r(s, a) is the reinforcement received after performing a in s, s' is the new state, β is a discount factor ($0 \le \beta < 1$) and a is the learning rate ($\alpha > 0$).

b. MDP and Q-learning Algorithm Markov games and Minmax-Q Algorithm

Let us consider a specialization of Markov games, which consists of two agents performing actions in alternating turns, in a zero-sum game. Let A be the set of possible actions that the playing agent A can choose from, and O be the set of actions for the opponent player agent O. r(s, o, a) is the immediate reinforcement agent A receives for performing action $a \in A$ in state $s \in S$ when its opponent agent O performs action $o \in O$.
The goal of agent A is to learn an optimal policy of actions that maximizes its expected cumulative sum of discounted reinforcements. However, learning this policy is very difficult, since it depends critically on the actions the opponent performs. The solution to this problem is to evaluate each policy with respect to the opponent's strategy that makes it look the worst [1]. This idea is the core of Minmax-Q algorithm, which is essentially very similar to Q-learning algorithm with a minmax replacing the max function in the definition of the state value.
For deterministic action policies, the value of a state $s \in S$ in a MG is:

$$V(s) = \max_{a \in A} \min_{o \in O} Q(s,a,o) \tag{15}$$

And Minmax-Q learning rule is:

$$Q(s,a,o) \leftarrow Q(s,a,o) + \alpha[r(s,a,o) + \beta V(s') - Q(s,a,o)] \tag{16}$$

where s is the current state, a is the action performed by agent A in s, o is the action performed by agent O in s, Q(s, a, o) is the expected discounted reinforcement for taking action a when Agent O performs o in state s, and continuing the optimal policy thereafter, r(s, o, a) is the reinforcement received by agent A, s' is the new state, β is a discount factor ($0 \le \beta < 1$) and α is the learning rate ($\alpha > 0$).
For non-deterministic action policies, a more general formulation of Minmax-Q has been formally defined elsewhere.

3.2 Reinforcement function based on knowledge

Reinforcement learning systems learn a mapping from situations to actions by trial-and-error interactions with a dynamic environment. The goal of reinforcement learning is defined using the concept of a reinforcement function, which is the exact function of future reinforcements the agent seeks to maximize. In other words, there exists a mapping from state/action pairs to reinforcements; after performing an action in a given state the learner agent will receive some reinforcement (reward) in the form of a scalar value. The agent learns to perform actions that will maximize the sum of the reinforcements received when starting from some initial state and proceeding to a terminal state.

Perhaps, design of reinforcement is the most difficult aspect of setting up a reinforcement learning system. The action performed by the learner not only receives an immediate reward but also transits the environment to a new state. Therefore, the learning has to consider both the immediate reward and the future reinforcement caused by the current action. Nowadays, much of reinforcement learning work uses two types of reward: immediate, and very delayed. In reinforcement learning system, immediate reinforcement, when available, is the most effective. And delayed reinforcement requires introduction of sub-goal so that learning is performed within time-limited. Reinforcement learning is a feedback algorithm, so it is not good for long-term goal but more effective to the near goals. A learner can introduce medium-term goals and distributing task so as to accelerate the learning rate and increase the learning efficiency.

In traditional reinforcement learning, the agent-environment interaction can be modeled as a MDP, in which agent and environment are synchronized finite state automata. However, in real-world, the environment and agent states change asynchronously, in response to events. Events take various amounts of time to execute: the same event (as perceived by the agent) can vary in duration under different circumstances and have different consequences. Reinforcement learning gives the reward to what are caused by and in control of the agent.

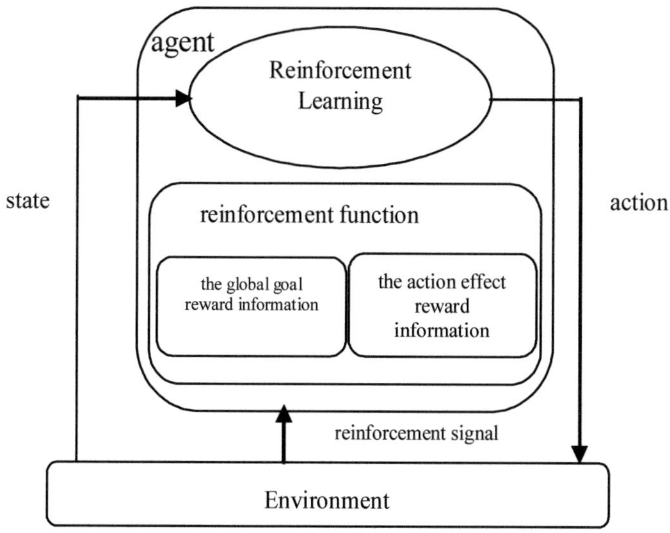

Fig. 5. Learning Model

Instead of encoding knowledge explicitly, reinforcement learning hides it in the reinforcement function which usually employs some ad hoc embedding of the semantics of the domain. We divide this reinforcement information involving domain knowledge into two types:

- The global goal's reward;
- The agent action effect's reward.

In each state, a learner agent chooses an appropriate action and performs it to environment, which is transited to a new state. On the one hand, the agent depends on the task to judge the environment and receives the global goal reward; on the other hand, based on the agent's domain knowledge about its action ability, it compares performance effect and obtains the reward of action. The reinforcement function that we design combines the global environment's reinforcement and the agent action's reinforcement. The reinforcement learning model with this reinforcement function is shown in Figure 5.

3.3 Experiments

a. Experimental Environment

We adopted the Robot Soccer to perform our experiments. Robot Soccer is a typical MAS: robots is the agents, the playground and ball are thought as environment.
State, actions of multi-agent learning are design as follows:

- S = {threat, sub-threat, sub-good, good};
- Home agents' A = {Shoot, Attack, Defend, More-defend};
- Opponent agents' O = {Shoot, Attack, Defend, More-defend}

In traditional reinforcement learning, reinforcement function is usually developed that reward is +1 if home team scored; reward is -1 if opponent team scored. Instead of it, we design the reinforcement function including two kinds of information: game goal reinforcement and robot's action effect reinforcement.
In play, game goal reinforcement information is the reward received by score of both sides. The rewards signal rs, is defined as:

$$r_s = \begin{cases} c, & \text{our team scored} \\ -c, & \text{opponent team scored} \\ 0, & \text{otherwise} \end{cases} \quad c > 0 \tag{17}$$

And, reinforcement information of the robot's action effect is that, after performing each action, the robot receives the reward signal ra, which involves the robot's domain knowledge about each action and evaluates the action effect.

$$r_a = \begin{cases} d & \text{action success} \\ 0 & \text{action unsuccesss} \end{cases} \quad d > 0, \tag{18}$$

The combination reinforcement function considers the two kinds of reward and sums them with weighting their values constants appropriately.

$$\begin{aligned} &R = \omega_s \bullet r_s + \omega_a \bullet r_a \\ &\omega_s, \omega_a \geq 0, \quad (\omega_s + \omega_a) = 1 \end{aligned} \tag{19}$$

Thus, the robot agent evaluates its policy using comprehensive reinforcement. With learning continually, the agent improves its policy and increases its ability.

b. Experimental Result

We use SimuroSot, one of simulation match provided by FIRA [11] to conduct the experiments. In experiments, In order to evaluate the effectiveness of the reinforcement function presented in this paper, we compare its performance against traditional reinforcement function.
traditional reinforcement function:

$$R = \begin{cases} +1 & \text{hom}\,e\ \textit{team scored} \\ \text{-}1 & \textit{opponent team scored} \end{cases} \tag{20}$$

reinforcement function based on knowledge:

$$R = \omega_s \bullet r_s + \omega_a \bullet r_a \tag{21}$$

There are two group experiments. In experiment 1, the home team uses the conventional Q-learning. In experiment 2, the home team uses the Minmax-Q algorithm of Markov Games. The opponent team uses fix strategy. The team size is 1.
The parameters used in the algorithms were set at: $\beta = 0.9$, initial value of $\alpha = 1.0$, α decline = 0.9. In Q-learning, initial value of Q-table = 0. In Minmax-Q algorithm, initial value of Q-table = 1.
In experiment, we define that the appropriate policy is: s1→a1,s2→a2, s3→a3, s4→a4. For Q-learning algorithm, we save several Q-values, which are $Q(s_1,a_1)$, $Q(s_2,a_2)$, $Q(s_3,a_3)$, $Q(s_4,a_4)$. And for Minmax-Q algorithm, we save Q-values, which are $\underset{o \in O}{Min}\, Q(s_1, a_1, o)$, $\underset{o \in O}{Min}\, Q(s_2, a_2, o)$, $\underset{o \in O}{Min}\, Q(s_3, a_3, o)$ and $\underset{o \in O}{Min}\, Q(s_4, a_4, o)$.
During more than 1000 steps learning, we analyze their results. Q-learning with the two kinds of reinforcement function all can converge to appropriate policy, but the former needs long time. In Minmax-Q algorithm, it can get to appropriate policy with knowledge-base reinforcement function, while it does not learn appropriate policy with traditional reinforcement function even if spending too long time. We choose the same Minmax-Q value to observe.
The results of Q-learning are shown in Figure 6. The results of Minmax-Q are shown in Figure 7. Thereinto, Figure 5(a) and Figure 6(a) are respectively the learning with traditional reinforcement function; Figure 5(b) and Figure 6(b) are respectively the learning with

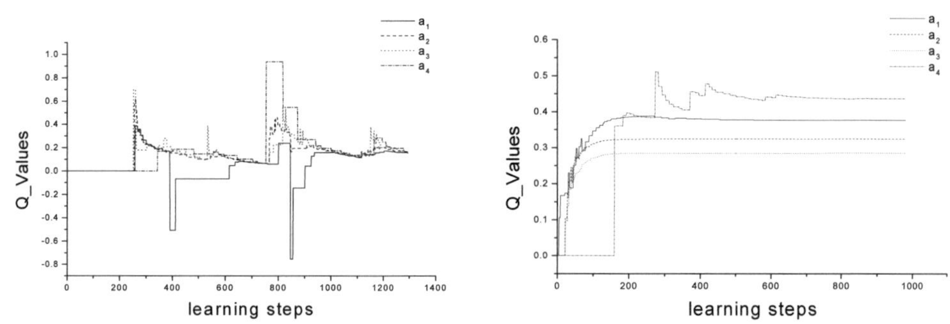

(a) (b)

Fig. 6 (a). Q-learning algorithm with the traditional reinforcement function; (b). Q-learning algorithm with the knowledge-base reinforcement function

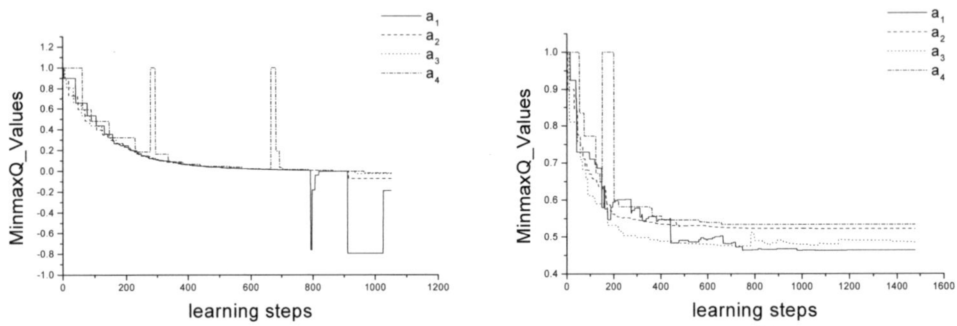

(a) (b)

Fig. 7 (a). Minmax-Q algorithm with the traditional reinforcement function; (b). Minmax-Q algorithm with the knowledge-base reinforcement function

knowledge-base reinforcement function. Obviously, we can observe that learning with traditional reinforcement function has worse convergence and still has many unstable factors at end of experiment, while the learning with knowledge-base reinforcement function converges rapidly and it gets to stable value about half time of experiment. Therefore, with the external knowledge (environment information) and internal knowledge (action effect information), multi-agent learning has better performance and effectivity.

3.4 Summary

When Multi-agent learning is applied to real environment, it is very important to design the reinforcement function that is appropriate to environment and learner. We think that the learning agent must take advantage of the information including environment and itself domain knowledge to integrate the comprehensive reinforcement information. This paper presents the reinforcement function based on knowledge, with which the learner not only pays more attention to environment transition but also evaluates its action performance each step. Therefore, the reinforcement information of multi-agent learning becomes more abundant and comprehensive, so that the leaning can converge rapidly and become more stable. From experiment, it is obviously that multi-agent learning with knowledge-base reinforcement function has better performance than traditional reinforcement. However, we should point out, how to design the reinforcement must depend on the application background of multi-agent learning system. Different task, different action effect and different environments are the key factors to influence multi-agent learning. Hence, differ from traditional reinforcement function; the reinforcement function is build by the characteristic based on real environment and learner action.

4. Distributed multi-agent reinforcement learning and its application in multi-robot

Multi-agent coordination is mainly based on agents' learning abilities under distributed environment ((Yang, X. M. Li, & X. M. Xu, 2001), (Y. Chang, T. Ho, & L. P. Kaelbling, 2003), (Kok, J. R. & Vlassis, N., 2006)). In this section, a multi-agent coordination based on distributed reinforcement learning is proposed. In this way, a coordination agent decomposes the global task of system into several sub-tasks and applies the central reinforcement learning to distribute these sub-tasks to task agents. Each task agent uses the individual reinforcement learning to choose its action and accomplish its sub-task.

4.1 Distributed reinforcement learning of MAS

Currently, research on distributed reinforcement learning of MAS mainly includes the central reinforcement learning (CRL), the individual reinforcement learning (IRL), the group reinforcement learning (GRL) and the social reinforcement learning (SRL) (Zhong Yu; Zhang Rubo & Gu Guochang, 2003).

The CRL aims at the coordinating mechanism of MAS and adopts the standard reinforcement learning algorithm to accomplish an optimal coordination. The distributed problem of the system is focused on and resolved by learning centrally. In a CRL, the whole state of MAS is the input and the action assignment of every agent is the output. The agents in CRL system are not the learning unit but an actuator unit to perform the orders of the learning unit passively. The structure of CRL is shown in Figure 8.

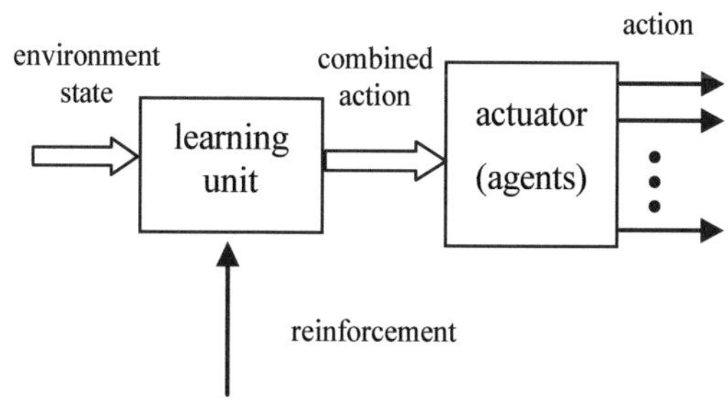

Fig. 8. the structure of CRL

In IRL, all agents are the learning units. They perceive the environment state and choose the actions to receive the maximized reward. An IRL agent does not care about other agents' states and only considers its reward to choose the action, so it is selfish and the learning system has difficulty in attaining the global optimal goal. However, the IRL has strong independence and is easy to add or reduce the agents dynamically. Also the number of agents has less effect on learning convergence. The structure of IRL is shown in Figure 9.

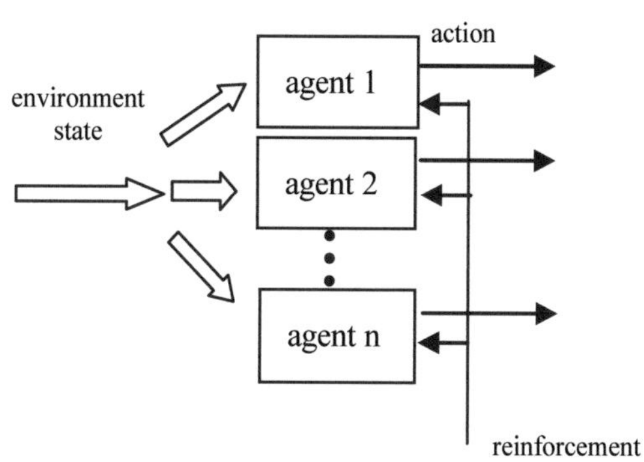

Fig. 9. the structure of IRL

The GRL regards all agents' states and actions as the combined states and actions. In a GRL, the Q-table of each agent maps the combined states into the combined actions. A GRL agent must consider other agents' states and choose its action based on the global reward. The GRL has an enormous state space and action space, so it would learn much more slowly as the number of agents grew, which is not feasible. The structure of GRL is shown in Figure 10.

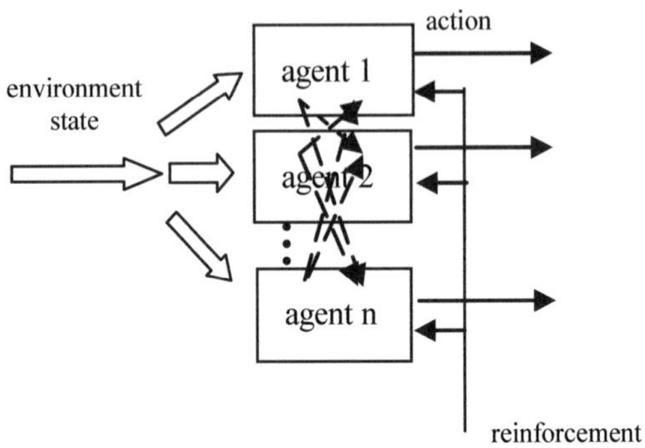

Fig. 10. the structure of GRL

SRL is thought as the extension of IRL. It is the combination of IRL, social models and economical models. The SRL simulates the individual interaction of human society and builds the social model or economical model. In SRL, the methodology of management and sociology is introduced to adjust the relation of agents and produces more effective communication, cooperation and competition mechanisms so as to attain the learning goal of the whole system.

4.2 Multi-agent coordination based on reinforcement learning

In this section, the multi-agent coordination based on distributed reinforcement learning is proposed, which is shown in Figure 11. This coordination method is a hierarchical structure: coordination level and behavioral level. The complicated task is decomposed and distributed to the two levels for learning.

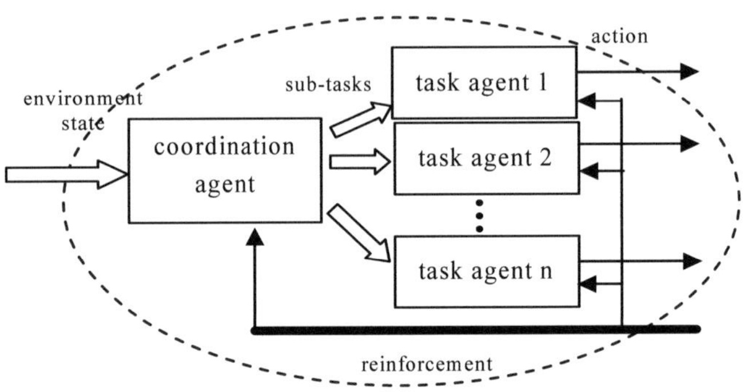

Fig. 11. the structure of multi-agent coordination based on distributed reinforcement learning

a. Coordination Level

Coordination level decomposes the complicated task into several sub-tasks firstly. Let $P = \{p_1, p_2, \ldots, p_m\}$ be a set of strategies of coordination agent, where $p_i\ (1 \le i \le m)$ is the element of the set of strategies and corresponds to the assignment of sub-tasks. Based on the environment state, coordination agent adopts CRL to choose the appropriate strategy and distributes the sub-tasks to task agents. The update for coordination agent's Q function can be written:

$$
\begin{aligned}
Q_p(s,p) &\leftarrow (1-\alpha_p)Q_p(s,p) \\
&+\alpha_p\left[r_p + \beta \max_{p' \in P} Q_p(s',p')\right]
\end{aligned}
\tag{22}
$$

where s is the current state, p is the strategy chosen by coordination agent in s, rp is the reward signal received by coordination agent, s′ is the next state, α_p is the learning rate of coordination agent, β is the discount factor.

b. Behavioral Level

In behavioral level, all task agents have a common internal structure. Let A be the action set of task agents. Each sub-task corresponding an action sub-set, $SA_k \subseteq A$, is assigned to a task agent. According to the sub-task, each task agent k ($1 \le k \le n$) adopts the IRL to choose its action, $a^k \in SA_k$, and performs it to environment. The update for Q function of task agent k is written:

$$
\begin{aligned}
Q^k(s,a^k) &\leftarrow (1-\alpha^k)Q^k(s,a^k) \\
&+\alpha^k\left[r^k + \beta \max_{a^k{}' \in st_k} Q_p(s',a^k{}')\right]
\end{aligned}
\tag{23}
$$

where s is the current state, ak is the action performed by task agent k in s, rk is the reinforcement signal received by task agent k, s′ is the next state, αk is the learning rate of task agent k, β is the discount factor.

c. Reinforcement assignment

The reinforcement assignment is that the reinforcement signal received from environment is assigned to all agents in distributed system according to the effective method. In this paper, we design a heterogeneous reinforcement function: global task reinforcement and sub-tasks' coordination effect reinforcement.

Coordination agent is responsible to decide the high-level strategies and focuses on the global task achievement. Simultaneously, it arranges the sub-tasks to all task agents. So its reinforcement information includes both the global task and sub-tasks' coordination effect. All task agents coordinate and cooperate so as to take their actions to accomplish the high-level strategies. So their learning is evaluated by sub-tasks' coordination effect.

4.3 Experiments and results

The SimuroSot simulation platform [10] is applied to the evaluation of our proposed method. In this simulation platform, the simulation system provides the environment information (ball's and all robots' position information), from which the strategic system makes decision to control each robot's action and perform it to the game.

In the distributed reinforcement learning system, the state set is defined to S = {threat, sub-threat, sub-good, good}. In the coordination level, the strategy set of coordination agent is defined to H = {hard-defend, defend, offend, strong-offend}. In the behavioral level, the action set of task agents is defined to A = {guard, resist, attack, shoot}.

The global goal of games is to encourage home team's scoring and avoid opponent team's scoring. The reward of global goal is defined:

$$r_g = \begin{cases} c, & our\ team\ scored \\ -c, & other\ team\ scored \\ 0, & otherwise \end{cases} \tag{24}$$
$$c > 0$$

The reinforcement of sub-tasks' coordination effect is to evaluate the home team's strategies, which includes the domain knowledge of each strategy. It is defined:

$$r_a = \begin{cases} d & strategy\ success \\ 0 & strategy\ unsuccess \end{cases} \tag{25}$$
$$d > 0,$$

Coordination agent sums the two kinds of reinforcement, weighting their values constants appropriately, so its reinforcement function, R_c, is defined:

$$R_c = \omega \bullet r_g + \upsilon \bullet r_a$$
$$\omega, \upsilon \geq 0, \quad (\omega + \upsilon) = 1 \tag{26}$$

Task agents cooperate and take their actions to accomplish the team strategies. Their reinforcement function, Rm, is defined: $R_m = r_a$

The parameters used in the algorithm are set at : β = 0.9, initial value of α = 1.0, α decline = 0.9, initial value of Q-table = 0.

There are two groups in experiments. The conventional reinforcement learning (group 1) and our proposed distributed reinforcement learning (group 2) are applied to the home team respectively. The opponent team uses random strategy. The team size is 2.

The results of group 1 are shown in Figure 12a and Figure 12b respectively. During the simulation, the convergence of Q-learning has worse performance. Two Robots cannot learn the deterministic action policies.

In group 2, Figure 13a shows the Q-value of the coordination agent, which convergent rapidly. From the Q's maximum, coordination agent can get the effective and feasible result. Figure 13b and Figure 13c describe two Robots' Q values respectively, which are convergent. Robots can get deterministic policy to choose actions.

4.4 Summary

With agents' coordination and cooperation, MAS adopts multi-agent learning to accomplish the complicated tasks that the single agent is not competent for. Multi-agent learning provides not only the learning ability of individual agent, but also the coordination learning of all agents. Coordination agent decomposes the complicated task into sub-tasks and adopts the CRL to choose the appropriate strategy for distributing the subtasks. Task agents adopt the IRL to choose the effective actions to achieve the complicated task. With application and experiments in robot soccer, this method has better performance than the conventional reinforcement learning.

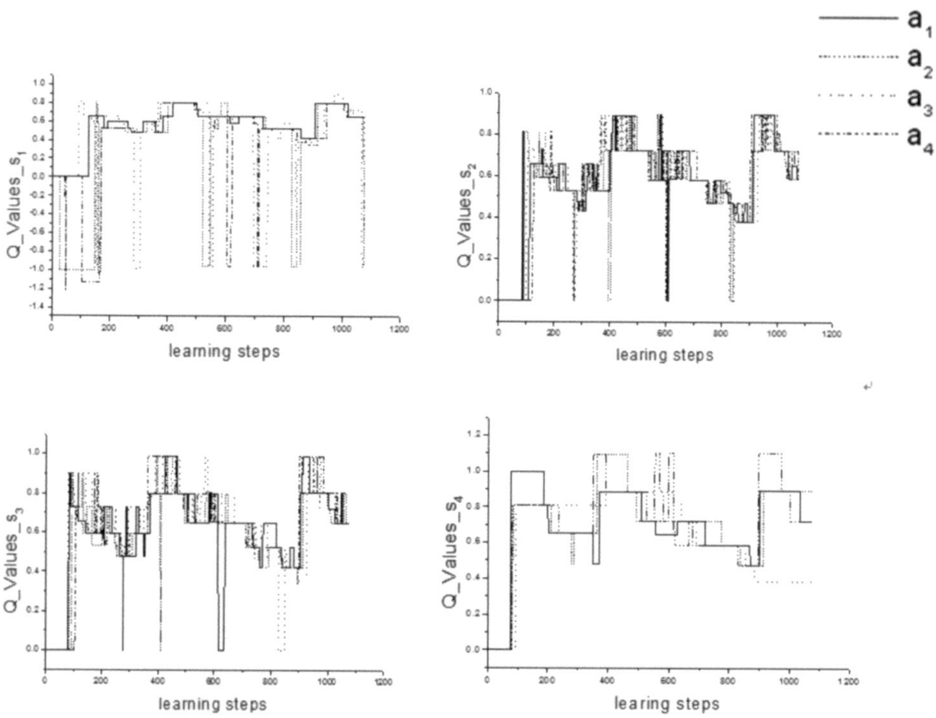

Fig. 12a. Q-values of Robot 1 in group 1

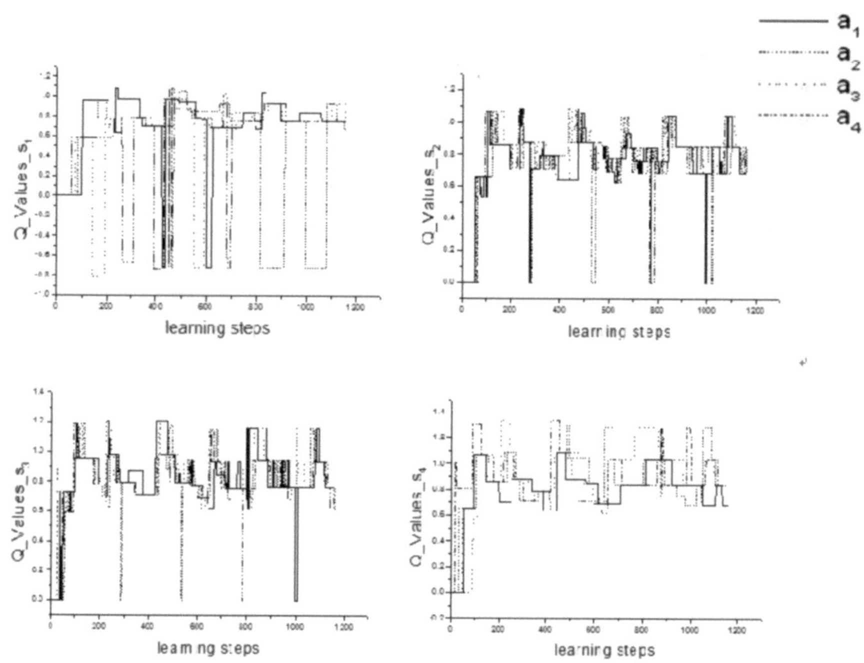

Fig. 12b. Q-values of Robot 2 in group 1

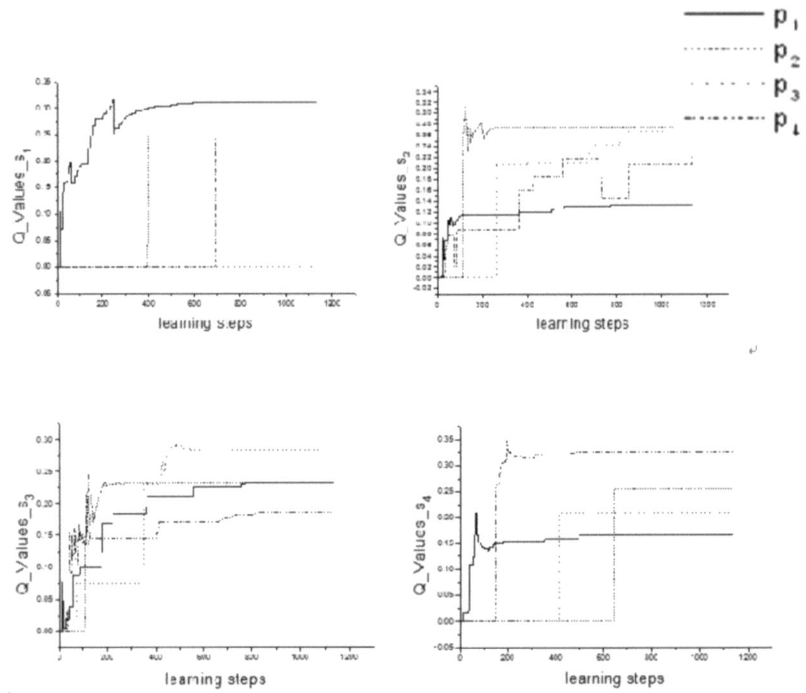

Fig. 13a. Q-values of coordination agent in group 2

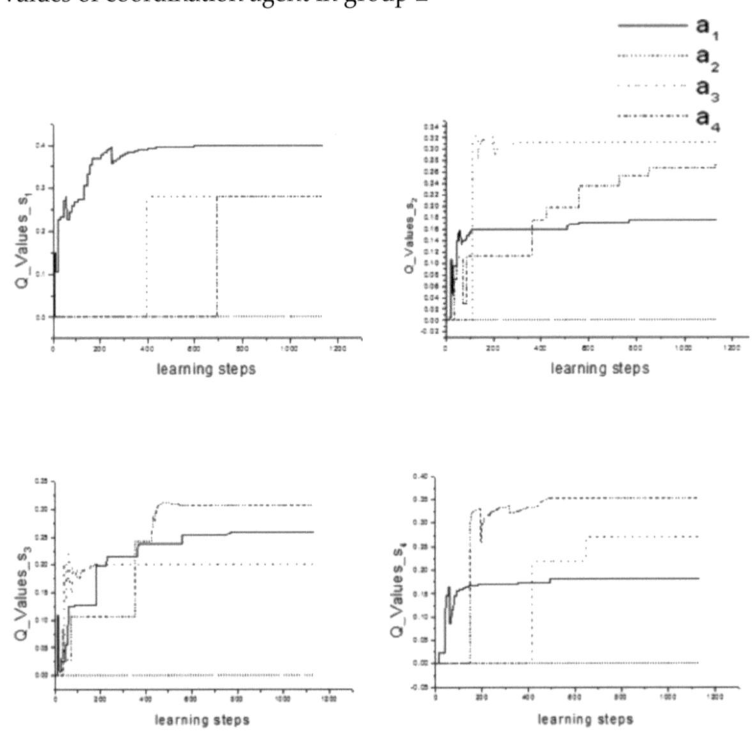

Fig. 13b. Q-values of Robot 1 in group 2

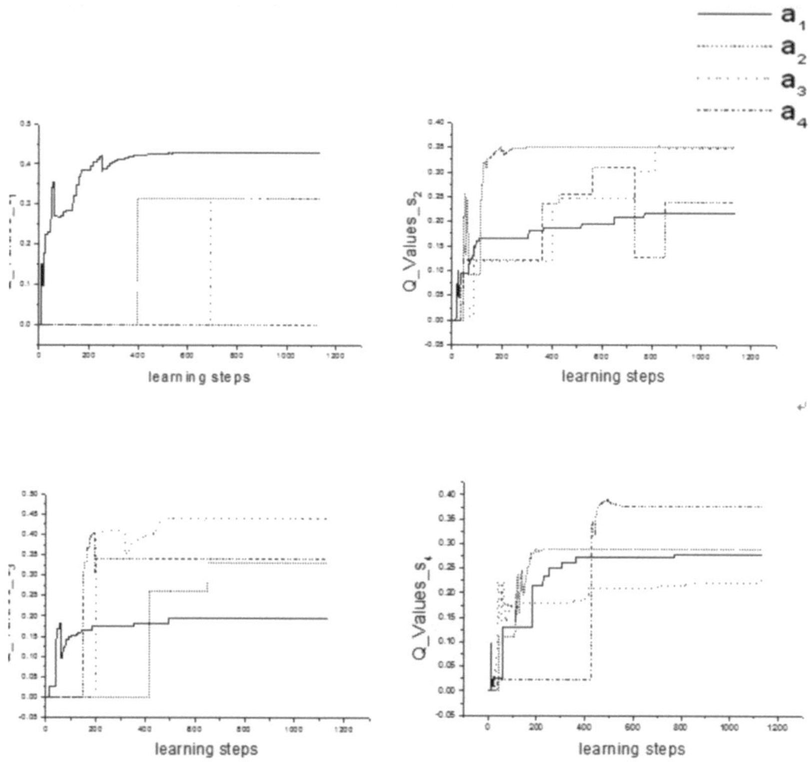

Fig. 13c. Q-values of Robot 2 in group 2

5. Multi-robot coordination framework based on Markov games

The emphasis of MAS enables the agents to accomplish the complicated tasks or resolve the complex problems with their negotiation, coordination and cooperation. Games and learning are the inherence mechanism of the agents' collaboration. On the one side, within rational restriction, agents choose the optimal actions by interacting each other. On the other side, based on the information of environment and other agents' actions, agents adopt the learning to deal with the special problem or fulfill the distributed task.

At present, research on multi-agent learning lacks the mature theory. Littman takes the games as the framework of multi-agent learning (M. L. Littman, 1994). He presents the Minmax Q-learning to resolve the zero-sum Markovgames, which only fit to deal with the agents' competition. The coordination of MAS enables the agents not only to accomplish the task cooperatively, but also to resolve the competition with opponents effectively. On the basis of Littman's multi-agent game and learning, we analyze the different relationship of agents and present a layered multi-agent coordination framework, which includes both their competition and cooperation.

5.1 Multi-agent coordination based on Markov games

Because of the interaction of cooperation and competition, all agents in the environment are divided into several teams. The agents are teammates if they are cooperative. Different agent teams are competitive. Two kinds of Markov games are adopted to cope with the different interaction: zero-sum games are used to the competition between different agent teams; team games are applied to the teammates' cooperation.

a. Team level: zero-sum Markov games

Zero-sum Markov games are a well-studied specialization of Markov games in which two agents have diametrically opposed goals. Let agent A and agent O be the two agents within zero-sum game. For $a \in A$, $o \in O$ (A and O are the action sets of agent A and agent O respectively) and $s \in S$ (S is the state set), R1(s, a, o) = - R2(s, a, o). Therefore, there is only a single reward function R1, which agent A tries to maximize and agent O tries to minimize. Zero-sum games can also be called adversarial or fully competitive for this reason.
Within a Nash equilibrium of zero-sum game, each policy is evaluated with respect to the opposing policy that makes it look the worst. Minmax Q-learning (M. L. Littman, 1994) is a reinforcement learning algorithm specifically designed for zero-sum games. The essence of minimax is that behave so as to maximize your reward in the worst case. The value function, V(s), is the expected reward for the optimal policy starting from state s. Q(s, a, o) is the expected reward for taking action a when the opponent chooses o from state s and continuing optimally thereafter.

$$V(s) = \max_{\pi \in PD(A)} \min_{o \in O} \sum_{a \in A} Q(s,a,o)\pi_a \tag{27}$$

The update rule for minimax Q-learning can be written:

$$\begin{aligned} Q(s,a,o) \leftarrow & (1-\alpha)Q(s,a,o) \\ & + \alpha(r + \beta V(s)) \end{aligned} \tag{28}$$

In MAS, there are several competitive agent-teams. Each of teams has a team commander to be responsible for making decision. Therefore, two teams' competition simplifies the competition between two Team-commanders, which adopt the zero-sum Markov games.

b. Member level: team Markov games

In team Markov games, agents have precisely the same goals. Supposed that there are n agents, for $a1 \in A1$, $a2 \in A2$,…, $an \in An$, and $s \in S$, R1(s, a1, a2,…,an) = R2(s, a1, a2,…,an) = …. Therefore, there is only a single reward function R1, which all agents try to maximize together. Team games can also be called coordination games or fully cooperative games for this reason.
Team Q-learning (Michael L. Littman., 2001) is a reinforcement learning algorithm specifically designed for team games. In team games, because every reward received by agent 1 is received by all agents, we have that Q1=Q2=…=Qn. Therefore, only one Q-function needs to be learned. The value function is defined:

$$V_1(s) = \max_{a_1,\dots a_n} Q_1(s,a_1,\dots,a_n) \tag{29}$$

The update rule for team Q-learning can be written:

$$\begin{aligned} Q_1(s,a_1,\dots,a_n) \leftarrow & (1-\alpha)Q_1(s,a_1,\dots,a_n) \\ & + \alpha(r_1 + \beta V_1(s)) \end{aligned} \tag{30}$$

In MAS, an agent team consists of the agents that have the same goal. Because of cooperation in a team, agents adopt team Markov game to cooperate each other to accomplish the task.
We present the multi-agent coordination framework shown in Figure 14. Based on the environment information and opponent information, Team commander applies zero-sum Markov game to make decision of the team level. According to team commander's strategies, member agents use the team Markov game to make the decision of member level, performing their actions to environment.

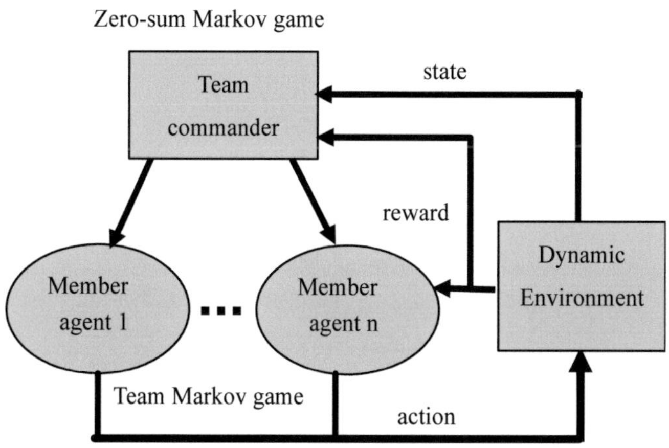

Fig. 14. Multi-agent coordination framework

Team commander's strategies aim at the environment and opponent team. Also, these strategies arrange different actions' choice scope to all member agents. Team commander decomposes the complex task to several strategies. Each of them divides member agents into different roles, which are according to basic skills of member agents. Each member agent carries out its skill by learning.
The decomposition of task and arrangement of roles are designed based on application system and domain knowledge. How to make decision and accomplish task is learned by multi-agent coordination framework.

5.2 Experiment and results

a. Experiment setup

Robot soccer is a typical MAS. SimuroSot simulation platform is applied to evaluate our proposed method. Ball and playground is environment. Robots are agents. We define the state set, S = {threat, sub-threat, sub-good, good}. The opponent team situation is defined to O = {hard-defend, defend, offend, strong-offend}. In the team commander, there is a team-level strategy set, H = {hard-defend, defend, offend, strong-offend}. Each member agent has the action set, A = {guard, resist, attack, shoot}. Each team level strategy corresponds to a team formation and arranges the roles of all member agents.
In multi-agent learning, traditional reinforcement function is usually developed that reward is +1 if the home team scored; reward is -1 if the opponent team scored. In order to accelerate learning, we design a heterogeneous reinforcement function, which reinforces multiple goals including global and local goals.

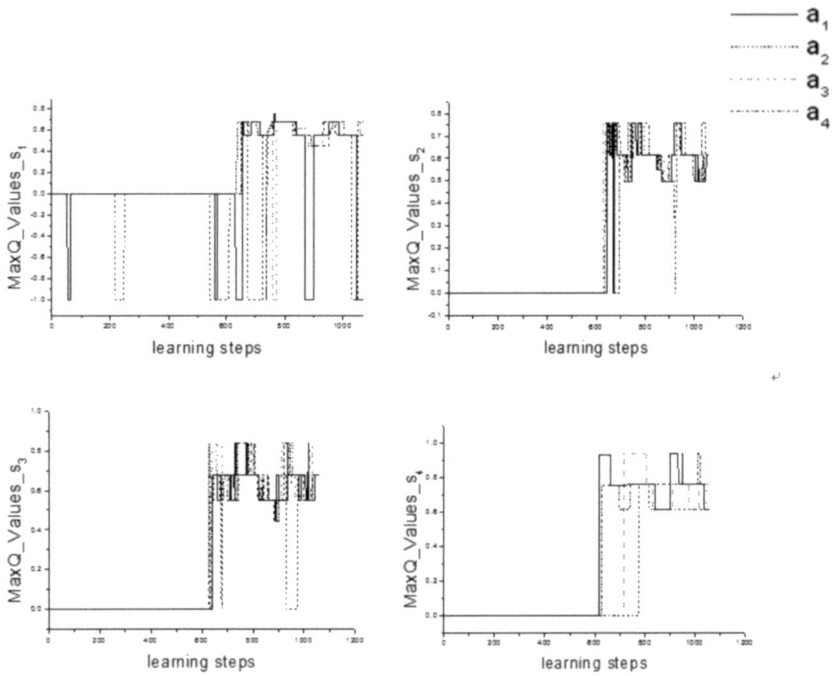

(a)

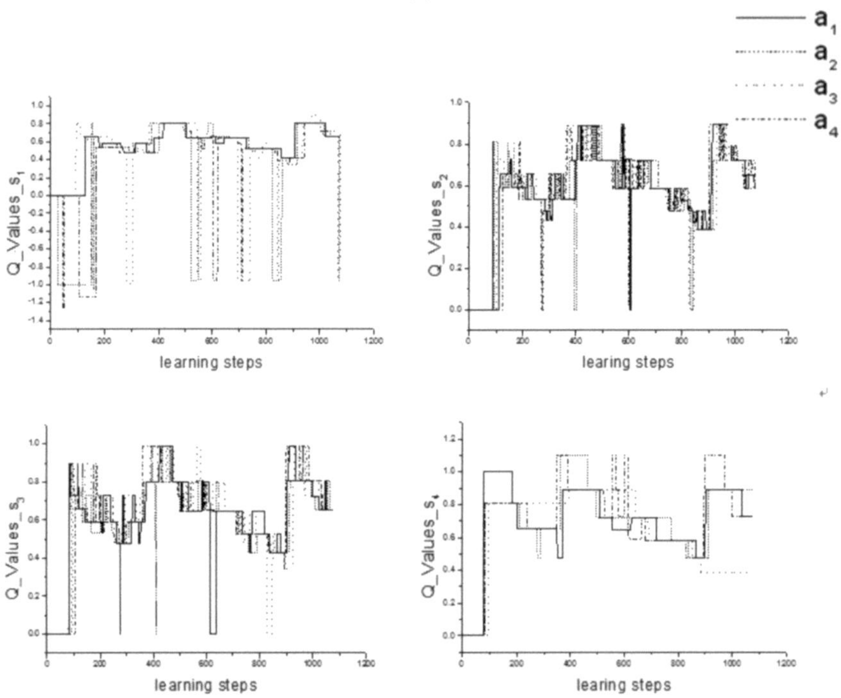

(b)

Fig. 15. Q-values of Robot 1, 2 in experiment 1

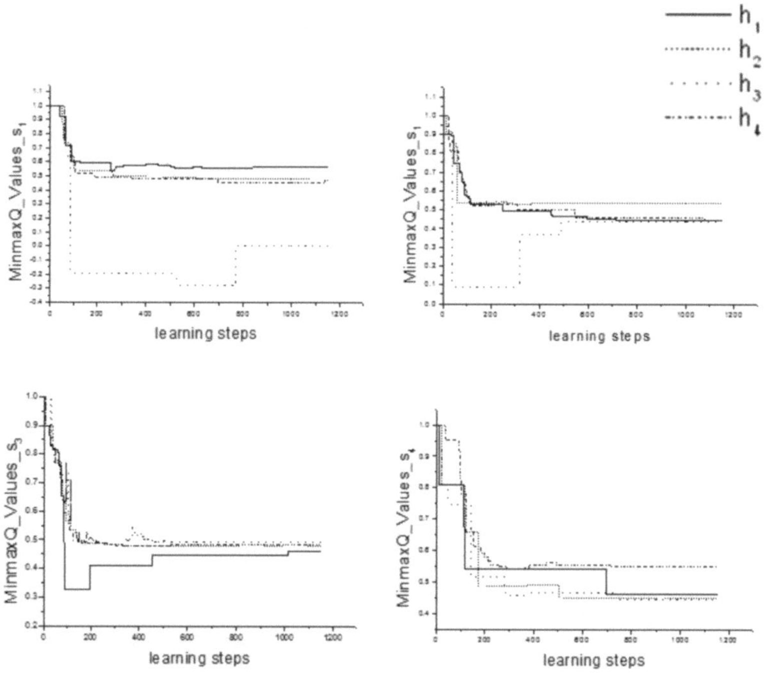

Fig. 16a. Q-values of Team commander in experiment 2

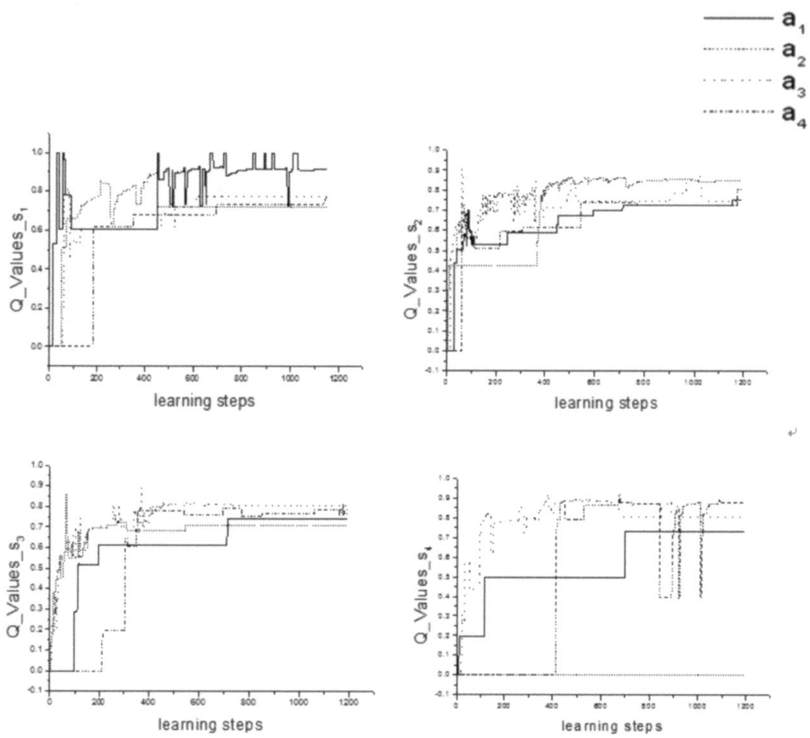

(b)

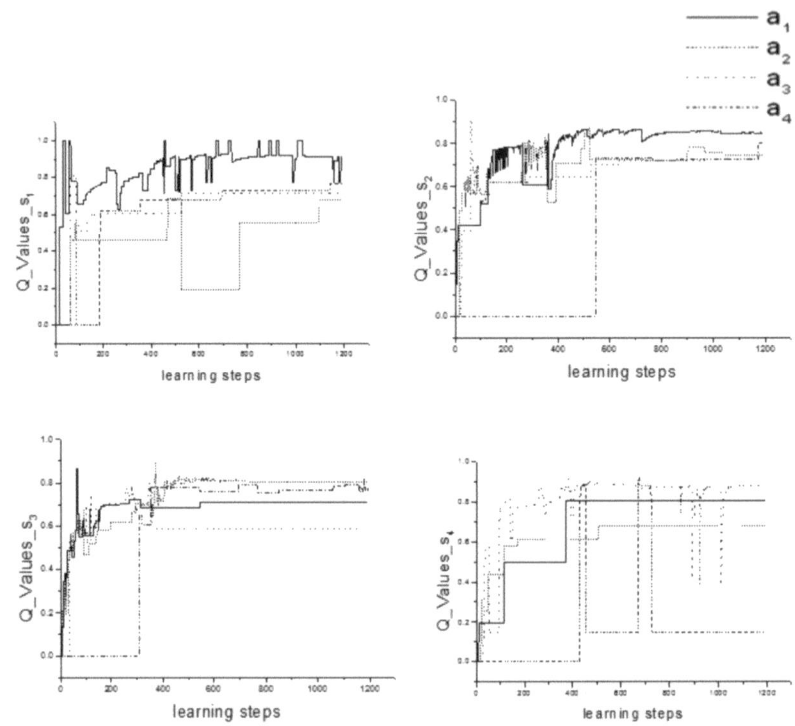

(c)

Fig. 16b-c. Q-values of Robot 1, 2 in experiment 2

The global goal of match is to encourage home team's scoring and avoid opponent team's scoring. The reward of global goal is defined:

$$r_g = \begin{cases} c, & our\ team\ scored \\ -c, & other\ team\ scored \\ 0, & otherwise \end{cases} \tag{31}$$

$$c > 0$$

The local goals are to achieve home team's cooperative strategies. This reinforcement includes the domain knowledge and evaluates member agents' cooperative effect. It is defined:

$$r_a = \begin{cases} d & strategy\ success \\ 0 & strategy\ unsuccess \end{cases} \tag{32}$$

$$d > 0,$$

Team commander sums the two kinds of reinforcement, weighting their values constants appropriately, so its reinforcement function, Rc, is defined:

$$R_c = \omega \bullet r_g + \upsilon \bullet r_a$$
$$\omega, \upsilon \geq 0, \quad (\omega + \upsilon) = 1 \tag{33}$$

In member level, team games focus on the cooperation of member agents. Its reinforcement function, Rm, is defined:

$$R_m = r_a \quad (33)$$

b. Results

There are two group experiments. In experiment 1, the home team uses the conventional Q-learning. In experiment 2, the home team uses our proposed method. The opponent team uses fix strategy. The team size is 2.

The results of experiment 1 are shown in Figure 4a and Figure 4b respectively. The learning of two Robots has worse convergence and still has many unstable factors at the end of experiment. In the results of experiment 2, Figure 5a shows zero-sum game performance of the team commander. The values of $\underset{o \in O}{Min} Q(s_i, h_j, o)$ (i, j = 1, 2, 3, 4) are recorded. They are convergent rapidly. Team commander gets the effective and rational strategy. Figure 5b and Figure 5c describe two Robots' Q values, $\underset{a \in A}{Min} Q(s_i, a_j, a)$ and $\underset{a \in A}{Min} Q(s_i, a, a_j)$ (i, j = 1, 2, 3, 4) respectively, which are convergent. Robots can get deterministic policy to choose actions.

5.3 Summary

In multi-agent environment, neglecting the agents' interaction of competition and cooperation, multi-agent learning can not acquire the better performance. This paper proposed a multi-agent coordination framework based on Markov game, in which team level adopts zero-sum game to resolve competition with opponent team and member level adopts team game to accomplish agents' cooperation. By applying the proposed method to Robot Soccer, its performance is better than the conventional Q-learning. However, this paper only discusses two agent teams' relationship. How to deal with the games and learning of multiple agent teams in multi-agent environment will confront with more challenges and difficulties.

6. References

Galina Rogova & Pierre Valin. (2005). Data fusion for situation monitoring, incident detection, alert and response management, Amsterdam, Washington, D.C.: IOS Press.

Dempster, A. P. (1967). Upper and Lower Probabilities Induced by a Multivalued Mapping. Ann. Math. Statist., vol. 38, pp. 325-339.

Shafer, G. (1976). A Mathematical Theory of Evidence, Princeton University Press.

Elouedi, Z.; Mellouli, K. & Smets, P. (2004). Assessing sensor reliability for multisensor data fusion within the transferable belief model. In: IEEE Transactions on Systems, Man, and Cybernetics, Vol: 34, Issue 2, Feb, pp.782- 787

Philippe Smets. (2005). Decision making in the TBM: the necessity of the pignistic transformation. International Journal of Approximate Reasoning, Vol 38, Issue 2, February, pp. 133-147.

Rogova G. (2003) Adaptive decision fusion by reinforcement learning neural network. In Distributed Reinforcement Learning For Decision-making In Cooperative Multi-agent Systems, Part 1, CUBRC Technical report prepared for AFRL, Buffalo, NY.

M. L. Littman. (2001). Value-function reinforcement learning in Markov games. Journal of Cognitive Systems Research, Vol. 2, pp.55-66,

Bowling M.; Veloso M. (2004). Existence of Multiagent Equilibria with Limited Agents. J of Artificial Intelligence Research, Vol. 22, Issue 2, pp.353-384

C. J. C. H. Watkons & P. Dayan. (1992). Q-leanign. Machine Learning, Vol. 8, Issue 3, pp.279-292.

M. J. Mataric (2001). Learning in behavior-based multi-robot systems: policies, models, and other agents. Journal of Cognitive Systems Research, Vol. 2, pp. 81-93,

Kousuke INOUE; Jun OTA; Tomohiko KATAYAMA & Tamio ARAI. (2000). Acceleration of Reinforcement Learning by A Mobile Robot Using Generalized Rules, Proc. IEEE int.Conf. Intelligent Robots and Systems, pp.885-890

W. D. Smart & L. P. Kaelbling. (2002). Effective reinforcement learning for mobile robots. in Proceedings of the IEEE International Conference on Robotics and Automation, Vol. 4, pp. 3404-3410.

Yang, X. M. Li & X. M. Xu (2001). "A suery of technology of multi-agent cooperation", Information and Control, Issue. 4, pp.337-342

Y. Chang; T. Ho & L. P. Kaelbling. (2003). Reinforcement learning in mobilized ad-hoc networks. Technical Report, AI Lab, MIT,

Kok, J. R. & Vlassis, N. (2006). "Collaborative multiagent reinforcement learning by payoff propagation", Journal of Machine Learning Research 7, pp.1789 -1828.

Zhong Yu; Zhang Rubo & Gu Guochang. (2003). Research On Architectures of Distributed Reinforcement Learning Systems. Computer Engineer and Application., Issue 11, pp.111-113 (in Chinese).

M. L. Littman. (1994). Markov Games as a Framework for Multi-agent Reinforcement Learning. Machine Learning , Vol. 11, pp.157-163.

19

Bio-Inspired Communication for Self-Regulated Multi-Robot Systems

Md Omar Faruque Sarker and Torbjørn S. Dahl
University of Wales, Newport
United Kingdom

1. Introduction

In recent years, the study of social insects and other animals has revealed that collectively, the relatively simple individuals in these self-organized societies can solve various complex and large problems using only a few behavioural rules (Camazine et al., 2001). In these self-organized systems, individual agents may have limited cognitive, sensing and communication capabilities, but they are collectively capable of solving complex and large problems, e.g., coordinated nest construction of honey-bees, collective defence of school fish from a predator attack. Since the discovery of these collective behavioural patterns of self-organized societies, scientists have also observed modulation of behaviours on the individual level (Garnier et al., 2007). One of the most notable self-regulatory processes in biological social systems is the *division of labour* (DOL) (Sendova-Franks & Franks, 1999) by which a larger task is divided into a number of small subtasks and each subtask is performed by a separate individual or a group of individuals. *Task-specialization* is an integral part of DOL where a worker does not perform all tasks, but rather specializes in a set of tasks, according to its morphology, age, or chance (Bonabeau et al., 1999). DOL is also characterized by *plasticity* which means that the removal of one group of workers is quickly compensated for by other workers. Thus distribution of workers among different concurrent tasks keeps changing according to the environmental and internal conditions of a colony.

In artificial social systems, like multi-agent or multi-robot systems, the term "division of labour" is often synonymous to "task-allocation" (Shen et al., 2001). In robotics, this is called *multi-robot task allocation* (MRTA) which is generally identified as the question of assigning tasks to appropriate robots considering changes in task-requirements, environment and the performance of other team members. The additional complexities of the distributed MRTA problem, over traditional MRTA, arise from the fact that robots have limited capabilities to sense, to communicate and to interact locally. In this chapter, we present this issue of DOL as a relevant self-regulatory process in both biological and artificial social systems. We have used the terms DOL and MRTA (or simply, task-allocation) interchangeably.

Traditionally, task allocation in multi-agent systems has been dominated by *explicit* and self-organized task-allocation approaches. Explicit approaches, e.g. intentional cooperation (Parker, 2008), use of dynamic role assignment (Chaimowicz et al., 2002) and market-based bidding approach (Dias et al., 2006) are intuitive, comparatively straight forward to design and implement and can be analysed formally. However, these approaches typically works well only when the number of robots are small (≤ 10) (Lerman et al., 2006). On the other hand bio-inspired self-organized task-allocation relies on the emergent group behaviours, such as emergent cooperation (Kube & Zhang, 1993), or adaptation rules (Liu et al., 2007). These solutions are more robust and scalable to large team sizes. However, they are difficult to design, to analyse formally and to implement in real robots. Existing research using this approach typically limit their focus on one specific global task (Gerkey & Mataric, 2004).

Within the context of the Engineering and Physical Sciences Research Council (EPSRC) project, "Defying the Rules: How Self-regulatory Systems Work", we have proposed to solve the above mentioned self-regulated DOL problem in an alternate way (Arcaute et al., 2008). Our approach is inspired from the studies of emergence of task-allocation in both biological and human social systems. We have proposed four generic requirements to explain self-regulation in those social systems. These four requirements are: *continuous flow of information*, *concurrency*, *learning* and *forgetting*. Primarily, these requirements enable an individuals actions to contribute positively to the performance of the group. In order to use these requirements for control on an individual level, we have developed a formal model of self-regulated DOL, called the *attractive field model* (AFM). Section 2 reviews our generic requirements of self-organization and AFM.

In biological social systems, communication among the group members and sensing the task-in-progress, are two key components of self-organized DOL. In robotics, existing self-organized task-allocation methods rely heavily upon local sensing and local communication of individuals for achieving self-organized task-allocation. However, AFM differs significantly in this point by avoiding the strong dependence on the local communications and interactions. AFM requires a system-wide continuous flow of information about tasks, agent states etc. but this can be achieved by using both centralized and decentralized communication modes under explicit and implicit communication strategies.

In order to enable continuous flow of information in our multi-robot system, we have implemented two types of sensing and communication strategies inspired by the self-regulated DOL found in two types of social wasps: *polistes* and *polybia* (Jeanne et al., 1999). Depending on the group size, these species follow different strategies for communication and sensing of tasks. Polistes wasps are called the *independent founders* in which reproductive females establish colonies alone or in small groups (in the order of 10^2), but independent of any sterile workers. On the other hand, polybia wasps are called the *swarm founders* where a swarm of workers and queens initiate colonies consisting of several hundreds to millions of individuals. The most notable difference in the organization of work of these two social wasps is: independent founders do not rely on any cooperative task performance while swarm founders interact with each-other locally to accomplish their tasks. The work mode of independent founders can be considered as *global sensing - no communication (GSNC)* where the individuals sense the task requirements throughout a small colony and do these tasks without communicating with each other. On the other hand, the work mode of swarm founders can be treated as *local sensing - local communication (LSLC)* where the individuals can only sense tasks locally due to large colony-size and they can communicate locally to exchange information, e.g. task-requirements (although their exact mechanism is unknown). In this chapter, we have used these two sensing and communication strategies to compare the performance of the self-regulated DOL of our robots under AFM.

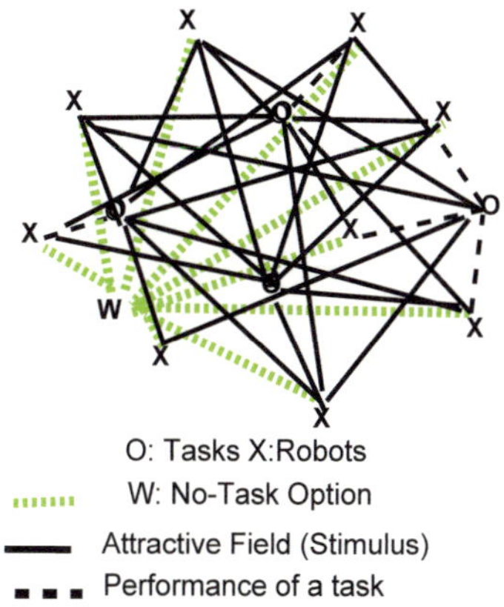

Fig. 1. The attractive filed model (AFM)

2. The attractive field model

Inspired from the DOL in ants, humans and robots, we have proposed the following necessary and sufficient set of four requirements for self-regulation in social systems.

Requirement 1: Concurrence. The simultaneous presence of several task options is necessary in order to meaningfully say that the system has organised into a recognisable structure. In task-allocation terms the minimum requirement is a single task as well as the option of not performing any task.

Requirement 2: Continuous flow of information. Self-organised social systems establish a flow of information over the period of time when self-organisation can be defined. The task information provides the basis on which the agents self-organise by enabling them to perceive tasks and receive feedback on system performance.

Requirement 3: Sensitization. The system must have a way of representing the structure produced by self-organisation, in terms of MRTA, which tasks the robots are allocated. One of the simplest ways of representing this information is an individual preference parameter for each task-robot combination. A system where each robot has different levels of preference or *sensitivity* to the available tasks, can be said to have to embody a distinct organisation through differentiation.

Requirement 4: Forgetting. When a system self-organises by repeated increases in individual sensitisation levels, it is also necessary, in order to avoid saturation, to have a mechanism by which the sensitisation levels are reduced or *forgotten*. Forgetting also allows flexibility in the system, in that the structure can change as certain tasks become important and other tasks become less so.

Building on the requirements for self-organised social systems, AFM formalises these requirements in terms of the relationships between properties of individual agents and of the system as a whole Arcaute+2008. AFM is a bipartite network, i.e. there are two different types of nodes. One set of nodes describes the sources of the attractive fields, the tasks, and the other set describes the agents. Edges only exist between different types of nodes and they encode the strength of the attractive field as perceived by the agent. There are no edges between agent nodes. All communication is considered part of the attractive fields. There is also a permanent field representing the *no-task* option of not working in any of the available tasks. This option is modelled as a random walk. The model is presented graphically in Fig. 1. The elements are depicted as follows. Source nodes (o) are tasks to be allocated to agents. Agent nodes (x) e.g., ants, humans, or robots. Black solid edges represent the attractive fields and correspond to an agent's perceived stimuli from each task. Green edges represent the attractive field of the ever present no-task option, represented as a particular task (w). The red lines are not edges, but represent how each agent is allocated to a single task at any point in time. The edges of the AFM network are weighted and the value of this weight describes the strength of the stimulus as perceived by the agent. In a spatial representation of the model, the strength of the field depends on the physical distance of the agent to the source. In information-based models, the distance can represent an agent's level of understanding of that task. The strength of a field is increased through the sensitisation of the agent through experience with performing the task. This elements is not depicted explicitly in Figure 1 but is represented in the weights of the edges. In summary, from the above diagram of the network, we can see that each of the agents is connected to each of the tasks. This means that even if an agent is currently involved in a task, the probability that it stops doing it in order to pursue a different task, or to random walk, is always non-zero.

AFM assumed a repeated task selection by individual agents. The probability of an agent choosing to perform a task is proportional to the strength of the task's attractive field, as given by Equation 1.

$$P_j^i = \frac{S_j^i}{\sum_{j=0}^{J} S_j^i} \quad where, \quad S_0^i = S_{RW}^i \tag{1}$$

Equation 1 states that the probability of an agent, i, selecting a task, j, is proportional to the stimulus, S_j^i, perceived from that task, with the sum of all the task stimuli normalised to 1.

The strength of an attractive field varies according to how sensitive the agent is to that task, k_j^i, the distance between the task and the agent, d_{ij}, and the *urgency*, ϕ_j of the task. In order to give a clear edge to each field, its value is modulated by the hyperbolic tangent function, *tanh*. Equation 2 formalises this part of AFM.

$$S_j^i = tanh\{\frac{k_j^i}{d_{ij} + \delta}\phi_j\} \tag{2}$$

Eqation 2, used small constant δ, called *delta distance*, to avoid division by zero, in the case when a robot has reached to a task.

Equation 3 shows how AFM handles the the no-task, or random walk, option. The strength of the stimuli of the random walk task depends on the strengths of the fields real tasks. In particular, when the other tasks have a low overall level of sensitisation, i.e., relatively weak fields, the strength of the random walk field if relatively high. On the other hand, when the agent is highly sensitised, the strength of the random walk field becomes relatively low. We use J to denote the number of real tasks. AFM effectively considers random walking as an ever present additional task. Thus the total number of tasks becomes $J + 1$.

$$S_{RW}^i = tanh\left\{1 - \frac{\sum_{j=1}^{J} S_j^i}{J+1}\right\} \tag{3}$$

A task j has an associated urgency ϕ_j indicating its relative importance over time. If an agent attends a task j in time step t, the value of ϕ_j will decrease by an amount $\delta_{\phi_{INC}}$ in the time-step $t + 1$. On the other hand, if a task has not been served by any of the agents in time-step t, ϕ_j

will increase by a different amount, $\delta_{\phi_{DEC}}$ in time-step $t+1$. This behaviour is formalised in Equations 4 and 5.

$$If\ the\ task\ is\ not\ being\ done:\ \phi_{j,t+1} \rightarrow \phi_{j,t}\ + \delta_{\phi_{INC}} \quad (4)$$

$$If\ the\ task\ is\ being\ done:\ \phi_{j,t+1} \rightarrow \phi_{j,t}\ - n\ \delta_{\phi_{DEC}} \quad (5)$$

Equation 4 refers to a case where no agent attends to task j and Equation 5 to the case where n agents are concurrently performing task j.

In order to complete a task, an agent needs to be within a fixed distance of that task. When an agent performs a task, it learns about it and this will increases the probability of that agent selecting that task in the future. This is done by increasing its sensitization to the task by a fixed amount, k_{INC}. The variable affinity of an agent, i, to a task, j, is called its *sensitization* to that task and is denoted k_j^i. If an agent, i, does not do a task j, k_j^i is decreased by a different fixed amount, k_{DEC}. This behaviour is formalised in Equations 6 and 7.

$$If\ task\ is\ done:\ k_j^i \rightarrow k_j^i\ +\ k_{INC} \quad (6)$$

$$If\ task\ is\ not\ done:\ k_j^i \rightarrow k_j^i\ -\ k_{DEC} \quad (7)$$

2.1 A robotic interpretation of AFM

The interpretation of AFM in a multi-robot system follows the above mentioned generic interpretation. Each robot is modelled as an agent and each task is modelled as a spatial location. The robots repeatedly select tasks and if the robot is outside a fixed task boundary, it navigates towards the task. If the robot is within the task boundary it remains there until the end of the time step when a new (or the same) task is selected. The distance between a task and a robot is simply the physical distance and the sensitivities are recorded as specific values on each robot. The urgency values of the tasks are calculated based on the number of robots attending each task and the updated urgency values are communicated to the robots.

The sensing of the distance between the tasks and robots as well as the communication of urgency values are non-trivial in a robotic system. Both the sensing and communication can be done either locally by the individual robots or centrally, through an overhead camera and a global communication network.

3. Communication in biological social systems

Communication plays a central role in self-regulated DOL of biological social systems. In this section, communication among social insects are briefly reviewed.

3.1 Purposes, modalities and ranges

Communication in biological societies serves many closely related social purposes. Most P2P communication include: recruitment to a new food source or nest site, exchange of food particles, recognition of individuals, simple attraction, grooming, sexual communication. In addition to that colony-level broadcast communication include: alarm signal, territorial and home range signals and nest markers (Holldobler & Wilson, 1990).

Biological social insects use different modalities to establish social communication, such as, sound, vision, chemical, tactile, electric and so forth. Sound waves can travel a long distance and thus they are suitable for advertising signals. They are also best for transmitting

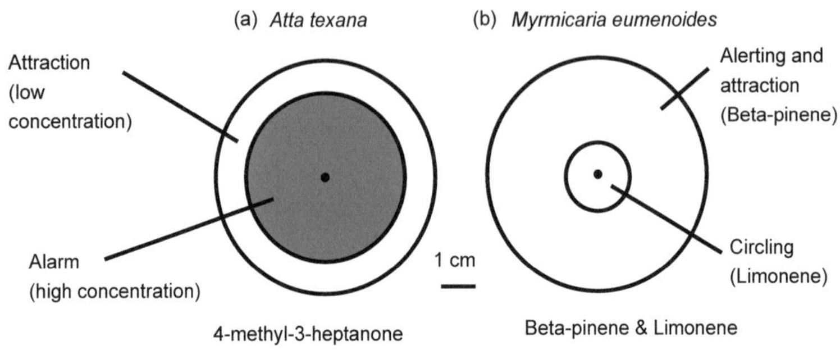

Fig. 2. Pheromone active space observed in ants, reproduced from Holldobler & Wilson (1990).

complicated information quickly (Slater, 1986). Visual signals can travel more rapidly than sound, but they are limited by the physical size or line of sight of an animal. They also do not travel around obstacles. Thus they are suitable for short-distance private signals.

In ants and some other social insects, chemical communication is predominant (Holldobler & Wilson, 1990). A pheromone is a chemical substance, usually a type of glandular secretion, used for communication within species. One individual releases it as a signal and others respond to it after tasting or smelling. Using pheromones individuals can code quite complicated messages in smells. If wind and other conditions are favourable, this type of signals emitted by such a tiny species can be detected from several kilometres away. Thus chemical signals are extremely economical of their production and transmission. But they are quite slow to diffuse away. But ants and other social insects manage to create sequential and compound messages either by a graded reaction of different concentrations of same substance or by blends of signals.

Tactile communication is also widely observed in ants and other species typically by using their body antennae and forelegs. It is observed that in ants touch is primarily used for receiving information rather than informing something. It is usually found as an invitation behaviour in worker recruitment process. When an ant intends to recruit a nest-mate for foraging or other tasks it runs upto a nest-mate and beats her body very lightly with antennae and forelegs. The recruiter then runs to a recently laid pheromone trail or lays a new one.

In underwater environment some fishes and other species also communicate through electric signals where their nerves and muscles work as batteries. They use continuous or intermittent pulses with different frequencies to learn about environment and to convey their identity and aggression messages.

3.2 Signal active space and locality

The concept of active space (AS) is widely used to describe the propagation of signals by species. In a network environment of signal emitters and receivers, active space is defined as the area encompassed by the signal during the course of transmission (McGregor & Peake, 2000). The concept of active space is described somewhat differently in case some social insects. In case of ants, this active space is defined as a zone within which the concentration of pheromone (or any other behaviourally active chemical substances) is at or above threshold concentration (Holldobler & Wilson, 1990).

Fig. 2 shows the use of active spaces of two species of ants: (a) *Atta texana* and (b) *Myrmicaria eumenoides*. The former one uses two different concentrations of *4-methyl-3-heptanone* to create attraction and alarm signals, whereas the latter one uses two different chemicals: *Beta-pinene* and *Limonene* to create similar kinds signals, i.e. alerting and circling. According to need, individuals regulate their active space by making it large or small, or by reaching their maximum radius quickly or slowly, or by enduring briefly or for a long period of time. From the precise study of pheromones it has been found that active space of alarm signal is consists of a concentric pair of hemispheres (Fig. 2). As an ant enters the outer zone, she is attracted inward toward the point source; when she next crosses into the central hemisphere she become alarmed. It is also observed that ants can release pheromones with different active spaces. Active space has strong role in modulating the behaviours of ants. For example, when workers of *Acanthomyops claviger* ants produce alarm signal due to an attack by a rival or insect predator, workers sitting a few millimetres away begin to react within seconds. However, those ants sitting a few centimetres away take a minute or longer to react. In many cases, ants and other social insects exhibit modulatory communication within their active space where many individuals involve in many different tasks. For example, while retrieving the large prey, workers of *Aphaeonogerter* ants produce chirping sounds (known as *stridulate*) along with releasing poison gland pheromones. These sounds attract more workers and keep them within the vicinity of the dead prey to protect it from their competitors. This communication amplification behaviour can increase the active space to a maximum distance of 2 meters.

3.3 Common communication strategies

In biological social systems, we can find all different sorts of communication strategies ranging from indirect pheromone trail laying to local and global broadcast of various signals. The most common four communication strategies are indirect, P2P, local and global broadcast communication strategies. The pheromone trail laying is one of the most discussed indirect communication strategy among various species of ants. This indirect communication strategy effectively helps ants to find a better food source among multiple sources, find shorter distance to a food source, marking nest site and move there etc. (Hughes, 2008). Direct P2P communication strategy is also very common among most of the biological species. This tactile form of communication is very effective to exchange food item, flower nectar with each-other or this can be useful even in recruiting nest-mates to a new food source or nest-site.

3.4 Roles of communication in task-allocation

Communication among nest-mates and sensing of tasks are the integral parts of the self-regulated DOL process in biological social systems. They create necessary preconditions for switching from one tasks to another or to attend dynamic urgent tasks. Suitable communication strategies favour individuals to select a better tasks. For example, Garnier et al. (2007) reported two worker-recruitment experiments on black garden ants and honey-bees. The scout ants of *Lasius niger* recruit uninformed ants to food source using a well-laid pheromone trails. *Apis mellifera* honey-bees also recruit nest-mates to newly discovered distant flower sources through waggle-dances. In the experiments, poor food sources were given first to both ants and honey-bees. After some time, rich food sources were introduced to them. It was found that only honey-bees were able to switch from poor source to a rich source using their sophisticated dance communication.

Table 1 presents the link between sensing the task and self-regulation of communication behaviours among ants and honey-bees. Here, we can see that communication is modulated based on the perception of task-urgency irrespective of the communication strategy of a particular species. Under indirect communication strategy of ants, i.e. pheromone trail-laying, we can see that the principles of self-organization, e.g. positive and negative feedbacks take

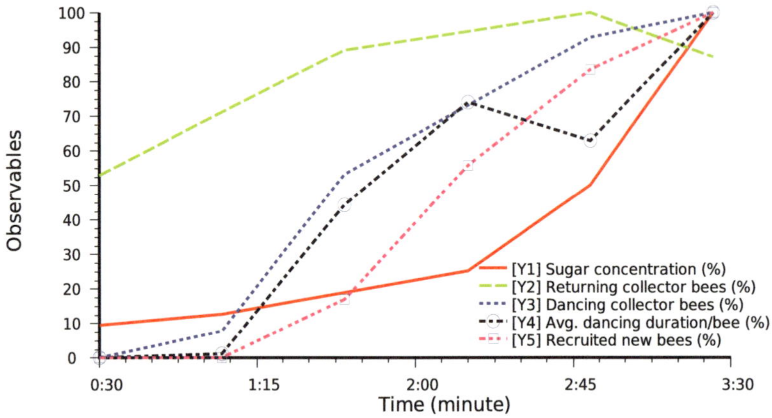

Fig. 3. Self-regulation in honey-bee's dance communication behaviours, produced after the results of Von Frisch (1967) honey-bee round-dance experiment performed on 24 August 1962.

place due to the presence of different amount of pheromones for different time periods. Initially, food source located at shorter distance gets relatively more ants as the ants take less time to return nest. So, more pheromone deposits can be found in this path as a result of positive feedback process. Thus, the density of pheromones or the strength of indirect communication link reinforces ants to follow this particular trail. Similarly, perception of task-urgency influences the P2P and broadcast communication strategies. *Leptothorax albipennis* ant take lees time in assessing a relatively better nest site and quickly return home to recruit its nest-mates (Pratt et al., 2002). Here, the quality of nest directly influences its intent to make more "tandem-runs" or to do tactile communication with nest-mates. We have already discussed about the influences of the quality of flower sources to honey-bee dance. Fig. 3 shows this phenomena more vividly. It has been plotted using the data from the honey-bee round-dance experiments of (Von Frisch, 1967, p. 45). In this plot, Y1 line refers to the concentration of sugar solution. This solution was kept in a bowl to attract honey-bees and the amount of this solution was varied from $\frac{3}{16}$M to 2M (taken as 100%). In this experiment, the variation of this control parameter influenced honey-bees' communication behaviours while producing an excellent self-regulated DOL.

Example event	Strategy	Modulation of communication upon sensing tasks
Ant's alarm signal by pheromones	Global broadcast	High concentration of pheromones increase aggressive alarm-behaviours
Honey-bee's round dance	Local broadcast	High quality of nectar source increases dancing and foraging bees
Ant's tandem run for nest selection	P2P	High quality of nest increases traffic flow
Ant's pheromone trail-laying to food sources	Indirect	Food source located at shorter distance gets higher priority as less pheromone evaporates and more ants joins

Table 1. Self-regulation of communication behaviours in biological social systems

In Fig. 3 Y2 line represents the number of collector bees that return home. The total number of collectors was 55 (taken as 100%). Y3 line plots the percent of collectors displaying round dances. We can see that the fraction of dancing collectors is directly proportional to the concentration of sugar solution or the sensing of task-urgency. Similarly, the average duration of dance per bee is plotted in Y4 line. The maximum dancing period was 23.8s (taken as 100%). Finally, from Y5 line we can see the outcome of the round-dance communication as the number of newly recruited bees to the feeding place. The maximum number of recruited bees was 18 (taken as 100%). So, from an overall observation, we can see that bees sense the concentration of food-source as the task-urgency and they self-regulate their round-dance communication behaviour according to their perception of this task-urgency. Thus, this self-regulated dancing behaviour of honey-bees attracts an optimal number of inactive bees to work.

Broadcast communication is one of the classic ways to handle dynamic and urgent tasks in biological social systems. It can be commonly observed in birds, ants, bees and many other species. Table 1 mentions about the alarm communication of ants. Similar to the honey-bee's dance communication, ants has a rich language of chemical communication that can produce words through blending of different glandular secretions in different concentrations. Fig. 2 shows how ants can use different concentrations of chemicals to make different stimulus for other ants. From the study of ants, it is clear to us that taking defensive actions, upon sensing a danger, is one of the highest-priority tasks in an ant colony. Thus, for this highly urgent task, ants almost always use their global broadcast communication strategy through their strong chemical signals and they make sure all individuals can hear about this task. This gives us a coherent picture of the self-regulation of biological species based on their perception of task-urgency.

3.5 Effect of group size on communication

The performance of cooperative tasks in large group of individuals also depends on the communication and sensing strategies adopted by the group. Depending on the group size, different kinds of information flow occur in different types of social wasps (Jeanne et al., 1999). Polistes independent founders are species in which reproductive females establish colonies alone or in small groups with about 10^2 individuals at maturity. Polybia swarm founders initiates colonies by swarm of workers and queens. They have a large number of individuals, in the order of 10^6 and 20% of them can be queen. In case of swarm founders information about nest-construction or broods food-demand can not reach to foragers directly. Among the swarm founders for nest construction. The works of *pulp foragers* and *water foragers* depend largely on their communication with *builders*. On the other hand, in case of independent founders there is no such communication and sensing are present among individuals.

The above interesting findings from social wasps have been linked up with the group productivity of wasps. Jeanne et al. (1999) reported high group productivity in case of LSLC of swarm founders. The per capita productivity was measured as the number of cells built in the nest and the weight of dry brood in grams. In case of independent founders this productivity is much lesser (max. 24 cells per queen at the time the first offspring observed) comparing to the thousands of cells produced by swarm founders. This shows us the direct link between high productivity of social wasps and their selection of LSLC strategy. These fascinating findings from wasp colonies have motivated us to test these communication and sensing strategies in a fairly large multi-robot system to achieve an effective self-regulated MRTA.

4. Communication in multi-robot systems

Communication plays an important role for any high-level interaction e.g. cooperation among a multi-robot team. Below we have described the dominant issues of communication among multi-robot teams with a focus on how communication can lead to produce effective MRTA solutions.

4.1 Rationale of communication

Communication in multi-robot system provides several major benefits. Robots can exchange potential information based on their spatial position and knowledge of past events. This, in turn, leads to improve perception over a distributed region without directly sensing it. In order to perform (or stop performing) certain tasks simultaneously or in a particular order, robots need to communicate, or signal, to each other. Communication enables robots to interact and negotiate their actions effectively.

4.2 Information content

Although communication provides several benefits for team-work it is costly to provide communication support in terms of hardware, firmware as well as run-time energy spent in communication. So robotic researchers carefully minimize the necessary information content in communications by using suitable communication protocols and high-level abstractions. The potential information contents that can be used in communication among robots are mainly:

- **Individual state:** ID number, battery level, task-performance statistics, etc.
- **Goal:** Location of target task or all tasks discovered.
- **Task-related state:** The amount of task completed.
- **Environmental state:** Free and blocked paths, level of interference found, any urgent event or dangerous changes found in the environment.
- **Intentions:** Detail plan for doing a task or sequences of selected actions.

4.3 Communication modalities

Robotic researchers typically use robot's on-board wireless radio, infra-red (IR), vision and sound hardware modules for robot-robot and robot-host communication. The reduction in price of wireless radio hardware chips e.g. wifi (ad-hoc WLAN 802.11 network) or Bluetooth makes it possible to use wireless radio communication widely. Inexpensive IR communication module is also typically built into almost all mobile robots due to its low-cost and suitability for ambient light and obstacle detection. IR can also be used for low bandwidth communication in short-ranges, e.g. keen-recognition. Most robots can also produce basic sound waves and detect it with their built-in speakers and on-board microphones.

4.4 Communication strategies

Whatever be the communication modalities of a multi-robot system, suitable strategies are required to disseminate information in a timely manner to a target audience that maximizes the effective task-completion and minimizes delays and conflicts. The complexities of communication strategies can be elaborated in terms of three independent aspects: organization, expressiveness and range of communication. These are described below.

Organization of communication structure
Communication in a multi-robot system can be organized using an external/internal central entity (e.g. a server PC, or a leader robot) or, a few leader robots, or by using decentralized or local schemes where every robot has the option to communicate with every other robot of the team. From a recent study of multi-robot flocking Çelikkanat et al. (2008) have shown that a mobile robot flock can be steered toward a desired direction through externally guiding some of its members, i.e. the flock relies on multiple leaders or information repositories. Note that here task-allocation is fully decentralized i.e. each robot selects its task, but the communication structure is hybrid; robots communicate with each other and with a centralized entity.

Expressiveness of communication
Communication in a multi-robot system can also be characterized its expressiveness or the degree of explicitness. In one extreme it can be fully implicit, e.g. stigmergic, or on the other end, it can be fully explicit where communication is done by a rich vocabulary of symbols and meanings. Researchers generally tend to stay in either end based on the robotic architecture and task-allocation mechanism used. However, both of these approaches can be tied together under any specific application. They are highlighted below.

1. **Explicit or direct communication:** This is also known as intentional communication. This is done purposefully by usually using suitable modality e.g. wireless radio, sound, LEDs. Because explicit communication is costly in terms of both hardware and software, robotic researchers always put extra attention to design such a system by analysing strict requirements such as communication necessity, range, content, reliability of communication channel (loss of message) etc.
2. **Implicit or indirect communication:** This is also known as indirect stigmergic communication. This is a powerful way of communication where individuals leave information in the environment. This method was adopted from the social insect behaviour, such as stigmergy of ants (leaving of small amount of pheromone or chemicals behind while moving in a trail).

Target recipients of message
The target recipient selection or determining the communication range or sometimes called radius of communication is an interesting issue in multi-robot system research. Researchers generally tries to maximize the information gain by using larger range. However, transmission power and communication interference among robots play a major role to limit this range. The following major instances of this strategy can be used.

- **Global broadcast:** where all robots in the team can receive the message.
- **Local broadcast:** where a few robots in local neighbourhood can receive the message.
- **Publish-subscribe:** where only the subscribed robots can receive the message.
- **Peer-to-peer:** where only the closest peer robot can receive the message.

4.5 Role of communication in MRTA

Although researchers in the field of multi-robot system have been adopting various communication strategies for achieving MRTA solutions in different task domains, very few studies correlate the role of communication with the effectiveness of MRTA. This is due to the fact that researchers usually adopt a certain task-allocation method and they limit their use of communication strategy to either explicit global/local broadcast (in most predefined task-allocation researches) or implicit/no communication (in most self-organized task-allocation researches). Here we have attempted to scrutinize how MRTA solutions have been affected by the variations in communication strategies.

Kalra & Martinoli (2007) empirically studied the comparative performance of MRTA under both predefined and self-organized approaches with event-driven simulations. They found that the accuracy of information is crucial for predefined market-based approach where every robot communicated with every other robot. In case of unreliable link, threshold-based approach performed same as market-based approach, but with less computational overhead. In case of varying robot's communication range, they found that market-based approach performed well for a short communication range where robots were able to communicate with less than a third of the total number of team-mates.

In order to pursue MRTA, robots can receive information from a centralised source (Krieger & Billeter, 2000) or from their local peers (Agassounon & Martinoli, 2002). This centralized communication system is easy to implement. However as we mentioned before, this system has disadvantage of a single point of failure and it is not scalable. On the other hand, uncontrolled reception of information from decentralized or local sources is also not free from drawbacks. If a robot exchanges signals with all other robots, it might get the global view of the system quickly and can select an optimal or near optimal task. This can produce a great improvement in overall performance of some types of tasks e.g., in area coverage Rutishauser et al. (2009). But this is also neither practical nor scalable for a typically large multi-robot system.

A potential alternate solution of this problem can be obtained by decreasing the number of message recipients on the basis of a local communication range. This means that robots are allowed to communicate only with those peers who are physically located within a pre-set distance. When this strategy is used for sharing task information among peers, MRTA can be more robust to the dynamic changes in the environment and energy-efficient (Agassounon & Martinoli, 2002). Simailar to this, Pugh & Martinoli (2009) reported a distributed multi-robot learning scenario with two cases: 1) robots were allowed to communicate with any two other robots (*Model A*) and 2) robots were allowed to communicate with all robots in a fixed radius (*Model B*). In simulation and real robotic experiments with 10 robots and communication ranges of 0.3 m, 1.0 m and 3.3 m, they showed that Model B performed better in intermediate communication range.

Many robotic researchers tried to use some forms of adaptation rules in local communication to avoid saturation of the communication channel, e.g. based on robot densities in a given area. Yoshida & Arai (2000) tried to formalize the suitable communication range based on spatial and temporal properties of information diffusion of a given communication channel. The major focus of this type of research is to measure the cost of communication based on some metrics, e.g. transmission time and collisions with other robots, and then regulate communication ranges dynamically. These ideas are attractive to maximize information gain in dynamic environment, but there is no point of doing communication if there is little or no task-requirement.

Oca et al. (2005) acknowledged the above fact within the context of their ant-based clustering experiments. They used two simple communication strategies: 1) simple memory sharing by robots (shared memory access) and 2) shared use of environment maps (global sensing). In both of these cases, it was found that communication is only useful when some initial random clustering phase was passed. The accuracy of shared information in highly dynamic environment was poor and did not carry any significant advantage. In case of local memory sharing by robots, they showed that sharing information within a limited number of robots produced more efficient clusters, rather than not sharing information at all in stigmergic communication mode. However, sharing memory in a large group is not a feasible communication strategy because of the huge latencies and interferences involved in the communication channel.

5. Validation of AFM under centralized communication strategy

In this section, in order to present the validation of AFM, we first describe our manufacturing shop floor scenario and then the centralized communication model along with its implementation under this scenario. Finally we present the experimental results that validates our model.

5.1 A manufacturing shop-floor scenario

By extending our interpretation of AFM in multi-robot system, we can set-up manufacturing shop-floor scenario. Here, each task represents a manufacturing machine that is capable of producing goods from raw materials, but they also require constant maintenance works for stable operations. Let W_j be a finite number of material parts that can be loaded into a machine j in the beginning of its production process and in each time-step, ω_j units of material parts can be processed ($\omega_j \ll W_j$). So let Ω_j^p be the initial production workload of j which is simply: W_j/ω_j unit. We assume that all machines are identical. In each time step, each machine always requires a minimum threshold number of robots, called hereafter as *minimum robots per machine* (μ), to meet its constant maintenance work-load, Ω_j^m unit. However, if μ or more robots are present in a machine for production purpose, we assume that, no extra robot is required to do its maintenance work separately. These robots, along with their production jobs, can do necessary maintenance works concurrently. For the sake of simplicity, here we consider $\mu = 1$.

Now let us fit the above production and maintenance work-loads and task performance of robots into a unit task-urgency scale. Let us divide our manufacturing operation into two subsequent stages: 1) *production and maintenance mode* (PMM), and 2) *maintenance only mode* (MOM). Initially a machine starts working in PMM and does production and maintenance works concurrently. When there is no production work left, then it enters into MOM. Fig. **??** illustrates this scenario for a single machine.

Under both modes, let α_j be the amount of workload occurs in a unit time-step if no robot serves a task and it corresponds to a fixed task-urgency $\Delta\phi_{INC}$. On the other hand, let us assume that in each time-step, a robot, i, can decrease a constant workload β_i by doing some maintenance work along with doing any available production work. This corresponds to a negative task urgency: $-\Delta\phi_{DEC}$. So, at the beginning of production process, task-urgency, occurred in a machine due to its production work-loads, can be encoded by Eq. 8.

$$\Phi_{j,INIT}^{PMM} = \Omega_j^p \times \Delta\phi_{INC} + \phi_j^{m0} \tag{8}$$

where ϕ_j^{m0} represents the task-urgency due to any initial maintenance work-load of j. Now if no robot attends to serve a machine, each time-step a constant maintenance workload of α_j^m will be added to j and that will increase its task-urgency by $\Delta\phi_{INC}$. So, if k time steps passes without any production work being done, task urgency at k^{th} time-step will follow Eq. 9.

$$\Phi_{j,k}^{PMM} = \Phi_{j,INIT}^{PMM} + k \times \Delta\phi_{INC} \tag{9}$$

However, if a robot attends to a machine and does some production works from it, there would be no extra maintenance work as we have assumed that $\mu = 1$. Rather, the task-urgency on this machine will decrease by $\Delta\phi_{DEC}$ amount. If ν_k robots work on a machine simultaneously at time-step k, this decrease will be: $\nu_k \times \Delta\phi_{DEC}$. So in such cases, task-urgency in $(k+1)^{th}$ time-step can be represented by:

$$\Phi_{j,k+1}^{PMM} = \Phi_{j,k}^{PMM} - \nu_k \times \Delta\phi_{DEC} \tag{10}$$

At a particular machine j, once $\Phi_{j,k}^{PMM}$ reaches to zero, we can say that there is no more production work left and this time-step k can give us the *production completion time* of j, T_j^{PMM}. Average production time-steps of a shop-floor with M machines can be calculated by the following simple equation.

$$T_{avg}^{PMM} = \frac{1}{M}\sum_{j=1}^{M} T_j^{PMM} \tag{11}$$

T_{avg}^{PMM} can be compared with the minimum number of time-steps necessary to finish production works, T_{min}^{PMM}. This can only happen in an ideal case where all robots work for production without any random walking or failure. We can get T_{min}^{PMM} from the total amount of work load and maximum possible inputs from all robots. If there are M machines and N robots, each machine has Φ_{INIT}^{PMM} task-urgency, and each time-step robots can decrease N $\times$ $\Delta\phi_{DEC}$ task-urgencies, then the theoretical T_{min}^{PMM} can be found from the following Eq. 12.

$$T_{min}^{PMM} = \frac{M \times \Phi_{INIT}^{PMM}}{N \times \Delta\phi_{DEC}} \tag{12}$$

$$\zeta_{avg}^{PMM} = \frac{T_{avg}^{PMM} - T_{min}^{PMM}}{T_{min}^{PMM}} \tag{13}$$

Thus we can define ζ_{avg}^{PMM}, average production completion delay (APCD) by following Eq. 13: When a machine enters into MOM, only μ robots are required to do its maintenance works in each time step. So, in such cases, if no robot serves a machine, the growth of task-urgency will follow Eq. 9. However, if ν_k robots are serving this machine at a particular time-step k^{th}, task-urgency at $(k+1)^{th}$ time-step can be represented by:

$$\Phi_{j,k+1}^{MOM} = \Phi_{j,k}^{MOM} - (\nu_k - \mu) \times \Delta\phi_{DEC} \tag{14}$$

By considering $\mu = 1$, Eq. 14 will reduces to Eq. 10. Here, $\Phi_{j,k+1}^{MOM}$ will correspond to the *pending maintenance work-load* of a particular machine at a given time. This happens due to the random task switching of robots with a no-task option (random-walking). Interestingly PMW will indicate the robustness of this system since higher PMW value will indicate the delay in attending maintenance works by robots. We can find the *average pending maintenance work-load* (APMW) per time-step per machine, χ_j^{MOM} (Eq. 15) and average PMW per machine per time-step, χ_{avg}^{MOM} (Eq. 16).

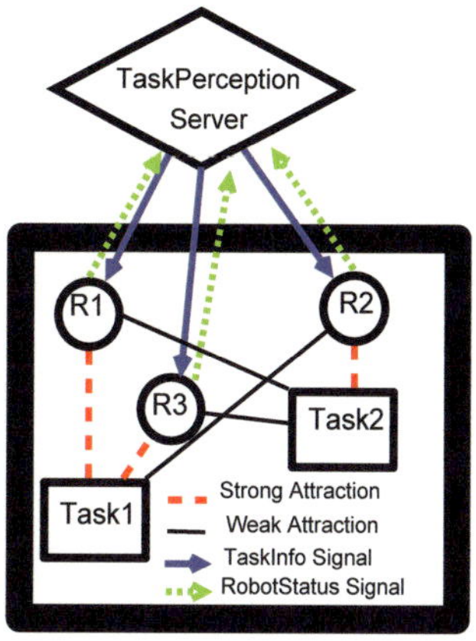

Fig. 4. A centralized communication scheme

$$\chi_j^{MOM} = \frac{1}{K}\sum_{k=1}^{K}\Phi_{j,k}^{MOM} \quad (15)$$

$$\chi_{avg}^{MOM} = \frac{1}{M}\sum_{j=1}^{M}\chi_j^{MOM} \quad (16)$$

5.2 Centralized communication model

AFM relies upon a system-wide continuous flow of information which can be realized using any suitable communication model. A simple centralized communication scheme is outlined in Fig. 4. In this model we have used bi-directional signal-based exchange of communication messages between a centralized *task perception server* (TPS) and a *robot-controller client* (RCC). The main role of TPS is to send up-to-date task-information to RCCs. This task-information mainly contains the location and urgency of all tasks which is used by the RCCs for running their task-allocation algorithm. The urgency value of each task is dynamically updated by TPS after receiving the status signals from the working robots of that particular task. Fig. 4 shows how three robots are attracted to two different tasks and their communications with TPS. We can characterize our communication model in terms of three fundamental issues of communication: i) message content, ii) communication frequency and iii) target message recipients (Gerkey & Mataric, 2001). AFM suggests the communication of task-urgencies among robots. This communication helps the robots to gain information that can be treated as "global sensing". However in this model robots do not communicate among themselves. Hence this model can be approximated as the GSNC strategy. Since in order to run the task-allocation algorithm robot-controllers need the distance information we also include the task position information in the message. Our centralized communication model is open to include any further information, such as time-stamp, in the message payload. In this model the frequency of signal emission depends on several issues, e.g. the rate at which the environment is changing, the bandwidth of communication medium. In case of time-extended tasks, robots can receive information less frequently and the bandwidth usage can be kept minimum. However under a fast changing environment relatively more bandwidth will be required. Finally the centralized communication model spread the attractive fields of all tasks globally by broadcasting information to all robots.

5.3 Experiment design

We have designed a set of manufacturing shop-floor scenario experiments for validating the effectiveness of our AFM in producing self-regulated MRTA. In our experiments we design the following observables.

- **Plasticity:** Within our manufacturing shop-floor context, plasticity refers to the collective ability of the robots to switch from doing no-task option (random-walking) to doing a task (or vice-versa) depending on the work-load present in the system. Here we expect to see that most of the robots would be able to engage in tasks when there would be high workloads (or task-urgencies). The changes of task-urgencies and the ratio of robots engaged in tasks can be good metrics to observe plasticity in MRTA.
- **Task-specialization:** Self-regulated MRTA is generally accompanied with task-specializations of agents. That means that few robots will be more active than others. From the interpretation of AFM, we can see that after doing a task a few times, a robot will soon be sensitized to it. Therefore, from the raw log of task-sensitization of robots, we can be able to find the pattern of task-sensitization of robots per task basis.
- **Quality of task-performance:** As discussed in Sec. 5.1 we can measure the quality of MRTA from the APCD. It first calculates the ideal minimum production time and then finds the delay in production process from the actual production completion data. Thus this will indicate how much more time is spent in the production process due to the self-regulation of robots.
- **Robustness:** In order to see if our system can respond to the gradually increasing workloads, we can measure APMW within the context of our manufacturing shop-floor scenario. This can show the robustness of our system. When a task is not being served by any robot for some time we can see that its urgency will rise and robots will respond to this dynamic demand.
- **Flexibility:** From the design of AFM, we know that robots that are not doing a task will be de-sensitized to it or forget that task. So at an overall low work-load (or task urgency), less robots will do the tasks and hence less robots will have the opportunity to learn tasks. From the shop-floor work-load data, we can confirm the presence of flexibility in MRTA.
- **Energy-efficiency:** In order to characterize the energy-efficiency in MRTA we can log the pose data of each robot that can give us the total translations occurred by all robots in our experiments. This can give us a rough indication of energy-usage by our robots.
- **Information flow:** Since AFM requires a system-wide continuous flow of information, we can measure the communication load to bench-mark our implementation of communication system. This bench-mark data can be used to compare among various communication strategies. Here we can measure how much task-related information, i.e. task-urgency, location etc. are sent to the robots at each time step.
- **Scalability:** In order to see the effects of scaling on MRTA, we have designed two group of experiments. Series A corresponds to a small group where we have used 8 robots, 2 tasks under an arena of 2 m^2. We have doubled these numbers in other experiments, i.e. 16 robots, 4 tasks under an arena of 4 m^2. This proportional design can give us a valuable insight about the effects of scaling on self-regulated MRTA.

In order to observe the self-regulated MRTA, we have designed our experiments to record the following observables in each time-step:
task-urgency of each task (ϕ),number of robots engaged in each task,task-sensitizations (k) of robots,pose data of robots and communication of task-information messages. Table 2 lists a set of common parameters of our experiments. The initial values of task urgencies correspond to 100 units of production work-load without any maintenance work-load as outlined in Eq. 8. For task-urgency (and task-sensitization) limits, we choose a limit of 0 and 1, where 0

Parameter	Value
Initial production work load/machine (Ω_j^p)	100 unit
Task urgency increase rate ($\Delta\phi_{INC}$)	0.005
Task urgency decrease rate ($\Delta\phi_{DEC}$)	0.0025
Initial sensitization (K_{INIT})	0.1
Sensitization increase rate (Δk_{INC})	0.03
Sensitization decrease rate (Δk_{DEC})	0.01

Table 2. Experimental parameters of Series A & B experiments

means no urgency (complete forgetting) of a task and 1 means maximum urgency (or full specialization) of that task. We choose a initial sensitization value of 0.1 for all tasks.

5.4 Implementation

As shown in Fig. 5, in our implementation there exists a centralized *TaskPerceptionServer* that is responsible for disseminating task information to RCCs. The contents of task information can be physical locations of tasks, their urgencies and so on. TaskPerceptionServer delivers this information by emitting *TaskInfo* signals periodically. For example, in a wireless network it can be a message broadcast. TaskPerceptionServer has another interface for catching feedback signals from robots. The *RobotStatus* signal can be used to inform TaskPerceptionServer about a robot's current task id, its device status and so on. TaskPerceptionServer uses this information to update relevant part of task information such as, task-urgency. This up-to-date information is sent in next TaskInfo signal. In order to track all robots in real-time, we have used SwisTrack (Lochmatter et al., 2008) with a 16-megapixel overhead GigE camera.

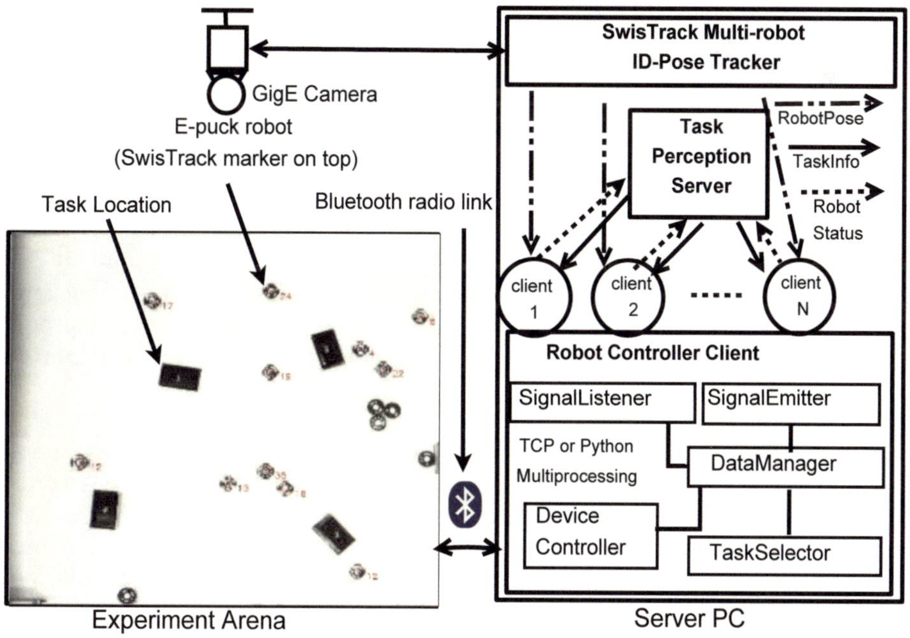

Fig. 5. Hardware and software setup

This set-up gives us the position, heading and id of each of the robots by processing the image frames at about 1 FPS. The interaction of the hardware and software of our system is illustrated in Fig. 5. For inter-process communication (IPC), we have used D-Bus technology (Pennington et al., 2010). We have developed an IPC component for SwisTrack that can broadcast id and pose of all robots in real-time over our server's D-Bus interface.
Apart from SwisTrack, we have implemented two major software modules: *TaskServer* and *RCC*. They are developed in Python with its state of the art *Multiprocessing*[1] module. This python module simplifies our need to manage data sharing and synchronization among different sub-processes. As shown in Fig. 5, RCC consists of four sub-processes. *SignalListener* and *SignalEmitter*, interface with SwisTrack D-Bus Server and TaskServer respectively. *TaskSelector* implements AFM algorithms for task selection . *DeviceController* moves a robot to a target task. Bluetooth radio link is used as a communication medium between a RCC and a corresponding e-puck robot. We have previously presented the detailed design and implementation of our of centralized communication model (Sarker & Dahl, 2010).

5.5 Results and discussions

Our AFM validation experiments were conducted with 8 and 16 robots, 4 tasks in an arena of 4 m^2 for about 40 minutes and averaged them over five iterations. For the sake of brevity, here we describe only the results of Series B experiments (with 16 robots).
In our experiments we have defined shop-floor work-load in terms of task urgencies. For example, Eq. 8 shows how we have calculated initial production work-load of our manufacturing shop-floor scenario. Fig. 6 shows the dynamic changes in task urgencies in one iteration. The fluctuations in this plot is resulted from the different levels of task-performance of our robots.
In order to measure the task-related work-loads on our system we have summed up the changes in all task-urgencies over time. We call this as *shop-floor work-load history* and formalized as follows. Let $\phi_{j,q}$ be the urgency of a task j at q^{th} step and $\phi_{j,q+1}$ be the task urgency of $(q+1)^{th}$ step. We can calculate the sum of changes in urgencies of all M tasks at $(q+1)^{th}$ step:

$$\Delta\Phi_{j,q+1} = \sum_{j=1}^{M} (\phi_{j,q+1} - \phi_{j,q}) \tag{17}$$

From Fig. 7 shows the dynamic shop-floor workload. Here, we can see that initially the sum of changes of task urgencies (shop-floor workload) is going towards negative direction. This implies that tasks are being served by a high number of robots. Fig. 9 shows that in production stage, when work-load is high, many robots are active in tasks and this ratio varies according to task urgency changes.
To measure the task performance in our manufacturing shop-floor scenario, we have calculated the APCD and APMW. For Series A we have got average production completion time 111 time-steps (555s) where sample size is 10 tasks, SD = 10 time-steps. According to Eq. 12, our theoretical minimum production completion time is 50 time-steps (250s). Eq. 13 gives us APCD, $\zeta = 1.22$. For Series B, we have got average production completion time 165 time-steps where sample size is 20 tasks, SD = 72 time-steps and APCD, $\zeta = 2.3$. For APMW, Series A experiments give us an average time length of 369 time-steps (1845s). In this period we have calculated APMW = 1 time-step with SD = 1 time-step and $\Delta\Phi_{INC} = 0.005$ per task

[1]http://docs.python.org/library/multiprocessing.html

per time-step. This shows a very low APMW (χ = 0.000235) implying a very high robustness of our system. For Series B experiments, we have got APMW, χ = 0.012756 which corresponds to the pending work of 3 time-steps where SD = 13 time-steps. This also tells us the robust task performance of our robots which can return to an abandoned task within a minute or so. We have measured the task-specialization of the robots based-on their peak value of sensitization. This maximum value represents how long a robot has repeatedly been selecting a particular task. Since tasks are homogeneous we have considered the maximum sensitization value of a robot among all tasks during an experiment run. This value is then averaged for all robots using the following equation.

$$K^G_{avg} = \frac{1}{N}\sum_{i=1}^{N}\max_{j=1}^{M}\left(k^i_{j,q}\right) \quad (18)$$

If a robot r_i has the peak sensitization value k^i_j on task j ($j \in M$) at q^{th} time-step, Eq. 18 calculates the average of the peak task-specialization values of all robots for a certain iteration of our experiments. We have also averaged the time-step values (q) taken to reach those peak values for all robots using the following equation.

$$Q^G_{avg} = \frac{1}{N}\sum_{i=1}^{N} q^i_{k=k_{max}} \quad (19)$$

In Eq. 19, $q^i_{k=k_{max}}$ represents the time-step of robot r_i where its sensitization value k reaches the peak k_{max} as discussed above. By averaging this peak time-step values of all robots we can have an overall idea of how many task-execution cycles are spent to reach the maximum task-specialization value K^G_{avg}. Based on Eq. 18 and Eq. 19, we have got the peak task-sensitization K^G_{avg} values: 0.40 (SD=0.08) and 0.30 (SD=0.03), and their respective time-step Q^G_{avg} values: 38 (SD=13) and 18 (SD=5) time-step. Here the robots in Series A had higher chances of task-specialization than that of Series B experiments. Fig. 8 presents the frequency of signalling task information by TaskServer. Since the duration of each time step is 50s long and TaskServer emits signal in every 2.5s, there is an average of 20 signals in each time-step.

From the above results, we have noted several aspects of self-regulated MRTA that expose the effectiveness of AFM. As we have pointed out that this self-regulated MRTA, as observed in biological and human social systems, needs to satisfy several important characteristics, particularly plasticity and task-specialization. In addition to satisfying those basic qualities, AFM has demonstrated many other aspects. Our self-regulated robots, driven by AFM, effectively handle the dynamic work-load in our manufacturing shop-floor. They can dynamically support the need to work on demanding tasks, if there any. The variations of active worker ratio shows this. We have observed the effect of scaling-up the robot team size. The system size of Series B is double of that of Series A in terms of robots, tasks and experiment arena. Keeping a fixed ratio of robot-to-task and task-to-arena we have intended to see the scaling effects in our experiments. Here we see that both systems can show sufficient self-regulated DOL, but task-performance of both systems varies significantly. For example, the value of APCD in Series B is higher by 1.08. This means that performance is decreased in Series B experiments despite having the resources in same proportion in both systems.

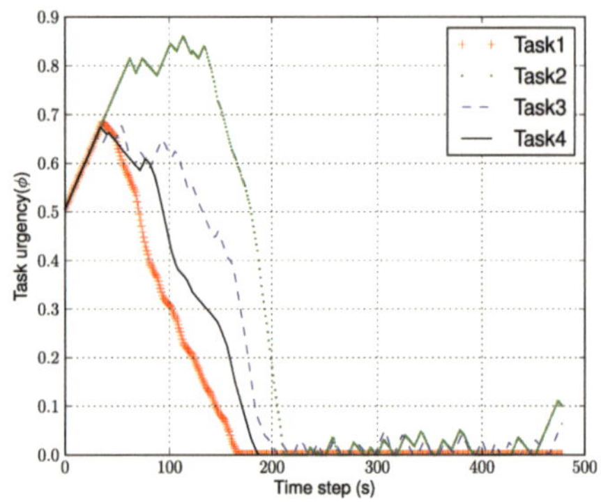

Fig. 6. Dynamic task-urgency changes.

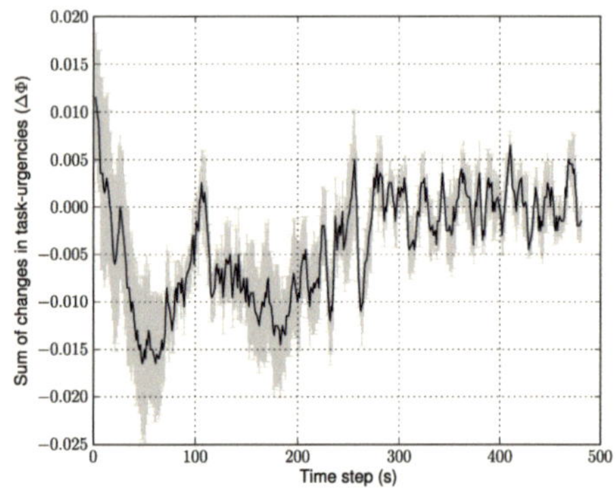

Fig. 7. Shop-floor workload history

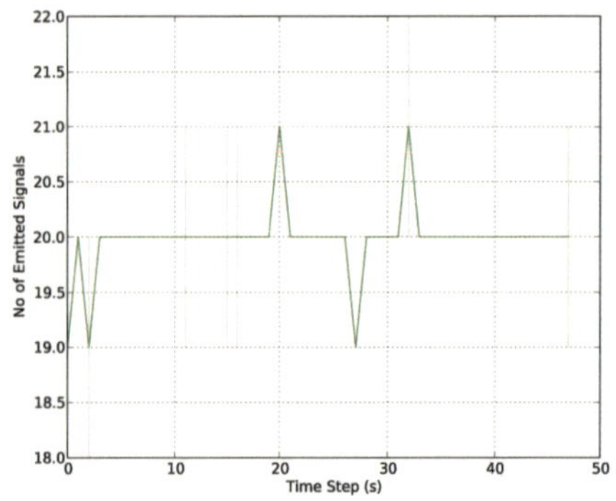

Fig. 8. Task server's task-info broadcasts

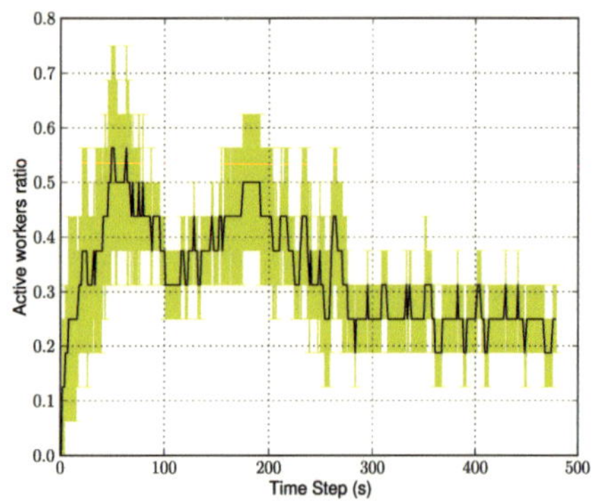

Fig. 9. Self-organized task-allocation

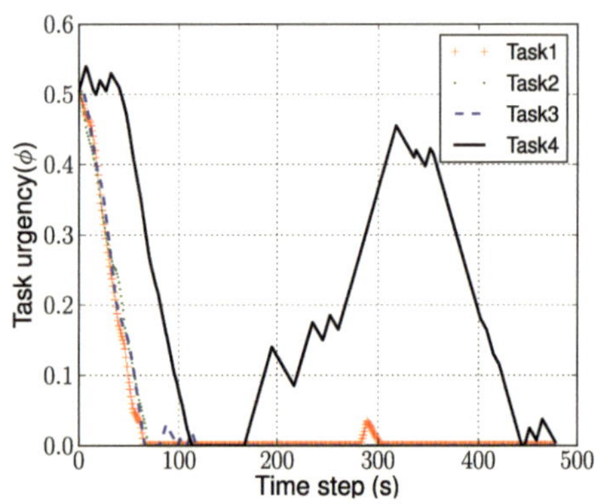

Fig. 10. Task-urgencies observed in Series D experiments

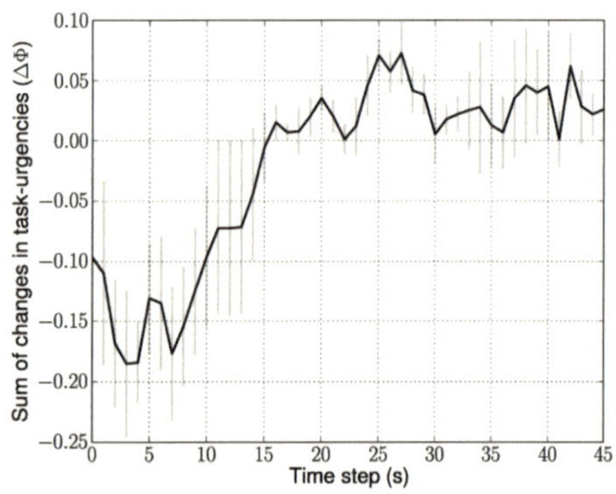

Fig. 11. Shop-floor work-load history of Series D experiments

6. Comparisons between local and centralized communication strategies

In most swarm robotic research local communication is considered as the one of the most critical components of the swarms where the global behaviours emerges from the local interactions among the individuals and their environment. In this study, we have used the concepts of pheromone active-space of ants to realize our simple LSLC scheme. Ants use various chemical pheromones with different active spaces (or communication ranges) to communicate different messages with their group members Holldobler & Wilson (1990). Ants sitting near the source of this pheromone sense and respond quicker than others who wander in far distances. Thus both communication and sensing occurs within a small communication range. We have used this concept of communication range or locality in our LPCM. A suitable range (or radius) of communication and sensing can be set at design time based on the capabilities of robots (Agassounon & Martinoli, 2002). Alternately they can also be varied dynamically over time depending on the cost of communication and sensing, e.g. density of peers, ambient noise in the communication channels, or even by aiming for maximizing information spread (Yoshida & Arai, 2000). In this study, we have followed the former approach. as our robots do not have the precise hardware to dynamically vary their communication and sensing ranges.

6.1 General characteristics of LPCM

Our LPCM relies on the local P2P communications among robots. we have assumed that robots can communicate to its nearby peers within a certain communication radius, r_{comm} and they can sense tasks within another radius r_{task}. They exchange communication signals reliably without any significant loss of information. A robot R_1 is a *peer* of robot R_2, if spatial distance between R_1 and R_2 is less than this r_{comm}. Similarly, when a robot comes within this r_{task} of a task, it can sense the status of this task. Although the communication and sensing range can be different based on robot capabilities, we have considered them same for the sake of simplicity of our implementation.

Local communication can also give robots similar task information as in centralized communication. In this case, it is not necessary for each robot to communicate with every other robot to get information on all tasks. Since robots can random walk and explore the environment we assume that for a reasonably high robot-to-space density, all tasks will be known to all robots after an initial exploration period. In order to update the urgency of a task, robots can estimate the number of robots working on a task in two ways: by either using their sensory perception (e.g. on-board camera) or doing local P2P communication with others.

Similar to our centralized communication model, we can characterize our local communication model in terms of message content, communication frequency and target recipients Gerkey & Mataric (2001). Regarding the issue of message content, our local communication model is open. Robots can communicate with their peers with any kind of message. Our local model addresses the last two issues very specifically. Robots communicate only when they meet their peers within a certain communication radius (r_{comm}). Although in case of an environment where robots move relatively faster the peer relationships can also be changed dynamically. But this can be manipulated by setting the signal frequency and robot to space density to somewhat reasonably higher value.

In terms of target recipients, our model differs from a traditional publish/subscribe communication model by introducing the concept of dynamic subscription. In a traditional

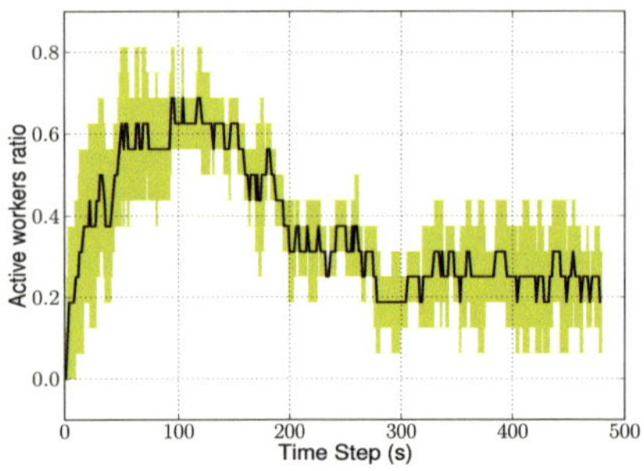

Fig. 12. Self-organized allocation of robots.

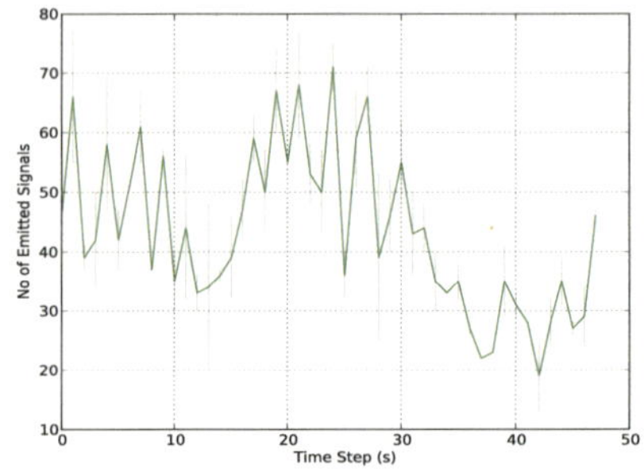

Fig. 13. Frequency of P2P signalling.

publish/subscribe communication model, subscription of messages happens prior to the actual message transmission. In that case prior knowledge about the subjects of a system is necessary (Gerkey & Mataric, 2001). But in our model this is not necessary as long as all robots uses a common addressing convention for naming their incoming signal channels.

6.2 Implementation

In order to implement LPCM, our centralized communication scheme has been converted into a decentralized one where robots can use local observation and communicate with peers about tasks to estimate task-urgencies. Under this implementation, we present an emulation of this scenario where robots do not depend entirely on TPS for estimating task-urgencies, instead they get task information from TPS when they are very close to a task (inside r_{task}) or from local peers who know about a task via TPS. The details implementation of LPCM and results can be found in Sarker (2010).

6.3 Results and discussions

For the sake of brevity, below we describe only the results from Series D experiments. Interested readers can find other results in Sarker (2010). The sample raw task-urgencies of Series D experiments are shown in Fig. 10. In this case, we can see that an unattended task, *Task4*, was not served by any robot for a long period and later it was picked up by some of the robots. The dynamic shop floor work-load is shown in Fig. 11. This shows similar work-load as experienced in Series B experiments.

The active worker ratios of Series D experiments are plotted in Fig. 12. Series C data shows us a large variation in this active worker ratios. From task-performance data of Series C we have got average production completion time 121 time-steps (605s) with SD = 36 time-steps (180s). For Series D, average production completion time is 123 time-steps (615s) with SD = 40 time-steps (200s). According to Eq. 12, our theoretical minimum production completion time is 50 time-steps (250s). The values of APCD are as follows. For Series C, $\zeta = 1.42$ and for Series D, $\zeta = 1.46$. For both series of experiments APCD values are very close.

For APMW, Series C experiments give us an average time length of 359 time-steps (1795s). In this period we calculated APMW and it is 5 time-steps with SD = 17 time-steps and $\chi = 0.023420$. For Series D experiments, from the average 357 time-steps (1575s) of maintenance activity of our robots per experiment run, we have got APMW, $\chi = 0.005359$ which corresponds to the pending work of 2 time-steps (10s) where SD = 7 time-steps. By applying Eq. 18 and Eq. 19 on our robots' task-sensitization statistics, we have got the

Series	Average translation (m)	SD
A	2.631	0.804
B	13.882	3.099
C	4.907	1.678
D	4.854	1.592

Table 3. Sum of translations of robots in Series A-D experiments.

peak task-sensitization K^G_{avg} values: 0.39 (SD=0.17) and 0.27 (SD=0.10), and their respective time-step Q^G_{avg} values: 13 (SD=7) and 11 (SD=5) time-step.

6.4 Comparisons

Results from Series C and Series D experiments show us many similarities and differences with respect to the results of Series A and Series B experiments. Both Series C and Series D experiments show similar APCD values: 1.42 and 1.46 respectively, which are significantly less than Series B experiment result (APCD = 2.3) and are close to Series A experiment result (APCD = 1.22). This means that for large group, task-performance is efficient under LSLC strategy (Series C and Series D) comparing with their GSNC counterpart (Series B).
Besides, in terms of task-specialization, the overall task-specialization of group in Series C (K^G_{avg} = 0.4) is closer to that of Series A experiments (K^G_{avg} = 0.39) and interestingly, the value of Series D (K^G_{avg} = 0.27) is much closer to that of Series B experiments (K^G_{avg} = 0.30). So task-specialization in large group under LSLC strategy shows higher performance than their GSNC counter part. Besides task-specialization happens much faster under LSLC strategy as we can see that the average time to reach peak sensitization values of the group, Q^G_{avg} in Series C is lower than that of Series A values by 25 time-steps.
We have aggregated the changes in translation motion of all robots over time following an approach similar to task-urgency aggregation as described in Sec. 5.5 and summarized in Table 3. From the robot motion profiles found in all four series of experiments, we have found that under LSLC strategy, robot translations have been reduced significantly. From this table we can see than Series C and Series D show about 2.8 times less translation than that in Series B experiments. The translation of 16 robots in Series C and Series D experiments are approximately double (1.89 times) than that of Series A experiments with 8 robots. Thus the energy-efficiency under LSLC strategy seems to be higher than that under GSNC strategy.
From the above results we can see that large group robots achieve better MRTA under LSLC strategy. The local sensing of tasks prevents them to attend a far-reaching task which may be more common under global sensing strategy. However, as we have seen in Fig. 10 some tasks can be left unattended for a long period of time due to the failure to discover it by any robot. For that reason we see that the values of APMW is slightly higher under LSLC strategy. But this trade-off is worth as LSLC strategy provides superior self-regulated MRTA in terms of task-performance, task-specialization and energy-efficiency.

7. Conclusion

This study has focused on reviewing bio-inspired communication strategies for self-regulated multi-robot systems with an emphasis on comparing two bio-inspired communication and sensing strategies in producing self-regulated MRTA by AFM, an interdisciplinary model of task-allocation. Under the GSNC strategy, AFM has produced the desired self-regulated MRTA among a group of 8 and 16 robots. This gives us the evidence that AFM can successfully solve the MRTA issue of a complex multi-tasking environment like a manufacturing shop-floor. Under the LSLC strategy, AFM can also produce the desired self-regulated MRTA for 16 robots with different communication and sensing ranges.

From our comparative results, we can conclude that for large group of robots, degradation in task-performance and task-specialization of robots are likely to occur under GSNC strategy that relies upon a centralized communication system. Thus GSNC strategy can give us better performance when the number of tasks and robots are relatively small. This confirms us the assertions made by some biologists that self-regulated DOL among small group of individuals can happen without any significant amount of local communications and interactions. However, our findings suggest that task-specialization can still be beneficial among the individuals of a small group which contradicts the claim that small groups only posses the generalist workers, but not the specialists.

On the other hand, LSLC strategy is more suitable for large group of individuals that are likely to be unable to perform global sensing and global communications with all individuals of the group. The design of communication and sensing range is still remained as a critical research issue. However, our results suggest that the idea of maximizing information gain is not appropriate under a stochastic task-allocation process, as more information causes more task-switching behaviours that lowers the level of task-specialization of the group. This might not be the case under a deterministic task-allocation scheme where more information leads to better and optimum allocations, but that is limited to a small group of individuals. Nevertheless, despite having the limited communication and sensing range, LSLC strategy helps to produce comparatively better task-allocation with increased task-specialization and significantly reduced motions or savings in energy e.g. battery power.

8. Future work

This study can possibly be extended in co-operative task performance where different individuals with variety of task-skills can interact with each other directly. In our experiments, no dynamic task has been introduced during the run-time of our experiments. But AFM can be applied to a more challenging environment with suddenly appearing (and disappearing) dynamic tasks. Moreover, some more research can be done in order to figure out how to optimize the initial experimental parameters, e.g. robots' task learning and forgetting rate. Moreover, real implementation of communication range should be achieved by using suitable on-board communication module, e.g. Wifi or IR, with relatively powerful robots. In our experiments, we have selected two fixed communication ranges that approximates LSLC strategy. However, much research is required to find optimum communication range as a property of self-regulation of individuals.

9. References

Agassounon, W. & Martinoli, A. (2002). Efficiency and robustness of threshold-based distributed allocation algorithms in multi-agent systems, *Proceedings of the first international joint conference on Autonomous agents and multiagent systems: part 3*, ACM, p. 1097.

Arcaute, E., Christensen, K., Sendova-Franks, A., Dahl, T., Espinosa, A. & Jensen, H. J. (2008). Division of labour in ant colonies in terms of attractive fields, *Ecol. Complexity* .

Bonabeau, E., Dorigo, M. & Theraulaz, G. (1999). *Swarm intelligence: from natural to artificial systems*, Oxford University Press.

Camazine, S., Franks, N., Sneyd, J., Bonabeau, E., Deneubourg, J. & Theraula, G. (2001). *Self-organization in biological systems*, Princeton, N.J. : Princeton University Press, c2001. What is self-organization? – How self-organization works – Characteristics of self-organizing systems – Alternatives to self-organization –.

Çelikkanat, H., Turgut, A. & Şahin, E. (2008). Guiding a robot flock via informed robots, *Distributed Autonomous Robotic Systems 8* pp. 215–225.

Chaimowicz, L., Campos, M. F. M. & Kumar, V. (2002). Dynamic role assignment for cooperative robots, *Robotics and Automation, 2002. Proceedings of the 2002 International Conference on Robotics and Automation (ICRA'02), 1:293-298.* 1.

Dias, M. B., Zlot, R. M., Kalra, N. & Stentz, A. (2006). Market-based multirobot coordination: A survey and analysis, *Proceedings of the IEEE* 94: 1257–1270.

Garnier, S., Gautrais, J. & Theraulaz, G. (2007). The biological principles of swarm intelligence, *Swarm Intelligence* 1(1): 3–31.

Gerkey, B. & Mataric, M. (2001). Principled communication for dynamic multi-robot task allocation, *Experimental Robotics VII* pp. 353–362.

Gerkey, B. P. & Mataric, M. J. (2004). A formal analysis and taxonomy of task allocation in multi-robot systems, *The International Journal of Robotics Research* 23: 939.

Holldobler, B. & Wilson, E. (1990). *The ants*, Belknap Press.

Hughes, D. (2008). *Sociobiology of communication: an interdisciplinary perspective*, Oxford University Press, USA.

Jeanne, R., Detrain, C., Deneubourg, J. L. & Pasteels, J. M. E. (1999). Group size, productivity, and information flow in social wasps, *Information processing in social insects* pp. 3–30.

Kalra, N. & Martinoli, A. (2007). A comparative study of market-based and threshold-based task allocation, *Distributed Autonomous Robotic Systems 7* pp. 91–101.

Krieger, M. & Billeter, J. (2000). The call of duty: Self-organised task allocation in a population of up to twelve mobile robots, *Robotics and Autonomous Systems* 30(1-2): 65–84.

Kube, C. R. & Zhang, H. (1993). Collective robotics: From social insects to robots, *Adaptive Behavior* 2: 189.

Lerman, K., Jones, C., Galstyan, A. & Mataric, M. J. (2006). Analysis of dynamic task allocation in multi-robot systems, *The International Journal of Robotics Research* 25: 225.

Liu, W., Winfield, A. F. T., Sa, J., Chen, J. & Dou, L. (2007). Towards energy optimization: Emergent task allocation in a swarm of foraging robots, *Adaptive Behavior* 15(3): 289–305.

Lochmatter, T., Roduit, P., Cianci, C., Correll, N., Jacot, J. & Martinoli, A. (2008). Swistrack-a flexible open source tracking software for multi-agent systems, *IEEE/RSJ International Conference on Intelligent Robots and Systems, 2008. IROS 2008*, pp. 4004–4010.

McGregor, P. & Peake, T. (2000). Communication networks: social environments for receiving and signalling behaviour, *Acta Ethologica* 2(2): 71–81.

Oca, M., Garrido, L. & Aguirre, J. (2005). Effects of Inter-agent Communication in Ant-Based Clustering Algorithms: A Case Study on Communication Policies in Swarm Systems, *MICAI 2005: Advances in Artificial Intelligence* pp. 254–263.

Parker, L. E. (2008). Distributed intelligence: Overview of the field and its application in multi-robot systems, *Journal of Physical Agents, special issue on multi-robot systems* 2(2): 5–14.

Pennington, H., Carlsson, A. & Larsson, A. (2010). D-bus specification.

Pratt, S., Mallon, E., Sumpter, D. & Franks, N. (2002). Quorum sensing, recruitment, and collective decision-making during colony emigration by the ant leptothorax

albipennis, *Behavioral Ecology and Sociobiology* 52(2): 117–127.
Pugh, J. & Martinoli, A. (2009). Distributed scalable multi-robot learning using particle swarm optimization, *Swarm Intelligence* 3(3): 203–222.
Rutishauser, S., Correll, N. & Martinoli, A. (2009). Collaborative coverage using a swarm of networked miniature robots, *Robotics and Autonomous Systems* 57(5): 517–525.
Sarker, M. & Dahl, T. (2010). Flexible Communication in Multi-robotic Control System Using HEAD: Hybrid Event-driven Architecture on D-Bus, *In Proc. of the UKACC International Conference on Control 2010 (CONTROL 2010)*, pp. 926–931.
Sarker, M. O. F. (2010). *Self-regulated Multi-Robot Task Allocation*, PhD thesis, University of Wales, Newport, UK.
Sendova-Franks, A. B. & Franks, N. R. (1999). Self-assembly, self-organization and division of labour', *Philosophical Transactions of the Royal Society of London B* 354: 1395–1405.
Shen, W., Norrie, D. H. & Barthes, J.-P. (2001). *Multi-agent systems for concurrent intelligent design and manufacturing*, Taylor & Francis, London.
Slater, P. J. B. (1986). *Animal behaviour*, Leisure Circle Wembley.
Von Frisch, K. (1967). *The dance language and orientation of bees*, Belknap Press of Harvard University Press.
Yoshida, E. & Arai, T. (2000). Performance analysis of local communication by cooperating mobile robots, *IEICE Transactions on Communications* 83(5): 1048–1059.

20

Multi-Robot Task Allocation Based on Swarm Intelligence

Shuhua Liu[1], Tieli Sun[1] and Chih-Cheng Hung[2]
[1]*Northeast Normal University*
[2]*Southern Polytechnic State University*
[1]*China*
[2]*USA*

1. Introduction

In the field of cooperative robotics, task allocation is an issue receiving much attention. When researchers design, build, and use cooperative multi-robot system, they invariably try to answer the question of which robot should execute which task. This is in fact a multi-robot task allocation problem (MRTA). The task allocation problem addresses the question of finding the task-to-robot assignments that optimize global cost or utility objectives. Finding an optimal task allocation, even in a relatively simplified case, is an NP-hard problem. Therefore, the majority of common approaches are approximate or heuristic in nature. Those approaches usually give suboptimal solutions. MRTA is a fundamental issue of the multi-robot systems, which embodies the high-level system organization and operation mechanism. The quality of task allocation algorithm directly affects the performance of multi-robot system. With an increase in the number of robots and difficulty of tasks within a system, the issue of task allocation has risen to prominence and become a key research topic in the multi-robot domain. In 2005, the International Conference on Robotics and Automation (ICRA 2005) set special panels on multi-robot task allocation, in which the latest research and the progress are discussed.
Gerkey and Mataric (2004) presented a particular taxonomy for the task allocation problem. It is described as follows:

- Single-task robots (ST) vs. multi-task robots (MT): ST means that each robot is capable of executing at most one task at a time, while MT means that some robots can execute multiple tasks simultaneously.
- Single-robot tasks (SR) and multi-robot tasks (MR): SR means that each task requires exactly one robot to achieve it, while MR means that some tasks can require multiple robots.
- Instantaneous (IA) and time-extended (TA) assignment: In the instantaneous assignment, robots do not plan for future allocations and are only concerned with the one task they are carrying out at the moment (or for which they are considering executing). In the time-extended assignment, robots have more information and can come up with longer-term plans involving task sequences or schedules.

Based on above categorization, there are eight types of task allocation combination. ST-SR-IA is the simplest, as it is actually a trivial instance of the Optimal Assignment Problem

(OAP). ST-MR-IA often appears in real world applications; that is, some tasks require the combined effort of multiple robots. These two types of tasks are also called loosely-coupled tasks and tightly-coupled tasks, respectively. Although some approaches for solving either loosely-coupled task or tightly-coupled task allocation have been proposed, few approaches for solving both loosely-coupled and tightly-coupled task allocation have been developed.

In this chapter, we present a task allocation mechanism based on swarm intelligence for the large-scale multi-robot system, with both loosely-coupled and tightly-coupled task allocation. The mechanism adopts a hierarchical architecture. At the high level, we employ an Ant Colony Algorithm to find optimal allocations. Namely, each ant performs a task allocation so as to choose an undertaker for every task. At the low level, each ant forms a task-oriented robot coalition to perform a tightly-coupled task. Ant colony optimization (ACO), the particle swarm and ant colony optimization (PSACO) and the quantum-inspired ant colony optimization (QACO) are adopted to form the coalition. Finally, the algorithm is implemented in the TeamBots simulation platform. Simulation results show that the proposed mechanism can effectively solve loosely-coupled and tightly-coupled task allocation in the large-scale multi-robot system.

2. Related work

Recently a number of solutions have been proposed in the literature to MRTA problems (Zhang & Liu, 2008). These include behaviour based approaches such as ALLCANCE (Parker, 1998), BLE (Werger & Mataric, 2000) and ASyMTRe(Tang & Parker, 2005). The advantage of these approaches possesses real-time, fault-tolerance and robustness; the solution, however, can only be locally optimal. The market-based approach is the current mainstream of task allocation methods. The representative method is CNP (Contract Network Protocol) which proposed by Smith (1980). Other typical examples include First-price auctions (Zlot et al, 2002), Dynamic Role Assignment (Chaimowicz et al, 2002), Traderbots (Dias, 2004), M+ (Botelho & Alami, 1999), MURDOCH (Gerkey & Mataric, 2002a) and DEMiR-CF (Sanem & Tucker, 2006). Because of better scalability, this method is particularly well-suited to the distributed robotic domain. Furthermore, it is guaranteed to produce optimal allocations, but robots must cooperate through explicit communication and more resource consumption. Once the communication is interrupted, the performance of this method will degrade significantly (Kalra & Martinoli, 2006). Therefore, it is suitable for small- to medium- scale task allocation problems. Derived from the behaviours of social insects, the swarm intelligence approach is exhibiting several good features such as self-organizing ability in unknown environments, and emergent and adaptive behaviours through simple interaction among individuals. Since cooperative individuals are distributed and there is no central control and global data in the group, the system will be more robust. The failure of one or several individuals will not affect the whole solution. Additionally, individuals cooperate through implicit communications. As the number of the individuals in the system increases, the amount of communication grows quite slowly. Therefore the swarm intelligence approach is the most suitable for distributed multi-robot systems and as such more and more researchers have applied it to the multi-robot task allocation, especially in dynamic environments. Ding et al. (2003) and Yang &Wang (2004) adopted Ant colony algorithm for multi-robot cooperation. Zhang et al. (2007) employed swarm intelligence for adaptive task assignment. Zhang & Liu (2008 b, 2009) and Liu & Zhang (2009, 2010) conducted intensive research on swarm intelligence and applied it to the task allocation of large-scale multi-robot system.

3. Architecture

Ant Colony Algorithm is a new intelligent optimization algorithm and first proposed by Colorni et al. (1992). In ant colony algorithm, each ant searches for solutions independently in the candidate solution space, and lays some pheromone on the found solution. The better the solution, the more pheromone the ant lays. A solution with higher pheromone has a much greater chance of being chosen, and consequently this gives a kind of positive feedback. Through this positive feedback, ants can eventually find the optimal solution. Via this process the algorithm effectively solves combinatorial optimization problems and performs especially well in solving complicated problems (Jiang et al, 2003; Xia et al, 2005).

The paper adopts a hierarchical architecture, as shown in Fig.1. At the high level, we employ the Ant Colony Algorithm to find optimal allocations. Let an ant denote a task; each ant forms its task allocation so as to choose an undertaker for every task. At the low level, each ant forms a task-oriented robot coalition to perform a tightly-coupled task by the ant colony optimization (ACO), the particle swarm and ant colony optimization (PSACO) and the quantum-inspired ant colony optimization (QACO). It is worth mentioning that the proposed mechanism can not only solve loosely-coupled task allocation, but also tightly-coupled task allocation because ants in the high level denote tasks instead of individual robots. Finally, simulation results give a performance comparison, and then conclusions follow.

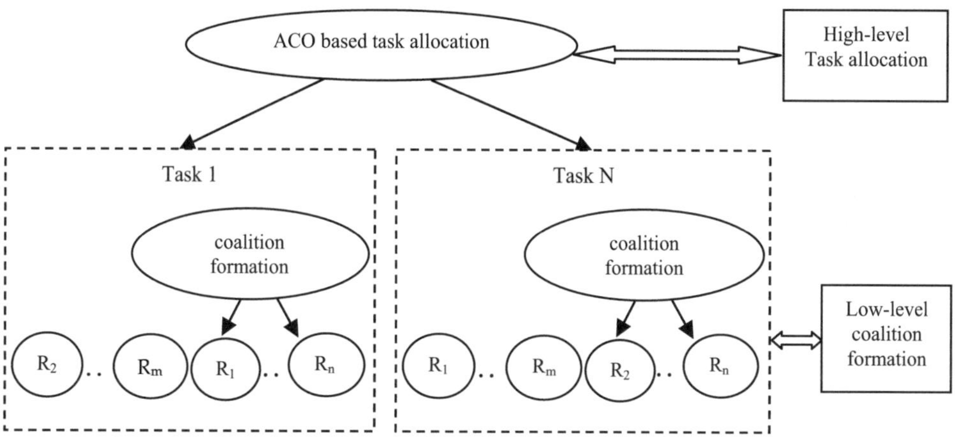

Fig. 1. Hierarchical architecture of the system

4. Key issues of robot coalition formation

4.1 Validity of robot coalition

Similar to agent coalition formation, robot coalition formation also tries to find the robot coalition with the greatest value that can complete a task *t*. A coalition may be formed by several arbitrary robots in the system. However, in order to obtain a satisfactory result, we must consider all or most of the combinations. Therefore it is a complex combinatorial optimization problem. In addition, although there are many similarities between agent coalition and robot coalition, there are also inherent differences which should not be overlooked.

Firstly, software agents are simply code fragments whose capabilities corresponding to software functionality and current data knowledge while robots are tangible entities that occupy physical space and whose capabilities correspond to sensors, actuators, etc. Multi-robot systems must handle real world sensory noise, full or partial robot failures, and communication latency or even loss of communications.

Secondly, agents are allowed to exchange resources, so the formed coalition freely redistributes resources amongst the members. However, this is not possible in a multiple-robot domain. Robot capabilities in handling sensors (camera, laser, sonar, or bumper) and actuators (wheels or gripper) cannot be autonomously exchanged. This implies that a robot coalition that simply possesses the adequate resources is not necessarily up to performing a given task, and other locational constraints have to be represented and met in order for the coalition to succeed.

Finally, correct resource distribution is an important issue in the robot coalition formation. The box-pushing task (Gerkey & Mataric, 2002 b) is used to illustrate this point. Three robots, two pushers (with one bumper and one camera) and one watcher (with one laser range finder and one camera) cooperate to complete the task. The total resource requirements are: two bumpers, three cameras and one laser range finder. However, this information is incomplete, as it does not accurately represent the constraints related to sensor locations. Correct task execution requires that the laser range finder and camera reside on a single robot while the bumper and laser range finder reside on different robots. Therefore each candidate coalition must be verified feasibly.

Checking the feasibility of robot coalition is a Constraint Satisfaction Problem (CSP). It is defined by a set of variables, a set of the domain values for each variable and a set of constraint relationships between variables, which is denoted as (V,D,C). Where V is the set of variables $\{V_1,\ldots,V_n\}$ which are resources and capabilities requirements, in box-pushing task, $V_1,\ldots,V_n$ are the bumper, camera and laser range finder. D is the set of the domain values which is the sum of the available robots possessing the required resources and capabilities, $D=\{D_1,\ldots,D_n\}$, where D_i is the limited domain of V_i's all possible values. C is the set of constraint relationships between variables, $C=\{C_1,\ldots,C_m\}$, each constraint includes a subset of V, that is $\{V_i,\ldots,V_j\}$ and a constraint relationship $R \subseteq D_i \times \ldots \times D_j$. For the box-pushing task, two types of constraints exist, the sensors and actuators must reside either on the same robot or on different robots. As shown in Fig. 2, locational constraints are represented as solid arcs (same robot) and dash arcs (different robot).

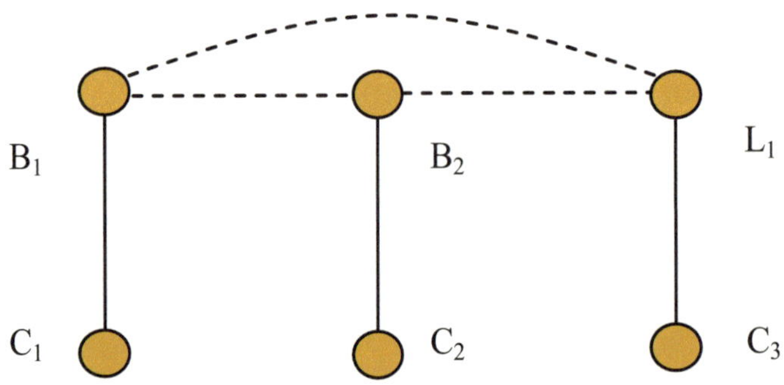

Fig. 2. Box-pushing task constraint graph

4.2 The evaluation criteria of robot coalition formation

Because robots are typically unable to redistribute their resources, it is possible that the coalition will have one or a few robots as main resource providers. This kind of coalition tends to be heavily dependent on these members for task execution that these dominating members become indispensable. Such coalitions should be avoided in order to improve fault tolerance. The coalition imbalance is defined as the degree of unevenness of resource contributions made by individual members to the coalition. The perfectly balanced coalition is where each member contributes equally (taskvalue/n) to the task. The Balance Coefficient (BC) quantifies the coalition imbalance level. The BC can be calculated as follows:

$$BC = \frac{\gamma_1 \times \gamma_2 \times \cdots \times \gamma_n}{\left[\frac{\text{taskvalue}}{n}\right]^n} \tag{1}$$

where $(\gamma_1,\gamma_2,\ldots,\gamma_n)$ is a resource distribution with a coalition C. For the coalitions of the same size, the higher BC, the more balanced the coalition is.

In general, larger coalitions imply that the average individual contribution and the capability requirements from each member are lower; thus larger coalitions are more balanced. However, larger coalitions have much more costs and therefore it is necessary to consider coalition balance and coalition size simultaneously. The Fault Tolerance Coefficient (FTC) metric can be used to solve this problem and it is defined as follows:

$$FTC = \delta BC + \mu f(n) \tag{2}$$

where $\delta+\mu=1$, $f(n)=1-e^{-\lambda n}$ is the function of coalition size. After a particular point, increasing n will not result in a significant increase to the function value. This means that enlarging coalition size does not yield improved performance when the number of robots increases beyond a threshold value. This, as one might imagine, is in accordance with a realistic robot application.

4.3 The description of robot coalition formation problem

1. The Ability Description of Robots

All robots in the system form a robot set $R=\{R_1,R_2,\ldots,R_n\}$. The ability vector of R_i is $B_{Ri}=(b_{i1},b_{i2},\ldots,b_{im})^T$, and the ability cost vector is $cost_{Ri}=(cost_{i1},cost_{i2},\ldots,cost_{im})^T$,where $cost_{ij}$ is the cost of the ability b_{ij}. When $b_{ij}=0$, it denotes R_i without the ability b_{ij}. The cost of R_i is $\sum_{j=1}^{m} cost_{ij} b_{ij}$, which has m kinds of abilities.

2. The Ability Description of Robot Coalition

Robot coalition is a set of robots in which robots can cooperate to complete a task. A coalition C is the nonempty subset of R. Based on the different ability attributes of the robots, there are different ability vectors of the coalition. For the additive capacity (such as handling, etc.), the ability of the coalition C is as follows:

$$B_C = \sum_{R_i \in C} B_{R_i} \tag{3}$$

For the merger capacity (such as video distance, etc.), the ability of the coalition C is as follows:

$$B_C = \bigcup_{R_i \in C} B_{R_i} \tag{4}$$

The cost of the coalition ability is defined as follows.
The additive capacity:

$$D(C) = \sum_{R_i \in C} \sum_{j=1}^{m} cost_{ij} b_{ij} \tag{5}$$

The merger capacity:

$$D(C) = \bigcup_{R_i \in C} \sum_{j=1}^{m} cost_{ij} b_{ij} \tag{6}$$

3. The Requirement Description of Task Capacity

There are *K* tasks, denoted by $T = \{t_1, t_2, \cdots, t_k\}$. The task *t* has the ability requirement vector: $B_t = (b_1, b_2, \cdots, b_m)^T$.
The essential condition for the coalition C to finish the task *t* is as follows：$B_C \geq B_t$.

4. The Definition of Coalition' s Income

We define a *reward* function which is a mapping from the set of tasks to the set of real numbers, denoted by *reward*: $T \to R^+$. A *cost* function is defined as *cost*: $C \to R^+$, which is a mapping from the set of coalitions to the set of real numbers. We consider two types of cost:

- A *coalition-inherent* cost measures the inherent cost (e.g., in terms of energy consumption or computational requirements) of using particular capabilities of the coalition. Here the main consideration is the consumption of the robot's ability to accomplish the tasks, including the communication between the robots in the coalition and the cost of the coalition ability. We denote it by *C_cost.*
- A *task-specific* cost measures cost according to task-related metrics, such as time, distance, etc. Here we mainly consider the distance. We denote the cost of the coalition performing the task by *T_cost.*

Thereby, the *cost* function of the coalition C performing task *t* is denoted as:

$$Cost(C,t) = \varpi_1 C\_cost + \varpi_2 T\_cost \tag{7}$$

where ϖ_1 and ϖ_2 are weighted coefficient of both the *coalition-inherent* cost and *task-specific* cost, $\varpi_1 > 0$, $\varpi_2 > 0$. According to the differences between agent coalitions and robot coalitions, the income of the robot coalition should be defined as:

$$Inc(C) = FTC \times [rew(t) - Cost(C,t)] \tag{8}$$

where FTC is the Fault Tolerance Coefficient, rew(t) is the reward after robots accomplish task *t*.

5. Low-level coalition formation

At the low level, we employ the ant colony optimization (ACO), the particle swarm and ant colony optimization (PSACO) and the quantum-inspired ant colony optimization (QACO) for the coalition formation. Their performance of forming robot coalition for tightly-coupled task is compared by simulation results.

5.1 Forming robot coalition by ant colony algorithm

Put m ants on n robots at random, the probability of ant k located on the Robot i choosing Robot j is defined as follows:

$$p_{ij}^{k} = \frac{\left[\tau_{ij}(t)\right]^{\alpha}\left[1/d_{ij}\right]^{\beta}}{\sum_{u \in J_k}\left[\tau_{ij}(t)\right]^{\alpha}\left[1/d_{iu}\right]^{\beta}}, j \in J_k \tag{9}$$

where J_k is the robot set that ant k has not chosen; $\tau_{ij}(t)$ is the quantity of pheromone remaining on the line between robot i and robot j; d_{ij} (i,j=1,2,…,n) is the distance between robot i and robot j, called communication cost; a and β control the relative weights of pheromone and communication cost. The ant will stop seeking a route when it arrives at a certain robot and finds that the current robot coalition can accomplish the task. When all ants have formed their task-oriented coalitions, one loop finishes. Then each candidate coalition is checked to verify its feasibility. Update the maximal income and the intensity of pheromone according to the following Equation.

$$\tau_{ij}(t+1) \leftarrow \rho\tau_{ij}(t) + \sum_{k=1}^{m} \Delta\tau_{ij}^{k} \tag{10}$$

Here $\Delta\tau_{ij}^{k}$ is the increment of the familiar degree between robot i and robot j given by ant k in this loop and it is defined as:

$$\Delta\tau_{ij}^{k} = \begin{cases} \dfrac{Inc(C_k)}{\sum_{k=1}^{m} C_k}, & \textit{if the coalition formed by ant k includes robot i and j} \\ 0, & \textit{others} \end{cases} \tag{11}$$

$Inc(C_k)$ is the income of the coalition formed by ant k. The optimal combination of parameters a, β and ρ in this algorithm can be determined by the experimental method. The program termination may be controlled by a fixed evolving generation or when the evolving trend is inconspicuous. The time complexity degree is $O(NC.m.n^2)$, NC is the number of loops.

5.2 Forming robot coalition by particle swarm and ant colony optimization

Particle Swarm Optimization (PSO) was proposed by Eberhart and Kennedy (1995). Inspired by foraging behaviours of birds, birds are viewed as particles of swarm and their motion is affected by their own velocity, best position of individual and population in the past. As a result, an optimal solution can be obtained in a complex solution space.
The system is initialized with a population of random particles and then the best solution can be found through iterations. In each time step, particles update their velocity and position by the following formula:

$$v_{k+1} = c_0 v_k + c_1(pbest_k - x_k) + c_2(gbest_k - x_k) \tag{12}$$

$$x_{k+1} = x_k + v_{k+1} \tag{13}$$

where, *pbest* denotes the optimal position of single particle, *gbest* denotes the optimal position of whole population, v_k is the velocity of the particle, x_k is the current position of the particle, c_0, c_1 and c_2 are weight coefficients.

1. Particle Swarm and Ant Colony Optimization (PSACO)

PSO is suitable for dealing with continuous optimal problems, but for discrete optimal problems it is difficult to express the velocity of a particle. Therefore, inspired by Genetic Algorithms, $c_0 v_k$ is viewed as variation operator, while $c_1(pbest_k - x_k) + c_2(gbest_k - x_k)$ is viewed as the crossover operator of current solution with the individual optimal value and the global optimal value respectively.

The PSACO takes an ant as a particle. Ants choose their cooperative ants based on their own information, *pbest* and *gbest*. Then the current coalition executes crossover operations with individual optimal coalition and global optimal coalition to form new coalition. Finally, the new coalition executes a variation operator.

The adopted crossover strategy is to choose a random position from the second string as a crossover point. In addition, the variation rule is constructed so as to choose a random position, if the variation bit is -1 (the robot is not chosen), its value is set 1 (the robot is chosen), and vice versa.

2. The PSACO Algorithm

The PSACO algorithm is described as follows:

Step 1. Initialization

Set $NC = 0$, $J_k = \{1, 2, \cdots, n\}$. Execute ACO to form m initial coalitions and then compute the fitness *Income0* of each coalition according to Eq. (8). Treat current fitness as the individual optimal value *ptbest* and treat current coalition as the individual optimal value coalition *pcbest*. Then, find the global optimal value *gtbest* and global optimal value coalition *gcbest* via *ptbest*.

Step 2. Put m ants on n robots randomly.

for $k = 1$ to m

{Initialize robot coalition consisting of robots which ants initially are located and delete these robots from J_k. Then calculate the capability vector B_{C_k} of each initial coalition.}

Step 3. for $k = 1$ to m

while ($B_{C_k} < B_t$)

{Choose a robot j according to probability $p_{ij}{}^k$ by Eq. (9) and put it into current coalition. Delete j form J_k. Increase the capability vector of coalitions. }

Step 4. for $k = 1$ to m

Coalition $C_0(k)$ formed by the *K-th* ant crossovers with *gcbest* thus produces $C_1^{'}(k)$, and then $C_1^{'}(k)$ crossovers with *pcbest* to produces $C_1^{''}(k)$. After the variation operator applied to $C_1^{''}(k)$, a new coalition $C_1(k)$ is formed. If $C_1(k)$ can perform the task, compute the fitness *Income*1 according to Eq. (8). If $Income1 > Income0$, the new value is accepted, otherwise keep $C_0(k)$ as the coalition of ant k. Update the values of *ptbest*, *pcbest*, *gtbest*, *gcbest*.

Step 5. Compute the coalition income $Inc(C_k)$ by Eq. (8) and save the best solution.
Step 6. Update the pheromone by Eqs. (10) & (11).
Step 7. Set $t = t+1$, $NC = NC+1$, $\Delta\tau_{ij} = 0$
Step 8. if ($NC < NC_{\max}$)

$J_k = \{1,2,\cdots,n\}$;

Goto Step 2.
Step 9. Output the optimal coalition and its income.

5.3 Forming robot coalition by quantum-inspired ant colony optimization

Quantum-Inspired evolutionary algorithm (QEA) was proposed by Kuk-Hyun Han (2002). It is based on the concept and principles of quantum computing (Grover, 1994) such as a quantum bit and superposition of states. QEA performs well even with a small population and without premature convergence as compared to the conventional genetic algorithm.
QEA is also characterized by the representation of the individual, the evaluation function, and the population dynamics. However, instead of using the binary, numeric and symbolic representation, QEA uses Q-bit as a probabilistic representation which is defined as the smallest unit of information. A Q-bit individual is defined by a string of Q-bits. The Q-bit individual has the advantage that can represent a linear superposition of states (binary solutions) in search space probabilistically. Thus, the Q-bit representation has a better characteristic of population diversity than other representations.

1. Encoding with Q-bits

A number of different representations can be used to encode the solutions onto individuals in evolutionary computation. QEA uses a new representation, called Q-bit, for a probabilistic representation. The representation is based on the concept of Q-bit; a Q-bit individual as well as a string of Q-bits are defined below.
Definition 1: A Q-bit is the smallest unit of information in QEA, which is defined with a pair of numbers (α,β) as

$$\begin{bmatrix} \alpha \\ \beta \end{bmatrix}$$

where $|\alpha|^2 + |\beta|^2 = 1$. $|\alpha|^2$ gives the probability that the Q-bit will be found in the '0' state and $|\beta|^2$ gives the probability that the Q-bit will be found in the '1' state.
A Q-bit may be in the '0' state, in the '1' state, or in a linear superposition of the two.
Definition 2: An individual Q-bit as a string of Q-bits is defined as

$$\begin{bmatrix} \alpha_1 \\ \beta_1 \end{bmatrix}\begin{matrix} \alpha_2 \\ \beta_2 \end{matrix}\begin{matrix} \cdots \\ \cdots \end{matrix}\begin{matrix} \alpha_m \\ \beta_m \end{matrix}\Bigg]$$

where $|\alpha_i|^2 + |\beta_i|^2 = 1, i = 1,2,...,m$.

The Q-bit representation has the advantage that it is able to represent a linear superposition of states. If there is, for instance, a three-Q-bit system with three pairs of amplitudes such as

$$\begin{bmatrix} \frac{1}{\sqrt{2}} & \frac{1}{\sqrt{2}} & \frac{1}{2} \\ \frac{1}{\sqrt{2}} & \frac{-1}{\sqrt{2}} & \frac{\sqrt{3}}{2} \end{bmatrix}$$

Then the states of the system can be represented as

$$\frac{1}{4}|000\rangle+\frac{\sqrt{3}}{4}|001\rangle-\frac{1}{4}|010\rangle-\frac{\sqrt{3}}{4}|011\rangle+\frac{1}{4}|100\rangle+\frac{\sqrt{3}}{4}|101\rangle-\frac{1}{4}|110\rangle-\frac{\sqrt{3}}{4}|111\rangle$$

The above result means that the probabilities to represent the states $|000\rangle,|001\rangle,|010\rangle,|011\rangle$ $,|100\rangle,|101\rangle,|110\rangle,|111\rangle$ are 1/16, 3/16, 1/16, 3/16, 1/16, 3/16, 1/16, and 3/16, respectively. Therefore, the three-Q-bit system contains the information of eight states.

Evolutionary computing with Q-bit representation has a better characteristic of population diversity than other representations, since it can represent linear superposition of states probabilistically. Only one Q-bit individual is enough to represent eight states, but in binary representation at least eight strings, (000), (001), (010), (011), (100), (101), (110), and (111) are needed.

2. Quantum-Inspired Ant Colony Optimization

Wang & Li (2007) proposed a novel quantum genetic algorithm for TSP. The basic idea of quantum-inspired ant colony optimization is to make ants which have quantum characteristics, that is, every ant is a quantum individual and encoded by the probability of choosing cooperative robots instead of Q-bit. The QACO is added to the corresponding observation process and repairing process (Han, 2002).

The probability coding is defined as:

$$\begin{bmatrix} P_0 \\ P_1 \end{bmatrix}$$

where $P_0+P_1=1$. The individual is denoted as:

$$q_k=\begin{bmatrix} p_{k_{10}} & p_{k_{20}} & p_{k_{j0}} & p_{k_{m0}} \\ p_{k_{11}} & p_{k_{21}} & p_{k_{j1}} & p_{k_{m1}} \end{bmatrix} \tag{14}$$

where $k=1,2,\cdots,n$, $j=1,2,\cdots,m$, $P_{k_{j1}}=P_{ij}^{\ k}$, $P_{k_{j0}}=1-P_{k_{j1}}$. The t-th generation population of QACO is denoted as: $Q(t)=\{q_1^{\ t},q_2^{\ t},\cdots,q_n^{\ t}\}$. $P(t)=\{X_1^{\ t},X_2^{\ t},\cdots,X_n^{\ t}\}$, where $X_k^{\ t}$ is the state of observing k-th individual, $X_k^{\ t}=\{x_{k1}^{\ t}x_{k2}^{\ t}\cdots x_{km}^{\ t}\}$, $x_{kj}^{\ t}$ is either 0 or 1. When its value is 0, it means that robot j is not chosen while the value 1 means robot j is chosen.

The algorithm of QACO is given as follows:

Step 1. Initialize $t=0$, $NC=0$, $NC_{\max}=N$, $numAnt=m$, $numRobot=n$, $\Delta\tau_{ij}=0$, $\tau_{ij}(0)=\tau_0$

Step 2. Put m ants on n robots randomly

for $k=1$ to m

for $j=1$ to n

{ if ant k starts from robot j, then $P_{k_{j1}}=1$. According to Eq. (9), calculate the probability of choosing cooperative robots, $P_{k_{j1}} = P_{ij}^{\ k}$, $P_{k_{j0}} = 1 - P_{ij}^{\ k}$ }

Step 3. Observe the individuals of $Q(t)$ and get the states $P(t)$.

Step 4. Check whether every state in $P(t)$ is a solution, if not then go to Step10 and repair it.

Step 5. According to Eq. (8), calculate the income $Inc(X_j^{\ t})$ of $X_j^{\ t}$.

Step 6. Save the optimization coalition b and its income $Inc(b)$.

Step 7. Update the pheromone by Eqs. (10) & (11).

Step 8. Set $t = t + 1$, $NC = NC + 1$, $\Delta\tau_{ij} = 0$

Step 9. If $(\mathrm{NC} < \mathrm{NC}_{\max})$ and not keep evolving for a long time then go to Step 2, else output the optimization coalition and its income.

Step 10. Repair the state which is not a solution through repairing process. If states in $P(t)$ are all solutions, then go to Step 5.

6. High-level task allocation

The following parameters are introduced; m denotes the number of ants, each task is denoted as node 0, and the candidate robots or robot coalition are labelled as node 1 to n. The probability that ant k moves from node 0 to node j is formulated below:

$$\mathrm{p_{ij}}^{\mathrm{k}} = \frac{\left[\tau_{\mathrm{ij}}(\mathrm{t})\right]^{\alpha}\left[1/\mathrm{cost_{ij}}\right]^{\beta}}{\sum\limits_{\mathrm{u}\in \mathrm{J_i}}\left[\tau_{\mathrm{iu}}(\mathrm{t})\right]^{\alpha}\left[1/\mathrm{cost_{iu}}\right]^{\beta}}, j \in J_i \tag{15}$$

where J_i is the set of candidate robots or robot coalition to task i, and $cost_{ij}$ is the cost of robots or robot coalition to finish task i. If the task can be completed by a single robot, the cost is both the distance of the robot to the task and its ability consumption. Otherwise, the cost Cost(C,t) is the cost of robot coalition to complete the task. For each ant k, the first task node in the task list is the beginning point for the optimization. After ant k chooses an undertaker, it moves to next task to choose an undertaker for next task, and so on. When ant k has chosen undertakers for all tasks, one task allocation is finished. When all ants have completed a solution, one cycle is completed. The solution with the maximal income is the optimal solution, and then updates the intensity of pheromone according to Eq. (10).
However, $\Delta\tau_{ij}^{\ k}$ is defined as follows:

$$\Delta\tau_{\mathrm{ij}}^{\ \mathrm{k}} = \frac{\mathrm{Q}}{\sum\limits_{\mathrm{k}=1}^{\mathrm{m}}\mathrm{cost_{kj}}}, \quad Q \text{ is a constant} \tag{16}$$

The detailed task allocation algorithm is as follows:

Step 1. Initialization

Set $t = 0, NC = 0, \tau_{ij}(0) = \tau_0, \Delta\tau_{ij} = 0, numTask = s, numAnt = m, numRobot = n$, the capability requirement of each task, capability vector and cost vector of each robot.

Step 2. for i=1 to s

for k=1 to m do

{Ant k starts from the first task and determines whether the current task i is a tightly-coupled task. If it is, then go to step 7, else choose an undertaker from

J_i according to p_{ij}^k by Eq. (15) and calculate the income. Then, ant k moves to next task and repeats the above process until all tasks have been allocated to undertakers.}

Step 3. Calculate total income of the task allocation formed by each ant. Then, update the maximal income and the allocation schema.

Step 4. For ant k=1 to m do
Update the intensity of pheromone $\tau_{ij}(t+1)$ according to Eqs. (10) & (16).

Step 5. Set $t=t+1, NC=NC+1, \Delta\tau_{ij}=0$.

Step 6. If ($NC<NC_{max}$) and (still keep evolving) then go to step 2
else output the allocation schema with the maximal income and stop the program.

Step 7. Call coalition formation algorithm ACO, PSACO and QACO to form a coalition for task i, then goto Step 2.

The allocating process is finished by the algorithm above. If current task is tightly-coupled, the high-level algorithm will call the low-level algorithm to form a coalition formation.

7. Deadlock elimination

Because robots are fully distributed in the system with equal status among them, it is likely to appear deadlock due to robots waiting each other at different task position. We employ a simple strategy to avoid the deadlock. Each robot has a task queue. Robots perform tasks in the same order as the tasks are allocated.

8. Simulation

In order to verify the effectiveness of proposed algorithms, we implement the algorithms in the TeamBots platform developed by Carnegie Mellon University and Georgia Institute of Technology. The implementation runs on a PC with M CPU 750, 1.8GHz Intel Pentium processor. Based on the transportation mission, there are some tasks in the environment. Some of them can be carried out by a single robot (loosely-coupled task) and the others must be completed by multiple robots (tightly-coupled task). Tables 1 and 2 list the capability of robots and task requirement.

According to Tables 1 and 2, we can find that tasks T1, T3, T6 and T9 must be completed by multiple robots. Simulation parameters are as follows:

The high-level ant colony size m=20, low-level colony size n=20, the maximal iteration number $NC_{max}=500$, $Q=1$, $rew(T_i)=1000$, $\delta=\mu=\lambda=0.5$, $\varpi_1=\varpi_2=1$, $\alpha=1.5$, $\beta=2$, and $\rho=0.9$

The task allocation algorithm was run 10 times. A comparison of three coalition formation algorithms is given in Fig. 3 and Table 3.

From Fig. 2 and Table 3, the following conclusions can be made:

1. The effectiveness of ACO is poor and it is easy to enter into premature convergence
2. The quality of PSACO is best, however, because each ant takes longer time than other two methods to finish a cycle, the runtime is relative long
3. QACO can find a good solution in a short time, so it is suitable for large-scale multi robots systems

Robot	Capacity	Cost	Robot	Capacity	Cost
R_0	1, 0, 1	1, 2, 1	R_8	3, 2, 1	2, 1, 3
R_1	1, 1, 1	1, 1, 2	R_9	3, 1, 1	2, 3, 2
R_2	2, 1, 2	2, 3, 1	R_{10}	2, 0, 1	1, 4, 3
R_3	1, 2, 1	3, 2, 1	R_{11}	1, 3, 3	2, 2, 1
R_4	0, 1, 1	1, 1, 1	R_{12}	2, 1, 3	1, 3, 1
R_5	1, 1, 2	2, 1, 1	R_{13}	0, 2, 1	3, 1, 2
R_6	0, 1, 1	3, 2, 3	R_{14}	1, 2, 3	4, 2, 1
R_7	2, 2, 1	3, 2, 1			

Table 1. Capacity vector and Cost Vector of Robots

Task	Capacity Required	Position	Task	Capacity requirement	Position
T_0	1 1 1	(13,10)	T_5	1 1 2	(15,0)
T_1	3 2 3	(0,0)	T_6	3 3 2	(0,-10)
T_2	1 2 1	(10,-10)	T_7	1 2 3	(20,-10)
T_3	3 3 1	(-10,10)	T_8	2 1 2	(20,20)
T_4	2 1 1	(-8,-3)	T_9	3 2 4	(20,0)

Table 2. Task requirement information

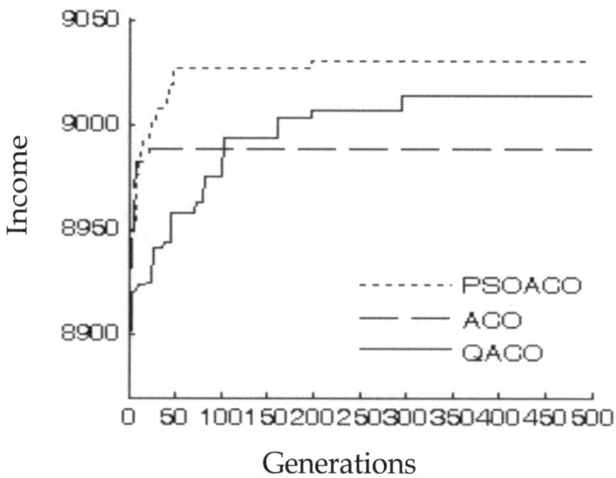

Fig. 3. Optimal evolution curves

Algorithm	Best (Generations)	Worst (Generations)	Average (Generations)	Average runtime (Sec)
ACO	9012	8953	8988	7.37
PSACO	9030	9030	9030	8.52
QACO	9022	8971	8997	3.75

Table 3. Results comparison among ACO, PSACO and QACO

9. Conclusion

This paper discusses the key issues of robot coalition formation. A task allocation mechanism based on swarm intelligence is proposed. This allocation method adopts a hierarchical architecture. At the high level, we employ Ant Colony Algorithm to find optimal allocations; each ant forms a task allocation so as to choose an undertaker for every task. At the low level, each ant forms a task-oriented robot coalition to perform a tightly-coupled task. ACO, PSACO and QACO are used to form the coalition. The algorithm is implemented in the TeamBots platform. Simulation results show that the proposed approaches can effectively achieve loosely-coupled and tightly-coupled task allocation in large-scale multi-robot systems. PSACO achieves the best solution, but its running time is the longest. On the other hand, although QACO is somewhat inferior to PSACO in the solution quality, its running time is only half of two other methods. Therefore, QACO is more suitable for the large-scale multi-robot system. Our future work is to improve the performance of algorithms and accelerate their convergence.

10. Reference

Botelho S. & Alami, R. (1999). M+: A scheme for multi-robot cooperation through negotiated task allocation and achievement. *Proceedings of IEEE International Conference on Robotics and Automation (ICRA '99)*, pp. 1234–1239, Detroit, Michigan, USA, May 1999.

Chaimowicz, L. et al(2002). Dynamic Role Assignment for Cooperative Robots, *Proceedings of the IEEE International Conference on Robotics and Automation*, pp. 293-298, Washington, America, May 2002.

Colorni, A.; Dorigo, M. & Maniezzo, V(1992). An investigation of some properties of an ant algorithm, *Proceedings of the Parallel Problem Solving from Nature Conference*, pp. 509-520, Brussels, Belgium, September,1992.

Dias, M. B. (2004). TraderBots: A New Paradigm for Robust and Efficient Multirobot Coordination in Dynamic Environments. *PhD thesis*, Robotics Institute, Carnegie Mellon University, January 2004.

Ding,Y.Y. et al (2003). Multi-Robot Cooperation Method Based on the Ant Algorithm, *Robot*, Vol. 25, No.5, pp. 414-418, 2003.

Eberhart R. C. & Kennedy, J.(1995) A new optimizer using particles s warm theory, *Proceedings of the Sixth International Symposium on Micro Machine and Human Science*, pp. 39-43, Nagoya,Japan,1995.

Gerkey, B. & Mataric, M.J. (2004). A formal analysis and taxonomy of task allocation in multi-robot systems. *International Journal of Robotics Research*, Vol. 23, No.9, pp.939-954, 2004.

Gerkey, B. & Mataric, M.J.(2002 a). Sold!: Auction methods for multirobot coordination. *IEEE Transactions on Robotics and Automation*, Vol. 18, No.5, pp. 758–786, 2002.

Gerkey, B. & Mataric, M.J. (2002 b). Pusher-watcher: An approach to fault-tolerant tightly-coupled robot coordination, *In Proceedings of IEEE International Conference on Robotics and Automation*, pp. 464-469, Washington, America, May 2002.

Grover, L K. (1994). Algorithms for quantum computation : discrete logarithms and factoring. *In Proceedings of the 35th Annual Symposium on Foundations of Computer Science*, New Jersey, November, 1994.

Han K. H. (2002). Quantum-Inspired Evolutionary Algorithm for a Class of Combinatorial Optimization, *IEEE Transactions on Evolutionary Computation*, Vol.6, No.6, pp.580-593, 2002.

Jiang, J.G. et al(2003).Solution to travelling agent problem based on improved ant colony algorithm, *Pattern Recognition and Artificial Intelligence*,Vol.16, No. 1, pp.6-12, 2003.

Kalra, N. & Martinoli, A. (2006). A Comparative Study of Market-Based and Threshold-based Task Allocation. *Proceedings of Distributed Autonomous Robotic Systems (DARS)*, Minnesota, USA, July 2006.

Liu, S. H. & Zhang Y.(2009). Multi-robot task allocation based on particle swarm and ant colony optimal , *Journal of Northeast Normal University*, Vol.41, No.4, pp. 68-72, 2009.

Liu, S. H. & Zhang Y.(2010). Multi-robot task allocation based on swarm intelligence, *Journal of Jilin University*, Vol.40, No.1, pp. 123-129, 2010.

Parker L. E. (1998). ALLIANCE : an architecture for fault tolerant multirobot cooperation, *IEEE Transactions on Robotics and Automation*, Vol.14, No.2, pp.220－240,1998.

Sanem, S.& Tucker, B.(2006). A Distributed Multi-Robot Cooperation Framework for Real Time Task Achievement, *Proceedings of Distributed Autonomous Robotic Systems*, Minnesota, USA, July 2006.

Smith R. G. (1980). The Contract Net Protocol: High level communication and control in a distributed problem solver. *IEEE Transaction on Computers*, 29, 12, pp. 1104-1113, 1980.

Tang, F. & Parker, L.E. (2005). ASyMTRe: Automated Synthesis of Multi-Robot Task Solution Through Software Reconfiguration, *Proceedings of IEEE International Conference on Robotics and Automation*, pp. 1501-1508, Barcelona, Spain, May 2005.

Wang Y. P. & Li Y. H. (2007). A Novel Quantum Genetic Algorithm for TSP, *Chinese Journal of Computers*, Vol.30, NO.5, pp. 748-755, 2007.

Werger, B. & Mataric, M.J.(2000). Broadcast of local eligibility: Behavior based control for strongly cooperative multi-robot teams, *In Proceedings of Autonomous Agents*, pp. 21-22, Barcelona, Spain, June 2000.

Xia, N. ; Jiang, J.G. & Wei, X. (2005). Searching for Agent coalition for single task using improved ant colony algorithm, *Journal of Computer Research and Development*, Vol.42, No.5, pp. 734-739, 2005.

Yang, D. &Wang, Z.(2004). Improved Ant Algorithm for Assignment Problem, *Journal of Tianjing University*, Vol.37, No.4, pp. 373-376, 2004.

Zhang, D.D. et al (2007). Adaptive task assignment for multiple mobile robots via swarm intelligence approach, *Robotics and Autonomous Systems*, Vol. 55, No.7 pp. 572-588, 2007.

Zhang, Y. & Liu, S. H. (2008 a). Survey of Multi-Robot Task Allocation. *CAAI Transactions on Intelligence Systems*, Vol.3, No.2, pp.115-120, 2008.

Zhang, Y. & Liu, S. H. (2008 b). Large-scale Multi-robot Task Allocation Based on Ant Colony Algorithm, *Proceedings of Chinese Control and Decision Conference*, pp.2057-2062, Yantai, China, July 2008.

Zhang Y. & Liu, S. H. (2009). A Quantum-Inspired Ant Colony Optimization for Robot Coalition Formation, *Proceedings of Chinese Control and Decision Conference,* pp.632-637, Guilin, China, June 2009.

Zlot, R. et al (2002). Multi-Robot Exploration Controlled by a Market Economy, *Proceedings of the IEEE International Conference on Robotics and Automation,* pp. 3016-3023, Washington, DC, May 2002.

21

Research on Multi-Robot Architecture and Decision-making Model

Li Shuqin[1] and Yuan Xiaohua[2]
Department of Computer Science,
[1]Beijing Information Science &Technology University, Beijing
[2]College of Information, Shanghai Ocean University, Shanghai
China

1. Introduction

Robot architecture (or controlling architecture) mainly describes robot combining modules, then relationship between modules and exchanging between robots. Up to now multi-robot architecture is one of the main topics in multi-agent and multi-robot research, and many researchers strive to design controlling architectures of excellent performance, and a few of them have already proposed some valid multi-robot architecture and given related simulation [Dias 2004], among which the famous are

- Architecture of GOPHER [Caloud et al. 1990] combined by four layers including decomposition and distribution of task, moving programming and execution control. In GOPHER a central task processing system (CTPS) take charge of task distribution.Every robot can learn its task from CTPS's announcment, use task distributing algorithm to determine its own role, and use a classical AI programming technique to realize its role. Although has successfully fulfilled tasks of box pushing and tracing, GOPHER prevent robot join other task before fulfilled its current task, and has not clearly proposed how robot can restore from error or failing, and how to make use of the limited sources and to define state role. These limitations have weakened robot in GOPHER to work well under dynamic environment.
- Distributive architecture of ALLIANCE [Parker 1998] was a behavior-based, fault-tolerant and self-adoptive multi-robot cooperative architecture. In ALLIANCE, individual robot used a behavior-based controller to select behavior based on a motivation model. Robot in ALLIANCE could not make fast and optimal response in dynamic environment. ALLIANCE has not considered optimal distribution of limited resources, did not allow dynamic assigning of new type tasks too. By far ALLIANCE has fulfilled tasks such as box pushing, disc collecting, and formation moving.
- Lueth and Laengle [Laengle et al. 1998] co-proposed a distributive controlling architecture of KAMARA team oriented to multi-robot cooperation. KAMARA is behavior fault-tolerance and error correction also. The architecture is based on universal concept of agent to respresent robot component. Agent take charge of communication, task programming and behavior selecting, and task executing. In KAMARA, agent without capability can not take part in consultation and being assigned any task.

KAMARA can not guarantee incapable agent fulfilling its task. And in addition, in KAMARA there is no optimal resource exploit also, so agent need to store all the resources, thus will lead to a calamitous increase of consultation.

- The famous controlling architecture STEAM [Tambe & Zhang 1997] was built on joint-intension and sharing programming. STEAM does not rely on special domain knowledge, thus is reusability. In order to reduce communication, based on decision-making theory, STEAM used a communication selecting mechanism to guarantee the realization of joint-intension although without any communication. Tambe and etc. have further designed a consultation-based model of CONSA based on STEAM.
- Noreils[Noreils 1993]proposed a three-layer hierarchical controlling architecture , in which programming layer divides task into little sub tasks and assigns sub tasks to a robot network, controlling layer organizes robot in task fulfilling, and function layer provides actually controlling. Noreils has report implement of this architecture in multi-robot cooperation of box pushing.
- Habib [Habib et al. 1992] proposed an AC-tRESS controlling architecture, in which a consultation mechanism allow robot to seek help from other robots when needed.
- Zhao,Y W. & Tan, D L [Zhao & Tan 1990] proposed a hybrid hierarchical architecture based on behavior decomposition.
- Tan-Min and etc. [Tan et al. 2005 ;Chao et al.2001] proposed a hybrid controlling architecture oriented to task-level cooperation of multi-robot system, which was combined by layers of system monitor, cooperative programmer, and behavior controlling.

Since hierarchical cooperation can reduce programming complication and improve system efficiency, the above architectures are almost hierarchical, but these architectures have not emphasized autonomical behavior decision-making.

We take for that in multi-robot system under highly dynamic environment, it is impossible and unpractical to rely on one controller to assign task and to make route programming for all robots, robot must has capability of autonomous, self-adaption, and cooperation, all the three are of the same importance and can not be lacked.

In this chapter, in order to emphasize the autonomical behavior decision-making, and for system modularity and robusticity, we propose a hybrid architecture based on five layers, among which decision-making is explicitly being presented as one laye. Since in our architecture, different layer send out different information, communication consumptioncan is largely reduced, and when exigency occurrs, robot needs not to wait for induction from high layer, thus the system is more effective and robustic.

Firstly we introduce the hybrid architecture in section 2. Then we design the decision-making module and develop a related algorithm in section 3. In section 4 we gave details on implement of our architecture in Garbage disposal under dangerous environment, and at last in section 5, we arrived at some chapter conclusions.

2. Hierarchical robot architecture based on behavior

Based on the advantage of existing robot architecture, considering characteristics of moving task of multi-robot in dynamic complex environments, emphasizing robot's capability of self-adaptive, autonomous decision-making and cooperation, and strengthening monitoring of robot also, we proposed a behavior-based five-layer hybrid architecture of hierarchical individual robot, which includes two modules and five layers as shown in figure 1.

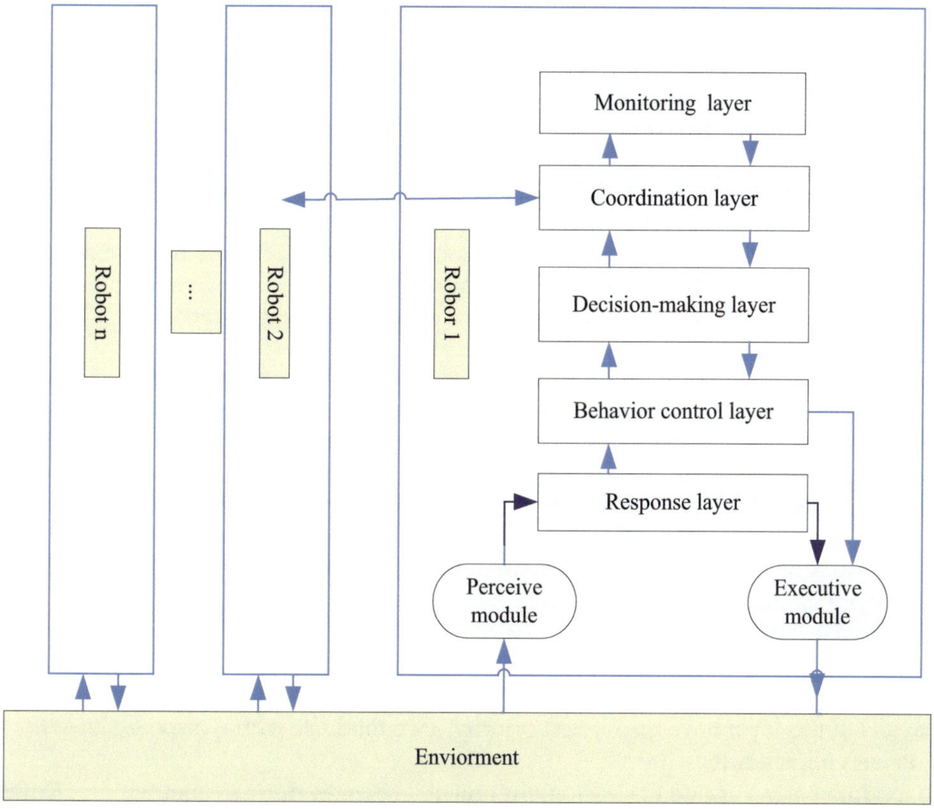

Fig. 1. Five-layer hybrid hierarchical robot architecture

Where the five layers are

1. **System Monitoring Layer**

Combined by monitoring modules, this layer watch if system state is abnormal. If it is, then halt task execution and send a message to behavior planning controller.

2. **Organization and coordination layer**

This layer mainly take charge of task management and make robot cooperation rules. It consists of seven modules as below

- Repository stores knowledge of environment, task, robot and experience. Robot knowledge are about other surrounding robot, especially robot's location, pose, and intension. Experiential knowledge are a set of examples, which robot canuse for reference when organizing, coordinating and programming.
- Update module periodically modify and update its interior organizing and coordinating database according to information it collected.
- Task decomposition module will partition system functions according to knowledge of tasks, and to build up robot organization model.
- Task assessment module will assesses the cost and befit of task fulfilling.
- Task assigning module. According to different robot role, this module assigns tasks using a cost contract network or of optimization.
- Communication module mainly transfers local layer information among robots.

- Cooperation module is the kernel controller in the layer. By exchanging with the same module of other robot,it sets up a hierarchical organization, and by cooperatively assessment, decomposition and assigning of task, it can fulfill task decomposition and assigning the subtasks quickly and rationally.

3. **Behavior decision-making layer**

This layer reflects robot autonomy and is mainly combined by behavior decision-making module and communication module. The first behavior decision-making module involves robot intention and realizes robot's cooperation intension. According to repository content and information from exchanging, this module autonomous search, reason and decide, produce joint behavior intension, that is, to choose a team to take part in. The second communication module mainly transfers information about behavior intension among robots.

4. **Behavior control layer**

This layer mainly takes charge of detail planning and executing of behavior decisions made by the above behavior decision-making layer. Behavior control layer is mainly combined by module of programming, coordination and communication. Programming module produce or select a recently behavior sequence according to tasks selected by behavior decision-making layer, when error or unexpected events occurring, programming module need to do reprogramming. Strategy coordination module coordinates robot moving to avoid collision and dead-lock as much as possible. Communication module transfers information about behavior programming and coordination.

5. **Response layer**

This layer is combined by response modules, and primarily give rapid response. In this layer there is a rule base which maps perceived information to some special behaviors. Behaviors of this layer have the highest priority. Two modules within response layer are

- **Perceiving module**

This module perceives and abstract environmental changes during robot moving Different kinds of information after abstracted will be loaded and processed in a related processing layer. For example if perceived some emergent, then information will be sent to response layer, from whose's response, behavior instruction will be sent to an Execute Module.

- **Execute module**

This module takes charge of actual behavior execution, such as avoiding obstacles, forward and backward movement, and etc.

In our architecture, time cost in decision-making layer is the longest. As refer to literature [Farinelli et al. 2003], time cost in response layer was about 10 ms, and that of higher layer was longer than 1min. In general, our proposed architecture has properties such as

- By setting a behavior decision-making layer to emphasize robot autonomous ability;
- Different layer will send out different information, thus can largely reduce communication consumption.
- When exigency occurring, robot can make response by itself, no need to wait decision from some higher layer, and
- System has modularity and robusticity.

3. Implement of behavior decision-making module

Robot can be taken as agent that has limited range of vision and communication, and certain autonomy. So robot in system has capabilities such as [Tang 2002, Xu 2004].

- Perceptive capability,it can perceive and adopt to the changes of environment.

- Communication capability, which is needed when robots consult for cooperation.
- Moving capability, which includes steering and moving in dynamic environment, such as climbing, cross country, paddle and etc. Moving capability can be represented by moving speed and direction.
- Behavior capability, which includes skills needed in task fulfilling, such as installing, maintaining, conveying, digging, site leveling out, attacking, scouting, computation, searching, and plotting and etc.
- Behavior decision-making capability, which is robot autonomy in behavior. In this chapter, this mainly refers that under multiple task condition, robot can decide to select a task team to join in according to information it collected.
- Real time response capability, which means that robot can response and take behaivior in emergency, such as avoiding obstacle and collision.
- Cooperation capability. In multi-robot system, robot must have capability of cooperation with others for task fulfilling.
- Capability of local programming, which means that robot can deduce other robot's intension, and according to this to plan behavior of its own.
- Organization capability, it refers that Leader robot can organize and coordinate robots with different skills to fulfill tasks together. And
- Learn capability. Individual robot must can learn from and adopt to complicate and changeful environment, thus to improve the running efficiency of the whole system.

The below studies are mainly related to robot decision-making module in our architecture. We firstly give definitions of robot intension, intension rule and role, then analyze factors influence robot behavior decision-making, at last propose a intension decision-making algorithm based on multiple dimension attributes.

3.1 Definition of intension

In dynamic environment, if can not fulfill some complicate task independently for lack of essential global environmental information or skills by itself, individual robot must has capability to choose a team to take part in, synthetically according to the environmental information collected by its perceptive system, intension of other robot within its communication range, and system runner's indirect instruction (called as joint intension), and through behavior programming to produce a series behavior to fulfill the intension .

Definition 1 Robot intension

Robot intension expresses robot's task selection at some time abiding by the intension rule defined as below.

Definition 2 Robot intension rule

There are two robot intension rules

- At a certain time intension only can be one, and
- intension must be of some certain stability and flexibility.

Here stability refers that intension can not change frequently, and flexibility is that intension can change in some special situation, such as robot encounter a new target, or intended task has being fulfilled, or motivation of one target disappeared. When accident comes forth in task fulfilling, individual robot should modify its intension also.

3.2 Definition of role

Because of robot's limited vision and communication capability, so in order to reduce communication, according to robot's knowledge of current task and the distance from the task, we give the definition of state role that can be referred to [Chaimowicz et al. 2002].

Definition 3 State role
In task fulfilling, the distance from robot to task and robot's responsibility are called state role, it is related to task in specified application. State roles can be converted dynamically. In our system, we set five state roles, including Explore, Leader, Approach, Attach and Arrived.
Definition 4 Leader
Leader is the first robot that arrives at task, and take charge of organizing of task fulfilling. To a given task, Leader should be the only. Represented by R_0, Leader can be described as $Find(first, goal\_T) \wedge Distance(R_0, goal\_T) \leq \rho$, where $\rho > 0$ is the nearest distance constant, and $goal\_T$ is goal of the task.
Definition 5 Arrived
Arrived is robot that had arrived at task location and waiting for fulfilling it, which can be described as
$Distance(R_0, goal\_T) \leq \rho + \varepsilon$, where $\varepsilon > 0$ is a small positive constant. In our below experiments, $\rho + \varepsilon$ is equal to robot vision radius.
Definition 6 Attach
Attach is the robot within R_0's communication range or R_0 can indirectly communicate with it, and it has already selected some task and already begin to move to. Attach can be described as $Distance(R, R_0) \leq R_0.Cap.Crange$.
Definition 7 Approach
Approach is also within R_0's communication range or R_0 can indirectly communicate with, Although Approach has got some task information, but it has not selected any task yet.
Definition 8 Explore
Explore are robot that move randomly in environment for searching task.
In system running, each robot will correspond to and execute one role at one moment. In dynamical environment robot's role can be reassigned, which include methods of Dynamical Assigning and Relocating. In Dynamical Assigning, robot can be assigned to a new role after it fulfilled a task. After all the tasks of one team having being fulfilled, the team will be dissolved, and Leader and Arriveds will be reassigned as Explore. When Leader is not competent, its role can be changed to Arrived also. In Relocating, robot stops executing its current role and start a new one, and in dynamic environment, robot can become the Leader through competition. Since in its moving, robot's team selection is continually changed and robot may serves different role, thus robot can reassign and relocate its role at any moment.
We prescribe that to the same task, role Relocating abide by the conversion order of Explore->Approach->Attach->Arrived->Leader.
Roles and their dynamically reassigning can be described in figure 2, in which a solid arrow represents Relocating, and dashed arrow represents Dynamical reassigning.
Since Explore does not send but only accept information, after selecting one team Approch only send application of team joining to task Leader, and Arrived does not send out any information, thus by role setting, communication in our system can be reduced largely.

3.3 Attributes related to joint intention making
It is key to decide intension in our five-layer architecture. Below we firstly analyze two kinds of factors that affect the autonomy of task selecting. One kind is indirect influencing factors produced by task, including main task attributes. The other kind is direct factors

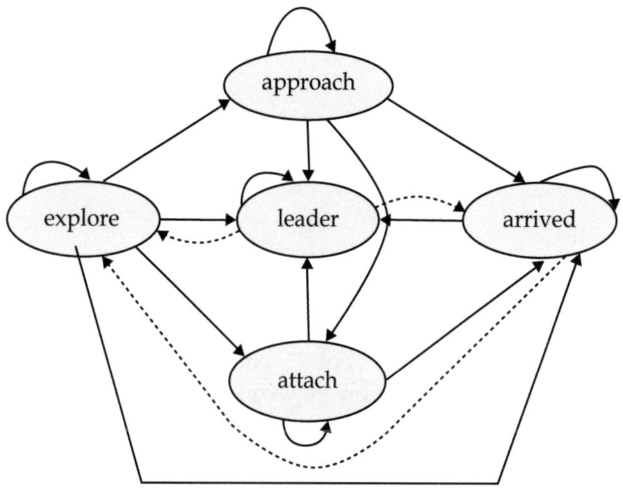

Fig. 2. Depict of role conversion

produced by robot itself, which include robot own capailitis. Below we give details about these two kinds of factors.

1. Indirect factors

Indirect factors are all kinds of attraction of task to surrounding robot, which including

- Skills need to fulfill task T_j

Represented by $TCap_j$, is the capability set need for fulfill task T_j. If robot has no $TCap_j$ it will be refused by task T_j.

- Benefits of task T_j

Represented by UL_j, is the total benefits from fulfilling of task T_j. The more UL_j, the larger attraction of task T_j.

- Least robot number needed for task T_j

Represented by $Tnum_j$, it the least robot number needed for task T_j.

- Complex degree of task T_j

Represented by pr_j, complex degree of task T_j is the integrated complex degree, its value is between 0 and 1. In muti-task enviromnet, different tasks have different complex degree.

Value of the above factors are set by system runner, and have no relation to system running time.

- Location of task

Location of task T_j at time t is represented by $TPlace_j(t)$, which can be fixed or changeable either, for example, when multiple robots are rounding up multiple targets, task location will change continuously.

- Number of robot taking part in task

Number of robot taking part in task T_j at time t is represented by $Cnum_j$. The smaller value of $Tnum_j$ - $Cnum_j$, the greater attraction of task T_j.

- Number of robot intend to take part in task

Number of robot intend to take part in task T_j at time t is represented by $Anum_j(t)$. The smaller of $Tnum_j$ - $Anum_j$, the more attraction of task T_j.

- Task priority

The priority of task T_j at time t is represented by $Pr_j(t)$. The higher of the priority $Pr_j(t)$, the more attraction of T_j.

2. Direct factors

Direct factors mainly include robot's own effect on task choosing, which include

- Robot capability

Cap_i is the capability set of robot R_i. If robot wants to take part in a task, it must has the capacity required by that task. Since there are more than one tasks, therefore we can define Q to represent if robot R_i has skills needed by task T_j.

$$Q : Cap \times T \rightarrow \{0,1\}$$

$Q(Cap_i,T_j)$=1 represents robot R_i has skills for task T_j. $Q(Cap_i,T_j)$=0 does not.

- Success rate

Ab_{ij} is the estimated success rate of robot R_i completing task T_j. As a machinery or equipment, robot will be aging and possibly go wrong, and possibly can not fulfill some task. According to its current situation, robot estimate an Ab_{ij}, $0 < Ab_{ij} \leq 1$. The larger Ab_{ij} the more confidence of robot to fulfill task T_j.

- Task attraction

Task has attraction to robot, which will reduce along with distance increasing[Parker 1999]. Using $Attr_i$ representing the attraction, *distance* (R_i,R_0) representing distance from Leader robot R_0 to robot R_i, and $0 <$ *distance* $(R_i,R_0) \leq 1$, then

$$Attr_i = \frac{k}{distance(R_i, R_0)}$$

Where constant k is the largest attraction. In order to discuss conveniently, let k=1. Therefore, $0 < Attr_{ii} \leq 1$. The larger $Attr_i$, the more task attraction.

- Current state role

According to whether robot R^i is within the communication of R_0 of one certain task T_j, we can set robot R_i to different role, which can be represented by Sta_{ij}. $Sta_{ij}=0$ represents role of Explore, Sta_{ij}=1 of Approach, Sta_{ij}=2 of Attach, Sta_{ij}=3 of Arrived, and Sta_{ij}=4 of Leader. When robot select task, it need to fully consider role property, and select the task in which robot's role can be of higher priority.

- Intending benefit of task completing

$RUL_j(t)$ is benefit expectation of fulfilling task T_j , which can be calculated by

$$RUL_j(t) = \frac{UL_j}{Tnum_j}$$

The larger $RUL_j(t)$, the more interesting robot feeling in task T_j.

- Communication amount

For data sharing, robots needs communication with each other. Communication amount Com_{ij} is the ratio of the observed robot number (R_v) to the total robot number in the team ($Tnum$), that is

$$Com_{ij} = \frac{R_v}{Tnum}$$

The larger Com_{ij}, the more time cost and less choosing interesting.

- Interesting factor

Int_{ij} is the interesting degree of robot R_i in task T_j, which can be calculated using

$$Int_{ij} = \frac{Times_{ij}}{\sum_i Times_{ij}}$$

Where $Times_{ij}$ is the total times robot R_i had chosen task T_j. From Int_{ij} we can induce the interesting of robot R_i in task T_j, and lead robot R_i to select T_j.

- Time factor

Take into account the continued influence of time interval R_i on the selection of task T_j, we induce a remember coefficient ξ. Denote the interval between that moment and current using Δ time, and according to Ebbinghaus forgetting curve , we can compute the remember rate of robot R_i selecting T_j

$$\xi_{ij} = ce^{\frac{b}{\Delta time}}$$

where b,c are some positive number. The above formula shows that the smaller Δ time, the less possibility of R_i forgetting T_j.

3.4 Decision-making model based on multi-attribute

Decision-making model based on multiple attributes is an important kind of that by multiple rules, which was usually used in fields such as military, economy and polity. This model can be used under condition that parts of tast attributes and weights have been known [Y 2003]. We can descrbe these attributes by a decision-making matrix.

1. Matrix of decision-making based on multiple attributes

Denote the selected attribute set as $Z = \{Z_1, Z_2, ..., Z_m\}$, the task set as $T = \{T_1, T_2, ..., T_m\}$, then the value of m attributes related to n tasks can be represented by a optimal matrix **X**

$$\mathbf{X} = \begin{bmatrix} X_{11} & X_{12} & \cdots & X_{1j} & \cdots & X_{1n} \\ \vdots & \vdots & & \vdots & \vdots & \vdots \\ X_{i1} & X_{i2} & \cdots & X_{ij} & \cdots & X_{in} \\ \vdots & \vdots & & \vdots & \vdots & \vdots \\ X_{m1} & X_{m2} & \cdots & X_{mj} & \cdots & X_{mn} \end{bmatrix}$$

Where X_{ij} represent the ith attribute value of task T_j. all element in matrix **X** are unprocessed primal data, has different physical meaning and usually different dimension, and value difference is larger, so **X** need to be nondimensionalized(or standardization), by transforming actually attribute value in **X** to relative value. To do this, we first divide attributes into benefit type and cost type, according to the influence of attribute value changing on task selecting. Benefit type is that benefit is large if attribute value is, this kind of attribute are also called positive ones. And cost type are that benefit is large and attribute value is small instead, this also be called as invert attributes. Then we can adapt the formula (1) and (2) in [Y 2003] to compute the standardized optimal attribute degree y_{ij} of benefit type by

$$y_{ij} = \frac{X_{ij}}{X_{i\max}}, \qquad X_{ij} \geq 0 \tag{1}$$

and of cost type by

$$y_{ij} = \frac{X_{i\min}}{X_{ij}}, \quad X_{ij} < 0 \tag{2}$$

In (1) and (2), $X_{i\ max}$ and $X_{i\ min}$ are the maximum and minimum of attribute i respectively. After the above standardization, we can get the relative optimal attribute degree matrix Y

$$\mathbf{Y} = \begin{bmatrix} y_{11} & y_{12} & \dots & y_{1j} & \dots & y_{1n} \\ \vdots & \vdots & & \vdots & \vdots & \vdots \\ y_{i1} & y_{i2} & \dots & y_{ij} & \dots & y_{in} \\ \vdots & \vdots & & \vdots & \vdots & \vdots \\ y_{m1} & y_{m2} & \dots & y_{mj} & \dots & y_{mn} \end{bmatrix}$$

2. Parameter determination

Weight coefficient is very important in our architecture, it can reflect how the attributes act on optimum seeking. By now there are subjective and objective methods to determine the weight. Here we adapt the first, and weight values are set by system runner beforehand, and denote the attribute weight vector w as $w = \{w_1, w_2, ..., w_m\}$, where W_i is the weight of attribute Z_i and w satisifies

$$\sum_{i=1}^{m} w_i = 1$$

3. Task selecting

In optimal take selecting there is some relativity, the final result is relative to the m attributes of n tasks. Here we take the chose task as a selecting project and for conveniently analysis and comparison, we set a best selecting project Y^+ and a worst one Y^-. In Y^+, all the relative optimal attribute degrees can reach their largest value, and in the worst one, it is on the contrary. Thus we have

$$Y^+ = (y_1^+, y_2^+, ...y_m^+)^T \text{ , and}$$

$$Y^- = (y_1^-, y_2^-, ...y_m^-)^T$$

Where $y_i^+ = \max_{1 \le j \le n}\{y_{ij}\}, y_i^- = \min_{1 \le j \le n}\{y_{ij}\}$ are the relative optimal attribute degree of attribute Z_i when select task T_j.

Since the existed n optional projects are commonly between Y^+ and Y^-. So we can not but compare every actual project with Y^+ and Y^-, and to search the nearest to $Y^+$and the farmost fromY^-. But it is harder even to do this. Therefore, we introduce a concept of weighted Euclidean distance, and use a relative closing degree to judge the distance from one project to Y^+ and Y^- and select the optimal project. The weighted Euclidean distance of project j to Y^+ and Y^-can be computed

$$D_j^+ = \sqrt{\sum_{i=1}^{m} w_i |y_{ij} - y_i^+|)^2}$$

$$D_j^- = \sqrt{\sum_{i=1}^{m} w_i |y_{ij} - y_i^-|)^2}$$

Where w_i is the attribute weight. Thus the relative closing degree of project j is

$$C_j = \frac{D_j^-}{D_j^+ + D_j^-} \qquad j = 1,2,...,n$$

It is clearly that $0 \le C_j \le 1$, and the larger C_j, project j be nearer to Y^+ and be better. As to Y^+, $C_j = 1$, and to Y^-, $C_j = 0$.

3.5 Behavior decision-making algorithms based on multiple attributes

Behavior Decision-Making in dynamic environment has properties such as robot's own autonomy and isomerism, variability of the dynamic environment, distribution of task, and task's own isomerism and variability. Thus in task executing, robots need to select a fitter task according to the exterior and interior on-line information, and make the whole system be in a changefully task assigning state. And just because of this, robot will dicover more than one task at one moment, and it must chose one team to participate in according to its knowledge about the task and by the judging of its own capability.

Recently, most algorithms for task choosing merely have considered whether robots fits task, or only have further considered the single attribute of distance from robot to task. In this research, according to analysis in the last section and at the precondition robot suit to task, by fully considering many factors such as task, environment and robot itself, combing attribute weight, and we propose a new robot behavior decision-making algorithm.

The main idea of our algorithm is that robot use greedy strategy to choose task, this also was called the one-step optimization. The algorithm idea is that, after every time interval Δt, in order to obtain information about other robots' current situation, tasks needed to perform, and situation of known tasks, robot will exchange with other robots within its communication range. Integrating the information, robot will firstly find out a set of tasks it competent for, then determine the relative attributes and weights, load the multiple attributes decision matrix, and at last choose target task. These details are shown in figure 3.

In the implement, robot state in system can be described by a septuple

$$R{=}def < id\_robot, Cap, State, Envir, Rec, Comm, Time>$$

Where

Id_robot is the unique ID of robot;

State is the current interior state of robot, which is represented by a quintuple (*Sta, Vic, θ, id_ros, SRole*), here *Sta* is robot's location, *Vic* and θ are robot's speed and direction of current moving, *id_ros* is the identifier of robot's chose task, and *SRole* is robot's current role. *id_ros*=0 represents that robot has not selected any task , accordingly *SRole* ='Explore';

Cap represents robot's capability, which can be described by a group of (*SRange, CRange, MV, AC, ST, REAC, CO, PL, OR, LE*), which are robot's vision radius, communication radius, and the ability of moving, behavior, behavior decision-making, real time reaction, cooperation, local programming, organization, and of learning respectively;

Envir is the state space set of robot's possible world, such as information of surrounding geographical environment, of obstacles and surrounding robots;

Rec are history records, which are combined by a tetred (T_j, $TSta_j$, Pre_j, $time_j$) of task T_j, where $TSta_j$ is the latest state, Pre_j represent the predecessor robot related to task T_j, that is the *ID* of the robot who apprize the latest information, and $time_j$ represents time when the robot come into learn task T_j;

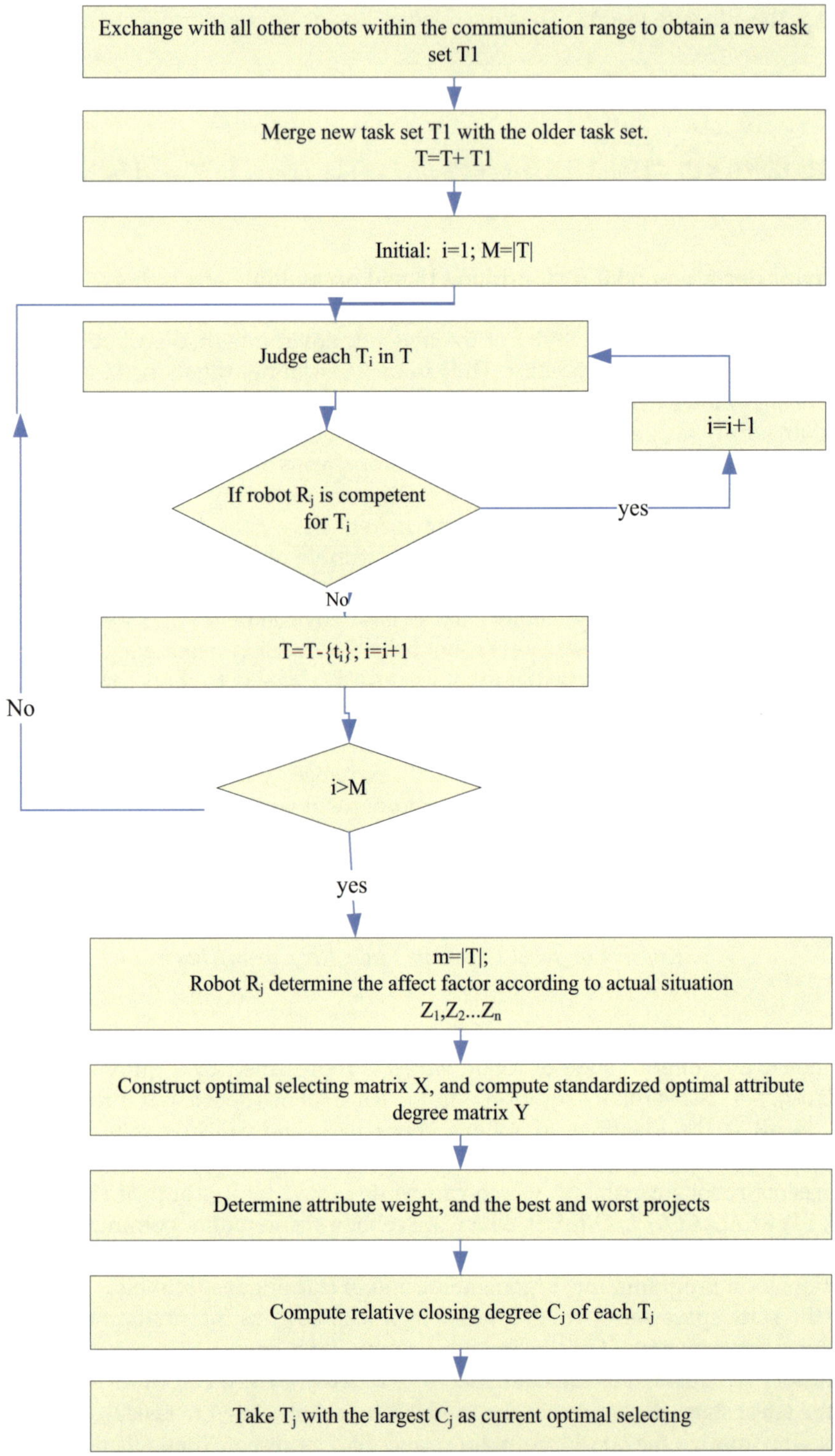

Fig. 3. Flow chart of behavior decision-making algorithm based on multiple attribute

Comm is robot communication language; And

Time is the time of updating record, which used in maintaining robot group.

The Algorithm in detail is described in below algorithm 1.

Algorithm 1: Behavior decision-making algorithm based on multiple attribute

/*Algorithm description: After every time interval Δt, robot R_i will update organizing or coordinating database and task information perceived by itself or obtained by communication, and choose one task*/

Step 1. Set i, $1 \le i \le m$

Step 2. R_i exchange with robot R_i within its communication range.

Step 3. if R_i find a new task in its vision range, then $R_i.Rec.Rv_i \leftarrow$ Leader; /*set R_i the Leader of the new task*/

Step 4. R_i judge if there are any other new tasks by analysis the received information, if there not any, R_i maintain its previous situation and goto 15. /*to maintain task's relative stability*/
/* below steps dealing with currently known tasks*/

Step 5. merge new task with the previous task set, set the counter count $\leftarrow$ 1, and set the known task number to M.

Step 6. according to robot's selected task, divide all robots into M class

Step 7. to each task, judge if it has been completed. if has, delete its information and goto 10.

Step 8. if the new task k is the same as the current task of R_i, then update the information of task k with its latest information. Set the *ID* of robot who giving new task information with u, and goto10

Step 9. if $R_i.Cap \subseteq T_j.TCap_j$, then add task T_j, add set *ID* of robot who giving new task information with u

Step 10. count$\leftarrow$count+1

Step 11. if $count\delta \le M$ then goto 7

Step 12. call the behavior decision-making algorithm based on multi-attributes, find the task whose intension function get the largest value by calculating $\max(U_{ij}(t))$.

Step 13. if $k == R_i.id\_ros$, then goto 15 /* to perform the same task as current*/
else R_i send a request to robot R_u for joining in task k.

Step 14. if R_i be accepted by task k, then set $R_i.id\_ros = k$.

Step 15. if $R_i.id\_ros <> 0$, then calculate the distance from robot R_i to Leader, and reassign R_i's role, then call the behavior programming module. Start and perform the behavior control module.

Hereon, robot uses a one-step optimal searching strategy to choose task. This has merits such as below

- After each moving step, robot will collect new information about tasks and environment, to avoid information outdated.
- Can find disabled robot. If one robot has not updated its information for a long time, then other robot take it being wrong and will inform this to Leader.
- By using the minimized task relationship, potential communication conflicts and time needed for conflicts solving can be reduced, thus system efficiency can be improved. In Algorithm 1 each step is the optimal, so it is fit for changeful dynamic environment in which it is difficult to make a wholly route programming.

4. Garbage disposal in dangerous environment and its implement

In this section, in a simulated cross-country environment, test result of multiple robots fulfilling garbage disposal through efficiently corporation was used to validate the efficiency of the proposed hierarchical controlling architecture and the decision-making algorithm.

4.1 Problem description

Multiple robots cooperatively performing garbage disposal was a loosely coupling problem, that is, robots separately search and dispose the garbage. There are two kinds of method to do this. In the first kind of method, robots of different labor division will cooperatively dig and bury garbage on the spot. In the other kind, robots firstly need to convey garbage to some specified center then to dispose. Here we take the two kinds as two works.

In system, there set three class of robots, in which class i are crane robots adept at pushing and convey object. Class ii are rooter robots adept at sapping. And class iii are conveyance robot. All the three kinds of robot have stored information of task, can perform functions such as task searching, organize, and coordinate. the first kind of task needs corporation of robot class I and ii, in which after robot of class ii fulfilling dig, one or more than one robot of class i will push garbage into the hole. And the second kind of task need the corporation of ii and iii, as that robot of class ii grasp and transfer garbage to robot class iii, and one or more robot of class iii will transfer garbage to an appointed location .

At system beginning, robots having capabilities of environment perceiving and behavior programming were dispersed randomly in the cross-country environment, and began to search garbage object. When find some garbage, robot will firstly judge whether it can dispose the garbage by itself, if can, then began to, otherwise it will take the garbage as a task and itself as the Lead, make sure numbers of three class robot needed according to task's size and property, and began to inform other robot to form a group. Without loss of generality, we assumed that task of the first kind need 1 robot of class ii and a few of class i, when robot number meet the required, robot of class ii will surround the task, which represent robots have disposed garbage jointly, and task has been completed. As to the second kind of task, we assume there need 1 robot of class i and a few of class iii, similarly all the needed robots must firstly come to the garbage, then they form a column team for garbage portage. After convey garbage to a target location, the task be completed.

In realization, the number of needed robot and of that around were labeled in a square bracket beside the task. Three colors as we listed above were used to indicate the founded, being performed and completed state of task respectively. If task is hung, then its needed robot number is 0.

4.2 Implement strategy

Form point of view of organization, robots can be divided into task Leader and collaborators. As manager of task, Leader will fulfill certain task also. Leader uses algorithm 2 below to build up a team, and also to fulfill task as soon as possible.

Algorithm 2: Leader select team member

Step 1. After tasks being announced, Leader begin to time and set i=0;

Step 2. Leader announces current tasks information to robots within its communication;

Step 3. Leader judge each answered robot R_i if it has competent to join the team. If it has not, goto 8;

Step 4. Leader read the capacity of R_i related to task T_j;

Step 5. if $Tnum_j(t) \geq Cnum_j(t)$, then announce the end of recruit, and goto 7

Step 6. announce robot R_i as one of pre-team member, and if $R_i.SRole = Arrived$ then $Cnum_j(t) = Cnum_j(t) + 1$; else if $R_i.SRole = Attach$ then $Anum_j(t) = Anum_j(t) + 1$;

Step 7. if there be $Tnum_j(t) \geq Cnum_j(t)$ (j=1，2，...，n), then goto 10;

Step 8. if it has not exceed the scheduled time, then i=i+1, and gotto 3;

Step 9. Leader announces the fail of formation;

Step 10. Leader determines final team members need for the task, and notifies all the selected members.

In system running, each robot corresponds to one of the five state roles. For a relative stable team, and reducing the unneeded cost of role exchanging, here we prescribe that only Explore, Approach and Attach can bid and select team, robot after having chosen task only send application to Leader of the task , and only Leader,Approach,Attach can announce their knowledge of tasks.

In system we abstract and define task as class, in which we emphasize task needed robot number, and the change of the number. The task class can be described as

```
class TARGET
{ CPoint m_Position;         //task location
  int m_nValue ;             //benift obtain from task completing
  int m_nComplax ;           //complex degree of task fulfilling
  int m_nPrior  ;            // priority of current task
  int m_type;                //kind of current task, m_ type =1 represent bury on the spot,
                             // m_type =2 represent transfer to a centralized spot then bury.
  int m_nNeedRobotNum1;             // needed robot number of type  I  for task fulfilling
  int m_nNeedRobotNum2;             // needed robot number of type II
  int m_nNeedRobotNum3;             // needed robot number of type III
  int m_nArrivedRobotNum1;          // arriveded robot number of I
  int m_nArrivedRobotNum2;          // arriveded robot number of II
  int m_nArrivedRobotNum3;          // arriveded robot number of III
  int m_nConfirmRobotNum1;          // robot number of type I chosen the task
  int m_nConfirmRobotNum2;          //robot number of type II chosen the task
  int m_nConfirmRobotNum3;          //robot number of type III chosen the task
  int m_nLeaderId;           // Leader ID
  bool m_bfinished;          //if task fulfilled
  Real BeginTime;            //task started(or discoveredd) time
  Real EndTime;              // task completed time
  CList<Cpoint, CPoint&> m_RoundPoint;   //coordinate of points surrounding the task.
        };
```

And robot in the system is another class, which is

```
class Robot
 { int RobotId;              //robot  ID
   Type m_nType;             //number represents robot's current state role, 0 as Explore, 1
                             //as Approach, 2 as Attach, and 3 as Leader
   Type Cap;                  //robot's capacity type
   int m_nViewDistance;      //robot's vision range
   int m_nComDistance;       //robot's communication range
```

```
    CPoint m_Position;        // robot's current location
    int m_nSpeed;             // robot's speed
    int m_nTargetId;  //robot's choosing task, value -1 represent it has not chosen any task.
    int m_nMaxValue;                  // upper limit of task benefit estimated by the robot
    int m_ObjectTarget[1501][1501];  //robot's known information about task, value -2
                              //represent no task , >=0 represent discovered some task,
                              //value -1 represent not discovered any task, and -3 represent
                              // having completed the task
    Char  m_Pa[n];            // information about robot's known teammate
    Real CuTime;              //time of current record
};
```

4.3 Implement strategy

In our system, robot adapt the controlling based on behavior, and behaviors can be divided into four kinds as below

- move_to_goal;
- maintain_formation, after chosen one task and but can not see the task directly, robot take this behavior lest diverge from the main direction;
- avoid_static_obstacle, robot takes this behavior lest it collides with obstacle;
- avoid_robots, robot takes this action lest it collides with other ones.

After chosen one task team, robot take that task's location as its moving target, and Leader will assign one role to it, this role correspond to robot location after task fulfilling. And after all robot members determined their task's location, the moving and coordination in robot team can be taken as the processing of team formation. Each robot need to determine its team's formation vector according to its surrounding condition, such as the location of task and other members, and the surrounding obstacle. Referring to formation vector constructing algorithm in [Dong et al. 2000; Chio et al. 2003; Balch & Arkin 1995; Balch & Hybinette 2000; Han 2003], we first prescribe some identifiers such as $R=\{R_1,R_2,\cdots R_n\}$ is a robot set with n members, $TARGET=\{T_1,T_2,\cdots T_n\}$ is a task set, $OBSTACLE=\{O_1,O_2,\cdots O_m\}$ is an obstacle set, and d_i is formation vector by which R_i can control its cooperation with other members thus to maintain the formation. Value in d_i can indicate robot R_i's driving power and moving direction.

By the above identifiers, Algorithm 3 of formation controlling during moving and coordination can be described as below.

Algorithm 3: Formation controlling algorithm

Step 1. Determining robot type.In the system robots are dividend into type ***A*** that can see the task directly, type ***B*** can see task indirectly, that is robot although can not see task itself, but can see other robots in its team, and type **C**, can not see task or any other robots.

Step 2. Using formula (3) to determine formation vector d_i

$$d_i=\begin{cases} K_1Q_i & R_i\in A\cup B \\ K_2Q_i^{'} & R_i\in C \end{cases} \tag{3}$$

Where K_1,K_2 are two controlling parameters, we will give their value in the simulation test. Q_i is a unit vector from robot R_i to other tasks or members, and $Q_i^{'}$ is a unit vector from R_i and normal to Q_i.

Step 3. judge if there are some obstacles or team members along each robot's formation vector d_i, and using result of formula (4) to weightedly sum up every robot's sub behavior, thus to modify their moving directions.

$$\begin{pmatrix} x_i^i \\ y_i^i \end{pmatrix} = \alpha\tau_t K_1 \begin{pmatrix} x_t^i \\ y_t^i \end{pmatrix} \Bigg/ \left\| \begin{pmatrix} x_t^i \\ y_t^i \end{pmatrix} \right\| + \beta\tau_{j,j\in R} K_1 \begin{pmatrix} x_j^i \\ y_j^i \end{pmatrix} \Bigg/ \left\| \begin{pmatrix} x_j^i \\ y_j^i \end{pmatrix} \right\|$$
$$+\gamma K_2 \begin{pmatrix} x_o^i \\ y_o^i \end{pmatrix} \Bigg/ \left\| \begin{pmatrix} x_o^i \\ y_o^i \end{pmatrix} \right\| + \sum_{k\in R\cup OBSTACLE} \delta_{ik} \left\{ \begin{pmatrix} x_k^i \\ y_k^i \end{pmatrix} - L \begin{pmatrix} x_k^i \\ y_k^i \end{pmatrix} \Bigg/ \left\| \begin{pmatrix} x_k^i \\ y_k^i \end{pmatrix} \right\| \right\} \quad (4)$$

In (4), $\left(x_i^i, y_i^i\right)^T$ be R_i 's moving direction during the current controlling cycle T_c. Coefficient α, β and γ can be

$$\begin{cases} \alpha = 1 & \beta = 0 & \gamma = 0, & R_i \in A \\ \alpha = 0 & \beta = 1 & \gamma = 0, & R_i \in B \\ \alpha = 0 & \beta = 0 & \gamma = 1, & R_i \in C \end{cases}$$

τ_i be the attraction force of task T_j on robot R_i, τ_j be inducing force of other robot R_j on R_i, and δ_{ik} be the exclusive force of obstacles or other robot on robot R_i. If distance from R_i to other robot or obstacle is less than some L, then $\delta_{ik} = \delta > 0$, otherwise there is no exclusive force, that is $\delta_{ik} = 0$.

Step 4. estimate robot R_i's $Position_i$ at next moment.

Step 5. R_i moves to $Position_i$. If $|Position_i\text{-}T_i| < \varepsilon$, then R_i directly arrived at task location T_i, and goto 2.

4.4 Simulation plateform

1. Simulated environment

The system uses a 1501×1501 pixels 2-dimensional cross-country simulation environment, which represent a 500×500 meters actual environment, value of pixel represent land-use type of actual environment, which can be road, lake, river, natural land Surface, fortification, sandlot, and plate. Surface such as grass and road can get through, and diked area such as lake, road, and fortification can not.

2. Development tool

We use Microsoft VC++ 6.0 as the development IDE.

3. Running plate

Our simulation need to run on operating system of Windows 2000/XP.

4. Functions of main module

The main function of out simulation software includes

- Display environment map with depth feeling of environmental information
- Map can zoomes in or out
- Provides convenient interface for system user
- Dynamically and intuitively shows the process of robot formation for task fulfill.

5. Contents in display area in program running

In our system running, robot type of Crane, Rooter and Transporter distribute randomly, and numbers of the three type robots are approximately equal. The three type robots are represented by symbols as

■ Crane
■ Rooter
■ Transporter

Two kinds of tasks are represented by circle and ellipse respectively, that is the 1'th task type using circle, and the second using ellipse. And according to time order, tasks are divided into three types, which we using three colors to express, that are

● Undiscovered task

● Discovered but not completed task

□ Completed task

6. Status area

In status area below display area, there displays the location, needed robot number, having recruited number of current task, and system running time.

4.5 Simulation of formation based on task

At the beginning, a few of tasks and robot randomly distribute in the cross-country environment. We suppose that robot know their location and can communicate faultlessly. Every robot has its own range of communication and vision and speed. And commonly communication range is large than that of vision, and vision range is larger than speed×per step time. System controlling parameters are set as in table 1. In the below demonstrating map, we use color to represent robot role conversion, and beside each task there is a square, in which robot number needed for task, and already recruited number are listed. Task such as being discovered, executed and completed are distinguished by different colors, and states being hang uses 0 needed robot number to express. the six below demonstration map show the whole formation process, including produce, building, programming and executing of cooperation.

Figure 4 is initial state of system running. There randomly distributes 6 tasks, represented by character of A to F, and 17 robots including 6 crane robots (in color of pink), 6 transfer robots (in red) and 5 rooter robots (in black).

Figure 5 is the system after running 1.75 s. Robot found 4 tasks including C, D, E and F, and task F needed transferred. In square bracket beside each task there labeled the number of robot needed and that of arrived.

Figure 6 shows system after running 2.406s. Task C has already been fulfilled, and task A and B been founded. Task B was hang, so its needed robot number is 0, two robots around B are moving towards other tasks. Task D needed one robot but around it there are two, the redundancy is mainly caused by errors in communication and time setting.

Figure 7 shows system after running 3.156s. Tasks A~D have been completed, robot number of task E already is 3, but that of task F have not changed. The black robot moving to task F found that F out of its capability, so left it to other task.

Figure 8 shows system after running 10.327s. Robot number of task E is 4, and that of task F unchanged, no other robot move to task F, thus deadlock came into being.

Figure 9 E and F shorting of robot, and within their communication no available ones, dead-lock occur.

4.6 Result analysis

1. Four strategies in the system

In the system we use four controlling strategies

T0, integrated controlling strategy combining autonomic and entire controlling model

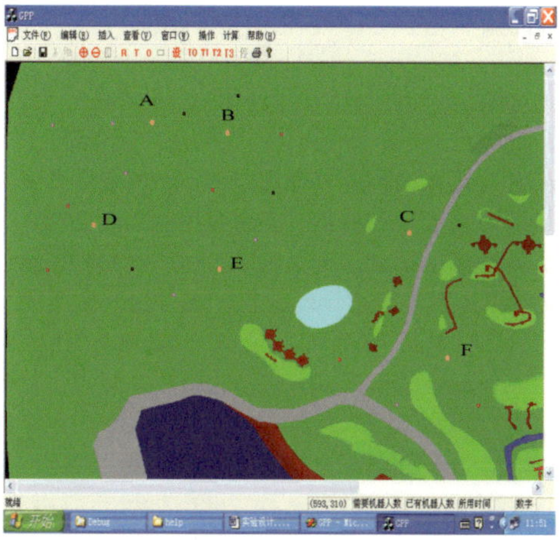

Fig. 4. Initial system state

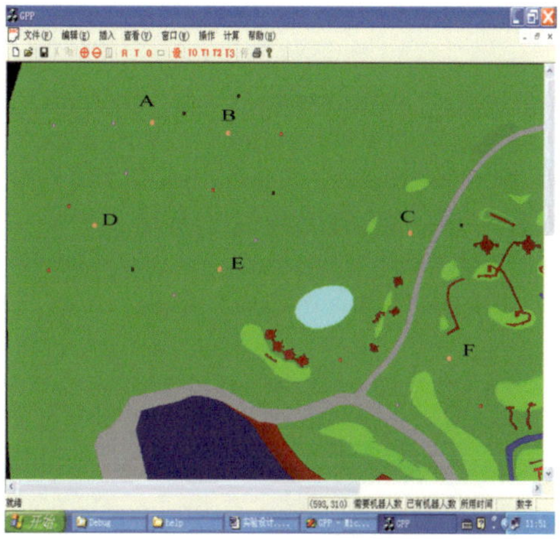

Fig. 5. System state after running 1.75s

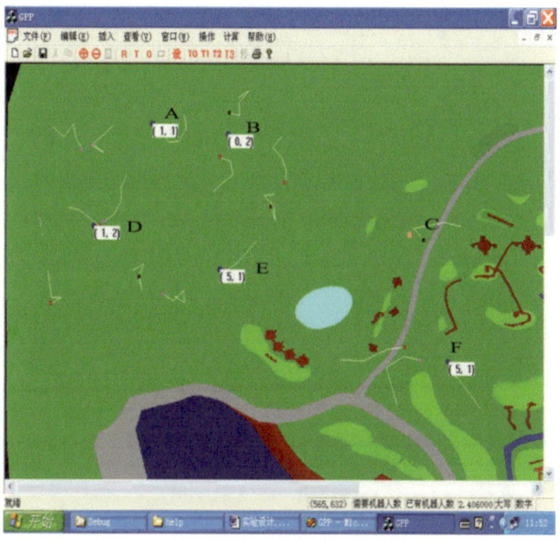

Fig. 6. System state after 2.406s

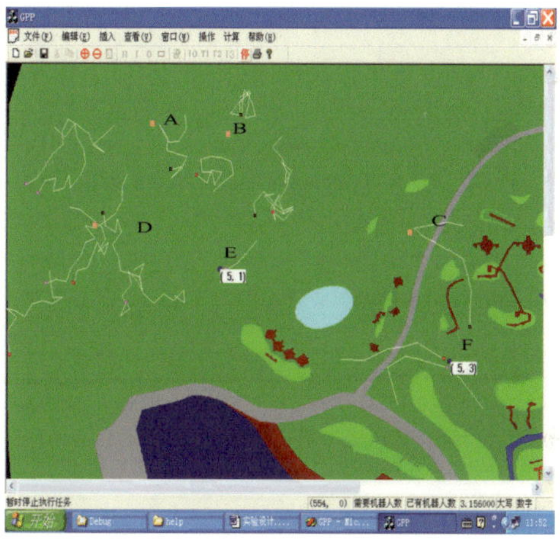

Fig. 7. System state after 3.156s

Fig. 8. System state after 10.327s

Fig. 9. E and F occur dead-lock

T1, integrated controlling strategy combining random and entire controlling model
T2, integrated controlling strategy combining autonomic and partial controlling model
T3, integrated controlling strategy combining random and partial controlling model.
Here autonomic controlling is that robot adapting behavior decision-making algorithm to select behaviour (to decide its role and team) based on multiple attributes proposed in this chapter, making using of information by watching by exchanging. Randomly controlling is that robot randomly select one team to join. And entire controlling is that in system there is a virtual robot, it can collect information of all the known tasks, including task location, task needed robot number, task's recruited robot number and arrived robot number, and set priority level to each task thus to induct robot's team selecting. Virtual robot also will check at intervals if dead-lock occurring (when all task's robot number have not satisfied but no robot in state of Explore, or all the remained robots are at state of Explore), if occurring, virtual robot must solve it by forcing some robot to take one role or take part in certain team. Interval of entire controlling will be determined by dead-lock occurring frequency at last time, if this frequency is high, then shorten the interval, otherwise, extend it.
Success times in our simulation are the times robot complete task by its own coordination without virtual robot's intervening. And completing number is robot's completing tasks under entire controlling plus limited intervening.
2. System parameter setting
To valid the proposed architecture in this chapter, here we set value of all the common parameters in table 1, other special parameters value of simulation will be set in respective test table. In table 1, unit of running time is ms (millisecond), and units of communication and vision range are pixel.

Parameter identifier	Parameter value	Parameter meaning
Range	40	Surrounding radius
τ_i	1	Attraction of task T_j on robot R_i
τ_j	1	Inducing power of robot R_j on R_i
K_1	20	Coefficient of attraction and inducing power
K_2	100	Coefficient of exclusive power
δ	100	Exclusive coefficient of obstacle to robot R_i

Table 1. System controlling parameter

3. Result and analysis
We give tests for five kinds of comparisons as below.
Test 1, test with same task number and different robot number, result is listed in table 2.
Test 2, test with same robot number and different task number, results is listed in table 3.
Test 3, test with different vision range, result is listed in table 4.
Test 4, test with different communication range, result is listed in table 5.
Test 5, Test with different time length per running step, result is listed in table 6.
Reasult in Table 2 shows that along with the increasing of robot numbers, total time needed for task fulfilling decreased, numbers of discovered tasks and completed tasks increased, and dead-lock number lessened.

Basic parameter value					
Robot number	Task number	Most robot number needed for task	Total loop number	Total time / time per step	Vision range / communication range
10	5	6	50	20000/500	50/100
Test result					
	Total time consume	Success times	Discovered task number	Completed number	Dead-lock number
T0	1075.454	12	163	168	435
T1	1110.5.2	8	184	122	496
T2	1058.156	16	180	156	304
T3	1111.434	8	178	118	476
Basic parameter value					
Robot number	Task number	Most robot number needed for task	Total loop number	Total time / time per step	Vision range / communication range
20	5	6	50	20000/500	50/100
Test results					
	Total time consume	Success times	Discovered task number	Completed number	Dead-lock number
T0	1193.84	14	217	185	289
T1	1071.517	15	225	224	174
T2	1473.213	19	240	213	223
T3	1565.595	2	224	133	220
Basic parameter value					
Robot number	Task number	Most robot number needed for task	Total loop number	Total time / time per step	Vision range / communication range
30	5	6	50	20000/500	50/100
Test result					
	Total time consume	Success times	Discovered task number	Completed number	Dead-lock number
T0	554.454	23	236	216	56
T1	652.22	23	240	230	72
T2	341.4	28	244	226	69
T3	305.233	28	241	227	83

Table 2. Results of test with same task number and different robot number

Value of basic parameters					
Robot number	Task number	Maximum needed robot number	Total loops	Total time / time per step	Vision range/ communication range
20	3	6	50	20000/500	50/100
Test result					
	Total time consuming	Success times	Discovered task number	Completed task number	Dead-lock number
T0	1179.749	26	137	126	88
T1	1140.765	23	136	121	194
T2	1084.253	36	138	136	78
T3	1066.696	37	137	137	96
Value of basic parameters					
Robot number	Task number	Maximum needed robot number	Total loops	Total time / time per step	Vision range/ communication range
20	4	6	50	20000/500	50/100
Test result					
	Total time consuming	Success times	Discovered task number	Completed task number	Dead-lock number
T0	821.091	29	170	164	197
T1	1253.700	25	163	163	348
T2	1122.657	29	165	151	246
T3	1122.08	33	167	152	198
Value of basic parameters					
Robot number	Task number	Maximum needed robot number	Total loops	Total time / time per step	Vision range/ communication range
20	5	6	50	20000/500	50/100
Test result					
	Total time consuming	Success times	Discovered task number	Completed task number	Dead-lock number
T0	1193.84	14	217	185	289
T1	1071.517	15	225	224	174
T2	1473.213	19	240	213	223
T3	1565.595	2	224	133	220

Table 3. Test results with same robot number and different task number

When recruited robot number far exceeds the needed number, having or hving not used entire controlling, the numbers of dead-locks and completed tasks is not different. The reason is that when robot number is large, possibility of dead-lock will reduce, then even not using the entire controlling, robot can fulfill task quickly by autonomic controlling.
If no more robot available, then although using entire controlling and bid algorithm based on intension, because of there are many weak intervening, which will reduce robot's autonomic capability, so robot only can discover less tasks. And if not using entire controlling intension-based algorithm, then system had to solve more dead-locks, thus will reduce robot's task discovering capability too.
Reasult in Table 3 shows that the more the task, the more the dead-lock, and the less completed task number and the higher time consuming.

Value of basic parameter		Test result					
Robot number	20						
Task number	3		Total time consuming	Success times	Discovered task number	Completed task number	Dead-lock number
Task's Maximum needed robot number	6	T0	1179.749	26	137	126	88
Total loops	50	T1	1140.765	23	136	121	194
Total time/ time per step	20000/ 500	T2	1084.253	36	138	136	78
Vision range/ communication range	50/100	T3	1066.696	37	137	137	96
		Test result					
Robot number	20						
Task number	3		Total time consuming	Success times	Discovered task number	Completed task number	Dead-lock number
Task's Maximum needed robot number	6	T0	506.72	14	64	64	74
Total loops	50	T1	553.316	12	62	62	91
Total time/ time per step	20000/ 500	T2	937.531	6	52	52	84
Vision range/ communication range	25/100	T3	702.733	5	40	40	74

Table 4. **Test** result of different vision range

Value of basic parameter		Test result					
Robot number	10						
Task number	3		Total time consuming	Success times	Discovered task number	Completed task number	Dead-lock number
Task's Maximum needed robot number	6	T0	774.366	28	123	118	317
Total loops	50	T1	1054.996	16	106	82	536
Total time/ time per step	20000/ 500	T2	849.47	22	114	108	398
Vision range/ communication range	50/100	T3	1125.786	18	100	78	492
		Test result					
Robot number	10						
Task number	3		Total time consuming	Success times	Discovered task number	Completed task number	Dead-lock number
Task's Maximum needed robot number	6	T0	839.421	16	114	107	422
Total loops	50	T1	950.795	7	107	75	182
Total time/ time per step	20000/ 500	T2	757.423	20	106	100	206
Vision range/ communication range	50/200	T3	750.513	21	110	88	425

Table 5. **Test** result of different communication range

Reasult in Table 4 shows that vision range is better to be large.
Reasult in Table 5 shows that as to communication range it is not the greater the better. The decreasing of completed task number along with the increasing of communication range in the result has illustrated this point.
Reasult in Table 6 illustrates that changing of time per step has no more influences on task fulfilling. But if adopting the entire controlling and intension-based bid recruiting algorithm jointly under a moderate ratio of robot number to total task number, then the total time consuming will reduce remarkably, and success time will increase remarkably.

Value of basic parameter		Test result					
Robot number	10						
Task number	3		Total time consuming	Success times	Discovered task number	Completed task number	Dead-lock number
Task's Maximum needed robot number	6	T0	774.366	28	123	118	317
Total loops	50	T1	1054.99	16	106	82	536
Total time/time per step	20000/500	T2	849.47	22	114	108	398
Vision range/communication range	50/100	T3	1125.78	18	100	78	492
		Test result					
Robot number	10						
Task number	3		Total time consuming	Success times	Discovered task number	Completed task number	Dead-lock number
Task's Maximum needed robot number	6	T0	787.652	24	122	112	300
Total loops	50	T1	1121.10	14	110	80	462
Total time/ time per step	20000/700	T2	893.756	22	114	104	404
Vision range/ communication range	50/100	T3	1086.30	17	94	75	502
		Test result					
Robot number	10						
Task number	3		Total time consuming	Success times	Discovered task number	Completed task number	Dead-lock number
Task's Maximum needed robot number	6	T0	798.72	28	124	120	296
Total loops	50	T1	1091.99	14	106	80	398
Total time/ time per step	20000/1000	T2	884.734	24	114	106	250
Vision range/ communication range	50/100	T3	1102.62	18	100	78	368

Table 6. **Test** result of different running time per step

4.7 Simulation conclusion

From the above comparisons we can found that the discovered and completed task number, and total time consuming are mainly affected by factors such as the adapted strategy, ratio of robot number to task number, range of vision and communication, and system total running time. Generally speaking, we can have these four conclusions

1. When existed robot number does not exceed the total needed robot number of all tasks, result by jointly adapting entire controlling and intension-based bidding algorithm is better than that neither strategy being used. But if the existed robot number is larger, adapting those two strategies will make system more complicate and less efficiency.
2. Using entire controlling and intension-based bidding algorithm jointly will induce some weak intervening. But if not using neither of the two strategies, then time consumed in dead-lock solving will increase, which will also reduce robot's efficiency.
3. Along with the increasing of robot number, task numbers discovered and completed will increase, and dead-lock number and total time consuming will decrease remarkably.
4. In searching, along with the increasing of vision range, number of completed tasks will increase largely. But along with increasing of communication, it is on the contrary.

So for the sake of efficiently fulfilling given tasks, the practicable solution is that besides jointly adapting entire controlling and intension-based bidding algorithm, we can set robot number the half of total needed robot number, and extend robot's vision as large as possible.

5. Conclusion

In this chapter, we firstly gave analysis on some typical architectures of robot system, and took for that in multi-robot system that oriented to task under a dynamic environment, the prominence should be given to robot capabilities of self-adopting, real time reaction, behaviour autonomic decision-making, and cooperation, especially to behavior autonomic selecting, but all this has not presented in the existed architectures. Therefore, we proposed a hybrid hierarchical controlling architecture of five layers, in which behavior decision-making as an independent module is expressed. And then we emphatically studied the implement of the behavior decision-making module. And at last, we used the effectively fulfilling of garbage disposal by robot's corporation in cross-country environment to validate the proposed hierarchical controlling architecture and decision-making algorithm. Simulation results showed that our architecture and algorithm are effective.

6. Acknowledgment

This research is sponsored by Scientific Research Common Program of Beijing Municipal Commission of Education (KM200910772011) and by the Funding Project for Academic Human Resources Development in Institutions of Higher Learning under the Jurisdiction of Beijing Municipality (PHR201007131).

7. References

Balch, T. & Arkin, R C.(1995). Motor Schema-based Formation Control for Multi-agent Robot Teams, *in Proceeding of the First International Conference on Multi-agent*

Systems, pp.10-15, ISBN 978-0262621021, San Francisco, June,1995, The MIT Press, Cambridge, Massachusetts (USA).

Balch, T & Hybinette, M. (2000). Social Potentials for Scalable Multi-Robot Formation, *IEEE International Conf. on Robotics and Automation*, pp. 73-80, ISBN 978-0780358867, April, 2000, IEEE, New York, NY (USA).

Caloud, P.; Choi, W., Latombe, J C.; Pape, C L. & Yim, M. (1990). Indoor automation with many mobile robots, *Proceeding of IEEE international Workshop on Intelligent Robotic system*, pp. 67-72, ISBN 90-247-3346-4, Ibaraki, Japan, July, 1990, IEEE, New York, NY (USA).

Cao, Z Q.; Zhang, B. & TAN, M. (2001). Individual Control Architecture for Multiple Robot System. *Robot*, Vol. 23, No. 5, 450-454, ISSN 1002-0446.

Chaimowicz, L.; Campos, M F M. & Kumar, V. (2002). Dynamic Role Assignment for Cooperative Robots, *Proceedings of the 2002 IEEE International Conference on Robotics and Automation*, pp. 293-298, ISBN 0-7803-7272-7, Washington,May, 2001, ,IEEE, New York, NY (USA).

Yue, C Y.(2003).*Decision-making Theory and Methods*, Science Press, ISBN 7-03-010816-7, Beijing, China.

Chio,T S. & Tarn, T J. (2003). Rules and Contral Strategies of Multi-Robot Team Moving in Hierarchical Formation. *IEEE International Conf. on Robotics and Automation*, pp. 2701-2706, ISBN 0-7803-7737-0, Taipei, Taiwan, September, 2003.

Dias, B. (2004). Trader Bots: *A New Paradigm for Robust and Efficient Multirobot Coordination in Dynamic Environments*, the Robotics Institute, Carnegie Mellon University, 2004.

Dong, S L.; Chen, W D. & Xi, Y G.(2000). Distributed Control System for Multi-robot Formation. *ROBOT*, Vol. 20, No.6, 433-438, ISSN 1002-0446.

Farinelli, A.; Scerri, P. & Tambe, M.(2003). Building Large-scale Robot Systems: Distributed Role Assignment in Dynamic, Uncertain Domains, *In AAMAS'03 Workshop on Resources, role and task allocation in multiagent systems,* ISBN 1-58113-683-8, Melbourne, Australia, July, 2003, ACM, New York, NY (USA) .

Habib,M K.; Asama,H. & Ishida Y.(1992). Simulation Environment for an Autonomous and Decentralized Multi-agent Robotic System, Proc. IROS'92, pp. l550-1557, ISBN 0780307372, Raleigh , NC (USA) , July 1992, IEEE, New York, NY (USA).

Han, X d.; HONG, B R. & MENG, W.(2003). Distrubuted Control for Generating Arbitrary Formation of Multiple Robots. Robot, Vol. 25, No. l, 66- 72, ISSN 1002-0446.

Laengle, T.; Lueth,T C.; Rembold,U. & Woern, H. (1998). A Distributed Control Architecture for Autonomous Mobile Robots-implementation of the Karlsruhe Multi-agent Robot Architecture (KAMARA). *Advanced Robotics*, Vol. 12, No.4, 411-431, ISSN 0169-1864.

Noreils,F R.(1993). Toward a Robot Architecture Integrating Cooperation between Mobile Robots: Application to Indoor Environmentm. *The International Journal of Robotics Research*, Vol. 12, No. 1, 79-98, ISSN 0278-3649.

Parker, L E.(1998) *ALLIANCE:* An Architecture for Fault Tolerant Multi-Robot Cooperation. *IEEE Transactions on Robotics and Automation*, Vol. 14, No.2, 220-240, ISSN 1042-296X.

Parker, L E.(1999). Cooperative Robotics for Multi-Target Observation. *Intelligent Automation and Soft Computing, special issue on Robotics Research at Oak Ridge National Laboratory,* Vol. 5 , No.1, 5-19, ISSN, 1079-8587.

Tambe M. & Zhang W.(1997). Towards Flexible Teamwork. *Journal of Artificial Intelligence Research*(JAIR), Vol. 7, No.1, 83-124, ISSN 1076 - 9757.

Tan, M.; Wang, S. & Cao, Z Q.(2005) *Multi-r*obot systems, Tsinghua University Press, ISBN 7302100950 , Beijing, China.

Tang, Z M. (2002) *Research on Essential Techniques for Mobile Intelligent Robot and Robot Team* [D].Nanjing university of science and technology, Nanjing, Jiangsu province, China.

Xu D. (2004). Research on Some Key Techniques for Multi-robot System. Applied Science and Technology. Vol. 7, No. 31, 37-39, ISSN 1009-671X.

Zhao, Y W. & Tan, D L. (1990). Study of Robot Architecture in Multiple Mobile Robots System. *Robots,* Vol. 21, No.6, 421-425, ISSN 1002-0446.

22

Auction and Swarm Multi-Robot Task Allocation Algorithms in Real Time Scenarios

José Guerrero and Gabriel Oliver
Universitat de les Illes Balears (Dep. of Mathematics and computer Science)
Spain

1. Introduction

A group of several autonomous robots (multi-robot system) can perform tasks that with only one of them would be impossible to carry out or would take much more time, moreover, they are more robust and even can be cheaper, etc than systems with a single robot. In general, the problems that have to be solved to benefit from all these advantages are divided into three main stages: task division/planning, task allocation and motion planning. Task division stage, consists on dividing the general and complex mission into simple tasks that can be carried out by a robot and, if it's necessary, scheduling those simpler goals. The task allocation step will select the best robot or group of robots to execute each goal. Finally, the motion planning issues involve the robots' motions coordination to get the assigned tasks. Although these steps have been explained as independent and sequential stages, they are tightly connected and the decisions made in one level affect the whole system performance. For example, in Zlot & Stentz (2006) the authors proposed a task allocation method that combined planning, task decomposition and task allocation. Although this and similar efforts can be found in the literature. Each one of these steps is still an open problem. This paper will be focused on multi robot task allocation (MRTA) issues, without taking into account the other problems. Task allocation is one of the main problems in multi-robot systems, very especially when the tasks must be executed before deadlines, that is, in real-time scenarios. In most cases this problem is an NP-hard problem, and therefore nowadays there is not any algorithm that in a reasonable computing time gives the optimal tasks allocation. Two main paradigms have been proposed in recent years to try to manage this problem in both real-time and non real-time scenarios: swarm and auction methods. At present, there does not exist any study that compares both strategies when the robots must carry out tasks with soft or hard real-time restrictions. Other works, for example Kalra & Martinoli (2006), compare auction and swarm methods but using tasks without deadlines. Therefore, the first objective of this work is to compare all those methods under different scenarios to identify the weak points of each paradigm when a deadline is assigned to the tasks.

Firstly, our work presents and study three auction-like strategies based on existing ones: Sequential Unordered Auction (SUA), Earliest Deadline First Auction (EDFA) and Sequential Best Pair Auction (SBPA). In all these cases there is a central auctioneer who receives the bids from all the robots and decides the allocation of the tasks. These strategies differ between them on the way the auctioneer announces the tasks to the robots and on the robots' answers are processed. Besides the auction methods, a classical swarm strategy has been taken into account. The results show that in most cases the most complex algorithm(SPBA) outperforms the other auction based procedures. Besides EDFA is better than the simple SUA strategy. Finally, swarm strategy is better than EDFA or SUA when the number of robots and tasks is not very large.

In Gerkey & Mataric (2004), the MRTA problem was divided using three axes: multi-task robots (MT) vs. single-task robots (ST) depending on whether multiple tasks can be assigned to the same robot or not. The second axes is single-robot tasks (SR) vs. multi-robot tasks (MR) where SR means that only one robot can be assigned to a task, while MR means that several robots (a coalition) can execute concurrently a task. The last axes is, instantaneous assignment (IA) vs. time-extended assignment (TE) where in IA the allocation is made without taking into account the future incoming tasks. In terms of this taxonomy, in this paper we focus on a ST-SR-IA and MT-SR-IA task allocation, our previous work Guerrero & Oliver (2010) was focused on ST-MR-IA approaches in real time scenarios. In MT-SR-IA, each single robot must have the capabilities for deciding how to schedule its assigned tasks. Thus, we extend the original MT category to take into account problems where a robot has the schedule several tasks. For example, in the MT-SR-IA strategy implemented in this work, each robot decides in what order it will visit its assigned goals, that is, the robot has to solve the traveling Salesman Problem (TSP). We have to note that the TSP is also an NP-Hard problem. The results of our experiments show that in a MT-SR-IA system the local planning made by each robot is more important than the algorithm used by the central auctioneer. From these results, this work presents a new MRTA algorithm called Earliest Deadline First Best Pair (EDFBP) which, depending on the robots' scheduling capabilities, uses a more (algorithmic) complex MRTA algorithm or it simplifies the task allocation process.

A classical foraging task has been used to verify our methods. In this mission each object have to be gathered before an specific deadline. The performance measure used to compare the systems is the number of tasks finished before their deadline. A simulator developed by the authors, called RoboSim, has been used to execute most of the experiments, this simulator allows to execute a great number of tests, with a very large number of robots in the colony in a very short time. Some experiments with less robots has also been carried out with the well known Player/Stage simulator Collett et al. (2005).

The rest of this paper is organized as follows: section 2 presents some relevant work in the field of multi-robot task allocation focused very specially on auction and swarm methods; section 3 shows a formal definition of the problem to solve and specifies the details of the real time foraging task; section 4 explains the algorithms implemented when only one task can be assigned to each robot; section 5 extends the algorithms already explained in section 4 to allow multiple tasks assigned to the same robot (MT tasks) ; section 6 shows the results of the experiments using the swarm SUA, EDFA and SBPA methods; section 7 explain the new EDFBP strategy and the experiments carried out to validate it; finally, section 8 exposes some conclusions and the future work of our research.

2. Related work

A lot of research has been done to solve the multi robot task allocation problem, but it is still an open issue. The proposed solutions can be classified into three main groups: centralized, negotiation and self organized system(swarm). In centralized methods there is a central agent who has all the information about the tasks, the robots, environment, etc. and takes all the decisions. The centralized algorithms can use classical optimization methods, like for example Linear Koes et al. (2005) or Dynamic programming, which get very good results in terms of number of tasks executed per time unit and of energy required by the robots, but they need too much computation time for being used in a dynamic environment. Some other centralized methods, like the best pair selection, use a greedy algorithm that produces a worse allocation but needs less time. This strategy has also been used for non centralized methods, like Broadcast Local Eligibility (BLE)Werger & Mataric (2000). In this work the SBPA is based in this concept, but on an environment where the robots use an auction to get the tasks. In the self organized or swarm systems each robot takes the decision by itself, without any kind of negotiation and executing very simple procedures like in Sahin et al. (2008). Probably, the most used swarm algorithms are the response threshold methods Agassounon & Martinoli (2002); Yang et al. (2009); Ferreira et al. (2010), where each robot has a stimuli associated with each task. When the level of the stimuli exceeds a threshold, the robot starts its execution. The pure threshold based systems, and in general the pure swarm systems, don't require any kind of communication mechanisms. Some studies like Ducatelle et al. (2009) studied how the communication can improve the performance of their swarm method for foraging like tasks. Nonetheless, a disadvantage of these systems is the interference produced when two or more robots decide to execute the same task, when this task can only be executed by a single robot. The swarm method proposed in this work does not use any kind of communication between robots and they will only be able to get information from a central auctioneer. Finally, the negotiation methods are a middle way solutions, among these methods the most used ones are the auction based solutions like for example Gerkey & Mataric (2002); Dias & Stentz (2003); Vig (2006). In this kind of systems, the robots act as self-interest agents and they bid for tasks. The robot with the highest bid wins the auction process and gets the task. The bids are adjusted to the robots' interest (capacity) to carry out the goal. Thus, the best robot for a specific task can be chosen, but they need communication mechanisms between robots.

In this paper we focus on auction and swarm systems. In Zheng et al. (2006) the authors used an auction method with sequential allocation, similar to the SUA method developed in this work, but they improve the sequential results using a prediction of futures assignments. Our improvements of the sequential auctions are based on real time concepts like EDF, or on reducing the algorithmic complexity with EDFBP method. Hybrid methods, which combine both auction and swarm approaches, has also been introduced by several authors like Zhang et al. (2007) or Dasgupta & Hoeing (2008). In all these cases only a single robot can be assigned to the same task (SR scenario). A lot of works allow has been done to solve the multi-robot assignment problem (MR problem) where tightly cooperation between robots is required to execute a task Jones (2009); Vig (2006); Service & Adams (2010); Zheng & Koenig (2008). MR problems are out of the scope of this work and they have been studied by the authors in Guerrero & Oliver (2010; 2004)

Very few work has been done to test swarm systems in real time scenarios, where the tasks must be executed before a deadline. In del Acebo & de-la Rosa (2008) the authors proposed a swarm method to solve conflicts between robots using a local planning and high communication skills to perform a local auction process. Hence, no learning algorithm was proposed to fit the algorithm's parameters that, as the authors pointed, affect dramatically the results. The swarm algorithm proposed in our work is much more simple in order to simplify the comparison with the other methods. Auction strategies have also been used in real time scenarios, for example, in Jones et al. (2006) the robots learnt what to bid to increase the number of tasks that fulfill a deadline. A great effort has

been done to solve the scheduling and allocation problem on multi-processors systems Pinedo (2008). Some of these works use the well known Earliest Deadline First (EDF) Goossens et al. (2002), the same method used in this work to decide in what order the tasks must be auctioned.
Finally, other works, like for example Kalra & Martinoli (2006), compare both auction and swarm without deadlines under different types of communication restrictions. The authors tried to use a classical response threshold algorithm, but in all cases the results with a deterministic selection were better. The same swarm strategy used in Kalra & Martinoli (2006) has been implemented to execute our swarm experiments.

3. General task description

In this section, we will formalize the task allocation problem previously sketched and we will explain the main problems that presents.
We have a set of tasks $T = \{t_1, t_2, ..., t_n\}$ and a set of robots $R = \{r_1, r_2, ..., r_m\}$ where in general $n \neq m$. Each task t_i has associated a set of characteristics $C_i = \{C_{i1}, C_{i2}, ..., C_{il}\}$, these characteristics can be, for example, the location of the task (x and y position), the amount of work to do (object's weight, area to clean, ...), etc. Each task i has a set of restrictions RT_i that must be satisfied by the robot or robots that will be assigned to it. Some examples of restrictions can be: number of robots that can simultaneously execute the task, sensorial skills that the robots must have, time restrictions like a deadline, etc. So, we want to find a task allocation function $A: T \rightarrow R$ that assigns to each task a set of robots in such way that robots' skill meet the task's restrictions taking into account the task's characteristics. We can also define a utility function $U: A \rightarrow \Re$ which given a task allocation returns its utility, that is, a real number that indicates how "good" is an allocation. Thus, our goal will be to find a A function that maximize the total utility U. In this work the utility function will be the number of tasks that fulfill its deadline.

3.1 Foraging task

To validate the algorithms, the classical like foraging task will be used. This task is defined as follows: some randomly placed robots have to pick up some randomly placed objects in the environment. New objects can arrive to the environment following a poisson distribution. There is also a central agent who knows the position of all the objects and will inform (broadcast) this information to all the robots. Each object to gather has a weight and each robot has a work capacity. The robot's work capacity is the amount of object's weight that the robot can process per time unit. The robots stops when it is near an object and starts to process the object for a time equals to *weight/work Capacity*. After this time, the robot goes back to its idle state and tries to get another task.
Each task has associated a utility (U), and a deadline time DL_i. DL_i is the time instant before which the task must be finished. The deadline time for a task will start its countdown just after the task appears in the environment. If the tasks' deadline has been met, then the group receives the utility of the task as a benefit. Otherwise, the task will disappear of the environment and no other robot will be able to execute it anymore. Then, our goal will be maximize the total utility, and thus, minimize the number of tasks executed after its deadline. In the experiments executed all the tasks had the same utility.

4. Implemented approaches for ST-SR-IA

In this section we will explain the four first approaches implemented in this work when only a task can be assigned simultaneously to a robot, that is, when the ST-SR-IA strategy is used. As it has been said, these strategies are: Sequential Best Pair Auction (SBPA), Earliest Deadline First Auction (EDFA), Serial Unordered Auction (SUA) and swarm. In all cases there will be a central auctioneer who will send the tasks information to the robots and decide what robot wins each task when the auction methods are executed.

4.1 Serial best pair auction: SBPA

We have used the classical best pair selection approach very similar to the selection method used in Broadcast of Local Eligibility (BLE) Werger & Mataric (2000) but into an auction process. Each time that a new task appears in the environment or when a robot finishes its execution, a central auctioneer starts a new auction round. The process followed by the auctioneer can be seen in algorithm 1. Firstly, it requests for a bid for each task to all the idle robots (lines 1-3). The idle robots (without any task assigned) bid using its expected time to finish the task, as long as they are able to execute the task before its deadline. Each robot uses its kinematic characteristics to know how much time it will need to finish a task. Then the auctioneer selects in each iteration the pair robot-task with the best execution time and notifies this election to the robot. This algorithm is similar to the studied in Gerkey & Mataric (2004).

The detailed analysis of the algorithmic complexity of our SBPA algorithm (algorithm 1) is as follows: let's n be the number of tasks (objects) and m the number of robots, then the complexity of the loop in lines 1-3 is $O(m)$. To find the best robot-task pair (line 5) it is required to test each robot and each task, but in each iteration a robot and a task are removed, therefore the complexity of the lines 1-8 is $O(\sum_{i=0}^{min(n,m)}(n-i)(m-i)))$. Thus, the total algorithmic complexity of the SBPA algorithm is $O(m+\sum_{i=0}^{min(n,m)}(n-i)(m-i))$. As it can also be seen, in each iteration the auctioneer sends a award message to a robot, therefore the cost of the communication system is equal to $O(m+min(n,m))$

Algorithm 1 SBPA algorithm for the ST approach

```
1: for all unassigned task t do
2:     Ask for a bid to all idle robots
3: end for
4: repeat
5:     Select the best robot-task pair (best bid).
6:     Send an award message to the selected robot
7:     Remove the task and the robot of the list
8: until There is no more unassigned robots or tasks
```

4.2 Earliest Deadline First Auction: EDFA

The earliest deadline first (EDF) is a very well known method in processors scheduling for real time environments. In these cases, the tasks (processes) are sorted by deadline, in such a way that the tasks with the nearest deadline are firstly processed. The same concept has been used in this work to implement the Earliest Deadline First Auction (EDFA) strategy, as it can be seen in algorithm 2. When a new task appears or when a robot becomes idle, the central auctioneer orders all the available tasks by deadline, and sends a request to all the robots for the first task, the task with the earliest deadline. Then, the robots that are able to finish the task before the deadline bid for the task using its expected execution time. Finally, the auctioneer selects the best robot (the robot who is able to finish the task first). If there are more tasks, the task with the next earliest deadline is selected and the process starts again.

Algorithm 2 EDFA algorithm for the ST approach

```
1: sort the list of tasks T by deadline (EDF)
2: for all task t in T do
3:     Ask for a bid to all idle robots
4:     Select the best bid
5:     Send an award message to the assigned robot
6: end for
```

Following the same reasoning as for the SBPA, the analysis of the EDFA complexity is as follows: let's n be the number of tasks and m the number of robots, then, the complexity for the sorting algorithm (line 1) is $O(nlog(n))$. Then, the auctioneer must check each robot's bid to get the best robot for a task, but we have to take into account that the robots already assigned to earlier objects does not need to be considered. Thus, in each iteration a robot is assigned to a task and the complexity will be equal to: $O(nlog(n)+\sum_{i=0}^{\min(n,m)}(m-i))$. The cost of the communication is similar to the already explained for SBPA algorithm.

4.3 Serial Unordered Auction: SUA

This is the more simple auction strategy implemented in this work. As the tasks arrive to the central auctioneer, it starts a new auction round for each one of them. That is, the task are processed in a sequential way, like in a FIFO cue. When an auction round is started, the robots bids for this task using its expected execution time, as long as the robot is able to finish the task before the deadline. Then, the robots send their bid to the auctioneer who selects as the auction winner the robot with the minor execution time. Finally, if there are more tasks, a new auction process is started again until all objects have been processed. Thus, the central auctioneer does not have to make any decision about the order the task must be offered to the robots.

The computational complexity analysis of this algorithm is as follows: let's n be the number of tasks and m the number of robots, then the auctioneer for each task has to check all the bids, that in the worst case will be equal to the number of robots. Following the same reasoning as in the EDFA algorithm, we can see that the complexity of this algorithm is $O(\sum_{i=0}^{\min(n,m)}(m-i))$. The communication complexity is the same as in the EDFA strategy.

4.4 Swarm

In the swarm strategy each robot makes the decision about what task it will process by itself, without taking into account any other robot. As new tasks arrive, the central auctioneer sends to all the robots the information about them. Then, each idle robot selects the nearest task to it as its next objective. To select a task the distance between the robot and the task must be lower than a value D, thus, we avoid assigning a robot to a very distant task. Other more complex strategies have been used, like response threshold, but, as was pointed in Kalra & Martinoli (2006) for tasks without deadlines, the nearest task first strategy outperform response threshold in all cases. The complexity of this selection algorithm is obviously $O(n)$ where n is the number of tasks. Here the complexity of the communication system is equals to $O(n)$ because the central auctioneer should send to all the robots the information of the n tasks. Table 5 summarizes the complexity of all the single task algorithms proposed in this work and includes a the new EDFBP method that will be explained later.

5. Multi-task per robot: MT-SR-IA approaches

In this section we will explain the MT-SR-IA strategy implemented for this work. In the MTSR- IA strategies the robots can have more than one assigned task, and therefore, they have to schedule all its objectives. In our case, each robot has an scheduling, P with the objects to gather, thus, this list is the path or plan that the robot will follow. When a robot receives a new offer to execute a task t it will try to add t in P creating a provisional scheduling $P' = P \cup t$, in such a way that the total length of P' is as short as possible and all tasks in P' meet the deadline. Then, the robot bids for t using the difference of expected time between P' and P, that is, the bid value $b(t)$ will be:

$$b(t) = \sum tExpected(t_{j-1}, t_j) \qquad (1)$$

where $tExpected(a, b)$ returns the expected time that the robots would need to go from task a to task b, the task t_0 is the initial position of the robot. Other bidding strategies has also been tested, like bid the total execution time of the new path, but the equation 1 provided the best results. The central auctioneer will select the best robot (the robot with the lowest b value) using any of the already explained strategies (SUA, EDFA or SBPA). Finally, provisional path P' is assigned to the selected robot.

The minimization of the path P' is a NP-Hard problem called the traveling salesman problem with deadlines in metric spaces, Δ-D_LTSP, where the path to minimize can not be a cycle. A lot of work has been done to try to solve the Δ-D_LTSP problem Bckenhauer et al. (2009); Bansal et al. (2004). In this paper the nearest neighbor strategy has been used to get P' from P and t, that is, the new task is inserted between each two tasks in the path P, and the shortest one is selected. If there is no way to create a new path P' that meets all the deadlines, the robot will not bid for the task. Let's n be the number of tasks in P, then to create P' we have to make $n + 1$ tests (places where insert the new task) and $n + 1$ more to verify that all tasks meet the deadline, therefore the complexity of this algorithm is $O(n^2)$. The complexity of this algorithm is quite low but its completeness is not bounded.

This new strategy involves that the algorithm 1 has to be updated. As it can be seen in algorithm 3, now after each assignment the central auctioneer has to ask for a bid to all the robots again (lines 2-4) because the bidding of a robot in one iteration will depend on the decisions made in the last assignment. The SUA and EDFA methods have also been modified, in such a way that now the auctioneer asks for bids before auctioning each task. Thus, the complexity from the communication point of view, has been increased in all cases. Now for EDFA and SUA, for each task the auctioneer has to send a broadcast request to all the robots (1 message), wait for the m bids (one for each robot) and finally send the award to the winner (1 message). Therefore the complexity of the communication is, in the worst case, $O(n * (m+2)) = O(nm)$. This is very similar for the SBPA method, but in each iteration of algorithm 3 the robot has to send a broadcast message requesting for the remaining tasks (1 message), this message will be much more longer than the sent in a EDFA or SUA strategy. Then, the auctioneer receives the bids from all the robots (m messages) and finally it sends the award to the winner (1 message). The complexity from the communication point of view will be $O(n * (m + 2)) = O(nm)$, the same as in EDFA or SUA, but we have to take into account that the length messages will be longer.

Algorithm 3 SBPA algorithm for the multi task approach (MT)

repeat
    for all unassigned unassigned task t **do**
        Ask for a bid to all robots
    end for
    Select the best robot-task pair (best bid).
    Send an award message to the assigned robot
until There is no more unassigned robots or tasks

As it is shown in table 1, can be easily seen the algorithmic complexity of the algorithms with MT assignment must be recalculated. In all cases, the complexity has increased compared to the single task assignment algorithms.

SUA	$O(nm)$
EDFA	$O(nlog(n) + nm)$
SBPA	$O(n + \sum_{i=0}^{n} m(n-i))$

Table 1. Complexity order of the algorithms introduced in this work in a multi task approach (MT). n is the number of tasks, m is the number of robots

6. ST-SR-IA and MT-SR-IA experiments

In this section we will show the results of the experiments carried out to study the behavior of the methods explained in sections 4 and 5, that is, the ST-SR-IA and MT-SR-IA approaches (SUA, EDFA, SBPA).

6.1 Experiments design: RobSim and Payer/stage simulator

We used a simulator, called RobSim, developed in our university to execute most of our experiments. RobSim is a simulator that allows to emulate the behavior of a very large population of robots and a huge number of tasks. After each time period the simulator updates the robots' positions and processes all the events happened in that period: new object in the environment, task executed successfully, expired task's deadline, etc . To speed up the simulation time, we assume that the robot can not collide with any other object in the environment and therefore, an obstacle avoidance algorithm is not needed. Thus, RobSim can be considered as a nonrealistic simulator but it is very useful tool to compare the global performance of the different tested strategies. To carry out more accurate experiments with

a less number of robots and tasks we have use the very well known and more realistic Player/Stage simulator.
We have executed in the RoboSim experiments with the foraging task already explained in 3.1. New objects to pick up appear in the environment following a poisson process with parameter λ, where λ is the average number of new tasks that will appear in the environment per time unit. Three different values of λ have been used: 0.05, 0.1, and 0.3. Moreover, the followings 5 different kinds of task sets were used:

- 1st Environment (Uniform Tasks): all tasks had the same weight (1 weight unit) and the same deadline time (250 time units)
- 2nd Environment (Weighted Tasks): all tasks had the same deadline time but their weights were generated following a uniform distribution between 1 and 70 weight units.
- 3th Environment (Random Deadline): all tasks had the same weight but the tasks' deadlines were generated according to a uniform distribution between 100 and 500 time units.
- 4th Environment (Hybrid Tasks): similar to the Random Deadline but with a probability of 0.2, the new task has not an associated deadline, that is, it has no time restrictions. Therefore, tasks with and without deadlines coexist in the same environment.
- 5th Environment (Tasks without deadline): there is no deadline assigned to any task, and its weight is equal to 1.

All robots in the colony had the same characteristics they move in a 160m.x160m.environment. The number of robots varied between 2 and 40. 1920 simulations were executed, each one lasting 10000 time units during which 270000 objects were processed.

6.2 Experiments with RoboSim

Here we will explain the main results of the experiments carried out with the RoboSim simulator over a large number of tasks and objects.
Figure 1(a) shows the total number of objects finished when no deadline is assigned to the tasks and with a $\lambda = 0.1$ and a $D = \infty$ for the swarm strategy. The planning methods means (5th. environment) the strategies with a MT-SR-IA strategy, that is, when the local path scheduling, explained in section 5, is performed. The total length covered by all the robots under the same environment is shown in figure 1(b). The EDF strategy has not been tested because without deadlines its results are equal to the SUA method ones. As it can be seen, when the ST-SR-IA (no planning) is used in SUA strategy the number of tasks finished is increased in a quasi lineal way with regards to the number of robots. This number of tasks is greater than swarm strategy if the number of robots is grater than 28. On the one hand, the SBPA method is not affected by the local planning, in both cases MT and ST the number of tasks is very similar. On the other hand, the planning clearly improves the SUA strategy results getting similar results as the SBPA method. For all strategies, except for swarm, there is a number of robots from which the total traveled path decreases. In the swarm system this total length increases lineally regards to the number of robots due to the interference between robots, produced when two or more robots select the same task simultaneously.
Figure 2(a) shows the total number of finished tasks with $\lambda = 0.05$ and figure 2(b) shows the total length traveled by all the robots in this same scenario. In this experiments the SUA

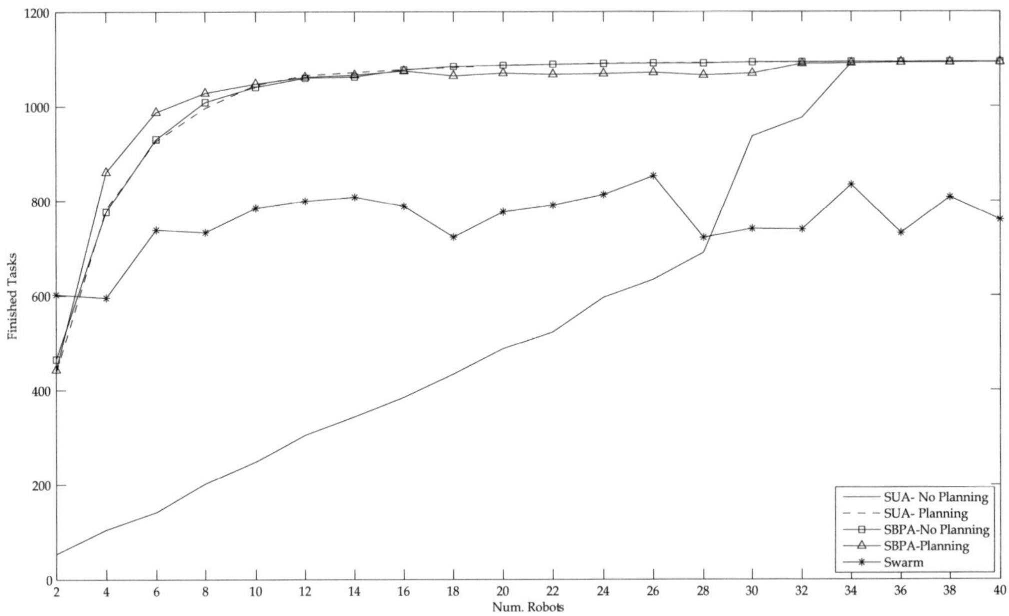

(a) Number of finished tasks.

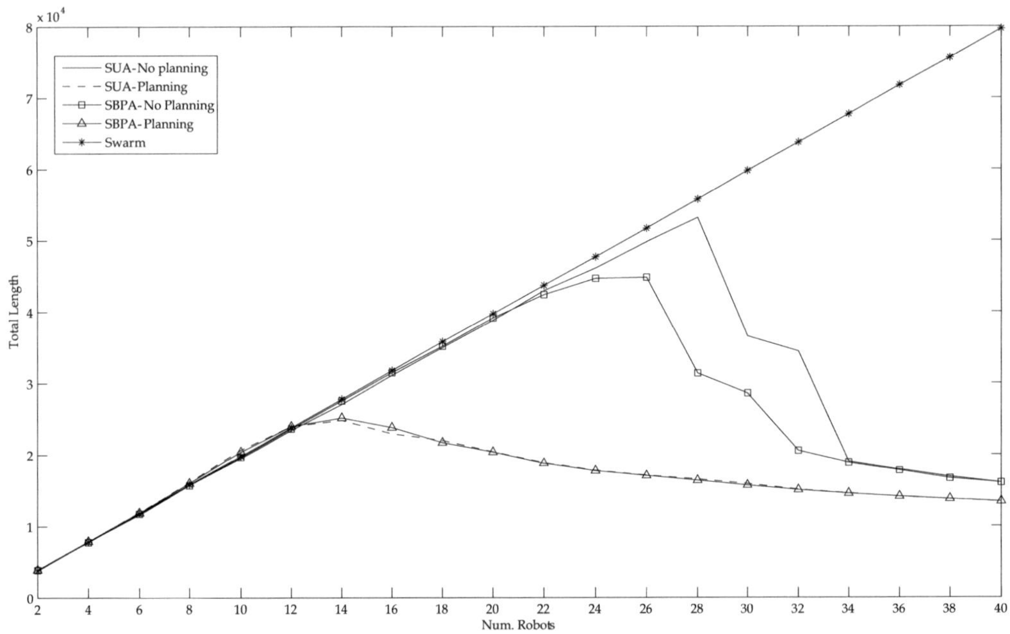

(b) Total length of the robots' path.

Fig. 1. Results without deadlines, with and without using planning. $\lambda = 0.1$

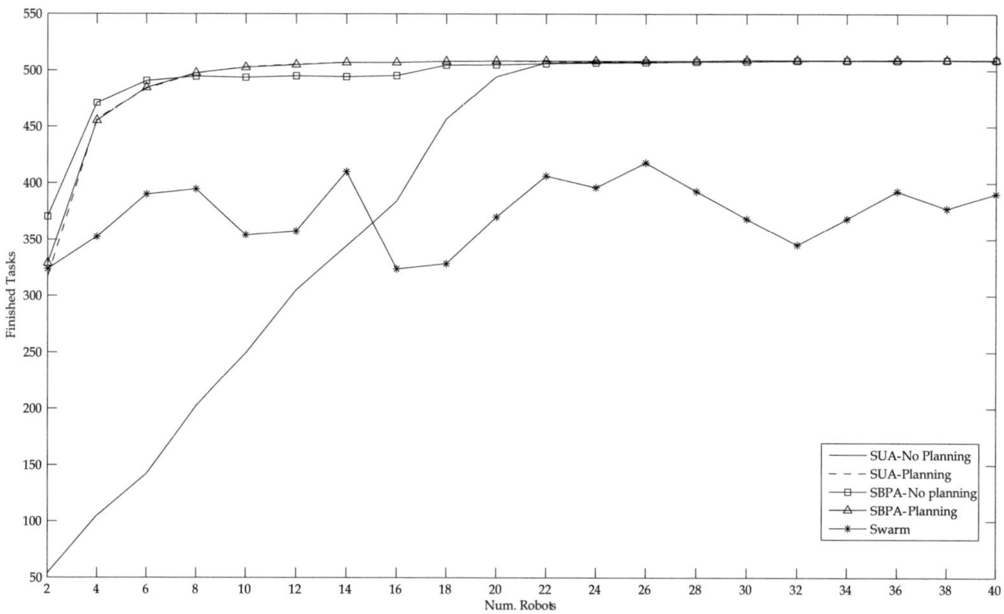

(a) Number of finished tasks.

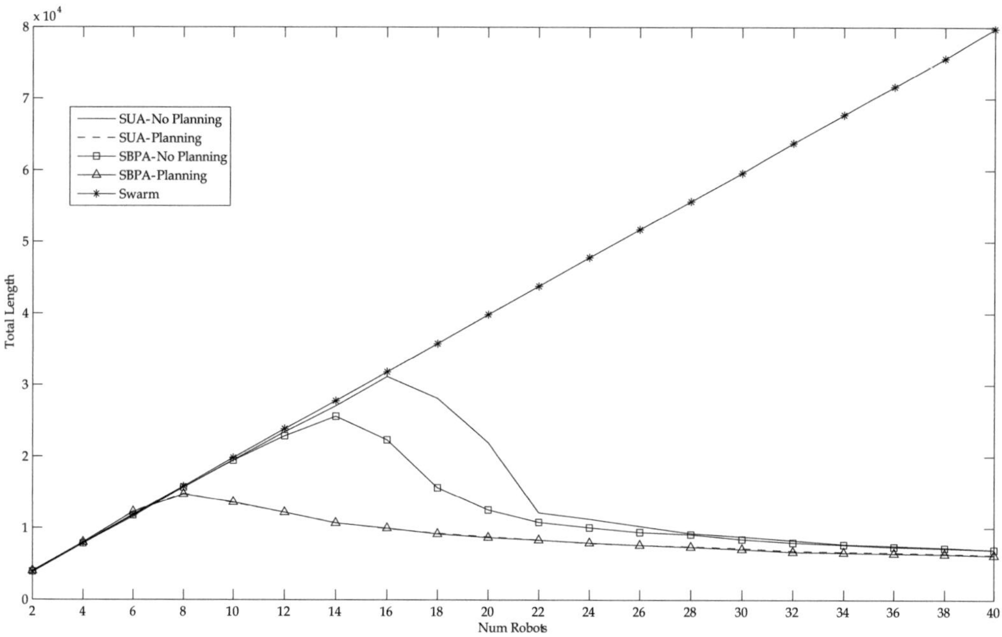

(b) Total length of the robots' path.

Fig. 2. Total length of the robots' path without deadlines with and without using planning. $\lambda = 0.05$

strategy outperforms swarm with less robot than when λ was equal to 0.1. Besides, the number of robots from which the robots' path length starts to decrease is also lower than in figure 1(b). The experiments carried out using tasks with deadlines (environments from 1st to 4th), show that all the strategies are very similar when the arrival ratio of tasks is low (low values of λ). Hence, we will focus on the scenarios with a high ratio of arrivals. Figure 3 shows the number of tasks executed before its deadline with $\lambda = 0.3$ and with two different set of tasks: environment 3 (random deadlines) and environment 4 (Hybrid Tasks). In both cases the SBPA without planning outperforms the planning version when the number of robots is low. In the 4th environment the number of robots from which the SBPA-planning is better than SBPA without planning is grater than in the 3th environment. This is because in the 3th environment all the tasks have a deadline, and in the 4th environment there are some tasks without time restriction. In any case, the behavior of the SUA and EDFA strategies is dramatically increased when the planning is used, therefore, in those cases the main key to improve the system is the use of a MT approach (planning).

6.3 Experiments with player/stage

In this section we will analyze in a deeper way the single task strategy (ST) when the number of robots is low. We will use the very realistic simulator Player/Stage, which will allow us to study the physical interference between robots, produced when 2 or more robots want to access to the same point of the space at the same time. The physical interference has already been studied by the authors in ST-MR-IA strategies Guerrero & Oliver (2010).

To execute our experiments we have several pioneer 3DX robots, which have become a standard research platform in robotics. The dimensions of the environment was 18mx18m and the maximum robots' velocity was 0.25m/s. The robots used this information to calculate the expected execution time and to decide if they were able to execute a task before the deadline. We used 200 objects randomly placed in each experiment and with a deadline time uniformly distributed between 12 and 70 seconds. When an object is gathered, it immediately appears another one in a random position, thus, the number of objects in the environment (*M*) is always the same. (*M*) is a parameter and its influence in the performance of the system will be tested in the experiments.

Table 2 shows the number of tasks that do not meet its deadline using the SBPA strategy, where *R* is the number of robots. In all cases, this auction algorithm is better than the swarm system, very specially when the number of robots is increased. For example, with 12 robots this benefit can be around 60%. Furthermore, the maximum distance (*D*) has not a great impact on the results, by contrast, Kalra & Martinoli (2006) showed that without deadline this parameter can be very important.

		R=4	R=8	R=12
D=9	M=5	67 (26%)	38 (38%)	18 (60%)
	M=10	90 (17%)	48 (46%)	48 (44%)
D=12	M=5	69 (39%)	35 (53%)	24 (63%)
	M=10	90 (29%)	56 (47%)	56 (47%)
D= ∞	M=5	78 (32%)	45 (46%)	24 (61%)
	M=10	87 (33%)	59 (46%)	68 (23%)

Table 2. Number of tasks that do not meet its deadline with the SBPA strategy, in brackets the percentage increase of tasks when swarm is used.

Tables 3 and 4 show the number of tasks that do not meet its deadline using SUA and EDFA, respectively. As it can be seen, in all cases the SBPA is better than both SUA and EDFA and, even in most cases, the swarm outperforms the SUA and EDFA results. The performance SUA/EDFA systems get better as the ratio between maximum distance and number of robots (R/D) increases. When there are a lot of robots with regards to the number of tasks, like for example if $D = 9$ and $R = 4$, the SUA/EDFA results are 17% worse than swarm, but with low values of $\frac{R}{D}$ the results are SUA/EDFA 14% better than swarm. Moreover, the EDFA seems to improve, in most cases the system performance, very especially for the worst SUA cases. We have to note that these results are partially similar to the already shown in figure 3 where for a low number of robots, the swarm strategy can outperform SUA and EDFA. In the RoboSim experiments the distance D was infinity, and therefore the $\frac{R}{D}$ ratio was the minimum possible.

		R=4	R=8	R=12
D=9	M=5	105 (-17%)	94 (-54%)	98(-118%)
	M=10	128 (-17%)	93 (-4%)	96 (-13%)
D=12	M=5	102 (11%)	85 (-13%)	89 (-39%)
	M=10	128 (-2%)	94 (11%)	89 (15%)
D= ∞	M=5	98 (14%)	84 (0%)	90 (-48%)
	M=10	122 (6%)	100 (9%)	88 (-13%)

Table 3. Number of tasks that do not meet its deadline with the SUA strategy. The percentage of increase when swarm is used appears in brackets.

		R=4	R=8	R=12
D=9	M=5	99 (-10%)	87 (-43%)	78 (-73%)
	M=10	135 (-24%)	87 (2%)	90 (-6%)
D=12	M=5	97 (15%)	81 (-8%)	91 (-42%)
	M=10	126 (0%)	97 (15%)	100 (-5%)
D= ∞	M=5	96 (16%)	94 (-12%)	85 (-39%)
	M=10	132 (-2%)	94 (8%)	96 (-9%)

Table 4. Number of tasks that do notmeet its deadlinewith the EDFA strategy. The percentage of increase when swarm is used appears in brackets.

7. Earliest Deadline First Best Pair method (EDFBP)

In this section we will propose a new auction like algorithm called Earliest Deadline First Best Pair (EDFBP), which is in a middle way between the EDFA and the SBPA. The objective of the EDFBP algorithm is to have the SBPA's performance but with a lower algorithmic cost. To achieve this goal, EDFBP follows the algorithm 4, where firstly the central auctioneer orders all the tasks by deadline (line 1). Then, it selects a subset of this tasks (line 2) and apply only over this subset the SBPA procedure (algorithm 1). In our case the total set of tasks (T) is split in several consecutive subsets using the β parameter (see algorithm 5). Thus, β is the percentage of the total number of tasks that will be processed as one unit by SBPA. When $\beta = 1$ the EDFBP will behave as a SBPA and when $\beta = 0$ it is a EDF algorithm.

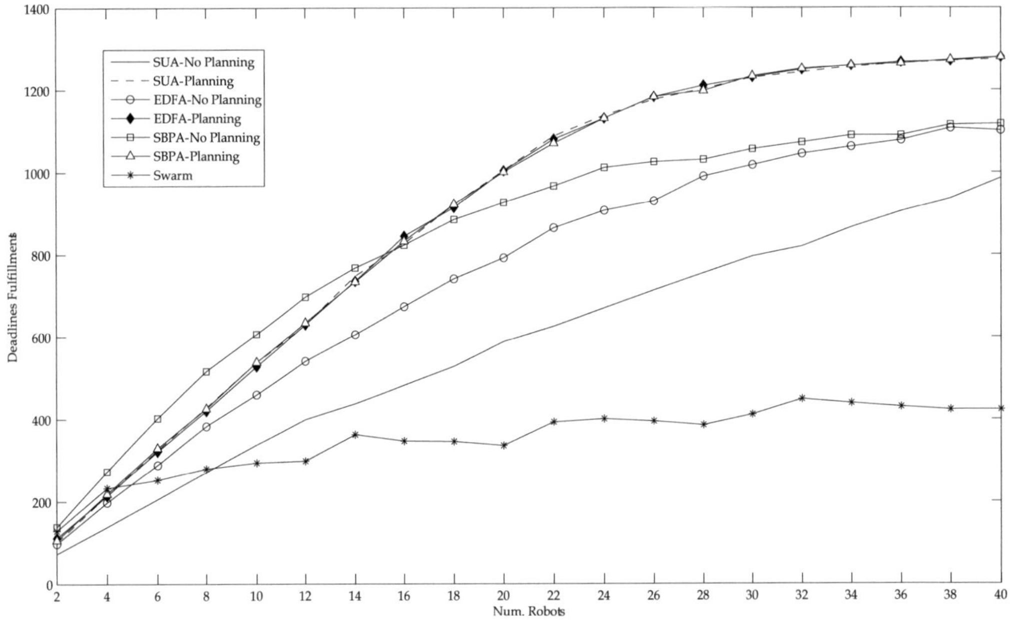

(a) 3th Environment (random deadlines)

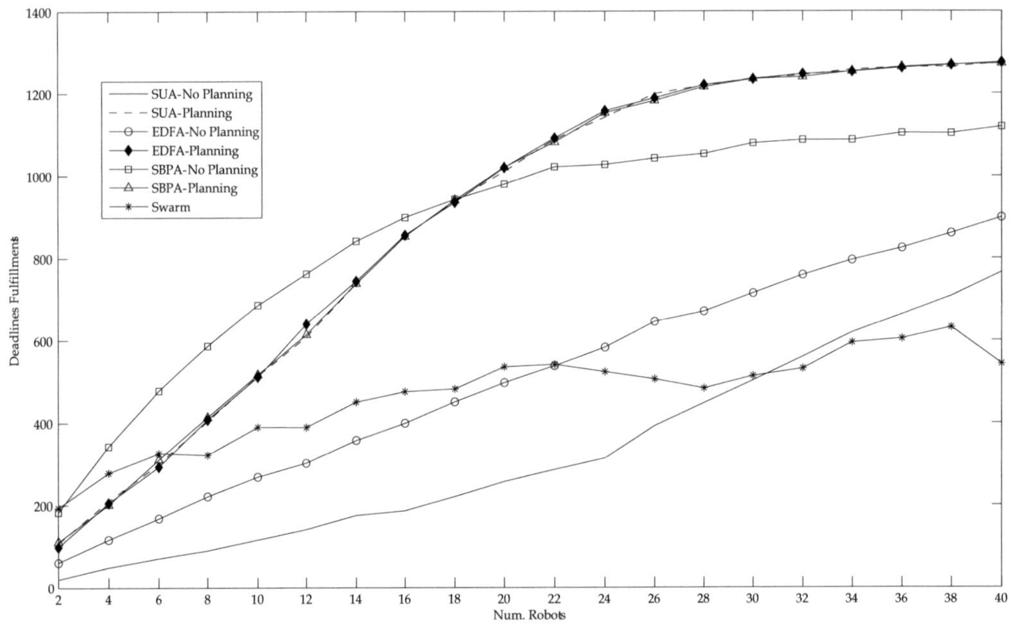

(b) 4th Environment (hybrid tasks)

Fig. 3. Deadlines fulfillments with $\lambda = 0.3$ and different environments.

The algorithmic complexity of the EDFBP can be easily gotten as follows: let's n be the number of tasks, m the number of robots and $r = \frac{1}{\beta}$. To simplify the process we will assume that all the partitions of T have the same number of tasks, and therefore $| TW |$ always has the same value. Following the same reasoning as in section 4.2, the ordering process (line 1) has a complexity equal to $O(nlong(n))$. Then, the SBPA algorithm is performed over $\frac{n}{r}$ tasks, and therefore its complexity must be equals to $O(\sum_{i=0}^{min(\frac{n}{r},m)} (\frac{n}{r} - i)(m-i))$. Thus, the total complexity of the EDFBP algorithm is equal to: $O(nlog(n) + r\sum_{i=0}^{min(\frac{n}{r},m)} (\frac{n}{r} - i)(m-i))$. It is easy to see that the complexity of the algorithm is in general lower than the complexity of the SBPA method and the lower value of β the greater algorithm complexity is.

Algorithm 4 EDFBP algorithm

Require: T=List of unassigned tasks
1: sort T by earliest deadline
2: **while** $T \neq \emptyset$ **do**
3: $TW \leftarrow tasksOfInterest(T)$
4: $SBPA\,(TW)$
5: $T \leftarrow T - TW$
6: **end while**

Algorithm 5 tasksOfInterest

Require: T=List of unassigned tasks
1: sort T by earliest deadline
2: $N \leftarrow MAX(1, \lceil \beta * |T| \rceil)$
3: $TInt \leftarrow T[0..N]$
4: **return** TInt

Figure 4(a) shows the results of some experiments carried out to validate the EDFBP with the 3th environment, the environment with random deadlines, and with the single task (ST) approach. The β values are expressed in percentage, thus the EDFBP (50%) means the results with $\beta = 0.5$. These results show that with only a $\beta = 0.5$, that is splitting the T table in two, the results are very similar to the the SBPA strategy. This similar performances has been achieved with a much lower algorithmic cost. Figure 4(b) shows the same results but using the 1st. environment, that is the environment with all tasks with the same deadline. In this case, the results of the different values of β are more similar between them than in the last figure, but, like in the 3th environment, when $\beta = 0.5$ SBPA and EDFBP show very similar results.

Figure 5 shows the total path traveled by all the robots in the same scenario as figure 4(b). As it can be seen there are no major differences between the 4 different strategies and can also be noted that the length is practically lineal with the number of robots. If we compare this results with an environment with a low λ value (see figure 1(b) or figure 2(b)), it can be seen that now there isn't any reduction in the length with regards to the number of robots, or at least, this reduction is not relevant with less than 40 robots.

8. Conclusion and future work

This work has studied how several different auction like algorithms and an swarm approach can carry out a set of tasks with an associated deadline. Three different auction methods has been proposed: SUA, EDFA, SBPA and a deterministic swarm approach. From the results of the experiments carried out, a forth method is also introduced, the EDFBP. The EDFBP is an hybrid between EDFA and SBPA, which, modifying a parameter β, can behave like a SUA or like a SBPA. A study of the algorithmic complexity has also been explained, the tables 5 and 1 show the order of complexity of all the methods studied. As it can be seen, the complexity of EDFBP can be fitted to be between SUA or SBPA.

Moreover, The results of the experiments show that in a single task scenario (ST), when only one task can be assigned to the same robot, the EDFA method outperforms the SUA and shows better results than a swarm approach when there are a lot of robots. In all cases the SBPA has better results than any other strategy. When the robots can have several task (MT approach) all the auction strategies have a similar performance.

The work presented has some challenging aspects to add and to improve. For the time being we are focused on finding a method to learn on-line the β parameter of the EDFBP strategy. New experiments with the Player/stage simulator using much more robots and poisson arrivals for tasks are under consideration too. This new kind of experiments will allow us a more accurate analysis about the effects of our algorithm on real robots and a better comparison with the RoboSim results. The algorithm to schedule tasks explained in section 5 is very simple, more complex and efficient methods should be tested. Some other futures improvements of our work could be: use an heterogeneous set of robots with different sensorial or computational characteristics, develop new methods to learn the expected execution time from the environment's and robot's characteristics or carry out new types of missions, for example cleaning the floor of a room or test our methods on the RoboCup Rescue simulator Kitano et al. (1999).

Swarm	$O(n)$
SUA	$O(\sum_{i=0}^{min(n,m)}(m-i))$
EDFA	$O(nlog(n)+\sum_{i=0}^{min(n,m)}(m-i))$
SBPA	$O(n+\sum_{i=0}^{min(n,m)}(n-i)(m-i))$
EDFBP	$O(nlog(n)+r\sum_{i=0}^{min(n,m)}(\frac{n}{r}-i)(m-i))$

Table 5. Complexity order of the algorithms introduced in this work in a single task environment (ST). n is the number of tasks, m is the number of robots and $r=\frac{1}{\beta}$

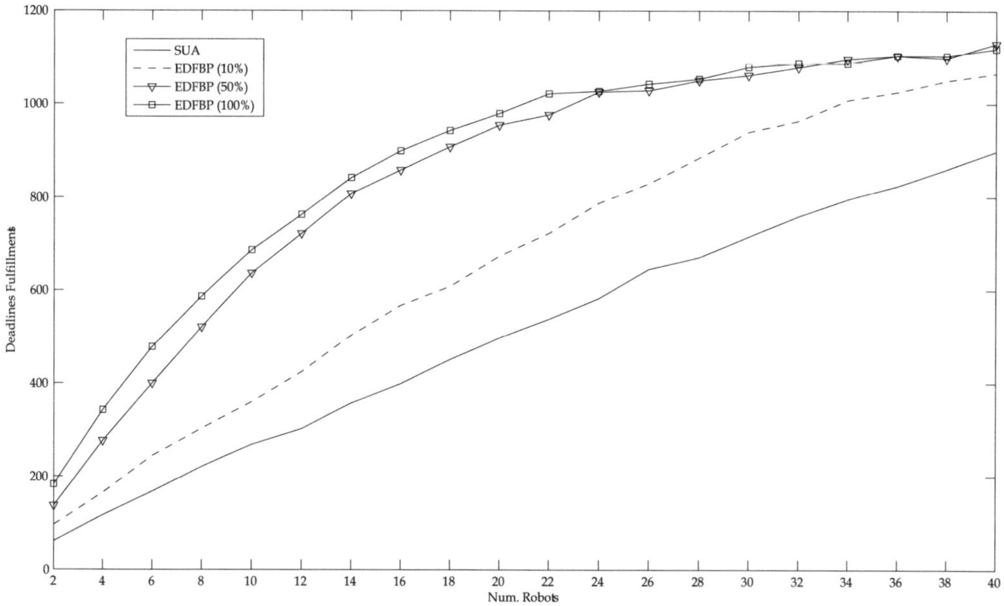

(a) 3th Environment (random deadline)

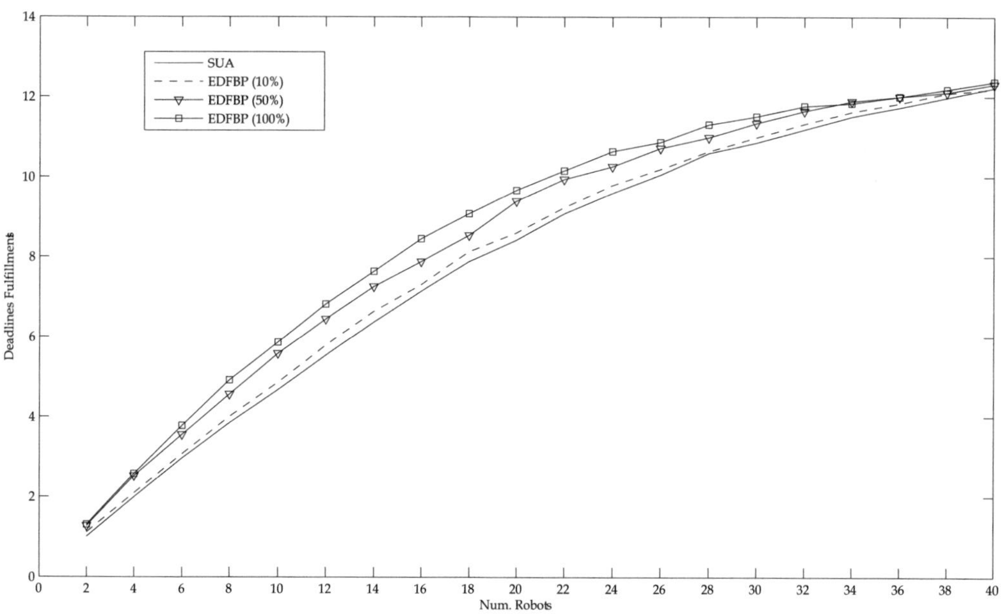

(b) 1th environment (all the tasks has the same deadline)

Fig. 4. Deadlines fulfillments with EDFBP $\lambda = 0.3$, different β values and different environments.

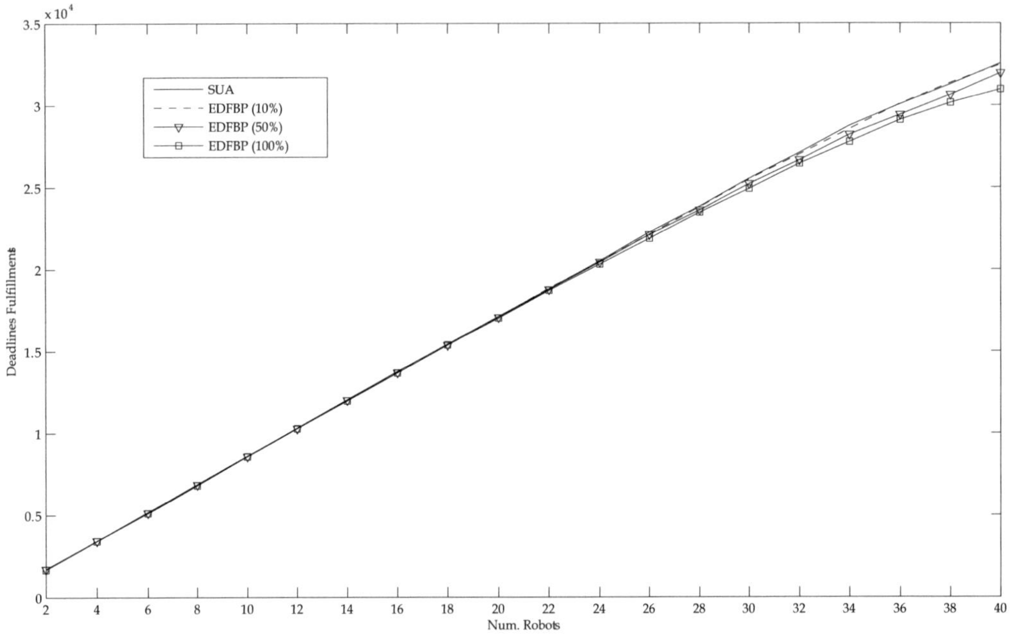

Fig. 5. Total Length with EDFBP λ = 0.3, 1th environment (all the tasks has the same deadline) and different β values.

9. Acknowledgment

This work has been partially supported by project DPI2008-06548-C03-02 and FEDER funding.

10. References

Agassounon, W. & Martinoli, A. (2002). Efficiency and robustness of threshold-based distributed allocation algorithms in multi-agent systems, *1st Int. Joint Conf. on Autonomous Agents and Multi-Agents Systems*, Bologna (Italy).

Bansal, N., Blum, A., Chawla, S. & Meyerson, A. (2004). Approximation algorithms for deadline-tsp and vehicle routing with time-windows, *Proc. of ACM STOC*, pp. 166–174.

Bckenhauer, H.-J., Kneis, J. & Kupke, J. (2009). Approximation hardness of deadline-tsp reoptimization, *Theoretical Computer Science* 410: 2241–2249.

Collett, T.-H., MacDonald, B. A. & Gerkey, B. P. (2005). "player 2.0: Toward a practical robot programming framework", *Proceedings of the Australasian Conference on Robotics and Automation (ACRA 2005)*, Sydney (Australia).

Dasgupta, P. & Hoeing, M. (2008). *Massively Multi-Agent Technology*, Vol. 5043/2008 of *Lecture Notes in Computer Science*, Springer Berlin / Heidelberg, chapter Dynamic Pricing Algorithms for task Allocation in multi-agent Swarms, pp. 64–79.

del Acebo, E. & de-la Rosa, J. L. (2008). Introducing bar systems: A class of swar intelligence optimization algorithms., *Proceedings of AISB 2008 Convention Communication, Interaction and Social Intelligence*, Aberdeen (Scotland).

Dias,M. & Stentz, A. (2003). Traderbots: A market-based approach for resource, role, and task allocation in multirobot coordination, *Technical Report CMU-RI-TR-03-19*, Carnegie Mellon University.

Ducatelle, F., Forster, A., Di-Caro, G. & Gambardella, L. (2009). Task allocation in robotic swarms: new methods and comparisons, *Technical report IDSIA-01-09*, Institute for Artificial Intelligence, Manno, Switzerland.

Ferreira, P. R., dosSantos, F. & et al. (2010). Robocup rescue as multiagent task allocation among teams: experiments with task interdependencies, *Autonomous Agents and Multi-Agent Systems* 20: 421–443.

Gerkey, B.-P. & Mataric,M. (2002). Sold!: Auction methods formulti-robot coordination, *IEEE Transactions on robotics and Automation, Special Issue on Multi-robot Systems* 18(5): 758- 768.

Gerkey, B.-P. & Mataric, M. (2004). A formal analysis and taxonomy of task allocation in multi-robot systems, *Intl. J. of Robotics Research* 23 (9): 939–954.

Goossens, J., Funk, S. & Baruah, S. (2002). Edf scheduling on multiprocessor platforms: some (perhaps) counterintuitive observations, *Proceedings of RealTime Computing Systems and Applications Symposium.*

Guerrero, J. & Oliver, G. (2004). Multi-robot task allocation method for heterogeneous tasks with priorities, *7th. International Symposium on Distributed Autonomous Robotic Systems*, Tolouse (France), pp. 311–317.

Guerrero, J. & Oliver, G. (2010). Amulti-robot auction method to allocate taskswith deadlines, *7th Symposium on Intelligent Autonomous Vehicles (IAV 2010)*, Lecce (Italy).

Jones, E. (2009). *Multi-Robot Coordination in Domains with Intra-path Constraints*, Phd thesis, The Robotics Institute- Carnegie Mellon University, Pittsburg, Pennsylvania (USA).

Jones, E., Dias, M. & Stentz, A. (2006). Learning-enhanced market-based task allocation for disaster response, *Technical Report CMU-RI-TR-06-48*, Carnegie Mellon University.

Kalra, N. & Martinoli, A. (2006). A comparative study of market-based and threshold-based task allocation, *8th Int. Symp. on Distributed Autonomous Robotic Systems.*

Kitano, H., Tadokoro, S., Noda, I. & et al. (1999). Robocup rescue: Search and rescue in large-scale disasters as a domain for autonomous agents research, *Proceedings of IEEE international conference on systems, man and cybernetics (SMC)*, Vol. 6, Tokyo (Japan), pp. 739–743.

Koes, M., Nourbakhsh, I. & Sycara, K. (2005). Heterogeneous multirobot coordination with spatial and temporal constraints, *Proceedings of the Twentieth National Conference o Artificial Intelligence (AAAI)*, AAAI Press, pp. 1292–1297.

Pinedo, M.-L. (2008). *Scheduling: Theory, Algorithms, and Systems*, 3th. edition edn, Springer.

Sahin, E., Girgin, S., Bayindir, L. & Turgut, A.-E. (2008). *Swarm Intelligence: Introduction and Applications*, Natural Computing Series, Springer Verlag, Berlin, Germany, chapter Swarm Robotics.

Service, T.-C. & Adams, J.-A. (2010). Coalition formation for task allocation: theory an algorithms, *Autonomous Agents and Multi-Agent Systems* .

Vig, L. (2006). *Multi-Robot Coalition Formation*, Phd thesis, Gratuate School of Vanderbilt University.

Werger, B. B. & Mataric,M. J. (2000). Broadcast of local eligibility for multi-target observation, *Distributed Autonomous Robotic Systems 4*, Knoxville, Tennessee, USA.

Yang, Y., Zhou, C. & Tin, Y. (2009). Swar robots task allocation based on response threshold model, *Proceedings of the 4th Intl. Conference on Autonomous Robots and Agents*, Willengton (New Zeland).

Zhang, D., Xie, G., Yu, J. & Wang, L. (2007). Adaptive task assignment for multiple mobile robots via swarm intelligence approach, *Robotics and Autonomous Systems* 55(7): 572- 588.

Zheng, X. & Koenig, S. (2008). Greedy approaches for solving task-allocation problems with coalitions, *In Proceedings of the AAMAS-08 Workshop on Formal Models and Methods for Multi-Robot Systems*, Estoril (Portugal), pp. 35–40.

Zheng, X., Koenig, S. & Tovey, C. (2006). Improving sequential single-item auctions, *Proceedings of the IEEE International Conference on Intelligent Robots and Systems (IROS)*, pp. pages 2238–2244.

Zlot, R. & Stentz, A. (2006). Market-based multirobot coordination for complex tasks, *Intl. J. of Robotics Research. Special Issue on the 4th Intl. Conference on Field and Service Robotics*, Vol. 25 (1).

23

Improving Search Efficiency in the Action Space of an Instance-Based Reinforcement Learning Technique for Multi-Robot Systems

Toshiyuki Yasuda and Kazuhiro Ohkura
Hiroshima University
Japan

1. Introduction

Recent years have witnessed growing interest in multi-robot system (MRS) research. To date, numerous research projects have been undertaken in various forms, such as robot soccer (Stone & Sutton, 2001), all-terrain operation (Mondada et al., 2003), box-pushing problems (Gerkey & Mataric, 2002), and many others. We can point out at least three advantages of an MRS over traditional single-robot systems (Stone & Veloso, 2000). The first is *parallel processing*, performed by autonomous and asynchronous robots in the system. The second is *robustness*, realized by redundancy: the system has more robots than required. The third is *scalability* in the sense that a robot can be added or removed from the system easily.

From the viewpoint of complex adaptive systems, it is important to coordinate cooperative behavior to solve a given task because a task is given simply to a robot group without sufficiently detailed specifications to solve it. The most popular approach to realize coordination is providing strategies for effective cooperation in advance in the form of behavior rules, roles, or communication protocols.

However, it is practically impossible to give hand-crafted behavior rules for all possible situations that a robot will encounter. This means that the performance is context-sensitive. One approach to this problem is giving the ability of acquiring cooperative behavior through experience to each robot by autonomous role development and assignment so that an MRS has the potential for system-level robustness.

We consider that a key factor would be how to give an *on-line* autonomous specialization mechanism to an MRS. This study introduces an approach that uses reinforcement learning (RL) to achieve autonomous specialization. To date, RL has not often been applied to an MRS because of the following two reasons. The first is that RL generates quite sensitive results for segmentation of the state space and the action space. When segmentation is inappropriate, RL often fails. Even if RL obtains a successful result, the achieved behavior might not be sufficiently robust. The second is that the RL theory is constructed on the assumption of a static environment (Sutton & Barto, 1998). Therefore, RL in a simple form can yield good results only when the environment is sufficiently static or stable for a robot to be able to assume that it is static.

We must therefore apply RL carefully to an MRS, so that learning robots cope with the dynamics in their environment resulting from the moves of other robots that are learning simultaneously.

To overcome these problems, we apply a novel RL algorithm that has a mechanism for segmenting continuous state space and continuous action space autonomously and simultaneously. We call this Bayesian-discrimination-function-based Reinforcement Learning (BRL). In addition, for supporting the stabilization of the dynamics in the learning problem for the RL, complementary information, *i.e.*, the prediction of the other robots' postures at the next time step is provided to the BRL by a learning neural network.
The remainder of this chapter is organized as follows: The target MRS is introduced in the second section. The third and fourth sections explain our design concept and our reinforcement learning controller details. The fourth section proposes an extended BRL for improving the robustness. The fifth section shows results of our experiments. Conclusions are given in the final section.

2. Task: cooperative carrying problem

Our target problem is a simple MRS composed of three autonomous robots, as shown in Fig. 1. This problem is called the *cooperative carrying problem* (CCP), and involves requiring the MRS to carry a triangular board from the start to the goal. A robot is connected to the different corners of the load so that it can rotate freely. A potentiometer measures the angle between the load and the robot's direction θ. A robot can perceive the potentiometer measurements of the other robots, as well as its own. All three robots have the same

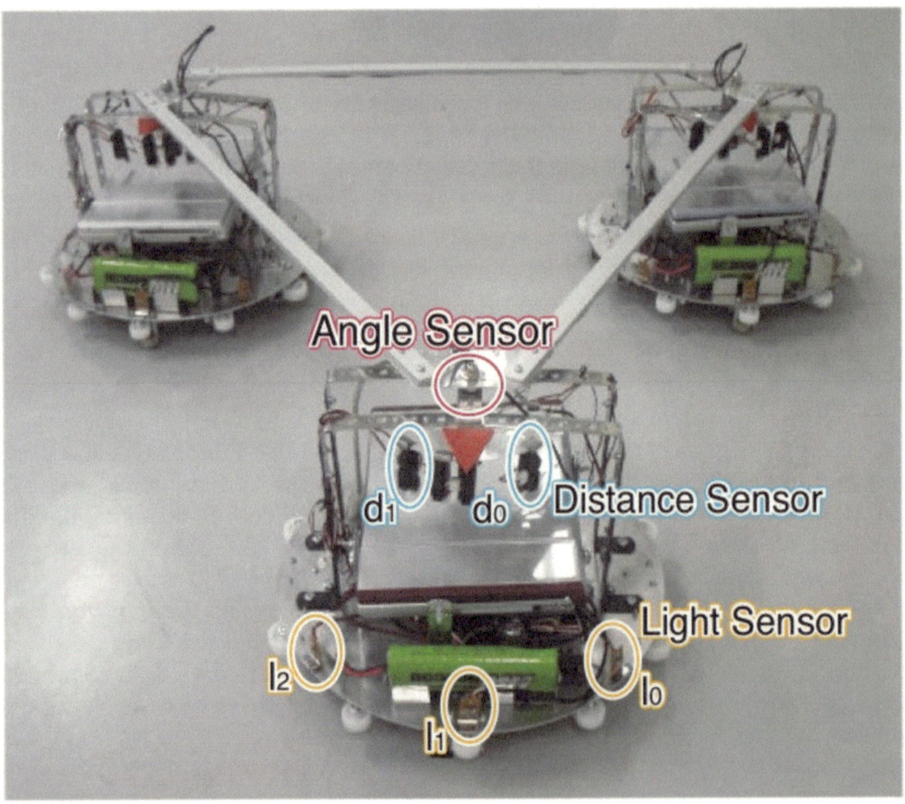

Fig. 1. Cooperative carrying problem, CCP

specifications. Each robot has two distance sensors d and three light sensors l. The greater d / l becomes, the nearer the distance to an obstacle or a light source. Each robot has two motors for rotating two omnidirectional wheels. A wheel provides powered drive in the direction it is pointing and passive coasting in an orthogonal direction at the same time.

The difficulties in this task can be summarized as follows:

- The robots have to cooperate with each other to move around.
- They begin with no predefined behavior rule sets or roles.
- They have no explicit communication functions.
- They cannot perceive the other robots through the distance sensors because the sensors do not have sufficient range.
- Each robot can perceive the goal (the location of the light source) only when the light is within the range of its light sensors.
- Passive coasting of the omnidirectional wheels brings a dynamic and uncertain state transition.

3. Reinforcement learning approach to CCP

3.1 Reinforcement learning in continuous space:

BRL: Overview

Our approach, called BRL, updates the classification only when such an update is required. A set of production rules is defined using Bayesian discrimination method, which is a well-known method of pattern classification (Dura & Hart, 1972). This method can assign an input, X, to the cluster, C_i, which has the largest posterior probability, max $\Pr(C_i|\boldsymbol{x})$. Here, $\Pr(C_i|\boldsymbol{x})$ indicates the probability calculated by Bayes' formula that a cluster, C_i, holds the observed input $\boldsymbol{x}$. Therefore, using this technique, a robot can select the most similar rule to the current sensory input. The learning procedure is overviewed as follows:

1. A robot perceives the current input data $\boldsymbol{x}$.
2. A robot selects the most similar rule from a rule set by using the Bayesian discrimination method. If a robot selects a rule, it executes the corresponding action $\boldsymbol{a}$. Otherwise, a robot executes an action randomly.
3. A robot is transferred to the next state and receives a reward r.
4. The utilities of all rules are updated according to r. The rules for which the utilities are below a certain threshold are removed.
5. The robot produces a new rule as the combination of the current input data and the executed action if a robot executed an action randomly. This executed rule is stored in the rule set.
6. Parameters of all the rules are updated by the interval estimation technique if a robot receives no penalty. Otherwise, a robot only updates the parameters of the selected rule.
7. Go to (1).

Rule Representation

The BRL operates on a set of rules R. A rule $rl \in R$ is defined as rl:=< v, u, $\boldsymbol{a}$, f, Σ, Φ>. In this expression, the state vector associated with rl is $\boldsymbol{v} = \{v_1,\dots,v_{nd}\}^{\mathrm{T}}$, where n_d is the number of inputs. The utility of rl is represented as u. The action vector is $\boldsymbol{a} = \{a_1,\dots,a_{na}\}^{\mathrm{T}}$, where n_a is the number of actuators. The prior probability is denoted as f. The covariance matrix is Σ = diag $\{\sigma_1,\dots,\sigma_{nd}\}$. The sample set associated with rl is $\Phi = \{\phi_1,\dots, \phi_{ns}\}^{\mathrm{T}}$, where n_s is the number of samples.

Action Selection

A rule in R is selected to minimize the risk of misclassification of the current input. The posterior probability $\Pr(C_i \mid \boldsymbol{x})$ is calculated as the risk of misclassification for each cluster; it is calculated by Bayes' Theorem:

$$\Pr(C_i \mid x) = \frac{\Pr(C_i)\Pr(x \mid C_i)}{\Pr(x)} \tag{1}$$

For finding the minimal risk, it is sufficient to calculate the posterior probability because all clusters have a common factor of $1/\Pr(\boldsymbol{x})$. The probability density function of the i-th rule's cluster is represented as the following.

$$\Pr(C_i \mid x) = \frac{1}{(2\pi)^{\frac{n_s}{2}} \mid \Sigma_i \mid^{\frac{1}{2}}} \cdot \exp\left\{\frac{-1}{2}(x - v_i)^{\mathrm{T}} \Sigma_i^{-1}(x - v_i)\right\} \tag{2}$$

The estimated value of g_i, the risk of misclassification of the input data $\boldsymbol{x}$ into the other clusters, is calculated as the following:

$$\begin{aligned} g_i &= -\log\{f_i \cdot \Pr(C_i \mid x)\} \\ &= \frac{1}{2}(x - v_i)^{\mathrm{T}} \Sigma_i^{-1}(x - v_i) - \log\left\{\frac{1}{(2\pi)^{\frac{n_s}{2}} \mid \Sigma_i \mid^{\frac{1}{2}}}\right\} - \log f_i \end{aligned} \tag{3}$$

After calculating g_i for all the rules, the winner rule, rl_w, is selected as that which has the minimal value of g_i. As mentioned in the learning procedure, the action in the rl_w is performed if g_i is lower than a threshold g_{th}. Otherwise, a random action is performed.

Temporal Credit Assignment

The respective utilities of the rules are updated using the following four strategies after the action is performed.

1. *Direct payoff distribution:* The direct payoff P is given to the winner rule. Two types of payoff are obtainable: reward (P>0) and punishment (P<0). The payoff is spread back along the sequence of the rules that triggered its actions with the discount rate γ.
2. *"Bucket brigade" like strategy:* The current winner rule, rl_w, hands over part of its utility Δu to the previous winner only when Δu is positive.
3. *Taxation:* A firing rule reduces its utility as $u_w \leftarrow (1 - c_f)\, u_w$.
4. *Evaporation:* All rules reduce their utilities at the evaporation rate $\eta < 1$ when the robot reaches the goal: $u_w \leftarrow \eta u_w$. A rule that has smaller utility than the threshold u_{min} is removed from the rule set R.

Updating Rule Set

The update phase is performed except when action by rl_w results in punishment. If a random action is taken (*i.e.* $g_w > g_{th}$), a new rule that is composed of the current sensory input, v_c, and the executed action, $\boldsymbol{a}_c$, is added to R. Parameters for the new rule are defined as follows.

$$v_c = \boldsymbol{x},\ \Sigma_c = \sigma_0^2\mathbf{I},\ \boldsymbol{a}_c = \boldsymbol{a}_w,\ u_c = u_0,\ f_c = f_0 \tag{4}$$

In those equations, σ_0, u_0 and f_0 are constants, **I** is a unit matrix. When the action in rl_w is performed as (*i.e.* $g_w \leq g_{th}$), all of its parameters are updated as follows. First, the sample set Φ_w is updated by adding the current sensory input to $\boldsymbol{x}$. Then, the sample mean $\boldsymbol{x} = \{x_1,..., x_{ns}\}^T$ and the sample variance $\mathbf{s}^2 = \{s_1^2,..., s_{ns}^2\}^T$ are estimated from the updated set Φ_w. The confidence intervals for X and s^2 are also updated. Subsequently, BRL determines whether any component of v and Σ is out of the range of the confidence intervals. If any component is outside of that range, the updates are conducted:

$$v_i \leftarrow v_i + \alpha(x_i - v_i) \tag{5}$$

$$\sigma_i^2 \leftarrow \sigma_i^2 + \alpha[s_i^2 - \sigma_i^2] \tag{6}$$

$$f_w \leftarrow f_w + \beta(1 - f_w) \tag{7}$$

where α and β are constants. For all other rules, the prior probabilities f_i are updated as follows:

$$f_i \leftarrow (1 - \beta)f_i \tag{8}$$

3.2 Reducing the dynamics in an environment

Related Work

To date, numerous reports that are related to the RL approach and that are applied to an MRS have been published. For instance, Tan (Tan, 1993), who examined the effects of sharing information, described that shared information is beneficial if it can be used efficiently. Asada et al. (Asada et al., 1999) and Ikenoue et al. (Ikenoue et al. 2002) proposed a vision-based RL method for acquiring cooperative behavior in a soccer-like game that includes two mobile robots: a shooter and a passer. To stabilize the learning process, Asada et al. introduced a method of global scheduling by limiting the number of learning agents to one and allowing the remaining agents to execute fixed policies that were acquired in the previous learning stage. Ikenoue et al. proposed a method of asynchronous policy renewal with one policy and one action value function. Elfwing et al. (Elfwing et al., 2004) added macro actions. Macro actions force an agent to execute the same primitive action for more than one time step to thereby stabilize learning and make action selection more predictable for other agents. Several studies have specifically addressed the internal model of other learning agents (Littman, 1994; Hu & Wellman, 1998; Nagayuki et al., 2000). In those models, agents learn through estimating others' actions, Q values, or policies.

To the best of our knowledge, no RL approaches have displayed autonomous specialization. Therefore, robots need well-designed states, actions, strategies, or roles for acquiring cooperative behavior. Achieving all of these goals simultaneously is a practical impossibility.

Our Approach

In this study, we adopt a mechanism for predicting the near-future state based on time-series sensory information. As related work, a memory-based method (Moore & Atkenson, 1993) and a decision-tree (Suzuki et al., 1999) have been proposed for dealing with non-Markovian characteristics in an MRS environment. However, the state space is expanded according to the length of the time series information; in the worst case, it is expanded indefinitely.

We consider that the state space expansion should be as little as possible.
Our research group has demonstrated that merely the nearest future state prediction is sufficient for stabilizing the dynamics in an RL space (Kawakami et al., 1999). In this study, although a continuous learning space is assumed, an identical approach is examined with a feed-forward neural network for predicting the average of the other robots' postures at the next time step. As shown in Fig. 2, BRL uses the output of the neural network as a sensory information input.

4. Extended BRL

4.1 Basic concept

We have some RL approaches that provide learning in continuous action spaces. An actor-critic algorithm built with function approximators has a continuous learning space and modifies actions adaptively (Doya, 2000; Peters & Schaal, 2008). This algorithm modifies policies based on TD-error at every time step. The REINFORCE algorithm theoretically also needs immediate reward (Williams, 1992). These approaches are not useful for tasks such as the navigation problem shown in Sec. 2, because the robot gets a reward only when it reaches the goal. BRL, however, proves to be robust against a delayed reward.
In the standard BRL, a robot performs a random search in its action space, and these random actions can produce unstable behavior. Therefore, reducing the chance of random actions may accelerate behavior acquisition and provide more robust behavior. Instead of performing a random action, BRL needs a function that determines action based on acquired knowledge.

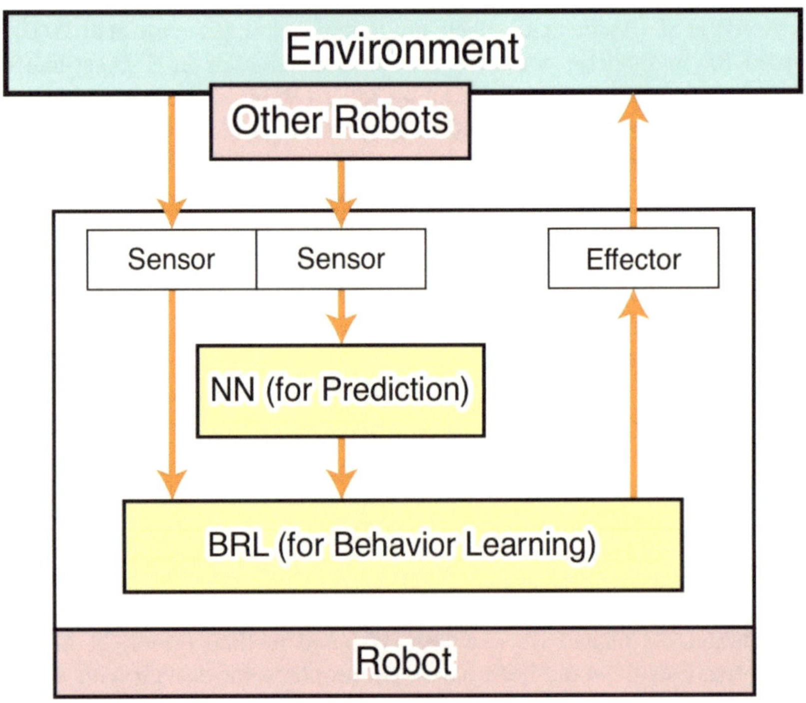

Fig. 2. Robot Controller

4.2 BRL with an adaptive action generator

To improve the search efficiency in a action space, in this paper, we introduce an extended BRL by modifying the learning procedure, Step (2) in Sec. 3. In this extension, instead of a random action, the robot performs a knowledge-based action when it encounters a new environment. To do this, we set a new threshold, P'_{th} ($< P_{th}$), and provide three cases for rule selection in Step (2) as follows:

- $g_w < g_{th}$: The robot selects the rule with g_w and executes its corresponding action $\boldsymbol{a}_w$.
- $g_{th} \leq g_w < g'_{th}$: The robot executes an action with parameters determined based on rl_w and other rules with misclassification risks within this range as follows:

$$a' = \sum_{l=1}^{n_r} \left(\frac{u_l}{\sum_{k=1}^{n_r} u_k} \cdot a_l \right) + N(0, \sigma), \tag{9}$$

  where n_r is the number of referred rules, and $N(0, \sigma)$ is a zero-centred Gaussian noise with variance σ. This action is regarded as an interpolation of previously-acquired knowledge.
- $g'_{th} \leq g_w$: The robot generates a random action.

In this rule selection, the first and third cases are the same as the standard BRL.

5. Experiments

5.1 Settings

Fig. 3 and 4 show the general views of the experimental environments for simulation and physical experiments, respectively. In the simulation runs, the field is a square surrounded by a wall. The physical robots are situated in a 3.6-meter-long and 2.4-meter-wide pathway. The task for the MRS is to move from the start to the goal (light source). All robots get a positive reward when one of them reaches the goal ($l_0 > thr_{goal} \vee l_1 > thr_{goal} \vee l_2 > thr_{goal}$). A robot gets a negative reward when it collides with a wall ($d_0 > thr_d \vee d_1 > thr_d$). We represent a unit of time as a *step*. A step is a sequence that allows the three robots to get their own input information, make decisions by themselves, and execute their actions independently. When the MRS reaches the goal, or when it cannot reach the goal within 200 steps in simulations and 100 steps in physical experiments, it is put back to the start. This time span is called an *episode*.

The settings of the robot controller are as follows.

Prediction Mechanism (NN)

The prediction mechanism attached is a three-layered feed-forward neural network that performs back propagation. The input of *i*-th robot is a short history of sensory information, $\boldsymbol{I}^i = \{\cos\theta_{t-2}, \sin\theta_{t-2}, \cos\psi^i_{t-2}, \sin\psi^i_{t-2}, \cos\theta_{t-1}, \sin\theta_{t-1}, \cos\psi^i_{t-1}, \sin\psi^i_{t-1}, \cos\theta_t, \sin\theta_t, \cos\psi^i_t, \sin\psi^i_t\}$, where $\psi^i_t = (\theta^j_t + \theta^k_t)/2$ ($i \neq j \neq k$). The output is a prediction of the posture of the other robots at the next time step $\boldsymbol{O}^i = \{ \cos\psi^i_{t+1}, \sin\psi^i_{t+1} \}$. The hidden layer has eight nodes.

Behavior Learning Mechanism (BRL)

The input is $\boldsymbol{x}^i = \{ \cos\theta_t, \sin\theta_t, \cos\psi^i_{t+1}, \sin\psi^i_{t+1}, d^i_0, d^i_1, l^i_0, l^i_1, l^i_2 \}$. The output is $\boldsymbol{a}^i = \{ m^i_{rud}, m^i_{th} \}$, where m^i_{rud} and m^i_{th} are the motor commands for the rudder and the throttle respectively. σ in Eq.(9) is 0.05. For the standard BRL, P_{th} = {0.012, 0.01}. For the extended BRL, P_{th} = 0.012 and P'_{th}= 0.01. The other parameters are shown in Table. 1. These values are the same as the recommended values in our journal (Yasuda et al., 2005).

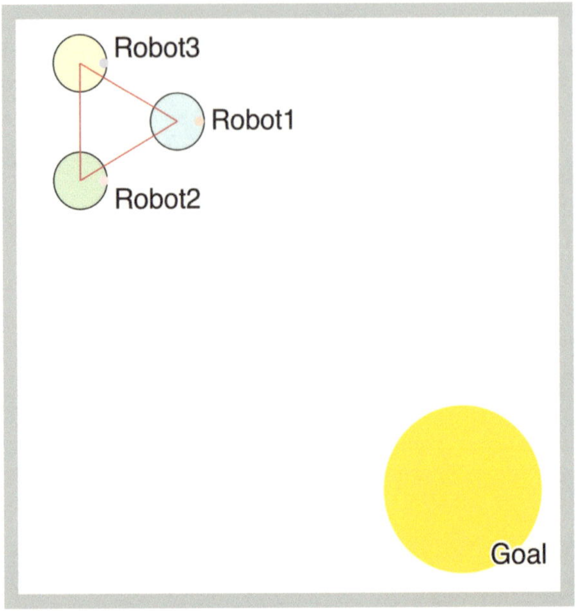

Fig. 3. Experimental environment (simulation)

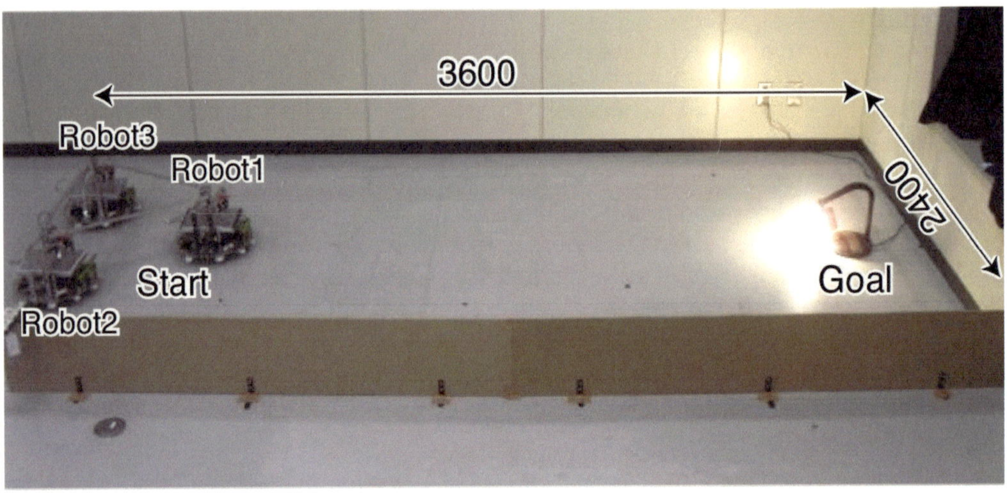

Fig. 4. Experimental environment (physical experiment)

5.2 Results: simulations

Fig. 5 shows the averages and the deviations of steps that the MRS takes by the end of each episode. In the early stages, the MRS requires a lot of trial and error and takes many steps to finish the episode. After such a trial and error process, the behavior of MRS becomes more stable and it takes fewer steps. An MRS with the standard BRL stably achieves the task within nearly constant steps after the 250th episode, and the extended BRL accomplishes this in 200 episodes. This means that, in terms of learning speed, the extended BRL outperforms the standard one.

Parameter		Value
n_{rl}^{max}	maximum size of the rules	100
n_s^{max}	maximum size of the samples	50
P	payoff (reward)	25.0
P	payoff (punishment)	-0.05u
u_0	initial utility	10.0
u_{min}	threshold for extinction	9.2
c_f	cost for an action	0.01
γ	distribution rate of utility	0.9
κ	utility spread rate	0.15
η	evaporation rate	0.98
f_0	initial prior probability	0.001
σ_0	initial variance	0.05
α	in eq (6)	0.001
β	in eqs (7) and (8)	0.0001

Table 1. BRL parameters

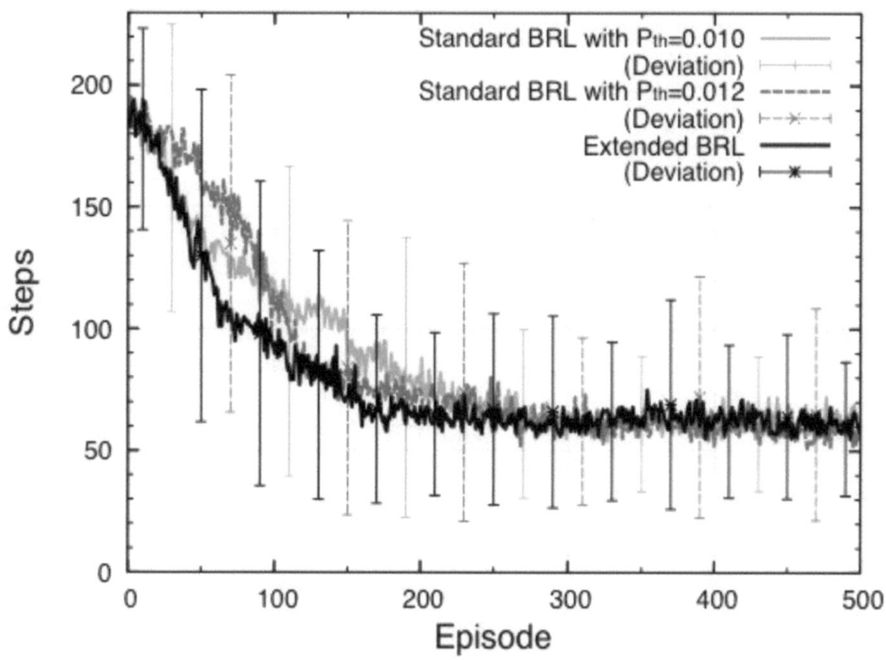

Fig. 5. Mean learning history for 50 simulations (three robots)

For the 50 independent runs, the MRS achieved different globally stable behavior as shown in Fig. 6. However, we found a common point that robots always achieved cooperative behavior by developing team play organised by a leader, a sub-leader and a follower. This implies that acquiring cooperative behavior always involved autonomous specialization. The extended BRL displayed higher adaptability, and yielded autonomous specialization faster than the standard BRL.

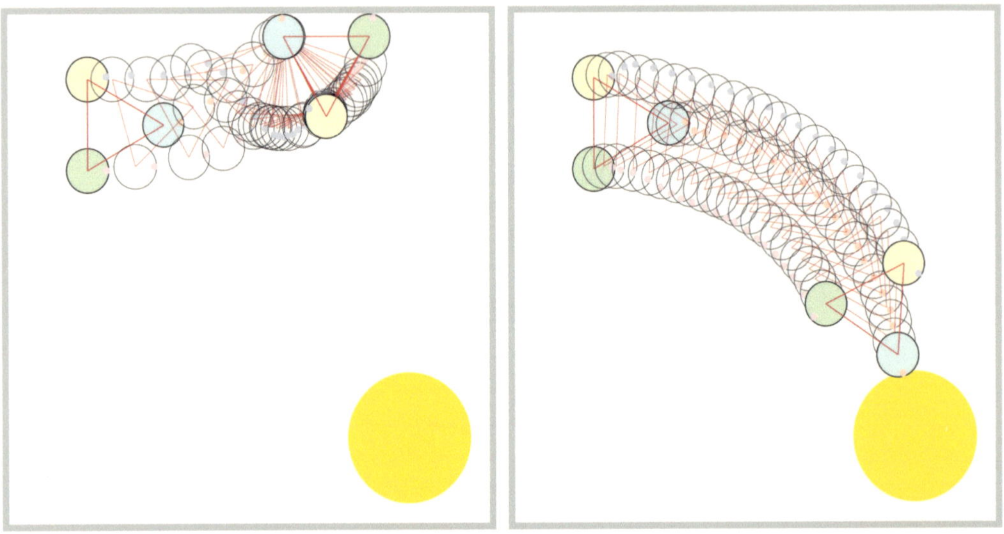

Fig. 6. Typical behavior in the early stage and acquired stable behavior (three robots)

Discussion

There is no significant difference in results in the learning performance of the BRLs for a three-robot CCP; therefore, we tested four- and five-robot CCP performance for more dynamic and complicated problems. The four robots use a square load, and the five robots have a pentagonal load. In these CCPs, ψ is the average of the angles between two neighbouring robots and the load. The other controller settings are the same as those for the three-robot CCP.

Figs. 7 and 8 show the average and the deviations of steps an MRS takes by the end of each episode. As the number of robots increases, we can find that the extended BRL provides increasingly better results than the standard BRL, although it requires more episodes before obtaining stable behavior as shown in Figs. 9 and 10. The extended BRL has a function for coordinating behavior as well as reducing the number of random actions that can result in unstable behavior. These results show that the extended BRL has a higher learning ability and is less dependent on the number of robots in the MRS. This implies that the extended BRL might have more scalability, which is one of the advantages of MRS over single-robot systems.

Although parameters that are more refined might provide better performance, parameter tuning is outside the scope, because BRL is designed for acquiring reasonable behavior as quickly as possible, rather than optimal behavior. In other words, the focal point of our MRS controller is not optimality but versatility. In fact, we obtain similar experimental results through experiments with an arm-type MRS similar to that in (Svinin et al., 2000) using the same parameter settings.

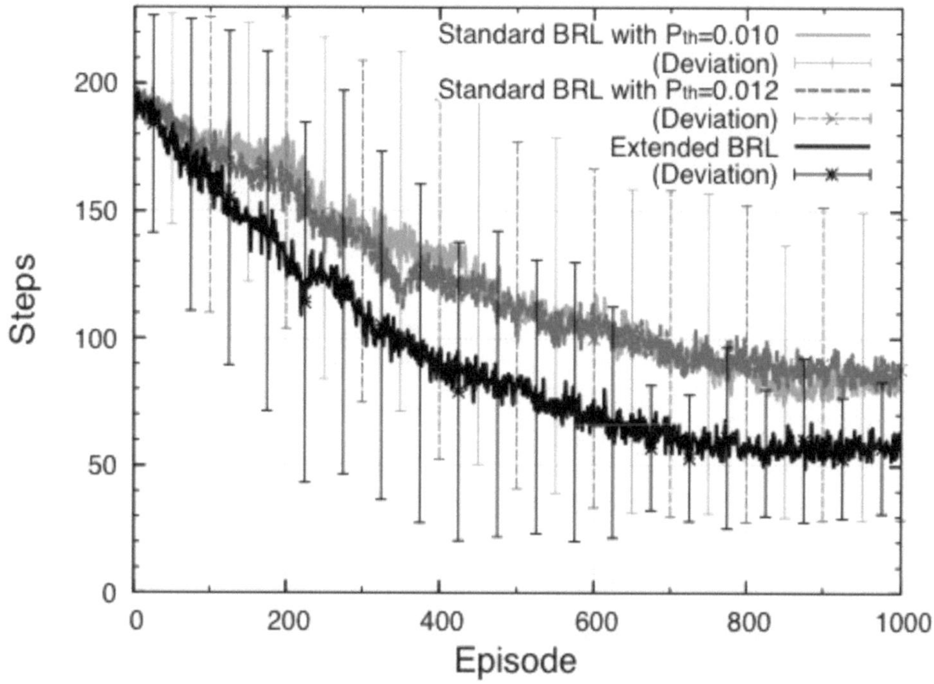

Fig. 7. Mean learning history for 50 simulations (four robots)

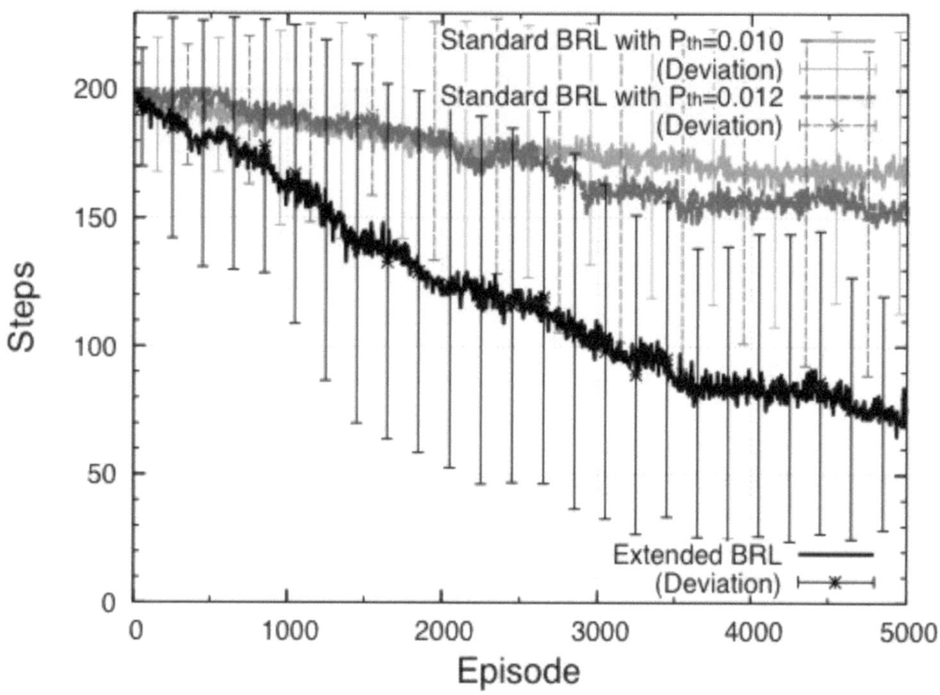

Fig. 8. Mean learning history for 50 simulations (five robots)

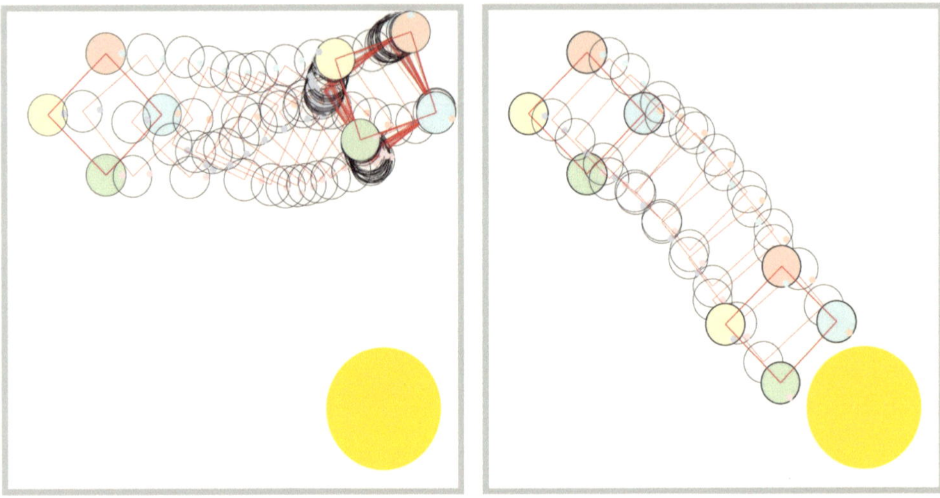

Fig. 9. Typical behavior in the early stage and acquired stable behavior (four robots)

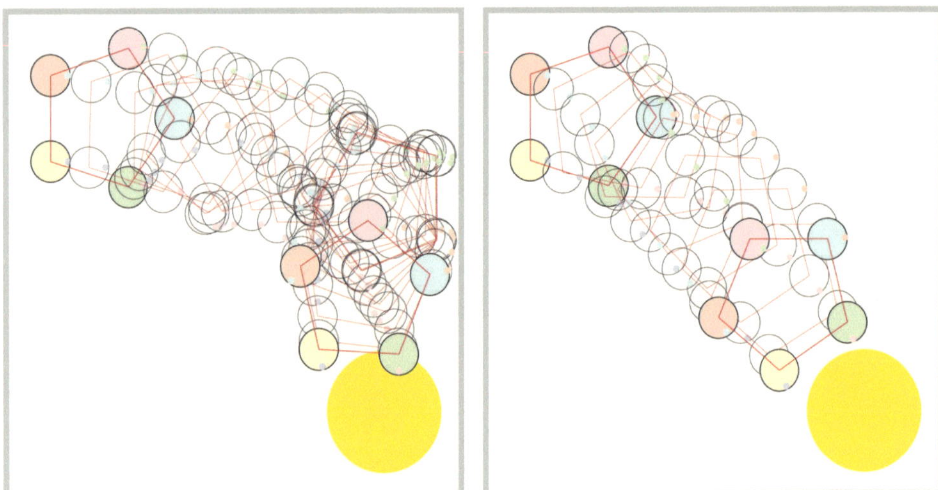

Fig. 10. Typical behavior in the early stage and acquired stable behavior (five robots)

5.3 Results: physical experiments

We conducted five independent experimental runs for each BRL. The standard BRL provided two successful results and the extended BRL provided four. Figs. 11 and 12 illustrate the best results of the physical experiments by the standard and the extende BRL, respectively. These figures illustrate the number of steps and punishments in each episode. Comparing these results shows that the extended BRL requires fewer episodes to learn behavior. The other successful results of the extended BRL show better performance than the best result of the standard BRL. The behavior of the extended BRL is also more stable than that of the standard, because the MRS with the standard BRL gets several punishments after learning goal-reaching behavior.

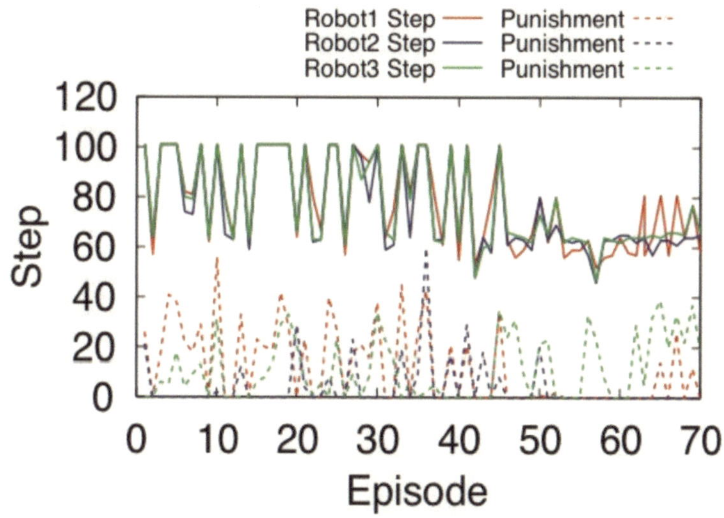

Fig. 11. Learning history: physical experiment (standard BRL)

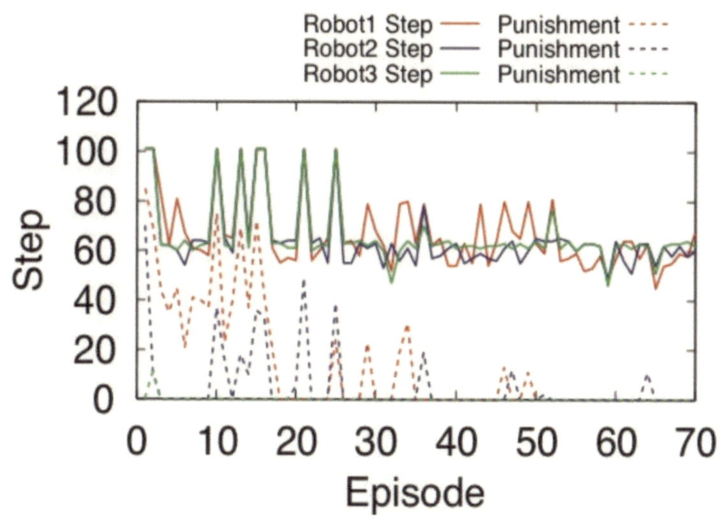

Fig. 12. Learning history: physical experiment (extended BRL)

Figs. 13 and 14 show examples of the behavior of the extended BRL. In the early stages, robots have no knowledge and function by trial and error. During this process, robots often collide with a wall and become immovable (Fig. 13). Then, some robots reach the goal and develop appropriate input-output mappings (Fig. 14). Observing the acquired behavior and investigating rule parameters, we found that the robots developed cooperative behavior, based on autonomous specialization.

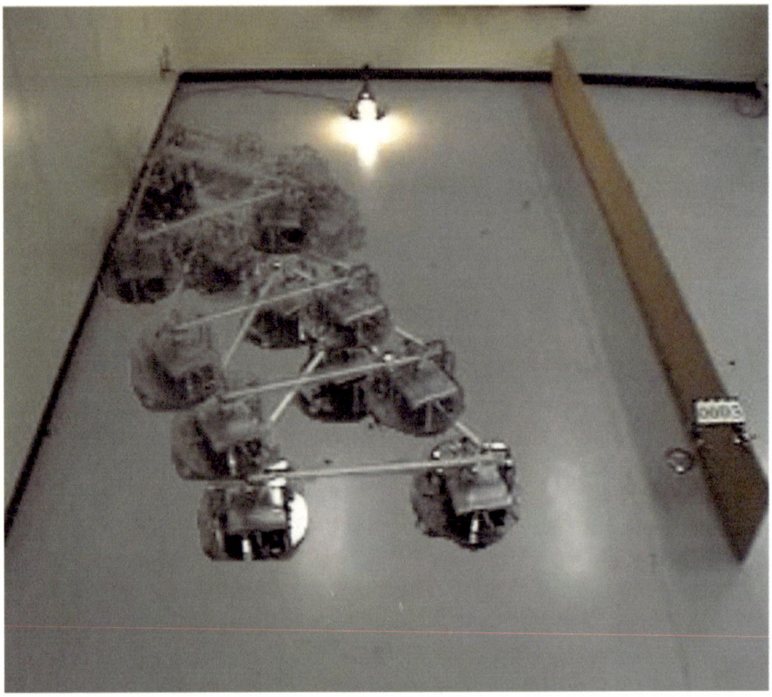

Fig. 13. An example of behavior in the early stage (extended BRL)

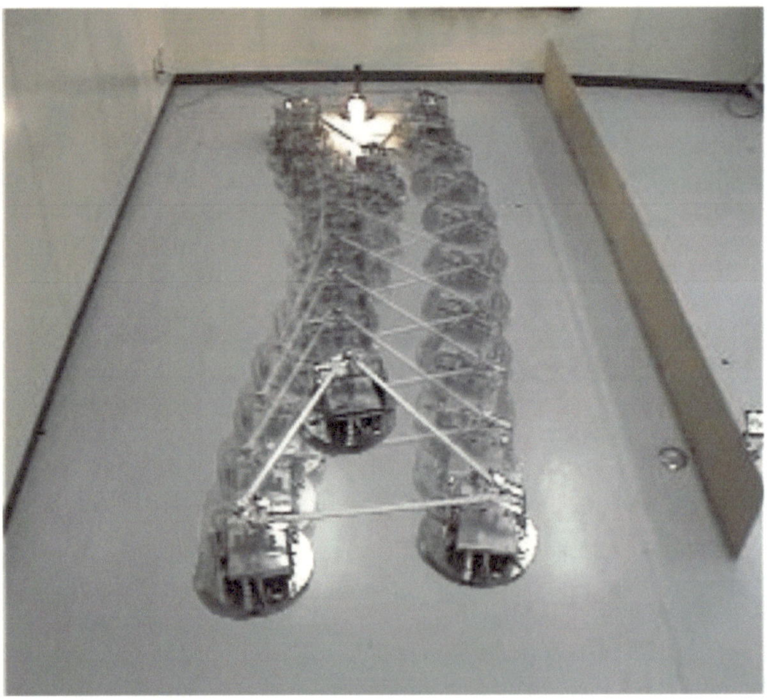

Fig. 14. An example of acquired behavior after successful learning (extended BRL)

6. Conclusions

We investigated the RL approach for the behavior acquisition of autonomous MRS. Our proposed RL technique, BRL, has a mechanism for autonomous segmentation of the continuous learning space, and proved effective for MRS through the emergence of autonomous specialization. For accelerated learning, we proposed an extension of BRL with a function to generate interpolated actions based on previously acquired rules. Results of the simulations and physical experiments showed that the MRS with an extended BRL did learn behavior faster than that with the standard BRL.

7. References

Stone, P. & Sutton, R.S. (2001). Scaling Reinforcement Learning toward RoboCup Soccer, *Proc. of the 18th International Conference on Machine Learning*, pp.537-544

Mondada, F., Guignard. A., Bonani, M., Floreano, D., Bar, D., & Lauria, M. (2003). SWARM-BOT: From Concept to Implementation, *Proc. of IEEE/RSJ International Conference on Intelligent Robot and Systems*, pp.1626-1631

Gerkey, B. & Mataric, M.J. (2002). Pusher-Watcher: An Approach to Fault-Tolerant Tightly Coupled Robot Coordination, *Proc. of IEEE International Conference on Robotics and Automation*, pp.464-469

Stone, P. & Veloso, M. (2000). Multiagent systems: survey from a machine learning perspective, *Autonomous Robots*, 8(3): pp. 345-383

Sutton R.S. & Barto, A.G. (1998). *Reinforcement Learning: An Introduction*, MIT Press

Duda, R.O. &Hart, P.E. (1972). *Pattern Classification and Scene Analysis*, Wiley-Interscience, N.Y.

Tan, M. (1993). Multi-Agent Reinforcement Learning: Independent vs. Cooperative Agents, *Proc. of the Tenth International Conference on Machine Learning*, pp.330-337

Asada, M., Uchibe, E. &Hosoda, K. (1999). Cooperative Behavior Acquisition for Mobile Robots in Dynamically Changing Real Worlds via Vision-Based Reinforcement Learning and Development, *Artificial Intelligence*, 110, pp.275-292

Ikenoue, S., Asada, M., & Hosoda, K. (2002). Cooperative Behavior Acquisition by Asynchronous Policy Renewal that Enables Simultaneous Learning in Multiagent Environment, *Proc. of IEEE/RSJ International Conference on Intelligent Robots and Systems*, pp.2728-2734

Elfwing, S., Uchibe, E., Doya, K. & Christensen, H.I. (2004). Multi-Agent Reinforcement Learning: Using Macro Actions to Learn a Mating Task", *Proc. of IEEE/RSJ International Conference on Intelligent Robots and Systems*, pp.3164-3169

Littman, M.L. (1994). Markov Games as a Framework for Multi-Agent Reinforcement Learning, *Proc. of Eleventh International Conference on Machine Learning*, pp.157-163

Hu, J. & Wellman, M.P. (1998). Multiagent Reinforcement Learning: Theoretical Framework and an Algorithm, Proc. of Fifteenth International Conference on Machine Learning, pp.242-250

Nagayuki, Y., Ishii, S. & Doya, K. (2000). Multi-Agent Reinforcement Learning: An Approach Based on the Other Agent's Internal Model, *Proc. of Fourth International Conference on Multi-Agent Systems*, pp.215-221

Moore, A.W. & Atkeson, C.G. (1993). Memory-Based Reinforcement Learning: Converging with Less Data and Less Real Time, *Machine Learning*, 13, pp.103-130

Suzuki, S., Tamura, T., & Asada, M. (1999). Learning from conceptual aliasing caused by direct teaching, *Proc. of the IEEE International Conference on Systems, Man, and Cybernetics*, pp.698-703

Kawakami, K., Ohkura, K., & Ueda, K. (1999) Adaptive Role Development in a Homogeneous Connected Robot Group, *Proc. of IEEE International Conference on Systems, Man and Cybernetics*, 3, pp. 251-256

Doya, K. (2000). Reinforcement Learning in Continuous Time and Space, *Neural Computation*, 12, 219-245

Peters, J. & Schaal, S. (2008). Natural actor critic, *Neurocomputing*, 71, 7-9, pp.1180-1190

Williams, R.J. (1992). Simple Statistical Gradient-Following Algorithms for Connectionist Reinforcement Learning, *Machine Learning*, 8, pp. 229-256

Yasuda, T. & Ohkura, K. (2005). Autonomous Role Assignment in Homogeneous Multi-Robot Systems. Journal of Robotics and Mechatronics, 17, 5, pp.596-604

Svinin, M.M., Kojima, F., Katada, Y., & Ueda, K. (2000). Initial Experiments on Reinforcement Learning Control of Cooperative Manipulations, *Proc. of IEEE/RSJ International Conference on Intelligent Robots and Systems*, pp.416-422

24

A Reinforcement Learning Technique with an Adaptive Action Generator for a Multi-Robot System

Toshiyuki Yasuda and Kazuhiro Ohkura
Hiroshima University
Japan

1. Introduction

A robust instance-based reinforcement learning (RL) approach for controlling autonomous multi-robot systems (MRS) is introduced in this chapter. Although RL has been proven to be an effective approach for behavior acquisition for an autonomous robot, it generates considerably sensitive results for the segmentation of the state and action spaces. This problem can yield severe results with increase in the complexity of the system. When segmentation is inappropriate, RL often fails. Even if RL obtains successful results, the achieved behavior might not be sufficiently robust. In conventional RL, human designers segment the state and action spaces by using implicit knowledge based on their personal experience, because there are no guidelines for segmenting the state and action spaces.

Two main approaches for solving the abovementioned problem and for learning in a continuous space have been discussed. One of the methods applies function-approximation techniques such as artificial neural networks to the Q-function. Sutton (Sutton, 1996) used CMAC and Morimoto and Doya (Morimoto & Doya, 2000) used Gaussian softmax basis functions for function approximation. Lin represented the Q-function by using multi-layer neural networks called Q-net (Lin, 1993). However, these techniques have the inherent difficulty that a human designer must properly design their neural networks before executing RL. The other method involves the adaptive segmentation of the continuous state space according to the robots' experiences. Asada et al. proposed a state clustering method based on the Mahalanobis distance (Asada et al., 1996). Takahashi et al. used the nearest-neighbor method (Takahashi et al., 1996). However, these methods generally require large learning costs for tasks such as the continuous update of data classifications every time new data arrives.

Our research group has proposed an instance-based RL method called the continuous space classifier generator (CSCG), which proves to be effective for behavior acquisition (Svinin et al., 2000). We have also developed a second instance-based RL method called Bayesian-discrimination-function-based reinforcement learning (BRL) (Yasuda et al., 2005). Our preliminary experiments proved that BRL, by means of adaptive segmentation of state and action spaces, exhibits better performance as compared to CSCG.

As we mentioned in the previous chapter, BRL has an extended form that accelerates the learning speed (Yasuda & Ohkura, 2010). Our focal point for the extension is the process of action searching. In a standard BRL, a robot performs a random action and stores an input-output pair as a new rule when it encounters a new situation. This random action sometimes produces one novel situation after another, which results in unstable behavior. In order to overcome this problem, we added a function that performs an action on the basis of acquired experiences. Our previous study demonstrated that MRSs that employ the extended BRL learn behaviors faster as compared to those that employ the standard BRL. In this chapter, we conduct further experiments in which a robot in an MRS is initialized after successful learning, and thus we investigate the robustness and relearning ability of the extended BRL.

The remainder of this chapter is organized as follows. In the next section, the target problem in this chapter and our concept of cooperative MRSs are introduced. Our design concept and the controller details are explained in Section 3. The results of our experiments are provided in Section 4. The conclusions are provided in Section 5.

2. Cooperative multi-robot systems

2.1 Cooperative transportation task

One of the challenging tasks in multi-robotics is object transportation. In this task, several robots move cooperatively to transport an object to a goal area in a static or dynamic environment. The object is sufficiently heavy and/or large so that no single robot can handle it.

Kosuge et al. adopted the feed back control method using the force sensors to achieve effective leading and following (Kosuge et al., 1997). Huntsberger et al. proposed a layered control architecture called CAMPOUT (Control Architecture for Multi-robot Planetary Outposts) that was tailored for extraterrestrial multi-robot systems (Huntsberger et al., 2004). CAMPOUT employs a leader-follower distributed control. Robots transport an object by lifting it in these approaches.

An alternative method of transporting object is pushing. Sen et al. used reinforcement learning techniques on a block pushing problem to show agents could learn coordinated behavior without any knowledge about each other (Sen et al., 1994). Kube and Zhang described a box-pushing task as a sequence of sub-tasks with separate controller designed for each step using finite state automata theory (Kube & Zhang, 1996). Here, 10 physical homogeneous robots achieved box-pushing without explicit communication. Parker proposed a behavior-based multi-robot architecture termed ALLIANCE that uses concepts of impatience/acquiescence to motivate behavior (Parker, 1998). ALLIANCE was validated in a pushing task by heterogeneous robots. Mataric et al. demonstrated box-pushing by two six-legged robots equipped with hand-coded sensing and behavior (Mataric et al., 1995). They demonstrated communication can produce performance improvements. They also developed that an auction-based task allocation system by using a publish/subscribe communication protocol (Gerkey et al., 2002). The system was validated in physical manipulation tasks by a watcher robot and two pusher robots. Wang and de Silva developed a controller comprised of reinforcement learning and genetic algorithms for object transportation by two robots (Wang & de Silva, 2008). A probabilistic arbitrator was used to select the winning output between reinforcement learning and genetic algorithms.

2.2 Autonomous specialization

MRSs aim to achieve *effective* cooperation by exploiting roles, behavior rules, or communication functions that are useful for the desired cooperation. However, it is practically impossible to give the hand-crafted factors for all possible situations that a robot will encounter. This means that the performance of conventional human scripted manipulation is restricted in a given condition.

One approach to this problem is giving an ability to acquire cooperative behavior through experience to each robot by autonomous role development and assignment. This provides an MRS with the potential for system-level robustness, i.e., *generalization capability*. We call this particular ability *autonomous specialization* in this chapter. Recently, based on evolutionary robotics (Harvey et al., 1997; Nolfi & Floreano, 2000), Quinn et al. (Quinn et al., 2002) and Baldassarre et al. (Baldassarre et al., 2003) applied artificial evolution to realize this ideal function. There has been also significant progress in the field of swarm robotics (Sahin & Spears, 2005). Here, a swarm is as a kind of MRSs where many simple physical autonomous robots perform a task without any global central controller. The collective behavior emerges due to interactions between simple autonomous robots and an environment. The concept of swarm robotics however does not include the behavior-learning mechanisms. To the best of our knowledge, generally effective behavior-learning mechanisms for swarm robotics have not been proposed yet.

From the view point of autonomous specialization, a homogeneous MRS for a task that require appropriate cooperation is explained in this chapter. Reinforcement learning with some extensions is adopted as a behavior-learning mechanism.

3. Approach

3.1 BRL: RL in continuous learning space

Our approach, called BRL, updates the classification only when such an update is required. A set of production rules is defined using Bayesian discrimination method, which is a well-known method of pattern classification (Dura & Hart, 1972). This method can assign an input, X, to the cluster, C_i, which has the largest posterior probability, max $\Pr(C_i \mid \boldsymbol{x})$. Here, $\Pr(C_i \mid \boldsymbol{x})$ indicates the probability calculated by Bayes' formula that a cluster, C_i, holds the observed input $\boldsymbol{x}$. Therefore, using this technique, a robot can select the most similar rule to the current sensory input. The learning procedure is overviewed as follows:

1. A robot perceives the current input data $\boldsymbol{x}$.
2. A robot selects the most similar rule from a rule set by using the Bayesian discrimination method. If a robot selects a rule, it executes the corresponding action $\boldsymbol{a}$. Otherwise, a robot executes an action randomly.
3. A robot is transferred to the next state and receives a reward r.
4. The utilities of all rules are updated according to r. The rules for which the utilities are below a certain threshold are removed.
5. The robot produces a new rule as the combination of the current input data and the executed action if a robot executed an action randomly. This executed rule is stored in the rule set.
6. Parameters of all the rules are updated by the interval estimation technique if a robot receives no penalty. Otherwise, a robot only updates the parameters of the selected rule.
7. Go to (1).

Action Selection and Rule Production

In BRL, a rule in the rule set is selected to minimize g_i, i.e. the risk of misclassification of the current input. We obtain g on the basis of the the posterior probability $\Pr(C_i \mid \boldsymbol{x})$. $\Pr(C_i \mid \boldsymbol{x})$ is calculated as an indicator of classification for each cluster by using Bayes' Theorem:

$$\Pr(C_i \mid x) = \frac{\Pr(C_i)\Pr(x \mid C_i)}{\Pr(x)} \tag{1}$$

A rule cluster of i-th rule, C_i, is represented by a v_i-centered Gaussian distribution with covariance Σ_i. Therefore, the probability density function of the i-th rule's cluster is represented by

$$\Pr(C_i \mid x) = \frac{1}{(2\pi)^{\frac{n_s}{2}} \mid \Sigma_i \mid^{\frac{1}{2}}} \cdot \exp\left\{\frac{-1}{2}(x - v_i)^{\mathrm{T}} \Sigma_i^{-1}(x - v_i)\right\} \tag{2}$$

A robot requires g_i instead of calculating Pr $(C_i \mid x)$, because no one can correctly estimate $\Pr(x)$ in Eq.(1) (the higher the value of $\Pr(C_i \mid x)$, the lower is the value of g_i). A robot must select a rule on the basis of only the numerator. The value of g_i is calculated as

$$\begin{aligned} g_i &= -\log\{f_i \cdot \Pr(C_i \mid x)\} \\ &= \frac{1}{2}(x - v_i)^{\mathrm{T}} \Sigma_i^{-1}(x - v_i) - \log\left\{\frac{1}{(2\pi)^{\frac{n_s}{2}} \mid \Sigma_i \mid^{\frac{1}{2}}}\right\} - \log f_i \end{aligned} \tag{3}$$

After calculating g_i for all the rules, the winner rule, rl_w, is selected as that which has the minimal value of g_i. As mentioned in the learning procedure, the action in the rl_w is performed if g_i is lower than a threshold g_{th} as shown in Fig. 1. Otherwise, a random action is performed.

3.2 Extended BRL with an adaptive action generator

Basic Concept

We have some RL approaches that provide learning in continuous action spaces. An actor-critic algorithm built with function approximators has a continuous learning space and

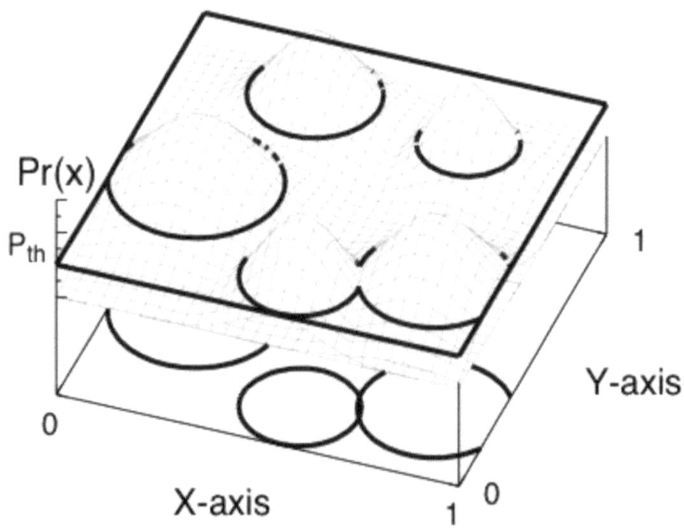

Fig. 1. State Space of the Standard BRL

modifies actions adaptively (Doya, 2000; Peters & Schaal, 2008). This algorithm modifies policies based on TD-error at every time step. Theoretically, the REINFORCE algorithm requires immediate rewards (Williams, 1992). These approaches are not useful for tasks such as transport tasks if a robot gets a reward only when the goal is achieved. However, BRL proves to be robust against a delayed reward.

In the standard BRL, a robot performs a random search in its action space; such random actions often resulted in instability in the global behavior of MRS in our preliminary experiments (Fig. 2). Therefore, reducing the chance of random actions may accelerate behavior acquisition and provide a more robust behavior. Instead of performing a random action, BRL requires a function that determines actions on the basis of acquired knowledge (Fig. 3).

Adaptation Based on Acquired Knowledge

To improve the search efficiency in a action space, in this paper, we introduce an extended BRL by modifying the learning procedure, Step (2) in the previous sub-section. In this extension, instead of a random action, the robot performs a knowledge-based action when it encounters a new environment. To do this, we set a new threshold, P'_{th} ($< P_{th}$) as shown in Fig. 4, and provide three cases for rule selection in Step (2) as follows:

- $g_w < g_{th}$: The robot selects the rule with g_w and executes its corresponding action $\boldsymbol{a}_w$.
- $g_{th} \leq g_w < g'_{th}$: The robot executes an action with parameters determined based on rl_w and other rules with misclassification risks within this range as follows:

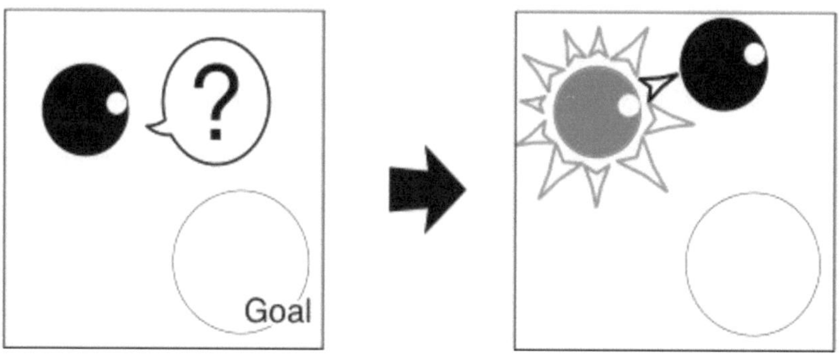

Fig. 2. BRL Robot that Executes a Random Action When it Encounters an Unknown Situation

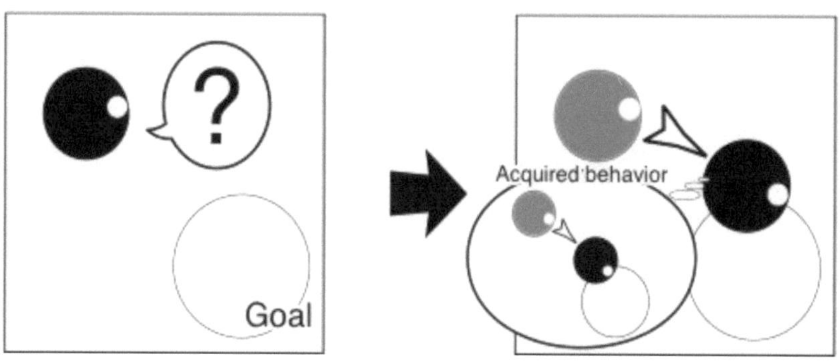

Fig. 3. Basic Idea of the Extended BRL; Generating an Action on the basis of Acquired Behavior

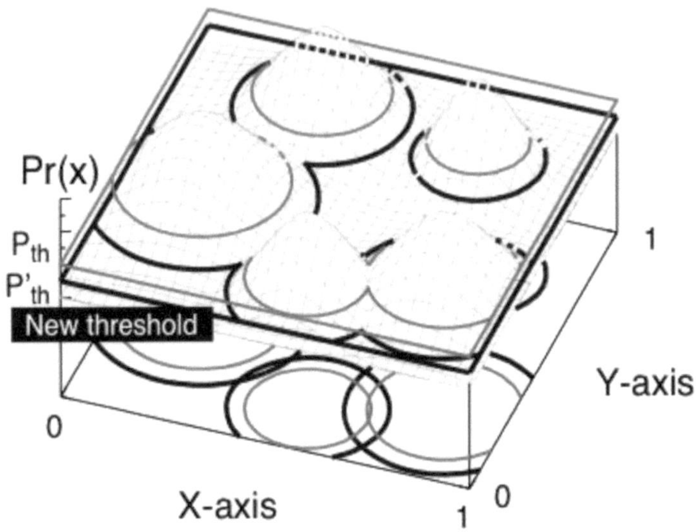

Fig. 4. State Space of the Extended BRL

$$a' = \sum_{l=1}^{n_r} \left(\frac{u_l}{\sum_{k=1}^{n_r} u_k} \cdot a_l \right) + N(0, \sigma), \tag{4}$$

where n_r is the number of referred rules, and $N(0, \sigma)$ is a zero-centred Gaussian noise with variance σ. This action is regarded as an interpolation of previously-acquired knowledge.

- $g'_{th} \leq g_w$: The robot generates a random action.

In this rule selection, the first and third cases are the same as the standard BRL.

4. Experiments

4.1 Problem settings

Our target problem is a simple MRS composed of three autonomous robots, as shown in Fig. 5. This problem is called the *cooperative carrying problem* (CCP), and involves requiring the MRS to carry a triangular board from the start to the goal. A robot is connected to the different corners of the load so that it can rotate freely. A potentiometer measures the angle between the load and the robot's direction θ. A robot can perceive the potentiometer measurements of the other robots, as well as its own. All three robots have the same specifications. Each robot has two distance sensors d and three light sensors l. The greater d / l becomes, the nearer the distance to an obstacle or a light source. Each robot has two motors for rotating two omnidirectional wheels (Fig. 6). A wheel provides powered drive in the direction it is pointing and passive coasting in an orthogonal direction at the same time.

The difficulties in this task can be summarized as follows:

- The robots have to cooperate with each other to move around.
- They begin with no predefined behavior rule sets or roles.
- They have no explicit communication functions.
- They cannot perceive the other robots through the distance sensors because the sensors do not have sufficient range.

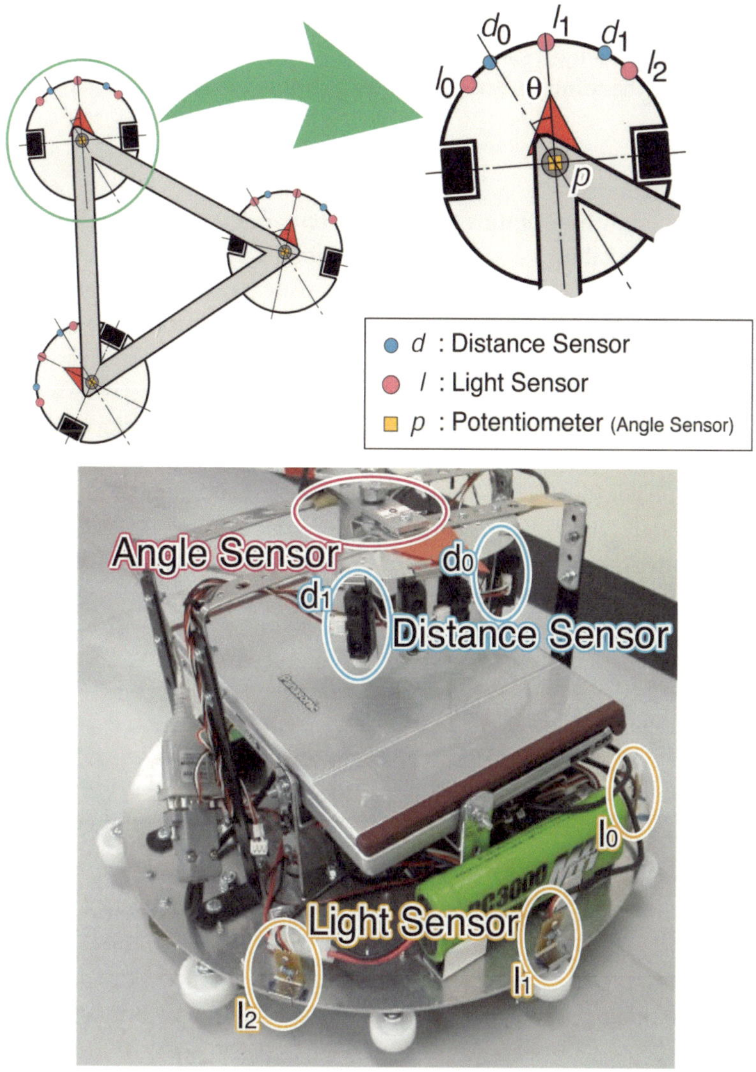

Fig. 5. Cooperative Carrying Task

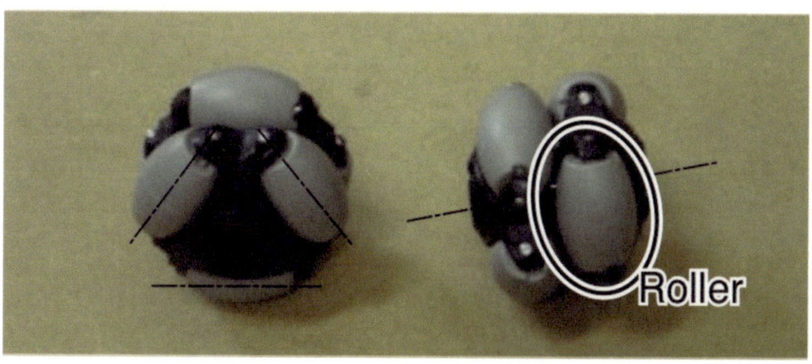

Fig. 6. Ominidirectional Wheel

- Each robot can perceive the goal (the location of the light source) only when the light is within the range of its light sensors.

Passive coasting of the omnidirectional wheels brings a dynamic and uncertain state transition.

4.2 Experimental settings

Fig. 7 shows the general views of the experimental environments for simulation and physical experiments. In the simulation runs, the field is a square surrounded by a wall. The physical robots are situated in a 3.6-meter-long and 2.4-meter-wide pathway. The task for the MRS is to move from the start to the goal (light source). All robots get a positive reward when one of them reaches the goal ($l_0 > thr_{goal} \vee l_1 > thr_{goal} \vee l_2 > thr_{goal}$). A robot gets a negative reward when it collides with a wall ($d_0 > thr_d \vee d_1 > thr_d$). We represent a unit of time as a *step*. A step is a sequence that allows the three robots to get their own input information, make decisions by themselves, and execute their actions independently. When the MRS reaches the goal, or when it cannot reach the goal within 200 steps in simulations and 100 steps in physical experiments, it is put back to the start. This time span is called an *episode*.

The robot controller comprises a prediction mechanism and abehavior learning algorithm. The settings for these two mechanisms are as follows.

Prediction Mechanism (NN)

The prediction mechanism attached is a three-layered feed-forward neural network that performs back propagation. The input of *i*-th robot is a short history of sensory information, $\boldsymbol{I}^i = \{\cos\theta_{t-2}, \sin\theta_{t-2}, \cos\psi^j_{t-2}, \sin\psi^j_{t-2}, \cos\theta_{t-1}, \sin\theta_{t-1}, \cos\psi^j_{t-1}, \sin\psi^j_{t-1}, \cos\theta_t, \sin\theta_t, \cos\psi^j_t, \sin\psi^j_t\}$, where $\psi^j_t = (\theta^j_t + \theta^k_t)/2$ ($i \neq j \neq k$). The output is a prediction of the posture of the other robots at the next time step $\boldsymbol{O}^i = \{\cos\psi^j_{t+1}, \sin\psi^j_{t+1}\}$. The hidden layer has eight nodes.

Behavior Learning Mechanism (BRL)

The input is $\boldsymbol{x}^i = \{\cos\theta_t, \sin\theta_t, \cos\psi^j_{t+1}, \sin\psi^j_{t+1}, d^i_0, d^i_1, l^i_0, l^i_1, l^i_2\}$. The output is $\boldsymbol{a}^i = \{m^i_{rud}, m^i_{th}\}$, where m^i_{rud} and m^i_{th} are the motor commands for the rudder and the throttle respectively. σ in Eq.(9) is 0.05. For the standard BRL, $P_{th} = \{0.012, 0.01\}$. For the extended BRL, $P_{th} = 0.012$ and $P'_{th} = 0.01$. The other parameter values are the same as the recommended values in our previous chapter.

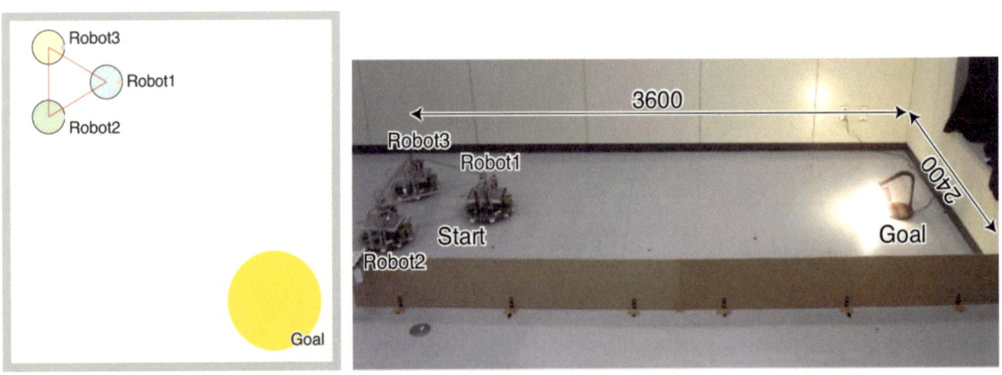

Fig. 7. Experimental Environment; (left) simulation, (right) physical experiment

We introduce a change in an environment by initializing one of the three robots. This may correspond to a situation in which a robot is replaced with a new one. Such changes occur when the MRS continuously reaches the goal for 100 consecutive episodes in the simulations and for 25 consecutive episodes in the physical experiments.

4.3 Results: simulations

We have investigated the improved performance of the extended BRL by means of three-/four-/five-robot CCP simulations in which robots must learn cooperative behavior from scratch in our previous work. In these experiments, we observed that robots always achieve cooperative behavior by developing team play organized by a leader, a sub-leader, and a follower. This implies that acquiring cooperative behavior always involves *autonomous specialization*.

The experiments in this section are conducted to observe the robustness of BRLs against a change in an environment. The MRS is disturbed in such a manner that one of the three robots is initialized immediately after a globally stable behavior is observed. Then, we count the number of episodes required for the MRS to relearn a new, stable behavior.

Mean performance for all 30 independent runs are illustrated in Fig. 8. The extended BRL, needs about twice as small number of the episodes as the standard BRL. On the other hand, Figs. 9-11 show the averages and the deviations in the number of episodes for the three roles of the initialized robot. For each roles, 10 independent runs are conducted. The difficulty in relearning is apparently different for each case. The most difficult cases are those in which the initialized robot is the leader of the team (Fig.9). If a leader robot is initialized, the robots require a large number of episodes to relearn a new, stable behavior; however, such cases show the largest difference among those employing BRLs. The extended BRL generates 50% better results as compared to the standard BRL. Since the acquired cooperative behavior possesses slight instability and the robots must coordinate their behaviors, particularly in a case in which a follower is initialized, the extended BRL provides a slightly worse result (Fig. 11). The improvement can be observed from the graphs for our proposed extensions. This implies that in terms of learning speed, the extended BRL outperforms the standard BRL.

4.4 Results: physical experiments

We conducted five independent experimental runs for each case employing the BRL. The standard BRL provided two successful results and theextended BRL provided four successful results from scratch (Yasuda & Ohkura, 2007).

Figs. 12-14 illustrate the learning results after one of the robots is initialized by using the best results in our preliminary experiments (Yasuda & Ohkura, 2007) for the standard and extended BRL. Before an environmental change, Robot1, Robot2, and Robot3 are the leader, sub-leader, and follower, respectively, in the experiments for both the BRLs. These figures illustrate the number of steps and punishments in each episode. Comparing these results shows that the extended BRL requires fewer episodes to newly develop a globally stable behavior. Similar to the simulation results, the case where a leader robot is initialized demonstrates the most significant difference. In this case, the standard BRL could not achieve a globally stable behavior and hence resulted in failure. In the other cases, the extended BRL required smaller number of episodes to relearn cooperative behavior. Further, the extended BRL is more stable than the standard BRL because the MRS with the standard BRL gets several punishments.

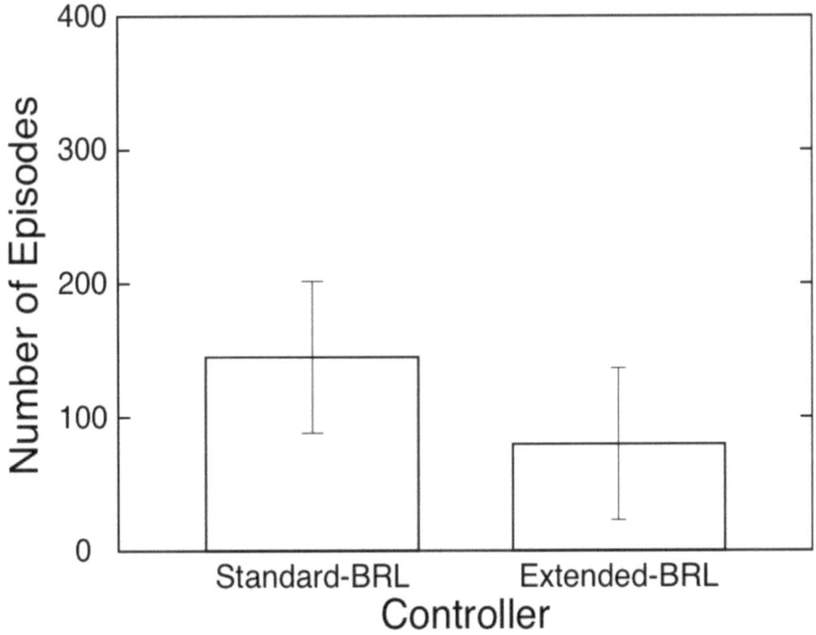

Fig. 8. Numbers of episodes required to relearn a behavior after an environmental change for all 30 independent runs.

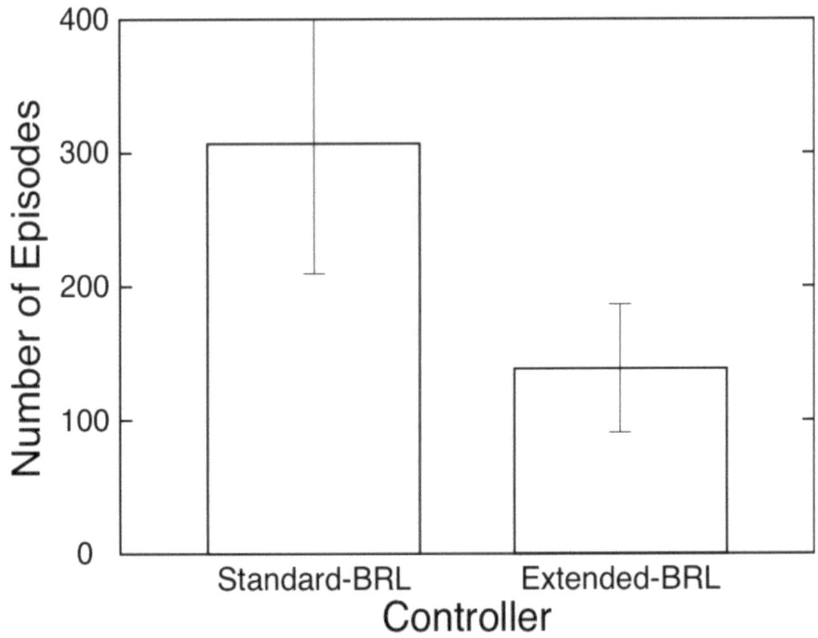

Fig. 9. Numbers of episodes required to relearn a behavior after an environmental change for 10 independent runs (a leader robot is initialized).

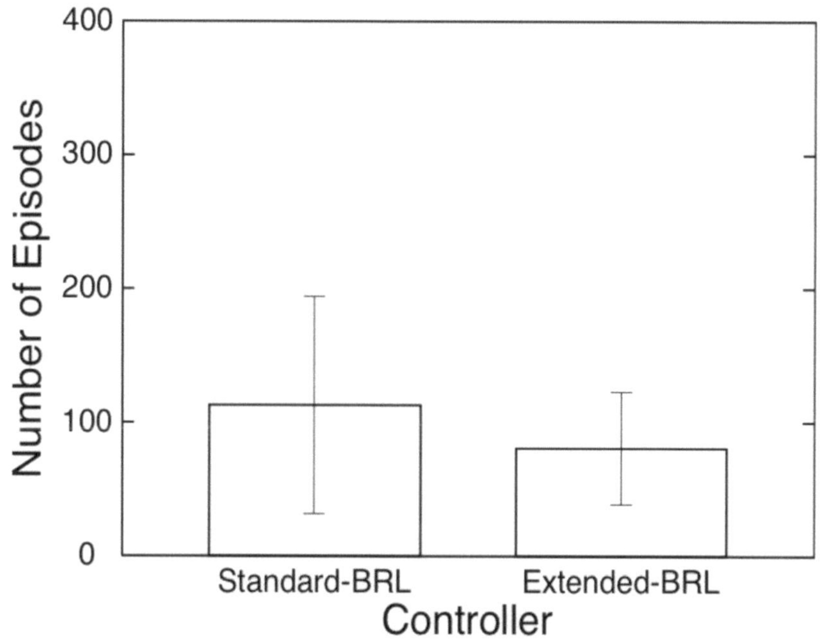

Fig. 10. Numbers of episodes required to relearn a behavior after an environmental change for 10 independent runs (a sub-leader robot is initialized).

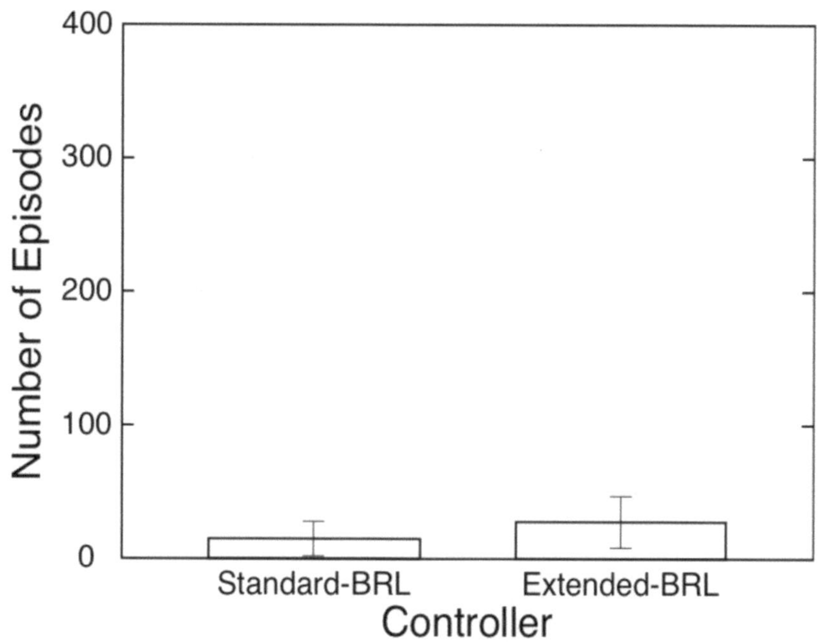

Fig. 11. Numbers of episodes required to relearn a behavior after an environmental change for 10 independent runs (a follower robot is initialized).

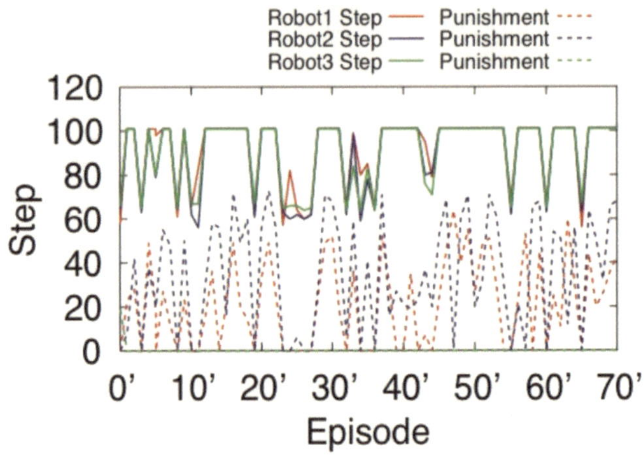

(a) Standard BRL

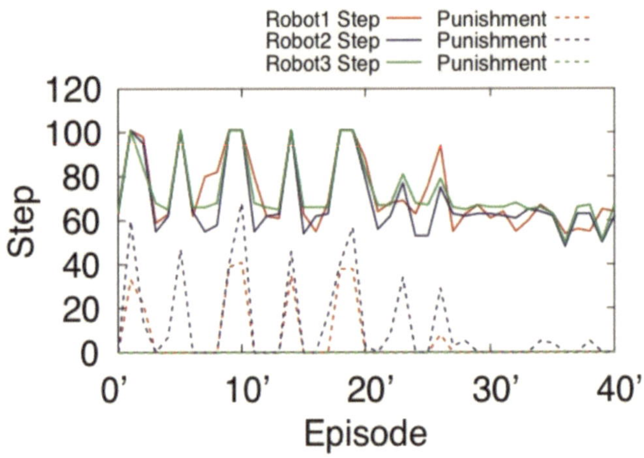

(b) Extended BRL

Fig. 12. Learning history after a leader is initialized

Fig. 15 shows examples of the stable behaviors acquired by the extended BRL, before and after Robot1 is initialized. Although an environmental change occurred for Robot2 and Robot3, the robots achieved a globally stable behavior similar to the behavior before initialization. The robots trooped right, left and right, and then reached the goal. By observing the rule parameters, we found that Robot1 learned to be another type of a leader and the other robots utilized some rules stored before initialization and the newly generated rules based on our extension.

Although parameters that are more refined might provide better performance, parameter tuning is outside the scope of this study because BRL is designed for acquiring a reasonable behavior as quickly as possible, rather than the optimal behavior. In other words, the focal point of our MRS controller is not optimality but versatility. In fact, we obtain similar experimental results through experiments with an arm-type MRS, similar to that in (Svinin et al., 2000), by using the same parameter settings.

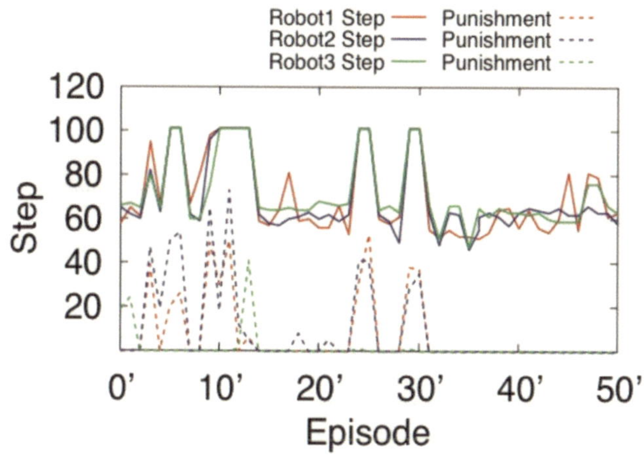

(a) Standard BRL

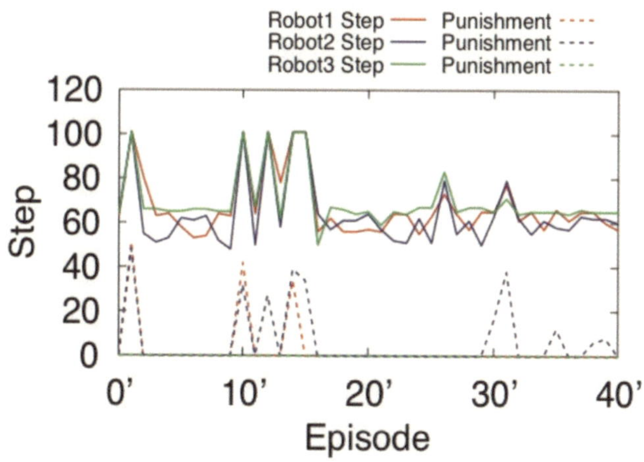

(b) Extended BRL

Fig. 13. Learning history after a sub-leader is initialized

5. Conclusion

We investigated an RL approach for the behavior acquisition of an autonomous MRS. Our proposed RL technique, BRL, has a mechanism for the autonomous segmentation of the continuous learning space, and it proves to be effective for an MRS through autonomous specialization. For improving the robustness of an MRS, we proposed an extension of BRL by adding a function to generate interpolated actions based on previously acquired rules.

The results of the simulations and physical experiments demonstrated that the MRS with the extended BRL relearns behaviors faster than that with the standard BRL, after an environmental change.

In the future, we plan to analyze the learning process in detail. We also plan to increase the number of sensors and adopt other expensive sensors such as an omnidirectional camera that will allow a robot to incorporate a variety of information, and thereby acquire more sophisticated cooperative behavior in more complex environments.

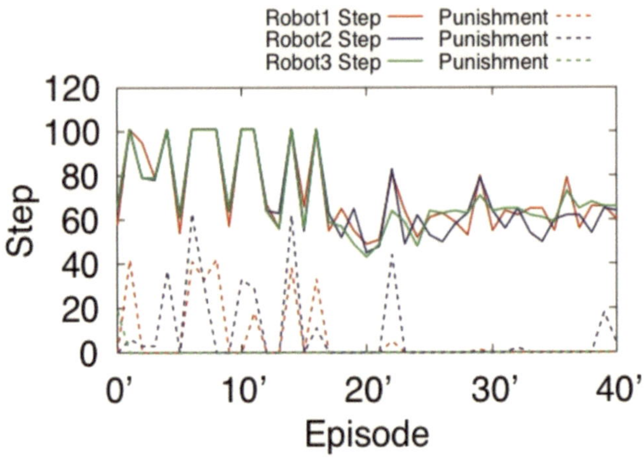

(a) Standard BRL

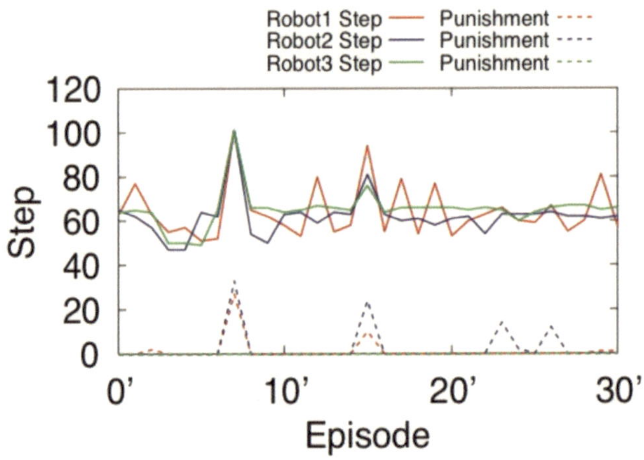

(b) Extended BRL

Fig. 14. Learning history after a follower is initialized

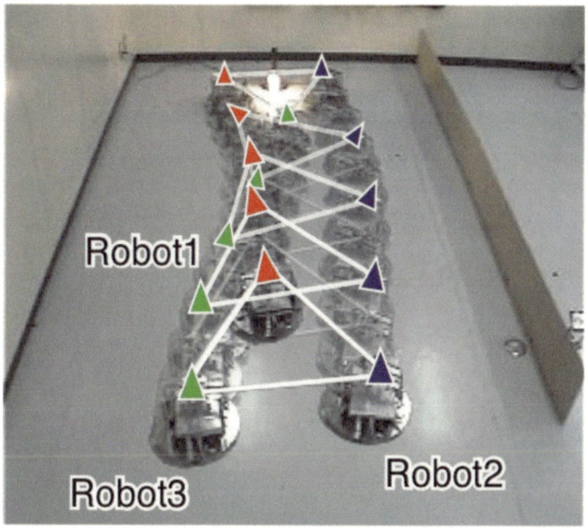

(a) Before Initializing Robot1

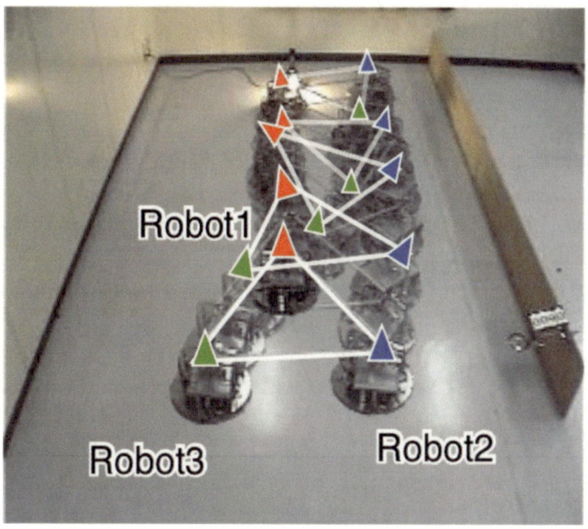

(b) After Successful Relearning

Fig. 15. Acquired Behavior by the Extended BRL

6. References

Sutton, R.S. (1996). Generalization in Reinforcement Learning: Successful Examples Using Sparse Coarse Coding. *Advances in Neural Information Processing Systems*, 8, pp. 1038-1044, MIT Press

Morimoto, J. & Doya, K. (2000). Acquisition of Stand-Up Behavior by a Real Robot using Hierarchical Reinforcement Learning for Motion Learning: Learning ``Stand Up'' Trajectories, *Proceedings of International Conference on Machine learning*, pp. 623-630

Lin, L.J. (1993). Scaling Up Reinforcement Learning for Robot Control, *Proceedings of the 10th International Conference on Machine Learning*, pp. 182-189

Asada, M., Noda, S. & Hosoda, K. (1996). Action-Based Sensor Space Categorization for Robot Learning, *Proceedings of IEEE/RSJ International Conference on Intelligent Robots and Systems*, pp. 1502-1509

Takahashi, Y., Asada, M., & Hosoda, K. (1996). Reasonable Performance in Less Learning Time by Real Robot Based on Incremental State Space Segmentation, *Proceedings of IEEE/RSJ International Conference on Intelligent Robots and Systems*, pp. 1518-1524

Svinin, M., Kojima, F., Katada, Y., and Ueda, K. (2000) Initial Experiments on Reinforcement Learning Control of Cooperative Manipulations, *Proceedings of IEEE/RSJ International Conference on Intelligent Robots and Systems*, pp. 416-422

Yasuda, T. and Ohkura, K. (2005) Autonomous Role Assignment in Homogeneous Multi-Robot Systems. Journal of Robotics and Mechatronics, 17, 5, pp. 596-604

Kosuge, K., Oosumi, T. & Chiba, K. (1997). Load Sharing of Decentralized-Controlled Multiple Mobile Robots Handling a Single Object, *Proceedings of the 1997 IEEE International Conference on Robotics and Automation*, pp.3373--3378

Hunstsburger, T.L., Trebi-Ollennu, A., Aghazarian, H. & Schenker, P.S. (2004). Distributed Control of Multi-Robot Systems Engaged in Tightly Coupled Tasks, *Autonomous Robotics*, 17, pp.79-92

Sen, I., Sekaran, M. & Hale, J. (1994). Learning to Coordinate without sharing information, *Proceedings of the Twelfth National Conference on Artificial Intelligence*, pp.426-431

Kube, C., Zhang, H. (1996) The use of perceptual cues in multi-robot box-pushing, *Proceedings of the 1996 IEEE International Conference on Robotics and Automation*, pp. 2085-2090

Parker, L. (1998) Alliance: an architecture for fault tolerant multirobot cooperation, *IEEE Transaction on Robotics and Automation*, 14, 2, pp.220-240

Mataric, M.J., Nilsson, M. & Simsarian, K. (1995). Cooperative Multi-Robot Box-Pushing, *Proceedings of International Conference on Intelligent Robots and Systems*, pp.556-561

Gerkey, B.P. & Mataric, M.J. (2002), Sold!: Auction methods for multi-robot coordination, *IEEE Transactions on Robotics and Automation, special issue on Advances in Multi-Robot Systems*, 18, 5, pp.758-786

Wang, Y. & de Silva, C.W. (2008). A machine-learning approach to multi-robot coordination, *Engineering Applications of Artificial Intelligence*, 21, pp.470-487

Harvey, I., Husbands, P., Cliff, D., Thompson, A., & Jakobi, N. (1997). Evolutionary Robotics: the Sussex Approach, *Robotics and Autonomous Systems*, 20, pp.205-224

Nolfi, S. & Floreano, D. (2000), Evolutionary Robotics, MIT Press

Quinn, M., Smith, L., Mayley, G. & Husbands, P. (2002). Evolving Team Behavior for Real Robots, *Proceedings of EPSRC/BBSRC International Workshop on Biologically-Inspired Robotics*, pp.217-224

Baldassarre, G, Nolfi, S. & Parisi, D. (2003), Evolution of collective behaviour in a team of physically linked robots, *Applications of Evolutionary Computing*, pp.581-592

Sahin, E. & Spears, W.M. (eds.) (2005). *Swarm Robotics*, LNCS 3342, Springer

Duda, R.O. &Hart, P.E. (1972). *Pattern Classification and Scene Analysis*, Wiley-Interscience, N.Y.

Doya, K. (2000). Reinforcement Learning in Continuous Time and Space, *Neural Computation*, 12, 219-245

Peters, J. & Schaal, S. (2008). Natural actor critic, *Neurocomputing*, 71, 7-9, pp.1180-1190

Williams, R.J. (1992). Simple Statistical Gradient-Following Algorithms for Connectionist Reinforcement Learning, *Machine Learning*, 8, pp. 229-256

Part 3

Modeling/Design

25

A Control Agent Architecture for Cooperative Robotic Tasks

Enrique González[1], Fernando De la Rosa[2], Alvaro Sebastián Miranda[1], Julián Angel[2] and Juan Sebastián Figueredo[1]
[1]*Pontificia Universidad Javeriana*
[2]*Universidad de los Andes*
Colombia

1. Introduction

In Robotics a multi-robot approach is mandatory when the performance, robustness needed or functionality cannot be fulfil with only one robot. In this context, cooperation is a very important aspect to be taken into account because it allows that a set of autonomous robots to achieve the task by adding their skills and resources. A natural approach to accomplish a multi-robot task is by decomposing it into cooperative actions, each one executed by a group of the robots where every robot takes a well defined role. To have an intentional cooperation level working with a Multi-Robot System (MRS), explicit mechanisms and control architectures have to be defined. In order to analyse or design a multi-robot system, it can be viewed as a Multi-Agent System (MAS) composed of physical agents. Many aspects have influence in the design of these complex systems in robotics: task decomposition, task allocation, role assignment, inter-agent interference and competition, agent cooperation, coordination, conflict resolution, negotiation and inter-agent communication.

Cooperation in the context of MAS has emerged to provide better use and performance of the agents and their capabilities. Following the approach proposed by Ferber (Ferber, 1999), cooperation can be seen as the conjunction of three components:

Collaboration: it is centered in task allocation. In order to assign which agent has to accomplish a specialized task, interaction protocols can be used. These dialogues allow to take into account not only the capabilities of the agents, but also their availability.

Coordination: it deals with the synchronization and planning issues. For this, it is necessary to determine at what time an agent should perform a task. The global team performance depends on providing good timing to each agent.

Conflict Resolution: usually agents share resources in a concurrent way, which easily can produce conflicts and even dead locks; thus it is necessary to incorporate mechanisms to prevent, avoid or solve conflicts.

Normally, these three components are obtained by the use of interaction protocols that define well structured dialogues between the cooperative agents. In just one sentence, cooperation is achieved by using collaboration, coordination and conflict resolution mechanisms supported by structured communications between agents.

In order to achieve cooperation, different architectures and techniques have been proposed, as shown in section 2. In this chapter, the Multi-Resolution Cooperation Control (MRCC) approach is presented, which proposes a control architecture for intentional cooperation distributing responsibilities on multiple levels by applying the multi-resolution principle. This principle implies a hierarchical decomposition of the MAS cooperative control, where each layer manages the decisions at different granularity and abstraction levels. The layers of decomposition are: the system level (the higher level) which determines the global strategy and affects the lower levels trying to cope with the team goals and to obtain a better global system performance. Then, the formation level, which aims to give structure to the team, defines zones and assigns structural roles. Next, the micro-social level creates agent societies charged of executing cooperative actions; each agent in a micro-society assumes one of the required cooperative roles. Finally, the agent level (the lower level) includes the individual control of agents acting to achieve role goals. The proposed control architecture is validated by means of a functional prototype developed to play robotic soccer. This experimental context is characterized by a high dynamic environment, with multiple situations and possible game actions where the robotic team cooperation and its performance are critical.

This chapter is organized in three parts described as follows. In the first part, some of the most relevant previous works about control architectures in multi-robot systems is presented; on one hand, the idea is to show how different approaches consider and combine the aspects involved in the design of multi-robot systems, and on the other hand, to show their application to specific problems. The next part, which includes several sections, explains our approach of control architecture MRCC for intentional robotics cooperation, the micro-social level is analyzed in detail; it also introduces the principal considerations of the validation of the approach in the context of robotic soccer. The chapter ends with the presentation of some results focused in the cooperative action mechanism and a final discussion.

2. Related work

In this section, a selection of outstanding works, which propose control architectures in mobile robotics, is presented. These works highlight the main problems and considerations in the design and implementation of these architectures in order to accomplish cooperative tasks with a group of autonomous mobile robots.

ACTRESS (acronym of ACTor-based Robot and Equipments Synthetic System) is a general architecture for robotics systems which are composed of multiple robots and other teams/components (Asama et al., 1989). Each element in the system is represented by means of the concept of *robotor* (robotic actor). A *robotor* has associated data, capabilities of processing, making decisions, movement, manipulation and message sending. A robotics system is composed of *robotors* with different structure and functionality which use a communication protocol in order to achieve the coordination among them. However, this work does not precise/define a mechanism for solving cooperative tasks. It presents experimental results of a system composed of two physical micromouses and one virtual micromouse executing an obstacle pushing task.

Mataric presents a multi-robot architecture based on (basic) behaviors (Mataric, 1995). The author affirms that, for each domain/task, it is possible to find a minimal set of behaviors which are necessary for achieving its objective. The combination of these behaviors in a robot (with concurrent execution or by exclusive selection) allows to generate more complex behaviors. Each behavior has associated a small set of activation rules (in some cases, only one rule). The collective behavior is the result of local interactions between robots when executing the basic behaviors in each robot. The main purpose is maximizing the synergy among multiple robots in order to achieve the objective of the task, minimizing the inter-agent interference. For the task, it is used a set of 20 mobile robots equipped with infrared and touch sensors, with a broadcast communication mechanism, limited to a distance. The behavior-based architecture was tested experimentally, evaluating the flocking collective behavior by concurrent execution of the basic behaviors avoidance, aggregation and wandering. Independently, the foraging collective behavior was evaluating by selective execution based on the basic behaviors avoidance, dispersion, following, homing, wandering, grasping and dropping.

ALLIANCE (Parker, 1998) is an architecture of distributed control and based on behaviors which supports fault tolerance, trusted and adaptable to small or medium team of heterogeneous robots (with uncertainty in their actions). The agents/robots have the capability of making decisions in an autonomous way according to the task to solving and the actions of the other robots. The architecture allows to solve missions composed of independent tasks in an adequate order in dynamic environments. Each agent has multiple sets of behaviors (competences), each set designed for solving a high level task. The activation of each set depends on the evaluation of a motivational behavior/model getting a positive numeric value. Whether this value is greater than a threshold value, the set of associated behaviors is activated. In this case, the rest of the sets of behaviors are inhibited. This evaluation is continually done in each robot and allows to adapt its behavior according to environmental changes, communication faults or fault(s) in any robot. The low level behaviours/abilities (e.g. collision avoidance) are always active. A robot periodically informs to the rest of robots, the task that it is solving/executing. The motivational behavior/model takes into account the sensorial information of the robot, the inter-robot communication, the inhibition of the other behaviors and the internal motivations. The internal motivations correspond to the *impatience* and to the *acquiescence*. The impatience allows a robot to deal with situations in which other robots fail. The acquiescence allows to deal with situations in which a robot decides to give up because it could not complete them in a determined time. In this way, a robot searches to participate in tasks where it could be more productive. The architecture does not provide an explicit coordination mechanism among the team members, in the case that it will be necessary. This architecture was tested experimentally in a hazardous waste cleanup mission with a team of 3 homogeneous robots, each robot equipped with infrared sensors, touch sensors and a gripper. For the mission, four independent tasks were identified: find-locations-methodical, find-locations-wander, move-spill(loc), and report-progress. In addition, the avoidance-obstacle is included as a low level behavior. There is a report of successful tests of the mission under different functioning conditions of the robots.

Simmons et al. propose a multi-robot system (MRS) for tasks where, an heterogeneous robot team and a mechanism of explicit coordination among the robots, are necessary in order to achieve the objective (Simmons et al., 2001)(Hershberger et al., 2002). The proposal is based on a layered architecture belonging to each robot. This architecture is composed of: (a) a superior planning layer for achieving high level objectives; (b) an executive intermediate layer for synchronizing agents, tasks sequences and monitoring the execution; and (c) a behavioral layer which is connected/related with sensors and actuators. There are connections between the layers robot's and also there are multi-robot connections. The architecture supports dynamic formations of the team. Each agent dynamically generates a task sub-tree. The decomposition of a task between the MRS, the time restrictions and the sub-objectives restrictions in the MRS are defined by using the Task Description Language (TDL). Each agent executes its role by using its task tree. A foreman agent facilitates the execution of cooperative actions constituting the group of robots and assigning their roles. Once the roles have been assigned, the foreman agent monitors and coordinates the robot actions during a cooperative action by means of explicit communication. The architecture was experimentally tested in the execution of a large-scale assembly, using 3 autonomous heterogeneous robots (a 6 DOF Robocrane, a roving eye and a 5 DOF mobile manipulator).

CS Freiburg (Weigel et al., 2002) is a winner team of middle-size robot league (F2000) of Robocup in 1998, 2000 and 2001 and, third place in 1999. The player's (local) perception is obtained by using a LRF Sick LMS200 sensor and a digital video camera. By using the LFR sensor information, each robot has the ability of auto-location in the play field. Additionally, filtering the information of the play field borders, it is possible to detect the other players in the LRF's field of view. The camera allows to detect the ball. Each robot resends its location estimation, the detection of other players and the estimation of the ball to a central processing node. This node uses a sensorial fusion model in order to obtain an estimation of players' location (distinguished by team) and of the ball (active elements). The team strategy is based on the concept of formation which defines positions of the robots in specific areas of the play field. The goalkeeper robot has a well-defined role. The three other robots have dynamic roles: a robot with the active role (related with a direct action on the ball), other has the strategic role (supports the defense) and the last one has the role of support (support to the defense or pass receiver). Each role additionally has a priority. The central node dynamically defines the formation and the roles assignment which communicates to the players. Each robot works in an autonomous way by using local information and information about the active elements (if it is available from the central node). The robot evaluates according to its role, the position most appropriated (preferred pose). Each robot does the path planning in order to achieve its appropriated position which is communicated to its team in order to avoid collisions. The solution of highest priority is the one of the active role. A player continually evaluates its estimation in order to carry out each possible role, taking into account its priority and communicates it to its team. In the case of possible conflicts for a role, there is a negotiation mechanism. Each player has an emergency strategy which assigns the preferred area in the play field, in case of the existence of communication problems; in this way, the team covers all the most important zones.

Lima and Custódio propose an architecture composed of 3 types of behaviors available in a team of robots: (a) organizational behaviors related to the roles in a team, (b) relational behaviors which depend on the relations in a team, and (c) individual behaviors related to individual abilities (Lima & Custódio, 2005). A behavior is based on the concept of operator. An operator implements actions which produce an individual or team behavior. A team behavior implies the establishment of commitments among participant agents; this establishment implies a communication process among the operators applied among the participant agents. The architecture considers 3 levels: (1) Organization team level where a strategy is defined for the team and its objective. A strategy consists in activating a subset of behaviors for each agent according its role. (2) Task coordination level where the sequence of appropriated behaviors is selected for executing the strategy and accomplishing the team objective. This level is in charge of the coordination of individual and team behaviors. The coordination uses mechanisms of event detection, validation of commitments and synchronization messages among the participants. (3) Behavior execution level where the basic/primitive functions are executed, taking into account the sensors and the actuators of each agent/robot. The implementation of a behavior is based on a finite state automaton, which is executed in one or multiple robots. An implementation of this architecture was done for robotic soccer where the pass is used as a team behavior. However, this architecture has limitations in tasks with strong coordination (coupling) among participants (e.g. team formations).

ETHNOS (acronym of Expert Tribe in a Hybrid Network Operating System) is a framework which allows to design distributed robotic applications (Sgorbissa, 2006). ETHNOS is composed of a set of services and characteristics that suit some tasks of mobile robotics: a distributed real-time operating system, a dedicated network communication protocol designed for both single robot and multi-robot systems; an object oriented Application Programming Interface (API) based on the C++ language. The control in ETHNOS is based on the concept of concurrent agents and experts in specific activities. These agents are process with real time restrictions and with priorities which can be distributed in a computer network. ETHNOS allows to execute these agents/robots with different conceptual solutions but they can integrate explicit communication and coordination capabilities, necessary in a multi-robot system. In the case of robotic soccer, the coordination in ETHNOS is based on the formation concept which has associated a set of roles, a role for each robot player which includes its activities/responsibilities and its position in the play field. The assignment of roles is dynamic according to the actual situation and the capabilities of each robot. This framework was tested by the Azzurra Robot Team composed of 5 different robot models, each one with its own control logics. This team won the second place in the middle-size robot league of Robocup (1999).

An architecture based on behaviors is the one proposed for a Multi-Robot System (MRS) in dynamic and unknown scenarios (Quiñonez et al., 2009). The behaviors are defined for a pursuit-evasion (surveillance) task between two robot teams. According to its objective, each team has associated a set of behaviors. These behaviors are represented in a state machine automaton. The autonomy and the decision making process of each robot are based on this automaton. The behaviors for each team are of two types: Navigation Behaviors (defining the movement possibilities) which consist of behaviors: searching robot, avoiding obstacle, unblocking, following robot and avoiding robot. The second type is the Communication Behaviors (by using an indirect mechanism based on traces/marks left by the "evaders") defined by the behaviors: releasing puck, following puck and avoiding puck. Each behavior is modeled by an artificial neural network and implemented by using evolutionary algorithms. There are some test results in simulation with 3 pursuers and 1 evader.

De la Rosa and Jimenez evaluate four multi-robots architectures based on behaviors with different levels of knowledge, coordination and organization of the robots (De la Rosa & Jimenez, 2009). Each of the architectures has a central process with information of the robots and of the scenario map. The relation of its behaviors is defined with a finite-state automaton which receives sensorial and central process information. A task of garbage collector is used in a scenario with obstacles, using 3 robots, each one equipped with 14 infrared sensors and a communication mechanism with the central process. The available behaviors in the robots are: search-garbage, recognize-detected-object (obstacle, garbage object or robot), avoid-obstacle and put-garbage-object. In the simplest architecture, each robot has the same logic of behaviors but does not know the existence of the others. The cooperative behavior is emergent. The central process is executed in order to carry each garbage found at the collecting site. In the second architecture, each robot has a different

logic of behaviors and keeps the function of the central process. In the third architecture, the robot logic with the best results with regard to the previous architecture is reused in each robot. The robots report their location to the central process and ask for the location of the other robots. This solution improves the task performance and minimizes the inter-robot interferences. In the last architecture, the logic of the robot is maintained with regard to the previous architecture. The central process uses a regular grid of the scenario map for registering the visit frequency of each cell. If there is not new found garbage during a time period, the central process guides the robots to the cells with minor visit frequency (i.e. with a high probability of finding garbage). Each of the architectures was tested in simulation for knowing its performance and obtaining a comparison between the architectures. However, the architectures do not provide an explicit cooperation mechanism.
As a summary of precedent works, the Table 1 shows a comparative analysis between some important concepts related to the multi-robot systems. The table includes the MRCC approach presented in this chapter.

	Layered Archit.	Coordination Mechanism	Inter-robot Communic.	Type of System	Role Concept	Formation Concept	Behavior-Based	Negotiation Mechanism
(Asama et al., 1989)			✓	Distributed				
(Mataric, 1995)			✓	Distributed			✓	
(Parker, 1998)			✓	Distributed			✓	
(Simmons et al., 2001)	✓	✓	✓	Distributed / Centralized	✓	✓		✓
(Weigel et al., 2002)		✓		Centralized	✓	✓	✓	✓
(Lima & Custódio, 2005)	✓	✓	✓	Centralized	✓	✓	✓	
(Sgorbissa, 2006)		✓	✓	Distributed	✓	✓		
(Quiñonez et al., 2009)				Distributed			✓	
(De la Rosa & Jimenez, 2009)				Distributed / Centralized			✓	
MRCC (Gonzalez et al., 2010)	✓	✓	✓	Distributed	✓	✓		✓

Table 1. Comparative analysis between related precedent works.

3. MRCC conceptual model

This section is focused on the application of the Multi-Resolution paradigm in the context of cooperative agents and robots. The conceptual model of Multi-Resolution Cooperation Control (MRCC) proposes that the cooperation control architecture be formed by a hierarchy of layers, each one dealing with goals of different level of abstraction. For the case of robotic soccer, the MRCC composed by 4 layers appears as a complete solution; in this section this specific model is explained; so far in the chapter, it will be shown how it is used in the context of cooperative soccer robots.

3.1 Resolution paradigm

One of the most interesting multi-resolution models was proposed by Meystel & Bathija in the context of path planning for mobile robots (Meystel & Bathija, 2002). In order to get to a goal point, a robot must evaluate a great number of possibilities when trying to choose the appropriate atomic movement action to execute; at this decision level the resulting search tree can be enormous. Besides, because of the information volume, the set of data obtained from the environment and the incertitude involved in its interpretation, a long term plan is almost impossible to follow without adjusting it; each a modification of the plan is required, a new complex planning procedure should be executed. Due these reasons, Meystel & Bathija proposed a hierarchical model that decomposed the problem space in different resolution layers in a recursive way. At higher levels a coarse grain is used, thus making the search tree smaller; the planning task becomes faster and produces a short path including the main milestones that the robot must traverse in order to get to the goal position. Once the coarse grain path has been determined, each step of this path is analyzed using a finer grain resolution; a new planning procedure is executed only in the area restricted by the precedent planning resolution level. In consequence, the low level search task is reduced; only the area defined by higher levels must be considered. In the lower level, the planning task is applied to the atomic movement action decision; however this task only considers the areas restricted by all the higher levels. Each layer acts as a parametric and limiting body for the next lower layer, in such a way, the problem passing each of the layers decreases its complexity. In conclusion, thanks to the use of resolution models a more efficient path planning execution is obtained. Moreover, the planning at low levels can wait until it is really required; thus, re-planning can be done at the adequate resolution level and in the right moment.

3.2 Resolution applied to agent cooperation

The MRCC aims to apply the paradigm of decomposing in resolution levels the control a set of robots performing a complex task. From a structural point of view, this problem has the same nature as path planning. At each moment, the control system selects the next action that each one of the robots must execute in order to achieve the goals of the team. At the low level, the search tree is too big; there are too many possible alternatives, not only for the variety of available actions, but also for the possible orders of concurrent execution of these actions.

MRCC use the multi-resolution paradigm by performing a goal based decomposition of the control system into layers. The higher layers are responsible for the general team's goals, while lower ones take into account more specific goals that usually involve a reduced number of agents. In the general model, the highest layer takes decisions analyzing the system as a whole; the lowest layer control each individual agent in order to comply with the goals and responsibilities of a specific role. The intermediate layers, restricted by higher ones, determine the roles that should be assigned to agents. Figure 1 illustrates this model.

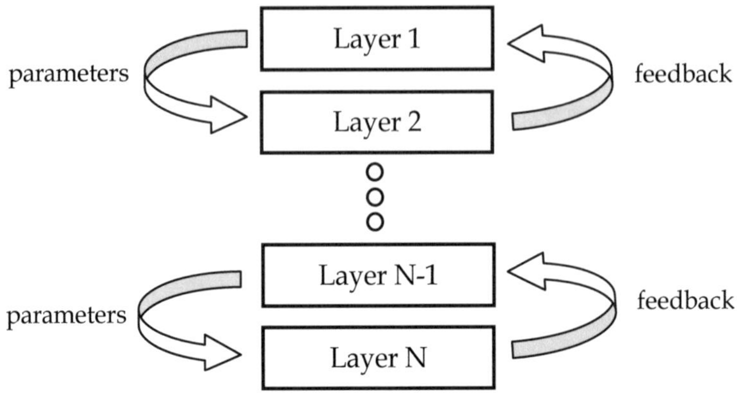

Fig. 1. General MRCC Model.

In other words, the concept of multi-resolution implies that a problem can be decomposed in different resolution layers without any restriction over the exact number of layers. In fact, the problem must be decomposed into as many layers as considered necessary, until reaching the desired atomic action decision level. MRCC being a result of the integration of cooperation control and multi-resolution gives the possibility to decompose the system into so many layers as wanted.

In general, there can be as many layers as desired. In practice, the system should have at least 3 layers; at least one intermediate must be present working as a bridge between the general goals and the individual ones. The relations inside the model refer to the connections and influences that exist between layers. The definition of parametric relation appears when a higher layer determines the guidelines that influences and restricts the way a lower layer takes decisions, so only a higher layer can do a parametric action over a lower layer. In the other side, the definition of feedback relation allows a lower layer to return information about the results obtained; this feedback can be used for the higher layer to make adjustments to its way of working. In a simple approach this relations can be established only by consecutive layers; however, in a more general approach, the parametric influences can be obtained from any of the higher layers, and the feedback information from any of the lower layers.

3.3 MRCC 4 layers

The first 3-layers MRCC proposed model includes the system, micro-social and agent layers. The intermediate micro-social layer aims to control the execution of cooperative actions between a reduced number of robots; at the agent level, robots assume cooperative roles assigned by the micro-social layer. This approach is suitable for robot teams where structuring the deployment of team members in the work space is not mandatory.

Afterward, a 4-layers MRCC model has been designed (Fig. 2), which tries to resolve the problems that were found in the precedent model. The first problem is the lack of overall structure of the MAS; the second one is that the agents don't get the robots to meet the required preconditions to start a cooperative action as often as desired. The function of the additional formation layer is to manage in a dynamic way structural roles associated to spatial regions. In order to solve the first problem, the control of team structure is incorporated into the system by raising negotiations between software agents, which represent spatial regions. Each region will control a reduced set of robots by assigning structural roles to them. If the goals linked to these roles are designated to make the robots achieve the preconditions of the cooperative actions, the second problem would be also solved.

Therefore, by including a formation layer between the micro-social and the system layers improves the detection of cooperation opportunities, and allows having a more detailed decomposition of the goals of the system. In this way, the resources are used in a more efficient way and the achievement of the team goals is assured to be more suitable. Moreover, the inclusion of this layer in the system, allows the use of the model in other application contexts. The control of more complex cooperative systems is now possible.

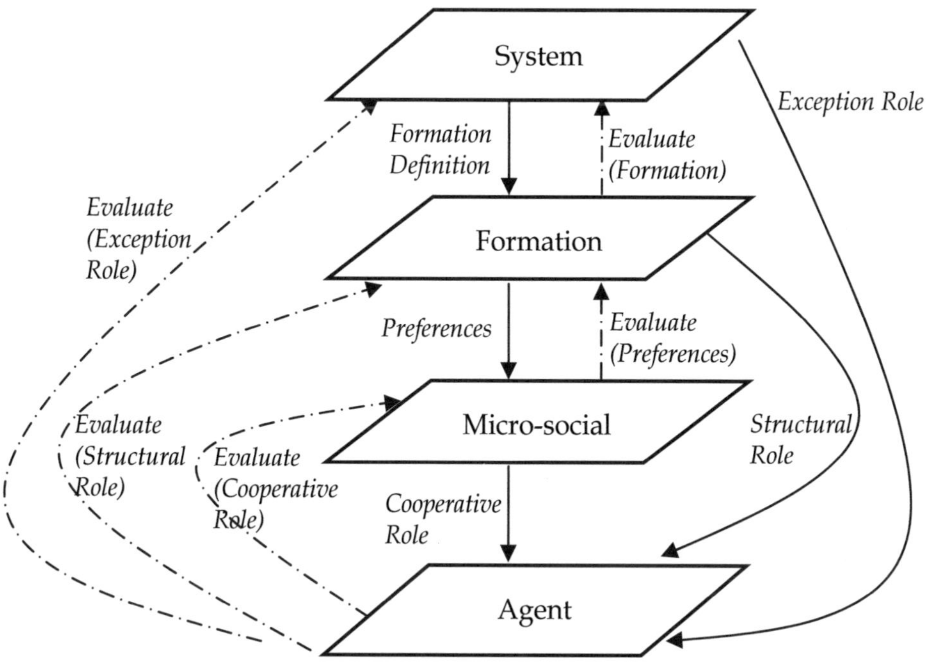

Fig. 2. The 4-layers MRCC Model.

A more precise description of each one of the layers in figure 2 is as follows:

System Layer: it is responsible for the decisions of the highest degree of abstraction (Gonzalez et al., 2007), where the global team goals are considered. It sends parametric influences to the lower layers; it is responsible for the general composition and the structure of the spatial regions of the formation level; it can also give more preference to some cooperative actions depending on the state of the team in relation to its goals. This layer can be seen as the coach of the team that takes strategic decisions.

Formation Layer: it manages a set of spatial regions in which actions take place; for each region a software agent aims to achieve a set of local goals. Robots can be assigned dynamically by a negotiation mechanism between regions as the goals of a region are not fulfilled. Inside a region, robots assume structural roles, which determine restrictions in the movement of a robot and also individual goals to accomplish. A structural role can be seen as a default role, assigned only when there are no opportunities to participate in a cooperative action.

Micro-social Layer: it is charged of the detection of opportunities to execute cooperative actions. Each robot includes a component that constantly monitors if the preconditions of any of the available cooperative actions are true. As an opportunity is detected, a negotiation protocol takes place between the concerned robots. If the negotiation succeeds, the action is executed by assigning cooperative roles to them.

Agent Layer: At this layer all the decisions taken at the formation and micro-social layers are transformed in actions performed by each individual agent according to the context and role assigned. Thus, each cooperative action of micro-social layer is carried out according to a number of roles that are assumed by an actor in a space of time. The appropriate role for an agent not only depends on the possibilities, the location and role it has assumed within the system (structuring), but also depends on the characteristics and abilities of the robot. If an agent is not involved in the execution of a cooperative action, its actions are guided by the structural role assigned by the formation level.

The concept of role is essential in the context of the MRCC. As explained by (Ch'ng & Padgham, 1998), a role can be defined as the set of responsibilities related to an agent, towards the objectives of the system. Moreover, according to what is mentioned in (Gonzalez et al., 2007), a role is a set of goals, skills and resources that enable an agent to perform specific tasks within the framework of collaborative action. Then, a role can be defined within the model as a set of elements (type of agent, responsibilities, skills, context and resources), assigned to an agent which allow to meet one or more individual goals aimed at supporting the objectives of the system. In the 4-layers model, there are 2 different kind of roles within the system, each associated with a specific aspect of the model, among them are:

Structural Role: According to Kendal defined in (Kendall, 1998) and (Kendall, 2000), and over the formation level, a structuring role is a set of defined characteristics to meet specific needs within a system. Among these needs are also found the interaction and fulfillment of responsibilities in the case of the formations level, compliance responsibilities in a spatial region.

Cooperative Role: The cooperative role is defined as the set of guidelines to be assigned to the agent to accomplish with part of the goals involved in the achievement of a cooperative action.

4. Dynamics of micro-societies

For the resolution and fulfillment of goals, it is possible to perform different actions on an individual basis, but depending on the context and situation, there may be events which need to be answered by one or more agents, in these situations the concept of cooperation is evident. In the MRCC model, the central mechanism to take advantage of these opportunities is the cooperative action execution control. In this section, a more detailed presentation of the procedure used in the micro-social level to manage cooperative actions is presented.

4.1 Cooperative actions

Cooperation in the context of multi-robot systems, and specifically when the multi-agent approach is used, refers to the interaction between players, performance improvement by making efficient use of team agent skills, and available resources (Weiss, 1999). This concept arises from the need to make a better use of the agents in a MAS and its features for both work together to meet their individual goals. In situations where cooperation occurs, each of the agents involved must perform a set of actions to be completed within a certain time. In other words, the actions must be conducted concurrently in order to reach the goals (Gonzalez et al., 2007). The construction of a cooperative action model is quite complex, and can become a really difficult scenario when put in a changing and dynamic environment; at each moment, the general context can change and the system as whole must react and make decisions. In such scenario, agents must perform actions, cooperate and share resources in a very dynamic and opportunistic fashion, what makes the problem too complex to be solved in an understandable, simple and effective way.

In the MRCC approach, the proposed solution is to decompose the problem in different perspectives or levels of resolution. In this way, the overall goals of the primary objective is handled at higher levels of abstraction, and a more specific level will be solved more detailed aspects of the problem. As seen in the precedent section, the micro-social layer plays an essential role to connect the decisions of the system level with the individual agent. In this connection, the central component is the cooperative action execution mechanism.

4.1.1 Cooperative action's components

A cooperative action aims to fulfill a particular goal by a reduced group of agents by detecting when a cooperation opportunity is present. Once an opportunity is detected, a cooperative strategy is applied, which involves specialized negotiation mechanisms and also action preemption control. In general, a cooperative action includes the following components:

Opportunity Detection: this mechanism is responsible for assessing whether there are conditions necessary for a cooperative action, either taking into account all possible agents involved or only those who are considered as actors of the cooperative action.

Synchronization protocol: This mechanism allows control of the negotiations that occur before the beginning of the execution of the cooperative action. It can be done in one direction or two directions, by, sending the request and response or simply by sending request and confidence in the acceptance and timing of the agents. It is possible to use more complex protocols as the 2PC (two phase commit protocol) proposed in the context of concurrent transactions.

Expropriation: This mechanism evaluates whether the actual action that an agent is performed should be preempted by another more promising cooperative action. There can be different ways of measure how promising an action is, and also different algorithms to make the expropriation decision.

Monitoring: It is the mechanism necessary for every agent to follow the evolution of action in relation with the changes in the environment, in order to detect the moment of completion of the action, whatever the outcome. The action must end properly in case of failure, but also when it succeeds.

Rating: it is a qualifier mechanism by which measures the performance of the implementation of the cooperative action. Its use is usually related to learning tasks and providing feedback to higher levels.

4.1.2 Phases of a cooperative action

A cooperative action requires an interaction that takes place between the involved parties to define the roles to be assumed for each on during its execution. Consequently, a cooperative action required to comply with certain steps that are presented below:

1. Opportunity detection to execute a cooperative action, comparing the current situation (context) with a state of ideal conditions required; in other words, a measure of the matching between the action preconditions and the actual environment is calculated. If the matching is high enough, the layer will try to establish a micro-society
2. Creation of a micro-society, through a negotiation protocol where agents are invited candidates to participate. The agent that has detected the opportunity send an invitation to the other agents that are candidates to have the roles associated to the cooperative action. While analyzing the invitation, action preemption can occur.
3. Once the micro-society has been created, the execution of the cooperative action is accomplished as each agent carries out its goals according to the role assigned in the context of the micro-society.
4. When an agent terminates its participation in a cooperative action, it must exit. Not all the agents should remain in the micro-society until the end of the action; if an agent has fulfilled the goals associated to his role, it is free to do other actions.
5. Completion of cooperative action as a whole when the action goal is met or when it is not possible to complete it. Thus, agents has to monitor the evolution of the action execution in order to detect any of possible end conditions. Once an end condition is reached, an end action protocol is performed between the agents that still participate in the micro-society.
6. Assessment results of the execution of the cooperative action are calculated that can be used for learning or feedback purposes.

Notice that these steps are performed in a distributed, concurrent and dynamic way, there is not a unique coordinator of the execution of an action. In fact, all agents must include components that work permanently to detect opportunities, reply to invitations, assume assigned cooperative roles and monitor action execution. This distributed approach is very well suited for multi-robot applications, where each cooperative agent is embodied in a robot.

These series of steps are carried out to define the beginning and end of a cooperative action. The way they are carried out cooperative actions is generally regulated by a higher level, which gives preference parameters and values to respond to the detected opportunities. In particular, these preferences are taken into account while applying the action preemption strategy.

4.2 Cooperative strategies

There are different negotiation protocols and preemption politics that can be used while following the different steps involved in the execution of a cooperative action. Therefore, there can be a great variety of mechanisms to create and end micro societies; a particular instance of such mechanism is called a "cooperation strategy". The team situation in relation to its goals and the environment are characteristics that should be taken into consideration when choosing or designing cooperation strategies. In brief, a cooperative strategy incorporates the management of the mechanisms required in the execution of a cooperative action. In order to have a clear conception of what a cooperative strategy is, three different ones are introduced in this section.

4.2.1 BCA – Bind-based Cooperative Actions

This strategy is inspired from the human relationships that lead to work as a team. The idea is that the partnerships between agents are built through the analysis of the previous results

obtained when trying to carry out a cooperative action. An action can end either by a failure or by success, and then strengthening or weakening the cooperation binds between the involved agents.
In the BCA strategy (Perez, 2008), the negotiation protocol is very simple, only the invitation message is sent from the agent that has detected the opportunity to the other candidates to participate. If the communication channel is not reliable, a reply message can be included in the protocol; the purpose of this second message is only to acknowledge the reception of the invitation, but not to inform if the invited agent would participate in the micro-society. The action preemption politic is based on an elitist approach. The "probability of success" of all possible actions is calculated, and then the action with the higher probability is selected. In order to make this calculation, not only the information available in the invited agent is taken into account, but also the information sent in the invitation. In this way, the preemption mechanism uses the perspective of both agents in relation with the candidate action.
This simple protocol is based in an optimistic approach; the agent that sends the invitation hopefully waits that the other agents will get into the cooperative action. The fact receiving an invitation makes an agent aware of an opportunity, provides information about the possible action and leads him to participate in the micro-society; however the agent is not forced to get in the action. A possible scenario occurs when the initiator agent starts acting applying its role, but other agents don't. In this case, the evolution of the action can derive in two alternatives. In the first, the individual actions of performed by the initiator agent lead to a situation that seen from the other agents make them obtain a better value for evaluation of the action, which finally makes them participate. The other alternative is that the initiator agent perceives that the calculated probability of success goes down, leading to the preemption of the action. In both cases, the system continues without any problem.

4.2.2 CCS - Commit Cooperation Strategy

The BCA strategy is fast and simple, but has two problems related to the commitment. First, the agents do not have commitment with the micro-societies; thus, agents can start to execute actions that don't contribute to real cooperative action, if not all the required agents participate the goals are not fulfilled. In the other hand, there is a lack of persistency in the execution of an action; if there are two or more actions that have a similar score in the probability of success, the agent can easily switch between them. It would be better if the agent try to stay longer doing the same action, having more commitment with the action that is currently executed.
The CCS strategy (Gonzalez et al., 2006) aims to solve these two problems. The protocol used is a 2PC (two-phase commit), as the one that is usually used in distributed transaction systems. This protocol produces a dialog that includes four messages between the initiator agent and each one of the invited agents. If the 2PC protocol succeeds, all agents have confirmed their participation, and also all know that the others have agreed. Thus, it is assured that all are going to assume the proposed role and start acting accordingly. Additionally, the action preemption politic gives more importance to the cooperative action that is currently executed. A threshold based mechanism is used to implement this politic.

4.2.3 CCNet - Cooperation Contract Net

The CCS strategy (Pachon & Ariza, 2007) solved the problems detected in the BCA one. However, the requirements to establish a micro-society are too high. Thus, it becomes harder to start cooperative actions; before starting, everything has to be almost perfect. As a result, when an action starts will probably lead to a success. Nevertheless, the problem is too few actions are initiated.

The CCNet strategy aims to obtain a balance between the former alternatives. In the negotiation step, the traditional and well known "contract net" protocol is used. As an agent receives an invitation, it evaluates a profit/cost function. It measures the profit obtained if the proposed action is selected and compares it against the cost of the preemption of the current action. All the invited agents send their values, and then the initiator agent makes a global evaluation. If this evaluation is good enough, the agent inform the others that the action will be executed; finally, the agents perform the as assigned role.

5. Validation model

The MRCC model is being validated through a practical implementation allowing setting up different experimental environments and protocols. In this section, the considerations to take into account in order to implement cooperative actions under the MRCC model are presented. Additionally, an introduction about how this model is being tested in the robot soccer domain is also included.

5.1 Elements of MRCC cooperative actions

In the precedent section the main concepts related to the execution of a cooperative action were introduced. The general internal architecture that is used to implement MRCC based agents was described in a precedent paper (Gonzalez et al., 2007). In this section, the key elements of this architecture that allow implementing in practice a cooperative action are explained.

<u>Matching:</u> It measures the similarity between the ideal and the current situations. A situation is defined from factors that should be considered in the cooperative action, such as object/agent positions, lengths, angles, etc.

<u>Mapping:</u> it makes all the decisions and calculations concerning the necessary actions that should be accomplished in order to reach the goal associated to a specific role.

<u>Parameters:</u> These are a set of input values that allow to specify the characteristics of matching and mapping functions. Thus, these parameters allow reusing the code of a cooperative action to achieve different goals.

<u>Role</u>: In practice a role is composed of mapping and matching functions and their parameters. The conjunction of these elements is used by the opportunistic detection mechanism and the decision component associated to a role (cooperative or structural).

<u>Cooperative action</u>: It aims to define the sets of roles that must participate to accomplish an action involved several agents; the role's matching is used to calculate if the cooperative action is suitable for the current situation or not.

Based on the above definitions, the process to create of a new cooperative action includes the following steps:

- To define the system's goal, so all the cooperative actions that will be defined in the system has to contribute to reach this goal.
- To define the action's objective which has to be aligned with the system's goal.
- To define all the roles needed in the action, as well as their matching and mapping functions.

- To identify how to calculate the cooperative action's matching, using the matching of each of its associated roles.
- To try, if possible, to reuse precedent roles, matching and mapping functions that already exist.

5.2 Study case: robotic soccer

Soccer is one of the most popular sports around the world; currently the FIFA has 208 members around the world (FIFA, 2010). Due to this popularity, intrinsic cooperation and dynamism of this sport did that different researchers get together and they created events where robotic soccer tournaments take place: Federation of International Robot-soccer Association (FIRA, 2010) and Robot World Cup Initiative (RoboCup, 2010). Each one of these events has its own rules and categories.

Despite the difference among categories, a team wishing to participate in any category, not only has to deal with the physical constrains of the category, but also with the inherent soccer problems as:

Limited communication: The existent communication systems are not reliable, due to some information could be lost when the transmission is occurring. Also the bandwidth of the channel is constraint by the technology, making that a message has to be cut in packets.

Best action vs. Time to find it: Often find the best action make necessary analyze all the possible actions and their consequence. However, this analysis requires time, but the soccer dynamism makes impossible to spend a lot of time to make a decision; for example, an action could be feasible in a certain moment but not later.

Limited resources: Two of the most important resources in soccer are the ball and the physical space. Robots occupy physical space, making sometimes impossible that a robot could receive the ball in an estimated position; especially when there are antagonist robots.

Cooperation: The speed that can reach the ball is always greater than the speed that any player could reach during the match. So, the team that takes advantage of this is the team that has most opportunity to win. This characteristic makes necessary to organize and coordinate the players.

5.3 Robot soccer examples

The success or failure of a robotic soccer team depends on the effectiveness and the appropriate number of cooperative actions that the system could perform according to the current match situation. The general goal of a robot soccer team is to win the game, which can be decomposed into two second level goals: score goals and avoid opponent goals. Therefore, it is important to create cooperative actions for both attacking and defending situations.

5.3.1 Building block

The goal of this cooperative action is to organize the robots in order to improve the team's defense. This is the base of other cooperative actions, because just changing the mapping and/or matching parameters, it is possible to obtain a variety of cooperative actions. In this action, the *neighborhood* defines the area where the agents will be taken into account to build the block; and the *figure* defines the geometric figure that the agents will be tried to form. This *neighborhood* is defined as a geometric figure, such as circle, rectangle, etc. The following concepts are used in this action:

Cardinality: the number of the agents that will be considered for the figure. If the number of the agents inside the neighborhood is less of this number, this action is not considered by the system. On the other hand, if the number is more than the cardinal number, this action will be penalized.
Triangular block is an example of this action, with the following characteristics(Fig. 3):
Neighborhood: the area where candidate agents are detected is rectangular.
Figure: the shape of the block formed by the agents is triangular.
Cardinality: requires 3 agents.
Number of roles: 3 instances of only one role is used, it knows how to go to the assigned point of the figure.
Mapping parameter: only one parameter is needed representing the ideal designed position for the roles, which can dynamically be changed by the system.
Role mapping: It aims to reach the point defined in the mapping parameter.
Role matching: The ideal situation is that each agent is over the desired position but not all the times happen this. Thus the Gaussian function is used to calculate the probability that an agent go to the desire position. The input for this function is the current position of the agent and the expected value of the Gaussian function is the ideal position where the agent is supposed to go, the variance is established by the programmer.
Matching parameters: These parameters are agent's positions P1, P2 and P3, the neighborhood area, the cardinality, the expected value and the variance.
Action matching: Initially, an agent calculates the probability to be in the desired position P1 (figure 3); if the probability is higher than a threshold then the agent gets all the teammates being in the neighborhood and estimates which agent is the best for each position. Once the best agents are established, then all probabilities are averaged to consolidate one action success probability.

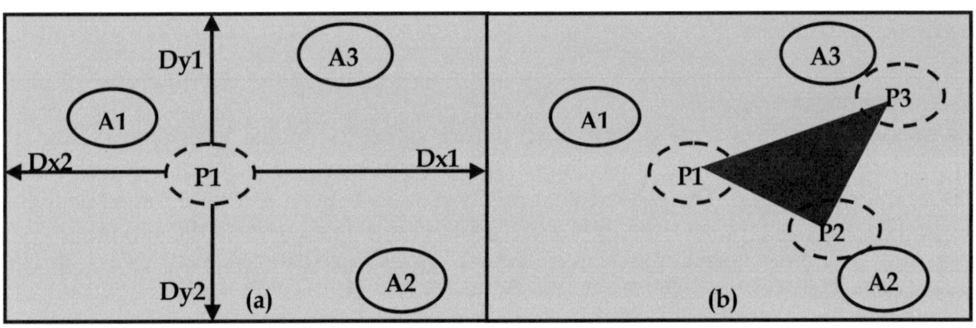

Fig. 3. Triangular block action. The point P1 is given in global coordinates, while points P2, P3, and the neighborhood are given as vectors from P1. A1, A2 and A3 are agents. a) The rectangular neighborhood definition, distances have not been equals. b) The points of the block which do no have to be in the neighborhood.

In the figure 3, it could be seen the concepts and definitions used for this action. Figure 4 shows the simulated results obtained for this action. It could be possible to change the role's mapping to obtain a block that follows the ball position, as in figure 5, where the idea is to take away from the ball but trying to maintain the triangular formation.

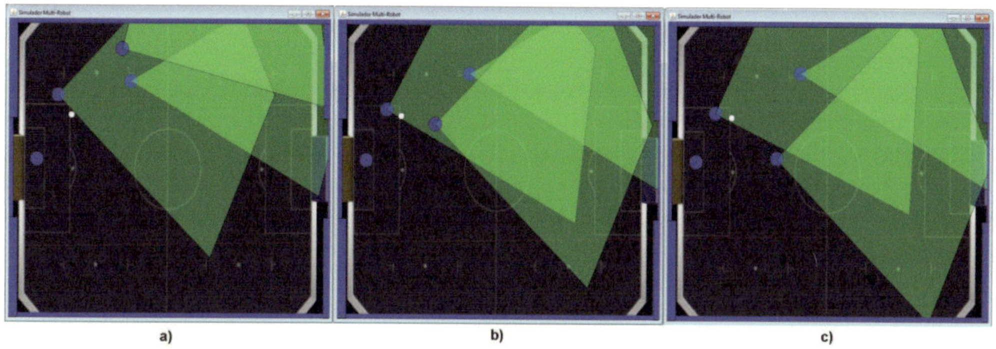

Fig. 4. Triangular block example. The blue spheres represent the robots, and the green area represents their vision area. a) The initial position of robots, b) how robots try to go to their position, and c) the final position.

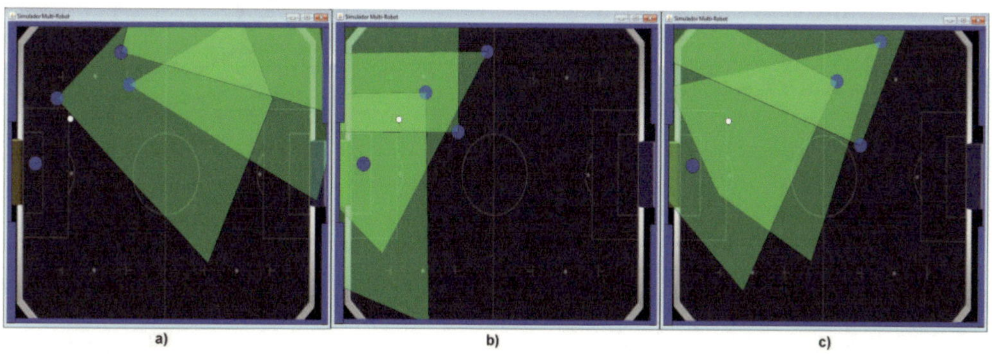

Fig. 5. Triangular block variation. The robots try to get as much distance as they can from the ball but trying to maintain the triangle. a) The initial position, b) forming the triangle, and c) the agents maintain the figure but they are taking away from the ball.

5.3.2 Pass

This action is one of the main plays to attack the opponent. It takes advantage of the velocity that the ball can reach when is kicked out by a player. The goal of this action is to send the ball to a teammate which is better positioned in order to score. This action has the following characteristics:

Number of roles: two roles are needed: passer and receiver.

Passer mapping parameter: It is the point where the player has to shoot the ball.

Passer role mapping: It calculates the point where the player has to kick the ball from the desired position.

Passer role matching: The ideal situation is that the agent is the closest teammate to the ball. If it is not the closest, it is not considered as a passer. The time needed for the closest opponent to the ball decreases the probability of the agent to be a passer. Additionally, this takes into account the angle that the agent has respect the opponent's goal (Fig. 6).

Receiver mapping parameter: It is the point where the player has to receive the ball.

Receiver role mapping: It tries to go to the point defined in the mapping parameter.

Receiver role matching: The ideal situation that all the opponents are not near to the ball trajectory, the receiver agent is close to the opponent's goal and the ball's trajectory is not

too large. Also, this function calculates the point where the agent has to receive the ball, as shown in figure 7.
<u>Matching parameters:</u> It is the distance from the receiver to the point and the parameters for the functions used in all matching.
<u>Action matching:</u> Initially, the agent calculates the probability to be a passer, if the probability is higher than a threshold then the agent get all the teammates and try to find which the best agent to receive the pass. Once the best agent is established, then all probabilities are averaged to consolidate one probability of success.

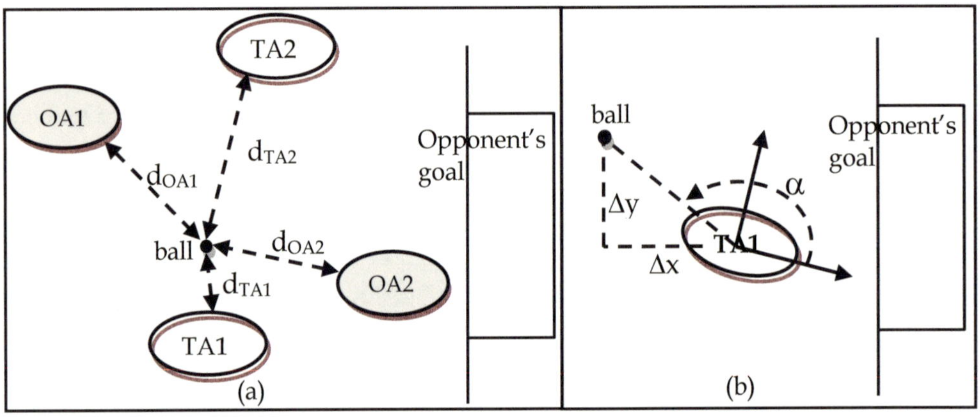

Fig. 6. Variables considered for passer role matching. a) Distance of all the agents to the ball. TA agents are teammates and OA agents are opponents. b) Orientation of the ball respect to the agent. If the agent is between the opponent's goal and the ball, the probability decreases.

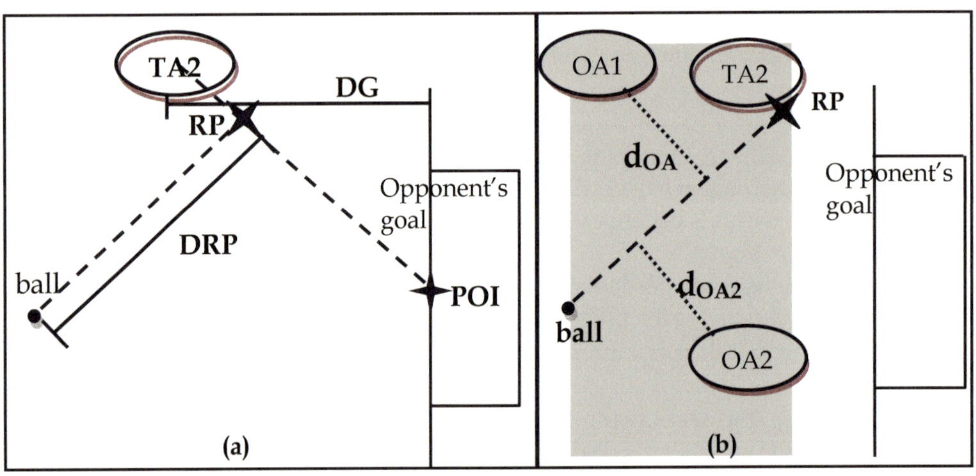

Fig. 7. Variables considered for a receiver agent. a) Calculation of the receiver point (RP) from the receiver's position to shoot the ball in direction of the point of interest (POI). DRP is the distance from the ball to RP and DG is the distance from the agent to the opponent's goal line. The probability to be a receiver is inversely proportional to the longer distance DG and DRP. b) Region to evaluate opponents near the ball's trajectory and their respective distance.

6. Simulation results

Below are shown two cases where MRCC was used as a cooperation control model. Over this model was implemented Commit bases Cooperation Strategy (CCS) (Gonzalez et al., 2006), Cooperative Contract NET (CCNET) (Pachon & Ariza, 2007), and Bind based Cooperative Actions (BCA) (Perez, 2008) as cooperation strategies. The two examples used to test MRCC were the Hunters–Prey problem and the robotic soccer.

6.1 Hunter-Prey problem

The hunters-Prey problem and the Robocup simulations were made using MRCC. A multirobot simulator has been built, where the agent control is implemented using the BESA agent framework (Gonzalez et al., 2003). The required mechanism to simulate the capture of preys has been added. The MRCC was used to manage the access to the physical world from the agents' brains, and also to facilitate the communication among them. Figure 8 shows a view of the simulator where agent systems are implemented and tested. Agents can be configured to have a limited field of view, which is represented by a triangle. Some simulation results were obtained after resolving this problem under different conditions (80 worlds of 12, 16, and 20 agents).

Fig. 8. Hunter-Prey simulation using MRCC.

The threshold to obtain the results was the time spent by the hunters to capture their prey. After analyzing the experimental results, it can be noticed that the number of built societies is greater when the number of hunters is superior to the number of the preys. In addition, when the number of agents increases, the number of micro-societies also increases proportionally. Also it was possible to observe that the success of the micro-societies is not related to the proportion between preys and hunters; but related to the number of conformed micro-societies, approaching the 50 percent of effectiveness.
The experiments have been run using the CCS approach (Gonzalez et al., 2006), and have been compared against an egoistic strategy, where hunters try to continuously persecute preys. The results show an increase in the performance when using the cooperative approach proposed by CCS. When analyzing the way micro-societies evolve, it was observed that the cooperative actions that involve more agents are very hard to achieve. In fact, the requirements imposed by the hard engagement of CSS are not easy to attain when

several agents are involved. However, it was observed that when a micro-society is established, there is a good probability of succeeding.

6.2 Robot soccer simulation

Pachon & Ariza show the results of the comparisons between CCS and Cooperative Contract NET (CCNET) as a strategy to create micro-societies using the MRCC model in order to organize robots that play soccer (Pachon & Ariza, 2007). Soccer simulations were made dividing a soccer field in sections and creating 4 different scenarios using CCS and CCNET (Fig 9).

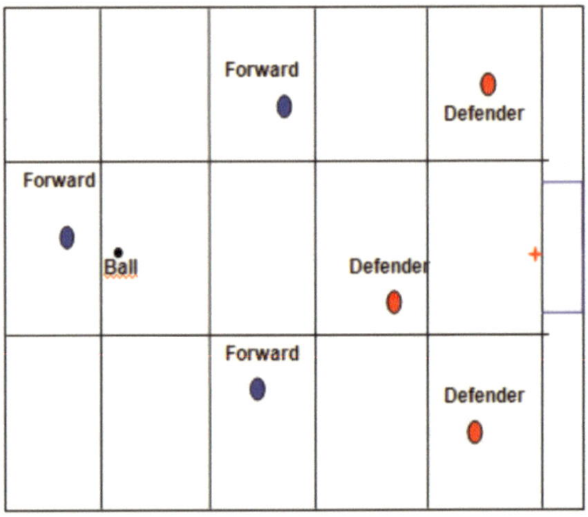

Fig. 9. Definition of micro-societies using CCS and CCNET applied to robotics soccer.

There was a greater attempt to set up micro-societies in CCNET. However, CCS was more effective in creating and implementing them. This allows the conclusion that CCS has higher rate to establish cooperation, but for robotic soccer CCNET is a better option to finish a cooperative action, which is a positive feature. Having a higher rate of dissolution of cooperative actions is desirable in a context of robot soccer, because the robots will have a faster response to change actions and/or roles in an environment where the scenarios change in a fast way.

About matching, both approaches, CCS and CCNET, had a similar response; the mean in both situations was similar. This can be explained because both approaches were calculating matching over geometrical calculi.

CCNet showed a higher goal rate due the adaptability this approach has to changes.

The cooperative action that was chosen most of the time by the agents was shooting to goal, due to the scenarios favored this move instead of passing the ball.

Due to some restrictions in the "view cone" of the agents, they had to choose to realize single-agent actions most of the time, because they were not able to see other team mates. And the actions that prevailed in this situation were defensive actions.

(Perez, 2008) uses the cooperation Strategy BCA (Bind Based Cooperative Actions) over MRCC to select cooperative actions. In this case the cooperative actions selected were 6 different types of soccer moves such as attacking, defending blocking, etc. The results of this approach consisted in proving how a group of agents can bind to and specific cooperative action due a preference factor, which is decided by the cooperative agents. Also a matching function works in this strategy that initiates cooperative actions. These actions are started only if a group of agents and the environment fill up the requirements to start such cooperative actions. Finally, the approaches CCS and BCA were tested and approach with machine learning.

7. Final discussion

Nowadays, a general trend is to use robots for more complex tasks. However, as complexity increases it is not viable to get the task done using a single robot. Even if we were able to build such a complex robot, there are situations where the use of several robots is mandatory. In fact, it is not viable to incorporate all the abilities and resources required for a complex task into a single robot. A better approach is to distribute these capacities into several specialized robots which could accomplish the task by adding their skills in a synergic fashion. Besides, there are many situations where the use of several robots will allow getting the work done in less time or in a more efficient way. Multi robot systems incorporate these properties: specialization and redundancy, which result in qualitative and quantitative gains in comparison with single robot approaches. Thus, multi robot systems are required to achieve complex tasks. Nevertheless, team control implies new problems to solve; a control strategy is required to determine who does what, at what moment and which resources can be used. Cooperation is the key, as it incorporates mechanisms to carry out: task allocation, synchronization and planning, and conflict resolution.

The MRCC, Multi-Resolution Cooperation Control, proposes a general solution to the cooperation control by decomposing it into a set of layers with different level of abstraction. The key idea is that higher levels influence the behavior of lower ones. The control complexity is split into the layers, each one is concerned with goals according to its abstraction plane. In general, there can be as many levels as required; an outline of the 4-level approach has been introduced. At the agent level, the lower one, individual teammates assume roles; these roles are assigned by the decision mechanisms included in the higher levels. The system level, the higher one, allocates exception roles in order to deal with special situations that affect the whole team. The formation level, through an organization based on zones, gives structural roles to agents. The micro-society level decides which agent should assume a cooperative role. In a similar fashion, the way cooperative actions take place and the structure of the formations are affected by the higher levels. Finally, the model also includes feedback interactions from lower levels to higher ones; thanks to this information, dynamic control and learning can be achieved.

This chapter was focused in the micro-social level. The central issue at this level is to execute cooperative actions, which aim to accomplish a goal between a selected and reduced set of agents. The detection of cooperative actions is based on an opportunistic approach. As an opportunity is detected a negotiation protocol allows to form a micro-society and specific cooperative roles are assigned to agents. This proactive mechanism is performed in a distributed way; each agent is looking for cooperation opportunities and invites others to form micro-societies. There is a balance between the autonomy of the agent and its commitment with the team. Each agent works in an autonomous fashion, there is not hierarchy between robots; but when the agent is required to assume a role, it changes its own goals for those of the role it has to play. At the end, what are more important are the team goals.

Actually, the MRCC has been implemented as a general cooperation framework. The case studies of hunters and preys and robot soccer have been studied and implemented. In the former one, a 3 layer MRCC model has been enough to have a good performance. However, in the soccer task, it is mandatory to incorporate the formation level. Experimental simulation trials have demonstrated the viability of the approach. Actual work includes the refinement of the formation level and the validation of the MRCC with real robots.

In the near future, it is expected to have a MRCC based team of robotic soccer participating in international competitions. The approach will be tested not only in competitions, where the desire of winning often leads to simplified assumptions of the problem and centralized control approaches. The MRCC operates in a real distributed system and is able to deal with restrictions concerning the sensor information available and of the communication capacity.

8. Acknowledgements

This work is product of the projects Cooperative Agents ("Cooperación en Sistemas MultiAgentes Aplicada a Robótica Móvil" and "Robótica Cooperativa Basada en Agentes Heterogéneos Aplicada a Educación en Tecnología") financed by the government of Colombia through COLCIENCIAS with the participation of Pontificia Universidad Javeriana, Universidad de los Andes, Maloka and Universidad del Norte. The authors thank the students and colleagues that have contributed to the development and testing of the architecture MRCC.

9. References

Asama, H.; Matsumoto, A. & Ishida, Y. (1989). Design of an Autonomous and Distributed Robot System: Actress, *Proceedings of IEEE/RSJ International Workshop on Intelligent Robots and Systems (IROS)*, pp. 283 - 290, Tsukuba - Japan, September 1989, IEEE and Robotics Society of Japan (RSJ).

Ch'ng, S. & Padgham, L. (1998). From Roles to Teamwork: A Framework and Architecture. *Applied Artificial Intelligence Journal*, Vol. 12, No. 2 - 3, (1998), page numbers (211-231), ISSN 1087-6545.

De la Rosa, F. & Jimenez, M.E. (2009). Simulation of Multi-robot Architectures in Mobile Robotics, *Proceedings of IEEE Electronics, Robotics and Automotive Mechanics Conference (CERMA)*, pp. 199 - 203, Cuernavaca - México, September 2009, IEEE.

Ferber, J. (1999). MultiAgent Systems: an Introduction to Distributed Artificial Intelligence, Ed. Addison Wesley, ISBN 978-0201360486.

FIFA. (2010). History of Football - The Global Growth. Available at: http://www.fifa.com/classicfootball/history/game/historygame4.html, July 2010.

FIRA. (2010). Federation of International Robot-soccer Association. Available at: http://www.fira.net/, July 2010.

Gonzalez, E.; Avila, J. & Bustacara, C. (2003). BESA: Behavior-oriented, Event-Driven and Social-based Agent Framework. *Proceedings of Parallel and Distributed Processing Techniques and Applications (*PDPTA), pp 1033-1039, Las Vegas - USA, June 2003, CSREA Press.

Gonzalez, E.; Vazquez, A.; Plata, A.; Montañez, L.; Perez, A. & Bustacara, C. (2006). CCS: Commit based Cooperation Strategy for MultiRobot Systems, *Proceedings of*

International Symposium on Robotics and Automation (ISRA), pp. 193 - 198, San Miguel - México, August 2006.

Gonzalez, E.; Perez, A.; Cruz, J. & Bustacara, C. (2007). MRCC: A Multi-Resolution Cooperative Control Agent Architecture, *Proceedings of IEEE/WIC/ACM Intelligent Agent Technology (IAT)*, pp. 391 - 394, San Francisco - USA, November 2007, IEEE.

Hershberger, D.; Simmons, R.; Singh, S.; Ramos, J. & Smith, T. (2002). Coordination of Heterogeneous Robots for Large-Scale Assembly, In: *Robot Teams: From Diversity to Polymorphism,* Balch, T. & Parker, L.E., (Ed.), page numbers (369-380), A K Peters Ltd, ISBN 1-56881-155-1.

Kendall, E.A. (1998). Agent Roles and Aspects, In: *Lecture Notes in Computer Science - Workshop on Aspect Oriented Programming - ECOOP 1998,* Goos, G.; Hartmanis, J. & van Leeuwen, J., (Ed.), Vol. 1543, page numbers (431-432), Springer, ISBN 978-3-540-65460-5.

Kendall, E.A. (2000). Role Modeling for Agent System Analysis, Design, and Implementation. *IEEE Concurrency,* Vol. 8, No. 2, (April 2000), page numbers (34-41), ISSN 1092-3063.

Lima, P.U. & Custódio, L.M. (2005). Multi-Robot Systems, In: *Innovations in Robot Mobility and Control,* Patnaik, S.; Jain, L.C.; Tzafestas, S.G.; Resconi, G. & Konar, A., (Ed.), Vol. 8, page numbers (1-64), Springer, ISBN 978-3-540-26892-5.

Mataric, M. (1995). Issues and Approaches in the Design of Collective Autonomous Agents. *Robotics and Autonomous Systems,* Vol. 16, No. 2 – 4, (December 1995), page numbers (321-331), ISSN 0921-8890.

Meystel, A. & Bathija, A. (2002). Multiresolutional Planning: Using the Randomized Tessellation of the State Space, *Proceedings of International Symposium on Robotics and Automation (ISRA)*, Toluca - México, September 2002.

Pachon, A. & Ariza, L. (2007). Cooperation Techniques based on Contract NET CCNET, Pontificia Universidad Javeriana, Bogotá - Colombia.

Parker, L. E. (1998). ALLIANCE: An Architecture for Fault Tolerant Multirobot Cooperation. *IEEE Transactions on Robotics and Automation,* Vol. 14, No. 2, (April 1998) page numbers (220-240), ISSN 1042-296X.

Perez, A. (2008). Learning Techniques in Multi Agent Systems applied to cooperation strategies. Master Thesis. Pontificia Universidad Javeriana, Bogotá - Colombia.

Quiñonez Y.; de Lope, J. & Maravall, D. (2009). Cooperative and Competitive Behaviors in a Multi-robot System for Surveillance Tasks, In: *Lecture Notes in Computer Science - Computer Aided Systems Theory - EUROCAST 2009,* Moreno-Díaz, R.; Quesada-Arencibia, A. & Pichler, F., (Ed.), Vol. 5717, page numbers (437-444), Springer, ISBN 978-3-642-04771-8.

RoboCup. (2010). RoboCup World Championship and Conference. Available at: http://www.robocup.org/, July 2010.

Sgorbissa, A. (2006). Multi-Robot Systems and Distributed Intelligence: The ETHNOS Approach to Heterogeneity, In: *Mobile Robotics, Moving Intelligence,* Buchli, J., (Ed.), page numbers (423-446), Pro Literatur Verlag, Germany / ARS, Austria, ISBN 3-86611-284-X.

Simmons, R.; Singh, S.; Hershberger, D.; Ramos, J. & Smith, T. (2001). First Results in the Coordination of Heterogeneous Robots for Large-Scale Assembly, In: *Lecture Notes in Control and Information Sciences,* Thoma, M. & Morari, M., (Ed.), Vol. 271, page numbers (323-332), Springer, ISBN 978-3-540-42104-7.

Weigel, T.; Gutmann, J.-S.; Dietl, M.; Kleiner, A. & Nebel, B. (2002). CS Freiburg: coordinating robots for successful soccer playing. *IEEE Transactions on Robotics and Automation,* Vol. 18, No. 5, (October 2002), page numbers (685-699), ISSN 1042-296X.

Weiss, G. (1999). Multiagent Systems: A Modern Approach to Distributed Artificial Intelligence, MIT Press, ISBN 978-0262232036.

26

Robot Teams and Robot Team Players

Gerard McKee and Blesson Varghese
School of Systems Engineering, University of Reading, Whiteknights Campus
Reading, Berkshire, RG6 6AY
United Kingdom

1. Introduction

Multi-robot systems are generally organized around the concept of a team, from teams of mobile robots for outdoor tasks such as surveillance to teams of smaller robot systems for competitions such as RoboCup (Balch & Parker, 2002; Schultz & Parker, 2002). Variants of this theme include small numbers of cooperating robots for transport tasks, such as two robots carrying an extended payload, which is the robot equivalent of a two-man team. In the majority of research the team structure is limited to a single team. In this chapter, we propose to explore a multi-team model for multi-robot systems, whereby multiple subsets of robots are drawn from a larger pool to form multiple teams. Each team has an assigned task that is to be distributed among the members of the team.

In the conventional model for robot teams, a task is broken into sub-tasks and each sub-task is allocated to members of the team through a negotiation process; individual robots can signup for one or more sub-tasks based on their ability to perform the sub-tasks. The set of robots which sign-up are essentially the team associated with the task. A limitation of this model is that it doesn't support the concept of multiple teams of robots, in which each team has a collective identity associated with a task it is to perform that is separate from the identity of other teams. However, multiple teams are a successful approach used in business and industry to organize work (Jelphs & Dickinson, 2008). The benefit of multiple teams is that work can be carried out in parallel, improving efficiency. Further, it is possible to reallocate robots between teams, a practice often used in business and industry to ensure that tasks are completed on time.

Introducing a multi-team framework in multi-robot systems can offer the same benefits. Moreover, in the conventional multi-robot team, robots can locally cooperate, effectively forming a sub-team. This is generally perceived as cooperation but not necessarily team based cooperation. However, the concept of forming and re-forming sub-teams may be useful in this context as well. Therefore, a model emerges in which a pool of robots provides a resource for creating multiple teams, each of which essentially can be seen as a pool of resources in its own right for creating further sub-teams when needed.

The chapter is organised as follows. The following section outlines the requirements for multiple robots working in multiple teams. The third section of the chapter proposes a model for multiple robots working in multiple teams, which we abbreviate as the MRMT model.The fourth section discusses the architecture in more detail, specifically the concepts of roles and targets and the communication requirements. The fifth section provides two case studies, motivated by space applications, to describe how the model can work in practice. The final section provides a summary and conclusions.

2. Requirements for multiple robots working in multiple teams

The term 'multi-robot systems' can be used to refer to a wide range of robotics systems incorporating more than one robot, including swarms of many robot systems and smaller numbers of robots in robot teams for competitions such as Robocup (Balch & Parker, 2002). The term is used in this chapter to refer to homogeneous or heterogeneous teams of mobile robot systems, including, for example, robot teams in the Middle Sized league of RoboCup and medium sized robots for surveillance operations in both open unstructured landscapes and structured outdoor and indoor environments. Such systems typically incorporate wireless Ethernet as the basis for communication, vision based sensing, an on-board computer, possibly a laptop, and hence the ability to support a significant level of autonomy as well as robot-robot and human-robot cooperation.

A set of two or more robot systems can be incorporated into a robot team to perform some task. The task can be broken out into subtasks, which can then be allocated to individuals members of the robot team (Choudhury et al., 2009; Parker, 1998). There are four issues concerned with the allocation of tasks to robots and the subsequent performance of the robot team in completing the tasks.

First, the allocation of tasks can be categorised based on whether the robot team is homogeneous or heterogeneous. In the former case, since the robots are all equally capable of performing any task the main issue is the distribution of the robots between the different tasks (e.g. (McLurkin & Yamins, 2005)). In the second case, since the robots are different, possibly overlapping in their capability, the key challenge is to match each task to a robot in the team capable of performing the task (e.g. (Mataric et al., 2003)). A number of strategies are available for such task allocation, including both centralised and distributed strategies and taking into account the capabilities of the robots, typically their sensing capabilities (e.g. (Estlin et al., 2005; Tsalatsanis et al., 2009)). Among the strategies include bidding strategies based on a market economy model whereby each robot bids for and is allocated a task based on comparing its bid with that of other robots (e.g. (Zlot et al., 2002)).

Second, during the performance of the task a robot may suffer partial (e.g. a sensor fails) or total failure which prevents it completing the task it has been assigned. The task must in this case be reallocated to another robot. A number of successful behaviour-based strategies have been developed for this purpose, whereby the other robots in the team recognise the failure and take over the task (Mataric et al., 2003; Parker, 1998). This work is explored largely in the context of fault tolerance.

Third, the behaviour of the robots needs to be coordinated in order to ensure the successful completion of the task. For example, in the ALLIANCE architecture the coordination operates to ensure that all tasks assigned to the team are completed (Parker, 1998). The coordination is through explicit communication, whereby each robot broadcasts its current state to the other robots, which can in turn determine whether a task is being completed successfully or should be reallocated. Communication has associated overheads, and algorithms have been explored which trade-off communication requirements (e.g. (Balch & Arkin, 1998; McLurkin & Yamins, 2005)).

Fourth, robot teams incorporate a number of interface types, the most common being the interface between the individual robots in a team, employing explicit communication via a wireless network to share task-related information. However, in some cases this communication is not direct robot-to-robot but via a server or base station (e.g. (Roussos et al., 2007)). In addition to these, the robot team may also be interfaced with one or more human operators to which the robots report task information that can be used to support task coordination (e.g. (Sugiyama et al., 2008)).

The adopted control architecture for many robot systems, either alone or working in a team is a hybrid comprising deliberative and behavioural components with the balance between the two determined by the task performed and the scale and number of robot systems (Balch & Parker, 2002; Bekey, 2005; Schultz & Parker, 2002). A multi-robot team also creates challenges in command and control, whether top-down, bottom-up, or a combination of these; and challenges and opportunities for human-robot interaction. These must be reflected in the capabilities incorporated in the robot architecture itself and in the global commands that need to be translated into actions for individual robots.

The above issues set requirements for the creation of robot architectures to support robots working in teams. The conventional architectures for the robots in a team do not actually support team working for two reasons. First, the conventional robot architectures work largely on the principle that a robot is first and foremost an individual and only secondly has the potential to be a member of a robot team. In this context, team working is designed in as effectively an afterthought. If robots are expected to be team players, however, then team working should be designed in from the ground up. This can be realised by ensuring that the architecture supports robot-robot cooperation in its command and control interfaces and explicitly treats the robot as a team player.

Second, the conventional approach to multi-robot teams assumes a single-team single-level approach. Specifically, a pool of robots is assumed which is essentially configured into a team without an explicit representation of a "team" within the multi-robot team. In other words, the robots have no notion that they are members of a team. In addition, there is no scope for a team of robots to organise into sub-teams. In cases where a subset of robots within a team needs to coordinate, the subset is treated as an exceptional circumstance rather than a natural feature of a more explicit model of team working.

In summary, therefore, a more useful architecture for team working will treat an individual robot as a team player, which means essentially that the robot knows it is a team player, and will incorporate an explicit recursive model of team working whereby a pool of robots can form into a set of teams and a team can form into sub-teams. In this context also tasks and roles are not only assigned to individual robots but also to teams.

3. The MRMT model

Having established the requirements for multi-robot multi-team working, we propose in this section to outline a model for the same. In order to present the model, we first need to establish some assumptions and terminology which will be used to define and explain the model. The following sub-section explains the concepts of macroscopic and microscopic commands, explicit and implicit communication, and roles and targets. The first is familiar from swarm robotics (Varghese & McKee, 2008), the second from cooperative robotics (Bouloubasis & McKee, 2005; Lam et al., 2003) and the third are definitions that we are introducing in order to articulate the model.

3.1 Command, communication and task assumptions

In multi-robot multi-team working we wish to draw the distinctions between commands which are issued to a team of robots as against commands which are issued to individual robots. This distinction is reflected in the distinction between macroscopic and microscopic commands (Varghese & McKee, 2009). Macroscopic (group) commands are issued to a team of robots and define a task or action that the team needs to perform as a group. Examples include commanding the team to pack more closely together or to move forward in a specified direction as a group. Microscopic (individual) commands are issued to individual robots, specifying for the robot a task or action that it needs to perform independent of the other robots in the team. Each robot can convert macroscopic commands to microscopic commands, reflecting its individual perspective on the group task. For example, a team of robots commanded as a group to fetch an object will each have been allocated specific grasp points on the object; each robot is required to interpret the fetch command in terms of its allocated grasp point.

In addition to interpreting group and individual commands, the robots in a team will need to share information with each other, and depending on the task this communication can be mediated explicitly or implicitly, which are terms from familiar to robotics. Explicit communication is a mode of communication in which the robots share information with each other via a wireless communications network. For example, the individual robots in a robot team performing a fetch operation will alert other team members when they have grasped their respective interfaces and therefore are ready to move. Implicit communication is a mode of communication in which the robots sense the action of other robots through the latter's action on the same target. For example, if one of a team of robots holding an object moves off, the other robots will sense the action that the move has on their respective grasp interfaces (implicit communication) and can react immediately (tight coupling) by moving off as well.

We propose, in addition, to draw a distinction between the roles that a robot performs in a team and the targets on which the roles are performed. Roles are associated with tasks and targets are associated with the objects to which the tasks are directed. An example of a role is to carry an object, while the object to be carried is an example of a target. Tasks assigned to a team can be classified on the basis of roles and targets as follows:

- Single Role
    - Single Target
    - Multiple Target
- Multiple Role
    - Single Target
    - Multiple Target

The extent to which implicit and explicit communication and also macroscopic and microscopic control should be exploited in each of the above categories is summarised in Table 1.

	Single Target	**Multiple Target**
Single Role	Macroscopic	Macroscopic & Microscopic
	Implicit	Explicit & Implicit
Multiple Role	Macroscopic & Microscopic	Microscopic
	Explicit & Implicit	Explicit

Table 1. Roles and Targets

In summary, single target scenarios tend to provide more scope for implicit communication and more macroscopic control, whereas multiple target scenarios tend to provide more scope for explicit communication and more microscopic control. In contrast, single role scenarios tend to provide more scope for implicit communication and more macroscopic control whereas multiple role scenarios tend to provide more scope for explicit communication and more microscopic control.

3.2 Components of the MRMT model

The Multi Robot Multi Team (MRMT) model that we are proposing comprises five components as well as a design for the lifecycle of a task under the model. The latter is described in section 4. The five aspects are (a) the concept of a universal robot set, from which robots are drawn to form one or more team, (b) teams, robots and their capabilities, (c) tasks, roles and targets, (d) role management and (e) command, control and communication. The definition of each of these aspects is provided in detail below and the key components of the architecture and their dependencies are summarised in figure 1.

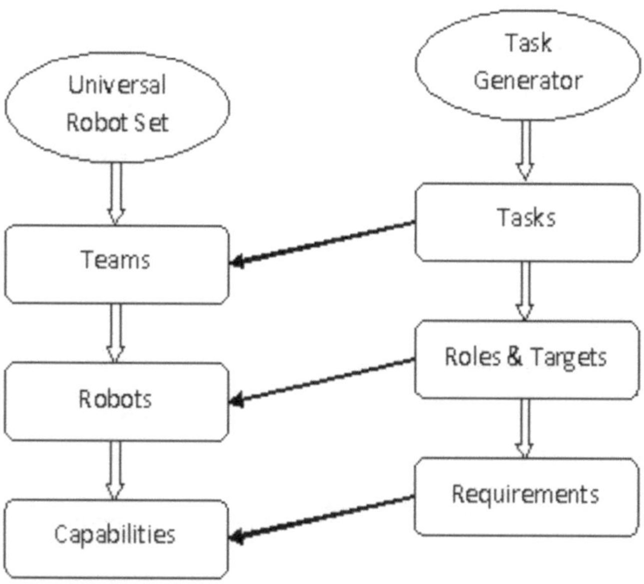

Fig. 1. Overview of the proposed MRMT architecture

a. Universal Robot Set (URS)
   - A pool of robots, referred to as the universal robot set (URS) is assumed from which robots can be drawn to form one or more robot teams.
   - Subsets of robots can be drawn from the universal set to form robot teams. A robot team may comprise zero, one, two or more robots. The first case represents the requirement for a team to perform a task but the robots may not need to be allocated immediately.
   - If multiple robot teams are drawn simultaneously from the universal set they are expected to be mutually exclusive; however it is possible for a robot to be a member of multiple robot teams simultaneously.

b. Teams, robots, capabilities
   - Robot teams are comprised of robots which possess mobility, manipulation, sensing, computing and instrumentation modules that determine their capabilities.

- In a modular framework a robot can swap in or out modules, and hence the selection of a robot to be a member of a team should take into account its potential configurations.
- The capabilities of a robot are determined also by its cognitive, deliberative and behavioural intelligence, which can also be swapped in or out to suit different roles.
- The set of capabilities that are collectively possessed by a robot team must satisfy the requirements of the task that the team is required to perform.

c. Tasks, roles, targets
- A task specifies the work that a robot team is to perform, specifically the goal to be achieved and the termination conditions to be satisfied.
- Tasks have associated implementation schemas. The schema sets out the roles that are required for the task, the targets of these roles, the plans for completing the task; and the requirements for the robotic systems to perform the roles including sensing, actuation, instrumentation, and cognitive, behavioural and deliberative intelligence components.
- Tasks are assigned to robot teams and roles and targets are assigned to robots within the team.
- The robots within the robot team must possess the capabilities required to satisfy the roles to which they are assigned.

d. Role Management
- Each robot possesses a Role Manager which has the responsibility for managing the allocation of roles to the robot and the robot's operation according to the role(s) it has been assigned.
- The Role Manager is responsible for either accepting an assigned role (top-down allocation) or negotiating on behalf of the robot to be assigned a role (bottom-up negotiation).
- The Role Manger incorporates mechanisms to ensure the appropriate interaction and scheduling of multiple roles, if multiple roles are assigned to a robot.
- Each robot possesses a Download Manager, a Configuration Manager, and a Task Manager.
- The Role Manager liaises with a Download Manager to ensure that the software required to support the role is downloaded and installed.
- The Role Manager liaises with a Configuration Manager to ensure that the modules appropriate to the roles are installed.
- The Role Manager liaises with the Task Manager to ensure that the robot executes the subtask associated with the role that has been allocated to the robot.

e. Command, Control and Communication
- The method a task schema proposes for performing a task places requirements on robot to robot command, control and communication. These are specified in the task schema and embodied in the software that implements the method.
- These requirements are stated in terms of
  - macroscopic and microscopic command & control
  - implicit and explicit communication
- In order to support these requirements the command structures for robot control need to be stated as group-type commands and each robot, in fulfilling the roles

and targets it has been assigned in a robot team, must possess a command, control and communication system that interprets these commands with respect to the individual robot's operations.

4. The lifecycle of a task

The previous section described the aspects and components of the MRMT model. This section illustrates the application of the model. To support the application of the model we propose a lifecycle for a task. This is described in the following sub-section. We then give examples to illustrate the application of the lifecycle for the four combinations of roles and targets from Table 1.

4.1 The design of the lifecycle

We propose a design for the lifecycle of a task in the MRMT model that comprises seven steps, from the inception of the task to its satisfactory completion and subsequent disbanding of the robot team as follows.

Step 1. *Generate the task to be performed.* The task may be generated manually or automatically, on the fly in response to real-time events or part of a predefined work schedule. The responsibility for the generation of tasks can be considered to be a role that could be carried out centrally or assigned to a robot in a robot team.

Step 2. *Assess the requirements for the task and determine a corresponding task schema.* The requirements can be used to index a schema library. A number of schemas may be available for completing the task. The selected schema may also incorporate rules for scaling it to meet the size and scope of the task.

Step 3. *Create a robot team and allocate the task and schema to the team.* A team object is created to represent the team that is required for the task. The task and the schema are then registered with the team object.

Step 4. *Populate the team with robots and assign roles and targets.* The allocation of robots to the robot team can follow a top-down centralised approach where roles are assigned to robots and the robots are therefore assigned to the team, a bottom-up negotiated approach where each of the robots negotiates for its position in the team, or a combination of these. In all cases the services offered by individual modules and robots (current and potential configurations of modules) must be considered. The responsibility for the creation of teams to perform a task can be considered to be a role. The role can be performed centrally or allocated to one or more of the robots in a team.

Step 5. *Install the appropriate robot configurations to support the assigned roles.* The modules (e.g. instruments) that are required by each robot to perform its allocated role on associated target are installed. The software to support the cognitive, deliberative and behavioural requirements for the task is downloaded, if required, and installed.

Step 6. *Perform the task until satisfactorily completed.* The task is performed according to the overall task plan and the plans associated with each role, as set out in the task schema. The task is completed when the goal has been achieved to the satisfaction of the individual robots and the robot team, which is also set out in the task schema.

Step 7. *Disband the robot team.* The set of robots are removed from the team and the team bject is removed.

4.2 Demonstration of the lifecycle

In section 3.1 we proposed classifying roles and targets into four categories, namely (a) Single Role, Single Target, (b) Single Role, Multiple Targets, (c) Multiple Roles, Single Targetand (d) Multiple Roles, Multiple Targets. We now demonstrate the application of the lifecycle model for example tasks relevant to space applications that fall under each of these categories.

4.2.1 Single role, single target

We select as an example, multiple robots cooperating to carry an object. One role is required, namely a carrier role. The target is the object to be carried and sub-targets are the grasp interfaces on the object to be carried. The carriers are responsible for collectively picking up the object, carrying the object to a destination and depositing or assembling the object. The robots will assess their resources and locations relative to the object to be carried and negotiate with each other for grasp interfaces. Each robot will approach and grasp its assigned grasp interfaces, avoiding obstacles and interference with other robots.

The robots will need to synchronise so that they lift the object together. This can exploit both explicit and implicit communication. The robots will need to coordinate during traversal, using primarily implicit communication, to ensure that the object to be transported is not dropped. The robots will need to synchronise to ensure that the object is set down or assembled safely. Each robot will need to ensure that it has the resources to perform its role and to evaluate satisfactory completion of its role.

The capabilities required by each robot include the identification and localization of target and sub-targets, planning and navigation functions, manipulation for object pick-up and transport, and grippers for the grasp interfaces. The robots will also require sensing and evaluation capabilities for task and sub-task completion.

4.2.2 Single role, multiple target

We select as an example, sample acquisition from multiple science sites. The task requires a single role, namely sample acquisition. The targets are a set of sites from which samples are to be taken; there are no sub-targets. The robots are responsible for navigating to an assigned target, taking a sample and returning the sample to a Lander. The robots will need to localize the target, generate a plan and navigate to the target following this plan. At the target the robots will deploy the sampling instrument, take the sample and stow it in a sample container. The robot will then be required to generate a plan and navigate back to the Lander and transfer the sample.

The robots will need to coordinate on the allocation of samples, taking account of their resources and locations with respect to the set of samples. A robot may be assigned a number of targets, which will require it to generate a plan to visit each of the targets before returning to the Lander. The robots will need to avoid interference with each other and avoid obstacles.

Each robot will need to ensure that it has the resources to perform its role and to evaluate satisfactory completion of its role. The robots must synchronise to ensure that the multiplesample acquisition task is completed successfully. If one or more targets have not been visited the robots will need to negotiate to assign the targets and acquire samples.

4.2.3 Multiple roles, single target

We select as an example, site preparation for construction of a human habitat. The roles include diggers, movers, and breakers. The target is a designated area that is to be leveled in preparation for infrastructure building. The robots will be working on sub-targets within this area, avoiding interference with each other. The diggers are responsible for digging and moving soil. The movers are responsible for moving small sized rocks. The breakers are responsible for breaking medium sized rocks into small sized rocks. It is assumed that the site has been selected such that it contains no large sized rocks and minimal numbers of medium sized rocks.

Each role, namely digging, moving and breaking will have associated sub-target types. Digging will include areas from which soil is to be removed and areas in which it is to be deposited. Moving will include the identities of small sized rocks to be moved and locations to which they are to be deposited. Breaking will include the identities of medium sized rocks to be broken apart. The robots filling each role type need to assess their locations and resources and negotiate (explicit communication) to assign each other sub-targets.

The robots will need to identify their respective sub-targets from the environment, navigate to these, perform the corresponding operations on the sub-targets and repeat for all sub targets until the site preparation task has been completed. The robots will also need to identify new sub-targets. For example, when a medium sized rock has been broken a new set of small sized rocks are created, which become new sub-targets for the movers. The movers can identify the new sub-targets through implicit communication (i.e., observation of the environment) or explicit communication (i.e., the breakers inform the movers). The diggers need to identify if new sub-targets that need levelling and new sub-targets that need filling.

The robots will need to coordinate. For example, small sized rocks can be used to fill a dip in the terrain prior to depositing soil. Therefore, the movers and diggers need to coordinate to ensure that this constraint is satisfied. In addition, the robots will need to avoid interference with each other and avoid obstacles. Each robot will need to ensure that it has the resources to perform its role and to evaluate satisfactory completion of its role. The robots must synchronise to ensure that the terrain is levelled before agreeing that the task has been satisfactorily completed.

4.2.4 Multiple roles, multiple targets

We select as an example, transportation of an object across unstructured terrain. The scenario includes three robot teams with associated roles, namely carriers, clearers, and scouters. The targets are an object that is to be transported (the carriers team), a path that is to be cleared (the clearers team), and open terrain through which a path is to be scouted (the scouters team). Sub-targets are respectively grasp points on the object to be transported, rocks that are to be removed from the path, and areas to be explored. The carriers are responsible for picking up an object to be transported, carrying it along a path and setting it down or assembling it at a destination. The clearers are responsible for clearing rocks from the path. The scouters are responsible for discovering a path to the site where the transported object is to be relocated.

The robots will need to identify their respective sub-targets from the environment, navigate to these, and perform the corresponding operations on the sub-targets until the object has been successfully transported to the destination. The requirements of the carrier team are similar to those described in the example above of multiple robots cooperating to carry an object. The requirements for the clearers team are similar to those for the movers team described in the example above of site preparation for construction of a human habitat. The scouters will need to collectively identify new sub-targets to explore in order to find a path to the destination. They will need to evaluate the suitability of the sub-targets for traversal and clearance.

The scouters will need to coordinate with each other to select a suitable path through the explored sub-targets. The scouters will need to communicate the selection to the clearers and also to the carriers. The clearers need to coordinate with the scouters and the carriers to confirm the path. Each robot will need to ensure that it has the resources to perform its role and to evaluate satisfactory completion of its role. The robots must synchronise to ensure that the task has been satisfactorily completed.

5. Case studies

In this section two extended scenarios are presented to illustrate the application of the MRMT model. The scenarios are labelled here as expedition robotics and transportation robotics. The expedition robotics scenario emphasises diversity of robot-robot cooperation with a specific focus on exploration, whereas the transportation robotics scenario emphasises cooperation between robot teams, as an extension of cooperation between robots in a single team.

5.1 Expedition robotics

This scenario comprises two robotic systems, a Carrier (Heavy-Duty UAV) Robot and a general purpose Runabout Robot. The Carrier Robot provides a transport vehicle for robots, robot spares and science instruments, while the Runabout provides a dexterous and highly mobile assistant to the Carrier. The following are the considerations of the scenario with respect to the proposed MRMT model.

5.1.1 Universal robot set

- The Carrier, the Runabout, and robots on the Carrier (e.g. mini-robots, micro-robots; small teams, swarms; surface, air, underground robots; and robots custom-built from modules).

5.1.2 Teams, robots, capabilities

- The Carrier Robot offers the following:
  - A charging station for the Runabout.
  - A charging station for the Runabout.
  - Crane hoist for lifting/deploying robots and instruments from Storage; can be stowed during long-distance traverse.
  - Storage Rack for instruments and robot spares.
  - A computational platform complementing the Runabout's onboard processing capabilities.
  - A heterogeneous pool of micro and mini robot systems with wheeled and legged mobility.
  - A Build and Change out station for assembling robot systems and hot-swapping robotic modules.
- The Runabout offers the following:
  - A high-dexterity mobility platform.
  - A mobile assistant to deploy science instruments from the Carrier.
  - A scouting capability to support navigation to science sites.
  - Ability to survey a science site in cooperation with the Carrier.

5.1.3 Tasks, roles, target

- Science Deployment Tasks
  - The Runabout carries an instrument pack from the Carrier to a selected location where it is deployed.
  - The Runabout carries one or more robots to selected deployment sites.
- Science Tasks
  - Sample acquisition task can be performed by the Runabout and/or Carrier-supplied robots and instruments.
  - Site surveys employing the Runabout and/or Carrier-supplied robots and instruments.
- These tasks can be generated locally, i.e. at the site by the robot systems (i.e. autonomously) or through cooperation between the Carrier and the Runabout working together to identify science targets. In the latter, the Runabout may fulfil the role of a roving eye for the Carrier.
- The task generation role can be located on the Carrier, using its powerful onboard computing capacity and/or located on the Runabout.

5.1.4 Role management

- The Carrier is assumed to house a server on which the task schema library is housed and the software modules to support the range of roles applicable to the tasks. The software is downloaded as required.
- The Carrier must support the configuration of the Runabout and other robot systems to support the roles required for the task.

5.1.5 Command, control, communication

- Most of the tasks will require explicit communication, since it is assumed that the Carrier houses assembly mechanisms for configuring robots and there is little requirement for tightly coupled cooperation such as for object transport.
- Much of the cooperation will be in terms of managing the loading and off-loading of robots and instruments between the Carrier and the Runabout with the help of the Crane Hoist.
- The Carrier and/or Runabout can issue group commands to robot teams.

5.2 Transportation robotics

This scenario comprises multiple robot teams, incorporating cooperation between robots within a team and between robot teams. Three robot teams are proposed including (a) a mover robot team, charged with cooperatively carrying an extended payload incorporating multiple grasp interfaces, (b) a clearing robot team, charged with clearing a path of obstacles for the mover robot team and (c) a scouting robot team, charged with scouting a path to a target site and hence guiding the clearing robot team and the mover robot team. The following are the considerations of the scenario with respect to the proposed MRMT model.

5.2.1 Universal robot set

- A heterogeneous set of robot systems to support lifting, clearing, exploring.

5.2.2 Teams, robots, capabilities

- Ability to lift objects, good mobility, custom purpose grippers/manipulators.
- Vision sensing for localisation, navigation and identifying objects to be cleared from the path.
- Planning and navigation software capability for autonomy.
- Information can be passed between the teams (team-based communication required).
- Robots can move between teams as resources become available and the subtasks become doable.
- In one scenario the task starts with all robots assigned to the scouting team; then as the task progresses some of these are reallocated to the clearer team, and then some of both of these to the mover team.

5.2.3 Tasks, roles, target

- Tasks include cooperative pickup, transport, assembly, clearance and scouting/ mapping.
- Roles include moving, clearing, scouting and guiding.

5.2.4 Role management

- The task script is pre-defined; a number of scripts can be assumed for the task, requiring selection and download.
- Role allocation is required, since different robots may perform different roles, and possibly a single robot may perform multiple roles simultaneously.
- Robots may be reassigned between teams.

5.2.5 Command, control, communication

- The mover team will require implicit communication.
- Synchronisation of the robots for initiation and completion of the task requires explicit communication.
- Explicit communication is required between the members of the scouter team.
- Guidance and command & control may be directed from the guide robots to clearers and movers.
- Macroscopic/microscopic command and conversion will be required.
- Inter-team communication will be explicit.

5.3 Summary

The two case studies, Expedition and Transportation Robotics, illustrate how the proposed MRMT model can be exploited in multi-robot multi-team working. The second scenario, in particular, illustrates the way in which the model supports multiple teams, including collaboration between teams and sharing of robots between teams. This builds on the idea that an individual robot is inherently a team player.

6. Conclusions

Conventional robot architectures applied to team robot systems treat the robots as individual systems and only then overlay a team-based perspective. This does not offer the flexibility of teams being able to organise themselves recursively into finer sub-teams and indeed leaves the whole idea of a team implicit. In this chapter, we have proposed a model, the Multi- Robot Multi-Team (MRMT) model, for multiple robots working in multiple teams. We have defined aspects and components to the model and presented a design for the lifecycle of a task. We have subsequently illustrated the application of the model in a set of four example applications and two extended scenarios using space robotics as the application domain. We propose, in conclusion, that the MRMT model offers a more flexible framework for robot teams since the individual robots are effectively designed from the ground up as team players.

7. References

Balch, T. & Arkin, R. (1998). Behaviour-Based Formation Control for Multi-Robot Teams, *IEEE Transactions on Robotics and Automation*, Vol. 14, No. 6, pp. 1-15.

Balch, T. & Parker, L. E. (2002). *Robot Teams: From Diversity to Polymorphism*, A. K. Peters, Ltd.

Bekey, G. A. (2005). Autonomous Robots from Biological Inspiration to Implementation and Control, *MIT Press.*

Bouloubasis, A. K. & McKee, G. T. (2005). Cooperative Transport of Extended Payloads, In: *Proceedings of International Conference on Advanced Robotics*, pp. 882-887.

Choudhury, B. B.; Biswal, B. B. & Mishra, B. B. (2009). Development of Optimal Strategies for Task Assignment in Multi-robot Systems, In: *Proceedings of the IEEE International Advanced Computing Conference.*

Estlin, T.; Gaines, D.; Fisher, F. & Castano, R. (2005). Coordination Multiple Rovers with Interdependent Science Objectives, In: *Proceedings of Fourth International Joint Conference on Autonomous Agents and Multiagent Systems*, pp. 879-886.

Jelphs, K. & Dickinson, H. (2008).Working in Teams (Better PartnershipWorking), *Policy Press.*

Lam, Y. K.; Wong, E. K.; & Loo, C. K. (2003). Explicit Communication in Designing Efficient Cooperative Mobile Robotic Systems. In: *Proceedings of the IEEE International Conference on Robotics and Automation.*

Mataric, M. J.; Sukhatme, G. S. & Ostergaard, E. H. (2003). Multi-Robot Task Allocation in Uncertain Environments, *Autonomous Robots*, Vol. 14, 2003, pp. 255-263.

McLurkin, J. & Yamins, D. (2005). Dynamic Task Assignment in Robot Swarms, *Robotics: Science and Systems*, Vol. 8, June 2005.

Parker, L. (1998). ALLIANCE: An Architecture for Fault Tolerant Multi-Robot Cooperation, *IEEE Transactions on Robotics and Automation*, Vol. 14, No. 2, April 1998, pp. 220-240.

Roussos, G.; Papadogkonas, D.; Taylor, J.; Airantzis, D.; Levene, M. & Zoumboulakis, M. (2007). Shared Memories: A Trial-based Coordination Server for Robot Teams. In: *Proceedings of the 1st International Conference on Robot Communication and Coordination*, Greece.

Schultz, A. C. & Parker, L. E. (2002). Multi-Robot Systems: From Swarms to Intelligent Automata, In: *Proceedings from the 2002 NRL Workshop on Multi-Robot Systems*, Kluwer Academic Publishers.

Sugiyama, H.; Sujioka, T. & Murata, M. (2008). Coordination of Rescue Robots for Real-Time Exploration Over Disaster Areas, In: *Proceedings of the 11th IEEE International Symposium on Object Oriented Real-Time Distributed Computing.*

Tsalatsanis, A.; Yalcin, A. & Valavanis, K. P. (2009). Optimized Task Allocation in Cooperative Robot Teams, In: *Proceedings of the 17th Mediterranean Conference on Control and Automation*, Thessaloniki, Greece, 2009, pp. 270–275.

Varghese, B. & McKee, G. T. (2008). A Mathematical Model, Implementation and Study of a Swarm Conglomerate and its Formation Control, In: *Proceedings of Towards Autonomous Robotic Systems*, Edinburgh, Scotland, pp. 156–162.

Varghese, B. & McKee, G. T. (2009). Investigating Feasible Tools for Swarm Pattern Transformation, In: *Proceedings of the 2nd International Conference on Robot Communication and Coordination*, Odense, Denmark.

Zlot, R.; Stentz, A.; Dias, M. B. & Thayer, S. A. T. S. (2002). Multi-Robot Exploration controlled by a Market Economy, In: *Proceedings of IEEE International Conference on Robotics and Automation*, 2002, pp. 3016–3023.

27

On the Problem of Representing and Characterizing the Dynamics of Multi-Robot Systems

Angélica Muñoz-Meléndez
INAOE
Mexico

1. Introduction

In the recent years, there has been a growing interest in the design and programming of multi-robot systems. This is mainly due to the potential advantages of these systems, such as physical deployment, redundancy and parallelism in sensing and actuation.

The interest of the collective robotics community has focused on the development of technology to support the interaction among single robots to achieve common goals, such as methods for inter-robot communication, kin recognition, sensor fusion, and information sharing. The outcomes of this research are seen to be of direct relevance to other fields involving the inter-operation of various software and physical components, such as sensor networks and ubiquitous computing.

In spite of all the progress made in collective robotics in the last years, a lot of work remains to be done both in describing and understanding the behavior of multi-robot systems without regard to their internal mechanisms. However, theoretical descriptions of the dynamics of multi-robot systems pose a considerable challenge to robot designers because they do not rely on well-established and quantitative laws of behavior. As a matter of fact, collective robotics suffers from a lack of descriptive and analytical tools for estimating the tendencies and evolution of the dynamics of multi-robot systems under a variety of conditions.

Some efforts have been made towards the theoretical understanding of multi-robot systems, such as the introduction of metrics for measuring specific aspects of multi-robot systems, e.g. diversity (Balch, 2000) and fluctuations from a steady state (Lerman et al., 2006), as well as attempts to describe the dynamics of multi-robot systems by using formal and semi-formal methodologies, e.g. ergodic dynamics (Shell et al., 2005).

In this work, various attempts to describe the dynamics of multi-robot systems are presented and discussed. Two large-scale measures, average flow and average activity, are namely introduced and applied in experiments of simulated foraging robots, in order to characterize the systems limits. These measures are supported on parameters of crowd behavior applied in mechanical statistics. In addition, based on a set of selected case studies we provide experimental evidence about the quantification of the performance of multi-robot systems.

This research aims at contributing to understand and characterize multi-robot dynamics, in order to generate a favorable framework to detect strengths and weaknesses in current designs.

2. The dynamics of multi-robot systems

By the dynamics of a multi-robot system we mean the set of influencing factors that produce the system's activity. This in turn is relevant because its association with systems change. Note that the dynamics of the system may be useful for its understanding and characterization.

The dynamics of a multi-robot system should represent the activity of the members of the system, in terms of the evolution of their behavior and interactions over time, as a whole. By characterizing a multi-robot system its designers may determine what sort of influences can be traced from multiple experiments using the system under different environmental circumstances, they also can find bounds on the expected performance of the system, and they can also study the system's sensitivity to changes in the population size or the population diversity, to mention but few tasks to undertake to answer some of the challenging questions in collective robotics.

It is worth mentioning that we use the concept of multi-robot system in a very general sense, meaning a group of autonomous or semi-autonomous robots. Thus, the category of multi-robot systems is a broad family comprising teams of homogeneous and heterogenous robots, of collaborative and "individualist" robots; modular robots with static or dynamic reconfiguration capabilities, to mention some examples. For extensive surveys and taxonomies of multi-robot systems, see (Dudek et al., 1996; Cao et al., 1997; Iocchi et al., 2001; Farinelli et al., 2004; Bayinder & Sahin, 2007).

A problem faced by roboticists to characterize the dynamics of a multi-robot system is the *sui generis* nature of choices of the system parameters that are directly measurable, on the one hand; and the available tools to measure the system's activity on the other hand.

The parameters of multi-robot systems, for both physical and simulated robots, that can be directly measurable are, for instance, the goal achievement rate (Tang & Parker, 2007), the average time (Parker, 1993; Couture-Beil & Vaughan, 2009) or steps (Sgorbissa & Arkin, 2003; Mataric et al., 1995) needed to reach a goal, the work distribution (Wawerla & Vaughan, 2010), the cost and use of common resources, such as recharging time (Sempé et al., 2002; Wawerla & Vaughan, 2008) or spatial occupation (Goldberg & Mataric, 1997; Likhachev & Arkin, 2000; Balch et al., 2001). These parameters indicate important aspects of the behavior and interaction of a multi-robot system, as such they will keep being indicators of the performance of the system under varied circumstances. However, parameters indicating the "projection" of the system in a wide variety of circumstances have been rarely measured in the context of multi-robot systems. An exception to that is probably the characterization of the system in terms of fluctuations from a steady state introduced by Lerman et al. (2006) (see section 3 for a detailed description of this work).

Concerning the available tools to measure the system's activity, there is a lot of different numerical tools that can be used for analyzing and assessing robot behavior. However, when the analysis focuses on group behavior issues there is no evidence to justify the use of specific tools. Descriptive statistics are useful tools to describe and summarize properties of data concerning multi-robot systems in a simple and understandable manner.

We consider that descriptive statistic tools can capture significant parameters of the performance of a multi-robot system, such as the mentioned directly measurable parameters, provided that a variety of "projections" of the system can be sized. These "projections" can be generated by a gradual exposure of the system to the variation of scenarios, as we show at the end of this work. These projections should reflect a scale-dependent picture of the multi-robot system, in terms of the selected measurable parameters.

3. Related work

Below we review two works that are closely related to the nature of our research and that deal with the problem of capturing in some way the dynamics of a multi-robot system.

Tucker Balch has been tackling the problem of defining quantitative metrics for multi-robot systems. He introduced a metric inspired by Shannon's information theory that he called "social entropy" that is applied to correlate how group member diversity affects learning in multi-robot systems (Balch, 1997). This metric is subsequently extended to a continuous measurement of diversity in robot groups by combining the previous social entropy with a measure of behavioral difference between individual robots. The extended metric, that is called the "hierarchic social entropy", is applied to investigate a more general question concerning how group member diversity impacts the whole system performance (Balch, 2000).

Diversity is measured by Balch from a behavioral perspective in such a way that perceptual states associated to robot behaviors are represented as binary patterns. These associations are then compared in order to quantify a behavioral difference between two robots. Social entropy and hierarchic social entropy look forward to the improvement of coarse-grain taxonomies that represent multi-robot systems as extreme points in a linear dimension. Balch reviews the flat taxonomy of multi-robot systems that considers two unique classes, homogeneous versus heterogeneous robots. And he proposes instead a more comprehensive taxonomy that holds various degrees of heterogeneity in multi-robot systems, represented as numerical values. An interesting finding regarding Balch's work is that diversity is not desirable *per se*, and that, for some tasks such as foraging, homogeneous robot teams perform better than diverse robot teams. Balch suggests that inherently cooperative tasks, such as robot soccer, are better performed by diverse teams than by homogeneous teams, whereas for more individualistic tasks such as foraging, the opposite performance is observed.

The measures proposed by Balch capture the composition of multi-robot systems in a precise way. At the same time these measures provide evidence that the performance of multi-robot systems is certainly related to their composition, and more precisely that this performance is affected by small differences in the behavioral profile of the members of the system. However we do not know in detail the evolution of the activity of a multi-robot system over time by applying these measures.

The research of Lerman et al. (2006) aims at representing and studying the dynamics of multi-robot systems. This work is closely related to our research in the sense that a global measure of the performance of a multi-robot system is calculated in spite of having incomplete information about that system and its environment. This measure is calculated from the observations of the environment made locally by each robot of the system and recorded onto its own memory. Memory is described by the authors as a rolling history window of finite length.

In the work of Lerman and her colleagues the performance of a multi-robot system is not only measured for characterization purposes. They also investigate how the number of observations, from the local perspective of each robot of the system, and the decisions made by robots from these observations affect the performance of the whole system. For that, transition probabilities between states are calculated by each robot from its individual history. The authors focus their analysis on a scenario of dynamic task allocation, a class of the general problem of task-allocation. The latter is described as the process of assigning individual robots to sub-tasks of a given system level task, whereas dynamic task allocation is the process of assigning robots to subtasks that may need to be continuously adjusted in response to changes in the task environment or group performance. In this scenario, robots decide their task allocation.

A mathematical model of a group of robots that apply previous mechanisms is also introduced, and theoretical predictions made by this model are compared with experimental results of a group of simulated foraging robots. By applying this mechanism, a steady state of the multi-robot system, as well as fluctuations or variations of the steady state are identified, in terms of the number of tasks or foraging objects, and the length of the history of robot observations. Simulated results fit very well with the theoretical results given by the model, which means that the dynamics of the system is well understood and can be captured in the proposed performance measure.

In this research we share the interest of Lerman and her colleagues in macroscopic approaches to study collective behavior in large systems. Our research focuses on homogeneous multi-robot systems.

4. Hands-on practice in representing the dynamics of multi-robot systems

In this section we summarize some efforts of our research group to describe the dynamics of multi-robot and multi-agent systems at various levels. It is worth mentioning that representing and characterizing the dynamics of both, simulated and physical multi-robot systems is far from being obvious. First, we present some examples that illustrate the representation of microscopic robot interactions using a case study approach. And second, we introduce a measure of global multi-robot performance based on ideas of crowd behavior applied in the field of mechanical statistics.

4.1 Microscopic interactions in small group size

The microscopic measurement of interaction among the members of a multi-robot system can be monitored directly throughout one or various experiments. These measurements are basically recordings of detailed observations of robots. These observations are important since based on them, robots are able to make decisions on how to behave. Microscopic measurements are adequate for small groups of robots, where interactions and their effect on robot decisions can be readily captured and traced. We present two cases of microscopic interaction recordings.

Case study 1- The representation of the dynamics is delimited by the nature of the task

The nature of the problem can give some indication of the system dynamics, and this is the case of multi-robot resource sharing applications. We have conducted an experimental study to investigate mechanisms for ensuring some degree of self-sufficiency (McFarland, 1995) in a small group of autonomous robots. The goal of this research was to enable three Pioneer mobile robots from ActivMedia© to remain in operation and efficiently share a charging station using simple mechanisms. A plot of the autonomy of robots during a period of one hour using different sharing strategies gives us a good idea about the interactions of the system, see Figure 1. It can be noticed in the plots that, even though robots manage and allocate a common resource, they might experience delays when accessing the charging station. This information was in fact very useful for defining better sharing strategies. For a detailed description of this work see Sempé et al. (2002).

A second example of representing the dynamics of systems in a multi-robot resource sharing scenario concerns the sharing of the environment. The problem of multi-robot exploration and mapping has been investigated under different approaches, such as multi-robot exploration with unknown start locations (Fox et al., 2006), or multi-robot localization

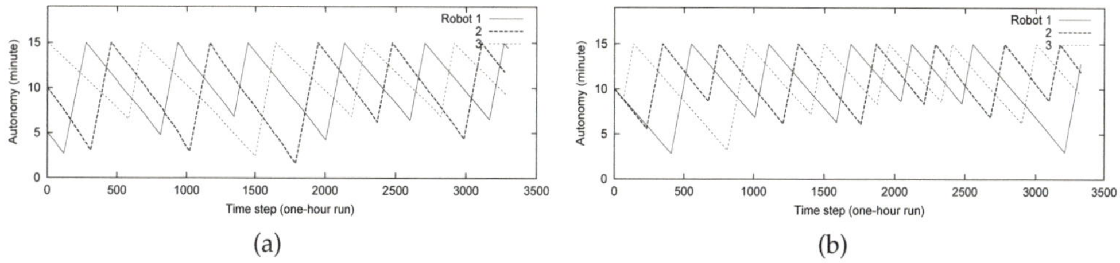

Fig. 1. Autonomy of three mobile robots sharing a charging station using a basic strategy with a 7.5-minute recharge threshold (a), and using an opportunistic strategy with a flexible recharge threshold (b) (Sempé et al., 2002).

based on encounters of pairs of robots (Roy & Dudek, 2000; Howard et al., 2006). We have conducted experiments of multi-robot exploration and mapping of known environments for map updating purposes. For that, a scheme for collective exploration was defined. This scheme enables robots to navigate and self-locate within an indoor environment, communicate to each other and with an external server, provide information to create local maps of their environment to be merged into a global map, and coordinate individual actions in order to explore autonomously the environment. A multi-robot system consisting of three micro mobile robots with very limited equipment was used in these experiments. The testing environment, and the local and global maps acquired by the robots are shown in Figures 2 and 3. Original and updated maps of the environment were also correlated in our work, in order to identify significant changes of the environment. These maps reflect properties of the environment as perceived by the robots, as well as a trace of their actions. Therefore, maps capture the dynamics of the system from the robot's perspective. For a detailed description of this work see (Méndez-Polanco, 2007; Méndez-Polanco & Muñoz-Meléndez, 2008).

Case study 2 - The representation of the dynamics is based on the system's behavior

Now we want to focus on the problem of representing the dynamics of a group of robots that require the performance of accurate physical maneuvers to operate, as it is the case of modular and self-assembling multi-robot systems (Mondada et al., 2003; Murata et al., 2002; Yim, 1994). In contrast to other applications of collective robotics in which isolated, even individualist autonomous robots can contribute to the successful operation of the whole system, a modular multi-robot system relies on the establishment and execution of agreements among its members. Therefore, a key aspect to trace in the dynamics of these systems is the way as their members reach agreements and coordinate their actions as a result, and that usually happens in very short periods of time. As we need a different approach to this problem we represent the dynamics of a modular system from a behavioral perspective.

Fig. 2. Environment used for the experiments of multi-robot exploration.

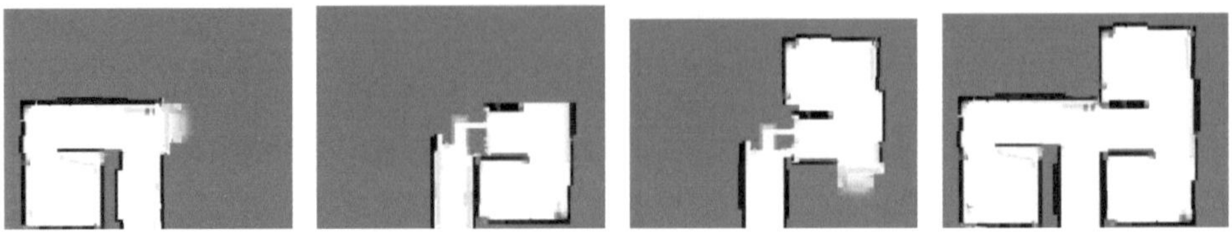

(a) (b) (c) (d)

Fig. 3. Local maps acquired by individual robots (a-c) and global map merged by the server (d) from data of the environment illustrated in Figure 2.

The Mini-trans system is a home-made multi-robot system prototype consisting of three mobile autonomous robots. It was developed in our laboratory of robotics as part of a master thesis (Jiménez-Velasco, 2006). The members of the Mini-trans system have very limited communication capabilities, based on simple devices such as near-IR photo-reflectors, photosensors, and LEDS. The whole system moves sequentially since a single robot is unable to pull or drag a motionless robot. For that, robots transmit messages to each other constantly in order to move collectively. Figure 4 shows a sequence of snapshots acquired during an experiment of collective exploration where various agreements were achieved by the robots. When there was enough space to go ahead, the supervisor stepped forward and a request to copy this movement was progressively propagated and executed from the head towards the tail of the formation. When an obstacle was perceived, a request to go backward was first propagated, followed by its execution from the tail towards the head of the formation. Figure 5 plots the behaviors executed by the robots during this experiment. The plot of behaviors captures the dynamics of the Mini-trans system. For a detailed description of this work see (Jiménez-Velasco, 2006; Jiménez-Velasco & Muñoz-Meléndez, 2006).

4.2 Global interactions

In this part we review some cases where the group size of multi-robot systems is greater than that presented in previous section. For groups of 20 or more robots, as well as for large-scale

(a) (b) (c)

(d) (e) (f)

Fig. 4. The Mini-trans system during an experiment of collective exploration where avoidance maneuvers where conducted (Jiménez-Velasco & Muñoz-Meléndez, 2006).

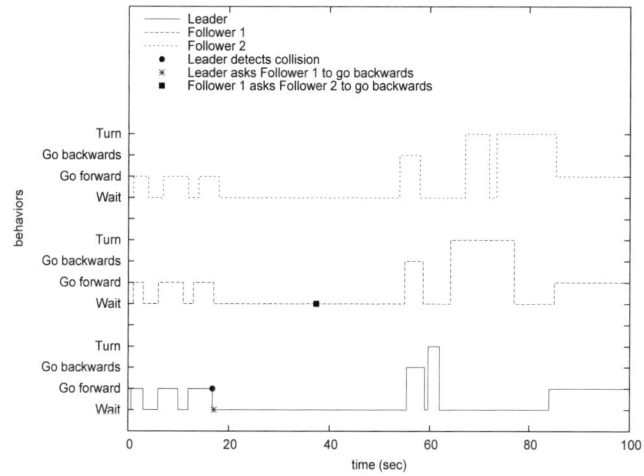

Fig. 5. Behaviors executed and time in which robots of the Mini-trans system send messages during the experiment illustrated in Figure 4 (Jiménez-Velasco & Muñoz-Meléndez, 2006).

repeated experiments it becomes necessary to provide a unique value that quantifies the global state of the system. We first represent the dynamics of a multi-robot system by summarizing the states of its members, then we represent the dynamics by considering flow aspects based on measures of crowd behavior applied in the field of mechanical statistics. As this section concerns extensive experiments, the selected case studies involve simulated multi-robot systems.

Case study 3 - The representation of the dynamics is based on the states of the system

We have studied the problem of collective coordinated motion that is required in applications of flocking (Reynolds, 1987), and generation and maintenance of spatial formations (Unsal & Bay, 1994; Belta & Kumar, 2001; Jakob Fredslund, 2002). In these applications, a group of autonomous robots or agents have to move while keeping a spatial arrangement. Since the acquisition of complete and accurate information about mobile robots in a formation, such as their pose or their speed, is too expensive or inaccesible, local perception based methods are well suited for applications involving multi-robot systems capable of collective coordinated motion.

We proposed and evaluated several robot classes with different capabilities of perception and action, and then we defined a set of organization principles for robots capable of collective coordinated motion using "communicative" robots, a class of robots able to transmit their orientation using color signals on their bodies. For evaluation purposes we recorded the states of the robots which can be in one of two possible states, follower or leader, according to their perception. When they are isolated, robots are in the state of leader, and when they have joined a formation they are in the state of follower. We plotted the number of robots in these states along an experiment in order to verify if the system converges into a single stable formation. Figure 6 shows a sequence of snapshots acquired during an experiment using 25 simulated robots, and Figure 7 plots the states of the robots during this experiment, where robots succeed to generate a formation. For a detailed description of this work see (León-Fernández, 2005; León-Fernández & Muñoz-Meléndez, 2007).

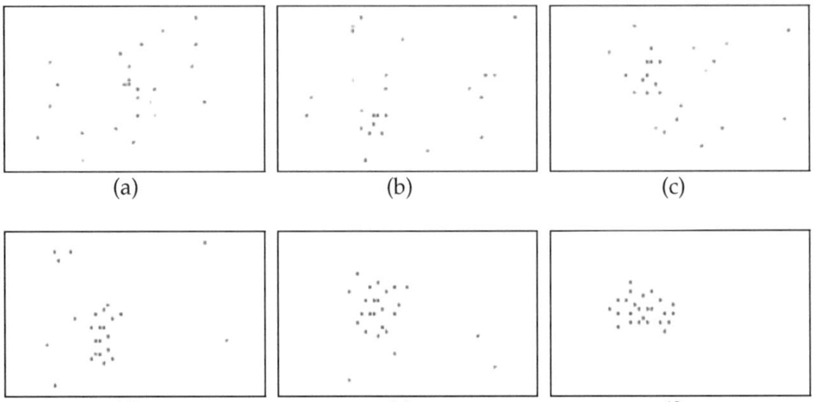

Fig. 6. Simulated robots while trying to gather together
(León-Fernández & Muñoz-Meléndez, 2007).

Case study 4 - The representation of the dynamics based on mechanical statistics metrics
In the previous cases we have succeeded in summarizing the state of a multi-robot system in such a way that its dynamics, in terms of its evolution towards the achievement of a goal, can be followed. Now we are interested in the large-scale replication of these experiments and measurements. We would like to investigate how scalable are the rules and the organizational principles underlying the previous applications, and if certain properties of the system can be characterized from a global measure of its dynamics.
We conducted a set of experiments of foraging robots increasing the population size from 2 robots (that occupy 0.1% of the size of the environment) up to 506 robots (that occupy 25% of the size of the environment), whose goal was to search and retrieve 1,012 pucks (that occupy 50% of the size of the environment) randomly distributed. The robots apply a reactive strategy to solve this problem, they search pucks randomly and carry them towards the center of the environment. Robots can perceive other robots and modify their speed when these encounters are detected, in order to avoid a collision.
Given the large number of experiments and robots, we applied metrics commonly used in the field of mechanical statistics to characterize the dynamics of crowds. The average speed for all crossing robots is calculated, as well as a measure concerning the individual

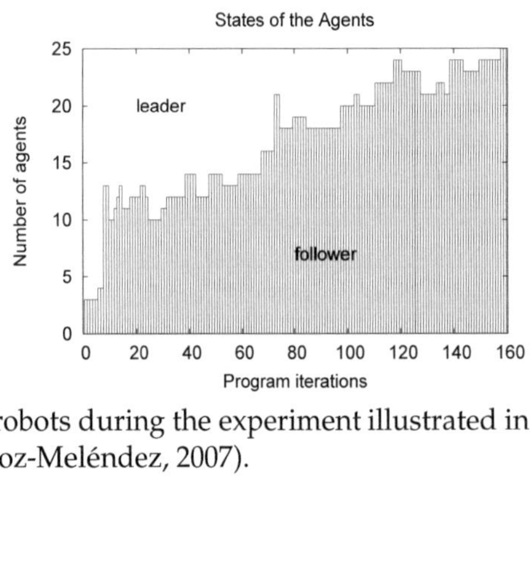

Fig. 7. States of flocking robots during the experiment illustrated in Figure 6
(León-Fernández & Muñoz-Meléndez, 2007).

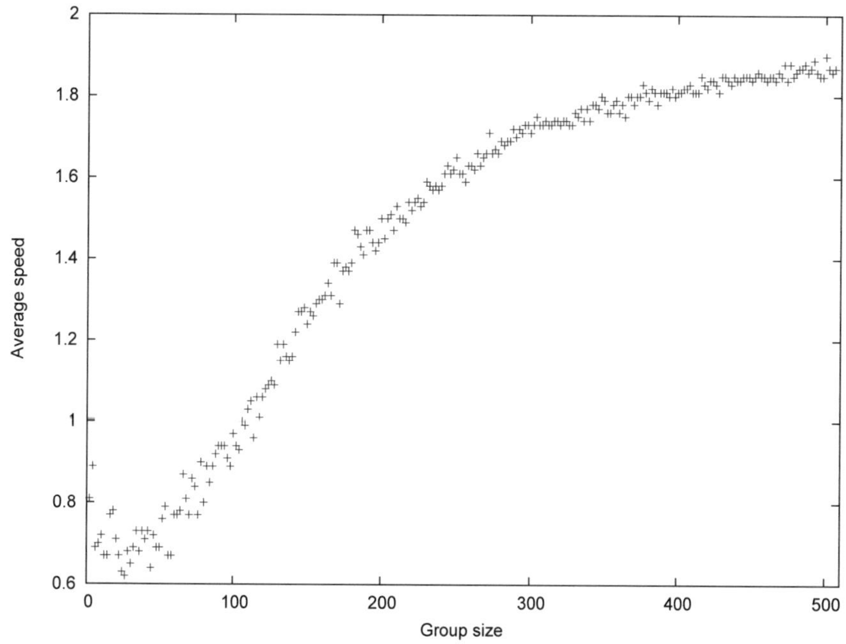

(a)

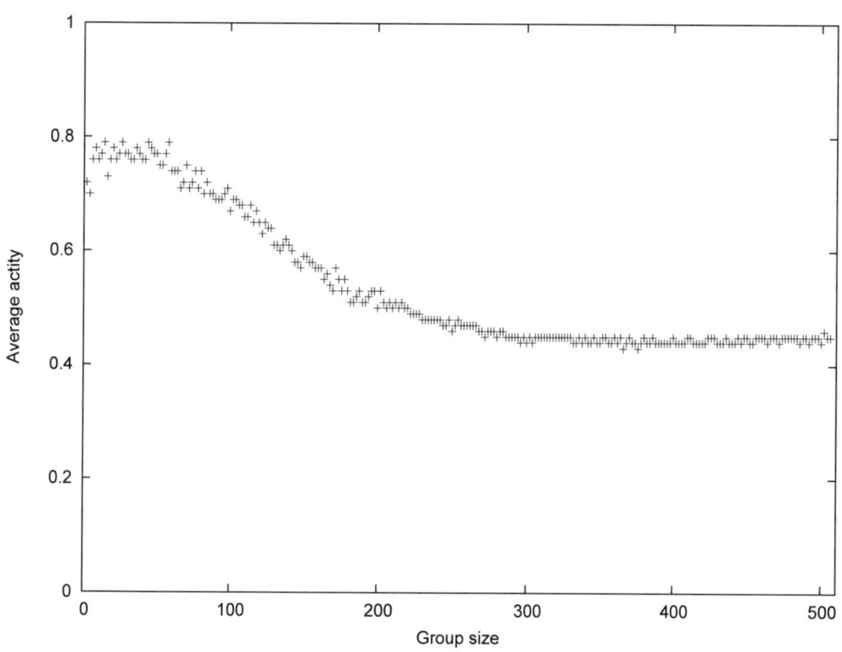

(b)

Fig. 8. Average speed (a) and average activity (b) of a foraging multi-robot system under different conditions of group size. The average speed is given in units of the simulation environment, where 1 unit is around 1m. The activity is a value between 0 and 1. All the experiments lasted 350 iterations of the program.

activity of robots. Activity is a value between 0 and 1 that is calculated from the local perception of each robot, where 0 means no activity in the perceptual field of the robot, and 1 means that a partner or a puck was perceived by the robot. Figure 8 plots the average speed and average activity recorded during 252 experiments where the population size was varied. From these measures we can conclude that this particular system behave as expected when the population size is increased up to 20% of the size of the environment (around 200 robots), for larger groups the activity remains stalled that is also reflected as an increase in the average speed of the robots that result from their useless wandering of the environment looking for pucks. Previous measures have exponential distributions, the average speed of robots exhibits an exponential growth whereas their average activity exhibits an exponential decay. Average speed summarizes the effect of robot decisions on their environment, and average activity summarizes the internal robot perception. Both measures change in proportion to the density of multi-robot groups. The task of foraging a number of pucks is quite beyond the capabilities of small groups consisting of less than 100 robots, as can be noticed in their slow speed and high level of activity. Mid-sized groups of around 200 robots and bigger groups retrieve pucks and move faster as a result of the "cleaning" of their environment. Note that the activity of groups consisting of more than 200 robots remains constant, since activity captures the permanent interaction among the robots. Activity and speed measured during large-scale repeated experiments provide a general idea of the performance of multi-robot systems, their evolution and the way as these systems are degraded. Specific design aspects such as the impact in robot dynamics of different robot controllers can also be analyzed by applying these metrics. The field of mechanical statistics has a well-trodden path to the understanding and characterization of crowd dynamics and the research on multi-robot systems can take advantage of its progress. A kinetic model of a multi-agent system for an application of pedestrian crowd simulation, as well as measures of speed and activity with inverse tendencies to those observed previously can be consulted in Rangel-Huerta & Muñoz-Meléndez (2010).

5. Conclusions

We described some efforts of our research group towards the theoretical understanding and characterization of homogeneous multi-robot systems. Event though collective robotics comprises a large diversity of applications, we analyzed a set of case studies and provided experimental results that illustrate that the dynamics of multi-robot systems can be represented in various applications. A lot of work remains to be done in order to represent and quantify the behavior, evolution and convergence of multi-robot systems in an effective and accurate manner. The experience gained in other fields such as, for instance, mechanical statistics should be considered in this effort. Representation and characterization of the dynamics and performance of multi-robot systems will certainly benefit the field of collective robots by providing design guidelines, good practices for roboticists, and standards of validation.

6. References

Balch, T. (1997). Social entropy: a new metric for learning multi-robot teams, *Proceedings of the 10th International Florida Artificial Intelligence Research Society Conference (FLAIRS-97*, pp. 272–277.

Balch, T. (2000). Hierarchic social entropy: an information theoretic measure of robot group diversity, *Autonomous Robots* 8(3): 209–237.

Balch, T., Khan, Z. & Veloso, M. (2001). Automatically tracking and analyzing the behavior of live insect colonies, *Proceedings of the 5th International Conference on Autonomous Agents*, pp. 521–528.

Bayinder, L. & Sahin, E. (2007). A review of studies in swarm robotics, *Turk Journal of Electronics and Engineering* 15(2): 115–147.

Belta, C. & Kumar, V. (2001). Motion generation for formations of robots: a geometric approach, *Proceedings of the IEEE International Conference on Robotics and Automation (ICRA)*, pp. 1245–1250.

Cao, Y. U., Fukunaga, A. S. & Kahng, A. B. (1997). Cooperative mobile robotics: antecedents and directions, *Autonomous Robots* 4: 226–234.

Couture-Beil, A. & Vaughan, R. T. (2009). Adaptive mobile charging stations for multi-robot systems, *Proceedings of the IEEE International Conference on Intelligent Robots and Systems (IROS'09)*, pp. 1363–1368.

Dudek, G., Jenkin, M. R. M., Milios, E. & Wilkes, D. (1996). A taxonomy for multi-agent robotics, *Autonomous Robots* 3.

Farinelli, A., Iocchi, L. & Nardi, D. (2004). Multi-robot systems: a classification focused on coordination, *IEEE Transactions on Systems, Man and Cybernetics - Part B* 34(5): 2015–2018.

Fox, D., andKurt Konolige, J. K., Limketkai, B., Schulz, D. & Stewart, B. (2006). Distributed multi-robot exploration and mapping, *Proceedings of the IEEE*, pp. 1325–1339.

Goldberg, D. & Mataric, M. (1997). Interference as a tool for designing and evaluating multi-robot controllers, *Proceedings of the 14th National Conference on Artificial Intelligence (AAAI-97)*, AAAI Press, pp. 637–642.

Howard, A., Parker, L. E. & Sukhatme, G. S. (2006). Experiments with a large heterogeneous mobile robot team: Exploration, mapping, deployment and detection, *The International Journal of Robotics Research* 25(5-6): 431–447.

Iocchi, L., Nardi, D. & Salerno, M. (2001). Reactivity and deliberation; a survey on multi-robot systems., *Balancing Reactivity and Social Deliberation in Multi-Agent Systems, From RoboCup to Real-World Applications*, Springer, pp. 9–34.

Jakob Fredslund, M. J. M. (2002). A general, local algorithm for robot formations, *IEEE Transactions on Robotics and Automation, special issue on Multi Robot Systems* 18(5): 837–846.

Jiménez-Velasco, M. G. (2006). *Design and implementation of a multi-robot system capable of self-assembling*, Master's thesis, Computer Science Department, INAOE. In Spanish.

Jiménez-Velasco, M. G. & Muñoz-Meléndez, A. (2006). Multi-robot motion coordination based on swing propagation, *Proceedings of the 7th International Conference on Computer Science (ENC'06)*, pp. 44–51.

León-Fernández, Y. (2005). *Generation and maintenance of spatial formations for collective robotics*, Master's thesis, Computer Science Department, INAOE. In Spanish.

León-Fernández, Y. & Muñoz-Meléndez, A. (2007). Investigación sobre los requisitos del movimiento colectivo coordinado en un sistema multi-agente, *Inteligencia Artificial. Revista Iberoamericana de Inteligencia Artificial* 11(34): 83–103.

Lerman, K., Jones, C., Galstyan, A. & Mataric, M. J. (2006). Analysis of dynamic task allocation in multi-robot systems, *International Journal of Robotics Research* 3(25): 225–242.

Likhachev, M. & Arkin, R. C. (2000). Robotic comfort zones, *Proceedings of SPIE Sensor Fusion andDecentralized Control in Robotic Systems III*, Vol. 4196, pp. 27–41.

Mataric, M. J., Nilsson, M. & Simsarin, K. T. (1995). Cooperative multi-robot box-pushing, *Proceedings of the IEEE/RSJ International Conference on Intelligent Robots and Systems 95 (IROS'95)*, Vol. 3, pp. 556–561.

McFarland, D. (1995). *The artificial life route to artificial intelligence: building embodied, situated agents*, Lawrence Erlbaum Ass., chapter Autonomy and self-sufficiency in robots, pp. 187–213.

Méndez-Polanco, J. A. (2007). *Local map fusion from the distributed perception of a robot team*, Master's thesis, Computer Science Department, INAOE. In Spanish.

Méndez-Polanco, J. A. & Muñoz-Meléndez, A. (2008). Collaborative robots for indoor environment exploration, *Proceedings of the 10th International Conference on Control, Automation, Robotics and Vision (ICARCV 2008)*.

Mondada, F., Guignard, A., Bonani, M., Bar, D., Lauria, M. & Floreano, D. (2003). Swarm-bot: from concept to implementation, *Proceedings of the 2003 IEEE/RSJ International Conference on Intelligent Robot and Systems (IROS 203)*, pp. 1626–1631.

Murata, S., Yoshida, E., Kamimura, A., Kurokawa, H., Tomita, K. & Kokaji, S. (2002). Mtran: A self-reconfigurable modular robot, *IEEE/ASME Transactions on Mechatronics* 7(4).

Parker, L. E. (1993). Designing control laws for cooperative agent teams, *Proceedings of the IEEE International Conference on Robotics and Automation (ICRA)*, Vol. 3, pp. 582–587.

Rangel-Huerta, A. & Muñoz-Meléndez, A. (2010). Kinetic theory of situated agents applied to pedestrian flow in a corridor, *Physica A: A Statistical Mechanics and its Applications* (389): 1077–1086.

Reynolds, C. (1987). Flocks, herds, and schools: A distributed behavioral model, *Computer Graphics* 21(4): 25–34.

Roy, N. & Dudek, G. (2000). Collaborative robot exploration and rendezvous. algorithms, performance bounds and observations, *Autonomous Robots* 11: 117–136.

Sempé, F., Muñoz, A. & Drogoul, A. (2002). Autonomous robots sharing a charging station with no communication: a case study, *in* A. H. et al. (ed.), *Distributed Autonomous Robotic Systems 5*, Springer-Verlag, pp. 91–100.

Sgorbissa, A. & Arkin, R. C. (2003). Local navigation strategies for a team of robots, *Robotica* 21(5): 461–473.

Shell, D. A., Jones, C. V. & Mataric, M. J. (2005). Ergodic dynamics by design: A route to predictable multi-robot systems, *Multi-robot systems: From swarms to intelligent automata*, pp. 291–297.

Tang, F. & Parker, L. E. (2007). A complete methodology for generating multi-robot task solutions using asymtre-d and market-based task allocation, *Proceedings of IEEE International Conference on Robotics and Automation (ICRA07)*, pp. 3351–3358.

Unsal, C. & Bay, J. S. (1994). Spatial self-organization in large populations of mobile robots, *IEEE International Symposium on Intelligent Control*, pp. 249–254.

Wawerla, J. & Vaughan, R. T. (2008). Optimal robot recharging strategies for time discounted labour, *Proceedings of the 11th International Conference on on the Simulation and Synthesis of Living Systems (Artificial Life XII)*, MIT Press, pp. 670–677.

Wawerla, J. & Vaughan, R. T. (2010). A fast and frugal method for team-task allocation in a multi-robot transportation system, *Proceedings of the IEEE International Conference on Robotics and Automation*.

Yim, M. (1994). *Locomotion with a unit modular reconfigurable robot*, PhD thesis, Deptartment of Mechanical Engineering, Stanford University.

28

Modeling, Simulation and Control of 3-DOF Redundant Fault Tolerant Robots by Means of Adaptive Inertia

Claudio Urrea and John Kern
Departamento de Ingeniería Eléctrica, DIE
Universidad de Santiago de Chile, USACH
Santiago, Chile

1. Introduction

Control systems that have the ability, in the one hand, to detect incipient failures in sensors and/or actuators and, in the other hand, to adapt quickly the control laws in order to preserve the specified performance in terms of production quality, safety, etc., are called fault-tolerant control systems (Blanke et al., 2001), (Blanke et al., 2006). This kind of systems have become increasingly important for manipulator robots, especially those performing in remote or dangerous zones, like outer space, underwater or nuclear environments. In this context, there is a growing need and interest in developing control systems that can operate in acceptable manners, even after the occurrence of failures, also being able to stop the process before irreparable damages arise (Bonivento et al., 2004).

In this work, modeling, simulation and control of industrial fault tolerant robots by means of adaptive inertia is presented. This study, initially developed for robots with n Degrees Of Freedom (DOF), includes the calculation of adaptive inertia parameters; which is particularized for planar systems with two and three rotational joints. The modeling of these systems considers kinematic and dynamic aspects of robots, including the dynamics of actuators and position sensors that, by employing MatLab/Simulink software, permits the simulation and results displaying of dynamic behavior of such systems in front of actuator failures.

2. Fault tolerant controller: adaptive inertia

The active fault tolerant control system proposed in this work is based on an adaptive control law, specifically: adaptive inertia (Lewis et al., 2004), (Siciliano & Khatib, 2008), (Ollero, 2001) then it is necessary to consider the manipulator dynamic model in the way expressed in equation (1) (Angeles, 2006), (Craig, 1986), (Spong et al., 2005), where the term corresponding to centrifugal and Coriolis forces is expressed through a matrix **Vm**.

$$\boldsymbol{\tau} = \mathbf{M}(q)\ddot{\mathbf{q}} + \mathbf{V}_{\mathrm{m}}(q,\dot{q})\dot{\mathbf{q}} + \mathbf{G}(q) + \mathbf{F}(\dot{q}) \tag{1}$$

Position, speed and acceleration errors, in terms of manipulator link coordinates, are shown in equations (2), (3) and (4), respectively.

$$\mathbf{e} = \mathbf{q_d} - \mathbf{q} \tag{2}$$

$$\dot{\mathbf{e}} = \dot{\mathbf{q}}_\mathbf{d} - \dot{\mathbf{q}} \tag{3}$$

$$\ddot{\mathbf{e}} = \ddot{\mathbf{q}}_\mathbf{d} - \ddot{\mathbf{q}} \tag{4}$$

Clearing link position q, its first and second derivative; from equations (2), (3) and (4), respectively we have:

$$\mathbf{q} = \mathbf{q_d} - \mathbf{e} \tag{5}$$

$$\dot{\mathbf{q}} = \dot{\mathbf{q}}_\mathbf{d} - \dot{\mathbf{e}} \tag{6}$$

$$\ddot{\mathbf{q}} = \ddot{\mathbf{q}}_\mathbf{d} - \ddot{\mathbf{e}} \tag{7}$$

Next, we define error auxiliar signal $\mathbf{r}$ and its derivative $\dot{\mathbf{r}}$, with respect to time, as shown in equations (8) and (9), respectively:

$$\mathbf{r} = \mathbf{\Lambda e} + \dot{\mathbf{e}} \tag{8}$$

$$\dot{\mathbf{r}} = \mathbf{\Lambda}\dot{\mathbf{e}} + \ddot{\mathbf{e}} \tag{9}$$

where:
$\mathbf{\Lambda}$: Definite positive diagonal matrix ($n \times n$ dimension).

$$\mathbf{\Lambda} = \begin{bmatrix} \lambda_1 & & & \\ & \lambda_2 & & \\ & & \ddots & \\ & & & \lambda_n \end{bmatrix} \tag{10}$$

Clearing the first and second derivatives from error in equations (8) and (9), respectively, we obtain:

$$\dot{\mathbf{e}} = \mathbf{r} - \mathbf{\Lambda e} \tag{11}$$

$$\ddot{\mathbf{e}} = \dot{\mathbf{r}} - \mathbf{\Lambda}\dot{\mathbf{e}} \tag{12}$$

Replacing equations (11) and (12) in equations (5), (6) and (7), we have:

$$\dot{\mathbf{q}} = \dot{\mathbf{q}}_\mathbf{d} - \mathbf{r} + \mathbf{\Lambda e} \tag{13}$$

$$\ddot{\mathbf{q}} = \ddot{\mathbf{q}}_\mathbf{d} - \dot{\mathbf{r}} + \mathbf{\Lambda}\dot{\mathbf{e}} \tag{14}$$

Replacing equations (13) and (14) in expression (1), we achieve:

$$\boldsymbol{\tau} = \mathbf{M}(q)(\ddot{\mathbf{q}}_\mathbf{d} - \dot{\mathbf{r}} + \boldsymbol{\Lambda}\dot{\mathbf{e}}) + \mathbf{V}_\mathbf{m}(q,\dot{q})(\dot{\mathbf{q}}_\mathbf{d} - \mathbf{r} + \boldsymbol{\Lambda}\mathbf{e}) + \mathbf{G}(q) + \mathbf{F}(\dot{q}) \tag{15}$$

Then:

$$\boldsymbol{\tau} = \mathbf{M}(q)(\ddot{\mathbf{q}}_\mathbf{d} + \boldsymbol{\Lambda}\dot{\mathbf{e}}) + \mathbf{V}_\mathbf{m}(q,\dot{q})(\dot{\mathbf{q}}_\mathbf{d} + \boldsymbol{\Lambda}\mathbf{e}) + \mathbf{G}(q) + \mathbf{F}(\dot{q}) - \mathbf{M}(q)\dot{\mathbf{r}} - \mathbf{V}_\mathbf{m}(q,\dot{q})\mathbf{r} \tag{16}$$

Making the following matching:

$$\mathbf{Y}(\cdot)\boldsymbol{\varphi} = \mathbf{M}(q)(\ddot{\mathbf{q}}_\mathbf{d} + \boldsymbol{\Lambda}\dot{\mathbf{e}}) + \mathbf{V}_\mathbf{m}(q,\dot{q})(\dot{\mathbf{q}}_\mathbf{d} + \boldsymbol{\Lambda}\mathbf{e}) + \mathbf{G}(q) + \mathbf{F}(\dot{q}) \tag{17}$$

where:

$$\mathbf{Y}(q,\dot{q},q_d,\dot{q}_d,\ddot{q}_d) = \begin{bmatrix} Y_{11} & Y_{12} & \cdots & Y_{1n} \\ Y_{21} & Y_{22} & \cdots & Y_{2n} \\ \vdots & \vdots & \ddots & \vdots \\ Y_{n1} & Y_{n2} & \cdots & Y_{nn} \end{bmatrix} \tag{18}$$

$\mathbf{Y}(\cdot)$: Regression matrix ($n \times n$ dimension).
$\boldsymbol{\varphi}$: Parameter vector ($n \times n$ dimension).
Equation (16) can be written in the following way:

$$\boldsymbol{\tau} = \mathbf{Y}(\cdot)\boldsymbol{\varphi} - \mathbf{M}(q)\dot{\mathbf{r}} - \mathbf{V}_\mathbf{m}(q,\dot{q})\mathbf{r} \tag{19}$$

The control torque is given by:

$$\boldsymbol{\tau} = \mathbf{Y}(\cdot)\hat{\boldsymbol{\varphi}} + \mathbf{K}_\mathbf{v}\mathbf{r} \tag{20}$$

where:
$\mathbf{K}_\mathbf{v}$: Definite positive diagonal matrix ($n \times n$ dimension).
$\hat{\boldsymbol{\varphi}}$: Parameter estimation vector ($n \times n$ dimension).
The update rule is expressed by:

$$\dot{\hat{\boldsymbol{\varphi}}} = -\dot{\tilde{\boldsymbol{\varphi}}} = \boldsymbol{\Gamma}\mathbf{Y}^T(\cdot)\mathbf{r} \tag{21}$$

where:
$\boldsymbol{\Gamma}$: Definite positive diagonal matrix ($n \times n$ dimension).

$$\boldsymbol{\Gamma} = \begin{bmatrix} \gamma_1 & & & \\ & \gamma_2 & & \\ & & \ddots & \\ & & & \gamma_n \end{bmatrix} \tag{22}$$

Replacing equation (21) into equation (20), we have:

$$\boldsymbol{\tau} = \mathbf{Y}(\cdot)\int \boldsymbol{\Gamma}\mathbf{Y}^T(\cdot)\mathbf{r} + \mathbf{K}_\mathbf{v}\mathbf{r} \tag{23}$$

Replacing equation (8) into equation (23), we have:

$$\boldsymbol{\tau} = \mathbf{Y}(\cdot)\int \boldsymbol{\Gamma}\mathbf{Y}^T(\cdot)(\boldsymbol{\Lambda}\mathbf{e} + \dot{\mathbf{e}}) + \mathbf{K}_\mathbf{V}\boldsymbol{\Lambda}\mathbf{e} + \mathbf{K}_\mathbf{V}\dot{\mathbf{e}} \tag{24}$$

3. Applications

3.1 Planar system with two rotational joints

3.1.1 Vm matrix for 2 DOF

To obtain the matrix of centrifugal and Coriolis forces in a planar system with two rotational joints, we must consider:

$$\mathbf{C}(\mathbf{q},\dot{\mathbf{q}}) = \mathbf{V_m}(\mathbf{q},\dot{\mathbf{q}})\dot{\mathbf{q}} \tag{25}$$

$$\mathbf{V_m} = \frac{1}{2}\left(\dot{\mathbf{M}} + \mathbf{U}^{\mathrm{T}} - \mathbf{U}\right) \tag{26}$$

$$\mathbf{U} = \left(\mathbf{I}\otimes\dot{\mathbf{q}}^{T}\right)\frac{\partial \mathbf{M}}{\partial \mathbf{q}} \tag{27}$$

where:

$\otimes$: Kronecker product.

Considering the expression given by (64) (Appendix A), and developing equations (26) and (27), we have:

$$\mathbf{V_m} = \begin{bmatrix} V_{m11} & V_{m12} \\ V_{m21} & V_{m22} \end{bmatrix} \tag{28}$$

$$\left(\mathbf{I}\otimes\dot{\mathbf{q}}^{\mathrm{T}}\right) = \begin{bmatrix} 1 & 0 \\ 0 & 1 \end{bmatrix} \otimes \begin{bmatrix} \dot{q}_1 & \dot{q}_2 \end{bmatrix} \tag{29}$$

$$\left(\mathbf{I}\otimes\dot{\mathbf{q}}^{T}\right) = \begin{bmatrix} \dot{q}_1 & \dot{q}_2 & 0 & 0 \\ 0 & 0 & \dot{q}_1 & \dot{q}_2 \end{bmatrix} \tag{30}$$

$$\frac{\partial \mathbf{M}}{\partial \mathbf{q}} = \begin{bmatrix} \dfrac{\partial \mathbf{M}}{\partial q_1} \\ \dfrac{\partial \mathbf{M}}{\partial q_2} \end{bmatrix} \tag{31}$$

$$\begin{aligned} V_{m11} &= -m_2 l_1 l_{c2} \sin\theta_2 \dot{\theta}_2 \\ V_{m12} &= -m_2 l_1 l_{c2} \sin\theta_2 \left(\dot{\theta}_1 + \dot{\theta}_2\right) \\ V_{m21} &= m_2 l_1 l_{c2} \sin\theta_2 \dot{\theta}_1 \\ V_{m22} &= 0 \end{aligned} \tag{32}$$

3.1.2 Regression matrix for 2 DOF

The regression matrix considering two degrees of freedom is expressed by:

$$\mathbf{Y} = \begin{bmatrix} Y_{11} & Y_{12} \\ Y_{21} & Y_{22} \end{bmatrix} \tag{33}$$

Calculation of regression matrix is developed in Appendix B, resulting in the components we can see in equation (34):

$$\begin{aligned}
Y_{11} &= \left(\frac{I_{1zz}}{m_1} + l_{c1}^2\right)\dot{Q}_1 \\
Y_{12} &= l_1^2\dot{Q}_1 + \left(\frac{I_{2zz}}{m_2} + l_{c2}^2\right)\left(\dot{Q}_1 + \dot{Q}_2\right) + y_A\left(2\dot{Q}_1 + \dot{Q}_2\right) - y_a\left(Q_2\left(\dot{\theta}_1 + \dot{\theta}_2\right) + Q_1\dot{\theta}_2\right) \\
Y_{21} &= 0 \\
Y_{22} &= y_a\dot{\theta}_1 Q_1 + y_A\dot{Q}_1 + \left(\frac{I_{2zz}}{m_2} + l_{c2}^2\right)\left(\dot{Q}_1 + \dot{Q}_2\right)
\end{aligned} \tag{34}$$

3.2 Planar system with three rotational joints

We will consider now the three first DOF of the robotic manipulator shown in figure 1.

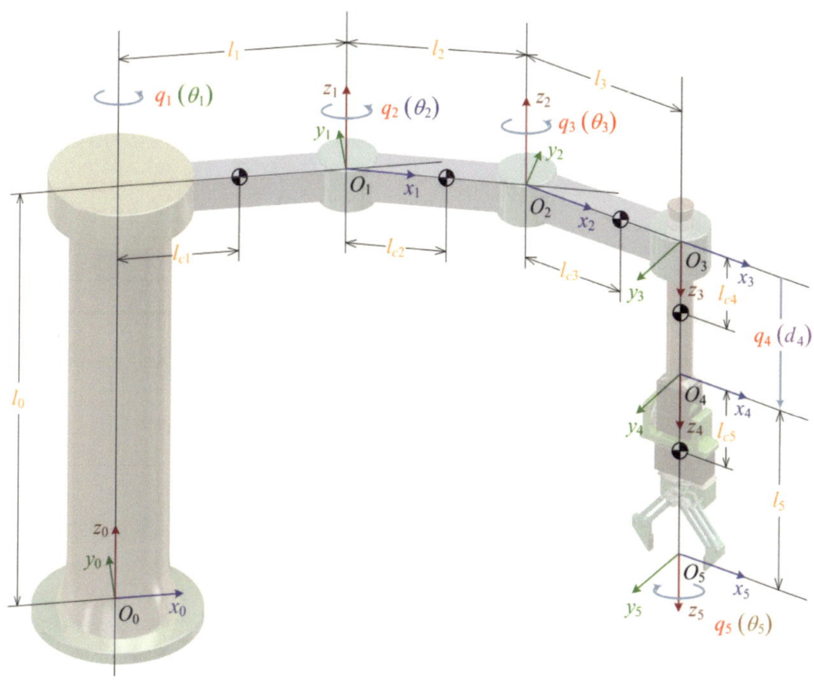

Fig. 1. Scheme of a redundant robotic manipulator of SCARA type

3.2.1 Vm matrix for 3 DOF3

From the development of expressions given by (26) and (27), considering three degrees of freedom, we get:

$$\mathbf{V_m} = \begin{bmatrix} V_{m11} & V_{m12} & V_{m13} \\ V_{m21} & V_{m22} & V_{m23} \\ V_{m31} & V_{m32} & V_{m33} \end{bmatrix} \tag{35}$$

$$\left(\mathbf{I}\otimes\dot{\mathbf{q}}^T\right) = \begin{bmatrix}1 & 0 & 0\\ 0 & 1 & 0\\ 0 & 0 & 1\end{bmatrix}\otimes\begin{bmatrix}\dot{q}_1 & \dot{q}_2 & \dot{q}_3\end{bmatrix} \tag{36}$$

$$\left(\mathbf{I}\otimes\dot{\mathbf{q}}^T\right) = \begin{bmatrix}\dot{q}_1 & \dot{q}_2 & \dot{q}_3 & 0 & 0 & 0 & 0 & 0 & 0\\ 0 & 0 & 0 & \dot{q}_1 & \dot{q}_2 & \dot{q}_3 & 0 & 0 & 0\\ 0 & 0 & 0 & 0 & 0 & 0 & \dot{q}_1 & \dot{q}_2 & \dot{q}_3\end{bmatrix} \tag{37}$$

$$\frac{\partial \mathbf{M}}{\partial \mathbf{q}} = \begin{bmatrix}\dfrac{\partial \mathbf{M}}{\partial q_1}\\ \dfrac{\partial \mathbf{M}}{\partial q_2}\\ \dfrac{\partial \mathbf{M}}{\partial q_3}\end{bmatrix} \tag{38}$$

The matrix of centrifugal and Coriolis forces for the three first degrees of freedom of the robot manipulator under study, can be expressed by means of equation (39) (see Appendix C):

$$\begin{aligned}
V_{m11} &= -\left(c_a + c_b\right)\dot{\theta}_2 - c_c\dot{\theta}_3 - c_d\left(\dot{\theta}_2 + \dot{\theta}_3\right)\\
V_{m12} &= -\left(c_a + c_b\right)\left(\dot{\theta}_1 + \dot{\theta}_2\right) - c_c\dot{\theta}_3 - c_d\left(\dot{\theta}_1 + \dot{\theta}_2 + \dot{\theta}_3\right)\\
V_{m13} &= -\left(c_c + c_d\right)\left(\dot{\theta}_1 + \dot{\theta}_2 + \dot{\theta}_3\right)\\
V_{m21} &= \left(c_a + c_b + c_d\right)\dot{\theta}_1 - c_c\dot{\theta}_3\\
V_{m22} &= -c_c\dot{\theta}_3\\
V_{m23} &= -c_c\left(\dot{\theta}_1 + \dot{\theta}_2 + \dot{\theta}_3\right)\\
V_{m31} &= c_c\left(\dot{\theta}_1 + \dot{\theta}_2\right) + c_d\dot{\theta}_1\\
V_{m32} &= c_c\left(\dot{\theta}_1 + \dot{\theta}_2\right)\\
V_{m33} &= 0
\end{aligned} \tag{39}$$

3.2.2 Regression matrix for 3 DOF

After obtaining the matrix of centrifugal and Coriolis forces **Vm** for the three first degrees of freedom under consideration, we proceed to calculate the corresponding regression matrix, whose form is expressed by means of equation (40):

$$\mathbf{Y} = \begin{bmatrix}Y_{11} & Y_{12} & Y_{13}\\ Y_{21} & Y_{22} & Y_{23}\\ Y_{31} & Y_{32} & Y_{33}\end{bmatrix} \tag{40}$$

The components of the regression matrix are developed in Appendix D, and the results can be expressed by:

$$Y_{11} = \left(I_{1zz}/m_1 + l_{c1}^2\right)\dot{Q}_1 \tag{41}$$

$$Y_{12} = -y_a\left(\dot{\theta}_2 Q_1 + \left(\dot{\theta}_1 + \dot{\theta}_2\right)Q_2\right) + \left(I_{2zz}/m_2 + l_1^2 + l_{c2}^2 + 2y_A\right)\dot{Q}_1 + \left(I_{2zz}/m_2 + l_{c2}^2 + y_A\right)\dot{Q}_2 \quad (42)$$

$$\begin{aligned} Y_{13} = & -\left(y_b + y_d\right)\left(\dot{\theta}_2 Q_1 + \left(\dot{\theta}_1 + \dot{\theta}_2\right)Q_2\right) - \left(y_c + y_d\right)\left(\dot{\theta}_3\left(Q_1 + Q_2\right) + \left(\dot{\theta}_1 + \dot{\theta}_2 + \dot{\theta}_3\right)Q_3\right) + \\ & \left(I_{3zz}/m_3 + l_1^2 + l_2^2 + l_{c3}^2 + 2\left(y_B + y_C + y_D\right)\right)\dot{Q}_1 + \left(I_{3zz}/m_3 + l_2^2 + l_{c3}^2 + y_B + 2y_C + y_D\right) \\ & \dot{Q}_2 + \left(l_{c3}^2 + y_C + y_D\right)\dot{Q}_3 \end{aligned} \quad (43)$$

$$Y_{21} = 0 \quad (44)$$

$$Y_{22} = y_a \dot{\theta}_1 Q_1 + \left(I_{2zz}/m_2 + \left(l_{c2}^2 + y_A\right)\right)\dot{Q}_1 + \left(I_{2zz}/m_2 + l_{c2}^2\right)\dot{Q}_2 \quad (45)$$

$$\begin{aligned} Y_{23} = & \left(y_b + y_d\right)\dot{\theta}_1 Q_1 - y_c\left(\dot{\theta}_3\left(Q_2 + Q_1 + Q_3\right) + \left(\dot{\theta}_1 + \dot{\theta}_2\right)Q_3\right) + \left(I_{3zz}/m_3 + l_2^2 + l_{c3}^2 + y_B + \right. \\ & \left. 2y_C + y_D\right)\dot{Q}_1 + \left(I_{3zz}/m_3 + l_2^2 + l_{c3}^2 + 2y_C\right)\dot{Q}_2 + \left(I_{3zz}/m_3 + l_{c3}^2 + y_C\right)\dot{Q}_3 \end{aligned} \quad (46)$$

$$Y_{31} = 0 \quad (47)$$

$$Y_{32} = 0 \quad (48)$$

$$\begin{aligned} Y_{33} = & y_d \dot{\theta}_1 Q_1 + y_c\left(\dot{\theta}_1 + \dot{\theta}_2\right)\left(Q_1 + Q_2\right) + \left(I_{3zz}/m_3 + l_{c3}^2 + y_C + y_D\right)\dot{Q}_1 + \left(I_{3zz}/m_3 + l_{c3}^2 + \right. \\ & \left. y_C\right)\dot{Q}_2 + \left(I_{3zz}/m_3 + l_{c3}^2\right)\dot{Q}_3 \end{aligned} \quad (49)$$

3.2.3 Inverse kinematics

When a failure arises in the robot manipulator, the fault tolerant controller must reconfigure itself, carrying out real-time calculation of the new inverse kinematics that is generated. In the case of adaptive inertia control, it is necessary to calculate, in addition to the new joint positions, the new joint speeds and accelerations.

The new position of joint three is given by equation (50):

$$\theta_{N3} = \arccos\left(\frac{x^2 + y^2 - l_v^2 - l_3^2}{2 l_v l_3}\right) - \theta_\gamma \quad (50)$$

The new joint speed and acceleration is given by equations (55) and (56), respectively.

$$u = \frac{x^2 + y^2 - l_v^2 - l_3^2}{2 l_v l_3} \quad (51)$$

$$\dot{u} = \frac{1}{l_v l_3}\left(x\dot{x} + y\dot{y}\right) \quad (52)$$

$$\ddot{u} = \frac{1}{l_v l_3}\left(\dot{x}^2 + \dot{y}^2 + x\ddot{x} + y\ddot{y}\right) \quad (53)$$

$$\theta_{N3} = \arccos(u) - \theta_\gamma \tag{54}$$

$$\dot{\theta}_{N3} = -\frac{\dot{u}}{\sqrt{1-u^2}} \tag{55}$$

$$\ddot{\theta}_{N3} = -\frac{\ddot{u}}{\sqrt{1-u^2}} - \frac{u\dot{u}^2}{\left(1-u^2\right)^{3/2}} \tag{56}$$

The new position of joint one is expressed by equation (57):

$$\theta_{N1} = \arctan\left(\frac{y}{x}\right) - \arctan\left(\frac{l_3 \sin\left(\theta_{N3}+\theta_\gamma\right)}{l_v + l_3\cos\left(\theta_{N3}+\theta_\gamma\right)}\right) - \theta_\beta \tag{57}$$

The new joint speed and acceleration is given by equations (62) and (63), respectively.

$$v = \frac{l_3 \sin\left(\theta_{N3}+\theta_\gamma\right)}{l_v + l_3\cos\left(\theta_{N3}+\theta_\gamma\right)} \tag{58}$$

$$\dot{v} = \frac{l_3}{l_v + l_3\cos\left(\theta_{N3}+\theta_\gamma\right)}\left(\frac{l_3 \sin\left(\theta_{N3}+\theta_\gamma\right)^2}{l_v + l_3\cos\left(\theta_{N3}+\theta_\gamma\right)} + \frac{\cos\left(\theta_{N3}+\theta_\gamma\right)}{l_v + l_3\cos\left(\theta_{N3}+\theta_\gamma\right)}\right)\dot{\theta}_{N3} \tag{59}$$

$$\begin{aligned}\ddot{v} = {} & \frac{l_3 \sin\left(\theta_{N3}+\theta_\gamma\right)}{\left(l_v + l_3\cos\left(\theta_{N3}+\theta_\gamma\right)\right)^2}\left(\frac{2l_3^2 \sin\left(\theta_{N3}+\theta_\gamma\right)^2}{l_v + l_3\cos\left(\theta_{N3}+\theta_\gamma\right)} + 3l_3\cos\left(\theta_{N3}+\theta_\gamma\right) - 1\right)\dot{\theta}_{N3}^2 + \\ & \frac{l_3}{l_v + l_3\cos\left(\theta_{N3}+\theta_\gamma\right)}\left(\frac{l_3 \sin\left(\theta_{N3}+\theta_\gamma\right)^2}{l_v + l_3\cos\left(\theta_{N3}+\theta_\gamma\right)} + \cos\left(\theta_{N3}+\theta_\gamma\right)\right)\ddot{\theta}_{N3}\end{aligned} \tag{60}$$

$$\theta_{N1} = \arctan\left(\frac{y}{x}\right) - \arctan(v) - \theta_\beta \tag{61}$$

$$\dot{\theta}_{N1} = \frac{x\dot{y} - \dot{x}y}{x^2+y^2} - \frac{\dot{v}}{1+v^2} \tag{62}$$

$$\ddot{\theta}_{N1} = \frac{2v\dot{v}^2}{\left(1+v^2\right)^2} - \frac{\ddot{v}}{\left(1+v^2\right)} + \frac{\left(x\ddot{y} - \ddot{x}y\right)}{\left(x^2+y^2\right)} + \frac{2\left(xy\left(\dot{x}^2-\dot{y}^2\right) - \dot{x}\dot{y}\left(x^2-y^2\right)\right)}{\left(x^2+y^2\right)^2} \tag{63}$$

3.2.4 Simulation curves

To obtain the different simulation curves for the proposed control system, by employing MatLab/Simulink software, we use the simulation diagrams presented in figure 2 and figure 3. The resulting curves are shown next:

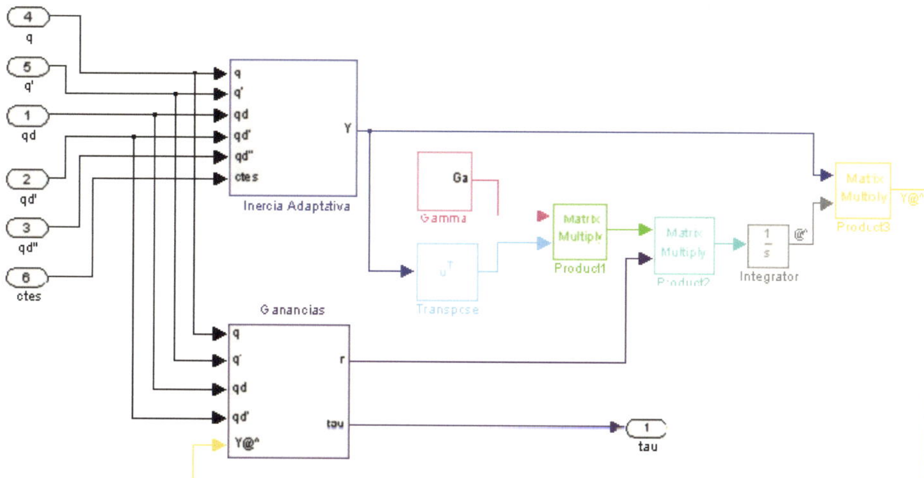

Fig. 2. Schematic diagram showing the block: adaptive inertia

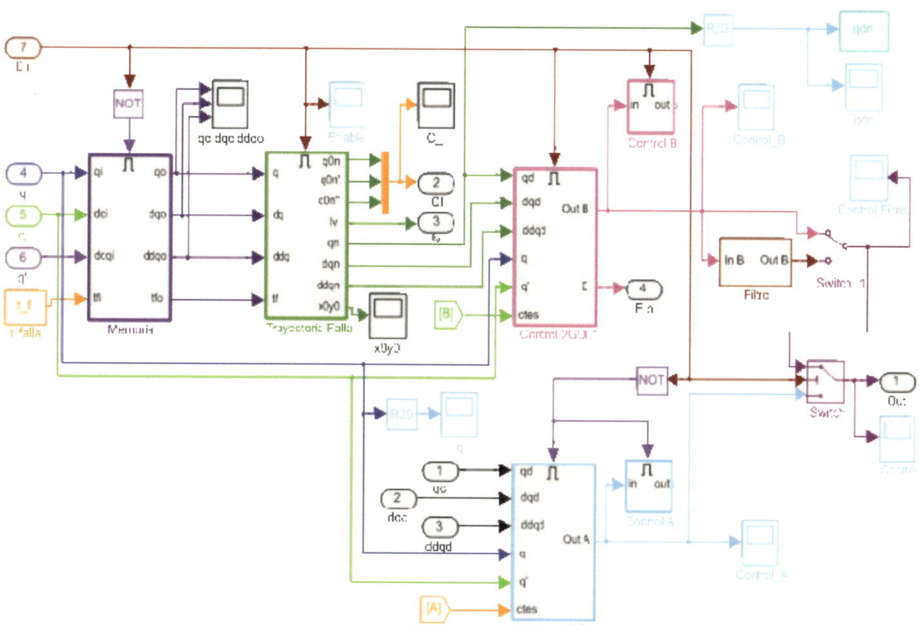

Fig. 3. Schematic diagram showing fault tolerant control stage: adaptive inertia

3.2.5 Results

After establishing the control laws by adaptive inertia to build fault tolerant control, we proceed to test such controller by means of the developed simulation tools. The obtained results are as follows:

Figures 4 and 5 show the test desired joint trajectory, along with the real obtained trajectory; and the test desired Cartesian trajectory along with the real obtained Cartesian trajectory. In absence of failures, we can see a good tracking of the desired trajectory.

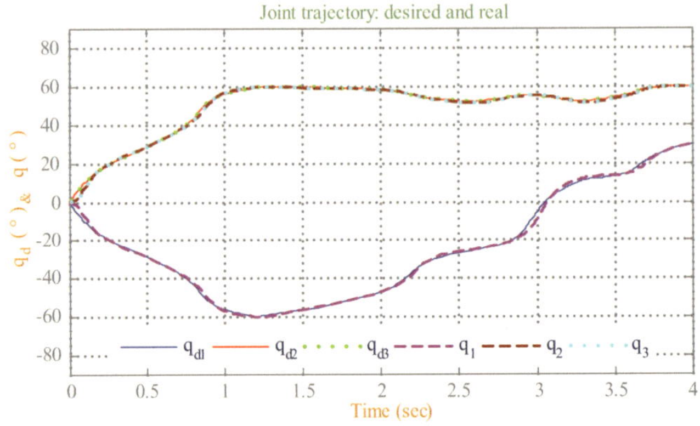

Fig. 4. Joint trajectory: desired and real

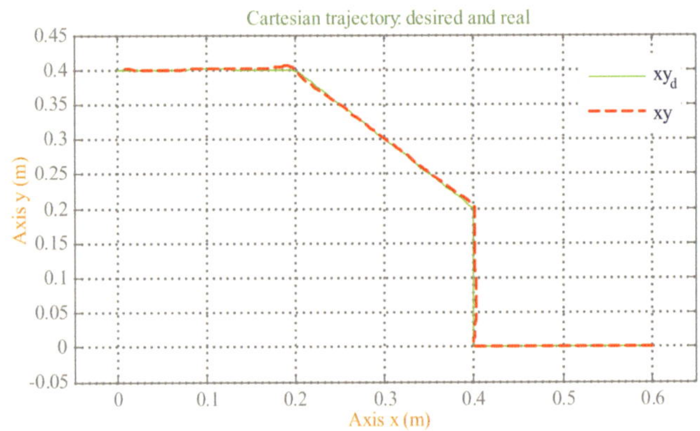

Fig. 5. Cartesian trajectory: desired and real

In figure 6 we can see the torques applied on each manipulator joint.

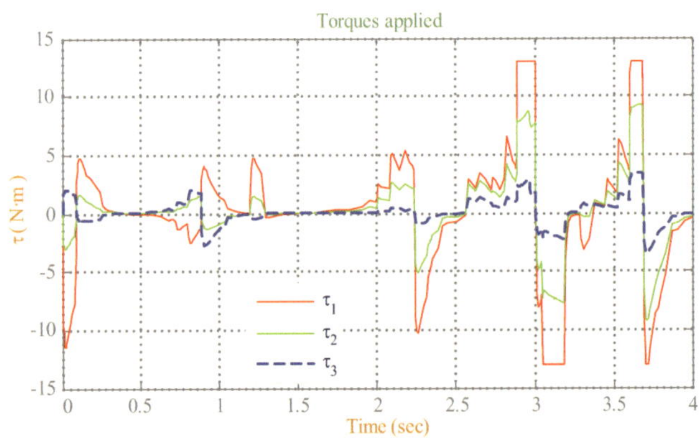

Fig. 6. Torques applied

We can notice that the greater applied torque, corresponding to joint 1, experiences saturation due to limitations inherent to the actuator.

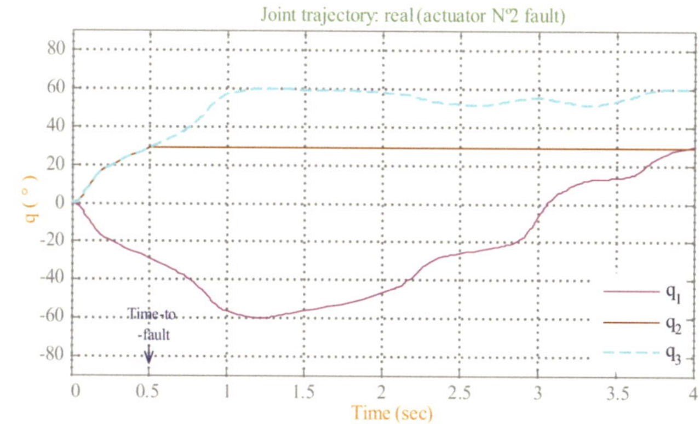

Fig. 7. Joint trajectory: real (failure in actuator N° 2)

Figure 7 shows manipulator real joint trajectory when actuator 2 is blocked at 0.5 sec from starting trajectory, and figure 8 shows a superposition of real and desired joint trajectories.

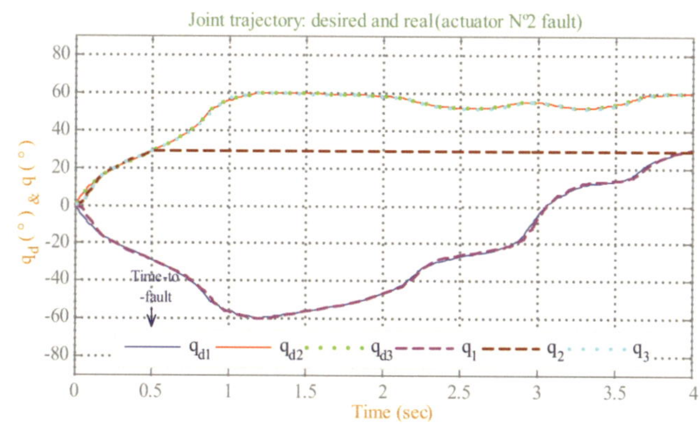

Fig. 8. Joint trajectory: desired and real (failure in actuator N° 2)

The real Cartesian trajectory suffers a remarkable deviation when failure arises in actuator 2 of the manipulator, as evidenced in figure 9.

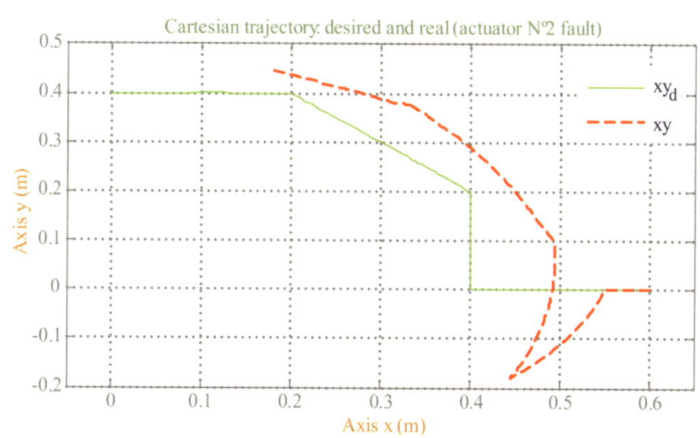

Fig. 9. Cartesian trajectory: desired and real (failure in actuator N° 2)

In figure 10 we can see torques applied to the robot when the controller has not corrected the fault yet (classic adaptive inertia controller: without fault tolerance).

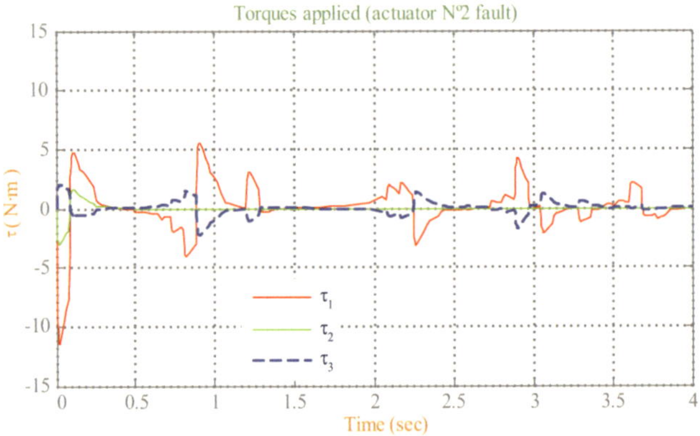

Fig. 10. Torques applied (failure in actuator N° 2)

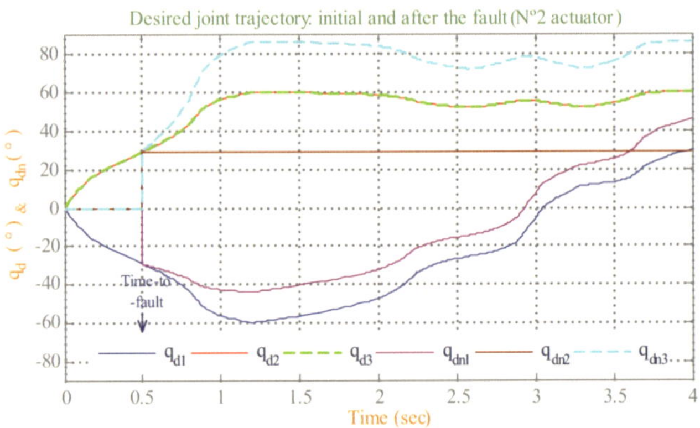

Fig. 11. Joint trajectory: desired, initial and after to failure (actuator N° 2)

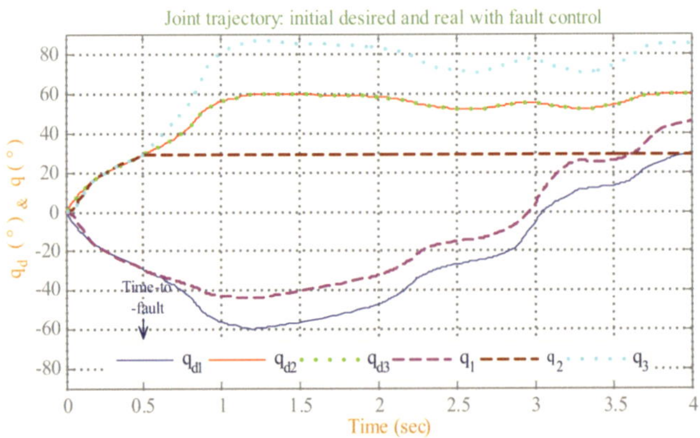

Fig. 12. Joint trajectory: desired, initial and real with fault control

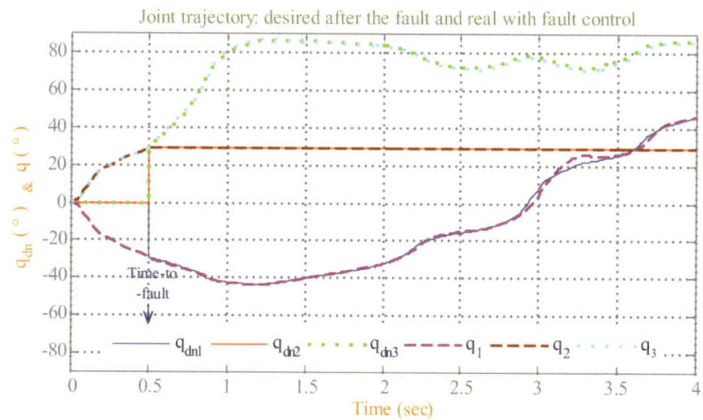

Fig. 13. Joint trajectory: desired, after the fault and real with fault control

In figure 11 we can see desired joint trajectories: initial and after to failure; in the last case, we can notice the increase in torques corresponding to joints 1 and 3, in order to compensate the failure in actuator 2.

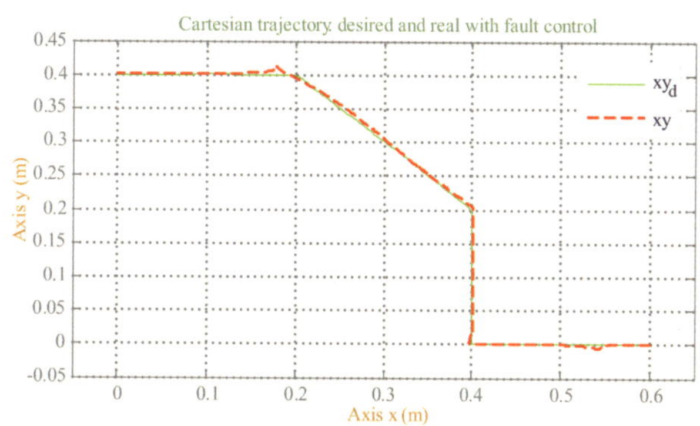

Fig. 14. Cartesian trajectory: desired and real with fault control

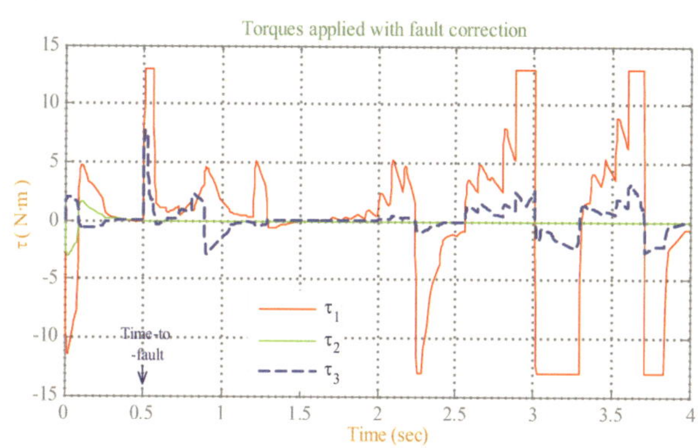

Fig. 15. Torques applied with fault correction

Figures 12 and 13 show desired, initial and real joint trajectories; and desired, after failure and real, respectively, with the application of fault tolerant control by employing adaptive inertia.

The effectiveness of fault tolerant control by adaptive inertia is evidenced in figure 14, where we can see the desired joint trajectory along with the real joint trajectory. We can notice a remarkable improvement in the desired trajectory tracking, in comparison with the performance under adaptive inertia classic control.
In figure 15 we notice an increase in needed torques applied to joints 1 and 3, in order to follow the desired trajectory in presence of a failure in actuator 2.
The obtained simulation curves show the better performance of the fault tolerant adaptive inertia controller when a failure arises (figure 14), in comparison with the classic adaptive inertia controller (figure 9). We can notice the influence of actuators as non-infinite torque generators in trajectory following when significant changes in joint position and speed are produced.

4. Conclusions

In this work we exposed the modeling and development of a fault tolerant controller by adaptive inertia, and the simulation of an industrial-type 3 DOF robot, including the application of a failure in an actuator. We presented the adaptive inertia parameter calculation, considering the manipulator kinematic and dynamic aspects. From the obtained results, we concluded that in absence of failures the classic adaptive inertia controller has a good tracking of the desired trajectory, as seen in figures 4 and 5. The greater torque applied to the manipulator, corresponding to joint 1, experiences saturation due to limitations inherent to the actuator, provided for the inclusion of its dynamics in the model. Classic adaptive inertia control, in presence of a failure (blocking) in actuator 2, experiences a detriment in its performance; in other words, the real Cartesian trajectory suffers a notorious deviation when a failure has been applied to the manipulator; this situation is evident in fig. 8, and in this context the torques applied to the robot decrease significantly, as shown in fig. 10. Fault tolerant control by adaptive inertia is effective in the occurrence of a fault: the real joint trajectory approaches to the desired joint trajectory, what is evident in figure 14. In order to compensate the immobility of failure in actuator 2 it is necessary an increase in torques corresponding to joints 1 and 3 (figure 15). We can notice the influence of actuators as generators of non-infinite torques in trajectory tracking when significant changes in joint position/speed occur. Concluding, fault tolerant control by adaptive inertia has a better performance in desired trajectory tracking, when compared with classic adaptive inertia control.

5. Acknowledgements

This work had the support of the Department for Scientific and Technologic Research of the Universidad de Santiago de Chile, by means of Project 060713UO, Santiago, Chile.

6. Further developments

Thanks to the development of this work, from the implemented simulation tools and the obtained results, fault tolerant control systems essays are being currently carried out, in order to apply them to actual robotic systems, with and without link redundancy, like the SCARA-type robots shown in figure 16 and figure 17, respectively.

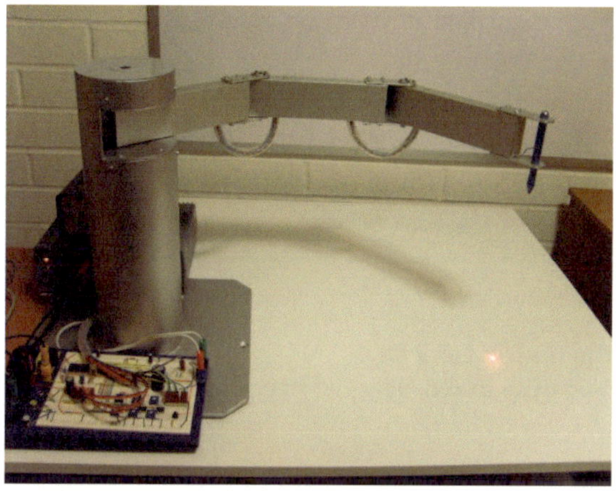

Fig. 16. SCARA-type redundant robot, DIE-USACH

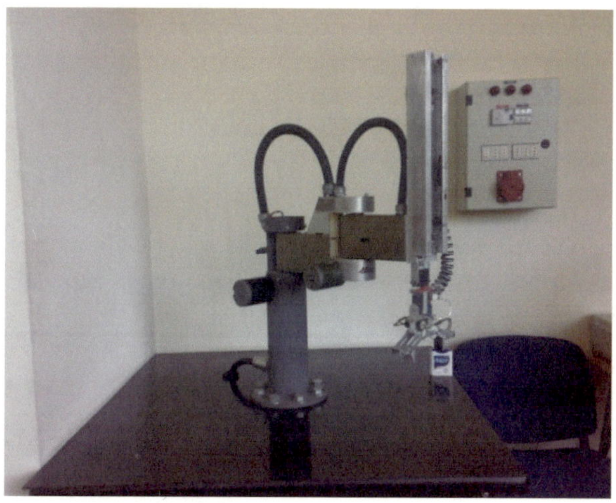

Fig. 17. SCARA-type robot, DIE-USACH

7. References

Angeles, J., 2006. *Fundamentals of Robotic Mechanical System: Theory, Methods, and Algorithms, Third Edition*. New York: Springer.

Blanke, M., Kinnaert, M., Lunze, J. & Staroswiecki, M., 2006. *Diagnosis and Fault-Tolerant Control 2nd Edition*. New York: Springer-Verlag Berlin Heidelberg.

Blanke, M., Staroswiecki, M. & Wu, E., 2001. Concepts and Methods in Fault-Tolerant Control. In *Arlington, VA, USA: American Control Conference. Proceedings of the 2001.*, 2001. Pearson Education.

Bonivento, C., Isidori, A., Marconi, L. & Paoli, A., 2004. Implicit Fault-Tolerant Control: Application to Induction Motors. *Automatica, vol. 40, N° 3*, p.355–371.

Craig, J., 1986. *Introduction to Robotics, Mechanics and Control*. Reading, Massachusetts: Addison-Wesley Publishing Company, Inc.

Lewis, F., Dawson, D. & Abdallah, C., 2004. *Robot Manipulator Control Theory and Practice.* New York: Marcel Dekker, Inc.
Ollero, A., 2001. *Robótica Manipuladores y Robots Móviles*. Barcelona, España: Marcombo, S.A.
Siciliano, B. & Khatib, O., 2008. *Handbook of Robotics*. Berlin, Heidelberg: Springer-Verlag.
Spong, M., Hutchinson, S. & Vidyasagar, M., 2005. *Robot Modeling and Control, First Edition.* New York: John Wiley & Sons, Inc.

8. Appendices

8.1 Appendix A: inertia matrix for 2 DOF

The inertia matrix considering two degrees of freedom is given by equation (64):

$$\begin{aligned}
\mathbf{M} &= \begin{bmatrix} M_{11} & M_{12} \\ M_{21} & M_{22} \end{bmatrix} \\
M_{11} &= I_{1zz} + I_{2zz} + m_1 l_{c1}^2 + m_2\left(l_1^2 + l_{c2}^2 + 2 l_1 l_{c2}\cos\theta_2\right) \\
M_{12} &= I_{2zz} + m_2\left(l_{c2}^2 + l_1 l_{c2}\cos\theta_2\right) \\
M_{21} &= I_{2zz} + m_2\left(l_{c2}^2 + l_1 l_{c2}\cos\theta_2\right) \\
M_{22} &= I_{2zz} + m_2 l_{c2}^2
\end{aligned} \tag{64}$$

8.2 Appendix B: regression matrix for 2 DOF

The regression matrix considering two degrees of freedom, is expressed by equation (33). Defining relationships (65) to (68) as:

$$Q_1 = \dot{q}_{d1} + \lambda_1 e_1 \tag{65}$$

$$Q_2 = \dot{q}_{d2} + \lambda_2 e_2 \tag{66}$$

$$\dot{Q}_1 = \ddot{q}_{d1} + \lambda_1 \dot{e}_1 \tag{67}$$

$$\dot{Q}_2 = \ddot{q}_{d2} + \lambda_2 \dot{e}_2 \tag{68}$$

The components of the matrix given by equation (33) can be calculated by means of expressions (69) to (70):

$$Y_{11} = \left.\frac{M_{11}\dot{Q}_1 + M_{12}\dot{Q}_2}{m_1}\right/_{m_2=0} + \left.\frac{V_{m11}Q_1 + V_{m12}Q_2}{m_1}\right/_{m_2=0} + \left.\frac{G_1}{m_1}\right/_{m_2=0} \tag{69}$$

$$Y_{12} = \left.\frac{M_{11}\dot{Q}_1 + M_{12}\dot{Q}_2}{m_2}\right/_{m_1=0} + \left.\frac{V_{m11}Q_1 + V_{m12}Q_2}{m_2}\right/_{m_1=0} + \left.\frac{G_1}{m_2}\right/_{m_1=0} \tag{70}$$

$$Y_{21} = \left.\frac{M_{21}\dot{Q}_1 + M_{22}\dot{Q}_2}{m_1}\right/_{m_2=0} + \left.\frac{V_{m21}Q_1 + V_{m22}Q_2}{m_1}\right/_{m_2=0} + \left.\frac{G_2}{m_1}\right/_{m_2=0} \tag{71}$$

$$Y_{22} = \left.\frac{M_{21}\dot{Q}_1 + M_{22}\dot{Q}_2}{m_2}\right/_{m_1=0} + \left.\frac{V_{m21}Q_1 + V_{m22}Q_2}{m_2}\right/_{m_1=0} + \left.\frac{G_2}{m_2}\right/_{m_1=0} \quad (72)$$

where:

$$\mathbf{G} = \begin{bmatrix} 0 \\ 0 \end{bmatrix} \quad (73)$$

With these considerations, the resulting regression matrix components are:

$$Y_{11} = \left(\frac{I_{1zz}}{m_1} + l_{c1}^2\right)\dot{Q}_1 \quad (74)$$

$$Y_{12} = l_1^2\dot{Q}_1 + \left(\frac{I_{2zz}}{m_2} + l_{c2}^2\right)\left(\dot{Q}_1 + \dot{Q}_2\right) + l_1 l_{c2}\cos\theta_2\left(2\dot{Q}_1 + \dot{Q}_2\right) - l_1 l_{c2}\sin\theta_2\left(Q_2\left(\dot{\theta}_1 + \dot{\theta}_2\right) + Q_1\dot{\theta}_2\right) \quad (75)$$

$$Y_{21} = 0 \quad (76)$$

$$Y_{22} = l_1 l_{c2}\sin\theta_2\,\dot{\theta}_1 Q_1 + l_1 l_{c2}\cos\theta_2\,\dot{Q}_1 + \left(\frac{I_{2zz}}{m_2} + l_{c2}^2\right)\left(\dot{Q}_1 + \dot{Q}_2\right) \quad (77)$$

Defining relationships (78) and (79) as:

$$y_a = l_1 l_{c2}\sin\theta_2 \quad (78)$$

$$y_A = l_1 l_{c2}\cos\theta_2 \quad (79)$$

The components Y_{12} and Y_{22} of the regression matrix can be expressed by:

$$Y_{12} = l_1^2\dot{Q}_1 + \left(\frac{I_{2zz}}{m_2} + l_{c2}^2\right)\left(\dot{Q}_1 + \dot{Q}_2\right) + y_A\left(2\dot{Q}_1 + \dot{Q}_2\right) - y_a\left(Q_1\dot{\theta}_2 + Q_2\left(\dot{\theta}_1 + \dot{\theta}_2\right)\right) \quad (80)$$

$$Y_{22} = y_a\,\dot{\theta}_1 Q_1 + y_A\,\dot{Q}_1 + \left(\frac{I_{2zz}}{m_2} + l_{c2}^2\right)\left(\dot{Q}_1 + \dot{Q}_2\right) \quad (81)$$

8.3 Appendix C: Vm matrix for 3 DOF

The **Vm** Matrix for 3 DOF is expressed by:

$$V_{m11} = -\left(m_2 l_1 l_{c2}\sin\theta_2 + m_3 l_1 l_2\sin\theta_2\right)\dot{\theta}_2 - m_3 l_2 l_{c3}\sin\theta_3\,\dot{\theta}_3 - m_3 l_1 l_{c3}\sin\left(\theta_2 + \theta_3\right)\left(\dot{\theta}_2 + \dot{\theta}_3\right) \quad (82)$$

$$V_{m21} = \left(m_2 l_1 l_{c2}\sin\theta_2 + m_3 l_1 l_2\sin\theta_2 + m_3 l_1 l_{c3}\sin\left(\theta_2 + \theta_3\right)\right)\dot{\theta}_1 - m_3 l_2 l_{c3}\sin\theta_3\,\dot{\theta}_3 \quad (83)$$

$$V_{m31} = m_3 l_2 l_{c3}\sin\theta_3\left(\dot{\theta}_1 + \dot{\theta}_2\right) + m_3 l_1 l_{c3}\sin\left(\theta_2 + \theta_3\right)\dot{\theta}_1 \quad (84)$$

$$V_{m12} = -\left(m_2 l_1 l_{c2}\sin\theta_2 + m_3 l_1 l_2\sin\theta_2\right)\left(\dot{\theta}_1 + \dot{\theta}_2\right) - m_3 l_2 l_{c3}\sin\theta_3\,\dot{\theta}_3 - m_3 l_1 l_{c3}\sin\left(\theta_2 + \theta_3\right)\left(\dot{\theta}_1 + \dot{\theta}_2 + \dot{\theta}_3\right) \quad (85)$$

$$V_{m22} = -m_3 l_2 l_{c3} \sin\theta_3 \dot{\theta}_3 \tag{86}$$

$$V_{m32} = m_3 l_2 l_{c3} \sin\theta_3 \left(\dot{\theta}_1 + \dot{\theta}_2\right) \tag{87}$$

$$V_{m13} = -\left(m_3 l_2 l_{c3} \sin\theta_3 + m_3 l_1 l_{c3} \sin\left(\theta_2 + \theta_3\right)\right)\left(\dot{\theta}_1 + \dot{\theta}_2 + \dot{\theta}_3\right) \tag{88}$$

$$V_{m23} = -m_3 l_2 l_{c3} \sin\theta_3 \left(\dot{\theta}_1 + \dot{\theta}_2 + \dot{\theta}_3\right) \tag{89}$$

$$V_{m33} = 0 \tag{90}$$

Defining the following relationships:

$$c_a = m_2 l_1 l_{c2} \sin\theta_2 \tag{91}$$

$$c_b = m_3 l_1 l_2 \sin\theta_2 \tag{92}$$

$$c_c = m_3 l_2 l_{c3} \sin\theta_3 \tag{93}$$

$$c_d = m_3 l_1 l_{c3} \sin\left(\theta_2 + \theta_3\right) \tag{94}$$

Replacing expressions (91) to (94) into equations (82) to (89), we arrive to:

$$V_{m11} = -\left(c_a + c_b\right)\dot{\theta}_2 - c_c\dot{\theta}_3 - c_d\left(\dot{\theta}_2 + \dot{\theta}_3\right) \tag{95}$$

$$V_{m21} = \left(c_a + c_b + c_d\right)\dot{\theta}_1 - c_c\dot{\theta}_3 \tag{96}$$

$$V_{m31} = c_c\left(\dot{\theta}_1 + \dot{\theta}_2\right) + c_d\dot{\theta}_1 \tag{97}$$

$$V_{m12} = -\left(c_a + c_b\right)\left(\dot{\theta}_1 + \dot{\theta}_2\right) - c_c\dot{\theta}_3 - c_d\left(\dot{\theta}_1 + \dot{\theta}_2 + \dot{\theta}_3\right) \tag{98}$$

$$V_{m22} = -c_c\dot{\theta}_3 \tag{99}$$

$$V_{m32} = c_c\left(\dot{\theta}_1 + \dot{\theta}_2\right) \tag{100}$$

$$V_{m13} = -\left(c_c + c_d\right)\left(\dot{\theta}_1 + \dot{\theta}_2 + \dot{\theta}_3\right) \tag{101}$$

$$V_{m23} = -c_c\left(\dot{\theta}_1 + \dot{\theta}_2 + \dot{\theta}_3\right) \tag{102}$$

$$V_{m33} = 0 \tag{103}$$

8.4 Appendix D: Regression matrix for 3 DOF

Defining relationships (104) and (105), and considering the relationships defined by means of equations (65) to (68), we have:

$$Q_3 = \dot{q}_{d3} + \lambda_2 e_3 \quad (104)$$

$$\dot{Q}_3 = \ddot{q}_{d3} + \lambda_3 \dot{e}_3 \quad (105)$$

$$Y_{11} = \frac{M_{11}\dot{Q}_1 + M_{12}\dot{Q}_2 + M_{13}\dot{Q}_3}{m_1}\Bigg/_{\substack{m_2=0\\m_3=0}} + \frac{V_{m11}Q_1 + V_{m12}Q_2 + V_{m13}Q_3}{m_1}\Bigg/_{\substack{m_2=0\\m_3=0}} + \frac{G_1}{m_1}\Bigg/_{\substack{m_2=0\\m_3=0}} \quad (106)$$

$$Y_{12} = \frac{M_{11}\dot{Q}_1 + M_{12}\dot{Q}_2 + M_{13}\dot{Q}_3}{m_2}\Bigg/_{\substack{m_1=0\\m_3=0}} + \frac{V_{m11}Q_1 + V_{m12}Q_2 + V_{m13}Q_3}{m_2}\Bigg/_{\substack{m_1=0\\m_3=0}} + \frac{G_1}{m_2}\Bigg/_{\substack{m_1=0\\m_3=0}} \quad (107)$$

$$Y_{13} = \frac{M_{11}\dot{Q}_1 + M_{12}\dot{Q}_2 + M_{13}\dot{Q}_3}{m_3}\Bigg/_{\substack{m_1=0\\m_2=0}} + \frac{V_{m11}Q_1 + V_{m12}Q_2 + V_{m13}Q_3}{m_3}\Bigg/_{\substack{m_1=0\\m_2=0}} + \frac{G_1}{m_3}\Bigg/_{\substack{m_1=0\\m_2=0}} \quad (108)$$

$$Y_{21} = \frac{M_{21}\dot{Q}_1 + M_{22}\dot{Q}_2 + M_{23}\dot{Q}_3}{m_1}\Bigg/_{\substack{m_2=0\\m_3=0}} + \frac{V_{m21}Q_1 + V_{m22}Q_2 + V_{m23}Q_3}{m_1}\Bigg/_{\substack{m_2=0\\m_3=0}} + \frac{G_2}{m_1}\Bigg/_{\substack{m_2=0\\m_3=0}} \quad (109)$$

$$Y_{22} = \frac{M_{21}\dot{Q}_1 + M_{22}\dot{Q}_2 + M_{23}\dot{Q}_3}{m_2}\Bigg/_{\substack{m_1=0\\m_3=0}} + \frac{V_{m21}Q_1 + V_{m22}Q_2 + V_{m23}Q_3}{m_2}\Bigg/_{\substack{m_1=0\\m_3=0}} + \frac{G_2}{m_2}\Bigg/_{\substack{m_1=0\\m_3=0}} \quad (110)$$

$$Y_{23} = \frac{M_{21}\dot{Q}_1 + M_{22}\dot{Q}_2 + M_{23}\dot{Q}_3}{m_3}\Bigg/_{\substack{m_1=0\\m_2=0}} + \frac{V_{m21}Q_1 + V_{m22}Q_2 + V_{m23}Q_3}{m_3}\Bigg/_{\substack{m_1=0\\m_2=0}} + \frac{G_2}{m_3}\Bigg/_{\substack{m_1=0\\m_2=0}} \quad (111)$$

$$Y_{31} = \frac{M_{31}\dot{Q}_1 + M_{32}\dot{Q}_2 + M_{33}\dot{Q}_3}{m_1}\Bigg/_{\substack{m_2=0\\m_3=0}} + \frac{V_{m31}Q_1 + V_{m32}Q_2 + V_{m33}Q_3}{m_1}\Bigg/_{\substack{m_2=0\\m_3=0}} + \frac{G_3}{m_1}\Bigg/_{\substack{m_2=0\\m_3=0}} \quad (112)$$

$$Y_{32} = \frac{M_{31}\dot{Q}_1 + M_{32}\dot{Q}_2 + M_{33}\dot{Q}_3}{m_2}\Bigg/_{\substack{m_1=0\\m_3=0}} + \frac{V_{m31}Q_1 + V_{m32}Q_2 + V_{m33}Q_3}{m_2}\Bigg/_{\substack{m_1=0\\m_3=0}} + \frac{G_3}{m_2}\Bigg/_{\substack{m_1=0\\m_3=0}} \quad (113)$$

$$Y_{33} = \frac{M_{31}\dot{Q}_1 + M_{32}\dot{Q}_2 + M_{33}\dot{Q}_3}{m_3}\Bigg/_{\substack{m_1=0\\m_2=0}} + \frac{V_{m31}Q_1 + V_{m32}Q_2 + V_{m33}Q_3}{m_3}\Bigg/_{\substack{m_1=0\\m_2=0}} + \frac{G_3}{m_3}\Bigg/_{\substack{m_1=0\\m_2=0}} \quad (114)$$

$$Y_{11} = \left(I_{1zz}/m_1 + l_{c1}^2\right)\dot{Q}_1 \quad (115)$$

$$\begin{aligned} Y_{12} =& -l_1 l_{c2}\sin\theta_2\,\dot{\theta}_2 Q_1 - l_1 l_{c2}\sin\theta_2\left(\dot{\theta}_1 + \dot{\theta}_2\right)Q_2 + \left(I_{2zz}/m_2 + l_1^2 + l_{c2}^2 + 2l_1 l_{c2}\cos\theta_2\right)\dot{Q}_1 + \\ &\left(I_{2zz}/m_2 + l_{c2}^2 + l_1 l_{c2}\cos\theta_2\right)\dot{Q}_2 \end{aligned} \quad (116)$$

$$\begin{aligned} Y_{13} =& -\Big(\big(l_1 l_2 \sin\theta_2 + l_1 l_{c3}\sin(\theta_2+\theta_3)\big)\dot{\theta}_2 + \big(l_2 l_{c3}\sin\theta_3 + l_1 l_{c3}\sin(\theta_2+\theta_3)\big)\dot{\theta}_3\Big)Q_1 + \\ & -\Big(\big(l_1 l_2 \sin\theta_2 + l_1 l_{c3}\sin(\theta_2+\theta_3)\big)\big(\dot{\theta}_1 + \dot{\theta}_2\big)\Big)Q_2 + \big(l_2 l_{c3}\sin\theta_3 + l_1 l_{c3}\sin(\theta_2+\theta_3)\big) \\ & \dot{\theta}_3 Q_2 - \big(l_2 l_{c3}\sin\theta_3 + l_1 l_{c3}\sin(\theta_2+\theta_3)\big)\big(\dot{\theta}_1 + \dot{\theta}_2 + \dot{\theta}_3\big)Q_3 + \Big(I_{3zz}/m_3 + l_1^2 + l_2^2 + l_{c3}^2 \\ & + 2l_1 l_2\cos\theta_2 + l_2 l_{c3}\cos\theta_3 + l_1 l_{c3}\cos(\theta_2+\theta_3)\big)\Big)\dot{Q}_1 + \Big(I_{3zz}/m_3 + l_2^2 + l_{c3}^2 + l_1 l_2\cos\theta_2 \\ & + 2l_2 l_{c3}\cos\theta_3 + l_1 l_{c3}\cos(\theta_2+\theta_3)\Big)\dot{Q}_2 + \Big(l_{c3}^2 + l_2 l_{c3}\cos\theta_3 + l_1 l_{c3}\cos(\theta_2+\theta_3)\Big)\dot{Q}_3 \end{aligned} \quad (117)$$

$$Y_{21} = 0 \tag{118}$$

$$Y_{22} = l_1 l_{c2} \sin\theta_2 \dot{\theta}_1 Q_1 + \left(I_{2zz}/m_2 + \left(l_{c2}^2 + l_1 l_{c2} \cos\theta_2 \right) \right) \dot{Q}_1 + \left(I_{2zz}/m_2 + l_{c2}^2 \right) \dot{Q}_2 \tag{119}$$

$$\begin{aligned} Y_{23} = & \left(l_1 l_2 \sin\theta_2 \dot{\theta}_1 + l_1 l_{c3} \sin(\theta_2 + \theta_3) \dot{\theta}_1 - l_2 l_{c3} \sin\theta_3 \dot{\theta}_3 \right) Q_1 - l_2 l_{c3} \sin\theta_3 \dot{\theta}_3 Q_2 - l_2 l_{c3} \sin\theta_3 \\ & \left(\dot{\theta}_1 + \dot{\theta}_2 + \dot{\theta}_3 \right) Q_3 + \left(I_{3zz}/m_3 + l_2^2 + l_{c3}^2 + l_1 l_2 \cos\theta_2 + 2 l_2 l_{c3} \cos\theta_3 + l_1 l_{c3} \cos(\theta_2 + \theta_3) \right) \\ & \dot{Q}_1 + \left(I_{3zz}/m_3 + l_2^2 + l_{c3}^2 + 2 l_2 l_{c3} \cos\theta_3 \right) \dot{Q}_2 + \left(I_{3zz}/m_3 + l_{c3}^2 + l_2 l_{c3} \cos\theta_3 \right) \dot{Q}_3 \end{aligned} \tag{120}$$

$$Y_{31} = 0 \tag{121}$$

$$Y_{32} = 0 \tag{122}$$

$$\begin{aligned} Y_{33} = & \left(l_2 l_{c3} \sin\theta_3 \left(\dot{\theta}_1 + \dot{\theta}_2 \right) + l_1 l_{c3} \sin(\theta_2 + \theta_3) \dot{\theta}_1 \right) Q_1 + l_2 l_{c3} \sin\theta_3 \left(\dot{\theta}_1 + \dot{\theta}_2 \right) Q_2 + \\ & \left(I_{3zz}/m_3 + l_{c3}^2 + l_2 l_{c3} \cos\theta_3 + l_1 l_{c3} \cos(\theta_2 + \theta_3) \right) \dot{Q}_1 + \left(I_{3zz}/m_3 + l_{c3}^2 + l_2 l_{c3} \right. \\ & \left. \cos\theta_3 \right) \dot{Q}_2 + \left(I_{3zz}/m_3 + l_{c3}^2 \right) \dot{Q}_3 \end{aligned} \tag{123}$$

Defining relationships (124) to (129), and considering the relationships defined in (78) and (79), we have:

$$y_b = l_1 l_2 \sin\theta_2 \tag{124}$$

$$y_c = l_2 l_{c3} \sin\theta_3 \tag{125}$$

$$y_d = l_1 l_{c3} \sin(\theta_2 + \theta_3) \tag{126}$$

$$y_B = l_1 l_2 \cos\theta_2 \tag{127}$$

$$y_C = l_2 l_{c3} \cos\theta_3 \tag{128}$$

$$y_D = l_1 l_{c3} \cos(\theta_2 + \theta_3) \tag{129}$$

29

Comparison of Identification Techniques for a 6-DOF Real Robot and Development of an Intelligent Controller

Claudio Urrea, Felipe Santander and Marcela Jamett
Departamento de Ingeniería Eléctrica, DIE
Universidad de Santiago de Chile, USACH
Santiago, Chile

1. Introduction

In their beginnings, control systems were developed out of a full knowledge of the mathematical model of the process to be controlled. Nowadays, however, the trend for advanced control systems points to the fact that they can be developed without a previous knowledge of the mathematical model of the system to be controlled, hence leading to advantages and drawbacks at the moment of their application (Craig, 2006). Amongst the most remarkable disadvantages we have the fact that the higher accuracy we ask the controller, the more response delay we have (Ogata, 1996). That is why, if we can get a good enough system description, control systems can be simplified, enhancing their accuracy as well as their speed (Pierro et al., 2008).

Advanced control techniques allow us an accurate control from a system predictor model, as the case of adaptive control techniques by reference model, studied in this chapter. An adaptive control system is a controller capable of modifying system's adjustable parameters generating an acting signal, in order to keep optimum performance independently from environmental modifications. Adaptive control can be represented through the following block diagram:

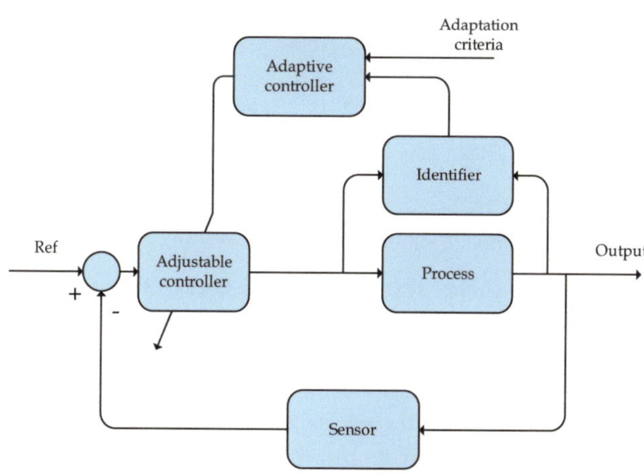

Fig. 1. Adaptive control block diagram

In the scheme we can notice the need of adaptive control for a model that allows to describe the system behavior.
There are several techniques for modeling a system when we have not information about the model, as well as techniques that allows to estimate interesting parameters in a model, approximating it to a specific system. These techniques are known as system identification techniques, which allows to create or approximate specific mathematic models in order to describe, predict or simulate a system (Ljung, 1999).
In the utilization of system identification methods we have to consider the dynamic nature of the system, since there are identification structures for models with linear and non-linear dynamics. Generally speaking, the knowledge of the system's dynamics is a previous or given information, or, in its absence, we can suspect the kind of structure that will describe in a better way the studied system. When starting any identification process, it is necessary to take three basic steps (Ljung, 1999):

1. To carry out an experiment in order to obtain a data set.
2. To choose a model to be adjusted.
3. To select from a set of candidate models a rule by which candidate models can be assessed using the data.

Henceforth, we follow with model estimation; as a general rule, those estimated models use to result acceptable after several iterations, where we must verify if the obtained model is the right one.

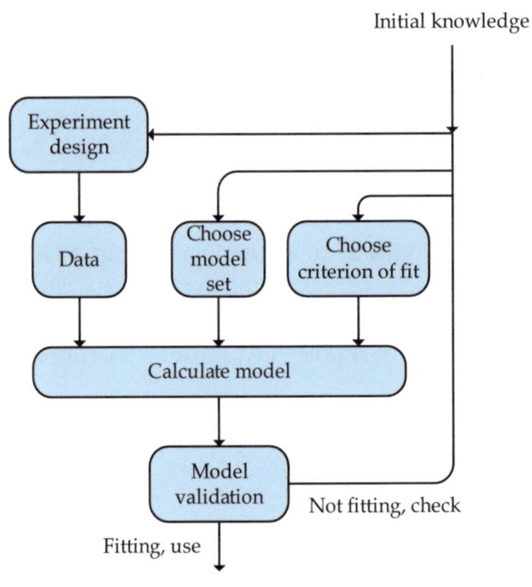

Fig. 2. System identification loop

In this chapter we will review many system identification techniques and adaptive control techniques; both kinds will be applied in the identification and control of a SCARA industrial manipulator. In order to do that, we will obtain a model efficiently representing the dynamics of a SCARA robot, through Hammerstein-Wiener Models. Those models will be verified by implementing several trajectory experiments applied on the system. This identification is carried out in the aim to implement Model Reference Adaptive Control (MRAC), improving in this way the general behavior of the system.

2. Linear system identification

During the modeling process there arise great problems concerning the choice of modelling methods, amongst others. It is here where studies on system identification are centered, basically looking to answer the question How to create the model for a specific system from measured data?
Concerning systems identification, when we talk about a system, we mean a process having inputs and outputs. Observed variables are simply known as outputs. Inputs that can be managed are known as inputs, and other inputs –that only can be measured- are known as measurable perturbations and, finally, there are inputs that cannot be measured, known as non measurable perturbations (Ljung, 1999). In this way, by means of mathematic methods, systems identification tries to model the global behavior of the studied system.
The most important identification techniques are divided into two major groups: linear identification techniques, and non-linear identification techniques. This classification of identification techniques is made because in the real field there are systems that can be approximated to linear or non-linear models.
The most popular system identification linear models family is the Black Box models group. This family of structures covers a total of 32 models. Black Box models base their identification capabilities in parameter adjustment of the polynomials that compose them. Those models are composed by 5 polynomials; depending on which polynomials are employed, it is the model at which the system is approximated to.
The BlackBox model is described in (1).

$$A(q)y(t)=\frac{B(q)}{F(q)}u(t)+\frac{C(q)}{D(q)}e(t) \tag{1}$$

Those polynomials are polynomials in q, that is an operator employed to specify that we are working with a discrete system, since the operator is q=z, corresponding to the operator of the z transform. In this way, the polynomials are defined in (2).

$$\begin{aligned} A(q)&=a_0+a_1q^{-1}+\cdots+a_{na}q^{-na}\\ B(q)&=b_0+b_1q^{-1}+\cdots+b_{nb}q^{-nb}\\ C(q)&=c_0+c_1q^{-1}+\cdots+c_{nc}q^{-nc}\\ D(q)&=d_0+d_1q^{-1}+\cdots+d_{nd}q^{-nd}\\ F(q)&=f_0+f_1q^{-1}+\cdots+f_{nf}q^{-nf} \end{aligned} \tag{2}$$

Through the adjustment of each one of the parameters, we achieve the approximation to the studied system. Those adjustable parameters use to be denoted as shown in (3).

$$\theta=[a_0\ldots a_{na} \quad b_0\ldots b_{nb} \quad f_0\ldots f_{nf}] \tag{3}$$

In some cases we observe that system dynamics has delays from input u(t) to output y(t) of n_k samples, therefore, some coefficients of the B(q) polynomial are managed as zero (4).

$$B(q)=b_{nk}q^{-nk}+\ldots+b_{nk+nb-1}q^{-nk-nb-1}=q^{-nk}B'(q) \tag{4}$$

In this way, the generalized model for the case with delays is shown in (5).

$$A(q)y(t)=q_{-nk}\frac{B'(q)}{F(q)}u(t)+\frac{C(q)}{D(q)}e(t) \quad (5)$$

For the sake of simplicity, it is usual to employ nk=1 and the expression shown in (1). Nevertheless, we could always arrive to a general form including the delays by replacing u(t) for u(t-nk+1).

In order to identify the parameters of the model proposed in (1) we employ a predictor with the form:

$$y(t|\theta)=\frac{D(q)B(q)}{C(q)F(q)}u(t)+\left[1-\frac{D(q)A(q)}{C(q)}\right]y(t) \quad (6)$$

This predictor is compared with the system real output and the error is minimized using some mathematic algorithm, commonly the least square method.

A practical summary of linear Black Box models appears in the scheme shown in fig. 3.

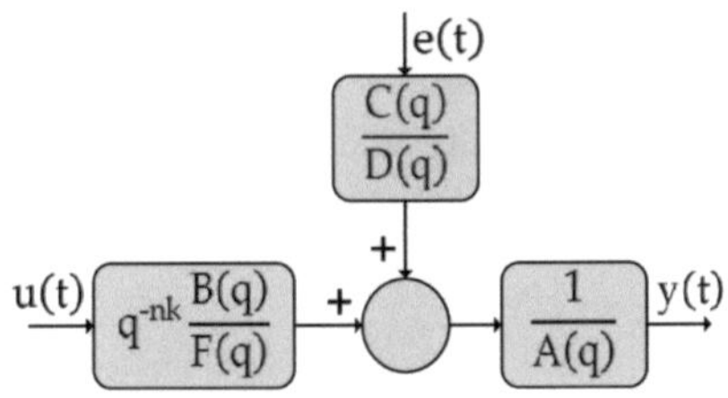

Fig. 3. General structure of linear Black-Box models

As already mentioned, depending on which polynomials are employed in expression (1) a different structure will be chosen. Generally speaking, the most employed structures for systems identification are summarized in table 1.

Employed Polynomials	Name of the model structure
B	FIR (Finite Impulse Response)
AB	ARX
ABC	ARMAX
AC	ARMA
ABD	ARARX
ABCD	ARARMAX
BF	OE (Output Error)
BFCD	BJ (Box-Jenkins)

Table 1. Most popular linear Black-Box models, as a special case of (1)

The model choice will rely on what is intended to be modeled. We will illustrate this situation through an example.

2.1 Example of model selection

Lets consider a DC servomotor having only viscous friction, described in fig. 4.

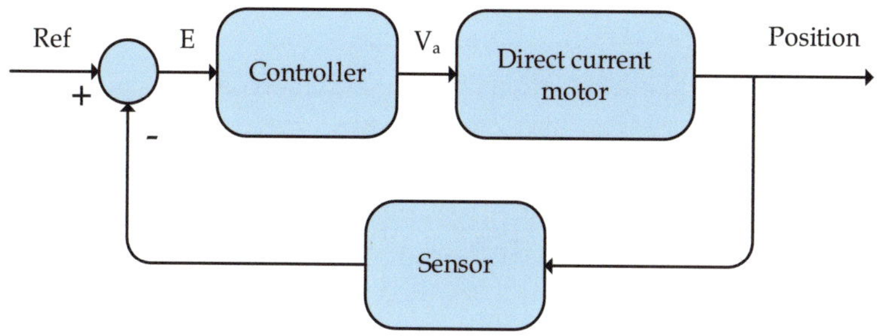

Fig. 4. Servomotor block diagram

The model of a DC motor in the domain of Laplace (Nyzen, 1999) is given by (7):

$$V_a(s)=\frac{1}{nk_m}\left[JLs^3+(JR+fL)s^2+(fR+k_mk_e)s\right]\Theta_m(s) \tag{7}$$

where:

V_a : DC motor input voltage.
R, L, k_e : Electric parameters of the equivalent circuit.
k_m : Motor characteristic torque constant.
n : Geartrain ratio.
F : Viscous friction constant.

It is important to remark that in the model shown in (7) it is included the phenomenon of friction in the joint driven by the servomotor, but only considering the linear part representing such phenomenon, without including the non-linear parts present in classic friction models, like the static friction one (Makkar, 2005).

Assuming an ideal sensor and a proportional integral controller, as shown in (8):

$$V_a(s)=k_p\left(1+\frac{k_I}{s}\right)E(s) \tag{8}$$

Linking equations (7) and (8) we have the equation that models the position with respect to the servomotor input voltage:

$$(r_1s^4+r_2s^3+r_3s^2+r_{41}s+r_5)\Theta(s)=(r_4s+r_5)U(s) \tag{9}$$

where:

$$r_1=\frac{JL}{nk_a}$$

$$r_2=\frac{(JR+fL)}{nk_a}$$

$$r_3=\frac{(fR+k_mk_e)}{nk_a}$$

$$r_4=k_p$$

$$r_5=k_pk_I$$

Using Euler's backward method, shown in (10), we can discretize (9), having:

$$s=\frac{1-z^{-1}}{T} \tag{10}$$

where:
T: Sample time.

$$\left[\frac{r_1'}{r_5'}z^{-4}+\frac{r_2'}{r_5'}z^{-3}+\frac{r_3'}{r_5'}z^{-2}+\frac{r_4'}{r_5'}z^{-1}+1\right]\Theta(z)=\left[\frac{r_6'}{r_5'}z^{-1}+\frac{r_7'}{r_5'}\right]U(z) \tag{11}$$

where:

$$r_1'=\frac{JL}{nk_aT^3}$$

$$r_2'=\frac{3JL}{nk_aT^3}+\frac{(JR+fL)}{nk_aT^2}$$

$$r_3'=\frac{-3JL}{nk_aT^3}-\frac{2(JR+fL)}{nk_aT^2}-\frac{(fR+k_mk_e)}{nk_aT}$$

$$r_4'=\frac{JL}{nk_aT^3}+\frac{(JR+fL)}{nk_aT^2}+k_p$$

$$r_5'=k_p$$

The model (11) can be represented and approximated through a linear Black-Box model of the ARX kind. This model only has A and B polynomials, therefore it can be a good linear approximation for a simplified servomotor, considering an A polynomial of order 3 and a B polynomial of order 1, as shown in (12) (Santander et al., 2010).

$$\left[A_3q^{-3}+A_2q^{-2}+A_1q^{-1}+1\right]y(t)=B(q)u(t)+e(t) \tag{12}$$

Assuming zero error, the model in (12) can be simply written as:

$$\left[A_3q^{-3}+A_2q^{-2}+A_1q^{-1}+1\right]y(t)=B(q)u(t) \tag{13}$$

2.2 Choice of excitation signal

In order to obtain a model describing in an efficient way a given system, we must take into account the applied excitation signal, since it will permit a better tracking of the behavior we desire to describe.

Lets consider again the example of a servomotor, in (13) it is clear that it can be described with an ARX model, but the choice of the signal that can capture in a better way its dynamics it's not a trivial issue, generally depending of the system behavior, and without clear rules to follow. For this example we carry out the identification process using three different excitation signals: PRBS (Pseudo Random Binary Signal), RBS (Random Binary Signal), and GCPS (Growing Constant Pulses Signal) (Santander et al., 2010).

Using excitation signals we can get the adjustment of A and B polynomials for each one of the cases presented in fig. 5, those models are then validated using a smooth trajectory –as shown in fig.6- and model errors are calculated using (14). Results are summarized in table 2.

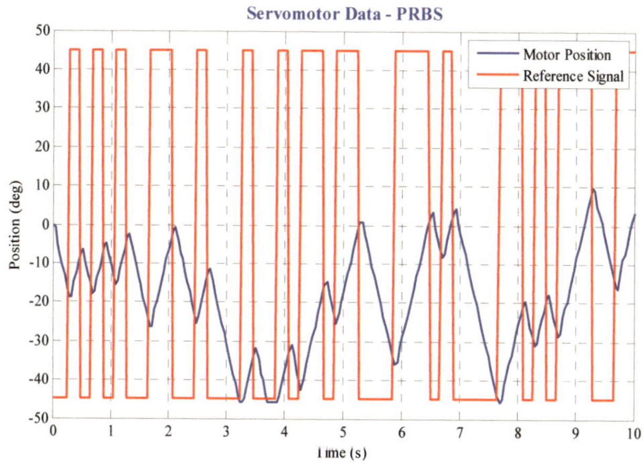

(a) PRBS excitation

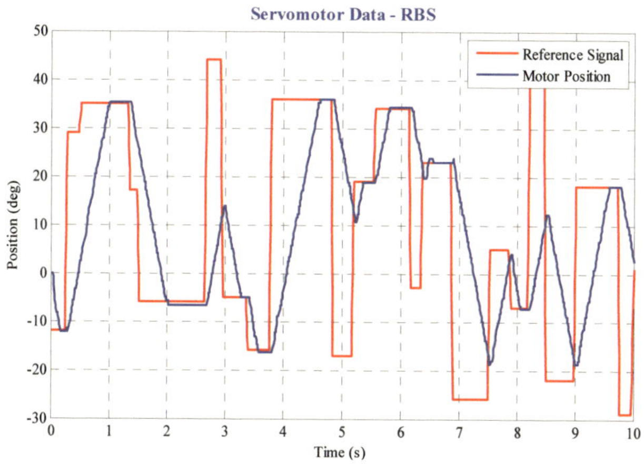

b) RBS excitation

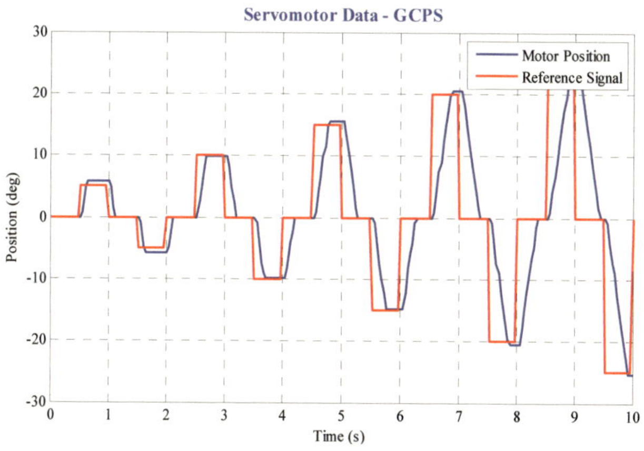

c) GCPS excitation

Fig. 5. HITEC HS-475HB servomotor data, with PRBS, RBS and GCPS excitations, respectively

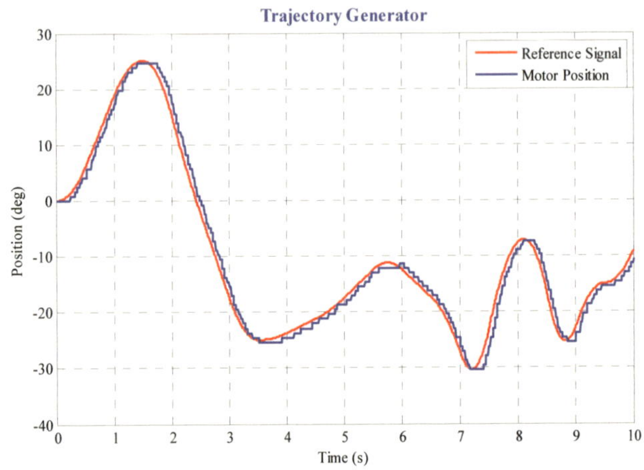

Fig. 6. Servomotor response when applying a smooth trajectory

$$error\% = \sqrt{\frac{\sum_{i=1}^{n}(o_i - p_i)^2}{\sum_{i=1}^{n} o_i^2}} \qquad (12)$$

where:
o_i: Motor observed values.
p_i: Predicted or identified values.

Signal	error %
PRBS	193.611%
RBS	29.968%
GCPS	16.475%

Table 2. Approximated ARX models verification results

We must remark that, for the specific case of the studied servomotor, the best excitation signal for servomotor identification is GCPS (Santander et al., 2010).

3. Wiener-Hammerstein models

The main objective of this chapter is the control of a SCARA robot, therefore we will focus on finding models that describe efficiently the dynamic behavior of robotic manipulators. It is important to notice that robot dynamic models are highly non-linear, due to the different coupling of their links, and also because of opposition to their movement, that is, friction. That is why approximation with linear methods is not enough for a SCARA robot, and therefore it is necessary to explore other options providing an efficient modeling of the robot. Amongst current and most valid options applied to robots, we find studies carried out for parameter estimation of direct dynamic models, using the non-linear function obtained by means of Lagrange-Euler or Newton-Euler methods (Gautier et al., 2008), (Olsen & Petersen, 2001). Even if the models obtained for describing robot dynamics are highly accurate, they require a vast amount of calculations and measurement of robot interesting variables, at least the measurement of torque applied on each robot link. But what happens when the studied system have not sensors for torque measurement? It is necessary the implementation of such system? Next we will review a modeling option that does not require this kind of sensors.

There is a great variety of methods for non-linear identification, covering many different points of view. Up to date, the application of any method is totally arbitrary: some methods that work with very good predictions in some cases, are completely useless in other cases. The non-linear identification techniques we will review now are the Wiener-Hammerstein models.

It is common to find systems whose dynamics can be properly described by linear systems, although having static nonlinearities from the input and/or output. These nonlinearities can be caused by phenomena like saturation, or others. In the studied case, the SCARA robot actuators are DC motors subject to friction forces, with highly non-linear characteristics, so it is a good option to apply this kind of models.

We talk about Hammerstein models when the static nonlinearity is found in the input, and Wiener models when the static nonlinearity is in the output, as shown here:

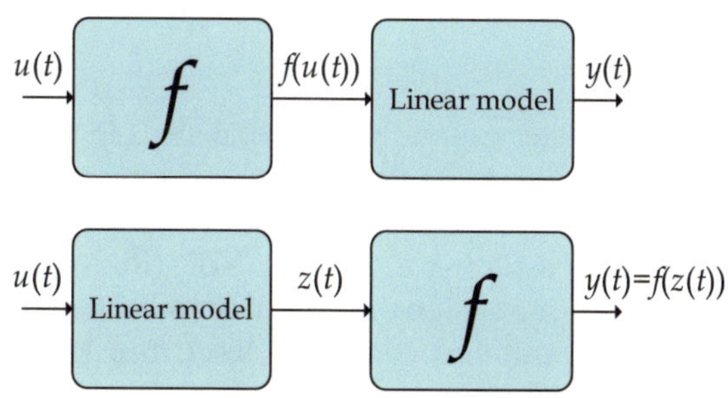

Fig. 7. Upper diagram: Hammerstein Model, Lower diagram: Wiener Model

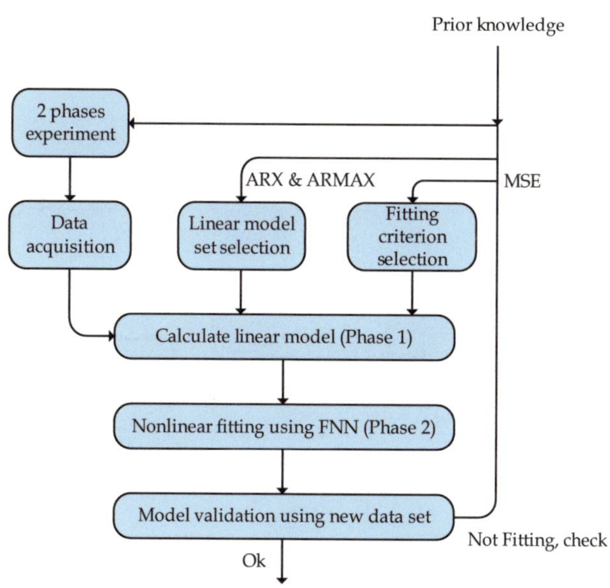

Fig. 8. System identification loop for Hammerstein-Wiener models

Function *f* presented in the model can be parameterized in terms of the physical parameters that compose it, like saturation level, or also in terms of another non-linear functions. In this way, if we assume a linear model G, the output predictor will be:

$$\hat{y}(t\,|\,\theta,\eta) = G(q,\theta) f(u(t),\eta) \tag{14}$$

For the case of modeling of the linear part we can use Black Box linear models, described in the previous section. The non-linear function employed for modeling can be any non-linear function that models and contributes to the improvement of the model. The most employed ones are: neural networks, fuzzy functions, tree partitioning, and others.

It is important to have in mind the kind of signal employed for function adjustment, since it must capture the system's nonlinear dynamics. It is advisable to employ a set of at least 10 chained independent trajectories for such identification (Gautier et al., 2008).

For the identification through Hammerstein-Wiener models we created a scheme that particularizes the general scheme of identification loop shown in fig. 2; in this scheme, Hammerstein-Wiener models are considered as the predetermined models to be employed.

4. Adaptive control

System identification and parameter estimation are vital steps in most control applications, as well as adaptive controllers by reference models and self-tuning controllers (Kasim, 2003). Adaptive control techniques can be divided mainly in two groups: Adaptive controllers by reference models (MRAC) and Self-tuning regulators (STR) (Rodríguez & Lopéz, 1996). The MRACs try to find, for a defined input signal, a closed-loop behavior given by the reference model. The STRs try to reach optimum control, subject to a kind of controller, getting information about the process and its signals. The advantages of the MRACs lie in their quick adaptation to a defined input, and in the simplicity of the stability treatment using non-linear systems stability theory. The STRs have the advantage of adapting to any case, particularly to non-measurable perturbations, having at the same time a modular structure, making it possible block programming. In the proposed work we decided to develop adaptive control by model of reference.

The most popular scheme of adaptive control is shown in fig. 9.

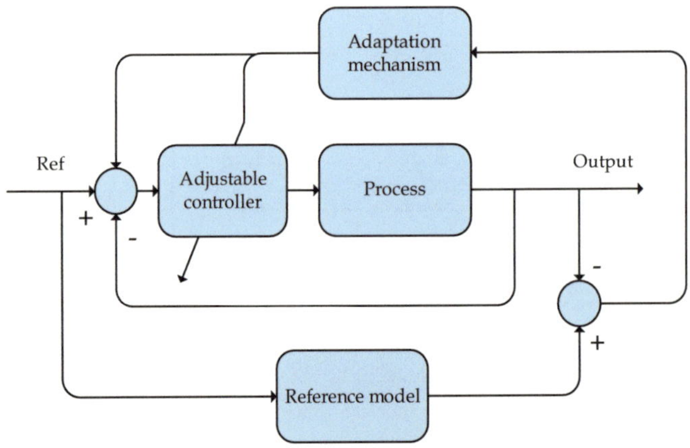

Fig. 9. MRAC scheme

One of the most important parts shown in the scheme in fig. 9 is the adaptation law. Generally speaking, adaptation laws employ Lyapunov's stability theory and Popov's hyperstability theory.

4.1 Adaptive control design

The method presented below is based in the utilization of sensibility models, so parameters can be adapted in the right way. The method deduction starts by setting the actuation index. Given a reference model Gref and an adjustable system Gadj(û), which we desire to follow the model for getting zero or minimum error in case or perturbations, we define:

$$J=\frac{1}{2}\int e^2 dt \ ; \ e=y_m - y_a \tag{15}$$

where:
y_m: Motor observed values.
y_a: Predicted or identified values.
û: Adjustable parameters.
By using the optimization rule by gradient, we obtain the adaptation rule:

$$\Delta\hat{u}(e,t)=-K grad(J)=-K\frac{\partial J}{\partial \hat{u}} \tag{16}$$

The variation of the adjustable parameter with respect to time will be:

$$\dot{\hat{u}}=\frac{\partial \hat{u}}{dt}=-K\frac{\partial}{\partial t}\left(\frac{\partial J}{\partial \hat{u}}\right) \tag{17}$$

Assuming a slow variation of the adaptation law:

$$\dot{\hat{u}}=\frac{\partial \hat{u}}{dt}=-K\frac{\partial}{\partial \hat{u}}\left(\frac{\partial J}{\partial t}\right)=-K\frac{\partial}{\partial \hat{u}}\left(\frac{1}{2}e^2\right)=-Ke\frac{\partial e}{\partial \hat{u}} \tag{18}$$

The adaptation rule presented in 18, is known as the MIT adaptation rule (Whitetaker et al., 1958).

$$\frac{\partial e}{\partial \hat{u}}=\frac{\partial (y_m - y_a)}{\partial \hat{u}}=\frac{\partial y_a}{\partial \hat{u}} \tag{19}$$

The partial derivative of y_a with respect to û is the sensibility of the adjustable system with respect to the parameter. In this case, the sensibility function is proportional to y_m, leading 19 to:

$$\dot{\hat{u}}=-Key_m \tag{20}$$

This rule has been very popular, although having some disadvantages we should take in consideration:

- When adjusting several parameters, it is required a great number of sensibility functions.
- The adaptation gain controls the adaptation speed: if it's too high, it can cause system unstability, and if it's too low, the adaptation will be slow.
- To obtain a good behavior between speed and stability, studies must be carried out through simulation.

5. Description of SCARA robot model

Next, we will make a brief description of the system on which identification and adaptive control techniques previously explained will be theoretically and practically applied. This system is a SCARA (Selective Compliant Assembly Robot Arm) robot with 6 DOF (Degree Of Freedom), whose construction is a cheap solution for design and implementation of this kind of systems, and that was developed by students of the Department of Electric Engineering of the Universidad de Santiago de Chile, for teaching and research purposes.

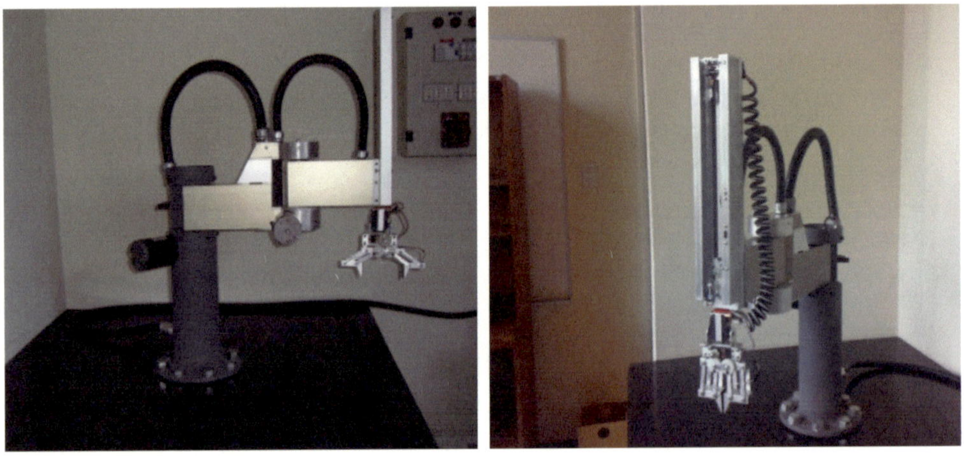

Fig. 10. Real employed SCARA system

The first three joints of this system are driven by DC motors controlled by signals provided by an interface implemented through the utilization of MatLab/Simulink software, and the other three joints are driven by servomotors. The SCARA system has an encoder in each one of the main joints, letting angular position readings for the first two rotational joints, and linear position readings for its prismatic joint, permitting the positioning of objects in space. The employed encoders were specifically designed and manufactured for this particular purpose. The last three actuators, located in the end of the robot's kinematic open chain, permit the driving of a clamp able to orientate objects in space. This clamp is endowed with pressure sensors in the tips.

It is important to remark that this robot, besides the non-linearities inherent to this kind of system, poses additional control challenges, due to mechanical building imperfections. One of the most important problems is the difference between absolute values of the torques required for rotate in either way each one of the first two joints, because of mechanical imperfections in the employed gear trains. Due to this, the rotation speeds to the left or right of those joints are not equal to the absolute values of the applied torques. That is why this system poses additional control challenges, compared with other SCARA robots currently available in the market, since for achieving a good performance, in theoretical and practical ways, it is necessary to investigate, develop and implement control algorithms allowing to obtain better intelligent controllers.

6. Hammerstein-Wiener models applied to the SCARA system

For the application of identification techniques it is necessary to gather data that capture the robot dynamics, requiring the concatenation of at least 10 different trajectories, so the identification process can be developed with a proper and sufficient amount of information. That is why excitation trajectories are generated and applied combining different dynamics, in order to obtain a good identification of the studied system (Janot et al., 2007), (Gautier et al., 2008), (Olsen & Petersen, 2001). The trajectories employed in this process are generated out of an interpolation or third degree, being known the final and initial position, and the initial and final times of the two first joints of the studied system. We look for capturing the non-linear dynamics of the robot, considering its total work range, from -135° to 135° for each joint. In order to capture the dynamics of the system's non-linear behavior, sudden changes in rotation way and speed are produced, and for doing that, 10 different trajectories are concatenated, as shown in fig. 11.

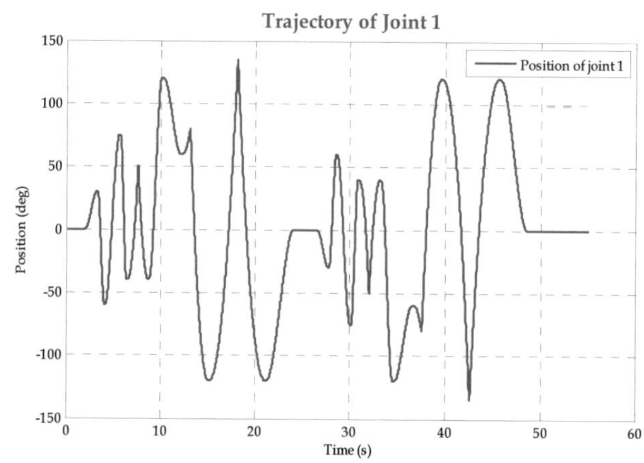

a) Trajectory applied in joint 1

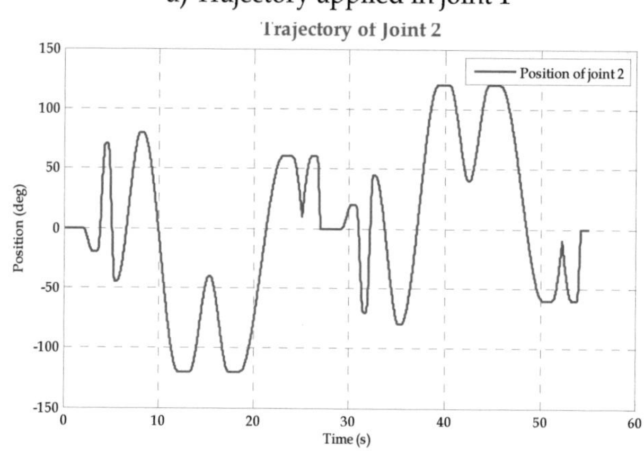

b) Trajectory applied in joint 2

Fig. 11. Trajectories applied in joints 1 and 2, respectively

The major dynamic complexities of this robot are found in its two first joints, therefore, the process of parameter identification is carried out on these joints only.

6.1 Linear models

Using data from the application of trajectories for both joints, black-box linear models for describing the system dynamics are proposed. In this regard, the following scheme is used:

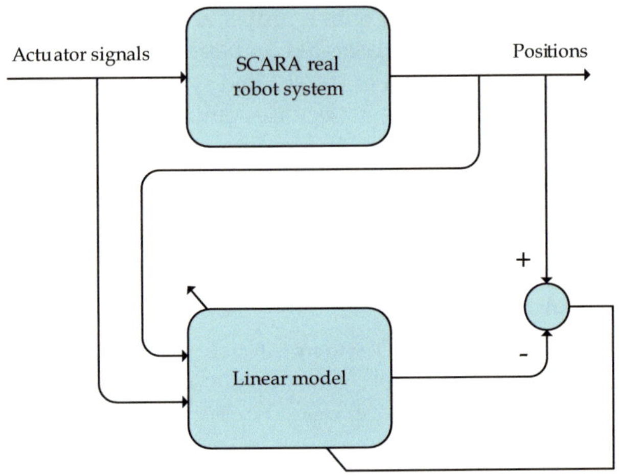

Fig. 12. Linear model adjustment scheme

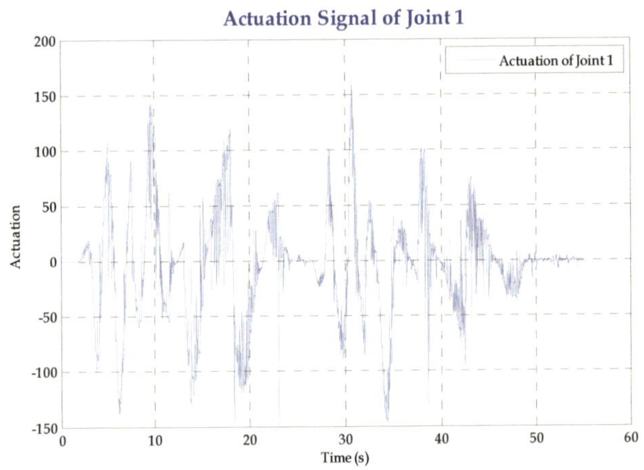

a) Actuation signal of joint 1

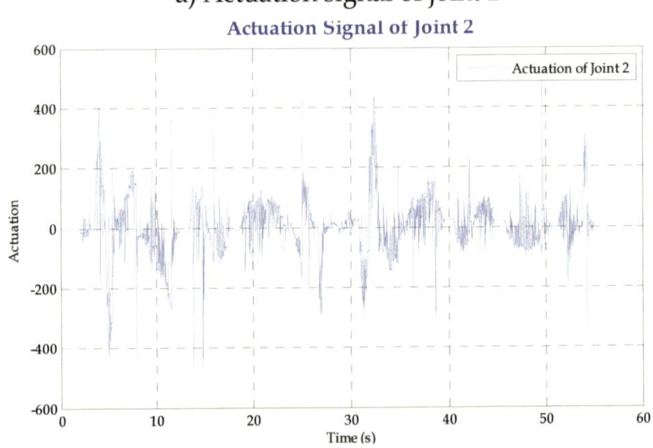

b) Actuation signal of joint 2

Fig. 13. SCARA robot actuator signals applied

The actuator signals applied to the SCARA robot for the trajectories shown in fig. 11 are used as input for adjusting the parameters of the polynomials in different linear models. The actuator signals are shown in fig. 13.

To select the most appropriate linear model for the identification of the different joints of the system under study, the model used in Example 2.1 can't be used, since it is highly complex and there is too much parameters uncertainty. Model selection and order of polynomials is done by selecting the simulation tests that best fits. Keep in mind that the linear model fit doesn't need to be too accurate, since this is used as part of a nonlinear model named Hammerstein-Wiener model.

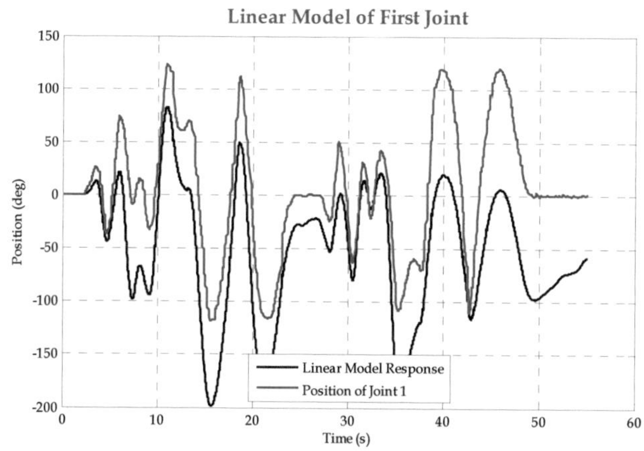

a) Linear model performance for joint 1

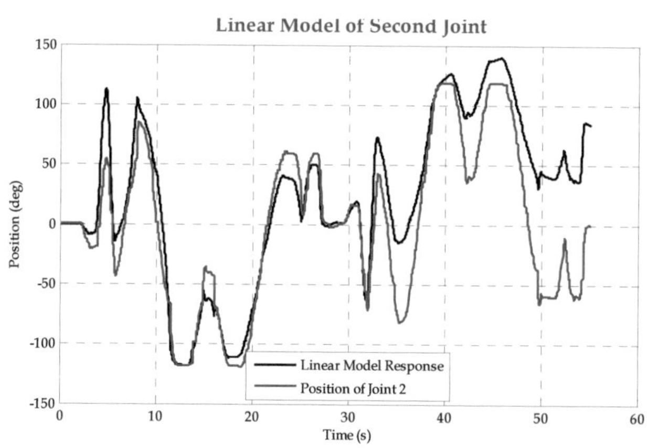

b) Linear model performance for joint 2

Fig. 14. Linear models performance for joints 1 and 2, respectively

To create linear models, actuator signals in both joints are used as inputs, and the joint position as a reference signal. For joint 1, the linear model that best fits is an ARMAX with A polynomial of order 3, the B polynomials of orders 4 and 2 respectively, and finally a C polynomial of order 2. The fitting percentage is 52.82%. For joint 2, the linear model that best fits is an ARX, with A polynomial of order 4, and B polynomials of order 5. The percentage fit of this model is 41.41%. Both models used a first order delay for the first actuator entry and a second order delay for the second actuator. The responses of both models are shown in the figure 14.

6.2 Hammerstein-Wiener models

From the previous linear models, the proposed nonlinear model can be completed. The realization of this model uses the following scheme:

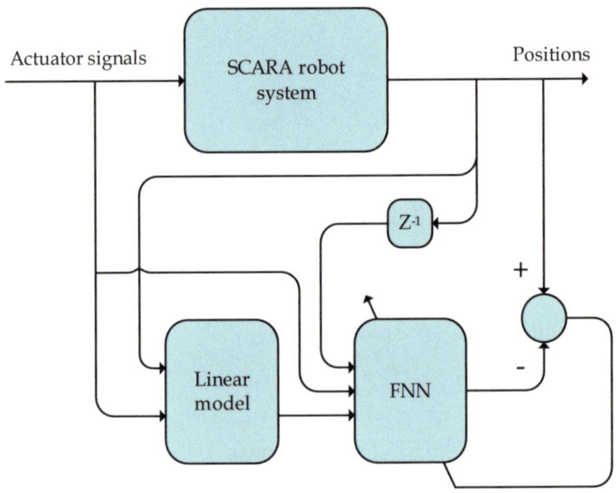

Fig. 15. Hammerstein-Wiener models fitting scheme

The nonlinear functions used are three-layered Feed forward Neural Networks (FNN). The FNN training results that correct the Hammerstein-Wiener model are shown below:

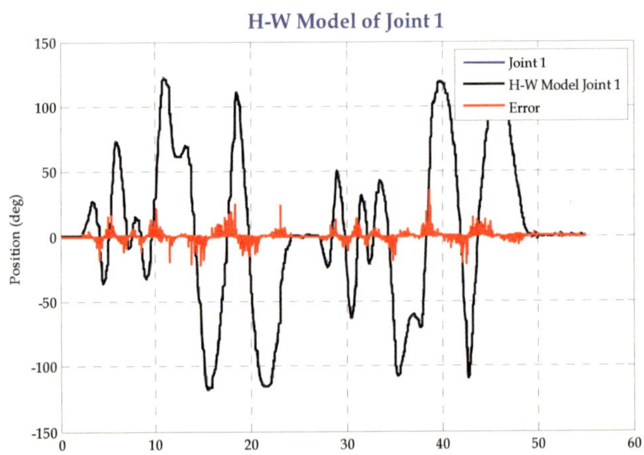

a) Hammerstein-Wiener model response for both joint 1

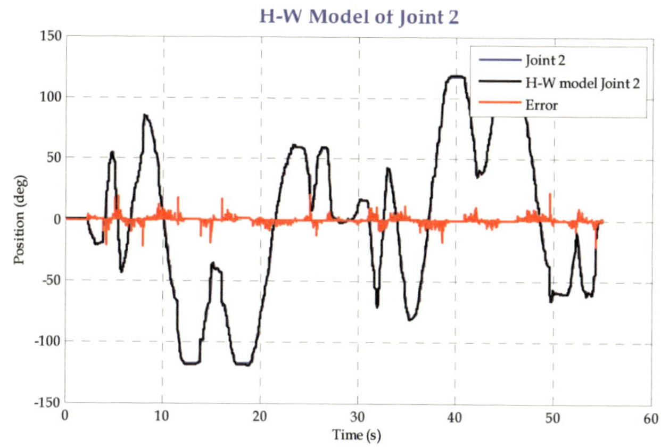

b) Hammerstein-Wiener model response for both joint 2

Fig. 16. Hammerstein-Wiener model response for both joints

6.3 Model implementation

The implementation of the obtained models is performed using MatLab/Simulink software, due to its simplicity in creating simulations, and in the fact that the studied robot is controlled through an interface created in it. The model implemented is the following:

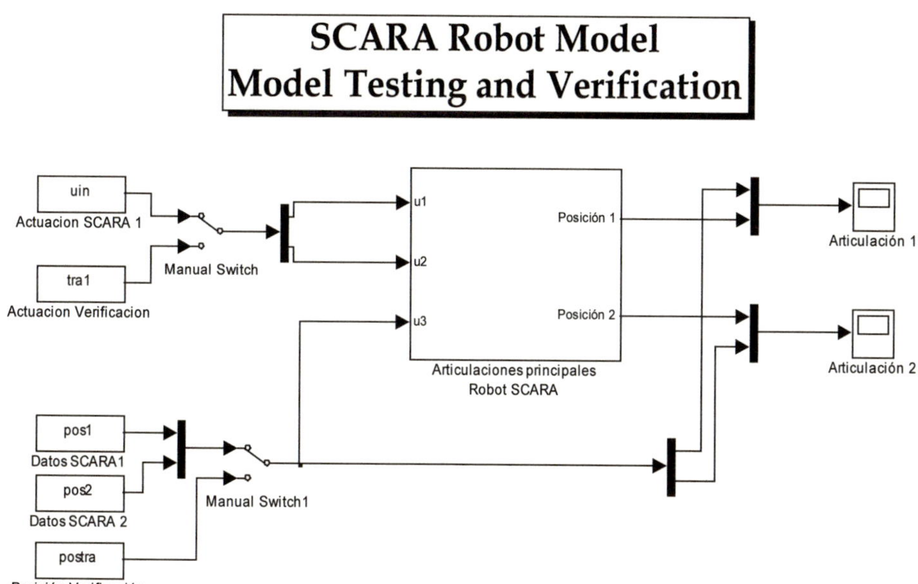

Fig. 17. Implemented model in MatLab/Simulink

The specific identification model is shown in figure 18.

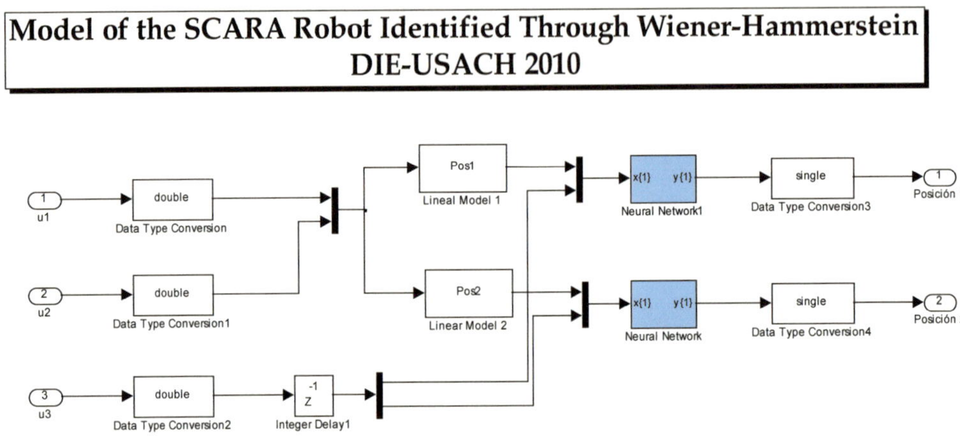

Fig. 18. Hammerstein-Wiener Model

6.4 Model validation

To ensure that the model obtained is a good representation of the joints of the SCARA system, another experiment is performed using a path different from that used for fitting, which allows evaluating the system behavior. The validation, implementing 3 different experiments, was carried out on-line. The scheme implemented in MatLab/Simulink used for controlling the SCARA robot and verifying the created model is shown below:

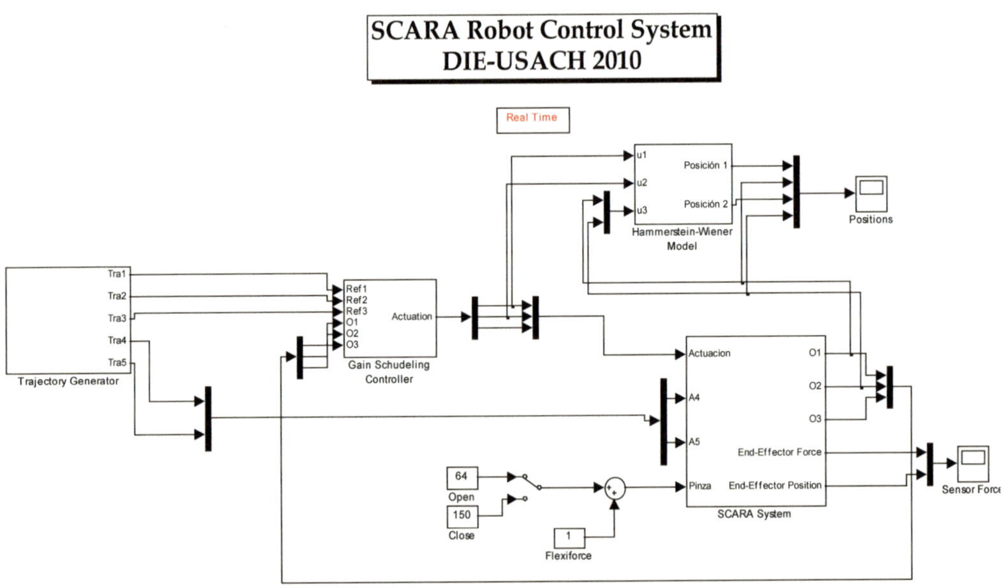

Fig. 19. Implemented control system

For the first verification experiment, we applied a trajectory to the first joint, keeping fixed the second joint.

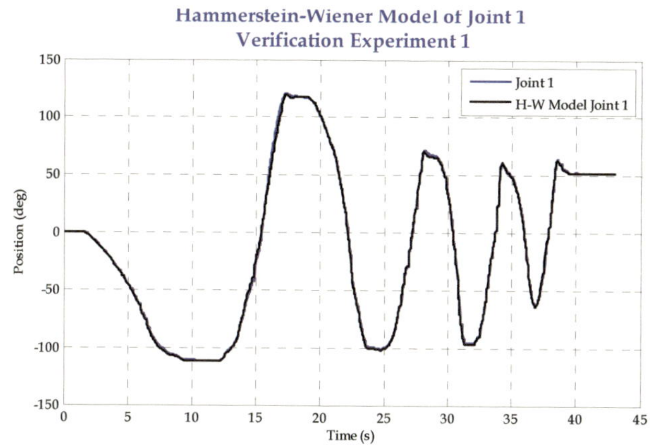

Fig. 20. Joint 1 verification; experiment 1

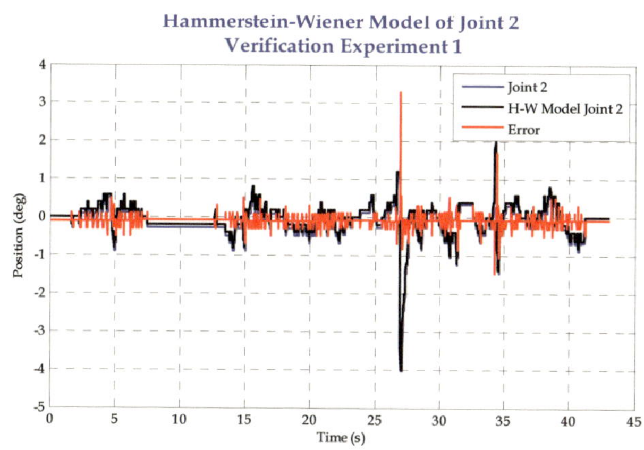

Fig. 21. Joint 2 verification; experiment 1

For the second experiment, we applied different trajectories to both joints, the verifications are shown next:

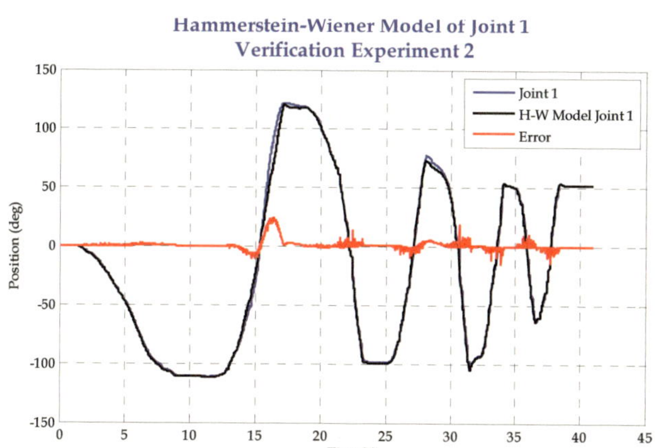

Fig. 22. Joint 1 verification; experiment 2

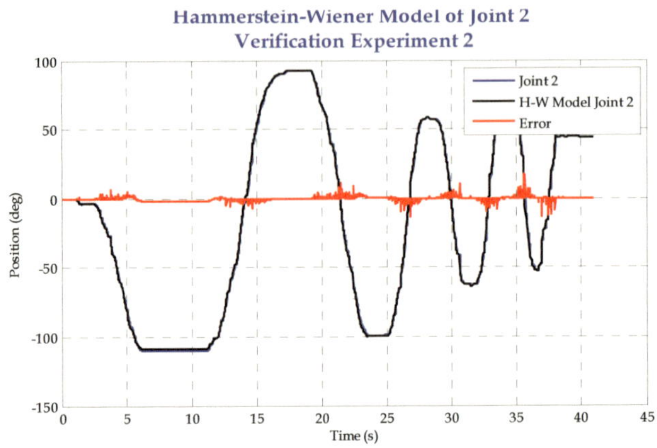

Fig. 23. Joint 2 verification; experiment 2

Finally, in order to carry out a most exigent test to the created model, we applied a PRBS signal as reference for the robot to be followed in its second joint, and a normal trajectory in the first joint. The results are shown below:

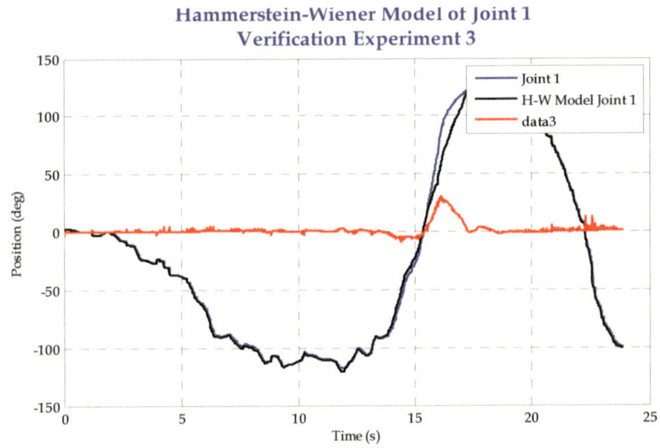

Fig. 24. Joint 1 verification; experiment 3

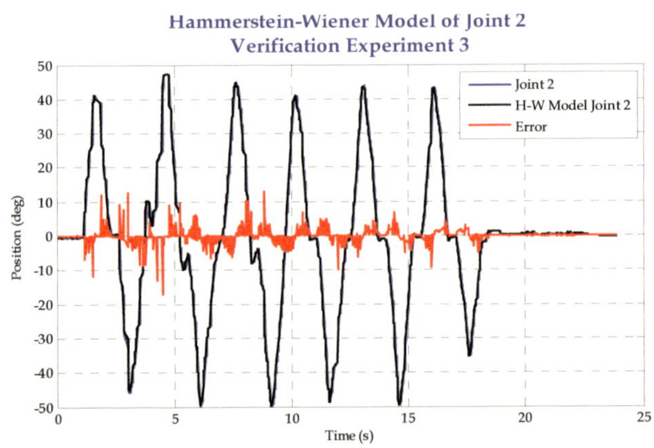

Fig. 25. Joint 2 verification; experiment 3

7. MRAC implementation

For the implementation of MRAC we will employ the sensibility theory presented in eq. 20. The implementation of such controller, using MatLab/Simulink software, is shown below:

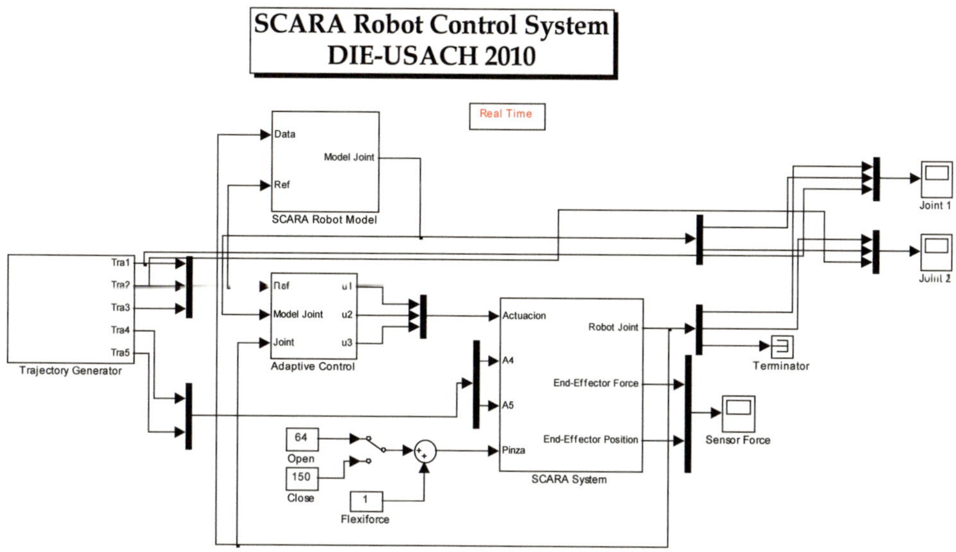

Fig. 26. MRAC Implementation

For the implementation of the sensibility theory we created three adaptation law blocks. Adaptive control makes parameter adjustment of a classic PID controller, as shown in the next figure:

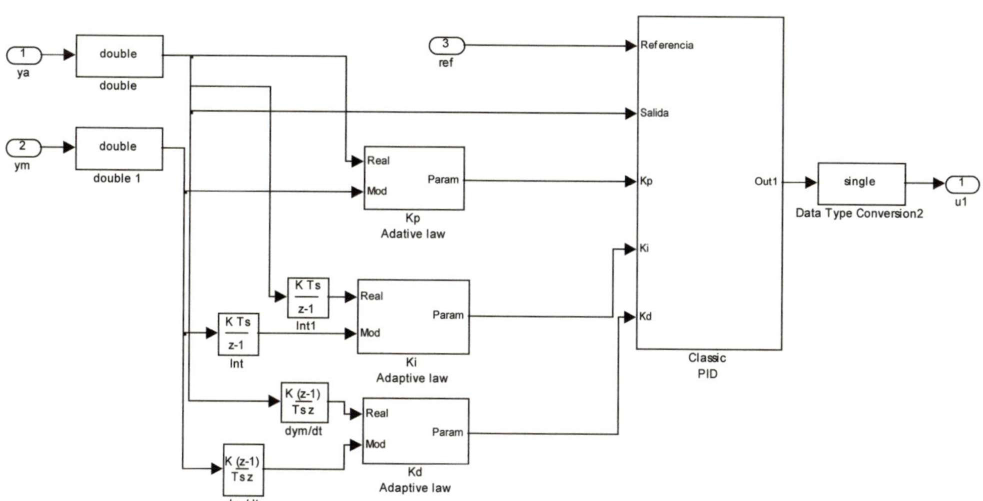

Fig. 27. Adaptive Controller

The adaptation laws were built accordingly to (Espinoza, 2009), and are shown in the figure below:

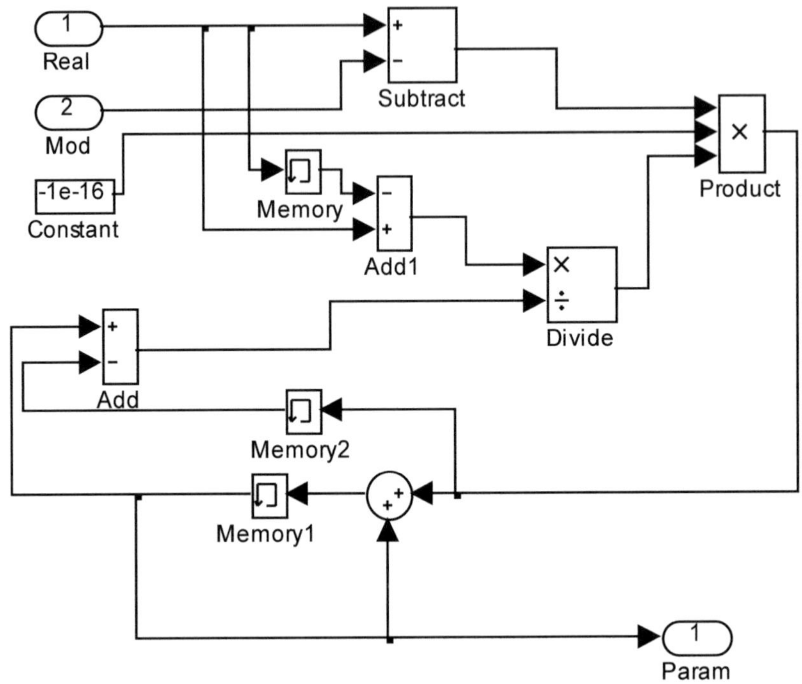

Fig. 28. Adaptive law

7.1 Results

Applying a step of 50° for the first joint and of -50° for the second joint, we obtain the following response of the system with adaptive controller:

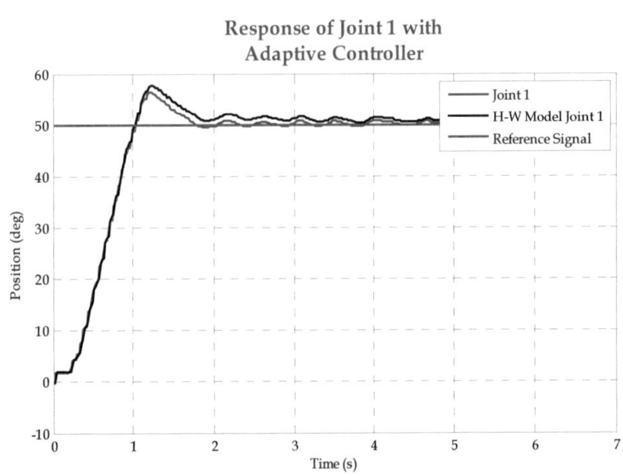

Fig. 29. Response to step, joint 1

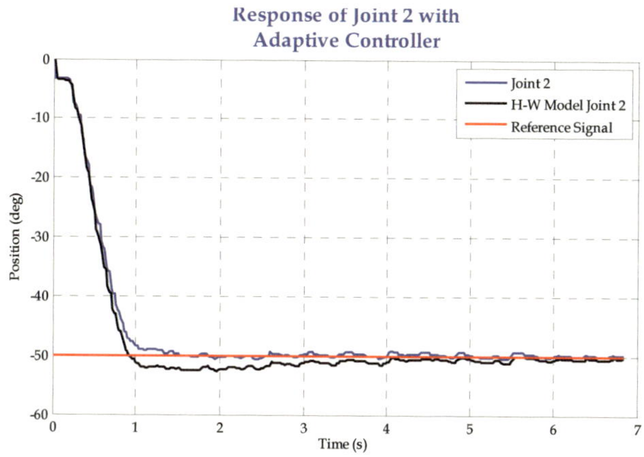

Fig. 30. Response to step, joint 2

Finally, we apply a trajectory for verifying the result obtained with the implemented controller.

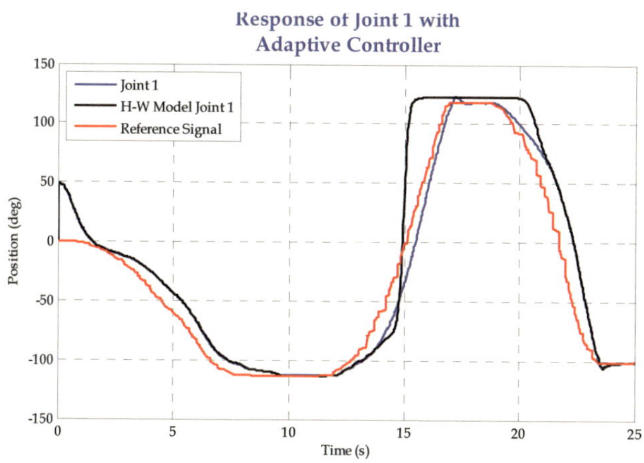

Fig. 31. Response of joint 1 to a trajectory

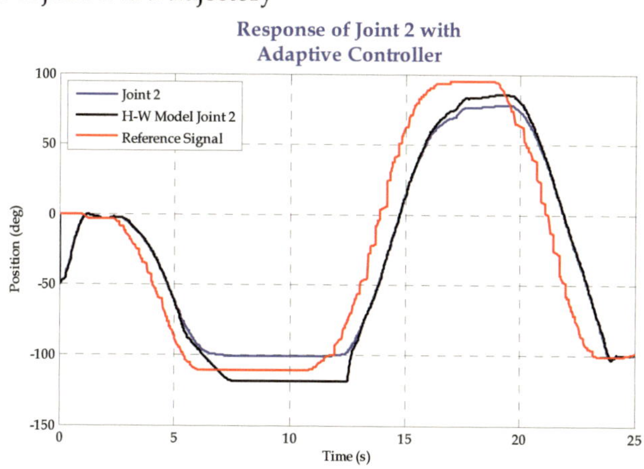

Fig. 32. Response of joint 2 to a trajectory

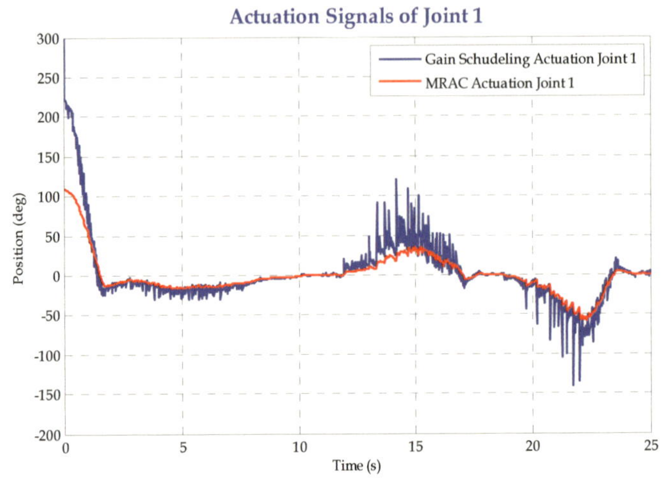

Fig. 33. Actuation signals of joint 1

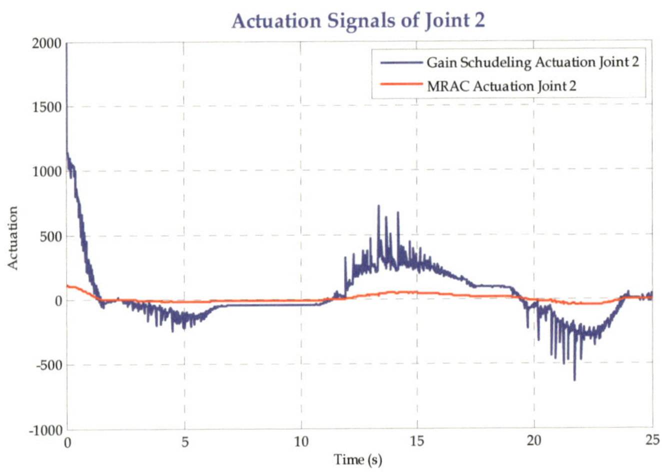

Fig. 34. Actuation signals of joint 2

8. Conclusions

Through the application of Hammerstein-Wiener models we can identify efficiently the dynamics of a real manipulator robot. For the application of those models, it is only necessary to know the position output of each joint and the robot's actuation signal.

We propose a new particular identification loop for Hammerstein-Wiener models, shown schematically in fig. 8, where we consider ARX or ARMAX linear models and a non-linear part composed by FNN. It is important to notice that for non-linear cases, the choice of linear model and the FNN configuration is obtained thanks to experimental developments, choosing the models better describing the studied system, from a set of identified models.

From the verification carried out for the obtained Hammerstein-Wiener models, we conclude that those models can capture the non-linear dynamics of the system; nevertheless, those models present little errors when more exigent trajectories are applied to the system, as in the case of PRBS trajectory (see fig. 25), due to the fact that the dynamics of the first two links is coupled, therefore, sudden movements in a joint cause unidentified perturbations in the adjacent joint.

An adaptive controller has been successfully implemented in a real system. Although we can notice some flaws in the identified model of the real robotic system, the adaptive controller follows closely the behavior of the model (see figs. 28 and 29). A remarkable aspect is that actuation signals obtained employing the adaptive controller are smoother than the ones obtained with the Gain Scheduling controller implemented first in the robotic system, both for the applied trajectories (see figs. 31 and 32), and their respective actuation signals (see figs. 33 and 34). The smoothing of actuation signals in both joints, as the case obtained in this work, leads to a decrease of oscillations in the joints, lower material fatigue and, therefore, a lower energy consumption for the robotic system.

9. Acknowledgements

This work had the support of the Department for Scientific and Technologic Research of the Universidad de Santiago de Chile, by means of Projects 060713UO and 060713JD, Santiago, Chile.

10. References

Angeles, J., 2006. *Fundamentals of Robotic Mechanical System: Theory, Methods, and Algorithms, Third Edition*. New York: Springer.

Blanke, M., Kinnaert, M., Lunze, J. & Staroswiecki, M., 2006. *Diagnosis and Fault-Tolerant Control 2nd Edition*. New York: Springer-Verlag Berlin Heidelberg.

Blanke, M., Staroswiecki, M. & Wu, E., 2001. Concepts and Methods in Fault-Tolerant Control. In *Arlington, VA, USA: American Control Conference. Proceedings of the 2001.*, 2001. Pearson Education.

Bonivento, C., Isidori, A., Marconi, L. & Paoli, A., 2004. Implicit Fault-Tolerant Control: Application to Induction Motors. *Automatica, vol. 40*, N° 3, pp.355–371.

Craig, J., 1986. *Introduction to Robotics, Mechanics and Control*. Reading, Massachusetts: Addison-Wesley Publishing Company, Inc.

Craig, J., 2006. *Robótica*. Pearson Education.

Espinoza, L., 2009. *Diseño e Implementación de un Simulador Gráfico de un Robot Bípedo de 14 Grados de Libertad*. Tesis de Ingeniería Civil en Electricidad. Santiago: Universidad de Santiago de Chile.

Gautier, M., Janot, A. & Vandanjon, P., 2008. A New Identification Method for Mechatronic Systems in closed-loop from only Control Data. *Proceedings of the 17th World Congress The International Federation of Automatic Control*, pp.498-503.

Janot, A. et al., 2007. Modeling and identification of a 3 DOF haptic interface. In *In Proceedings of the IEEE International Conference on Robotics and Automation*. Roma, Italia, 2007.

Kasim, A., 2003. Multi-Models Adaptive Controller for Multivariable Systems. *Proceedings of The 3rd IEEE International Workshop on System-on-Chip for Real-Time Applications*.

Lewis, F., Dawson, D. & Abdallah, C., 2004. Robot Manipulator Control Theory and Practice. New York: Marcel Dekker, Inc.

Ljung, L., 1999. *System Identification, Theory for the User*. Prentice Hall PTR.

Makkar, C., Dixon W., Sawyer W. & Hu, G., 2005. A New Continuously Differentiable Friction Model for Control Systems Design.

Nyzen, R., 1999. *Analysis and Control of an Eight Degree-of-Freedom Manipulator*. Tesis de Magister, Ohio University.

Ogata, K., 1996. *Ingeniería de Control Moderna*. Pearson Education.

Ollero, A., 2001. *Robótica Manipuladores y Robots Móviles*. Barcelona, España: Marcombo, S.A.

Olsen, M. & Petersen, H., 2001. A New Method for Estimating Parameters of a Dynamic Robot Model. *IEEE Transaction on Robotics and Automation*, 17(1), pp.95-100.

Pierro, P., Monje, C. & Balaguer, C., 2008. Modelling and Control of the Humanoid Robot RH-1 for Collaborative Tasks. *IEEE RAS/RSJ Conference on Humanoids Robots*.

Rodríguez, F. & Lopéz, M., 1996. *Control Adaptivo y Robusto*. Sevilla, España: Universidad de Sevilla.

Santander, F., Urrea, C. & Jamett, M., 2010. Identificación de Sistemas Aplicada a Servomotores. *Congreso de la Asociación Chilena de Control Automático ACCA*.

Siciliano, B. & Khatib, O., 2008. *Handbook of Robotics*. Berlin, Heidelberg: Springer-Verlag.

Spong, M., Hutchinson, S. & Vidyasagar, M., 2005. *Robot Modeling and Control, First Edition*. New York: John Wiley & Sons, Inc.

Whitetaker, H., Yamron, J. & Kezer, A., 1958. Design of model reference Adaptive Control System for Aircraft. *Report R-164 Intrumentation Laboratory MIT*.